Right Triangles

Pythagorean Theorem

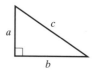

$$c^2 = a^2 + b^2$$

45°-45°-90° Triangle

$$c = a\sqrt{2}$$

$$c = 2a$$
$$b = a\sqrt{3}$$

Interest Formulas

Simple Interest (I)

$I = Prt$
P = principal
r = rate of interest
t = number of time periods

$A = P + I$
A = sign interest amount
$I = A - P$
I = interest

Compounded Amount (A)

$A = P(1 + r)^t$
P = principal
r = interest rate per time period
t = number of time periods

Compounded Continuously Amount (A)

$A = Pe^{rt}$
P = principal
r = annual interest rate compounded continuously
t = number of years
$e \approx 2.718$ (irrational number)

Temperature Formulas

Fahrenheit Temperature (F)

$F = \dfrac{9}{5}C + 32$ C = Celsius temperature

Celsius Temperature (C)

$C = \dfrac{5}{9}(F - 32)$ F = Fahrenheit temperature

Other Formulas

Distance Traveled Formula

$d = rt$
d = distance traveled
r = rate (speed)
t = time traveled

Vertical Position Formula

$s = -16t^2 + v_0t + s_0$
s = position in feet above ground level
t = time in seconds
v_0 = initial velocity in feet per second
s_0 = initial position in feet above ground level

Distance between Two Points Formula

$d = \sqrt{(x_2 - x_1)^2 + (y_2 - y_1)^2}$
(x_1, y_1) and (x_2, y_2) are coordinates of two points

Pendulum Formula

$T = 2\pi\sqrt{\dfrac{L}{32}}$
T = time of period (in seconds)
L = length in feet of suspension

Voltage Formula

$V = IZ$
V = total voltage in volts
I = current in amperes
Z = impedance in ohms

Quadratic Formula

$x = \dfrac{-b \pm \sqrt{b^2 - 4ac}}{2a}$
a, b, and c are real numbers
$a \neq 0$ and $ax^2 + bx + c = 0$

Products of Polynomials

Two Binomial Factors (FOIL Method)
$(a + b)(c + d) = ac + ad + bc + bd$

Squaring a Binomial
$(a + b)^2 = a^2 + 2ab + b^2$
$(a - b)^2 = a^2 - 2ab + b^2$

Sum and Difference of the Same Two Terms
$(a + b)(a - b) = a^2 - b^2$

Other Special Products
$(a + b)(a^2 - ab + b^2) = a^3 + b^3$
$(a - b)(a^2 + ab + b^2) = a^3 - b^3$

Experiencing Algebra

JoAnne Thomasson
Pellissippi State Technical Community College

Bob Pesut
Pellissippi State Technical Community College

Prentice Hall
Upper Saddle River
New Jersey 07458

Acquisitions Editor: Karin E. Wagner
Editor-in-Chief: Jerome Grant
Editorial Director: Tim Bozik
Associate Editor-in-Chief, Development: Carol Trueheart
Associate Editor, Math/Statistics Media: Audra J. Walsh
Editorial Assistant/Supplements Editor: Kate Marks
Text Design and Project Management: Elm Street Publishing Services, Inc.
Senior Managing Editor: Linda Mihatov Behrens
Executive Managing Editor: Kathleen Schiaparelli
Assistant Vice President of Production and Manufacturing: David W. Riccardi
Marketing Manager: Jolene Howard
Manufacturing Buyer: Alan Fischer
Manufacturing Manager: Trudy Pisciotti
Art Director: Maureen Eide
Associate Creative Director: Amy Rosen
Director of Creative Services: Paula Maylahn
Assistant to Art Director: John Christiana
Art Manager: Gus Vibal
Art Editor: Grace Hazeldine
Cover Designer: Daniel Conte
Cover Photo: H. Kuwajima/Photonica/IMA USA, Inc.
Photo Researcher: Diana Gongora
Photo Research Administrator: Melinda Reo
Art Studio: Scientific Illustrators

© 1999 by Prentice-Hall, Inc.
Simon & Schuster / A Viacom Company
Upper Saddle River, New Jersey 07458

Printed in the United States of America

10 9 8 7 6 5 4 3 2 1

ISBN 0-13-974478-9

Student edition ISBN 0-13-761248-6

Prentice-Hall International (UK) Limited, *London*
Prentice-Hall of Australia Pty. Limited, *Sydney*
Prentice-Hall Canada, Inc., *Toronto*
Prentice-Hall Hispanoamericana, S.A., *Mexico*
Prentice-Hall of India Private Limited, *New Delhi*
Prentice-Hall of Japan, Inc., *Tokyo*
Simon & Schuster Asia Pte. Ltd., *Singapore*
Editoria Prentice-Hall do Brasil, Ltda., *Rio de Janeiro*

Thanks to our spouses and families
for their encouragement and support
while writing this text.

Jack	*Gretchen*
Tracy	*Lauren*
Tommy	*Katherine*
Shawn	*Tracy*
Cameron	*Jim*
J.T.	*B.P.*

Contents

15

Exponential and Logarithmic Functions 1118

Preface

Our goal in developing *Experiencing Algebra* is to implement a new approach to teaching and learning developmental mathematics. This approach is based upon our ten years of teaching and research experience, and it combines a traditional approach with the reform movements presented in the National Council of Teachers of Mathematics (NCTM) and American Mathematical Association of Two-Year Colleges (AMATYC) standards. The NCTM student goals state that in our present technological society, students should learn to value mathematics, reason and communicate mathematically, become confident of their mathematical abilities, and become mathematical problem solvers. In addition, the AMATYC standards for intellectual development state that students will model real-world situations, connect mathematics with other disciplines, and use appropriate technology. We determined that a new textbook approach was needed to achieve these goals. We also decided that all students should have a graphing calculator on the first day of class and use this calculator on a daily basis.

Project Development

Experiencing Algebra is the culmination of more than ten years of work by the authors, reviewers, answer-checkers, editors, class-testers, and students. This project began in 1987 with the establishment of the Remedial/Developmental Mathematics Department at Pellissippi State Technical Community College. Since that time, the mathematics faculty has regularly reviewed and implemented changes in the two developmental algebra courses offered. In the spring of 1991, graphing calculators were included in the curriculum. Research in the summer and fall of that year indicated significantly positive results for students who used graphing calculators on a daily basis.

Research projects on activities such as writing across the curriculum and collaborative learning have also positively impacted student attitudes. However, our faculty could find no satisfactory text books that could be used with these activities, which led to the writing of this book. During the development of this text, we incorporated changes resulting from research studies with students of developmental mathematics. These changes include more emphasis on mathematical modeling of real-world situations, especially situations relevant to School-to-Career projects.

Approach

We have carefully written *Experiencing Algebra* in a positive manner to help students build confidence in their ability to do algebra. After completing the course, students should be able to:

- model real-world situations
- reason mathematically and develop convincing mathematical arguments
- use an appropriate method, numeric, graphic, or algebraic, to solve problems
- connect algebra to other disciplines
- communicate mathematics

- use appropriate technology
- work collaboratively in groups

To teach these skills, we introduce a problem-solving procedure in Chapter 5 and use this approach throughout the text. Numeric, graphic, and algebraic approaches to problem solving are described, and students are encouraged to choose the appropriate method to solve their problems. Every section of the text addresses real-world situations, so students can see reasons for learning algebra and can connect what they learn to other disciplines, both within and outside mathematics. Students are asked to discover mathematical ideas on their own, to develop mathematical reasoning skills, and to communicate their results. We then explain these results mathematically to reinforce the concepts students have found.

Content

Experiencing Algebra is written for a two-semester course in beginning and intermediate algebra. However, it is also flexible enough for use in a one-semester course. Topics for both courses are covered with a minimal amount of repetition. In **Chapters 1 and 2**, we introduce the set of real numbers, develop the properties of the real-number system, and present the rules for operations on real numbers. We complete these numeric topics with discussions of integer exponents, scientific notation, radicals and rational exponents.

After completing the numeric foundation, we introduce variables, algebraic expressions, and equations in **Chapter 3**. At this point we discuss all the geometric and other formulas used in the text. This early introduction allows us to integrate geometric applications and other applications throughout the book. In **Chapter 4**, we discuss additional topics needed for the study of algebra: ordered pairs, relations, functions and graphs. This early discussion of functions supports the structure of the remainder of the text, which focuses on the study of various families of functions.

Chapters 5, 6, 7, and 8 cover topics related to linear functions. In **Chapter 5**, we begin the explicit study of algebra by solving linear equations in one variable and absolute-value equations. Here and throughout the text, we teach how to solve equations numerically, graphically, and algebraically. **Chapter 6** focuses on linear equations in two variables and functions. **Chapter 7** presents methods for solving systems of linear equations in two variables, emphasizing solution by graphing, by substitution, and by elimination. Inequalities and solutions of linear inequalities are discussed in **Chapter 8**. The first eight chapters can be used as a beginning algebra text.

We designed Chapter 9 as the first chapter in the second semester of study, allowing for a review of graphical methods and the concept of a function. The remainder of the text follows a standard pattern, consisting of the introduction of a family of functions; a summary of rules for operating with the expressions that define the functions; and presentation of methods for solving related equations numerically, graphically, and algebraically. We follow this pattern for discussing polynomial functions in **Chapter 9**, polynomial expressions in **Chapter 10**, and polynomial equations and inequalities in **Chapter 11**. In Chapter 11, we solve quadratic equations numerically, graphically, and algebraically by factoring, by completing the square, and by using the quadratic formula. This arrangement allows for closure on quadratic equations and enables the student to choose an appropriate method for solving equations by examining the equation given. In **Chapter 12,** we describe rational functions, operations with rational expressions, and the solution of rational equations. We complete the coverage of radical functions, expressions, and equations in **Chapter 13**, along with functions, expressions, and equations having rational exponents.

We include a separate **Chapter 14** on the complex number system, describing equations in one variable with complex solutions. This chapter is designed to stand alone or to be incorporated into previous chapters, if desired. Finally, **Chapter 15** is a discussion of inverse functions, exponential functions, and logarithmic functions. It also includes properties of exponents and logarithms and methods for solving exponential equations and logarithmic equations in one variable.

Pedagogy

Use of Technology

Graphing calculators allow students the freedom to explore and experiment with mathematical ideas. Using graphing calculators helps boost student confidence and increase motivation. Skills such as estimation, computation, graphing, and data analysis can be developed and reinforced by use of the calculator. When students are relieved of tedious computations, they can focus on processes instead. They can also go beyond the limitations of traditional paper-and-pencil work and deal directly with real-world numbers.

Students should learn not only how to use technology, but also learn when to use technology. This text assumes that all students have a TI-83 graphing calculator available for use at all times. This requirement will minimize the amount of time necessary for the instructor to demonstrate particular calculator functions. **Technology** boxes in this text, especially in early chapters, present the keystrokes required to produce selected TI-83 calculator screens. Additional calculator activities and instructions are included in the **Experiencing Algebra the Calculator Way** activities.

Multiple Approaches

Throughout the text, concepts are developed using *numeric*, *graphic*, *algebraic*, and *verbal* approaches. The *numeric* presentation emphasizes tables of values, either constructed manually or by using a calculator. *Graphic* techniques follow naturally from the numeric methods. The *algebraic* approach is introduced and supported by the other methods. Students are encouraged to decide which approach is the most appropriate for solving particular problems. They are also challenged to express *verbal* solutions, both *orally* and in writing.

Interactive and Collaborative Learning

We believe students should learn to read, write, and speak mathematically. We have written this text at a level that developmental readers can understand. Several features of this book ask students to write mathematically, including the **Discovery** sets, the **Experiencing Algebra the Checkup Way** exercises at the end of each objective, the **Experiencing Algebra the Write Way** exercises in each of the section's **Problem Sets**, the **Reflections** in each **Chapter Review**, and the **Chapter Tests**.

Eventually, whatever their careers, students will be expected to work together in groups. With this in mind, we have provided **Experiencing Algebra the Group Way** collaborative activities at the end of each section. **Discovery** sets, a key pedagogical feature, may also be completed in groups or pairs instead of alone. **Experiencing Algebra the Calculator Way** activities often provide additional opportunities for collaborative learning.

Experiencing Mathematics

The graphing calculator enables students to explore and experiment with mathematical ideas as they discover algebraic concepts in the **Discovery** sets. After a student discovers a concept, the accompanying text explains why the concept is true. Students develop a sense of ownership of the algebraic principles through this discovery process. As a result, students acquire a better understanding of the reasoning behind the mathematics.

To help students keep a positive attitude toward mathematics while experiencing algebra, we provide frequent **Helping Hands** to reinforce student skills. Students review their skills at the end of each chapter in the **Mixed Review** as well as every four to five chapters in the **Cumulative Review**. In addition, each **Chapter Test** begins with a **Test-Taking Tip** designed to further bolster students' confidence and improve their ability to perform well on tests.

Connection with Other Experiences

For a meaningful experience in this course, students must connect the algebra being taught with the world around them. To help students make this connection, we begin each section of each chapter with a real-world **Application** and solve this application before the section ends. Each section also presents a list of section objectives, one of which is to model real-world situations using concepts discussed in that section. **Experiencing Algebra the Calculator Way**, **Experiencing Algebra the Group Way**, and **Experiencing Algebra the Write Way** activities in each section's **Problem Set** often connect the concepts to disciplines and fields outside mathematics, as well as to areas of applied mathematics such as geometry, probability, and statistics.

Supplements for the Instructor

Printed Supplements

Instructor's Edition

• Instructor answer section at the end of the text includes answers to every exercise in the text.

Instructor's Solution Manual

• Solutions to even-numbered "Exercise Way" exercises at the end of every section.
• Solutions to every (even and odd) exercise found in the Chapter Reviews, Chapter Tests, and Cumulative Reviews.
• A graphing calculator reference for the TI-83 presents a collection of keystrokes for quick reference.

Instructor's Test Manual
- Six Chapter Tests per chapter (two multiple-choice, four free-response).
- Four Final Exams (two multiple-choice, two free-response) covering chapters 1 through 8.
- Four Final Exams (two multiple-choice, two free-response) covering chapters 1 through 15.

Media Supplements

TestPro4 Computerized Testing
- Algorithmically driven, text-specific testing program.
- Networkable for administering tests and capturing grades on-line.
- Edit and add your own questions—create nearly unlimited number of tests and drill worksheets.

Companion Website
- www.prenhall.com/thomasson

Supplements for the Student

Printed Supplements

Student's Solution Manual
- Solutions to odd-numbered "Exercise Way" exercises at the end of every section exercises.
- Solutions to every (even and odd) "Calculator Way" exercise at the end of every section.
- Solutions to every (even and odd) exercise found in the Chapter Reviews, Chapter Tests and Cumulative Reviews.
- A graphing calculator reference for the TI-83 presents a collection of keystrokes for quick reference.

New York Times Supplement
- Have your instructor contact their local Prentice Hall sales representative.

How to Study Mathematics
- Have your instructor contact their local Prentice Hall sales representative.

Internet Guide
- Have your instructor contact their local Prentice Hall sales representative.

Media Supplements

MathPro4 Computerized Tutorial
- Keyed to each section of the text for text-specific tutorial exercises and instruction.
- Includes Warm-up Exercises and graded practice Problems.
- Algorithmically driven and fully networkable.
- Have your instructor contact their local Prentice Hall sales representative—also available for purchase for home use.

Videotape Series

Companion Website
- www.prenhall.com/thomasson

Acknowledgments

This text was completed with the help of many individuals who offered us encouragement, suggestions, and criticisms. We would like to thank the following individuals who reviewed the text.

Thomas Blackburn	*Northeastern Illinois University*
Steve Boettcher	*Scottsdale Community College*
Barbara Buoy	*Illinois State University*
Celeste Carter	*Richland College*
Delaine Cochran	*Indiana University—Southeast*
Faye Dang	*Joliet Junior College*
Barbara Edwards	*Oregon State University*
Mary Monroe-Ellis	*Pellissippi State Technical Community College*
William Ferguson	*Columbus State Community College*
Jeanne Fitzgerald	*Phoenix College*
Toni Fountain	*Chattanooga State Technical Community College*
Edward Gallo	*Ivy Tech State College*
Ruth Ann Henke	*Southern Illinois University—Edwardsville*
Tracey Hoy	*College of Lake County*
Diane Johnson	*Humboldt State University*
Aimee Martin	*Amarillo College*
Katherine Nickell	*College of DuPage*
Barbara Peck	*Charles County Community College*
Kathy Presley	*Lewis and Clark Community College*
Mike Scroggins	*Lewis and Clark Community College*
Colin Max Sheppard	*Arizona Western College*
Melody Shipley	*North Central Missouri College*
Mark Sigfrids	*Kalamazoo Valley Community College*
Bonnie Simon	*Nangatuck Valley Community—Technical College*
Helen Smith	*South Mountain Community College*
William Smith	*Lewis and Clark Community College*
Karl Zilm	*Lewis and Clark Community College*

To the students, who participated in the various research projects and class tests: your involvment has been invaluable. To the mathematics faculty and Regina Moore at Pellissippi State Technical Community College who supported us in this project, we offer our thanks. In particular, Caroline Best, Beth Krepps, Mary Monroe-Ellis, and Dougal Moore did an outstanding job in class testing the text. Ms. Best, Ms. Krepps, Ms. Moore, and Glenda Taylor assisted in checking solutions.

We would like to thank the editorial, production, and marketing staff at Prentice Hall for their patience, assistance, and contributions to this project. From the first time that we proposed this project to Karin Wagner, senior acquisitions editor, she has been unwavering in her support. David Chelton, developmental editor, buoyed our spirits throughout this project as he assisted us through the developmental process.

Special thanks to the Demand Copy Center who prepared materials for our class tests; to Laurel Technical Services for their work on developing test banks, solutions manuals, and other support activities; to Frank Weihenig and the staff at Prepare Inc. for their timely composition efforts; and to Michele Heinz and the staff at Elm Street Publishing Services for their editorial support.

JoAnne Thomasson
Bob Pesut

Rational Numbers

I n this chapter, we introduce rational numbers and show how to work with numerical expressions that use them. In our daily lives, we often have to evaluate expressions containing rational numbers—for example, finding the current balance in a checking account, comparing costs of items on sale, or deciding whether we have enough gas in the car to get home. We discuss how to perform operations on rational numbers to evaluate situations such as these.

Mathematically, debts (or deficits) are written as negative numbers. We will use information about the U.S. national debt to illustrate operations with rational numbers in each section of this chapter. In 1790, Alexander Hamilton, who was the first Secretary of the Treasury, estimated the national debt to be about $70 million. It has fluctuated up and down (mostly up) ever since then. By 1992, the national debt had reached approximately $4.083 trillion. Believe it or not, mathematically speaking, the national debt is a rational number.

1.1 Rational Numbers and the Number Line

Objectives

1 Identify a number as a member of the set of natural numbers, whole numbers, integers, or rational numbers.

2 Write a rational-number representation for a verbal description.

3 Graph rational numbers on a number line.

4 Determine the order of rational numbers and use the symbols $=$, $<$, and $>$ to complete an equation or inequality.

5 Evaluate the absolute value of a rational number.

6 Evaluate the opposite of a rational number.

Application

In 1992, the U.S. national debt was about $4.083 trillion. Write a rational-number representation for this amount.

After completing this section, we will discuss this application further. See page 14.

---

1 Identifying Rational Numbers and Their Subsets

A **set** is a group or collection of objects. The objects, which we call **members** or **elements** of the set, could be anything, such as state capitals in the United States, basketball players who have scored over 40,000 points in their careers, or stars in the sky. In mathematics, we often discuss sets of numbers.

A set with no members is called an **empty set** or **null set**. For example, the set of basketball players who have scored over 40,000 points in their careers is an empty set.

If it is possible to list all members of a set, it is called a **finite set**, such as the state capitals in the United States. If it is not possible to list all members of a set, it is called an **infinite set**, such as the set of stars in the sky.

We indicate a set by enclosing its members in a pair of braces: {}. If the set is infinite, we include enough members to show the pattern of the set. Then we add three dots, called an **ellipsis**, to indicate that the pattern continues. Examples of sets of numbers are

$A = \{\ \}$ Empty set A (no members)

$B = \{1, 3, 5, 7, 9\}$ Finite set B (odd numbers between 0 and 10)

$C = \{1, 3, 5, \ldots\}$ Infinite set C (odd numbers greater than or equal to 1)

A set that is contained in another set is called a **subset**. In the three previous sets, set B is a subset of set C. In this section, we discuss the set of rational numbers and several of its subsets.

To visualize these sets, we use a **number line**. We construct a number line by drawing a line and labeling equally spaced intervals with numbers in consecutive order. If all possible numbers in the set cannot be written on the line, an arrow placed on the end of the line indicates that the numbers continue in the same pattern.

The first set of numbers we consider is the set N of **natural numbers**, also called **counting numbers**.

$N = \{1, 2, 3, \ldots\}$

A number line representation of natural numbers looks like this:

If we extend the set of natural numbers by including 0 as an element, we have the set W of **whole numbers**.

$$W = \{0, 1, 2, 3, \ldots\}$$

A number line representation of whole numbers is as follows:

To extend the set of whole numbers, we include the opposites of all the natural numbers. The opposite of a natural number is a negative number and is written with a negative sign, $-$, in front of the number.

The opposite of 1 is negative 1 or -1.
The opposite of 2 is negative 2 or -2.

The opposites of all natural numbers form a set of negative numbers, $\{-1, -2, -3, \ldots\}$, or since the order does not matter, $\{\ldots, -3, -2, -1\}$. If we combine this set of negative numbers with the set of whole numbers, we have the set Z of **integers**.

$$Z = \{\ldots -3, -2, -1, 0, 1, 2, 3, \ldots\}$$

We can represent the integers on a number line like this:

If we examine the number line of integers, we see a space between each pair of consecutive integers. The numbers located between each pair include fractions and decimals. Fractions are simply ratios of integers, while some decimals are equivalent to fractions. We can name many fractions and decimals between 0 and 1, such as $\frac{1}{8}, \frac{1}{4}, \frac{1}{3}, 0.5, \frac{2}{3}, 0.75,$ and $\frac{7}{8}$.

In fact, if we could name and locate all fractions and decimals between 0 and 1, the entire space between 0 and 1 would appear to be filled with numbers.

We can extend the set of integers by including all fractions and their decimal equivalents. This gives us the set R of **rational numbers**.

> Rational numbers are numbers that can be written as a ratio of integers, excluding the possibility of a zero denominator.

All integers are rational numbers because we may write them with a denominator of 1. For example,

$$6 = \frac{6}{1} \qquad -5 = \frac{-5}{1}$$

All terminating decimals are rational numbers. For example,

$$0.25 = \frac{25}{100} = \frac{1}{4} \qquad 0.9 = \frac{9}{10} \qquad 0.85 = \frac{85}{100} = \frac{17}{20}$$

All repeating decimals are rational numbers. For example,

$$0.3333\ldots = \frac{1}{3} \qquad 0.5454\ldots = \frac{6}{11} \qquad 0.8333\ldots = \frac{5}{6}$$

Other forms of decimals will be discussed later.

All of these examples of rational numbers are written in fractional notation in simplest form. **Fractional notation** (in simplest form) is a form of a rational number written as a ratio of an integer numerator to a nonzero integer denominator, with the numerator and denominator having no common factors other than 1. For example,

$$\frac{3}{4} \frac{\text{numerator}}{\text{denominator}}$$ is fractional notation in simplest form because 3 and 4 are integers that have no common factors other than 1.

In summary, since the set of rational numbers includes all possible ratios of integers (excluding a denominator of 0), it includes all integers, which includes all whole numbers, which includes all counting numbers.

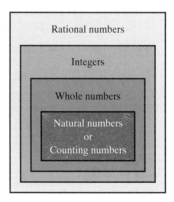

EXAMPLE 1 Identify the possible sets of numbers (that is, natural numbers, whole numbers, integers, or rational numbers) to which the number belongs.

a. 123   **b.** 0   **c.** -386 **d.** 36.25   **e.** $-\dfrac{28}{3}$

Solution

a. natural number, whole number, integer, rational number
b. whole number, integer, rational number
c. integer, rational number
d. rational number
e. rational number ∎

Experiencing Algebra the Checkup Way

In exercises 1–4, consider the following numbers, which may belong to one or more of the subsets of the rational numbers.

$$15, \ -3, \ 0, \ \frac{1}{3}, \ \frac{6}{3}, \ \frac{8}{3}, \ -\frac{5}{3}, \ 1 \text{ billion}, \ -15.4, \ 25.75, \ -180$$

1. Which of these numbers are natural numbers?
2. Which are rational numbers?
3. Which are integers?
4. Which are whole numbers?
5. Write a short definition of the following terms: *set*; *empty set*; *finite set*; *infinite set*.
6. Define the following sets of numbers: the integers; the whole numbers; the natural numbers; the rational numbers.

---

2 Writing Rational Numbers

Positive and negative numbers occur in all kinds of everyday situations. For example, positive rational numbers are used to represent gains and negative rational numbers are used to represent losses.

EXAMPLE 2

In football, a team has four downs in order to gain 10 yards and retain possession of the ball. On first down at the 50-yard line, the team gains 4 yards. On second down, the team gains $2\frac{3}{4}$ yards. On the next two downs, the team loses 2 yards and loses $3\frac{1}{2}$ yards, respectively.

Write a rational number representing each of these possessions and enter each number on your calculator.

Solution

$$4 \text{ yard gain} = \text{ positive } 4 = 4$$

$$2\frac{3}{4} \text{ yard gain} = \text{ positive } 2\frac{3}{4} = 2\frac{3}{4}$$

$$2 \text{ yard loss} = \text{ negative } 2 = -2$$

$$3\frac{1}{2} \text{ yard loss} = \text{ negative } 3\frac{1}{2} = -3\frac{1}{2}$$

Note: The calculator returns improper fractions for mixed numbers. That is, the mixed number $2\frac{3}{4}$ is represented as the improper fraction $\frac{11}{4}$, and $-3\frac{1}{2}$ is represented as $-\frac{7}{2}$. Directions for changing an improper fraction to a mixed number are given in "Experiencing Algebra the Calculator Way" in this section.

TECHNOLOGY

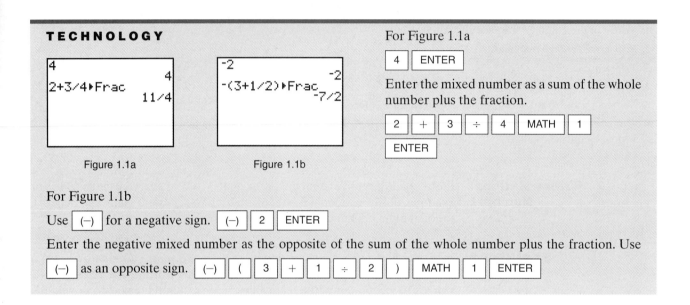

Figure 1.1a   Figure 1.1b

For Figure 1.1a

| 4 | ENTER |

Enter the mixed number as a sum of the whole number plus the fraction.

| 2 | + | 3 | ÷ | 4 | MATH | 1 |
| ENTER |

For Figure 1.1b

Use | (–) | for a negative sign. | (–) | 2 | ENTER |

Enter the negative mixed number as the opposite of the sum of the whole number plus the fraction. Use | (–) | as an opposite sign. | (–) | (| 3 | + | 1 | ÷ | 2 |) | MATH | 1 | ENTER |

Another example of positive and negative numbers representing everyday situations occurs in defining geographic elevations. Sea level separates positive and negative elevations.

EXAMPLE 3 The elevation of a body of water is the height of the surface of the water above sea level. Lake Superior has an elevation of 600 feet above sea level, while Lake Maracaibo has an elevation of 0 feet above sea level. The Caspian Sea has an elevation of 92 feet below sea level and Lake Titicaca has an elevation of 2.37 miles above sea level.

Write these elevations as rational numbers.

600 ft

Sea level

Lake Superior

Solution

600 feet above sea level $=$ positive 600 $=$ 600
0 feet above sea level $=$ 0
92 feet below sea level $=$ negative 92 $=$ -92
2.37 miles above sea level $=$ positive 2.37 $=$ 2.37 ∎

 Experiencing Algebra the Checkup Way

On the Celsius temperature scale, 0 degrees is defined as the temperature at which water freezes under standard atmospheric conditions.

Write a rational-number representation for the following Celsius temperatures and enter each number on your calculator.

1. The temperature is 12 degrees below freezing.

2. The temperature is 36 degrees above freezing.

3. The temperature is $5\frac{1}{2}$ degrees below freezing.

4. The temperature is 18.75 degrees above freezing.

3 Graphing Rational Numbers

Earlier, we used a number line to visualize sets of numbers. We can also use a number line to understand relationships between numbers. To construct a number line, draw a line and locate a position for the number 0. At equally spaced intervals, locate positions for the integers. Place positive integers in increasing order to the right of 0. Place negative integers in decreasing order to the left of 0. Since we cannot place all integers on the number line, place arrows on the ends of the number line to indicate that the line continues farther than drawn.

To **graph**, or **plot**, a number on a number line, we place a dot at its location. For example, graph -2 and 3 on a number line.

EXAMPLE 4 Graph 2, $\frac{3}{4}$, -1.5, $\frac{7}{4}$, and $-2\frac{1}{4}$ on a number line.

Solution

2 is located 2 units to the right of 0.
$\frac{3}{4}$ is located $\frac{3}{4}$ units to the right of 0.
-1.5 is located 1.5 units to the left of 0, or 0.5 $\left(\frac{1}{2}\right)$ unit to the left of -1.
$\frac{7}{4}$ is located $1\frac{3}{4}$ units to the right of 0, or $\frac{1}{4}$ unit to the left of 2.
$-2\frac{1}{4}$ is located $2\frac{1}{4}$ units to the left of 0, or $\frac{1}{4}$ unit to the left of -2 ∎

Experiencing Algebra the Checkup Way

1. Graph the following numbers on a number line.

$$-2,\ 4.75,\ 7,\ -5\frac{1}{4},\ 0,\ -8.6,\ 3\frac{1}{3},\ \frac{3}{5},\ -\frac{1}{3}$$

2. Describe what a number line is and how it is used.

---

4 Ordering Rational Numbers

Two numbers have the same value if they are located in the same position on a number line. For example, 3.5 and $3\frac{1}{2}$ have the same location on the number line.

$$3\frac{1}{2}$$

Therefore, they have the same value, or are **equal** to each other.

$$3.5 = 3\frac{1}{2} \qquad \text{or} \qquad 3.5 \text{ is equal to } 3\frac{1}{2}.$$

Numbers that are not of equal value can be placed in size order by comparing their locations on a number line. The farther a number is located to the right, the larger the number is. The farther a number is located to the left, the smaller the number is. We use **inequality (order) symbols** of greater than, $>$, and less than, $<$, to write these statements. For example, use $>$ or $<$ to compare

$$7 \underline{\hspace{1cm}} 2$$
$$2 \underline{\hspace{1cm}} 7.$$

In comparing 7 and 2 on a number line, we notice that 7 is to the right of 2; therefore, 7 is greater than 2.

$$7 > 2$$

We can also see that 2 is to the left of 7. Therefore, 2 is less than 7.

$$2 < 7$$

Helping Hand We can think of the inequality symbol as an arrow pointing to the smaller number.

The two inequalities, $7 > 2$ and $2 < 7$, are **equivalent**, or mean the same thing. To write equivalent inequalities, the numbers are exchanged and the inequality symbol is reversed. (The arrow is still pointing to the smaller number.)

EXAMPLE 5   Use $>, <,$ or $=$ to compare the following numbers.

a. 3 _____ 4.5   **b.** 2 _____ −5   **c.** 3 _____ 0

d. 0 _____ $-\dfrac{1}{2}$ **e.** −6 _____ −2   **f.** $-1\dfrac{1}{4}$ _____ −1.25

Solution

a. 3 $\underline{<}$ 4.5   3 is to the left of 4.5. Therefore, $3 < 4$.

b. 2 $\underline{>}$ −5   2 is to the right of −5. Therefore, $2 > -5$.

c. 3 $\underline{>}$ 0   3 is to the right of 0. Therefore, $3 > 0$.

d. 0 $\underline{>}$ $-\dfrac{1}{2}$ 0 is to the right of $-\frac{1}{2}$. Therefore, $0 > -\frac{1}{2}$.

e. −6 $\underline{<}$ −2   −6 is to the left of −2. Therefore, $-6 < -2$.

f. $-1\dfrac{1}{4}$ $\underline{=}$ −1.25 $-1\frac{1}{4}$ and −1.25 are located in the same position on the number line. Therefore, the numbers are equal.

A calculator can test whether an inequality or equation is true or false. The calculator returns a 0 for a false statement and a 1 for a true statement. To do this, enter the statement in your calculator and then press ENTER. All of the answers in the solution are true, so the calculator returns a 1 for all of them. The checks for Examples 6a, 6b, and 6f are shown in Figure 1.2. ∎

TECHNOLOGY

Figure 1.2

For Figure 1.2
The inequality symbols and the equal symbol are under the TEST menu.

Helping Hand Rounding errors can occur in calculations, so at times the calculator may return 0 for false when the statement is true and 1 for true when the statement is false. For example, $333.333333 = \frac{1000}{3}$ returns 0 for false, but

$333.3333333 = \frac{1000}{3}$, which is the calculator's limit of decimal places, returns 1 for true. In fact, both statements are false.

EXAMPLE 6   Write equivalent order relations for the following statements.

a. $0.6 < 0.85$ **b.** $-2 > -3\frac{1}{2}$ **c.** $-0.5 = -\frac{1}{2}$

Solution

a. $0.85 > 0.6$ Exchange the numbers and replace $<$ with $>$.

b. $-3\frac{1}{2} < -2$ Exchange the numbers and replace $>$ with $<$.

c. $-\frac{1}{2} = -0.5$ Exchange the numbers. The $=$ does not change. ∎

Experiencing Algebra the Checkup Way

Use one of the symbols $>$, $<$, or $=$ to compare the two numbers.

1. $0 \_\_\_\_ -2$ **2.** $-1\frac{1}{2} \_\_\_\_ 1\frac{1}{2}$ **3.** $1\frac{1}{2} \_\_\_\_ 1.5$ **4.** $-2.3 \_\_\_\_ -3.5$

Use your calculator to determine whether each statement is true or false.

5. $\frac{1}{2} > \frac{3}{4}$ **6.** $\frac{3}{2} < 1.5$ **7.** $\frac{27}{3} = 9$

Write an equivalent order relation for each statement.

8. $5 < 15$ **9.** $6 > -2$ **10.** $2.75 = \frac{11}{4}$

---

5   Evaluating Absolute Values

We are now ready to consider mathematical expressions. An **expression** is a combination of numbers and mathematical operations. (By a mathematical operation we mean addition, subtraction, multiplication, or division.) The quantity $2 + 3$ is a mathematical expression, as is the quantity 2×3. We **evaluate** expressions by finding their numerical value. The first expression has a value of 5, and the second expression has a value of 6.

The distance (number of units) a number is from 0 on the number line is called the **absolute value** of the number. The absolute value of a number is always nonnegative (positive or zero) because distance is always measured in nonnegative units.

To write an absolute value expression, enclose the number in a set of vertical bars, $|\ |$. Do not confuse these bars with parentheses, ( ), brackets, [ ], or braces, { }. For example, the absolute value of 6 is written $|6| = 6$. The absolute value of -6 is written $|-6| = 6$.

EXAMPLE 7   Evaluate.

a. $|34|$ b. $|-16|$

c. $|3.5|$ d. $\left|-\dfrac{1}{2}\right|$ e. $|0|$

Solution

a. $|34| = 34$ 34 is 34 units from 0.

b. $|-16| = 16$ -16 is 16 units from 0.

c. $|3.5| = 3.5$ 3.5 is 3.5 units from 0.

d. $\left|-\dfrac{1}{2}\right| = \dfrac{1}{2}$ $-\dfrac{1}{2}$ is $\dfrac{1}{2}$ unit from 0.

e. $|0| = 0$ 0 is 0 units from 0.

The checks for Examples 7a, 7b, and 7d are shown in Figure 1.3. ∎

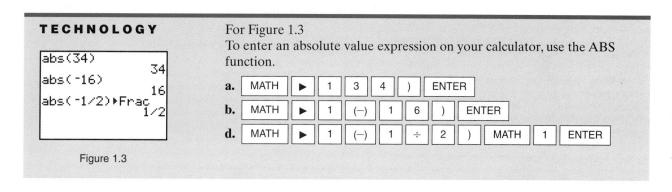

TECHNOLOGY

```
abs(34)
                    34
abs(-16)
                    16
abs(-1/2)▶Frac
                   1/2
```

Figure 1.3

For Figure 1.3
To enter an absolute value expression on your calculator, use the ABS function.

a. | MATH | ▶ | 1 | 3 | 4 |) | ENTER |

b. | MATH | ▶ | 1 | (−) | 1 | 6 |) | ENTER |

d. | MATH | ▶ | 1 | (−) | 1 | ÷ | 2 |) | MATH | 1 | ENTER |

EXAMPLE 8   Mount McKinley is 20,320 feet above sea level. Rounded to the nearest 10 feet, the depth of Agulhas Basin in the Indian Ocean is the same distance below sea level.

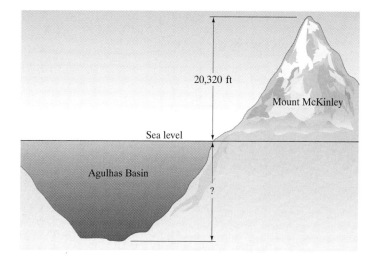

20,320 ft

Sea level

Mount McKinley

Agulhas Basin

?

Write an expression, using an absolute value symbol and a rational number, to represent the distance Agulhas Basin is from sea level. Evaluate the expression.

Solution

The absolute value symbol means the distance from 0, or in this case, sea level. Therefore, the distance, in feet, Agulhas Basin is from sea level is $|-20,320|$ or 20,320 feet. Agulhas Basin's elevation is 20,320 feet below sea level. ∎

Experiencing Algebra the Checkup Way

In exercises 1–4 evaluate.

1. $|-15|$ **2.** $|-3.3|$ **3.** $\left|\dfrac{2}{7}\right|$ **4.** $\left|-\dfrac{5}{3}\right|$

5. According to *The Book of Lists*, the coldest temperature recorded on Earth was at Vostok, Antarctica, registering 126.9°F below zero. Write an expression, using an absolute value symbol and a rational number, to represent the number of degrees Fahrenheit that this temperature is away from zero.

6. Write the keystrokes needed to find the following absolute value: $\left|-3\frac{3}{4}\right|$.
What is the result?

7. What does the absolute value of a number represent?

---

6 Evaluating Opposites   Two numbers with different signs but the same absolute value, meaning the same distance from 0, are called **opposites**. The opposite of a positive number is a negative number. The opposite of a negative number is a positive number. To write an opposite expression, enclose the expression in a set of parentheses, ( ), with a negative sign in front of it. In the preceding discussion, 6 and −6 are both 6 units from 0; therefore, 6 and −6 are opposites. For example, the opposite of 6 is written $-(6) = -6$. The opposite of −6 is written $-(-6) = 6$.

EXAMPLE 9   Evaluate.

a. $-(71)$ **b.** $-(-19)$ **c.** $-(0)$

d. $-\left(1\dfrac{1}{2}\right)$ **e.** $-\left|-\dfrac{3}{4}\right|$ **f.** $-(-(75))$

Solution

a. $-(71) = -71$ −71 is the same distance from 0 as 71.

b. $-(-19) = 19$ 19 is the same distance from 0 as −19.

c. $-(0) = 0$ 0 is the same distance from 0 as 0.

d. $-\left(1\dfrac{1}{2}\right) = -1\dfrac{1}{2}$ $-1\frac{1}{2}$ is the same distance from 0 as $1\frac{1}{2}$.

e. $-\left|-\dfrac{3}{4}\right| = -\dfrac{3}{4}$ Evaluate the absolute value of $-\frac{3}{4}$ and obtain $\frac{3}{4}$. Then take the opposite of $\frac{3}{4}$ and obtain $-\frac{3}{4}$.

f. $-(-(75)) = 75$ Evaluate the opposite of 75 and obtain -75. Next, the opposite of -75 is 75. In other words, the opposite of the opposite of a number is the number itself.

 Helping Hand When evaluating an expression with more than one set of parentheses, you should always work from the inside out. This procedure will be explained in more detail later.

The checks for Example 9 are shown in Figure 1.4a and Figure 1.4b. ∎

TECHNOLOGY

```
-(71)
              -71
-(-19)
               19
-(0)
                0
```

Figure 1.4a

```
-(1+1/2)▶Frac
              -3/2
-abs(-3/4)▶Frac
              -3/4
-(-(75))
               75
```

Figure 1.4b

To enter an opposite of an expression on the calculator, use $(-)$ and a pair of parentheses, $(\ )$.

Enter $\boxed{(-)}$ $\boxed{(}$ the number $\boxed{)}$.

For Figure 1.4a

a. $\boxed{(-)}$ $\boxed{(}$ $\boxed{7}$ $\boxed{1}$ $\boxed{)}$ $\boxed{\text{ENTER}}$

b. $\boxed{(-)}$ $\boxed{(}$ $\boxed{(-)}$ $\boxed{1}$ $\boxed{9}$ $\boxed{)}$ $\boxed{\text{ENTER}}$

c. $\boxed{(-)}$ $\boxed{(}$ $\boxed{0}$ $\boxed{)}$ $\boxed{\text{ENTER}}$

For Figure 1.4b

d. $\boxed{(-)}$ $\boxed{(}$ $\boxed{1}$ $\boxed{+}$ $\boxed{1}$ $\boxed{\div}$ $\boxed{2}$ $\boxed{)}$ $\boxed{\text{MATH}}$ $\boxed{1}$ $\boxed{\text{ENTER}}$

The improper fraction form of the mixed number $-1\frac{1}{2}$ is shown for Example 8d.

e. $\boxed{(-)}$ $\boxed{\text{MATH}}$ $\boxed{\blacktriangleright}$ $\boxed{1}$ $\boxed{(-)}$ $\boxed{3}$ $\boxed{\div}$ $\boxed{4}$ $\boxed{)}$ $\boxed{\text{MATH}}$ $\boxed{1}$ $\boxed{\text{ENTER}}$

f. $\boxed{(-)}$ $\boxed{(}$ $\boxed{(-)}$ $\boxed{(}$ $\boxed{7}$ $\boxed{5}$ $\boxed{)}$ $\boxed{)}$ $\boxed{\text{ENTER}}$

EXAMPLE 10 Human body temperature is about 98°F. According to the *Guinness Book of World Records*, the coldest inhabited place is the Siberian village of Oymyakon, with an unofficial recorded temperature that is the opposite of the human body temperature. Write and evaluate an expression for the temperature of Oymyakon.

Solution

Oymyakon has a temperature that is the opposite of the human body temperature, 98°F. Therefore, an expression for the temperature is $-(98)$ or -98. The unofficial temperature in Oymyakon is -98°F. ∎

Application

In 1992, the U.S. national debt was about \$4.083 trillion. Write a rational number representation for this amount.

Discussion

A debt corresponds to a negative number. Therefore, the national debt in 1992 corresponds to −\$4,083,000,000,000 or −\$4.083 trillion. ∎

Experiencing Algebra the Checkup Way

In exercises 1–6, evaluate.

1. $-\left(3\frac{1}{3}\right)$

2. $-\left(-\frac{1}{2}\right)$

3. $-(-(15))$

4. $-|35|$

5. $-\left|-\frac{4}{7}\right|$

6. $-|0|$

7. Between 1980 and 1990, the population of Lowell, Massachusetts, increased by 11.9 percent. The population of Cleveland, Ohio, had the opposite change. Write and evaluate an expression for the percentage change in Cleveland's population.

8. What does the term *opposites* mean when referring to numbers? What symbol is used to indicate the opposite of a number?

PROBLEM SET 1.1

Experiencing Algebra the Exercise Way

Identify the possible sets of numbers (natural, whole, integer, or rational) to which each number belongs.

1. a. -15 **b.** 29   **c.** 1 million   **d.** $\frac{3}{7}$

2. a. 278   **b.** $-15\frac{2}{3}$ **c.** 5 billion   **d.** -14.2

3. a. 0   **b.** 12.75   **c.** $2\frac{4}{9}$ **d.** -8.35

4. a. $\frac{9}{3}$ **b.** -199 **c.** $-\frac{11}{15}$ **d.** 0.009

In exercises 5–10, write a rational-number representation for each situation.

5. In a poker game, a player wins \$3.00. On the second hand, the player wins \$1.75. On the next two hands, the player loses \$2.00 and \$1.25 respectively.

6. Stock investments are measured in fractions of full dollar amounts. On Monday, S & S stock rose $1\frac{1}{8}$ points; on Tuesday it dropped $\frac{3}{4}$ points; on Wednesday it dropped 2 points; on Thursday it rose $1\frac{7}{8}$ points; and on Friday it rose $1\frac{3}{4}$ points.

7. In managing a bank account, if funds are present in the account, the account is "in the black." If the account is "in the red," the account owes money. An account is in the red for \$345.67.

8. In 1988 the world record for running a marathon was established at 2 hours, 6 minutes, and 50 seconds. If a runner finishes a marathon in a longer time than this record, the time is recorded as a positive number of seconds above the record. If a runner beats this record, the time is recorded as a negative time below the record. A runner beats this record by 17 seconds.

9. On a true/false test, an instructor awards 5 points for every correct answer, deducts 5 points for each incorrect answer, and deducts 2 points for each unanswered question. A student answers a question correctly; a student answers a question incorrectly; a student leaves a question unanswered.

10. In the game of Hearts, at the end of the game, each heart won by a person counts as 1 point, but the player holding the queen of spades loses 13 points. A player has won 2 hearts at the end of the game; a player has the queen of spades at the end of the game.

11. On the number line, between what two integers would you graph the rational number $\frac{17}{3}$?

12. On the number line, between what two integers would you graph the rational number $-\frac{3}{2}$?

13. Graph the following numbers on a number line.

$$-2, \ 1.5, \ \frac{1}{2}, \ -3.5, \ \frac{9}{4}, \ -1\frac{1}{4}, \ -\frac{4}{5}, \ 4$$

14. Graph the following numbers on a number line.

$$\frac{7}{2}, \ -2.25, \ -1.5, \ 0.5, \ 2, \ -2\frac{1}{4}, \ -1, \ -\frac{1}{5}$$

Use one of the symbols $>$, $<$, or $=$ to compare the two numbers.

15. -9 _____ -5

16. -7 _____ -4

17. 0 _____ -6

18. 0 _____ 11

19. 5 _____ 3

20. 12 _____ 9

21. $-\frac{1}{2}$ _____ $-\frac{2}{5}$

22. $-\frac{1}{3}$ _____ $-\frac{2}{7}$

23. $\frac{3}{7}$ _____ $\frac{7}{10}$

24. $\frac{3}{8}$ _____ $\frac{2}{7}$

25. $2\frac{3}{5}$ _____ $-2\frac{3}{5}$

26. $-4\frac{3}{7}$ _____ $4\frac{3}{7}$

27. $1\frac{4}{5}$ _____ 1.8

28. $2\frac{2}{5}$ _____ 2.4

29. -3.7 _____ -5.8

30. -6.2 _____ -4.6

31. 1.7 _____ 3.2

32. 4.1 _____ 3.9

Use your calculator to determine whether each statement is true or false.

33. $32 < 45$

34. $91 > 96$

35. $-13 > -7$

36. $-5 < -7$

37. $0 < -9$

38. $0 > -12$

39. $\frac{2}{3} > \frac{5}{7}$

40. $\frac{3}{5} > \frac{5}{8}$

41. $-\frac{1}{6} < -\frac{6}{7}$

42. $-\frac{4}{9} < -\frac{9}{13}$

43. $\frac{5}{4} > 1.25$

44. $1.8 > \frac{9}{5}$

45. $\frac{1}{15} > 0.15$

46. $5.7 > \frac{5}{7}$

47. $-4.6 > -4.7$

48. $-8.3 < -8.4$ **49.** $1.87 > 1.89$ **50.** $3.75 < 3.76$

Write an equivalent order relation for each statement.

51. $0.7 > 0.295$ **52.** $-2.56 < 0.06$ **53.** $-5 < -1$

54. $25 > 24$ **55.** $\dfrac{2}{5} = 0.4$ **56.** $-0.86 = -\dfrac{43}{50}$

In exercises 57–74, evaluate.

57. $|15.34|$ **58.** $|25|$ **59.** $|-15.34|$

60. $|-25|$ **61.** $\left|-\left(-3\dfrac{1}{3}\right)\right|$ **62.** $|-(-25)|$

63. $\left|-\left(-\left(-3\dfrac{1}{3}\right)\right)\right|$ **64.** $|-(-(-25))|$ **65.** $-|23|$

66. $-|25|$ **67.** $-|-23|$ **68.** $-|-25|$

69. $-(15)$ **70.** $-\left(\dfrac{1}{2}\right)$ **71.** $-(-25)$

72. $-(-35)$ **73.** $-\left(-\left(-\dfrac{3}{2}\right)\right)$ **74.** $-\left(-\left(-\dfrac{5}{4}\right)\right)$

75. In 1993, the 10th-ranked company on the Fortune 500 list was Texaco, reporting a profit of $712 million. At the same time, the 36th-ranked company, AlliedSignal, reported an opposite value as a loss. Write and evaluate an expression for the loss.

76. In comparing the performance of equity fund groups, Capital Appreciation Funds reported a gain of 8.28% in its 1992 returns. At the same time, Health/Biotechnology Funds reported an opposite value as a loss. Write and evaluate an expression for the loss.

Experiencing Algebra the Calculator Way

Use your calculator to determine whether each order relation is true or false.

1. $-193,987 < -194,879$ **2.** $\dfrac{123}{579} > \dfrac{296}{978}$ **3.** $15\dfrac{11}{19} < 15\dfrac{9}{16}$

4. $\dfrac{119}{250} > 0.476$ **5.** $-\dfrac{149}{275} < -\dfrac{356}{567}$ **6.** $-13.0987 > -13.0879$

7. $-\dfrac{129}{500} = -0.2585$ **8.** $12.368 = \dfrac{1546}{125}$ **9.** $|-1.5| = 1.5$

10. $|-1.5| = -1.5$ **11.** $\left|-\dfrac{3}{2}\right| = -1.5$ **12.** $\left|-\dfrac{3}{2}\right| = 1.5$

13. $|-4| = -4$ **14.** $-|4| = -4$

Experiencing Algebra the Group Way

1. It's a good idea to get to know your classmates so that you can work together on some of your mathematics assignments. Take a few minutes of class time now to introduce yourself to four other students in the class. Tell those students something about your past experiences with mathematics, and one personal fact about yourself. If you feel comfortable doing so, exchange phone numbers in case you would like to discuss your mathematics work over the phone. This will also help you in case you miss a class and need to find out what was discussed or assigned for that day.

2. Draw an enlarged representation of the number line from −1 to 1, with 10 increments between each integer, as shown.

Then graph the following numbers on the number line.

$$-0.9, \ 0.75, \ \frac{4}{5}, \ -\frac{3}{10}, \ \frac{5}{8}, \ \frac{3}{13}, \ -\frac{7}{9}, \ 0.333\ldots, \ -0.62$$

Explain to the class how you positioned the plotted points.

Experiencing Algebra the Write Way

How do you feel about mathematics? Has it always been an easy subject for you or have you always struggled with it? This is your chance to tell your instructor about your feelings toward the subject. Write a short letter to your instructor about your feelings toward math. In the letter, be sure to give reasons for your feelings—either good or bad past experiences with a math class, a math instructor, or whatever. Suggest to your instructor what would be helpful to you and what would cause you problems in this class. Describe any personal situations that might affect your study of mathematics, such as work, family responsibilities, or course load. Explain how you plan to handle these situations.

1.2 Addition

Objectives
1 Discover the rules for addition of rational numbers.
2 Illustrate the rules for addition of rational numbers.
3 Evaluate the sum of rational numbers.
4 Model real-world situations using a sum of rational numbers.

Application

The ceiling on the U.S. national debt in 1981 was $1.08 trillion. In 1990, the ceiling was raised an additional amount of $3.07 trillion. Determine the new national debt ceiling in 1990.

After completing this section, we will discuss this application further. See page 25.

When we add two rational numbers, we obtain a **sum**. The numbers that we add are called **addends**. We will find these terms helpful as we discuss the rules for adding rational numbers.

$$8 \ + \ 4 \ = 12$$
addend + addend = sum

1 Discovering Addition Rules

In this text, we use the calculator to do simple problems quickly so that we can use the results to discover rules of mathematics. The rules of mathematics do not depend on the calculator, and the rules we discover are more basic and fundamental in mathematics than calculator operations. In fact, the people who designed and built your calculator used these rules to do so.

When we add two rational numbers, we might have any of four possible combinations. The two numbers may be both positive, or both negative, or a positive and a negative, or a negative and a positive. In order to discover rules for adding these combinations, complete the following sets of exercises with your calculator. (Remember to use the $\boxed{(-)}$ for a negative number.)

D I S C O V E R Y   1

Adding Two Positive Rational Numbers

Evaluate each expression and compare the results obtained in the left column to the corresponding results in the right column.

1. a. $6 + 2 = $ _____   **b.** $|6| + |2| = $ _____

2. a. $3 + 9 = $ _____   **b.** $|3| + |9| = $ _____

3. a. $1.2 + 2.5 = $ _____   **b.** $|1.2| + |2.5| = $ _____

4. a. $\dfrac{1}{2} + \dfrac{1}{4} = $ _____   **b.** $\left|\dfrac{1}{2}\right| + \left|\dfrac{1}{4}\right| = $ _____

Write in your own words a rule for writing the sum of two positive rational numbers.

In the column on the left, we add two positive rational numbers. Each sum results in a positive number. In the column on the right, we add the absolute values of the addends. The results are the same as on the left.

D I S C O V E R Y   2

Adding Two Negative Rational Numbers

Evaluate each expression and compare the results obtained in the left column to the corresponding results in the right column.

1. a. $-6 + (-2) = $ _____   **b.** $|-6| + |-2| = $ _____

2. a. $-3 + (-9) = $ _____   **b.** $|-3| + |-9| = $ _____

3. a. $-1.2 + (-2.5) = $ _____   **b.** $|-1.2| + |-2.5| = $ _____

4. a. $-\dfrac{1}{2} + \left(-\dfrac{1}{4}\right) = $ _____   **b.** $\left|-\dfrac{1}{2}\right| + \left|-\dfrac{1}{4}\right| = $ _____

Write in your own words a rule for writing the sum of two negative rational numbers.

In the column on the left, we add two negative rational numbers. Each sum results in a negative number. In the column on the right, we add the absolute values of the addends. The results are the opposite of those on the left.

D I S C O V E R Y   3

Adding a Positive and a Negative Rational Number

Evaluate each expression and compare the results obtained in the left column to the corresponding results in the right column.

1. a. $6 + (-2) = $ _____   **b.** Since $|6| > |-2|$, then

$|6| - |-2| = $ _____

Continued

2. a. $3 + (-9) =$ _____   **b.** Since $|-9| > |3|$, then
$$|-9| - |3| =$$ _____

3. a. $1.2 + (-2.5) =$ _____   **b.** Since $|-2.5| > |1.2|$, then
$$|-2.5| - |1.2| =$$ _____

4. a. $\dfrac{1}{2} + \left(-\dfrac{1}{4}\right) =$ _____   **b.** Since $\left|\dfrac{1}{2}\right| > \left|-\dfrac{1}{4}\right|$, then
$$\left|\dfrac{1}{2}\right| - \left|-\dfrac{1}{4}\right| =$$ _____

Write in your own words a rule for writing the sum of a positive and a negative rational number.

    In the column on the left, we add a positive and a negative rational number. Each sum results in a number whose sign is the same as the sign of the addend with the larger absolute value. In the column on the right, we subtract the smaller absolute value addend from the larger absolute value addend. The results are the same as the absolute value of the sum in the left column.

D I S C O V E R Y   4

Adding a Negative and a Positive Rational Number
Evaluate each expression and compare the results obtained in the left column to the corresponding results in the right column.

1. a. $-6 + 2 =$ _____   **b.** Since $|-6| > |2|$, then
$$|-6| - |2| =$$ _____

2. a. $-3 + 9 =$ _____   **b.** Since $|9| > |-3|$, then
$$|9| - |-3| =$$ _____

3. a. $-1.2 + 2.5 =$ _____   **b.** Since $|2.5| > |-1.2|$, then
$$|2.5| - |-1.2| =$$ _____

4. a. $-\dfrac{1}{2} + \dfrac{1}{4} =$ _____   **b.** Since $\left|-\dfrac{1}{2}\right| > \left|\dfrac{1}{4}\right|$, then
$$\left|-\dfrac{1}{2}\right| - \left|\dfrac{1}{4}\right| =$$ _____

Write in your own words a rule for writing the sum of a negative and a positive rational number.

    In the column on the left, we add a negative and a positive rational number. Each sum results in a number whose sign is the same as the sign of the addend with the larger absolute value. In the column on the right, we subtract the smaller absolute value addend from the larger absolute value addend. The results are the same as the absolute value of the sum on the left.

    The preceding discoveries suggest the following rules for addition.

Addition of Rational Numbers
To add two rational numbers with like signs (both positive or both negative):

- Add the absolute values of the addends.
- The sign of the sum is the sign of the addends.

(Continued)

To add two rational numbers with unlike signs (one positive and one negative):

- Subtract the smaller absolute value addend from the larger absolute value addend.
- The sign of the sum is the sign of the addend with the larger absolute value.

To add 0 and any rational number, the result is the rational number.

Experiencing Algebra the Checkup Way

1. When adding two rational numbers with like signs, what will be the sign of the result? What do you do with the absolute values of the addends?

2. When adding two rational numbers with unlike signs, what will be the sign of the result? What do you do with the absolute values of the addends?

---

2 Illustrating Addition Rules

To help you understand the addition rules we have just discovered, let's add rational numbers by using a number line. This will help you visualize how the signs of the addends determine the sign of the sum. We will do the first exercise in each of the previous discovery sets on a number line.

Adding Two Positive Rational Numbers   To add two rational positive numbers, such as $6 + 2$, we begin at 0 and move in the positive direction (to the right) 6 units on the number line. We then move in the positive direction (to the right) 2 units on the number line. The resulting position on the number line represents the sum of the two numbers, which is 8 in this case. This is positive because both moves were in the positive direction. The absolute value of this sum is the sum of the absolute values of the addends, because both moves were in the same direction from 0.

Addition: $6 + 2$

Adding Two Negative Rational Numbers   To add two negative rational numbers, such as $-6 + -2$, we begin at 0 and move in the negative direction (to the left) 6 units on the number line. We then move in the negative direction (to the left) 2 units on the number line. The resulting position on the number line represents the sum of the two numbers, which is -8 in this case. This is negative because both moves were in the negative direction. The absolute value of this sum is the sum of the absolute values of the addends, because both moves were in the same direction from 0.

Addition: $-6 + -2$

Adding a Positive and a Negative Rational Number   To add a positive rational number and a negative rational number, such as $6 + -2$, we begin at 0 and move in the positive direction (to the right) 6 units on the number line.

We then move in the negative direction (to the left) 2 units on the number line. The resulting position on the number line represents the sum of the two numbers, which is 4 in this case. This is positive because although the moves were in opposite directions, the larger move was in the positive direction. The absolute value of this sum is the difference in the absolute values of the addends, because the moves were in different directions and overlapped each other.

Addition: $6 + -2$

Adding a Negative and a Positive Rational Number   To add a negative rational number and a positive rational number, such as $-6 + 2$, we begin at 0 and move in the negative direction (to the left) 6 units on the number line. We then move in the positive direction (to the right) 2 units on the number line. The resulting position on the number line represents the sum of the two numbers, which is -4 in this case. This is negative because although the moves were in opposite directions, the larger move was in the negative direction. The absolute value of this sum is the difference in the absolute values of the addends, because the moves were in different directions and overlapped each other.

Addition: $-6 + 2$

   Experiencing Algebra the Checkup Way

In exercises 1–4, use number lines to illustrate the additions.

1. $2 + 3$ **2.** $-1 + (-2)$ **3.** $5 + (-3)$ **4.** $-7 + 3$

5. Explain how you would move on the number line when adding a positive addend to a number.

6. Explain how you would move on the number line when adding a negative addend to a number.

7. How is the sign of the sum of two numbers determined when both addends are positive numbers? What if both addends are negative numbers? What if one addend is a positive number and the other is a negative number?

---

3   Evaluating Sums of Rational Numbers

We are now ready to use the addition rules we have discovered and illustrated. Let's begin with examples of integers to prepare us for the more complicated exercises that follow.

EXAMPLE 1   Add.

a. $8 + (-2)$ **b.** $-6 + (-5)$
c. $-7 + 3$ **d.** $-8 + 12$

Solution

a. $8 + (-2) = 6$ Unlike signs: The sum is positive because $|8| > |-2|$ and 8 is positive. The absolute value of the sum is $|8| - |-2| = 6$. Therefore, the sum is positive 6.

b. $-6 + (-5) = -11$ Like signs: The sum is the same sign as the addends; negative. The absolute value of the sum is $|-6| + |-5| = 11$. Therefore, the sum is negative 11.

c. $-7 + 3 = -4$ Unlike signs: The sum is negative because $|-7| > |3|$ and -7 is negative. The absolute value of the sum is $|-7| - |3| = 4$. Therefore, the sum is negative 4.

d. $-8 + 12 = 4$ Unlike signs: The sum is positive because $|12| > |-8|$ and 12 is positive. The absolute value of the sum is $|12| - |-8| = 4$. Therefore, the sum is positive 4.

The checks for Example 1 are shown in Figure 1.5a and Figure 1.5b. ∎

TECHNOLOGY

Figure 1.5a

Figure 1.5b

For Figure 1.5a

Note: Negative numbers may be entered without the ( ). The parentheses are written in the exercise simply to separate the plus sign and the negative sign for clarity, and serve no mathematical purpose.

a. | 8 | | + | | (−) | | 2 | | ENTER |

b. | (−) | | 6 | | + | | (−) | | 5 | | ENTER |

For Figure 1.5b

c. | (−) | | 7 | | + | | 3 | | ENTER |

d. | (−) | | 8 | | + | | 1 | | 2 | | ENTER |

EXAMPLE 2   Add.

a. $-4.89 + 6.4$

b. $-12.5 + (-2)$

c. $-8.9 + 0$

d. $\dfrac{1}{2} + \left(-\dfrac{2}{3}\right)$

e. $-1\dfrac{2}{3} + 2\dfrac{3}{5}$

Solution

a. $-4.89 + 6.4 = 1.51$ Unlike signs: The sum is positive because $|6.4| > |-4.89|$ and 6.4 is positive. The absolute value of the sum is $|6.4| - |-4.89| = 1.51$. Therefore, the sum is positive 1.51.

b. $-12.5 + (-2) = -14.5$ Like signs: The sum is the same sign as the addends: negative. The absolute value of the sum is $|-12.5| + |-2| = 14.5$. Therefore, the sum is negative 14.5.

c. $-8.9 + 0 = -8.9$ We are adding a rational number and 0. The sum is the number itself, -8.9.

d. $\dfrac{1}{2} + \left(-\dfrac{2}{3}\right) =$ Unlike signs:

$\dfrac{3}{6} + \left(-\dfrac{4}{6}\right) = -\dfrac{1}{6}$ First, convert the fractions to their lowest common denominator, $\frac{1}{2} = \frac{3}{6}$ and $-\frac{2}{3} = -\frac{4}{6}$. The sum is negative because $\left|-\frac{4}{6}\right| > \left|\frac{3}{6}\right|$ and $-\frac{4}{6}$ is negative. The absolute value of the sum is $\left|-\frac{4}{6}\right| - \left|\frac{3}{6}\right| = \frac{1}{6}$. Therefore, the sum is negative $\frac{1}{6}$.

e. $-1\dfrac{2}{3} + 2\dfrac{3}{5} =$ Unlike signs:

$-1\dfrac{10}{15} + 2\dfrac{9}{15} =$ First, convert the fractions to their lowest common denominator, 15.

$-\dfrac{25}{15} + \dfrac{39}{15} = \dfrac{14}{15}$ Then, convert the mixed numbers to improper fractions. The sum is positive because $\left|\frac{39}{15}\right| > \left|\frac{-25}{15}\right|$ and $\frac{39}{15}$ is positive. The absolute value of the sum is $\left|\frac{39}{15}\right| - \left|\frac{-25}{15}\right| = \frac{14}{15}$. Therefore, the sum is positive $\frac{14}{15}$.

The checks for Example 2 are shown in Figure 1.6a and Figure 1.6b. ∎

TECHNOLOGY

Figure 1.6a

Figure 1.6b

For Figure 1.6a

For Figure 1.6b
Note: Enter fractions in sets of parentheses for proper grouping and ease in reading. Mixed numbers are written as addition expressions. Negative mixed numbers have the negative sign outside the parentheses.

To evaluate expressions with more than one addition symbol perform the operations in order, left to right. That is, find the sum of the first two numbers and add it to the third number. Add the resulting sum to the next number and keep going until you have added all the numbers.

EXAMPLE 3 Evaluate.

a. $13 + 15 + (-17) + 14 + (-16)$
b. $-2.5 + 3 + (-7.83) + 14.6$
c. $-\dfrac{3}{4} + \left(-\dfrac{1}{2}\right) + \dfrac{2}{3} + \dfrac{1}{4}$

Solution

a. $13 + 15 + (-17) + 14 + (-16) =$ Add the numbers left to right.
$28 + (-17) + 14 + (-16) =$
$11 + 14 + (-16) =$
$25 + (-16) = 9$

b. $-2.5 + 3 + (-7.83) + 14.6 =$ Add the numbers left to right.
$.5 + (-7.83) + 14.6 =$
$-7.33 + 14.6 = 7.27$

c. $-\dfrac{3}{4} + \left(-\dfrac{1}{2}\right) + \dfrac{2}{3} + \dfrac{1}{4} =$ First find a common denominator for all fractions.

$-\dfrac{9}{12} + \left(-\dfrac{6}{12}\right) + \dfrac{8}{12} + \dfrac{3}{12} =$ Add left to right.

$-\dfrac{15}{12} + \dfrac{8}{12} + \dfrac{3}{12} =$

$-\dfrac{7}{12} + \dfrac{3}{12} =$

$-\dfrac{4}{12} = -\dfrac{1}{3}$ Reduce answer.

Another way to do Example 4a is to determine the sum of the positive numbers and the sum of the negative numbers.

$$13 + 15 + 14 = 42$$
$$-17 + -16 = -33$$

Then add these results.

$$42 + -33 = 9$$

Check Examples 4b and 4c with this method. ■

 Experiencing Algebra the Checkup Way

Add.

1. $-43 + 77$ **2.** $-8.75 + 3$ **3.** $0 + 4.5$

4. $-1\dfrac{1}{3} + \left(-2\dfrac{2}{3}\right)$ **5.** $\dfrac{-5}{7} + \dfrac{3}{4}$

In exercises 6–7 evaluate.

6. $21 + 14 + (-16) + 43 + (-19)$ **7.** $\dfrac{-1}{2} + \left(\dfrac{-3}{4}\right) + \dfrac{1}{8} + \left(\dfrac{-1}{12}\right)$

8. When using your calculator to add fractions or mixed numbers, it is advisable to enclose the number in parentheses. Explain why this is so.

4 Modeling the Real World   The addition rules for rational numbers are the same rules that govern situations involving addition in our daily lives. Situations that involve totals or balances, such as totaling an amount spent in a store or balancing a bank account, can be written as rational expressions. Once we've decided how to represent real data as rational expressions, we add the expressions and obtain a sum.

EXAMPLE 4 Joe opened a new bank account with a deposit of $250.00. He wrote checks for $35.68, $68.50, and $112.72 before making another deposit for $250.00. Write and evaluate a sum to represent the amount of money in Joe's account after these transactions.

Solution

We want to write an addition expression. Deposits into a bank account represent positive numbers. Checks written on an account represent negative numbers. Therefore, we have the addition problem:

deposit + wrote check + wrote check + wrote check + deposit
250.00 + (−35.68) + (−68.50) + (−112.72) + 250.00

If we add two numbers at a time, as we would in our checkbook, we have

$$250.00 + (-35.68) = 214.32$$
$$214.32 + (-68.50) = 145.82$$
$$145.82 + (-112.72) = 33.10$$
$$33.10 + 250.00 = 283.10$$

Or, we can add all positive numbers (deposits) and all negative numbers (amount of checks) and then find the sum of the results.

$$250.00 + 250.00 = 500.00$$
$$-35.68 + (-68.50) + (-112.72) = -216.90$$
$$500.00 + (-216.90) = 283.10$$

Joe had $283.10 in his account after the transactions. ∎

Application

The ceiling on the U.S. national debt in 1981 was $1.08 trillion. In 1990, the ceiling was raised an additional amount of $3.07 trillion. Determine the new national debt ceiling in 1990.

Discussion

A debt corresponds to a negative number. Therefore, the national debt ceiling in 1981 corresponds to −1.08 and the additional debt translates to −3.07 (measured in trillions of dollars). The new national debt ceiling corresponds to the sum of these numbers.

debt + debt
−1.08 + (−3.07) = −4.15

This translates into a ceiling on the national debt of $4.15 trillion or $4,150,000,000,000. ∎

✓ Experiencing Algebra the Checkup Way

Bob opened an account with a deposit of $455.76. He then wrote checks for $12.56, $35.78, $255.65, and $267.87. He's afraid he has overdrawn his account, and may need to make a deposit. Write and evaluate a sum to determine his balance. What is the minimum amount, if any, he must deposit in order not to have his account overdrawn?

PROBLEM SET 1.2

 Experiencing Algebra the Exercise Way

Add.

1. $-7 + 9$

2. $-17 + 29$

3. $0 + (-13)$

4. $-15 + 0$

5. $-19 + (-12)$

6. $-22 + (-36)$

7. $15 + (-15)$

8. $-8 + 8$

9. $52 + (-13)$

10. $12 + (-45)$

11. $32 + (-579)$

12. $703 + (-21)$

13. $2.7 + 3.96$

14. $0.06 + 3.1$

15. $1.2 + (-2.5)$

16. $-5.5 + 2.7$

17. $-2.73 + 4.1$

18. $3.9 + (-1.81)$

19. $-1.1 + (-2.27)$

20. $-3.5 + (-7.9)$

21. $-1.25 + 0$

22. $0 + (-23.5)$

23. $1.23 + (-1.23)$

24. $2.7 + (-2.7)$

25. $-\dfrac{3}{5} + \left(-\dfrac{1}{2}\right)$

26. $-\dfrac{1}{4} + \left(-\dfrac{3}{7}\right)$

27. $-\dfrac{7}{9} + \dfrac{1}{6}$

28. $-\dfrac{3}{8} + \dfrac{1}{12}$

29. $\dfrac{2}{3} + \left(-\dfrac{2}{9}\right)$

30. $\dfrac{5}{6} + \left(-\dfrac{1}{3}\right)$

31. $\dfrac{2}{3} + 0$

32. $0 + \left(-\dfrac{3}{4}\right)$

33. $\dfrac{1}{3} + \left(-\dfrac{1}{3}\right)$

34. $-\dfrac{3}{7} + \dfrac{3}{7}$

35. $-2\dfrac{3}{4} + 3\dfrac{2}{3}$

36. $-1\dfrac{4}{5} + 4\dfrac{2}{3}$

37. $1 + \left(-4\dfrac{3}{4}\right)$

38. $2 + \left(-4\dfrac{1}{2}\right)$

Add.

39. $-13 + (-25) + (-26)$

40. $-52 + (-41) + (-5)$

41. $17 + (-23) + (-16) + 13$

42. $32 + (-55) + (-14) + 72$

43. $1 + (-2.3) + (-5.71)$

44. $4.3 + (-2.31) + (-9)$

45. $-\dfrac{1}{2} + \dfrac{1}{3} + \left(-\dfrac{1}{4}\right)$

46. $\dfrac{2}{5} + \left(-\dfrac{1}{2}\right) + \left(-\dfrac{3}{4}\right)$

47. $1124 + (-923) + 2305 + (-1156) + (-109)$

48. $3562 + (-901) + (-805) + (-3231) + 1020$

Write and evaluate a sum to represent each of the following situations. Interpret the result.

49. Lindsay's parents opened a college savings account at the credit union. The initial deposit was $1500. For each of the next 3 months they deposited $150. However, they withdrew $75 for a savings bond, $500 for a stock investment opportunity, and $200 for a municipal bond. The credit union paid the account $12 in interest for the 3-month period. What is the net balance of Lindsay's account?

50. At her birth, Mallory's grandparents opened a savings account for her by making an initial deposit of $500. Mallory's parents added deposits of $75, $50, and $100, received as gifts from relatives. Her parents withdrew $125 to make a premium payment on a new insurance policy. The bank added $35 interest at the end of the first year. What is the balance in the account?

51. According to the 1990 census, the second largest county in the United States was Cook County, Illinois. However, the county experienced a drop in population of 148,561 from its 1980 census of 5,253,628 people. What was the 1990 census for this county?

52. According to the 1990 census, the largest drop in population for the top 50 counties occurred in Wayne County, Michigan, which lost 226,156 people from its 1980 census of 2,337,843 people. What was the 1990 census for this county?

53. Heath is quarterbacking a football game. On his first play, he runs for a gain of 8 yards. On the next play, he is sacked for a loss of $4\frac{3}{4}$ yards. On the third play, he passes for a gain of $22\frac{1}{2}$ yards. What is the net gain or loss on these three plays?

54. In scoring a touchdown, Heath ran the following plays: He ran for a gain of $5\frac{1}{4}$ yards, was sacked for a loss of $6\frac{1}{2}$ yards, completed a pass of 32 yards, and ran $2\frac{1}{4}$ yards into the end zone. What was his net yardage for this drive?

55. Karin is a saleswoman with a weekly quota of $5000 in sales. She keeps track of her sales by noting how much she is above her quota (a positive number) or how much she is below her quota (a negative number). Last month her weekly sales in relation to her quota were: $255 below, $375 above, $575 below, and $1525 above. What was Karin's overall standing for the month in terms of her quota? Is she above or below quota? How can you tell?

56. For 6 weeks, Karin's sales in relation to her quota were: $385 above, $285 above, $555 below, $405 below, $265 above, and $575 above. She keeps track of her sales by noting sales above quota as a positive number and sales below quota as a negative number. What was her overall performance in sales? Is she above quota for the 6-week period or below?

57. On a diet and exercise program, Beth lost 2.5 pounds the first week, gained 1.25 pounds the next week, then lost 1.8 pounds the next week, and lost 2.5 pounds the last week. What was her overall change in weight over the 4 weeks?

58. Brett went on a diet and exercise program. He lost 3.5 pounds the first week, lost 2.6 pounds the second week, gained 2.25 pounds the next week, and stayed the same the fourth week. What was his overall change in weight over the 4 weeks?

59. On an extended auto trip, Liu drove her car 378 miles the first day, 322 miles the second day, and 218 miles the third day. What was the total distance of the trip?

60. On a bike tour in Vermont, a troop of bikers traveled 33.6 miles the first day, 25.9 miles the second day, and 28.3 miles the third day. What was the total distance of the tour?

61. Julio started a poker game with 25 identical poker chips. On the first hand he won 8 more chips. On the second hand he lost 12 chips. On the third hand he won 17 chips. How many chips did he have at the end of the third hand?

62. Julianne started the day with $72.38 in a petty-cash box. She paid out $5.95 for coffee and $12.75 for a birthday cake. She collected a total of $35.00 from the office staff for their monthly contributions to the fund. She spent $7.81 for miscellaneous paper products for the office kitchen. What was the balance of the petty-cash fund at the end of the day?

63. A cookie recipe requires $\frac{1}{2}$ cup of granulated sugar, $\frac{1}{4}$ cup of brown sugar, 1 cup of sifted all-purpose flour, 1 cup of semisweet chocolate pieces, and $\frac{1}{2}$ cup of chopped nuts. How many cups of dry ingredients does the recipe use?

64. A quilting pattern requires $1\frac{1}{4}$ yards of solid blue material, $\frac{3}{4}$ yard of yellow floral material, $\frac{1}{2}$ yard of green floral material, and $2\frac{1}{4}$ yards of navy plaid material. How many yards of material does the pattern use?

 ## Experiencing Algebra the Calculator Way

A. Converting an Improper Fraction to a Mixed Number

When performing operations with mixed numbers, some calculators may present the result as an improper fraction. If the calculator does not provide an option to convert the improper fraction to a mixed number, the following procedure may be used.

    1. Convert the improper fraction to a decimal by dividing on the calculator.
    2. Subtract the integer part of the decimal (left of the decimal point) from the decimal on the calculator.
    3. Convert the remaining part of the decimal (right of the decimal point) to a fraction on the calculator.
    4. Add the integer part back to the fraction part to obtain the mixed number.

For example, convert the improper fraction $\frac{43}{15}$ to a mixed number.

    1. $\frac{43}{15}$ is 2.86666666 ... .
    2. $2.8666666666 \ldots - 2 = 0.8666666666 \ldots$
    3. $0.8666666666 \ldots$ MATH | 1 | ENTER yields $\frac{13}{15}$.
    4. $\frac{13}{15}$ added to 2 yields $2\frac{13}{15}$.

```
43/15
          2.866666667
Ans-2
           .8666666667
Ans►Frac
                 13/15
```

Convert the following improper fractions to mixed numbers using this approach.

1. $\dfrac{55}{7}$ **2.** $-\dfrac{295}{113}$ **3.** $\dfrac{1227}{487}$ **4.** $-\dfrac{108}{19}$

B. Using the Calculator to Perform Operations

Practice entering the following calculations into your calculator. Express your answers in fractional notation or round decimals to the nearest thousandth as appropriate.

1. $-\dfrac{171}{92} + \left(-\dfrac{170}{33}\right)$ **2.** $\dfrac{171}{92} + \left(-\dfrac{170}{33}\right)$ **3.** $-\dfrac{171}{92} + \dfrac{170}{33}$

4. $\dfrac{171}{92} + \dfrac{170}{33}$ **5.** $15\dfrac{17}{19} + 21\dfrac{13}{17}$ **6.** $15\dfrac{17}{19} + \left(-21\dfrac{13}{17}\right)$

7. $-15\dfrac{17}{19} + 21\dfrac{13}{17}$ **8.** $-15\dfrac{17}{19} + \left(-21\dfrac{13}{17}\right)$ **9.** $437.925 + (-108.0065)$

10. $-437.925 + (-108.0065)$ **11.** $-437.925 + 108.0065$ **12.** $437.925 + 108.0065$

13. $893,475 + 1,093,007$ **14.** $-893,475 + 1,093,007$ **15.** $893,475 + (-1,093,007)$

16. $-893,475 + (-1,093,007)$

Experiencing Algebra the Group Way

In your group, analyze the exercises in Part B of "Experiencing Algebra the Calculator Way." In exercises 1–4, what is the same? What is different? What pattern exists for the solutions to these four exercises? State what this analysis has taught you. Verify your conclusions by doing the same for exercises 5–8; for exercises 9–12; and for exercises 13–16. Report your findings to the class.

Experiencing Algebra the Write Way

In this section, we introduced the concept of adding as an operation that can be explained by movement along the number line. Discuss how this illustration either helped you to understand the concept of addition or confused you. Give reasons for your stance. Can you think of other methods for explaining the operation of addition? Try to describe one other example for understanding addition.

1.3   Subtraction

Objectives
1 Discover the rules for subtraction of rational numbers.
2 Illustrate the rules for subtraction of rational numbers.
3 Evaluate the difference of rational numbers.
4 Evaluate combinations of sums and differences.
5 Model real-world situations using a difference of rational numbers.

Application

In the last year of the Civil War, the U.S. national debt was $2.68 billion. The debt fell $1.53 billion in the next few years. Determine the new national debt after this fall.

After completing this section, we will discuss this application further. See page 37.

When two rational numbers are subtracted, we obtain a **difference**. The numbers that we subtract are called the **minuend** and **subtrahend**. We do not use these terms often, but they are useful for describing the process of subtraction.

$$10 \quad - \quad 4 \quad = \quad 6$$
minuend $-$ subtrahend $=$ difference

---

1   Discovering Subtraction Rules

Once again, we will use the calculator to explore the rules underlying mathematical operations. This time, we investigate the subtraction of rational numbers.

When we subtract two rational numbers, we might have any of four combinations. The two numbers may be both positive, or both negative, or a positive number and a negative number, or a negative number and a positive number. However, in the discoveries, we combine the last two combinations. Complete the following sets of exercises with your calculator. (Remember to use the ⎡(−)⎤ for a negative number and ⎡ − ⎤ for subtraction.)

DISCOVERY 5

Subtracting Two Positive Rational Numbers

Evaluate each expression and compare the result obtained in the left column to the corresponding results in the right column.

1. **a.** $6 - 2 =$ _____   **b.** $6 + (-2) =$ _____
2. **a.** $3 - 9 =$ _____   **b.** $3 + (-9) =$ _____
3. **a.** $1.2 - 2.5 =$ _____   **b.** $1.2 + (-2.5) =$ _____
4. **a.** $\dfrac{1}{2} - \dfrac{1}{4} =$ _____   **b.** $\dfrac{1}{2} + \left(\dfrac{-1}{4}\right) =$ _____

Write in your own words a rule for writing the difference of two positive rational numbers.

In the column on the left, we subtract two positive rational numbers. In the column on the right, we add the minuend and the opposite of the subtrahend. The results are the same in both columns.

DISCOVERY 6

Subtracting Two Negative Rational Numbers

Evaluate each expression and compare the results obtained in the left column to the corresponding results in the right column.

1. **a.** $-6 - (-2) =$ _____   **b.** $-6 + 2 =$ _____
2. **a.** $-3 - (-9) =$ _____   **b.** $-3 + 9 =$ _____
3. **a.** $-1.2 - (-2.5) =$ _____   **b.** $-1.2 + 2.5 =$ _____
4. **a.** $\dfrac{-1}{2} - \left(\dfrac{-1}{4}\right) =$ _____   **b.** $\dfrac{-1}{2} + \dfrac{1}{4} =$ _____

Write in your own words a rule for writing the difference of two negative rational numbers.

In the column on the left, we subtract two negative rational numbers. In the column on the right, we add the minuend and the opposite of the subtrahend. Again, the results are the same in both columns.

DISCOVERY 7

Subtracting Combinations of Positive and Negative Rational Numbers

Evaluate each expression and compare the results obtained in the left column to the corresponding results in the right column.

1. **a.** $6 - (-2) =$ _____   **b.** $6 + 2 =$ _____
2. **a.** $-3 - 9 =$ **b.** $-3 + (-9) =$ _____
3. **a.** $1.2 - (-2.5) =$ _____   **b.** $1.2 + 2.5 =$ _____
4. **a.** $\dfrac{-1}{2} - \dfrac{1}{4} =$ _____   **b.** $\dfrac{-1}{2} + \left(\dfrac{-1}{4}\right) =$ _____

Write in your own words a rule for writing the difference of a positive and a negative rational number.

In the column on the left, we subtract a positive and a negative rational number. In the column on the right, we add the minuend and the opposite of the subtrahend. Once again, the results are the same in both columns.

Note that the same rule was used to describe each of the three preceding discoveries. In fact, the same rule is used for all subtraction involving rational numbers.

> *Subtraction of Rational Numbers*
> To subtract two rational numbers, add the minuend to the opposite of the subtrahend.

Experiencing Algebra the Checkup Way

1. Explain how you would subtract two rational numbers.
2. Define the terms *minuend* and *subtrahend*.

---

2 Illustrating Subtraction Rules

To help you understand the addition rules we discovered, we added using a number line. Let's do the same for subtraction. This will help you visualize the rules. We will subtract the first exercise in each of the previous discovery sets on a number line.

Subtracting Two Positive Rational Numbers To subtract two positive rational numbers, such as $6 - 2$, we begin at 0 and move in the positive direction (to the right) 6 units on the number line. We then take away a positive 2, which results in a move in the negative direction (to the left) 2 units on the number line. The resulting position on the number line represents the difference of the two numbers, which is 4 in this case.

Subtraction: $6 - 2$

Subtracting Two Negative Rational Numbers To subtract two negative rational numbers, such as $-6 - (-2)$, we begin at 0 and move in the negative direction (to the left) 6 units on the number line. We then take away a negative 2, which results in a move in the positive direction (to the right) 2 units on the number line. The resulting position on the number line represents the difference of the two numbers, which is -4 in this case.

Subtraction: $-6 - (-2)$

Helping Hand Note carefully that subtracting a negative number results in a move in the positive direction on the number line. In this course we will often see that a double negative equals a positive.

Subtracting Combinations of Positive and Negative Rational Numbers To subtract a positive rational number and a negative rational number, such as $6 - (-2)$, we begin at 0 and move in the positive direction (to the right) 6 units on the number line. We then take away a negative 2, which results in a move in the positive direction (to the right) 2 units on the number line. The resulting position on the number line represents the difference of the two numbers, which is 8 in this case.

Subtraction: $6 - (-2)$

 ## Experiencing Algebra the Checkup Way

In exercises 1–4, use a number line to illustrate the subtractions.

1. $2 - 3$ **2.** $-1 - (-2)$ **3.** $5 - (-3)$ **4.** $-7 - 3$

5. Explain how you would move on the number line when subtracting a positive subtrahend from a number.

6. Explain how you would move on the number line when subtracting a negative subtrahend from a number.

---

3 Evaluating Differences We are now ready to use the subtraction rules we have discovered and illustrated. We first perform subtraction on integers in order to prepare ourselves for the more complicated problems that follow.

EXAMPLE 1 Subtract.

     a. $8 - 12$ **b.** $-9 - (-6)$
     c. $-7 - 3$ **d.** $4 - (-12)$

Solution

a. $8 - 12 =$ Change the subtraction to addition and take the opposite
       $8 + (-12) = -4$ of 12. Then add.

b. $-9 - (-6) =$ Change the subtraction to addition and take the opposite
       $-9 + 6 = -3$ of -6. Then add.

c. $-7 - 3 =$ Change the subtraction to addition and take the opposite
     $-7 + (-3) = -10$ of 3. Then add.

d. $4 - (-12) =$ Change the subtraction to addition and take the opposite
       $4 + 12 = 16$ of -12. Then add.

The checks for Example 1 are shown in Figure 1.7a and Figure 1.7b. ∎

TECHNOLOGY

Figure 1.7a

Figure 1.7b

For Figure 1.7a

Note: Negative numbers may be entered without the ( ) because the parentheses are written in the problem only to separate the minus sign and negative sign for clarity in reading.

a. | 8 | − | 1 | 2 | ENTER |

b. | (−) | 9 | − | (−) | 6 | ENTER |

For Figure 1.7b

c. | (−) | 7 | − | 3 | ENTER |

d. | 4 | − | (−) | 1 | 2 | ENTER |

EXAMPLE 2 Subtract.

a. $9.6 - (-3.8)$

b. $0 - (-8.9)$

c. $\dfrac{-3}{4} - \left(\dfrac{-1}{2}\right)$

d. $\dfrac{-2}{5} - \dfrac{1}{3}$

Solution

a. $9.6 - (-3.8) =$
$\qquad 9.6 + 3.8 = 13.4$ Add the opposite of −3.8.

b. $0 - (-8.9) =$
$\qquad 0 + 8.9 = 8.9$ Add the opposite of −8.9.

c. $\dfrac{-3}{4} - \left(\dfrac{-1}{2}\right) =$ Add the opposite of $\frac{-1}{2}$.

$\qquad \dfrac{-3}{4} + \dfrac{1}{2} =$ Change to the lowest common denominator (LCD) of 4 and 2.

$\qquad \dfrac{-3}{4} + \dfrac{2}{4} = \dfrac{-1}{4}$

d. $\qquad \dfrac{-2}{5} - \dfrac{1}{3} =$ Add the opposite of $\frac{1}{3}$.

$\qquad \dfrac{-2}{5} + \left(\dfrac{-1}{3}\right) =$ Change to the LCD of 5 and 3.

$\qquad \dfrac{-6}{15} + \left(\dfrac{-5}{15}\right) = \dfrac{-11}{15}$

The checks for Example 2 are shown in Figure 1.8a and Figure 1.8b. ∎

To evaluate expressions with more than one subtraction symbol perform the operations in order, left to right. That is, change all the subtractions to additions and change all the numbers except the first to their opposites.

TECHNOLOGY

```
9.6--3.8
          13.4
0--8.9
           8.9
```

Figure 1.8a

```
(-3/4)-(-1/2)▶Fr
ac
            -1/4
(-2/5)-(1/3)▶Fra
c
          -11/15
```

Figure 1.8b

For Figure 1.8a

a. [9] [.] [6] [−] [(−)] [3] [.] [8]
[ENTER]

b. [0] [−] [(−)] [8] [.] [9] [ENTER]

For Figure 1.8b

Note: Enter fractions in sets of parentheses for proper grouping and ease in reading.

c. [(] [(−)] [3] [÷] [4] [)] [−] [(] [(−)] [1] [÷] [2] [)] [MATH] [1] [ENTER]

d. [(] [(−)] [2] [÷] [5] [)] [−] [(] [1] [÷] [3] [)] [MATH] [1] [ENTER]

EXAMPLE 3 Evaluate.

a. $19 - 7 - (-17) - 32 - (-26)$

b. $-2.6 - 4 - (-6.73) - 8.6$

c. $\dfrac{-3}{4} - \left(\dfrac{-2}{3}\right) - \left(\dfrac{1}{6}\right) - \left(\dfrac{1}{4}\right)$

Solution

a. $19 - 7 - (-17) - 32 - (-26) =$ Rewrite as addition.
$19 + (-7) + 17 + (-32) + 26 =$ Add left to right.
$12 + 17 + (-32) + 26 =$
$29 + (-32) + 26 =$
$-3 + 26 = 23$

b. $-2.6 - 4 - (-6.73) - 8.6 =$ Rewrite as addition.
$-2.6 + (-4) + 6.73 + (-8.6) =$ Add left to right.
$-6.6 + 6.73 + (-8.6) =$
$0.13 + (-8.6) = -8.47$

c. $\dfrac{-3}{4} - \left(\dfrac{-2}{3}\right) - \left(\dfrac{1}{6}\right) - \left(\dfrac{1}{4}\right) =$ Rewrite as addition. Change to the LCD of 12.

$\dfrac{-3}{4} + \dfrac{2}{3} + \left(-\dfrac{1}{6}\right) + \left(-\dfrac{1}{4}\right) =$ Add left to right. Reduce to lowest terms.

$\dfrac{-9}{12} + \dfrac{8}{12} + \left(\dfrac{-2}{12}\right) + \left(\dfrac{-3}{12}\right) =$

$\dfrac{-1}{12} + \left(\dfrac{-2}{12}\right) + \left(\dfrac{-3}{12}\right) =$

$\dfrac{-3}{12} + \left(\dfrac{-3}{12}\right) =$

$\dfrac{-6}{12} = \dfrac{-1}{2}$

Another way to do Example 3a is to change all subtractions to equivalent additions and then determine the sum of the positive numbers and the sum of the negative numbers.

$$19 + 17 + 26 = 62$$
$$-7 + (-32) = -39$$

Next add these results.

$$62 + (-39) = 23$$

Check Examples 3b and 3c with this method. ■

 Experiencing Algebra the Checkup Way

Subtract.

1. $12 - 36$

2. $-43 - (-77)$

3. $-8.75 - 3$

4. $0 - 4.5$

5. $-\dfrac{5}{7} - \dfrac{3}{4}$

6. $-1\dfrac{1}{3} - \left(-2\dfrac{2}{3}\right)$

Evaluate.

7. $21 - 14 - (-16) - 43 - (-19)$

8. $-4.3 - 11 - (-5.85) - 5.9$

9. $-\dfrac{1}{2} - \left(-\dfrac{3}{4}\right) - \dfrac{1}{8} - \left(-\dfrac{1}{12}\right)$

---

4 Evaluating Sums and Differences

To perform addition and subtraction operations in the same exercise, first change all subtractions to equivalent additions. Then add all the numbers by the addition rules.

EXAMPLE 4 Evaluate.

a. $-32 + 48 - 16 + (-12) - (-26)$
b. $7.3 - 4.23 + 5 - (-7.9) + (-8.75)$
c. $\dfrac{-2}{3} + \left(\dfrac{-1}{6}\right) + \dfrac{3}{8} - \dfrac{5}{12}$

Solution

a.
$$-32 + 48 - 16 + (-12) - (-26) =$$ Rewrite subtraction as addition.
$$-32 + 48 + (-16) + (-12) + 26 =$$ Add left to right·
$$16 + (-16) + (-12) + 26 =$$
$$0 + (-12) + 26 =$$
$$-12 + 26 = 14$$

b.
$$7.3 - 4.23 + 5 - (-7.9) + (-8.75) =$$ Rewrite subtraction as addition.
$$7.3 + (-4.23) + 5 + 7.9 + (-8.75) =$$ Add left to right.
$$3.07 + 5 + 7.9 + (-8.75) =$$
$$8.07 + 7.9 + (-8.75) =$$
$$15.97 + (-8.75) = 7.22$$

c.
$$\dfrac{-2}{3} + \left(\dfrac{-1}{6}\right) + \dfrac{3}{8} - \dfrac{5}{12} =$$ Rewrite subtraction as addition.

$$\dfrac{-2}{3} + \left(\dfrac{-1}{6}\right) + \dfrac{3}{8} + \left(\dfrac{-5}{12}\right) =$$ Change to the LCD of 24.

$$\frac{-16}{24} + \left(\frac{-4}{24}\right) + \frac{9}{24} + \left(\frac{-10}{24}\right) = \qquad \text{Add left to right.}$$
$$\frac{-20}{24} + \frac{9}{24} + \left(\frac{-10}{24}\right) =$$
$$\frac{-11}{24} + \left(\frac{-10}{24}\right) =$$
$$\frac{-21}{24} = \frac{-7}{8} \qquad \text{Reduce to lowest terms.} \blacksquare$$

Experiencing Algebra the Checkup Way

In exercises 1–3, evaluate.

1. $-13 + 52 - (-2) - 13 + (-21)$

2. $\dfrac{1}{4} + \left(-\dfrac{3}{5}\right) - \left(-\dfrac{1}{2}\right) - \dfrac{3}{10} + \left(-\dfrac{3}{20}\right)$

3. $12.3 + (-11.5) - 3.7 - (-23.1) + 2$

4. When an expression contains both addition and subtraction of rational numbers, what can you do to ease the burden of evaluating it?

---

5   Modeling the Real World

The subtraction rules for rational numbers apply to situations in our daily lives. We must decide how to represent real data as rational expressions involving subtraction. Then, we subtract the expressions and obtain a difference.

EXAMPLE 5

Lorenzo is the owner of a handcrafted furniture business. He is balancing his account records of transactions for the day. He took in three sales: $123.00, $798.00, and $563.00. He paid out to suppliers $699.38 for wood and $76.93 for varnish. He also received a credit from the phone company for $12.75 for an overpayment of his last bill. What are his net earnings for the day?

Solution

We begin with the sum of the positive numbers that represent amounts taken in from sales. We subtract from these positive numbers the amount paid out to each supplier. A credit is a return of an amount paid out. We subtract (a return) a negative amount (amount paid out).
   Therefore, we have an expression

$$\overset{\text{sales}}{123.00} + \overset{\text{sales}}{798.00} + \overset{\text{sales}}{563.00} - \overset{\text{supplies}}{699.38} - \overset{\text{supplies}}{76.93} - \overset{\text{credit}}{(-12.75)}$$

First, change all subtractions to additions and the number following each subtraction symbol to its opposite. Note that subtracting a credit is the same as adding a positive amount.

$$123.00 + 798.00 + 563.00 + (-699.38) + (-76.93) + 12.75$$

Next, add all the positive numbers and all of the negative numbers, and find the sum of the two results.

$$123.00 + 798.00 + 563.00 + 12.75 = 1496.75$$
$$-699.38 + (-76.93) = -776.31$$
$$1496.75 + (-776.31) = 720.44$$

Lorenzo had net earnings of $720.44 for the day. ∎

Application

In the last year of the Civil War, the U.S. national debt was $2.68 billion. The debt fell $1.53 billion in the next few years. Determine the new national debt after this fall.

Discussion

A debt corresponds to a negative number. Therefore, a debt of $2.68 billion corresponds to −$2.68 billion and a debt of $1.53 billion corresponds to −$1.53 billion. Translate "fell" into a subtraction sign. The result is

$$\overset{\text{debt}}{-2.68} \overset{}{-} \overset{\text{debt}}{(-1.53)} = -2.68 + 1.53 = -1.15$$

This translates into a national debt of $1.15 billion or $1,150,000,000. ∎

Experiencing Algebra the Checkup Way

At the start of the month, Beverly's checking account showed a balance of $897.63. During the month, she added to her account by making two deposits, one for $355.00 and another for $572.00. During the same month, she decreased her account by making two withdrawals, one for $120.00 and another for $300.00. She wrote three checks for $185.23, $104.50, and $231.97. However, she stopped payment on the last check, thereby subtracting the deduction from her account. The bank charged $10.00 to stop payment on the check. Write an addition and subtraction problem to represent these transactions.

What is the current balance in Beverly's account?

PROBLEM SET 1.3

Experiencing Algebra the Exercise Way

Subtract.

1. $-7 - 9$ **2.** $-17 - 29$ **3.** $0 - (-13)$

4. $-15 - 0$ **5.** $-19 - (-12)$ **6.** $-22 - (-36)$

7. $15 - (-15)$ **8.** $-8 - 8$ **9.** $52 - (-13)$

10. $12 - (-45)$ **11.** $32 - 579$ **12.** $703 - 21$

13. $1.2 - (-2.5)$ **14.** $-5.5 - 2.7$ **15.** $-2.73 - 4.1$

16. $3.9 - (-1.81)$ **17.** $-1.1 - (-2.27)$ **18.** $-3.5 - (-7.9)$

19. $-1.25 - 0$ **20.** $0 - (-23.5)$ **21.** $1.23 - (-1.23)$

22. $2.7 - (-2.7)$ **23.** $2.7 - 3.96$ **24.** $0.06 - 3.1$

25. $-\dfrac{3}{5} - \left(-\dfrac{1}{2}\right)$ **26.** $-\dfrac{1}{4} - \left(-\dfrac{3}{7}\right)$ **27.** $-\dfrac{7}{9} - \dfrac{1}{6}$

28. $-\dfrac{3}{8} - \dfrac{1}{12}$

29. $\dfrac{2}{3} - \left(-\dfrac{7}{9}\right)$

30. $\dfrac{5}{6} - \left(-\dfrac{1}{3}\right)$

31. $\dfrac{2}{3} - 0$

32. $0 - \left(-\dfrac{3}{4}\right)$

33. $\dfrac{1}{3} - \left(-\dfrac{1}{3}\right)$

34. $-\dfrac{3}{7} - \dfrac{3}{7}$

35. $\dfrac{3}{7} - 3$

36. $\dfrac{3}{5} - 2$

37. $1\dfrac{5}{6} - \dfrac{1}{3}$

38. $1\dfrac{7}{8} - \dfrac{3}{4}$

39. $-5 - \left(-1\dfrac{4}{5}\right)$

40. $-7 - \left(-3\dfrac{2}{3}\right)$

41. $3\dfrac{2}{3} - 5$

42. $4\dfrac{1}{4} - 6$

43. $-13 - (-25) - (-26)$

44. $-52 - (-41) - (-5)$

45. $17 - (-23) - (-16) - 13$

46. $32 - (-55) - (-14) - 72$

47. $1.2 - (-2.31) - (-5.7)$

48. $4.3 - (-2.3) - (-9.72)$

49. $5 - (-7) - (-2.3)$

50. $17 - (-26.2) - 8$

51. $-\dfrac{1}{2} - \dfrac{1}{3} - \left(-\dfrac{1}{4}\right)$

52. $\dfrac{2}{3} - \left(-\dfrac{2}{3}\right) - \left(-\dfrac{3}{4}\right)$

53. $1124 - (-924) - 2305 - (-1156) - (-109)$

54. $3562 - (-901) - (-805) - (-3231) - 1020$

Evaluate.

55. $23 + 56 - 34 + (-12) - 68 - (-31)$

56. $132 - (-239) + (-141) - 53 + 75 - 18$

57. $1\dfrac{1}{5} - 2\dfrac{3}{10} + \dfrac{4}{5} - \left(-\dfrac{7}{10}\right) + \left(-\dfrac{3}{5}\right)$

58. $1\dfrac{1}{3} + 2\dfrac{3}{5} - 5\dfrac{2}{3} - \left(-1\dfrac{2}{5}\right) + \dfrac{4}{15}$

59. $3.75 - 1.2 + (-1.09) - (-0.76) + 13.13$

60. $-1.08 + 5.7 - (-0.05) - 4.37 + (-1.11) - 2$

Write and evaluate an expression. Interpret the results.

61. According to the *Guinness Book of World Records*, the greatest temperature range in the world occurs in Siberia. Temperatures at Verkhoyansk have ranged from $-90°F$ to $98°F$. What is the range of these temperatures? (Range is calculated as the high value minus the low value.)

62. The greatest temperature variation recorded in one day occurred at Browning, Montana, from $44°F$ to $-56°F$, on January 23–24, 1916. What was the range of temperatures that day?

63. The mean surface temperature of the Moon during the lunar day has been reported to be $130°C$, and at night $-180°C$. What is the change in mean surface temperatures from lunar day to night?

64. The mean surface temperature of the planet Mercury has been reported to be $350°C$ during the day and $-170°C$ during the night. What is the change in mean surface temperature during these times?

65. The highest point in the United States is Mount McKinley in Alaska, which has an elevation of 20,320 feet above sea level. The lowest point in the United States is Death Valley in California,

which has an elevation of 282 feet below sea level (−282 feet). Find the difference between the highest point and the lowest point.

66. The highest point in the state of Louisiana is Driskill Mountain, which has an elevation of 163 meters above sea level. The lowest point in Louisiana is New Orleans, which has an elevation of 2 meters below sea level. Find the difference between these highest and lowest points.

67. At the start of the month, Rolanda had $420.35 in her checking account. She made two deposits of $185.00 and $75.00. She made two withdrawals of $50.00 and $120.00. She wrote two checks for $12.55 and $110.76. The bank deducted a monthly service charge of $5.50. What is her current balance?

68. Daryl had a beginning balance of $485.26 in his checking account. He made one deposit of $325.00 and three withdrawals of $50.00, $40.00, and $10.00. He wrote three checks for $175.00, $14.59, and $35.76. The bank deducted a service charge of $3.75. What is the current balance?

69. Betty had a full canister of flour when she started baking pastries for a church bazaar. The canister held 20 cups of flour. For the first recipe, she used $2\frac{1}{2}$ cups of flour; for the second, she used $1\frac{2}{3}$ cups of flour; the next used 1 cup of flour; and the fourth used $2\frac{1}{4}$ cups of flour. How many cups of flour were left in the canister?

70. In a fabric store, a bolt of fabric had $15\frac{3}{4}$ yards of fabric on it. The first sale from the bolt was an order for $1\frac{1}{2}$ yards of fabric. The next order was for 3 yards of fabric, followed by orders for $2\frac{3}{4}$ yards and $\frac{2}{3}$ yard of fabric. How many yards of fabric remain on the bolt?

71. A petty-cash fund started with $25.00. The fund custodian paid out $5.75 for lunchroom supplies and collected a total of $15.00 from the staff to add to the fund. She then paid $12.50 for a flower arrangement for an employee and $4.50 for greeting cards. She added to the fund $2.35 that was in the coffee contributions bowl. What is the current balance of the petty-cash fund?

72. A storage tank was filled to its capacity of 25 gallons of liquid fertilizer. During the course of the day, one employee used 12.5 gallons of fertilizer from the tank. A second employee used 8.25 gallons of fertilizer from the tank. An additional supply of 15 gallons of fertilizer was added to the tank, after which an employee used 5.5 gallons of fertilizer from the tank. How much liquid fertilizer remains in the tank?

73. Rosie makes and sells T-shirts. On one morning, she sold three shirts at $19.95 each, paid $25.00 to purchase dyes, paid the light bill of $59.27, and refunded the price of one shirt that was the wrong size. What was the net cash flow that morning?

74. Richard runs a bookstore. In one hour he sold a book for $39.95, another for $27.95, and a third for $19.99. He paid out $175.00 for the monthly rent, and paid $29.95 to the newspaper to run an advertisement for him. A customer returned a book for a refund of $14.95. What was the net cash flow for that hour?

Experiencing Algebra the Calculator Way

Use the calculator to perform the following operations. Express your answers in fractional notation or round decimals to the nearest thousandth as appropriate.

1. $-\dfrac{171}{92} - \left(-\dfrac{170}{33}\right)$
2. $\dfrac{171}{92} - \left(-\dfrac{170}{33}\right)$
3. $-\dfrac{171}{92} - \dfrac{170}{33}$
4. $\dfrac{171}{92} - \dfrac{170}{33}$

5. $15\dfrac{17}{19} - 21\dfrac{13}{17}$
6. $15\dfrac{17}{19} - \left(-21\dfrac{13}{17}\right)$
7. $-15\dfrac{17}{19} - 21\dfrac{13}{17}$
8. $-15\dfrac{17}{19} - \left(-21\dfrac{13}{17}\right)$

9. $437.925 - (-108.0065)$
10. $-437.925 - (-108.0065)$
11. $-437.925 - 108.0065$
12. $437.925 - 108.0065$
13. $893,475 - 1,093,007$
14. $-893,475 - 1,093,007$
15. $893,475 - (-1,093,007)$
16. $-893,475 - (-1,093,007)$

Experiencing Algebra the Group Way

An interesting application of the skills of adding and subtracting numbers occurs in the reading of parts diagrams for a machine shop. Many times the diagrams list only the essential measurements, and assume that the user of the diagram can obtain the remaining measurements through addition and subtraction. The drawing in Figure 1.9 is an example of such a diagram. It is a drawing of a part called a taper, which a machinist may have to produce. All measurements are in inches. In your group, discuss how you would determine the lengths of A, B, and C in the drawing. Then find the lengths.

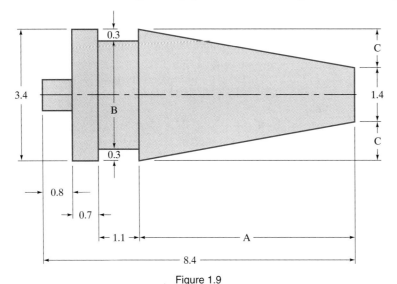

Figure 1.9

Experiencing Algebra the Write Way

Review this section and write a short description of the various combinations of positive and negative numbers that can occur in a subtraction problem. (You should have four different combinations listed.) Illustrate each combination with an example of your own making. Then explain how you would perform each subtraction and illustrate by solving the examples you created. Summarize your results by restating the rule for subtracting rational numbers.

1.4 Multiplication

Objectives
1 Discover the rules for multiplication of two rational numbers.
2 Illustrate the rules for multiplication of two rational numbers.
3 Evaluate the product of two rational numbers.
4 Discover the rules for multiplication of three or more rational numbers.
5 Evaluate the product of three or more rational numbers.
6 Model real-world situations using a product of rational numbers.

Application

Fifty-two percent of the U.S. national debt consists of marketable loans such as bills, notes, and bonds that can be traded. In 1990, the national debt ceiling was $4.15 trillion. Determine the amount of the debt ceiling that is made up of marketable loans.

After completing this section, we will discuss this application further. See page 49.

When two rational numbers are multiplied, we obtain a **product**. The numbers that we multiply are called **factors**. We will use these terms as we discuss multiplying rational numbers.

$$6 \times 3 = 18$$
factor × factor = product

Sometimes we use a dot, • for multiplication instead of an ×. The previous example would then be written as

$$6 \cdot 3 = 18$$
factor • factor = product

Another way to write a multiplication problem, especially when using decimals, is to place the factors in parentheses with no sign between them. The previous example would then be written as

$$(6)(3) = 18$$
(factor)(factor) = product

1 Discovering Multiplication Rules

As before, we use the calculator to perform mathematical operations so we can discover the rules that govern these operations. In this case, we want to discover the rules for multiplication of rational numbers.

When we multiply two rational numbers, we might have any of the same four possible combinations as before. That is, the two numbers may be both positive, or both negative, or a positive and a negative, or a negative and a positive. We will combine these possibilities into two more general combinations. The two numbers may have like signs; that is, they may be both positive or both negative. The two numbers may have unlike signs; one number is positive and one number is negative. Complete the following sets of exercises with your calculator.

DISCOVERY 8

Multiplying Two Rational Numbers with Like Signs
Evaluate each expression and compare the results obtained in the left column to the corresponding results in the right column.

1. a. $6 \cdot 2 =$ _____   **b.** $|6| \cdot |2| =$ _____

2. a. $-6 \cdot (-2) =$ _____   **b.** $|-6| \cdot |-2| =$ _____

3. a. $-1.2 \cdot (-2.5) =$ _____   **b.** $|-1.2| \cdot |-2.5| =$ _____

4. a. $\dfrac{1}{2} \cdot \dfrac{1}{4} =$ _____   **b.** $\left|\dfrac{1}{2}\right| \cdot \left|\dfrac{1}{4}\right| =$ _____

Write in your own words a rule for writing the product of two rational numbers with like signs.

In the column on the left, we multiply two rational numbers with like signs. Each product results in a positive number. In the column on the right, we multiply the absolute values of the factors. The results are the same as on the left.

DISCOVERY 9

Multiplying Two Rational Numbers with Unlike Signs
Evaluate each expression and compare the results obtained in the left column to the corresponding results in the right column.

1. a. $6 \cdot (-2) =$ _____   **b.** $|6| \cdot |-2| =$ _____

2. a. $-6 \cdot 2 =$ _____   **b.** $|-6| \cdot |2| =$ _____

3. a. $1.2 \cdot (-2.5) =$ _____   **b.** $|1.2| \cdot |-2.5| =$ _____

4. a. $\dfrac{-1}{2} \cdot \dfrac{1}{4} =$ _____   **b.** $\left|\dfrac{-1}{2}\right| \cdot \left|\dfrac{1}{4}\right| =$ _____

Write in your own words a rule for writing the product of two rational numbers with unlike signs.

In the column on the left, we multiply two rational numbers with unlike signs. Each product results in a negative number. In the column on the right, we multiply the absolute values of the factors. The results are the opposite of those on the left.

The preceding discoveries suggest the following rules for multiplication.

Multiplication of Rational Numbers
To multiply two rational numbers with like signs (both positive or both negative):

• Multiply the absolute values of the factors.
• The sign of the product is positive.

To multiply rational numbers with unlike signs (one positive and one negative):

• Multiply the absolute values of the factors.

> • The sign of the product is negative.
>
> To multiply 0 and any rational number, the result is 0.

 ## Experiencing Algebra the Checkup Way

1. When multiplying two rational numbers that have like signs, what will be the sign of the product?
2. When multiplying two rational numbers that have unlike signs, what will be the sign of the product?
3. When multiplying a rational number by 0, what will the product be?

---

2 Illustrating Multiplication Rules

To visualize the rules of multiplication that we have just discovered, we need to remember that multiplication is a shortcut for repeated addition. If we work the first two examples in the preceding discovery sets, the result is

$$6 \cdot 2 = 2 + 2 + 2 + 2 + 2 + 2 = 12$$
six two's

$$6 \cdot (-2) = (-2) + (-2) + (-2) + (-2) + (-2) + (-2) = -12$$
six negative two's

A problem occurs when we try to use this reasoning for multiplying a negative times a positive.

$$-6 \cdot 2 = \quad \text{How do we write two a negative six times?}$$

Let's look at the following pattern and see if we can deduce that this product is really -12.

$$4 \cdot 2 = 8$$

first factor decreases by one $\qquad$ $3 \cdot 2 = 6$ $\qquad$ product decreases by two

$$2 \cdot 2 = 4$$
$$1 \cdot 2 = 2$$
$$0 \cdot 2 = 0$$
$$-1 \cdot 2 = -2$$
$$-2 \cdot 2 = -4$$
$$-3 \cdot 2 = -6$$
$$-4 \cdot 2 = -8$$
$$-5 \cdot 2 = -10$$
$$-6 \cdot 2 = \underline{\quad\quad} \quad \text{(Using the preceding pattern, this answer must be } -12.)$$

Therefore, $-6 \cdot 2 = -12$.

The same problem occurs when we try to multiply two negative numbers.

$$-6 \cdot (-2) = \quad \text{How do we write negative two a negative six times?}$$

Let's look at the following pattern and see if we can deduce that this product is really 12.

$$4(-2) = -8$$

first factor decreases by one $3(-2) = -6$ product increases by two

$$2(-2) = -4$$
$$1(-2) = -2$$
$$0(-2) = 0$$
$$-1(-2) = 2$$
$$-2(-2) = 4$$
$$-3(-2) = 6$$
$$-4(-2) = 8$$
$$-5(-2) = 10$$
$$-6(-2) = \underline{}$$ (Using the preceding pattern, this answer must be 12.)

Therefore, $-6(-2) = 12$.

 Experiencing Algebra the Checkup Way

In exercises 1–2, complete the sequences for multiplying signed numbers.

1. $4(4) =$
$4(3) =$
$4(2) =$
$4(1) =$
$4(0) =$
$4(-1) =$
$4(-2) =$
$4(-3) =$

2. $-4(4) =$
$-4(3) =$
$-4(2) =$
$-4(1) =$
$-4(0) =$
$-4(-1) =$
$-4(-2) =$
$-4(-3) =$

3. In exercise 1, we started with the product of two positive integers and established a pattern by changing the multiplier. What does the pattern indicate about the product of two numbers with opposite signs?

4. In exercise 2, we started with the product of two integers with opposite signs and established a pattern by changing the multiplier. What does the pattern indicate about the product of two negative numbers?

---

3 Evaluating Products of Two Rational Numbers   We are now ready to use the multiplication rules we have discovered and illustrated. Once again, we begin with examples of integers.

EXAMPLE 1   Multiply.

a. $8(-2)$ **b.** $-6(-5)$
c. $-7 \cdot 3$ **d.** $8 \cdot 12$

Solution

a. $8(-2) = -16$ Unlike signs: The product is negative. The product of the absolute values of the factors is $|8| \cdot |-2| = 16$. Therefore, the product is negative 16.

b. $-6(-5) = 30$ Like signs: The product is positive. The product of the absolute values of the factors is $|-6| \cdot |-5| = 30$. Therefore, the product is positive 30.

c. $-7 \cdot 3 = -21$ Unlike signs: The product is negative. The product of the absolute values of the factors is $|-7| \cdot |3| = 21$. Therefore, the product is negative 21.

d. $8 \cdot 12 = 96$ Like signs: The product is positive. The product of the absolute values of the factors is $|8| \cdot |12| = 96$. Therefore, the product is positive 96.

The checks for Example 1 are shown in Figure 1.10a and Figure 1.10b. ∎

TECHNOLOGY

```
8*-2
              -16
-6*-5
              30
```

Figure 1.10a

```
-7*3
              -21
8*12
              96
```

Figure 1.10b

For Figure 1.10a

a. [8] [×] [(–)] [2] [ENTER]

b. [(–)] [6] [×] [(–)] [5] [ENTER]

For Figure 1.10b

c. [(–)] [7] [×] [3] [ENTER]

d. [8] [×] [1] [2] [ENTER]

EXAMPLE 2   Multiply.

a. $(-4.89)(6.4)$ **b.** $(-12.5)(-2)$ **c.** $(-8.9)(0)$

d. $\dfrac{1}{2} \cdot \dfrac{-1}{3}$ **e.** $-1\dfrac{2}{3} \cdot 2\dfrac{3}{5}$

Solution

a. $(-4.89)(6.4) = -31.296$ Unlike signs: The product is negative. The product of the absolute values of the factors is $|-4.89| \cdot |6.4| = 31.296$. Therefore, the product is negative 31.296.

b. $(-12.5)(-2) = 25$ Like signs: The product is positive. The product of the absolute values of the factors is $|-12.5| \cdot |-2| = 25$. Therefore, the product is positive 2.5.

c. $(-8.9)(0) = 0$ The product of a number and 0 is 0.

d. $\dfrac{1}{2} \cdot \dfrac{-1}{3} = \dfrac{-1}{6}$ Unlike signs: The product is negative. The product of the absolute values of the factors is $|\frac{1}{2}| \cdot |\frac{-1}{3}| = \frac{1}{6}$. Therefore, the product is negative $\frac{1}{6}$.

e. $-1\dfrac{2}{3} \cdot 2\dfrac{3}{5} =$ Unlike signs: The product is negative.

$\dfrac{-5}{3} \cdot \dfrac{13}{5} =$ Change the mixed numbers to improper fractions and multiply. The product of the absolute values of the factors is $|\frac{-5}{3}| \cdot |\frac{13}{5}| = \frac{65}{15}$. Therefore, the product is negative $\frac{65}{15}$.

$\dfrac{-65}{15} =$

$\dfrac{-13}{3} = -4\dfrac{1}{3}$ Reduce the fraction and change to a mixed number.

The checks for Example 2 are shown in Figure 1.11a and Figure 1.11b. ∎

TECHNOLOGY

```
-4.89*6.4
            -31.296
-12.5*-2
                 25
-8.9*0
                  0
```

Figure 1.11a

```
(1/2)*(-1/3)▶Fra
c
               -1/6
-(1+2/3)*(2+3/5)
▶Frac
              -13/3
```

Figure 1.11b

For Figure 1.11a

Note: Even though it is correct to do so, there is no need to place the numbers in parentheses. Enter the numbers with the multiplication sign between them for faster entry.

a. | (−) | 4 | . | 8 | 9 | × | 6 | . | 4 |
| ENTER |

b. | (−) | 1 | 2 | . | 5 | × | (−) | 2 |
| ENTER |

c. | (−) | 8 | . | 9 | × | 0 | ENTER |

For Figure 1.11b

Note: Enter fractions in sets of parentheses for proper grouping and ease in reading.

d. | (| 1 | ÷ | 2 |) | × | (| (−) | 1 | ÷ | 3 |) | MATH | 1 | ENTER |

e. | (−) | (| 1 | + | 2 | ÷ | 3 |) | × | (| 2 | + | 3 | ÷ | 5 |) | MATH | 1 | ENTER |

Experiencing Algebra the Checkup Way

In exercises 1–7, multiply.

1. $36 \cdot 2$

2. $-56 \cdot (-4)$

3. $-\dfrac{1}{3} \cdot \left(-\dfrac{3}{4}\right)$

4. $(-7.2)(0.02)$

5. $-1\dfrac{1}{3} \cdot \dfrac{1}{4}$

6. $12 \cdot (-8)$

7. $2\dfrac{1}{4} \cdot \left(-1\dfrac{1}{3}\right)$

8. Write the keystrokes needed to perform the following multiplication: $\left(-2\frac{3}{7}\right) \cdot \left(3\frac{5}{8}\right)$
What is the result?

9. When multiplying two numbers with the same sign, what will be the sign of the product?

10. When multiplying two numbers with unlike signs, what will be the sign of the product?

---

4 Discovering Rules for Multiple Factors

We again use the calculator to perform mathematical operations so we can discover underlying rules. In this case, we want to discover the rules for multiplication of multiple factors. Complete the following sets of exercises with your calculator.

DISCOVERY 10

Multiplying Three or More Rational Numbers

Evaluate each expression and compare the results obtained in the left column to the corresponding results in the right column.

Continued

1. one negative factor

    a. $-6 \cdot 3 \cdot 4 \cdot 1 = $ ____   **b.** $|-6| \cdot |3| \cdot |4| \cdot |1| = $ ____

2. two negative factors

    a. $-6 \cdot (-3) \cdot 4 \cdot 1 = $ ____   **b.** $|-6| \cdot |-3| \cdot |4| \cdot |1| = $ ____

3. three negative factors

    a. $-6 \cdot (-3) \cdot (-4) \cdot 1 = $ ____   **b.** $|-6| \cdot |-3| \cdot |-4| \cdot |1| = $ ____

4. four negative factors

    a. $-6 \cdot (-3) \cdot (-4) \cdot (-1) = $ ____   **b.** $|-6| \cdot |-3| \cdot |-4| \cdot |-1| = $ ____

Write in your own words a rule for writing the product of three or more rational numbers.

In the column on the left, we multiply three or more rational numbers. An even number of negative factors results in a positive product and an odd number of negative factors results in a negative product. In the column on the right, we multiply the absolute value of the factors. The results are the same as the absolute value of the product on the left.

D I S C O V E R Y   11

Multiplying Three or More Rational Numbers with 0 as a Factor or Factors

Evaluate each expression.

1. $-5 \cdot 0 \cdot 4 \cdot 1 = $ _____

2. $-5 \cdot 0 \cdot 0 \cdot 1 = $ _____

3. $-5 \cdot 0 \cdot 0 \cdot 0 = $ _____

Write in your own words a rule for writing the product of three or more rational numbers with 0 as a factor or factors.

Multiplying with one or more factors of 0 always results in 0.

The preceding discoveries suggest the following additional rules for multiplication.

> *Multiplication of Rational Numbers*
> To multiply rational numbers with an even number of negative factors:
>
> - Multiply the absolute values of the factors.
> - The sign of the product is positive.
>
> To multiply rational numbers with an odd number of negative factors:
>
> - Multiply the absolute values of the factors.
> - The sign of the product is negative.
>
> To multiply rational numbers with a 0 factor, the result is 0.

These rules are simply an extension of the rules of multiplication of two rational numbers.

Experiencing Algebra the Checkup Way

1. When multiplying two or more rational numbers, how can you determine what the sign of the product will be?

2. When multiplying two or more rational numbers, when will the product be 0?

---

5 Evaluating Products of Three or More Rational Numbers

We are now ready to use the multiplication rules we have just discovered.

EXAMPLE 3 Multiply.

a. $(-6)(8)(-3)(-5)$

b. $(1.5)(-2.3)(-7)$

c. $\left(\dfrac{1}{3}\right)\left(\dfrac{-5}{8}\right)\left(\dfrac{-5}{7}\right)$

d. $(-380)(257)(0)(25)$

Solution

a. $(-6)(8)(-3)(-5) = -720$ — This is an odd number of negative factors (three). The product is negative. Multiply the absolute values of the factors from left to right.

b. $(1.5)(-2.3)(-7) = 24.15$ — This is an even number of negative factors (two). The product is positive. Multiply the absolute values of the factors from left to right.

c. $\left(\dfrac{1}{3}\right)\left(\dfrac{-5}{8}\right)\left(\dfrac{-5}{7}\right) = \dfrac{25}{168}$ — This is an even number of negative factors (two). The product is positive. Multiply the absolute values of the factors from left to right.

d. $(-380)(257)(0)(25) = 0$ — A factor of 0 results in a product of 0. ∎

 ## Experiencing Algebra the Checkup Way

Multiply. Check using your calculator.

1. $(-2)(3)(-1)(-2)(4)$

2. $(2)(-2)(-3)(10)(5)$

3. $(125)(-341)(0)(-534)$

4. $\left(-\dfrac{1}{5}\right)\left(-\dfrac{5}{7}\right)\left(-\dfrac{7}{9}\right)\left(-\dfrac{9}{11}\right)$

5. $\left(1\dfrac{5}{7}\right)\left(-3\dfrac{5}{9}\right)\left(-\dfrac{3}{4}\right)\left(-\dfrac{2}{3}\right)$

6. $(12)(-13)(0)(-56)(39)$

7. $\left(\dfrac{2}{3}\right)\left(-\dfrac{6}{7}\right)(0)\left(-\dfrac{4}{9}\right)(0)\left(-\dfrac{3}{8}\right)(0)$

8. $(2.5)(-3.5)(0)(5.6)(0)(3.9)$

---

6 Modeling the Real World

In our daily lives, many situations can be expressed as products of rational numbers. Whenever there is a repeated process, such as writing a check for the same amount several weeks in a row, or paying rent every month for a year, we may represent the amount as a multiplication expression. Also, when we take a "percentage of" or "fractional part of" a value, we write a multiplication expression. In these cases, the rules for multiplication of rational numbers may be applied to obtain a product.

EXAMPLE 4

Sara buys a *Young and Lively* magazine each week at the supermarket for $2.50. How much would she save if she got a subscription of $32.50 for 16 weeks?

Solution

If Sara spends $2.50 for 16 magazines, she spends

$$2.50 \cdot 16 = 40.00.$$

Sara spends $40.00 at the supermarket for 16 magazines.

If the subscription costs $32.50, the difference of the cost at the supermarket and the subscription is

$$40.00 - 32.50 = 7.50.$$

Sara would save $7.50 if she purchased a subscription. ■

EXAMPLE 5

Determine the number of seconds in 1 week.

Solution

We need to know the following measurements of time:

$$60 \text{ seconds} = 1 \text{ minute}$$
$$60 \text{ minutes} = 1 \text{ hour}$$
$$24 \text{ hours} = 1 \text{ day}$$
$$7 \text{ days} = 1 \text{ week}$$

To find the number of seconds in 1 week, we find the product of

$$(60)(60)(24)(7) = 604{,}800.$$

There are 604,800 seconds in 1 week. ■

Application

Fifty-two percent of the U.S. national debt consists of marketable loans such as bills, notes, and bonds that can be traded. In 1990, the national debt ceiling was $4.15 trillion. Determine the amount of the debt ceiling that is made up of marketable loans.

Discussion

A debt corresponds to a negative number. Therefore, the national debt ceiling of $4.15 trillion may be represented as -4.15. If 52% of this debt consists of marketable loans, determine the amount of the debt ceiling that is made up of marketable loans by multiplying the debt ceiling by the percentage, written as a decimal.

$$52\% \text{ of } -4.15 = 0.52 \times -4.15 = -2.158.$$

This translates into a national debt of $2.158 trillion in marketable loans, or $2,158,000,000,000. ∎

Experiencing Algebra the Checkup Way

1. Sara earns $215 a week working as a produce clerk at the local market. How much does her paycheck show as gross earnings if she is paid every 4 weeks?

2. Lorraine buys lottery tickets each week for a year (52 weeks). She buys the same amount each week—3 Instant Game tickets at $3 each, 2 Big Jackpot tickets at $4 each, and 2 Monster Millions tickets at $5 each. How much would she have to win during the year in order to break even?

PROBLEM SET 1.4

Experiencing Algebra the Exercise Way

Multiply.

1. $45\cdot(-3)$
2. $56\cdot(-4)$
3. $-32\cdot(-4)$
4. $-55\cdot(-11)$
5. $-25\cdot5$
6. $-3\cdot3$
7. $51\cdot3$
8. $16\cdot8$
9. $0\cdot(-15)$
10. $-2\cdot0$
11. $(0.88)(-1.1)$
12. $4(-0.25)$
13. $(-1.7)(-0.2)$
14. $(-34.2)(-2)$
15. $(24.3)(0.3)$
16. $(0.5)(10)$
17. $(-0.25)(50)$
18. $(-5.7)(0.19)$
19. $\left(\dfrac{2}{5}\right)\left(\dfrac{25}{48}\right)$
20. $\left(\dfrac{11}{17}\right)\left(\dfrac{2}{3}\right)$
21. $\left(1\dfrac{2}{3}\right)\left(-\dfrac{3}{4}\right)$
22. $\left(\dfrac{4}{5}\right)\left(-\dfrac{20}{21}\right)$
23. $\left(-\dfrac{1}{3}\right)\left(-\dfrac{3}{7}\right)$
24. $\left(-1\dfrac{1}{5}\right)\left(-\dfrac{5}{6}\right)$
25. $\left(-\dfrac{4}{7}\right)\left(\dfrac{3}{16}\right)$
26. $\left(-\dfrac{15}{17}\right)\left(\dfrac{5}{9}\right)$
27. $(0)\left(-3\dfrac{5}{19}\right)$
28. $\left(-\dfrac{2}{3}\right)(0)$
29. $(-1.11)(0)$
30. $(0)(-2.357)$

Determine the sign of the product. Do not carry out the multiplication.

31. $(-55)(21)(-3)(-15)(27)(32)(41)(-23)$
32. $(-55)(21)(-3)(-15)(27)(-32)(-41)(-23)$
33. $(-5.6)(13.9)(65.2)(-3.9)(1.6)(0.03)(-4.6)(-4.7)(-1.7)$
34. $(-5.6)(13.9)(65.2)(-3.9)(1.6)(0.03)(-4.6)(4.7)(-1.7)$
35. $(39)(-1.2)(9)(17)(-3.5)(22)(3.5)(9.9)$
36. $(39)(-1.2)(-9)(17)(-3.5)(-22)(3.5)(-9.9)$
37. $\left(-\dfrac{7}{12}\right)\left(-2\dfrac{4}{11}\right)\left(\dfrac{5}{8}\right)\left(\dfrac{21}{10}\right)\left(-\dfrac{9}{13}\right)\left(5\dfrac{2}{7}\right)$
38. $\left(\dfrac{7}{12}\right)\left(2\dfrac{4}{11}\right)\left(\dfrac{5}{8}\right)\left(\dfrac{21}{10}\right)\left(-\dfrac{9}{13}\right)\left(5\dfrac{2}{7}\right)$

Multiply.

39. $(-2)(-3)(-4)(-10)(20)$
40. $(-5)(-4)(6)(-100)(-5)$
41. $\left(-\dfrac{1}{5}\right)\left(-\dfrac{2}{3}\right)\left(-\dfrac{4}{5}\right)\left(\dfrac{1}{2}\right)$
42. $\left(-\dfrac{5}{7}\right)\left(\dfrac{14}{25}\right)\left(-\dfrac{2}{5}\right)\left(\dfrac{1}{3}\right)$
43. $(5.2)(-0.1)(-2.2)$
44. $(-2.9)(-1.1)(0.2)$
45. $\left(\dfrac{1}{3}\right)(-2)(4.2)(5)$
46. $(1.3)(0)(-2.5)(-4.3)$
47. $(5)(-6.8)\left(\dfrac{1}{2}\right)(0)$
48. $(-5)(-6.2)\left(\dfrac{1}{2}\right)(-3)$

49. $(14)(0)(-35)(0)(-312)$ **50.** $(-1.4)(0)(3.76)(0)(-45.2)$

Write and evaluate a multiplication expression for each situation.

51. Steve pays \$225 per month for rent. How much does he pay in a year?

52. Tricia pays off an interest-free loan from her father with \$65 each week for 13 weeks. How much was the loan?

53. The deductions from Sara's paycheck typically amount to 22% of her gross pay. If she grosses \$645 every 2 weeks, how much can she expect to have deducted? Deductions are represented by negative numbers. Over a 12-week period, what can she expect her total deduction to be?

54. Ron bets a total of \$5 per race, with nine races each day at the horse track. Bets are represented as negative numbers, since this is money he pays out. If he attends a week's worth of races (6 days, since the horses don't race on Monday), how much money will he bet in the week?

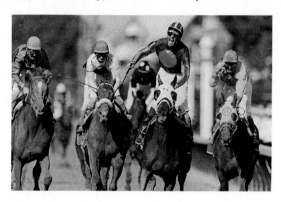

55. During a football game, Heath is sacked four times, with an average loss of $4\frac{1}{2}$ yards each time. How many total yards did Heath lose on these four sacks?

56. Each time JoAnne makes a person-to-person call, she is charged a service charge of \$1.75, which is a negative number. What will be the charge for five such calls?

57. A track athlete trains by running 4.5 miles each day. How many miles will she run in 4 weeks?

58. An athlete trains with weights for $1\frac{1}{4}$ hours each day. How many hours of training will he complete in 2 weeks?

59. In a military parade, soldiers are lined up in groups of 20 rows with 25 soldiers in each row. How many soldiers are in a group?

60. At a wedding reception, guests are seated eight to a table. If there are 22 full tables of guests, how many guests are at the reception?

61. A Labor Day parade has 10 rows of antique cars in it. Each row has three cars passing side by side. Each car has four people riding in it, with two in the front seat and two in the back seat. How many people are riding in the antique cars?

62. A military parade has 12 rows of battle tanks lined up with four tanks in a row. Each tank has a crew of three soldiers in it. How many soldiers are riding in the tanks?

63. Sammy is paid 5 cents for each flyer he distributes. He can distribute 40 flyers per hour. He is permitted to distribute flyers for $1\frac{1}{2}$ hours each weekday. He does so on three weekdays. How much will he earn for the work?

64. Melanie earns 25 cents for her scout troop for each box of cookies she sells. She averages 20 boxes of cookies sold each time she works at the cookie booth in the local mall. She is permitted to work the cookie booth six different times. How much money did she make for her troop?

65. Millie wants to buy cabinets to hold her CD collection. She can afford to buy four cabinets. Each cabinet has three drawers, and each drawer holds 20 CDs. How many CDs will she be able to store in the cabinets?

66. Omar buys five bookcases for his library. Each case has five shelves, and each shelf holds 24 average-sized books. How many books can Omar expect to store on the bookcases?

67. George averages 50 miles per hour on his business trip. He drives approximately $8\frac{1}{2}$ hours each day and his drive takes him 4 days to complete. Approximately how many miles did George drive to get to his destination?

68. Michele hikes for $9\frac{1}{2}$ hours per day on the Appalachian Trail. She hikes at an average pace of $1\frac{3}{4}$ miles per hour. How far can she hike in 5 days?

69. A grocery store receives a shipment of canned vegetables. The vegetables arrive in cases with 24 cans in each case. Each can of vegetables will retail for 59 cents. If the grocery store receives 14 cases of vegetables, what will be the total retail value of the shipment?

70. A distributor packages cleaner concentrate in 12-ounce bottles. The concentrate is packaged 18 bottles to a case. An order for 12 cases of concentrate is received. It costs the distributor 35 cents per ounce to obtain the concentrate. What costs will the distributor incur to obtain the concentrate for this order?

71. Drucilla agrees to pay back money she borrowed from her parents at the rate of $100 per month. She projects that it will take her $2\frac{3}{4}$ years to pay off the loan. How much will Drucilla pay her parents?

72. Keith has an annuity that pays him $175 per month. How much money will he receive from the annuity in 10 years?

73. Special commemorative bottles of Kangaroo Kola are being produced for the year 2000 Olympic Games. Each commemorative bottle of soda contains 8 fluid ounces of beverage. The bottles are packed 6 to a carton, and the cartons are packed 4 to a case. An order has been placed for 24 cases of the soda. How many fluid ounces must be produced to fill the order?

74. Commemorative cans of Kangaroo Kola are being produced for the year 2000 Olympic Games. Each can contains 12 fluid ounces. The cans are packed 12 to a carton, and the cartons are packed 4 to a case. An order has been placed for 18 cases of the soda. How many fluid ounces must be produced to fill this order?

 Experiencing Algebra the Calculator Way

Use your calculator to evaluate the following exercises. Express your answers in fractional notation or round decimals to the nearest thousandth as appropriate.

1. $\left(-\dfrac{171}{92}\right)\left(-\dfrac{170}{33}\right)$

2. $\left(\dfrac{171}{92}\right)\left(-\dfrac{170}{33}\right)$

3. $\left(-\dfrac{171}{92}\right)\left(\dfrac{170}{33}\right)$

4. $\left(\dfrac{171}{92}\right)\left(\dfrac{170}{33}\right)$

5. $\left(15\dfrac{17}{19}\right)\left(21\dfrac{13}{17}\right)$

6. $\left(15\dfrac{17}{19}\right)\left(-21\dfrac{13}{17}\right)$

7. $\left(-15\dfrac{17}{19}\right)\left(21\dfrac{13}{17}\right)$

8. $\left(-15\dfrac{17}{19}\right)\left(-21\dfrac{13}{17}\right)$

9. $(437.925)(-108.0065)$

10. $(-437.925)(-108.0065)$

11. $(-437.925)(108.0065)$

12. $(437.925)(108.0065)$

13. $(893)(1,093)$

14. $(-893)(1,093)$

15. $(893)(-1,093)$

16. $(-893)(-1,093)$

Experiencing Algebra the Group Way

A. Brainstorming Key Words for Multiplication

Being able to recognize words, phrases, or situations that imply mathematical operations will increase your skills in solving word problems. Brainstorm within your group to produce the lists described. Compare your lists with the lists from other groups to see which group produced the largest lists.

1. List as many words or phrases as you can that imply multiplication.
2. List examples of multiplication situations that occur in everyday life.

B. A Thought-Provoking Multiplication Exercise

Multiply:

$$111{,}111{,}111 \cdot 111{,}111{,}111$$

In your group, discuss the significance of the answer and what it illustrates about multiplication.

Experiencing Algebra the Write Way

In this section, it was stated that multiplication is just a shortcut way of performing repeated addition. Explain what this statement means. Illustrate it by presenting an example in which you choose a number and then add it to itself repeatedly, starting with a sum of two numbers, then three, and working up to five repetitions of the number. Use your illustration to explain what multiplication can represent.

1.5 Division

Objectives
1. Discover the rules for division of rational numbers.
2. Illustrate the rules for division of rational numbers.
3. Evaluate the quotient of rational numbers.
4. Evaluate combinations of products and quotients.
5. Model real-world situation using a quotient of rational numbers.

Application

In 1790, the first U.S. national debt was announced as $70 million. In 1840, the national debt had been reduced to $4 million. Determine the average debt reduction per year.

After completing this section, we will discuss this application further. See page 65.

When two rational numbers are divided, we obtain a *quotient*. The numbers we divide are called the *dividend* and the *divisor*. We will use these terms when discussing division of rational numbers.

$$15 \div 3 = 5$$

dividend ÷ divisor = quotient

Using a long-division symbol, this example would be written as

$$3\,\overline{)15} = 5$$

divisor)dividend = quotient

A fraction bar also means division. The previous example would then be written as

$$\frac{15}{3} = 5$$

$$\frac{\text{dividend}}{\text{divisor}} = \text{quotient}$$

---

1 Discovering Division Rules

When we divide two rational numbers, we might have any of four combinations, as before. In the case of division, we want to combine these four possibilities into the same two more general combinations, like and unlike signs, as we did for the multiplication rules. We will add two discoveries for the rules of division involving 0. The results in these two additional discoveries will be different from the previous discoveries we have completed. Complete the following sets of exercises with your calculator.

DISCOVERY 12

Dividing Two Rational Numbers with Like Signs
Evaluate each expression and compare the results obtained in the left column to the corresponding results in the right column.

1. a. $8 \div 2 = $ _____ **b.** $|8| \div |2| = $ _____
2. a. $-8 \div (-2) = $ _____ **b.** $|-8| \div |-2| = $ _____
3. a. $-1.2 \div (-2.5) = $ _____ **b.** $|-1.2| \div |-2.5| = $ _____
4. a. $\dfrac{1}{2} \div \dfrac{1}{4} = $ _____ **b.** $\left|\dfrac{1}{2}\right| \div \left|\dfrac{1}{4}\right| = $ _____

Write in your own words a rule for writing the quotient of two rational numbers with like signs.

In the column on the left, we divide two rational numbers with like signs. Each quotient results in a positive number. In the column on the right, we divide the absolute values of the dividend and divisor. The results are the same as on the left.

DISCOVERY 13

Dividing Two Rational Numbers with Unlike Signs
Evaluate each expression and compare the results obtained in the left column to the corresponding results in the right column.

1. a. $8 \div (-2) = $ _____ **b.** $|8| \div |-2| = $ _____
2. a. $-8 \div 2 = $ _____ **b.** $|-8| \div |2| = $ _____
3. a. $1.2 \div (-2.5) = $ _____ **b.** $|1.2| \div |-2.5| = $ _____
4. a. $\dfrac{-1}{2} \div \dfrac{1}{4} = $ _____ **b.** $\left|\dfrac{-1}{2}\right| \div \left|\dfrac{1}{4}\right| = $ _____

Write in your own words a rule for writing the quotient of two rational numbers with unlike signs.

In the column on the left, we divide two rational numbers with unlike signs. Each quotient results in a negative number. In the column on the right, we divide the absolute values of the dividend and divisor. The results are the opposite of those on the left.

D I S C O V E R Y   14

Dividing a Rational Number by 0

Evaluate each expression.

1. $8 \div 0 = $ _____

2. $-8 \div 0 = $ _____

3. $-3.4 \div 0 = $ _____

4. $\dfrac{1}{2} \div 0 = $ _____

Write in your own words a rule for dividing a rational number by 0.

Dividing a nonzero rational number by 0 results in an error on the calculator. That is, the quotient cannot be found when the divisor is 0. We call this quotient **undefined**. Therefore, there is no rule for dividing a rational number by 0, and we write the results as "undefined."

D I S C O V E R Y   15

Dividing 0 by a Rational Number

Evaluate each expression.

1. $0 \div 2 = $ _____

2. $0 \div (-5) = $ _____

3. $0 \div 1.7 = $ _____

4. $0 \div \dfrac{3}{4} = $ _____

5. $0 \div 0 = $ _____

Write in your own words a rule for dividing 0 by a rational number other than 0.

Dividing 0 by any rational number other than 0 results in 0. Dividing 0 by 0 results in an error (the quotient is indeterminate).

Helping Hand "Undefined" and "indeterminate" do not mean the same thing. This will be explained in the next section.

The preceding discoveries suggest the following rules for division.

Division of Rational Numbers
To divide two rational numbers with like signs (both positive or both negative):

- Divide the absolute values of the numbers.
- The sign of the quotient is positive.

To divide two rational numbers with unlike signs (one positive and one negative):

- Divide the absolute values of the numbers.
- The sign of the quotient is negative.

To divide 0 by a nonzero rational number, the result is 0.
To divide a rational number by 0 is undefined.
To divide 0 by 0 is indeterminate.

Experiencing Algebra the Checkup Way

1. When two rational numbers with like signs are divided, what will be the sign of the quotient?
2. When two rational numbers with different signs are divided, what will be the sign of the quotient?
3. What is the result of dividing 0 by a nonzero rational number?
4. What is the result of dividing a nonzero rational number by 0?
5. What is the result of dividing 0 by 0?

2 Illustrating Division Rules

To visualize the rules of division that we have just discovered, we need to remember that division is related to multiplication. Therefore, we can write any division expression as a related multiplication expression. For example,

$$12 \div 4 = 3$$
dividend ÷ divisor = quotient

may be written as

$$4 \cdot 3 = 12$$
divisor quotient = dividend

If we use this fact, then we can find a quotient by completing a multiplication expression. We will work examples from the previous discovery sets to understand this concept.

$8 \div 2 = $ ____ is related to $2 \cdot$ ____ $= 8$.
The missing quotient must be 4.

$-8 \div -2 = $ ____ is related to $-2 \cdot$ ____ $= -8$.
The missing quotient must be 4.

$8 \div -2 = $ ____ is related to $-2 \cdot$ ____ $= 8$.
The missing quotient must be -4.

$-8 \div 2 =$ _____ is related to $2 \cdot$ _____ $= -8$.

The missing quotient must be -4.

$8 \div 0 =$ _____ is related to $0 \cdot$ _____ $= 8$.

The missing quotient cannot be found because 0 times any number results in 0, not 8. Therefore, we say the quotient is undefined.

$0 \div 2 =$ _____ is related to $2 \cdot$ _____ $= 0$.

The missing quotient must be 0.

$0 \div 0 =$ _____ is related to $0 \cdot$ _____ $= 0$.

The missing quotient could be any number. Since it is impossible to determine only one number that correctly completes this statement, we say the quotient is indeterminate.

 Experiencing Algebra the Checkup Way

1. Use the relationship between multiplication and division to explain why the quotient of two numbers with different signs must be a negative result.

2. Use the relationship between multiplication and division to explain why the quotient of two numbers with the same signs must be a positive result.

3. Use the relationship between multiplication and division to explain why a nonzero number divided by 0 must be undefined.

4. Use the relationship between multiplication and division to explain why 0 divided by a nonzero number must be 0.

3 Evaluating Quotients

We are now ready to use the division rules we have discovered and illustrated. Let's begin with examples of integers.

EXAMPLE 1 Divide.

a. $8 \div (-4)$

b. $-6 \div (-2)$

c. $\dfrac{-9}{3}$

d. $\dfrac{18}{-2}$

Solution

a. $8 \div (-4) = -2$ Unlike signs: The quotient is negative. The quotient of the absolute values of the numbers is $|8| \div |-4| = 2$. Therefore, the quotient is negative 2.

b. $-6 \div (-2) = 3$ Like signs: The quotient is positive. The quotient of the absolute values of the numbers is $|-6| \div |-2| = 3$. Therefore, the quotient is positive 3.

c. $\dfrac{-9}{3} = -3$ Unlike signs: The quotient is negative. The quotient of the absolute values of the numbers is $|-9| \div |3| = 3$. Therefore, the quotient is negative 3.

d. $\dfrac{18}{-2} = -9$ Unlike signs: The quotient is negative. The quotient of the absolute values of the numbers is $|18| \div |-2| = 9$. Therefore, the quotient is negative 9.

The checks for Example 1 are shown in Figure 1.12a and Figure 1.12b. ■

TECHNOLOGY

Figure 1.12a

Figure 1.12b

For Figure 1.12a

a. $\boxed{8}$ $\boxed{\div}$ $\boxed{(-)}$ $\boxed{4}$ $\boxed{\text{ENTER}}$

b. $\boxed{(-)}$ $\boxed{6}$ $\boxed{\div}$ $\boxed{(-)}$ $\boxed{2}$ $\boxed{\text{ENTER}}$

For Figure 1.12b

c. $\boxed{(-)}$ $\boxed{9}$ $\boxed{\div}$ $\boxed{3}$ $\boxed{\text{ENTER}}$

d. $\boxed{1}$ $\boxed{8}$ $\boxed{\div}$ $\boxed{(-)}$ $\boxed{2}$ $\boxed{\text{ENTER}}$

Now we are ready to divide two integers with the dividend smaller than the divisor. The result is a fraction or an equivalent decimal.

EXAMPLE 2   Divide.

a. $\dfrac{3}{4}$ **b.** $\dfrac{-3}{-4}$ **c.** $\dfrac{3}{-4}$ **d.** $\dfrac{-3}{4}$

Solution

In these examples, the only differences in the quotients are their signs.

The absolute values of the quotients are the same for each example because we are dividing the same absolute values for the dividend and divisor, 3 and 4. The quotient of 3 divided by 4 is preferably written as a fraction, $\frac{3}{4}$, or it may be written as an equivalent decimal, 0.75.

a. $\dfrac{3}{4} = \dfrac{3}{4}$ or 0.75 Like signs: The quotient is positive.

b. $\dfrac{-3}{-4} = \dfrac{3}{4}$ or 0.75 Like signs: The quotient is positive.

c. $\dfrac{3}{-4} = -\dfrac{3}{4}$ or -0.75 Unlike signs: The quotient is negative.

d. $\dfrac{-3}{4} = -\dfrac{3}{4}$ or -0.75 Unlike signs: The quotient is negative.

Enter these examples on your calculator to check, in the same manner as in previous examples. ■

Figure 1.13a

Figure 1.13b

 Helping Hand *Note*: In Examples 2a and 2b, $\frac{3}{4} = \frac{-3}{-4} = \frac{3}{4}$. In Examples 2c and 2d, $\frac{3}{-4} = \frac{-3}{4} = -\frac{3}{4}$.

$\frac{-3}{4}$ or $-\frac{3}{4}$ is the *preferred* way to write these fractions. If we remember that the denominator of a fraction denotes the number of equal parts the whole is divided into, a negative denominator would not make sense.

EXAMPLE 3 Divide.

a. $(1.2) \div (-3)$ **b.** $\dfrac{-4.89}{0.6}$ **c.** $\dfrac{-12}{-0.8}$

d. $(-8.9) \div (0)$ **e.** $\dfrac{0}{-0.34}$

Solution

a. $(1.2) \div (-3) = -0.4$
     Unlike signs: The quotient is negative. The quotient of the absolute values of the numbers is $|1.2| \div |-3|$ $= 0.4$. Therefore, the quotient is negative 0.4.

b. $\dfrac{-4.89}{0.6} = -8.15$
     Unlike signs: The quotient is negative. The quotient of the absolute values of the numbers is $|-4.89| \div |0.6| = 8.15$. Therefore, the quotient is negative 8.15.

c. $\dfrac{-12}{-0.8} = 15$
     Like signs: The quotient is positive. The quotient of the absolute values of the numbers is $|-12| \div |-0.8|$ $= 15$. Therefore, the quotient is positive 15.

d. $(-8.9) \div (0) =$ undefined
     The quotient for a rational number divided by 0 is undefined.

e. $\dfrac{0}{-0.34} = 0$
     The quotient for 0 divided by a rational number other than 0 is 0.

The checks for Example 3 are shown in Figure 1.14a, Figure 1.14b, and Figure 1.14c. ■

TECHNOLOGY

```
1.2/-3
           -.4
-4.89/.6
        -8.15
-12/-.8
          15
```

```
ERR:DIVIDE BY 0
1:Quit
2:Goto
```

```
0/-.34
            0
```

| Figure 1.14a | Figure 1.14b | Figure 1.14c |

Note: Even though it is correct to do so, there is no need to place the numbers in parentheses; enter the numbers with the division sign between them for faster entry. It is also not necessary to enter a 0 if it is the whole number part of the decimal, as in the divisor of Example 3b.

For Figure 1.14a

a. | 1 | . | 2 | ÷ | (−) | 3 | ENTER |

b. | (−) | 4 | . | 8 | 9 | ÷ | . | 6 | ENTER |

c. | (−) | 1 | 2 | ÷ | (−) | . | 8 | ENTER |

For Figure 1.14b

d. | (−) | 8 | . | 9 | ÷ | 0 | ENTER |

Note: A calculator error occurs for this division. Press | ENTER | to quit the error screen and return to the default screen.

For Figure 1.14c

e. | 0 | ÷ | (−) | . | 3 | 4 | ENTER |

Before we divide fractions, we must remember that to divide proper fractions, we change the division symbol to a multiplication symbol and change the divisor to its reciprocal. We then multiply the results.

Let's review the term "reciprocal." **Reciprocals** are two numbers whose product is 1. Therefore, $\frac{5}{8}$ and $\frac{8}{5}$ are reciprocals because $\frac{5}{8} \cdot \frac{8}{5} = 1$. To find a reciprocal for a given number, interchange the numerator and denominator of the number. Remember that the denominator of an integer is 1.

EXAMPLE 4 Find the reciprocals for the following numbers.

a. $\dfrac{3}{4}$ b. $\dfrac{-5}{7}$ c. 3   d. $1\dfrac{2}{3}$

Solution

	Number	Reciprocal	
a.	$\dfrac{3}{4}$	$\dfrac{4}{3}$	Interchange the numerator, 3, and the denominator, 4. The result is $\frac{4}{3}$.
b.	$\dfrac{-5}{7}$	$\dfrac{-7}{5}$	Interchange the numerator, −5, and the denominator, 7. The result is $\frac{7}{-5}$ or $\frac{-7}{5}$.

c. $3 = \dfrac{3}{1}$ $\dfrac{1}{3}$ The denominator of an integer is 1. Therefore, $3 = \frac{3}{1}$. Interchange the numerator, 3, and the denominator, 1. The result is $\frac{1}{3}$.

d. $1\dfrac{2}{3} = \dfrac{5}{3}$ $\dfrac{3}{5}$ Change the mixed number to an improper fraction. Then interchange the numerator, 5, and the denominator, 3. The result is $\frac{3}{5}$. ∎

EXAMPLE 5   Divide.

a. $\dfrac{1}{2} \div \dfrac{-1}{3}$

b. $\dfrac{-3}{4} \div \dfrac{-1}{2}$

c. $\dfrac{-3}{5} \div \dfrac{1}{3}$

d. $-1\dfrac{2}{3} \div 2\dfrac{3}{5}$

e. $\dfrac{2}{3} \div 3$

Solution

a. $\dfrac{1}{2} \div \left(\dfrac{-1}{3} \right) =$ Change division to multiplication and change the divisor to its reciprocal. Use the rules of multiplication. The quotient is negative $\frac{3}{2}$.

$\dfrac{1}{2} \cdot \left(\dfrac{-3}{1} \right) = \dfrac{-3}{2}$

b. $\dfrac{-3}{4} \div \left(\dfrac{-1}{2} \right) =$ Change division to multiplication and change the divisor to its reciprocal. Use the rules of multiplication. The quotient is positive $\frac{3}{2}$.

$\dfrac{-3}{4} \cdot \left(\dfrac{-2}{1} \right) =$

$\dfrac{6}{4} = \dfrac{3}{2}$

c. $\dfrac{-3}{5} \div \dfrac{1}{3} =$ Change division to multiplication and change the divisor to its reciprocal. Use the rules of multiplication. The quotient is negative $\frac{9}{5}$.

$\dfrac{-3}{5} \cdot \dfrac{3}{1} = \dfrac{-9}{5}$

d. $-1\dfrac{2}{3} \div 2\dfrac{3}{5} =$ Change the mixed numbers to equivalent improper fractions. Change the division to multiplication and change the divisor to its reciprocal. Use the rules of multiplication. The quotient is negative $\frac{25}{39}$.

$\dfrac{-5}{3} \div \dfrac{13}{5} =$

$\dfrac{-5}{3} \cdot \dfrac{5}{13} = \dfrac{-25}{39}$

e. $\dfrac{2}{3} \div 3 =$ Change the whole number to a fraction, $3 = \frac{3}{1}$. Change the division to multiplication and change the divisor to its reciprocal, $\frac{1}{3}$. Use the rules of multiplication. The quotient is positive $\frac{2}{9}$.

$\dfrac{2}{3} \cdot \dfrac{3}{1} =$

$\dfrac{2}{3} \cdot \dfrac{1}{3} = \dfrac{2}{9}$

Enter fractions in sets of parentheses for proper grouping and ease in reading. ∎

TECHNOLOGY

Figure 1.15a

Figure 1.15b

Figure 1.15c

For Figure 1.15a

a. (1 ÷ 2) ÷ ((−) 1 ÷ 3) MATH 1 ENTER

b. ((−) 3 ÷ 4) ÷ ((−) 1 ÷ 2) MATH 1 ENTER

For Figure 1.15b

c. ((−) 3 ÷ 5) ÷ (1 ÷ 3) MATH 1 ENTER

d. (−) (1 + 2 ÷ 3) ÷ (2 + 3 ÷ 5) MATH 1 ENTER

For Figure 1.15c

e. (2 ÷ 3) ÷ 3 MATH 1 ENTER

 Experiencing Algebra the Checkup Way

Divide.

1. a. $-14 \div 7$ **b.** $18 \div (-9)$ **c.** $\dfrac{-12}{-4}$ **d.** $\dfrac{63}{-21}$

2. a. $\dfrac{3}{5}$ **b.** $\dfrac{-3}{5}$ **c.** $\dfrac{3}{-5}$ **d.** $\dfrac{-3}{-5}$

3. a. $36.9 \div (-9)$ **b.** $\dfrac{-18}{-0.5}$ **c.** $0 \div (-13.257)$

Find the reciprocals.

4. a. $\dfrac{7}{8}$ **b.** $-\dfrac{7}{9}$ **c.** $1\dfrac{4}{5}$ **d.** -5

In exercise 5, divide.

5. a. $\dfrac{3}{7} \div 2$ **b.** $-\dfrac{1}{3} \div \left(-\dfrac{3}{4}\right)$ **c.** $\left(2\dfrac{1}{4}\right) \div \left(-1\dfrac{1}{3}\right)$ **d.** $-\dfrac{1}{5} \div 0$

6. Write the keystrokes needed to perform the following division: $-2\dfrac{3}{7} \div \left(3\dfrac{5}{8}\right)$

What is the result?

7. What does the term *reciprocals* mean?

4 Evaluating Products and Quotients

To perform multiplication and division operations in the same problem, perform the operations in order from left to right.

EXAMPLE 6 Evaluate.

a. $-32 \div (-4) \cdot 2 \cdot (-16) \div 8$

b. $(-3.6) \div (9)(-4.76) \div (-0.2)$

c. $\left(\dfrac{-2}{3}\right) \div \left(\dfrac{1}{3}\right) \div \left(\dfrac{-1}{4}\right)\left(\dfrac{3}{8}\right)$

Solution

a.
$$-32 \div (-4) \cdot 2 \cdot (-16) \div 8 =$$
$$8 \cdot 2 \cdot (-16) \div 8 =$$
$$16 \cdot (-16) \div 8 =$$
$$-256 \div 8 = -32$$

Perform operations from left to right.

b.
$$(-3.6) \div (9)(-4.76) \div (-0.2) =$$
$$-0.4(-4.76) \div (-0.2) =$$
$$1.904 \div (-0.2) = -9.52$$

Perform operations from left to right.

c.
$$\left(\dfrac{-2}{3}\right) \div \left(\dfrac{1}{3}\right) \div \left(\dfrac{-1}{4}\right)\left(\dfrac{3}{8}\right) =$$
$$\left(\dfrac{-2}{3}\right) \cdot \left(\dfrac{3}{1}\right) \cdot \left(\dfrac{-4}{1}\right)\left(\dfrac{3}{8}\right) =$$
$$\dfrac{72}{24} = 3$$

Change division to multiplication and write the fractions following the division signs (the divisors) as their reciprocals. Perform multiplication rules from left to right. ∎

Helping Hand Some calculators use implied multiplication. This means that if two numbers are written together without a sign between them, the multiplication is completed first, not in order from left to right.

See whether your calculator uses implied multiplication by working Example 6b. Enter the example as it appears and then enter the example by inserting a multiplication sign between the numbers to indicate multiplication. The parentheses do not need to be entered. The results should be the same.

The calculator used in Figure 1.16 does not use implied multiplication, because both answers are equal.

TECHNOLOGY

For Figure 1.16

Figure 1.16

Experiencing Algebra the Checkup Way

In exercises 1–3, evaluate. Check your results using the calculator.

1. $(-12)(-3) \div (-6)(15) \div 9(25) \div (-2)$

2. $\left(\frac{3}{4}\right)\left(-\frac{1}{3}\right) \div \left(-\frac{3}{4}\right)\left(1\frac{1}{5}\right) \div (-6)$

3. $(-18.9) \div (-9)(2.24) \div (-0.4)$

4. Explain what the term *implied multiplication* means.

5. When using a calculator to perform a string of multiplications and divisions, explain how you can guard against implied multiplication giving the wrong result.

---

5 Modeling the Real World

Practical situations involving division are often indicated by the word *per*, as in calculating sales income per month, or calories eaten per day. Finding an average also involves dividing the sum of numbers by the count of the numbers added.

EXAMPLE 7

Thomas had a balance in his checking account on Monday of $145.21, on Tuesday of $497.86, on Wednesday of $344.32, on Thursday of $129.87, and on Friday an overdraw of $37.65.

Write and evaluate a division expression to represent the average daily balance in his account for this week.

Solution

To find the average, first find the total of the balances and then divide the result by the number of balances added, 5.

balance + balance + balance + balance + overdraw

$145.21 + 497.86 + 344.32 + 129.87 + (-37.65) = 1079.61$

$1079.61 \div 5 = 215.922 \approx 215.92$ when rounded to the nearest cent.

The average daily balance in Thomas's account was $215.92. ∎

 Helping Hand When rounding we use the symbol $\approx$ to mean "approximately equal to."

EXAMPLE 8

Dollyland amusement park had 750,000 visitors in one 6-day period. How many visitors should be expected in one 31-day month?

Solution

First, determine the number of visitors per day. To do this, divide the total number of visitors, 750,000, by the number of days, 6.

$$\frac{750,000}{6} = 125,000$$

The average number of visitors per day for the 6-day period was 125,000.

To determine the number of visitors expected in a 31-day month, multiply the average number per day by 31 days.

$$125,000 \cdot 31 = 3,875,000$$

The number of visitors expected in a 31-day month is 3,875,000. ∎

Application

In 1790, the first U.S. national debt was announced as $70 million. In 1840, the national debt had been reduced to $4 million. Determine the average debt reduction per year.

Discussion

A debt corresponds to a negative number. Therefore, the amount, in millions of dollars, of the national debt reduction is the difference of the two debt amounts, in millions of dollars.

$$\overset{\text{debt}}{-70} - \overset{\text{debt}}{(-4)} = -70 + 4 = -66$$

The national debt reduction was 66 million dollars.

To determine the average debt reduction per year, divide the amount of the national debt reduction, in millions of dollars, by the number of years. $(1840 - 1790 = 50 \text{ years})$

$$-66 \div 50 = -1.32$$

This translates into an average debt reduction of $1.32 million per year or $1,320,000. ∎

Experiencing Algebra the Checkup Way

1. During the winter, weather forecaster Marti reported the daily low temperature for one week as follows:

   Monday: 11°   Tuesday: −4°   Wednesday: 8°   Thursday: −2°

   Friday: 0°   Saturday: 4°   Sunday: 12°

   Determine the average daily low temperature for the week. Round your answer to one decimal place.

2. Napoleon sent a message from Rome to Paris using a semaphore system (signaling with flags from mountaintop to mountaintop). It took approximately 4 hours to send the message a distance of 700 miles. At the same rate, how far could you send a message in $2\frac{1}{2}$ hours, using the same system?

PROBLEM SET 1.5

Experiencing Algebra the Exercise Way

Divide.

1. $45 \div (-3)$ **2.** $56 \div (-4)$ **3.** $-32 \div (-4)$ **4.** $-55 \div (-11)$

5. $51 \div 3$ **6.** $16 \div 2$ **7.** $0 \div (-15)$ **8.** $0 \div 12$

9. $18 \div (-18)$ **10.** $-33 \div 33$ **11.** $26 \div (-0.13)$ **12.** $-54 \div 0.6$

13. $-1.7 \div (-0.2)$ **14.** $-34.2 \div (-2)$ **15.** $24.3 \div 0.3$ **16.** $0.5 \div 10$

17. $-2.7 \div (-2.7)$ **18.** $3.4 \div (-3.4)$

19. $\dfrac{-25}{5}$ **20.** $\dfrac{-3}{3}$ **21.** $\dfrac{-16}{0}$

22. $\dfrac{-2}{0}$ **23.** $\dfrac{0.88}{-1.1}$ **24.** $\dfrac{4}{-0.25}$

25. $\dfrac{-5.7}{19}$

26. $\dfrac{-0.25}{50}$

27. $\dfrac{2}{5} \div \dfrac{25}{48}$

28. $\dfrac{11}{17} \div \dfrac{2}{3}$

29. $1\dfrac{2}{3} \div \left(-\dfrac{3}{4}\right)$

30. $2\dfrac{1}{5} \div \left(-\dfrac{1}{3}\right)$

31. $\dfrac{6}{7} \div \left(-\dfrac{18}{19}\right)$

32. $\dfrac{4}{5} \div \left(-\dfrac{20}{21}\right)$

33. $-\dfrac{1}{3} \div \left(-\dfrac{3}{7}\right)$

34. $-\dfrac{2}{5} \div \left(-\dfrac{5}{9}\right)$

35. $-1\dfrac{1}{4} \div \left(-\dfrac{4}{5}\right)$

36. $-1\dfrac{1}{5} \div \left(-\dfrac{5}{6}\right)$

37. $-\dfrac{4}{7} \div \dfrac{3}{16}$

38. $-\dfrac{15}{17} \div \dfrac{5}{9}$

39. $0 \div \left(-3\dfrac{5}{19}\right)$

40. $0 \div \left(1\dfrac{7}{8}\right)$

41. $\dfrac{3}{5} \div 0$

42. $\dfrac{1}{2} \div 0$

43. $-\dfrac{2}{3} \div \left(-\dfrac{2}{3}\right)$

44. $-\dfrac{2}{3} \div \dfrac{3}{2}$

45. $\dfrac{8}{9} \div 4$

46. $-\dfrac{7}{8} \div 2$

47. $14 \div \left(-\dfrac{1}{3}\right)$

48. $-21 \div \dfrac{3}{2}$

49. $\dfrac{0}{1.3}$

50. $\dfrac{-5.7}{0}$

Evaluate.

51. $(-15)(4) \div (-3)(12) \div 3(-10)$

52. $(-40) \div (-8)(9)(-12)$

53. $(-3.3)(2.7) \div (-11)(0.6)$

54. $(15.5) \div (-0.5)(-3.3) \div 11$

55. $\left(\dfrac{2}{3}\right)\left(-\dfrac{5}{8}\right) \div \left(-\dfrac{5}{16}\right)$

56. $\left(\dfrac{7}{22}\right) \div \left(-\dfrac{7}{11}\right)\left(-\dfrac{1}{2}\right)(4)$

Write and evaluate a division expression to represent each situation. Interpret the results.

57. Peyton ran four plays to score a touchdown for his football team. On the first play he threw a pass for a gain of 20 yards. On the second play he was sacked for a loss of $3\frac{1}{2}$ yards. On the third play he ran for a gain of $8\frac{3}{4}$ yards. On the fourth play he ran 12 yards to score a touchdown. What was his average gain per play?

58. On one set of plays in a football game, Andy threw a pass for a gain of 16 yards. He then ran a play and gained 3 more yards. On the next play he was sacked for a loss of 7 yards. On the next play he was sacked again for a loss of $6\frac{1}{2}$ yards. What was his average yardage per play for this series?

59. Students were asked to evaluate Professor Chips using the following scale:

The following scores were recorded for him:

   3.5, 2.0, 0.5, −1.5, −2.5, 3.5, 4.0, −4.0, 3.5, 2.5, 3.5

Determine the average rating received by Professor Chips. Round your answer to two decimal places.

60. Miss Bundy had a total rating of 75 points from 20 student evaluations, using the scale described in exercise 59. What is the average of the 20 evaluations? Mr. Rooney had a total rating of -18.75 points for 15 student evaluations. What is the average of the 15 evaluations?

61. A military parade includes a marching unit that has 364 soldiers in it. If the parade limits the group to marching in 26 rows, how many soldiers will march in each row?

62. A contingent of 54 antique cars is to appear in a parade. If the cars are arranged three in a row for the parade, how many rows of cars will there be?

63. Michaela plans to drive from Atlanta to New Orleans, a trip of 479 miles. If she drives an average of 60 miles per hour, how long will it take her to drive to New Orleans, excluding stops?

64. Thelma and Louise plan to drive from El Paso, Texas, to Salt Lake City, a trip of 868 miles. If the trip is to be completed in 14 hours, what must be their average speed for the drive?

65. A distributor has 3200 cans of soda pop on hand. If the cans are packaged into 12-can packs, how many full packs will the distributor have?

66. A supermarket has 1450 bottles of soda pop packed into 8-bottle cartons. How many full cartons does the market have?

67. Al's car averages 19.4 miles to a gallon of gas. If Al plans to drive from Nashville, Tennessee, to Washington, D.C., a distance of 659 miles, approximately how many gallons of gas will he use?

68. Al completes his car trip of 659 miles, and finds that he has used 38 gallons of gas. What was his gas mileage for the trip?

69. How many 40-fluid-ounce bottles of fabric softener can be filled from a production run of 47,500 fluid ounces, assuming none is lost to spillage?

70. How many 98-ounce boxes of laundry detergent can be filled from a production run of 2800 pounds of detergent, assuming none is lost to spillage? (Note: Each pound of detergent is equivalent to 16 ounces of detergent.)

71. To promote a town fund-raiser, Smallville sets up a clock that ticks off the seconds until the event begins. If the clock starts at 16,000,000 seconds, how many days will it be until the event kicks off?

72. Pioneer Village uses a clock to tick off the seconds until its bicentennial celebration will begin. If the clock starts at 20,000,000 seconds, how many weeks will it be until the event kicks off?

73. Anita borrows $850 from her mother for college expenses. If she agrees to pay back the money at $35 per week, how many weeks will it take for her to pay off the loan, assuming her mother does not charge her any interest?

74. Sonya decides to save for college rather than borrow money. If she can save $45 a week, how many weeks will it take her to save $1200 for college expenses?

75. Billie wants to buy cabinets to hold her CD collection. She owns 335 CDs. If each cabinet has three drawers and each drawer holds 20 CDs, how many cabinets will she need to buy in order to store her entire collection?

76. Bruce has a collection of 650 LPs (long-playing records). He will buy record cabinets to store his collection. Each cabinet has three shelves, and each shelf holds 125 LPs. How many cabinets will Bruce need to buy for his collection?

77. In 1992, the industry with the most advertising expenditures was the automotive industry, which spent $1,035,900,000 for the 12-month period. If this amount was evenly distributed throughout the year, what would you estimate was the expenditure for a 3-month quarter?

78. Aerialist Philippe Petit walked a 1350-foot-long tightrope between the twin towers of the World Trade Center in New York City in a time of 50 minutes. At the same rate of speed, how many minutes would you expect him to take to walk a tightrope of 1000 feet?

Experiencing Algebra the Calculator Way

Use your calculator to evaluate the following exercises. Express your answers in fractional notation or round decimals to the nearest thousandth as appropriate.

1. $-\dfrac{171}{92} \div \left(-\dfrac{17}{3}\right)$

2. $\dfrac{171}{92} \div \left(-\dfrac{17}{3}\right)$

3. $-\dfrac{171}{92} \div \dfrac{17}{3}$

4. $\dfrac{171}{92} \div \dfrac{17}{3}$

5. $15\dfrac{17}{19} \div \left(21\dfrac{13}{17}\right)$

6. $15\dfrac{17}{19} \div \left(-21\dfrac{13}{17}\right)$

7. $-15\dfrac{17}{19} \div \left(21\dfrac{13}{17}\right)$

8. $-15\dfrac{17}{19} \div \left(-21\dfrac{13}{17}\right)$

9. $\dfrac{437.925}{-108.0065}$

10. $\dfrac{-437.925}{-108.0065}$

11. $\dfrac{-437.925}{108.0065}$

12. $\dfrac{437.925}{108.0065}$

13. $893 \div 1093$

14. $-893 \div 1093$

15. $893 \div (-1093)$

16. $-893 \div (-1093)$

Experiencing Algebra the Group Way

Many fields of work use division in their everyday activities. Following are examples of some applications. First solve each exercise. Then try to come up with a related application either from the same field of work or from another field.

1. Health Sciences: If the human heart pumps 4 liters of blood in 90 seconds, how many liters are pumped in 60 seconds?

2. Nursing Management: The case load in a hospital ward is 15 patients for 2 nurses. How many nurses are required for a ward of 70 patients?

3. Surgery: The mortality rate for a surgical procedure is seven deaths for every 2500 operations. How many deaths would you expect if 12,000 of these operations are performed per year?

4. Drafting: A computer-aided design (CAD) operator can plot 3 drawings in 20 minutes. How long will it take to plot 17 drawings of the same size and detail?

5. Construction: A metal joint 8 feet long requires 45 rivets. How many rivets are required in a joint 5 feet long?

6. Trades: The weight of 10 gallons of fuel oil is 71 pounds. What is the weight of 225 gallons of fuel oil?

7. Heating and Cooling: A 768-square-foot living space requires a 5-ton air conditioner. What size air conditioner would be required for an 1100-square-foot living space?

8. Utilities: A city utility bill of $44.25 includes $22.50 for water, $9.75 for sewer, and $12.00 for trash disposal. If a customer makes a partial payment of $25.00, how much should be credited to each department, if the payment is prorated?

9. Legal: An attorney determines that child support payments are proportioned as $100 for every $350 earned. If a client makes $50,000 a year, how much should he contribute for child support?

10. Forestry: A survey showed that out of 2500 vehicles traveling into a national park area, 300 visited the park. Current data indicate that the area receives an average of 3850 vehicles daily. Assuming the same proportion will visit the park, how many vehicles can the park expect to see each day?

Experiencing Algebra the Write Way

An important skill in being successful in mathematics is the ability to recognize words that indicate a mathematical operation. The following words are different ways to indicate the operation of division: *halved, ratio of, quotient of, divided, equally apportioned, per, average*. Pick three of these words, or suggest other words that indicate the operation of division, and write three sentences using these words, indicating a division operation. Then write division expressions that reflect the sentences and evaluate them.

CHAPTER 1 | Summary

After completing this chapter, you should be able to define in your own words the following key terms and rules.

Terms
set
members
elements
empty set
null set
finite set
infinite set
ellipsis
subset
number line
natural numbers
counting numbers
whole numbers
integers
rational numbers

fractional notation
graph
plot
equal
inequality symbol
order symbol
equivalent
expression
evaluate
absolute value
opposites
sum
addends
difference
minuend
subtrahend

product
factor
quotient
dividend
divisor
undefined
indeterminate
reciprocals

Rules
Addition of rational numbers
Subtraction of rational numbers
Multiplication of rational numbers
Division of rational numbers

CHAPTER 1 | Review

Reflections

1. In mathematics, what is a set? What is the difference between a finite set and an infinite set?

2. What is a rational number? What types of numbers are included in the set of rational numbers?

3. What is a number line? How is it used to help us understand the order relations among numbers?

4. Explain what is meant by the absolute value of a number.

5. What is meant by the opposite of a number?

6. How do you use absolute values to add two numbers with like signs, and with unlike signs? How do you use absolute values to subtract two numbers that may have like or unlike signs?

7. How do you use absolute values to multiply two numbers that have like or unlike signs? How do you use absolute values to divide two such numbers?

Express your answers in fractional notation or round decimals to the nearest thousandth as appropriate.

1.1

1. Identify the possible sets of numbers (natural numbers, whole numbers, integers, rational numbers) to which the following numbers belong.

$$-15, \ 1000, \ 0, \ -2000, \ 13, \ -\frac{15}{17}, \ 12.97, \ 3\frac{5}{8}, \ \frac{12}{4}$$

2. Professional golfer Peter Putter had the following scores: 3 above par in the first round, even par in the second round, 2 below par in the third round, and 1 above par in the fourth round. Write a rational number representation for each of the scores.

3. Graph the following numbers on a number line.

$$-1.1, \quad \frac{3}{4}, \quad -2\frac{1}{2}, \quad 0, \quad 2.5, \quad 1\frac{1}{2}, \quad 4, \quad -3$$

Use one of the symbols $>$, $<$, or $=$ to compare the two numbers.

4. -7 _____ -9

5. -0.54 _____ -0.65

6. $\frac{3}{11}$ _____ $\frac{1}{3}$

7. -329 _____ -115

8. $\frac{13}{45}$ _____ $\frac{4}{9}$

9. $\frac{27}{75}$ _____ 0.36

10. 2035 _____ 491

11. 12.304 _____ 12.344

12. -28 _____ 13

13. $-\frac{23}{79}$ _____ $\frac{13}{47}$

14. 0.056 _____ -0.197

15. 331 _____ -331

16. $\frac{23}{17}$ _____ $-\frac{17}{23}$

17. -0.34 _____ 0.17

18. -1.34 _____ -1.04

19. $-\frac{3}{4}$ _____ $-\frac{5}{8}$

Use your calculator to determine whether each statement is true or false.

20. $-4\frac{1}{3} > -5\frac{1}{2}$

21. $\frac{13}{23} < \frac{51}{91}$

22. $-408 > -513$

Write an equivalent order relation for each statement.

23. $-23 > -49$

24. $\frac{252}{529} < \frac{13}{17}$

25. $-34.58 = -\frac{1729}{50}$

Evaluate.

26. $-\left|-\frac{17}{33}\right|$

27. $\left|-(-67)\right|$

28. $-\left|-16.85\right|$

29. $-\left(-\left(-\left(-5\frac{1}{2}\right)\right)\right)$

30. $-(-32.698)$

31. $-(-(-(257)))$

1.2

Add.

32. $-27 + 13$

33. $-16 + (-22)$

34. $35 + (-19)$

35. $-1123 + (-3406)$

36. $82.56 + (-43.7)$

37. $-5\frac{2}{9} + 4\frac{5}{9}$

38. $18 + \left(-1\frac{1}{3}\right)$

39. $\frac{102}{43} + \left(-\frac{29}{75}\right)$

40. $235{,}407 + (-571{,}004)$

41. $12.097 + 1.92$

42. $\frac{32}{77} + \frac{50}{99}$

43. $-3.57 + (-41.098)$

44. $23{,}596 + 143{,}271$

45. $-49.071 + 105.399$

46. $-\frac{103}{345} + \left(-\frac{21}{115}\right)$

47. $0 + (-123)$

Evaluate.

48. $53 + (-97) + 33 + 50 + (-83) + (-101)$

49. $\dfrac{1}{8} + \dfrac{5}{6} + \left(-\dfrac{2}{3}\right) + \left(-\dfrac{7}{12}\right) + \left(-\dfrac{5}{2}\right)$

Write and evaluate an addition expression for each situation. Interpret the result.

50. Willy has a sales quota of $5000 per week. He was $650 above quota the first week, $250 below quota the second week, $1200 above quota the third week, and $700 below quota the fourth week. What was his overall standing at the end of the 4-week period?

51. In physics, a vector quantity is completely specified by a magnitude (number of units) and a direction. A vector pointing to the east is positive, while one pointing to the west is negative. A resultant vector for two vectors in opposite directions is found by adding them, taking account of their opposite signs. What is the resultant of two vectors if one vector is pointing to the east with a magnitude of 65 km and the other is pointing west with a magnitude of 100 km?

1.3

Subtract.

52. $-35 - (-61)$

53. $-\dfrac{3}{8} - \dfrac{4}{7}$

54. $15.6 - 18$

55. $0 - 3.97$

56. $-2.3 - (-2.3)$

57. $3\dfrac{5}{9} - 5\dfrac{2}{9}$

58. $\dfrac{23}{112} - \dfrac{19}{24}$

59. $4,079,321 - 7,056,902$

60. $-473 - 2091$

61. $-\dfrac{34}{75} - \left(-\dfrac{203}{275}\right)$

62. $101.02 - (-23.9)$

63. $553 - (-392)$

64. $2\dfrac{26}{27} - \left(-5\dfrac{1}{27}\right)$

65. $1\dfrac{61}{125} - 1.488$

66. $3.5 - 4.7 - (-8.2) - (-10.1) - 4.9 - (-16.7)$

67. $1 - 2 - (-3) - (-4) - 5 - 6 - (-7) - 8 - (-9)$

68. $\dfrac{3}{2} - \dfrac{1}{4} - \left(-\dfrac{8}{3}\right) - \dfrac{5}{6} - \left(-\dfrac{7}{2}\right) - 3$

69. $31 - 16 + (-23) - 45 - (-37) + 52 + (-83)$

Evaluate.

70. $3.7 - 6.83 + 5.5 + (-9.02) - 0.8 - (-15.2)$

71. $\dfrac{4}{5} - \dfrac{7}{3} + \dfrac{8}{9} - \left(-\dfrac{4}{15}\right) + \left(-\dfrac{2}{3}\right) + 3$

Write and evaluate an addition/subtraction expression for each situation. Interpret the result.

72. Cleta had a beginning balance in her checking account of $735.66. She wrote checks for $276.12, $187.05, and $68.57. She made deposits of $75.00, $185.00, and $50.00. The bank deducted a monthly service charge of $4.65 and also charged her $12.00 for her order of blank checks. What was the closing balance on her account?

73. The highest point in California is the top of Mount Whitney, with an elevation of 14,494 feet. The lowest point is in Death Valley, with an elevation of -282 feet. What is the difference in elevation between these two points?

74. John bought shares of stock at $22\frac{1}{2}$ per share and sold them at $28\frac{1}{4}$. What was his gain per share on the investment?

1.4

Multiply.

75. $(-13)(-6)$

76. $(21)(-5)$

77. $\left(-7\dfrac{2}{5}\right)\left(-\dfrac{5}{7}\right)$

78. $\left(-3\dfrac{1}{5}\right)\left(\dfrac{5}{16}\right)$

79. $(23.05)(-0.04)$

80. $0 \cdot (-11)$

81. $(-1) \cdot 25$

82. $(-34)(20)$

83. $(-2357)(1037)$

84. $\left(\dfrac{23}{171}\right)\left(\dfrac{33}{230}\right)$

85. $(-2.04)(-4.12)$

86. $2905 \cdot 1197$

87. $(13.902)(4.387)$

88. $(-763)(-924)$

89. $\dfrac{-13}{29} \cdot \dfrac{58}{169}$

90. $(-2.101)(3.337)$

91. $765 \cdot (-835)$

92. $(43.996)(0)$

93. $(-32)(20)(-1)(5)(-2)(10)$

94. $(-1.1)(0.2)(-4)(-10)(-0.8)$

95. $\left(-\dfrac{1}{3}\right)\left(\dfrac{6}{7}\right)\left(-\dfrac{14}{15}\right)\left(-\dfrac{25}{8}\right)$

96. $(-54)(21)(0)(32)(0)(-25)$

Write and evaluate a multiplication expression for each situation. Interpret the result.

97. A distributor packages cleanser in 14-ounce cans. The cans are packaged 36 to a case. An order is received for 16 cases. How many ounces of cleanser will be required to process the order, given that no waste occurs?

98. Find the bill for the labor of a remodeling project if the labor was calculated for 22.5 hours at $45 per hour.

1.5

Divide.

99. $220 \div (-4)$

100. $-78 \div (-3)$

101. $-26{,}320 \div (-112)$

102. $\dfrac{5}{9} \div \left(\dfrac{-2}{3}\right)$

103. $-10.557 \div 2.3$

104. $0 \div 25$

105. $-2 \div 0$

106. $-13.7 \div (-1)$

107. $749.82645 \div (-35.65)$

108. $-\dfrac{23}{356} \div \dfrac{46}{89}$

109. $-1{,}363{,}443 \div 2539$

110. $\dfrac{143{,}883}{657}$

111. $\dfrac{-87}{121} \div \dfrac{-58}{99}$

112. $\dfrac{65}{323} \div \dfrac{91}{247}$

113. $7.32864 \div 1.056$

114. $90{,}258 \div (-307)$

Evaluate.

115. $(-25) \div (-5)(12)(-3) \div (-9)(-5)$

116. $(4.2)(-3.2) \div (1.6)(0.2) \div (-0.4)(-2.2)$

117. $\left(\dfrac{5}{12}\right)\left(-\dfrac{6}{25}\right) \div \left(-\dfrac{3}{10}\right)\left(\dfrac{15}{17}\right) \div \left(-\dfrac{5}{13}\right)$

Write and evaluate a division expression for each situation. Interpret the result.

118. In David's statistics class, grades are reported as the number of points above (positive) or below (negative) the class average. His scores on five tests are: 10 points above; 5 points below; 8 points above; 1 point above; and 12 points below. Calculate his average. Is it above or below the class average?

119. A landlord finds that six similar apartments in his neighborhood rent for $625, $690, $620, $590, $630, and $660 per month. Based on the average of these, what would be a fair monthly rent for the landlord to charge for his apartments?

120. Clarence records his gasoline usage on a trip from Louisville, Kentucky, to Cleveland, Ohio, to see the Rock and Roll Hall of Fame. He uses 18.7 gallons of gas to drive 345 miles. What was his average mileage for the trip?

CHAPTER 1	Mixed Review

Express your answers in fractional notation or round decimals to the nearest thousandth as appropriate.

Evaluate.

1. $-\left|\dfrac{9}{25}\right|$

2. $|-(-102)|$

3. $-|-(-3.7)|$

4. $-\left(-\left(-\left(4\dfrac{6}{7}\right)\right)\right)$

5. $-(0.085)$

6. $-(-(-(-7)))$

7. $-549 + (-908)$

8. $3.07 + (-2.9)$

9. $-1\dfrac{4}{13} + 2\dfrac{1}{2}$

10. $-\dfrac{1}{8} + \left(-1\dfrac{1}{4}\right)$

11. $1260 + 1111$

12. $-67,853 + 80,000$

13. $0.005 + 0.05$

14. $\dfrac{17}{65} + \dfrac{8}{91}$

15. $-9.678 + (-9.678)$

16. $-34.07 - (-31.97)$

17. $-576 - (-394)$

18. $-\dfrac{4}{13} - \dfrac{7}{39}$

19. $0.52 - 3$

20. $0 - \dfrac{3}{11}$

21. $-4.07 - (-5.1)$

22. $\dfrac{13}{25} - \dfrac{2}{5}$

23. $\dfrac{3}{17} - \left(-\dfrac{5}{34}\right)$

24. $1,000,000 - 1,000$

25. $-21 - 453$

26. $-\dfrac{4}{9} - \left(-\dfrac{47}{81}\right)$

27. $15.07 - (-0.907)$

28. $4500 - (-45)$

29. $\left(-\dfrac{12}{55}\right)\left(-\dfrac{5}{6}\right)$

30. $\left(-4\dfrac{3}{7}\right)\left(\dfrac{14}{31}\right)$

31. $(0.09)(-0.06)$

32. $0 \cdot (-8.05)$

33. $(-45) \cdot 65$

34. $(-1)(-88)$

35. $(-767)(-11)$

36. $\left(\dfrac{17}{72}\right)\left(\dfrac{9}{34}\right)$

37. $(-31.6)(-1.001)$

38. $4000 \cdot 1200$

39. $(121.3)(12.1)$

40. $(-111)(0)$

41. $\dfrac{-1175}{-5}$

42. $\dfrac{4}{13} \div \left(-\dfrac{12}{13}\right)$

43. $-18.87 \div 5.1$

44. $0 \div 0$

45. $-21 \div 0$

46. $(56.8) \div (-1)$

47. $-9.02 \div (-1.1)$

48. $\dfrac{-8}{55} \div \left(\dfrac{-4}{17}\right)$

49. $\dfrac{-16,281}{243}$

50. $5.5 \div 2.2$

51. $\dfrac{184,008}{902}$

52. $\dfrac{2}{5} \div \dfrac{56}{75}$

53. $-\dfrac{1}{5} - \left(-\dfrac{2}{9}\right)$

Use one of the symbols $>$, $<$, or $=$ to compare the two numbers.

54. 75 _____ 59

55. 3.54 _____ 3.65

56. $\dfrac{31}{51}$ _____ $\dfrac{10}{17}$

57. -142 _____ -105

58. $-\dfrac{21}{59}$ _____ $-\dfrac{29}{59}$

59. $\dfrac{3}{8}$ _____ 0.375

60. −35 _____ 71

61. −9.05 _____ −9.07

62. −3.7 _____ 0.53

63. $-\dfrac{6}{7}$ _____ $\dfrac{3}{7}$

64. 0 _____ −197

65. 31 _____ 0

In exercises 66–80, evaluate.

66. $2.56 + (-3.78) + 0.5 + 9.882 + (-1.05) + (-0.009)$

67. $\dfrac{5}{7} + \dfrac{3}{5} + \left(-\dfrac{1}{2}\right) + \left(-\dfrac{23}{35}\right) + \left(-\dfrac{7}{10}\right)$

68. $17.6 - 0.9 - (-12.7) - (-28.4) - 25.8 - (-21.4)$

69. $-45 - 88 - (-74) - (-90) - 65 - 71 - (-27) - 53 - (-48)$

70. $\dfrac{5}{6} - \dfrac{11}{30} - \left(-\dfrac{3}{5}\right) - \dfrac{14}{15} - \left(-\dfrac{9}{2}\right) - 1$

71. $57 - 61 + (-32) - 54 - (-73) + 25 + (-38)$

72. $7.3 - 38.6 + 5.5 + (-2.09) - 8 - (-2.51)$

73. $\dfrac{3}{7} - \dfrac{17}{21} + \dfrac{11}{14} - \left(-\dfrac{5}{6}\right) + \left(-\dfrac{35}{42}\right) + 7$

74. $(-55)(12)(-2)(9)(-3)(1)$

75. $(-3.2)(0.6)(-5)(-100)(-0.1)$

76. $\left(-\dfrac{14}{22}\right)\left(\dfrac{8}{21}\right)\left(-\dfrac{11}{4}\right)\left(-\dfrac{3}{5}\right)$

77. $(-11.2)(3.1)(0)(-9.4)(-1)(-7.5)$

78. $(-15) \div (-3)(22)(-4) \div (-8)(-7)$

79. $(13.1)(-4.2) \div (2.62)(0.5) \div (-0.7)(-1.1)$

80. $\left(\dfrac{9}{14}\right)\left(-\dfrac{7}{18}\right) \div \left(-\dfrac{3}{4}\right)\left(\dfrac{6}{7}\right) \div \left(-\dfrac{1}{21}\right)$

81. Graph the following numbers on a number line.

$$3.6, \quad -\dfrac{2}{3}, \quad 2\dfrac{1}{2}, \quad 0, \quad -2.7, \quad -3\dfrac{2}{3}$$

In exercises 82–84, write an equivalent order relation for each statement.

82. $76 > 75$

83. $-\dfrac{2}{5} < \dfrac{1}{7}$

84. $0.52 = \dfrac{13}{25}$

85. In business mathematics, profit is defined as the difference of revenue less expenses. For the following situations, determine the profit, and state whether the business experienced a gain or a loss.

   a. The business had revenues of $275,000 and expenses of $183,000.

   b. The business had revenues of $695,000 and expenses of $710,000.

86. During a 4-week period, a stock experienced weekly fluctuations in price as follows: increased by $5\frac{3}{8}$ points; decreased by $1\frac{5}{8}$ points; decreased by $3\frac{3}{4}$ points; no change in points. Find the average weekly change in stock prices for the 4-week period. Interpret the average to show whether the stock had an average increase or a decrease over the 4-week period.

87. The film *Who Framed Roger Rabbit?* has the longest list of credits of any film, with 763 names. It takes $6\frac{1}{2}$ minutes to run the credits. On the average, how many credits run each minute?

88. A 10-gallon hat actually holds only $\frac{3}{4}$ gallon of water. How many gallons of water will fill ten 10-gallon hats?

89. In *Star Trek*, Captain Kirk had 430 people in his crew. Captain Picard, his successor, had 1012 crew and civilians under his command. How many more people did Captain Picard command?

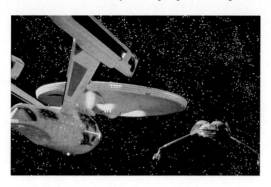

90. In the National Football League, the home team is required to provide 24 new footballs for each game. If the league has 28 teams, and if each team plays eight home games a season, how many footballs are needed?

CHAPTER 1 | Test

Test-Taking Tips

Changing the rate and pattern of your breathing to a deep, slow pattern will calm your body and ease your mind. Before you start a test, take at least three deep, slow breaths and blow out as much air as you can. It will help relax you and clear your mind for the test.

Consider the following numbers.

$$0, \ -\frac{1}{3}, \ 15, \ -4\frac{1}{5}, \ 0.546, \ -17$$

1. Which numbers are natural numbers?

2. Which numbers are whole numbers?

3. Which numbers are integers?

4. Which numbers are rational numbers?

Use one of the symbols >, <, or = to compare the numbers.

5. $\dfrac{4}{9}$ _____ $\dfrac{5}{6}$

6. -18 _____ -23

7. $\dfrac{17}{25}$ _____ 0.68

Write an equivalent order relation for each statement.

8. $\dfrac{5}{16} > \dfrac{1}{4}$

9. $-3.2 < -2.3$

10. $\dfrac{3}{50} = 0.06$

In exercises 11–32, evaluate. Express your answers in the same form as the original exercise wherever possible, and round decimals to the nearest thousandth.

11. $|-13.37|$

12. $-(-20)$

13. $-|-20|$

14. $59 + (-95)$

15. $-\dfrac{17}{95} + \dfrac{4}{19}$

16. $4.378 - 7.98$

17. $\left(-\dfrac{3}{4}\right)\left(-\dfrac{8}{15}\right)$

18. $-6985 - (-2576)$

19. $45.78 \cdot (-1)$

20. $(-37{,}562)(456)$

21. $-413.9 + (-597.65)$

22. $-819 \div (-9)$

23. $-\dfrac{44}{57} \div \dfrac{11}{19}$

24. $15.9 \div 0$

25. $0 \div (-53)$

26. $2\dfrac{3}{7} \div 1\dfrac{3}{14}$

27. $-12.05 - 2.4$

28. $(-23)(-4)(0)(-17)(0)(-45)$

29. $\left(-\dfrac{5}{6}\right)\left(-\dfrac{3}{7}\right)\left(\dfrac{1}{2}\right)\left(-\dfrac{2}{15}\right)$

30. $4.3 + (-0.1) - (-2) + (-1.1)$

31. $3\dfrac{2}{3} \div 4\dfrac{1}{9} \cdot \left(-7\dfrac{4}{11}\right)$

32. $(-42)(22) \div 77(-4) \div (-16)$

33. Graph the following numbers on a number line. Label the points.

$$-3.5,\ 3,\ \dfrac{1}{2},\ 2\dfrac{3}{4},\ -1\dfrac{1}{2}$$

34. Sally opened a checking account with an initial deposit of $500.00. She wrote checks for $123.75, $56.80, and $95.87. She made an additional deposit of $250.00. Write an addition statement to represent what her account balance would be. What is the current balance of her account?

35. Regina has 24% of her gross pay deducted for withholding and other expenses. She earns $675 per week as her gross pay. Write a multiplication expression to find out how much will be deducted from her weekly pay. What will her deduction be?

36. Explain how you would determine the sign of the product of two rational numbers.

37. How would you determine the sign of the product of three or more rational numbers?

Real Numbers

2

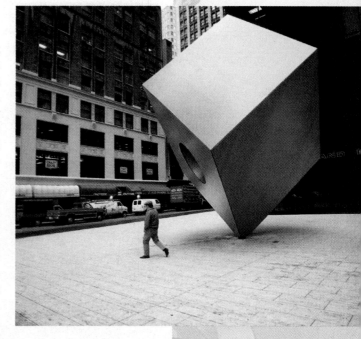

I n Chapter 1, we discussed the rational numbers, which can be expressed as a ratio of two integers. In this chapter, we introduce the irrational numbers, which cannot be expressed as a ratio of integers. Together, these two categories of numbers make up the real number system. We will examine the properties of real numbers and investigate the order of operations on them. We will also evaluate expressions containing exponents and radicals, which often include irrational numbers.

Irrational numbers occur frequently in quite simple geometric situations. For example, suppose you draw a square measuring exactly 1 foot on each side. What is the length of the diagonal of the square? You will find that though this line is easy to draw, we cannot express it as a rational number, because it is an irrational number. Similarly, if you draw a cube whose edge is exactly 1 foot long, you will not be able to express its major diagonal in terms of a rational number, because it is an irrational number. In mathematics, some numbers make a great deal of sense, but they are still irrational.

2.1 Exponential Expressions with Integer Exponents

Objectives

1 Evaluate exponential expressions with integer exponents greater than 1.

2 Evaluate exponential expressions with integer exponents of 1 and 0.

3 Evaluate exponential expressions with integer exponents less than 0.

4 Model real-world situations using exponential expressions with integer exponents.

Application

In the town of Marostica in northern Italy, a game of chess is played every 2 years using live people as pieces. The event celebrates a game played in 1454 between two suitors for a lady's hand, in which the winner could claim the lady as his bride. The board on which the living chess game is played measures 8 squares by 8 squares, and each square measures 10 feet by 10 feet. What is the area of the board?

After completing this section, we will discuss this application further. See page 88.

1 Evaluating Exponential Expressions with an Integer (>1) Exponent

When a number is repeated as a factor, it may be written in exponential form instead of as a multiplication problem. For example,

$$\underbrace{2 \cdot 2 \cdot 2 \cdot 2 \cdot 2 \cdot 2}_{\text{6 factors}} = 2^6$$

The repeated factor is the **base** of the expression. The number of times it is repeated as a factor is written as an **exponent**. That is,

$$\underbrace{2 \cdot 2 \cdot 2 \cdot 2 \cdot 2 \cdot 2}_{\text{2 repeated 6 times}} = \underset{\text{base}^{\text{exponent}}}{2^6}$$

The base is 2 and the exponent is 6.

In the preceding example, $2 \cdot 2 \cdot 2 \cdot 2 \cdot 2 \cdot 2$ is called an **expanded form** and 2^6 is called an **exponential form** or an **exponential expression**.

For the moment, we will examine expressions with integer exponents greater than 1 and with bases that are positive numbers or 0.

EXAMPLE 1   Write in exponential form.

   a. $4 \cdot 4 \cdot 4 \cdot 4 \cdot 4$

   b. $1 \cdot 1 \cdot 1 \cdot 1$

   c. $(0.2)(0.2)(0.2)(0.2)(0.2)(0.2)$ **d.** $\dfrac{2}{5} \cdot \dfrac{2}{5} \cdot \dfrac{2}{5}$

Solution

a. $4 \cdot 4 \cdot 4 \cdot 4 \cdot 4 = 4^5$

4 is a factor 5 times.
4 is the base and 5 is the exponent.

b. $1 \cdot 1 \cdot 1 \cdot 1 = 1^4$

1 is a factor 4 times.
1 is the base and 4 is the exponent.

c. $(0.2)(0.2)(0.2)(0.2)(0.2)(0.2) = 0.2^6$

0.2 is a factor 6 times. 0.2 is the base and 6 is the exponent.

d. $\dfrac{2}{5} \cdot \dfrac{2}{5} \cdot \dfrac{2}{5} = \left(\dfrac{2}{5}\right)^3$

$\frac{2}{5}$ is a factor 3 times.
$\frac{2}{5}$ is the base, written in parentheses, and 3 is the exponent. ∎

To evaluate an exponential expression, write it in expanded form and then multiply the factors. For example,

$$2^2 = 2 \cdot 2 = 4$$

Therefore, $2^2 = 4$.   This is read:
2 (raised) to the second power is 4.
or: 2 squared is 4.

$$2^3 = 2 \cdot 2 \cdot 2 = 8$$

Therefore, $2^3 = 8$.   This is read:
2 (raised) to the third power is 8.
or: 2 cubed is 8.

$$2^6 = 2 \cdot 2 \cdot 2 \cdot 2 \cdot 2 \cdot 2 = 64$$

Therefore, $2^6 = 64$.   This is read:
2 (raised) to the sixth power is 64. (All powers except 2 and 3 are read in this manner.)

EXAMPLE 2   Write in expanded form and evaluate.

   a. 4^2

   b. 1.5^3

   c. $\left(3\dfrac{1}{4}\right)^2$

   d. 0^4

   e. $\left(9\dfrac{1}{3}\right)^5$

Solution

a. $4^2 = 4 \cdot 4 = 16$

4 is repeated as a factor 2 times.

b. $1.5^3 = (1.5)(1.5)(1.5) = 3.375$

1.5 is repeated as a factor 3 times.

c. $\left(3\dfrac{1}{4}\right)^2 = \left(3\dfrac{1}{4}\right)\left(3\dfrac{1}{4}\right)$

$3\frac{1}{4}$ is repeated as a factor 2 times.

$$= \left(\dfrac{13}{4}\right)\left(\dfrac{13}{4}\right) = \dfrac{169}{16}$$

d. $0^4 = 0 \cdot 0 \cdot 0 \cdot 0 = 0$

0 is repeated as a factor 4 times.

e. $\left(9\frac{1}{3}\right)^5 = \left(\frac{28}{3}\right)\left(\frac{28}{3}\right)\left(\frac{28}{3}\right)\left(\frac{28}{3}\right)\left(\frac{28}{3}\right)$ $9\frac{1}{3}$ is repeated as a factor 5 times.

$$= \frac{17{,}210{,}368}{243}$$

To evaluate an exponential expression on your calculator, it is not necessary to enter it in expanded form. The calculator has special keys for exponents.

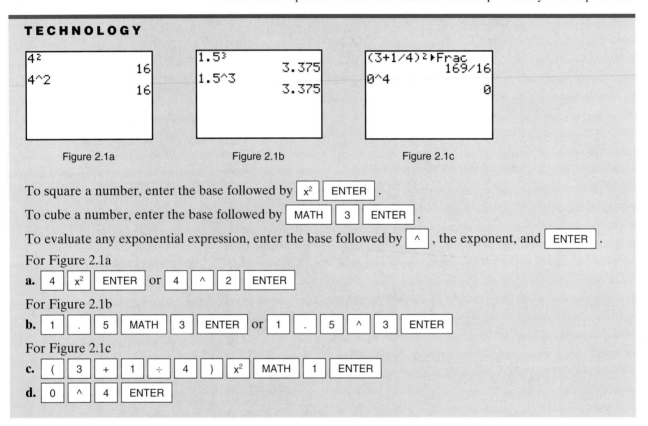

Figure 2.1a   Figure 2.1b   Figure 2.1c

To square a number, enter the base followed by $\boxed{x^2}$ $\boxed{\text{ENTER}}$.

To cube a number, enter the base followed by $\boxed{\text{MATH}}$ $\boxed{3}$ $\boxed{\text{ENTER}}$.

To evaluate any exponential expression, enter the base followed by $\boxed{\wedge}$, the exponent, and $\boxed{\text{ENTER}}$.

For Figure 2.1a

a. $\boxed{4}$ $\boxed{x^2}$ $\boxed{\text{ENTER}}$ or $\boxed{4}$ $\boxed{\wedge}$ $\boxed{2}$ $\boxed{\text{ENTER}}$

For Figure 2.1b

b. $\boxed{1}$ $\boxed{.}$ $\boxed{5}$ $\boxed{\text{MATH}}$ $\boxed{3}$ $\boxed{\text{ENTER}}$ or $\boxed{1}$ $\boxed{.}$ $\boxed{5}$ $\boxed{\wedge}$ $\boxed{3}$ $\boxed{\text{ENTER}}$

For Figure 2.1c

c. $\boxed{(}$ $\boxed{3}$ $\boxed{+}$ $\boxed{1}$ $\boxed{\div}$ $\boxed{4}$ $\boxed{)}$ $\boxed{x^2}$ $\boxed{\text{MATH}}$ $\boxed{1}$ $\boxed{\text{ENTER}}$

d. $\boxed{0}$ $\boxed{\wedge}$ $\boxed{4}$ $\boxed{\text{ENTER}}$

Due to the calculator's limitations, some fractions will be displayed as a decimal. To check your answer for 2e, enter the fraction answer and compare the decimal values. ■

If the repeated factor in an exponential expression is a negative number, write the factor in parentheses as the base. For example,

$$\underbrace{-2\cdot-2\cdot-2\cdot-2\cdot-2\cdot-2}_{-2\text{ repeated 6 times}} = \underset{\text{base}^{\text{exponent}}}{(-2)^6}$$

The parentheses are very important here. If no parentheses are used, the base is not considered to be a negative number. For example,

-2^6 means the opposite of "2 to the sixth power."

$$-(2)^6 = -(2\cdot2\cdot2\cdot2\cdot2\cdot2) = -64$$

$(-2)^6$ means "-2 to the sixth power."

$$(-2)^6 = -2\cdot-2\cdot-2\cdot-2\cdot-2\cdot-2 = 64$$

Therefore, $(-2)^6 \neq -2^6$ because $(-2)^6 = 64$ and $-2^6 = -64$.

We see that $(-2)^6 = 64$, which is a positive number. Do all negative bases raised to an exponent greater than 1 give positive numbers? Let's try a few cases to see. Complete the following set of exercises with your calculator.

DISCOVERY 1

Exponential Expressions with Negative Number Bases
Evaluate each expression.

1. $(-2)^2 =$ ____   **2.** $(-2)^3 =$ ____
3. $(-2)^4 =$ ____   **4.** $(-2)^5 =$ ____

Write in your own words a rule for determining the sign when evaluating an exponential expression with a negative base.

The sign of an exponential expression with a negative base is negative if the exponent is an odd number (such as 3 and 5) and is positive if the exponent is an even number (such as 2 and 4).

Evaluating Exponential Expressions with an Integer Exponent Greater Than 1
To evaluate an exponential expression with an integer exponent greater than 1, determine the product of its expanded form.
   If the base is positive, the product is positive.
   If the base is negative:

- The product is positive if the exponent is even.
- The product is negative if the exponent is odd.

If the base is 0, the product is 0.

To understand this rule, remember the rule for multiplication, which states that an even number of negative factors results in a positive product and an odd number of negative factors results in a negative product.

$$(-2)^3 = -2 \cdot -2 \cdot -2 \quad = \quad -8$$

3 negative factors (odd number)   negative product

$$(-2)^4 = -2 \cdot -2 \cdot -2 \cdot -2 = \quad 16$$

4 negative factors (even number)   positive product

EXAMPLE 3   Write in expanded form and evaluate.

a. $(-4)^2$ **b.** $(-9)^3$ **c.** $-(-1.8)^5$
d. $\left(-\dfrac{3}{4}\right)^4$ **e.** $(-1)^6$ **f.** -1^6

Solution

a. $(-4)^2 = -4 \cdot -4 = 16$
b. $(-9)^3 = -9 \cdot -9 \cdot -9 = -729$
c. $-(-1.8)^5 = -(-1.8 \cdot -1.8 \cdot -1.8 \cdot -1.8 \cdot -1.8) = 18.89568$

d. $\left(-\dfrac{3}{4}\right)^4 = \left(-\dfrac{3}{4}\right)\left(-\dfrac{3}{4}\right)\left(-\dfrac{3}{4}\right)\left(-\dfrac{3}{4}\right) = \dfrac{81}{256}$

e. $(-1)^6 = (-1)(-1)(-1)(-1)(-1)(-1) = 1$

f. $-1^6 = -(1 \cdot 1 \cdot 1 \cdot 1 \cdot 1 \cdot 1) = -1$

The checks for examples 3e and 3f are shown in Figure 2.2. ∎

TECHNOLOGY

```
(-1)^6
                1
-1^6
               -1
```

For Figure 2.2

e. ((−) 1) ^ 6 ENTER

f. (−) 1 ^ 6 ENTER

Figure 2.2

 Experiencing Algebra the Checkup Way

Write in exponential form.

1. $3 \cdot 3 \cdot 3 \cdot 3 \cdot 3 \cdot 3 \cdot 3$

2. $\left(\dfrac{2}{3}\right)\left(\dfrac{2}{3}\right)\left(\dfrac{2}{3}\right)\left(\dfrac{2}{3}\right)$

Write in expanded form and evaluate.

3. $(1.3)^2$

4. 0^6

5. $\left(\dfrac{2}{5}\right)^5$

Evaluate and compare the results of each part.

6. a. $(-6)^2$ **b.** -6^2

7. a. $(-6)^3$ **b.** -6^3

8. Write the keystrokes needed to find $(-2\frac{1}{3})^4$. What is the result expressed as a fraction? What is the result expressed as a decimal, rounded to two places?

9. Explain the meaning of the terms *base* and *exponent* in an exponential expression.

10. When the base of an exponential expression is negative, how can you tell whether the value of the exponential expression will be positive or negative?

---

2 Evaluating Exponential Expressions with an Exponent of 1 or 0

The expanded form of an expression with an exponent of 1 or 0 is not obvious. We need to find a second method for evaluating such expressions. Complete the following sets of exercises with your calculator.

DISCOVERY 2

Expressions with an Exponent of 1

Evaluate each expression.

1. $3^1 =$ ____　　　　**2.** $(-3)^1 =$ ____　　　　**3.** $2.4^1 =$ ____

4. $\left(\dfrac{1}{2}\right)^1 =$ ____　　　　**5.** $0^1 =$ ____

Write in your own words a rule for evaluating an exponential expression with an exponent of 1.

An exponential expression with an exponent of 1 results in the base number.

DISCOVERY 3

Expressions with an Exponent of 0

Evaluate each expression.

1. $3^0 =$ ____　　　　**2.** $(-3)^0 =$ ____　　　　**3.** $2.4^0 =$ ____

4. $\left(\dfrac{1}{2}\right)^0 =$ ____　　　　**5.** $0^0 =$ ____

Write in your own words a rule for evaluating an exponential expression with an exponent of 0.

An exponential expression with an exponent of 0 and a nonzero base is 1. If the base is 0 and the exponent is 0, the expression is indeterminate.

> *Evaluating Exponential Expressions with an Exponent of One or Zero*
> The value of an exponential expression with an exponent of 1 is equal to the base number.
>   The value of an exponential expression with an exponent of 0 is
>
> • 1 if the base is not 0.
>
> • indeterminate if the base is 0.

To visualize these rules, examine the following pattern:

$$3^4 = 3 \cdot 3 \cdot 3 \cdot 3$$

Exponent
decreases
by 1.

$$3^3 = 3 \cdot 3 \cdot 3 \qquad \text{Divide by 3.}$$
$$3^2 = 3 \cdot 3$$
$$3^1 = \underline{\quad}$$
$$3^0 = \underline{\quad}$$

Using the preceding pattern, $3^1 = \underline{\ 3\ }$ and $3^0 = \underline{\ 1\ }$. (If we divide by 3, we get 1.)

EXAMPLE 4　Evaluate.

a. 18^0　　　　　　　**b.** $(-18)^0$　　　　　　　**c.** -18^0

d. $(-15)^1$　　　　　　**e.** -15^1

Solution

a. $18^0 = 1$ **b.** $(-18)^0 = 1$ **c.** $-18^0 = -1$

d. $(-15)^1 = -15$ **e.** $-15^1 = -15$ ∎

 ## Experiencing Algebra the Checkup Way

Evaluate. Check your results on the calculator.

1. 7^1 **2.** $(-7)^1$ **3.** -7^1 **4.** 7^0 **5.** $(-7)^0$ **6.** -7^0

---

3 Evaluating Exponential Expressions with a Negative Integer Exponent and a Nonzero Base

If an exponential expression has a negative exponent, it is impossible to determine the number of times to repeat the base when writing in expanded form. Therefore, we must discover an alternative method to evaluate these exponential expressions. Complete the following sets of exercises with your calculator.

DISCOVERY 4

Nonzero Integer Bases with Negative Integer Exponents
Evaluate each expression and compare the results obtained in the left column to the corresponding results in the right column.

1. a. $2^{-1} = $ ____   **b.** $\left(\dfrac{1}{2}\right)^1 = $ ____

2. a. $2^{-2} = $ ____   **b.** $\left(\dfrac{1}{2}\right)^2 = $ ____

3. a. $2^{-3} = $ ____   **b.** $\left(\dfrac{1}{2}\right)^3 = $ ____

4. a. $(-2)^{-1} = $ ____   **b.** $\left(\dfrac{-1}{2}\right)^1 = $ ____

5. a. $(-2)^{-2} = $ ____   **b.** $\left(\dfrac{-1}{2}\right)^2 = $ ____

6. a. $(-2)^{-3} = $ ____   **b.** $\left(\dfrac{-1}{2}\right)^3 = $ ____

Write in your own words a rule for evaluating an exponential expression with a nonzero integer base and a negative integer exponent.

In the column on the left, we evaluate an exponential expression with a nonzero integer base and a negative integer exponent. In the column on the right, we evaluate an exponential expression consisting of a base that is the reciprocal of the base on the left and an exponent that is the opposite of the exponent on the left. The results are the same in both columns.

DISCOVERY 5

Fraction Bases with Negative Integer Exponents
Evaluate each expression and compare the results obtained in the left column to the corresponding results in the right column.

1. a. $\left(\dfrac{1}{2}\right)^{-1} = $ ____   **b.** $2^1 = $ ____

Continued

2. a. $\left(\dfrac{1}{2}\right)^{-2} = $ ____ **b.** $2^2 = $ ____

3. a. $\left(\dfrac{1}{2}\right)^{-3} = $ ____ **b.** $2^3 = $ ____

4. a. $\left(\dfrac{-1}{2}\right)^{-1} = $ ____ **b.** $(-2)^1 = $ ____

5. a. $\left(\dfrac{-1}{2}\right)^{-2} = $ ____ **b.** $(-2)^2 = $ ____

6. a. $\left(\dfrac{-1}{2}\right)^{-3} = $ ____ **b.** $(-2)^3 = $ ____

Write in your own words a rule for evaluating an exponential expression with a fraction base and a negative integer exponent.

In the column on the left, we evaluate an exponential expression with a fraction base and a negative integer exponent. In the column on the right, we evaluate an exponential expression consisting of a base that is the reciprocal of the base on the left and an exponent that is the opposite of the exponent on the left. We see that the results are the same in both columns.

Note: The same rule was used for each of the previous procedures. Therefore, the same rule is used for evaluating all exponential expressions with a nonzero base and a negative integer exponent.

Notice that a number raised to the -1 power results in the reciprocal of the number itself. This is important enough that the calculator has a special key that can be used for this exponent.

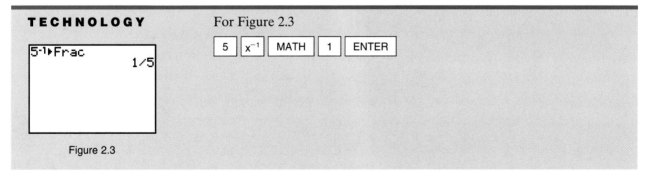

TECHNOLOGY

```
5⁻¹▸Frac
            1/5
```

Figure 2.3

For Figure 2.3

| 5 | x^{-1} | MATH | 1 | ENTER |

It is impossible to evaluate an exponential expression with a negative exponent and a zero base, because if we take the reciprocal of 0 we obtain $\frac{1}{0}$, which is undefined.

Evaluating Exponential Expressions with a Negative Integer Exponent
To evaluate an exponential expression with a nonzero base and a negative integer exponent:

- Rewrite the expression as the reciprocal of the base with the opposite of the exponent.
- Evaluate the new expression.

An exponential expression with a zero base and a negative integer exponent is undefined.

To visualize these rules, examine the following pattern we began in the last objective:

$$3^4 = 3 \cdot 3 \cdot 3 \cdot 3$$

Exponent decreases by 1.

$$3^3 = 3 \cdot 3 \cdot 3 \qquad \text{Divide by 3.}$$
$$3^2 = 3 \cdot 3$$
$$3^1 = 3$$
$$3^0 = 1$$
$$3^{-1} = \underline{\qquad}$$
$$3^{-2} = \underline{\qquad}$$

Using the preceding pattern, $3^{-1} = \frac{1}{3}$ and $3^{-2} = \frac{1}{9}$.

EXAMPLE 5 Write an equivalent exponential expression having a positive exponent. Evaluate.

a. 4^{-3} **b.** $(-2)^{-4}$ **c.** $\left(\frac{2}{3}\right)^{-3}$

d. $\left(-3\frac{1}{4}\right)^{-2}$ **e.** $-(0.3)^{-3}$ **f.** $-(-0.3)^{-3}$

Solution

a. $4^{-3} = \left(\frac{1}{4}\right)^3 = \frac{1}{64}$ Reciprocal of 4 is $\frac{1}{4}$.

b. $(-2)^{-4} = \left(-\frac{1}{2}\right)^4 = \frac{1}{16}$ Reciprocal of -2 is $-\frac{1}{2}$.

c. $\left(\frac{2}{3}\right)^{-3} = \left(\frac{3}{2}\right)^3 = \frac{27}{8}$ Reciprocal of $\frac{2}{3}$ is $\frac{3}{2}$.

d. $\left(-3\frac{1}{4}\right)^{-2} = \left(\frac{-13}{4}\right)^{-2}$ Change the base to the improper fraction $\frac{-13}{4}$.

$= \left(\frac{-4}{13}\right)^2 = \frac{16}{169}$ Reciprocal of $\frac{-13}{4}$ is $\frac{-4}{13}$.

e. $-(0.3)^{-3} = -\left(\frac{3}{10}\right)^{-3}$ Write the base as a fraction, $\frac{3}{10}$.

$= -\left(\frac{10}{3}\right)^3 = \frac{-1000}{27}$ Reciprocal of $\frac{3}{10}$ is $\frac{10}{3}$.

f. $-(-0.3)^{-3} = -\left(\dfrac{-3}{10}\right)^{-3}$ Write the base as a fraction, $\frac{-3}{10}$.

$\qquad\qquad = -\left(\dfrac{-10}{3}\right)^{3} = \dfrac{1000}{27}$ Reciprocal of $\frac{-3}{10}$ is $\frac{-10}{3}$.

The checks for Example 5 are shown in Figure 2.4a and Figure 2.4b. ∎

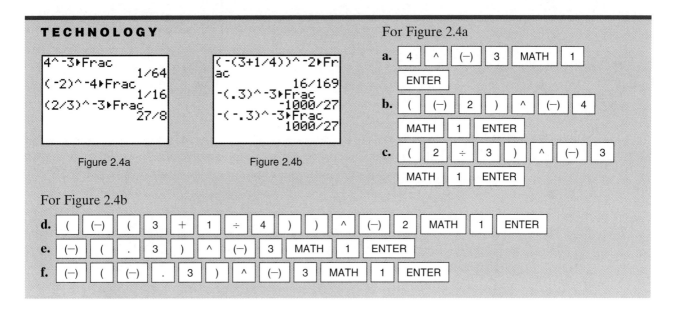

Figure 2.4a

Figure 2.4b

Experiencing Algebra the Checkup Way

In exercises 1–6, write an equivalent exponential expression having a positive exponent. Evaluate.

1. 3^{-3}

2. -3^{-3}

3. $-(-3)^{-3}$

4. $(0.5)^{-4}$

5. $\left(\dfrac{3}{4}\right)^{-3}$

6. $\left(-1\dfrac{3}{7}\right)^{-2}$

7. Write the keystrokes needed to determine the following exponential expression, in fraction form: $(-3\frac{1}{3})^{-4}$.
What is the result? If the calculator result was not a fraction, can you explain why?

8. What is the effect of a negative exponent on an exponential expression?

9. If an exponential expression has a negative exponent, what is the restriction on the value of its base?

4 Modeling the Real World   Evaluating the areas and the volumes of geometric figures requires evaluating exponential expressions. To determine the area of a square, we square the length of its side. The length of a side consists of a unit of measurement, as well as a number. Therefore, if the number is squared, the unit of measurement is also squared. For example, if we have a square of side 1 ft, the area is 1 ft².

To determine the volume of a cube, we cube the length of each edge. As before, we cube the number and the unit of measurement. For a cube of edge 1 ft, the volume is 1 ft³.

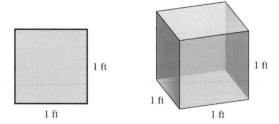

1 ft

1 ft

1 ft

1 ft

1 ft

EXAMPLE 6 Johana has a square piece of material to use for a small tablecloth that is $\frac{3}{4}$ yard on a side. Determine the area of the tablecloth.

Solution

To determine the area of the tablecloth, square the length of the side, $\frac{3}{4}$ yard.

$$\left(\frac{3}{4}\,\text{yd}\right)^2 = \left(\frac{3}{4}\,\text{yd}\right)\left(\frac{3}{4}\,\text{yd}\right) = \frac{9}{16}\,\text{yd}^2$$

The area of the tablecloth is $\frac{9}{16}$ square yard.

Helping Hand In this course, as long as we remember that the unit of measurement is squared, we do not need to write the unit of measurement in the problem. However, *always* remember to include the unit of measurement squared in the answer.

Application

In the town of Marostica in northern Italy, a game of chess is played every 2 years using live people as pieces. The event celebrates a game played in 1454 between two suitors for a lady's hand, in which the winner could claim the lady as his bride. The board on which the living chess game is played measures 8 squares by 8 squares, and each square measures 10 feet by 10 feet. What is the area of the board?

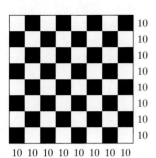

10
10
10
10
10
10
10
10

10 10 10 10 10 10 10 10

Discussion

To find the area of the board, first find the area of each individual square on the board by squaring the length of its side. This gives us $10 \cdot 10$, or 10^2. Then, multiply this area by the number of squares on the board.

Since there are 8 squares in a row and 8 rows of squares, multiply 8 times 8 to find the total number of squares, or $8 \cdot 8 = 8^2$.

Therefore, the total area is

$$\left(10^2\right)\left(8^2\right) = 6400$$

The area of the board is 6400 ft^2. ∎

 ## Experiencing Algebra the Checkup Way

Joshua builds a toy box in the shape of a cube. The inside edge of the toy box measures 18 inches on a side. Determine the volume of the box.

18 in.   18 in.

18 in.

PROBLEM SET 2.1

 ## Experiencing Algebra the Exercise Way

Write in exponential form.

1. $15 \cdot 15 \cdot 15 \cdot 15 \cdot 15 \cdot 15$

2. $(-31)(-31)(-31)(-31)$

3. $\left(-\frac{1}{5}\right)\left(-\frac{1}{5}\right)\left(-\frac{1}{5}\right)\left(-\frac{1}{5}\right)$

4. $\left(\frac{4}{7}\right)\left(\frac{4}{7}\right)\left(\frac{4}{7}\right)\left(\frac{4}{7}\right)\left(\frac{4}{7}\right)$

5. $(3.7)(3.7)(3.7)$

6. $(-2.2)(-2.2)(-2.2)(-2.2)$

7. $0 \cdot 0 \cdot 0 \cdot 0 \cdot 0 \cdot 0 \cdot 0$

8. $1 \cdot 1 \cdot 1 \cdot 1 \cdot 1 \cdot 1 \cdot 1$

Determine the resulting sign of the exponential expression. Do not evaluate.

9. $(-55)^8$ **10.** $(-85)^{12}$ **11.** -55^8 **12.** -85^{12}

13. $(-55)^5$ **14.** $(-85)^7$ **15.** -55^5 **16.** -85^7

Write in expanded form and evaluate.

17. 3^4 **18.** 2^6 **19.** $(-3)^4$ **20.** $(-2)^6$

21. -3^4 **22.** -2^6 **23.** $-(-3)^4$ **24.** $-(-2)^6$

25. $(-4)^3$ **26.** $(-3)^5$ **27.** $-(-4)^3$ **28.** $-(-3)^5$

Evaluate.

29. $(-2.5)^2$ **30.** $(-0.4)^2$ **31.** $-(0.5)^3$ **32.** $-(0.3)^3$

33. $-\left(-\dfrac{3}{7}\right)^2$ **34.** $-\left(-\dfrac{2}{3}\right)^4$ **35.** $\left(1\dfrac{1}{3}\right)^3$ **36.** $\left(1\dfrac{1}{2}\right)^3$

37. 0^8 **38.** 0^5 **39.** 1^{32} **40.** 1^{10}

41. $(-1)^{29}$ **42.** $(-1)^9$ **43.** $(-1)^{122}$ **44.** $(-1)^{12}$

Use your calculator to evaluate; round your answers to three decimal places or use fractional notation.

45. $(-79)^4$ **46.** $(-31)^4$ **47.** $(-1.08)^5$ **48.** $(-1.5)^3$

49. $\left(-\dfrac{2}{3}\right)^6$ **50.** $\left(-\dfrac{3}{4}\right)^4$ **51.** $\left(\dfrac{5}{6}\right)^5$ **52.** $\left(\dfrac{8}{9}\right)^3$

53. $(-37)^5$ **54.** $(-87)^5$ **55.** $(2.24)^6$ **56.** $(0.05)^2$

57. $-\left(3\dfrac{2}{11}\right)^4$ **58.** $-\left(-5\dfrac{12}{17}\right)^6$ **59.** $-\left(7\dfrac{21}{29}\right)^7$ **60.** $-\left(-6\dfrac{19}{21}\right)^9$

Evaluate.

61. 1256^1 **62.** $\left(-\dfrac{4}{17}\right)^1$ **63.** $-(13.06)^1$ **64.** $-\left(-3\dfrac{16}{37}\right)^1$

65. 1256^0 **66.** $(-34.601)^0$ **67.** -4721^0 **68.** $-\left(-8\dfrac{12}{55}\right)^0$

Write an equivalent exponential expression having a positive exponent. Evaluate.

69. 7^{-2} **70.** 8^{-2} **71.** $\left(\dfrac{2}{3}\right)^{-4}$ **72.** $\left(\dfrac{1}{2}\right)^{-4}$

73. $(-0.2)^{-2}$ **74.** $(-0.4)^{-2}$ **75.** -11^{-2} **76.** -12^{-2}

77. $(-12)^{-1}$ **78.** $(-11)^{-1}$ **79.** $-(-97)^{-1}$ **80.** $-(-52)^{-1}$

Use your calculator to evaluate; round your answers to three decimal places or use fractional notation.

81. $-\left(-\dfrac{5}{6}\right)^{-4}$ **82.** $-\left(-\dfrac{3}{7}\right)^{-4}$ **83.** $-(2.06)^{-4}$ **84.** $-(0.35)^{-4}$

85. $-\left(2\dfrac{2}{9}\right)^{-2}$ **86.** $-\left(-1\dfrac{1}{8}\right)^{-4}$ **87.** $\left(-\dfrac{2}{7}\right)^{-3}$ **88.** $(3.02)^{-5}$

89. $\left(1\dfrac{1}{5}\right)^{-3}$ **90.** $-\left(6\dfrac{2}{7}\right)^{-3}$ **91.** $-\left(-5\dfrac{4}{11}\right)^{-3}$ **92.** $-\left(-5\dfrac{1}{12}\right)^{-1}$

Write and evaluate an exponential expression for each application.

93. The barbecue pit for a luau is a cube that measures 3.5 feet on a side. What is the volume of the pit?

94. A cubic block of ice measures 15 inches on a side. What is its volume?

95. Aladdin's magic carpet is square and measures 6.5 feet on each of its four sides. How many square feet will it cover?

96. A square canvas sheet measures 4.25 yards on a side. How much ground will it cover?

97. The square base of the Great Pyramid, the tomb of Pharaoh Cheops, measures 755 feet on each of its four sides. What is the area of ground covered by the pyramid?

98. Three squares are nested, one within another. The innermost square is to be painted light blue. It measures 6 feet on a side. The middle square is to be painted white, and measures 10 feet on a side. The outer square is to be painted dark blue, and measures 15 feet on a side. How many square feet of surface will be painted with each color?

 Experiencing Algebra the Calculator Way

Use your calculator to evaluate. Express your answers as fractions or round decimals to the nearest thousandth as appropriate.

1. 17^6

2. -17^6

3. $(-17)^6$

4. 17^5

5. -17^5

6. $(-17)^5$

7. $-(-24)^6$

8. $-\left(\dfrac{2}{9}\right)^4$

9. $\left(-\dfrac{2}{9}\right)^4$

10. $(12.89)^4$

11. $-(12.89)^4$

12. $(-0.56)^4$

13. $-(-0.56)^4$

14. $-\left(3\dfrac{5}{6}\right)^4$

15. $\left(-4\dfrac{1}{4}\right)^4$

16. $-\left(-4\dfrac{1}{4}\right)^4$

17. $\left(-\dfrac{4}{7}\right)^7$

18. $-\left(-\dfrac{4}{7}\right)^7$

19. $(-4.076)^7$

20. $-(-4.076)^7$

21. $\left(2\dfrac{2}{7}\right)^5$

22. $-\left(-3\dfrac{2}{3}\right)^7$

23. $\left(-7\dfrac{19}{21}\right)^3$

24. $\left(-17\dfrac{21}{37}\right)^6$

 Experiencing Algebra the Group Way

Study the results for the exercises in "Experiencing Algebra the Calculator Way."

1. Consider the exercises that do not have a negative sign outside the parentheses. Some of these exercises have positive results and some have negative results. Can you tell why? Discuss the patterns. You should be able to state the rule that operates here to determine the sign.

2. Now consider the exercises that have a negative sign outside the parentheses. You might have thought that all the results would be negative, but they aren't. Some are negative and some are positive again. Can you tell why? Again, discuss the patterns to see that two things are happening. What are the two rules operating here that determine the sign?

3. Generalize what you have learned. How does the exponent affect the sign of the result? How does the sign in front of the expression affect the result?

Share what you have learned with the class.

Experiencing Algebra the Write Way

1. In "Experiencing Algebra the Calculator Way," explain why exercises 1 and 3 yield the same answer. Explain why exercises 5 and 6 yield the same answer. Explain the different effects of having a negative base in an exponential expression when the exponent is an even number or when it is an odd number.

2. Evaluate.

   a. 3^{-2} **b.** $(-3)^{-2}$ **c.** $\left(\dfrac{1}{3}\right)^{-2}$ **d.** $\left(-\dfrac{1}{3}\right)^{-2}$

   e. 3^{-3} **f.** $(-3)^{-3}$ **g.** $\left(\dfrac{1}{3}\right)^{-3}$ **h.** $\left(-\dfrac{1}{3}\right)^{-3}$

   Study the results for these eight exercises. Notice that many of the results are reciprocals of each other or opposites of each other. Try to explain in writing when you can expect to find results that are opposites of each other and when you can expect to find results that are reciprocals of each other.

2.2 Scientific Notation

Objectives

1 Write equivalent scientific notation, given standard notation.

2 Write equivalent scientific and standard notation, given calculator notation.

3 Write and evaluate numerical representations for real-world data and express the results in the desired notation.

Application

Common table salt consists of atoms of the elements sodium (Na) and chlorine (Cl), arranged with alternate atoms at the corners of a cube. The distance between neighboring atoms is 4.12×10^{-12} meters. Write this distance in standard notation.

After completing this section, we will discuss this application further. See page 96.

Numbers are usually written in **standard notation**. For example,

   5,000,000

   −3,458,000,000

   0.000034

However, very large and very small numbers are often written in scientific notation. **Scientific notation** is an expression written as the product of a number whose absolute value is between 1 and 10, including 1, and an integer power of 10. We call the number whose absolute value is between 1 and 10 the **numerical factor**.

Standard Notation	*Scientific Notation*
	numerical factor $\times$ 10$^{\text{integer exponent}}$
$5{,}000{,}000 =$	5×10^6
$-3{,}458{,}000{,}000 =$	-3.458×10^9
$0.000034 =$	3.4×10^{-5}

Since calculators display a limited number of digits, very large and very small numbers are written in an abbreviated scientific notation. We will call this form calculator notation. **Calculator notation** is a display consisting of the numerical factor followed by "E" followed by the integer exponent of 10.

Standard Notation	*Calculator Notation*
	numerical factor E integer exponent
$5{,}000{,}000 =$	$5 \text{ E}6$
$-3{,}458{,}000{,}000 =$	$-3.458 \text{ E}9$
$0.000034 =$	$3.4 \text{ E} - 5$

---

1   Writing Equivalent Scientific Notation from Standard Notation

Writing Numbers in Scientific Notation from Standard Notation
To write a number whose absolute value is 10 or greater in scientific notation, write a product of a numerical factor and an exponential expression.

- The numerical factor is determined by moving the decimal point to the left so that the resulting number has an absolute value between 1 and 10, including 1.
- The exponential expression consists of a base 10 and a positive exponent that is the number of places the decimal was moved.

To write a number whose absolute value is less than 1 in scientific notation, write a product of a numerical factor and an exponential expression.

- The numerical factor is determined by moving the decimal point to the right so that the resulting number has an absolute value between 1 and 10, including 1.
- The exponential expression consists of a base 10 and a negative exponent that has an absolute value of the number of places the decimal was moved.

To write a number whose absolute value is between 1 and 10, including 1, in scientific notation, write a product of a numerical factor and an exponential expression.

- The numerical factor is the number itself.
- The exponential expression consists of a base 10 and an exponent of 0.

For example,

$$245{,}000{,}000 = 2.45 \times 10^8$$

Move the decimal between the 2 and the 4. (8 places to the left)   The exponent of 10 is 8.

$$0.00000032 = 3.2 \times 10^{-7}$$

Move the decimal between the 3 and the 2. (7 places to the right)   The exponent of 10 is −7.

 Helping Hand In scientific notation, numbers with absolute values greater than or equal to 10 have positive exponents. Numbers with absolute values less than 1 have negative exponents.

EXAMPLE 1 Write in scientific notation.

a. 65,780,000,000,000   **b.** −65,780,000,000,000
c. .00000000002895   **d.** −0.00000000002895

Solution

a. $65{,}780{,}000{,}000{,}000 = 6.578 \times 10^{13}$ The decimal was moved to the left 13 places.

b. $-65{,}780{,}000{,}000{,}000 = -6.578 \times 10^{13}$ The decimal was moved to the left 13 places.

c. $0.00000000002895 = 2.895 \times 10^{-11}$ The decimal was moved to the right 11 places.

d. $-0.00000000002895 = -2.895 \times 10^{-11}$ The decimal was moved to the right 11 places.

The calculator will automatically display very large or small numbers in calculator notation. ■

 Experiencing Algebra the Checkup Way

Write exercises 1–4 in scientific notation.

1. 5,000,000   **2.** −15,890,000   **3.** 0.000367   **4.** −0.0000005037

5. When you write a number in scientific notation, under what conditions will the exponent of 10 be a positive number, and under what conditions will it be a negative number?

6. If a negative number is written in scientific notation, where is the negative sign placed in the result?

2 Writing Numbers in Equivalent Notations

Writing Numbers in Scientific Notation from Calculator Notation
To write a number in scientific notation, write a product of a numerical factor and an exponential expression.

- The numerical factor is the number displayed before the "E."
- The exponential expression consists of a base 10 and an exponent whose value is the number after the "E."

For example,

$$3.86 \, E7 = 3.86 \times 10^7$$

3.86 is the numerical factor.
7 is the exponent.

$$7.4 \, E - 5 = 7.4 \times 10^{-5}$$

7.4 is the numerical factor.
−5 is the exponent.

Writing Numbers in Standard Notation from Scientific Notation
To write a number in standard form if the exponent is positive:

- Move the decimal point in the numerical factor to the right the number of places the exponent denotes (its value).

To write a number in standard form if the exponent is negative:

- Move the decimal point in the numerical factor to the left the number of places the exponent denotes (its value).

If the exponent is 0, a number in standard form is simply the numerical factor.

The previous examples in standard notation are the following:

$$3.86 \times 10^7 = 38,600,000$$

Move the decimal 7 places to the right.

$$7.4 \times 10^{-5} = 0.000074$$

Move the decimal 5 places to the left.

EXAMPLE 2 Write in scientific notation and standard notation.

a. 5.76 E14 **b.** −5.76 E14
c. 1.4 E − 16 **d.** −1.4 E − 16

Solution

a. $5.76 \, E14 = 5.76 \times 10^{14} = 576,000,000,000,000$

Move the decimal 14 places to the right.

b. $-5.76 \, E14 = -5.76 \times 10^{14} = -576,000,000,000,000$

Move the decimal 14 places to the right.

c. $1.4\,\text{E} - 16 = 1.4 \times 10^{-16} = 0.00000000000000014$

Move the decimal 16 places to the left.

d. $-1.4\,\text{E} - 16 = -1.4 \times 10^{-16} = -0.00000000000000014$

Move the decimal 16 places to the left. ∎

Experiencing Algebra the Checkup Way

Write exercises 1–4 in scientific notation and standard notation.

1. 6.5 E7   **2.** −8.33 E13   **3.** 9.3 E − 3   **4.** −3.12 E − 4

5. When writing a number in standard notation from scientific notation, explain how the decimal point is placed.

---

3 Modeling the Real World

Scientific notation is used most of the time when dealing with very large and very small numbers. You will find it very common in areas such as astronomy, which deals with large distances and huge masses; environmental science, which deals with global populations and resources; biology and chemistry, which deal with very small cells and molecules; economics, which deals with large amounts of money and financial data; and most other areas of science.

EXAMPLE 3

The world population in 1991 was estimated to be 5,423,000,000. Write a numerical representation of this amount in scientific notation.

Solution

$$5{,}423{,}000{,}000 = 5.423 \times 10^9$$

Move the decimal to the left 9 places to obtain a number between 1 and 10. Therefore, the exponent of 10 is 9. ∎

EXAMPLE 4

The lightest atom, hydrogen, weighs 1.7×10^{-24} grams. Write the weight of two hydrogen atoms in standard notation.

Solution

$$2(1.7 \times 10^{-24}) = 2(0.0000000000000000000000017)$$
$$= 0.0000000000000000000000034 \text{ grams}$$

Move the decimal to the left 24 places. ∎

Application

Common table salt consists of atoms of the elements sodium (Na) and chlorine (Cl), arranged with alternate atoms at the corners of a cube. The distance between neighboring atoms is 4.12×10^{-12} meters. Write this distance in standard notation.

Discussion

$$4.12 \times 10^{-12} = 0.00000000000412$$

Move the decimal to the left 12 places.

The distance between neighboring atoms is 0.00000000000412 meters. ∎

Experiencing Algebra the Checkup Way

1. The speed of light in a vacuum is accepted to be 2.99792458×10^8 meters per second. Write a numerical representation of this number in standard notation. What do you think would be a useful approximation to this number?

2. The amount of heat needed to change 125 grams of water at 100°C to steam at 100°C is about 67,400 calories. Write a numerical representation, in scientific notation, of the number of calories needed to change twice as much water to steam.

PROBLEM SET 2.2

 ## Experiencing Algebra the Exercise Way

Write in scientific notation.

1. 23,450,000,000
2. 18,300,000,000,000,000,000
3. −203,415,000,000,000
4. −15,395,000,000,000,000,000
5. 0.0000000176
6. 0.000000000000013
7. −0.000006591
8. −0.00000000072193
9. 3.6943
10. 9.98031
11. −4.7502
12. −1.40001

Write in scientific notation and standard notation.

13. 6.3 E17
14. 3.076 E8
15. −7.1103 E5
16. −1.005 E11
17. −3.7 E − 5
18. −8.405 E − 7
19. 1.966 E − 2
20. 5.555 E − 6
21. 4.356 E0
22. 6.055 E0
23. −9.95 E0
24. −8.103 E0

Write exercises 25–36 in standard notation.

25. 2.7×10^7
26. 5.47×10^9
27. -4.005×10^6
28. -8.9905×10^8
29. 4.056×10^{-7}
30. 6.66×10^{-5}
31. -3.0303×10^{-4}
32. -5.11×10^{-9}
33. 1.26×10^0
34. 3.69×10^0
35. -4.5×10^0
36. -8.81×10^0

37. In 1992, it was reported that the GNP (gross national product) of the United Kingdom was equivalent to 1.024769×10^{12} U.S. dollars. Write this amount in standard notation.

38. In 1992, the GNP of India was reported to be equivalent to 2.71638×10^{11} U.S. dollars. Write this amount in standard notation.

39. From exercises 37 and 38, determine by how many U.S. dollars the GNP of the United Kingdom exceeded that of India. Write your answer both in scientific notation and in standard notation.

40. From exercises 37 and 38, determine the ratio of the GNP of India to that of the United Kingdom. Express your answer both in scientific notation and in standard notation.

41. In 1992, according to the *Statistical Abstract of the United States*, there were 14,438,000 crimes reported. The population of the United States in 1992 was reported to be 255,458,000. Write these numbers in scientific notation. Then determine the ratio of the number of crimes to the number of people in the population. Interpret your answer.

42. In 1992, according to the *Statistical Abstract*, 23,800 murders were reported. Write this number in scientific notation. Using the population figure in exercise 41, determine the ratio of the number of murders to the number of people in the population. Interpret your answer.

43. In 1990, the American Indian population was reported to be 1,878,285. The total U.S. population in 1990 was reported to be 248,700,000. Write the two numbers in scientific notation. What percentage of the U.S. population were American Indian?

44. In 1990, there were 2,177,000 deaths reported in the United States. Write this number in scientific notation. Using the number from exercise 43, what percentage of the U.S. population does this represent?

45. The U.S. population in 1993 was reported to be 258,245,000. If the average American drinks 1 cup of fruit juice each day, how many cups of juice will be consumed in a year? Express your answer in scientific and standard notation.

46. In 1992, the per capita consumption of fresh fruits in the United States was 98.7 pounds per year. If this same number applies in 1993, how many total pounds of fresh fruit will be consumed? Use the population figure from exercise 45. Express your answer in scientific and standard notation.

47. Research by Hallmark Cards Incorporated reported that the number of Christmas cards expected to be sold in 1996 was 2.65×10^9. Write this number in standard notation and interpret the result.

48. Hallmark Cards Incorporated research indicates that Valentine's Day is the second busiest card-giving occasion. In 1996, they estimate that 9.25×10^8 cards were sold. Write this number in standard notation and interpret the result.

49. The pyramids at Giza are the most colossal funeral monuments ever built. Each weighs over 6,000,000 tons. Convert this weight to pounds, given that 1 ton equals 2000 pounds. Write the answer in scientific notation.

50. The Egyptians had to move about 2,000,000 blocks of stone to build the Great Pyramid. Write this number in scientific notation.

51. The Great Wall of China is the only human-built structure that can be seen from the space shuttle with the naked eye. When completed, the wall was over 3700 miles long. Convert this length to feet, given that 1 mile equals 5,280 feet. Write the answer in scientific notation.

52. The Grand Coulee Dam on the Columbia River in the state of Washington contains 10,979,641 cubic yards of concrete. Write this number in scientific notation.

 Experiencing Algebra the Calculator Way

1. In physics, the study of the thermal properties of matter involves special numbers. For example, the number of molecules in 1 mole is given by Avogadro's number, N_A, which is approximately equal to 6.023×10^{23}. Enter this number into your calculator.

   a. What does the calculator notation read?

   b. How would you write this number in standard notation?

   c. Which is the easier way to write the number and why?

   d. Multiply this number by 200, and write the calculator notation.

   e. Convert the result in exercise 1d to scientific notation.

2. The population of the world in 1994 was estimated to be 5,642,151,000.

   a. Write this number in scientific notation.

b. Enter the number into your calculator and write the calculator notation for it.

c. If the world population triples, what will the population be, in scientific notation?

d. Write this result in standard notation.

Experiencing Algebra the Group Way

You will become more comfortable with scientific notation and calculator notation through use. To help you do so, work together to complete the following table.

Number	Standard Notation	Scientific Notation	Calculator Notation
One-thousandth			
One-hundredth			
One-tenth			
One			
Ten			
One hundred			
One thousand			
Ten thousand			
One hundred thousand			
One million			
Ten million			
One hundred million			
One billion			
One trillion			
One quadrillion			
One quintillion			
One sextillion			
One septillion			
One octillion			
One nonillion			
One decillion			

After you have completed the table, write as many examples as you can for each of the numbers. Compare your results with those of the other groups.

Experiencing Algebra the Write Way

Review the results of "Experiencing Algebra the Group Way." Explain the relationship between the number of zeroes in the number and the value of the exponent in scientific notation for the numbers listed there.

2.3 Radical Expressions and Real Numbers

Objectives

1 Evaluate square-root expressions.

2 Evaluate radical expressions other than square roots.

3 Graph a real number on a number line.

4 Model real-world situations using radical expressions.

Application

Television screens are usually designated by the length of the diagonal from one corner to the opposite corner. This length can be calculated from the lengths of the sides of the screen. The length of the diagonal is the square root of the sum of the squares of two adjacent sides. How long is the diagonal of a square TV screen that measures 15 inches on a side?

After completing this section, we will discuss this application further. See page 107.

1 Evaluating Square Roots

Previously, we discussed squaring a number, such as $3^2 = 9$. The result 9 is called a perfect square. A **perfect square** is defined to be the result of squaring a rational number. Examples of perfect squares are $0, 1, 4, \frac{1}{9}, \frac{4}{25}$, and 0.36, because

$$0 = 0^2, 1 = 1^2, 4 = 2^2, \frac{1}{9} = \left(\frac{1}{3}\right)^2, \frac{4}{25} = \left(\frac{2}{5}\right)^2, \text{ and } 0.36 = (0.6)^2.$$

If we need to reverse this operation—that is, go from the square of a number back to the number itself—we take the **square root** of a number. Thus, 3 is the square root of 9 because $3^2 = 9$. However, -3 is also a square root of 9 because $(-3)^2 = 9$. We call 3 the **positive root** or **principal root**. We call -3 the **negative root**. The notation for this is

$\sqrt{9} = 3$ This is read:
                    The positive square root of 9 is 3.

$-\sqrt{9} = -3$ This is read:
                    The negative square root of 9 is negative 3.

All perfect squares except 0 have two roots. The perfect square 0 has only one root, $\sqrt{0} = 0$, because 0 is neither positive nor negative.

Now let's find the square roots of numbers that are not perfect squares. There are two different possibilities: positive numbers and negative numbers.

First, let's find a value for the square root of a positive rational number that is not a perfect square. Remember, perfect squares are $1, 4, 9$, and so on. A number such as 2 is between the perfect squares 1 and 4. Therefore, the value of $\sqrt{2}$ should be between the values of $\sqrt{1} = 1$ and $\sqrt{4} = 2$. In order to find a value for $\sqrt{2}$, we must determine what number to square that results in 2. Complete the following set of exercises to discover the square root of 2.

D I S C O V E R Y   6

**Square Root of a Positive Rational Number
That Is Not a Perfect Square**

Since $\sqrt{1} = 1$ and $\sqrt{4} = 2$, we know that $\sqrt{2}$ is not an integer but must be a number between 1 and 2. Therefore, if we try to determine a decimal number for $\sqrt{2}$, we might try the following patterns:

1. Evaluate the following exponential expressions on a calculator. Stop when you find a value over 2.

$(1.1)^2 = $ ____ $(1.6)^2 = $ ____

$(1.2)^2 = $ ____ $(1.7)^2 = $ ____

$(1.3)^2 = $ ____ $(1.8)^2 = $ ____

$(1.4)^2 = $ ____ $(1.9)^2 = $ ____

$(1.5)^2 = $ ____

Therefore, $\sqrt{2}$ must be between ____ and ____.

2. Add another decimal place to the numbers. Stop evaluating when you find a value over 2.

$(1.41)^2 = $ ____ $(1.46)^2 = $ ____

$(1.42)^2 = $ ____ $(1.47)^2 = $ ____

$(1.43)^2 = $ ____ $(1.48)^2 = $ ____

$(1.44)^2 = $ ____ $(1.49)^2 = $ ____

$(1.45)^2 = $ ____

Therefore, $\sqrt{2}$ must be between ____ and ____.

We could continue this pattern and never find a terminating or repeating decimal equal to $\sqrt{2}$. On a calculator, we find that $\sqrt{2}$ is given by 1.414213562. If we check, we get $(1.414213562)^2 = 1.999999999$. This is a close approximation, but not exactly 2. In fact, we cannot find a rational number whose square is exactly equal to 2.

The fact that we cannot find a rational number whose square is equal to 2 means that we can never express such a number as a ratio of integers. In other words, the value of $\sqrt{2}$ is not a rational number because we cannot write it as a ratio of integers. Therefore, we call $\sqrt{2}$ an irrational number. An **irrational number** is a number that cannot be written as a ratio of integers. **Real numbers** are the set of all rational and irrational numbers.

Now, let's find the square root of a negative number that is not a perfect square, such as -9. In order to find a value for $\sqrt{-9}$, we must determine what number to square in order to obtain -9. Since squaring a positive number results in a positive number $(3 \cdot 3 = 9)$ and squaring a negative number results in a positive number $(-3 \cdot -3 = 9)$, we know we cannot find a real number whose square is -9 (a negative number). Therefore, $\sqrt{-9}$ cannot be evaluated in the real number system. However, we will introduce the *complex number system*, in which we can evaluate $\sqrt{-9}$, in Chapter 14.

Evaluating Square Roots

To evaluate the positive or principal root of a positive number that is a perfect square:

- Determine the positive number whose square results in the perfect square.

To evaluate the positive or principal root of a positive number that is not a perfect square:

- Determine the positive number whose square results in an approximate value for the number. A calculator may be needed to find this number.

To evaluate the negative root of a positive number that is a perfect square:

- Determine the negative number whose square results in the perfect square.

To evaluate the negative root of a positive number that is not a perfect square:

- Determine the negative number whose square results in an approximate value for the number. A calculator may be needed to find this number.

The positive and negative square roots of a negative number are not defined among the real numbers.

The square root of 0 is 0.

EXAMPLE 1 Evaluate.

a. $\sqrt{64}$ b. $\sqrt{1.44}$ c. $\sqrt{\dfrac{4}{9}}$

d. $-\sqrt{25}$ e. $\sqrt{-25}$

Solution

a. $\sqrt{64} = 8$ The positive square root of 64 is 8.

b. $\sqrt{1.44} = 1.2$ The positive square root of 1.44 is 1.2.

c. $\sqrt{\dfrac{4}{9}} = \dfrac{2}{3}$ The positive square root of $\frac{4}{9}$ is $\frac{2}{3}$.

d. $-\sqrt{25} = -5$ The negative square root of 25 is −5.

e. $\sqrt{-25}$ is not a real number.   There is no real number whose square is −25 (a negative number).

The checks for Example 1 are shown in Figure 2.5a, Figure 2.5b, and Figure 2.5c.

Note: Example 1e results in an error because it is not a real number. ∎

EXAMPLE 2 Determine between what two integers the values of the following square roots lie. Then estimate the square roots on your calculator.

a. $\sqrt{3}$ b. $-\sqrt{5}$ c. $\sqrt{99}$

TECHNOLOGY

| Figure 2.5a | Figure 2.5b | Figure 2.5c |

For Figure 2.5a

a. 2nd √ 6 4) ENTER

b. 2nd √ 1 . 4 4) ENTER

c. 2nd √ 4 ÷ 9) MATH 1 ENTER

For Figure 2.5b

d. (−) 2nd √ 2 5) ENTER

For Figure 2.5c

e. 2nd √ (−) 2 5) ENTER

Calculator Solution

a. $\sqrt{3}$ is between $\sqrt{1} = 1$ and $\sqrt{4} = 2$ or approximately 1.732050808.

b. $-\sqrt{5}$ is between $-\sqrt{4} = -2$ and $-\sqrt{9} = -3$ or approximately −2.236067977.

c. $\sqrt{99}$ is between $\sqrt{81} = 9$ and $\sqrt{100} = 10$ or approximately 9.949874371. ∎

 Experiencing Algebra the Checkup Way

Evaluate.

1. $\sqrt{49}$ **2.** $\sqrt{0.81}$ **3.** $\sqrt{\dfrac{25}{36}}$ **4.** $-\sqrt{16}$ **5.** $\sqrt{-16}$

6. Write the keystrokes needed to evaluate $\sqrt{\dfrac{144}{169}}$. What is the result?

In exercises 7 and 8, determine between what two integers the value of each square root lies. Then estimate, using your calculator.

7. $\sqrt{17}$ **8.** $-\sqrt{15}$

9. Explain the difference between the principal root of a number and the negative root of a number.

10. What is meant by an irrational number?

2 Evaluating Radical Expressions

The square root of a number, defined in the first part of this section, is one example of a radical expression. In the example $\sqrt{9}$, the symbol $\sqrt{}$ is called a **radical sign**, and 9 is the **radicand**. The expression $\sqrt{9}$ is a **radical expression**.

We also can define roots to correspond to exponents larger than 2. For example, we may want to reverse cubing a number and call it a cube root. In order to use the same notation as with square roots, we will need to add an index to the radical sign. An **index** is the power we are reversing. To write a cube root, in which we are reversing a power of 3, we would write the following:

$$\sqrt[3]{64} \qquad \text{What number multiplied as a factor 3 times is 64?}$$
$$\overset{\text{index}}{}\sqrt{\text{radicand}}$$

To evaluate $\sqrt[3]{64}$, we determine that $4^3 = 64$. Therefore, 4 is the cube root of 64. There is only one possible cube root.

$$\sqrt[3]{64} = 4 \qquad \begin{array}{l}\text{This is read:} \\ \text{The cube root of 64 is 4.}\end{array}$$

Other powers are written in the same manner. For example, to reverse $3^5 = 243$, we would write

$$\sqrt[5]{243} = 3 \qquad \begin{array}{l}\text{This is read:} \\ \text{The fifth root of 243 is 3.}\end{array}$$

> **Evaluating Radical Expressions**
> The value of a radical expression with an even index and a positive radicand is a positive number.
>   The value of a radical expression with an even index and a negative radicand is not defined among the real numbers.
>   The value of a radical expression with an odd index and a positive radicand is a positive number.
>   The value of a radical expression with an odd index and a negative radicand is a negative number.
>   The value of a radical expression with a radicand of 0 is 0.

EXAMPLE 3 Evaluate, rounding to the nearest thousandth.

a. $\sqrt[3]{-27}$ **b.** $\sqrt[3]{30}$ **c.** $\sqrt[4]{625}$
d. $\sqrt[4]{-625}$ **e.** $-\sqrt[4]{625}$ **f.** $\sqrt[4]{1.44}$
g. $\sqrt[3]{\dfrac{1}{27}}$

Solution

a. $\sqrt[3]{-27} = -3$ **b.** $\sqrt[3]{30} \approx 3.107232506 \approx 3.107$
c. $\sqrt[4]{625} = 5$ **d.** $\sqrt[4]{-625}$ is not a real number.
e. $-\sqrt[4]{625} = -5$ **f.** $\sqrt[4]{1.44} \approx 1.095445115 \approx 1.095$
g. $\sqrt[3]{\dfrac{1}{27}} = \dfrac{1}{3}$

The checks for Example 3 are shown in Figure 2.6a, Figure 2.6b, and Figure 2.6c. *Note:* Example 3d results in an error because it is not a real number. ∎

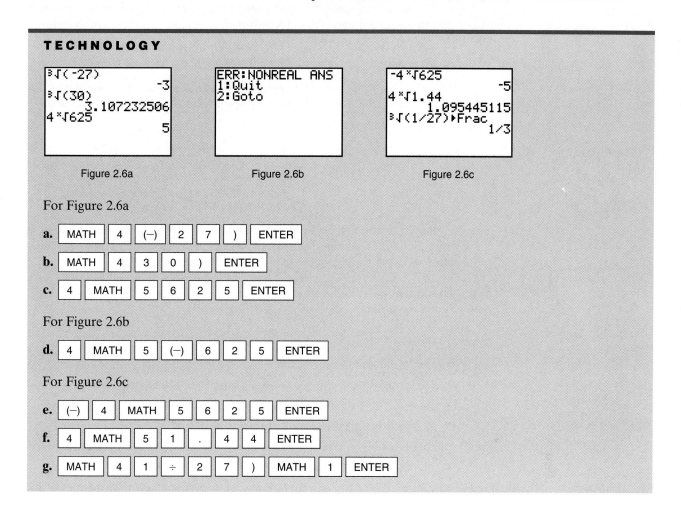

Figure 2.6a   Figure 2.6b   Figure 2.6c

For Figure 2.6a

a. [MATH] [4] [(−)] [2] [7] [ )] [ENTER]

b. [MATH] [4] [3] [0] [ )] [ENTER]

c. [4] [MATH] [5] [6] [2] [5] [ENTER]

For Figure 2.6b

d. [4] [MATH] [5] [(−)] [6] [2] [5] [ENTER]

For Figure 2.6c

e. [(−)] [4] [MATH] [5] [6] [2] [5] [ENTER]

f. [4] [MATH] [5] [1] [.] [4] [4] [ENTER]

g. [MATH] [4] [1] [÷] [2] [7] [ )] [MATH] [1] [ENTER]

 Experiencing Algebra the Checkup Way

In exercises 1–7, evaluate, rounding to the nearest thousandth.

1. $\sqrt[3]{100}$ **2.** $\sqrt[4]{81}$ **3.** $\sqrt[3]{-64}$ **4.** $\sqrt[4]{-81}$

5. $-\sqrt[4]{81}$ **6.** $\sqrt[3]{\dfrac{8}{125}}$ **7.** $\sqrt[4]{39.0625}$

8. Define what is meant by the index of a radical expression and the radicand of a radical expression.

9. What is the name of the symbol that is used to indicate the root of a number?

3 Graphing Real Numbers

In the first section of this text, we discussed the set of rational numbers. A rational number is any number that may be written as a ratio of integers, excluding a zero denominator. We located these rational numbers as points on a number line. However, there are points on a number line that we did not identify. These are the irrational numbers. Irrational numbers are numbers that cannot be written as a ratio of integers.

The set of real numbers is the set of all rational and irrational numbers that make up a number line. Examples of irrational numbers are as follows:

0.13133133313333 ...	(Only terminating and repeating decimals can be written as rational numbers.)
π	$\pi \approx 3.141592654$. The value of π is defined to be the ratio of the circumference of a circle to its diameter. (This decimal representation continues without terminating or repeating.)
$\sqrt{2}$	$\sqrt{2} \approx 1.414213562$ (This decimal representation continues without terminating or repeating.)
$-\sqrt{2}$	$-\sqrt{2} \approx -1.414213562$ (This decimal representation continues without terminating or repeating.)
$\sqrt[3]{5}$	$\sqrt[3]{5} \approx 1.709975947$ (This decimal representation continues without terminating or repeating.)

Just as in the first section, we can graph irrational numbers on our real-number line. To do this, we need to evaluate the irrational number to determine its approximate value, in order to place it correctly.

EXAMPLE 4 Graph the real numbers 3, $\sqrt{3}$, $-\sqrt{3}$, $\sqrt{36}$, $\sqrt[3]{3}$, and π on a number line. Label the points.

Solution

3 is located 3 units to the right of 0.

$\sqrt{3} \approx 1.732050808$, which is approximately 1.7 units to the right of 0.

$-\sqrt{3} \approx -1.732050808$, which is approximately 1.7 units to the left of 0.

$\sqrt{36} = 6$, which is 6 units to the right of 0.

$\sqrt[3]{3} \approx 1.44224957$, which is approximately 1.4 units to the right of 0.

$\pi \approx 3.141592654$, which is approximately 3.1 units to the right of 0.

In summary, we have now discussed the entire set of real numbers with its subsets. We have identified natural numbers, whole numbers, and integers as subsets of rational numbers. However, rational numbers are not a subset of irrational numbers. They are mutually exclusive sets: any number that belongs to one set does not belong to the other set. To visualize this relationship, see Figure 2.7.

 Experiencing Algebra the Checkup Way

1. Graph the following real numbers on a number line. Label the points.

$\sqrt{16}, -\sqrt{4}, \sqrt{70}, -\sqrt{60}, 5, -\pi, 1.767676..., \sqrt{0}$

2. Name all the types of numbers that form subsets of the real numbers.

3. Explain the difference between irrational numbers and rational numbers.

Real numbers

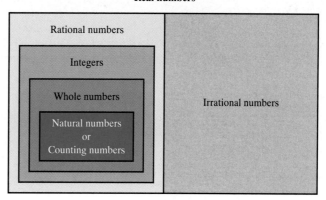

Figure 2.7

---

4   Modeling the Real World

Several common geometric applications involve radical expressions. For example, the length of a side of a square is found by taking the square root of the area of the square.

EXAMPLE 5

The area of a square carpet remnant is $42\frac{1}{4}$ square feet. Determine the dimensions of the carpet.

Calculator Solution

To determine the length of the equal sides, we take the square root of the area. According to the calculator screen, each side of the carpet measures $\frac{13}{2}$ feet. Therefore, the dimensions of the carpet remnant are $6\frac{1}{2}$ feet by $6\frac{1}{2}$ feet. ■

Application

Television screens are usually designated by the length of the diagonal from one corner to the opposite corner. This length can be calculated from the lengths of the sides of the screen. The length of the diagonal is the square root of the sum of the squares of two adjacent sides. How long is the diagonal of a square TV screen that measures 15 inches on a side?

Discussion

The length of the diagonal is the square root of the sum of the squares of two adjacent sides. Therefore, the length of the diagonal is

$$\sqrt{15^2 + 15^2} = \sqrt{450} \approx 21.21.$$

The diagonal of a square TV screen measuring 15 inches on a side is approximately 21 inches. ■

15 in.

15 in.

Experiencing Algebra the Checkup Way

The area of a square tablecloth is $33\frac{1}{16}$ square feet. Find the length of a side.

PROBLEM SET 2.3

Experiencing Algebra the Exercise Way

Evaluate.

1. $\sqrt{36}$ **2.** $\sqrt{81}$ **3.** $\sqrt{256}$ **4.** $\sqrt{324}$

5. $-\sqrt{25}$ **6.** $-\sqrt{49}$ **7.** $\sqrt{0.64}$ **8.** $\sqrt{0.81}$

9. $\sqrt{\dfrac{49}{81}}$ **10.** $\sqrt{\dfrac{64}{121}}$ **11.** $-\sqrt{\dfrac{16}{9}}$ **12.** $-\sqrt{\dfrac{36}{49}}$

13. $\sqrt{1}$ **14.** $-\sqrt{1}$ **15.** $-\sqrt{0}$ **16.** $\sqrt{0}$

17. $\sqrt{-16}$ **18.** $\sqrt{-100}$

Determine between what two integers the values of the following square roots lie. Then estimate the square roots using your calculator.

19. $\sqrt{10}$ **20.** $\sqrt{22}$ **21.** $-\sqrt{3}$ **22.** $-\sqrt{14}$

Evaluate, rounding your answers to the nearest thousandth.

23. $-\sqrt{1200}$ **24.** $-\sqrt{2170}$ **25.** $\sqrt{10.5}$ **26.** $\sqrt{50.1}$

27. $-\sqrt{\dfrac{1}{10}}$ **28.** $\sqrt{\dfrac{11}{17}}$ **29.** $\sqrt{5\dfrac{8}{13}}$ **30.** $\sqrt{8\dfrac{2}{5}}$

31. $-\sqrt{2.5}$ **32.** $-\sqrt{0.4}$

Evaluate exercises 33–58; express your answers in fractional notation or round decimals to the nearest thousandth as appropriate.

33. $\sqrt[3]{64}$ **34.** $\sqrt[3]{8}$ **35.** $\sqrt[3]{1728}$ **36.** $\sqrt[3]{9261}$

37. $\sqrt[3]{1234}$ **38.** $\sqrt[3]{4321}$ **39.** $\sqrt[3]{-125}$ **40.** $\sqrt[3]{-64}$

41. $-\sqrt[4]{1296}$ **42.** $-\sqrt[4]{625}$ **43.** $\sqrt[6]{17}$ **44.** $\sqrt[5]{-328}$

45. $\sqrt[4]{-1296}$ **46.** $\sqrt[6]{-729}$ **47.** $\sqrt[5]{-12.7}$ **48.** $\sqrt[7]{-289.5}$

49. $\sqrt[4]{11.3}$ **50.** $\sqrt[6]{130.5}$ **51.** $\sqrt[3]{\dfrac{1}{8}}$ **52.** $\sqrt[5]{\dfrac{32}{3125}}$

53. $\sqrt[5]{-\dfrac{32}{3125}}$ **54.** $\sqrt[3]{-\dfrac{729}{1331}}$ **55.** $-\sqrt[3]{2\dfrac{5}{7}}$ **56.** $-\sqrt[4]{3\dfrac{2}{9}}$

57. $\sqrt[5]{-7\dfrac{19}{32}}$ **58.** $\sqrt[4]{50\dfrac{46}{81}}$

59. Graph the following numbers on a number line. Label the points.

$$\sqrt{25}, -\sqrt{45}, \sqrt{\dfrac{9}{16}}, -\sqrt{16}, -\sqrt{\dfrac{8}{3}}, \sqrt[3]{8}, \sqrt{75}$$

60. Graph the following numbers on a number line. Label the points.

$$-\sqrt{9}, \sqrt{-63}, -\sqrt{\dfrac{7}{3}}, \sqrt{17}, \sqrt{\dfrac{25}{4}}, \sqrt{64}, \sqrt[3]{-64}$$

61. A square carpet has an area of 182.25 square feet. What are the dimensions of the carpet?

62. What are the dimensions of a square garden that covers an area of 349.69 square feet?

63. Jennie is putting in a flower garden in her backyard. The garden will be rectangular, with a length of 8 feet and a width of 5 feet. She wants to divide it in half diagonally with landscaping logs. How many feet of logs does she need for the diagonal? (In order to figure this, Jennie must square the length and width, add the two squares, and then take the square root of the sum.)

5 ft

8 ft

64. Jennie decides to enlarge her flower garden from exercise 63. She plans to have a length of 15 feet and a width of 8 feet. Now how many feet of logs does she need for the diagonal?

65. An electrical engineer must calculate the current (in amperes) of a 3-phase household electrical system as equal to the power delivered (in kilowatts) divided by the voltage (in volts) times $\sqrt{3}$. If the power is 120 kilowatts, and the line carries 400 volts, calculate the current.

$$\text{Current} = \frac{120}{400\sqrt{3}}.$$

66. In exercise 65, refigure the current if the power is 100 kilowatts and the line carries 200 volts.

67. A car left a skid mark of 50 feet before crashing. Based on research data, police estimated the speed of the car (in miles per hour) as $2\sqrt{5 \cdot 50}$. What is the estimated speed of the car?

68. The estimated speed of a car that left a skid mark of 120 feet, using the same calculation method as in exercise 67, is $2\sqrt{5 \cdot 120}$. What is this speed?

69. When the pavement is wet, police adjust the calculations in exercises 67 and 68. They estimate the speed of a car that left a 300-foot skid mark to be $(3.25)\sqrt{300}$. What is the speed?

70. If a car left a 450-foot skid mark on wet pavement, police would estimate its speed as $(3.25)\sqrt{450}$. Was the car going faster than the speed limit of 65 mph?

71. If a nozzle has a diameter of 1.5 inches, and the static pressure of the water is 40 pounds per square inch, then the flow rate of water through the nozzle is calculated as $(2.97)(1.5^2)\sqrt{40}$ gallons per minute. What is this flow rate?

72. Using the calculation method from exercise 71, the flow rate of water through a 2-inch nozzle at 50 pounds per square inch is calculated as $(2.97)(2^2)\sqrt{50}$ gallons per minute. What would this flow rate equal?

Experiencing Algebra the Calculator Way

Use your calculator to evaluate the following. Express your answers in fractional notation or round decimals to the nearest thousandth as appropriate.

1. $\sqrt{351,649}$

2. $\sqrt[3]{-13,312,053}$

3. $\sqrt{\dfrac{1681}{2601}}$

4. $\sqrt{695.798884}$

5. $\sqrt[3]{-\dfrac{512}{729}}$

6. $\sqrt[5]{1,160,290,625}$

7. $\sqrt{-24,025}$

8. $-\sqrt{24,025}$

9. $\sqrt[5]{14,539.33568}$

10. $\sqrt{\pi}$

11. $\sqrt{1999}$

12. $\sqrt{\dfrac{2}{3}}$

Experiencing Algebra the Group Way

Fill out the chart, completing all columns and rows.

Number n	Square n^2	Cube n^3	Fourth Power n^4	Fifth Power n^5
1	1	1	1	1
2	4	8	16	32
3	9	27	81	
4	16	64		
5	25			
6	36			
7				
8				
9				
10				
11				
12				

Using the chart, determine the following:

a. $\sqrt[5]{248,832}$

b. $\sqrt[4]{6561}$

c. $\sqrt[3]{216}$

d. $\sqrt{121}$

Use the chart to explain to the class the relationship between raising a number to a power and taking a root of a number.

List as many examples you can find for numbers involving squares, cubes, fourth powers, and fifth powers. Compare the results of your group with those of the rest of the class.

Experiencing Algebra the Write Way

In some radical expressions, the radicand may be negative or positive. In other radical expressions, the radicand must always be positive. Describe the conditions that determine when either situation may apply.

2.4 Exponential Expressions with Rational Exponents

Objectives
1 Discover the relationship of exponential expressions with rational exponents to radical expressions.

2 Evaluate exponential expressions with rational exponents.

3 Model real-world situations using exponential expressions with rational exponents.

Application

For his final performance, circus performer The Great Fallenda walks down a thin wire stretched diagonally from the top corner of the Big Top to the opposite corner on the ground. The Big Top is roughly in the shape of a cube, 100 feet on each side. If the length of the diagonal of a cube is equal to the square root of the sum of the squares of the three edges of the cube, how far does Fallenda have to walk?

After completing this section, we will discuss this application further. See page 113.

1 Discovering Exponential Expressions with Rational Exponents

We have discussed both exponential expressions and radical expressions in this chapter. There is a relationship between these two types of expressions. Let's see if we can discover this relationship with our calculators. Complete the following set of exercises with your calculator. (Remember to put the fractional exponent in parentheses.)

DISCOVERY 7

Radical and Rational Exponent Expressions
Evaluate each expression and compare the results obtained in the left column to the corresponding results in the right column.

1. a. $\sqrt{3} = $ ____   **b.** $3^{1/2} = $ ____

2. a. $\sqrt[3]{3} = $ ____   **b.** $3^{1/3} = $ ____

3. a. $\sqrt[4]{3} = $ ____   **b.** $3^{1/4} = $ ____

4. a. $\sqrt{-3} = $ ____   **b.** $(-3)^{1/2} = $

5. a. $\sqrt[3]{-3} = $ ____   **b.** $(-3)^{1/3} = $ ____

6. a. $\sqrt[4]{-3} = $ ____   **b.** $(-3)^{1/4} = $ ____

Continued

Write in your own words a rule for writing a radical expression as an exponential expression.

In the column on the left, we evaluate a radical expression. In the column on the right, we evaluate an exponential expression, consisting of a base that is the same as the radicand of the radical expression on the left, with an exponent that is the reciprocal of the index of the radical expression on the left. The results are the same in both columns.

> *Writing an Equivalent Exponential Expression*
> *for a Radical Expression*
> To write an equivalent exponential expression for a radical expression:
>
> • Write the radicand as the base.
> • Write the reciprocal of the index as the exponent.

We will explain this rule further later in this text, after we have discussed rules for simplifying exponential expressions.

Experiencing Algebra the Checkup Way

1. How can you rewrite the square root of a real number as an equivalent exponential expression?
2. How can you rewrite the cube root of a real number as an equivalent exponential expression?
3. How can you rewrite any root of a real number as an equivalent exponential expression?

2 Evaluating Expressions with Rational Exponents

We are now ready to write an equivalent exponential expression for a radical expression.

EXAMPLE 1 Write an equivalent exponential expression and evaluate. Express your answers rounded to the nearest thousandth.

a. $\sqrt[4]{81}$ b. $\sqrt[4]{-81}$ c. $\sqrt[5]{16,807}$
d. $\sqrt[5]{-16,807}$ e. $\sqrt[3]{83}$ f. $-\sqrt[3]{83}$

Solution

a. $\sqrt[4]{81} = 81^{1/4} = 3$
b. $\sqrt[4]{-81} = (-81)^{1/4}$ is not a real number.
c. $\sqrt[5]{16,807} = 16,807^{1/5} = 7$
d. $\sqrt[5]{-16,807} = (-16,807)^{1/5} = -7$
e. $\sqrt[3]{83} = 83^{1/3} \approx 4.362070671 \approx 4.362$
f. $-\sqrt[3]{83} = (-83)^{1/3} \approx -4.362070671 \approx -4.362$

First, enter the radical expression in your calculator as in previous examples. Then, to check equivalence, enter the exponential expression in your calculator. The check for Example 1a is shown in Figure 2.8. ■

EXAMPLE 2 Write an equivalent exponential expression and evaluate. Express your answers rounded to the nearest thousandth.

a. $\sqrt[4]{1.21}$ b. $\sqrt[5]{\dfrac{3}{4}}$

TECHNOLOGY

```
4 ˣ√81
               3
81^(1/4)
               3
```

Figure 2.8

For Figure 2.8

| 4 | MATH | 5 | 8 | 1 | ENTER |

| 8 | 1 | ^ | (| 1 | ÷ | 4 |) | ENTER |

Calculator Solution

a. $\sqrt[4]{1.21} = 1.21^{1/4} \approx 1.048808848 \approx 1.049$

b. $\sqrt[5]{\dfrac{3}{4}} = \left(\dfrac{3}{4}\right)^{1/5} \approx 0.9440875113 \approx 0.944$ ∎

✔ Experiencing Algebra the Checkup Way

Write an equivalent exponential expression and evaluate. Express your answers rounded to the nearest thousandth. Check your work with your calculator.

1. $\sqrt[4]{256}$ **2.** $\sqrt[5]{243}$ **3.** $\sqrt[4]{-256}$ **4.** $\sqrt[5]{-243}$

5. $\sqrt[3]{25}$ **6.** $\sqrt[3]{-25}$ **7.** $\sqrt[4]{2.8561}$ **8.** $\sqrt[4]{\dfrac{16}{81}}$

9. $\sqrt[4]{1.95}$ **10.** $\sqrt[5]{\dfrac{4}{9}}$

---

3   Modeling the Real World

Another common geometric application that involves radical expressions is the volume of a cube. The length of a side of a cube is found by taking the cube root of the volume of the cube, or by raising the volume to the one-third power.

EXAMPLE 3

The volume of a cubic box is equal to 857.375 cubic inches. Determine the dimensions of the cube.

Calculator Solution

To determine the length of a side of the cube, take the cube root of the volume.

$$\sqrt[3]{857.375} \text{ or } (857.375)^{1/3} = 9.5$$

The dimensions of the cubic box are 9.5 inches by 9.5 inches by 9.5 inches. ∎

Application

For his final performance, circus performer The Great Fallenda walks down a thin wire stretched diagonally from the top corner of the Big Top to the opposite corner on the ground. The Big Top is roughly in the shape of a cube, 100 feet on each side. If the length of the diagonal of a cube is equal to the square root of the sum of the squares of the three edges of the cube, how far does Fallenda have to walk?

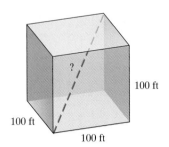

100 ft

100 ft

100 ft

Discussion

The length of the diagonal of a cube is equal to the square root of the sum of the squares of the three edges of the cube. Therefore, the length of the diagonal is

$$\sqrt{100^2 + 100^2 + 100^2}$$
$$= \sqrt{10,000 + 10,000 + 10,000}$$
$$= \sqrt{30,000} \text{ or } 30,000^{1/2}$$
$$\approx 173.21$$

Fallenda walks approximately 173 feet. ■

 ## Experiencing Algebra the Checkup Way

1. A fish tank at the local zoo must have a volume of 343 cubic feet in order to comfortably accommodate *Pisciraris*, a rare fish. Find the dimensions of the tank if it is designed in the shape of a cube.

2. Old MacDonald built a chicken coop in the shape of a cube, measuring 8.5 feet on a side. He wants to install a diagonal walkway in the coop so that the chickens can walk from one corner of the floor to the opposite corner of the ceiling, which has a ledge for them to perch upon. If the length of the diagonal of a cube is equal to the square root of the sum of the squares of the three edges of the cube, how long should the diagonal walkway be?

PROBLEM SET 2.4

 ## Experiencing Algebra the Exercise Way

Write an equivalent exponential expression and evaluate. Express your answers in fractional notation or round decimals to the nearest thousandth as appropriate.

1. $\sqrt[3]{27}$
2. $\sqrt[3]{125}$
3. $\sqrt[3]{-27}$
4. $\sqrt[3]{-125}$
5. $-\sqrt[3]{27}$
6. $-\sqrt[3]{125}$
7. $-\sqrt[3]{-27}$
8. $-\sqrt[3]{-125}$
9. $-\sqrt[4]{256}$
10. $-\sqrt[6]{729}$
11. $\sqrt[4]{-256}$
12. $\sqrt[6]{-729}$
13. $\sqrt[5]{250}$
14. $\sqrt[5]{200}$
15. $\sqrt[3]{-39.304}$
16. $-\sqrt[3]{39.304}$
17. $\sqrt[4]{-5.6}$
18. $-\sqrt[4]{-5.6}$
19. $\sqrt[5]{75.85}$
20. $-\sqrt[5]{-75.85}$
21. $\sqrt[3]{\dfrac{64}{343}}$
22. $\sqrt[3]{\dfrac{125}{512}}$
23. $\sqrt[4]{\dfrac{12}{13}}$
24. $\sqrt[4]{\dfrac{5}{6}}$
25. $\sqrt[5]{\dfrac{1}{243}}$
26. $\sqrt[5]{\dfrac{1}{32}}$
27. $\sqrt{289}$
28. $\sqrt{961}$
29. $\sqrt[5]{-1024}$
30. $\sqrt[5]{-7776}$
31. $\sqrt[4]{187.4161}$
32. $\sqrt[4]{133.6336}$
33. $\sqrt[4]{\dfrac{16}{2401}}$
34. $\sqrt[4]{\dfrac{625}{4096}}$
35. $\sqrt[3]{6859}$
36. $\sqrt[3]{12,167}$
37. $-\sqrt[4]{4096}$
38. $-\sqrt[4]{14,641}$
39. $-\sqrt[4]{4.85}$
40. $-\sqrt[4]{14.51}$
41. $\sqrt{\dfrac{841}{1225}}$
42. $\sqrt{\dfrac{1089}{1369}}$
43. $\sqrt[4]{614,656}$
44. $\sqrt[4]{20,736}$

45. $\sqrt[3]{-5832}$

46. $\sqrt[3]{-13{,}824}$

47. $\sqrt[5]{-5.55}$

48. $\sqrt[5]{-12.03}$

49. $\sqrt[5]{-2\frac{1}{7}}$

50. $\sqrt[5]{-3\frac{5}{9}}$

51. $\sqrt[5]{3125}$

52. $\sqrt[5]{32{,}768}$

53. $-\sqrt{841}$

54. $-\sqrt{3025}$

55. $\sqrt[3]{-17.576}$

56. $\sqrt[3]{-6.859}$

57. $-\sqrt[4]{3\frac{3}{5}}$

58. $-\sqrt[4]{4\frac{8}{15}}$

Write a radical expression and an equivalent exponential expression and evaluate. (Remember that the side of a cube is equal to the cube root of its volume, and that the side of a square is equal to the square root of its area.)

59. Find the dimensions of a cube-shaped bank vault that has a volume of 125 cubic yards.

60. A cube-shaped room has a volume of 91.125 cubic meters. What are its dimensions?

61. Instructions for planting a shrub require that a hole be dug in the shape of a cube with a volume of 3 cubic feet. What are the dimensions of the hole?

62. A pit for a luau is shaped like a cube with a volume of 15 cubic feet. What are the dimensions of the pit?

63. A card table has a surface in the shape of a square with an area of 12 square feet. What are the dimensions of the surface?

64. A square goldfish pond has a surface area of 50 square feet and a depth of 2 feet. What are the dimensions of the pond?

65. The Taj Mahal is one of the most beautiful buildings in the world. It is designed with a high central dome surrounded by small chambers arranged about two intersecting axes so that all four sides of the center structure are the same length. The center structure covers an area of about 377,000 square feet. What is the length of a side of this structure?

66. For the Taj Mahal, described in exercise 65, what is the length of the diagonal of the center structure, measured from one corner to the opposite corner? (Recall that the length of the diagonal of a square is the square root of the sum of the squares of its two adjacent sides.)

67. St. Peter's Basilica in Vatican City has a dome above the papal altar that spans an area of about 19,400 square feet. The radius of this domed area is the distance from the center of the circle to its outer edge. To find the radius of this circular area, you must divide the area by the mathematical constant π and then take the square root of the quotient. What is the radius of this domed area?

68. One of the largest domes ever constructed is in the Louisiana Superdome. The area of floor covered by the dome measures about 363,000 square feet. Use the calculation method in exercise 67 to determine the radius of the domed area.

 ## Experiencing Algebra the Calculator Way

First, write an equivalent exponential expression for each radical expression. Then, use your calculator to evaluate both the radical expression and the exponential expression. The two results should agree. Express your answers in fractional notation or round decimals to the nearest thousandth as appropriate.

1. $\sqrt[5]{57,392}$

2. $-\sqrt[4]{37,652}$

3. $\sqrt[3]{\pi}$

4. $\sqrt{13\frac{15}{19}}$

5. $\sqrt[7]{-23\frac{15}{17}}$

6. $\sqrt[3]{\frac{2197}{3375}}$

7. $\sqrt[4]{299,821.9536}$

8. $\sqrt{0.1}$

9. $\sqrt[5]{\frac{1}{5}}$

 ## Experiencing Algebra the Group Way

Consider the following radical expressions:

1. $\sqrt{1225}$

2. $\sqrt[3]{42,875}$

3. $\sqrt{-1225}$

4. $\sqrt[3]{-42,875}$

Write an equivalent exponential expression for each. Then, enter the four radical expressions into your calculator and record the results. Next, enter the four exponential expressions into the calculator and record the results. Do the results agree with each other? They should if they were entered correctly. Exercise 3 should have given you an error message on the calculator, stating that there is a "NONREAL ANS." This will be discussed further in later chapters.

From what you have learned in this chapter, discuss why exercise 3 does not have a real-number answer. For now, you should note that the calculator is consistent in handling the two types of expressions. If you cannot evaluate a radical using your calculator because it violates some condition we have studied, the same will be true when you try to evaluate its equivalent exponential expression using your calculator. Point out this fact as you present the results of this exercise to the class and explain why exercise 3 had no real-number answer.

 ## Experiencing Algebra the Write Way

Study the results from "Experiencing Algebra the Exercise Way" in this section, and answer the following questions.

1. When converting from a radical to an equivalent exponential expression, what part of the radical becomes the base of the exponential expression?

2. During the conversion to an equivalent exponential expression, what part of the radical becomes the exponent of the exponential expression?

3. Recall the conditions when the radicand can be negative. What would you say about the condition when the base of an exponential expression can be negative? That is, what has to be true about the rational exponent in order for the base to be negative?

4. What does a negative sign in front of a radical expression do? When converting to an exponential expression, where does this negative sign appear?

2.5 Properties of Real Numbers and Order of Operations

Objectives

1 Identify the identity properties of 0 and 1, the multiplication properties of -1 and 0, and the inverse properties for addition and subtraction.

2 Discover, identify, and illustrate the commutative and associative laws for addition and multiplication.

3 Discover, identify, and illustrate the distributive law of multiplication over addition and subtraction.

4 Discover order of operations and evaluate expressions using order of operations.

5 Model real-world situations using expressions and evaluate them using order of operations.

Application

The Haunted House of Horrors has seven rooms. Celia's Cell is shaped like a cube, 8 feet on each side. Dracula's Dining Room is twice the size of Celia's Cell, plus 24 cubic feet. Bluebeard's Bedroom is three times the size of Celia's Cell, less 36 cubic feet. Kaptain Kidd's Kitchen is half the size of Bluebeard's Bedroom, exactly. Perilous Pauline's Parlor is the same size as Kaptain Kidd's Kitchen and Celia's Cell together. Frankenstein's Fiery Foyer is as large as Kaptain Kidd's Kitchen, plus 50 cubic feet. And finally, Gruesome Gary's Garage (yikes!) is one-third as large as Frankenstein's Fiery Foyer and Perilous Pauline's Parlor, less 12 cubic feet. How big is each room? How big is the Haunted House of Horrors?

After completing this section, we will discuss this application further. See page 132.

In previous sections, we have written equivalent expressions for real numbers. In this section, we discuss properties of real numbers that will help us write additional equivalent expressions and understand the ones we have already written. These properties will be useful later on, when we study algebra. We will find that we can discuss properties of a real number even if we don't know its value. In fact, we will sometimes be able to use these properties to figure out the value of an unknown number from information about it.

1 Identifying Identity, Multiplication, and Inverse Properties

The first property we discuss is the identity property of 0. We have already seen that adding 0 to any rational number results in the number itself. This is also true for irrational numbers. In other words, when we add 0 to any real number, the number's "identity" does not change. Therefore, 0 is called the **additive identity**.

> *Identity Property of 0*
> The sum of a real number and 0 is the number itself.

For example,

$$6 + 0 = 6$$
$$0 + -6 = -6$$

Helping Hand Subtracting 0 from a real number also results in the number itself. However, subtracting a real number from 0 does not result in the number itself. For example,

$$6 - 0 = 6$$
$$0 - 6 = -6$$

We also have seen the identity property of 1. Any real number multiplied by 1 results in the number itself. Therefore, 1 is called the **multiplicative identity**.

> *Identity Property of 1*
> The product of a real number and 1 is the real number itself.

For example,

$$6 \cdot 1 = 6$$
$$1 \cdot 6 = 6$$

Helping Hand Dividing a real number by 1 also results in the number itself. However, dividing 1 by a real number does not result in the number itself. For example,

$$6 \div 1 = 6$$
$$1 \div 6 = \frac{1}{6}$$

The identity property of 1 is used in writing equivalent fractions. For example, write $\frac{5}{8}$ as an equivalent fraction with a denominator of 16.

$$\frac{5}{8} = \frac{?}{16}$$

$$\frac{5}{8} \cdot 1 = \frac{?}{16} \qquad \text{Identity property of 1}$$

$$\frac{5}{8} \cdot \frac{2}{2} = \frac{10}{16} \qquad \text{Rewrite 1 as } \frac{2}{2}.$$

$$\frac{5}{8} = \frac{10}{16}$$

Multiplying a real number by -1 is an extension of this identity property. The result of the product of a real number and -1 is the opposite of the number itself.

> *Multiplication Property of -1*
> The product of a real number and -1 is the opposite of the number itself.

For example,

$$6 \cdot -1 = -(6) = -6$$
$$-1 \cdot 6 = -(6) = -6$$

We will apply this property in reverse later in this text, in the form

$$-(6) = (-1)(6)$$

The multiplication property of 0 is another property we discussed previously. The result of multiplying any real number by 0 is 0.

> *Multiplication Property of 0*
> The product of a real number and 0 is 0.

For example,

$$6 \cdot 0 = 0$$
$$0 \cdot -6 = 0$$

 Helping Hand Dividing 0 by any nonzero real number results in 0. Dividing 0 by 0 is indeterminate. However, dividing a nonzero real number by 0 is undefined.

$$0 \div 6 = 0$$
$$6 \div 0 \text{ is undefined.}$$
$$0 \div 0 \text{ is indeterminate.}$$

Another property we use in addition is the additive inverse property. When adding on a number line, we always begin at 0. This property enables us to write an expression (sum) that results in returning to 0. We must add a real number and its opposite to obtain this result. Therefore, the opposite is sometimes called the **additive inverse** of a real number.

> *Additive Inverse Property*
> The sum of a real number and its opposite, or additive inverse, is 0.

For example,

$$6 + (-6) = 0$$
$$-6 + -(-6) = 0$$

Multiplication also has an inverse, which results in a value of 1. Multiplying a real number by its reciprocal, sometimes called its **multiplicative inverse**, results in 1.

> *Multiplicative Inverse Property*
> The product of a nonzero real number and its reciprocal, or multiplicative inverse, is 1.

For example,

$$6 \cdot \frac{1}{6} = 1$$
$$-6 \cdot \frac{-1}{6} = 1$$

A major error in mathematics is to confuse the opposite of a number with the reciprocal of a number. Review the following table to make sure you understand the difference.

Number	Opposite (additive inverse)	Reciprocal (multiplicative inverse)
6	−6	$\dfrac{1}{6}$
−6	6	$\dfrac{-1}{6}$
$\dfrac{3}{2}$	$\dfrac{-3}{2}$	$\dfrac{2}{3}$
$\dfrac{-3}{2}$	$\dfrac{3}{2}$	$\dfrac{-2}{3}$

 Helping Hand The sign of the reciprocal of a number is always the same as the sign of the number itself.

EXAMPLE 1   Identify the properties used to write the following equivalent expressions.

a. $\dfrac{10}{15} \div \dfrac{5}{5} = \dfrac{2}{3}$ **b.** $(-3)\left(-\dfrac{1}{3}\right) = 1$

c. $\dfrac{3}{4} + \dfrac{0}{5} = \dfrac{3}{4}$ **d.** $\dfrac{-1}{2} + \dfrac{1}{2} = 0$

e. $(0.2)(0) = 0$ **f.** $-(3) = (-1)(3)$

Solution

a. $\dfrac{10}{15} \div \dfrac{5}{5} = \dfrac{2}{3}$ Identity property of 1

b. $(-3)\left(-\dfrac{1}{3}\right) = 1$ Multiplicative inverse property

c. $\dfrac{3}{4} + \dfrac{0}{5} = \dfrac{3}{4}$ Identity property of 0

d. $\dfrac{-1}{2} + \dfrac{1}{2} = 0$ Additive inverse property

e. $(0.2)(0) = 0$ Multiplication property of 0

f. $-(3) = (-1)(3)$ Multiplication property of −1 ∎

EXAMPLE 2   Complete the following table.

Number	2	$\dfrac{2}{3}$	−5	$\dfrac{-6}{7}$
Opposite				
Reciprocal				

Solution

Number	2	$\frac{2}{3}$	-5	$\frac{-6}{7}$
Opposite	-2	$\frac{-2}{3}$	5	$\frac{6}{7}$
Reciprocal	$\frac{1}{2}$	$\frac{3}{2}$	$\frac{-1}{5}$	$\frac{-7}{6}$

✔ Experiencing Algebra the Checkup Way

In exercises 1–6, match each expression with the appropriate property.

1. ___ $\left(\frac{8}{9}\right)\cdot\left(\frac{2}{2}\right)=\frac{16}{18}$

2. ___ $\left(\frac{8}{9}\right)\cdot\left(\frac{9}{8}\right)=1$

3. ___ $(4.5)\cdot 0=0$

4. ___ $15\cdot(-1)=-15$

5. ___ $14+(-14)=0$

6. ___ $-3+0=-3$

a. Identity property of 0 (or additive identity)

b. Identity property of 1 (or multiplicative identity)

c. Multiplicative property of -1

d. Multiplicative property of 0

e. Additive inverse

f. Multiplicative inverse

7. Complete the table.

Number	4	-17	$\frac{5}{7}$	$-\frac{8}{9}$
Opposite				
Reciprocal				

8. How can you obtain the opposite of a real number?

9. How can you obtain the reciprocal of a real number?

10. What is the difference between the opposite of a real number and the reciprocal of a real number?

2 Identifying Commutative and Associative Laws   Now we need to discuss the order in which we use mathematical operations to evaluate our expressions. First we will look at changing the order of two real numbers in expressions involving each of the four operations. Complete the following set of exercises with your calculator.

DISCOVERY 8

Operations with Two Real Numbers in Different Orders

Evaluate each expression and compare the results obtained in the left column to the corresponding results in the right column.

1. a. $-6 + (-2) =$ ____   **b.** $-2 + (-6) =$ ____
2. a. $-6 + 2 =$ ____   **b.** $2 + (-6) =$ ____
3. a. $-6 - (-2) =$ ____   **b.** $-2 - (-6) =$ ____
4. a. $-6 - 2 =$ ____   **b.** $2 - (-6) =$ ____
5. a. $-6 \cdot (-2) =$ ____   **b.** $-2 \cdot (-6) =$ ____
6. a. $-6 \cdot 2 =$ ____   **b.** $2 \cdot (-6) =$ ____
7. a. $-6 \div (-2) =$ ____   **b.** $-2 \div (-6) =$ ____
8. a. $-6 \div 2 =$ ____   **b.** $2 \div (-6) =$ ____

Write in your own words a law for changing the order of two real numbers when adding, subtracting, multiplying, and dividing.

In the column on the left, we perform the arithmetic operations with two real numbers. In the column on the right, we change the order of the two real numbers and then perform the same arithmetic operations. The results are the same when addition and multiplication operations are performed. Therefore, changing the order of real numbers when addition or multiplication operations are performed results in equivalent values. However, changing the order of real numbers when subtraction or division operations are performed results in different values.

Commutative Law for Addition
Changing the order of two real-number addends does not change the sum.

For example,

$$6 + 2 = 2 + 6$$
$$2 + (-3) = -3 + 2$$

Commutative Law for Multiplication
Changing the order of two real-number factors does not change the product.

For example,

$$6 \cdot 2 = 2 \cdot 6$$
$$2 \cdot (-3) = -3 \cdot 2$$

In order to group three real numbers, it may be necessary to use more than one set of grouping symbols. It is customary to use a set of parentheses ( ) within a set of brackets [ ] within a set of braces { }. To evaluate such an expression, perform the operations within the innermost grouping symbol first. For example, evaluate

$$\left[-6 + (-2)\right] + 3 = -8 + 3 = -5$$

On your calculator, enter all grouping symbols as parentheses.

Now what happens if we change the grouping of three real numbers when evaluating expressions with the same operation? Let's see. Complete the following set of exercises with your calculator.

D I S C O V E R Y   9

Operations with Three Real Numbers in Different Groupings
Evaluate each expression and compare the results obtained in the left column to the corresponding results in the right column.

1. a. $\left[-6 + (-2)\right] + 3 =$ ____   **b.** $-6 + (-2 + 3) =$ ____

2. a. $-6 + (2 + 3) =$ ____   **b.** $(-6 + 2) + 3 =$ ____

3. a. $\left[-6 - (-2)\right] - 3 =$ ____   **b.** $-6 - (-2 - 3) =$ ____

4. a. $-6 - (2 - 3) =$ ____   **b.** $(-6 - 2) - 3 =$ ____

5. a. $\left[-6 \cdot (-2)\right] \cdot 3 =$ ____   **b.** $-6 \cdot (-2 \cdot 3) =$ ____

6. a. $-6 \cdot (2 \cdot 3) =$ ____   **b.** $(-6 \cdot 2) \cdot 3 =$ ____

7. a. $\left[-6 \div (-2)\right] \div 3 =$ ____   **b.** $-6 \div (-2 \div 3) =$ ____

8. a. $-6 \div (2 \div 3) =$ ____   **b.** $(-6 \div 2) \div 3 =$ ____

Write in your own words a law for changing the grouping of three real numbers when adding, subtracting, multiplying, and dividing.

In the column on the left, we perform the arithmetic operations with three real numbers. In the column on the right, we change the grouping of the three real numbers by moving the parentheses and then perform the same arithmetic operations. The results are the same when addition and multiplication operations are performed. Therefore, changing the grouping of real numbers when addition and multiplication operations are performed results in equivalent values. However, changing the grouping of real numbers when subtraction and division operations are performed results in different values.

> *Associative Law for Addition*
> Changing the grouping of three real-number addends does not change the sum.

For example,

$$(6 + 2) + 3 = 6 + (2 + 3)$$
$$6 + \left[2 + (-3)\right] = (6 + 2) + (-3)$$

> *Associative Law for Multiplication*
> Changing the grouping of three real-number factors does not change the product.

For example,

$$(6 \cdot 2) \cdot 3 = 6 \cdot (2 \cdot 3)$$
$$-6(2 \cdot 3) = (-6 \cdot 2)3$$

Combining the commutative and associative laws for addition allows us to add real numbers in any order, as we did in sections 1.2 and 1.3. Also, the commutative and associative laws for multiplication allow us to do the same for multiplication, as we did in sections 1.4 and 1.5.

Helping Hand When we add or multiply three real numbers, it is useful to distinguish between the use of the commutative and associative laws. The numbers contained within the grouping symbols are the same, but in a different order, when we use the commutative law. However, the numbers contained in the grouping symbols are different when we use the associative law. For example,

$(3 + 2) + 5 = (2 + 3) + 5$ uses the commutative law because the numbers contained in the grouping symbol in each expression are 3 and 2, but they are in a different order in each expression.

$(3 + 2) + 5 = 3 + (2 + 5)$ uses the associative law because the numbers contained in the grouping symbols in the left expression are 3 and 2 and the numbers contained in the grouping symbols in the right expression are 2 and 5. *Note:* It appears that the grouping symbol shifted to the right when comparing the left expression to the right expression.

EXAMPLE 3   Identify the laws used to write the following equivalent expressions.

   a. $5 + (-2) = -2 + 5$ **b.** $2 + (5 + 3) = 2 + (3 + 5)$
   c. $2 + (5 + 3) = (2 + 5) + 3$ **d.** $6(-2 + 5) = (-2 + 5)(6)$
   e. $6(-2 \cdot 5) = [6 \cdot (-2)]5$

   Solution

   a. $5 + (-2) = -2 + 5$ Commutative law for addition
   b. $2 + (5 + 3) = 2 + (3 + 5)$ Commutative law for addition
   c. $2 + (5 + 3) = (2 + 5) + 3$ Associative law for addition
   d. $6(-2 + 5) = (-2 + 5)(6)$ Commutative law for multiplication
   e. $6(-2 \cdot 5) = [6 \cdot (-2)]5$ Associative law for multiplication ■

EXAMPLE 4   Write equivalent expressions for the following expressions, using the commutative laws.

   a. $4 + (-2)$ **b.** $-2(-5)$ **c.** $3(5 + 4)$

   Solution

   a. $4 + (-2) = -2 + 4$ Change the order of the addends.
   b. $-2(-5) = -5(-2)$ Change the order of the factors.
   c. $3(5 + 4) = (5 + 4)3$ Change the order of the factors.
   $\quad\quad\quad = 3(4 + 5)$ Change the order of the addends.

To check equivalence of the expressions, enter each expression separately on your calculator. *Note:* This does not check for using the proper law. The check for Example 4c is shown in Figure 2.9. ■

```
3*(5+4)
            27
(5+4)*3
            27
3*(4+5)
            27
```

Figure 2.9

EXAMPLE 5   Write equivalent expressions for the following expressions, using the associative laws.

   a. $5(6 \cdot 3)$ **b.** $-6 + (3 + 2)$ **c.** $-1(2 \cdot 6)$

Figure 2.10

Solution

a. $5(6 \cdot 3) = (5 \cdot 6)3$ Change the grouping symbols.

b. $-6 + (3 + 2) = (-6 + 3) + 2$ Change the grouping symbols.

c. $-1(2 \cdot 6) = (-1 \cdot 2)6$ Change the grouping symbols.

To check equivalence of the expressions, enter each expression separately on your calculator. *Note:* This does not check for using the proper law. The check for example 5a is shown in Figure 2.10. ∎

Experiencing Algebra the Checkup Way

Match each expression with the appropriate law.

1. ____ $2 + 7 = 7 + 2$

2. ____ $(7 \cdot 3) \cdot 5 = 7 \cdot (3 \cdot 5)$

3. ____ $2 + (3 + 8) = (2 + 3) + 8$

4. ____ $7 \cdot (-8) = (-8) \cdot 7$

a. Associative law for addition

b. Associative law for multiplication

c. Commutative law for multiplication

d. Commutative law for addition

Write an equivalent expression using the commutative laws. Check for equivalence using your calculator.

5. $-11 + (-42)$ **6.** $4(5 + 9)$ **7.** $125 \cdot (-102)$

Write an equivalent expression using the associative laws. Check for equivalence using your calculator.

8. $-4 + (-3 + 11)$ **9.** $-5 \cdot \left[-3 \cdot (-2) \right]$

10. What is the result if you apply the commutative law to a difference or a quotient?

11. What is the result if you apply the associative law to a difference or a quotient?

Identifying the Distributive Law

All of the properties previously described in this section have dealt with only one operation at a time, such as all addition or all multiplication. The next property involves both multiplication and addition. Complete the following set of exercises with your calculator.

DISCOVERY 10

Combining Multiplication and Addition

Evaluate each expression and compare the results obtained in the left column to the corresponding results in the right column.

1. a. $2(6 + 4) =$ ____   **b.** $2(6) + 2(4) =$ ____

2. a. $-2(-6 + 4) =$ ____   **b.** $-2(-6) + (-2)(4) =$ ____

Write in your own words a rule for combining multiplication and addition.

In the column on the left, we multiply a sum of real-number addends by a real-number factor. In the column on the right, we multiply each addend by the real-number factor and then add the results. The results are the same in both columns.

This rule is one of the four parts to the distributive law.

> *Distributive Laws*
> *Multiplication over Addition*
> The product of a real-number factor and a sum of real-number addends is the same as the sum of the products of the factor and each addend.

Multiplication over Subtraction
The product of a real-number factor and a difference of real numbers is the same as the difference of the products of the factor and the minuend less the product of the factor and the subtrahend.

Division over Addition
The quotient of a real-number divisor and a sum of real-number addends is the same as the sum of the quotients of the divisor and each addend.

Division over Subtraction
The quotient of a real-number divisor and a difference of real numbers is the same as the difference of the quotients of the divisor and the minuend less the quotient of the divisor and the subtrahend.

Examples of this property are as follows:

$$5(6 + 3) = 5(6) + 5(3)$$
$$5(6 - 3) = 5(6) - 5(3)$$
$$\frac{6 + 4}{2} = \frac{6}{2} + \frac{4}{2}$$
$$\frac{12 - 6}{3} = \frac{12}{3} - \frac{6}{3}$$

The reverse of the distributive property is called **factoring**. Some examples of factoring are

$$4(3) + 4(2) = 4(3 + 2)$$ The real-number factor, 4, is called the **common factor** of the addends.

$$2(3) - 2(4) = 2(3 - 4)$$ The common factor of the addends is 2.

Combining the multiplication property of -1 and the distributive law results in a very important property. The following example illustrates this.

$$-(3 + 6) = -1(3 + 6)$$ Multiplication property of -1 (in reverse)
$$= -1(3) + (-1)(6)$$ Distributive law
$$= -(3) + \left[-(6)\right]$$ Multiplication property of -1

In this example, we see that the opposite of a sum of real numbers is the same as the sum of the opposite of each addend. For example,

$$-(3 + 6) = -(9) = -9 \ \text{ and } \ -(3) + \left[-(6)\right] = -3 + (-6) = -9$$

Opposite of a Sum Property
The opposite of a sum of real numbers is the same as the sum of the opposites of each addend.

For example,

$$-(-4 + 6) = -(-4) + \left[-(6)\right] = 4 + (-6) \text{ or } 4 - 6$$

Note: This is also true for taking the opposite of a difference. For example,

$$-(3 - 6) = -(3) - \left[-(6)\right] = -3 + 6$$

EXAMPLE 6   Write an equivalent expression for the following expressions, using the distributive law or opposite of a sum property.

a. $9(3 + 4)$ **b.** $(4 + 2)3$ **c.** $\dfrac{15 + 5}{5}$

d. $-(3 + 6)$ **e.** $-(-2 + 4)$ **f.** $(5 - 2)(-6)$

Solution

a. $9(3 + 4) = 9(3) + 9(4)$

Distributive law
Multiply each addend by the factor 9.

b. $(4 + 2)3 = 4(3) + 2(3)$

Distributive law
Multiply each addend by the factor 3.

c. $\dfrac{15 + 5}{5} = \dfrac{15}{5} + \dfrac{5}{5}$

Distributive law
Divide each addend by the divisor 5.

d. $-(3 + 6) = -(3) + \left[-(6)\right]$ or $-3 - 6$

Opposite-of-a-sum property
Take the opposite of each addend.

e. $-(-2 + 4) = -(-2) + \left[-(4)\right]$ or $2 - 4$

Opposite-of-a-sum property
Take the opposite of each addend.

f. $(5 - 2)(-6) = 5(-6) - 2(-6)$

Distributive law
Multiply the minuend and subtrahend by the factor, −6. ∎

EXAMPLE 7   Factor the following expressions by writing an equivalent expression, using the distributive law in reverse.

a. $2(4) + 2(3)$ **b.** $2(4) - 2(3)$
c. $-2(4) - 2(-3)$ **d.** $-2(4) - 2(3)$

Solution

a. $2(4) + 2(3) = 2(4 + 3)$ The common factor is 2.
b. $2(4) - 2(3) = 2(4 - 3)$ The common factor is 2.
c. $-2(4) - 2(-3) =$
    $-2(4) + (-2)(-3) =$ Rewrite as addition.
      $-2(4 + (-3)) = -2(4 - 3)$ The common factor is −2.
      Rewrite as subtraction.

d. $-2(4) - 2(3) =$ Rewrite as addition.
    $-2(4) + (-2)(3) = -2(4 + 3)$ The common factor is −2. ∎

Experiencing Algebra the Checkup Way

Use the distributive law or the opposite-of-a-sum property to write an equivalent expression. Enter both expressions on your calculator to check for equivalence.

1. $5(3 + 7)$ **2.** $(4 + 18)(-7)$ **3.** $(17 - 25)5$ **4.** $\dfrac{-46 + 62}{2}$

5. $-(5 + 9)$ **6.** $-(-5 + 9)$

Factor by writing an equivalent expression using the distributive law in reverse.

7. $5(12) + 5(17)$ **8.** $13(17) - 13(22)$ **9.** $-6(7) - 6(11)$ **10.** $-12(11) - 12(-14)$

11. Explain the terms *factoring* and *common factor*.

---

4 Evaluating Expressions using Order of Operations

We are now ready to evaluate expressions that involve all operations. To do this we must establish a few rules, so that we all obtain the same results. Complete the following set of exercises to discover the order of operations for addition, subtraction, multiplication, and division.

DISCOVERY 11

Order of Operations

Consider the expression $6 \div 2 + 1 \cdot 3 - 5$. Complete the following possible methods of evaluation.

1. Evaluate in order from left to right.
2. First, evaluate all addition and subtraction in order from left to right. Then, evaluate all multiplication and division in order from left to right.
3. First, evaluate all multiplication and division in order from left to right. Then, evaluate all addition and subtraction in order from left to right.
4. Enter the expression on your calculator.

Write a rule for the order of operation by comparing the calculator value and the values in exercises 1, 2, and 3.

The calculator result is 1. The result of the third set of directions resulted in 1. Therefore, the calculator is programmed to evaluate the expression in the same order as described in the third set of directions; it performed all multiplication and division before addition and subtraction. The calculator evaluated the expression according to the **order of operations**.

In addition to basic arithmetic operations, we use parentheses, brackets, braces, absolute value symbols, fraction bars, and radicals as grouping symbols. These grouping symbols change the order of operations of the arithmetic operations (addition, subtraction, multiplication, and division). To evaluate an expression involving grouping symbols, perform the operations within the grouping symbols first. If more than one pair of grouping symbols is present, perform the innermost operation first.

Order of Operations
To evaluate an expression, perform operations in the following order:

- Perform all operations within grouping symbols. If more than one grouping symbol is present, perform the innermost first and work outward.
- Evaluate exponents and roots.
- Evaluate multiplication and division from left to right.
- Evaluate addition and subtraction from left to right.

A phrase we can use to help us remember the correct order of operations is "Please Excuse My Dear Aunt Sally." The first letter of each word corresponds to an operation. That is,

Please	Parentheses or groupings
Excuse	Exponents and roots
My	Multiply $\Big\}$ and
Dear	Divide
Aunt	Add $\Big\}$ and
Sally	Subtract

EXAMPLE 8 Evaluate using the order of operations.

a. $15 + 7 - 6 \div 3 - 2 \cdot 8$ **b.** $-12(-3) - 6(4) + 8$

c. $4(-3 + 6) - 7(8 - 2)$ **d.** $-(3^2 - 7) + 8(-2 - 4)$

e. $\dfrac{16 - 2^2 + 3}{3 + 2}$ **f.** $2\{[2(3 - 4) + 7] - 8\} + 3(-5)$

g. $-\sqrt{25} + 11$ **h.** $-|3.5 - 4.26 - 5|$

Solution

a.
$$15 + 7 - \underline{6 \div 3} - 2 \cdot 8 = \qquad \text{Divide.}$$
$$\underline{15 + 7} - \quad 2 \quad - 2 \cdot 8 = \qquad \text{Multiply.}$$
$$\underline{15 + 7} - \quad 2 \quad - \underline{16} = \qquad \text{Add.}$$
$$\underline{\quad 22 \quad} - \quad 2 \quad - 16 = \qquad \text{Subtract.}$$
$$20 \quad - 16 = 4 \qquad \text{Subtract.}$$

b.
$$\underline{-12(-3)} - 6(4) + 8 = \qquad \text{Multiply.}$$
$$36 \quad - \underline{6(4)} + 8 = \qquad \text{Multiply.}$$
$$\underline{36 \quad - \quad 24} + 8 = \qquad \text{Subtract.}$$
$$12 \quad + 8 = 20 \qquad \text{Add.}$$

c.
$$4(\underline{-3 + 6}) - 7(8 - 2) = \qquad \text{Add within parentheses.}$$
$$4(\quad 3 \quad) - 7(\underline{8 - 2}) = \qquad \text{Subtract within parentheses.}$$
$$\underline{4(3)} - 7(\quad 6 \quad) = \qquad \text{Multiply.}$$
$$12 - \underline{7(6)} \qquad = \qquad \text{Multiply.}$$
$$12 - \quad 42 \qquad = -30 \qquad \text{Subtract.}$$

d.
$$-(\underline{3^2} - 7) + 8(-2 - 4) = \qquad \text{Evaluate exponent.}$$
$$-(\underline{9 - 7}) + 8(-2 - 4) = \qquad \text{Subtract within parentheses.}$$
$$-(\quad 2 \quad) + 8(\underline{-2 - 4}) = \qquad \text{Subtract within parentheses.}$$
$$\underline{-(2)} + 8(\quad -6 \quad) = \qquad \text{Take the opposite. (Multiply by } -1.)$$
$$-2 + \underline{8(-6)} \qquad = \qquad \text{Multiply.}$$
$$-2 + \quad -48 \qquad = -50 \qquad \text{Add.}$$

e.
$$\dfrac{16 - 2^2 + 3}{3 + 2} = \qquad \text{Evaluate exponent.}$$
$$\dfrac{16 - 4 + 3}{3 + 2} = \qquad \text{Subtract.}$$
$$\dfrac{12 + 3}{3 + 2} = \qquad \begin{array}{l}\text{Add both groups separated}\\\text{by fraction bar.}\end{array}$$
$$\dfrac{15}{5} = 3 \qquad \text{Divide.}$$

f. $2\{[2(3-4)+7]-8\}+3(-5) =$ Subtract within parentheses.

$2\{[2(\underline{\ -1\ })+7]-8\}+3(-5) =$ Multiply.

$2\{[\ \underline{\ -2\ }\ +7]-8\}+3(-5) =$ Add within brackets.

$2\{\ \underline{\ \ \ \ 5\ \ \ \ }\ -8\}+3(-5) =$ Subtract.

$2\{\ \underline{\ -3\ }\}+3(-5) =$ Multiply.

$\underline{\ -6\ }-\underline{\ 15\ } = -21$ Subtract.

g. $-\sqrt{25+11} =$ Add within radical.

$-\sqrt{36} = -6$

h. $-|3.5-4.26-5| =$ Subtract within absolute values.

$-|-5.76| =$ Evaluate the absolute value.

$-(5.76) = -5.76$ Take the opposite (multiply by -1).

When entering these examples on your calculator, it may be necessary to add additional parentheses for grouping. Remember to use parentheses for all grouping symbols. The checks for Example 8e, 8f, and 8g are shown in Figure 2.11. ∎

TECHNOLOGY

```
(16-2²+3)/(3+2)
                3
2((2(3-4)+7)-8)+
3(-5)
               -21
-√(25+11)
                -6
```

Figure 2.11

For Figure 2.11

It is necessary to enclose the numerator in a set of parentheses, as well as the denominator.

e.

ENTER

Use parentheses in place of brackets.

f. 2 ((2 (3 − 4) + 7) − 8)

+ 3 ((−) 5)   ENTER

Enclose the radicand in a set of parentheses.

g. (−) 2nd √ 2 5 + 1 1) ENTER

✓ Experiencing Algebra the Checkup Way

In exercises 1–8, evaluate, using the order of operations.

1. $11+9-4\div2-3\cdot4$

2. $-6(-5)-2(3)+7$

3. $5(-4+7)-3(9-5)$

4. $-(4^3-15)+6(-5-3)$

5. $\dfrac{27-4^2+5}{7+1}$

6. $[8(4-7)+9]-2$

7. $-\sqrt{9+16}$

8. $-2\{4[3-(5-7)]+6\div3\}+7(-3)$

9. What does the memory device "Please Excuse My Dear Aunt Sally" help you to remember? Explain.

---

5 Modeling the Real World

When using real numbers to evaluate real-world data, the same rules for order of operations apply. Be careful in determining what grouping symbols, if any, are needed to correctly describe the situation, since grouping symbols can change the order of operations. It is often a good idea to check your answer and see whether it seems reasonable to you. For example, if you calculate an average test score and your answer is higher than any of the individual scores, you've made an error somewhere.

EXAMPLE 9   Gretchen wants to find her grade average for algebra class. Her first test grade was 73. She was not very happy with the grade, so she studied very hard. Her next test grade was 13 points more than the first test grade. Her third test grade was 91. On her final test, Gretchen scored 1 point less than her third test grade. Write an expression for Gretchen's grade average. Evaluate the expression.

Solution

first grade $= 73$
second grade $= 73 + 13$
third grade $= 91$
fourth grade $= 91 - 1$

To find the average, add the grades and divide by the number of grades added. Therefore, an expression for Gretchen's average is

$$\frac{73 + (73 + 13) + 91 + (91 - 1)}{4} = \qquad \text{Simplify parentheses.}$$

$$\frac{73 + 86 + 91 + 90}{4} = \qquad \text{Add.}$$

$$\frac{340}{4} = 85 \qquad \text{Divide.}$$

Gretchen's algebra average was 85. ∎

EXAMPLE 10   Alex the Train Man is 5 years old. His mother is 9 times Alex's age plus 2. His father is 12 times Alex's age less 4. Brother Brian is half of his father's age plus 3. Uncle Buncle is as old as Brother Brian and Alex together. Auntie Nan is younger than Uncle Buncle by 4 years. Determine the age of Alex and each member of his family.

Solution

Alex's age $\quad\quad = 5$
Alex's mother's age $= 9 \cdot 5 + 2$
$\quad\quad\quad\quad\quad\quad = 45 + 2 = 47$
Alex's father's age $\;= 12 \cdot 5 - 4$
$\quad\quad\quad\quad\quad\quad = 60 - 4$
$\quad\quad\quad\quad\quad\quad = 56$
Brother Brian's age $= \dfrac{1}{2}(56) + 3$
$\quad\quad\quad\quad\quad\quad = 28 + 3$
$\quad\quad\quad\quad\quad\quad = 31$
Uncle Buncle's age $\;= 31 + 5$
$\quad\quad\quad\quad\quad\quad = 36$
Auntie Nan's age $\quad = 36 - 4$
$\quad\quad\quad\quad\quad\quad = 32$

Alex is 5 years old, his mother is 47, his father is 56, Brother Brian is 31, Uncle Buncle is 36, and Auntie Nan is 32. ∎

Application

The Haunted House of Horrors has seven rooms. Celia's Cell is shaped like a cube, 8 feet on each side. Dracula's Dining Room is twice the size of Celia's Cell, plus 24 cubic feet. Bluebeard's Bedroom is three times the size of Celia's Cell, less 36 cubic feet. Kaptain Kidd's Kitchen is half the size of Bluebeard's Bedroom, exactly. Perilous Pauline's Parlor is the same size as Kaptain Kidd's Kitchen and Celia's Cell together. Frankenstein's Fiery Foyer is as large as Kaptain Kidd's Kitchen, plus 50 cubic feet. And finally, Gruesome Gary's Garage (yikes!) is one-third as large as Frankenstein's Fiery Foyer and Perilous Pauline's Parlor, less 12 cubic feet. How big is each room? How big is the Haunted House of Horrors?

Discussion

Size of:

Celia's Cell	$= 8^3 = 512$
Dracula's Dining Room	$= 2 \cdot 8^3 + 24$
	$= 2 \cdot 512 + 24$
	$= 1024 + 24 = 1048$
Bluebeard's Bedroom	$= 3 \cdot 8^3 - 36$
	$= 3 \cdot 512 - 36$
	$= 1536 - 36 = 1500$
Kaptain Kidd's Kitchen	$= \dfrac{1}{2}(1500) = 750$
Perilous Pauline's Parlor	$= 750 + 512 = 1262$
Frankenstein's Fiery Foyer	$= 750 + 50 = 800$
Gruesome Gary's Garage	$= \dfrac{1}{3}(800 + 1262) - 12$
	$= \dfrac{1}{3}(2062) - 12$
	$= 687\dfrac{1}{3} - 12$
	$= 675\dfrac{1}{3}$

The sizes of the rooms are as follows:

Celia's Cell	$= 512 \text{ ft}^3$
Dracula's Dining Room	$= 1048 \text{ ft}^3$
Bluebeard's Bedroom	$= 1500 \text{ ft}^3$
Kaptain Kidd's Kitchen	$= 750 \text{ ft}^3$
Perilous Pauline's Parlor	$= 1262 \text{ ft}^3$
Frankenstein's Fiery Foyer	$= 800 \text{ ft}^3$
Gruesome Gary's Garage	$= 675\dfrac{1}{3} \text{ ft}^3$

The Haunted House of Horrors is a total of $6547\frac{1}{3} \text{ ft}^3$. ∎

Experiencing Algebra the Checkup Way

1. In tracking the closing price of a stock for a week, Judy noted that the closing price was $71.00 on Monday. The price increased by $0.50 on Tuesday, was $69.50 on Wednesday, dropped by $0.25 on Thursday, and closed at $72.00 on Friday. Write an expression for the average closing price of the stock for the week. Evaluate the expression.

2. The manager of a road-show production of a Broadway play was charting the distances from New York City to the cities in which the show would be appearing. They would be going to Philadelphia, which is 100 miles from New York; Boston, which is 6 miles more than twice the distance to Philadelphia; Baltimore, which is 10 miles less than the distance to Boston; Chicago, which is the sum of the distances to Baltimore and Boston plus four times the distance to Philadelphia; Cleveland, which is 72 miles more than one-half the distance to Chicago; and Los Angeles, which is 52 miles less than six times the distance to Cleveland. Find the distances, and then find the distance between the closest and farthest cities on the tour.

PROBLEM SET 2.5

 ## Experiencing Algebra the Exercise Way

The properties and laws of the real-number system studied in this section are:

a. Identity property of 0   **b.** Identity property of 1

c. Multiplication property of -1 **d.** Multiplication property of 0

e. Additive inverse property   **f.** Multiplicative inverse property

g. Commutative law for addition   **h.** Commutative law for multiplication

i. Associative law for addition   **j.** Associative law for multiplication

Identify which property or law of the real-number system is used to write the following equivalent expressions.

1. $35 \cdot 1 = 35$

2. $\left(\dfrac{4}{5}\right)\left(\dfrac{5}{4}\right) = 1$

3. $-1 \cdot 250 = -250$

4. $-17 + 0 = -17$

5. $\left(\dfrac{3}{7}\right)\left(\dfrac{7}{3}\right) = 1$

6. $0 \cdot (-21) = 0$

7. $\left(\dfrac{3}{5}\right)\left(\dfrac{3}{3}\right) = \dfrac{9}{15}$

8. $53 \cdot (-1) = -53$

9. $57 + 0 = 57$

10. $-55 + 55 = 0$

11. $48 + (-48) = 0$

12. $\left(\dfrac{6}{7}\right)\left(\dfrac{2}{2}\right) = \dfrac{12}{14}$

13. $0 \cdot 556 = 0$

14. $1 \cdot (-7) = -7$

15. $7 + 11 = 11 + 7$

16. $3 + (1 + 5) = (3 + 1) + 5$

17. $52 \cdot 21 = 21 \cdot 52$

18. $46 + (-9) = -9 + 46$

19. $(5 \cdot 8) \cdot 4 = 5 \cdot (8 \cdot 4)$

20. $(-3) \cdot 4 = 4 \cdot (-3)$

21. $14 + \left[(-5) + 17\right] = \left[14 + (-5)\right] + 17$

22. $-35 \cdot \left[(-21) \cdot 18\right] = \left[-35 \cdot (-21)\right] \cdot 18$

Complete the tables in exercises 23 and 24.

23.

Number	12	-3	-6.2	3.5	$\dfrac{5}{9}$	$-\dfrac{3}{5}$
Opposite						
Reciprocal						

24.

Number	24	-5	-1.5	4.2	$\dfrac{6}{7}$	$-\dfrac{8}{11}$
Opposite						
Reciprocal						

Write an equivalent expression using the commutative laws of real numbers. Check for equivalence on your calculator.

25. $-4.33 + 1.9$ **26.** $\dfrac{15}{99} + \dfrac{4}{11}$ **27.** $58(-65)$ **28.** $\left(4\dfrac{1}{3}\right)\left(5\dfrac{2}{3}\right)$

Write an equivalent expression using the associative laws of real numbers. Check for equivalence on your calculator.

29. $5.6\big[(-3.7)(1.1)\big]$ **30.** $(40 \cdot 35) \cdot 17$ **31.** $\left(\dfrac{5}{13} + \dfrac{8}{13}\right) + \dfrac{1}{13}$ **32.** $-35 + \big[-54 + (-99)\big]$

Write an equivalent expression using the distributive law of real numbers. Check for equivalence on your calculator.

33. $\left(\dfrac{3}{8}\right)\left(\dfrac{5}{7} - \dfrac{1}{9}\right)$ **34.** $-23(31 + 25)$ **35.** $2.7(-1.5 + 3.2)$ **36.** $\left(1\dfrac{1}{4}\right)\left(5\dfrac{1}{2} - 3\dfrac{1}{8}\right)$

37. $\dfrac{217 - 175}{7}$ **38.** $\dfrac{-78 + 108}{6}$

Write an equivalent expression using the opposite-of-a-sum property of real numbers. Check for equivalence on your calculator.

39. $-(15 + 19.3)$ **40.** $-(5.7 + 0.06)$ **41.** $-\left(-\dfrac{6}{7} - \dfrac{5}{9}\right)$ **42.** $-(-51 - 19)$

43. $-\left(1\dfrac{1}{7} - 2\dfrac{1}{5}\right)$ **44.** $-(89 - 17)$ **45.** $-(19.37 + 15.043)$ **46.** $-\left(2\dfrac{1}{4} + 3\dfrac{5}{8}\right)$

Factor, using the distributive law of real numbers in reverse. Check for equivalence on your calculator.

47. $15(17) + 15(21)$ **48.** $81(22) + 81(4)$ **49.** $-3(14) - 3(21)$ **50.** $-13(21) - 13(16)$
51. $-6(12) - 6(-13)$ **52.** $-5(45) - 5(-7)$ **53.** $-3(15) + (-3)(17)$ **54.** $-2(38) + (-2)(15)$

Evaluate, using the order of operations. Check your answers on your calculator.

55. $-(6^2 - 12) + 5(-3 - 8)$ **56.** $-(8^2 - 15) + 4(-9 - 11)$

57. $[4(7-5)+2]-9$

58. $[6(8-2)+1]-7$

59. $-\sqrt{36+64}$

60. $-\sqrt{81+144}$

61. $\dfrac{18-4^2+7}{2+1}$

62. $\dfrac{25-3^3+14}{1+5}$

63. $2.7+5.6-16\div4-3\cdot2$

64. $2.2+(-1.5)-27\div9+5\cdot3$

65. $3(-4)-(5)(6)+4$

66. $-9(-4)-(8)(12)+22$

67. $(4.3)3-5(1.6)+42.9\div3$

68. $2(3.4)-(4.1)(2)+16.8\div2.1$

69. $-5(39-4^2)-2(23-11)$

70. $-6(100-9^2)-(15-23)$

71. $4(15-8)+31(14-11)$

72. $7(22-19)+16(12-14)$

73. $-|5.2-31.3+3.95|$

74. $-\left|3\dfrac{1}{3}-7\dfrac{5}{6}+1\dfrac{1}{2}\right|$

75. $6^2+12\div(-2)-12\cdot(-4)$

76. $4^3+57\div(-3)-7\cdot(-3)$

77. $\left(\dfrac{2}{3}\right)^2\div\left(\dfrac{1}{3}+\dfrac{1}{2}\right)\cdot\left(\dfrac{8}{9}\right)$

78. $\left(\dfrac{3}{4}\right)^2\div\left(\dfrac{1}{2}+\dfrac{1}{6}\right)\cdot\left(\dfrac{2}{5}\right)$

79. $\left(\dfrac{1}{5}\right)\cdot\left(\dfrac{15}{22}\right)\div\left(\dfrac{1}{11}+\dfrac{1}{33}\right)-\left(\dfrac{1}{3}\right)^2$

80. $\left(\dfrac{1}{3}\right)\cdot\left(\dfrac{6}{7}\right)\div\left(\dfrac{1}{7}+\dfrac{1}{2}\right)-\left(\dfrac{1}{3}\right)^2$

81. $100-(24+7^2-5)\cdot3+102\div2$

82. $214-(5+11^2-16)\cdot4+55\div11$

83. $2\{3[5-2(3+4)]+9\div3\}-9(-8)$

84. $15(7)-5\{3[8+2(5-9)]-14\div7\}$

85. $\dfrac{29+3-2^3}{2^2+2^3}$

86. $\dfrac{15+3\cdot9-6}{5+2^2}$

87. $15-\sqrt{2^2+3\cdot7}$

88. $-\sqrt{9^2+19}+3\cdot6$

89. $\dfrac{4+3\cdot9-5^2-2\cdot3}{6^2-5}$

90. $\dfrac{15-2^4+1^2}{3\cdot9-5^2}$

91. $\dfrac{8^2+3\cdot12}{5-4\cdot6+2\cdot3^2+1^2}$

92. $\dfrac{45-7\cdot5}{3^3-1+2\cdot19-8^2}$

Write and evaluate a mathematical expression for the following situations.

93. A passing grade for a math test is a grade of 80. Holly scored 7 points above passing on the first test, scored an 80 on the second test, was 12 points above passing on the third test, was 4 points below passing on the fourth test, and scored a 100 on the last test. What was Holly's average grade on the tests?

94. In Monica's science class, a grade of 75 is passing. She scored 10 points above passing on the first test, 5 points below passing on the second test, and 16 points above passing on the third test; she received a 95 and an 80 on the last two tests. What was Monica's average on the tests?

95. Estrelita had a sales quota of $500 per week. Over a 4-week period, she was $175 above quota the first week, $125 below quota the second week, $45 above quota the third week, and $110 below quota the fourth week. What were the average weekly sales for Estrelita?

96. Karen's sales quota was $3500 per month. During the first quarter of the year, she was $850 below quota the first month, $1200 above quota the second month, and right on quota the third month. Determine Karen's average monthly sales during the quarter.

97. Marilyn went on a diet and exercise regimen. When she started the program, she weighed 168 pounds. At the end of 12 weeks on the program, her weight had dropped to 136 pounds. What was her average weekly change in weight?

98. Brian went on a weight training program to get into shape for sports. At the start of the program, he weighed 195 pounds. At the end of 8 weeks, he weighed 210 pounds. What was his average weekly change in weight?

99. The list of the top ten record singles of all time has three songs each with worldwide sales of 7 million records. They are "Can't Buy Me Love" by the Beatles; "Do They Know It's Christmas" by Band Aid; and "We Are the World" by USA for Africa. "I Will Always Love You" by Whitney Houston has sold 0.5 million less than twice the number of any of these. One of the top-selling singles is "White Christmas" by Bing Crosby, which has sold 2 million more than four times as many singles as "Can't Buy Me Love." How many records have been sold of each of these singles? What is the total for all of them?

100. A top-selling single of all time is "Rock around the Clock" by Bill Haley and the Comets. The record has sold 3 million less than twice the number of copies of Elvis Presley's "It's Now or Never," which is one of the four top-selling singles. "It's Now or Never," has surpassed Elvis's other top seller, "Hound Dog," by 1 million sales. "Hound Dog" is tied with Paul Anka's "Diana" with sales of 9 million singles. How many of each of these records has been sold? What is the difference in sales between the highest and lowest selling singles of those records listed here?

Experiencing Algebra the Calculator Way

Use your calculator to evaluate. Express your answers in fractional notation or round decimals to the nearest thousandth as appropriate.

1. $1085 + 57[273(480 - 575) - (-1233)] - (-857 + 654) + 56^2$

2. $\dfrac{15}{17} - \left(-\dfrac{19}{23} + \dfrac{7}{2}\right) - \dfrac{5}{3}\left[\dfrac{8}{15}\left(\dfrac{2}{3} - \dfrac{7}{9}\right) - \dfrac{14}{17}\right] + \left(\dfrac{7}{3}\right)^2$

3. $[11.98644 \div (-2.36)]^2(5.76 - 3.1^3) + (15.75)^{-2}$

4. $\sqrt{(2.35)^3 - \left(\dfrac{11}{19}\right)^2}$

5. $\dfrac{57^2 - 31(15 + 17) - 47(-53)}{14(31) - 29^2 + 15^3}$

6. $\dfrac{57^2 - 43(-59)}{36^2 - 54(2^2)(6)}$

7. $\dfrac{15}{32}\sqrt{14(56)^3 - 2[56 - 7(2)^3]}$

8. $\dfrac{14 + 2(-3 + 5)}{5 + 2^2} + 3$

9. $\dfrac{5 \cdot 125 - 6 \cdot 115}{2 \cdot 7^2 - (5 \cdot 18 + 2^3)}$

10. $\dfrac{7 \cdot 35 - 5 \cdot 7^2}{425 - 4^3}$

Experiencing Algebra the Group Way

A. *Evaluate.*

1. $\dfrac{35 + 77}{7}$

2. $\dfrac{1}{7}(35 + 77)$

3. $\dfrac{1}{7}(35) + \dfrac{1}{7}(77)$

4. $\dfrac{35}{7} + \dfrac{77}{7}$

You should notice that all the results are the same. The expressions must be equivalent. While this is not a proof, but simply an illustration, the problems demonstrate a relationship between division and multiplication by reciprocals. In your discussion group, explain what this relationship is, and explain how the first exercise relates to each of the other three.
Construct a similar illustration in which you divide the difference of two numbers by a real number. Present your findings to the class.

B. *You have learned several properties of real numbers. Use these properties of real numbers to evaluate. See which group can evaluate these the fastest (and with the fewest errors).*

1. $101 + (-101)$

2. $-1\dfrac{4}{5} + 1\dfrac{4}{5}$

3. $-0.09 + 0.09$

4. $0 + (-135)$

5. $0 + \dfrac{24}{37}$

6. $0.001 + 0$

7. $156 \cdot 1$

8. $1 \cdot (2.95)$

9. $1 \cdot \left(\dfrac{5}{13}\right)$

10. $\left(-\dfrac{3}{5}\right)(-1)$

11. $(-1)(-11.2)$

12. $(-1)(-1)$

13. $39(-1)$

14. $\left(1\dfrac{5}{8}\right) \cdot 0$

15. $0 \cdot (-44)$

16. $(8.03) \cdot 0$

17. $15 \cdot \left(\dfrac{1}{15}\right)$

18. $\left(1\dfrac{7}{9}\right)\left(\dfrac{9}{16}\right)$

19. $(4.8)\left(\dfrac{5}{24}\right)$

20. $(-1.2)\left(-\dfrac{5}{6}\right)$

Experiencing Algebra the Write Way

In this section, you learned several important terms. You must be sure that you remember them and that you do not get them confused. To help reinforce your understanding, explain in your own words what the following terms mean: *opposite*, *reciprocal*, *distributive law of multiplication over addition* (and *over subtraction*), *commutative law*, and *associative law*. Include a numerical example of each term in your discussions.

CHAPTER 2 | Summary

After completing this chapter, you should be able to define in your own words the following key terms, properties, and rules.

Terms
base
exponent
expanded form
exponential form
exponential expression
standard notation
scientific notation
numerical factor
calculator notation
perfect square
square root
positive root
principal root
negative root
irrational number
real number
radical sign

radicand
radical expression
index
additive identity
multiplicative identity
additive inverse
multiplicative inverse
factoring
common factor
order of operations

Properties
Identity property of 0
Identity property of 1
Multiplication property of -1
Multiplication property of 0
Additive inverse property
Multiplicative inverse property

Commutative law for addition
Commutative law for multiplication
Associative law for addition
Associative law for multiplication
Distributive laws
Opposite-of-a-sum property
The order of operations

Rules
Evaluating exponential expressions
Evaluating square roots
Evaluating radical expressions
Writing an equivalent exponential
    expression for a radical expression
Order of operations

CHAPTER 2 | Review

Reflections
1. What do we mean by the expanded form of an exponential expression?
2. If the base of an exponential expression is a negative number, when will the expression result in a positive number and when will it result in a negative number?
3. In an exponential expression, what is the effect of a negative integer exponent? What is the effect of a zero exponent? What is the effect of an exponent equal to 1?
4. What is scientific notation and why is it useful?
5. What is the principal root of a number?
6. When will a radical expression have a positive value? When will it have a negative value? When will it not have a value in the set of real numbers?
7. How can a radical expression be rewritten as an exponential expression?
8. How does the set of real numbers differ from the set of rational numbers?
9. What do the commutative laws for real numbers allow you to do?
10. What do the associative laws for real numbers allow you to do?
11. What do the distributive laws for real numbers allow you to do?
12. Why is it important to follow the order of operations when evaluating a mathematical expression?

Express your answers in fractional notation or decimals to the nearest thousandth as appropriate.

2.1
Write in exponential form.

1. $12 \cdot 12 \cdot 12 \cdot 12 \cdot 12 \cdot 12 \cdot 12 \cdot 12 \cdot 12 \cdot 12$

2. $\left(\frac{5}{11}\right)\left(\frac{5}{11}\right)\left(\frac{5}{11}\right)\left(\frac{5}{11}\right)\left(\frac{5}{11}\right)$

3. Determine the resulting sign of the expression. Do not evaluate.

    a. $(-87)^{14}$ **b.** -87^{14} **c.** $-(-87)^{14}$ **d.** $(-87)^{19}$ **e.** -87^{19} **f.** $-(-87)^{19}$

Evaluate.

4. 2^8 **5.** $(1.2)^2$ **6.** $\left(1\frac{1}{3}\right)^3$ **7.** 0^{10}

8. 1^{15} **9.** $(-3)^5$ **10.** $(-3)^4$ **11.** $(-0.2)^3$

12. $\left(-1\frac{1}{3}\right)^2$ **13.** $(-1)^{18}$ **14.** $(-1)^{21}$

Use your calculator to evaluate.

15. $(-33)^5$ **16.** $\left(-2\frac{1}{3}\right)^5$ **17.** $(0.47)^6$ **18.** $(-56)^4$

19. $\left(-\frac{3}{4}\right)^6$ **20.** $-\left(-2\frac{1}{3}\right)^4$

Evaluate.

21. 15^0 **22.** $(-15)^0$ **23.** -15^0 **24.** 15^1

25. -15^1 **26.** $(-15)^1$ **27.** 1^0 **28.** 0^0

29. 1^1 **30.** 0^1 **31.** $(229,384)^0$ **32.** $(3.079)^1$

33. $\left(\frac{13}{23}\right)^0$ **34.** $(229,384)^1$

Write an equivalent expression having a positive exponent, and evaluate.

35. $(-12)^{-2}$ **36.** -12^{-2} **37.** $56,439^{-3}$ **38.** $(-9)^{-3}$

39. -9^{-3} **40.** $\left(-2\frac{3}{8}\right)^{-1}$ **41.** $\left(1\frac{3}{4}\right)^{-2}$ **42.** 1^{-9}

43. $(-1)^{-9}$ **44.** $(1.8)^{-3}$ **45.** $\left(\frac{7}{8}\right)^{-3}$

Write and evaluate an exponential expression for exercises 46 and 47.

46. A square flower garden measures 7.5 feet on a side. A flower catalog offers a variety of plants to fill an area up to 60 square feet. Will there be enough plants to fill the garden?

47. A storage bin in the shape of a cube measures 2.5 feet on a side. How many cubic feet of mulch will fit in the bin if it is piled level with the top of the bin?

2.2
Write in scientific notation.

48. 0.000000189 **49.** $189,000,000,000,000,000$ **50.** -0.00056 **51.** $-27,085,000,000$

Write exercises 52–55 in scientific notation and standard notation.

52. 5.89 E11   **53.** 4.02 E -7 **54.** -1.3 E7   **55.** -7.093 E -5

56. In 1992, the gross national product (GNP) of the United States was reported as $5,904,822,000,000. Write this number in scientific notation.

57. In 1992, the GNP of the Solomon Islands was reported as 2.37×10^8 U.S. dollars. Write this number in standard notation. Using the information in exercise 56, by how many dollars does the U.S. GNP exceed this amount?

58. Red blood cells of mammals measure about 8×10^{-6} meters in diameter. Write this number in standard notation.

59. Michael Jackson's album *Thriller* is one of the world's best-selling albums of all time. It has sold over 40,000,000 copies. Write this number in scientific notation.

2.3
Evaluate.

60. $\sqrt{81}$

61. $\sqrt{0.64}$

62. $\sqrt{\dfrac{9}{25}}$

63. $-\sqrt{49}$

64. $\sqrt{-16}$

65. $\sqrt{1.2769}$

66. $-\sqrt{470.89}$

67. $-\sqrt{\dfrac{576}{1369}}$

68. $\sqrt{2\dfrac{6}{11}}$

69. $\sqrt{15}$

70. $\sqrt{-1.2}$

71. $\sqrt[4]{81}$

72. $\sqrt[3]{0.125}$

73. $\sqrt[4]{\dfrac{16}{81}}$

74. $\sqrt[3]{-27,000}$

75. $\sqrt[5]{-1}$

76. $-\sqrt[4]{13.0321}$

77. $-\sqrt[5]{10}$

78. Graph the following numbers on a number line. Label the points.

$9, \sqrt{9}, -\sqrt{16}, \sqrt{18}, -\sqrt{68}, \pi, -\sqrt{7.29}, \sqrt[3]{140}$

79. The diamond in a baseball field is a square-shaped plot that has an area of 729 square meters. What are the dimensions of the diamond?

80. A box for facial tissues is designed as a cube that will be marketed as a bathroom boutique design. The box has a volume of $91\frac{1}{8}$ cubic inches. What are the dimensions of the box?

2.4
In exercises 81–86, write equivalent exponential expressions. Evaluate both expressions.

81. $\sqrt[4]{16}$

82. $\sqrt[4]{-16}$

83. $-\sqrt{9}$

84. $\sqrt[5]{-3\dfrac{53}{1024}}$

85. $\sqrt[7]{-123}$

86. $\sqrt[5]{20}$

87. A square window fan measures 21.5 inches on a side. What is the length of the diagonal from one corner to the opposite corner of the fan's face? (Recall that the length of the diagonal is the square root of the sum of the squares of two adjacent sides of the square.)

2.5
In exercises 88–98, match each expression with the appropriate property.

88. _____ $85 \cdot (-1) = -85$

89. _____ $3(1 + 5) = 3 \cdot 1 + 3 \cdot 5$

90. _____ $\left(\dfrac{3}{7}\right)\left(\dfrac{7}{3}\right) = 1$

91. _____ $-6.7 + 0 = -6.7$

92. _____ $(2 \cdot 4) \cdot 7 = 2 \cdot (4 \cdot 7)$

93. _____ $\left(\dfrac{2}{5}\right)\left(\dfrac{4}{4}\right) = \dfrac{8}{20}$

94. _____ $15 \cdot 0 = 0$

95. _____ $6 \cdot 4 = 4 \cdot 6$

a. Additive identity

b. Multiplicative identity

c. Multiplication property of -1

d. Multiplication property of 0

e. Additive inverse

f. Multiplicative inverse

g. Commutative law for addition

h. Commutative law for multiplication

96. ____ $2.3 + (-2.3) = 0$ **i.** Associative law for addition

97. ____ $12 + 7 = 7 + 12$ **j.** Associative law for multiplication

98. ____ $(5 + 1) + 3 = 5 + (1 + 3)$ **k.** Distributive law

99. Complete the table.

Number	8	−12	$\dfrac{3}{17}$	$-\dfrac{5}{3}$
Opposite				
Reciprocal				

Write an equivalent expression using the commutative laws, and then check for equivalence on your calculator.

100. $-33.05 + 12.4$ **101.** $\left(1\dfrac{9}{10}\right)\left(2\dfrac{4}{19}\right)$

Write an equivalent expression using the associative laws, and then check for equivalence on your calculator.

102. $132 + (-207 + 391)$ **103.** $\left(\dfrac{3}{7} \cdot \dfrac{14}{15}\right) \cdot \dfrac{5}{9}$

Write an equivalent expression using the distributive law or the opposite-of-a-sum property, and then check for equivalence on your calculator.

104. $-2.6(-1.9 + 3.2)$ **105.** $\dfrac{5}{6}\left(\dfrac{-3}{5} - \dfrac{4}{15}\right)$ **106.** $\dfrac{1687 - 1372}{7}$ **107.** $-(2.7 + 3.09)$

108. $-(-296 - 132)$ **109.** $-\left[14.2 - (-10.9)\right]$ **110.** $-\left[32 + (-51)\right]$

Factor. Check for equivalence.

111. $21(18) + 21(47)$ **112.** $5(19) - 5(17)$

Evaluate exercises 113–121, using the order of operations.

113. $17 + 31 - 20 \div 2 - 15 \cdot (-3)$ **114.** $-2(-4.8) - 5(1.7) + 9.2$ **115.** $41(-73 + 65) - (52 - 46)$

116. $-(27 - 4^2) - 16(-5 - 3)$ **117.** $\dfrac{191 + 104 - 11^2}{5^2 + 3^3 - 46}$ **118.** $\left[15 + 21(14 - 18)\right] - 7^2$

119. $22 - \sqrt{9^2 - 45}$ **120.** $\dfrac{8 \cdot 9 - 2 \cdot 6^2}{125 - 7^2}$ **121.** $\dfrac{78 - 3 \cdot 17}{5^2 - 4 \cdot 6 - 1^3}$

122. Sandi buys an area rug that measures 6 feet on each side. She will use the rug in a room that measures 12 feet by 14 feet. If the area of the room is the product of its length times its width, write an expression and evaluate it to find how much of the floor will not be covered by the rug.

123. Mary is making a tablecloth for a rectangular table. The tablecloth measures 7 feet by 5 feet. Mary will buy lace to sew around the edge of the tablecloth and also to crisscross it diagonally. Write an expression and evaluate it to find how much lace Mary will need to trim the edge of the tablecloth and to sew the two diagonals. (Remember that the diagonal is equal to the square root of the sum of the squares of the two sides of the tablecloth.)

124. On the first day of the week, the daily high temperature was 77°. The next day, the daily high rose by 4 degrees. The third day, the daily high was 68°. The fourth day, it dropped by 6 degrees. The fifth day, the daily high registered 82°. Write an expression and evaluate it to determine the average daily high temperature for these five days.

125. Following a diet and exercise program, Richard went from a weight of 227 pounds to a weight of 185 pounds in 20 weeks. Write an expression and evaluate it to determine his average weekly weight change.

CHAPTER 2 | **Mixed Review**

Express your answers in fractional notation or round decimals to the nearest thousandth as appropriate.
Write in exponential form and evaluate.

1. $(-9)(-9)(-9)(-9)(-9)(-9)(-9)$

2. $(-5.5)(-5.5)(-5.5)(-5.5)$

Write in scientific notation and calculator notation.

3. 0.00000475

4. $355,400,000,000,000,000$

5. -0.000092

6. $-100,505,000$

Write in scientific notation and standard notation.

7. $1.12\ \text{E}9$

8. $7.94\ \text{E}-12$

9. $-6.876\ \text{E}4$

10. $-2.35\ \text{E}-7$

Write equivalent exponential expressions and evaluate both expressions.

11. $\sqrt[3]{2197}$

12. $\sqrt[5]{32}$

13. $\sqrt[4]{-81}$

14. $\sqrt[5]{-125}$

15. $\sqrt[3]{-\dfrac{64}{125}}$

16. $-\sqrt{121}$

17. $\sqrt[4]{10}$

18. $-\sqrt[4]{4521.2176}$

Factor. Check for equivalence on your calculator.

19. $42(15)-42(23)$

20. $-31(12)-31(42)$

Evaluate exercises 21–90.

21. $25+63-48\div 3-22\cdot(-8)$

22. $-3.4(-1.1)-7(2.6)+14.3$

23. $2-\{4[3+2(7-5)]-18\div 3\}$

24. $-(34-7^2)-21(-8-4)$

25. $\dfrac{412+204-4^2}{5^2+35}$

26. $[651+18(21-19)]-5^2$

27. $96-\sqrt{11^2-21}$

28. $\dfrac{10\cdot 25-2\cdot 5^3}{275-3^5}$

29. $\dfrac{35-6\cdot 22}{6^3-4\cdot 50-4^2}$

30. 13^2

31. $(3.4)^7$

32. $\left(2\dfrac{1}{5}\right)^2$

33. 0^{35}

34. 1^{25}

35. $(-5)^3$

36. $(-5)^4$

37. $(-3.34)^5$

38. $\left(-1\dfrac{2}{5}\right)^3$

39. $(-1)^{24}$

40. $(-1)^{35}$

41. 3^4

42. $-\left(\dfrac{1}{3}\right)^5$

43. $(-2.1)^4$

44. 22^0

45. $(-22)^0$

46. -22^0

47. 22^1

48. -22^1

49. $(-22)^1$

50. -1^0

51. 0^0

52. -1^1

53. 0^1

54. $(2,333,145)^0$

55. $(65.02)^1$

56. $(-0.84)^0$

57. $(2,333,145)^1$

58. $\left(\dfrac{79}{95}\right)^0$

59. $\left(-\dfrac{11}{65}\right)^1$

60. $(-0.0004)^0$

61. 20^{-2}

62. $(-20)^{-2}$

63. -20^{-2}

64. 6^{-3}

65. $(-6)^{-3}$

66. -6^{-3}

67. $\left(1\dfrac{3}{5}\right)^{-2}$

68. 1^{-7}

69. $(-1)^{-7}$

70. $\sqrt{2500}$

71. $\sqrt{-400}$ **72.** $-\sqrt{400}$ **73.** $\sqrt{4.5369}$ **74.** $\sqrt{\dfrac{16}{289}}$

75. $-\sqrt{\dfrac{441}{1444}}$ **76.** $\sqrt{5\dfrac{4}{9}}$ **77.** $\sqrt{1.44}$ **78.** $-\sqrt{\dfrac{5}{400}}$

79. $-\sqrt{2235.6}$ **80.** $\sqrt[3]{-64}$ **81.** $\sqrt[4]{\dfrac{81}{16}}$ **82.** $-\sqrt[3]{274.625}$

83. $\sqrt[4]{3\dfrac{13}{81}}$ **84.** $-\sqrt[5]{25}$ **85.** $\sqrt[3]{\dfrac{1}{3}}$ **86.** $\sqrt[4]{2.56}$

87. $\sqrt[3]{-2\dfrac{5}{7}}$ **88.** $\sqrt[5]{\dfrac{243}{1024}}$ **89.** $-\sqrt[4]{6.5536}$ **90.** $-\sqrt[4]{2\dfrac{113}{256}}$

91. Graph the following numbers on a number line. Label the points.

$$-7,\ \sqrt{7},\ -\sqrt{7},\ \sqrt{25},\ \sqrt[3]{0},\ \sqrt{81},\ -\sqrt{64},\ \sqrt{\dfrac{9}{25}}$$

92. Complete the table.

Number	24	−15	$\dfrac{4}{9}$	$-\dfrac{5}{8}$
Opposite				
Reciprocal				

93. A square porch measures 14 feet on a side. Write an exponential expression and evaluate it to find the area of the porch floor.

94. A fruit cellar is shaped like a cube and measures 6 feet on a side. Write an exponential expression and evaluate it to find the volume of the cellar.

95. In 1960, it was reported that 1,176,946,000 acres of U.S. farmland were being utilized. Write scientific notation for this number.

96. In 1990, 9.87×10^8 acres of farmland were being utilized in the United States. Write standard notation for this number.

97. A square tarpaulin has an area of 300 square feet. Write a radical expression for its dimensions and an equivalent exponential expression, and evaluate both expressions.

98. A child's treehouse is shaped like a cube and has a volume of 343 cubic feet. Write a radical expression for its dimensions and an equivalent exponential expression, and evaluate both expressions.

99. Katie had four prints of various sizes framed. She was charged $35 for the first frame, the second was $8 more, the third was $52 and the fourth was $16 less. Write an expression and find the average cost per framed print.

100. Cecilia's annual salary in 1990 was $22,675. Six years later, her salary was $32,800. Write an expression to find her average yearly increase in salary for the period.

CHAPTER 2 | Test

Write in scientific notation.

1. 5,239,000,000,000,000

2. -0.00000203

Write in standard notation.

3. 5.07 E6

4. $-1.04\ \mathrm{E} - 8$

5. Graph the following numbers on a number line. Label the points.

$$-\sqrt{16},\ \sqrt{15.2},\ \sqrt{25},\ -\sqrt{\frac{49}{4}},\ \sqrt{7}$$

Write an equivalent exponential expression. Evaluate.

6. $-\sqrt[3]{117{,}649}$

7. $\sqrt[6]{\dfrac{4096}{729}}$

Match each expression with the appropriate property.

8. _____ $\dfrac{13}{15} \cdot \dfrac{3}{3} = \dfrac{39}{45}$

    a. Additive identity

9. _____ $15 + (-15) = 0$

    b. Multiplicative identity

10. _____ $45 + 0 = 45$

    c. Additive inverse

Evaluate exercises 11–31.

11. $(1.5)^2$

12. 3^4

13. $\left(\dfrac{4}{3}\right)^4$

14. 1^9

15. 0^{12}

16. $(-4)^3$

17. $(-4.008)^1$

18. $\left(\dfrac{55}{81}\right)^0$

19. 1^1

20. 0^0

21. $\left(-\dfrac{3}{8}\right)^{-2}$

22. $(-3)^0$

23. $-\sqrt{196}$

24. $\sqrt{\dfrac{36}{121}}$

25. $-\sqrt{3.6}$

26. $\sqrt[6]{\dfrac{262{,}144}{729}}$

27. $\sqrt[4]{7\dfrac{58}{81}}$

28. $-\left[51.3 - (-20.9)\right]$

29. $\dfrac{-609 + 928}{29}$

30. $\sqrt[3]{17^2 - 6 \cdot 12 - 1} + 126 \div 9$

31. $\dfrac{2(5^2 + 3^2) - 8^2 - 2^2}{3.65}$

32. A flower garden in the shape of a square measures 9.5 feet on a side. A catalog offers an assortment of flowers to fill a garden that has 68 square feet of space. Write an expression and find the amount of excess space the garden will have.

33. The GNP of Switzerland was 2.49×10^{11} U.S. dollars in 1992. During the same time, the GNP of Romania was 2.49×10^{10} U.S. dollars. By how much did the GNP of Switzerland exceed that of Romania? Write your answer in scientific notation and in standard notation.

34. How can you rewrite an exponential expression so that it has no negative exponents?

35. How can you rewrite a radical expression as an exponential expression?

Variables, Expressions, Equations, and Formulas

I n the previous two chapters, we described the set of
real numbers and the rules of arithmetic that apply
to real numbers. In this chapter, we generalize arithmetic by introducing algebra. We define variables,
algebraic expressions, and equations, and we discuss geometric formulas and other formulas. As before, we use
real-world data in each discussion.

The word *algebra* comes from the Arabic word *al-jabr*,
which appears in the title of one of the earliest algebra
books known. The book was written about 825 A.D.,
which is about the same time as the setting for the sto-
ries of the Arabian Nights. The book's author was an
astronomer and mathematician named Muhammed ibn Musa al-Khwarizmi, and
the full title may be translated as "the science of restoring and reduction." We
will see in this chapter how the Arabian mathematicians solved equations by
moving terms around ("restoring") and combining like terms ("reduction").

3.1 Variables and Algebraic
Expressions

3.2 Algebraic Addition and
Subtraction

3.3 Algebraic Multiplication and
Division

3.4 Equations

3.5 Formulas and Geometry

3.6 More Formulas

3.1   Variables and Algebraic Expressions

Objectives

1 Translate word expressions into algebraic expressions.

2 Translate algebraic expressions into word expressions.

3 Evaluate algebraic expressions.

4 Model real-world situations using algebraic expressions.

Application

The area of a rectangular figure is found by multiplying its length by its width. Write an algebraic expression for the area of a rectangle.

A rectangular oriental rug has dimensions of 60 inches by 96 inches. Use the area expression to determine the area the rug covers.

After completing this section, we will discuss this application further. See page 153.

Algebra is the branch of mathematics that generalizes arithmetic by using variables to range over numbers. In particular, algebra is the use of symbols to stand for unknown quantities and the evaluation of these quantities by applying elementary operations of arithmetic. Algebra is closely connected to geometry, which is the branch of mathematics that studies properties and relationships of plane and solid figures. We will discuss applications of algebra and geometry in each section of this chapter.

1   Translating Word Expressions

In the first two chapters, we worked with **numeric expressions**, which are combinations of numbers and mathematical operations, such as

$$14 + 5, \quad -28 - 3, \quad 23 \cdot 5, \quad 45 \div (-5).$$

In algebra, we work with algebraic expressions. Examples of algebraic expressions are

$$14 + x, \qquad y - 3, \qquad 23a, \qquad \frac{s}{t}.$$

In an algebraic expression, we use letters as symbols. A symbol representing only one number is called a **constant**. A symbol that can represent more than one number is called a **variable**. In the expression $14 + x$, 14 is a constant and x is a variable. We define an **algebraic expression** as an expression containing variables.

In this section, we will translate word expressions into algebraic expressions. In order to do this, we need to know that certain words translate into operation symbols. Table 3.1 lists examples of these words and their translation.

TABLE 3.1

Addition (+)	Subtraction (−)	Multiplication (·)	Division (÷)
add	subtract	multiply	divide
sum	difference	product	quotient
plus	minus	times	divided by
increased by	decreased by	multiplied by	divided into
more than	less than	of	per
total	less	twice	ratio
	taken from	double	
	net	triple	

To write an algebraic expression:

- Define the variable or variables.
- Translate the words into numbers and symbols.

For example, translate into an algebraic expression the word expression "add some number and 5."

Let $x =$ some number. Define a variable.
(We chose x but it could have been another symbol.)

$x + 5$ "Add" translates into +.

 Helping Hand If you have trouble writing an algebraic expression, you can change it to a numeric expression by substituting a number for the variable. Write the numeric expression. Then change the number back to the variable for an algebraic expression. For example, "add some number and 5" can be "add 3 and 5." Therefore, we have the numeric expression $3 + 5$. Then change to the algebraic expression $x + 5$.

EXAMPLE 1 Translate each word expression into an algebraic expression.

a. 12 more than some number.
b. 4 less than some number.
c. 4 less some number.

Solution

a. Let x = some number.   Define a variable.

$x + 12$ "More than" translates into addition. Be careful of the order.

b. Let y = some number.   Define a variable.

$y - 4$ "Less than" translates into subtraction. Be careful of the order of the subtraction expression.

c. Let n = some number.   Define a variable.

$4 - n$ "Less" translates into subtraction. Be careful of the order of the subtraction expression. ∎

 Helping Hand Be sure you understand the difference in the order of the subtraction expressions for Examples 1b and 1c.

EXAMPLE 2   Translate the word expression "half of the sum of two numbers" into an algebraic expression.

Solution

Let a = first number   Define two variables.
b = second number

$$\frac{1}{2} \cdot (a + b) \quad \text{or} \quad \frac{1}{2}(a + b)$$ "Of" translates into multiplication. "Sum" translates into addition. ∎

 Helping Hand You may omit the times sign in multiplication expressions involving parentheses.

EXAMPLE 3   The volume of a rectangular box is the product of its length, width, and height measurements. Write an algebraic expression for the volume of a rectangular box.

Solution

Let L = length   Define three variables.
W = width
H = height

$L \cdot W \cdot H$ or LWH "Product" translates into multiplication. ∎

 Helping Hand You may omit the times sign in multiplication expressions involving variables.

 ## Experiencing Algebra the Checkup Way

In exercises 1–4, translate each word expression into an algebraic expression.

1. The sum of a number and 13.

2. Twice the sum of two numbers.

3. 6 less than the product of a number and 8.

4. 6 less the product of a number and 8.

5. The area of a parallelogram (a four-sided figure, with opposite sides parallel) is the product of its height and its base measurements. Write an algebraic expression for the area.

6. What is the difference between basic arithmetic and algebra?

---

2   Translating Algebraic Expressions

Sometimes we need to translate an algebraic expression into an appropriate word expression. Most of the time, more than one translation will be correct.

EXAMPLE 4   Translate the algebraic expression $5x$ into a word expression.

Solution

There are several possibilities. Four of these are:

> Multiply 5 and a number.
> The product of 5 and a number.
> 5 times a number.
> 5 multiplied by a number. ∎

EXAMPLE 5   Translate the algebraic expression $3x + 7$ into a word expression.

Solution

Three possibilities are:

> The product of 3 and a number, increased by 7.
> 7 more than 3 times a number.
> The sum of a number tripled and 7. ∎

EXAMPLE 6   An algebraic expression for the perimeter of (or distance around) a rectangular figure is given by $2L + 2W$, where $L =$ length and $W =$ width. Write a word expression for the perimeter of a rectangular tablecloth.

Solution

Two possibilities are:

> The sum of twice the length and twice the width.
> 2 times the length plus 2 times the width. ∎

 Experiencing Algebra the Checkup Way

In exercises 1 and 2, translate each algebraic expression into a word expression.

1. $-27y$ **2.** $2x - 25$

3. The perimeter of a triangle is given by $a + b + c$, where a is the length of the first side, b is the length of the second side, and c is the length of the third side. Write a word expression for the perimeter of a triangle.

---

3   Evaluating Algebraic Expressions

An algebraic expression can have different values, depending on what value the variable has. To determine the value for the expression, we **substitute** the value of the variable into the expression. For instance, if the variable x has the value 5, then the expression $2x$ has the value 10. If x has the value -3, then the expression $2x$ has the value -6. This process is called **evaluating** the algebraic expression. For expressions with more than one variable, substitute the given value of each variable into the expression and evaluate.

To evaluate an algebraic expression:

- Substitute the given values for the variables.
- Evaluate the resulting numeric expression, using order of operations.

To evaluate an algebraic expression on your calculator:

- Store the given values for the variables.
- Enter the calculator's notation for a line return.
- Enter the expression in terms of the variables.

For example, evaluate $x + 12$ for $x = -2$.

$$x + 12 = -2 + 12 \quad \text{Substitute } -2 \text{ for } x$$

$$= 10 \qquad \text{Add.}$$

Note: While the calculator steps are shown, this example, which is not very difficult, should be completed mentally or with paper and pencil.

TECHNOLOGY

Figure 3.1

For Figure 3.1
Store the given value for the variable.

| (−) | 2 | STO▶ | ALPHA | X | or | (−) | 2 | STO▶ | X, T, θ, n |

Enter the calculator's notation for a line return.

| ALPHA | : |

Enter the expression in terms of the variable.

| ALPHA | X | + | 1 | 2 | ENTER | or | X, T, θ, n | + | 1 | 2 |
| ENTER |

EXAMPLE 7 Evaluate $m^2 - \frac{n}{2}$ for

a. $m = 3$ and $n = 12$.   **b.** $m = \frac{3}{4}$ and $n = 2$.

Solution

a. $m^2 - \dfrac{n}{2} = 3^2 - \dfrac{12}{2}$ Substitute 3 for *m* and 12 for *n*.

$$= 9 - 6 \qquad \text{Use order of operation.}$$

$$= 3$$

b. $m^2 - \dfrac{n}{2} = \left(\dfrac{3}{4}\right)^2 - \dfrac{2}{2}$ Substitute $\frac{3}{4}$ for m and 2 for n.

$\qquad\qquad = \dfrac{9}{16} - \dfrac{2}{2}$ Use order of operation.

$\qquad\qquad = \dfrac{9}{16} - \dfrac{16}{16}$

$\qquad\qquad = \dfrac{-7}{16}$

The check for Example 7 is shown in Figure 3.2.

TECHNOLOGY

Figure 3.2

For Figure 3.2

a. | 3 | | STO▶ | | ALPHA | | M | | ALPHA | | : | | 1 | | 2 | | STO▶ | | ALPHA |

| N | | ALPHA | | : | | ALPHA | | M | | x² | | − | | ALPHA | | N | | ÷ | | 2 |

| ENTER |

b. To change the previous entry without having to reenter all the above, press | 2nd | | ENTRY |, then use the arrow keys to move over the →. Then | 2nd | | INS | | ÷ | | 4 | and use the arrow keys to move over the 1. Press | DEL | and use the arrow keys to move to the end | MATH | | 1 | | ENTER |.

EXAMPLE 8   For $x = 3$, evaluate

a. x **b.** $-x$ **c.** $-(-x)$

d. x^2 **e.** $-x^2$

Solution

a. x for $x = 3$

$\quad x = 3$ Substitute 3 for x.

b. $-x$ for $x = 3$

$\quad -x = -(3) = -3$ Substitute 3 for x.
   The opposite of 3 is −3.

c. $-(-x)$ for $x = 3$

$\quad -(-x) = -(-(3)) = 3$ Substitute 3 for x.
   The opposite of the opposite of 3 is 3.

d. x^2 for $x = 3$

$\quad x^2 = (3)^2 = 9$ Substitute 3 for x.

e. $-x^2$ for $x = 3$

$\quad -x^2 = -(3)^2 = -(9) = -9$ Substitute 3 for x.
   The opposite of 9 is −9.

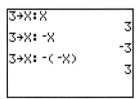

Figure 3.3a

Figure 3.3b

The check for Example 8 is shown in Figure 3.3a and Figure 3.3b. ∎

EXAMPLE 9 For $x = -3$, evaluate

a. x **b.** $-x$ **c.** $-(-x)$

d. x^2 **e.** $-x^2$

Solution

```
-3→X:X
                    -3
-3→X: -X
                     3
-3→X: -(-X)
                    -3
```

```
-3→X:X²
                     9
-3→X: -X²
                    -9
```

a. x for $x = -3$

$\qquad x = -3$ Substitute -3 for x.

b. $-x$ for $x = -3$

$\qquad -x = -(-3) = 3$ Substitute -3 for x.
                                      The opposite of -3 is 3.

c. $-(-x)$ for $x = -3$

$\qquad -(-x) = -(-(-3)) = -3$ Substitute -3 for x.
                                      The opposite of the opposite of -3 is -3.

d. x^2 for $x = -3$

$\qquad x^2 = (-3)^2 = 9$ Substitute -3 for x.

e. $-x^2$ for $x = -3$

$\qquad -x^2 = -(-3)^2 = -(9) = -9$ Substitute -3 for x.
                                      The opposite of 9 is -9.

Use your calculator to check your results. ■

✓ Experiencing Algebra the Checkup Way

1. Evaluate $x - 23$ for $x = 75$

2. Evaluate $x^2 + 2xy + y^2$ for

    a. $x = 3$ and $y = 1$ **b.** $x = \dfrac{3}{5}$ and $y = -1$

3. For $a = 12$, evaluate

    a. $2a$ **b.** $-2a$ **c.** $-(-2a)$ **d.** $2a^2$ **e.** $-2a^2$

4. For $a = -12$, evaluate

    a. $2a$ **b.** $-2a$ **c.** $-(-2a)$ **d.** $2a^2$ **e.** $-2a^2$

5. Write the keystrokes needed to store the value for the variable and to evaluate the expression $3x + 15$ for $x = -12$.
What is the result?

6. What does it mean to evaluate an algebraic expression?

---

4 Modeling the Real World

Algebraic expressions are very helpful for evaluating properties of geometric figures, such as areas and perimeters. For example, once you know the expression for the perimeter or area of a rectangle in terms of the lengths of its sides, you can evaluate the perimeter or area of any rectangle, no matter how big or small, given the lengths of its sides. Always remember that whatever operations you perform on the numbers when evaluating the expression must also be performed on the units of measurement involved.

EXAMPLE 10   The perimeter of a rectangle is found by doubling the sum of its length and width. Write an algebraic expression for finding the perimeter and evaluate the expression for a rectangular rug that is 9 feet by 12 feet.

Solution

Let $L =$ length   Define two variables.
   $W =$ width

$2(L + W)$ "Double" translates into 2 times.
         "Sum" translates into addition.

An expression for the perimeter is $2(L + W)$ feet.

$2(L + W) = 2(9 + 12)$ Substitute 9 for L and 12 for W.

$\qquad = 42$ Simplify.

The perimeter of the rug is 42 feet. ∎

Application   The area of a rectangular figure is found by multiplying its length by its width. Write an algebraic expression for the area of a rectangle.

A rectangular oriental rug has dimensions of 60 inches by 96 inches. Use the area expression to determine the area the rug covers.

Discussion

Let $L =$ length   Define two variables.
   $W =$ width

LW Multiply length times width.

An expression for the area is LW square inches.

$LW = 96 \cdot 60$ Substitute values for L and W.

$\quad = 5760$ Simplify.

The rug covers an area of 5760 square inches. ∎

 ## Experiencing Algebra the Checkup Way

The area of a triangle is one-half the product of the measures of its base and its height. Write an algebraic expression to represent this area. Then evaluate the expression for a triangle with a height of 10 inches and a base of 7 inches.

PROBLEM SET 3.1

 ## Experiencing Algebra the Exercise Way

In exercises 1–20, translate each word expression into an algebraic expression.

1. The difference of 25 and a number.

2. The difference of a number and 25.

3. Three-fourths of a number.

4. 25 percent of a number.

5. The quotient of a number divided by 15.

6. The quotient of 55 divided by a number.

7. The product of 2.5 and a number, less the quotient of 19.59 divided by the number.

8. The square of a number, increased by the product of 3 times the number.

9. The product of 12 and a number, decreased by 25.

10. 3 subtracted from the product of a number and 8.

11. The sum of two numbers, increased by 2 times the product of the numbers.

12. 80 more than triple a number.

13. The total of three numbers, divided by 3.

14. One-third of the difference of a number less 5.

15. 5 less than twice a number.

16. 4 more than the product of a number and 5.

17. 6 more than one-third of a number.

18. The product of a number and 3, less the quotient of 10 divided by the number.

19. Double a number divided by the sum of the number and 5.

20. The product of two numbers less 8.

21. At a charity fund-raiser, adult tickets were sold for $6 each and children's tickets were sold for $2 each. Write an algebraic expression for the total amount of money raised from the sale of tickets.

22. On a production line, a machine can fill 3300 bottles of soda pop each hour. Write an algebraic expression for the total number of bottles filled after a production run of a given number of hours.

23. Katie works part-time at two different jobs. The first job pays her $9.50 per hour, while the second job pays her $12.25 per hour. Write an algebraic expression for the money she will earn on both jobs if she works a certain number of hours on the first and a different number of hours on the second.

24. Pablo receives a commission of $200 for each personal computer system he sells and a commission of $50 for each piece of ancillary equipment he sells. He has a fixed monthly expense of $750. Write an algebraic expression for his net income if he sells a certain number of computer systems and a different number of pieces of ancillary equipment.

In exercises 25–38, translate each algebraic expression into a word expression.

25. $x + 27$

26. $b - 8$

27. $\dfrac{35}{a}$

28. $a + b + c$

29. $\dfrac{3}{5} \cdot z$

30. $\dfrac{x}{y} + 3$

31. $t - 12.50$

32. $\dfrac{2}{3} m + \dfrac{1}{3} n$

33. $14 - 5z$

34. $2\pi r$

35. $3.14d$

36. $-25 - \dfrac{y}{12}$

37. $\dfrac{1}{2}(L + H)$

38. $a^2 + b^2$

39. An algebraic expression for the average of three grades is given by $(a + b + c) \div 3$, where the letters represent the three grades. Write a word expression for the average of the grades.

40. The gas mileage of a car is given by $(e - b) \div g$, where e is the ending odometer reading, b is the beginning odometer reading, and g is the gallons of gas used. Write a word expression for the gas mileage of a car.

Evaluate $3x + 5$ for

41. $x = -5$

42. $x = -13$

43. $x = \dfrac{2}{3}$

44. $x = 2\dfrac{2}{3}$

45. $x = -2.7$

46. $x = -1.06$

Evaluate $18 - 3z$ for

47. $z = -12.07$

48. $z = -0.9$

49. $z = 23$

50. $z = 33$

51. $z = -\dfrac{5}{6}$

52. $z = -5\dfrac{4}{9}$

Evaluate $\frac{1}{2}bh$ *for*

53. $b = 56$ and $h = 14$

54. $b = 12.8$ and $h = 10.5$

55. $b = \frac{8}{5}$ and $h = \frac{16}{3}$

56. $b = 12$ and $h = 11$

57. $b = 6.8$ and $h = 4.2$

58. $b = \frac{4}{3}$ and $h = \frac{5}{2}$

Evaluate $x^2 + 2x + 9$ *for*

59. $x = -7$

60. $x = -8$

61. $x = 2.5$

62. $x = 1.6$

Evaluate $\sqrt{4x^2 - 20x + 25}$ *for*

63. $x = 3$

64. $x = 5$

65. $x = -4$

66. $x = -1$

Evaluate $|4.5 - 3.1b|$ *for*

67. $b = 2$

68. $b = 3$

69. $b = -2$

70. $b = -3$

Evaluate $\frac{x^2 + 2x + 1}{x + 1}$ *for*

71. $x = -3$

72. $x = -1$

73. $x = 3$

74. $x = 1$

75. At a high school play, adult tickets sold for $4.00 each and children's tickets sold for $0.75 each. Write an algebraic expression for the total revenue from the sale of the tickets. Evaluate the expression for a situation in which 150 adult tickets and 200 children's tickets were sold.

76. The daily charge for renting a car is $45.00, and the charge per mile driven is $0.35. Write an algebraic expression for the total charge to rent a car for a given number of days and for driving it a certain number of miles. Evaluate the expression for renting the car for 5 days and driving it 600 miles.

77. The distance around a circle (the circumference) is calculated as the product of π and the diameter of the circle. Write the algebraic expression needed to find the circumference of a circle. Evaluate the expression for a circular wading pool with a diameter of 12 feet. Round your answer to the nearest tenth.

78. The circumference of a circle is calculated as the product of π and twice the radius of the circle. Write the algebraic expression needed to find the circumference of a circle. Evaluate the expression for a circular dining table with a radius of 3 feet. Round your answer to the nearest tenth.

 Experiencing Algebra the Calculator Way

As algebraic expressions become more complex, and the values of the variables become more difficult to work with, the calculator can be used to ease the burden of evaluating expressions and to avoid calculation error. With this in mind, use your calculator to perform the following evaluations.

1. Evaluate $\frac{a + 15}{b - 10}$ for

a. $a = 120$ and $b = 150$

b. $a = 275$ and $b = 13$

c. $a = 16$ and $b = 375$

2. Evaluate πr^2 for

a. $r = 19$

b. $r = 23.76$

c. $r = 0.05$

d. $r = \frac{7}{8}$

e. $r = 3\frac{5}{9}$

f. $r = 100$

3. Evaluate $\sqrt{a^2 + b^2}$ for

a. $a = 120$ and $b = 160$

b. $a = 3$ and $b = 4$

c. $a = 2.4$ and $b = 3.2$

d. $a = 1$ and $b = 1$

e. $a = \frac{3}{5}$ and $b = \frac{4}{5}$

f. $a = \sqrt{5}$ and $b = \sqrt{11}$

4. Evaluate $\dfrac{4x^2 - 28x + 49}{2x - 7}$ for

   a. $x = 7$ **b.** $x = -2$ **c.** $x = -\dfrac{9}{2}$ **d.** $x = 7.5$ **e.** $x = 0$ **f.** $x = \dfrac{7}{2}$

5. Evaluate $\left| \dfrac{x - 250}{2x + 100} \right|$ for

   a. $x = 10$ **b.** $x = 100$ **c.** $x = 1000$ **d.** $x = 10{,}000$ **e.** $x = -50$ **f.** $x = 250$

Experiencing Algebra the Group Way

Evaluating Expressions with Opposites

Evaluate $-3a + b - c$ *for*

   1. $a = 2, \quad b = 10, \quad c = 20$ **2.** $a = -2, \quad b = -10, \quad c = -20$

   3. $a = -2, \quad b = 10, \quad c = -20$ **4.** $a = 2, \quad b = -10, \quad c = 20$

You should see that the results for exercises 1 and 2 are opposites of each other. Do you know why? You should also see that the results for exercises 3 and 4 are opposites of each other. Do you know why? Did everyone in the group get the same answer? If not, can you see where the error was? These exercises should illustrate one very important consideration when you are evaluating algebraic expressions. Can you see what that consideration is? Can you suggest ways that you can avoid erroneous results when this situation is present? After discussing this in your group, present what you have learned to the class.

Evaluating Expressions with Exponents and Groupings

Evaluate $a^2 + b^2$ *for*

   1. $a = 7$ and $b = 9$ **2.** $a = 0.8$ and $b = 0.6$ **3.** $a = \dfrac{9}{5}$ and $b = \dfrac{12}{5}$

   4. $a = 6$ and $b = 5$ **5.** $a = 0.4$ and $b = 0.3$ **6.** $a = \dfrac{15}{7}$ and $b = \dfrac{8}{7}$

Now evaluate $(a + b)^2$ *for the values used in exercises 1–6.*

  The results are different. Discuss the differences between the two expressions, $a^2 + b^2$ *and* $(a + b)^2$*. Can you suggest why they yield different results when evaluated for the same values of the variables?*

Experiencing Algebra the Write Way

Evaluate the three algebraic expressions

     $x^2, \quad (-x)^2, \quad$ and $\quad -x^2$

for $x = 4$ and $x = -4$. Explain how the negative sign and the parentheses affect the result. Now consider the three algebraic expressions

     $x^3, \quad (-x)^3, \quad$ and $\quad -x^3$

for $x = 4$ and $x = -4$. Evaluate these expressions and consider the results you obtain. Were they similar to what you saw earlier? What is different? Write an explanation of what causes a different result in the second set of evaluations as compared to the first. For which situations should you be watchful when evaluating algebraic expressions?

3.2 Algebraic Addition and Subtraction

Objectives
1 Understand the terminology associated with algebraic expressions.
2 Simplify algebraic expressions by collecting like terms.
3 Simplify algebraic expressions involving addition and subtraction.
4 Model real-world situations using algebraic expressions involving addition and subtraction.

Application

To find the surface area of a rectangular solid, add the areas of all the surfaces. Write an expression for the surface area of a rectangular solid.

A microwave oven is packed in a box (a rectangular solid). The box has dimensions of 25 inches by 20 inches by 18 inches. Determine the amount of wrapping paper needed to gift-wrap the box for a present (that is, the surface area of the box, assuming no waste or overlap of paper).

After completing this section, we will discuss this application further. See page 164.

1 Terminology of Algebraic Expressions

In the previous section, we evaluated algebraic expressions. At times we will not know the values for the variables in an expression. However, we would like to write the algebraic expression in its simplest equivalent form even when we don't know the values of the variables. We call this **simplifying** an algebraic expression.

Before we begin simplifying, we need to define words used with algebraic expressions. The **terms** of an algebraic expression are its addends. For example, the expression $x + y$ has two terms, and the expression $x^2 + 3x - 1$ has three terms. There are two types of terms. A constant term represents only one value. Variable terms represent more than one value because they contain one or more variables, and variables represent different values at different times. For example, the algebraic expression $6x^2 + 7x - 5$ can be written as a sum: $6x^2 + 7x + (-5)$. Therefore, it has three terms: $6x^2$, $7x$, and -5. The constant term is -5 and the variable terms are $6x^2$ and $7x$.

Grouping symbols affect the number of terms of an expression. The algebraic expression $6x^2 + (7x - 5)$ has two terms, because it can be written as a sum of $6x^2$ and $(7x - 5)$.

Helping Hand To determine the number of terms of an algebraic expression, identify the parts of the expression separated by plus or minus signs that are not inside grouping symbols.

EXAMPLE 1 Complete the table.

Algebraic Expression	Number of Terms	Terms
a. $6x^2 + 7x - 5$		
b. $-x^2y - 9xy + x$		
c. $-8x^2 + (7x - 4)$		

Solution

a. There are three terms. The terms are $6x^2$, $7x$, and -5.

b. There are three terms. The terms are $-x^2y$, $-9xy$, and x.

c. There are two terms. The terms are $-8x^2$ and $(7x - 4)$. ■

The **numeric coefficient** (often called the *coefficient*) is the numeric factor (sign and number) in a term. For example, in the expression $6x^2 + 7x - 5$, the numeric factors of the terms are 6, 7, and -5, respectively.

EXAMPLE 2 Complete the table.

Algebraic Expression	Coefficients of Terms
a. $6x^2 + 7x - 5$	
b. $-x^2y - 9xy + x$	
c. $-8x^2 + (7x - 4)$	

Solution

a. $6x^2 + 7x - 5$
The coefficients are 6, 7, and -5.

b. $-x^2y - 9xy + x = -1x^2y - 9xy + 1x$
The coefficients are -1, -9, and 1.

c. $-8x^2 + (7x - 4) = -8x^2 + 1(7x - 4)$
The coefficients are -8 and 1. ■

Terms are called **like terms** if they are constant terms or contain the same variables with the same exponents. The expression $6x^2 + 7x - 5$ has no like terms. Notice that the variable terms both have the same variable, x, but the variables have different exponents. However, in the expression $6x^2 + 7x^2 - 5$ there are two like terms, $6x^2$ and $7x^2$, because both variable terms have the same variables with the same exponents.

EXAMPLE 3 Complete the table.

Algebraic Expression	Like Terms
a. $6x^2 + 7x - 5$	
b. $6x^2 + 7x^2 - 5$	
c. $x^2 + 4 - y^2 + 6$	
d. $6x^2 + 7xy - 8x + 4x - y^2 - 5$	
e. $5(x + y) - 2(x + y)$	

Solution

a. There are no like terms.

b. The like terms are $6x^2$ and $7x^2$.

c. The like terms are 4 and 6.

d. The like terms are $-8x$ and $4x$.

e. The like terms are $5(x + y)$ and $-2(x + y)$. ∎

Experiencing Algebra the Checkup Way

Complete the tables.

Algebraic Expression	Number of Terms	Terms
1. $4x^2 - 3x + 7$		
2. $5x^2 + 3xy - 2y^2 + 11$		
3. $2(x - 4) - 6x + 12$		

Algebraic Expression	Coefficients of Terms
4. $12x^2 - 17x + 29$	
5. $-2.3y^2 + 1.6xy - 4.1x^2$	
6. $5(a + 2b) - (a + 2b)$	

Algebraic Expression	Like Terms
7. $3y^2 + 9y + 8$	
8. $3(p + q) + 13 - 5(p + q) - 6$	
9. $3x^2 + 3xy + 6y^3 - 5x + 7y - 2$	

10. How can you identify the terms of an algebraic expression?

11. When are two terms of an algebraic expression like terms?

2 Simplifying by Collecting Like Terms

Now we are ready to simplify algebraic expressions. In order to simplify an algebraic expression, we **collect like terms**. That is, we combine similar terms mathematically. In order to do this we will use the distributive law and factor out the common variables in the like terms. For example,

$$3x + 4x = (3 + 4)x \quad \text{Factor out the common factor of } x.$$
$$= 7x \quad \text{Add.}$$

In simplifying a more complicated algebraic expression, first use the associative and commutative properties for addition to rearrange the terms before combining like terms. For example,

$$
\begin{aligned}
6x^2 + 8x &- 7x^2 + x - 2 \\
= 6x^2 + (-7x^2) &+ 8x + x \quad - 2 \quad &\text{Rearrange terms.} \\
= [6 + (-7)]x^2 &+ (8 + 1)x - 2 \quad &\text{Factor.} \\
= -1x^2 &+ 9x \quad - 2 \quad &\text{Simplify.} \\
= -x^2 &+ 9x \quad - 2 \quad &\text{It is not necessary to write the } -1 \text{ coefficient.}
\end{aligned}
$$

 Helping Hand We must be careful with the signs of the coefficients when we rearrange the terms.

To simplify an algebraic expression by collecting like terms:

• Rearrange terms, if needed.
• The sum of the coefficients of the like terms is the coefficient of the simplified term.
• The common variable factor for the variable terms does not change in the simplified expression.

It is not necessary to write a coefficient of 1 or −1 with a variable term. Also, it is not necessary to write a variable term with a coefficient of 0 or a constant term of 0.

EXAMPLE 4 Simplify.

a. $5x + 7x$ **b.** $2x + x$

c. $6y - y$ **d.** $3x + 6x - 9x$

Solution

a. $5x + 7x = 12x$ Add coefficients 5 and 7.

b. $2x + x = 3x$ Add coefficients 2 and 1.

c. $6y - y = 5y$ Add coefficients 6 and −1.

d. $3x + 6x - 9x = 0$ Add coefficients 3, 6, and −9. The result is $0x$ or 0. ∎

EXAMPLE 5 Simplify.

a. $2a^3 + 3a^2 - a^3 + a^2 - 3$ **b.** $2.3xy - 4.4x + 2xy + 6.56x$

c. $\dfrac{1}{2}x + \dfrac{3}{4}x - \dfrac{2}{3}x^2 - x^2$

Solution

a.　　$2a^3 + 3a^2 - a^3 + a^2 - 3$

$= 2a^3 - a^3 \quad + 3a^2 + a^2 - 3$　　Rearrange terms.

$= 1a^3 \qquad\quad + \quad 4a^2 \quad - 3$　　Collect like terms.

$= a^3 \qquad\qquad + \quad 4a^2 \quad - 3$　　It is not necessary to write the 1 coefficient.

b.　　$2.3xy - 4.4x + 2xy + 6.56x$

$= 2.3xy + 2xy - 4.4x + 6.56x$　　Rearrange terms.

$= 4.3xy \qquad\qquad + \qquad 2.16x$　　Collect like terms.

c.　　$\dfrac{1}{2}x + \dfrac{3}{4}x - \dfrac{2}{3}x^2 - x^2$

$= \dfrac{2}{4}x + \dfrac{3}{4}x - \dfrac{2}{3}x^2 - \dfrac{3}{3}x^2$　　Find the least common denominator for like terms.

$= \dfrac{5}{4}x - \dfrac{5}{3}x^2$　　Collect like terms. ∎

Experiencing Algebra the Checkup Way

Simplify exercises 1–7.

1. $12x + 23x$　　　　**2.** $z + 11z$　　　　**3.** $15a - a$　　　　**4.** $2b + b - 3b$

5. $4x^3 + 3x^2 - 5x + 3 - 2x^3 - x^2 + x - 3$　　　　**6.** $1.7xy + 2.5xz - 3.9yz + 4.3xy - 2.5xz + 1.9yz$

7. $\dfrac{7}{3}x + \dfrac{1}{3}y - \dfrac{1}{4}x + \dfrac{3}{4}y$　　　　**8.** What does it mean to collect like terms?

---

3 Simplifying Algebraic Expressions with Addition and Subtraction

Algebraic expressions may have parentheses. Therefore, in order to simplify these expressions, we must apply the properties we learned in Chapter 2 to remove the parentheses. For example,

$4y + 2 \;\; + (3y - 1)$

$= 4y + 2 \;\; + \;\; 3y - 1$　　Remove parentheses first.

$= 4y + 3y + \;\; 2 - 1$　　Rearrange.

$= 7y \qquad\quad + \quad 1$　　Collect like terms.

To simplify algebraic expressions involving addition:

- Remove parentheses.
- Collect like terms of the resulting expression.

EXAMPLE 6　Simplify.

a. $6x + (2x - 4)$　　　　**b.** $6x + 5 + (2x - 4)$

c. $(6x + 2y + 5) + (2x - y - 4)$

Solution

a. $6x + (2x - 4)$

$= (6x + 2x) \quad - 4$ Associative law for addition

$= \quad 8x \quad\quad - 4$ Combine like terms.

b. $6x + 5 + (2x - 4)$

$= 6x + 5 + 2x - 4$ Remove parentheses first.

$= 6x + 2x + 5 - 4$ Commutative and associative laws for addition

$= \quad 8x \quad + \quad 1$ Combine like terms.

c. $(6x + 2y + 5) + (2x - y - 4)$

$= 6x + 2y + 5 + 2x - y - 4$ Remove parentheses first.

$= 6x + 2x + 2y - y + 5 - 4$ Commutative and associative laws for addition

$= \quad 8x \quad + \quad y \quad + \quad 1$ Combine like terms. ■

In order to simplify algebraic expressions with subtraction signs before parentheses, we need to remember the opposite-of-a-sum (or difference) property. That is, $-(4x + 2) = -4x - 2$. Therefore,

$7x - (4x + 2)$

$= 7x - 4x \quad - 2$ Opposite-of-a-sum property

$= \quad 3x \quad - 2$ Combine like terms.

In another example,

$7x - 5 - (4x + 2)$

$= 7x - 5 - 4x - 2$ Opposite-of-a-sum property

$= 7x - 4x - 5 - 2$ Commutative and associative laws for addition

$= \quad 3x \quad - \quad 7$ Combine like terms.

To simplify algebraic expressions involving subtraction:

- Remove parentheses first by taking the opposite of the terms within them.
- Collect like terms of the resulting expression.

EXAMPLE 7   Simplify.

a. $-(2x - 4)$ **b.** $6x - (2x - 4)$

c. $6x + 5 - (2x - 4)$ **d.** $(6x + 2y + 5) - (2x + y - 4)$

Solution

a. $-(2x - 4) = -2x + 4$ Opposite-of-a-sum (or difference) property

b. $6x - (2x - 4)$

$= 6x - 2x + 4$ Opposite-of-a-sum (or difference) property

$= 4x \quad + 4$ Combine like terms.

c. $6x + 5 - (2x - 4)$

$= 6x + 5 - 2x + 4$ Opposite-of-a-sum (or difference) property

$= 6x - 2x + 5 + 4$ Commutative and associative laws for addition

$= 4x \quad + \quad 9$ Combine like terms.

d. $(6x + 2y + 5) - (2x + y - 4)$

$= 6x + 2y + 5 - 2x - y + 4$ Opposite-of-a-sum (or difference) property

$= 6x - 2x + 2y - y + 5 + 4$ Commutative and associative law for addition

$= \quad 4x \quad + \quad y \quad + \quad 9$ Combine like terms. ∎

 ## Experiencing Algebra the Checkup Way

Simplify.

1. $3a + (5 - 5a)$

2. $1.7b + 3.6 + (4.2b - 9.6)$

3. $(x^2 + 3x + 7) + (3x^2 - x + 5)$

4. $-(3a + 5)$

5. $2.3x + 4.5 - (1.9x - 6.7)$

6. $(5y - 13) - (2y - 27)$

4 Modeling the Real World   When you use algebraic expressions to represent real data, the same rules apply for combining like terms and simplifying. The old saying is that you can't add apples and oranges; you also can't add x and x^2, or length and area.

If you've handled units correctly, they can help you sort out like terms from unlike terms. That is, you can't add feet to square feet or subtract square feet from cubic feet. Each different kind of unit is associated with a different kind of term.

EXAMPLE 8   The perimeter of a geometric figure is the sum of the lengths of the sides of the figure.

a. Write an expression for the perimeter of a rectangular room. Evaluate the expression to find the length of baseboard needed for a rectangular room 15 feet by $8\frac{1}{2}$ feet.

b. Write an expression for the perimeter of a rectangular room that has two doorways, each 3 feet across. Evaluate the expression to find the length of baseboard needed for a rectangular room 15 feet by $8\frac{1}{2}$ feet.

15 ft $8\frac{1}{2}$ ft

Solution

a. The perimeter of a rectangular room is the sum of its length, width, length, and width.

Let L = length
W = width

$L + W + L + W = 2L + 2W$ Collect like terms.

Therefore, an expression for the perimeter is $2L + 2W$ feet.
Evaluating $2L + 2W$ for $L = 15$ and $W = 8\frac{1}{2}$,

$$2L + 2W = 2(15) + 2\left(8\frac{1}{2}\right)$$ Substitute.

$$= 30 + 17$$ Evaluate.
$$= 47$$

47 feet of baseboard are needed for the room.

b. The perimeter of a rectangular room with two doorways is the sum of its length, width, length, and width, minus the length of each doorway.

Let L = length
W = width

$L + W + L + W - 3 - 3 = 2L + 2W - 6$ Collect like terms.

Therefore, an expression for the perimeter is $2L + 2W - 6$ feet.
Evaluating $2L + 2W - 6$ for $L = 15$ and $W = 8\frac{1}{2}$,

$$2L + 2W - 6 = 2(15) + 2\left(8\frac{1}{2}\right) - 6$$ Substitute.

$$= 30 + 17 - 6$$ Evaluate.
$$= 41$$

41 feet of baseboard is needed for the room. ∎

Application

To find the surface area of a rectangular solid, add the areas of all the surfaces. Write an expression for the surface area of a rectangular solid.

A microwave oven is packed in a box (a rectangular solid). The box has dimensions of 25 inches by 20 inches by 18 inches. Determine the amount of wrapping paper needed to gift-wrap the box for a present (that is, the surface area of the box, assuming no waste or overlap of paper).

Discussion

Let L = length
W = width
H = height

The rectangular solid has six surfaces. The top and bottom each have the same area of LW. The front and back each have an area of LH. Each of the two sides has an area of WH. An expression for the surface area is found by adding these terms:

$$LW + LW + LH + LH + WH + WH = 2LW + 2LH + 2WH.$$

Therefore, an expression for the surface area is $2LW + 2LH + 2WH$ square inches.
Evaluating $2LW + 2LH + 2WH$ for $L = 25$, $W = 20$, and $H = 18$:

$$2LW + 2LH + 2WH = 2(25)(20) + 2(25)(18) + 2(20)(18)$$ Substitute.

$$= 1000 \quad + \quad 900 \quad + \quad 720$$ Evaluate.
$$= 2620$$

To wrap the microwave oven, 2620 square inches of wrapping paper are needed. ■

Experiencing Algebra the Checkup Way

1. Write an expression for the perimeter of a triangular garden. Evaluate the expression to find the total length of border tiles needed to surround a triangular garden that is 9 feet by 12 feet by 15 feet.

2. A cube is a rectangular solid with all edges measuring the same length. Write an expression for its surface area. A box in the shape of a cube is used to ship a television set. Use the expression to find the surface area of the box, which measures 27 inches along each edge.

PROBLEM SET 3.2

Experiencing Algebra the Exercise Way

Without simplifying, (a) determine the number of terms, (b) list the coefficient of each term, and (c) identify like terms, for each expression.

1. $12x - 11$
2. $3a + 4b + 13$
3. $-15y + 12z - y + 9$
4. $3x + 5z - 2 + x + 3z - 6$
5. $2x^2 - 6x + x + 12$
6. $3y^5 + y^3 - y + 1 + 4y^3$
7. $3.4a - 11.2b - 0.3a$
8. $\frac{2}{5}m + \frac{1}{10}n - \frac{3}{10}m + \frac{1}{5}n$
9. $2m + 3(n - 5) + 6(n - 5)$
10. $3(p + q) - 2(p + q) - 7p - q$
11. $x^2 + 3xy - y^2 + 7$
12. $a^2 - b^2 + 6ab - 3$

Simplify.

13. $27x + 44x$
14. $17v + 29v$
15. $17a + a$
16. $q + 86q$
17. $5x + 9 - 13x + 17 - 12 + 9x$
18. $22a + 31 - 12a + 51 + 27 + 42a$
19. $2x^3 + 7x^2 - 2x + 8 - x^3 - 7x^2 + 3x - 2$
20. $5h^3 + 2h^2 + h - 10 - 4h^2 + 2h^3 - h + 1$
21. $5 - xy + 2yz + 5xz - 17 + xy - 12yz$
22. $-18mn - 23 + 16np + 37mp + 21np + 42mn$
23. $3.05a + 6.29b - 1.18a + 0.49b$
24. $19.92z - 47.08x + 3.076x - 2.572z$
25. $\frac{1}{6}x + \frac{2}{9} - \frac{2}{3}x + \frac{5}{18}$
26. $\frac{3}{4}z - \frac{5}{16} + \frac{7}{8}z + \frac{17}{32}$
27. $6x^3 + 3x^2y - 5xy^2 + 3y^3 - 5x^2y + xy^2 + x^3 + 6y^3$
28. $9d^5 - 7d^3e^2 + 8d^2e^3 - 15e^5 + 6d^2e^3 - 3d^3e^2 + d^5 - e^5$
29. $\frac{5}{7}x + \frac{1}{6}y + \frac{5}{6}x - \left(-\frac{2}{7}y\right)$
30. $-\frac{7}{11}a + \frac{10}{11}b - \frac{5}{9}a - \left(-\frac{4}{9}b\right)$
31. $9.35a^2 - 4.31b^2 + 2.35ab - 1.61 + 4.39a^2 - 5.77b^2 + 10.06$
32. $16.7m^3 + 21.9n^2 - 23.9mn + 12.6m^3 - 31.1n^2 + 15.7mn$
33. $35a^3 - 41b^3 + 5ab - 11 + 4a^2 - 7b^2 + 16$
34. $7m^3 + 29n^2 - 29mn + 16m^2 - 11n^3 + 15mn$
35. $15a + 14b - 12 + 3a + 9 - 8b - 17a - 6b$
36. $3x^2 + 5x - 2 - 3x^2 - 4x + 3$
37. $8w + (7w - 5)$
38. $2k + (12k - 17)$
39. $5.3x + 1.4 + (3.4 - 1.7x)$
40. $1.9y + 3.7 + (4.8y - 7.9)$
41. $(45x - 112) + (21x + 33)$
42. $(48 - 22t) + (12t - 23)$
43. $-(29d - 7c)$
44. $-(57r - 22t)$
45. $4.9z + 1.8 - (2.6z + 0.5)$
46. $1.2x + 8.8 - (0.5x + 13.2)$
47. $(235 - 12y) - (307 + 31y)$
48. $(483z - 79) - (12 - 235z)$
49. $(x + y + 4z) - (2x - 5y + z)$
50. $(41a + 21b + c) - (a - 12b - 13c)$
51. $25z - (12z + 7)$
52. $104p - (320p - 114)$
53. $-(1.8y - 3.5z) + (4.1y - 2.7z)$

54. $-(2.07t + 5.2r) + (0.15t - 7.6r)$ **55.** $(a + b) - (a + b) + (a + b) - (a + b)$

56. $(x - y) + (x - y) + (x - y) - (x - y)$ **57.** $(-x + y) + (x - y)$

58. $-(a - b) - (-a + b)$ **59.** $(a + 5b) - (-a + 5b)$ **60.** $-(5m - 10n) + (-5m - 10n)$

Write an expression for each situation. Then simplify and evaluate.

61. Willy wants to fence in his backyard, which is rectangular in shape. The fence will be attached to the long side of his house, which is 65 feet long. The fence will have a 3-foot gate in it. How many feet of fencing will he need for a yard that is 250 feet by 400 feet?

62. Joshua wants to trim the edge of a table with aluminum stripping. How many inches of stripping will he need if the rectangular top of the table measures 60 inches by 48 inches?

63. Rusty is making a cubical box out of sheets of balsa wood. Each edge of the box measures 7 inches. How many square inches of balsa wood will he need for the box, ignoring any waste?

64. Tammy wants to wrap a box with silver foil paper. The box is in the shape of a cube and measures 14 inches along the edge. How many square inches of foil paper will she need, ignoring any waste?

65. Carl's Carpet Cleaners charges a fee of $20.00 per visit plus a charge of $1.55 per square yard of carpeting. The materials used for the cleaning average $0.65 per square yard of carpeting cleaned, and the cost of each trip averages $6.50. How much net profit will the carpet cleaners realize on a job involving a certain number of square yards of carpeting? What is the net profit if a job requires cleaning 250 square yards of carpeting?

66. Pete's Plumbing Company charges $35.00 for each visit to a home. Pete charges $55.00 an hour for himself and his helper to work on the job. He pays his helper $25.00 an hour. The trip to the house costs him an average of $12.00. What is the net amount of money he makes after expenses for a job taking a given number of hours? What are the net earnings if the job takes 3.5 hours?

67. Snail Mail Delivery charges $5.00 plus $1.50 per ounce to deliver a letter overnight. The company figures it costs them a fixed cost of $2.25 for each letter delivered. What is the net profit for a letter weighing a certain number of ounces? What is the net profit if the letter weighs 4 ounces?

68. Tillie's Typing Service charges $10.00 plus $2.00 per page for each manuscript Tillie types. On the average, she spends $3.00 per manuscript on setup and $0.50 per page on supplies. What is her net return on typing a manuscript of a given number of pages? What will be the net return for a manuscript of 112 pages?

69. Laurie purchases some compact discs at $9.99 each. The sales clerk adds a 5% sales tax to the cost of each disc. Write an algebraic expression for the total cost of the purchase. Laurie pays with a $50.00 bill. What is an algebraic expression for her change? If Laurie buys 3 compact discs, what is her cost? What is her change?

70. Mary Lynne paints and sells T-shirts. The shirts cost her $4.50 each. After she paints them, she sells them at craft shows for $15.00 each. She spends $18.50 for the paint kit that she uses for all the T-shirts she paints and sells. What is an algebraic expression for her net return on all the shirts she paints and sells? What is Mary Lynne's net return if she sells 22 shirts at the show?

71. At a charity fund-raiser dinner, adults were charged $15.00 for each admission and children were charged $7.00 for each admission. The caterer charged the committee $6.00 for each adult meal served and $2.50 for each child meal served. Write an algebraic expression for the amount of money made at the dinner. Determine the amount of money made at the dinner if 75 adults and 40 children attended.

72. A charter bus company charges adults $45 and senior citizens $35 for a day tour. The company figures that its average expense for each person taking the trip is $14.50. Write an algebraic expression for the amount of money made on the tour. Evaluate the expression to determine the amount of money the company will make if 23 adults and 9 senior citizens take the trip.

Experiencing Algebra the Calculator Way

Simplify. Use your calculator to help you combine coefficients of like terms.

1. $12.078x + 2.093 - 17.42x - 13.9035$

2. $(2579x - 4302) - (1087x - 306)$

3. $\dfrac{10}{13}x - \dfrac{5}{52}y - \dfrac{17}{20}x - \dfrac{7}{13}y$

4. $\left(2\dfrac{11}{25}\right)x + 5\dfrac{17}{30} - \left(3\dfrac{13}{15}\right)x - 3\dfrac{23}{75}$

5. $(1.0009x + 0.0004) - (0.0909x - 1.0031)$

6. $-(935.3376x + 701.315) - (83.027x - 581.9534)$

7. $3.995x + 12.083 - 2.995x - 9.083$

Experiencing Algebra the Group Way

Discuss exercises 1–11 to see that you understand the differences illustrated, and explain the differences to the class.

1. How many terms are there in $3x + y - 2$, as compared to $3x + (y - 2)$?

Are the following pairs of terms like terms? Explain your answer.

2. $12x^4y^3z^2$ and $-15x^4y^3z^2$

3. $3x$ and x^3

4. $5x^4y^3z^2$ and $5x^2y^3z^4$

5. $-3x$ and $3x$

6. $5x$ and $5y$

7. $(a + b)$ and $-(a + b)$

8. $(a + b)$ and $(b + c)$

9. $(a + b)$ and $(b + a)$

10. xy and $\dfrac{x}{y}$

11. $2xy$ and $-5yx$

Experiencing Algebra the Write Way

1. Consider the following two terms: $3a^4b^3$ and $4a^4b^3$. Are the two terms like terms? Explain.

2. Now consider the following two terms: $3a^4b^3$ and $4a^3b^4$. Are the two terms like terms? Explain.

3. What should you look for in order to find like terms?

3.3 Algebraic Multiplication and Division

Objectives

1 Simplify algebraic expressions involving multiplication and division.

2 Simplify algebraic expressions involving mixed operations.

3 Model real-world situations using algebraic expressions involving multiplication and division.

Application

The area of a trapezoid is sometimes written as $\frac{1}{2}h(b + B)$, where h is the height of the trapezoid, B is the length of the base, and b is the length of the top. Write an equivalent form for this expression.

Great Wall of China

The Great Wall of China has a trapezoidal cross-section, with average dimensions of base 25 feet, top 20 feet, and height 30 feet. Use the equivalent form for the area of a trapezoid to determine the area of a cross-section of the wall.

After completing this section, we will discuss this application further. See page 172.

1 Simplifying Algebraic Expressions with Multiplication and Division

In the previous section, we simplified algebraic expressions that involved parentheses with addition and subtraction signs. Now we will simplify expressions that involve multiplication and division.

In order to simplify algebraic expressions with multiplication, we need to remember the commutative and associative laws for multiplication and the distributive law. For example,

$$6(3x) = (6 \cdot 3)x \qquad \text{Associative law for multiplication}$$
$$= 18x$$

$$6y(3x) = (6 \cdot 3)yx \qquad \text{Commutative and associative laws}$$
$$= 18xy \qquad \text{Multiply. Rearrange variables in alphabetical order.}$$

In products involving variables, we multiply numeric coefficients and arrange variable factors in alphabetical order.

To multiply an algebraic expression involving more than one term, we use the distributive law. For example,

$$3(4x - 1) = 3(4x) - 3(1) \qquad \text{Distributive law}$$
$$= 12x \quad - \quad 3 \qquad \text{Multiply.}$$

To simplify algebraic expressions involving multiplication:

- Remove the parentheses by using the distributive law.
- Simplify multiplication by using the associative and commutative laws for multiplication.

EXAMPLE 1 Simplify.

a. $7(8xy)$ **b.** $6(4a + 2)$

c. $-2(3y - 2)$ **d.** $3x(2y + 5x)$

Solution

a. $7(8xy) = (7 \cdot 8)xy$ Associative law for multiplication

     $= 56xy$ Multiply.

b. $6(4a + 2) = 6(4a) + 6(2)$ Distributive law

     $= (6 \cdot 4)a + 6(2)$ Associative law for multiplication

     $= 24a + 12$ Multiply.

c. $-2(3y - 2) = -2(3y) - (-2)(2)$ Distributive law

     $= (-2 \cdot 3)y - (-2)(2)$ Associative law for multiplication

     $= -6y + 4$ Multiply.

d. $3x(2y + 5x) = 3x(2y) + 3x(5x)$ Distributive law

     $= (3 \cdot 2)xy + (3 \cdot 5)xx$ Commutative and associative laws for multiplication

     $= 6xy + 15x^2$ Multiply. Rewrite xx as x^2. ∎

To simplify algebraic expressions with division, we need to remember that division may be written as a multiplication expression. Therefore, the same rules used in multiplication are used in division. For example,

$$\frac{24x}{8} = 24x \div 8 \quad \text{Rewrite as division.}$$

$$= 24x \cdot \frac{1}{8} \quad \text{Rewrite as multiplication.}$$

$$= 24 \cdot \frac{1}{8} \cdot x \quad \text{Commutative law for multiplication}$$

$$= 3x \quad \text{Multiply.}$$

Therefore, in dividing expressions with variable terms by a number, we divide the numeric coefficient of the term by the number.

To divide an algebraic expression involving more than one term, we use the distributive law. For example,

$$\frac{6x - 12}{3} = (6x - 12) \div 3 \quad \text{Rewrite as division.}$$

$$= (6x - 12) \cdot \frac{1}{3} \quad \text{Rewrite as multiplication.}$$

$$= \frac{6x}{3} - \frac{12}{3} \quad \text{Distributive law}$$

$$= 2x - 4 \quad \text{Divide.}$$

We see that the division and multiplication steps are not necessary. We can use the distributive law with the original division expression. For example,

$$\frac{6x - 12}{3} = \frac{6x}{3} - \frac{12}{3} \quad \text{Distributive law}$$

$$= 2x - 4 \quad \text{Divide.}$$

To simplify algebraic expressions involving division:

- Remove the parentheses or grouping symbols by using the distributive law.
- Simplify division by rewriting as multiplication and then using the commutative and associative laws for multiplication.

Algebraic expressions may involve division by a variable, such as $\dfrac{24xy}{x}$.

Remember, division by 0 is undefined or indeterminate. Therefore, *in this text, we will assume the variable denominator does not represent values for which the expression is undefined or indeterminate.*

EXAMPLE 2 Simplify.

a. $\dfrac{32xy}{14y}$ **b.** $\dfrac{\frac{1}{16}a}{4}$ **c.** $\dfrac{20y - 16z + 9}{2}$

Solution

a. $\dfrac{32xy}{14y} = 32xy \div 14y$ Rewrite as division.

$= 32 \cdot x \cdot y \cdot \dfrac{1}{14y}$ Rewrite as multiplication.

$= \dfrac{32}{14} \cdot x \cdot \dfrac{y}{y}$ Associative and commutative laws for multiplication

$= \dfrac{16}{7} \cdot x \cdot 1$ Simplify.

$= \dfrac{16x}{7}$ Multiply.

b. $\dfrac{\frac{1}{16}a}{4} = \dfrac{1}{16}a \div 4$ Rewrite as division.

$= \dfrac{1}{16}a \cdot \dfrac{1}{4}$ Rewrite as multiplication.

$= \dfrac{1}{64}a$ Multiply.

c. $\dfrac{20y - 16z + 9}{2} = \dfrac{20y}{2} - \dfrac{16z}{2} + \dfrac{9}{2}$ Distributive law

$= 10y - 8z + \dfrac{9}{2}$ Divide. ∎

Experiencing Algebra the Checkup Way

Simplify exercises 1–6.

1. $12(6ab)$ **2.** $9(2x + 5)$ **3.** $-2x(3x + 4y)$

4. $\dfrac{44ab}{8b}$ **5.** $\dfrac{\frac{3}{4}x}{3}$ **6.** $\dfrac{14x + 21y - 56}{7}$

7. Explain how the associative and commutative laws of real numbers enable you to perform multiplication and division of algebraic expressions.

8. How does the distributive law help you multiply and divide algebraic expressions involving grouping?

2 Simplifying Algebraic Expressions with Mixed Operations

In order to simplify algebraic expressions involving mixed operations, use the properties of real numbers and order of operations.

EXAMPLE 3 Simplify.

a. $2(3x + 4y) + 5(2x - y)$

b. $4(2a - b) - (6a + 10b)$

c. $-2(7x + 4y + z) - 3(-6y + 4z)$

d. $[10(x + 2) - 5] + [4(2x - 6) + 8]$

e. $3\{[2(3x - 4) + 7] - [2(5x + 1) - 6]\}$

f. $\dfrac{5(2x + 4) - 7(x + 2)}{2x - (3x + 3) + x}$

Solution

a. $2(3x + 4y) + 5(2x - y)$
$= 6x + 8y \quad + 10x - 5y$ Distributive law
$= 16x + 3y$ Combine like terms.

b. $4(2a - b) - (6a + 10b)$
$= 8a - 4b \quad - 6a - 10b$ Distributive law
$= 2a - 14b$ Combine like terms.

c. $-2(7x + 4y + z) \quad - 3(-6y + 4z)$
$= -14x - 8y - 2z \quad + 18y - 12z$ Distributive law
$= -14x + 10y - 14z$ Combine like terms.

d. $[10(x + 2) - 5] + [4(2x - 6) + 8]$
$= [10x + 20 - 5] \; + [8x - 24 + 8]$ Distributive law
$= [10x + 15] \qquad + [8x - 16]$ Combine like terms.
$= 10x + 15 \qquad + 8x - 16$ Remove brackets (addition).
$= 18x - 1$ Combine like terms.

e. $3\{[2(3x - 4) + 7] - [2(5x + 1) - 6]\}$
$= 3\{[6x - 8 + 7] \quad - [10x + 2 - 6]\}$ Distributive law
$= 3\{[6x - 1] \qquad - [10x - 4]\}$ Combine like terms
$= 3\{6x - 1 \qquad - 10x + 4\}$ Opposite-of-a-sum property
$= 3\{-4x + 3\}$ Combine like terms.
$= -12x + 9$ Distributive law

f. $\dfrac{5(2x + 4) - 7(x + 2)}{2x - (3x + 3) + x}$

$= \dfrac{10x + 20 - 7x - 14}{2x - 3x - 3 + x}$ Apply the distributive law in numerator and the opposite-of-a-sum property in the denominator.

$= \dfrac{3x + 6}{-3}$ Combine like terms.

$= \dfrac{3x}{-3} + \dfrac{6}{-3}$ Distributive law

$= -x - 2$ Divide. ∎

Experiencing Algebra the Checkup Way

Simplify exercises 1–6.

1. $3(6p + 7q) + 4(8p - 5q)$

2. $2(3x - 5) - (5x + 3)$

3. $-4(5a + 2b + c) - 2(-a + 3b)$

4. $[3(2y - 3) + 14] + [-4 + 7(-2y + 6)]$

5. $4\{[2(7p - 3) + 6] - [9(p - 4) - 15]\}$

6. $\dfrac{9(3x - 7) - 8(6x + 12)}{x - 2(3x + 2) + 1 + 5x}$

7. An algebraic expression may have groupings nested within one another, such as in exercise 4. When this occurs, how should you proceed to remove the grouping symbols?

---

3 Modeling the Real World

Many algebraic expressions used to describe real-world situations can be simplified using the associative or distributive laws. In fact, you will find that calculations are often easier to do if you first simplify the algebraic expression before substituting numbers, instead of substituting numbers first and then trying to simplify.

EXAMPLE 4

The perimeter of a rectangular figure is sometimes expressed as twice the sum of its length and width. Write an algebraic expression for the perimeter. Write an equivalent expression without using parentheses. Evaluate each expression to find the amount of fringe needed to finish the edges on a rectangular tablecloth if the tablecloth measures 52 inches by 90 inches. (Both answers should be the same.)

Solution

Let $L = $ length   Define two variables.
    $W = $ width

The expressions would be

$2(L + W)$ Twice the sum translates into 2 times the sum. The sum is addition, with the length and width as addends.

$= 2L + 2W$ Use the distributive law.

To evaluate the expressions, substitute the values for the variables and use the order of operations to determine the result.

$$2(L + W) = 2(52 + 90) \quad \text{or} \quad 2L + 2W = 2(52) + 2(90)$$
$$= 2(142) \qquad\qquad\qquad = 104 + 180$$
$$= 284 \qquad\qquad\qquad\quad = 284$$

284 inches of fringe are needed to finish the edges of the tablecloth. ∎

Application

The area of a trapezoid is sometimes written as $\frac{1}{2}h(b + B)$, where h is the height of the trapezoid, B is the length of the base, and b is the length of the top. Write an equivalent form for this expression.

The Great Wall of China has a trapezoidal cross-section, with average dimensions of base 25 feet, top 20 feet, and height 30 feet. Use the equivalent form for the area of a trapezoid to determine the area of a cross-section of the wall.

Discussion

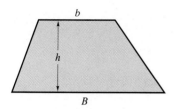

$$\frac{1}{2}h(b + B) = \frac{1}{2}hb + \frac{1}{2}hB \quad \text{Distribute } \tfrac{1}{2}h.$$

The area of a trapezoid is $\frac{1}{2}hb + \frac{1}{2}hB$.

To determine the area of the cross-section of the Great Wall of China, substitute 25 for B, 20 for b, and 30 for h.

$$\frac{1}{2}hb + \frac{1}{2}hB = \frac{1}{2}(30)(20) + \frac{1}{2}(30)(25)$$
$$= 300 + 375$$
$$= 675$$

The area of the cross-section of the Great Wall of China is about 675 square feet. ∎

Experiencing Algebra the Checkup Way

A rectangular desktop has a length that measures 25 inches more than its width. Write an expression for the perimeter of the desktop in terms of its width, W. Then write an equivalent expression without using parentheses. What will the perimeter be if the width of the desktop is 30 inches?

PROBLEM SET 3.3

Experiencing Algebra the Exercise Way

Simplify exercises 1–78.

1. $31(2xy)$ **2.** $16(31rs)$ **3.** $(-120a)(8b)$ **4.** $(-5x)(121y)$

5. $-55(-4mn)$ **6.** $(15n)(-0.2m)$ **7.** $-4.3(-0.7st)$ **8.** $-0.02(13.6xy)$

9. $-\dfrac{16}{27}\left(\dfrac{15}{24}cd\right)$ **10.** $-\dfrac{8}{15}\left(\dfrac{5}{12}mn\right)$ **11.** $12(4a + 7)$ **12.** $65(2x + 5)$

13. $-15(2x + 3)$ **14.** $-12(5z + 1)$ **15.** $-4(-5z - 14)$ **16.** $-2(-a - 205)$

17. $2.2(3.5x - 7.3)$ **18.** $3.6(1.1a - 0.8)$ **19.** $-8(-4.2z - 5)$ **20.** $-7(-3.5a - 15)$

21. $\dfrac{36}{49}\left(-\dfrac{7}{6}m + \dfrac{49}{72}\right)$ **22.** $\dfrac{5}{8}\left(-\dfrac{12}{55}z + 6\right)$ **23.** $-4\left(-\dfrac{5}{12}b + \dfrac{3}{16}\right)$ **24.** $-7\left(\dfrac{5}{14}y - \dfrac{20}{21}\right)$

25. $-\dfrac{2}{3}\left(-\dfrac{5}{8}d - \dfrac{9}{16}\right)$ **26.** $-\dfrac{1}{10}\left(-40x - \dfrac{5}{7}\right)$ **27.** $3x(5x + 4y)$ **28.** $x(6x + 12y)$

29. $-12d(-3c - 7d)$ **30.** $-4x(-5x - 7y)$ **31.** $-0.9m(-2.2m + 3.6n)$ **32.** $-0.7z(-8.3y + 4.9z)$

33. $-\dfrac{3}{5}a\left(\dfrac{15}{17}a + b\right)$ **34.** $-\dfrac{7}{10}m\left(-\dfrac{5}{21}m + n\right)$ **35.** $\dfrac{3}{8}m(m - 4n)$ **36.** $\dfrac{5}{16}b(a - 8b)$

37. $\dfrac{108p}{9}$ **38.** $\dfrac{98x}{7}$ **39.** $\dfrac{-138x}{46}$ **40.** $\dfrac{-244z}{61}$

41. $\dfrac{-58z}{-29}$ **42.** $\dfrac{-124b}{-62}$ **43.** $\dfrac{5.4c}{-2.7}$ **44.** $\dfrac{46.8m}{-15.6}$

45. $\dfrac{-\frac{1}{2}x}{2}$ **46.** $\dfrac{\frac{5}{12}y}{-3}$ **47.** $\dfrac{-\frac{2}{3}a}{-4}$ **48.** $\dfrac{-\frac{9}{4}b}{-3}$

49. $\dfrac{120xy}{24y}$

50. $\dfrac{80ab}{16b}$

51. $\dfrac{-1.9rs}{9.5r}$

52. $\dfrac{-3.6xy}{1.5y}$

53. $\dfrac{12.321pqr}{-1.11pr}$

54. $\dfrac{-65.8abc}{-2.8bc}$

55. $\dfrac{-\frac{5}{9}mn}{5n}$

56. $\dfrac{\frac{4}{7}cd}{-4d}$

57. $\dfrac{36x + 60}{12}$

58. $\dfrac{-90m - 45n}{15}$

59. $\dfrac{20.4b - 3.4c}{-6.8}$

60. $\dfrac{-2.88m + 9.6n}{-9.6}$

61. $\dfrac{96a + 24b - 120c}{8}$

62. $\dfrac{-75x - 20y + 125z}{5}$

63. $11(-3a + 2b - 4c) - 8(5a - 7b + 2c)$

64. $-31(x - 7y + 9z) + 5(-4x + 7y + 6z)$

65. $-4.6(2x - 5y) + 9.9(5x - 3y)$

66. $16.2(5p - 3q) - 3.8(4p - 8q)$

67. $\dfrac{3}{8}\left(-\dfrac{4}{9}p - \dfrac{2}{9}q\right) + \dfrac{2}{3}\left(\dfrac{7}{8}p - \dfrac{6}{7}q\right)$

68. $-\dfrac{5}{16}\left(\dfrac{2}{5}a + \dfrac{8}{15}b\right) - \dfrac{2}{3}\left(\dfrac{1}{2}a - \dfrac{1}{6}b\right)$

69. $[15 - 2(3x + 6y - 10) + 4x] + [6x + 2(8y - 12)]$

70. $-[23x + 5(2x - 6y) + 9] + [4y - 3(6x + y) - 10]$

71. $2[-5a + 3(2b - 4c) + 15] - [7(2a + 6b - c) + 12]$

72. $-4[5(6x + 4y) + 7z - 22] - [55 - 3(x + y - z)]$

73. $6\{2[x + 2(3y - 4z)] - [x - y + 3(y + 2z)]\}$

74. $2\{3[a + 2(b - 4c) + 3b] - [a + 2(b + c) + 6c]\}$

75. $\dfrac{8(5a + 7c) - 6(2a + 4c)}{4}$

76. $\dfrac{3(x + 2y) + 5(3x - 9y)}{3}$

77. $\dfrac{2.6m + 3(1.2m - 2.6n) - (4.8m + 7.4n) - 1.6n}{3m + 2(-2m + 1) + m}$

78. $\dfrac{2(1.1a + 4.6b) - 3(5.72a - 6.2b)}{(a + 1) - (a - 1)}$

79. Write an algebraic expression for the surface area of a box whose length is twice its width, and whose height is equal to its width. Write an equivalent expression without using parentheses. Evaluate the expression for a box that is 2 feet wide.

80. A carton has a length that is triple its width and a height that is one-half its width. Write an algebraic expression for the carton's surface area. Write an equivalent expression without parentheses. Evaluate the expression when the width is 12 inches.

81. Shirley and Joan file an expense report for a business trip. Shirley rented a car for several days. The charge for rental was $35.00 per day plus $0.20 per mile driven. Each was given a daily budget for food and lodging of $120.00 per day and a miscellaneous total trip allowance of $50.00. Write an algebraic expression for their total trip expense. Simplify to an equivalent expression without parentheses. Evaluate the expression if their trip lasted 4 days and they drove 625 miles.

82. On a business trip, Jim and Dave rented a car at $33.00 per day plus $0.25 per mile. Each of the men was allowed $95.00 per day for food and lodging. They were each given a miscellaneous spending allowance for the trip of $75.00. Write an algebraic expression for the total trip expense. Simplify to an equivalent expression without parentheses. Evaluate the expression if the trip was for 3 days and the distance covered was 750 miles.

83. On a business trip, Margaret drove a rental car for $30.00 per day and $0.22 per mile. Patricia flew to the destination at a cost of $450.00, and was met by Margaret on the first day of the trip. Each woman received a daily allowance of $85.00 for food and lodging. The miscellaneous spending allowance was $50.00 apiece. Write an algebraic expression for the total trip expense. Simplify to an equivalent expression without parentheses. Evaluate the expression if the trip lasted two days and Margaret drove a distance of 375 miles.

84. On their business trip, Jules and Malcolm both flew to their destination at a cost of $195.00 each. They then rented a car at a cost of $35.00 per day and $0.36 per mile. The men each had a daily food and lodging allowance of $125.00, and were allowed $30.00 each for miscellaneous expenses. Write an algebraic expression for the total trip expense. Simplify to an equivalent expression without parentheses. Evaluate the expression if the trip lasted 4 days and they drove 225 miles.

85. Franklin's Electrical Services sends two electricians and three apprentices out to wire a house. Each electrician is paid $38.00 per hour, and then $22.00 is added to their pay for travel expenses. The three apprentices working with the crew are each paid $16.00 per hour, but are not given the travel payment. Write an algebraic expression for the cost of the total job. Simplify to an equivalent expression without parentheses. Evaluate the expression if the job took 7 hours to complete.

86. Green's Lawn Service has quoted a price of $29.95 per application to fertilize lawns in a neighborhood. Several homes in the neighborhood agree to hire the service. They contract for three treatments for the season. In addition, the homeowners all agree to one application of a lime treatment for $19.95 each. Write an algebraic expression for the total price of caring for the neighborhood lawns. Simplify to an equivalent expression without parentheses. Evaluate the expression if 24 homes in the neighborhood subscribe to the service.

Experiencing Algebra the Calculator Way

Simplify. Use your calculator to help with the arithmetic.

1. $-679(138x - 349y) + 903(287x + 423y)$

2. $\dfrac{1173.04a + 2147.893b}{23.65}$

3. $27.12[39.675(x - 41.56) - 21.876(y - 22.7)] + 109.35[30.4(x + 33.9) + 43.76(y - 52.7)]$

4. $\left(3\dfrac{5}{12}\right)\left[\left(4\dfrac{1}{2}\right)x - \left(3\dfrac{3}{5}\right)y\right]$

5. $\dfrac{12.0832abc}{2.36b}$

6. $\dfrac{-2102.17yz}{41.3yz}$

7. $\dfrac{-34.155xyz}{-2.07xz}$

8. $\dfrac{\dfrac{5}{12}y}{-\dfrac{15}{16}}$

9. $\dfrac{-\dfrac{2}{5}ab}{\dfrac{3}{5}ab}$

10. $\dfrac{\dfrac{3}{5}xy}{-\dfrac{2}{5}x}$

11. $\dfrac{-5bc}{-\dfrac{5}{7}b}$

12. $\dfrac{-\dfrac{5}{21}x + \dfrac{15}{49}y}{-\dfrac{5}{7}}$

Experiencing Algebra the Group Way

Students often confuse addition and subtraction rules with the multiplication and division rules of algebra. Simplify the following expressions, where possible, and discuss within your group the differences in the exercises.

1. $2x + 8x$

2. $(2x)(8x)$

3. $2x - 8x$

4. $\dfrac{2x}{8x}$

5. $2x + 8y$

6. $(2x)(8y)$

7. $2x - 8y$

8. $\dfrac{2x}{8y}$

9. $3(9x + 6)$

10. $3 + (9x + 6)$

11. $3 - (9x + 6)$

12. $\dfrac{9x + 6}{3}$

13. $x(9x + 6)$

14. $x + (9x + 6)$

15. $x - (9x + 6)$

16. $\dfrac{9x + 6}{x}$

Experiencing Algebra the Write Way

To be sure you understand how to use the commutative, associative, and distributive laws in simplifying expressions, write a paragraph explaining what each of the three laws permits you to do in this respect. In each paragraph, include an example that shows how the law is applied.

3.4 Equations

Objectives

1 Identify expressions and equations.

2 Determine whether a number is a solution of an algebraic equation.

3 Write equations for word statements.

4 Model real-world situations using equations.

Application

The area of a rectangle is the product of its length and width. The perimeter of a rectangle is the sum of twice its length and twice its width. For a particular rectangular playground, its area is numerically equal to its perimeter. Write an equation to represent this statement.

After completing this section, we will discuss this application further. See page 185.

1 Identifying Expressions and Equations

In the first part of this text we discussed expressions. To review, a numeric expression is a combination of numbers and mathematical operations. An algebraic expression is a combination of numbers, variables, and mathematical operations. We evaluate these expressions by finding a numeric value for the expression. If the expression contains variables, we first substitute a value for each of the variables and then find a numeric value for the expression.

In this section we will make a mathematical statement by combining two expressions with an equal symbol. This kind of statement is called an equation. Therefore, an **equation** is a mathematical statement that two expressions have the same (or equal) value. For example,

combining two numeric expressions

$$2 + 3 = 9 - 4$$

$$14 - (-3) + 8(4) \div 2 = (-5)(-6) + 7$$

combining two algebraic expressions

$$4x - 3 = 3x + 2$$

$$3x + 2y - z = 2x - y + 2z$$

It is very important to understand the difference between an expression and an equation.

EXAMPLE 1

Determine whether each of the following is an expression or an equation.

a. $6 + x - y + 3z$ **b.** $2x - 3y = 5 + x$ **c.** $P = a + b + c$

Solution

a. $6 + x - y + 3z$ is an expression.   (There is no equality.)

b. $2x - 3y = 5 + x$ is an equation.   (There is equality.)

c. $P = a + b + c$ is an equation.   (There is equality.) ∎

Experiencing Algebra the Checkup Way

In exercises 1–6, determine whether each of the following is an expression or an equation.

1. $3x + 6 = 17$ **2.** $5x - 35$ **3.** $2L + 2W$ **4.** $-6x - 18 = 0$

5. $\frac{1}{3}x + 3 = 2$ **6.** $2.3a + 1.5b$

7. Explain the difference between an algebraic expression and an algebraic equation.

---

2 Determining Solutions of Algebraic Equations

Equations may be true or false. If the two expressions have the same value, then the equation is true. If the two expressions have different values, the equation is false.

To determine whether a numeric equation is true:

- Evaluate both expressions in the equation.
- Determine whether the expressions are equal.

If the expressions are equal, the equation is true. If the expressions are not equal, the equation is false.

An alternative method to determine whether a numeric equation is true is to use the TEST function on your calculator.

- Enter the equation on the calculator as it appears.

The calculator will give a result of 1 if the equation is true and a result of 0 if the equation is false.

 Helping Hand On some calculators, a true statement may result in a 0 for false if the calculator is working with nonterminating decimals or with certain fractions. In this case, evaluate both expressions separately and determine whether the expressions are equal.

For example, determine whether the following equation is true or false.

$$\frac{2 + 3 = 9 - 4}{5 \quad | \quad 5}$$

Both expressions, $2 + 3$ and $9 - 4$, have the same value, 5. Therefore, the equation is true. This should not need to be evaluated on a calculator.

Here is a second example, taken from the preceding part of this section.

$$
\begin{array}{rl}
14 - (-3) + 8(4) \div 2 =& (-5)(-6) + 7 \\
\hline
14 + 3 \quad + 8(4) \div 2 \;\Big|& \quad 30 \quad\quad + 7 \\
14 + 3 \quad + 32 \div 2 \;\;& \quad\quad 37 \\
14 + 3 \quad + 16 \;\;& \\
33 \;\;& \\
\end{array}
$$

The two expressions have different values ($33 \neq 37$). Therefore, the equation is false. (Did you notice this when you first saw this equation? It's not always easy to tell.)

On a calculator, as shown in Figure 3.4, the display of 0 means the equation is false.

TECHNOLOGY

```
14-(-3)+8*4/2=-5
*-6+7
                    0
```

For Figure 3.4

| 1 | 4 | − | (| (−) | 3 |) | + | 8 | × | 4 | ÷ | 2 |

| 2nd | TEST | 1 | (−) | 5 | × | (−) | 6 | + | 7 | ENTER |

Figure 3.4

EXAMPLE 2 Determine whether each equation is true or false.

a. $6 + 4(2) - (-3) = -3(-5) + 16 \div 8$

b. $-30 \div 5(-2) + 6 = (4.2)(5) - 3 + 1$

c. $\dfrac{1}{2} + \left(-\dfrac{2}{3}\right) + \dfrac{3}{4} = \dfrac{6}{12} + \left(-\dfrac{8}{12}\right) + \dfrac{9}{12}$

d. $\dfrac{5}{9} - \dfrac{3}{7} = \dfrac{50}{63} - \dfrac{2}{3}$

Solution

a. $6 + 4(2) - (-3) = -3(-5) + 16 \div 8$

$$\begin{array}{ccc|cc}
6 + & 8 & + 3 & 15 & + 2 \\
& 17 & & & 17
\end{array}$$

The equation is true because $17 = 17$.

b. Before we complete this example, remember the rules of order of operations. That is, when multiplication and division occur in the same expression, perform them in order from left to right. Also, remember that some calculators use implied multiplication and you must insert a multiplication sign as you enter an expression.

$$-30 \div 5(-2) + 6 = (4.2)(5) - 3 + 1$$

$$\begin{array}{cc|c}
-6(-2) & + 6 & 21 \quad - 3 + 1 \\
12 & + 6 & 19 \\
& 18 &
\end{array}$$

Perform division before multiplication.

The equation is false because $18 \neq 19$.

c. $\dfrac{1}{2} + \left(-\dfrac{2}{3}\right) + \dfrac{3}{4} = \dfrac{6}{12} + \left(-\dfrac{8}{12}\right) + \dfrac{9}{12}$

$$\begin{array}{cc|c}
\dfrac{6}{12} + \left(-\dfrac{8}{12}\right) + \dfrac{9}{12} & & \dfrac{7}{12} \\
\dfrac{7}{12} &
\end{array}$$

The equation is true because $\dfrac{7}{12} = \dfrac{7}{12}$.

d.

$$\frac{5}{9} - \frac{3}{7} = \frac{50}{63} - \frac{2}{3}$$

$$\frac{35}{63} - \frac{27}{63} \ \bigg| \ \frac{50}{63} - \frac{42}{63}$$

$$\frac{8}{63} \ \bigg| \ \frac{8}{63}$$

The equation is true because $\dfrac{8}{63} = \dfrac{8}{63}$.

Use your calculator to check your results.

a. The display of 1 in Figure 3.5 means the equation is true.

TECHNOLOGY

```
6+4*2-( -3)= -3* -5
+16/8
                   1
```

Figure 3.5

For Figure 3.5

| 6 | + | 4 | × | 2 | − | (| (−) | 3 |) |

| 2nd | TEST | 1 | (−) | 3 | × | (−) | 5 | + | 1 | 6 | ÷ | 8 |

| ENTER |

---

b. Remember that some calculators need a multiplication sign between 5 and -2.

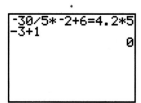

```
-30/5* -2+6=4.2*5
-3+1
                   0
```

The display of 0 means the equation is false.

c.
```
(1/2)+( -2/3)+(3/
4)=(6/12)+( -8/12
)+(9/12)
                   1
```

The display of 1 means the equation is true.

d.
```
(5/9)-(3/7)=(50/
63)-(2/3)
                1
(5/9)-(3/7)
        .126984127
(50/63)-(2/3)
        .126984127
```

This results in 1 for true.

However, on some calculators, this will result in 0. Evaluate both expressions separately to verify that the equation is true. This results in the same value for both expressions. Therefore, the equation is true. ∎

If the expressions in an equation contain a variable, we need to substitute a value for the variable in order to be able to evaluate the expressions. However, not all values of the variable will make the equation true. If there is a value for the variable that makes a true equation, that value is called a **solution** of the equation.

> *Solution of an Algebraic Equation*
> A solution of an algebraic equation is a value for the variable that will result in a true equation.

To determine whether a number is a solution of an algebraic equation:

- Substitute the possible solution for the variable.
- Evaluate both expressions in the equation.
- Determine whether the expressions are equal.

If the expressions are equal, then the value substituted for the variable is a solution.

To determine on your calculator whether a number is a solution of an algebraic equation:

- Assign the possible solution to the variable.
- Enter each expression separately.
- Determine whether the expressions are equal.

If the expressions are equal, then the value substituted for the variable is a solution.

An alternative method to determine on your calculator whether a number is a solution of an algebraic equation:

- Assign the possible solution to the variable.
- Enter the calculator's notation for a new line.
- Enter the equation.

The calculator will determine whether the equation is true and return a 1 to denote a solution or a 0 to denote a nonsolution.

Note: On some calculators, a solution may result in a 0 for false if the calculator is working with nonterminating decimals (fractions). In this case, evaluate both expressions separately and visually check for equivalence.

For example, determine whether $x = 5$ is a solution of $4x - 3 = 3x + 2$.

$$\begin{array}{c|c}
4x \quad - 3 = & 3x \quad + 2 \\
\hline
4(5) - 3 & 3(5) + 2 \\
20 \ - 3 & 15 \ + 2 \\
17 & 17
\end{array}$$ Substitute 5 for x.

Since $17 = 17$, the equation is true for $x = 5$. Therefore, 5 is a solution of the equation.

On a calculator, as shown in Figure 3.6a, each expression results in 17. Therefore, 5 is a solution.

The result is 1 in Figure 3.6b, which indicates that the equation is true when x is 5; therefore, 5 is a solution.

TECHNOLOGY

Figure 3.6a

Figure 3.6b

For Figure 3.6a
Store the given value for the variable.

| 5 | STO▸ | X, T, θ, n |

Enter the calculator's notation for a line return.

| ALPHA | : |

Enter each expression separately.

| 4 | X, T, θ, n | $-$ | 3 | ENTER |
| 3 | X, T, θ, n | $+$ | 2 | ENTER |

For Figure 3.6b
Store the given value for the variable.

| 5 | STO▸ | X, T, θ, n |

Enter the calculator's notation for a line return.

| ALPHA | : |

Enter the equation.

| 4 | X, T, θ, n | $-$ | 3 | 2nd | TEST | 1 | 3 | X, T, θ, n | $+$ | 2 | ENTER |

EXAMPLE 3 Determine whether the given value is a solution of the equation.

a. $6x + 3 = 8x - 1$ for $x = 2$
b. $4(x - 2) + 7x = 6x + 2x + 5x$ for $x = -4$
c. $8 - 3a^2 - (a + 6) = (a + 2) - 2(2a + 4)$ for $a = 1$

Solution

a. $6x + 3 = 8x - 1$ for $x = 2$

$$\begin{array}{c|c}
6x \ + 3 = & 8x \ - 1 \\
\hline
6(2) + 3 & 8(2) - 1 \\
12 \ + 3 & 16 \ - 1 \\
15 & 15
\end{array}$$ Substitute 2 for x.

The solution is 2 because $15 = 15$.

b. $4(x - 2) + 7x = 6x + 2x + 5x$ for $x = -4$

$$
\begin{array}{c|c}
4(x - 2) \quad + 7x & = \quad 6x \quad + \quad 2x \quad + \quad 5x \\
\hline
4[(-4) - 2] + 7(-4) & 6(-4) + 2(-4) + 5(-4) \\
4\,(-6) \qquad\quad + 7(-4) & -24 + (-8) \ + (-20) \\
-24 \qquad\qquad + (-28) & -52 \\
-52 &
\end{array}
$$

The solution is -4 because $-52 = -52$.

c. $8 - 3a^2 - (a + 6) = (a + 2) - 2(2a + 4)$ for $a = 1$

$$
\begin{array}{c|c}
8 - \quad 3a^2 - (a + 6) & = (a + 2) - 2(2a + 4) \\
\hline
8 - 3(1)^2 - (1 + 6) & (1 + 2) - 2[2(1) + 4] \\
8 - \quad 3 \ - \quad 7 & 3 \qquad - 2(\ 2 \ + 4) \\
-2 & 3 \qquad - 2(\ 6\ ) \\
& 3 \qquad - 12 \\
& -9
\end{array}
$$

The solution is not 1 because $-2 \neq -9$.

Use your calculator to check your results.

a. In Figure 3.7, 1 means true. The solution is 2.

TECHNOLOGY

`2→X:6X+3=8X−1`
`                           1`

Figure 3.7

For Figure 3.7

| 2 | STO▶ | X, T, θ, n | ALPHA | : | 6 | X, T, θ, n | + | 3 |

| 2nd | TEST | 1 | 8 | X, T, θ, n | − | 1 | ENTER |

b.
`-4→X:4(X−2)+7X=6`
`X+2X+5X`
`                           1`

1 means true. The solution is -4.

c. Remember to enter the variable using the alpha key.

0 means false. The solution is not 1. ∎

 ## Experiencing Algebra the Checkup Way

Determine whether each equation is true or false.

1. $5(3.8) - 9 + 6 \cdot 5 = -25 \div 5(-7) + 8$

2. $-2(-6) + 24 \div 4 = 3 + 7(2) - (-1)$

3. $\dfrac{4}{9} + \dfrac{2}{5} = \dfrac{8}{15} + \dfrac{1}{3}$

4. $\dfrac{1}{2} \cdot \dfrac{1}{3} + \dfrac{1}{5}\left(-\dfrac{5}{6}\right) = \dfrac{1}{4} \cdot \dfrac{1}{2} + \dfrac{1}{3}\left(-\dfrac{3}{8}\right)$

In exercises 5–7, determine whether the given value is a solution of the equation.

5. $5(2x - 6) + 9 = x + 15$ for $x = 4$

6. $3x - 5 = 8x - 2$ for $x = -\dfrac{3}{5}$

7. $3c^2 + 5c - 2 = 0$ for $c = 2$

---

3 Writing Equations from Word Statements

In solving real-life mathematics problems, we often need to write equations from word statements. To do this, we translate each expression into numbers and symbols, as we did in previous sections. The only difference is that we now equate the two expressions by using an equal symbol.

Some words and expressions that translate into an equal symbol are:

> equals, is equal to, is the same as, results in, is, was, will be, becomes, gives, is equivalent to

To write an equation from a word statement:

- Define the variable or variables.
- Write two algebraic expressions for the word expressions.
- Join the expressions with an equal symbol.

For example,

> The sum of twice a number and 3 is the same as the difference of 3 times the number and 5.

Let $n = $ a number.   First define a variable.

$$\underset{\text{Sum of twice a number and 3}}{2n + 3} \qquad \underset{\text{is the same as}}{=} \qquad \underset{\substack{\text{Difference of three times}\\\text{the number and 5}}}{3n - 5}$$

EXAMPLE 4   Write an equation for each word statement.

a. The sum of the product of -8 and -2 and the quotient of -72 and 9 is equal to the difference of 14 and 6.

b. The difference of twice a number and 4 results in the sum of one-half the number and 5.

Solution

a. The sum of the product of -8 and -2 and the quotient of -72 and 9 is equal to the difference of 14 and 6.

$$-8(-2) + \frac{-72}{9} \qquad = \qquad 14 - 6$$

"Sum" means addition.   is equal to   "Difference" means subtraction.
The first addend is a product, $-8(-2)$.
The second addend is a quotient, $\frac{-72}{9}$.

b. The difference of twice a number and 4 results in the sum of one-half the number and 5.
Let $x =$ the number.

$$2x - 4 \qquad = \qquad \frac{1}{2}x + 5$$

"Difference" means subtraction.   results in   "Sum" means addition.
"Twice a number" means $2x$.   "One-half the number" means $\frac{1}{2}x$. ∎

 ## Experiencing Algebra the Checkup Way

Write an equation for each word statement.

1. 2 times the quotient of 21 divided by 3 is equal to the sum of 2 and the product of 4 and 3.
2. 3 times the sum of a number and 4 is equal to 4 times the number.

---

4 Modeling the Real World

One of the most important steps in solving real-world mathematical problems of any kind is correctly translating the given word statements into mathematical equations. This is usually the first step in solving problems in physics and chemistry, medicine and biology, economics and business, ecology and computer science—in fact, any area of human activity that involves mathematical relationships. You need to learn various concepts in these fields so that you know what variables and relationships are available to you. But once you have the right equation, you can usually figure out what you know and what you need to find in order to solve the problem.

EXAMPLE 5

In 1905, Albert Einstein suggested his famous equation that relates energy and mass. The theory of relativity states that "energy equals mass multiplied by the velocity of light squared." Write an equation for this famous relationship, using E for energy, m for mass, and c for the velocity of light.

Solution

Let $E =$ energy   Define the variables.
     $m =$ mass
     $c =$ velocity of light

$$E \qquad = \qquad mc^2$$

Energy   equals   Mass multiplied by the velocity of light squared ∎

EXAMPLE 6 The area of a triangle is the product of one-half its base and its height. Write an equation for this statement.

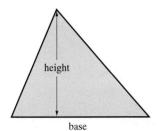

height

base

Solution

Let A = area
 b = base
 h = height

$$A = \frac{1}{2}bh \qquad \text{"Product" means multiply.} \quad \blacksquare$$

Application

The area of a rectangle is the product of its length and width. The perimeter of a rectangle is the sum of twice its length and twice its width. For a particular rectangular playground, its area is numerically equal to its perimeter. Write an equation to represent this statement.

Discussion

Let L = length   Define two variables.
 W = width

An expression for area is LW.   "Product" means multiply.

An expression for the perimeter is $2L + 2W$.   "Sum" means addition.

Therefore, the equation is $LW = 2L + 2W$. $\blacksquare$

Experiencing Algebra the Checkup Way

The area of a circle is equal to the product of the mathematical constant π and the square of the radius of the circle, which is the distance from the center of the circle to the outer edge. Write an equation for this area.

PROBLEM SET 3.4

Experiencing Algebra the Exercise Way

Determine whether each item is an expression or an equation.

1. $3x - 15 = 6$

2. $5x + 9 - 2x$

3. $15x^3 + 7x^2 - 2x + 4$

4. $3x^2 - 6x + 1 = 0$

5. $0.5x^2 - 2.8 = 0.7$

6. $1.8x^2 - 7.6x - 0.3$

7. $\frac{2}{3}x + \frac{6}{7} = 0$

8. $\frac{4}{9}x^3 - \frac{5}{7}$

9. $\frac{4}{9}x^2 - \frac{3}{5}x - \frac{1}{4}$

10. $\frac{1}{2} = \frac{x}{15}$

Determine whether each equation is true or false.

11. $7 + 15 = 2 \cdot 11$

12. $45 + 2^2 = 7(9 - 2)$

13. $4 \cdot 7 = 5 + 24$

14. $5(8 - 2) = 4^2 + 2 \cdot 8$

15. $\frac{1}{7} + \frac{2}{3} = \frac{6}{7} - \frac{1}{3}$

16. $\frac{4}{9} + \frac{2}{3} = \left(\frac{2}{3}\right)\left(1\frac{2}{3}\right)$

17. $\frac{1}{2} + \frac{1}{3} = \frac{2}{3} + \frac{1}{6}$

18. $\frac{3}{5} + \frac{2}{3} = \frac{5}{8}$

19. $3.7 - 4.8 = 1.7 - 0.6$

20. $5.8 + 1.01 = 6.9$

21. $4.9 + 1.2 = 8.4 - 2.2$

22. $4.6 + 2.4 - 7 = 0$

23. $2(16 - 5) = 3(19 - 12)$

24. $3(19 - 25) = -2(6 + 3)$

25. $\dfrac{2}{3} + \dfrac{3}{2} = 2$

26. $\dfrac{12}{13} - \dfrac{1}{8} = \dfrac{10}{13}$

Determine whether the given value is a solution of the equation.

27. $2x + 4 = 10$ for $x = 3$

28. $-3a - 2 = -16$ for $a = 6$

29. $5y - 7 = 9$ for $y = 3$

30. $-12z + 15 = 50$ for $z = -3$

31. $6a + 5 = 3a + 17$ for $a = 3$

32. $5p + 16 = 6p - 12$ for $p = 28$

33. $9z - 23 = 6z - 29$ for $z = -2$

34. $8a + 26 = -5a + 39$ for $a = 1$

35. $3(x - 5) + 9 = 4(6x - 5) - 7$ for $x = 1$

36. $5y + 2(y - 7) = 6 + 3(y - 1)$ for $y = 4$

37. $2[3(x - 4) - 6] + x = 3x$ for $x = 8$

38. $3x - [5(2x + 1) + 3] = x$ for $x = -1$

39. $x^2 + 5 = 33 - 3x$ for $x = 4$

40. $2x^2 - 20 = 3x + 34$ for $x = 7$

Write an equation for each word statement.

41. The sum of 7 and the product of 6 and 5 is equivalent to the sum of the product of 3 and 7 added to the square of 4.

42. The quotient of 21 divided by the opposite of 3 is equivalent to the difference of 8 less 15.

43. The sum of a number and 6 is 15.

44. 5 less than twice a number equals the sum of the number and 2.

45. The product of 2 and a number is 12.

46. The quotient of a number divided by 12 is 2200.

47. The difference of the square of a number less 21 is equal to 100.

48. Double a number less 100 is equivalent to the sum of the number and 50.

49. Twice the sum of a number and the square of 5 is equal to the sum of the number and 100.

50. Half of a number increased by 60 is 200.

51. Twice the sum of a number and 2 is equal to the sum of 4 and the product of 2 times the number.

52. 3 times the difference of a number less 6 is equal to the difference of triple the number less 18.

53. The sum of 17 and the quotient of a number divided by 2 is equal to the sum of 4 and the product of 3 and the number.

54. The sum of the square of a number and the number is equivalent to twice the number.

55. The perimeter of a semicircular sector is equal to the diameter added to the product of π and the radius (this product is one-half the circumference of a circle).

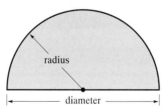

56. The average rate of speed is equal to the distance traveled divided by the time for travel.

57. The interest, I, paid on a continuously compounded loan is equal to the difference of the compounded amount, A, less the principal, P.

58. The total amount of a loan, A, is the sum of the principal, P, plus the interest, I.

 Experiencing Algebra the Calculator Way

Use your calculator to determine whether each equation is true or false.

1. $4 - 6 \cdot 3 + 28 \div 7 = 16 \div 4 + 2(-16 + 9)$

2. $14 \div 2 + 6 \cdot 3 - 2^2 = 5^2 - 2^2$

3. $4(8 + 7 \cdot 3) - 100 = 5 + 3(2 \cdot 6 - 20)$

4. $-7(-5 + 4) + 20 \div 5 = -2(3^2 + 1) + 19$

5. $13\left(\dfrac{1}{5} + \dfrac{3}{7}\right) = 11\left(\dfrac{3}{5} + \dfrac{1}{7}\right)$

6. $\dfrac{1}{2}\left(\dfrac{2}{3} + \dfrac{4}{7}\right) - \dfrac{3}{7} = 1 - \dfrac{17}{21}$

7. $\dfrac{3}{4} \div \dfrac{1}{2} + 2\left(\dfrac{3}{8}\right) - 1\dfrac{1}{4} = \dfrac{1}{2}$

8. $\dfrac{1}{3} - \dfrac{5}{7} \div \dfrac{5}{3} + 6\left(\dfrac{1}{7}\right) - 2\dfrac{1}{3} = -1\dfrac{4}{7}$

9. $1.2 - 3(4.7) + 6.5 \div 5 = -3(3.2) + 2(4.3 - 2.4 - 2.9)$

10. $-1.2 + 4.7 - 6.9 \div 2.3 = 3(5.6) - 4(4.2 - 0.5)$

11. $5.7 \div 3 + 7(-1.2) = -2(3.3)$

12. $2(2.7) - 5.8 \div 2 = 7.8 \div 3 - 0.1$

13. $269.1 \div 7.5 = 13.8(2.6)$

Use your calculator to determine whether the given value is a solution of the equation.

14. $5z + 13 = 2z - 6$ for $z = -6\dfrac{1}{3}$

15. $15x - 2 = x - 7$ for $x = -\dfrac{2}{7}$

16. $15x - 13 = 6(2x + 7) + x$ for $x = 27.5$

17. $3z + 20 = 5 - 3(z - 4)$ for $z = -0.5$

Experiencing Algebra the Group Way

Each member of the group should use the TEST function of his or her calculator to test whether each numeric equation is true or false.

1. $16 \div 4(2) = 8$ **2.** $16 \div 4 \cdot 2 = 8$ **3.** $16 \div 4(2) = 2$ **4.** $16 \div 4 \cdot 2 = 2$

Now check the equations without using your calculator, being sure to follow order of operations. You should see that equations 1 and 2 are true and that equations 3 and 4 are false. However, some calculators indicate that equations 2 and 3 are true. How can this be? Compare your results in your group and discuss to be sure you worked the problems correctly.

These equations illustrate the importance of implied multiplication, which is a feature of many calculators. When you indicate multiplication without using the multiplication key, many calculators are designed to perform the multiplication before applying the rules for order of operation. In equations 1 and 3 the multiplication is implied multiplication, since it is indicated by parentheses rather than by a multiplication key. Therefore the multiplication may be done before the division by some calculators, even though the division occurs first in operating from left to right. That is why some calculators determine that equation 1 is false and equation 3 is true. If your calculator gave you incorrect results, you must be careful that you always use a multiplication key to indicate multiplication, unless you wish the multiplication to take precedence over order of operations.

Now check the following equations, being on the alert for implied multiplication.

5. $1 + 27 \div 3(-3) = -26$

6. $1 + 27 \div 3(-3) = -2$

7. $45 - 56 \div 7(2) + 8 = 49$

8. $45 - 56 \div 7(2) + 8 = 37$

9. $\dfrac{3}{5} + \dfrac{5}{6} \div \left(\dfrac{5}{9}\right)\left(\dfrac{7}{12}\right) = \dfrac{111}{35}$

10. $\dfrac{3}{5} + \dfrac{5}{6} \div \left(\dfrac{5}{9}\right)\left(\dfrac{7}{12}\right) = \dfrac{59}{40}$

11. $10 + 42 \div 7 \cdot x = 4x$, where $x = 3$

12. $10 + 42 \div 7x = 4x$, where $x = 3$

Compare your results within your group, to be sure that implied multiplication was not an obstacle to your solution.

Experiencing Algebra the Write Way

1. In "Experiencing Algebra the Group Way," the concept of implied multiplication is discussed. Check to see whether the handbook that came with your calculator discusses this concept. If it does, try to explain what the handbook is telling you. If it does not, check to see whether your calculator uses implied multiplication by working the "Experiencing Algebra the Group Way" exercises. Then explain what precautions you must take when entering a mathematical expression into your calculator. Remember that you can check for this property of your calculator by working the exercises with pencil and paper and comparing your result with the calculator result.

2. In this section, you were instructed on the difference between expressions and equations, and the difference between numeric and algebraic forms of each. Write a short description of what is meant by a numeric expression, an algebraic expression, a numeric equation, and an algebraic equation. Describe the defining difference between an expression and an equation, and between numeric and algebraic forms. Give your own examples of each of these four forms.

3.5 Formulas and Geometry

Objectives

1 Evaluate two-dimensional geometric formulas.
2 Evaluate three-dimensional geometric formulas.
3 Evaluate angle formulas.
4 Evaluate the Pythagorean theorem.
5 Evaluate geometric formulas with real-world data.

Application

Janice is painting a rectangular toy box with dimensions $3\frac{1}{2}$ feet by 2 feet by $1\frac{1}{2}$ feet. She needs to determine the outside surface area in order to know how much paint to buy. Determine the surface area of the toy box.

After completing this section, we will discuss this application further. See page 196.

In Example 6 of section 3.4, we wrote a special type of equation called a formula. A **formula** is an equation used to find a numeric value for an unknown variable. We know the values for all the variables in the formula except one. For example, the formula in Example 6 may be used to find the area, A, of a triangle when the base, b, and height, h, are known.

$$A = \frac{1}{2}bh \quad \text{for } b = \text{base and } h = \text{height}$$

To find a numeric value for the area, A, we substitute values for b and h. We say we *evaluate* the formula.

To evaluate a formula:

* Write the formula.
* Substitute the values for the variables.
* Evaluate the expression containing the substituted values.

To evaluate a formula on your calculator:

* Store the known value for the first variable.
* Enter the calculator's notation for a line return.
* Repeat these two steps if more than one variable is known.
* Enter the expression to be evaluated.

For example, evaluate $A = \frac{1}{2}bh$ for $b = 12$ inches and $h = 5$ inches.

$$A = \frac{1}{2}bh \qquad \text{Write the formula.}$$

$$A = \frac{1}{2}(12)(5) \qquad \text{Substitute.}$$

$$A = 30 \text{ square inches} \qquad \text{Evaluate.}$$

The area of the triangle is 30 square inches.

On your calculator, as shown in Figure 3.8, the area of the triangle is 30 square inches.

```
12→B:5→H:(1/2)BH
                30
```

Figure 3.8

For Figure 3.8

Store values for the variables, separated by line returns.

| 1 | 2 | STO▶ | ALPHA | B | ALPHA | : | 5 | STO▶ | ALPHA | H |
| ALPHA | : |

Enter the expression to be evaluated.

| (| 1 | ÷ | 2 |) | ALPHA | B | ALPHA | H | ENTER |

1 Evaluating Two-Dimensional Geometric Formulas

Two-dimensional figures have properties of perimeter (circumference) and area. **Perimeter**, P, is the distance around a closed two-dimensional figure. **Circumference**, C, is the distance around a circle. **Area**, A, is the amount of surface covered by a two-dimensional figure.

The following are the two-dimensional figures we will use in this text.

Triangle

$$P = a + b + c$$

$$A = \frac{1}{2} bh$$

Rectangle

$$P = 2L + 2W$$

$$A = LW$$

Square

$$P = 4s$$

$$A = s^2$$

Parallelogram

$$A = bh$$

$$P = 2a + 2b$$

Trapezoid

$$A = \frac{1}{2} h(b + B)$$

$$P = a + b + c + B$$

Circle

$$d = 2r$$

$$r = \frac{1}{2}d$$

$$C = \pi d \quad \text{or} \quad C = 2\pi r$$

$$A = \pi r^2$$

EXAMPLE 1 Find the perimeter of a square that measures $6\frac{1}{4}$ inches on a side.

Solution

$$P = 4s \qquad \text{Write the formula.}$$

$$P = 4\left(6\frac{1}{4}\right) \qquad \text{Substitute.}$$

$$P = 4\left(\frac{25}{4}\right) \qquad \text{Evaluate.}$$

$$P = 25$$

The perimeter is 25 inches.
    As shown in Figure 3.9, the perimeter is 25 inches. ∎

TECHNOLOGY

```
6+1/4→S:4S
              25
```

For Figure 3.9

| 6 | + | 1 | ÷ | 4 | STO▶ | ALPHA | S | ALPHA | : | 4 | ALPHA |

| S | ENTER |

Figure 3.9

EXAMPLE 2 Find the area of a circle with a radius of 5 feet.

Solution

$$A = \pi r^2 \qquad \text{Write the formula.}$$

$$A = \pi(5)^2 \qquad \text{Substitute.}$$

$$A = 25\pi \qquad \text{Evaluate.}$$

$$A \approx 25(3.14) \qquad \text{Evaluate. } \textit{Note: } \pi \approx 3.14.$$

$$A \approx 78.5$$

The area is 25π square feet, or approximately 78.5 square feet.
    As shown in Figure 3.10, the area is approximately 78.5 square feet. ∎

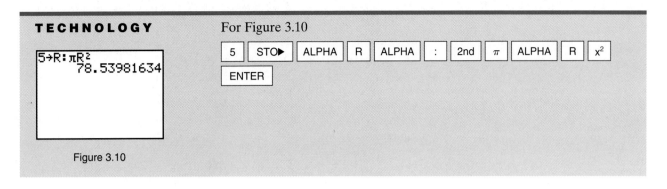

TECHNOLOGY

```
5→R: πR²
        78.53981634
```

Figure 3.10

For Figure 3.10

| 5 | STO▶ | ALPHA | R | ALPHA | : | 2nd | π | ALPHA | R | x² |

| ENTER |

```
π
     3.141592654
```

Helping Hand The calculator value is more precise because the noncalculator value for π we used was rounded to two decimal places. To be as precise as the calculator, we would need to use a value for π with more decimal places. To determine this value, we can enter π on the calculator. It will display a value for π rounded to nine decimal places.

✓ Experiencing Algebra the Checkup Way

1. Find the area of a parallelogram whose base measures 3.5 inches and whose height measures 2 inches.
2. Find the circumference of a circle with a diameter of 4.8 inches. Round your answer to the nearest hundredth. Write the keystrokes needed to evaluate the formula using your calculator and state the calculator result without rounding the answer.
3. What is a formula?
4. What is the difference between the perimeter of a two-dimensional figure and the area of a two-dimensional figure?

2 Evaluating Three-Dimensional Geometric Formulas

Three-dimensional figures have properties of volume and surface area. **Volume**, V, is the amount of space enclosed in a three-dimensional figure. **Surface area**, S, is the total area of all exposed surfaces of a three-dimensional figure. The following are the three-dimensional figures we will use in this text.

Rectangular solid

$V = LWH$

$S = 2LW + 2WH + 2LH$

Cube

$V = s^3$

$S = 6s^2$

Right circular cylinder

$$V = \pi r^2 h$$
$$S = 2\pi r^2 + 2\pi r h$$

Sphere

$$V = \frac{4}{3}\pi r^3$$
$$S = 4\pi r^2$$

Right circular cone

$$V = \frac{1}{3}\pi r^2 h$$
$$S = \pi r \sqrt{r^2 + h^2} + \pi r^2$$

Right pyramid

$$V = \frac{1}{3}Bh \quad \text{where}$$

$B =$ area of the base

EXAMPLE 3   Find the volume of a sphere with a radius of 3.4 meters.

Solution

$$V = \frac{4}{3}\pi r^3 \qquad \text{Write the formula.}$$

$$V = \frac{4}{3}\pi (3.4)^3 \qquad \text{Substitute.}$$

$$V = \frac{4}{3}\pi (39.304) \qquad \text{Evaluate.}$$

$$V \approx 52.405\pi$$
$$V \approx 52.405(3.14) \qquad \text{Evaluate. \textit{Note:} } \pi \approx 3.14.$$
$$V \approx 164.553$$

The volume is approximately 164.553 cubic meters.

Use your calculator to find that the volume is approximately 164.636 cubic meters. The calculator value is more precise because the noncalculator value for π was rounded to only two decimal places. ∎

EXAMPLE 4 Find the surface area of a rectangular solid with dimensions 32 inches by 45 inches by 26 inches.

W = 45 in.

H = 26 in.

L = 32 in.

Figure 3.11

H = 45 in.

W = 32 in.

L = 26 in.

Figure 3.12

Solution

$$S = 2LW + 2WH + 2LH$$ Write the formula.
$$S = 2(32)(45) + 2(45)(26) + 2(32)(26)$$ Substitute.
$$S = 2880 + 2340 + 1664$$ Evaluate.
$$S = 6884$$

The surface area is 6884 square inches.

It does not matter which measurement we use for L, W, and H. For example, we could have viewed the rectangular solid in Figure 3.11 in a different orientation, as in Figure 3.12.

Now we can substitute 26 for L, 32 for W, and 45 for H. The surface area remains the same. (Try it for yourself.) ∎

 Experiencing Algebra the Checkup Way

1. Find the volume and surface area of a cube that measures 3.7 inches on a side.
2. Find the volume and surface area of a cylindrical can with a height of 4 inches and a radius of 2.5 inches. Round your answers to the nearest hundredth.
3. What is the difference between the surface area of a three-dimensional figure and its volume?

3 Evaluating Angle Formulas

An **angle** is a geometric figure formed by two line segments extending from a common point. An angle can be measured by a unit of measurement called a degree (°). One degree is $\frac{1}{360}$ of a complete circle.

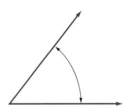

A **right angle** is an angle whose measure is 90°.

90°

If the sum of the measures of two angles is 90°, we say the angles are **complementary angles**.

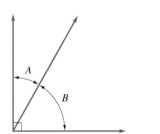

Complementary angles

$$A + B = 90°$$

or

$$A = 90° - B$$

If the sum of the measures of two angles is 180°, we say the angles are **supplementary angles**.

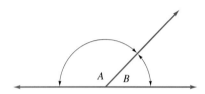

Supplementary angles

$$A + B = 180°$$

or

$$A = 180° - B$$

A triangle contains three angles. The sum of the measures of the three angles is 180°.

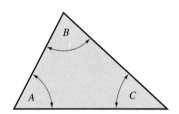

Sum of the angle measures in a triangle

$$A + B + C = 180°$$

or

$$A = 180° - (B + C)$$

EXAMPLE 5 Find the measure of the third angle in the following triangle.

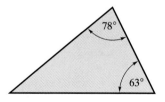

Solution

$$A = 180° - (B + C) \qquad \text{Write the formula.}$$
$$A = 180° - (63° + 78°) \qquad \text{Substitute.}$$
$$A = 180° - 141° \qquad \text{Evaluate.}$$
$$A = 39°$$

The third angle measures 39°. ∎

Experiencing Algebra the Checkup Way

1. One angle of a triangle measures 28 degrees and another angle measures 97 degrees. What is the measure of the third angle of the triangle?
2. Two angles are complementary. One angle measures 59 degrees. What is the measure of the other angle?
3. Explain the difference between complementary and supplementary angles.

4 Evaluating the Pythagorean Theorem

A special triangle that occurs frequently in all areas of mathematics is a triangle containing a right angle (one that measures 90°). Therefore, we call the triangle a **right triangle**. The side opposite the right angle is the **hypotenuse**. The other two sides are the **legs** of the right triangle.

The **Pythagorean theorem** states a relationship for the lengths of the legs and hypotenuse of a right triangle.

> *Pythagorean Theorem*
>
> $$c^2 = a^2 + b^2, \quad c = \text{length of hypotenuse}$$
> $$a = \text{length of first leg}$$
> $$b = \text{length of second leg}$$
>
> or
>
> $$c = \sqrt{a^2 + b^2}$$

The importance of the Pythagorean theorem lies in the fact that it applies to all right triangles, regardless of size and regardless of what acute angles are involved. Right triangles are extrememly common and important in all areas of mathematics, especially trigonometry and calculus. The Pythagorean theorem is a powerful tool in these cases; it helps us establish relationships among lengths that intersect each other at right angles, like the legs of a right triangle.

EXAMPLE 6

Find the length of the hypotenuse of a right triangle whose legs measure 12 cm and 10 cm.

Solution

$$c = \sqrt{a^2 + b^2} \qquad \text{Write the formula.}$$
$$= \sqrt{(12)^2 + (10)^2} \qquad \text{Substitute.}$$
$$= \sqrt{144 + 100} \qquad \text{Evaluate.}$$
$$= \sqrt{244}$$
$$\approx 15.62$$

The hypotenuse is $\sqrt{244}$ cm, or approximately 15.62 cm. ∎

Experiencing Algebra the Checkup Way

1. Find the length of the hypotenuse of a right triangle whose legs measure 15 cm and 8 cm.
2. What must be true about a triangle before you can apply the Pythagorean theorem to relate the lengths of its sides?

5 Modeling the Real World

Many objects in the real world are not perfect geometric shapes. For instance, the Earth is a little wider at the equator than it is through the North and South Poles, so it is not exactly a sphere. And most rooms in a house tend to be a little out of perfect alignment, and so are not exactly rectangular solids. But we can usually approximate real objects by geometrical shapes and use the formulas for volumes, areas, and perimeters introduced earlier in this section. The errors involved in these approximations are often small enough for us to ignore.

EXAMPLE 7

North Pole

Equator

South Pole

a. The equatorial diameter of the Earth is approximately 12,756.34 km. Determine its equatorial circumference (assuming the Earth is a sphere).
b. The polar diameter of the Earth is approximately 12,713.54 km. Determine its polar circumference.
c. What is the difference between the equatorial circumference and the polar circumference?
d. Although the difference in Example 7c seems large, it is not large in comparison to the size of the circumferences. Determine what percentage of the equatorial circumference is the difference.

Calculator Solution

a. The equatorial diameter:

$$C = \pi d$$

$$C \approx \pi(12,756.34)$$

$$C \approx 40,075.224$$

The equatorial circumference is approximately 40,075.224 km.

b. The polar diameter:

$$C = \pi d$$

$$C \approx \pi(12,713.54)$$

$$C \approx 39,940.764$$

The polar circumference is approximately 39,940.764 km.

c. The difference is $40{,}075.224 - 39{,}940.764 = 134.460$ km.
d. Let x = percentage

percentage	of	equatorial circumference	is	difference
x	$\cdot$	40,075.224	$=$	134.460
			$x =$	0.003355 or 0.34%

The difference is less than 1% of the equatorial circumference. Therefore, approximating the Earth as a sphere is a reasonable approximation for most purposes. A more accurate model would be necessary for calculating the orbit of a satellite. ∎

Application

Janice is painting a rectangular toy box with dimensions $3\frac{1}{2}$ feet by 2 feet by $1\frac{1}{2}$ feet. She needs to determine the outside surface area in order to know how much paint to buy. Determine the surface area of the toy box.

Discussion

$$S = 2LW + 2WH + 2LH$$ Write the formula.

$$S = 2\left(3\frac{1}{2}\right)(2) + 2(2)\left(1\frac{1}{2}\right) + 2\left(3\frac{1}{2}\right)\left(1\frac{1}{2}\right)$$ Substitute.

$$S = 14 + 6 + 10\frac{1}{2}$$ Evaluate.

$$S = 30\frac{1}{2}$$

Janice will need enough paint to cover $30\frac{1}{2}$ square feet.   ∎

Experiencing Algebra the Checkup Way

1. The equatorial diameter of the planet Mercury is approximately 4880 km. Determine the equatorial circumference of Mercury, assuming the planet is a sphere.

2. How many square inches of plywood are needed to make a packing crate measuring 20 inches by 14 inches by 12 inches, ignoring scrap?

PROBLEM SET 3.5

Experiencing Algebra the Exercise Way

Find the area and perimeter of each two-dimensional geometric figure.

1. A triangle has a base of 39 inches, a height of 24 inches, and sides of 40 inches and 25 inches.

2. A triangle has a height of 16 millimeters, a base of 75 millimeters, and sides of 20 and 65 millimeters.

3. A rectangle has a length of 6 centimeters and a width of 4 centimeters.

4. A rectangle's length is 8 feet and its width is 5 feet.

5. A square's sides each measures $2\frac{1}{2}$ feet.

6. A square has sides measuring 5.6 meters each.

7. A parallelogram has a base of 68 meters, a height of 45 meters, and a side of 53 meters.

8. The base of a parallelogram measures 95 inches, its height measures 39 inches, and its side measures 89 inches.

9. A trapezoid has a height of 8 feet, a small base measuring 2 feet and a large base measuring 23 feet. The other two sides measure 10 feet and 17 feet.

10. The height of a trapezoid is 24 centimeters, the small base measures 8 centimeters, the large base measures 47 centimeters, and the other two sides have lengths of 25 centimeters and 40 centimeters.

11. A circle has a radius of $5\frac{1}{4}$ inches. Round your answers to the nearest tenth.

12. The radius of a circle measures $2\frac{3}{4}$ feet. Round your answers to the nearest tenth.

Find the volume and surface area of each three-dimensional geometric solid.

13. A box has a length of 5 feet, a width of 3 feet, and a height of 1 foot.

14. A chest has a width of 4 feet, a length of 6 feet, and a height of 3 feet.

15. A cube has a side measuring 7.5 inches.

16. Each side of a cube measures 8.2 centimeters.

17. A right circular can has a height of 5 inches and a diameter of 3 inches. Round your answers to the nearest tenth.

18. A can of vegetable shortening has a height of 6 inches and a diameter of 5 inches. Round your answers to the nearest tenth.

19. A sphere has a diameter of 20 centimeters. Round your answers to the nearest whole number.

20. A ball has a radius of 5 inches. Round your answers to the nearest whole number.

21. A right cone has a height of 0.75 feet and a radius of 0.25 feet. Round your answers to the nearest thousandth.

22. A right cone's height measures 8 centimeters and its radius measures 2 centimeters. Round your answer to the nearest hundredth.

Find the volume of each pyramid.

23. A right pyramid has a height of 15 centimeters and a square base with each side measuring 8 centimeters.

24. The height of a right pyramid is 4 feet and its triangular base has a height of 2 feet and a base of 3 feet.

Find the required measure of each angle.

25. Two angles are complementary. One angle measures 65 degrees. Find the measure of the other angle.

26. An angle measures 71 degrees. What is its complement?

27. Two angles are supplementary. One angle measures 65 degrees. Find the measure of the other angle.

28. What is the supplement of an angle that measures 124 degrees?

29. Two angles of a triangle measure 33 degrees and 68 degrees. Find the measure of the other angle.

30. One angle of a triangle measures 47 degrees and another angle measures 88 degrees. What is the measure of the third angle?

Find the length of the hypotenuse of each right triangle.

31. The legs of a right triangle measure 40 inches and 42 inches.

32. One leg of a right triangle measures 16 meters and the other leg measures 30 meters.

33. The legs of a right triangle measure 6 centimeters and $2\frac{1}{2}$ centimeters.

34. The legs of a right triangle measure $\frac{7}{36}$ yards and $\frac{2}{3}$ yards.

35. The legs of a right triangle measure 4.81 millimeters and 6 millimeters.

36. One leg of a right triangle measures 6.37 meters and the other leg measures 11.16 meters.

Solve.

37. John wants to order outdoor carpeting to cover his patio, which has the shape of a trapezoid. The two bases measure 12 feet and 15 feet and the height measures 14 feet. How many square feet of space will he need to cover?

38. A corner of Ginger's yard is fenced in as a dog pen. The corner is shaped as a right triangle with legs of 9 feet and 12 feet. How many square feet of space are contained in the triangle? What is the perimeter of the triangle?

39. Gretchen made a square tablecloth measuring 52 inches on a side. What is the area of coverage? How much fringe material will she need for the perimeter?

40. Karen Ann made a circular tablecloth with a diameter of 8 feet. What is the area of the tablecloth? How much lace material will she need for the edging of the tablecloth?

41. Linda marked off a rectangular plot for a flower garden. The plot was 8.5 feet wide and 12 feet long. How many square feet of sod did she have removed to make the garden? She placed a border of landscaping bricks around the garden. How many linear feet did she need to order for the border?

42. Marcos built a square raised deck in his yard. The deck was 15 feet on a side. How many square feet of space did the deck contain? He wants to run latticework around the deck, leaving 4 feet along one side for stairs. How many feet of latticework will he need for this?

43. Linda decides to put a fountain opposite her flower garden. She has designed a circular area of greenery with the fountain in the center. The circular area has a radius of 5 feet. What is the square footage of this area? How many feet will the border be?

44. A wine cellar in the basement of Castle Mullaney has an odd shape, with the floor in the shape of a trapezoid. The front wall is the large base, measuring 16 feet. The back wall is the small base, measuring 12 feet. The distance between the two walls (the height of the trapezoid) measures 8 feet. What is the area of the floor of the wine cellar?

45. A lot in a subdivision has the shape of a parallelogram. The front side of the lot (the base) measures 220 feet and the perpendicular distance to the back (the height) measures 250 feet. What is the total square footage of the lot?

46. Rick wants to pour a concrete driveway that will be rectangular, with a length of 30 feet and a width of 12 feet. How many square feet of driveway will he have? How many feet of timber will he need to make the frame for pouring the driveway?

47. Jim built a toy box for his grandson. He made the box 4 feet long, 2 feet wide, and 2 feet high. How many cubic feet of toys will the box hold? Jim painted all six sides of the exterior with a high-gloss enamel. How many square feet of surface area did he paint? (He did not paint the interior, since he lined it with canvas.) If one pint of paint covers 20 square feet, how many pints of paint did Jim need for one coat?

48. A cheese ball has a diameter of 4 inches. How many cubic inches of cheese does the ball contain? The outside of the cheese ball is dusted with crushed pecans. How many square inches of pecans cover the cheese ball?

49. A cylindrical barrel is used to store waste oil collected at an express oil-service station. The barrel measures 4 feet high and has a radius of 1 foot. How many cubic feet of space does the barrel contain? If the side, bottom, and top are to be painted with a noncorrosive coating, how many square feet of surface area will need to be painted?

50. A cube of ice is to be carved into a swan. The cube measures 2.5 feet on a side. How many cubic feet of ice does it contain? What is the total surface area of the cube of ice?

51. Danny bought a spherical tank to store propane gas for his outdoor grill. The tank was listed as having a radius of 10 inches. How many cubic inches of propane gas will the tank hold? How many square inches of surface area does the tank have? Round your answers to the nearest tenth.

52. A packing crate is rectangular, with a width of 2 feet, a length of 4 feet, and a height of 2 feet. What is the volume of the crate? How many square feet of wood does the outer surface contain?

53. Tracy constructed a doll display case out of clear acrylic panes. She built it in the shape of a cube. If the case is 18 inches on a side, how many cubic inches of space does the case contain? How many square inches of acrylic does the surface of the cube measure?

54. The crystal base of a table lamp has the shape of a right circular cylinder, with a height of 20 inches and a radius of 4 inches. How many cubic inches of colored pellets will it take to fill the cylinder? What is the surface area of the base before any holes are made in it?

55. A paperweight is shaped as a right pyramid with a height of 7 inches and a square base measuring 3.5 inches on a side. What is the volume of the paperweight?

56. A cake-decorating kit has a squeeze bag in the shape of a right cone. The bag has a height of 9 inches and a radius of 3 inches. What is the volume of the bag?

57. Three holes will be bored into a steel plate. They form a triangle, with one angle measuring 30 degrees and another measuring 65 degrees. What is the measure of the third angle?

58. Three stakes in the ground mark off a triangular plot. One angle of the plot measures 55 degrees and another measures 65 degrees. What is the measure of the third angle?

59. The pitch of a roof measures the angle that the roof makes with a horizontal line. The angle that the roof makes with a vertical line is the complement of the pitch. What is the pitch of the roof if its complement measures 50 degrees?

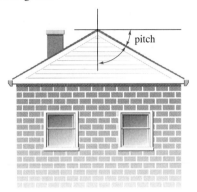

60. A ramp connects a loading dock to a driveway. The ramp forms a 70-degree angle with the vertical edge of the dock. The angle the ramp forms with the horizontal driveway is the complement of this angle. What is the measure of the angle formed with the horizontal driveway?

61. A guy wire forms two angles with the ground. The angles are supplementary. If one of the angles measures 45 degrees, what is the measure of the other angle?

62. An anchoring rope on a tent forms two supplementary angles with the ground. If one of the angles measures 60 degrees, what is the measure of the other angle?

63. The Pythagorean theorem is often used in construction to be sure a corner is square. What would the diagonal measurement have to be if the two sides of a corner measure 6 feet and 8 feet?

64. One side of a corner measures 5 feet. The other side of the corner measures 12 feet. What must the diagonal measure be in order for the corner to be a right angle?

Experiencing Algebra the Calculator Way

It is possible to write a calculator program to perform calculations for the geometric formulas. As an example, enter the following steps on your calculator. You will have created a program to calculate the area, circumference, and diameter of a circle when the radius is entered into the calculator.

| PRGM | ▶ | ▶ | ENTER | C | I | R | C | L | E | ENTER |

| PRGM | ▶ | 3 | 2nd | ALPHA | " | R | A | D | I | U | S | ? | " | ENTER |

| PRGM | ▶ | 1 | ALPHA | R | ENTER |

| 2nd | π | ALPHA | R | x² | STO▶ | ALPHA | A | ENTER |

| 2 | 2nd | π | ALPHA | R | STO▶ | ALPHA | C | ENTER |

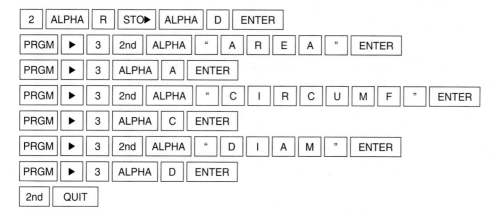

If you have entered the program correctly, you should see the displays shown in Figures 3.13a and 3.13b.

| Figure 3.13a | Figure 3.13b |

To run the program, perform the following steps:

Enter PRGM 1 , where "1" is the number of the program in your list.

Press ENTER , and the calculator will ask for a value for the radius.

Enter a value, then press ENTER .

The calculator will display the three measures.

To run the program for another value of the radius, press ENTER .

Then, repeat the preceding steps.

To quit, enter 2nd QUIT .

As a check, if you stored a value of 3 for the radius, the calculator should have displayed an area of 28.2743388, a circumference of 18.84955592, and a diameter of 6. You can use this program as a model to develop other programs for the various formulas presented in this section.

Experiencing Algebra the Group Way

According to the formula $C = \pi d$, the distance around a circle is equal to the product of its diameter and the real number π. The diameter is the distance across the circle in a straight line from one point on the circle through the center of the circle to a point on the opposite side of the circle. Test this out in your group by carrying out the following experiment.

1. Wrap a string around the top of a circular wastepaper can. Lay the string on a yardstick to see how long the distance is.

2. Place the string across the top of the wastepaper can through the center of its circle, marking the distance, and measure the string.

3. Check your formula to see whether the distance around is approximately equal to the product of π and the diameter.

Have each person in your group do the measurement and the calculation. Your answers will not agree exactly, since there will be some error in measurement. But they should be close to each other.

You could turn the expression around and say that π is the ratio of the circumference divided by the diameter. See how closely your measurements approximate π this way. You may want to average all of the group approximations of π to get a single estimate. Is it close to the calculator value for π? This is, in fact, the way many ancient cultures first estimated π. You can find other circular objects and repeat the experiment. You should always come up with values of π close to 3.14159....

To make the project even more interesting, have each member of the group bring a circular object into class (a can of fruit, an oatmeal box, a cup, a bucket, and so on) and repeat the experiment.

Experiencing Algebra the Write Way

In this section, you learned formulas that are used to measure various properties of two-dimensional and three-dimensional geometric shapes. Write a short definition of what is meant by two-dimensional and three-dimensional shapes. Discuss what can be measured for each, and illustrate your discussion with examples. Explain what distinguishes one from the other.

3.6 More Formulas

Objectives
1 Evaluate interest formulas.
2 Evaluate temperature conversion formulas.
3 Evaluate distance-traveled formulas.
4 Evaluate the vertical-position formula.
5 Evaluate the pendulum formula.
6 Evaluate formulas using real-world data.

Application

Roger plans to borrow $2347 for his freshman year expenses. The bank has a special compounded interest rate of $8\frac{1}{4}\%$ per year for school loans. Roger's uncle has offered to lend the same amount for 9% per year simple interest. Determine the best choice for Roger if he intends to pay off the loan after 4 years of college.

After completing this section, we will discuss this application further. See page 208.

Algebraic formulas are used to describe many relationships aside from the properties of geometric figures. In this section we briefly present some common and important formulas you are likely to see in a variety of applications.

1 Evaluating Interest Formulas

Interest, I, is the amount of money a lender charges for borrowing money. In order to determine the amount of interest, we need to know the **principal**, P, or amount borrowed, the **interest rate**, r, and the period of **time**, t, for which the loan is made.

Interest may be calculated by several different methods. **Simple interest** is interest based on the principal alone; that is, the amount borrowed. **Compound interest** is based on taking the interest accumulated in one time period and adding it to the principal for determining the interest in the next time period. **Continuously compounded interest** is the case of regular compound interest with very short periods, so that the addition of interest occurs on a continuous basis.

Simple interest (I)

$$I = Prt$$ P = principal, r = rate of interest, t = number of time periods

$$A = P + I$$ A = simple interest amount, P = principal, I = interest

Compounded amount (A)

$$A = P(1 + r)^t$$ P = principal, r = interest rate per time period, t = number of time periods

$$I = A - P$$ I = interest, A = compounded amount, P = principal

Continuously compounded amount (A)

$$A = Pe^{rt}$$ P = principal, r = annual interest rate compounded continuously, t = number of years, $e \approx 2.718$ (irrational number)

$$I = A - P$$ I = interest, A = continuously compounded amount, P = principal

EXAMPLE 1   Find the compounded amount for a principal of $1000 borrowed at a rate of $6\frac{1}{4}\%$ per year for 2 years.

Solution

$P = \$1000, r = 0.0625 \left(6\frac{1}{4}\%\right), t = 2$ years

$A = P(1 + r)^t$	Write the formula.
$A = 1000(1 + 0.0625)^2$	Substitute.
$A = 1000(1.0625)^2$	Evaluate.
$A \approx 1128.91$	

```
1000→P:.0625→R:2
→T:P(1+R)^T
        1128.90625
```

The compounded amount is approximately $1128.91. ∎

EXAMPLE 2   Find the continuously compounded amount for a principal of $1000 borrowed at a rate of $6\frac{1}{4}\%$ per year for 2 years.

Solution

$P = \$1000, e \approx 2.718, r = 0.0625 \left(6\frac{1}{4}\%\right), t = 2$ years

$A = Pe^{rt}$	Write the formula.
$A \approx (1000)(2.718)^{(0.0625)2}$	Substitute.
$A \approx 1133.13$	Evaluate.

The continuously compounded amount is approximately $1133.13.

The calculator has a key for the irrational number e. When we use the calculator value, our answer will be slightly different. Remember, this was also the case when we used the calculator value for π. The continuously compounded amount is approximately $1133.15. ∎

```
1000→P:.0625→R:2
→N:Pe^(NR)
        1133.148453
```

Experiencing Algebra the Checkup Way

1. Find the simple interest on a loan of $10,000 at a rate of interest of 8.5% per year for 2 years.
2. Find the continuously compounded amount of a loan of $10,000 at a rate of interest of 8.5% for 2 years. Find the interest on this continuously compounded loan.

---

2 Evaluating Temperature Conversion Formulas

Two of the most common scales used to measure temperature are the Celsius (C) and Fahrenheit (F) scales. These two scales are defined by assigning 0 degrees Celsius (0°) or 32 degrees Fahrenheit (32°) to the freezing point of water, and 100°C or 212°F to the boiling point of water.

Sometimes it is useful to convert temperatures measured on one scale to the other scale. The following formulas enable us to do this.

Celsius to Fahrenheit   Fahrenheit to Celsius

$$F = \frac{9}{5}C + 32 \qquad\qquad C = \frac{5}{9}(F - 32)$$

EXAMPLE 3 The average human body temperature is 98.6°F. Convert this to a Celsius temperature.

Solution

$$C = \frac{5}{9}(F - 32) \qquad \text{Write the formula.}$$

$$C = \frac{5}{9}(98.6 - 32) \qquad \text{Substitute.}$$

$$C = 37 \qquad\qquad\qquad \text{Evaluate.}$$

The average human body temperature is 37°C. ∎

Experiencing Algebra the Checkup Way

1. Scientists believe the temperature at the center of the Earth's core could be 7200°F. Convert this to a Celsius temperature.
2. When the astronauts landed on the Moon, they found a world that was airless, waterless, and devoid of life. Temperatures there range from up to 134°C on the bright side of the moon to −170°C on the dark side. Convert these to Fahrenheit temperatures.

3 Evaluating Distance-Traveled Formulas

Another formula we will use often allows us to find the distance traveled, d, if we are given the rate (speed), r, and time traveled, t.

Distance traveled (d)

$$d = rt \quad r = \text{rate (speed)}, t = \text{time traveled}$$

Two related formulas are $r = \frac{d}{t}$ and $t = \frac{d}{r}$.

EXAMPLE 4   Find the distance you travel after $2\frac{1}{2}$ hours on an interstate highway with the cruise control of your Jaguar XJE set at 65 miles per hour.

Solution

$$d = rt \qquad \text{Write the formula.}$$

$$d = (65)\left(2\frac{1}{2}\right) \qquad \text{Substitute.}$$

$$d = 162\frac{1}{2} \qquad \text{Evaluate.}$$

You traveled $162\frac{1}{2}$ miles on the interstate. ∎

Experiencing Algebra the Checkup Way

Find the distance traveled if Charlotte drives at an average rate of 50 miles per hour for $3\frac{1}{2}$ hours.

4 Evaluating the Vertical-Position Formula

The vertical-position formula is used to find the height in feet, s, of an object that is dropped or projected upward into the air after time in seconds, t, when the initial velocity in feet per second, v_0, and initial height in feet, s_0, are known.

Position in feet above ground level (s)

$$s = -16t^2 + v_0 t + s_0$$

t = time in seconds

v_0 = initial velocity in feet per second

s_0 = initial position in feet above ground level

Helping Hand This formula must only be used with the measurements of height in feet, time in seconds, and velocity in feet per second. A different formula is needed for other units of measurement.

EXAMPLE 5   Find the position after 2 seconds of a water balloon dropped from a hotel window 100 feet high.

Solution

$$s = -16t^2 + v_0 t + s_0 \qquad \text{Write the formula.}$$
$$s = -16(2)^2 + 0(2) + 100 \qquad \text{Substitute. } v_0 = 0 \text{ because the object was}$$
$$s = 36 \qquad \qquad \text{dropped.}$$

The water balloon was 36 feet above the ground after 2 seconds. ∎

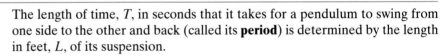

Experiencing Algebra the Checkup Way

Find the height of an apple 5 seconds after it is hurled upward at a speed of 10 feet per second from the top of a 500-foot tower.

---

5 Evaluating the Pendulum Formula

The length of time, T, in seconds that it takes for a pendulum to swing from one side to the other and back (called its **period**) is determined by the length in feet, L, of its suspension.

Pendulum formula

$$T = 2\pi \sqrt{\dfrac{L}{32}} \qquad T = \text{time of period, } L = \text{length in feet of suspension}$$

Helping Hand This formula must only be used with the measurements of length in feet and time in seconds. A different formula is needed for other units of measurement.

EXAMPLE 6   Find the time in seconds that is required for a pendulum in a grandfather clock to swing back and forth if it is suspended 3.25 feet.

Solution

Because of the mathematical constant π and the square root, this calculation is best performed using your calculator.

```
3.25→L:2π√(L/32)
        2.002380281
```

$$T = 2\pi \sqrt{\dfrac{L}{32}} \qquad \text{Write the formula.}$$

$$T = 2\pi \sqrt{\dfrac{3.25}{32}} \qquad \text{Substitute.}$$

$$T \approx 2.002 \qquad \text{Evaluate.}$$

The time required to swing back and forth is approximately 2.002 seconds. ∎

Experiencing Algebra the Checkup Way

Find the time of the period of a pendulum if it is suspended 6.5 feet. (Note that this is twice the length of the pendulum in Example 6, but the time is not twice the time.)

6   Modeling the Real World

The formulas presented in this section are common in many different situations. Sometimes we can simplify complicated situations by modeling them as pendulums or as vertically falling objects and then using these formulas. Remember to be careful about what system of units you are using and then carry out the same operations on the units as you do on the variables.

EXAMPLE 7

a. Fossils of *Tyrannosaurus rex* show its leg length to be about 10 feet. Determine the length of time in seconds during which the leg completed one back-and-forth swing—that is, one stride of the leg.
b. The fossil record also shows that the distance between *Tyrannosaurus rex* footprints of the same leg is about 13 feet. Determine the dinosaur's walking speed.

Solution

a. We will model the leg motion as a pendulum with $L = 10$ feet.

$$T = 2\pi\sqrt{\frac{L}{32}} \qquad \text{Write the formula.}$$

$$T = 2\pi\sqrt{\frac{10}{32}} \qquad \text{Substitute.}$$

$$T \approx 3.512 \text{ seconds}$$

The *Tyrannosaurus rex* completed one stride in approximately 3.512 seconds. Note that the leg was not a true pendulum because the dinosaur could have swung it faster or slower due to its own effort.

b. Use the formula for rate, r, listed as related to the distance-traveled formula.

$$r = \frac{d}{t}$$ Write the formula.

$$r = \frac{13}{3.512}$$ Substitute.

$$r = 3.702 \text{ feet per second}$$ Evaluate.

The *Tyrannosaurus rex*'s walking speed was approximately 3.702 feet per second. ∎

Application

Roger plans to borrow $2347 for his freshman year expenses. The bank has a special compounded interest rate of $8\frac{1}{4}\%$ per year for school loans. Roger's uncle has offered to lend the same amount for 9% per year simple interest. Determine the best choice for Roger if he intends to pay off his loan after 4 years of college.

Discussion

Compounded amount

$$A = P(1 + r)^t$$
$$A = 2347(1 + 0.0825)^4$$
$$A \approx 3222.74$$

Simple interest amount

$$I = Prt$$
$$I = (2347)(0.09)(4)$$
$$I = 844.92$$

$$A = P + I$$
$$A = 2347 + 844.92$$
$$A = 3191.92$$

```
2347→P:.0825→R:4
→T:P(1+R)^T
          3222.735846
```

```
2347→P:.09→R:4→T
:PRT
               844.92
2347+844.92
             3191.92
```

Roger would pay the bank $3222.74 and his uncle $3192.92.
Roger's best choice would be his uncle's offer of 9% simple interest. ∎

✓ Experiencing Algebra the Checkup Way

1. The distance from Steve's heel to his hip is about 3 feet. Determine the length of time in seconds during which his leg does one back-and-forth swing, or one stride. The distance between footprints of Steve's same leg is about 6 feet. Determine his walking speed. How does this speed compare with the *Tyrannosaurus rex*'s speed in Example 7?

2. Pete has three choices for a college loan. He can borrow $2000 at 10% simple interest for 2 years, payable at the end of the 2 years. Alternatively, he can borrow $2000 at 9.5% interest, compounded annually, payable at the end of 2 years. His third option is to borrow $2000 at 0.75% interest, compounded monthly, payable at the end of 2 years. Which of the three options should Pete choose?

PROBLEM SET 3.6

Experiencing Algebra the Exercise Way

1. JoAnne borrowed $2500 for 1 year at 6.5% simple interest to buy a laptop computer. How much interest did she pay?

2. Jack borrowed $5500 for 1 year at 7% simple interest to buy a used pickup truck. Find the interest on the loan.

3. JoAnne could have borrowed $2500 for 1 year at 0.6% per month, compounded monthly. Was this a better deal than paying simple interest for one year at 6.5%, as in exercise 1?

4. Jack considered borrowing $5500 for 1 year at 0.6% per month, compounded monthly. Was this a better deal than paying 7% simple interest for one year, as in exercise 2?

5. JoAnne could have borrowed $2500 for 1 year at 6.5% continuously compounded interest. Of the three options described in exercises 1, 3, and 5, which was the best choice for JoAnne?

6. Jack could have borrowed $5500 for 1 year at 6.6% continuously compounded interest. Which of the three options described in exercises 2, 4, and 6 is best for Jack?

7. How much simple interest is earned on $500 at 7% annual interest rate for 1 month ($\frac{1}{12}$ of a year)?

8. What will be the simple interest and total amount of $100 invested at an 8% annual interest rate for 3 months ($\frac{1}{4}$ of a year)?

9. How much simple interest would be paid on a loan of $1200 at 8% annual interest rate for 6 months?

10. What is the simple interest on a loan of $2400 at a 12% annual interest rate for 6 months?

11. Steve invested $2000 at 9% for 2 years. Interest is compounded annually. How much interest did he earn?

12. Sharona invested $6000 at 8% for 3 years, with interest compounded annually. Find the interest she earned.

13. Chauncie invested $4000 at 7% interest for 5 years, with interest compounded annually. What was her interest?

14. Chelsea invested $1800 for 4 years with interest compounded annually at 6%. Find her interest.

15. Interest is sometimes compounded semi-annually. Thus, if the annual interest rate is 8%, the account earns 4% semiannually. What will the earnings be if $3000 is invested at 4% semiannually for $1\frac{1}{2}$ years (that is, for three time periods)?

16. Interest is sometimes compounded quarterly, so that an annual rate of 6% earns 1.5% quarterly. What will the earnings be if $2000 is invested at 1.5% quarterly for $3\frac{1}{2}$ years?

17. Interest is continuously compounded on an investment of $1800 at 5% for 2 years. What is the interest?

18. Interest is continuously compounded on an investment of $1400 at 7% for 4 years. Find the interest.

19. An investment of $3000 earns interest continuously at 6% per year. The investment is kept for $4\frac{1}{2}$ years. Calculate the interest.

20. Interest is continuously compounded at 8% per year. An investment of $5000 is kept for $6\frac{1}{2}$ years. What is the interest?

21. Weather station KLOW in Seattle reported a daily low temperature of 25°C. What is the corresponding Fahrenheit temperature?

22. Todd the Weather Guy reported a daily high temperature of 31°C in Atlanta. Convert to the corresponding Fahrenheit temperature.

23. Marti told her friend that the high temperature for the day in Miami was 92°F. Convert this to Celsius measure.

24. The weather channel reported that the low temperature for the day in Boston was 66°F. What was the corresponding Celsius temperature?

25. At sea level, the boiling point of water is 100°C. What is the corresponding Fahrenheit temperature?

26. The melting point of gold is 1063°C. Convert to Fahrenheit temperature.

27. In Denver, the boiling point of water is 95°C. Convert to Fahrenheit temperature.

28. The boiling point of gold is 2966°C. What is the corresponding Fahrenheit temperature?

29. The melting point of mercury is −37.97°F. What is the corresponding Celsius temperature?

30. The boiling point of mercury is 673.84°F. Convert to Celsius temperature.

31. The average high temperature in Rio de Janeiro in January is 84°F. What is the Celsius temperature?

32. The average low temperature in Rio de Janeiro in January is 73°F. Convert to Celsius temperature.

33. The drive from home to college took $9\frac{1}{2}$ hours at an average speed of 55 miles per hour. What was the distance covered?

34. The drive to the beach took 8.25 hours at an average speed of 62 miles per hour. How many miles was the trip?

35. In 1911, Ray Harroun won the first Indianapolis 500, with an average speed of 74.602 miles per hour, in 6 hours, 42 minutes, and 8 seconds. At this speed, how far did he drive in the first 3 hours of the race?

36. In 1995, Jacques Villeneuve won the Indianapolis 500, with an average speed of 153.616 miles per hour, in 3 hours, 15 minutes, and 18 seconds. At this speed, how far did he drive in the first 3 hours of the race?

37. What is the position of a custard pie 3 seconds after it is dropped from a height of 200 feet?

38. Find the position of a banana 5 seconds after it is dropped from the top of the Empire State Building, a height of 1250 feet.

39. What is the position of a baseball 3 seconds after it is hurled upward at a speed of 25 feet per second from a height of 200 feet?

40. Find the position of a firecracker 4 seconds after it is hurled upward at a speed of 40 feet per second from a height of 100 feet.

41. How long will it take a yo-yo that has unwound to swing back and forth if it is on a string that is 3 feet long?

42. If a fishing sinker is tied to a 4-foot-long string, how long will it take to swing back and forth?

43. What is the period of a pendulum that has a length of $2\frac{1}{4}$ feet?

44. A pendulum has a length of $3\frac{2}{3}$ feet. What is its period?

45. How many seconds is the period of a pendulum with a length of 0.75 feet?

46. What is the period of a pendulum with a length of 2.8 feet?

47. The distance between Eydie's heel and her hip is about 2.5 feet. Determine the number of seconds of her stride, the time it takes for a leg to do one back-and-forth swing. The distance between footprints of her same leg is about 4 feet. What is Eydie's walking speed?

48. Gargantua, the latest movie monster, has a leg length of about 25 feet. What is the time for him to take a stride? The distance between his running footprints for the same leg is about 60 feet. How fast is he running?

Experiencing Algebra the Calculator Way

Complete the table to show how much money is earned if $80,000 is invested and is continuously compounded at 8.5% per year in the given number of years.

Number of Years (*n*)	Amount Earned (*A*)	Interest = *A* − $80,000
5	$122,367	$42,367
10		
15		
20		
25		
30		

The results of this table should surprise you. In 30 years, an investment of $80,000 can grow to over a million dollars, if the investor can find an opportunity such as this one! Other investments in which you regularly add to your investment also have surprising results. The mathematics that models these situations is very useful, and many people have profited by understanding this.

Experiencing Algebra the Group Way

In probability and statistics, other important formulas occur that you can practice using. The formulas are significantly different from those you have seen so far, and it may be easier to practice with them in a group setting. Discuss the formulas in your group to make sure you understand what they require you to do operationally. Then work together to apply the formulas to the exercises listed below.

Permutations, *P*, count the number of different orderings possible when *r* objects are selected from a set of *n* objects. (Note that this count assumes the ordering of the objects **is** important.)

$$P = \frac{n!}{(n-r)!},$$

where *n*! means *factorial* and is defined as

$$n! = n(n-1)(n-2)(n-3)\cdots 3\cdot 2\cdot 1,$$

which means the product of *n* with all the positive integers less than *n*.

Combinations, *C*, count the number of different compositions possible when *r* objects are selected from a set of *n* objects. (Note that this count assumes that the ordering of the objects **is not** important.)

$$C = \frac{n!}{(n-r)!r!},$$

again involving factorial calculations.

Try using these formulas to solve the following exercises. To help with the calculations, try writing the factorial multiplications in expanded form, and then see which factors divide out.

1. Use the permutation formula to figure out in how many ways you can pick the top three finalists from a beauty pageant that has 10 contestants in it. *Note:* Order is important.

2. Use the combination formula to figure how many different ways you can order a pizza if you can choose any three toppings from a selection of eight toppings. *Note:* Order is not important.

3. How many different frozen yogurt parfaits are possible if you are allowed to choose any 3 toppings from an offering of 12 toppings?

4. A student must pick 4 courses out of a list of 12 required courses for registration. If the courses can be scheduled in any order, use the permutation formula to find out how many different possible schedules the student could construct.

5. Five boys in Tiffan's kindergarten class want to play the three wise men in the Christmas play. How many different ways can Tiffan select and assign the boys to the three roles in the play? (*Hint:* Is order important in this calculation?)

6. Kari must select 4 students out of her science class of 18 students to serve as lab assistants. How many different ways can she do this? (*Hint:* Is order important in this calculation?)

7. In her recipe box, Debra has 18 different recipes for *hors d'oeuvres*. She wants to serve 6 of these for a party. How many different ways can she select 6 recipes to serve? (*Hint:* Will the order of selection affect the calculation?)

8. In a class of 15 students, 3 students will be elected to serve as class president, vice president, and secretary. How many different ways can the slate of officers be formed? (*Note:* Order of selection is important. Can you explain why?)

Experiencing Algebra the Write Way

Many of the formulas presented in this section come from applications in finance or in the sciences. Try to find a reference for one of the sets of formulas in either a business textbook or a science textbook. When you find a reference, make a copy of the pages with the examples presented, and note the call number of the text. Then write a short description of what you have found, being sure to reference the text's title, authors, publisher, and call number. Assess whether or not the author presents the material in such a way as to be helpful or not. Would you recommend this reference to your classmates to help them better understand the application of the formulas? Attach the copy of the pages you are referencing to your writeup.

CHAPTER 3 | **Summary**

After completing this chapter, you should be able to define in your own words the following key terms and rules.

Terms
numeric expression
constant
variable
algebraic expression
substitute
evaluate
simplify
terms
numeric coefficient
like terms
collecting like terms
equation
solution
formula
perimeter

circumference
area
volume
surface area
angle
right angle
complementary angles
supplementary angles
right triangle
hypotenuse
legs
Pythagorean theorem
interest
principal
interest rate
time

simple interest
compounded interest
continuously compounded interest
period

Rules
Writing algebraic expressions
Evaluating algebraic expressions
Collecting like terms
Simplifying algebraic expressions
Determining whether a numeric
    equation is true
Determining a solution of an algebraic
    equation
Writing equations
Evaluating formulas

| CHAPTER 3 | Review |

Reflections

1. What does it mean to evaluate an algebraic expression? What does it mean to simplify an algebraic expression?
2. What are the terms of an algebraic expression? What are like terms in an algebraic expression?
3. What is the difference between an algebraic expression and an algebraic equation?
4. How do you know whether the given values for the variables in an algebraic equation represent a solution to the equation?
5. What are formulas and why do we use them?
6. What properties of two-dimensional figures are usually represented by formulas?
7. What properties of three-dimensional figures are usually represented by formulas?
8. For what do we use the Pythagorean theorem? Are there any limits to its use?
9. Explain the differences in the three types of interest: simple interest, compounded interest, and continuously compounded interest.

3.1

Translate each word expression into an algebraic expression.

1. 4 more than the product of a number and 55.
2. The product of 4 more than a number and 55.
3. Three-fourths of the sum of a number and 35.
4. The sum of three-fourths of a number and 35.
5. 20 less than twice a number.
6. 20 less twice a number.
7. The total cost of a car is the sum of the down payment of $2500 and the product of monthly payments of $275 for n months.
8. Pat's hourly rate of pay for a job is the quotient of his total earnings of $650 divided by the hours he worked, h.
9. A telephone salesperson is paid $200 per week plus $5.50 for every customer who purchases the product. What is the weekly pay if k customers agree to purchase?

Translate each algebraic expression into a word expression.

10. $5 + x$
11. $8 - 6n$
12. $9x \div 6$
13. $\frac{2}{3}(x - 75)$
14. $x^2 + y$
15. xyz

Evaluate $5x - 25$ for

16. $x = 8$
17. $x = -4.6$

Evaluate $\sqrt{6x + 10}$ for

18. $x = 9$
19. $x = -1$

Evaluate $\dfrac{12y - 84}{6y + 36}$ for

20. $y = 9$
21. $y = -6$

Evaluate $|2x^2 - 45x - 75|$ for

22. $x = 0.1$
23. $x = 10$

Evaluate exercises 24–26 for $x = -15$.

24. x^2 **25.** $-x^2$ **26.** $(-x)^2$

27. Sandi establishes a special savings account to save for a vacation. She deposits a bonus of $1200 she received, and then she saves $75 per month. Write an algebraic expression for her savings after a given number of months. Evaluate the expression for the savings available after 12 months. Will she have enough to pay for a Caribbean cruise package, which is $1995, all expenses paid?

3.2

Without simplifying the algebraic expressions, complete the tables.

Algebraic Expression	Number of Terms	Terms
28. $3x^2 - 16x + 35$		
29. $5x + 12 - 3y - 16$		
30. $2(x + 1) - 4(y + 2) - 4$		
31. $a^2 + 2ab + b^2$		

Algebraic Expression	Coefficients of Terms	Like Terms
32. $3x - 2y + 4x + 9y$		
33. $2a^2 - a + 3a^2 - 5a^3$		
34. $2.4x + 5.1 + 6.2x$		
35. $4(a + b) - 2(a + b) + 2a$		

Simplify.

36. $6c - 17c$

37. $2.4z + 1.7z - 3.9z$

38. $17x + 51 + 26x - 86 - 19x - 7$

39. $\frac{3}{4}x + \frac{5}{8}y - \frac{2}{3}x + \frac{1}{4}y$

40. $15x^2 - 14xy + 12y^2 - 23 + 42xy - 7y^2 + 21 - 6x^2$

41. $-(19p - 21)$

42. $4a + 6 - (a - 1)$

43. $(3a + 4b) - (-2a - 6b) + (a - b) - (-a + b)$

Write an expression for each situation. Then simplify and evaluate.

44. Lincoln School students are selling cans of salted peanuts and cans of bridge mix for a fundraiser. The peanuts cost $1.25 per can and the bridge mix costs $1.50 per can. The school will sell both for $2.75 per can. What is the net profit for selling a certain number of cans of peanuts and a different number of cans of bridge mix? Evaluate the net profit if the school sells 220 cans of peanuts and 480 cans of bridge mix.

45. At the Summer Olympics gift shop, Katie bought some commemorative pins for $5 each. The clerk added 6% sales tax to the cost. Katie paid with a $20 bill. If Katie bought a certain number of pins, what was her change? Determine Katie's change if she bought 3 pins.

46. Margaret buys unfinished frames, which she decorates and sells. She pays $3.25 for each frame. After she decorates them, she sells them at craft fairs for $12.00 each. She spends $52.65 for paint and lace to decorate the frames, which is enough for all the frames she can make and sell. Write an algebraic expression for her net profit, given that she can sell all the frames she makes. What will her net profit be if she makes and sells 32 frames?

3.3
Simplify exercises 47–59.

47. $14(5ab)$

48. $-2(-4.1m)$

49. $-2a(3.8a - 4.7b)$

50. $-\dfrac{5}{12}\left(\dfrac{6}{7}x - \dfrac{4}{15}y\right)$

51. $2x(3x - 17y)$

52. $\dfrac{-123m}{-3}$

53. $\dfrac{\frac{15}{16}z}{-5}$

54. $\dfrac{36.6ab}{2}$

55. $\dfrac{-308.88ab}{4b}$

56. $\dfrac{27a - 36b + 18c}{9}$

57. $12(7x + 9y) + 15(3x - 7y)$

58. $3\big[-2(x + 3y) - 5\big] - \big[3(2x + y) + 16\big]$

59. $\dfrac{25(2a - 6b) + 5(4b - 3c) + 75}{4a - 2(2a - 3) - 1}$

60. In gym class, Tom can do x pushups without stopping. His friend Charles can do 5 less than twice the number Tom can do. Jim can do 7 more than Tom can do. Write an algebraic expression for the number of pushups each can do. Then write an algebraic expression for the total number of pushups all three students can do. Simplify this expression. What is the total if Tom can do 45 pushups?

61. Drucilla and Esmeralda attended a mathematics conference. Drucilla rented a car at $45.00 per day and $0.20 per mile. Each woman received a daily allowance for lodging and meals of $125.00 and a miscellaneous spending allowance of $20.00 per day. Write an algebraic expression for the total cost of the trip. Simplify the expression. What is the cost of a trip that took 4 days if the distance covered was 345 miles?

3.4
Determine whether each item is an expression or an equation.

62. $2x + 7y - x$

63. $5x = 3y - x$

64. $\dfrac{1}{x + 2} = \dfrac{5}{2x - 1}$

65. $2.4a + 1.7 - 3.9 + 1.1a$

Determine whether each equation is true or false.

66. $17 - 3 \cdot 4 = 20 \cdot 2 - 6^2$

67. $2(3.5) - 3(0.7) = 2.5 + 2(1.2)$

68. $3 + 5(9 - 8) + 6 \cdot 5 = 4 + 6(12 - 8) + 45 \div 9 + 5$

69. $\dfrac{2}{3} + 5\left(\dfrac{1}{6} - \dfrac{2}{9}\right) = \dfrac{4}{9} - 3\left(\dfrac{2}{3} - \dfrac{17}{18}\right)$

Determine whether the given value is a solution of the equation.

70. $15y - 35 = 12$ for $y = 3$

71. $8a + 2(3a - 7) = 11a - 32$ for $a = -6$

72. $x^3 - 25x = 2x^2 - 3x - 35$ for $x = 5$

73. $2(x - 3.4) = x - 5$ for $x = 1.8$

74. $x - \dfrac{2}{3} = -\dfrac{1}{9}$ for $x = \dfrac{4}{9}$

Write an equation for each word statement.

75. The sum of 3 and twice the difference of 27 less 15 is equal to the cube of 3.

76. The sum of 5 and the product of 4 and a number is equivalent to the sum of 65 and the quotient of the number divided by 4.

3.5
Find the area and perimeter of each two-dimensional figure.

77. A triangle has a base of 26 m, a height of 16 m, and sides of 22 m and 20 m.

78. A rectangle has a width of 20 inches and a length of 44 inches.

79. A square measures 15 cm on a side.

80. A parallelogram has a base of 10.0 m, a height of 6.5 m, and a side of 7.0 m.

81. The height of a trapezoid is 70 yards, the small base is 110 yards, the large base 160 yards, and the other two sides measure 75 yards and 80 yards.

82. A circle has a radius of 12.2 feet.

In exercises 83–87, find the volume and surface area of each three-dimensional figure.

83. A box has a length of 35 inches, a width of 9 inches, and a height of 21 inches.

84. A cubical carton measures 14.6 cm on each side.

85. A right circular cylinder has a height of 54 inches and a radius of 18 inches.

86. A ball has a radius of 32.6 cm.

87. A right circular cone has a height of 7 cm and a radius of 4 cm.

88. A pyramid has a square base measuring 5 inches on a side and a height of 8 inches. Find its volume.

89. Two angles are supplementary. One angle measures 58 degrees. What is the measure of the other angle?

90. Two angles are complementary. One angle measures 58 degrees. What is the measure of the other angle?

91. One angle of a triangle measures 67 degrees. Another angle of the triangle measures 88 degrees. What is the measure of the third angle of the triangle?

92. A right triangle has legs measuring 20 inches and 21 inches. Find the length of the hypotenuse.

93. The legs of a right triangle measure 5.39 and 29.4 centimeters. What is the length of the hypotenuse?

94. Dan wants to purchase sod for his backyard. The yard is rectangular, with a width of 60 feet and a length of 85 feet. How much sod should he order? If he fences in the yard, how many linear feet of fencing should he order, if he plans a 3-foot gate and attaches the fence to the back of the house, which measures 35 feet across?

95. Amelia marks off a circular plot in the yard for a garden. The plot has a radius of 8 feet. In the center she places a circular tile on which a birdbath will sit. The tile has a diameter of 2 feet. How many square feet of the garden will there be for the flowers?

96. Big Ed's Pizza Shop offers 10-inch (diameter) pizzas for $6.75 or 14-inch pizzas for $13.50. Since two of the 10-inch pizzas cost as much as one 14-inch pizza, which is a better deal, two 10-inch pizzas or one 14-inch pizza?

97. A garden shop delivers a truckload of mulch. The bed of the truck measures 8 feet by 5 feet by 2 feet high. How many cubic feet of mulch will the truck hold?

98. What is the surface area of a spherical storage tank with a diameter of 6 feet?

99. In a right triangle, one angle is a 90-degree angle and the other two angles are complementary. If one of these angles measures 40 degrees, what is the measure of the other angle?

100. In squaring off the corners of a room, a builder notes that one wall of the room measures 18 feet long and the other wall measures 13.5 feet long. What must the diagonal measure in order for the corner to be square (that is, a 90-degree angle)?

3.6

101. Find the simple interest on a loan of $850 at 12.5% per year for one year. What is the total amount of the loan, including the interest?

102. Find the compound interest on an investment of $15,000, with an annual rate of interest of 8.5% for a period of 6 years. What is the amount of interest earned on this investment?

103. Find the continuously compounded amount of savings of $10,000 deposited for 12 years, with a continuously compounded interest rate of 5.5%. What is the amount of interest earned on this savings plan?

104. Convert 50°C to Fahrenheit temperature.

105. Convert 80°F to Celsius temperature.

106. LuAnn's automobile trip took $5\frac{3}{4}$ hours of driving time, with an average speed of travel of 62 miles per hour. What was the distance traveled?

107. What is the position after 3 seconds of a wedding bouquet dropped from a window 180 feet above the ground?

108. An arrow is shot upward from ground level with a velocity of 96 feet per second. What is the height of the arrow after 2 seconds? What is the height after 3 seconds? What is the height after 4 seconds? What is the height after 5 seconds?

109. What is the period of a pendulum that has a length of 6 feet?

110. If you had the choice to invest $1000 at 8% simple interest for 2 years, or at 7% interest compounded annually for 2 years, which would be the better investment?

CHAPTER 3   Mixed Review

Without simplifying the algebraic expressions, complete the tables.

Algebraic Expression	Number of Terms	Terms
1. $12x + y - z + 23$		
2. $3(a - 2) + 5(b - 4) + 75$		
3. $12 - 7x + 14x - 18 + x$		

Algebraic Expression	Coefficients of Terms	Like Terms
4. $x - 2y - 5 + 4x - y + 6$		
5. $b^2 + 2b - 3b^2 + 6b + b^3$		

Evaluate for $x = -18$.

6. $3x$ **7.** $-3x$ **8.** $-(-3x)$ **9.** $-(-(-3x))$

10. x^2 **11.** $-x^2$ **12.** $(-x)^2$ **13.** $-(-x)^2$

Evaluate $\sqrt{12y + 20}$ for

14. $y = 8$ **15.** $y = -\dfrac{1}{3}$ **16.** $y = -5$

Evaluate $\dfrac{7x + 84}{2x - 3}$ for

17. $x = -12$ **18.** $x = 3$ **19.** $x = 1.5$

Determine whether each equation is true or false.

20. $3 + 5 \cdot 12 = 7(3 + 6)$ **21.** $38 - 2 \cdot 11 = (1 + 3)^2$

22. $5.9 + 3.6(8.7 - 3.1) + 7(6.3) = 100 - 3(8.52) - 4.3$

23. $\dfrac{25 + 5(14 - 2 \cdot 9) - 33(85 - 5 \cdot 7)}{100 - 5 \cdot 13} = -5 \cdot 9 - 2(50 - 7^2)$

Determine whether the given value is a solution of the equation.

24. $3x - 7 = x + 1$ for $x = 4$

25. $5x + 17 = 10x + 5$ for $x = 3$

26. $3x + 17 = 2(x - 5)$ for $x = -27$

27. $2.1x - 1.9 = 0.6x - 4.6$ for $x = -1.8$

28. $\dfrac{3}{4}\left(x - \dfrac{8}{9}\right) = \dfrac{1}{2}\left(x + \dfrac{2}{3}\right)$ for $x = 5\dfrac{1}{3}$

29. $3x^2 - 6x - 10 = x^2 + x - 5$ for $x = -5$

Simplify.

30. $12h + 9h - 4h$

31. $6m + 22 - m - 12 + 3m$

32. $3x - 35 + 4y - 5x - 6y + 7x + 27 + 17y + 22x$

33. $3x^4 + 5x - 7x^2 + 12x^4 - 17x - 34x + x^3 - 1$

34. $(6.2a + 5.3b) + (4.7a - 1.9b)$

35. $-(27y - 15)$

36. $5g + 8 - (g + 4)$

37. $(-2x + 4y - 7z) - (-x + 6y + 8z)$

38. $-14x(3y)$

39. $\dfrac{15}{22}\left(\dfrac{11}{25}a + \dfrac{33}{50}b\right)$

40. $\dfrac{-115.388z}{-4.55}$

41. $\dfrac{104x - 156y + 221z}{13}$

42. $\dfrac{\dfrac{21}{25}uv}{-3u}$

43. $\dfrac{-18x + 24y - 36z}{-6}$

44. $4(3.9x - 11.1y) + 7(2.9x - 0.7y)$

45. $12\big[-3(2a - 5b) + 9\big] + 8\big[-9(a + 13) - 6(b - 12)\big]$

46. $\dfrac{14.4(2x + 5) - 21.6(5x - 2) + 7.2(x - 1)}{3x - 4(x + 8) + x + 34.4}$

In exercises 47–48, translate each word expression into an algebraic expression.

47. 2 times the sum of a number and 50, decreased by one-half of the number.

48. 11 more than one-fourth of a number.

49. Write an equation for the following word statement: The sum of the square of a number and twice the number is equal to the number increased by 306.

50. Lakeetha charges a flat fee of $225 plus an hourly fee of $45 for consulting services while writing computer programs for a hospital auditing system. Write an algebraic expression for the amount of money she will make for one of her consulting contracts. How much will she earn for this assignment if she spends 120 hours developing the program?

51. Carmen sets up a savings account with an initial deposit of $500. She has $145 direct-deposited to the account each week. She has the bank automatically deduct $15 per week from her savings account for a Christmas club account. Write an algebraic expression for the amount of money she has in the savings account after n weeks. How much money has been deposited into the checking account after 15 weeks? If she withdrew $625 during this period, what is the balance of her account?

52. In a sales competition, each salesperson receives a flat fee of $100 plus $25 for each appliance sold. Beatrice has sold x appliances. Marie sold 5 less than twice what Beatrice sold. Ann sold one-half of what Beatrice sold. Magdalene sold the same as Beatrice.

    a. Write algebraic expressions for the number of appliances sold by each salesperson.

    b. Then write algebraic expressions for the amount of money each salesperson earned during the competition.

    c. Now combine these to obtain one algebraic expression for the total amount of money earned by the women.

    d. Simplify this expression.

    e. What was the total money earned if Beatrice sold 20 appliances?

53. Fuad wants to buy sod to landscape the backyard. The sod is sold in 1-square-foot pieces. He measures his yard and finds that it is in the shape of a trapezoid, with the short base measuring 120 feet and the long base measuring 200 feet. The depth of the yard between the two bases (that is, the height of the trapezoid) measures 100 feet. How many square feet of sod must he order?

54. Chum bought a circular aboveground swimming pool for his backyard. The pool has a radius of 10 feet. If he fills the pool to a depth of 4.5 feet, how many cubic feet of water will the pool hold?

55. If the temperature reads 96°F, what is the Celsius reading?

56. How much money will you have if you invest $18,500 at an interest rate of 5.5% compounded annually over a period of 10 years?

57. What is the distance traveled if Randy bicycled for 1.25 hours at an average speed of 13 miles per hour?

58. The legs of a right triangle measure 95 millimeters and 168 millimeters. What is the length of the hypotenuse?

59. Find the volume and surface area of a circular tuna fish can that has a height of 1.5 inches and a radius of 1.625 inches.

60. From a height of 6 feet, a tennis ball is shot upward with an initial velocity of 80 feet per second. What is the position of the ball 1 second later; 2 seconds later; 3 seconds later; 4 seconds later; 5 seconds later?

Translate each algebraic expression into a word expression.

61. $\frac{2}{3}x + 25$ **62.** $7(n - 45) + 15$

In exercises 63–66, determine whether each item is an equation or an expression.

63. $6x + 3 = 2(x - 5)$ **64.** $6x + 3 - 2(x - 5)$

65. $\dfrac{5}{2x - 1} + \dfrac{7}{x + 2}$ **66.** $2.4x - 1.8 = 4.9 - 1.7x$

67. What is the measure of the complementary angle of an angle that measures 85 degrees?

68. An angle measures 43 degrees. What is the measure of its supplementary angle?

69. Find the measure of the third angle of a triangle if the other two angles measure 31 degrees and 58 degrees.

CHAPTER 3 | **Test**

Test-Taking Tips

When you take a test, start out by first reading the instructions. Many students don't do this, and after working on a test for a while, find that they have not done what was asked for on the test. It is also good advice not to do more than has been asked. When you go beyond the instructions, you waste valuable time. You also open yourself up to make more mistakes, and the grader may deduct points for erroneous results, even though they were not required.

In exercises 1 and 2, translate each word expression into an algebraic expression.

1. The quotient of a number divided by 12.

2. The quotient of 12 divided by a number.

3. Write an algebraic expression for the total cost of a purchase when 8% sales tax is added to the selling price of x dollars. What will the total cost be if the selling price is $15.00?

4. Translate the algebraic expression $a^2 - b$ into a word expression.

Evaluate each algebraic expression for the given value.

5. $\sqrt{4x^2 - 20x + 25}$ for $x = 2$

6. $\dfrac{-18x + 54}{x - 8}$ for $x = -1$

Evaluate for $x = -6$.

7. x^2

8. $-x^2$

9. $(-x)^2$

Without simplifying, consider the algebraic expression

$$y^3 - 5y^2 + 15y - 3 + 7y^2 - 12 + 4y + 6y^3$$

10. How many terms are in the expression?

11. List the variable terms.

12. List the constant terms.

13. List the coefficients of the terms.

14. List the like terms.

Simplify exercises 15–18.

15. $\dfrac{2}{3}x + \dfrac{5}{6}y - \dfrac{8}{9} + \dfrac{1}{6}x + \dfrac{7}{9}y + \dfrac{1}{3}$

16. $-(5p + 2q) - (-9p + q) + (p + q) - (-p - q)$

17. $\dfrac{25x - 45}{-5}$

18. $2a(3a + 6b - 8c)$

In exercises 19 and 20, determine if the given value is a solution of the equation.

19. $-7x - 4 = 6x + 9$ for $x = -2$

20. $8x^2 + 40x + 45 = 2x^2 - 2x - 27$ for $x = -4$

21. Orhan builds a tool box that is 4 feet long, 2 feet wide, and 1.5 feet high. What is the volume of the box? What is the outside surface area?

22. If Tracy makes a single deposit of $2000 into an IRA account that continuously compounds interest at 5.5% annually, how much will the account contain in 40 years?

23. What does the supplementary angle of a 78-degree angle measure?

24. Find the hypotenuse of a right triangle whose legs measure 20 and 48 inches.

25. What is the Fahrenheit temperature if the Celsius temperature is 25°C?

26. Explain the difference between the area and the perimeter of a two-dimensional figure.

Relations, Functions, and Graphs

4

In Chapter 3, we saw that giving a value to one or two variables in an algebraic expression or equation usually determines the value of other variables. For example, if we know the values of the length and width of a rectangle, then we can find its area. There is a relationship among these variables that is expressed in the equation. That is, changing the value of one variable in an equation, such as length, might change the value of another variable, such as width or area, required for the equation to remain true.

In this chapter, we will examine the different kinds of relationships among variables in algebraic equations. We will see that this examination often tells us more information than we can get by simply evaluating expressions. To help us visualize these kinds of relationships, we will introduce the concept of the graph of an equation, and show how it translates an algebraic equation into a picture we can see.

As usual, we will present several types of real-world situations that illustrate the ideas in the chapter. One application is the relationship between the weight of a first-class letter and the cost to mail it in the United States. In early 1998, a letter weighing 1 ounce or less cost $0.32 to be delivered. The U.S. Postal Service charged an additional $0.23 for each additional ounce or part of an ounce, up to 11 ounces. We will study several different ways to describe this relationship between weight and cost as well as other relationships that involve the U.S. Postal Service, by using tables, equations, and graphs.

4.1 Tables of Values, Ordered Pairs, and Relations

Objectives
1 Create tables of values for given data.
2 Write ordered pairs for given data.
3 Identify the domain and range of a relation.
4 Create tables of values for real-world data.

Application

In early 1998, a letter mailed first-class cost $0.32 for the first ounce and $0.23 for each additional ounce or part of an ounce. Complete a table of values used by a postal clerk.

Weight	Cost
≤ 1 oz	
≤ 2 oz	
≤ 3 oz	
≤ 4 oz	
≤ 5 oz	
≤ 6 oz	
≤ 7 oz	
≤ 8 oz	
≤ 9 oz	
≤ 10 oz	
≤ 11 oz	

After completing this section, we will discuss this application further. See page 231.

1 Creating Tables of Values

Sometimes we need to evaluate a formula or equation more than once. It is often convenient to organize this information in a table of values. A **table of values** is a table with at least two columns. One column lists the values substituted for the variable. A second column lists the values obtained for the unknown variable when the formula is evaluated. For example, suppose a biologist needs to convert Celsius temperatures into Fahrenheit temperatures. Instead of using the conversion formula each time, she decides to make a reference table of all temperatures she is using. A portion of this table will look like the following:

Celsius Temperature (°C)	Fahrenheit Temperature (°F)
20	68
21	69.8
22	71.6
23	73.4

To complete the next three entries in the table, we will extend the table to include a third column (to show our work). The first column is labeled with the independent variable. The **independent variable** is the variable for which we are substituting values. The second column is labeled with the formula or equation we are evaluating. The third column is labeled with the dependent variable. The **dependent variable** is the variable that is determined by the substitution. We refer to the information in the table as **data**.

To construct a table of values, set up a three-column table.

- The first column is labeled with the independent variable.
- The second column is labeled with the formula or equation needed to find the unknown variable.
- The third column is labeled with the dependent variable.

Complete the table.

- Enter a number in the first column.
- Substitute this value in the formula or equation in the second column and evaluate the results.
- Enter the results in the third column.

For example, complete the next three entries in the Celsius-to-Fahrenheit temperature table.

°C	$F = \dfrac{9}{5}C + 32$	°F
24	$F = \dfrac{9}{5}(24) + 32$ $F = 75.2$	75.2
25	$F = \dfrac{9}{5}(25) + 32$ $F = 77$	77
26	$F = \dfrac{9}{5}(26) + 32$ $F = 78.8$	78.8

You can also construct a table of values using your calculator. To construct a table of values on a calculator:

- Rename the independent variable as x and the dependent variable as y.
- Enter the formula or equation in the first y.

Set the calculator to generate the table.

- Set up a minimum value and increments.
- Set the size of increments being added to the minimum number.
- Set the calculator to perform the evaluations automatically.

View the table.

An alternative method is to set up the calculator to ask for the *x*-values.

- Ignore the minimum value and increments.
- Set the calculator to ask for the *x*-values.
- Set the calculator to perform the evaluations automatically.

View the table.

- Enter values for *x*.

For example, complete the next three entries in the Celsius-to-Fahrenheit temperature table using your calculator.

Given $F = \frac{9}{5}C + 32$, rewrite as $y = \frac{9}{5}x + 32$ (*x* replaces *C* and *y* replaces *F*).

TECHNOLOGY

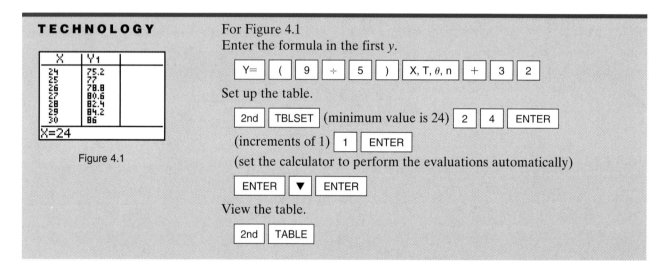

Figure 4.1

For Figure 4.1
Enter the formula in the first *y*.

| Y= | (| 9 | ÷ | 5 |) | X, T, θ, n | + | 3 | 2 |

Set up the table.

| 2nd | TBLSET | (minimum value is 24) | 2 | 4 | ENTER |

(increments of 1) | 1 | ENTER |

(set the calculator to perform the evaluations automatically)

| ENTER | ▼ | ENTER |

View the table.

| 2nd | TABLE |

EXAMPLE 1 **a.** Complete the following table.

°C	$F = \dfrac{9}{5}C + 32$	°F
−30		
−20		
−10		
0		
10		
20		
30		

b. Construct a table of values for the circumference of a circle, given {5, 10, 15, 20, 25} as the set of values for the diameter, *d*.
c. Construct a table of values for $y = 3x$, given {0, 5, 7} as the set of values for *x*.

Solution

a.

°C	$F = \dfrac{9}{5}C + 32$	°F
-30	$F = \dfrac{9}{5}(-30) + 32$ $F = -22$	-22
-20	$F = \dfrac{9}{5}(-20) + 32$ $F = -4$	-4
-10	$F = \dfrac{9}{5}(-10) + 32$ $F = 14$	14
0	$F = \dfrac{9}{5}(0) + 32$ $F = 32$	32
10	$F = \dfrac{9}{5}(10) + 32$ $F = 50$	50
20	$F = \dfrac{9}{5}(20) + 32$ $F = 68$	68
30	$F = \dfrac{9}{5}(30) + 32$ $F = 86$	86

b.

d	$C = \pi d$	C
5	$C = \pi(5)$ $C \approx 15.708$	15.708
10	$C = \pi(10)$ $C \approx 31.416$	31.416
15	$C = \pi(15)$ $C \approx 47.124$	47.124
20	$C = \pi(20)$ $C \approx 62.832$	62.832
25	$C = \pi(25)$ $C \approx 78.54$	78.54

c.

x	$y = 3x$	y
0	$y = 3(0)$ $y = 0$	0
5	$y = 3(5)$ $y = 15$	15
7	$y = 3(7)$ $y = 21$	21

Use your calculator to check your tables.

a. $F = \dfrac{9}{5}C + 32$ **b.** $C = \pi d$ **c.** $y = 3x$

$y = \dfrac{9}{5}x + 32$ $y = \pi x$ ∎

TECHNOLOGY

Figure 4.2a

Figure 4.2b

Figure 4.2c

For Figure 4.2a
Enter the formula.

Y= (9 ÷ 5) X, T, θ, n + 3 2

Set up the table (minimum value −30 and increments of 10)

2nd TBLSET (−) 3 0 ENTER 1 0 ENTER ENTER ▼ ENTER

View the table.

2nd TABLE

For Figure 4.2b
Enter the formula.

Y= 2nd π X, T, θ, n

Set up the table (minimum value 5 and increments of 5)

2nd TBLSET 5 ENTER 5 ENTER ENTER ▼ ENTER

View the table.

2nd TABLE

For Figure 4.2c
Use the ask mode.

Y= 3 X, T, θ, n 2nd TBLSET ▼ ▼ ▶ ENTER ▼ ENTER 2nd TABLE

0 ENTER 5 ENTER 7 ENTER

Experiencing Algebra the Checkup Way

In exercises 1–2, construct a table of values for each equation and check your results on your calculator.

1. Calculate Celsius temperatures for Fahrenheit temperatures, using the formula $C = \frac{5}{9}(F - 32)$, given {86, 77, 68, 59, 50, 41, 32} as the set of values for F.

2. Calculate the compounded amount A for an investment of $5000 at an interest rate of 1.25% per quarter, $A = 5000(1.0125)^t$, given {4, 8, 12, 16, 20} for the number of quarters, t.

3. Construct a table of values of $a = -6b + 7$, given {−3, −2, −1, 0, 1, 2, 3} as the set of values for b.

4. What is a table of values and how can it help you when working with an equation or formula?

---

2 Writing Ordered Pairs Another way to organize the data contained in an equation is to write ordered pairs. An **ordered pair** consists of two numbers in parentheses, separated by a comma. The first number in the ordered pair is the value of the independent variable. The second number in the ordered pair is the value of the dependent variable. The order of the numbers is very important.

For example, the previous temperature conversion table yields the following ordered pairs:

°C	°F	(C, F)
20	68	(20, 68)
21	69.8	(21, 69.8)
22	71.6	(22, 71.6)
23	73.4	(23, 73.4)

Ordered pairs are a common and useful way of organizing data for the purpose of graphing an equation, as we will see in section 4.2.

EXAMPLE 2 Write ordered pairs for the data found in Example 1.

Solution

a. $(-30, -22), (-20, -4), (-10, 14), (0, 32), (10, 50), (20, 68), (30, 86)$

b. $(5, 15.708), (10, 31.416), (15, 47.124), (20, 62.832), (25, 78.54)$

c. $(0, 0), (5, 15), (7, 21)$ ■

Experiencing Algebra the Checkup Way

1. Write ordered pairs for the data found in exercises 1–3 of the previous "Experiencing Algebra the Checkup Way."

2. When writing an ordered pair for a set of data, why is the order of the numbers important?

3 Identifying the Domain and Range of a Relation

A set of ordered pairs is a **relation**. For example:

The set T of ordered pairs the biologist used for temperature conversion

$$T = \{(20, 68), (21, 69.8), (22, 71.6), (23, 73.4)\}$$

is a relation.

The list of ordered pairs in a relation can be a finite or infinite list. A **finite** list has a definite number of ordered pairs. An example of a finite list of ordered pairs is

$$A = \{(1, 1), (1, 2), (1, 3)\}.$$

An **infinite** list does not have a definite number of ordered pairs. An example of an infinite list of ordered pairs is

$$B = \{\dots, (-2, -1), (-1, 0), (0, 1), (1, 2), (2, 3), \dots\}.$$

A relation can also be written as an equation with two variables. We can use the equation to determine the ordered pairs by substituting into the equation a value for the independent variable and determining a value for the dependent variable. An equation can also represent a finite set of ordered pairs or an infinite set of ordered pairs. For example:

$y = 2x$ for $x = \{1, 2, 3\}$ is a relation of a finite set of ordered pairs, $\{(1, 2), (2, 4), (3, 6)\}$.

$y = 3x + 5$ is a relation of an infinite set of ordered pairs. We are not given a set of values for the independent variable x. Therefore, we can replace x with any number that will result in a real-number value for the dependent variable y.

Some examples of the ordered pairs for $y = 3x + 5$ are $(1, 8)$, $\left(\frac{2}{3}, 7\right)$, and $(-3.5, -5.5)$. Since we can choose any real-number value for x, we cannot describe any pattern of ordered pairs, and cannot indicate the relation by an infinite list of ordered pairs. In this case, the equation is more convenient than a list of ordered pairs to describe the relation.

The set of all possible values for the independent variable is called the **domain** of the relation. The set of all possible values for the dependent variable is called the **range** of the relation. For example, using the previous relations,

$$T = \{(20, 68), (21, 69.8), (22, 71.6), (23, 73.4)\}$$

Domain 20   21   22   23
Range   68   69.8   71.6   73.4

The domain is $\{20, 21, 22, 23\}$.
The range is $\{68, 69.8, 71.6, 73.4\}$.

$A = \{(1, 1), (1, 2), (1, 3)\}$
The domain is $\{1\}$.
The range is $\{1, 2, 3\}$.

$B = \{ \dots, (-2, -1), (-1, 0), (0, 1), (1, 2), (2, 3), \dots \}$
The domain is $\{ \dots, -2, -1, 0, 1, 2, \dots \}$ or all integers.
The range is $\{ \dots, -1, 0, 1, 2, 3, \dots \}$ or all integers.

$y = 2x$ for $x = \{1, 2, 3\}$
The domain is $\{1, 2, 3\}$.
The range is $\{2, 4, 6\}$.

$y = 3x + 5$
The values for replacing x are not restricted. The domain is the set of all real numbers.
When x is replaced by a real number, the result is a real number. The range is the set of all real numbers.

EXAMPLE 3   Determine the domain and range for the following relations, assuming that x is the independent variable and y is the dependent variable.

a. $\{(1, 3), (2, 5), (6, 5)\}$ **b.** $\{(1, 2), (2, 2), (3, 2), \dots \}$

c. $y = 3x + 2$ **d.** $y = \sqrt{x - 4}$

e. $y = \dfrac{3}{x}$

f. $C = 2\pi r$, where the dependent variable, C, is the circumference of a circle and the independent variable, r, is the radius.

Solution

a. domain $\{1, 2, 6\}$
   range $\{3, 5\}$ There is no need to write more than one 5.

b. domain $\{1, 2, 3, \dots\}$ or all counting numbers
   range $\{2\}$

c. domain   all real numbers
   range   all real numbers

d. The square root of a negative number is not a real number. Therefore, the value of the radicand, $x - 4$, must be greater than or equal to 0. This is true for all real numbers greater than or equal to 4.
   domain   all real numbers ≥ 4
   The principal root, $\sqrt{x - 4}$, is always positive or 0.
   range   all real numbers ≥ 0

e. Division by 0 is undefined. Therefore, x cannot equal 0.
   domain   all real numbers $\neq 0$
   Evaluate $\frac{3}{x}$ by substituting all real numbers except 0 for x. The results will be real numbers except 0.
   range   all real numbers $\neq 0$

f. The radius must be a positive number or 0.
   domain   all real numbers ≥ 0
   The circumference must be a positive number or 0.
   range   all real numbers ≥ 0 ∎

Experiencing Algebra the Checkup Way

In exercises 1–6, determine the domain and range for each relation. Assume x is the independent variable.

1. $\{(5, 15), (10, 30), (15, 45)\}$

2. $\{(0, 4), (1, 6), (2, 8), (3, 10), \ldots\}$

3. $y = x + 15$

4. $y = \sqrt{x + 4}$

5. $y = \dfrac{8}{x + 1}$

6. $A = s^2$, where A is the area of a square whose side measures s units.

7. When speaking about the domain and the range of a relation, what do we mean?

8. What is the difference between a finite list of ordered pairs and an infinite list of ordered pairs?

---

4 Modeling the Real World

Real-life situations can often be modeled as relations. However, some relations are more convenient to describe by tables of values, other relations can best be described by sets of ordered pairs, and others are most appropriately described by equations. You need to be familiar with all these forms of relations in order to describe a situation in the most useful manner.

EXAMPLE 4

Awesome Rent-A-Car charges $20.99 per day plus $0.20 per mile for each mile or part of a mile over 150 miles.

a. Write an equation for the charge, c, in terms of x miles or parts of miles over 150.

b. Complete the following table:

Number of Miles over 150 (x)	Cost for a One-Day Rental (c)
100	
101	
102	

c. List the ordered pairs found in the table in part (b).

Solution

a. The charge, c, is one day's rental ($20.99) plus $0.20 per x mile or part of a mile over 150:

$$c = 20.99 + 0.20x$$

b. Add an extra column to show your work.

Number of Miles over 150 (x)	c = 20.99 + 0.20x	Cost for a One-Day Rental (c)
100	c = 20.99 + 0.20(100) c = 40.99	40.99
101	c = 20.99 + 0.20(101) c = 41.19	41.19
102	c = 20.99 + 0.20(102) c = 41.39	41.39

Y1 = 20.99 + 0.20x

X	Y1	
100	40.99	
101	41.19	
102	41.39	
103	41.59	
104	41.79	
105	41.99	
106	42.19	

X=100

c. (100, 40.99), (101, 41.19), (102, 41.39)

Use your calculator to check your table. ∎

Application

In early 1998, a letter mailed first-class cost $0.32 for the first ounce and $0.23 for each additional ounce or part of an ounce. Complete a table of values used by a postal clerk.

Weight	Cost
≤ 1 oz	
≤ 2 oz	
≤ 3 oz	
≤ 4 oz	
≤ 5 oz	
≤ 6 oz	
≤ 7 oz	
≤ 8 oz	
≤ 9 oz	
≤ 10 oz	
≤ 11 oz	

Discussion

Let $c =$ cost to mail a first-class letter
      $x =$ the number of additional ounces or part of an ounce over 1 ounce

The cost, c, is $0.32 plus $0.23 per ounce or part of an ounce over 1 ounce.

$$c = 0.32 + 0.23x$$

Note: x is 1 less than the total number of ounces.

Add two columns to show your work.

Weight	x	$c = 0.32 + 0.23x$	Cost
≤ 1 oz	0	$c = 0.32 + 0.23(0)$ $c = 0.32$	0.32
≤ 2 oz	1	$c = 0.32 + 0.23(1)$ $c = 0.55$	0.55
≤ 3 oz	2	$c = 0.32 + 0.23(2)$ $c = 0.78$	0.78
≤ 4 oz	3	$c = 0.32 + 0.23(3)$ $c = 1.01$	1.01
≤ 5 oz	4	$c = 0.32 + 0.23(4)$ $c = 1.24$	1.24
≤ 6 oz	5	$c = 0.32 + 0.23(5)$ $c = 1.47$	1.47
≤ 7 oz	6	$c = 0.32 + 0.23(6)$ $c = 1.70$	1.70
≤ 8 oz	7	$c = 0.32 + 0.23(7)$ $c = 1.93$	1.93
≤ 9 oz	8	$c = 0.32 + 0.23(8)$ $c = 2.16$	2.16
≤ 10 oz	9	$c = 0.32 + 0.23(9)$ $c = 2.39$	2.39
≤ 11 oz	10	$c = 0.32 + 0.23(10)$ $c = 2.62$	2.62

Y1 = 0.32 + 0.23x

X	Y1	
0	.32	
1	.55	
2	.78	
3	1.01	
4	1.24	
5	1.47	
6	1.7	

X=0

Use your calculator to check your table. ∎

Experiencing Algebra the Checkup Way

Sven attended a teachers' conference. His school reimbursed him $410 for plane fare, $95 per day for lodging, and $36 per day for meals.

1. Write an equation for the total reimbursement, r, in terms of the number of days, n, for the trip.
2. Construct a table showing the possible reimbursements for a trip that lasts from 2 through 5 days.
3. List the ordered pairs found in the table for exercise 2.

PROBLEM SET 4.1

Experiencing Algebra the Exercise Way

Express your answers in fractional form or round decimals to the nearest thousandth, as appropriate.
Construct a table of values, given each set of values for x.

1. $y = 5x + 4$, given $\{-2, -1, 0, 1, 2, 3\}$ for x.
2. $y = -8x - 6$, given $\{-3, -2, -1, 0, 1\}$ for x.

3. $y = \dfrac{3}{5}x - 2$, given $\{-15, -10, -5, 0, 5, 10, 15\}$ for x.　　**4.** $y = \dfrac{7}{9}x + 3$, given $\{-18, -9, 0, 9, 18, 27, 36\}$ for x.

5. $y = 2.3x + 1.6$, given $\{-2, -1, 0, 1, 2\}$ for x.　　**6.** $y = -4.8x - 9.2$, given $\{-3, -1, 0, 1, 3\}$ for x.

7. $y = \dfrac{1}{3}(x + 7)$, given $\{-1, -4, -7, -10, -13\}$ for x.　　**8.** $y = \dfrac{1}{6}(x - 2)$, given $\{-10, -4, 2, 8, 14\}$ for x.

Write a table of values for each equation. Select five values for the independent variable in each table.

9. $y = 6x - 8$　　　**10.** $y = -11x + 15$　　　**11.** $y = \dfrac{2}{7}x - 2$　　　**12.** $y = -\dfrac{3}{8}x + 5$

13. $y = -4.6x + 2.1$　　　**14.** $y = 10.6x - 0.8$　　　**15.** $y = \dfrac{1}{4}(3x - 2)$　　　**16.** $y = \dfrac{3}{8}(x - 5)$

Write a table of values for each equation with the given domain.

17. $y = 12x - 13$, where x is an even integer between -4 and 4.

18. $y = -9x + 12$, where x is an odd integer between -3 and 3.

19. $z = \dfrac{1}{3}y + 5$, where y is an integer multiple of 3 between -6 and 6.

20. $p = \dfrac{7}{8}q - 4$, where q is an integer multiple of 8 between -16 and 16.

21. $a = 14.2b + 5.7$, for a domain of integer values between -2 and 2.

22. $m = 1.9n - 3.7$, for a domain of integer values between -3 and 1.

23. $y = 2x^2 + 3x + 1$, with a domain of $\{-3, -2, -1, 0, 1, 2, 3\}$.

24. $y = -3x^2 + 11x - 10$, with a domain of $\{-2, -1, 0, 1, 2, 3, 4\}$.

25. $y = (2x - 3)(3x + 4)$, for integer values of x between -2 and 2.

26. $y = (4x + 1)(-x + 2)$, for integer values of x between 5 and 10.

27. $y = \dfrac{3x + 7}{x - 1}$, for odd integer values of x between -3 and 3.

28. $y = \dfrac{-5x + 2}{-x + 3}$, for odd integer values of x between -1 and 5.

Write tables of values for these formulas with their domains.

29. The volume of a box whose width is 2 feet, whose length is 4 feet, and whose height takes on the values $\{1, 3, 5, 7, 9\}$ feet.

30. The volume of a cube whose edge measures $\{1, 2, 3, 4, 5, 6\}$ feet.

31. The simple interest earned on an investment of $5000 invested at 4.5% simple interest for a time t, where t starts at 1 year and is repeatedly increased by 1 year until it reaches 12 years.

32. The simple interest on a loan of $3000 at a rate of interest of 7% for a time t, where t starts at 1 year and is incremented by 2 years until it reaches 15 years.

33. Ohm's law in electricity is $I = V \div R$, where I is current (measured in amperes), V is voltage (measured in volts), and R is resistance (measured in ohms). Find the current when the voltage is 9 volts and the resistance assumes values from 1 ohm to 9 ohms in increments of 1 ohm.

34. Ohm's law in electricity may also be stated as $V = I \cdot R$, where V is voltage (measured in volts), I is current (measured in amperes), and R is resistance (measured in ohms). Find the voltage when the current is 5 amps and the resistance varies as a natural number between 1 and 10 ohms.

Write ordered pairs.

35. $y = 1.2x + 4$, when $x = -2, -1, 0, 1, 2$.　　**36.** $y = 6 - 0.3x$, when $x = -4, -2, 0, 2, 4$.

37. $q = 1 - p$, when $p = \dfrac{1}{6}, \dfrac{1}{5}, \dfrac{1}{4}, \dfrac{1}{3}, \dfrac{1}{2}$.　　**38.** $S = \dfrac{n(n + 1)}{2}$, when $n = 1, 2, 3, 4, 5$.

39. The perimeter of a square when the side measures 2, 4, 6, 8, 10 inches.

40. The change received when paying with a $10.00 bill for a purchase of $4.00, $6.00, $8.00, $9.50.

Determine the domain and range for each relation. Assume that x is the independent variable.

41. $R = \{(3, 15.8), (5, 17.8), (7, 19.8), (9, 21.8)\}$
42. $U = \{(11, 8), (15, 12), (19, 16), (23, 20)\}$
43. $S = \{(4, -3), (4, -1), (4, 1), (4, 3), \dots\}$
44. $H = \{(3, -1), (2, -1), (1, -1), (0, -1), (-1, -1), \dots\}$
45. $T = \{\dots, (2, -2), (2, -1), (2, 0), (2, 1), (2, 2), \dots\}$
46. $I = \{\dots, (-2, 0), (-1, 0), (0, 0), (1, 0), (2, 0), \dots\}$
47. $y = 4x - 5$ for $x = \{2, 4, 6\}$
48. $y = 3x + 5$ for $x = \{10, 20, 30\}$
49. $y = 6 - x$
50. $y = -x - 8$
51. $y = x^2 + 1$
52. $y = x^2 - 2$
53. $y = \sqrt{x - 2}$
54. $y = \sqrt{x + 2}$
55. $y = \dfrac{6}{x - 2}$
56. $y = \dfrac{10}{4 - x}$

57. $V = s^3$, where s is the measure of the side of a cube whose volume is V.

58. $d = 65t$, where d is the distance traveled in miles when driving for t hours.

In Exercises 59–62, decide on the best method to describe each relation (table of values, ordered pairs, or an equation). Then provide the description. Note: *The vertical-position formula and the distance-traveled formula were introduced in Chapter 3.*

59. A diver jumped off a 50-foot cliff. Describe his position t seconds after the jump.

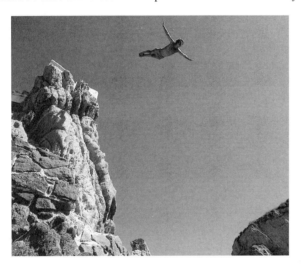

60. A toy rocket is shot upward from the ground with an initial velocity of 10 feet per second. What is its position t seconds after launch?

61. Rebecca is traveling on the interstate highway at a constant speed of 65 mph. What is the distance traveled at the end of each hour for a 4-hour trip?

62. David is driving his truck between two turnpike entrances that are 195 miles apart. What is his speed, to the nearest mile per hour, if he completes the trip in 2.5 hours, 2.75 hours, 3 hours, 3.25 hours, or 3.5 hours? (The Highway Patrol could use this information to determine whether David exceeded the speed limit on his trip.)

Experiencing Algebra the Calculator Way

Use your calculator to construct a table for each relationship.

1. $y = 2.75x - 15.8$, with a domain of $\{-250, -200, -150, -100, -50, 0, 50, 100, 150, 200, 250\}$.

2. $y = 3x^3 + 5x^2 + 7x + 9$, where $x = -5, -\sqrt{15}, -\pi, -3, -2, \sqrt[3]{-3}, 0, 2, \pi, \sqrt{10}$.

3. $y = (2x + 1)^4$, for x beginning at 25 and increasing by 5, up to and including 50.

4. The surface area of an 8-inch-tall cylinder as the radius increases from 2 inches, in units of 0.5 inches, up to and including 5 inches.

5. The compounded amount, A, of a principal of $12,000 invested at an annual rate of interest of 7.5% for t years, where t assumes integer values from 1 to 12 years.

6. The continuously compounded amount earned when a principal of $12,000 is invested at a continuously compounded interest rate of 7.5% for n years, where n assumes integer values from 1 to 12 years.

Experiencing Algebra the Group Way

Collaborate on the best way to approach the following exercises. Discuss how you would carry out the exercises in your group, and then complete them.

1. Use your calculator to construct a table of roots of the integers from 1 to 10. In the table, list the integer values as the domain in the leftmost column, and then list a column for each of the following roots: the square root, the cube root, the fourth root, and the fifth root. Round decimals to the nearest thousandth. Present the table to the class and share ways in which the calculator's table feature eased the effort in constructing the table.

2. In Chapter 3, statistical formulas were presented for calculating permutations and combinations (see "Experiencing Algebra the Group Way" in section 3.6). Use these formulas and your calculator to set up a table for the following situations.

   a. The number of permutations when there are 4 objects and the number of objects used varies from 1 to 4.

   b. The number of combinations when there are 4 objects and the number of objects used varies from 1 to 4.

Experiencing Algebra the Write Way

In using your calculator to construct a table of values, you may program the calculator to choose the values for the independent variable, or you may program the calculator to prompt you to enter the values you wish. Explain how you would do each of these. Then give an example of when you might choose to use each of the two methods.

4.2 Rectangular Coordinate System and Graphing

Objectives
1 Construct a coordinate plane.
2 Graph relations.
3 Identify the domain and range for a relation from its graph.
4 Interpret graphs of real-world data.

Application

The number of pounds of mail handled by the U.S. Postal Service has fluctuated over the years from 1990 to 1994.[1] Graph the relation illustrated in the

---

[1] *Source:* U.S. Postal Service, Annual Report of the Postmaster General.

following table. Determine the domain and range for this relation. Describe in words the meaning of these values.

Year	Weight (in billions of pounds)
1990	18.826
1991	18.340
1992	18.368
1993	19.598
1994	20.976

After completing this section, we will discuss this application further. See page 251.

1 Constructing a Rectangular Coordinate System

We have seen how to organize data in a table of values and in sets of ordered pairs. A third way to organize data is in a two-dimensional graph. In Chapter 1, we graphed numbers on a real-number line. Now we want to graph ordered pairs, consisting of two numbers. We use a **rectangular coordinate system** or **Cartesian coordinate system**. The word *Cartesian* comes from the name of the great French philosopher and mathematician René Descartes (1596–1650). Sometimes, we simply refer to the system as a **coordinate plane**. A coordinate system combines two real-number lines, perpendicular to each other and intersecting at 0 on each line. Remember, perpendicular lines are lines that intersect at right angles (90°).

The horizontal number line is called the **x-axis**. The vertical number line is called the **y-axis**. These two lines intersect at a point called the **origin**. We place an arrow at the end of each of the axes to indicate its positive direction.

We can draw lines perpendicular to the axes through the locations of all the integers on the two number lines. This network of lines forms a rectangular grid. This grid is divided by the x-axis and y-axis into four regions called **quadrants**. The quadrants are labeled with roman numerals in a counterclockwise direction, beginning with the upper right-hand region.

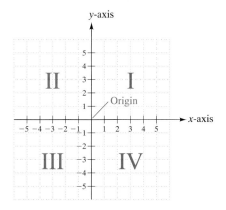

We can set up a coordinate plane on the calculator. The calculator has several choices of screens built in for us to use. We will call these screens *default* screens. We can also set the screen to a setting other than the default ones. We will need to change calculator screens at times in order to better view a picture.

The following are default calculator coordinate planes. Below each screen in parentheses is the window setting. It is written in the form

(*x* minimum value, *x* maximum value, *x* scale, *y* minimum value, *y* maximum value, *y* scale, *x* resolution)

A shorter version may not include the *x* scale, *y* scale, or *x* resolution:

(*x* minimum value, *x* maximum value, *y* minimum value, *y* maximum value)

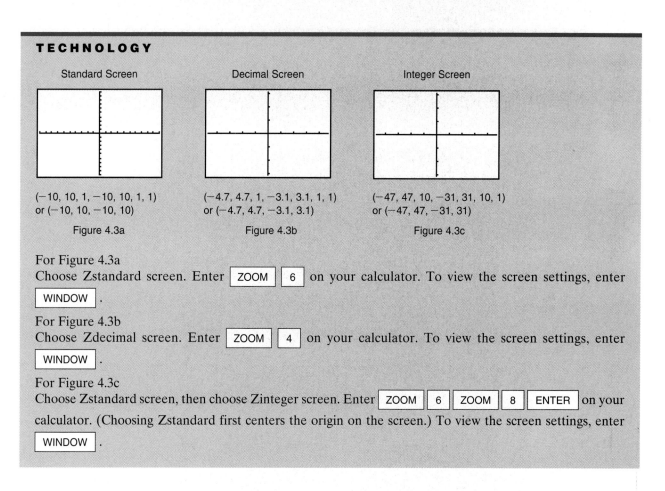

TECHNOLOGY

Standard Screen

Decimal Screen

Integer Screen

(−10, 10, 1, −10, 10, 1, 1)
or (−10, 10, −10, 10)

Figure 4.3a

(−4.7, 4.7, 1, −3.1, 3.1, 1, 1)
or (−4.7, 4.7, −3.1, 3.1)

Figure 4.3b

(−47, 47, 10, −31, 31, 10, 1)
or (−47, 47, −31, 31)

Figure 4.3c

For Figure 4.3a
Choose Zstandard screen. Enter ZOOM 6 on your calculator. To view the screen settings, enter WINDOW .

For Figure 4.3b
Choose Zdecimal screen. Enter ZOOM 4 on your calculator. To view the screen settings, enter WINDOW .

For Figure 4.3c
Choose Zstandard screen, then choose Zinteger screen. Enter ZOOM 6 ZOOM 8 ENTER on your calculator. (Choosing Zstandard first centers the origin on the screen.) To view the screen settings, enter WINDOW .

The default screens may not give us a good picture. We can change the default calculator settings. One method is to multiply all numbers in the current default setting, such as doubling the integer screen, as shown in Figure 4.4.

Another possibility is to change the settings to values of our choice. For example, set the screen to the following setting, as shown in Figure 4.5:

$$(-20, 20, 10, -100, 100, 10, 1)$$

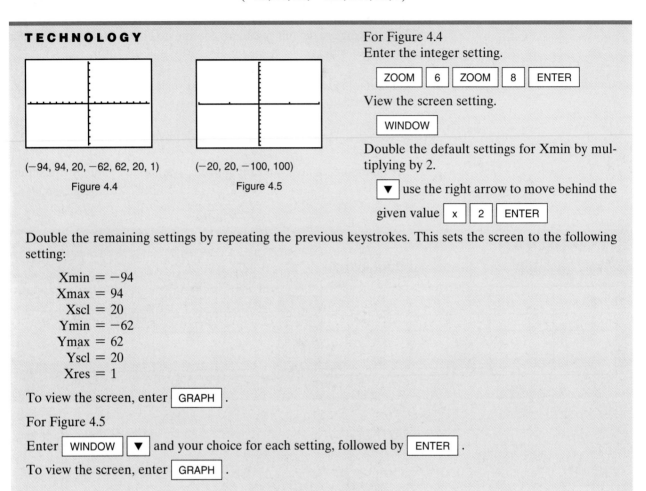

TECHNOLOGY

(−94, 94, 20, −62, 62, 20, 1)

Figure 4.4

(−20, 20, −100, 100)

Figure 4.5

For Figure 4.4
Enter the integer setting.

| ZOOM | 6 | ZOOM | 8 | ENTER |

View the screen setting.

| WINDOW |

Double the default settings for Xmin by multiplying by 2.

| ▼ | use the right arrow to move behind the given value | x | 2 | ENTER |

Double the remaining settings by repeating the previous keystrokes. This sets the screen to the following setting:

$$Xmin = -94$$
$$Xmax = 94$$
$$Xscl = 20$$
$$Ymin = -62$$
$$Ymax = 62$$
$$Yscl = 20$$
$$Xres = 1$$

To view the screen, enter | GRAPH | .

For Figure 4.5

Enter | WINDOW | ▼ | and your choice for each setting, followed by | ENTER | .

To view the screen, enter | GRAPH | .

Unless otherwise stated in this text, first use the default screen for integers.

integer—used for large numbers
$(-47 \leq x \leq 47 \quad$ and $\quad -31 \leq y \leq 31)$

If the numbers are small, use the default decimal calculator screen.

decimal—used for small numbers
$(-4.7 \leq x \leq 4.7 \quad$ and $\quad -3.1 \leq y \leq 3.1)$

EXAMPLE 1 **a.** Construct a coordinate plane on graph paper and label, in increments of 1, the x-axis from −4 to 4 and the y-axis from −3 to 3. This is very similar to the decimal screen on your calculator. On your calculator, set up a default decimal screen.

b. Construct a coordinate plane on graph paper. Label the x-axis from −141 to 141 in increments of 30. Label the y-axis from −124 to 124 in increments of 40. This is a multiple of the integer screen on your calculator. On your calculator, set up an integer screen and then enter the multiples needed.

Solution

a.

b.

 Helping Hand Be very careful to number lines, not the spaces between the lines.

The calculator display for Example 1 is shown in Figure 4.6a and Figure 4.6b. ∎

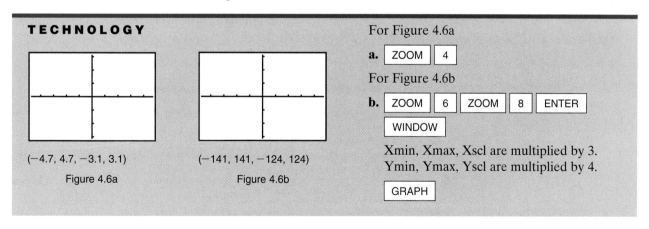

TECHNOLOGY

(−4.7, 4.7, −3.1, 3.1)

Figure 4.6a

(−141, 141, −124, 124)

Figure 4.6b

For Figure 4.6a

a. ZOOM 4

For Figure 4.6b

b. ZOOM 6 ZOOM 8 ENTER

WINDOW

Xmin, Xmax, Xscl are multiplied by 3.
Ymin, Ymax, Yscl are multiplied by 4.

GRAPH

 Experiencing Algebra the Checkup Way

1. Construct a coordinate system on graph paper and label the *x*-axis from −10 to 10 and the *y*-axis from −10 to 10, both in increments of 1 unit. To what setting on the ZOOM button of your

calculator does this scale compare? What are the keystrokes needed to obtain this setting? On your calculator, set up the screen and check the window format to see that you have selected correctly.

2. Construct a coordinate system on graph paper and label the x-axis from -50 to 50 and the y-axis from -30 to 30, both in increments of 10 units. To what setting on the ZOOM button of your calculator does this scale compare? What are the keystrokes needed to obtain this setting? On your calculator, set up the screen and check the window format to see that you have selected correctly.

3. Write a short definition of each of the following terms:
   a. coordinate plane **b.** axes **c.** origin **d.** quadrants

4. List the default choices on your calculator for graphing within the Cartesian coordinate system and explain what each setting does for graphing.

---

2 Graphing Relations

Locations in the coordinate plane are written as ordered pairs. The numbers in an ordered pair are called the **coordinates** of the point at that location. Each coordinate corresponds to the distance of the point from the x-axis or y-axis. The first number in the ordered pair is called the **x-coordinate**. This corresponds to the distance of the point from the y-axis, which we measure along the x-axis. Similarly, the second number in the ordered pair is called the **y-coordinate**, which corresponds to the distance of the point from the x-axis, as measured along the y-axis.

To graph an ordered pair (or plot a point,) we place a dot at its location on the coordinate plane.

- First, locate the x-coordinate on the x-axis.
- Second, locate the y-coordinate on the y-axis.
- Place a dot at the intersection of the two lines that are perpendicular to the axes and that go through these locations on the axes.
- Label the point with its name or coordinates.

For example, to graph the ordered pair $A(2, 3)$, locate the x-coordinate, 2, on the x-axis and the y-coordinate, 3, on the y-axis. The intersection of the two lines through these locations is the location of the dot for the ordered pair $(2, 3)$. Label the point by its name, A.

There are two ways to plot points on a calculator. To graph an ordered pair from the text or default screen:

- Choose the DRAW command.
- Enter the first coordinate value, followed by a comma.
- Enter the second coordinate value, followed by a closing parenthesis.

To graph an ordered pair from the graph screen:

- Enter the DRAW command.
- Use the arrow keys to move to the location of the point (the coordinates are on the bottom of the screen). Enter the coordinates.

For example, graph $(2, 3)$ on a decimal screen, as shown in Figure 4.7.

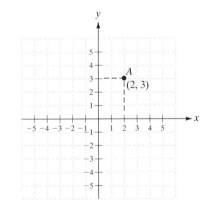

EXAMPLE 2   Graph and label each set of ordered pairs on a coordinate plane and check on your calculator decimal screen.

a. $A(1, 3)$ and $B(3, 1)$ **b.** $C(-2, 3)$ and $D(3, -2)$

c. $E(2, 0)$ and $F(0, 2)$

Solution

a.

b.

c.

■

TECHNOLOGY

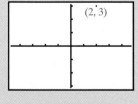

$(-4.7, 4.7, -3.1, 3.1)$

Figure 4.7

For Figure 4.7
Set the decimal screen.

| ZOOM | | 4 |

To plot from the graph screen:
Enter the DRAW command.

| 2nd | | DRAW | | ▶ | | 1 |

Use the arrow keys to locate the point and enter the coordinates, | ENTER |.

To clear the graph screen, enter | 2nd | | DRAW | | 1 |.

To plot from the text screen: Quit the graph screen.

| 2nd | | QUIT |

Enter the DRAW command.

| 2nd | | DRAW | | ▶ | | 1 |

Enter the first coordinate, followed by a comma.

| 2 | | , |

Enter the second coordinate, followed by a closing parenthesis.

| 3 | |) | | ENTER |

The checks for Example 2a and Example 2b are shown in Figure 4.8a and Figure 4.8b. The calculator is not used to check Example 2c because the points lie on the axes and cannot be seen on the calculator screen.

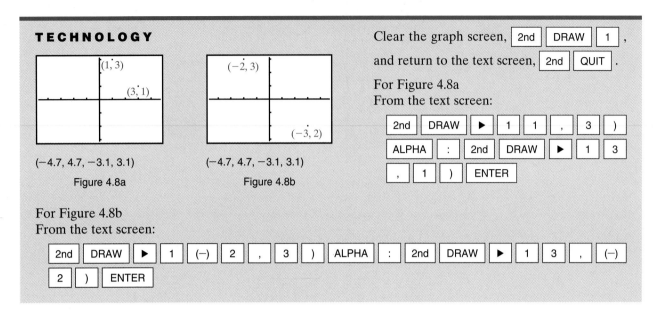

TECHNOLOGY

$(-4.7, 4.7, -3.1, 3.1)$

Figure 4.8a

$(-4.7, 4.7, -3.1, 3.1)$

Figure 4.8b

Clear the graph screen, [2nd] [DRAW] [1],

and return to the text screen, [2nd] [QUIT].

For Figure 4.8a
From the text screen:

[2nd] [DRAW] [▶] [1] [1] [,] [3] [)]

[ALPHA] [:] [2nd] [DRAW] [▶] [1] [3]

[,] [1] [)] [ENTER]

For Figure 4.8b
From the text screen:

[2nd] [DRAW] [▶] [1] [(−)] [2] [,] [3] [)] [ALPHA] [:] [2nd] [DRAW] [▶] [1] [3] [,] [(−)]

[2] [)] [ENTER]

EXAMPLE 3 Using the given graph, state the coordinates of the graphed points.

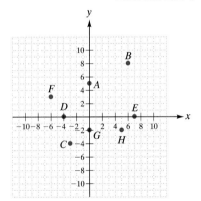

Solution

$A\ (0, 5)$ $B\ (6, 8)$ $C\ (-3, -4)$ $D\ (-4, 0)$

$E\ (7, 0)$ $F\ (-6, 3)$ $G\ (0, -2)$ $H\ (5, -2)$ ∎

At times it may be necessary to locate a point in the coordinate plane approximately, without actually plotting it. For such cases, it is useful to know how the coordinates of points vary from one quadrant to another and what coordinates correspond to points located on the axes. Complete the following sets of exercises on your calculator.

DISCOVERY 1

Signs of the Coordinates in Each Quadrant

Set your calculator to the integer screen setting. Use your arrow keys to locate five points in each of the following quadrants. Write the ordered pairs.

Quadrant I	*Quadrant II*	*Quadrant III*	*Quadrant IV*
(____,____)	(____,____)	(____,____)	(____,____)
(____,____)	(____,____)	(____,____)	(____,____)
(____,____)	(____,____)	(____,____)	(____,____)
(____,____)	(____,____)	(____,____)	(____,____)
(____,____)	(____,____)	(____,____)	(____,____)

Write a rule for a condition on the signs of the coordinates in each quadrant.

In quadrant I, both coordinates are positive; in quadrant II, the x-coordinate is negative and the y-coordinate is positive; in quadrant III, both coordinates are negative; and in quadrant IV, the x-coordinate is positive and the y-coordinate is negative.

D I S C O V E R Y   2

Location of the Zero Coordinate on the Axes
Set your calculator to the integer screen setting. Use your arrow keys to locate five points on each of the axes. Write the ordered pairs.

x-Axis   *y-Axis*
(____,____)   (____,____)
(____,____)   (____,____)
(____,____)   (____,____)
(____,____)   (____,____)
(____,____)   (____,____)

Write a rule for a condition on the numbers in an ordered pair for any point on the x-axis or the y-axis.

On the x-axis, the y-coordinate is always 0, and on the y-axis, the x-coordinate is always 0.

> *Signs of Coordinates in the Plane*
> In quadrant I, the x-coordinate is always positive and the y-coordinate is always positive.
> In quadrant II, the x-coordinate is always negative and the y-coordinate is always positive.
> In quadrant III, the x-coordinate is always negative and the y-coordinate is always negative.
> In quadrant IV, the x-coordinate is always positive and the y-coordinate is always negative.
> On the x-axis, the y-coordinate is always 0.
> On the y-axis, the x-coordinate is always 0.

EXAMPLE 4   Determine the location of the following points by quadrant or by axis.

a. $(24, 39)$ **b.** $(-24, 39)$ **c.** $(24, -39)$
d. $(-24, -39)$ **e.** $(0, 39)$ **f.** $(-24, 0)$

Solution

a. quadrant I   Coordinates are $(+, +)$.
b. quadrant II   Coordinates are $(-, +)$.
c. quadrant IV   Coordinates are $(+, -)$.
d. quadrant III   Coordinates are $(-, -)$.
e. y-axis   The x-coordinate is 0.
f. x-axis   The y-coordinate is 0. ■

Now we know how to locate a point, represented by an ordered pair, on the coordinate plane. Our next step is to graph a set of ordered pairs—that is, a relation—on the coordinate plane. In fact, since we have shown how to represent a relation by a set of ordered pairs, a table of values, or an equation, we can graph any of these forms in the same fashion.

To graph a relation:

- In list form, plot each ordered pair in the relation.
- In table form, write a set of ordered pairs and plot each ordered pair.
- In equation form, set up a table of values to determine the ordered pairs. For an infinite domain set, we can find only a sample of the ordered pairs. In this case, a smooth curve connecting the pairs is usually added to complete the graph. An arrow should be placed at the end of the curve to denote that the pattern continues.

EXAMPLE 5 Graph each relation.

a. $A = \{(1, 1), (1, 2), (1, 3)\}$

b. $B = \{\dots, (-2, -1), (-1, 0), (0, 1), (1, 2), (2, 3), \dots\}$

c. $y = 2x$ for $x = \{1, 2, 3\}$

d. $y = 2x + 3$

Solution

a. Plot the ordered pairs.

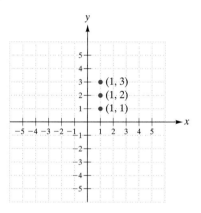

b. Plot the ordered pairs. Use an arrow to indicate the graph continues.

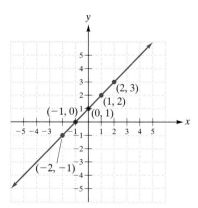

c. In order to graph the relation $y = 2x$ for $x = \{1, 2, 3\}$, we set up a table of values and graph the ordered pairs.

x	$y = 2x$	y
1	$y = 2(1)$ $y = 2$	2
2	$y = 2(2)$ $y = 4$	4
3	$y = 2(3)$ $y = 6$	6

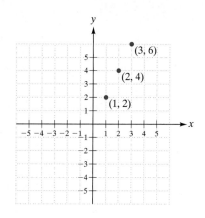

d. If a relation is represented using an equation such as $y = 2x + 3$ and the values for x are not given, we find a set of sample ordered pairs. We choose values for x in the domain of the relation. For example, we can choose $x = 1, 1.25, 1\frac{1}{2}$, and 2 and set up a table of values.

x	$y = 2x + 3$	y
1	$y = 2(1) + 3$ $= 5$	5
1.25	$y = 2(1.25) + 3$ $y = 5.5$	5.5
$1\frac{1}{2}$	$y = 2\left(1\frac{1}{2}\right) + 3$ $y = 2\left(\frac{3}{2}\right) + 3$ $y = 6$	6
2	$y = 2(2) + 3$ $y = 7$	7

When we graph the sample ordered pairs, we see a straight line being formed. In fact, if we could graph all the ordered pairs that satisfy this relation, a solid line would be formed. Therefore, to complete the graph of the relation, draw a line through the points graphed. An arrow denotes that the pattern continues. ∎

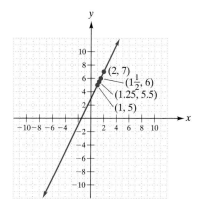

There are several ways to graph a relation on your calculator. The following procedures describe graphing relations in the form of ordered pairs (finite or infinite sets) or equations.

To graph a relation that is a finite set of ordered pairs:

- Enter the ordered pairs individually.

To graph a relation that is an infinite set of ordered pairs with an integer domain:

- Determine an equation which relates the second coordinate to the first coordinate.
- Set the calculator to dot mode.
- Set the calculator to an integer screen.
- Enter the rule into the calculator.
- Graph the relation.

To graph a relation defined as an equation:

- Set the calculator to the desired screen.
- Enter the equation into the calculator.
- Graph the relation.

EXAMPLE 6 Graph each relation on your calculator.

a. $A = \{(1, 1), (1, 2), (1, 3)\}$

b. $B = \{\ldots, (-2, -1), (-1, 0), (0, 1), (1, 2), (2, 3), \ldots\}$

c. $y = 2x + 3$

Calculator Solution

a. Graph on your calculator decimal screen, as shown in Figure 4.9.

b. We can graph the given ordered pairs as in Example 2. However, to graph the ordered pairs not listed, we must tell the calculator the pattern. We see that the second coordinate is one more than the first coordinate. Therefore, to write an equation, let $x =$ the first coordinate and $y =$ the second coordinate. Then $y = x + 1$.

Graph on your calculator integer screen as shown in Figure 4.10.

c. See graph in Figure 4.11. ∎

TECHNOLOGY

(−4.7, 4.7, −3.1, 3.1)

Figure 4.9

$y_1 = x + 1$

(−47, 47, −31, 31)

Figure 4.10

$y_1 = 2x + 3$

(−47, 47, −31, 31)

Figure 4.11

For Figure 4.9

| ZOOM | 4 | 2nd | QUIT |

| 2nd | DRAW | ▶ | 1 | 1 | , | 1 |) | ALPHA | : | 2nd | DRAW | ▶ | 1 | 1 | , | 2 |) |

| ALPHA | : | 2nd | DRAW | ▶ | 1 | 1 | , | 3 |) | ENTER |

For Figure 4.10
Choose dot mode.

| MODE | ▼ | ▼ | ▼ | ▼ | ▶ | ENTER |

Set the calculator to an integer screen.

| ZOOM | 6 | ZOOM | 8 | ENTER |

Enter the expression into the calculator.

| Y= | X, T, θ, n | + | 1 |

Graph the relation.

| GRAPH |

For Figure 4.11
Set the calculator to connect mode.

| MODE | ▼ | ▼ | ▼ | ▼ | ENTER |

Set the calculator to an integer screen.

| ZOOM | 6 | ZOOM | 8 | ENTER |

Enter the expression into the calculator.

| Y= | 2 | X, T, θ, n | + | 3 |

Graph the relation.

| GRAPH |

✓ **Experiencing Algebra the Checkup Way**

In exercises 1–4, graph and label each set of ordered pairs on a coordinate plane and check on your calculator integer screen.

1. $E(-5, -6)$ and $F(-6, -5)$

2. $G(3, -3)$ and $H(-3, 3)$

3. In exercises 1–2, what is the effect of swapping the two values of the coordinate pair? What is the effect of having a negative sign on the x-coordinate? What is the effect of having a negative sign on the y-coordinate?

4. State the coordinates of the graphed points in Figure 4.12.

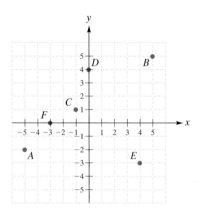

Figure 4.12

5. Determine the location of each point by quadrant or by axis.

a. $(-16, 95)$ **b.** $(123, 135)$ **c.** $(0.001, -1.009)$ **d.** $\left(-3\frac{1}{3}, -2\frac{1}{5}\right)$

e. $(0, 0)$ **f.** $(-3.6, 0)$ **g.** $\left(0, \frac{2}{9}\right)$

Graph each relation.

6. $R = \{(-2, 4), (0, 4), (3, 4), (7, 4)\}$ **7.** $y = -2x$ for $x = \{-2, 0, 2\}$

8. $y = -3x + 5$ **9.** $H = \{\dots, (-2, 6), (-1, 3), (0, 0), (1, -3), (2, -6), \dots\}$

3 Identifying the Domain and Range

We can determine the domain and range of a relation directly from its graph.

To determine the domain of a relation from its graph, examine the graph to see what values of the independent variable (the x-coordinates) are used to draw the graph.

To determine the range of a relation from its graph, write a set of the values of the dependent variable (the y-coordinates) used in the graph.

For example, determine the domain and range of the relation whose graph is shown in Figure 4.13.

We see that the graph includes points for every possible value for x as indicated below. The domain is the set of all real numbers.

Figure 4.13

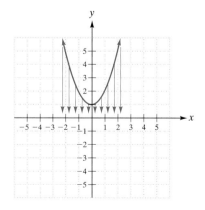

We see that the possible *y*-values are all greater than or equal to 1 as indicated below. The range is the set of all real numbers ≥ 1.

$Y1 = x^2 + 1$

$(-47, 47, -31, 31)$

$Y1 = x^2 + 1$

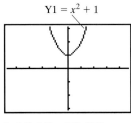

$(-4.7, 4.7, -3.1, 3.1)$

To determine the domain and range of a relation from a calculator graph, trace the graph. The coordinates of the points plotted are displayed on the screen. The *x*-coordinates will be in the domain and the *y*-coordinates will be in the range. (A table of values is also helpful.) However, the calculator window (or table setup) will determine the values displayed. These sample coordinates will only help us determine the domain and range.

For example, determine the domain and range of the relation graphed in Figure 4.13, which in equation form is $y = x^2 + 1$. Graph this relation on a calculator and confirm the domain and range found.

On an integer screen, we obtain all integers for the domain and integers greater than or equal to 1 for the range. On a decimal screen, we obtain positive and negative decimal values for the domain and decimal values greater than or equal to 1 for the range.

It is impossible to see the coordinates of all the points on the graph, but the graph does give us a sample of numbers to confirm that the domain is the set of all real numbers and the range is the set of all real numbers ≥ 1. A table of values can also be used to confirm this.

EXAMPLE 7   Determine the domain and range of each relation.

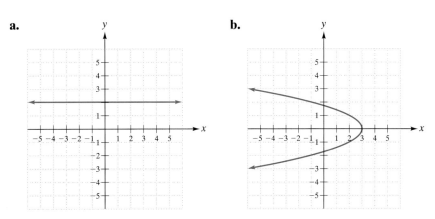

a.

b.

Solution

a. domain   all real numbers
    range   {2}
b. domain   all real numbers ≤ 3
    range   all real numbers ∎

EXAMPLE 8   On your calculator, graph each relation and determine the domain and range.

a. $y = 3x$ **b.** $y = \sqrt{x}$

Calculator Solution

a.   Y1 = 3x

(−47, 47, −31, 31)

    domain   all real numbers
    range   all real numbers

b.   Y1 = $\sqrt{x}$

(−47, 47, −31, 31)

    domain   all real numbers ≥ 0
    range   all real numbers ≥ 0 ∎

 ## Experiencing Algebra the Checkup Way

Determine the domain and range of each relation.

1.

2.

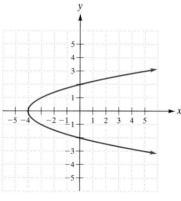

Graph each relation on your calculator and determine the domain and range.

3. $y = -2x + 5$ **4.** $y = \sqrt{-x}$

4   Modeling the Real World   Graphs are an important tool to help us visualize real-world relations. However, you should be aware that real situations sometimes impose restrictions on the domain and range of relations. For example, if the independent variable is time, then the domain must be limited to nonnegative numbers, since time can't be negative. If the dependent variable is the height of a ball above the ground, then the range is also nonnegative numbers, since the ball won't fall through the ground and keep going. It's a good idea to get into the habit of checking the domain and range of real-world relations in this way, and make sure you're looking at values that make sense.

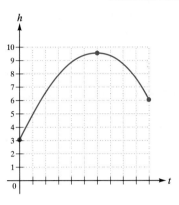

Figure 4.14

EXAMPLE 9   John throws a ball to his father. The relationship between time t (in seconds) and height h (in feet) of the ball is illustrated in the graph in Figure 4.14, with the horizontal axis representing time t (in seconds) and the vertical axis representing height h (in feet) of the ball.

a. Determine the domain and range of the relation. Describe what each set of values represents.

b. Assuming John's father caught the ball 1 second after John threw it, determine the height at which the ball was caught.

Solution

a. The domain of the relation is the set of all real numbers between and including 0 and 1. This represents the time (in seconds) the ball was in the air.

     The range of the relation is the set of all real numbers between and including 3 and 9.5. This represents the height (in feet) reached by the ball.

b. According to the graph, when $t = 1$ second, $h = 6$ feet. This is the ordered pair $(1, 6)$. Therefore, John's father caught the ball at a height of 6 feet. ∎

Application   The number of pounds of mail handled by the U.S. Postal Service has fluctuated over the years from 1990 to 1994.[1] Graph the relation illustrated in the following table. Determine the domain and range for this relation. Describe in words the meaning of these values.

Year	Weight (in billions of pounds)
1990	18.826
1991	18.340
1992	18.368
1993	19.598
1994	20.976

Discussion

Let $x =$ the number of years after 1990.

    $y =$ the total weight (in billions of pounds) of the mail.

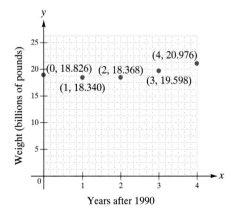

Years after 1990

[1] *Source:* U.S. Postal Service, Annual Report of the Postmaster General.

The domain is {0, 1, 2, 3, 4} or the number of years after 1990.
The range is {18.340, 18.368, 18.826, 19.598, 20.976} or the different weights (in billions of pounds) of mail. ∎

 Experiencing Algebra the Checkup Way

A quality-control engineer recorded the numbers of nondefective parts produced on an assembly line that produced 75 parts per day. The data for each day are shown in Figure 4.15. Determine the domain and the range for the relation. Describe in words the meaning of these values.

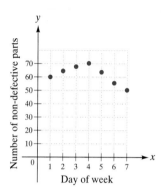

Figure 4.15

PROBLEM SET 4.2

 Experiencing Algebra the Exercise Way

Graph and label each ordered pair on a coordinate plane.

1. $A(-7, -5)$ and $B(-5, -7)$ **2.** $C(-2, -4)$ and $D(-4, -2)$
3. $E(4, 9)$ and $F(9, 4)$ **4.** $G(2, 6)$ and $H(6, 2)$
5. $I(-5, 5)$ and $J(5, -5)$ **6.** $K(-4, 4)$ and $L(4, -4)$
7. $M(2, -1)$ and $N(-1, 2)$ **8.** $O(3, -4)$ and $P(-4, 3)$
9. $Q(3, -1)$ and $R(-3, 1)$ **10.** $S(2, -7)$ and $T(-2, 7)$
11. $U(-8, -2)$ and $V(8, 2)$ **12.** $W(3, 5)$ and $X(-3, -5)$
13. $A(1.2, 2.4)$ **14.** $B(3.4, 1.2)$ **15.** $C(-4.5, -2.6)$ **16.** $D(-3.6, -2.5)$
17. $E(-2.4, 2.1)$ **18.** $F(4.1, -2.4)$ **19.** $G(1.8, -2.7)$ **20.** $H(-2.7, 1.8)$

Determine the location of each point by quadrant or by axis. Do not graph.

21. $(-21, 35)$ **22.** $(-33, -35)$ **23.** $(4, 96)$ **24.** $(28, -92)$
25. $(-3, -19)$ **26.** $(-75, 22)$ **27.** $(0, -31)$ **28.** $(94, 0)$
29. $(90, -100)$ **30.** $(2, 29)$ **31.** $(24, 0)$ **32.** $(0, -36)$
33. $(-19, 0)$ **34.** $(0, 0)$ **35.** $(0.05, 1.003)$ **36.** $(-2.09, 8.6)$

37. State the coordinates of the graphed points in Figure 4.16.
38. State the coordinates of the graphed points in Figure 4.17.

Figure 4.16

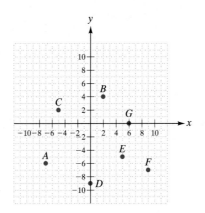

Figure 4.17

39. $(0, 3.7)$

40. $(-9.3, 0)$

41. $\left(\dfrac{13}{27}, -\dfrac{11}{19}\right)$

42. $\left(-\dfrac{57}{105}, -\dfrac{17}{21}\right)$

43. $\left(-\dfrac{53}{100}, -\dfrac{39}{100}\right)$

44. $\left(\dfrac{20}{33}, 0\right)$

45. $\left(0, \dfrac{28}{51}\right)$

46. $\left(3\dfrac{1}{7}, -1\dfrac{4}{5}\right)$

Graph each relation.

47. $A = \{(-3, -3), (-2, -2), (-1, -1), (0, 0), (1, 1), (2, 2), (3, 3)\}$

48. $B = \{(-2.5, -2), (-1.5, -1), (-0.5, 0.5), (0.5, 1), (1.5, 2)\}$

49. $C = \{(-4, 4), (-2, 2), (0, 0), (2, -2), (4, -4)\}$

50. $D = \{(0, 2), (1, 3), (2, 4), (3, 5), (4, 6)\}$

51. $E = \{(5, -3), (5, -1), (5, 1), (5, 3)\}$

52. $F = \{(-4, -2), (-2, -2), (0, -2), (2, -2), (4, -2)\}$

53. $G = \{\dots, (-2, -1), (-1, 0), (0, 1), (1, 2), (2, 3), \dots\}$

54. $H = \{\dots, (-2, 3), (-1, 2), (0, 1), (1, 0), (2, -1), \dots\}$

55. $I = \{\dots, (-2, -6), (-1, -5), (0, -4), (1, -3), (2, -2), (3, -1), \dots\}$

56. $J = \{\dots, (-4, -2), (-2, -1), (0, 0), (2, 1), (4, 2), \dots\}$

57. $y = 12x - 15$

58. $y = 14x$

59. $y = -10x + 9$

60. $y = -x - 1$

61. $y = \dfrac{1}{2}x + 3$

62. $y = -\dfrac{3}{4}x + 5$

63. $y = -\dfrac{2}{3}x - 2$

64. $y = \dfrac{2}{5}x + \dfrac{1}{5}$

65. $y = 2x^2 - 5$

66. $y = -3x^2 - 1$

67. $y = |2x|$

68. $y = |-4x|$

Determine the domain and the range for each relation.

69.

70.

71.

72.

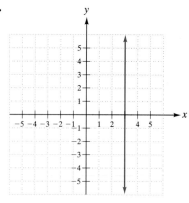

For each of the following applications, determine the domain and the range of the relation. Then describe what each set of values represents.

73. Figure 4.18 shows the political party identification of the adult population. Consider the line for Democratic Party identification as the relation of interest.

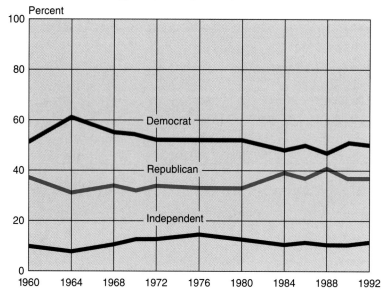

Political Party Identification of the Adult Population: 1960 to 1992

(Democrat and Republican parties include individuals identifying themselves as strong, weak, or independent.)

Source: Chart prepared by the U.S. Bureau of the Census.

Figure 4.18

74. Figure 4.19 shows violent crime rates in the United States. Consider the line for aggravated assault as the relation of interest.

75. An egg is dropped from a height of 100 feet. Figure 4.20 shows the distance of the egg from the ground in relation to the time after it is dropped.

76. Figure 4.21 represents the relation between the length of a pendulum and the period of the pendulum, which is the time it takes to complete its arc swing.

Violent and PropertyCrime Rates: 1960 to 1992

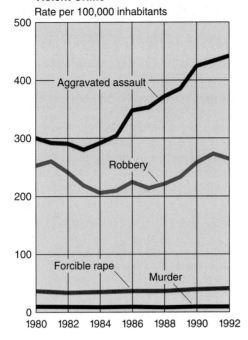

Violent Crime

Rate per 100,000 inhabitants

Source: Chart prepared by U.S. Bureau of the Census

Figure 4.19

Figure 4.20

Figure 4.21

 Experiencing Algebra the Calculator Way

A. Comparing View Screens on the Calculator

To give you an idea of what the various screen settings mean, first draw a coordinate plane on a large sheet of graph paper. Place the origin of the coordinate system in the middle of the graph paper and mark the x-axis in units of 5, from −50 to 50. Also mark the y-axis in units of 5, from −35 to 35. Make the graph as large as the paper will allow. You will use this graph to draw boxes for the various calculator settings.

Clear the [Y=] screen. Then set your calculator to the decimal setting, ZDecimal, option 4.

Press [WINDOW] to view the setting's limits. Plot the limits on the graph and draw a box. This box represents the portion of a graphed relation you can view with this setting.

Now set the calculator to the standard setting, ZStandard, option 6. Press $\boxed{\text{WINDOW}}$ to view this setting's limits. Plot the limits on the same graph and draw another box. This box represents the portion of a graphed relation you can view with this setting. You should see that you can view much more of a graphed relation with this setting.

Next set the calculator to the integer setting, ZInteger, option 8. Be sure to press $\boxed{\text{ENTER}}$ after choosing option 8 in order to move to the new setting. Press $\boxed{\text{WINDOW}}$ to view this setting's limits. Plot these limits on the same graph and draw a third box. This box represents the portion of a graphed relation you can view with this setting. Once again, you should see that you can view much more of a graphed relation with this setting.

So if you use a larger setting, you see more of a graph. However, if you use a smaller setting, you may see more detail in a smaller portion of the graph. It's up to you to become familiar enough with these settings in order to make a decision on which setting you should use. Be aware that there are other settings you can use. You can set the screen to any setting you choose, and you can also zoom in or zoom out on a setting to see more detail or more of the graph. Try the various settings on the following equations, and decide which is best for viewing them.

1. $y = 2x - 3$ **2.** $y = 2x^2 - 3x + 1$ **3.** $y = 2x^3 - 3x^2 + x - 4$

B. Transferring Graphs from the Calculator to Paper

Set your calculator screen to the decimal setting. Then graph the following relations on this setting. Find the coordinate pairs for the domain of $\{-2, -1, 0, 1, 2\}$. Now plot the points on graph paper using the coordinate plane. Then sketch the graph connecting these points.

1. $y = 0.6x - 1.2$ **2.** $y = -0.5x + 2.2$ **3.** $y = |x| - 2$
4. $y = |x - 2|$ **5.** $y = x - 2$

6. Write the keystrokes needed to enter exercises 3–5 into your calculator. What is the important difference that distinguishes these three exercises? Pay attention to this important difference as you use this calculator method.

Experiencing Algebra the Group Way

Graph each relation on your calculator, using the decimal screen setting. Determine the domain and the range.

1. $y = \dfrac{1}{x - 2}$ **2.** $y = |x - 4|$

For the first exercise, what value of x is excluded from the domain of the relationship? What value of y is excluded from the range of the relationship? See if you can find any feature of the equation that would have helped you determine these excluded values.

For the second exercise, notice that the domain includes all real numbers. But what value of the domain corresponds to a value of 0 in the range? Can you find any feature of the equation that would have helped you determine this value of the domain? Now, what is unusual about the range? Can you explain why the range has this property?

Now use the TABLE function to view these two functions, using integer values between -10 and 10. Do the tables illustrate the restrictions on the domain and on the range?

Share your findings with the class. You will work with these features later in this book.

Experiencing Algebra the Write Way

In this section, you learned that sometimes a graph is a finite set of points; at other times the graph is an infinite set of unconnected points; and at still other times the graph is an infinite set of points represented by a line. Explain what must be true about the domain and range of the relation for each type of graph to occur. In your explanation, give an example of a relation that yields each type of graph.

4.3   Functions and Function Notation

Objectives

1 Determine whether relations written in list form are functions.

2 Determine whether relations written in equation form are functions.

3 Determine whether relations represented as graphs are functions.

4 Evaluate functions written in function notation.

5 Use real-world data to determine functions.

Application

The number of pounds of first-class mail per capita delivered by the U.S. Postal Service is given in the following table for the years 1990 through 1994.[1]

Year	Weight (in pounds)
1990	14
1991	14
1992	14
1993	14
1994	14

Write a set of ordered pairs for the data. Graph the relation. Is this relation a function?

After completing this section, we will discuss this application further. See page 268.

---

1   Identifying Functions from Ordered Pairs

A special type of relation that we frequently use in mathematics is a function. A **function** is a relation in which every element in the domain corresponds to only one element in the range.

A relation written in list form,

$$M = \{(1, 2), (2, 4), (3, 5), (4, 6)\},$$

is a function because we match every element in the domain, {1, 2, 3, 4}, to only one element in the range, {2, 4, 5, 6}.

Domain   *Range*
1 ⟶ 2
2 ⟶ 4
3 ⟶ 5
4 ⟶ 6

[1] *Source*: U.S. Postal Service, Annual Report of the Postmaster General.

A relation written in list form,

$$N = \{(1, 2), (1, 3), (2, 4)\},$$

is not a function because we match one element, 1, in the domain {1, 2} to more than one element, 2 and 3, in the range {2, 3, 4}.

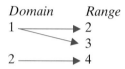

Domain   *Range*
1 ————→ 2
         ↘ 3
2 ————————→ 4

EXAMPLE 1   Determine whether each relation is a function.

a. $\{(3, 6), (-3, -6), (5, 10), (-5, -10)\}$

b. $\{(3, 6), (-3, 6), (5, 10), (-5, 10)\}$

c. $\{(3, 6), (3, -6), (5, 10), (-5, -10)\}$

Solution

a. $\{(3, 6), (-3, -6), (5, 10), (-5, -10)\}$ is a function because every element in the domain corresponds to only one element in the range. The first coordinate is not repeated in the set of ordered pairs.

b. $\{(3, 6), (-3, 6), (5, 10), (-5, 10)\}$ is a function because every element in the domain corresponds to only one element in the range. The first coordinate is not repeated in the set of ordered pairs. The repeated elements in the range, 6 and 10, do not matter.

c. $\{(3, 6), (3, -6), (5, 10), (-5, -10)\}$ is not a function because an element in the domain, 3, corresponds to two elements in the range, 6 and −6. The first coordinate, 3, is repeated in the set of ordered pairs. ■

✓ Experiencing Algebra the Checkup Way

In exercises 1–4, determine whether each relation is a function.

1. $A = \{(-2, 3), (-1, 5), (0, 7), (1, 5), (2, 3)\}$

2. $B = \{(-3, 5), (-1, 5), (1, 5), (3, 5)\}$

3. $C = \{(-3, 2), (-1, 3), (-1, -3), (-3, -2)\}$

4. $D = \{(2, -1), (2, 0), (2, 1), (2, 2)\}$

5. What should you look for in a relation to determine whether the relation is a function?

---

2 Identifying Functions from Equations   Relations are often written as equations. The relation $y = x^2$, in equation form, is a function because every element in the domain of the function, all real numbers, corresponds to only one element in the range. That is, if we set up a table of values for the equation and substitute an element of the domain into the equation, the result is only one value. Sample ordered pairs are $(1, 1)$, $(-1, 1)$, $(2, 4)$, $\left(\frac{1}{2}, \frac{1}{4}\right)$, and so on.

To determine whether a relation written as an equation is a function:

- Determine the domain of the relation.
- Determine the range of the relation.
- Determine that each element in the domain corresponds to only one element in the range.

EXAMPLE 2 Determine whether each relation is a function. Use x as the independent variable and y as the dependent variable.

a. $x = y^2$ b. $y = 2x + 5$

c. $|y| = x$ d. $y = \sqrt{x - 4}$

Solution

a. $x = y^2$ is not a function. The domain of the relation is all real numbers greater than or equal to 0. The range is all real numbers. Each element in the domain other than 0 corresponds to two elements in the range. For example, if $x = 1$, then there are two values for y, 1 and -1. Sample ordered pairs are $(1, 1)$, $(1, -1)$, $(2, \sqrt{2})$, $(2, -\sqrt{2})$, and so on.

b. $y = 2x + 5$ is a function. The domain of the function is all real numbers. The range is all real numbers. Each element in the domain corresponds to a single element in the range. Sample ordered pairs are $(1, 7)$, $(2, 9)$, $(3, 11)$, and so on.

c. $|y| = x$ is not a function. The domain is all real numbers greater than or equal to 0. The range is all real numbers. Each element in the domain other than 0 corresponds to two elements in the range. Sample ordered pairs are $(1, 1)$, $(1, -1)$, $(2, 2)$, $(2, -2)$, and so on.

d. $y = \sqrt{x - 4}$ is a function. The domain is all real numbers greater than or equal to 4. The range is all real numbers greater than or equal to 0. Sample ordered pairs are $(5, 1)$, $(6, \sqrt{2})$, $(7, \sqrt{3})$, and so on. ∎

Experiencing Algebra the Checkup Way

In exercises 1–5, determine whether each relation is a function. Use x as the independent variable and y as the dependent variable.

1. $y = -4x - 7$ **2.** $y = x^2 + 3$ **3.** $y^2 = 4x + 16$ **4.** $y = |x|$

5. $y = -\sqrt{x + 2}$

6. When checking an equation to see whether it is a function, what should you be checking?

3 Identifying Functions from Graphs

Relations are sometimes represented as graphs. Therefore, a function may be represented as a graph. For example, the following graph is a graph of a function.

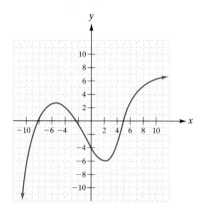

We need to determine a method for deciding whether a relation represented as a graph is a function. Complete the following set of exercises.

D I S C O V E R Y   3

Graphs of Functions

The following are graphs of functions. Draw a vertical line through more than one point on the graph, if possible.

1.

2.

3.

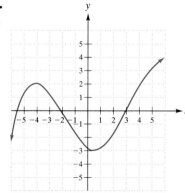

Continued

Write a rule for determining a function from the graph of a relation by drawing a line through points on the graph.

Check your rule on the following two graphs of relations that are not functions.

4.

5.

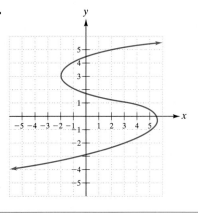

In the set of functions, a vertical line does not cross the graph of a function more than once. In the check, we see that a vertical line crossed the graphs of the relations that were not functions more than once.

Vertical Line Test
If a vertical line can be drawn such that it intersects the graph of a relation more than once, the graph does not represent a function. If it is not possible to draw such a vertical line, then the graph represents a function.

We know that this rule is a valid test because if we graph two distinct ordered pairs with the same x-coordinate, they will lie on the same vertical line, and a function does not have two ordered pairs with the same x-coordinate. For example, graph the relation $\{(4, 3), (4, -5)\}$, which is not a function.

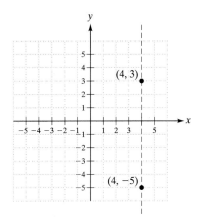

Examples of applying the vertical line test are given in the following figures.

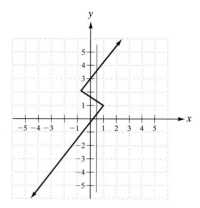

This graph represents a function. All possible vertical lines cross the graph only once.

This graph does not represent a function. The drawn vertical line is one of many such lines that cross the graph more than once.

EXAMPLE 3 Determine whether each graph represents a function.

a.

b.

c.

d.

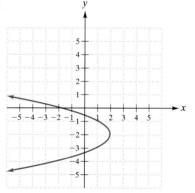

Solution

Open dots in a graph mean that the values corresponding to the dots are not part of the relation graphed.

a. The graph represents a function because all possible vertical lines cross the graph only once.
b. The graph does not represent a function because the graph consists of vertical lines.
c. The graph represents a function because all possible vertical lines cross the graph only once.
d. The graph does not represent a function because a vertical line can be drawn to cross the graph more than once. ∎

Since a function is a kind of relation, it may be graphed in the same manner as a relation. For example, $y = x^2$ is a function, as shown in Figure 4.22.

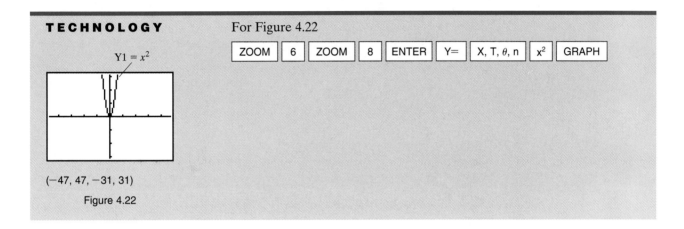

TECHNOLOGY

$Y1 = x^2$

$(-47, 47, -31, 31)$

Figure 4.22

For Figure 4.22

ZOOM 6 ZOOM 8 ENTER Y= X, T, θ, n x² GRAPH

EXAMPLE 4 Graph each function on a decimal screen on your calculator.

a. $y = 2x + 1$ **b.** $y = x^2 - 1$

Calculator Solution

The solutions for Example 4 are shown in Figure 4.23a and Figure 4.23b. ∎

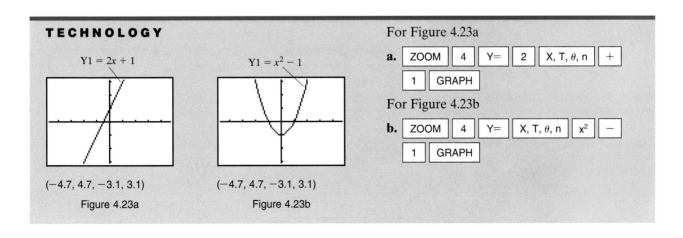

TECHNOLOGY

$Y1 = 2x + 1$

$(-4.7, 4.7, -3.1, 3.1)$

Figure 4.23a

$Y1 = x^2 - 1$

$(-4.7, 4.7, -3.1, 3.1)$

Figure 4.23b

For Figure 4.23a

a. ZOOM 4 Y= 2 X, T, θ, n +
1 GRAPH

For Figure 4.23b

b. ZOOM 4 Y= X, T, θ, n x² −
1 GRAPH

Experiencing Algebra the Checkup Way

Determine whether each graph represents a function.

1.

2.

3.

4.

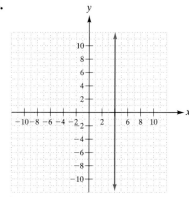

In exercises 5–6, graph each function on a decimal screen on your calculator.

5. $y = 2 - 3x^2$ **6.** $y = 3x - 2$

7. Summarize how to check the graph of a relation to determine whether it is a function.

---

4 Function Notation   A function is a relation, so it may be represented in all of the same ways as a relation. That is, a function may be written as a list of ordered pairs, in an equation form, or as a graph. However, there is a notation specific to functions called function notation. **Function notation** is written as an equation with the name of the function, the name of the independent variable in parentheses, and an expression to be evaluated to determine the dependent variable. For example, to write the relation $y = x + 2$ in function notation,

$$y = x + 2 \quad \text{Relation}$$
$$f(x) = x + 2 \quad \text{Function notation}$$

This is read: f of x equals x plus 2.

$$u = 3t - 5 \quad \text{Relation}$$
$$g(t) = 3t - 5 \quad \text{Function notation}$$

This is read: g of t equals $3t$ minus 5.

Caution: The notation $f(x)$ does not mean multiplication of f by x.

Helping Hand Function notation is very similar to the equation form of a relation. The difference is that in function notation the y is replaced with the name of the function and the name of the independent variable in parentheses.

We can evaluate a function written in function notation just as we evaluate a function written as an equation to determine ordered pairs.

To evaluate a function for a number:

- Substitute the number for the independent variable in the equation.
- Perform the indicated operations.

To evaluate a function for an algebraic expression:

- Substitute the expression for the independent variable in the equation.
- Simplify the expression.

For example, evaluate the function $y = x + 2$ for $x = 3$.

Given $f(x) = x + 2$, find $f(3)$.   Function notation

$f(3) = 3 + 2$ Substitute 3 for the variable, x.

$f(3) = 5$ Evaluate.

The ordered pair is written $(x, f(x))$ or $(3, 5)$.

Given $g(t) = 3t - 5$, find $g(-2)$.

$g(-2) = 3(-2) - 5$ Substitute -2 for the variable, t.

$g(-2) = -6 - 5$ Evaluate.

$g(-2) = -11$

Given $g(t) = 3t - 5$, find $g(a)$.

$g(a) = 3(a) - 5$ Substitute the expression for the variable, t.

$g(a) = 3a - 5$

Given $g(t) = 3t - 5$, find $g(a + 1)$.

$g(a + 1) = 3(a + 1) - 5$ Substitute the expression $a + 1$ for the variable, t.

$g(a + 1) = 3a + 3 - 5$ Distribute and simplify.

$g(a + 1) = 3a - 2$

To evaluate a function for a number on your calculator:

- Rewrite the function notation into an equation form in terms of x, if needed.
- Enter the expression for the function in the first y.
- Recall the function by name.
- Evaluate the function for the number. Enter the number to be substituted for the independent variable in parentheses.

Note: In "Experiencing Algebra the Calculator Way" at the end of this section, a second procedure is discussed.

We cannot evaluate a function for an algebraic expression on a calculator.

In the following calculator example, given $f(x) = x + 2$, find $f(3)$, as shown in Figure 4.24.

$y = x + 2$ Rewrite in equation form (change $f(x)$ into y).

TECHNOLOGY

```
Y₁(3)
              5
```

Y1 = x + 2

Figure 4.24

For Figure 4.24
Enter the expression in Y1.

| Y= | X, T, θ, n | + | 2 | 2nd | QUIT |

Recall the function by name.

| VARS | ▶ | 1 | 1 |

Enter the number to be substituted for the independent variable.

| (| 3 |) | ENTER |

We cannot evaluate $g(a)$ and $g(a + 1)$ on a calculator because we are evaluating a function for an algebraic expression.

EXAMPLE 5   Evaluate each function for the given number or expression.

a. Given $f(x) = x^2 + x + 5$, find $f(2)$ and $f(-2)$.
b. Given $g(v) = \sqrt{v + 7}$, find $g(8)$ and $g(-8)$.
c. Given $f(x) = x - 4$, find $f(a)$ and $f(a + h)$.

Solution

a. Given $f(x) = x^2 + x + 5$, find $f(2)$ and $f(-2)$.

$$f(2) = (2)^2 + 2 + 5 \qquad f(-2) = (-2)^2 + (-2) + 5 \qquad \text{Substitute.}$$
$$f(2) = 4 + 2 + 5 \qquad f(-2) = 4 + (-2) + 5 \qquad \text{Evaluate.}$$
$$f(2) = 11 \qquad f(-2) = 7$$

b. Given $g(v) = \sqrt{v + 7}$, find $g(8)$ and $g(-8)$.

$$g(8) = \sqrt{8 + 7} \qquad g(-8) = \sqrt{-8 + 7} \qquad \text{Substitute.}$$
$$g(8) = \sqrt{15} \qquad g(-8) = \sqrt{-1} \qquad \text{Evaluate.}$$
$$g(8) \approx 3.873 \qquad g(-8) \text{ is not a real number.}$$

c. Given $f(x) = x - 4$, find $f(a)$ and $f(a + h)$.

$$f(a) = a - 4 \qquad f(a + h) = (a + h) - 4 \qquad \text{Substitute.}$$
$$f(a + h) = a + h - 4 \qquad \text{Simplify.}$$

Use your calculator to check your results.

a. Given $f(x) = x^2 + x + 5$, find $f(2)$ and $f(-2)$. See Figure 4.25.
b. Given $g(v) = \sqrt{v + 7}$, find $g(8)$ and $g(-8)$. See Figures 4.26a and 4.26b.
c. Given $f(x) = x - 4$, find $f(a)$ and $f(a + h)$.

These expressions cannot be evaluated on a calculator. ■

Experiencing Algebra the Checkup Way

In exercises 1–3, evaluate each function for the given number or expression.

1. Given $f(x) = \sqrt{21 - 15x}$, find $f(4)$ and $f(-4)$.
2. Given $h(z) = 3z^3 - 2z^2 + 4z - 8$, find $h(1)$, $h(0)$, and $h(-1)$.

TECHNOLOGY

Y1 = x^2 + x + 5

Figure 4.25

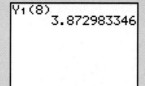

Y1 = $\sqrt{x + 7}$

Figure 4.26a

Y1 = $\sqrt{x - 7}$

Figure 4.26b

For Figure 4.25
To evaluate $f(2)$ on your calculator, enter the expression in Y1 and quit the screen.

| Y= | X, T, θ, n | x^2 | + | X, T, θ, n | + | 5 | 2nd | QUIT |

Evaluate the function in Y1 for $x = 2$.

| VARS | ▶ | 1 | 1 | (| 2 |) | ENTER |

To evaluate $f(-2)$, recall the last entry | 2nd | ENTRY |, move the cursor over the 2, and insert a negative
sign | 2nd | INS | (−) | ENTER |.

For Figure 4.26a
To evaluate $g(8)$ on your calculator, enter the expression in Y1 and quit the screen.

| Y= | 2nd | $\sqrt{\ }$ | X, T, θ, n | + | 7 |) | 2nd | QUIT |

Evaluate the function in Y1 for $x = 8$.

| VARS | ▶ | 1 | 1 | (| 8 |) | ENTER |

For Figure 4.26b
To evaluate $g(-8)$, recall the last entry and insert a negative sign. The result is an error on the calculator
because -8 is not in the domain of the function.

3. Given $g(x) = 4x - 8$, find $g(b)$, $g(1)$, and $g(b + 1)$.

4. Explain what the notation $f(x)$ means.

5. When can a function be evaluated using your calculator?

---

5 Modeling the Real World

Many important relations in business, science, social studies—in fact, almost any area of activity—are functions. We can write functions and evaluate them just as we've learned in this section. Remember, though, to keep in mind what the function value represents in terms of the original situation.

EXAMPLE 6

Dougal plans to decorate sweatshirts. The paint costs $14.75. The sweatshirts cost $7.14 each.

a. Write a cost function, $C(x)$, for the cost of x sweatshirts.
b. Determine the cost of two sweatshirts using the cost function in part (a).

Y1 = 14.75 + 7.14x

Solution

a. Let x = the number of sweatshirts decorated.
The cost is 14.75 plus 7.14 times the number of sweatshirts, x.
$C(x) = 14.75 + 7.14x$
b. To find the cost of two sweatshirts, find $C(2)$.
$C(2) = 14.75 + 7.14(2)$
$C(2) = 29.03$

Two sweatshirts cost Dougal $29.03 to produce. ■

Application

The number of pounds of first-class mail per capita delivered by the U.S. Postal Service is given in the following table for the years 1990 through 1994.[1]

Year	Weight (in pounds)
1990	14
1991	14
1992	14
1993	14
1994	14

Write a set of ordered pairs for the data. Graph the relation. Is this relation a function?

Discussion

Let x = the number of years after 1990
y = the weight in pounds of first-class mail per capita (per person)

The ordered pairs are (0, 14), (1, 14), (2, 14), (3, 14), (4, 14).
The relation is a function because every element in the domain corresponds to only one element in the range. Also, in viewing the graph, all possible vertical lines would intersect the graph once. ■

 Experiencing Algebra the Checkup Way

The charge for renting a chain saw is $10 per day or fraction of a day, with a $5 fixed fee for resharpening the saw.

1. Write a function to represent the charge for renting the saw for d days.

2. Determine the cost of renting the saw for 4 days.

[1] *Source:* U.S. Postal Service, Annual Report of the Postmaster General.

PROBLEM SET 4.3

Experiencing Algebra the Exercise Way

Determine whether each relation is a function.

1. $A = \{(-2, 1), (-2, 3), (2, -3), (2, -1)\}$

2. $B = \{(1.2, 2.4), (1.4, 2.8), (1.6, 3.2), (1.8, 3.6)\}$

3. $C = \{(1.1, 1.1), (2.2, 2.2), (3.3, 3.3), (4.4, 4.4), (5.5, 5.5)\}$

4. $D = \{(1, 9), (2, 8), (3, 7), (4, 6), (5, 5)\}$

5. $E = \{(6, -1), (6, -3), (6, -5), (6, -7)\}$

6. $F = \left\{ \left(\frac{1}{2}, 2\right), \left(\frac{1}{2}, 3\right), \left(\frac{1}{2}, 4\right), \left(\frac{1}{2}, 5\right) \right\}$

7. $G = \left\{ \left(-1, \frac{2}{3}\right), \left(-2, \frac{2}{3}\right), \left(-3, \frac{2}{3}\right), \left(-4, \frac{2}{3}\right) \right\}$

8. $H = \{(8, -2), (7, -2), (6, -2), (5, -2), (4, -2)\}$

Determine whether each relation is a function. Use x as the independent variable and y as the dependent variable.

9. $y = 22x - 11$

10. $y = -45x + 12$

11. $y = 13x^2 + 4$

12. $x = y^2 - 1$

13. $y^2 = 16x + 25$

14. $x^2 = -y - 9$

15. $y = 25x + 125$

16. $y = -2.3x - 5.5$

17. $y = 6x^3 + 4x^2 + 2x$

18. $y = -x^3 + 27$

19. $y^2 = 25 - x^2$

20. $y^2 = 1 - 0.25x^2$

21. $y = |-3x - 18|$

22. $y = |-3x| - 18$

23. $y = \sqrt{2x^2 + 4x + 1}$

24. $y = -\sqrt{4x^2 - 4x + 1}$

25.

26.

27.

28.

29.

30.

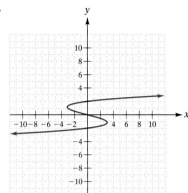

Evaluate each function for the given number or expression.
   Given $f(x) = 20x + 12$, find

31. $f(5)$

32. $f(50)$

33. $f(-7)$

34. $f(-17)$

35. $f(2.4)$

36. $f(-2.4)$

37. $f\left(-\dfrac{1}{4}\right)$

38. $f\left(\dfrac{1}{10}\right)$

39. $f(a)$

40. $f(-a)$

41. $f(a + 2)$

42. $f(-a + 2)$

43. $f(a - 4)$

44. $f(4 - a)$

45. $f(a + b)$

46. $f(b + a)$

Given $h(x) = 2x^2 - 4x + 5$, find

47. $h(7)$

48. $h(1)$

49. $h(-4)$

50. $h(-1)$

51. $h(-1.1)$

52. $h(0.1)$

53. $h\left(-\dfrac{2}{5}\right)$

54. $h\left(\dfrac{2}{5}\right)$

55. $h\left(2\dfrac{3}{5}\right)$

56. $h\left(-7\dfrac{1}{2}\right)$

57. $h(b)$

58. $h(-b)$

Given $g(x) = |-3x + 9|$, find

59. $g(5)$

60. $g(0)$

61. $g(-5)$

62. $g(-1)$

63. $g(4.5)$

64. $g(0.1)$

65. $g(-4.5)$

66. $g(-0.01)$

67. $g\left(\dfrac{2}{3}\right)$

68. $g\left(-\dfrac{2}{3}\right)$

69. $g\left(-4\dfrac{2}{3}\right)$

70. $g\left(4\dfrac{2}{3}\right)$

Given $F(x) = \sqrt{x + 15}$, find

71. $F(85)$

72. $F(34)$

73. $F(-6)$

74. $F(-11)$

75. $F(-25)$

76. $F(-100)$

77. $F(5.25)$

78. $F(6.16)$

79. $F\left(-2\dfrac{3}{4}\right)$

80. $F\left(2\dfrac{16}{25}\right)$

81. Goodbuy Television's production process for manufacturing television sets has a fixed cost of $1500 for setting up a production run. Materials and labor to produce their sets cost $35 per television. Write a cost function for a production run. What is the cost of a production run that produces 400 televisions?

82. Creaky Car Company is considering setting up a new line in its production plant. The setup cost for each run on the line is estimated to be $25,000. The cost of materials and labor to produce parts is $550 per unit. Write a cost function for a production run. If the company can produce 3000 units on one run of the line, what will be the cost of production?

83. Fixed costs associated with selling CD players amount to $470 for advertising and counter space. The players retail for $125 each. Write a net revenue function for selling the players. What is the net revenue after expenses when 400 players are sold?

84. Truck rental costs to deliver parts to a customer average $185 per delivery. The parts are sold for $1200 per lot. Write a net revenue function for one shipment of a given number of lots. What will be the net revenue for one delivery of 50 lots of parts to a customer?

85. A Musical Mastery bus tour has 25 seats to sell. Each seat on the tour costs $175. However, in order to entice more customers to sign up for the tour, the company advertises that it will reduce the price $3 for each filled seat on the bus. Write a revenue function, given that a certain number of customers sign up for the tour. How much revenue will the company collect if 22 customers make reservations for the tour? (*Hint:* First write an expression for the cost of a seat, then multiply this expression by the number of seats reserved in order to obtain an expression for the total revenue.)

86. The landlord of Midrose Place has rental property with 40 apartments to rent. In the past, a rent of $375 per apartment has been low enough that all the apartments will be rented. For each $25 increase in rent, one additional apartment will become vacant. Write a function for the total monthly rental receipts if he raises the rent a given integer multiple of $25. What will be the total monthly rental receipts if the landlord raises the rent $75?

87. Recycled CDs Incorporated offers a choice of five used CDs for $25, with each additional CD costing $4. Write a cost function for purchasing a given number of CDs that is five or more. What will be the cost of buying 12 used CDs?

88. Comix Collectors Club offers a sale of 10 comics for $35 with each additional comic selling for $1.50. Write a cost function for purchasing a given number of comics that is 10 or more. What will be the cost of purchasing 18 comics?

89. Trucks-4-U offers to rent a truck for a dropoff fee of $39 plus a daily rental fee of $25. Write a cost function for renting a truck for a given number of days. What will be the charge for renting the truck for 3 days?

90. Susie Seller is paid $475 per week plus a commission of $165 for each major furniture sale she completes. Write a pay function for her week's pay, given that she completes a certain number of major sales. What will her week's pay be if she makes four major sales this week?

91. Handi Parking charges a fee of $2.50 plus $1.00 for each half-hour of parking. Write a cost function for parking a given number of half-hour increments. What is the charge for parking a car for $3\frac{1}{2}$ hours?

92. Party Palace rents a party room for $140 per evening, and charges $18.50 per person for food and refreshments. Write a cost function to rent the room for a party for a given number of guests. What will be the charge for a party of 75 guests?

 Experiencing Algebra the Calculator Way

The table function of your calculator is helpful when a function is to be evaluated repeatedly. As an example, if

$$f(x) = x^3 + x^2 + x + 1,$$

this expression can be stored in the calculator and the table feature can be used to generate evaluations as needed. The keystrokes for this follow.

| Y= | X, T, θ, n | ^ | 3 | + | X, T, θ, n | x² | + | X, T, θ, n | + | 1 | 2nd | QUIT |

| 2nd | TBLSET | ▼ | ▼ | ▶ | ENTER | 2nd | QUIT | 2nd | TABLE |

To evaluate the function for a given value, enter the value into the calculator and press | ENTER | .
Thus $f(-5) = -104$. Use this setup to find the following values of this function.

1. $f(65)$ 2. $f(-83)$ 3. $f(\pi)$

4. $f(\sqrt{2})$ 5. $f(5634)$ 6. $f(-\pi)$

Given $F(x) = \sqrt{x^2 + 8x + 16}$, find

7. $F(-8)$ **8.** $F(0)$ **9.** $F(-4)$

10. $F(0.8)$ **11.** $F(-6.3)$ **12.** $F\left(\dfrac{3}{4}\right)$

Given $h(x) = \dfrac{5}{x-5}$, *find*

13. $h(10)$ **14.** $h(-5)$ **15.** $h(20)$

16. $h(5.5)$ **17.** $h(5)$ **18.** $h\left(\dfrac{1}{5}\right)$

Experiencing Algebra the Group Way

Another area of study of functions has to do with the property of symmetry. Work the following examples and exercises in your group to come to an understanding of what this property entails.

If a function has the property that $f(-x) = f(x)$, the function is said to be symmetric about the y-axis. In other words, suppose you replace the independent variable by its opposite and simplify the resulting expression. If this resulting expression is the same as the original expression, then the function is symmetric about the y-axis. When you look at the graph of such a function, the portion of the graph to the left of the y-axis is a mirror image of the portion to the right of the y-axis.

As an example, $f(x) = x^2$ is symmetric about the y-axis because

$$f(-x) = (-x)^2 = x^2 = f(x).$$

Use this test to see whether the following functions are symmetric about the y-axis. Check by graphing each function on your calculator and looking to see whether the property is present.

1. $f(x) = 5x^2 - 6$ **2.** $h(x) = 5x^2 - 6x$ **3.** $c(x) = x^3$
4. $g(x) = -x^3$ **5.** $p(x) = 4x^4 + 2x^2 + 1$ **6.** $q(x) = x^4 + x^3 + x^2 + x + 1$

Present the results of your study to the class.

Experiencing Algebra the Write Way

"A function is always a relation, but a relation is not always a function." Discuss this statement, explaining what it means and why it is true. Include examples to illustrate your explanation.

4.4 Analyzing Graphs

Objectives
1 Identify the intercepts of graphs.
2 Identify the maxima and minima of graphs.
3 Identify the intersection of two graphs.
4 Analyze graphs containing real-world data.

Application The amount of revenue taken in by the U.S. Postal Service has not always covered the total expenditures of the service for a given year.[1] A set of ordered pairs that represent the relation between the number of years after 1987 and the revenue (in millions of dollars) is

[1] *Source:* U.S. Postal Service, Annual Report of the Postmaster General.

$$\{(0,\ 32{,}297),\ (1,\ 35{,}939),\ (2,\ 38{,}920),\ (3,\ 40{,}074),\ (4,\ 44{,}202),$$
$$(5,\ 47{,}105),\ (6,\ 47{,}986),\ (7,\ 49{,}576)\}.$$

A set of ordered pairs that represent the relation between the number of years after 1987 and the total expenditures (in millions of dollars) is

$$\{(0,\ 32{,}520),\ (1,\ 36{,}119),\ (2,\ 38{,}370),\ (3,\ 40{,}490),\ (4,\ 43{,}291),$$
$$(5,\ 45{,}653),\ (6,\ 46{,}322),\ (7,\ 48{,}455)\}.$$

Use the data points to graph a line for each relation on the same coordinate plane. Determine the approximate intersection points of the two graphs and interpret their significance.

  After completing this section, we will discuss this application further. See page 283.

  Now we want to analyze a graph of a relation or a function by visually determining its characteristics. We first need to define several terms that will help us describe the graph.

1 Identifying Intercepts

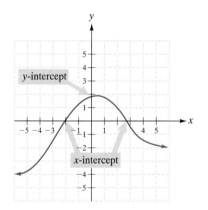

A graph may or may not cross the x-axis. If it does, it may cross the x-axis once or several times. An **x-intercept** is the location where the graph crosses the x-axis. There may be more than one x-intercept for a function. Similarly, a **y-intercept** is the location where the graph crosses the y-axis. There may be more than one y-intercept for a relation, but not for a function.

  In section 4.2, we discovered that the y-coordinate is 0 for all points located on the x-axis. Therefore, the x-intercept will always have a y-coordinate of 0. Similarly, the x-coordinate of a point located on the y-axis is 0. The y-intercept must have an x-coordinate of 0.

EXAMPLE 1 Use the following graphs in order to complete the sentences.

a.

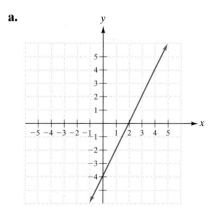

The x-intercept is ____. The y-intercept is ____.

b.

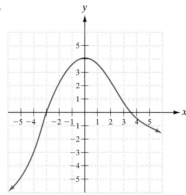

The *x*-intercepts are ____ and ____. The *y*-intercept is ____.

Solution

a. The *x*-intercept is $(2, 0)$. The *y*-intercept is $(0, -4)$.

b. The *x*-intercepts are $(-3, 0)$ and $\left(\frac{7}{2}, 0\right)$. The *y*-intercept is $(0, 4)$. ∎

To determine the *y*-intercept on your calculator:

- Trace the graph to find the *y*-intercept. The *y*-intercept has an *x*-coordinate of 0.
- If the *y*-intercept cannot be found by tracing, choose VALUE under the CALC function and ask for the *x*-value of 0.

 Helping Hand On the integer screen or decimal screen, the calculator's first trace coordinates are the *y*-intercept of the first graphed relation. The up or down arrow will move to the other graphed *y*-intercepts.

To determine the *x*-intercepts on your calculator:

- Trace the graph to find the *x*-intercept. The *x*-intercepts have a *y*-coordinate of 0.
- If the cursor skips the *x*-intercepts on a graph, choose ZERO under the CALC function.

EXAMPLE 2 Graph each function on your calculator. Then complete the sentence.

a. $y = x^2 - 1$ (Use decimal screen.)
The *x*-intercepts are ____ and ____. The *y*-intercept is ____.

b. $f(x) = x^3 + 4.05x^2 + 3.15x$ (Use decimal screen.)
The *x*-intercepts are ____, ____ and ____. The *y*-intercept is ____.

Calculator Solution

a. The *x*-intercepts are $(-1, 0)$ and $(1, 0)$.

The *y*-intercept is $(0, -1)$.

See Figure 4.27.

b. The x-intercepts are $(0, 0)$, $(-3, 0)$, and $(-1.05, 0)$.
The y-intercept is $(0, 0)$.
See Figure 4.28.

TECHNOLOGY

Y1 = $x^2 - 1$

$(-1, 0)$ $(1, 0)$

$(-4.7, 4.7, -3.1, 3.1)$

Figure 4.27

Y1 = $x^3 + 4.05x^2 + 3.15x$

$(-1.05, 0)$

$(-3, 0)$ $(0, 0)$

$(-4.7, 4.7, -3.1, 3.1)$

Figure 4.28

For Figure 4.27

a. | ZOOM | 4 | Y= | X, T, θ, n | x^2 | $-$ |
    | 1 | GRAPH |

For Figure 4.28

b. | ZOOM | 4 | Y= | X, T, θ, n | MATH | 3 |
    | + | 4 | . | 0 | 5 | X, T, θ, n | x^2 | + |
    | 3 | . | 1 | 5 | X, T, θ, n | GRAPH |

One of the x-intercepts cannot be found by tracing the graph. That is, the cursor passes over the x-intercept. This means that the x-intercept does not have coordinates with decimal values in the tenths place, which is the screen we are viewing. To find the x-intercepts, use the CALC function. To do this, trace the graph to the left side of the intercept (called lower bound). Press 2nd CALC 2 ENTER . Move the cursor to the right of the intercept (called upper bound) using the right arrow key. Press ENTER . Move the cursor as close to the intercept as possible using the left arrow key. Press ENTER . The calculator will display the coordinates of the x-intercept.

✓ Experiencing Algebra the Checkup Way

Determine the x-intercepts and the y-intercepts of each graph.

1.

2.

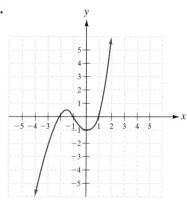

In exercises 3–4, graph each function on your calculator and determine the x-intercepts and the y-intercepts.

3. $y = x^2 - 4$ **4.** $y = 2x + 1$

5. If the graph of a relation has x-intercepts and y-intercepts, where do they occur?

6. Which coordinate of an x-intercept has a value of 0? Which coordinate of a y-intercept has a value of 0? What are the particular values of the coordinates of an x-intercept or a y-intercept?

2 Determining Maxima and Minima

A function is said to be **increasing** if the function values increase as the values for the independent variable increase. A function is said to be **decreasing** if the function values decrease as the values for the independent variable increase. A function is **constant** if the function values do not change as the values for the independent variable increase. We can visualize this by viewing a graph. Complete the following set of exercises on your calculator.

DISCOVERY 4

Determining Increasing and Decreasing Functions

1. Graph $f(x) = x^2 - 4x$ on an integer window.
2. Viewing the graph from left to right, we see that the graph first _____ and then _____. (Insert *falls* or *rises*.)
3. Trace the function to determine the following function values.

   $f(-2) =$ ____ $f(-1) =$ ____ $f(0) =$ ____

   $f(1) =$ ____ $f(2) =$ ____ $f(3) =$ ____

   $f(4) =$ ____ $f(5) =$ ____ $f(6) =$ ____

4. We see that the function values first _____ and then _____ as the x-values increase. (Insert *decrease* or *increase*.)

Write a rule to determine from a graph whether a function is increasing or decreasing.

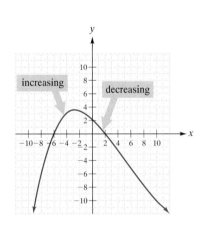

Viewing the graph from left to right, we see that it is first falling and then rising. We see that as the x-values increase, the function values decrease and then increase. Therefore, visually a function is decreasing if the graph is falling to the right and is increasing if the graph is rising to the right.

To determine an increasing, decreasing, or constant function from its graph, view the graph from left to right.

- If the graph is rising, the function values are increasing.
- If the graph is falling, the function values are decreasing.
- If the graph is neither rising nor falling, the function values are constant.

For example, in the graph to the left, we see that the function increases for all x-values less than -3 because the graph is rising. The function decreases for x-values greater than -3 because the graph is falling.

EXAMPLE 3   Use the following graph to complete the sentences.

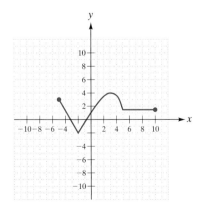

a. The function is increasing between the x-values of ____ and ____.

b. The function is decreasing between the x-values of ____ and ____ as well as between ____ and ____.

c. The function is constant between the x-values of ____ and ____.

Solution

a. The function is increasing between the x-values of -2 and 3.

b. The function is decreasing between the x-values of -5 and -2 as well as between 3 and 5.

c. The function is constant between the x-values of 5 and 10. ∎

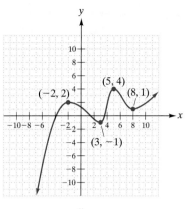

A function value is called a **relative maximum** (plural, *maxima*) if it is larger than the function values of its neighboring points. A function value is called a **relative minimum** (plural, *minima*) if it is smaller than the function values of its neighboring points. To determine a relative maximum or minimum visually, we determine the function values of the high points (relative maxima) or the low points (relative minima). A function may have more than one relative maximum or minimum. For example, see the graph to the left.

We see that the graph has two high points, at $(-2, 2)$ and $(5, 4)$. Therefore, the relative maxima are the function values 2 and 4. We know that these are the relative maxima because a maximum value of a function must be found at a point where the function values stop increasing and begin to decrease.

The graph has two low points, at $(3, -1)$ and $(8, 1)$. The relative minima are -1 and 1. We know that these are the relative minima because a minimum value of a function must be found at a point where the function values stop decreasing and begin to increase.

If a function is always increasing or always decreasing, it has no relative maximum or minimum. For example, see the graph to the left.

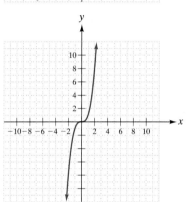

EXAMPLE 4 Use the following graph to answer the questions.

a. Determine the relative maxima of the graphed function.
b. Determine the relative minima of the graphed function.

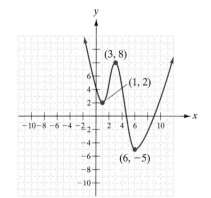

Solution

a. The relative maximum is 8, the function value of the high point $(3, 8)$.
b. The relative minima are 2 and -5, the function values of the low points $(1, 2)$ and $(6, -5)$. ∎

To determine the relative maxima of a function on your calculator:

• Trace the graph to the highest (maximum) function value.

or

• Use MAXIMUM under the CALC function, to calculate the maximum value.

To determine the relative minima of a function on your calculator:

• Trace the graph to the lowest (minimum) function value.

or

• Use MINIMUM under the CALC function, to calculate the minimum value.

EXAMPLE 5 Graph each function on the indicated window. Use the graph to determine the x-values for which the function is increasing and decreasing. Also, determine any relative maxima and minima.

a. $y = |x|$; decimal window

b. $g(x) = x^3 + 2x^2 - 4x + 4$; $(-4.7, 4.7, 1, -31, 31, 10, 1)$

c. $y = -x^2 + 8x - 2$; integer window

Calculator Solution

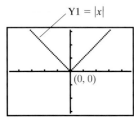

Y1 = |x|

(0, 0)

$(-4.7, 4.7, -3.1, 3.1)$

a. See the graph to the left.
   increasing—x-values greater than 0
   decreasing—x-values less than 0
   relative minimum of 0

b. See Figure 4.29.
   increasing—x-values less than -2
                     x-values greater than 0.667
   decreasing—x-values between -2 and 0.667
   relative maximum of 12
   relative minimum of 2.519

TECHNOLOGY

Y1 = $x^3 + 2x^2 - 4x + 4$

$(-2, 12)$

$(0.6, 2.519)$

$(-4.7, 4.7, -31, 31)$

Figure 4.29

For Figure 4.29

The low point of the graph cannot be found by tracing. The calculator will estimate a minimum function value between two given values called the left bound (smallest number) and the right bound (largest number). Choose MINIMUM under the CALC function by pressing [2nd] [CALC] [3]. Move the cursor to the left of the minimum point.

Press [ENTER]. Move to the right of the minimum point. Press [ENTER].

Move as close to the minimum point as possible and press [ENTER].

To check the high point found by tracing, choose MAXIMUM under the CALC function by pressing [2nd] [CALC] [4]. The calculator will estimate a maximum function value between two given values called the left bound (smallest number) and the right bound (largest number). Move the cursor to the left of the maximum point and press [ENTER]. Move the cursor to the right of the maximum point and press [ENTER]. Move as close to the maximum point as possible and press [ENTER].

Y1 = $-x^2 + 8x - 2$

(4, 14)

$(-4.7, 4.7, -3.1, 3.1)$

c. See the graph to the left.
   increasing—x-values less than 4
   decreasing—x-values greater than 4
   relative maximum of 14 ∎

Experiencing Algebra the Checkup Way

1. In Figure 4.30,

   a. between what values of x is the function increasing?

   b. between what values of x is the function decreasing?

   c. between what values of x is the function constant?

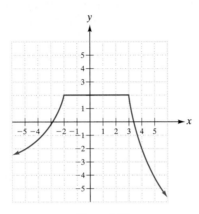

Figure 4.30

2. In Figure 4.31,

   a. what are the relative maxima and where do they occur?

   b. what are the relative minima and where do they occur?

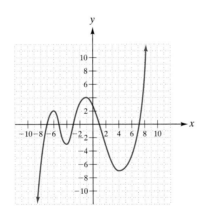

Figure 4.31

In exercises 3–5, use your calculator to determine (a) between what x-values each function is increasing, (b) between what x-values each function is decreasing, (c) the relative maxima, and (d) the relative minima. Use the indicated window.

   3. $y = -|x + 1|$; decimal screen

4. $y = 1 - 4x + 2x^2$; decimal screen

5. $y = 3x^4 - 14x^3 + 54x - 3$; $(-4.7, 4.7, 1, -62, 62, 20, 1)$

6. What does it mean to say that a function is increasing or decreasing over a certain part of the domain?

7. Define *relative maximum* and *relative minimum*.

---

3 Determining Intersections

The **intersection** of two graphs is the location where the two graphs cross. There may be more than one point of intersection. The intersection point is significant because the x-values of the two graphs are equal and the y-values of the two graphs are equal. This will turn out to be important as we continue in our discussions.

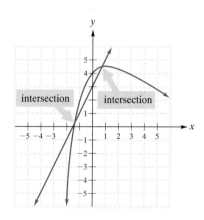

EXAMPLE 6 The point of intersection of the graphs below is ____.

Solution

The point of intersection of the graphs is $(-2, -5)$. ∎

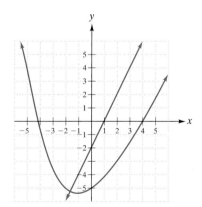

To determine on your calculator the intersection of two graphs:

- Trace one graph to the point of intersection. Check the intersection by using the up and down arrows to move between the graphs. If the x- and y-coordinates remain the same for both graphs, the cursor is on the intersection point.
- If the cursor skips the intersection, choose INTERSECT under the CALC function.

EXAMPLE 7 Graph the functions on the indicated window. Determine the point of intersection.

a. $y = 2x$ and $y = x + 1$ (Use decimal screen.)
b. $y = 3x - 5$ and $y = x + 2$ (Use integer screen.)

Calculator Solution

a. The point of intersection of the graphs is $(1, 2)$. See Figure 4.32.
b. The point of intersection of the graphs is $(3.5, 5.5)$. See Figure 4.33. ∎

TECHNOLOGY

Y1 = 2x

Y2 = x + 1

X=1   Y=2

(−4.7, 4.7, −3.1, 3.1)

Figure 4.32

Y2 = x + 2

Y1 = 3x − 5

Intersection
X=3.5   Y=5.5

(−47, 47, −31, 31)

Figure 4.33

For Figure 4.32

a. | ZOOM | 4 | Y= | 2 | X, T, θ, n | ▼ |
| X, T, θ, n | + | 1 | GRAPH |

To find the intersection, use | TRACE | and the left and right arrows. To move between the graphs, use the up and down arrows. Move between the graphs at the point of intersection to check the accuracy of your answer.

For Figure 4.33

b. | ZOOM | 6 | ZOOM | 8 | ENTER | Y= | 3 | X, T, θ, n | − | 5 | ▼ | X, T, θ, n | + | 2 | GRAPH |

The coordinates of the intersection are not integers. To find the intersection, use the CALC function. To do this, trace the graph to the closest location to the intersection and press | 2nd | CALC | 5 | ENTER |. Move the cursor to the closest location on the other graph by using the left or right arrow. Press | ENTER |. Choose this location as your guess by pressing | ENTER |. The calculator will display the coordinates of the intersection.

Experiencing Algebra the Checkup Way

1. Determine the point or points of intersection of the graphs in Figure 4.34.

Figure 4.34

In exercises 2–3, find the point or points of intersection of the graphs of the two functions.

2. $y = 2x - 15$ and $y = -2x + 5$ **3.** $y = 1.5(x - 1)$ and $y = x^2 - 4$

4. What is the term for the location at which two graphs cross? What is important about the coordinates of the point of crossing?

4 Modeling the Real World

We have seen that graphs are a very important way of representing functions that model real-world situations. One reason for this is that they make it easier to visualize things such as maximum and minimum values of functions or intersections of functions. However, remember that when dealing with real-world situations, the answers you get must make practical sense as well as mathematical sense. For example, suppose your function represents the number of T-shirts you need to sell to make a profit, and you find that your profit is a maximum if you sell 7.89 T-shirts. This means that you need to sell 8 T-shirts, since fractions of a T-shirt are not part of your sales model.

EXAMPLE 8

Figure 4.35 illustrates the height of a butterfly for x seconds after noon in terms of y feet above the ground.

Determine the times for which the function y is increasing, decreasing, and constant. Determine the maximum height above the ground.

Solution

The function is increasing for times between 0 seconds to 4 seconds after noon.

The function is decreasing for times between 4 seconds and 6 seconds after noon.

The function is constant for times between 6 seconds and 8 seconds.

The relative maximum of the function is 9 feet. ∎

Time in seconds

Figure 4.35

EXAMPLE 9

Dougal plans to decorate sweatshirts and sell them for a profit. She spends $14.75 for paint. The sweatshirts cost $7.14 each. The appliques cost $3.96 per shirt. She plans to sell the shirts for $20.00 each.

a. Write a cost function, $C(x)$, for the cost of the x sweatshirts.
b. Write a revenue function, $R(x)$, for the amount collected from the sale of x sweatshirts.
c. Graph the cost and revenue functions on a calculator. Use the following settings for your window: (0, 10, 1, 0, 62, 10, 1). Determine the intersection of the two graphs. Interpret the meaning of the coordinates of the intersection.

Solution

a. Let $x =$ the number of sweatshirts.
The sweatshirts cost $7.14 per sweatshirt, or $7.14x$.
The appliques cost $3.96 per sweatshirt, or $3.96x$.
The paint costs $14.75.

$$C(x) = 7.14x + 3.96x + 14.75 \quad \text{or} \quad C(x) = 11.10x + 14.75$$

b. The sweatshirts sell for $20.00 each, or $20.00x$.

$$R(x) = 20.00x \quad \text{or} \quad R(x) = 20x$$

Y2 = 20x

Y1 = 11.10x + 14.75

Intersection
X=1.6573034 Y=33.146067

(0, 10, 0, 62)

c. The intersection of the graphs is (1.657, 33.146). Therefore, Dougal must make and sell approximately 1.657 sweatshirts for approximately $33.15 in order to break even (equal cost and revenue). Actually, Dougal must make and sell 2 sweatshirts, since it is impossible to sell 1.657 sweatshirts. ∎

Application

The amount of revenue taken in by the U.S. Postal Service has not always covered the total expenditures of the service for a given year.[1] A set of ordered pairs that represent the relation between the number of years after 1987 and the revenue (in millions of dollars) is

$$\{(0,\ 32{,}297),\ (1,\ 35{,}939),\ (2,\ 38{,}920),\ (3,\ 40{,}074),\ (4,\ 44{,}202),$$
$$(5,\ 47{,}105),\ (6,\ 47{,}986),\ (7,\ 49{,}576)\}.$$

A set of ordered pairs that represent the relation between the number of years after 1987 and the total expenditures (in millions of dollars) is

$$\{(0,\ 32{,}520),\ (1,\ 36{,}119),\ (2,\ 38{,}370),\ (3,\ 40{,}490),\ (4,\ 43{,}291),$$
$$(5,\ 45{,}653),\ (6,\ 46{,}322),\ (7,\ 48{,}455)\}.$$

Use the data points to graph a line for each relation on the same coordinate plane. Determine the approximate intersection points of the two graphs and interpret their significance.

Discussion

The graphs intersect at approximately (1.5, 37,000), (2.5, 39,000), and (3.5, 42,000). When $x = 0$ and $x = 1$ (in 1987 and 1988), the expenditures exceeded the revenue. When $x \approx 1.5$ (in 1989), the revenue overtook the expenditures. When $x \approx 2.5$ (in 1990), the expenditures began to exceed the revenue. When $x \approx 3.5$ (in 1991), the revenue began to exceed the amount of expenditures and has continued to do so for the data given. ■

Experiencing Algebra the Checkup Way

To promote a bus tour, a company advertises a price of $55 per person, and offers a discount per person of $1 times the number of seats on the bus that are sold. Let x represent the number of seats sold for the tour.

1. Write an expression for the cost of each seat.

2. Write a revenue function that represents the total revenue received for selling x seats.

Graph the revenue function on your calculator and answer the following questions. Use a window of (0, 94, 10, 0, 930, 150, 1).

3. For what values of x is the function increasing?

4. For what values of x is the function decreasing?

5. For what value of x is the revenue at a maximum?

6. How many seats should be sold to maximize revenue?

7. What is the maximum revenue the company can realize for the tour?

---

[1] *Source:* U.S. Postal Service, Annual Report of the Postmaster General.

PROBLEM SET 4.4

Experiencing Algebra the Exercise Way

Use each graph to determine the following:

   a. *x*-intercepts   **b.** *y*-intercepts

   c. *x*-values for which the function is increasing

   d. *x*-values for which the function is decreasing

   e. relative maxima   **f.** relative minima

1.

2.

3.

4.

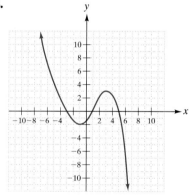

Graph each function and determine the x-intercepts and the y-intercepts.

5. $y = 3x - 6$

6. $y = 4x + 8$

7. $y = \dfrac{1}{2}x + 1$

8. $y = \dfrac{2}{3}x + 4$

9. $y = 1.2x - 6$

10. $y = 0.2x + 1$

11. $f(x) = -12x + 24$

12. $F(x) = 15x - 45$

13. $f(x) = 9x + 15$

14. $G(x) = -8x + 36$

15. $y = x^2 - 9$

16. $y = x^2 - 16$

17. $y = x^2 + 6x + 9$

18. $y = x^2 - 4x + 4$

19. $y = 4x^2 + 4x + 1$

20. $y = 4x^2 - 12x + 9$

21. $g(x) = x^2 + 10x - 3$

22. $f(x) = 0.4x^2 - 0.4x - 6.5$

23. $H(x) = x^2 - 5x - 24$

24. $g(x) = 2x^2 + 13x - 70$

25. $y = x^3 + x^2 - 2x$

26. $y = x^3 + 4x^2 + 3x$

27. $f(x) = x^3 + 2x^2 - x - 2$

28. $f(x) = x^3 + x^2 - 4x - 4$

29. $h(x) = |x| - 6$

30. $f(x) = |2x| - 6$

31. $y = |2x - 3| - 1$

32. $y = 5 - |3x + 1|$ **33.** $y = |x^2 - 2| - 1$ **34.** $y = |x^2 - 3| - 1$

Graph each function. Use the graph to determine the x-values for which the function is increasing and the x-values for which the function is decreasing. Also determine any relative minima and relative maxima.

35. $y = 2x + 8$ **36.** $y = 4 - x$ **37.** $f(x) = 3 - 2x$

38. $g(x) = x - 2$ **39.** $y = 1 - x^2$ **40.** $y = x^2 + 1$

41. $g(x) = x^2 + 4x + 3$ **42.** $h(x) = 4x - 5 - x^2$ **43.** $y = |x + 3|$

44. $y = |x| + 3$ **45.** $f(x) = x^3 + 2x^2 - x - 2$ **46.** $p(x) = -x^3 - x^2 + 4x - 4$

Given each pair of functions, find the point or points of intersection of their graphs.

47. $y = 3x - 5$ and $y = -2x + 15$ **48.** $y = x - 7$ and $y = -x + 9$

49. $f(x) = 2x + 7$ and $g(x) = -x + 1$ **50.** $f(x) = -x - 3$ and $g(x) = 2x$

51. $y = -5x + 2$ and $y = 3x + 8$ **52.** $y = -4x$ and $y = -x + 8$

53. $r(x) = 5x - 7$ and $c(x) = 12$ **54.** $p(x) = 5$ and $q(x) = -3x + 14$

55. $y = 3$ and $y = -x^2 + 4$ **56.** $y = x^2 - 16$ and $y = 9$

57. $f(x) = 2x^2 - 4x + 5$ and $g(x) = 4x - 1$ **58.** $m(x) = -2x^2 - 8x - 2$ and $n(x) = 2x + 6$

59. $y = \dfrac{1}{4}x^2 - 2$ and $y = \dfrac{1}{2}x$ **60.** $y = \dfrac{1}{3}x^2 - 6$ and $y = x$

61. $y = |x| - 5$ and $y = 2$ **62.** $y = |2x + 8| - 12$ and $y = 4$

For the following exercises, write a function that represents each situation; graph the function; determine for which values of the independent variable the function is increasing and for which values the function is decreasing; and find any relative minima or relative maxima.

63. To operate her craft booth, Jillie has a fixed daily expense of $50. She collects a net revenue of $5 on each craft sold (that is, items are priced to sell at $5 above wholesale cost). Write a function for the net daily profit after expenses are subtracted from revenue, when x items are sold. Use a window of (0, 94, 10, 0, 620, 100, 1).

64. Sierra starts college with a scholarship of $50,000. She withdraws $5000 per semester for tuition and expenses. Write a function representing the amount of money remaining in the scholarship fund after x semesters of withdrawals. Use a window of (0, 18.8, 2, 0, 62,000, 10,000, 1).

65. A promotion to sell laboratory equipment to a school offers each item for $400. However, if the school buys more than one piece of equipment, the price for each piece will be reduced by the product of $10 times the number of pieces sold, up to a maximum sale of 25 pieces. Write a function for the total cost of purchasing x pieces of equipment. Use a window of (0, 94, 10, 0, 6200, 1000, 1). (*Hint:* First write a function for the price of each piece sold, then multiply this function by x to obtain the cost function.)

66. Roadrunners Bus Company charges $100 per person for a weekend bus excursion. To promote reservations, they offer to reduce the price per person by the product of $1 times the number of people who take the trip. The bus can hold up to 65 people. Write a function for the total revenue if x people take the trip. Use a window of (0, 94, 10, 0, 6200, 1000, 1).

Write a function for each situation and use it to answer the questions asked.

67. Charlie's Container Company can build containers at a cost of $4 per container, with a setup cost of $50 per run. The company sells the containers for $10 each.

   a. Write a cost function for the cost of making x containers in one run.

   b. Write a revenue function for the revenue received for selling x containers.

   c. Graph the two functions on the same coordinate plane and determine the point of intersection. Use a window of (0, 9.4, 1, 0, 124, 20, 1).

   d. Interpret what this point of intersection tells you.

68. Jim's Carvings, Incorporated, pays a carver $12 per carving plus a bonus of a $100 for signing up to supply carvings to the company. The company retails the carvings for $24 each.

  a. Write a cost function for the cost of obtaining x carvings from a carver.

  b. Write a revenue function for the money received from selling x carvings.

  c. Graph the two functions and locate the point of intersection of the graphs. Use a window of (0, 18.8, 2, 0, 620, 100, 1).

  d. What does the point of intersection indicate?

69. Tatyana's employers make a deal with her to encourage her in her college work. They offer her a bonus of $200 plus $50 for each credit hour with a passing grade. Alternatively, if she prefers, instead of the $200, they will pay her $75 for each credit hour with a passing grade.

  a. Write functions to represent how much Tatyana will receive under each offer if she receives x credit hours with passing grades.

  b. Graph the two functions on the same coordinate plane and determine the point of intersection. Use a window of (0, 18.8, 2, 0, 930, 150, 1).

  c. Explain what the point of intersection means to Tatyana.

70. Dandylawn Mowing Service offers Khalid a job. The service gives him a choice of two payment methods. He can earn a base pay of $25 per week plus $10 for each lawn he mows, or he can earn $15 per lawn mowed with no base pay.

  a. Write functions to represent how much Khalid will receive under each payment plan if he mows x lawns a week.

  b. Graph the two functions on the same coordinate plane and determine the point of intersection. Use a window of (0, 9.4, 1, 0, 124, 20, 1).

  c. What does the point of intersection represent to Khalid?

 Experiencing Algebra the Calculator Way

Graph the following two functions, using the integer setting for the coordinate screen.

$$y = \frac{2}{3}x^2 - 6 \quad \text{and} \quad y = -2x - 6$$

Can you tell by looking at the screen how many times the line crosses the graph? It is difficult to see, but it does cross twice. Try changing the setting using the ZOOM button. First try $\boxed{\text{ZOOM}}\ \boxed{4}$. Is this better? Can you find the points of intersection using this graph? Now try $\boxed{\text{ZOOM}}\ \boxed{6}$. Is this better? If not, try $\boxed{\text{ZOOM}}\ \boxed{8}\ \boxed{\text{ENTER}}$. You will learn more about the $\boxed{\text{ZOOM}}$ button later, but you should see that it can help you better see the graph if you learn how to vary the setting. Remember, you can't get lost when you experiment with the $\boxed{\text{ZOOM}}$ key. You can always get back to the integer setting simply by first pressing $\boxed{\text{ZOOM}}\ \boxed{6}$, waiting until the graph is drawn, and then pressing $\boxed{\text{ZOOM}}\ \boxed{8}\ \boxed{\text{ENTER}}$ to go to the integer setting.

  Experiment with the ZOOM setting to find the points of intersection of each pair of functions.

  1. $g(x) = \frac{1}{3}x + 3 \quad \text{and} \quad f(x) = \frac{1}{4}x^2 - 4$ **2.** $y = |x| - 6 \quad \text{and} \quad y = -|x| + 4$

  3. $y = x^2 - 18 \quad \text{and} \quad y = -x^2 + 54$

 Experiencing Algebra the Group Way

Often, several people working together on an application problem can reach a solution that is difficult to find working alone. Sometimes this is referred to as synergy. As an example, working in groups may make solving the following problems easier.

When you graph a function and find its relative maximum, you are said to be maximizing the function. The following applications ask you to maximize an area. Do this by writing a function to represent the area and then graphically finding the relative maximum.

1. Find the dimensions that maximize the area of a rectangular dog pen built from a 50-foot roll of fencing.

2. Find the dimensions that maximize the area of a rectangular dog pen built from a 50-foot roll of fencing and built using a house as one side.

3. Find the dimensions that maximize the area of a rectangular dog pen built from a 50-foot roll of fencing and a 4-foot gate, and built using a house as one side.

Experiencing Algebra the Write Way

In analyzing graphs of functions, we stated that there may be more than one x-intercept for a function, but that there may not be more than one y-intercept for a function. Explain what we mean when we refer to x-intercepts or y-intercepts, and then explain why a function can have several x-intercepts but only one y-intercept. (*Hint:* Think about the vertical line test for checking to see whether a graph is the graph of a function.) Draw an example of a function that has two x-intercepts; three x-intercepts; four x-intercepts.

CHAPTER 4	Summary

After completing this chapter, you should be able to define in your own words the following key terms and rules.

Terms

		Rules
table of values	origin	Constructing a table of values
independent variable	quadrants	Writing ordered pairs
dependent variable	coordinates	Graphing an ordered pair (or plotting
data	x-coordinate	a point)
ordered pair	y-coordinate	Graphing relations
relation	function	Determining the domain and range of
finite	vertical line test	a relation from a graph
infinite	function notation	Determining a function from a
domain	x-intercept	relation written in list form
range	y-intercept	Determining a function from a
rectangular coordinate system	increasing	relation written as an equation
Cartesian coordinate system	decreasing	Determining a function from the
coordinate plane	constant	graph of a relation
x-axis	relative maximum	Evaluating functions
y-axis	relative minimum	
	intersection	

CHAPTER 4	Review

Reflections

1. What is the difference between a dependent variable and an independent variable?

2. Explain the importance of order in an ordered pair of values.

3. In mathematics, what is a relation? What is the domain of a relation? What is the range of a relation?

4. Describe the Cartesian coordinate system, and discuss its use.

5. What is a function? Are all relations functions? Explain.

6. What is an intercept of a graph?

7. Describe what a relative minimum or a relative maximum of a graph represents.

8. When two relations are graphed on the same coordinate system, what is the significance of any points of intersection?

4.1

Construct a table of values for each equation, given the set of values for the independent variable.

1. $b = -2a + 7$, given $\{-3, -2, -1, 0, 1, 2, 3\}$ for a.

2. $y = \frac{2}{3}x + 4$, given $\{9, 6, 3, 0, -3, -6, -9\}$ for x.

3. $y = 0.4x - 1.2$, given $\{-3, -2, -1, 0, 1, 2, 3\}$ for x.

4. $a = 3b^2 - 2b + 5$, given $\{-2, -1, 1, 2\}$ for b.

5. $y = 5x^3 - 3x^2 + 2x - 22$, given $\{-18, -7, 0, 6, 21, 22.5\}$ for x.

6. $y = |x^2 - 6x + 5|$, given $\{-2, -1, 0, 1, 2, 3\}$ for x.

7. $y = 3.6x^2 + 1.5x - 14.2$, given $\{-2.7, -1.9, -0.6, 0, 0.8, 1.5, 2.4\}$ for x.

Construct a table of values for each equation. Select five values for the independent variable, x, in each table.

8. $y = 12x - 21$

9. $y = -1.6x + 4.5$

10. $y = \frac{3}{2}x - 6$

11. $y = |2x - 9|$

Construct a table of values for each equation with the given domain.

12. $y = (5x + 2)(x - 4)$, for odd integer values of x between -5 and 5.

13. $y = \frac{3}{5}x + 8$, where x is an integer multiple of 5 between -20 and 20.

14. $y = 17.1x - 12.9$, where x is an integer value between -4 and 4.

15. $y = 3x^2 - 5x + 17$, with a domain of $\{-6, -2, 0, 3, 8, 11\}$.

Construct a table of values for each application with the given domain.

16. The area of a circle for even integer values of the radius between 2 and 12 inches.

17. The volume of a right circular cylinder with a radius of 6 centimeters and a height that takes on the values of $\{3, 6, 9, 12\}$ inches.

18. The measure of the third angle of a right triangle with one angle measuring $\{10, 20, 30, 40, 45\}$ degrees.

19. The compounded amount of an investment of $2000 at a rate of interest of 6% for t years, where t assumes integer values between 1 and 5.

20. The Celsius temperature when the temperature assumes values of $\{-23, -14, 0, 41, 50, 59, 100\}$ degrees Fahrenheit.

21. The distance traveled at a rate of 65 miles per hour for integer values of time between 1 and 8 hours.

Write ordered pairs.

22. $y = 7 - 3x$, when $x = -10, -5, 0, 5, 10$.

23. $y = \sqrt{x + 8}$, when $x = -8, -7, -4, 1, 8$.

24. $d = \frac{2}{3}c - 1$, when $c = -6, -3, 0, 3, 6$.

25. The radius of a circle whose diameter measures $2, 4, 6, 8,$ and 10 inches.

Determine the domain and the range for each relation. Assume that x is the independent variable.

26. $P = \{(1, 2), (3, 6), (5, 10), (7, 14), (9, 18)\}$

27. $C = \{\ldots, (-6, 6), (-4, 4), (-2, 2), (0, 0), (2, -2), (4, -4), (6, -6), \ldots\}$

28. $y = 4(x + 5) - 1$ for $x = \{-5, -4, -3, -2, -1\}$

29. $y = x^2 + 2.5$

30. $y = \sqrt{5 + x}$

31. $y = \frac{12}{1 - x}$

32. y is the sum of 5 and the product of x and 4.

33. $T = 2\pi\sqrt{\frac{L}{32}}$, where T is the time period for a pendulum that has a suspension of L feet (L is the independent variable).

4.2

Graph and label each ordered pair on a coordinate plane.

34. $A(3, 2)$ **35.** $B(4, -3)$ **36.** $C(-3, 2)$

37. $D(-4, -3)$ **38.** $E(0, 5)$ **39.** $F(-5, 0)$

Using Figure 4.36, identify the ordered pair corresponding to each plotted point.

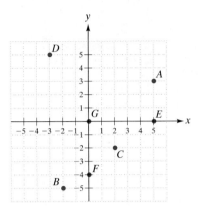

Figure 4.36

40. $A(\ ,\ )$ **41.** $B(\ ,\ )$ **42.** $C(\ ,\ )$ **43.** $D(\ ,\ )$

44. $E(\ ,\ )$ **45.** $F(\ ,\ )$ **46.** $G(\ ,\ )$

Using Figure 4.36, state the quadrant in which each plotted point lies, or the axis on which the point lies.

47. A **48.** B **49.** C **50.** D

51. E **52.** F **53.** G

Graph each relation.

54. $S = \{(0, -4), (1, -3), (2, -2), (3, -1), (4, 0), (5, 1)\}$ **55.** $y = 2x - 3$ for $x = \{-1, 0, 1, 2, 3, 4\}$

56. $y = 3 - 2x$ **57.** $T = \{(-5, 3), (-3, 3), (-1, 3), (1, 3), (3, 3), (5, 3)\}$

Determine the domain and range for each relation. Assume x is the independent variable.

58.

59.

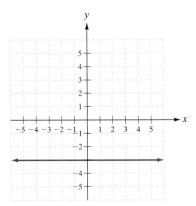

60. $y = 6x - 5$ **61.** $y = \sqrt{8 - 4x}$ **62.** $y = x^2 + 6x + 9$ **63.** $y = -x^2$

For each application, determine the domain and range, and interpret the values.

64. In Figure 4.37, energy supply and disposition are shown. Consider the line for consumption as the relation of interest.

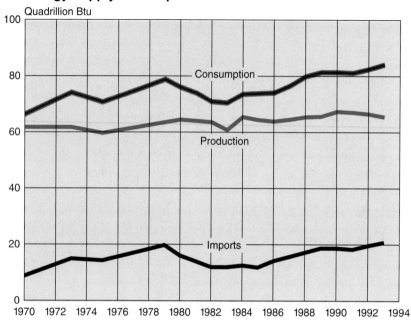

Energy Supply and Disposition: 1970 to 1993

Source: Chart prepared by U.S. Bureau of the Census. For data, see table 920.

Figure 4.37

65. A child-care center charges $40 per week for caring for a child. The charges for additional children from the same family can be determined using the chart shown in Figure 4.38.

66. In Figure 4.39, the area of a square is graphed in relation to the length of a side.

Figure 4.38

Figure 4.39

4.3

Determine whether each relation is a function. Assume x is the independent variable.

67. $S = \{(-2, 3), (-1, 5), (0, 7), (-1, 9), (-2, 11)\}$

68. $T = \{(-2, 3), (-1, 5), (0, 7), (1, 5), (2, 3)\}$

69. $y = x^2 - 10$

70. $y^2 = x - 10$

71. $y = 4$ for all x

72. $x = 2$ for all y

Determine whether each graph represents a function.

73.

74.

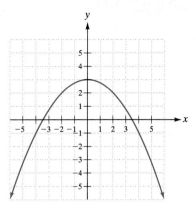

Evaluate each function for the given number or expression.

Given $f(x) = -4x + 13$, *find*

75. $f(13)$

76. $f(-21)$

77. $f(2.5)$

78. $f(-3.7)$

79. $f(a + 3)$

80. $f(-b)$

Given $g(x) = 5x^2 + x - 4$, *find*

81. $g(3)$

82. $g(-2)$

83. $g(0.5)$

84. $g(a)$

85. $g(-a)$

86. $g\left(-\dfrac{1}{4}\right)$

Given $S(x) = \sqrt{2x + 3}$, *find*

87. $S(3)$

88. $S(11)$

89. $S(59)$

Write a function to represent each application and evaluate it for the conditions listed.

90. A production process requires $4500 to set up for a production run. The cost of labor and materials to produce a single widget is $17. What is the cost of producing 1200 widgets on one production run?

91. A car rental firm charges $50 per rental plus $25 per day. What is the cost of a car rental for 4 days?

92. A learning institute will conduct a training session at your company for a fee of $1500 plus a charge of $125 per person attending. What will be the charge for a training session for 20 employees?

93. Dmitri charges $1.50 to paint faces at a church carnival. He purchased his supplies for $15.00. How much profit will he make for the church if he paints 135 faces?

4.4

94. Use the graph to determine the following:

   a. x-intercepts

   b. y-intercepts

   c. x-values for which the function is increasing

   d. x-values for which the function is decreasing

   e. relative maxima

   f. relative minima

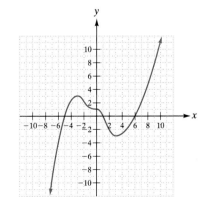

Graph each function and determine the x-intercepts and the y-intercepts.

95. $y = 3x + 9$ **96.** $y = 6 - x$ **97.** $y = \dfrac{3}{4}x - 9$

98. $y = x^2 - 0.36$ **99.** $y = |x| - 4$

Graph each function. Determine the values of x for which the function is increasing and the values of x for which it is decreasing. Also determine any relative minima and relative maxima.

100. $y = 4x - 3$ **101.** $h(x) = 6 - 2x$ **102.** $y = 3 - x^2$

103. $y = |x| + 2$ **104.** $f(x) = |x^2 - 1|$

What are the points of intersection of the graphs of each pair of functions?

105. $y = 2x - 2$ and $y = -\dfrac{1}{3}x + 5$ **106.** $y = x^2 - 6$ and $y = x$

107. $f(x) = |x + 5|$ and $g(x) = 2$

Write a function to represent each application, graph the function, and determine the values of x for which the function is increasing and decreasing.

108. The selling price of a horn switch wiring harness for a car is listed at $10.45. Write a revenue function when x harnesses are sold.

109. A bank account has a beginning balance of $216.00. There is no activity in the account except for a monthly service charge of $4.50. Write a function to represent the balance of the account after x months of inactivity.

110. An office contracts to buy a maximum of eight desks. The price of the first desk is $325, with each additional desk priced $15 lower than the previous desk's price. Let x represent the number of additional desks purchased after the first one. Write a function for the total cost of purchasing $x + 1$ desks, where x assumes values from 0 to 7. Use a window of (0, 9.4, 1, 0, 3100, 500, 1).

Write a function for each application and use it to answer the questions.

111. Hans can choose to receive a tuition reimbursement stipend of $400 plus $65 per credit hour for each credit hour passed, or he can instead choose to receive $100 per credit hour passed without a stipend.

    a. Write functions to represent how much Hans will receive under each option.

    b. Graph the two functions and determine the point of intersection. Use a window of (0, 18.8, 1, 0, 3100, 500, 1).

    c. What does the point of intersection represent to Hans?

112. The cost of production includes a setup cost of $500 plus a cost of $12 per item for labor and materials. The finished items sell for $25 each.

    a. Write functions to represent the total cost and total revenue associated with producing and selling x items.

    b. Graph the two functions and determine the point of intersection. Use a window of (0, 94, 10, 0, 1550, 500, 1).

    c. Interpret the point of intersection in business terms.

CHAPTER 4	**Mixed Review**

Given $f(x) = -x + 9$, *find*

1. $f(9)$ **2.** $f(-9)$ **3.** $f(1.8)$

4. $f(-2.7)$ **5.** $f(-b)$ **6.** $f(h + 1)$

Given $g(x) = x^2 - 3x - 4$, *find*

7. $g(4)$ **8.** $g(-1)$ **9.** $g(1.5)$

10. $g(v)$ **11.** $g(-v)$ **12.** $g\left(-\dfrac{2}{3}\right)$

Given $S(x) = \sqrt{6x - 8}$, *find*

13. $S(4)$ **14.** $S(12)$ **15.** $S(44)$

Determine whether each relation is a function. Assume x is the independent variable.

16. $P = \{(3, 8), (2, 6), (1, 4), (0, 2), (-1, 0)\}$ **17.** $Q = \{(2, -3), (2, -2), (2, -1), (2, 0), (2, 1)\}$

18. $y = x^2 + 5$ **19.** $y^2 = x + 5$ **20.** $y = -4$ for all x

Graph each function and determine the x-intercepts and the y-intercepts. Determine the values of x for which the function is increasing and the values of x for which it is decreasing. Also determine any relative minima and relative maxima.

21. $y = 5x - 10$ **22.** $y = 8 - 2x$ **23.** $y = 4.8x - 1.2$

24. $y = \dfrac{2}{5}x + 4$ **25.** $y = x^2 - 1.21$ **26.** $y = 2 - |x|$

Determine the points of intersection of the graphs of each pair of functions.

27. $y = 2x + 2$ and $y = -2x - 10$ **28.** $y = x^2$ and $y = 3x$

29. $f(x) = |2x|$ and $g(x) = x + 3$

Determine the domain and the range for each relation. Assume x is the independent variable.

30. $A = \{(2, 1), (4, 2), (6, 3), (8, 4), (10, 5)\}$

31. $B = \{\ldots, (-6, 3), (-4, 3), (-2, 3), (0, 3), (2, 3), (4, 3), (6, 3), \ldots\}$

32. $y = x^2$ for $x = \{-5, -4, -3, -2, -1\}$ **33.** $y = x^2 - 1.5$

34. $y = \sqrt{x - 8}$ **35.** $y = \dfrac{4}{x^2}$ **36.** $y = 7 - x$

37. $y = \sqrt{6 - 2x}$ **38.** $y = x^2 - 2x + 1$ **39.** $y = -x^2 + 3$

Write ordered pairs.

40. $y = 12 - 8x$, when $x = -6, -3, 0, 3, 6$.   **41.** $y = \sqrt{10 - 3x}$, when $x = 3, 2, 1, 0, -1, -2$.

42. $t = \dfrac{4}{7}s + 5$, when $s = -7, 0, 7, 14, 21$.

Construct a table of values for each relation.

43. $y = (3x - 5)(2x + 1)$, for even integer values of x between -4 and 4.

44. $y = \dfrac{3}{4}x - 5$, where x is an integer multiple of 4 between -12 and 12.

45. $y = 15.8 - 4.7x$, where x is an integer value between -3 and 3.

46. $y = 4x^2 - 17x - 15$, with a domain of $\left\{-2, -\dfrac{3}{4}, 0, \dfrac{3}{4}, 5\right\}$.

47. $y = x^3 + x^2 + x + 1$, given $\{-15, -5, 0, 5, 15, 25\}$ for x.

48. $y = |1 - 2x - 3x^2|$, given $\{-6, -3, 0, 3, 6, 9\}$ for x.

49. $y = 4.6x^2 + 2.8x + 10.4$, given $\{-3.7, -2.2, -0.7, 0, 0.8, 2.3, 3.8\}$ for x.

Construct a table of values for each relation. Select three values for the independent variable, x, in each table.

50. $y = 17 - 5x$ **51.** $y = 4.5x - 1.6$ **52.** $y = \dfrac{1}{4}x + 3$ **53.** $y = |3x - 10|$

54. Write ordered pairs for the circumference of a circle whose radius measures $\frac{1}{4}, \frac{1}{2}, 1, \frac{3}{2}$, and 2 inches.

Construct a table of values for each relation.

55. The area of a square for odd integer values of the length of a side between 1 and 7 feet.

56. The volume of a box with a length of 2 feet, a width of 1 foot, and a height that measures $\{1, 1.25, 1.5, 1.75, 2\}$ feet.

57. The measure of the second of two supplementary angles, where one angle measures $\{30, 60, 90, 120, 150\}$ degrees.

58. The simple interest on an investment of $2000 at a rate of interest of 6% for t years, where t assumes integer values between 1 and 5.

59. The Fahrenheit temperature when the temperature assumes values of $\{-10, -5, 0, 5, 10, 15, 20, 25\}$ degrees Celsius.

Write a function to represent each application and evaluate it for the conditions listed.

60. The setup costs for a production run are $2500. The labor and materials needed to produce a single production item cost $12. What will be the total cost of a production run of 1650 items?

61. A rental firm charges $15 to rent a grinder plus $2 for each hour of rental. What is the cost for renting the grinder for 10 hours?

62. A caterer will arrange an awards luncheon for your employees. He charges $275.00 to rent his party room and $9.50 per person for the luncheon. What will be the charge for a luncheon for 135 employees?

63. A charity basketball game charges $4 admission. Expenses for the game total $185. What is the net profit if the basketball game attracts 310 admissions?

Write a function to represent each application, graph the function, and determine the values of x for which the function is increasing and decreasing.

64. A storage tank holds 250 gallons of fluid when full. The tank dispenses fluid at a rate of 3.5 gallons per minute. Write a function for the amount of fluid remaining in a tank that was full after x minutes of dispensing fluid.

65. Jillian's grandparents deposited $1000 into a savings account at her birth. From then on, they deposited $50 per month into the account. Write a function for the total amount deposited into the account by her grandparents after x months.

66. The perimeter of a rectangle is fixed at 200 feet. If x represents the width of the rectangle, the length is $100 - x$. Write a function to represent the area of the rectangle. Use a window of $(0, 141, 15, 0, 3100, 500, 1)$.

Write a function for each application and use it to answer the questions.

67. A contest winner has the option of receiving $25,000 cash initially plus an annual payment of $5000 per year, or no initial cash payment but an annual payment of $6000 per year.
    a. Write functions to represent how much money the winner will receive under each option.
    b. Graph the two functions and determine the point of intersection. Use a window of $(0, 37.6, 4, 0, 248,000, 4000, 1)$.
    c. What does the point of intersection represent to the winner?

68. A retailer purchases appliances at a cost of $22 per appliance plus a total shipping charge of $600 for each lot ordered. She then sells the appliances for $75 apiece.

  a. Write functions to represent her total acquisition cost for a lot of x appliances, and for her total revenue for selling x appliances.

  b. Graph the two functions and determine the point of intersection. Use a window of $(0, 47, 5, 0, 3100, 500, 1)$.

  c. Interpret the point of intersection in terms of business decisions.

| CHAPTER 4 | Test |

Test-Taking Tips

Before you start a test, you should "dump your brain." By this, we mean that you should use scratch paper to list all the important information that you will need for the test—formulas, terms, tips, and so on. This gives you something to refer to while taking the test. Then you should scan the test questions, and pick out those problems that you think will be the easiest to do. Do those problems first. It will accomplish two things. First, it will allow you to expend your energies on the parts that you know best while you are still fresh. Secondly, it will build your confidence while taking the test, and will help you relax knowing that you can do the work. Save the difficult problems for last. Even then, don't spend a lot of time on any one question. If you can't seem to get a handle on it, go on to another question. Your subconscious will continue to work on the question, and when you return to it, you may find the solution will come easily.

1. Construct a table of values for $y = 2x^2 + 17x - 9$, given $\{-9, 0, 3\}$ as the set of values for x.

Consider the relation $y = |2x|$, where x is the independent variable.

2. Graph the relation.

3. What is the domain of the relation?

4. What is the range of the relation?

5. Is this relation a function? Justify your answer.

6. For what values of x is the relation increasing?

7. For what values of x is the relation decreasing?

8. What are the relative maxima of the relation?

9. What are the relative minima of the relation?

10. What are the x-intercepts of the relation?

11. What are the y-intercepts of the relation?

12. Identify the coordinates of the points in Figure 4.40.

$A \ (\quad , \quad), B \ (\quad , \quad), C \ (\quad , \quad), D \ (\quad , \quad), E \ (\quad , \quad)$

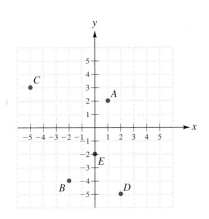

Figure 4.40

13. In Figure 4.40, in which quadrant does point D lie?

In exercises 14–17, for the function $f(x) = \frac{1}{2}x + 6$, find

14. $f(4)$ **15.** $f(-6)$ **16.** $f(2a - 2)$ **17.** $f(-b)$

18. A production process has a setup cost of $450.00. The cost of labor and materials to produce a single item is $21.50. Write a function to represent the cost of producing x items in one production run.

19. For the production process described in exercise 18, what is the cost of producing 250 items in one production run?

20. Find the intersection of the graphs of $y = 3x - 10$ and $y = -x - 2$.

21. What is meant by the term *ordered pair*, and why is the word *ordered* important?

CHAPTERS 1–4 | **Cumulative Review**

Consider the following real numbers.

$$-\frac{2}{3}, \quad 0, \quad 12, \quad 1\frac{4}{5}, \quad -0.33, \quad \sqrt{7}$$

1. Which numbers are whole numbers?

2. Which numbers are integers?

3. Which numbers are rational numbers?

4. Which numbers are irrational numbers?

Use one of the symbols $>$, $<$, or $=$ to compare the numbers.

5. $\frac{3}{8} \underline{\quad} \frac{1}{3}$ **6.** $\frac{2}{3} \underline{\quad} 0.66$ **7.** $-2.8 \underline{\quad} -1.6$

8. Graph the following numbers on a number line. Label the points.

$$-3.1 \quad -\frac{1}{2} \quad 2\frac{3}{4} \quad \sqrt{5} \quad -\sqrt{25}$$

Evaluate. Express your answers in fractional notation or round decimals to the nearest thousandth as appropriate.

9. $-28 + 13$ **10.** $4.8 - 7.36$ **11.** $-87 \div (-29)$

12. $-\frac{5}{8} - \frac{2}{3}$ **13.** $-2\frac{3}{4} \div 1\frac{3}{7}$ **14.** $\left(-\frac{2}{3}\right)\left(\frac{3}{8}\right)\left(-\frac{7}{16}\right)\left(\frac{9}{10}\right)$

15. $(12.96)(-4.8)$ **16.** $(14)(0)(5)(-6)$ **17.** $(-12)(16) \div 4(-2)$

18. $14 + (-7) + 22 - 16 - (-18)$ **19.** $-[3.8 - (-2.4)]$

20. $\dfrac{2(3^2 + 7) - 2^5}{3 \cdot 18}$ **21.** $-|12 - 20|$ **22.** $\sqrt{\dfrac{16}{25}}$

23. $-\sqrt{1.2}$ **24.** $\sqrt{-16}$ **25.** $\sqrt[3]{1\dfrac{13}{81}}$

26. 14^0 **27.** 1^{12} **28.** 0^0

29. -8^4 **30.** $(-8)^4$ **31.** $\left(\dfrac{3}{4}\right)^{-2}$

Write in scientific notation.

32. 0.00000305 **33.** $-4,235,600$

Write in standard notation.

34. 3.56 E-2

35. 6.78 E8

36. Write an equivalent exponential expression for $\sqrt[4]{3125}$. Evaluate both expressions.

37. Evaluate the expression $\sqrt{-x^2 + 5x - 2}$ for $x = 3$.

38. Consider the algebraic expression $a^3 - 2a^2 + a - 2a^3 + 7a - 5$.

    a. How many terms are in the expression?

    b. List the variable terms.

    c. List the constant terms.

Simplify exercises 39–40.

39. $-(3y + 2z) + (4y - 2z) - (-3y - 5z)$

40. $\dfrac{3}{4}x + \dfrac{5}{8}y - \dfrac{1}{16} - \dfrac{3}{4}x + \dfrac{1}{8}y - \dfrac{5}{6}$

41. Determine whether -2 is a solution of the equation $-x^2 + 3x + 8 = -3x$.

Consider the relation $y = 2x^2 + 3$, where x is the independent variable.

42. Graph the relation.

43. What is the domain of the function? What is the range of the function?

44. Is this relation a function? Justify your answer.

45. Determine the x-values for which the relation is increasing.

46. Determine the relative minima, if possible.

47. For the function $f(x) = \frac{1}{3}x - 5$, find

    a. $f(9)$ **b.** $f(a + h)$

48. Determine the volume of a rectangular solid with a length of 3.5 feet, a width of 2.25 feet, and a height of 1.75 feet.

49. Kelsie invests $500 for 4 years with interest compounded annually at 5.5%. Find her interest. Use the formula for the compounded amount A, $A = P(1 + r)^t$.

50. The Christmas House produces Christmas decorations. The setup cost for a certain ornament is $35.00. The cost of labor and materials per ornament is $2.80. Write a cost function to represent the cost of producing x ornaments in one production run. What is the cost of producing 150 ornaments in one production run?

5

Linear Equations in One Variable

I n Chapter 4 we saw how to describe relations using tables, equations, and graphs. In this chapter we present methods for solving equations—that is, using the description of a relation to find values of a variable that make the equation true. We work in this chapter with linear equations in one variable, which have fewer complications than more general kinds of equations. However, the three different methods we present—numeric, graphic, and algebraic—will apply to other kinds of equations in later chapters, as well as to solving real-world problems.

Speaking of real-world problems, we will examine in this chapter the relationship between a person's level of educational attainment and his or her monthly income. Our data come from the Bureau of the Census, U.S. Department of Commerce, in reports comparing monthly mean incomes for White, Black, and Hispanic populations, as well as for male and female populations.[1]
The general trends shown in these reports are not surprising. They document that a person can expect additional income for each higher level of education attained. Also, males earn more, on average, than do females at all levels of educational attainment, and Caucasians earn more than African-Americans or Hispanics at each level. We will not attempt to solve problems of social inequality in this course, but we will use these data to illustrate methods of solving mathematical equations.

[1] *Source:* "Education and Income, 1993," *The World Almanac and Book of Facts 1994.*

5.1 Solving Equations Numerically and Graphically

Objectives
1 Identify linear equations in one variable.
2 Solve linear equations numerically.
3 Solve linear equations graphically.
4 Model real-world situations using linear equations and solve numerically or graphically.

Application

The U.S. Bureau of the Census reported that the average of the mean monthly income for Caucasians, African-Americans, and Hispanics with B.S. degrees is $2150 (rounded to the nearest dollar).[1] If Caucasians have a mean income of $2552 and African-Americans have a mean income of $2002, determine the mean income for Hispanics.

After completing this section, we will discuss this application further. See page 314.

1 Linear Equations in One Variable

In this text we will be solving various kinds of equations. In this chapter we will solve **linear equations in one variable**. These equations can be written in a particular (standard) form.

> *Standard Form for a Linear Equation in One Variable*
> A linear equation in one variable (linear equation) is an equation that can be written in the form
>
> $ax + b = 0$, where a and b are real numbers and $a \neq 0$.

For example,

Standard form: $ax + b = 0$
1. $2x + 5 = 0$
2. $2x - 5 = 6$
3. $x + 2 + 3(x - 4) = 3x - 8$

The first equation is in the exact form $ax + b = 0$, where $a = 2$ and $b = 5$. The last two equations can be written in this form with algebraic manipulations that we will learn later in this chapter. Note that the variable x is raised to the first power. This *must* be the case for a linear equation in one variable.

Examples of nonlinear equations that contain variables raised to powers other than 1, variables in denominators of fractions, and roots of variables are listed here. We will solve these equations later in this text.

1. $2x^2 = 4$ *x* raised to the second power

2. $\dfrac{2}{x} + 1 = 0$ *x* in the denominator of a fraction

3. $2\sqrt{x} + 5 = x - 3$ *x* in the radicand of a radical expression

Until we learn algebraic manipulations, we will identify a linear equation in one variable, x, as an equation consisting of two expressions. Each of these

[1] *Source:* "Education and Income, 1993," *The World Almanac and Book of Facts 1994.*

expressions can be simplified to the form $ax + b$, where $a \neq 0$ in at least one of the expressions and the coefficient a is not the same in each expression. Using the previous linear examples,

Form: $ax + b$ $ax + b$

1. $2x + 5 = 0x + 0$

2. $2x + (-5) = 0x + 6$

3. $4x + (-10) = 3x + (-8)$

These equations are called linear equations because the graphs of the functions defined by the two expressions in the equation turn out to be straight lines. Let's test this statement on the calculator. Complete the following set of exercises with your calculator.

D I S C O V E R Y 1

Graphs of Functions Defined by Expressions in a Linear Equation
Graph on an integer screen the following functions, determined from the given linear equation.

1. $3x - 8 = 6$

     $Y1 = 3x - 8$ $Y2 = 6$

2. $-2x + 5 = -3x - 4$

     $Y1 = -2x + 5$ $Y2 = -3x - 4$

Describe the characteristic of the graph of the function defined by the expression in Y1.
Describe the characteristic of the graph of the function defined by the expression in Y2.

Graph on an integer screen the following functions, determined from the given nonlinear equation.

3. $\dfrac{2}{x} + x^3 = x$

     $Y1 = \dfrac{2}{x} + x^3$ $Y2 = x$

Describe the characteristic of the graph of the function defined by the expression in Y1.
Describe the characteristic of the graph of the function defined by the expression in Y2.

For linear equations, we see that the graphs of the functions defined by the expressions are straight lines.

For example, the equation $-2x + 5 = 8$ is a linear equation. The graph of the function $y = -2x + 5$ and the graph of the function $y = 8$ are both straight lines.

$(-47, 47, -31, 31)$

$(-47, 47, -31, 31)$

The equation $2x^2 = 4$ is not linear because the graph of the function $y = 2x^2$ is not a straight line, but a curve.

$(-47, 47, -31, 31)$

$(-47, 47, -31, 31)$

EXAMPLE 1   Identify each equation as linear or nonlinear.

a. $5x + (x - 2) = 3(x - 2)$ **b.** $x + 5 = x^3 - 2x$

c. $\sqrt[4]{x + 2} = 3x - 7$ **d.** $\dfrac{x}{5} + 3 = 6x$

Solution

a. Linear, because the equation simplifies to $6x - 2 = 3x - 6$.

b. Nonlinear, because x has an exponent of 3.

c. Nonlinear, because the radical expression has a variable in its radicand.

d. Linear, because the equation simplifies to $\frac{1}{5}x + 3 = 6x$.

Check your results graphically on your calculator. You may graph the expression on the left side of the equation and the expression on the right side of the equation using the same window.

a.

$(-47, 47, -31, 31)$

Linear, because the functions graphed are both straight lines.

b.

$$(-47, 47, -31, 31)$$

Nonlinear, because the graph of the function Y2, defined by the expression containing x^3, is not a straight line.

c.

$$(-10, 10, -10, 10)$$

Nonlinear, because the graph of the function Y1, defined by the radical expression containing a variable in the radicand, is not a straight line.

d.

$$(-47, 47, -31, 31)$$

Linear, because the functions graphed are both straight lines. ∎

Experiencing Algebra the Checkup Way

In exercises 1–5, identify each equation as linear or nonlinear.

1. $5x - (x - 7) = x - 5$

2. $4.1x - 2.3 = 5.3x^2 + 0.6$

3. $\dfrac{1}{7}x - \dfrac{3}{7} = \dfrac{5}{14}x + \dfrac{1}{2}$

4. $2x + 8 = \sqrt{x} + 1$

5. $\dfrac{1}{x^2} + 12 = 5$

6. What is meant by the standard form of a linear equation in one variable?

2 Solving Equations Numerically

Previously, we determined whether a number was a solution of an equation by substituting the number for the variable and evaluating the two resulting expressions in the equation. If the expressions were equivalent, then the number substituted was called a solution. The set of all possible solutions is called a **solution set**. For example, given $2x + 3 = x + 5$, determine whether 0 is a solution.

$$\begin{array}{c|c}
\multicolumn{2}{c}{2x + 3 = x + 5} \\
\hline
2(0) + 3 & 0 + 5 \\
0 + 3 & 5 \\
3 &
\end{array}$$

Substitute 0 for x.

Simplify.

Therefore, 0 is not a solution because the resulting values for the expressions, 3 and 5, are not equal.

To find a solution of the equation $2x + 3 = x + 5$, we could continue to substitute values for x until we find a number that results in equivalent values for each expression in the equation. To do this, it is convenient to use a table. You can see what we mean by trying the following "Discovery" exercise.

DISCOVERY 2

Numerical Solutions

To solve the equation $2x + 3 = x + 5$, complete the extended table of values shown and compare the values obtained.

x	$2x + 3$	$=$	$x + 5$	
0	3		5	$3 < 5$
1				
2				
3				
4				

Write a rule to determine the solution of an equation from a table of values.

The solution is the number in the first column, which, when substituted for the variable, results in two equal expressions.

> *Solving a Linear Equation Numerically*
> To solve a linear equation numerically:
> Set up an extended table of values.
>
> - The first column is labeled with the independent variable.
> - The second column is labeled with the expression on the left side of the equation.
> - The third column is labeled with the expression on the right side of the equation.
>
> Complete the table.
>
> - Substitute values for the independent variable.
> - Evaluate the second and third columns.

- Continue until values for the two expressions (the numbers in the second and third columns) are equal.

The value for the independent variable (the number in the first column) substituted to find these equivalent expressions is the solution.

For example, solve $2x + 3 = x + 5$ numerically for integer solutions.

A sample table to determine an integer solution follows:

x	$2x + 3$	$= x + 5$	
1	$2(1) + 3$	$1 + 5$	$5 < 6$
	$2 + 3$	6	
	5		
2	$2(2) + 3$	$2 + 5$	$7 = 7$
	$4 + 3$	7	
	7		
3	$2(3) + 3$	$3 + 5$	$9 > 8$
	$6 + 3$	8	
	9		
4	$2(4) + 3$	$4 + 5$	$11 > 9$
	$8 + 3$	9	
	11		

When 2 is substituted for the variable x, the two expressions are equivalent ($7 = 7$). Therefore, 2 is the solution of the linear equation $2x + 3 = x + 5$.

Note that in comparing the values obtained for the two expressions, the first expression is less than the second expression when $x = 1$ (a value less than the solution) but greater than the second expression when $x = 3$ and $x = 4$ (values greater than the solution).

To solve a linear equation numerically for integer solutions on your calculator:

- Rename the independent variable as x.

Set up the table.

- Set up the first column for the independent variable by setting a minimum integer value and increments of 1 for integers. Set the calculator to automatically perform the evaluations.
- Set up the second column of the table to be the expression on the left. Enter the left expression of the equation in Y1.
- Set up the third column of the table to be the right expression. Enter the expression on the right of the equation in Y2.

View the table.

- Move beyond the screen to view additional rows by using the up and down arrows.

The solution is the x-value that results in equal Y1 and Y2 values.

For example, solve $2x + 3 = x + 5$ numerically for integer solutions on a calculator.

As shown in Figure 5.1c, the solution is 2 because when $x = 2$, Y1 and Y2 have equal values.

TECHNOLOGY

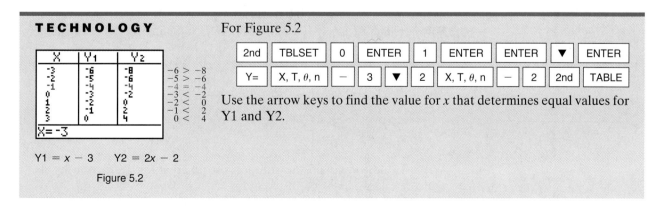

Figure 5.1a   Figure 5.1b   Figure 5.1c

For Figure 5.1a

| 2nd | | TBLSET | | 1 | | ENTER | (minimum number in table was 1)

| 1 | | ENTER | (independent variable values are increasing by 1)

| ENTER | | ▼ | | ENTER | (auto settings)

For Figure 5.1b
Y1 $= 2x + 3$ and Y2 $= x + 5$.

| Y= | | 2 | | X, T, θ, n | | + | | 3 | | ▼ | | X, T, θ, n | | + | | 5 |

For Figure 5.1c

| 2nd | | TABLE | results in the table.

EXAMPLE 2   Solve numerically.

a. $x - 3 = 2x - 2$ **b.** $3a + 5 = 2a$

c. $6x - (4x + 3) = 7 - 3x$

Calculator Numeric Solution

a. Let Y1 $= x - 3$ Y2 $= 2x - 2$.
As shown in Figure 5.2, the solution is -1 because when -1 is substituted for the variable x in both expressions, the results are equivalent, $-4 = -4$.

TECHNOLOGY

For Figure 5.2

| 2nd | | TBLSET | | 0 | | ENTER | | 1 | | ENTER | | ENTER | | ▼ | | ENTER |

| Y= | | X, T, θ, n | | − | | 3 | | ▼ | | 2 | | X, T, θ, n | | − | | 2 | | 2nd | | TABLE |

Use the arrow keys to find the value for x that determines equal values for Y1 and Y2.

Y1 $= x - 3$ Y2 $= 2x - 2$

Figure 5.2

Y1 = 3x + 5   Y2 = 2x

Figure 5.3

Y1 = 6x − (4x + 3)   Y2 = 7 − 3x

Figure 5.4

b. Rewrite the equation in terms of x, $3x + 5 = 2x$.

Let Y1 = 3x + 5   Y2 = 2x.

A sample table is shown in Figure 5.3.

The solution is -5 because when -5 is substituted for the variable a in both expressions, the results are equivalent, $-10 = -10$.

c. A sample table is shown in Figure 5.4.

The solution is 2 because when 2 is substituted for the variable x in both expressions, the results are equivalent, $1 = 1$. ∎

The linear equations in Example 2 have only one integer solution. This is not always true. Try solving the following equations with your calculator.

DISCOVERY 3

Linear Equations with Noninteger Solutions

$(5x + 4) - 2(3x + 1) = 2(x - 7)$ does not have an integer solution. Complete the table of values and compare the values obtained.

x	$(5x + 4) - 2(3x + 1) = 2(x - 7)$		
3	-1	-8	$-1 > -8$
4			
5			
6			
7			

Write a rule to determine when the solution of the equation is between two integers given in the table.

The expression on the left is greater than the expression on the right for x-values of 3, 4, and 5. The expression on the left is less than the expression on the right for x-values of 6 and 7. Therefore, the expression on the left is equal to the expression on the right at some x-value between 5 and 6. The solution is noninteger. (We will need a different method to find this solution.)

DISCOVERY 4

Linear Equations with No Solution

Solve $2x + 5 = 2x + 10$ numerically by completing the table of values and compare the values obtained.

x	$2x + 5 = 2x + 10$	
0		
1		
2		
3		

Write a rule to explain the solution of the equation from viewing its table of values.

The expression on the left is always 5 less than the expression on the right. The two expressions will never be equal. The equation does not appear to have a solution. Such an equation is called a contradiction. A **contradiction** is an equation with no solution.

Helping Hand The equation $2x + 5 = 2.0000001x + 10$ looks as if it has no solution when we examine a table of values. The table has a constant difference of 5 between the expressions on the left and right. However, other methods will give us a noninteger solution. This emphasizes the need to know other methods to check our findings.

D I S C O V E R Y   5

Linear Equations with Many Solutions

Solve $2x + 5 = (x + 3) + (x + 2)$ numerically by completing the table of values and compare the values obtained.

x	$2x + 5 = (x + 3) + (x + 2)$
0	
1	
2	
3	

Write a rule to explain the solution of the equation from viewing its table of values.

The two expressions are equal for every value of the independent variable evaluated. (This is also true for any other real-number value chosen for x.) The solution set of the equation is all real numbers. Such an equation is called an identity. An **identity** is an equation for which all permissable replacements of the variable result in a true equation.

EXAMPLE 3 Solve numerically for an integer solution, if possible.

  a. $4(x - 2) = 4x - 8$ **b.** $3x + 4 = 2x + (x + 10)$
  c. $4 - 5x - (3x + 2) = 7 - x$

Calculator Numeric Solution

a.

X	Y₁	Y₂
0	-8	-8
1	-4	-4
2	0	0
3	4	4
4	8	8
5	12	12
6	16	16

X=0

$$-8 = -8$$
$$-4 = -4$$
$$0 = 0$$
$$4 = 4$$
$$8 = 8$$
$$12 = 12$$
$$16 = 16$$

Y1 = 4(x − 2)   Y2 = 4x − 8

The expressions are always equal. The solution set is all real numbers. The equation is an identity.

b.

X	Y₁	Y₂
0	4	10
1	7	13
2	10	16
3	13	19
4	16	22
5	19	25
6	22	28

X=0

$$4 < 10$$
$$7 < 13$$
$$10 < 16$$
$$13 < 19$$
$$16 < 22$$
$$19 < 25$$
$$22 < 28$$

Y1 = 3x + 4   Y2 = 2x + (x + 10)

The difference in the values of the two expressions is always the same, 6. The expressions will never be equal. Therefore, there is no solution. The equation is a contradiction.

c.

X	Y₁	Y₂	
-2	18	9	$18 > 9$
-1	10	8	$10 > 8$
0	2	7	$2 < 7$
1	-6	6	$-6 < 6$
2	-14	5	$-14 < 5$
3	-22	4	$-22 < 4$
4	-30	3	$-30 < 3$

X=-2

$Y1 = 4 - 5x - (3x + 2)$ $Y2 = 7 - x$

The expression on the left is greater than the expression on the right for $x = -1$ and less than the expression on the right for $x = 0$. The solution is noninteger and between -1 and 0. ∎

> *Numerical Solutions of a Linear Equation*
> To solve numerically a linear equation for integer solutions, set up an extended table of values. One of four possibilities will occur:
>
> **An integer solution exists.** The solution is the integer in the first column that corresponds to equal values in the second and third columns.
> **A noninteger solution exists.** In the second and third columns, the values change in order from less than to greater than or from greater than to less than. The noninteger solution is between the two integers in the first column that correspond to this change.
> **No solution exists.** In the second and third columns, all of the differences in the values are the same.
> **An infinite number of solutions exist.** In the second and third columns, all of the corresponding values are equal.

In conclusion, a linear equation may be solved numerically using a table of values. However, if the solution is noninteger, it will be difficult to find by this method.

Experiencing Algebra the Checkup Way

Solve exercises 1–4 numerically for an integer solution, if possible.

1. $3x + 6 = 0$ **2.** $2x + 2(x + 4) = 4x + 8$

3. $2b - 5 = 10 - 3b$ **4.** $x - 1 + 3(x + 1) = 4(x + 2)$

5. If a linear equation in one variable is a contradiction or an identity, what do you know about its solutions?

6. When attempting to solve a linear equation numerically for integer solutions, what result indicates that the equation may be an identity or a contradiction?

---

3 Solving Equations Graphically

A second method to solve an equation is to graph two functions. The functions to be graphed are written using each expression in the equation as a rule for one of the functions. For example, for the equation $2x + 3 = x + 5$, we write the two functions $y_1 = 2x + 3$ and $y_2 = x + 5$. Try it yourself in the next "Discovery" exercise. Complete the following exercise on your calculator.

DISCOVERY 6

Graphical Solutions

To solve the equation $2x + 3 = x + 5$, graph the functions $Y1 = 2x + 3$ and $Y2 = x + 5$. Label the point of intersection of the graphs.

Write a rule to determine the solution of an equation from the graph of the two functions.

Write a rule to determine the numeric value of each expression when the equation is evaluated at its solution.

The solution, 2, of the equation $2x + 3 = x + 5$ is the x-coordinate of the point of intersection. The y-coordinate of the point of intersection, 7, is the value of each expression in the equation when x is replaced by the solution, 2.

> *Solving a Linear Equation Graphically*
> To solve a linear equation graphically:
>
> - Write two functions using each expression in the equation as a rule.
> - Graph both functions on the same coordinate plane by plotting points found in the table of values and connecting the points with a line, to include all values in the domains of the functions.
> - Determine the point of intersection.
>
> The solution of the equation is the x-coordinate of the point of intersection of the two graphs.
>
> The y-coordinate of the point of intersection of the two graphs is the value obtained for both expressions when the equation is evaluated with the solution.

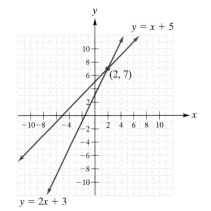

For example, solve $2x + 3 = x + 5$ graphically.

The solution is 2, because the x-coordinate of the intersection is 2, as shown in the figure to the left.

To solve a linear equation graphically on your calculator:

- Rename the independent variable as x.
- Set the screen to the desired settings.
- Enter the expression on the left side of the equation in Y1.
- Enter the expression on the right side of the equation in Y2.
- Graph.
- Find the point of intersection. Trace the graph of one of the functions by using the left and right arrow keys. Locate the point of intersection. The up and down arrow keys move the cursor between graphs. Check the point of intersection by using these keys. The coordinates of the intersection point will be the same for both graphed functions.
- If an intersection cannot be found by tracing, or if you want to check the coordinates found by tracing, use Intersect under the CALC function.

The solution of the equation is the x-coordinate of the point of intersection of the two graphs.

The y-coordinate of the point of intersection of the two graphs is the value obtained for both expressions when the equation is evaluated at the solution.

For example, solve $2x + 3 = x + 5$ graphically.

As shown in Figure 5.5, the solution is 2, because the x-coordinate of the intersection is 2.

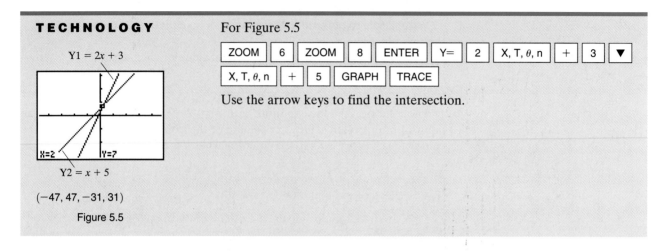

T E C H N O L O G Y

Y1 = 2x + 3

Y2 = x + 5

$(-47, 47, -31, 31)$

Figure 5.5

For Figure 5.5

| ZOOM | 6 | ZOOM | 8 | ENTER | Y= | 2 | X, T, θ, n | + | 3 | ▼ |

| X, T, θ, n | + | 5 | GRAPH | TRACE |

Use the arrow keys to find the intersection.

EXAMPLE 4   Solve graphically.

a. $3a + 5 = 2a$ **b.** $6x - (4x + 3) = 7 - 3x$

Calculator Graphic Solution

a. To graph using your calculator, change the variable a to x.

Y1 = 3x + 5

Y2 = 2x

$(-47, 47, -31, 31)$

The solution is -5, because the x-coordinate of the intersection is -5.

b. When using your calculator to graph, do not simplify the expressions on the left side or right side of the equation.

Y2 = 7 - 3x

Y1 = 6x - (4x + 3)

$(-47, 47, -31, 31)$

The solution is 2, because the x-coordinate of the intersection is 2. ∎

EXAMPLE 5 $(5x + 4) - 2(3x + 1) = 2(x - 7)$ does not have an integer solution. Use the Intersect function on your calculator to find an approximate solution.

Calculator Graphic Solution

As shown in Figure 5.6, the solution is approximately 5.333. ∎

TECHNOLOGY

$Y1 = (5x + 4) - 2(3x + 1)$
$Y2 = 2(x - 7)$

$(-47, 47, -31, 31)$

Figure 5.6

For Figure 5.6
Define the two expressions as rules for functions and enter into your calculator, as in previous examples.

| ZOOM | 6 | ZOOM | 8 | ENTER | Y= | (| 5 | X, T, θ, n | + |

| 4 |) | − | 2 | (| 3 | X, T, θ, n | + | 1 |) | ▼ | 2 | (|

| X, T, θ, n | − | 7 |) | GRAPH | TRACE |

Use the arrow keys to find the intersection. This is not possible, so enter

| 2nd | CALC | 5 | ENTER | ENTER | ENTER | .

Remember that linear equations may be contradictions or identities. Solving linear equations graphically may also result in these possibilities, as the next "Discovery" exercises show. Complete the following sets of exercises on your calculator.

DISCOVERY 7

Linear Equations with No Solution
Solve graphically the previous example of a linear equation with no solution, $2x + 5 = 2x + 10$. Sketch the graph.

Write a rule to determine graphically when a linear equation has no solution.

The two graphs do not appear to intersect. Therefore, there is no ordered pair common to both functions, which means that there is no solution of the equation. The equation is a contradiction (the lines are parallel).

Helping Hand The graphs of two functions may appear to be parallel when they are not. For example, if we graphically solve $2x + 5 = 2.000001x + 10$, the lines appear parallel when they are not. However, if we move between the two graphs with the up and down arrows, we can see that the difference in the y-coordinates is not constant for all x-coordinates.

DISCOVERY 8

Linear Equation with Many Solutions
Solve graphically the previous example of a linear equation with a solution of all real numbers, $2x + 5 = (x + 3) + (x + 2)$. Sketch the graph.

Write a rule to determine graphically when a linear equation has a solution of all real numbers.

There is only one graph on the screen. Actually, there are two graphs, but they are the same line. Therefore, all ordered pairs on the graph are common to both functions and all their x-coordinates are solutions of the equation. The solution set is all real numbers (the domain of the functions graphed). The equation is an identity (the lines coincide).

EXAMPLE 6 Solve graphically.

a. $4(x - 2) = 4x - 8$　　　　**b.** $3x + 4 = 2x + (x + 10)$

Calculator Graphic Solution

Define the two expressions as rules for functions and enter into your calculator, as in previous examples.

a.

$(-47, 47, -31, 31)$

The two graphs are the same. The expressions, when simplified, are the same. The equation is an identity. The solution set is all real numbers.

b.

$(-47, 47, -31, 31)$

The two graphs do not intersect. The difference in the values of the two expressions is always the same, 6. The expressions will never be equal. The equation is a contradiction. Therefore, there is no solution. ∎

Graphical Solutions of a Linear Equation
To solve a linear equation graphically, graph the two functions defined by the expressions on the left and right sides of the equation. One of three possibilities will occur:

One solution exists. The graphs intersect. The solution is the x-coordinate of the point of intersection.
No solution exists. The graphs are parallel.
An infinite number of solutions exist. The graphs coincide.

In conclusion, we can solve a linear equation graphically by graphing two functions. When using a calculator, we can use this method to find noninteger solutions.

 Experiencing Algebra the Checkup Way

Solve exercises 1–3 graphically.

1. $3x - 1 = 6 - 4x$

2. $(a - 1) + (a - 3) = 2(a - 2)$

3. $(x + 1) + (3x + 4) = 3(x - 1) + x$

4. $5(x + 1) = 4(x - 1) - (x - 2)$

5. When solving a linear equation in one variable graphically, how do you obtain the solution?

6. When solving graphically, how can you tell if the equation is an identity or a contradiction?

---

4   Modeling the Real World

Linear equations in one variable are very common descriptions of real-world situations. In practical terms, you don't always need to solve these equations—for example, you may know that a $20 bill is going to cover the cost of filling your car with gasoline at your local service station, regardless of whether it will take 12 gallons, 13 gallons, or whatever your gas tank will hold. But if you need to know how much money you'll need for gas when driving across the country, or if you're comparing costs of two different car rental plans, the equation-solving methods discussed in this section can help you make the right decision.

EXAMPLE 7   Jacques rented a carpet shampooer for $28.50 per day, including all supplies. Jill rented a floor buffer for $18.25 per day, plus $20.50 for the wax. They kept the shampooer and buffer for the same number of days and both spent the same amount. Determine how many days the shampooer and buffer were rented and the amount each person spent.

X	Y1	Y2
1	28.5	38.75
2	57	57
3	85.5	75.25
4	114	93.5
5	142.5	111.75
6	171	130
7	199.5	148.25

X=2

Y1 = 28.50x
Y2 = 18.25x + 20.50

Y2 = 18.25x + 20.50
Y1 = 28.50x

Intersection
X=2 _____ Y=57

(0, 7, 0, 134)

Calculator Numeric Solution

Let x = the number of days rented

The shampooer rental was $28.50 per day for x days, or $28.50x$. The buffer rental was $18.25 per day for x days plus $20.50, or $18.25x + 20.50$.

$$28.50x = 18.25x + 20.50$$

Set up a table of values as shown in the figure to the left.

The solution is 2 because $x = 2$ corresponds to the value of 57, where Y1 and Y2 are equal. The shampooer and buffer were rented for 2 days. Jacques and Jill both spent $57.00.

Calculator Graphic Solution

Graph the two functions Y1 $= 28.50x$ and Y2 $= 18.25x + 20.50$ as shown in the figure to the left.

The solution is 2 because 2 is the x-coordinate of the point of intersection. The shampooer and buffer were rented for 2 days. Jacques and Jill both spent $57.00. ∎

Application

The U.S. Bureau of the Census reported that the average of the mean monthly income for Caucasians, African-Americans, and Hispanics with B.S. degrees is $2150 (rounded to the nearest dollar).[1] If Caucasians have a mean income of $2552 and African-Americans have a mean income of $2002, determine the mean income for Hispanics.

$$Y1 = \frac{2552 + 2002 + x}{3}$$

$$Y2 = 2150$$

Intersection
X=1896 _____ Y=2150

(0, 4700, 0, 3100)

Discussion

Let d = the mean income for Hispanics

To determine the average, 2150, add the three mean incomes and divide by 3.

$$\frac{2552 + 2002 + d}{3} = 2150$$

The graphical solution of this equation is seen in the graph to the left.

The solution is the x-coordinate of the intersection, 1896. Hispanics with a B.S. degree can expect to earn $1896 per month (on the average). ∎

✔ **Experiencing Algebra the Checkup Way**

1. The cost of producing decorated baskets consists of a setup cost of $150 for materials and a cost of $5 per basket for labor. The baskets sell for $20 each. Determine the number of baskets for which the cost of production equals the revenue received.

2. Phillipe scored 83, 88, 91, 90, and 92 on his first five algebra exams. He is trying to earn an average of 90 in the course. What is the score he must get on the next test to achieve an average of 90?

PROBLEM SET 5.1

 Experiencing Algebra the Exercise Way

Identify each equation as linear or nonlinear.

1. $6x - 55 = x + 72$ **2.** $5(x - 3) = -(2x - 1)$ **3.** $4x^2 + 5 = 2x - 6$ **4.** $70x - 48 = 150x + 102$

5. $\frac{7}{9}z - \frac{2}{3} = 0$ **6.** $4.7x^2 - 5.3 = 4.4x + 0.7$ **7.** $\sqrt[3]{4x + 16} = 27$ **8** $x^{1/3} = 64$

[1] *Source*: "Education and Income, 1993," *The World Almanac and Book of Facts 1994.*

9 $3(2x - 5) = x + 3(x - 9)$

10. $235x - 476 = 0$

Solve numerically for an integer solution, if possible.

11. $2x - 7 = 35 - x$

12. $4z + 7 = 3z + 12$

13. $3(2x + 11) = 3(5 + x)$

14. $3(x + 10) = -2(x + 5)$

15. $6.8a + 4.3 = 2.6a + 33.7$

16. $\frac{1}{2}(x + 6) = \frac{1}{4}(x + 16) - 1$

17. $7(x + 10) + 15 = 6(x + 15) + (x - 5)$

18. $3(x - 4) = 2(x + 6) - 3(x + 7)$

19. $(a - 4) - (a + 4) = (a + 3) - (a - 2)$

20. $4(x + 1) - 2(x + 3) = 3(x + 1) - (x + 3)$

21. $3.5(z - 1) = 7(0.5z + 0.6) + 2$

22. $2(2.9x - 2.3) = 4.6(x - 1) + 1.2x$

23. $\frac{4}{5}(x - 1) = 6\left(\frac{1}{15}x - \frac{1}{10}\right)$

24. $\frac{1}{2}(x + 1) + \frac{1}{4}(x + 1) = \frac{3}{4}(x + 1)$

Solve graphically.

25. $x + 6 = 9 + 2x$

26. $(4x - 1) + (x - 6) = 3(2x + 1) - (x + 10)$

27. $(x + 4) + (x + 2) = (x - 1) + (x - 3)$

28. $2x - 8 = x - 6$

29. $2(x + 3) = 3(x - 1) - (x - 9)$

30. $2 - 3x = 4 - x$

31. $1.7x - 22.2 = 13.8 - 0.7x$

32. $5(0.5x + 0.3) = 0.1(25x + 15)$

33. $2.2(x - 1) + 1.7x = 3.5(x + 1) + 0.4x$

34. $7.3x + 23.7 = 2.6x - 13.9$

35. $\frac{4}{5}x + \frac{1}{5} = \frac{1}{5}x + 2$

36. $\frac{17}{24}x + \frac{1}{3} = \frac{1}{4}x + \frac{2}{3}$

37. $\frac{2}{3}(x + 1) - \frac{1}{3} = \frac{1}{3}(x + 1) + \frac{1}{3}x$

38. $\frac{4}{13}x + \frac{17}{4} = \frac{4}{13}x - \frac{7}{2}$

Solve each real-world application numerically or graphically.

39. The Rent-a-Ride car rental company will lease a compact car for $49.95 per day, with unlimited mileage. The Rent-R-Wheels car rental company offers the same car for $29.95 per day plus $0.25 per mile. Determine the number of miles driven that will make the cost of a one-day rental the same for the two offers.

40. Ercille has the choice of paying a flat fee of $25.00 to have a paper typed, or of paying a fee of $10.00 plus $0.75 per page to have the paper typed. How many pages must the paper be in order to pay the same price for both offers?

41. A shoe factory has a daily setup cost of $280. The cost of materials and labor for each pair of shoes produced is $8. The factory sells the shoes at wholesale for $22 a pair. How many pairs of shoes should be produced each day to break even (to have the cost of production equal the revenue from sales)?

42. Handyman Pete offers to paint your garage for $149. Handywoman Gladys offers to do the same job for $45 plus $13 per hour. How many hours will it take Gladys to complete the job if she can do it for the same cost as Pete?

43. On a business trip, Ingrid spent $28, $19, $22, and $27 for meals during the first 4 days of the trip. How much can she spend on the fifth day if she must keep her average daily expense for meals at $25?

44. For the first 4 weeks of her diet, Caitlin lost 3 pounds, 2 pounds, 3 pounds, and 1 pound. How much must she lose during the fifth week in order to average a loss of 2 pounds per week?

45. An area rug is 3 feet longer than its width. What are its dimensions if the perimeter of the rug is 26 feet?

46. Mr. Castorini is fitting a piece of pipe into a water line. He must bend the pipe so that one end is four times as long as the other end. How long is each end if the total length of the pipe is 14 inches long?

47. Charlene will paper a room for a setup charge of $25 plus $9 per roll of wallpaper, and $5 per roll to pay her assistant. Greta does not have an assistant and will do the same work for a setup charge of $25 plus $14 per roll, claiming that she can work faster and more efficiently alone. How many rolls of paper will the job require if Charlene's charge and Greta's charge for the job are the same?

48. Handi-Man Rentals will rent an auger for a flat fee of $20 plus $12 per hour. Tool-Time Rentals will rent the same auger for a flat fee of $25 plus $12 per hour. For what number of hours will the total rental be the same for the two firms?

 Experiencing Algebra the Calculator Way

A. Using the Zoom Feature to Find Intersection Points

Use your calculator to solve exercises 1 and 2 graphically, using the integer screen setting. Even though the lines do not cross on the integer screen, the lines look as if they will cross if extended. You can still use the intersection method to find the solution. Experiment with other screen settings to see if you can see the intersection point. Press ZOOM 3 ENTER to see more of the graph. Afterward, be sure to reset to the integer screen before attempting the second exercise.

   1. $10x - 156 = 108 - 2x$ **2.** $9.2x + 55.8 = 1.4x - 37.8$

In exercises 3 and 4, use the standard screen setting, ZOOM 6 , to graph each equation as two functions. The lines do not show up on the screen since they are outside the domain and range shown. To see the lines after graphing with the standard screen, repeatedly use the zoom-out feature, ZOOM 3 ENTER , until the lines appear. Now trace toward the point of intersection, and then use the CALC key to find the intersection.

   3. $7x + 450 = 2x + 1700$ **4.** $12x + 800 = 8x - 1200$

Always reset your screen selection after you have used the ZOOM feature, before starting another exercise.

B.   Using the Test Key to Solve Linear Equations Numerically

When storing the left and right side of the equation in Y1 and Y2, you can also store the condition
Y1 = Y2 in Y3. Do this by moving the cursor down to Y3 after entering the functions for Y1 and Y2.

Then enter | VARS | ▶ | 1 | 1 | 2nd | TEST | 1 | VARS | ▶ | 1 | 2 | . Now when you
scan the table to find a solution, you can scan the column for Y3, and when you find a row containing
a 1, this means that the equation Y1 = Y2 is true, and the value of *x* for this row is the solution to
the equation. Try this additional step on some of the exercises in this section.

Experiencing Algebra the Group Way

*When using the numerical method to solve a linear equation in one variable, a table of integer values is
constructed. When searching through the table for a solution, one of four things can happen. These are
shown in the following list. Discuss the four possibilities in your group and match the solution
outcomes with the table characteristics to summarize the four situations that can occur.*

Solution Outcomes	*Table Characteristics*
1. No solutions	**a.** Only one pair of table values are equal.
2. One integer solution	**b.** All table pairs have a constant difference.
3. One noninteger solution	**c.** All table pairs are pairwise equal.
4. Solution is all real numbers	**d.** None of the above happens.

*When graphically solving a linear equation in one variable, one of the three situations in the following
list can occur. Discuss these in your group and match the solution outcomes with the table
characteristics to summarize the three situations that can occur.*

Solution Outcomes	*Graphical Characteristics*
5. No solutions	**a.** Coinciding lines, appearing as one line.
6. One solution	**b.** Parallel lines.
7. Solution is all real numbers	**c.** Intersecting lines.

*Find an example of each of the four table situations and of each of the three graphical situations from
the exercises.*

Experiencing Algebra the Write Way

In this section, you have learned a numerical (table of values) method and a graphical (intersection)
method to solve a linear equation in one variable. Describe conditions under which you would
choose to use one or the other method to solve a problem. In what order would you choose to use the
methods? Which method do you prefer and why?

5.2   Solving Equations Using Addition and Multiplication

Objectives   1   Discover and illustrate the addition property of equations.

2   Solve linear equations algebraically using the addition property of equations.

3   Discover and illustrate the multiplication property of equations.

4   Solve linear equations algebraically using the multiplication property
of equations.

5   Model real-world situations using linear equations and solve algebraically.

Application

The U.S. Bureau of the Census reports that Caucasians with a high school diploma have mean monthly earnings that are $496 more than the mean monthly earnings of Caucasians who have not graduated from high school.[1] If a high school graduate expects to earn an average of $1405 monthly, what can a high school dropout expect to earn?

After completing this section, we will discuss this application further. See page 329.

We have defined equivalent expressions in the previous chapters of this text to be two expressions with the same value. Similarly, **equivalent equations** are two equations that have exactly the same solutions. In order to write equivalent equations, we will need to know certain properties.

---

1 The Addition Property of Equations

The addition property of equations is used to write equivalent equations. Let's see if we can discover how it works. Complete the following set of exercises.

D I S C O V E R Y 9

Addition Property of Equations

Given the equation $7 = 7$, add 2 to both expressions.

$$\frac{7 = 7}{\begin{array}{c|c} 7 + 2 & 7 + 2 \\ 9 & 9 \end{array}}$$

1. Given the equation $7 = 7$, add -2 to both expressions.

$$\frac{7 = 7}{|}$$

2. Given the equation $6 + 1 = 4 + 3$, add 2 to both expressions.

$$\frac{6 + 1 = 4 + 3}{|}$$

3. Given the equation $6 + 1 = 4 + 3$, add -2 to both expressions.

$$\frac{6 + 1 = 4 + 3}{|}$$

Write a rule for the addition property of equations.

In each of the preceding exercises, we began with an equation and added the same number to both expressions. The resulting expressions remained equal in value.

This property holds true for subtraction as well, because subtraction is defined to be adding the opposite of a number.

[1] *Source*: "Education and Income, 1993," *The World Almanac and Book of Facts 1994.*

> *Addition Property of Equations*
> Given expressions a, b, c,
>
> $$\text{if } a = b, \text{ then } a + c = b + c \text{ and } a - c = b - c.$$

To illustrate why the addition property is true, we can think of an equation as a balanced scale. Each expression weighs the same amount. If an equal weight is added to or subtracted from each side of a balanced scale, the scale will remain balanced. The same is true of a balanced equation. That is, if an expression is added to or subtracted from the equal expressions, the expressions remain equal.

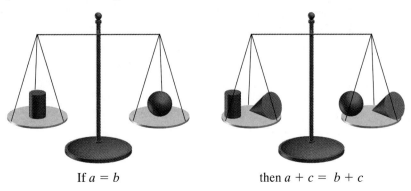

If $a = b$ then $a + c = b + c$

EXAMPLE 1   Write an equivalent equation using the addition property.

     a. Given the equation $4 - 3 = 1$, add 3 to both expressions.
     b. Given the equation $2 + 5 = 10 - 3$, subtract 5 from both expressions.
     c. Given the equation $x - 3 = 12$, add 3 to both expressions.
     d. Given the equation $2t = t + 9$, subtract t from both expressions.

Solution

a. $4 - 3 = 1$

     $4 - 3 + 3 = 1 + 3$ Add 3 to both expressions.

            $4 = 4$ Simplify.

b. $2 + 5 = 10 - 3$

     $2 + 5 - 5 = 10 - 3 - 5$ Subtract 5 from both expressions.

            $2 = 2$ Simplify.

c. $x - 3 = 12$

     $x - 3 + 3 = 12 + 3$ Add 3 to both expressions.

            $x = 15$ Simplify.

d. $2t = t + 9$

     $2t - t = t + 9 - t$ Subtract t from both sides.

            $t = 9$ Simplify. ∎

Experiencing Algebra the Checkup Way

In exercises 1–3, write an equivalent equation using the addition property.

1. Given $455 + 236 = 691$, subtract 236 from both expressions.
2. Given $a - 15.86 = 29.07$, add 15.86 to both expressions.
3. Given $2p - \dfrac{3}{4} = p - \dfrac{1}{8}$, subtract p from both expressions.
4. What operations can be performed on an equation, according to the addition property of equations?

---

2 Solving Linear Equations Using Addition

We are now ready to use the addition property of equations to solve algebraically a linear equation consisting of algebraic expressions. Our goal is to find a value for the variable that will make the equation true.

Let's begin with a simple equation, $x - 3 = 5$. We know that the solution of the equation is 8 because if we replace x with 8, the result is $5 = 5$, a true equation. Therefore, we begin with $x - 3 = 5$ and should end with the equation $x = 8$ (the solution). The step in the middle involves the addition property.

Solve $x - 3 = 5$.

We want to isolate the variable x on one side of the equation to determine the solution. To do this, we want to eliminate the term -3. Therefore, we must add the opposite of the term, 3, to -3 and obtain 0. However, we must add the same value to both sides of the equation in order to produce an equivalent equation.

$$x - 3 = 5$$
$$x - 3 + 3 = 5 + 3 \qquad \text{Add 3 to both sides.}$$
$$x = 8 \qquad \text{Combine like terms.}$$

The solution is 8.

Similarly, solve $x + 3 = 5$.

We want to isolate the variable term x on one side of the equation to determine the solution. To do this, we want to eliminate the term 3. We must add the opposite of the term, -3 (or subtract 3), to 3 and obtain 0. We must add (or subtract) the same value to both sides of the equation.

$$x + 3 = 5$$
$$x + 3 - 3 = 5 - 3 \qquad \text{Subtract 3 from both sides.}$$
$$x = 2 \qquad \text{Combine like terms.}$$

The solution is 2.

Solving a Linear Equation Using the Addition Property of Equations
To solve a linear equation using the addition property, first simplify both expressions in the equation. Then isolate the variable on one side of the equation:

- Add a term if a term is subtracted from the variable, and then combine like terms.

or

- Subtract a term if a term is added to the variable, and then combine like terms.

Check the solution by substitution, solving numerically, or solving graphically.

For example, solve $x + 12 = 25$.

$$x + 12 = 25$$
$$x + 12 - 12 = 25 - 12 \qquad \text{Subtract 12 from both sides.}$$
$$x = 13 \qquad \text{Combine like terms.}$$

The solution is 13.

There are three possible methods to check the solution 13.

1. Substitute.

$$\frac{x + 12 = 25}{13 + 12 \ \Big| \ 25}$$
$$25$$

The solution is 13.

2. Solve numerically.

Y1 = x + 12   Y2 = 25

X	Y₁	Y₂
7	19	25
8	20	25
9	21	25
10	22	25
11	23	25
12	24	25
13	25	25

X=13

The solution is 13.

3. Solve graphically.

Y2 = 25

X=13   Y=25

Y1 = x + 12

$(-47, 47, -31, 31)$

The solution is 13.

EXAMPLE 2 Use the addition property of equations to solve each equation algebraically. Check your solution by the stated method.

a. $x + 4 + 7 = 8$
Check by substituting the solution into the original equation.

b. $5 + (x - 7) = 9$
Check by solving the equation numerically.

c. $14 = (3x - 5) - (2x + 4)$
Check by solving the equation graphically.

Algebraic Solution

a. $x + 4 + 7 = 8$
$$x + 11 = 8 \qquad \text{Combine like terms.}$$
$$x + 11 - 11 = 8 - 11 \qquad \text{Subtract 11 from both sides.}$$
$$x = -3$$

The solution is -3.

```
-3→X:X+4+7=8
                    1
```

Y1 = 5 + (x − 7)   Y2 = 9

Y1 = 14

X=23   Y=14

Y2 = (3x − 5) − (2x + 4)

(−47, 47, −31, 31)

Check by substitution.

$$\begin{array}{r|l} x + 4 + 7 = 8 & \\ \hline -3 + 4 + 7 & 8 \\ 8 & 8 \end{array}$$

Substitute −3 for x.

Simplify.

The solution, −3, checks because 8 = 8.

b. $5 + (x − 7) = 9$

$\quad\quad 5 + x − 7 = 9$ Remove parentheses.

$\quad\quad\quad\quad x − 2 = 9$ Combine like terms.

$\quad x − 2 + 2 = 9 + 2$ Add 2 to both sides.

$\quad\quad\quad\quad\quad x = 11$ Combine like terms.

The solution is 11.

Check by solving numerically on a calculator.
The solution, 11, checks because 9 = 9.

c. $\quad\quad 14 = (3x − 5) − (2x + 4)$

$\quad\quad 14 = 3x − 5 − 2x − 4$ Remove parentheses.

$\quad\quad 14 = x − 9$ Combine like terms.

$14 + 9 = x − 9 + 9$ Add 9 to both sides.

$\quad 23 = x \quad \text{or} \quad x = 23$

The solution is 23.

Check by solving graphically on your calculator.
The solution, 23, checks because the point of intersection is (23, 14). ∎

  Experiencing Algebra the Checkup Way

In exercises 1–4, use the addition property of equations to solve each equation algebraically. Check your solutions.

1. $x + 25 = 56$

2. $\left(\dfrac{1}{3}x + \dfrac{3}{5}\right) + \left(\dfrac{2}{3}x − \dfrac{1}{5}\right) = \dfrac{4}{7}$

3. $6b − (5b + 12) = 3$

4. $8 − (5 − x) = 25$

5. What does it mean to solve a linear equation by isolating the variable? How does the addition property of equations enable you to do this?

3 The Multiplication Property of Equations   Another property of equations involves multiplication. It is very similar to the addition property of equations, which is not too surprising since multiplication is based on repeated additions of numbers. Let's see if we can discover how the multiplication property works. Complete the following set of exercises.

DISCOVERY 10

Multiplication Property of Equations

Given the equation $7 = 7$, multiply both expressions by 2.

$$
\begin{array}{c|c}
\multicolumn{2}{c}{7 = 7} \\
\hline
7 \cdot 2 & 7 \cdot 2 \\
14 & 14
\end{array}
$$

1. Given the equation $7 = 7$, multiply both expressions by -2.

$$
\begin{array}{c}
7 = 7 \\
\hline
 \\
|
\end{array}
$$

2. Given the equation $6 + 1 = 4 + 3$, multiply both expressions by 2.

$$
\begin{array}{c}
6 + 1 = 4 + 3 \\
\hline
 \\
|
\end{array}
$$

3. Given the equation $6 + 1 = 4 + 3$, multiply both expressions by -2.

$$
\begin{array}{c}
6 + 1 = 4 + 3 \\
\hline
 \\
|
\end{array}
$$

Write a rule for the multiplication property of equations.

In each of the preceding exercises, we began with an equation and multiplied both expressions by the same number. The resulting expressions remained equal in value.

This property holds true for division as well, because division is defined to be multiplying by the reciprocal of a number.

Multiplication Property of Equations
Given expressions *a, b, c,*

if $a = b$, then $a \cdot c = b \cdot c$ and $a \div c = b \div c$ (when $c \neq 0$).

To illustrate why the multiplication property is true, we can think of an equation as a balanced scale. Each expression weighs the same amount. If a weight is multiplied by a value on each side of a balanced scale, the scale remains balanced. The same is true of a balanced equation. That is, if each expression is multiplied by an equal expression, the resulting expressions remain equal.

If $a = b$ then $a \cdot c = b \cdot c$

EXAMPLE 3   Write an equivalent equation using the multiplication property.

a. Given the equation $4 - 3 = 1$, multiply both expressions by 3.
b. Given the equation $4 + 11 = 18 - 3$, divide both expressions by -3.
c. Given the equation $4x = 12$, divide both expressions by 4.
d. Given the equation $\dfrac{1}{2}x = 9$, multiply both expressions by 2.

Solution

a. $4 - 3 = 1$

$3(4 - 3) = 3(1)$ Multiply both expressions by 3.

$12 - 9 = 3$ Distribute.

$3 = 3$ Simplify.

b. $4 + 11 = 18 - 3$

$\dfrac{4 + 11}{-3} = \dfrac{18 - 3}{-3}$ Divide both expressions by -3.

$\dfrac{15}{-3} = \dfrac{15}{-3}$ Simplify.

$-5 = -5$

c. $4x = 12$

$\dfrac{4x}{4} = \dfrac{12}{4}$ Divide both expressions by 4.

$x = 3$ Simplify.

d. $\dfrac{1}{2}x = 9$

$2\left(\dfrac{1}{2}x\right) = 2(9)$ Multiply both expressions by 2.

$x = 18$ Simplify. ∎

✓ Experiencing Algebra the Checkup Way

In exercises 1–3, write an equivalent equation using the multiplication property.

1. Given $12.4 + 11.7 = 24.1$, multiply both expressions by 2.
2. Given $9x = -8.1$, divide both expressions by 9.

3. Given the equation $-\dfrac{1}{3}z = \dfrac{5}{9}$, multiply both expressions by -3.

4. Explain what the multiplication property of equations enables you to do in order to obtain equivalent equations.

---

4 Solving Linear Equations Using Multiplication

We are now ready to use the multiplication property of equations to solve a linear equation, such as $3x = 15$. We know that the solution of the equation is 5 because if we replace x with 5, the result is $15 = 15$, a true equation. Therefore, we begin with $3x = 15$ and should end with the equation $x = 5$ (the solution). The step in the middle involves the multiplication property.

Solve $3x = 15$.

We want to isolate the variable x on one side of the equation to determine the solution. To do this, we want to eliminate the factor of 3. Therefore, we must divide by 3 and obtain a factor of 1. However, we must divide both sides of the equation by the same value in order to produce an equivalent equation.

$$3x = 15$$

$$\frac{3x}{3} = \frac{15}{3} \quad \text{Divide both sides by 3.}$$

$$x = 5 \quad \text{Simplify.}$$

The solution is 5.

Similarly, solve $\frac{x}{3} = 5$.

$$3\left(\frac{x}{3}\right) = 3(5) \quad \text{Multiply both sides by 3.}$$

$$x = 15 \quad \text{Simplify.}$$

The solution is 15.

Solving a Linear Equation Using The Multiplication Property of Equations

To solve a linear equation using the multiplication property, first simplify both expressions in the equation. Then isolate the variable on one side of the equation:

- Multiply by an algebraic expression if the variable is divided by an algebraic expression.

or

- Divide by an algebraic expression if the variable is multiplied by an algebraic expression.

Check the solution by substitution, solving numerically, or solving graphically.

EXAMPLE 4 Use the multiplication property of equations to solve each equation algebraically. Check your solution.

    a. $4x + 5x = 72$ **b.** $46 = (4x + 3) + 3(2x - 1)$

    c. $\dfrac{3}{4}x = 9$ **d.** $0.22x = -2.4$ **e.** $-x = 9$

Algebraic Solution

a. $4x + 5x = 72$

$$9x = 72 \qquad \text{Combine like terms.}$$

$$\frac{9x}{9} = \frac{72}{9} \qquad \text{Divide both sides by 9.}$$

$$x = 8 \qquad \text{Simplify.}$$

The solution is 8.

Check by substitution.

$$\begin{array}{c|c} 4x + 5x & = 72 \\ \hline 4(8) + 5(8) & 72 \qquad \text{Substitute 8 for } x. \\ 32 + 40 & \qquad \text{Simplify.} \\ 72 & \end{array}$$

b. $46 = (4x + 3) + 3(2x - 1)$

$$46 = 4x + 3 + 6x - 3 \qquad \text{Remove parentheses and distribute.}$$

$$46 = 10x \qquad \text{Combine like terms.}$$

$$\frac{46}{10} = \frac{10x}{10} \qquad \text{Divide both sides by 10.}$$

$$4.6 = x \quad \text{or} \quad x = 4.6$$

The solution is 4.6.

Check by solving graphically on a calculator.
    The integer setting $(-47, 47, -31, 31)$ will not result in two graphs because the range is not large enough for the equation Y1 $= 46$ to be seen. Therefore, we need to double the range of the integer screen.
    As shown in Figure 5.7, the solution checks.

TECHNOLOGY

Y1 $= 46$

Intersection
X=4.6   Y=46

Y2 $= (4x + 3) + 3(2x - 1)$

$(-47, 47, -62, 62)$

Figure 5.7

For Figure 5.7
To double the range of an integer screen, enter | WINDOW | | ▼ | | ▼ | | ▼ |

| ▶ | | ▶ | | ▶ | | x | | 2 | | ▼ | | ▶ | | ▶ | | x | | 2 | . Now graph and calculate the point of intersection.

c. $\dfrac{3}{4}x = 9$

$\dfrac{3}{4}x \div \dfrac{3}{4} = 9 \div \dfrac{3}{4}$ Divide both sides by $\frac{3}{4}$.

$x = \dfrac{9}{1} \cdot \dfrac{4}{3}$ Simplify.

$x = \dfrac{36}{3}$

$x = 12$

The solution is 12.

The check is left for you.

   Note: This example could have been solved in a different way. Dividing by a fraction is equivalent to multiplying by the fraction's reciprocal. For example,

$\dfrac{3}{4}x = 9$

$\dfrac{3}{4}x \cdot \dfrac{4}{3} = 9 \cdot \dfrac{4}{3}$ Multiply both sides by the reciprocal of $\frac{3}{4}$ or $\frac{4}{3}$.

$x = 12$ Simplify.

The solution remains 12.

d. $0.22x = -2.4$

$\dfrac{0.22x}{0.22} = \dfrac{-2.4}{0.22}$ Divide both sides by 0.22.

$x \approx -10.909$ Simplify.

The solution is about -10.909.

The check is left for you.

e. $-x = 9$ The coefficient of $-x$ is -1.

$\dfrac{-x}{-1} = \dfrac{9}{-1}$ Divide both sides by -1.

$x = -9$ Simplify.

The solution is -9.

The check is left for you. ∎

✓ Experiencing Algebra the Checkup Way

Use the multiplication property of equations to solve each equation algebraically. Check your solutions.

1. $\dfrac{x}{2} = 14$

2. $-3.6x = 3.6$

3. $5x - 6x = 325$

4. $\dfrac{5}{11}x = -15$

5. $-4a = -\dfrac{8}{15}$

6. $8(5x + 12) - 3(32 - 4x) = 260$

5 Modeling the Real World

Solving linear equations using addition and multiplication properties of equations is the first big step in using the power of algebra to solve real-world problems. We will see this throughout the rest of this chapter. Remember, as in all real-world problem solving, whatever operation you do on a number must also be done on the number's unit of measurement. You know that $24 \div 4 = 6$, but remember that 24 sq ft $\div 4$ ft $= 6$ ft.

EXAMPLE 5

Two sides of a triangular flower bed are planned to be 13.6 m and 24.2 m. If Neerahda has 50 m of edging, what is the longest possible length she can make the third side without changing the existing two lengths?

Algebraic Solution

Let L = length of the third side

The distance around the flower bed, or the perimeter of the triangle, is the sum of the three sides. Therefore,

13.6 m L 24.2 m

$$L + 13.6 + 24.2 = 50$$
$$L + 37.8 = 50 \qquad \text{Combine constant terms.}$$
$$L + 37.8 - 37.8 = 50 - 37.8 \qquad \text{Subtract 37.8 from both sides.}$$
$$L = 12.2 \qquad \text{Simplify.}$$

The longest possible side is 12.2 m. ∎

EXAMPLE 6

David's small dog needs a pen with an area of 156 square feet for proper exercise. David wants to use 12 feet of the back of his house as the width of the pen. If he is constructing a rectangular pen, what is the needed length?

Algebraic Solution

Let L = length of the pen

L

12 ft

The area formula is $A = LW$.

$$156 = L \cdot 12 \qquad \text{Substitute known values.}$$
$$\frac{156}{12} = \frac{L \cdot 12}{12} \qquad \text{Divide both sides by 12.}$$
$$13 = L$$

The length will be 13 feet. ∎

EXAMPLE 7   How many liters of a 45% alcohol solution should a nurse use to obtain a solution containing 100 liters of alcohol?

Algebraic Solution

Let L = number of liters of 45% alcohol solution.

Since the amount of alcohol in the solution is 45% of L liters, an expression for this would be $0.45L$. This must equal 100 liters.

$$0.45L = 100$$

$$\frac{0.45L}{0.45} = \frac{100}{0.45} \qquad \text{Divide both sides by 0.45.}$$

$$L \approx 222.222 \qquad \text{Simplify.}$$

The nurse will need approximately 222.22 liters of the 45% solution. ■

Application

The U.S. Bureau of the Census reports that Caucasians with a high school diploma have mean monthly earnings that are $496 more than the mean monthly earnings of Caucasians who have not graduated from high school.[1] If a high school graduate expects to earn an average of $1405 monthly, what can a high school dropout expect to earn?

Discussion

Let a = average monthly earnings without graduation.

An expression for the average amount earned after graduation is $a + 496$.

$$a + 496 = 1405$$

$$a + 496 - 496 = 1405 - 496 \qquad \text{Subtract 496 from both sides.}$$

$$a = 909$$

The solution is 909. Therefore, a Caucasian person expects to earn $909 per month, on the average, without graduating from high school. ■

Experiencing Algebra the Checkup Way

Solve algebraically.

1. Total attendance at a baseball game was 472 people. If 257 admissions were children, how many adult admissions were there?

2. After writing a check for 124.95, Ayse had a balance in her checking account of $793.04. What was her balance before she wrote the check?

3. Cheryl plans to put a square flower garden in her backyard. She has 38 linear feet of landscaping bricks to use to border the garden. What will be the length of each side?

4. A triangle has an area of $8\frac{1}{4}$ square feet. If its base measures three feet, what is its height?

[1] *Source*: "Education and Income, 1993," *The World Almanac and Book of Facts 1994.*

PROBLEM SET 5.2

 Experiencing Algebra the Exercise Way

Use the addition property of equations to solve algebraically.

1. $x + 33 = 51$

2. $y + 73 = -31$

3. $75 = a - 41$

4. $x - 123 = -47$

5. $-4.91 = y + 3.07$

6. $a - 0.153 = -4.759$

7. $a - \dfrac{13}{18} = \dfrac{5}{6}$

8. $y - \dfrac{1}{6} = -\dfrac{1}{6}$

9. $27 + (x - 13) = 11$

10. $8 = (12 + a) - 54$

11. $(13.9 + x) + 0.88 = -2.07$

12. $(x - 14.75) - 10.5 = -2.65$

13. $\left(x - \dfrac{3}{10}\right) - \dfrac{2}{5} = -3\dfrac{1}{2}$

14. $4\dfrac{1}{2} = \left(\dfrac{5}{14} + b\right) - \dfrac{3}{7}$

15. $(5x - 2) - (4x + 7) = 27$

16. $42 = (36x - 21) - (35x + 60)$

17. $\left(\dfrac{1}{3}x + \dfrac{1}{8}\right) + \left(\dfrac{3}{4} + \dfrac{2}{3}x\right) = -\dfrac{3}{16}$

18. $\left(\dfrac{5}{7}z + \dfrac{3}{5}\right) - \left(\dfrac{3}{10} - \dfrac{2}{7}z\right) = \dfrac{13}{15}$

19. $(3x + 76) - (2x - 45) = 31$

20. $(16x + 15) - (15x + 16) = -1$

Use the multiplication property of equations to solve algebraically. Round decimal answers to the nearest thousandth.

21. $-324 = -4y$

22. $7x = -434$

23. $-5.1x = 0.102$

24. $-3.7y = 13.69$

25. $-3\dfrac{1}{3}x = -1\dfrac{1}{3}$

26. $\dfrac{1}{5}a = -3\dfrac{1}{5}$

27. $\dfrac{x}{4} = 1.22$

28. $\dfrac{x}{17.3} = -4$

29. $-x = 57$

30. $-x = -16\dfrac{1}{5}$

31. $57 = 2x + 17x$

32. $4a - 5a = -17$

33. $18.22x - 12.9x = -12.76$ **34.** $-121 = 2.2x + 9.9x$

35. $\dfrac{5}{14} = \dfrac{9}{14}a + \dfrac{3}{7}a$

36. $\dfrac{1}{5}x - \dfrac{1}{7}x = -\dfrac{2}{49}$

37. $2(3x + 6) + 3(x - 4) = 126$

38. $(a + 17) - (2a + 17) = 41$

39. $2.2(x + 3.7) + 7.4(x - 1.1) = 60.48$

40. $4.8(a + 3) + 2.4(a - 6) = -7.2$

41. $3\left(\dfrac{1}{2}x - \dfrac{3}{4}\right) - 18\left(x - \dfrac{1}{8}\right) = 0$

42. $\dfrac{1}{4}(x + 2) - \dfrac{1}{6}(x + 3) = -\dfrac{1}{12}$

Solve algebraically.

43. A box of Flakies cereal is marked to contain 10 servings of 1 cup each. Four servings have been used so far. How many servings remain in the box?

44. Jerome's diet limits his daily intake to 1200 calories. If Jerome has taken diet drinks for breakfast and lunch, each containing 250 calories, how many calories can he have for the remainder of the day?

45. Chuck's net paycheck was $1784.26 and the deductions amounted to $567.32. What was his gross pay? (*Hint:* Gross pay less deductions equals net pay.)

46. A jacket that originally sold for $129.95 was marked down to a sale price of $88.49. What was the amount of the markdown?

47. A recipe calls for $5\frac{1}{2}$ cups of flour. Glenda has $3\frac{3}{4}$ cups of flour in her canister. How much flour must she borrow from a neighbor to make the recipe?

48. In order to control overtime costs, Acme Industries limits its employees to 12 hours of overtime per week. If Ali has worked $3\frac{1}{3}$ hours of overtime on Monday and $4\frac{1}{4}$ hours of overtime on Wednesday, how many overtime hours remaining in the week can he work to reach the limit?

49. Tameka was charged $54.32 for a dress that was priced at $49.95. She had forgotten that sales tax would be added to the selling price. How much money in sales tax did Tameka pay on the purchase?

50. Employment for the Tennessee Valley Authority was officially recorded as 51,714 employees in 1980. By 1992, the employment for this federal agency had dropped to 19,493 employees. What was the amount of reduction in the workforce over this 12-year period?

51. A rectangular room measures 18 feet by 22 feet. Karla has 35 feet of wallpaper border to put around the room at the ceiling. How much more border must she buy in order to complete the job? If she buys 2 rolls of border that contain 20 feet each, will she have enough?

52. The selling price of a house is $125,000. A down payment of $32,000 is required to purchase the home. How much of a loan will be needed to purchase the home?

53. At an amateur talent contest, 264 of the paid admissions were adults. This represented 55% of the total number of paid admissions. How many paid admissions were there?

54. What was the selling price of a suit if the 8.75% sales tax amounted to $21.88?

55. If Erika's class receives $2.50 for each packet of gourmet coffee they sell, how many packets must they sell if they wish to make $1450 to purchase a computer?

56. How many months will it take to pay off a loan of $3150 (interest already included) if monthly payments are $175?

57. Jane and her two children received $45,240 as their portion of a probated estate. If they received $\frac{3}{5}$ of the estate, how much was the estate worth?

58. Angelo was charged $4.49 for $\frac{3}{4}$ pounds of baked ham. What was the selling price per pound of the ham?

59. The floor in Colonel Mustard's library is in the shape of a parallelogram. The base of the parallelogram from one end of the library to the other is 20 feet. If the covering on the floor is 350 square feet, what is the perpendicular distance (height) across the library?

60. In designing a rectangular storage bin, the base is limited to measurements of 6 feet long by 4 feet wide. How high must the bin be if it must hold 120 cubic feet?

61. A cylindrical tank is needed to hold 300 cubic feet of water. If the radius of the tank is 4 feet, what must its height be, rounded to the nearest foot?

62. What is the radius (rounded to the nearest inch) of a circle that has a circumference of 100 inches?

63. How much must you place into savings if you wish to earn $864 in simple interest at 4.5% over 3 years?

64. What was the average speed for a trip of 855 miles that took 13 hours to complete?

65. If each of five partners in a firm earned $12,730 last quarter in profits, what was the firm's quarterly profits?

66. If seven people share a lottery prize, and each receives $6,570,000, what was the jackpot, rounded to the nearest million dollars?

67. Connie earned $40.50 commission on her sales for Monday. If her commission is 3% of sales, what were her sales for that day?

68. Kitty receives 4% commission on sales of her records. If she received $4800 in commissions last year, what was the value of her record sales?

 Experiencing Algebra the Calculator Way

Write a linear equation to represent each situation and solve algebraically, using your calculator. See Chapter 3 for the formulas used in these exercises.

1. A circular fence is to be placed around a swimming pool area. The radius of the area enclosed will be 75 feet. Two gates will be placed at opposite ends of the pool. Each gate measures 5 feet wide. How many linear feet of fencing will be required to surround the area? Round your answer to the nearest tenth of a foot.

2. Katie borrows $8,000 at 4% interest compounded annually for a period of 5 years. How much interest will she pay on the loan?

3. A circle has a diameter of 25.8 inches. By how many inches is the circumference larger than the diameter?

4. How much money (to the nearest dollar) was invested at 4.5% interest, continuously compounded for 3 years, if the amount in the account at the end of the 3 years is $7325?

5. If a stock account grew by $531\frac{1}{4}$ points for 250 shares of stock, what was the increase per share of stock?

6. How many pieces of tubing, each measuring $5\frac{3}{8}$ inches long, can be cut from a piece measuring $34\frac{1}{2}$ inches long?

7. If a car averages 18.5 miles per gallon for highway driving, approximately how many gallons of fuel will be needed for a trip of 220 miles?

8. In laying brick, a rule of thumb is that 6.5 bricks are needed for each square foot of wall. How many square feet of wall can be constructed from a pallet containing 800 bricks?

9. The label on a package of Choc-o-Block cookies states that one serving of the cookies contains 2.5 grams of fat, which represents 4% of the daily recommended amount of fat. Using this information, calculate the daily recommended amount of fat.

10. A bakery states that one serving of its Sweetie-Goo cookies contains 3 grams of fat, representing 5% of the daily recommended amount of fat. Calculate the daily recommended amount from this information. Does this agree with the result in problem 9? If not, how do you explain the difference?

11. To measure the velocity of water flow in a stream, a ball is thrown into the stream and the time it takes to travel 250 feet is measured. Using the formula $d = rt$, find the speed (in feet per second) if the ball took 15 seconds to travel the 250 feet.

Experiencing Algebra the Group Way

You have learned how to solve equations using the following methods:

Numerically. Construct a table of values and search for the value that makes the left side and right side of the equation equal.

Graphically. Graph the left and right sides of the equation as two separate functions and search for the intersection point.

Algebraically. Isolate the variable by

1. adding the same term to both sides of the equation if the term is subtracted from the variable,

2. subtracting the same term from both sides of the equation if the term is added to the variable,

3. multiplying both sides of the equation by the same number if the number is dividing the variable, or

4. dividing both sides of the equation by the same number if the number is multiplying the variable.

Discuss solving the following exercises using the preceding methods in the order listed.

1. $x + 345{,}762 = 760{,}918$ 2. $a - 47{,}658 = -12{,}405$ 3. $\dfrac{x}{475} = 60{,}800$ 4. $0.0265x = 0.0025811$

Which of the methods is the easiest, most direct method for solving the equations? If you are not able to find the solution using any one method, can you explain why not?

Experiencing Algebra the Write Way

You have learned two properties of equations that can be used to help you solve linear equations algebraically: the addition property and the multiplication property. Explain how you would decide when to use each of the properties. In your explanation, state what characteristic you would look for in an equation that would signal the property to use. There are four different characteristics of an equation to consider. In your explanation, give examples of equations with each of the characteristics.

5.3 Solving Equations Using a Combination of Properties

Objectives   1 Solve linear equations algebraically using a combination of properties of equations.

2 Model real-world situations using linear equations and solve algebraically.

Application   The U.S. Bureau of the Census reports that a Hispanic person with an M.S. degree earns an average of $656 more per month than twice the salary of a Hispanic person with only a high school diploma.[1] If a Hispanic person with an M.S. degree earns \$2840 monthly, what are the average monthly earnings of a Hispanic high school graduate?

After completing this section, we will discuss this application further. See page 341.

1 Using Combinations of Properties of Equations

The addition property and the multiplication property are the keys to solving all linear equations. Now that we have mastered the basics, we are ready to solve more complicated linear equations. In order to do this, we will need to apply combinations of the properties of equations. Since there are several different ways to solve linear equations, we will set up a few rules so that at least in the beginning we are doing the same steps. When we become more sure of ourselves, we may do these steps in different orders and obtain the same results.

> *Solving a Linear Equation Using a Combination of Properties of Equations*
> To solve a linear equation using a combination of properties of equations:
>
> * Simplify both expressions in the equation (preferably without fractions).
> * Isolate the variable to one side of the equation (preferably the left side) by using the addition property of equations.
> * Use the addition property of equations to isolate the constants on the other side (preferably the right side).
> * Use the multiplication property of equations to reduce the coefficient of the variable to 1.
>
> Check the solution by substitution, solving numerically, or solving graphically.

For example, solve $2x + 3 = 7$.

$$2x + 3 = 7 \qquad \text{The expressions are simplified.}$$
$$2x + 3 - 3 = 7 - 3 \qquad \text{Subtract 3 from both sides to isolate the variable term.}$$
$$2x = 4 \qquad \text{Simplify.}$$
$$\frac{2x}{2} = \frac{4}{2} \qquad \text{Divide both sides by 2 to reduce the coefficient to one.}$$
$$x = 2$$

The solution is 2.

The process of simplifying equations by performing operations on both sides that will isolate the variable on one side is the basis of solving all equations, not just linear ones. Therefore, this process is important to remember.

EXAMPLE 1 Use a combination of the properties of equations to solve algebraically. Check your solutions.

a. $2x - 3 = 7$ **b.** $6x + 5 = 2x + 25$ **c.** $5x + 4 = 2(3x - 8)$

---

[1] *Source:* "Education and Income, 1993," *The World Almanac and Book of Facts 1994.*

Algebraic Solution

a.
$$2x - 3 = 7$$

$2x - 3 + 3 = 7 + 3$ Add 3 to both sides.

$$2x = 10$$ Simplify.

$$\frac{2x}{2} = \frac{10}{2}$$ Divide both sides by 2.

$$x = 5$$ Simplify.

The solution is 5.

The check is left to you.

b.
$$6x + 5 = 2x + 25$$

$6x + 5 - 2x = 2x + 25 - 2x$ Subtract 2x from both sides.

$$4x + 5 = 25$$ Simplify.

$4x + 5 - 5 = 25 - 5$ Subtract 5 from both sides.

$$4x = 20$$ Simplify.

$$\frac{4x}{4} = \frac{20}{4}$$ Divide both sides by 4.

$$x = 5$$ Simplify.

The solution is 5.

The check is left to you.

c.
$$5x + 4 = 2(3x - 8)$$

$$5x + 4 = 6x - 16$$ Distribute.

$5x + 4 - 6x = 6x - 16 - 6x$ Subtract 6x from both sides.

$$-x + 4 = -16$$ Simplify.

$-x + 4 - 4 = -16 - 4$ Subtract 4 from both sides.

$$-x = -20$$ Simplify.

$$\frac{-x}{-1} = \frac{-20}{-1}$$ Divide both sides by −1 (the coefficient of x).

$$x = 20$$ Simplify.

The solution is 20.

The check is left to you. ■

The linear equations in the last section and in Example 1 of this section all have one solution. However, from the first section in this chapter we know that this is not always the case. Linear equations may be contradictions or identities. Let's see what happens when we apply our rules in these cases. Complete the following set of exercises.

DISCOVERY 11

Linear Equations with No Solution
Solve algebraically the previous example of a linear equation with no solution, $2x + 5 = 2x + 10$.
Write a rule to explain the solution of the equation.

When we attempt to isolate the variable term to one side of the equation, the variable term is eliminated from both sides of the equation. The result is a false equation. Therefore, there is no solution. The equation is a contradiction.

DISCOVERY 12

Linear Equations with Many Solutions
Solve algebraically the previous example of a linear equation with many solutions, $2x + 5 = (x + 3) + (x + 2)$.
Write a rule to explain the solution of the equation from the preceding steps.

When we attempt to isolate the variable term to one side, the variable term is eliminated. The result is a true equation. Therefore, the solution set is all real numbers. The equation is an identity.

EXAMPLE 2 Solve algebraically.

    a. $4(x - 2) = 4x - 8$ **b.** $3x + 4 = 2x + (x + 10)$

Algebraic Solution

a.

$$4(x - 2) = 4x - 8$$
$$4x - 8 = 4x - 8 \qquad \text{Distribute 4.}$$
$$4x - 8 - 4x = 4x - 8 - 4x \qquad \text{Subtract } 4x \text{ from both sides.}$$
$$-8 = -8 \qquad \text{Simplify.}$$

Since this is a true equation, the solution is all possible values for x, or the set of all real numbers. The original equation is an identity.

b.

$$3x + 4 = 2x + (x + 10)$$
$$3x + 4 = 2x + x + 10 \qquad \text{Remove parentheses.}$$
$$3x + 4 = 3x + 10 \qquad \text{Simplify.}$$
$$3x + 4 - 3x = 3x + 10 - 3x \qquad \text{Subtract } 3x \text{ from both sides.}$$
$$4 = 10 \qquad \text{Simplify.}$$

Since this is a false equation, there is no solution. The original equation is a contradiction. ∎

If an equation has fractional coefficients in the terms, we must be very careful in applying these rules. For example,

$$\frac{3}{4}x + \frac{5}{6} = \frac{5}{3}$$

$$\frac{3}{4}x + \frac{5}{6} - \frac{5}{6} = \frac{5}{3} - \frac{5}{6} \qquad \text{Subtract } \tfrac{5}{6} \text{ from both sides.}$$

$$\frac{3}{4}x = \frac{10}{6} - \frac{5}{6} \qquad \text{Simplify and change to LCD.}$$

$$\frac{3}{4}x = \frac{5}{6} \qquad \text{Simplify.}$$

$$\frac{4}{3}\left(\frac{3}{4}x\right) = \frac{4}{3}\left(\frac{5}{6}\right) \qquad \text{Multiply both sides by } \tfrac{4}{3}.$$

$$x = \frac{10}{9}$$

The solution is $\frac{10}{9}$.

If an equation has several fractional coefficients in the terms, the multiplication property of equations allows us to solve an equation in an easier way than dealing with the fractions. To clear fractional (decimal) coefficients from terms in an equation, multiply by the least common denominator for all the fractional coefficients. For example,

$$\frac{3}{4}x + \frac{5}{6} = \frac{5}{3}$$

$$12\left(\frac{3}{4}x + \frac{5}{6}\right) = 12\left(\frac{5}{3}\right) \qquad \text{Multiply both sides by 12 (LCD of all the fractional coefficients).}$$

$$12\left(\frac{3}{4}x\right) + 12\left(\frac{5}{6}\right) = 12\left(\frac{5}{3}\right) \qquad \text{Distribute 12.}$$

$$9x + 10 = 20 \qquad \text{Simplify.}$$

$$9x + 10 - 10 = 20 - 10 \qquad \text{Subtract 10 from both sides.}$$

$$9x = 10 \qquad \text{Simplify.}$$

$$\frac{9x}{9} = \frac{10}{9} \qquad \text{Divide both sides by 9.}$$

$$x = \frac{10}{9}$$

The solution remains $\frac{10}{9}$.

EXAMPLE 3 Solve algebraically. Check your solutions.

a. $\dfrac{-2}{3}x + \dfrac{7}{5} = \dfrac{-5}{6}x$

b. $\dfrac{3}{8}\left(x + \dfrac{1}{4}\right) = \dfrac{5}{6}x + 2$

c. $0.25x - 2.75 = 0.1x + 2$

Algebraic Solution

a.
$$\frac{-2}{3}x + \frac{7}{5} = \frac{-5}{6}x$$

$$30\left(\frac{-2}{3}x + \frac{7}{5}\right) = 30\left(\frac{-5}{6}x\right) \qquad \text{Multiply both sides by 30 (LCD).}$$

$$30\left(\frac{-2}{3}x\right) + 30\left(\frac{7}{5}\right) = 30\left(\frac{-5}{6}x\right) \qquad \text{Distribute 30.}$$

$$-20x + 42 = -25x \qquad \text{Simplify.}$$

$$-20x + 42 + 20x = -25x + 20x$$ Add 20x to both sides because the right expression did not have a constant term and this will save steps.

$$42 = -5x$$ Simplify.

$$\frac{42}{-5} = \frac{-5x}{-5}$$ Divide both sides by −5.

$$\frac{-42}{5} = x$$ Simplify.

The solution is $\frac{-42}{5}$.

The check is left to you.

b. $\dfrac{3}{8}\left(x + \dfrac{1}{4}\right) = \dfrac{5}{6}x + 2$

 Helping Hand The first fraction in the expression on the left is a factor, not a term. It will be simpler if we distribute before we eliminate the fractions.

$$\frac{3}{8}x + \frac{3}{32} = \frac{5}{6}x + 2$$ Distribute.

$$96\left(\frac{3}{8}x + \frac{3}{32}\right) = 96\left(\frac{5}{6}x + 2\right)$$ Multiply both sides by 96 (LCD).

$$96\left(\frac{3}{8}x\right) + 96\left(\frac{3}{32}\right) = 96\left(\frac{5}{6}x\right) + 96(2)$$ Distribute.

$$36x + 9 = 80x + 192$$ Simplify.

$$36x + 9 - 80x = 80x + 192 - 80x$$ Subtract 80x from both sides.

$$-44x + 9 = 192$$ Simplify.

$$-44x + 9 - 9 = 192 - 9$$ Subtract 9 from both sides.

$$-44x = 183$$ Simplify.

$$\frac{-44x}{-44} = \frac{-183}{-44}$$ Divide both sides by −44.

$$x = \frac{183}{44}$$ Simplify.

The solution is $\frac{183}{44}$.

The check is left to you.

c. $0.25x - 2.75 = 0.1x + 2$

 Helping Hand Decimals are equivalent to fractions. The LCD is determined by the place values of each decimal.

$$100(0.25x - 2.75) = 100(0.1x + 2)$$ Multiply both sides by 100 (LCD).

$$100(0.25x) - 100(2.75) = 100(0.1x) + 100(2)$$ Distribute.

$$25x - 275 = 10x + 200$$ Simplify.

$$25x - 275 - 10x = 10x + 200 - 10x$$ Subtract 10x from both sides.

$$15x - 275 = 200$$ Simplify.

$$15x - 275 + 275 = 200 + 275 \qquad \text{Add 275 to both sides.}$$
$$15x = 475 \qquad \text{Simplify.}$$
$$\frac{15x}{15} = \frac{475}{15} \qquad \text{Divide both sides by 15.}$$
$$x \approx 31.667 \qquad \text{Simplify.}$$

The solution is approximately 31.667.

The check is left to you. ∎

> *Algebraic Solutions of Linear Equations*
> To solve a linear equation algebraically, use the properties of equations to isolate the variable. One of three possibilities will occur:
>
> **One solution exists.**
> **No solution exists.** The solving process results in a contradiction.
> **An infinite number of solutions exist.** The solving process results in an identity.

 Experiencing Algebra the Checkup Way

In exercises 1–7, use a combination of the properties of equations to solve algebraically. Check your solutions.

1. $-5x + 7 = -8$ **2.** $2x - 5 = 4(x + 2)$ **3.** $6(x - 3) + 23 = 6x + 5$

4. $x + 5(2x - 7) = 10(x + 4) + (x + 5)$ **5.** $\dfrac{3}{4}x + \dfrac{1}{5} = \dfrac{1}{2}x - \dfrac{11}{15}$

6. $\dfrac{1}{2}\left(x + \dfrac{3}{4}\right) = \dfrac{1}{3}x - \dfrac{1}{8}$ **7.** $1.2x - 4 = 0.8x + 1.2$

8. If a linear equation has parentheses in it, what should you do first when attempting to solve it?

9. If a linear equation has coefficients that are fractions or decimals, what can you do to make the equation easier to solve?

---

2 Modeling the Real World

Real-world situations tend to be complicated. But many situations can be expressed or approximated by linear equations, and now we know all we need to know in order to solve them. Remember that once you've solved an equation, you will need to look at your solution and see if it makes sense in terms of the original situation. Is it possible to have a negative solution? Is a fractional result realistic? Don't forget to ask yourself these kinds of questions.

EXAMPLE 4

The Brown family plans to rent a car to take a trip. The cost of the car rental is $18.50 per day and an additional $0.20 per mile. If the family budget allows for car rental costs of $100.00 per day, how many miles is the maximum the family can drive per day and stay within their budget?

Algebraic Solution

Let m = maximum number of miles traveled per day

$$18.50 + 0.20m = 100.00$$
$$18.50 + 0.20m - 18.50 = 100.00 - 18.50 \qquad \text{Subtract 18.50 from both sides.}$$

$$0.20m = 81.50 \qquad \text{Simplify.}$$

$$\frac{0.20m}{0.20} = \frac{81.50}{0.20} \qquad \text{Divide both sides by 0.20.}$$

$$m = 407.5 \qquad \text{Simplify.}$$

The family can drive a maximum of 407.5 miles each day to stay within the budget of $100.00 per day. ■

EXAMPLE 5   Charles plans to sell flower boxes for $5.00 each. He estimates that the cost of the wood is $3.25 per flower box. The other materials needed cost $1.75 per flower box. An advertisement costs $3.50. Determine the break-even point (that is, determine when the revenue and the cost are equal).

Algebraic Solution

Let x = number of flower boxes
  The revenue is $5.00 per flower box, or $5.00x$.
  The cost is $3.25 per flower box plus $1.75 per flower box plus $3.50, or $3.25x + 1.75x + 3.50$.

$$5.00x = 3.25x + 1.75x + 3.50$$

$$5.00x = 5.00x + 3.50 \qquad \text{Simplify.}$$

$$5.00x - 5.00x = 5.00x + 3.50 - 5.00x \qquad \text{Subtract 5.00x from both sides.}$$

$$0 = 3.50$$

This is a contradiction. There is no solution. Charles will not break even.
  If Charles examines his estimates, he will see that the cost of wood and materials is $5.00 per flower box, his selling price. Therefore, when he adds the cost of the advertisement to the cost of the wood and materials, his cost exceeds his selling price. He must raise the price of his flower boxes in order to break even. ■

EXAMPLE 6   A pharmacist needs a 40% alcohol solution. If she plans to mix 30 cubic centimeters (cc) of a 20% alcohol solution with a 70% alcohol solution, how many cc of the 70% solution does she use? How many cc are in the 40% solution?

Algebraic Solution

Let x = number of cc of 70% alcohol solution
    $x + 30$ = number of cc in 40% alcohol solution

The 40% solution is a mixture of the 20% alcohol solution and the 70% alcohol solution. Therefore, we add the amount of alcohol in the 20% solution, which is 20% of 30, and the amount of alcohol in the 70% solution, which is 70% of x. The result is the amount of alcohol in the 40% solution, 40% of $(x + 30)$.

$$0.2(30) + 0.7x = 0.4(x + 30)$$

$6 + 0.7x = 0.4x + 12$ Simplify.

$6 + 0.7x - 0.4x = 0.4x + 12 - 0.4x$ Subtract 0.4x from both sides.

$6 + 0.3x = 12$ Simplify.

$6 + 0.3x - 6 = 12 - 6$ Subtract 6 from both sides.

$0.3x = 6$ Simplify.

$$\frac{0.3x}{0.3} = \frac{6}{0.3}$$ Divide both sides by 0.3.

$x = 20$ Simplify.

The pharmacist needs 20 cc of the 70% alcohol solution. The result will be 50 cc of the needed 40% alcohol solution. ∎

Application

The U.S. Bureau of the Census reports that a Hispanic person with an M.S. degree earns an average of $656 more per month than twice the salary of a Hispanic person with only a high school diploma.[1] If a Hispanic person with an M.S. degree earns $2840 monthly, what are the average monthly earnings of a Hispanic high school graduate?

Discussion

Let $x =$ average monthly earnings of a Hispanic person with a high school diploma only

$2x + 656 =$ average monthly earnings of a Hispanic person with an M.S. degree

$$2x + 656 = 2840$$

$2x + 656 - 656 = 2840 - 656$ Subtract 656 from both sides.

$2x = 2184$ Simplify.

$$\frac{2x}{2} = \frac{2184}{2}$$ Divide both sides by 2.

$x = 1092$ Simplify.

A Hispanic high school graduate can expect to earn an average of $1092 monthly. ∎

Experiencing Algebra the Checkup Way

Solve algebraically.

1. A furniture store advertises that you may purchase a bedroom suite with a down payment of $50, no interest charges, and 36 months to pay the balance. How much will the monthly payments be if the bedroom suite sells for $2750?

2. Gladys is offered a job to help prepare handcrafted baskets for a bazaar. She will be paid $50.00 per day plus $5.00 per item sold. She must purchase all of her supplies herself. For each day's

[1] *Source:* "Education and Income, 1993," *The World Almanac and Book of Facts 1994.*

order, she buys $35.00 worth of dried flowers and $15.00 worth of ribbon. In addition, each basket costs her $3.75 and each basket lining costs her $1.25. Determine her break-even point.

3. If x cubic centimeters (cc) of a 40% alcohol solution is mixed with 20 cc of a 70% alcohol solution, a 60% alcohol solution is obtained. How many cc of the 40% alcohol solution were used?

PROBLEM SET 5.3

 Experiencing Algebra the Exercise Way

Solve algebraically. If necessary, round decimal answers to one more decimal place than that shown in the original exercise.

1. $4x + 8 = 0$
2. $-x - 41 = 3$
3. $-3x + 7 = 7$
4. $36 = 6x + 9$

5. $15.17 = 5.9x - 4.3$
6. $-4.22x - 0.4 = -21.5$
7. $6.1 = -0.55a + 6.1$
8. $3.05y + 0.09 = 31.2$

9. $-9.2x - 4.3 = -70.6$
10. $-6.3p + 1.5 = -4.8$
11. $-\frac{5}{9}b + \frac{11}{12} = \frac{23}{36}$
12. $\frac{5}{12}z + \frac{1}{6} = \frac{4}{9}$

13. $-2\frac{2}{3}z - 3\frac{1}{2} = -8\frac{5}{6}$
14. $-\frac{1}{9}y - \frac{5}{18} = -\frac{1}{6}$
15. $5x + 6 = x + 126$
16. $-5x - 18 = 2x - 4$

17. $27x - 49 = -12x - 10$
18. $2x + 17 = 17 - 4x$

19. $156z - 210 = 47z + 662$
20. $728a + 958 = 116a - 878$

21. $4x - (3x + 5) = x - 5$
22. $7x + 4 = 3x + 2(2x + 2)$

23. $6x - (x + 1) = 5x + 7$
24. $6x + (2x + 7) = 2(4x + 9)$

25. $5(0.3x + 8.7) = 1.5x + 43.5$
26. $3.4x + 8.8 = 0.2(17x + 5)$

27. $5.5x = 1.2x + 3.3(x - 2)$
28. $0.2x - 1.4 = 0.2(x - 7)$

29. $\frac{3}{4}x + 6 = \frac{1}{2}x + \frac{1}{4}x$
30. $\frac{1}{3}x + \frac{3}{5} = \frac{1}{2}x - \frac{2}{5}$

31. $3x - \frac{1}{4} = \left(x + \frac{1}{2}\right) + \left(2x + \frac{1}{3}\right)$
32. $\frac{3}{8}x + 2 = \frac{1}{8}x + 4$

33. $11x - 12 = 7(3x - 6) - 2(x + 9)$
34. $2(2x - 9) + 3(3x - 4) = 4(x - 3) + 9(x - 2)$

35. $7x - 5(3x + 9) = -2(4x + 35)$
36. $5(x + 3) - 2x = 2(x + 11) - (2x - 23)$

Use the multiplication property of equations to clear the fractions from each equation. Then solve algebraically.

37. $\frac{1}{4}x + \frac{5}{9} = \frac{5}{6}$
38. $\frac{3}{7}x + 2 = \frac{3}{4}x - 1$
39. $3x + \frac{1}{4} = 2x + \frac{7}{36}$

40. $\frac{9}{11}y - \frac{17}{22} = \frac{4}{11}y + \frac{1}{22}$
41. $\frac{2}{5}b - 12 = \frac{2}{3}b + 20$
42. $\frac{7}{9}x - 15 = \frac{4}{9}x - 37$

43. $\frac{3}{4}\left(x + \frac{4}{5}\right) = -\frac{7}{8}x - \frac{2}{5}$
44. $\frac{3}{4}\left(20p + \frac{1}{2}\right) = 13p - \frac{3}{8}$

Use the multiplication property of equations to clear the decimals from each equation. Then solve algebraically.

45. $0.05x + 10.5 = 0.15x - 0.25$
46. $0.01x + 0.11 = 0.47 - 0.09x$
47. $21.1x + 0.46 = 10.9x + 0.46$

48. $-1.05x - 15.41 = 2.55x - 47.09$
49. $15.2y - 175.43 = -2.4y - 176.31$
50. $81 = 0.5(120 - x) + 0.8x$

Solve algebraically.

51. Happy Harpo's car rental firm offers a weekly special for vacationers; you can rent a car for 7 days, paying $49.95 plus a charge of $0.12 per mile. If you have budgeted $200 for travel, how many miles is the maximum you would be able to drive in 1 week under this plan?

52. Elegant Eydie's car rental firm will rent you a luxury car for $119.95 per week and $0.22 per mile. If you budgeted $500 for a week's travel, how many miles is the maximum you could drive?

53. A furniture store will carry your loan without interest for 24 months on any purchase, if you pay $200 down. What would the monthly payments be for a living-room set selling for $2252?

54. During a special promotion, Frugal Fannie's furniture company offers to carry your loan without interest for 30 months, with no down payment required. Not only that, but they will give you an instant rebate on the purchase to apply to the account of $150. What would the monthly charges be on a purchase of $4350?

55. If 4 liters of a 10% vinegar solution is mixed with x liters of a 30% vinegar solution, the result is a 25% vinegar solution. How many liters of the 30% vinegar solution were mixed?

56. Five gallons of a 10% glucose solution is mixed with x gallons of a 40% glucose solution to obtain a 20% glucose solution. How many gallons of the 40% glucose solution were used?

57. Gina learned that her average weekly earnings are $25.00 more than twice her brother's average weekly earnings. If her weekly earnings average $730.10, what are her brother's average weekly earnings?

58. Dean's stock investments yielded a profit for the year that was $3565 less than 1.5 times his profit last year. If his profit this year was $9917, what was his profit last year?

59. Acme Sales pays each member of its sales staff $150 per week plus a commission of 10% of their sales. Out of this, the salespeople must pay expenses, which average 2% of sales. On the other hand, Mega Sales pays each of its salespeople $200 per week plus a commission of 6% of their sales. They are also given an additional 2% of sales to cover their expenses. For what level of sales will the two companies pay the same weekly amount to their salespeople?

60. During its festival promotion, the Discount Mall will rent a booth to retailers for $285 plus a daily charge of $25. They also add to this a daily charge of $20 for janitorial and other support. A license to sell at the Discount Mall costs $15. At the same time, the Christmas Mall next door will rent a booth to retailers for $255 plus a daily charge of $45. There is no charge for support labor, and a license to sell at the Christmas Mall costs $45. Find the number of days for which the two rental options have the same total cost.

61. The sales force at a car dealership has a choice of two pay plans. The first plan pays the salesperson $300 per week plus 4% of the total sales for the week. The second plan pays the salesperson $700 per week plus 4% of the total sales in excess of $10,000. For what value of sales will the two pay plans be equal?

62. The Flexi-Rental car rental firm will rent a car with a choice of rental plans. The first plan charges $39.50 plus $0.20 per mile. The second plan charges $49.50 plus $0.20 per mile for every mile over 100 miles. For what number of miles will the two plans cost the same?

Experiencing Algebra the Calculator Way

Write a linear equation to represent each application. Then use your calculator to assist you with the arithmetic while solving the linear equation algebraically.

1. A door-to-door cosmetics salesperson is charged a 3.75% fee on total sales plus $25.00 to participate in the program. If the fee for one month was $49.48, what were the total sales for that month?

2. A nurse must administer 620 grains of a medication to a patient. She has one 200-grain tablet that she must use, and the remainder is in 120-grain tablets. How many of the 120-grain tablets must she administer?

3. A carpenter wants to create a $4\frac{1}{4}$-inch-thick tabletop by layering sheets of different woods on a 2-inch base. The sheets are each $\frac{3}{4}$ inches thick. How many sheets of wood does he need?

Experiencing Algebra the Group Way

In your group, assign each member one of the three methods for solving exercises 1 and 2:

Numerically (table of values)
Graphically (intersection of lines)
Algebraically (properties of equations)

Each member of the group should solve the equations using the assigned method. Keep track of the times it takes to find the solutions and the methods used.

1. $5678x + 12,752 = 1,432,252$ 2. $0.00065x - 0.00016 = 0.00764$

After everyone in the group has found the solutions, discuss among yourselves which method was the easiest, most direct method for solving the equations. If you were not able to find the solution using any particular method, can you explain why not?

Experiencing Algebra the Write Way

At the beginning of this section, you were told that you should follow a few rules in solving linear equations, using a combination of properties of equations. The rules first suggested that you use the addition property to isolate the variable to one side of the equation and the constant term to the other side, and then use the multiplication property to complete the solution. Explain the advantages of solving in this order, as opposed to using the multiplication principle first. Describe difficulties you might encounter in reversing the order. Since every rule has its exceptions, describe situations in which you might want to apply the multiplication principle first. (*Hint:* There are some examples in this section where the multiplication principle was used first.) Finish your discussion by explaining in your own words the steps you will follow in applying these properties of equations to solve a linear equation, and illustrate with an example.

5.4 Solving Equations for a Variable

Objectives   1 Solve equations for a variable.

2 Model real-world situations using linear equations and solve.

Application   Data analyzed from a U.S. Bureau of the Census report indicate that the average monthly earnings of a male with a B.S. degree, y, in terms of the average monthly earnings of a male high school graduate,[1] x, can be found using the equation $y = \frac{7}{4}x - \frac{31}{4}$. Find an equation to determine the average monthly earnings of a male high school graduate in terms of the average monthly earnings of a male with a B.S. degree.

After completing this section, we will discuss this application further. See page 350.

[1] *Source:* "Education and Income, 1993," *The World Almanac and Book of Facts 1994.*

1 Solving Equations for a Variable

We defined *formula* in an earlier chapter. A formula is a statement equating an unknown variable with an expression that can be evaluated to find a value for the unknown variable. For example, $A = LW$ is a formula used to find a value for the variable A (area) when values for L (length) and W (width) are known for a rectangle.

If $L = 12$ feet and $W = 6$ feet, then

$$A = LW$$
$$A = 12 \cdot 6 \qquad \text{Substitute.}$$
$$A = 72 \text{ square feet.} \qquad \text{Evaluate.}$$

However, we may know values for A and W but not for L. If $A = 48$ square feet and $W = 8$ feet, then

$$A = LW$$
$$48 = L \cdot 8 \qquad \text{Substitute.}$$
$$\frac{48}{8} = \frac{L \cdot 8}{8} \qquad \text{Divide both sides by 8.}$$
$$6 = L \qquad \text{Simplify.}$$
$$\text{or} \quad L = 6 \text{ feet.}$$

If this type of evaluation must be repeated several times, then we need a new formula for L in terms of A and W. That is, we need to solve the formula $A = LW$ for the variable L. We do this by using the same properties of equations that we used in the last two sections.

Solving an Equation (Formula) for a Variable
To solve an equation for a variable using the properties of equations:

- Clear the equation of fractions.
- Isolate the term(s) involving the desired variable to one side of the equation using the addition property of equations.
- Use the addition property of equations to collect all the other terms to the other side.
- Collect like terms in both expressions. If the terms containing the desired variable are unlike, factor out the desired variable.
- Use the multiplication property of equations to reduce the coefficient of the desired variable to 1.

Helping Hand Since we are using the same process we have previously learned, with the difference being that we are using variables instead of numbers, we can substitute numbers for the variables and solve the equation first. This will help us "see" the steps to use for the variables.

For example, given $A = LW$, solve for L.

$$A = LW$$
$$\frac{A}{W} = \frac{LW}{W} \qquad \text{Divide both sides by } W.$$
$$\frac{A}{W} = L \quad \text{or} \quad L = \frac{A}{W} \qquad \text{Simplify.}$$

We now have a formula for L in terms of A and W.

Helping Hand The conventional form for writing an equation (formula) is to write the variable solved for on the left side of the equation. Remember that in Chapter 1 we wrote equivalent order relations. For equations, we simply exchange the expressions on each side of the equation.

EXAMPLE 1 Solve each formula for the indicated variable.

a. Perimeter of a rectangle, $P = 2L + 2W$, for L.

b. Area of a triangle, $A = \dfrac{1}{2}bh$, for b.

c. Average of three grades, $A = \dfrac{a + b + c}{3}$, for c.

d. Area of a trapezoid, $A = \dfrac{1}{2}hb + \dfrac{1}{2}hB$, for h.

Solution

a. Perimeter of a rectangle, $P = 2L + 2W$, for L.

$$P = 2L + 2W$$
$$P - 2W = 2L + 2W - 2W \qquad \text{Subtract } 2W \text{ from both sides.}$$
$$P - 2W = 2L \qquad \text{Simplify.}$$
$$\frac{P - 2W}{2} = \frac{2L}{2} \qquad \text{Divide both sides by 2.}$$
$$\frac{P - 2W}{2} = L \quad \text{or} \quad L = \frac{P - 2W}{2} \qquad \text{Simplify.}$$

We could continue to simplify this by dividing out the expression and obtaining $L = \frac{P}{2} - W$.

b. Area of a triangle, $A = \dfrac{1}{2}bh$, for b.

$$A = \frac{1}{2}bh$$
$$2A = 2\left(\frac{1}{2}bh\right) \qquad \text{Multiply both sides by 2 to clear the fraction.}$$
$$2A = bh \qquad \text{Simplify.}$$
$$\frac{2A}{h} = \frac{bh}{h} \qquad \text{Divide both sides by } h.$$
$$\frac{2A}{h} = b \quad \text{or} \quad b = \frac{2A}{h} \qquad \text{Simplify.}$$

c. Average of three grades, $A = \dfrac{a + b + c}{3}$, for c.

$$A = \frac{a + b + c}{3}$$
$$3A = 3\left(\frac{a + b + c}{3}\right) \qquad \text{Multiply both sides by 3 to clear the fraction.}$$

$$3A = a + b + c$$ Simplify.

$$3A - a - b = a + b + c - a - b$$ Subtract a and b from both sides.

$$3A - a - b = c$$ Simplify.

$$\text{or} \quad c = 3A - a - b$$

d. Area of a trapezoid, $A = \dfrac{1}{2}hb + \dfrac{1}{2}hB$, for h.

$$A = \frac{1}{2}hb + \frac{1}{2}hB$$

$$2A = 2\left(\frac{1}{2}hb + \frac{1}{2}hB\right)$$ Multiply both sides by 2 to clear the fractions.

$$2A = 2\left(\frac{1}{2}hb\right) + 2\left(\frac{1}{2}hB\right)$$ Distribute.

$$2A = hb + hB$$ Simplify.

$$2A = h(b + B)$$ Since we are solving for h, which is a factor in two unlike terms, we factor out the common factor of h.

$$\frac{2A}{b + B} = \frac{h(b + B)}{b + B}$$ Divide both sides by $(b + B)$.

$$\frac{2A}{b + B} = h$$ Simplify.

$$\text{or} \quad h = \frac{2A}{b + B}$$ ∎

EXAMPLE 2 Solve for x.

a. $y = 2x + 4$ **b.** $y = \dfrac{2}{3}x - \dfrac{3}{4}$

Solution

a. $$y = 2x + 4$$

$$y - 4 = 2x + 4 - 4$$ Subtract 4 from both sides.

$$y - 4 = 2x$$ Simplify.

$$\frac{y - 4}{2} = \frac{2x}{2}$$ Divide both sides by 2.

$$\frac{y - 4}{2} = x$$ Simplify.

$$\text{or} \quad x = \frac{y - 4}{2}$$ Write in conventional form.

$$x = \frac{y}{2} - \frac{4}{2}$$ Distribute.

$$x = \frac{y}{2} - 2$$ Simplify.

$$x = \frac{1}{2}y - 2$$ Simplify: $\frac{y}{2} = \frac{1y}{2} = \frac{1}{2} \cdot \frac{y}{1} = \frac{1}{2}y$.

b.
$$y = \frac{2}{3}x - \frac{3}{4}$$

$$12y = 12\left(\frac{2}{3}x - \frac{3}{4}\right)$$ Multiply both sides by 12 to clear the fractions.

$$12y = 12\left(\frac{2}{3}x\right) - 12\left(\frac{3}{4}\right)$$ Distribute.

$$12y = 8x - 9$$ Simplify.

$$12y + 9 = 8x - 9 + 9$$ Add 9 to both sides.

$$12y + 9 = 8x$$ Simplify.

$$\frac{12y + 9}{8} = \frac{8x}{8}$$ Divide both sides by 8.

$$\frac{12y + 9}{8} = x$$ Simplify.

or $$x = \frac{12y + 9}{8}$$ Write in conventional form.

$$x = \frac{12y}{8} + \frac{9}{8}$$ Distribute.

$$x = \frac{3}{2}y + \frac{9}{8}$$ Simplify.   ∎

EXAMPLE 3   Solve for y.

a. $3x - y = 6$ **b.** $4x + 2y = 6$ **c.** $-3x - 2y = 9$

Solution

a.
$$3x - y = 6$$

$$3x - y - 3x = 6 - 3x$$ Subtract 3x from both sides.

$$-y = 6 - 3x$$ Simplify.

$$\frac{-y}{-1} = \frac{6 - 3x}{-1}$$ Divide both sides by −1.

$$y = -6 + 3x$$ Distribute and simplify.

or $$y = 3x - 6$$ Rearrange the expression on the right with the variable term first.

 Helping Hand The conventional form for writing an equation when y is equated to an expression containing a variable term and a constant term is to write the right side of the equation with the expression having the variable term followed by the constant term.

b.
$$4x + 2y = 6$$

$$4x + 2y - 4x = 6 - 4x$$ Subtract 4x from both sides.

$$2y = 6 - 4x$$ Simplify.

$$\frac{2y}{2} = \frac{6 - 4x}{2}$$ Divide both sides by 2.

$$y = 3 - 2x \qquad \text{Distribute and simplify.}$$

or $\;\; y = -2x + 3 \qquad$ Rearrange the expression on the right with the variable term first.

c. $\qquad -3x - 2y = 9$

$$-3x - 2y + 3x = 9 + 3x \qquad \text{Add } 3x \text{ to both sides.}$$

$$-2y = 9 + 3x \qquad \text{Simplify.}$$

$$\frac{-2y}{-2} = \frac{9 + 3x}{-2} \qquad \text{Divide both sides by } -2.$$

$$y = -\frac{9}{2} - \frac{3}{2}x \qquad \text{Distribute and simplify.}$$

or $\;\; y = -\frac{3}{2}x - \frac{9}{2} \qquad$ Rearrange the expression on the right with the variable term first. ■

Experiencing Algebra the Checkup Way

Solve each formula for the indicated variable.

1. Area of a triangle, $A = \dfrac{1}{2} bh$, for h.

2. Average of four grades, $A = \dfrac{a + b + c + d}{4}$, for a.

3. $y = \dfrac{3}{5}x - \dfrac{1}{2}$ for x.

Solve for y.

4. $44x + 22y = 55$

5. $y + 5 = \dfrac{7}{3}(x + 6)$

---

2 Modeling the Real World

Many important formulas are used to describe real-world relationships in geometry, science, business—just about any subject you can think of. But once you understand how to solve a formula for any variable, you don't need to memorize all the different forms of the same equation. For example, if you know that speed is defined as distance traveled divided by the time of travel, $r = \frac{d}{t}$, you can solve for d and come up with the distance formula, $d = rt$. If you remember the formula for Celsius temperature in terms of Fahrenheit temperature, $C = \frac{5}{9}(F - 32)$, then you can solve for Fahrenheit temperature in terms of Celsius, $F = \frac{9}{5}C + 32$. Rearranging formulas in this way is a very useful skill to have.

EXAMPLE 4 Linda's class wants to decorate and sell T-shirts. Linda can buy the T-shirts for $4 each and the paint for $12.

a. Write an equation for the cost, c to decorate x T-shirts.

b. Use this equation to find a new equation for the number of T-shirts, x, in terms of the cost, c.

c. Use the equation obtained in part b to determine the number of T-shirts the class can make for $150.

Solution

a. Let c = total cost

x = number of T-shirts decorated

$c = 4x + 12$

b. Solve $c = 4x + 12$ for x.

$$c = 4x + 12$$

$$c - 12 = 4x + 12 - 12 \qquad \text{Subtract 12 from both sides.}$$

$$c - 12 = 4x \qquad \text{Simplify.}$$

$$\frac{c - 12}{4} = \frac{4x}{4} \qquad \text{Divide both sides by 4.}$$

$$\frac{1}{4}c - 3 = x \qquad \text{Simplify.}$$

$$x = \frac{1}{4}c - 3 \qquad \text{Write in conventional form.}$$

c. $x = \dfrac{1}{4}c - 3$

$$x = \frac{1}{4}(150) - 3 \qquad \text{Substitute the known values.}$$

$$x = 34.5$$

Note: It is not possible to make the 0.5 shirt. To stay within the budget, Linda cannot round up to 35 shirts. Therefore, Linda's class can make 34 shirts and stay within the budget. ∎

Application

Data analyzed from a U.S. Bureau of the Census report indicate that the average monthly earnings of a male with a B.S. degree, y, in terms of the average monthly earnings of a male high school graduate,[1] x, can be found using the equation $y = \frac{7}{4}x - \frac{31}{4}$. Find an equation to determine the average monthly earnings of a male high school graduate in terms of the average monthly earnings of a male with a B.S. degree.

Discussion

$$y = \frac{7}{4}x - \frac{31}{4}$$

$$4y = 4\left(\frac{7}{4}x - \frac{31}{4}\right) \qquad \text{Multiply both sides by 4.}$$

$$4y = 7x - 31 \qquad \text{Distribute.}$$

$$4y + 31 = 7x - 31 + 31 \qquad \text{Add 31 to both sides.}$$

$$4y + 31 = 7x \qquad \text{Simplify.}$$

$$\frac{4y + 31}{7} = \frac{7x}{7} \qquad \text{Divide both sides by 7.}$$

$$\frac{4y + 31}{7} = x \qquad \text{Simplify.}$$

[1] *Source:* "Education and Income, 1993," *The World Almanac and Book of Facts 1994.*

$$x = \frac{4y + 31}{7}$$ Write in conventional form.

$$x = \frac{4}{7}y + \frac{31}{7}$$ Distribute.

An equation to determine the earnings of a male high school graduate, x, in terms of the earnings of a male with a B.S. degree, y, would be $x = \frac{4}{7}y + \frac{31}{7}$. ∎

Experiencing Algebra the Checkup Way

Happy Harpo's car rental firm offers a weekly special for vacationers; you can rent a car for 7 days, paying $49.95 plus a charge of $0.12 per mile.

1. Write an equation for the cost of renting the car and driving x miles during the week.
2. Use the equation to find a new equation for the number of miles driven, x, in terms of the cost, c.
3. Use the equation in exercise 2 to find how many miles is the maximum you can drive if your vacation budget is $200. (Compare your answer to exercise 51 in section 5.3.)
4. Use the equation to find how many miles is the maximum you can drive if your budget is $150; if your budget is $250; if your budget is $500.

PROBLEM SET 5.4

Experiencing Algebra the Exercise Way

Solve each formula for the indicated variable.

1. The perimeter of a square, $P = 4s$, for s.
2. The area of a parallelogram, $A = bh$, for b.
3. The circumference of a circle, $C = \pi d$, for d.
4. The circumference of a circle, $C = 2\pi r$, for r.
5. The volume of a rectangular solid, $V = LWH$, for L.
6. The volume of a rectangular solid, $V = LWH$, for W.
7. The surface area of a rectangular solid, $S = 2LW + 2LH + 2WH$, for L.
8. The surface area of a rectangular solid, $S = 2LW + 2LH + 2WH$, for H.
9. The volume of a cylinder, $V = \pi r^2 h$, for h.
10. The surface area of a cylinder, $S = 2\pi r^2 + 2\pi rh$, for h.
11. Fahrenheit temperature, $F = \frac{9}{5}C + 32$, for C.
12. Celsius temperature, $C = \frac{5}{9}(F - 32)$, for F.
13. Simple interest, $I = Prt$, for P.
14. Simple interest, $I = Prt$, for r.
15. Compound amount, $A = P(1 + i)^t$ for P.
16. Continuously compounded amount, $A = Pe^{rt}$, for P.
17. Velocity of an object falling from rest, $v = gt$, where g is the acceleration and t is the time, for g.
18. Velocity of an object falling from rest, $v = gt$, for t.
19. Current in a circuit, $I = \frac{V}{R}$, where V is the voltage and R is the resistance, for R.
20. Einstein's law of mass-energy equivalence, $E = mc^2$, where c is a constant (the speed of light), for m, the mass.
21. From statistics, the standardized variable, $z = \frac{x - m}{s}$, for m, the mean.
22. Standardized variable, $z = \frac{x - m}{s}$, for s, the standard deviation.

Solve for y.

23. $4x + 3y = 0$ **24.** $5x + 15y = 0$ **25.** $-5x + 10y = 0$ **26.** $6x - 18y = 0$

27. $-x - y = 0$ **28.** $-x + y = 0$ **29.** $5x + 4y = 20$ **30.** $-4x - 4y = 12$

31. $-x - y = 7$ **32.** $13x - y = 13$ **33.** $7x - 14y = -28$ **34.** $8x + 7y = -56$

35. $-x + y = -1$ **36.** $-21x + 7y = -14$ **37.** $y - 5 = 4(x - 6)$ **38.** $y - 1 = -4(x - 3)$

39. $y + 6 = -2(x - 7)$ **40.** $y - 8 = 3(x + 9)$ **41.** $y + 2 = -1(x + 4)$ **42.** $y + 12 = -5(x + 10)$

43. $y - 4 = \dfrac{2}{3}(x + 9)$ **44.** $y + 6 = -\dfrac{3}{4}(x - 8)$ **45.** $y + \dfrac{5}{9} = -\dfrac{2}{3}\left(x - \dfrac{1}{3}\right)$ **46.** $y - \dfrac{7}{18} = \dfrac{4}{9}\left(x - \dfrac{1}{2}\right)$

In exercises 47–56, solve for x.

47. $y = 5x + 15$ **48.** $y = -x - 1$ **49.** $y = -2x + 8$ **50.** $y = 9x - 27$

51. $y = -\dfrac{6}{7}x + 8$ **52.** $y = \dfrac{4}{11}x - 5$ **53.** $y = \dfrac{5}{9}x - \dfrac{2}{3}$ **54.** $y = -\dfrac{1}{4}x + \dfrac{11}{12}$

55. $y = mx + b$ **56.** $y - a = m(x - b)$

57. With a down payment of $200, Jenny purchased a living-room suite, agreeing to make monthly payments of $85, with no interest charges, until the balance is paid up. Write an equation for Jenny's total payments, P, to pay off the bill in m months. Find a new equation for the number of months needed to pay off the bill. How long will it take to pay off a purchase of $2240? How long will it take to pay off a purchase of $1200?

58. Richard charges a flat fee of $75.00 per job plus $35.00 per hour to do interior painting. Write an equation for the total cost, c, of a job that takes h hours to complete. Find a new equation for the number of hours worked on a particular job that costs c dollars. How many hours did Richard work if the job costs $495.00? How many hours did he work if the job costs $652.50?

59. Mildred is planning a Halloween party for her kindergarten class. She has already spent $12.50 on decorations for the room. Write an equation for her total cost of the party, T, if she spends c dollars for favors and treats on each of the 22 students in the class. Find a new equation for the amount of money she can spend on each child to spend T dollars on the party. How much can she spend on each child if she has $35.00 for the party? How much can she spend on each child if she has $50.00 for the party?

60. The soccer team is planning a fund-raiser to buy equipment and uniforms for its team. The equipment will cost $175. Write an equation for the total amount needed, T, if the team spends c dollars for each uniform, given that there are 14 members on the team. Find a new equation for the amount spent on each uniform if they are limited to spending T dollars total. How much will each team member receive for uniforms if they raise $675? How much will each team member receive if they raise $1000?

61. Ted's boss's weekly earnings average $75 more than three times Ted's average weekly earnings. Write an equation for his boss's average weekly earnings, B, in terms of Ted's weekly earnings, T. Find a new equation for Ted's weekly earnings if we know what his boss's earnings are. What are Ted's weekly earnings if his boss averages $725 per week? What are Ted's weekly earnings if his boss averages $1275 per week?

62. In a gender discrimination suit, it was alleged that the average hourly wage of male employees was $0.75 less than 1.5 times the average hourly wage of female employees. Write an equation for the average hourly wage of male employees, M, given that the average hourly wage of female employees is F dollars. Find a new equation for the average hourly wage of female employees if the average hourly wage of male employees is known. What would be the average hourly wage of female employees if male employees average $12.45 per hour? What would be the average hourly wage for females if the male employees average $21.00 per hour?

63. You can rent a tree stump grinder for a flat fee of $75 plus $65 per day. Write an equation to represent the total cost, C, of renting the equipment for d days. Find a new equation for the number of days you can rent the equipment for a fixed cost, C. For how many days can the equipment be rented if you want to limit the total cost to $250? For how many days' rental will the cost be limited to $400?

64. Carol is taking a motor trip for her vacation. She has already driven 50 miles from Juneau. If she averages 60 miles per hour, write an equation for her total distance traveled, D, after driving h hours. Find a new equation for the number of driving hours remaining if the total distance of the trip is known. How many driving hours remain if the total distance is about 630 miles to Fairbanks? How many driving hours remain if the total distance is about 560 miles to Anchorage?

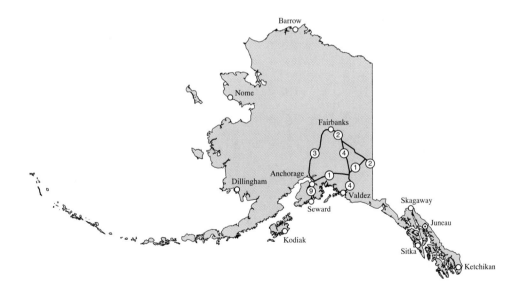

65. A storage bin must be built to fit into a corner of a shed. The bin is limited to being 3 feet wide and 5 feet long. Write an equation for the volume of the bin, V, in terms of its height, h. Find a new equation for the height of the bin in terms of its volume. What should the height be if the volume of the bin must be 60 cubic feet? What should the height be if the volume of the bin must be 100 cubic feet?

66. For the storage bin in exercise 65, write an equation for the total surface area, S, of the bin (including a bottom, top, and four sides) if the width is 3 feet, the length is 5 feet, and the height is h feet. Find a new equation for the height if the total surface area is known. What is the height if the total surface area is 86 square feet? What is the height if the total surface area is 120 square feet?

Experiencing Algebra the Calculator Way

An investment of P dollars continuously compounded for t years at an annual interest rate of r percent will accrue to an amount A, calculated as

$$A = Pe^{rt}.$$

Use this formula to write a new equation for the principal, P, in terms of the amount accrued and the time and interest rate. Find the amount to be invested, P, if you want to have $10,000 at the end of 5 years and the interest rate is 4.5%. Complete the following table of different investment strategies using the formula you wrote for P.

A	t	r	P
$10,000	5	4.5%	
$10,000	7	4.5%	
$10,000	10	4.5%	
$10,000	12	4.5%	
$25,000	5	7%	
$25,000	7	7%	
$25,000	10	7%	
$25,000	12	7%	

Experiencing Algebra the Group Way

Review the table you constructed in "Experiencing Algebra the Calculator Way." Using the formula repeatedly, you can begin to strategize on various investment options. In your group, discuss the effect of varying each of the variables as they influence the amount needed for an investment in order to obtain some accrued amount. The table holds accrued amount, A, and interest rate, r, constant, while varying the number of years. What is the influence of the variable year? Now have your group construct a new table by varying the interest rate while keeping the amount and number of years constant. What is the influence of the variable interest? Finally, construct a table in which you hold the number of years and interest rate constant and vary the amount to be accrued. What is the influence of the variable amount?

This exercise should impress your group with the value of the algebraic method to understand a real-world phenomenon. It is an example of mathematical modeling and is a powerful technique to understand complex relationships. Share your examples with the class.

Experiencing Algebra the Write Way

In this section, you learned to take a formula and, by applying the properties of equations, write a new formula by solving for one of the variables. Discuss reasons why you would want to use this technique. Illustrate your reasons with an example in which you start with one of the formulas you have worked with, and use it to solve for another variable. Explain why you are solving for the variable; that is, give reasons for needing to solve for another variable. Complete your example by specifying some values for the variables in the formula and calculating the value for the variable for which you solved initially.

5.5 More Real-World Models

Objectives
1 Model real-world situations involving consecutive integers.
2 Model real-world situations involving geometric figures.
3 Model real-world situations involving interest.
4 Model real-world situations involving a percentage of increase/decrease.

Application

The U.S. Bureau of the Census reports that the total expected average monthly income for a male with some high school education and a female with some college education is $2231.[1] If the male earns $1 more than the female, determine the two monthly incomes.

After completing this section, we will discuss this application further. See page 363.

We now know three methods for solving a linear equation: numeric, graphic, and algebraic. We have also solved real-world models with each of these methods. However, numerous other types of models can be solved with these methods.

In this section, we will discuss other types of real-world models involving linear equations. We will also examine some classic algebra exercises that are common in traditional algebra texts. These exercises are not as applicable to the real world as previous exercises in this text, but the ideas needed to solve them will help strengthen your problem-solving skills.

Remember, there is no set way to work all exercises. Also, once a linear equation is written for an exercise, it may be solved with any of the methods we have learned.

[1] *Source:* "Education and Income, 1993," *The World Almanac and Book of Facts 1994.*

Modeling Real-World Situations
To model a real-world situation:

- Read and understand the situation. A drawing is often helpful.
- Define a variable for the unknown quantity. Define other quantities in terms of the variable, if possible.
- Write an equation with the information given.
- Solve the equation, either numerically, graphically or algebraically.
- Check the solution.
- Write an answer for the question asked, using complete sentences.

The following examples are types of situations that require a linear equation for their solution.

1   Consecutive-Integer Models

We discussed the set of integers in Chapter 1. Remember,

$$Z = \{ \dots, -3, -2, -1, 0, 1, 2, 3, \dots \}.$$

Now we need to define new terminology that is used in this section. **Consecutive integers** are integers in increasing order with no integers between them. **Consecutive even integers** are even integers in increasing order with no even integers between them. **Consecutive odd integers** are odd integers in increasing order with no odd integers between them. For example,

1, 2, 3, 4 are consecutive integers.
−2, 0, 2, 4 are consecutive even integers.
−7, −5, −3, −1 are consecutive odd integers.

Consecutive integers may be represented with variables. For example, write consecutive integers in terms of the first integer.

Let $x =$ the first integer.
The first consecutive integer is written as x.
The second consecutive integer is 1 more than the first, or $x + 1$.
The third consecutive integer is 1 more than the second, or $(x + 1) + 1$ or $x + 2$.
The fourth consecutive integer is 1 more than the third, or $(x + 2) + 1$ or $x + 3$.

Write consecutive even integers in terms of the first even integer.

Let $x =$ the first even integer.
The first consecutive even integer is written as x.
The second consecutive even integer is 2 more than the first, or $x + 2$.
The third consecutive even integer is 2 more than the second, or $(x + 2) + 2$ or $x + 4$.
The fourth consecutive even integer is 2 more than the third, or $(x + 4) + 2$ or $x + 6$.

Write consecutive odd integers in terms of the first odd integer.

Let $x =$ the first odd integer.
The first consecutive odd integer is written as x.
The second consecutive odd integer is 2 more than the first, or $x + 2$.

The third consecutive odd integer is 2 more than the second, or $(x + 2) + 2$ or $x + 4$.

The fourth consecutive odd integer is 2 more than the third, or $(x + 4) + 2$ or $x + 6$.

 Helping Hand Note that the only difference in the consecutive even and odd integer representation is the beginning definition for the variable, x, because both even and odd integers are every other integer.

EXAMPLE 1   Del is wiring an electrical appliance and has to cut a wire into three pieces. The first piece must be an integer length and each consecutive piece must be 1 inch longer than the preceding one. He measures the wire to be 27 inches. What are the lengths of the three pieces of wire?

Algebraic Solution

The wire is to be cut into three consecutive integer lengths.

$$\text{Let} \quad x = \text{integer length of the first piece}$$
$$x + 1 = \text{integer length of the second piece}$$
$$x + 2 = \text{integer length of the third piece}$$

The sum of the integers will be 27 inches, which is the total length.

$$x + (x + 1) + (x + 2) = 27$$

$3x + 3 = 27$	Simplify.
$3x + 3 - 3 = 27 - 3$	Subtract 3 from both sides.
$3x = 24$	Simplify.
$\dfrac{3x}{3} = \dfrac{24}{3}$	Divide both sides by 3.
$x = 8$	Simplify.

Find the other integers (lengths of pieces) by substituting the solution in the other expressions:

Second piece: $x + 1 = 8 + 1 = 9$
Third piece: $x + 2 = 8 + 2 = 10$

To check the solution, we first determine that the values are consecutive integers. Then we total the lengths to see if the sum is 27 inches: $8 + 9 + 10 = 27$. Therefore, the solution is correct.

The three pieces should be cut 8, 9, and 10 inches in length.

Numeric Solution

$$Y1 = x + (x + 1) + (x + 2) \qquad Y2 = 27$$

A calculator table of values for the numeric solution of 8 is shown to the left. ∎

X	Y₁	Y₂
2	9	27
3	12	27
4	15	27
5	18	27
6	21	27
7	24	27
8	27	27

X=8

Experiencing Algebra the Checkup Way

1. The sum of three consecutive even integers is 42. Find the integers.

2. Jim is building a scale model for his architecture class. He has a 25-inch piece of balsa wood that he wants to cut into five pieces so that each piece is 1 inch longer than the preceding piece. What are the five lengths he needs to cut?

3. What are the differences in the terms *consecutive integers*, *consecutive even integers*, and *consecutive odd integers*?

---

2 Geometric-Formula Models

Geometric formulas are helpful in all kinds of everyday situations. You often need to use these formulas whenever you have to find a measurement of a length, an angle, or an area. The measurement you want to find is your unknown variable, and the geometric formula is the linear equation you want to solve. You will find that a diagram of the situation can help you set up the equation correctly.

EXAMPLE 2 Tonya is designing a triangular flag. She wants the second angle to measure twice the first angle, and the third angle to measure the same as the second. This will make two sides of equal length. (From her geometry class, she remembers that the sides opposite two equal angles will be equal in measurement.) Find the angle measurements she must use.

Algebraic Solution

A figure will help us see the triangular flag.

Let d = measure of the first angle
$2d$ = measure of the second angle
$2d$ = measure of the third angle

Remember that the sum of the measures of the angles in a triangle is 180 degrees.

$$d + 2d + 2d = 180$$
$$5d = 180 \quad \text{Simplify.}$$
$$\frac{5d}{5} = \frac{180}{5} \quad \text{Divide both sides by 5.}$$
$$d = 36 \quad \text{Simplify.}$$

Find the other two angles' measure by substituting the solution into the expression $2d$.

$$2d = 2(36) = 72$$

To check the solution, we add the three angle measures to see if we get 180: $36 + 72 + 72 = 180$. We also check to see if the second and third angles both measure twice the first angle measurement. The solution is correct.

Tonya should measure 36 degrees for one angle and 72 degrees for the other two angles.

Numeric Solution

$$Y1 = x + 2x + 2x \qquad Y2 = 180$$

A calculator table of values for the numeric solution of 36 is shown to the left. ∎

X	Y₁	Y₂
30	150	180
31	155	180
32	160	180
33	165	180
34	170	180
35	175	180
36	180	180

X=36

EXAMPLE 3   Menta is stringing lights for a dance. She plans to string lights from the center of the room and attach each string to the wall. The light string will form two angles with the wall. One angle measurement is twice the measurement of the other angle. Determine the angle measurements.

Algebraic Solution

A figure will help us see the light arrangements.

Let x = one angle measurement
      $2x$ = the other angle measurement

The two angles are supplementary angles, the sum of which is $180°$.

$$x + 2x = 180$$
$$3x = 180$$
$$\frac{3x}{3} = \frac{180}{3}$$
$$x = 60$$

One angle is $60°$ and the other angle is $2x = 2(60)$ or $120°$.
    To check the solution, see that one angle measurement is twice the other and their sum is 180.

wall

x

lights

$2x$

Y1 = $x + 2x$

Y2 = 180

Intersection
X=60   Y=180

(0, 100, 0, 250)

Graphic Solution

A calculator graph for the graphic solution of 60 is shown to the left. ∎

EXAMPLE 4   Shawn wants to add baseboards to his study. He measures the dimensions of his study and finds that the perimeter is 47 feet. When Shawn arrives at the home-repair store, he discovers a "manager's special" on carpet. He decides to carpet the floor of his study before adding the baseboards. However, he does not have the room's dimensions. All he can remember is that the rectangular study has a perimeter of 47 feet and the length is $4\frac{1}{2}$ feet more than the width. Determine the area of the floor in the study.

Algebraic Solution

A figure will help us see the problem.

Let x = width of study
      $x + 4\frac{1}{2}$ = length of study

To find the area of the floor, Shawn must know the dimensions of the study. He can find them by using the perimeter formula for a rectangle.

x

$x + 4\frac{1}{2}$

$$P = 2L + 2W$$
$$47 = 2\left(x + 4\frac{1}{2} \right) + 2(x) \qquad \text{Substitute.}$$
$$47 = 2x + 9 + 2x \qquad \text{Distribute.}$$
$$47 = 4x + 9 \qquad \text{Simplify.}$$
$$47 - 9 = 4x + 9 - 9 \qquad \text{Subtract 9 from both sides.}$$
$$38 = 4x \qquad \text{Simplify.}$$

$$\frac{38}{4} = \frac{4x}{4}$$ Divide both sides by 4.

$$9\frac{1}{2} = x$$ Simplify.

The width is $9\frac{1}{2}$ feet. To find the length, substitute the solution in the expression, $x + 4\frac{1}{2} = 9\frac{1}{2} + 4\frac{1}{2} = 14$. The length is 14 feet. To check this solution, we check the perimeter formula,

$P =$	$2L$	$+$	$2W$
47	$2(14)$	$+$	$2\left(9\frac{1}{2}\right)$
	28	$+$	19
		47	

The solution checks. The study dimensions are $9\frac{1}{2}$ feet by 14 feet.

The area of the rectangular floor is found by substituting the dimensions for the variables in the area formula.

$$A = LW$$

$$A = (14)\left(9\frac{1}{2}\right)$$

$$A = 133 \text{ square feet}$$

The area of the floor is 133 square feet.

Graphic Solution

Note: The graphic solution for the width is 9.5 or $9\frac{1}{2}$ feet as shown in the figure to the left. ∎

Y2 = 2(x + 4½) + 2x   Y1 = 47

(0, 50, 0, 100)

 Experiencing Algebra the Checkup Way

1. The second angle of a triangle measures twice the first angle. The third angle measures 20 degrees more than the first angle. What does each angle measure?

2. Carlos is building a sandbox for his son, making it triangular to fit in a corner of the patio. He wants two sides to be of equal length and the third side to be 1.5 feet longer than the others. If he has enough material for a perimeter of 12 feet, how long will each side be?

3 Interest Models   We saw in section 3.6 that there are several ways to calculate interest on a loan. Compound interest involves exponential functions, but simple interest is a linear relationship. Situations involving calculations of interest or principal at various rates of interest are very common and important in business and finance.

EXAMPLE 5   Dennis is building a trailer. He plans to sell it for $2500 when he is finished. He is borrowing the money needed to build the trailer from his father. His father charges 18% simple interest for 1 year. What is the most Dennis can borrow and know he will have enough to pay his father at the end of 1 year?

Algebraic Solution

Using the simple interest formula,

$$I = PRT$$
$$I = P(0.18)(1) \quad P = \text{amount borrowed}, R = 0.18, T = 1$$
$$I = 0.18P$$

Dennis will need to repay the amount borrowed, P, plus simple interest, $0.18P$. The maximum amount should be $2500.

$$P + 0.18P = 2500$$
$$1.18P = 2500 \quad \text{Combine like terms.}$$
$$\frac{1.18P}{1.18} = \frac{2500}{1.18} \quad \text{Divide both sides by 1.18.}$$
$$P \approx 2118.64$$

To check this solution, add the amount borrowed plus interest to see if we get 2500.

$$2118.64 + 0.18(2118.64) \approx 2500 \text{ (rounded to the nearest cent).}$$

Therefore, the solution is correct.

Dennis can borrow $2118.64 from his father and repay it at the end of one year.

$Y1 = x + 0.18x$
$Y2 = 2500$

Intersection
X=2118.6441 Y=2500

(0, 2500, 0, 3500)

Graphic Solution

The graphic solution of 2118.64 is shown to the left. ∎

EXAMPLE 6 Nygen received an inheritance of $10,000 from his great-uncle's estate. He invested part of the money in a simple-interest account paying 9% annually. The remainder of the money he invested in a savings account paying 4.75% simple interest annually. If he earned $815 at the end of one year, how much did he invest in each account?

Algebraic Solution

Let a = amount invested at 9% interest
$10,000 - a$ = amount invested at 4.75% interest

Use the simple-interest formula to determine the amount of interest for each account.

9% account	4.75% account	
$I = PRT$	$I = PRT$	
$I = a(0.09)(1)$	$I = (10,000 - a)(0.0475)(1)$	Substitute.
$I = 0.09a$	$I = (10,000 - a)(0.0475)$	Simplify.
	$I = 475 - 0.0475a$	Distribute.

The sum of the interest is $815.

$$0.09a + (475 - 0.0475a) = 815$$
$$0.0425a + 475 = 815 \quad \text{Simplify.}$$
$$0.0425a + 475 - 475 = 815 - 475 \quad \text{Subtract 475 from both sides.}$$

$$0.0425a = 340 \qquad \text{Simplify.}$$

$$\frac{0.0425a}{0.0425} = \frac{340}{0.0425} \qquad \text{Divide both sides by 0.0425.}$$

$$a = 8000 \qquad \text{Simplify.}$$

The amount deposited in the 9% account is $8000.
The amount deposited in the 4.75% account is

$$10{,}000 - a = 10{,}000 - 8000 = 2000.$$

To check, determine the amount of interest from each account. Their sum is 815.

$$(0.09)(8000) + (0.0475)(2000) = 720 + 95 = 815$$

Nygen deposited $8000 in the 9% account and $2000 in the 4.75% account.

Y1 = 0.09x + (475 − 0.0475x)
Y2 = 815

Intersection
X=8000   Y=815

(0, 10000, 0, 1000)

Graphic Solution

The graphic solution of 8000 is shown to the left. ∎

Experiencing Algebra the Checkup Way

1. When applying for a short-term loan at many firms, you must ask for the amount plus simple interest at the time you apply. If you apply for a loan of $3000 that includes the interest at 9% simple interest for 1 year, how much money will you actually receive? How much interest was paid on the loan?

2. Zeke would like to borrow $5000 at simple interest for 1 year. He is not able to borrow the total amount from one loan agency, so he must borrow part of it at 7% simple interest and the remainder at 8.5% simple interest. If his total interest payment is to be $365, how much will he borrow at each interest rate?

---

4 Percentage-of-Increase/Decrease Models

One of the most common linear relations in business and consumer finances involves calculating the percentage increase or decrease of some value. The value may be a cost, a sales price, a profit, or some other quantity. In any case, the method of calculating the increased/decreased value (or the calculation of the value before the increase/decrease) is the same.

EXAMPLE 7

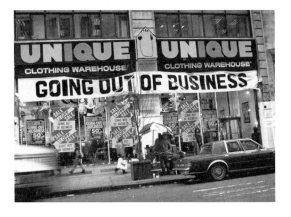

Latonya is moving her dress shop to a higher-rent neighborhood. Her rent now is $825 per month and her new rent will be $891 per month. She wants to mark up all of her merchandise the same amount as her rent increase, rounding all prices to the nearest $0.05. Latonya paid an outside consultant to do the markup. After the markup, she decided to check the price of a dress. Its new price was $63.75. What was the approximate price before markup?

Algebraic Solution

The amount of increase in rent is $891 - 825 = 66$.

$$\text{percentage increase} = \frac{\text{amount of increase}}{\text{original amount}} = \frac{66}{825} = 0.08 \quad \text{or} \quad 8\%.$$

Let $x =$ the original price of the dress
   $0.08x =$ amount of increase (8% of the original amount)

The new price, 63.75, will be the original price plus the increase.

$$x + 0.08x = 63.75$$
$$1.08x = 63.75 \qquad \text{Combine like terms.}$$
$$\frac{1.08x}{1.08} = \frac{63.75}{1.08} \qquad \text{Divide both sides by 1.08.}$$
$$x \approx 59.03$$

To check the solution, add the original amount and the increase to see if we get 63.75.

$$59.03 + 0.08(59.03) \approx 63.75$$

The solution checks. The dress was originally priced at about $59.03.

$Y2 = 63.75 \quad Y1 = x + 0.08x$

Intersection
X=59.02778 Y=63.75

(0, 100, 0, 100)

Graphic Solution

The graphic solution of 59.03 is shown to the left. ∎

Application

The U.S. Bureau of the Census reports that the total expected average monthly income for a male with some high school education and a female with some college education is $2231.[1] If the male earns 1 dollar more than the female, determine the two monthly incomes.

Discussion

Since the male earns $1 more than the female, we have a consecutive-integer problem.

Let $x =$ the female's income
   $x + 1 =$ the male's income

The sum of the incomes is $2231.

$$x + (x + 1) = 2231$$
$$2x + 1 = 2231 \qquad \text{Combine like terms.}$$
$$2x + 1 - 1 = 2231 - 1 \qquad \text{Subtract 1 from both sides.}$$
$$2x = 2230 \qquad \text{Simplify.}$$

[1] *Source:* "Education and Income, 1993," *The World Almanac and Book of Facts 1994.*

$$\frac{2x}{2} = \frac{2230}{2}$$ Divide both sides by 2.

$$x = 1115$$ Simplify.

The solution to the equation is 1115. Therefore, the two monthly incomes are $1115 and $1116. ∎

Experiencing Algebra the Checkup Way

Tillie's Travel Agency adds a 10% surcharge for handling motel reservations for your firm. If the charge for a room is $68.75, what was the charge before the surcharge was added?

PROBLEM SET 5.5

Experiencing Algebra the Exercise Way

1. A patient's medication is to be increased in consecutive even-integer dosages in three administrations, for a total of 24 grains of medication. How many grains of medication will be administered each time?

2. A patient's medication is to be decreased in consecutive integer amounts over five administrations for a total of 70 cc of medication. How many cc will be administered each time?

3. A lottery has four stages of winning. At each stage, the number of winners is increased in consecutive odd numbers. If there are a total of 24 prizes, how many will be awarded at each stage?

4. Lottery winnings will be distributed over a 5-day period, with the number of winners each day increasing by consecutive even integers. If the lottery will distribute 30 prizes, how many will be awarded each day?

5. An instructor ranks her eight students according to level of classroom participation, and then assigns them consecutive integer numbers as grades. If the total points for the eight students is 676, what were the lowest and highest grades given?

6. A movie rating scale has five categories, ranging from "strongly dislike" to "strongly like." Consecutive even integers are assigned left to right so that the sum of the integers is 0. What are the five numbers to be assigned to the scale?

7. The second angle of a triangle measures 10 degrees more than the first, and the third angle measures 10 degrees more than the second. How much does each angle measure?

8. A triangle has two equal angles and a third angle that is 30 degrees smaller. What do the angles measure?

9. The sides of an equilateral triangle are all of equal length. What is the length of a side if the perimeter of the triangle is $29\frac{1}{4}$ inches?

10. The second side of a triangle is twice as long as the first side. The third side is 1 centimeter shorter than the second side. If the perimeter is $11\frac{1}{2}$ centimeters, how long is each side?

11. By definition, an isosceles triangle has at least two sides of equal length. What are the lengths of its sides if the third side is two-thirds as long as each of the equal sides, and the perimeter is 16 feet?

12. If the third side of an isosceles triangle is half as long as each of the equal sides, and the perimeter is 38 meters, how long is each side?

13. The perimeter of a rectangle is 400 yards. What are its dimensions if the length is 30 yards more than the width?

14. If the perimeter of a square is 1 inch, what are its dimensions?

15. The width of a rectangle is 55% of the length. What are its dimensions if the perimeter is 294.5 centimeters?

16. The length of a rectangle is 2 inches more than twice its width. If its perimeter is 52 inches, what are the dimensions of the rectangle?

17. Karl wants to build a dog run for his German shepherd. He wants the length of the run to be five times as long as the width. If he has 96 feet of fencing, what should the dimensions of the dog run be? How many square feet of yard will the run cover?

18. See exercise 17. If Karl builds a square dog run with the fencing, how long would each side be? Will this give him more square feet of yard for the dog run than in exercise 17?

19. See exercise 17. If Karl uses an existing fence for his dog run, he will only need to run fencing along three sides, using the existing fence for the fourth side (a length). With his 96 feet of fencing, and still keeping the length as five times the width, what will the dimensions of the dog run become? How does the area of this run compare with that in exercise 17?

20. See exercise 19. If Karl were to build a square dog run and use the existing fence for one of the sides, how long would each of the three other sides be? What would the area of this run be?

21. Brit is making a poster. She wants to draw a triangle on the poster in which the first angle is three times as large as the second angle, and the third angle is 5 degrees smaller than the second angle. What will each angle measure?

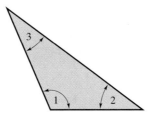

22. See exercise 21. Brit must draw a second triangle on her poster. Now the second angle is twice as large as the first angle. The third angle is three times as large as the first angle. What does each angle measure?

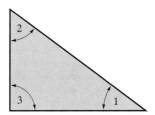

23. E-Z Loan Agency writes a loan agreement stipulating that the agency will be reimbursed for the amount to be borrowed plus simple interest. What is the amount of money borrowed if $4500 is to be paid back on a 1-year simple-interest loan at 12.5% interest? How much interest was paid on the loan?

24. E-Z-R Loan Agency writes a loan agreement stipulating that $1308 is to be repaid for a simple-interest loan for one year at 9%. How much is being borrowed? How much interest is being paid on the loan?

25. A mutual fund will pay 9% simple interest on an investment for 1 year. If you want to receive $5000 at the end of the investment year, how much must you invest?

26. An investment fund offers 12% simple interest on an investment for 1 year. How much should be invested to receive $12,500 at the end of the year?

27. A wise and successful businessman wants to establish an endowment of $500,000 with a community college. (What a great guy!) He invests money into a simple-interest account for a year. If the account pays 10% simple interest, how much should he invest, rounded to the nearest thousand dollars, in order to be able to establish the endowment?

28. A municipal bond earns 7.8% simple interest annually. How much should be invested in order to have $8000 at the end of the year?

29. Megan received $15,000 from a probated estate. She invested part of the money in a simple-interest account paying 8% and the rest in another simple-interest account paying 6.5%. If she earned $1117.50 in interest at the end of the year, how much did she invest in each account?

30. Zach received $15,000 from his great-great-grandfather's estate. He invested part of his money in a corporate bond that paid 9.2% simple interest annually, and the rest in a savings account paying 3.5% simple interest annually. If he earned $952.20 in one year, how much did he invest in each?

31. The Bedrock Savings and Loan Company will pay 7% simple interest on an investment of P dollars for one year. Write an equation for the total amount, A, in a savings account after 1 year. Find a new equation for the amount to be invested if you know the amount desired after 1 year. How much should be invested if you wish to have $1350 in an account at the end of the year? How much should be invested if you desire to have $2500 at the end of the year?

32. Friendly Dan's Loan Agency charges 11% simple interest on a loan. Write an equation for the total payback, P, if you take out a loan of L dollars for one year. Find a new equation for the amount of money borrowed if the total amount of the payback is known. How much will you receive as a loan if the payback is $1332? How much will you receive as a loan if the payback is $800?

33. The sale price of a dress that was reduced by 20% is $68. What was the original selling price of the dress?

34. The sale price of a CD player is $110.49 after a reduction of 15%. What was the original selling price? What was the amount of the reduction?

35. A boutique sells all of its items at a 60% markup over the cost of the items from their suppliers. If an item sells for $19.95, what was the cost to the boutique?

36. An antiques dealer purchases a restored radio and resells it for $350, which represents a 75% markup of the cost. How much did the dealer pay for the radio?

37. An artist notices that the item she sold to a boutique for $9.50 is selling for $17.10. What is the markup percentage at this boutique?

38. If an antiques dealer sells a vintage radio for $385 and paid $275 for it, what was the markup percentage?

39. A TV set is on sale for $195. The store claims this is a 25% savings over the regular price. What is the regular price of the TV?

40. A pro shop has its golf clubs on sale, with 20% off the regular price. If a golf club is on sale for $59, what is the regular price of the club?

41. Slippery Sam claims he can save you 35% of the suggested retail price (SRP) of a car. If he is willing to sell you the car for $12,500, what should the SRP be?

42. What would be the suggested retail price (SRP) of a car that is on sale for $8995 if this represents a 15%-off sale?

43. A clothing store reduces the original price of a coat by 10% for a sale. Write an equation for the sale price of the coat, y, if the original price is x dollars. Find a new equation for the original price if the sale price is known. What is the original price of a coat that is on sale for $53.96? What is the original price of a coat that is on sale for $98.95?

44. In the country of Erehwon, the sales tax on a purchase is 8.75%. Write an expression for the total cost of a sale, *y*, if the subtotal before tax is *x* dollars. Find a new equation for the subtotal if the total cost including tax is known. What is the subtotal when the total cost is $27.19? What is the subtotal when the total cost is $143.55?

45. Denzel received a cost-of-living increase. His new hourly wage is $13.75 per hour. If the cost of living index was 2.2%, what was his hourly wage before the increase?

46. Joan received a 6% merit increase, which raised her annual salary to $32,500. What was her salary before the increase?

47. For large parties, many restaurants automatically add a 15% gratuity to the bill, rather than allowing the customers to add their own gratuity. If the total bill including gratuity is $143.24, what was the bill before the gratuity was added?

48. What is the cost before gratuity of a dinner party if the bill plus 15% gratuity is $262.95? How much was the gratuity?

Experiencing Algebra the Calculator Way

A rectangle whose length and width hold the golden ratio, $G = \dfrac{\sqrt{5} - 1}{2}$, is considered to be uniquely pleasing to the eye. Many philosophers, artists, and mathematicians have been intrigued by it. To apply the ratio, the width of a rectangle should be G times the length. What should the width and length be for such a rectangle if the perimeter must be 323.61 inches?

1. Draw a picture and label it.

2. Define a variable.

3. Label the picture using the variable. Do not use rounded-off values for G. (Since you have a calculator, there is no reason to compound the round-off error by doing so.)

4. Write an expression for the perimeter and set it equal to the value given in order to obtain an equation.

5. Solve the equation for the length.

6. Find the width.

(*Hint:* You may want to store the expression for G, and key in the letter for calculations.)

7. Check to see that the perimeter is in fact 323.61 inches.

Experiencing Algebra the Group Way

Using the golden ratio, G (see "Experiencing Algebra The Calculator Way"), complete the following table of values for a rectangle whose width and length hold the golden ratio. (*Hint:* Begin by storing the expression for G in the calculator. Then set Y1 equal to Gx and Y2 equal to the calculation formula for the perimeter, in terms of G and x. Finally, use the Table feature of the calculator to obtain the values needed for the table.)

Length	Width	Perimeter
5 cm		
10 cm		
15 cm		
20 cm		
25 cm		
30 cm		
35 cm		
40 cm		

Each member of the group picks a different setting from the table and constructs a rectangle with the dimensions selected. Do the rectangles in fact appear aesthetically pleasing? Measure the perimeters and check to see that your calculations of perimeters are correct.

If you mark off a square in your rectangle, with a side as one of the widths of the rectangle, the resulting inner rectangle also has dimensions in the golden ratio. You can continue marking off squares in each inner rectangle to obtain another golden rectangle. The picture you generate should be an aesthetically pleasing modern artwork. If you want to get fancy, you can color each of the squares with primary colors and create a colorful work of art! The golden ratio can be tried with other geometric shapes also.

Experiencing Algebra the Write Way

1. In the preceding exercises, the golden ratio was introduced as a classical principle that has been studied by mathematicians and others because of its aesthetic appeal. It was used in architecture, with the classic application being the Parthenon, whose dimensions fit the ratio in many places. Renaissance writers called it the "divine proportion." Find a reference that discusses this principle, and write a short summary of your findings. Be sure to document your source.

2. Many business mathematics textbooks use the techniques presented here to solve application problems. Find one textbook that presents an illustration of a business application similar to the problems presented here. It may be a problem dealing with cost-of-living increases, markups or markdowns in selling prices, investments, and so on. Make a photocopy of the page in the text discussing the application. Write a one-paragraph critique of the illustration. In your critique, state whether you think the author did a good job in presenting the illustration. Was it clear or was it confusing? If it was not a good presentation, suggest what you might have done to present the example differently. Turn in your critique with the photocopy and the library call number of the textbook.

5.6 Solving Linear Absolute Value Equations

Objectives
1 Identify linear absolute value equations in one variable.
2 Solve linear absolute value equations numerically.
3 Solve linear absolute value equations graphically.
4 Solve linear absolute value equations algebraically.
5 Model real-world situations using linear absolute value equations and solve.

Application

The U.S. Bureau of the Census reports that the difference in the average monthly salary of a male and a female with a B.S. degree is $1537.[1] If a female expects to earn $1698 dollars monthly, determine a male's expected monthly salary.

After completing this section, we will discuss this application further. See page 380.

In this section we will solve a linear equation in one variable that contains an absolute value expression. Before we begin, we need to review the definition of absolute value. An absolute value expression is defined to be the distance of the expression from 0 (section 1.1). For example, $|3| = 3$ and $|-3| = 3$. Remember, the result is always nonnegative.

1 Linear Absolute Value Equations in One Variable

> *Standard Form for a Linear Absolute Value Equation in One Variable*
> A linear absolute value equation in one variable is an equation written in the form $|ax + b| = c$, where a and b are real numbers and $a \neq 0$.

For example,

Standard form: $|ax + b| = c$

1. $|2x + 3| = 5$
2. $|2x + 3| - 6 = 5$
3. $4|2x + 3| = 0$

The first equation is in the exact form $|ax + b| = c$ with $a = 2$, $b = 3$, and $c = 5$. The last two equations can be solved for the absolute value expression by using the properties of equations. For example,

$|2x + 3| - 6 = 5$ or $|2x + 3| = 11$ Add 6 to both sides of the equation.

$4|2x + 3| = 0$ or $|2x + 3| = 0$ Divide both sides of the equation by 4.

These equations are called **linear absolute value equations in one variable** because of the characteristics of the graphs of the functions defined by the two expressions in the equation. To see what we mean, let's graph some absolute value expressions on the calculator. Complete the following set of exercises on your calculator.

---

[1] *Source:* "Education and Income, 1993," *The World Almanac and Book of Facts 1994.*

DISCOVERY 13

Graphs of the Functions Defined by Expressions in a Linear Absolute Value Equation

Graph on an integer screen the following functions, determined from the given linear absolute value equation.

1. $|2x + 3| = 5$

   $Y1 = |2x + 3|$ $Y2 = 5$

2. $|2x - 3| = -5$

   $Y1 = |2x - 3|$ $Y2 = -5$

   Explain the characteristic of the graphs of the functions defined by an absolute value expression, Y1.
   Explain the characteristic of the graphs of the functions defined by a constant, Y2.

Graph on an integer screen the following functions, determined from the given linear absolute value equation.

3. $|2x + 3| - 6 = 5$

   $Y1 = |2x + 3| - 6$ $Y2 = 5$

4. $4|2x + 3| = 0$

   $Y1 = 4|2x + 3|$ $Y2 = 0$

   Explain the characteristic of the graphs of the functions defined by an absolute value expression, Y1.
   Explain the characteristic of the graphs of the functions defined by a constant, Y2.

For the linear absolute value equations in the form $|ax + b| = c$, the graph of the function defined by the absolute value expression is a V-shaped graph formed by two straight lines, and the graph of the constant function is a line. For the linear absolute value equations not in $|ax + b| = c$ form, the graph of the function defined by the expression containing the absolute value expression is formed by straight lines.

For example, the equation $|-2x + 5| = 8$ is a linear absolute value equation. The graph of the function $Y1 = |-2x + 5|$ is a V-shaped graph made up of two lines. The graph of the function $Y2 = 8$ is a line.

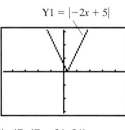

$Y1 = |-2x + 5|$

$(-47, 47, -31, 31)$

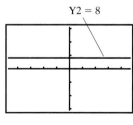

$Y2 = 8$

$(-47, 47, -31, 31)$

EXAMPLE 1   Identify each equation as a linear absolute value equation or a nonlinear absolute value equation.

a. $3|x - 4| - 6 = 9$ **b.** $-|3x - 5| + 8 = 0$ **c.** $|2x^3 + 3| = 5$

Algebraic Solution

a. $3|x - 4| - 6 = 9$ Linear absolute value, because it simplifies to $|x - 4| = 5$.

b. $-|3x - 5| + 8 = 0$ Linear absolute value, because it simplifies to $|3x - 5| = 8$.

c. $|2x^3 + 3| = 5$ Nonlinear absolute value, because the *x* term is raised to the third power.

Check your results graphically on your calculator.

a. $Y1 = 3|x - 4| - 6$

$Y2 = 9$

$(-47, 47, -31, 31)$

Linear absolute value, because the functions graphed both consist of straight lines.

b. $Y2 = 0$

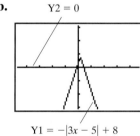

$Y1 = -|3x - 5| + 8$

$(-47, 47, -31, 31)$

Note: The graph of $Y2 = 0$ is the *x*-axis.

Linear absolute value, because the functions graphed both consist of straight lines.

c. $Y1 = |2x^3 + 3|$

$Y2 = 5$

$(-10, 10, -10, 10)$

Nonlinear absolute value, because the functions graphed are not both made up of straight lines. The graph of the function defined by the absolute value expression is not a line, but a curve. ∎

We will solve linear absolute value equations using the three methods we used with linear equations: numerically, graphically, and algebraically.

Experiencing Algebra the Checkup Way

In exercises 1–4, identify each equation as a linear absolute value equation or a nonlinear absolute value equation.

1. $9 - 2|2x + 1| = 8$ **2.** $-2 = |3 - x|$ **3.** $|5 - 2x^2| = 10$ **4.** $|x| = 1$

5. What does the absolute value of a number represent?

6. What distinguishes a linear absolute value equation from one that is nonlinear?

---

2 Solving Equations Numerically

First, let's solve linear absolute value equations numerically. We will use a calculator to see what happens in tables for three linear absolute value equations. Complete the following set of exercises on your calculator.

D I S C O V E R Y   1 4

Solving a Linear Absolute Value Equation Numerically

Solve each equation numerically by completing the given table of values.

1. $|x| = 3$

x	$|x|$	3
−5		
−4		
−3		
−2		
−1		
0		
1		
2		
3		
4		
5		

Solution: _____

2. $|x| = -3$

x	$|x|$	−3
−5		
−4		
−3		
−2		
−1		
0		
1		
2		
3		
4		
5		

Solution: _____

3. $|x| = 0$

x	$|x|$	0
−5		
−4		
−3		
−2		
−1		
0		
1		
2		
3		
4		
5		

Solution: _____

Write a rule for the number of solutions of a linear absolute value equation when the absolute value expression equals a positive number, a negative number, and 0.

In the first table, when the absolute value expression equals a positive number, there are two solutions of the equation. In the second table, when the absolute value expression equals a negative number, there is no solution of the equation. In the third table, when the absolute value expression equals 0, there is one solution of the equation.

> *Number of Solutions of a Linear Absolute Value Equation*
> To determine the number of solutions of a linear absolute value equation, write the equation in the form $|ax + b| = c$.

- If the constant, c, is positive, there are two solutions.
- If the constant, c, is negative, there are no solutions.
- If the constant, c, is 0, there is one solution.

We know this is true because the absolute value of a positive number and its opposite (a negative number) equal the same positive number. Hence, two solutions are possible if c is a positive number. However, an absolute value cannot equal a negative number. Hence, no solution is possible if c is negative. Also, the absolute value of 0 equals 0. Hence, there is only one solution possible if c is 0.

EXAMPLE 2 Determine the number of solutions and solve numerically.

    a. $|x + 4| = 3$ **b.** $|x + 4| = -3$ **c.** $|x + 4| = 0$

Calculator Numeric Solution

a. There are two solutions, because the absolute value expression equals positive 3.

    As shown in Figure 5.8, the solutions are -7 and -1, because Y1 and Y2 equal 3 when $x = -7$ and $x = -1$.

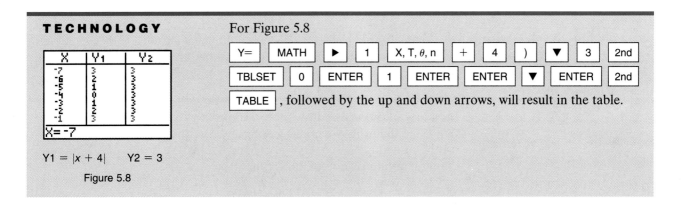

TECHNOLOGY

Y1 = $|x + 4|$ Y2 = 3

Figure 5.8

For Figure 5.8

| Y= | MATH | ▶ | 1 | X, T, θ, n | + | 4 |) | ▼ | 3 | 2nd |

| TBLSET | 0 | ENTER | 1 | ENTER | ENTER | ▼ | ENTER | 2nd |

TABLE , followed by the up and down arrows, will result in the table.

b. There is no solution, because the absolute value expression is equal to a negative number.

Y1 = $|x + 4|$ Y2 = -3

There is no solution, because Y1 and Y2 are never equal.

c. There is one solution, because the absolute value expression equals 0.

X	Y1	Y2
-4	0	0
-3	1	0
-2	2	0
-1	3	0
0	4	0
1	5	0
2	6	0

X= -4

Y1 = |x + 4| Y2 = 0

The solution is −4, because Y1 and Y2 equal 0 when $x = -4$. ∎

In conclusion: To solve a linear absolute value equation numerically, use a table of values. However, if the solution is noninteger, it will be difficult to find by this method.

Experiencing Algebra the Checkup Way

In exercises 1–3, state the number of solutions for each equation and solve numerically.

1. $|x - 9| = 1$ **2.** $|x - 9| = -1$ **3.** $|x - 9| = 0$

4. How can you tell how many solutions a linear absolute value equation will have, without actually solving for them?

---

3 Solving Equations Graphically Now we will graphically solve the previous linear absolute value equations to confirm the solutions. Complete the following set.

DISCOVERY 15

Solving a Linear Absolute Value Equation Graphically

Solve the following equations graphically. Use the tables of values found in the previous "Discovery" exercises. Sketch the graph and label the point(s) of intersection of the graphs.

1. $|x| = 3$ **2.** $|x| = -3$ **3.** $|x| = 0$

Solution: _____   Solution: _____   Solution: _____

Write a rule for the number of solutions of a linear absolute value equation when the absolute value expression equals a positive number, a negative number, and 0.

These results confirm the previously found rule for the number of solutions that can be found for a linear absolute value equation. We examine the number the absolute value expression is equated to. If the number is positive, two solutions can be found. If the number is negative, no solution can be found. If the number is 0, then one solution can be found.

EXAMPLE 3   Solve graphically.

   a. $|x + 4| = 3$ **b.** $|x + 4| = -3$ **c.** $|x + 4| = 0$

Calculator Graphic Solution

   a. As shown in Figure 5.9, the solutions are -7 and -1, because the graphs intersect at $(-7, 3)$ and $(-1, 3)$.

TECHNOLOGY

$(-47, 47, -31, 31)$

Figure 5.9

For Figure 5.9

, followed by the arrow keys, will result in the graph.

b.

$(-47, 47, -31, 31)$

There is no solution, because the graphs do not intersect.

c.

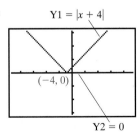

The solution is -4, because the graphs intersect at $(-4, 0)$. ∎

EXAMPLE 4   Solve graphically.

   a. $|2x| + 8 = 8$ **b.** $\left|\dfrac{x - 2}{3}\right| = 5$ **c.** $3|-2x + 1| - 6 = 9$

Calculator Graphic Solution

a.

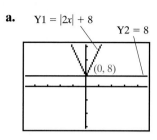

$(-47, 47, -31, 31)$

The solution is 0.

b.

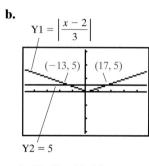

$(-47, 47, -31, 31)$

The solutions are -13 and 17.

c.

$(-47, 47, -31, 31)$

The solutions are -2 and 3. ∎

In conclusion: To solve a linear absolute value equation graphically, graph two functions defined by the expressions in the equation. When using your calculator, you may use this method to find noninteger solutions.

 Experiencing Algebra the Checkup Way

Solve exercises 1–5 graphically.

1. $|3x + 1| = 4$

2. $|3x| + 1 = 4$

3. $\left| \dfrac{x + 1}{2} \right| = 3$

4. $|x + 8| + 6 = 1$

5. $2| - 3x + 2| - 3 = 11$

6. How do you determine the solutions to a linear absolute value equation when solving the equation graphically?

4 Solving Equations Algebraically

We are now ready to solve linear absolute value equations algebraically. We begin with the rule found in the previous part of this section.

> *Solving a Linear Absolute Value Equation Algebraically*
> First, determine the number of solutions of an absolute value equation by writing it in the form $|ax + b| = c$.
>
> - If the constant, c, is positive, there are two solutions.
> - If the constant, c, is negative, there are no solutions.
> - If the constant, c, is 0, there is one solution.
>
> Second, write and evaluate an equation or equations needed to find the solution(s).
>
> - If there are two solutions, then
>
> $$ax + b = c \quad \text{or} \quad ax + b = -c.$$
>
> - If there is one solution, then
>
> $$ax + b = c.$$

For example, $|x| = 3$ has two solutions because the absolute value expression is equal to a positive number. The two solutions are found when the expression within the absolute value symbols, x, equals -3 or 3. Therefore, $x = -3$ or $x = 3$.

$|x| = -3$ has no solution because the absolute value expression equals a negative number.

$|x| = 0$ has one solution because the absolute value expression equals 0. The one solution is found when the expression within the absolute value symbols, x, equals 0. Therefore, $x = 0$.

EXAMPLE 5   Solve algebraically.

a. $|x + 4| = 3$ **b.** $|x + 4| = -3$ **c.** $|x + 4| = 0$

Algebraic Solution

a. $|x + 4| = 3$

There are two solutions because the absolute value expression equals a positive number.

$$
\begin{array}{ccc}
x + 4 = 3 & \text{or} & x + 4 = -3 \\
x + 4 - 4 = 3 - 4 & & x + 4 - 4 = -3 - 4 \\
x = -1 & & x = -7
\end{array}
$$

The two solutions are -1 and -7.

The check is left for you.

b. $|x + 4| = -3$

There is no solution because the absolute value expression equals a negative number.

c. $|x + 4| = 0$

There is one solution because the absolute value expression equals 0.

$$x + 4 = 0$$
$$x + 4 - 4 = 0 - 4$$
$$x = -4$$

The solution is -4.
The check is left for you. ∎

EXAMPLE 6 Solve algebraically. (Remember to isolate the absolute value expression first.)

a. $|2x| + 8 = 8$ **b.** $\left|\dfrac{x-2}{3}\right| = 5$ **c.** $3|-2x + 1| - 6 = 9$

Algebraic Solution

a. $|2x| + 8 = 8$

$|2x| + 8 - 8 = 8 - 8$ Subtract 8 from both sides to isolate the absolute value expression.

$|2x| = 0$ Simplify.

$2x = 0$ Rewrite for one solution.

$\dfrac{2x}{2} = \dfrac{0}{2}$ Divide both sides by 2.

$x = 0$ Simplify.

The solution is 0.
The check is left for you.

b. $\left|\dfrac{x-2}{3}\right| = 5$

$\dfrac{x-2}{3} = 5$ or $\dfrac{x-2}{3} = -5$ Rewrite for two solutions.

$3\left(\dfrac{x-2}{3}\right) = 3(5)$ $3\left(\dfrac{x-2}{3}\right) = 3(-5)$ Multiply both sides by 3.

$x - 2 = 15$ $x - 2 = -15$ Simplify.

$x - 2 + 2 = 15 + 2$ $x - 2 + 2 = -15 + 2$ Add 2 to both sides.

$x = 17$ $x = -13$ Simplify.

The solutions are 17 and -13.
The check is left for you.

c. $3|-2x + 1| - 6 = 9$

$3|-2x + 1| - 6 + 6 = 9 + 6$ Add 6 to both sides to isolate the absolute value expression.

$3|-2x + 1| = 15$ Simplify.

$\dfrac{3|-2x + 1|}{3} = \dfrac{15}{3}$ Divide both sides by 3.

$|-2x + 1| = 5$ Simplify.

$-2x + 1 = 5$ or $-2x + 1 = -5$ Rewrite for two solutions.

$-2x + 1 - 1 = 5 - 1$ $-2x + 1 - 1 = -5 - 1$ Subtract 1 from both sides.

$$-2x = 4 \qquad\qquad -2x = -6 \qquad \text{Simplify.}$$
$$\frac{-2x}{-2} = \frac{4}{-2} \qquad\qquad \frac{-2x}{-2} = \frac{-6}{-2} \qquad \text{Divide both sides by } -2.$$
$$x = -2 \qquad\qquad x = 3 \qquad \text{Simplify.}$$

The solutions are -2 and 3.
The check is left for you. ∎

Experiencing Algebra the Checkup Way

Solve exercises 1–6 algebraically.

1. $|x - 9| = 0$ **2.** $|3x + 1| = 4$ **3.** $|3x| + 1 = 4$

4. $\left|\dfrac{x + 1}{2}\right| = 3$ **5.** $|x + 8| + 6 = 1$ **6.** $2|-3x + 2| - 3 = 11$

7. Describe how you would algebraically solve a linear absolute value equation.

5 Modeling the Real World

Linear absolute value equations can describe several kinds of real-world situations. In particular, absolute values are used to describe the size, or magnitude, of many quantities that can be positive or negative in direction. This includes distance, speed, force, and other so-called vector quantities. Absolute values can also describe the magnitude of financial transactions, without regard to whether the money is a credit (positive) or a debit (negative). However, remember that when you solve linear absolute value equations, the answers you get must make sense in terms of the real situation. Sometimes you have to throw away an answer because it doesn't describe the physical situation correctly.

EXAMPLE 7

A plastic disposable hospital bowl is advertised to have an outer diameter of 5.146 inches with a tolerance (allowance for error) of plus or minus 0.015 inch. What is the least and greatest possible length of the diameter?

TOP VIEW

5.146″

Algebraic Solution

Let $x =$ the actual length of the diameter

Since we do not know which length is greater, the actual length or the length given on the package, we will take the absolute value of the difference of the lengths and equate it to the absolute value of the tolerance.

$$|x - 5.146| = |\pm 0.015|$$
$$|x - 5.146| = 0.015 \qquad \text{Take the absolute value of the right side.}$$

Write equations for the two possible solutions.

$$x - 5.146 = 0.015$$
$$x - 5.146 + 5.146 = 0.015 + 5.146$$
$$x = 5.161$$

or

$$x - 5.146 = -0.015$$
$$x - 5.146 + 5.146 = -0.015 + 5.146$$
$$x = 5.131$$

The greatest diameter measurement is 5.161 inches. The least diameter measurement is 5.131 inches. ∎

Application

The U.S. Bureau of the Census reports that the difference in the average monthly salary of a male and a female with a B.S. degree is $1537.[1] If a female expects to earn $1698 monthly, determine a male's expected monthly salary.

Discussion

Let $x =$ a male's expected monthly salary

Since we are not told which salary is greater, we will need to take the absolute value of the difference.

$$|1698 - x| = 1537$$

| $1698 - x = 1537$ | or | $1698 - x = -1537$ |

$$1698 - x - 1698 = 1537 - 1698 \qquad 1698 - x - 1698 = -1537 - 1698$$

$$-x = -161 \qquad\qquad -x = -3235$$

$$\frac{-x}{-1} = \frac{-161}{-1} \qquad\qquad \frac{-x}{-1} = \frac{-3235}{-1}$$

$$x = 161 \qquad\qquad x = 3235$$

It is unlikely that the male's expected monthly salary is $161. Therefore, we conclude that the male's monthly expected salary is $3235.

Since we are not told which salary is greater, we will need to take the absolute value of the difference. However, since we are taking the absolute value, we can also subtract the expected salaries in a different order. Instead of $|1698 - x|$, we can use $|x - 1698|$.

Let $x =$ a male's expected monthly salary

$$|x - 1698| = 1537$$

| $x - 1698 = 1537$ | or | $x - 1698 = -1537$ |

$$x - 1698 + 1698 = 1537 + 1698 \qquad x - 1698 + 1698 = -1537 + 1698$$

$$x = 3235 \qquad\qquad x = 161$$

As we said before, it is unlikely that the male's expected monthly salary is $161. Therefore, we conclude that the male's monthly expected salary is $3235.

Note: We can see why we obtain the same solution if we notice that $1698 - x$ is the opposite of $x - 1698$ (the sign of each term is the opposite of the corresponding term). The absolute value of an expression and the absolute value of its opposite are equal. ∎

Experiencing Algebra the Checkup Way

An auto manufacturer designs a sports car to comfortably seat a driver who is 6 feet tall (72 inches), give or take 3 inches. Another way of stating this is that the absolute value of the difference between 72 inches and a person's height, h, in inches, equals 3. Write a linear absolute value equation and solve it to find the greatest and smallest heights for drivers who will comfortably sit in the car.

[1] *Source:* "Education and Income, 1993," *The World Almanac and Book of Facts 1994.*

PROBLEM SET 5.6

Experiencing Algebra the Exercise Way

Solve numerically.

1. $|x + 6| = 3$

2. $|x - 7| = 9$

3. $|-x| = 13$

4. $-|x| = 13$

5. $|-x + 3| = 2$

6. $|-x + 2| = 5$

7. $|2x + 6| = 4$

8. $|8x - 4| = 4$

9. $|-4x - 12| = 0$

10. $|-3x - 3| = 0$

Solve graphically.

11. $|x| = 9$

12. $|-x| = 9$

13. $|x + 1| = 3$

14. $|x - 3| = 1$

15. $|6x + 6| = 12$

16. $|3x - 9| = 6$

17. $|-x - 1| = 1$

18. $|-4x - 8| = 4$

19. $|x + 21| = 26$

20. $|x - 19| = 29$

21. $|-x - 19| = 22$

22. $|-x - 1| = 18$

23. $|x - 2.17| = 6.09$

24. $|-x + 22.83| = 0.899$

25. $\left|x + \dfrac{2}{5}\right| = \dfrac{11}{15}$

26. $\left|x + \dfrac{7}{8}\right| = 6\dfrac{9}{16}$

27. $2|x - 15| + 25 = 15$

28. $3|2x + 12| + 14 = 14$

29. $7|x - 32| + 21 = 21$

30. $4|3x - 6| + 19 = 13$

31. $3|x + 5| - 7 = 4$

32. $3|2x - 5| - 16 = 2$

Solve algebraically.

33. $|x| = 138$

34. $|z| = 2400$

35. $|a| = -512$

36. $|m| = 0.009$

37. $|b| = 41.67$

38. $|s| = -22\dfrac{17}{21}$

39. $|c| = 14\dfrac{5}{9}$

40. $|x| = \dfrac{11}{12}$

41. $|x + 578| = 286$

42. $|z + 303| = 471$

43. $|x - 721| = 1942$

44. $|x - 651| = 124$

45. $5|x - 29| - 46 = 74$

46. $4|2x - 18| - 16 = 84$

47. $2|x + 41| + 96 = 48$

48. $3|x + 62| + 76 = 32$

49. $\left|\dfrac{x - 14}{7}\right| = 8$

50. $\left|\dfrac{2x + 3}{5}\right| = 14$

51. $|-3x - 6| - 18 = -6$

52. $|-2x - 16| - 34 = -17$

53. $-4|x + 12| = -16$

54. $-3|-2x + 8| = -15$

Write a linear absolute value equation for each situation and solve.

55. The maximum depth of Lake Superior differs from that of Lake Michigan by 410 feet. If Lake Michigan has a maximum depth of 923 feet, what are the possible values for the maximum depth of Lake Superior? Given that Lake Superior is deeper, what is its maximum depth?

56. The largest lake in the world is the Caspian Sea, which was incorrectly called a sea by the Romans because of its salty water. One of the most beautiful lakes in the world is Lake Baikal in Russia. The difference in maximum depths of these two lakes is 1952 feet. Given that Lake Baikal has a maximum depth of 5315 feet, what are the possible values for the maximum depth of the Caspian

Sea? Given further that Lake Baikal is the deepest lake in the world, what is the maximum depth of the Caspian Sea?

57. Ralph Raffish manufactures sports clothes to fit the average male height, give or take 6 inches. If the average male is 5 feet 9 inches tall, what are the maximum and minimum heights the clothes will fit?

58. Rexus Luxury Cars designs its cars to comfortably seat a driver whose height differs by 4 inches from the average height of buyers of the cars. If the average height of buyers of the cars is established by a customer survey to be 6 feet 1 inch, what are the limits on heights of drivers the car would comfortably seat?

59. A political survey reports that 42% of the voters support an issue, with a margin of error of 3%. What are the minimum and maximum percentages that may occur?

60. A poll of voters reports that 48% of the voters support unification of the city and county charters, with a margin of error of 4.5%. If this poll is accurate, what are the minimum and maximum percentages that could occur in the election?

61. If a bathroom scale has a margin of error of 2 pounds, what is the range for Dee's actual weight if she reads a weight of 132 pounds?

62. A scale in a meat market has an allowable margin of error of 0.05 pound. What is the range of weights for a 1-pound package of hamburger read on the scale?

63. The tolerance in cutting a piece of pipe is $\frac{1}{4}$ inch. What are the possible lengths of a piece of pipe that is to be cut to a length of $5\frac{1}{2}$ inches?

64. A metal rod is to be cut to a length of 25.5 inches, with a tolerance of 0.125 inches. What are the possible lengths of the rod?

65. The most extreme score in a set of test scores differs from the average by 22 points. If the average of the test scores is 71 points, what are the possible values for the extreme score?

66. The range of scores for a test was 28 points. If one of the extreme scores was 66, what are the possible limits for the scores? (Note that 66 could be either the highest score or the lowest score on the test.)

67. The difference in the ages of Barbra and her movie co-star is 12 years. If Barbra's age is 47, what are the possible pairs of values for their ages?

68. The difference in sales of two brands of soda pop averages 2,500,000 bottles per month. If one brand sells 12,100,000 bottles of soda pop per month, what are the possible values for the monthly sales of the other brand?

 Experiencing Algebra the Calculator Way

Solve graphically.

1. $|x + 2| = |x - 3|$

2. $3|x + 2| - 5 = 3|x + 2| + 5$

3. $|x + 6| - 9 = -|x + 3| + 8$

4. $|x + 2| = -3x + 8$

5. $|x + 3| + |x - 3| = 15$

Could you have solved any of these exercises algebraically? If so, which ones? For those you could not solve algebraically, why not?

Experiencing Algebra the Group Way

In your group, discuss the differences in the equations for exercises 1–3. Would you expect the equations to have the same solutions? Discuss what is the best method for solving each equation: numerically, graphically, or algebraically. Then have each member of the group pick a method and try to solve each equation by that method. Be sure that each method will be tried by at least one member of the group. Solve the equations. Check your solutions.

1. $|x + 5| = |x| + 5$ **2.** $|x + 5| = -|x + 5|$ **3.** $|x| + 5 = -|x| + 5$

Discuss what you have learned from this activity.

- Describe the solutions to exercise 1. What is unusual about this exercise? Does it have none, one, two, or more solutions? Can you explain why it has the unusual solution?
- Could exercise 2 be solved algebraically? What is unusual about the solution(s) to this exercise?
- Could exercise 3 be solved algebraically? What is unusual about the solution(s) to this exercise?

What seemed to be the easiest method to solve the equations?

Next discuss the best method to solve the equation in exercise 4. Then have members of the group try to solve the equation each way.

4. $\left|\dfrac{1}{2}x + 2\right| = |2x| + 8$

What can you say about the solutions to exercise 4? What method was the easiest to use for this equation?

Experiencing Algebra the Write Way

You have seen three ways to solve linear absolute value equations: numerically, graphically, and algebraically. Which method did you prefer? Write a brief summary of which methods you prefer and why. Try to think of situations in which you would be forced to use one method over another. The calculator and group exercises provide examples in which you might have to use one method to find a solution. Describe, in your own words, what you should look for in deciding which method to use. You should conclude that not all methods will always work.

CHAPTER 5 | Summary

After completing this chapter, you should be able to define in your own words the following key terms, definitions, properties, and rules.

Terms
linear equation in one variable
solution set
contradiction
identity
equivalent equations
consecutive integers
consecutive even integers
consecutive odd
  integers
linear absolute value equation in one
  variable

Definitions
Standard form for a linear equation in
  one variable
Standard form for a linear absolute
  value equation in one variable

Properties
Addition property of equations
Multiplication property of equations

Rules
Solving a linear equation numerically

Solving a linear equation graphically
Solving a linear equation using the
  addition property of equations
Solving a linear equation using the
  multiplication property of equations
Solving a linear equation using a
  combination of properties of
  equations
Solving an equation for a variable
Modeling real-world situations
Solving a linear absolute value
  equation algebraically

CHAPTER 5	Review

Reflections

1. Explain how the addition property of equations is used to solve a linear equation in one variable.

2. Explain how the multiplication property of equations is used to solve a linear equation in one variable.

3. How can you graphically solve a linear equation in one variable?

4. How can you numerically solve a linear equation in one variable?

5. Explain how you can tell that a linear equation in one variable has no solution.

6. Explain how you can tell that a linear equation in one variable has many solutions.

7. How does a linear absolute value equation in one variable differ from a linear equation in one variable?

8. What must you do differently when algebraically solving a linear absolute value equation in one variable as compared to solving a linear equation in one variable?

5.1

Identify each equation as linear or nonlinear.

1. $4x^2 - 2x + 1 = 0$
2. $5x + 3 = x - 4$
3. $5.7x - 8.2(x + 4.6) = 0$
4. $\sqrt{x} + 2 = 3x - 6$
5. $\frac{1}{8}x + \frac{3}{4} = \frac{11}{16}$
6. $\frac{3}{x} + 5 = 12x$

Solve numerically for an integer solution if possible.

7. $4x + 7 = 2x - 5$
8. $2.4x - 9.6 = 4.8$
9. $\frac{3}{5}x - \frac{7}{10} = \frac{1}{5}x + \frac{1}{2}$
10. $14x + 12 = 11(x - 5) + 60$
11. $3(x - 2) - 1 = 4(x - 1) - (x + 3)$
12. $2(2x + 1) + x = 3(2x - 1) - (x + 1)$

Solve graphically.

13. $2x - 2 = -x + 4$
14. $\frac{1}{2}x - 2 = -\frac{1}{3}x - \frac{11}{3}$
15. $(x + 3) + (x + 1) = 3(x + 1) - (x - 1)$
16. $(x + 6) - 3(x + 1) = (2x + 5) - 2(2x + 3)$
17. $1.2x + 0.72 = -2.1x + 8.64$

18. Theresa offers to rake and clean the wooded area of your back yard for a flat fee of $90, or for a fee of $25 plus $6.50 for each hour worked. Determine how many hours of work will make the two offers equivalent.

19. A church receives weekly donations of $2200, $1750, and $1885 for the first three weeks of the month. How much do they need to receive in the fourth week to meet their average weekly goal of $2000 in donations?

20. Two sides of a triangular worktable surface are of equal length. The third side measures 3 feet longer than each of the other two sides. If the perimeter of the surface is 26.25 feet, what are the lengths of each side?

5.2

Solve algebraically.

21. $41 + x = 67$
22. $y - \frac{7}{13} = \frac{11}{39}$
23. $5 - (2 - x) = 1$
24. $0.59(z - 1) + 0.41(z + 2) = 3.163$
25. $-4x = 272$
26. $45.86z = -1765.61$
27. $\frac{a}{7} = 15$
28. $\frac{4}{5}x = \frac{64}{125}$
29. $15x - 16x = -12$
30. $-y = 2.98$
31. $4(2x - 6) + 6(x + 4) = 49$

Write an equation for each situation and solve algebraically.

32. Total attendance at a benefit luncheon was 247 people. If 189 of these purchased tickets, how many tickets were given as complimentary passes?

33. If a graduating class had 154 males, representing 55% of the class, how many students graduated in total?

34. Students at an elementary school are selling coupon books for $15 each as a fund-raiser. If the goal of the school is to raise $80,000 for a computerized classroom, how many books must they sell?

35. Miyoshi was to receive $\frac{3}{7}$ of the proceeds from the sale of an estate. If she received $18,270, what was the total of the proceeds of the sale?

5.3

Solve algebraically.

36. $3x + 7 = 4x + 21$

37. $14 - 2x = 5x$

38. $8.7x + 4.33 = -2.4x - 33.41$

39. $6.8z - 9.52 = 0$

40. $\frac{3}{8}x + \frac{1}{2} = \frac{3}{4}$

41. $\frac{5}{7}a + \frac{11}{14} = \frac{2}{7}a$

42. $2(x + 5) - (x + 6) = 2(x + 2) - x$

43. $3(x - 4) + 2(x + 1) = 5x + 10$

Write an equation for each situation and solve algebraically.

44. Your business trip allows $250.00 reimbursement for car rental. If you rent a car for a flat fee of $49.95 per week plus $0.22 per mile, what are the maximum miles you can drive without exceeding your allowance?

45. Acme Industries invests $150,000 in new equipment, which they will depreciate evenly over a 7-year period. At the end of that time, they expect to sell the equipment for scrap for $25,000. What will the annual depreciation for the equipment be? (*Hint:* Depreciation plus scrap value equals the investment.)

46. One contractor offers to paint your home for a fee of $175 plus $35 per hour. Another contractor offers to do the same job for $100 plus $40 per hour. For what number of hours will the two offers be the same?

5.4

Solve exercises 47–50 for the indicated variable.

47. $A = \frac{1}{2}h(b + B)$ for h

48. $S = 2LW + 2WH + 2LH$ for W

49. $6x + 7y = 42$ for x

50. $\frac{3}{4}x - \frac{5}{8}y = \frac{11}{12}$ for y

51. An annuity will pay you $6,000 immediately and an annual payment of $8000. Write an equation for the total amount, A, that you will receive from the annuity over n years. Use the equation to solve for n, the number of years the annuity will last for a particular amount. Use the new equation to find how long the annuity will last if the amount is $78,000. How long will the annuity last if the amount is $126,000?

5.5

52. Rob was cutting three lengths of wire from a 3-foot piece. He can't find the instructions that tell how many inches each piece should measure, but he remembers that they were consecutive even integers. What are the lengths he should cut?

53. What would the lengths be for the previous exercise if the lengths were consecutive integers instead of consecutive even integers?

54. Noah wants to build a rectangular holding pen for some animals. He wants the length of the pen to be three times the width. He will install two gates on the pen at opposite ends. One gate is 4 feet wide and the other is 6 feet wide. If he has 230 feet of fencing, what should the dimensions of the pen be?

6 ft

4 ft

55. For how many years should you invest $5000 at 7.5% simple interest per year, if you want to earn $2250 in interest?

56. How much should you invest at 7.5% simple interest if you want to earn $2250 in 3 years?

57. A discount store listed the retail price of a suit as $249. The sale price on the suit was $210. The sale was advertised as a 20%-off sale. Was the store being honest about the sale? Explain your answer by determining what the retail price should be, calculated from the sale price.

58. If the markup on a signed art print is 30%, and the print sells for $32.50, how much was the artist paid for it?

5.6
Solve.

59. $|x| = 23$ **60.** $|x| = -12$ **61.** $|c| = 0$ **62.** $|a - 7| = 0$

63. $|-b + 12| = 4$ **64.** $|c - 2| = -4$ **65.** $|2x - 7| = 8$ **66.** $2|x - 7| - 4 = 8$

67. $5|2x - 7| + 10 = 8$ **68.** $2\left|\dfrac{x - 1}{2}\right| - 5 = -2$

Write a linear absolute value equation to represent each situation and solve.

69. The tolerance on a machining job is 0.04 mm. If the basic dimension on the part is 62.79 mm, what are the permissible limits on the part?

70. A voter survey shows that 49% of the voters are in favor of a consolidation proposal with a margin of error of 4%. What are the limits on the percentage of voters who favor the proposal?

CHAPTER 5 | **Mixed Review**

Solve graphically.

1. $3(x + 2) - 2(x - 1) = (2x + 5) - (x - 3)$ **2.** $(2x + 1) - (3x - 7) = (x + 5) - 2(x - 2)$

3. $x + 1 = 2x + 5$ **4.** $\dfrac{1}{3}x + 3 = 6 - \dfrac{2}{3}x$

5. $1.2x - 6.12 = -2.2x + 4.42$

Solve each equation numerically for an integer solution.

6. $4x - 5 = 7 - 2x$ **7.** $14(x + 6) - 17 = 12(x + 5)$

8. $1.5x + 5.5 = -2.4x - 6.2$ **9.** $2(2x - 3) + 3(x + 1) = 6(x - 1) + (x + 3)$

10. $\dfrac{1}{3}x + \dfrac{14}{3} = \dfrac{5}{2} - \dfrac{3}{4}x$

11. $4(x - 2) - (x - 1) = 3x + 1$

Identify each equation as linear or nonlinear.

12. $5 - \dfrac{3}{7}x = \dfrac{2}{3}x + 2$ **13.** $2x - 4 = 1 + \dfrac{9}{x}$ **14.** $-2x^3 + 3x = x - 5$

15. $15 = 2(x - 7) - (x - 2)$ **16.** $3.9(x - 1.2) - 6.7x = 0$ **17.** $\sqrt[3]{x + 1} - 5 = 4x$

Solve algebraically.

18. $\dfrac{z}{29} = -12$ **19.** $\dfrac{5}{22} = \dfrac{25}{33}y$ **20.** $59a = 1888$ **21.** $-174.243 = 2.41x$

22. $2.3x - 3.3x = 14$ **23.** $-b = 14.59$ **24.** $3(x - 8) + 8(x + 3) = 77$ **25.** $z + 193 = -251$

26. $\dfrac{13}{17} + a = \dfrac{5}{51}$ **27.** $0.92(x - 2) + 0.08(x + 1) = 5.73$

28. $6.2x + 5.67 = 4.9x + 16.98$ **29.** $24.96 - 3.9a = 0$

30. $\dfrac{2}{3}x - \dfrac{3}{4} = -\dfrac{5}{6}$ **31.** $\dfrac{4}{9}y + \dfrac{11}{18} = \dfrac{5}{6}y$ **32.** $7x - 4 = 3x + 20$ **33.** $7x = 15 - 3x$

34. $2(x + 2) + (x + 1) = 5(x + 1) - 2x$ **35.** $4(2x - 1) = 3(2x + 1) + 2(x + 1)$

Solve.

36. $|2x + 6| = 0$ **37.** $|4 - z| = 4$ **38.** $|2x - 1| = -4$

39. $|5x + 2| = 12$ **40.** $5|x - 7| = 15$ **41.** $3\left|\dfrac{x + 1}{4}\right| - 9 = -6$

42. $|x| = 31$ **43.** $|x| = -29$ **44.** $|-a| = 0$

Solve each equation for the indicated variable.

45. $1.2x - 2.4y = 0.36$ for x

46. $\dfrac{1}{9}x + \dfrac{2}{3}y = \dfrac{1}{6}$ for y

47. $S = 2\pi r^2 + 2\pi rh$ for h

48. $I = PRT$ for P

Write a linear absolute value equation for each situation and solve.

49. The difference in the heights of the Peachtree Center and the Nation's Bank Building, both in Atlanta, is 170 feet. If the Peachtree Center is 853 feet high, what are the two possible heights for the Nation's Bank Building? Given that the Peachtree Center is not as tall, which height is the correct height for the Nation's Bank Building?

50. An instructor decides to give grades of C to student scores that differ from the class average by 5 points. If the class average is 72 points, what are the limits for a C grade?

Write a linear equation for each situation and solve.

51. If the sales tax on a purchase was $5.41, which represents 8.25% tax, what was the subtotal of the purchases before taxes? What was the total bill, including sales tax?

52. Chuck was given an advance of $5,650 for developing software for a publishing firm. This represented $\frac{2}{5}$ of the total amount he would receive for his work. How much money does he expect to earn in total for this project?

53. A part-time employee earns $13.25 per hour working in a science laboratory. If her gross earnings last year were $16,562.50, how many hours did she work?

54. A newspaper delivery service pays its employees $15.00 per day plus $0.25 for each house along the delivery route. How many houses does an employee need on the route in order to earn $45.00 per day?

55. Equipment purchased for $250,000 is to be sold for a scrap value of $15,000 after 20 years. What will be the annual depreciation rate for the equipment? (*Hint:* Depreciation plus scrap value equals investment.)

56. Laurie wants to buy a personal computer. She has saved $985. If the computer sells for $1399, how much more does she needs to save before she can buy the computer?

57. Instructions for a model plane kit require a piece of balsa wood to be cut into four pieces, each being 1 inch longer than the previous piece. If the wood is 26 inches long, how long will each piece be?

58. In exercise 57, what lengths would the strips be if each piece were 2 inches longer than the preceding piece, allowing for 2 inches of scrap?

59. If an inkjet printer was marked down 15% to a sale price of $259.95, what was the price before the markdown?

60. At what simple-interest rate should you invest $8000 for 3 years in order to earn $1560 in interest?

61. How much should you invest at 4.5% simple interest for a year to earn $562.50 in interest?

62. The length of a room is one and one-half times its width. If the perimeter of the room is 84 feet, what are its dimensions?

63. If the price of a television set with 8.75% sales tax was $325.16, what was the price before tax for the set? How much was the sales tax?

64. A plumber charges you $40.00 per visit, plus $22.50 for each hour worked on a job. Write an equation for the total amount, A, that you will pay for a job that requires h hours of labor. Use the equation to solve for h, the hours worked in terms of the total amount for the job. Use the new equation to find how many hours a job costing $208.75 lasted. If the plumber is paid $85.00, for how long did he work?

65. A designer rug is rectangular, with diagonals running from one corner to the opposite corner. If the diagonal makes a 35-degree angle with the length of the rug, how large an angle does it make with the width of the rug?

CHAPTER 5 | **Test**

Test-Taking Tips

When reviewing for an exam, list all the major concepts the exam will cover. Locate exercises that illustrate each of the concepts. Think of how you would recognize them if they were randomly ordered on the exam. Spend more of your study time on those exercises where you know you are weak. Seek out additional exercises in the text that you have not worked for extra practice. Try to find someone to study with so that you can help each other with your weaknesses. If you can't work some exercises that you have tried, see your instructor or go to a tutoring center well before test time to seek help from them. If you do this, the exam should not be a surprise to you, it won't throw you, and your confidence level will be high.

Identify each equation as linear or nonlinear.

1. $3.14x + 9.07 = 5.72x$

2. $5x = 12 + \dfrac{19}{x}$

3. $4x + 21 = 5x^2$

4. $4(x - 6) = 3(5 - x) + 12$

Solve.

5. $2(2x - 5) - 2(2 - x) = 6(x + 1) + 1$

6. $2(x + 5) = -3(x + 1) - 2$

7. $1.41(x + 5.08) + 1.17x + 0.00102 = -3.46x - 5.39334$

8. $(x + 1) - 4(x - 1) = 3(2 - x) - 1$

9. $\dfrac{4}{5}x + \dfrac{31}{10} = \dfrac{-4}{3}x + \dfrac{41}{6}$

10. $|x + 3| = 7$

11. $3|2x - 9| + 14 = 5$

Write a linear equation for each situation and solve.

12. A piece of wire measures 45 inches. For splicing purposes, it will be cut into three pieces, each of which is 1 inch longer than the preceding piece. In what lengths should the three pieces be cut?

13. Ricardo's dad is loaning him the money to buy a used car, which sells for $2470. Ricardo will use the $850 he has saved as a down payment and plans to pay his dad back in 12 months. His dad will not charge him any interest on the loan. What will be Ricardo's monthly payment to his dad?

14. If a stereo is on sale at 25% off the retail price, and its sale price is $179.95, what was the price before it went on sale?

15. Solve $P = 2L + 2W$ for W, where P is the perimeter of a rectangle with length L and width W. Use the formula to find the width of a rectangle whose length is 14.8 inches and whose perimeter measures 44.8 inches.

16. The second angle of a triangle is 10 degrees larger than the first angle. The measure of the third angle equals the sum of the measures of the other two angles. Find the size of each angle.

17. The margin of error in a voter poll is 3%. If the survey suggests that 52% of the voters support a new tax levy, what are the limits on the true percentage of voters who will support the levy?

18. Fruit drinks are a mixture of fruit juice and water. How many liters of a drink containing 60% apple juice must be mixed with 500 liters of a drink containing 20% cranberry juice to make a drink containing 50% cranberry/apple juice?

19. Annie works at the Book City bookstore. She was offered a choice of payment plans. She could earn $1500 per month, or she could earn $1200 per month plus 4% of all her sales for the month. For what value of sales would the two pay plans be equal?

20. Serene Landscaping will clear the wooded area behind Candise's house for a labor charge of $12 per hour and a flat fee of $50 to haul away the brush. Evergreen Yard Service offers to do the same job for a labor charge of $15 per hour and no extra charge for hauling away the brush. For what number of hours will the two plans cost the same?

21. Describe how to solve a linear equation in one variable graphically. Explain in detail how to locate the solution.

6

Linear Equations and Functions in Two Variables

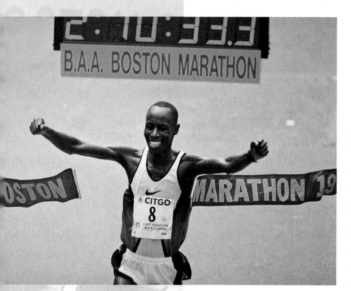

I n Chapter 5 we studied linear equations in one variable, learning to solve them by substituting a suitable value for the variable. In this chapter we examine linear equations in two variables and discuss methods for solving them. Some of the same ideas we learned before will apply here, too, such as solving equations numerically and graphically as well as algebraically. But we will also see several new ideas, such as the slope of a line, which is a very important and powerful tool in analyzing equations. With these tools we will be able to study the relationships between two lines and between two equations. As a result, we will learn how to write linear equations to predict new information. This is an important use of basic mathematics in the real world.

One important application of linear situations is the description of an object's motion. We saw in Chapter 3 that the distance an object travels at constant average speed is a function of time. We return to this application in this chapter and show that we can analyze it as a linear equation in two variables. This is an important mathematical relationship that can be used (with certain changes) for things such as planning when to launch rockets to meet up with an orbiting space station, or determining how long it will take to catch up with someone who has a head start on you, or even finding out whether you can catch someone at all.

6.1 Graphing Using Ordered Pairs

Objectives

1 Identify linear equations in two variables.

2 Determine whether an ordered pair is a solution of a linear equation in two variables.

3 Graph linear equations in two variables using a set of ordered pairs.

4 Determine solutions of a linear equation in two variables from its graph.

5 Model real-world situations using linear graphs.

Application

Ercille runs 10 kilometers three times a week for exercise. She tries to keep a steady pace, according to her wristwatch, of 6 minutes per kilometer. The graph shows her distance from home as a function of time for 1 hour. Determine three ordered pairs from the graph and explain the meaning of the numbers.

After completing this section, we will discuss this application further. See page 405.

1 Linear Equations in Two Variables

In the last chapter, we solved linear equations in one variable. We used this type of equation when solving a problem with one unknown quantity or a problem that can be written in terms of one unknown quantity. For example,

$$-4x + 25 = (x + 37) - 14$$

is a linear equation in one variable. However, if we need to solve a problem with two unknown quantities, then we may use a **linear equation in two variables**.

> *Standard Form for a Linear Equation in Two Variables*
> The standard form for a linear equation in two variables is $ax + by = c$, where $a, b,$ and c are real numbers and a and b are not both equal to 0.

For example, standard form is $ax + by = c$.

$2x + 5y = 2$	$a = 2$	$b = 5$	$c = 2$
$x - y = 0$	$a = 1$	$b = -1$	$c = 0$
$2x = 7$	$a = 2$	$b = 0$	$c = 7$
$-3y = 1$	$a = 0$	$b = -3$	$c = 1$

Note: The last two equations, when either $a = 0$ or $b = 0$, result in linear equations in one variable, which we discussed in Chapter 5. In this chapter, they are treated as special cases of linear equations in two variables.

Helping Hand Remember that an equation is linear only if the variable term has an exponent of 1.

The relation $y = -2x + 5$ is a linear equation in two variables because it can be rearranged by the properties of equations into the standard form. For example,

$$y = -2x + 5$$
$$y + 2x = -2x + 5 + 2x \quad \text{Add } 2x \text{ to both sides.}$$
$$y + 2x = 5 \quad \text{Simplify the right side.}$$
$$2x + y = 5 \quad \text{Rearrange the left side.}$$

All linear equations in two variables are relations. The relation $y = -2x + 5$ is also a function. Therefore, it may be written in function notation as $f(x) = -2x + 5$ and is called a **linear function**. (Remember, not all relations are functions.)

These equations are called linear equations because the graphs of the relations are straight lines. For example, the graph of $y = -2x + 5$ is linear as shown in the figure to the left.

Y1 = 2x + 5

(−47, 47, −31, 31)

EXAMPLE 1 Identify each equation as linear or nonlinear. Express each linear equation in standard form and determine values for a, b, and c.

a. $2x^2 + 3y = 4$ **b.** $y = -3x$

c. $x = 0$ **d.** $y = 2x + \sqrt{5}$

Solution

a. $2x^2 + 3y = 4$ is a nonlinear equation, because the x term is squared.

b. $y = -3x$ is a linear equation in two variables. Writing the equation in standard form,

$$y = -3x$$
$$y + 3x = -3x + 3x$$
$$y + 3x = 0$$
$$3x + y = 0$$

Therefore, $a = 3$, $b = 1$, and $c = 0$.

c. $x = 0$ is a linear equation in two variables. It is written in standard form as $1x + 0y = 0$. Therefore, $a = 1$, $b = 0$, and $c = 0$.

d. $y = 2x + \sqrt{5}$ is a linear equation in two variables. Writing the equation in standard form,

$$y = 2x + \sqrt{5}$$
$$-2x + y = \sqrt{5}$$

Therefore, $a = -2$, $b = 1$, and $c = \sqrt{5}$.

Helping Hand Be careful to examine an equation with a radical expression. If the radical has a radicand containing a variable term, the equation will be nonlinear. However, if the radicand contains only a constant term, the equation will be linear.

Check your results for parts a, b, and d on your calculator. First solve for y and then graph the equation. Note that you cannot graph part c on your calculator.

a. Y1 $= \frac{2}{3}x^2 + \frac{4}{3}$

$(-47, 47, -31, 31)$

b. Y1 $= -3x$

$(-47, 47, -31, 31)$

d. Y1 $= 2x + \sqrt{5}$

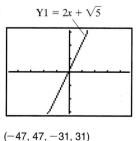

$(-47, 47, -31, 31)$ ∎

✓ Experiencing Algebra the Checkup Way

In exercises 1–7, identify each equation as linear or nonlinear. Express each linear equation in standard form and determine values for a, b, and c.

1. $x = 3y^2 + 12$

2. $2x + 4 = 5y - 3$

3. $x = -\frac{3}{8}$

4. $y = 8.2x - 3.6$

5. $y = x^2 - 2x + 6$

6. $\sqrt{3}x = \sqrt{2}y$

7. $3\sqrt{x} + 2y = 0$

8. Why is the equation $ax + by = c$ called a linear equation?

---

2 Determining Ordered-Pair Solutions

We solve a linear equation in one variable by substituting a value for the variable. If the result is a true statement, then the value is a **solution**. Similarly, we determine a solution of a linear equation in two variables by substituting values for each of the two variables (an ordered pair). If the result is a true statement, then the ordered pair is a solution of the equation. We say the solution satisfies the equation.

> *Solution of a Linear Equation in Two Variables*
> An ordered pair (x, y) is a solution of a linear equation in two variables if the values of its coordinates, when substituted for their corresponding variables, result in a true equation.

To determine whether an ordered pair is a solution of a linear equation in two variables:

- Substitute the values of the variables.
- Evaluate the resulting expressions.

If the expressions are equal, the ordered pair is a solution.

To determine on your calculator whether an ordered pair is a solution of a linear equation in two variables:

- Store the values of the variables.
- Enter the expressions on the left and right sides of the equation separately.

If the resulting values are equal, the ordered pair is a solution.
An alternative method on some calculators is to:

- Store the values of the variables.
- Enter the entire equation.

The calculator will return 1 for true and 0 for false. A true equation means the ordered pair is a solution.

 Helping Hand Sometimes the calculator may return a 0 for false due to rounding errors. Then we need to evaluate each expression separately to check for equality. Therefore, if the equation or possible solution contains fractions, this alternative method may not be reliable.

For example, given $x - y = 3$, determine whether $(4, 1)$ is a solution.

$$\frac{x - y = 3}{4 - 1 \ \big| \ 3}$$
$$3$$

Therefore, $(4, 1)$ is a solution because the resulting values for both expressions are 3.
On your calculator, store the values and enter the expressions on the left and right sides, as shown in Figure 6.1.
The resulting expressions are equal in value, $3 = 3$, so $(4, 1)$ is a solution. *Note:* The right side did not need to be entered, as it did not need to be evaluated.

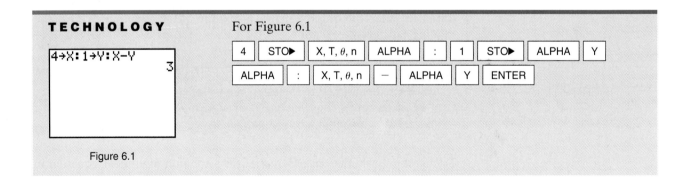

TECHNOLOGY

`4→X:1→Y:X−Y`
                    `3`

Figure 6.1

For Figure 6.1

| 4 | STO▶ | X, T, θ, n | ALPHA | : | 1 | STO▶ | ALPHA | Y |

| ALPHA | : | X, T, θ, n | − | ALPHA | Y | ENTER |

A second method on a calculator is to store the values and enter the entire equation, as shown in Figure 6.2.
The result is 1, which means the statement is true. Therefore, $(4, 1)$ is a solution.

As a second example, given $f(x) = 2x - 7$, determine whether $(0, 7)$ is a solution.

TECHNOLOGY

Figure 6.2

$$\begin{array}{c|c} f(x) = & 2x - 7 \\ \hline 7 & 2(0) - 7 \\ & 0 - 7 \\ & -7 \end{array}$$

Therefore, $(0, 7)$ is not a solution because the resulting values, 7 and -7, are not equal.

On your calculator, use y for $f(x)$, store the values for x and y, and enter the equation.

The result is 0, which means the statement is false. Therefore, $(0, 7)$ is not a solution.

EXAMPLE 2 Determine whether each ordered pair is a solution of the given linear equation.

a. $2x + 3y = 5; (6, -2)$ **b.** $f(x) = \dfrac{1}{2}x + 4; (4, 6)$

c. $x = 5; (5, -3)$

Solution

a.
$$\begin{array}{c|c} 2x + 3y & = 5 \\ \hline 2(6) + 3(-2) & 5 \\ 12 + (-6) & \\ 6 & \end{array}$$

Since $6 \ne 5$, $(6, -2)$ is not a solution.

b. $f(x) = \dfrac{1}{2}x + 4$

$$\begin{array}{c|c} & \\ \hline 6 & \dfrac{1}{2}(4) + 4 \\ & 2 + 4 \\ & 6 \end{array}$$

Since $6 = 6$, $(4, 6)$ is a solution.

c.
$$\begin{array}{c|c} x & = 5 \\ \hline 5 & 5 \end{array}$$

Since $5 = 5$, $(5, -3)$ is a solution.

Note: Since there is no *y*-variable in this equation, it is also a linear equation in one variable. Any *y*-coordinate in the ordered pair will satisfy the equation, as long as the *x*-coordinate is 5.

Check your results on your calculator.

a. As shown in Figure 6.3, the result is 0, which means the statement is false. $(6, -2)$ is not a solution.

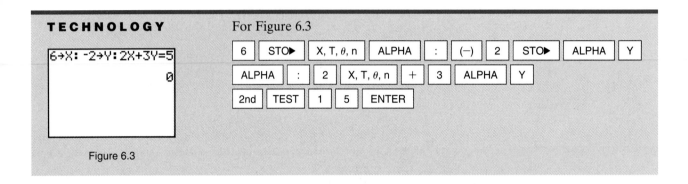

Figure 6.3

Enter parts (b) and (c) in the same manner. Each result is a solution.

b.   **c.**

 Experiencing Algebra the Checkup Way

In exercises 1–6, determine whether each ordered pair is a solution of the given linear equation.

1. $-3a - b = 13; (2, 7)$ **2.** $f(x) = -\dfrac{1}{4}x + 2; (8, 0)$

3. $3y = 10; \left(3, 3\dfrac{1}{3}\right)$ **4.** $1.7x - 2.3y = 12.66; (1.9, -4.1)$

5. Explain what is meant by the solution of a linear equation in two variables.

---

3 Graphing by Using Ordered Pairs

Some linear equations in one variable have more than one solution. A linear equation in two variables always has more than one solution. To determine the solutions of a linear equation in two variables, we will use a table of values, as we did with relations.

To determine solutions of a linear equation in two variables, *x* and *y*:

Set up an extended table of values.

- Label the first column *x*.
- Label the second column with the equation.
- Label the third column *y*.

Complete the table.

- Substitute values for x.
- Solve for y.

The x-value and its resulting y-value are coordinates of an ordered-pair solution.
To determine on your calculator solutions of a linear equation in two variables:

Set up a table of values.

- Solve the equation for y.
- Enter the equation in Y1.
- Use the TABLE feature of the calculator to generate a table.

Determine the possible solutions by viewing the table. Remember that it is possible to change the table setup. A good minimum number to start with is 0. Use an increment of 1 for integers. Other integer solutions are seen by using the up and down arrows.
For example, given $x - y = 3$, determine three integer solutions.

Set up a table of values. Choose any permissible value for x, the independent variable, and obtain a value for y, the dependent variable, by solving the equation. We will use 0, 1, and 2 for x-values.

x	$x - y = 3$	y
0	$0 - y = 3$ $-y = 3$ $\dfrac{-y}{-1} = \dfrac{3}{-1}$ $y = -3$	-3
1	$1 - y = 3$ $1 - y - 1 = 3 - 1$ $-y = 2$ $\dfrac{-y}{-1} = \dfrac{2}{-1}$ $y = -2$	-2
2	$2 - y = 3$ $2 - y - 2 = 3 - 2$ $-y = 1$ $\dfrac{-y}{-1} = \dfrac{1}{-1}$ $y = -1$	-1

Therefore, $(0, -3)$, $(1, -2)$, and $(2, -1)$ are three possible solutions of the linear equation in two variables $x - y = 3$.

 Helping Hand The equation in the center column in the table was solved for y on each row. It would be easier to solve the equation for y before setting up the table.

For example,

$$x - y = 3$$
$$x - y - x = 3 - x$$
$$-y = 3 - x$$
$$\frac{-y}{-1} = \frac{3 - x}{-1}$$
$$y = -3 + x \quad \text{or} \quad y = x - 3$$

x	$y = x - 3$	y
0	$y = 0 - 3$ $y = -3$	-3
1	$y = 1 - 3$ $y = -2$	-2
2	$y = 2 - 3$ $y = -1$	-1

The same ordered pairs are obtained with fewer steps.

On your calculator, enter the equation in Y1, set up the table for integers, and view the table. The result is a table of possible integer ordered-pair solutions, as shown in Figure 6.4.

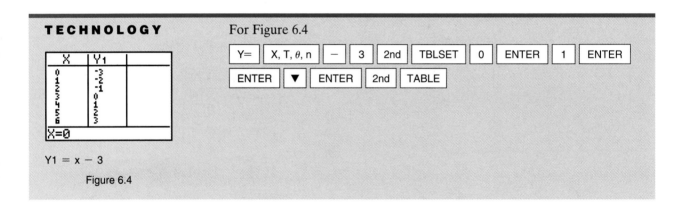

TECHNOLOGY

For Figure 6.4

| Y= | X, T, θ, n | − | 3 | 2nd | TBLSET | 0 | ENTER | 1 | ENTER |

| ENTER | ▼ | ENTER | 2nd | TABLE |

Y1 = x − 3

Figure 6.4

EXAMPLE 3   Determine three solutions of each equation, using a table of values.

a. $2x + y = 3$ **b.** $p(x) = \dfrac{2}{3}x + 1$ **c.** $y = -2$

Solution

a. Solve for y.

$$2x + y = 3$$
$$2x + y - 2x = 3 - 2x$$
$$y = 3 - 2x$$
$$y = -2x + 3$$

Set up a table. Choose any number for x. We'll use 0, 1, and 2.

x	$y = -2x + 3$	y
0	$y = -2(0) + 3$ $y = 3$	3
1	$y = -2(1) + 3$ $y = 1$	1
2	$y = -2(2) + 3$ $y = -1$	-1

Therefore, $(0, 3)$, $(1, 1)$, and $(2 -1)$ are three possible solutions of the linear equation.

b. $p(x) = \dfrac{2}{3}x + 1$

Set up a table. Choose any number for x. We'll use multiples of 3—that is, $-3, 0$, and 3—because we are multiplying these numbers by a fraction with a denominator of 3. The result will be an integer.

x	$p(x) = \dfrac{2}{3}x + 1$	$p(x)$
-3	$p(x) = \dfrac{2}{3}(-3) + 1$ $p(x) = -2 + 1$ $p(x) = -1$	-1
0	$p(x) = \dfrac{2}{3}(0) + 1$ $p(x) = 1$	1
3	$p(x) = \dfrac{2}{3}(3) + 1$ $p(x) = 2 + 1$ $p(x) = 3$	3

Therefore, $(-3, -1)$, $(0, 1)$, and $(3, 3)$ are three possible solutions of the linear equation (function).

c. $y = -2$

Set up a table. Choose any number for x. We'll use 0, 1, and 2.

x	$y = -2$	y
0	$y = -2$	-2
1	$y = -2$	-2
2	$y = -2$	-2

Therefore, $(0, -2)$, $(1, -2)$, and $(2, -2)$ are three possible solutions of the linear equation.

Check your results on your calculator.

a. Solve for y as before. Let $Y1 = -2x + 3$, as shown in Figure 6.5.

TECHNOLOGY

Figure 6.5

For Figure 6.5

Y= | (−) | 2 | X, T, θ, n | + | 3 | 2nd | TBLSET | 0 | ENTER | 1
ENTER | ENTER | ▼ | ENTER | 2nd | TABLE

The result is a table of possible integer ordered pairs.

b. Rewrite $p(x)$ as $y = \frac{2}{3}x + 1$. Let $Y1 = \frac{2}{3}x + 1$, as shown in Figure 6.6.

TECHNOLOGY

Figure 6.6

For Figure 6.6

Y= | (| 2 | ÷ | 3 |) | X, T, θ, n | + | 1 | 2nd | TBLSET | (−)
3 | ENTER | 3 | (multiples of 3)
ENTER | ENTER | ▼ | ENTER | 2nd | TABLE

X	Y1
0	-2
1	-2
2	-2
3	-2
4	-2
5	-2
6	-2

X=0

c. Let $Y1 = -2$. ∎

The preceding linear equations in two variables have an infinite number of possible ordered-pair solutions. In order to illustrate these solutions, we will use a graph. Remember that

1. every solution of an equation can be represented by a point on its graph; and
2. every point on a graph represents a solution of its equation.

To graph a linear equation in two variables using ordered pairs:

• Graph at least two ordered-pair solutions found in a table of values.
• Connect the points with a straight line.

A third ordered pair can be used for a check point. Label the coordinates of the points graphed.

To graph a linear equation in two variables on your calculator:

• Solve the equation for y.
• Enter the expression in Y1.
• Select a viewing screen and graph.

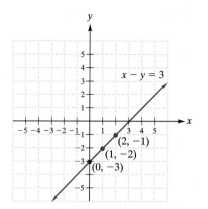

For example, graph the equation $x - y = 3$.

Solve for y.

$$y = x - 3$$

Graphing the ordered pairs found in the previous table gives three points: $(0, -3)$, $(1, -2)$, $(2, -1)$. Connecting the points with a straight line will locate other possible solutions.

On your calculator, enter the expression in Y1 and graph on an integer screen, as shown in Figure 6.7.

TECHNOLOGY

Y1 $= x - 3$

$(-47, 47, -31, 31)$

Figure 6.7

For Figure 6.7

| Y= | X, T, θ, n | − | 3 | ZOOM | 6 | ZOOM | 8 | ENTER |

EXAMPLE 4 Graph the linear equation $-x + y = 1$.

Solution

Solve the equation for y.

$$-x + y = 1$$
$$-x + y + x = 1 + x$$
$$y = 1 + x$$
$$y = x + 1$$

Set up a table of values. Choose values for x. We'll use -1, 0, and 1.

x	$y = x + 1$	y
-1	$y = -1 + 1$ $y = 0$	0
0	$y = 0 + 1$ $y = 1$	1
1	$y = 1 + 1$ $y = 2$	2

Graph the ordered pairs and connect with a straight line.

To check on your calculator, solve for y as before.

$$y = x + 1$$

Let $Y1 = x + 1$, as shown in Figure 6.8. ∎

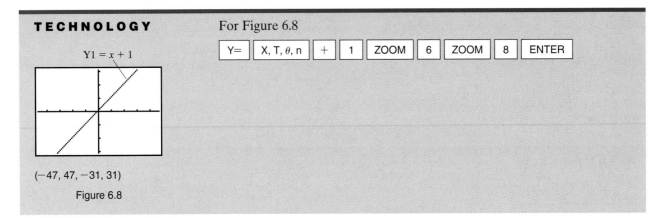

TECHNOLOGY

$Y1 = x + 1$

For Figure 6.8

| Y= | X, T, θ, n | + | 1 | ZOOM | 6 | ZOOM | 8 | ENTER |

$(-47, 47, -31, 31)$

Figure 6.8

 Experiencing Algebra the Checkup Way

Determine three solutions of each equation using a table of values.

1. $y = 6$ **2.** $4x - y = 1$ **3.** $g(x) = \dfrac{3}{5}x + 2$ **4.** $y = -1.5x - 4$

In exercises 5–6, graph each linear equation.

5. $x + y = 4$ **6.** $h(x) = -\dfrac{2}{3}x + 5$

7. How many solutions are there for a linear equation in two variables?

---

4 Determining Solutions of a Linear Equation in Two Variables from Its Graph

Since a graph represents solutions of an equation, we can determine possible solutions of a linear equation in two variables from its graph. To determine these solutions, we must determine the coordinates of points on the graph. To determine some of these solutions from the graph on a calculator, trace the graph. The coordinates of the traced points are displayed on the screen. The window setting will determine the points traced.

For example, determine integer solutions of the linear equation in two variables $x - y = 3$, shown on the following graph.

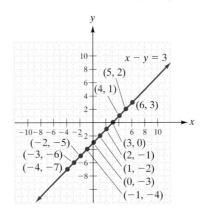

On your calculator, enter the equation solved for y, $y = x - 3$, graph using the integer screen, and trace the graph to obtain possible solutions, as shown in Figure 6.9.

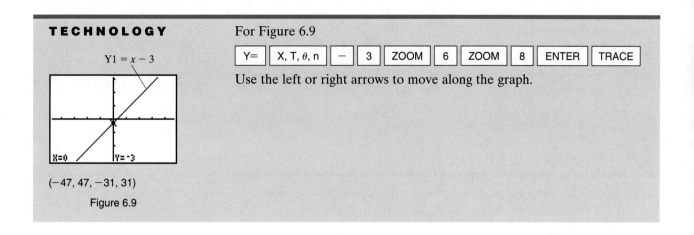

TECHNOLOGY

Y1 = x − 3

$(-47, 47, -31, 31)$

Figure 6.9

For Figure 6.9

| Y= | X, T, θ, n | − | 3 | ZOOM | 6 | ZOOM | 8 | ENTER | TRACE |

Use the left or right arrows to move along the graph.

EXAMPLE 5   Determine possible integer solutions of the linear equation in two variables shown on the following graph.

Solution

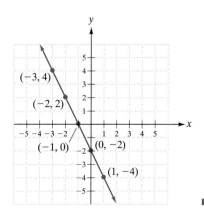

EXAMPLE 6 Graph $-3x + 2y = 1$ on your calculator integer screen and trace to find possible solutions.

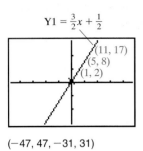

Y1 $= \frac{3}{2}x + \frac{1}{2}$

(11, 17)
(5, 8)
(1, 2)

$(-47, 47, -31, 31)$

Calculator Solution

Solve for y.

$$-3x + 2y = 1$$

$$y = \frac{3}{2}x + \frac{1}{2}$$

 Experiencing Algebra the Checkup Way

In exercises 1–2, determine three solutions of each linear equation from a graph.

1. $x + y = -2$ **2.** $y = -\frac{3}{4}x + 4$

3. How do you determine solutions of a linear equation in two variables from its graph?

5 Modeling the Real World

Graphs of linear equations in two variables are very useful for representing real-world data. Why? Because you need only two ordered pairs of data to determine the straight-line graph of the equation. Then you can use the graph to determine additional data that satisfy your original equation. So you go easily from knowing two solutions of the equation to knowing as many solutions as you want.

An important point to keep in mind is that real-world data often have practical limitations. A linear equation may be accurate for a period of time, but then the situation may change. This is why the domain and range of a function are so important—they tell you when the relationship is valid and when it is not.

EXAMPLE 7 Mike began his new job as supervisor on a lamp production line. The week before he began, the crew produced 25 lamps. During his first week, 30 lamps were produced. During the second week of Mike's supervision, 35 lamps were produced.

a. Let $x =$ the number of weeks Mike had supervised
     $y =$ the number of lamps produced during the week
Write three ordered pairs from the information given.

b. Assuming the same scenario continues, graph a linear representation of the lamp production.

c. Using the graph, predict what the weekly production would be during week 5.

d. Using the graph, predict what the weekly production would be during the 15th week. Is this reasonable to expect? Explain.

Solution

a. (0, 25), (1, 30), (2, 35)

b.

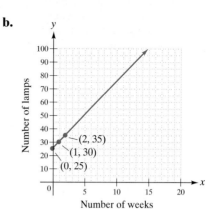

c.. The point (5, 50) is on the graph. Therefore, 50 lamps would be produced during week 5.

d.. The point (15, 100) is on the graph. Therefore, 100 lamps would be produced during the 15th week. This is unlikely unless additional people are hired or new equipment is added. The prediction capabilities are limited in this scenario. ∎

Application

Ercille runs 10 kilometers three times a week for exercise. She tries to keep a steady pace, according to her wristwatch, of 6 minutes per kilometer. The graph shows her distance from home as a function of time for 1 hour. Determine three ordered pairs from the graph and explain the meaning of the numbers.

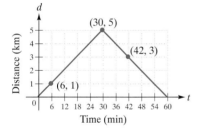

Discussion

A sample of three ordered pairs is as follows:

(6, 1)   After 6 minutes, Ercille is 1 kilometer from home.
(30, 5)   After 30 minutes, Ercille is 5 kilometers from home.
(42, 3)   After 42 minutes, Ercille is 3 kilometers from home.

Note: For the first 30 minutes, Ercille is increasing the distance from her home. For the last 30 minutes, Ercille is decreasing her distance from home. At 60 minutes, Ercille has arrived home. ∎

✓ Experiencing Algebra the Checkup Way

1. Dan's Delivery Service charges $3 to deliver a package weighing 1 pound. The charge for a package weighing 3 pounds is $7, while the charge for delivering a package weighing 5 pounds is $11. Let x = the weight of the package and y = the delivery charge.

a. Write three ordered pairs from the information given.

b. Assuming a linear relationship exists, graph the relation given by the information.

c. Using the graph, predict what the cost would be for a package weighing 8 pounds.

d. What would you say are limitations on the domain of the relation? Do you think Dan would put a limit on the weight of packages he delivers, or would you expect this relationship to continue for all possible weights of packages? Would the range of the relation have any limits? Explain.

2. Tom's Trucking Service makes nonstop round trips from its home base in Cincinnati to Chicago, a round trip of approximately 600 miles. His trucks average 60 miles per hour. The following graph tracks the distance the truck is from home base as a function of time since departure. Determine three ordered pairs from the graph. Explain the meaning of the ordered pairs.

Travel time (hr)

PROBLEM SET 6.1

Experiencing Algebra the Exercise Way

Identify each equation as linear or nonlinear. Express each linear equation in standard form, and determine values for a, b, and c.

1. $5x + 7y = 35$

2. $\sqrt{3}\, x + 2y = 6$

3. $-4\sqrt{x} + y = 8$

4. $8x + 3y = -24$

5. $6x^2 + 2y = 12$

6. $x^2 + y^2 = 1$

7. $y = \dfrac{5}{6} x - 2$

8. $y = 5x + 10$

9. $x - 2y + 1 = x - 4y + 9$

10. $3y - 2x = 15 - 7x - 3y$

11. $2x - 5 = 0$

12. $7y = 2y + 14$

13. $4.2x + 0.3y = 1.4$

14. $4.5y - 1.5x = 10.5$

Determine whether each ordered pair is a solution of the given equation.

15. $2x - 3y = 11;\ (5, 7)$

16. $4x + 2y = 2;\ (-3, 7)$

17. $-2x + y = 2;\ \left(\dfrac{1}{2}, 3\right)$

18. $8x + 7y = 9;\ \left(\dfrac{3}{4}, -\dfrac{3}{7}\right)$

19. $m(x) = 2.4x + 3.8;\ (3, 11)$

20. $n(x) = 7.2x - 2.4;\ (2, -12)$

21. $y = -6.4x + 10.4;\ (4, -4)$

22. $y = 15.8 - 7.6x;\ (3, -7)$

23. $y = 5;\ (11, 5)$

24. $6y - 42 = 0;\ (6, 6)$

25. $-4x = 12;\ (-3, 9)$

26. $2x + 8 = 4;\ (2, 3)$

27. $y = -2;\ (4, -5)$

28. $y = 7;\ (3, 7)$

29. $x = 15;\ (3, 15)$

30. $x = -6;\ (-6, 19)$

31. $x - 4y = 7;\ (18.6, -2.9)$

32. $x + y = 6;\ (2.8, 3.2)$

Using a table of values, determine three solutions of each linear equation.

33. $x - 6y = 12$

34. $x + 7y = 21$

35. $y = -\dfrac{5}{8} x + 1$

36. $y = \dfrac{7}{8} x - 4$

37. $p(x) = \dfrac{4x + 1}{3}$

38. $q(x) = \dfrac{2x - 3}{5}$

39. $y = 8$

40. $4y - 16 = 0$

41. $y = 2.6x - 4.2$ **42.** $y = 6.8x - 3.4$

In exercises 43–56, graph each equation. Then determine three solutions from the graph.

43. $2x + y = 3$ **44.** $5x - y = 6$ **45.** $5x - 3y = 6$ **46.** $8x + 7y = 9$

47. $r(x) = -\dfrac{3}{4}x + 4$ **48.** $s(x) = \dfrac{5}{6}x - 3$ **49.** $y = 2.8x - 1.6$ **50.** $y = 4.7 - 1.9x$

51. $y = \dfrac{3x - 5}{2}$ **52.** $y = \dfrac{3x - 2}{5}$ **53.** $3x + y - 4 = x + 2y - 3$

54. $7x - 2y + 8 = 5x - 3y + 1$ **55.** $5y = -20$ **56.** $3y + 7 = 25$

57. An assembly line is used to pack boxes of candy. When only one person is available, the assembly line cannot operate. When two people are working, they can pack 5 boxes per minute. When 4 people are working, they can pack 15 boxes per minute.

   a. Let x be the number of persons working the assembly line and let y be the number of boxes of candy packed per minute. Write three ordered pairs from the information given.

   b. Assuming the relation continues for other numbers of workers, graph the information.

   c. Use the graph to predict how many boxes per minute would be packed by a crew of 5 people.

   d. Are there any limitations on the domain and range of this relation? Is it reasonable to assume that as the number of workers increases, the number of boxes packed per minute could still be estimated using this graph? Explain your answer.

58. On an examination, Alex missed none of the questions and received a score of 100. Beth missed 6 questions and scored an 85. Chiyo missed 10 questions and scored 75.

   a. Let x be the number of questions missed, and let y be the score on the test. Write three ordered pairs from the information given.

   b. Assuming a linear relation, graph the information.

   c. Use the graph to predict what score students will receive if they miss 12 questions on the test.

   d. For what domain would it make sense to use this relation?

59. Speedy Delivery agrees to pay Stephanie a flat fee of $25 per day plus $8 for each package she delivers. If x represents the number of deliveries she makes in a day, and $p(x)$ represents the total amount paid to Stephanie that day, then $p(x) = 8x + 25$.

   a. How much would Stephanie earn if she made 7 deliveries in a day?

   b. Should she be paid $60 for 5 deliveries?

   c. If Stephanie were available one day to make deliveries, but no deliveries were made, how much would she be paid?

   d. What limits would you place on the domain or range of this equation to represent Stephanie's earnings?

60. Mr. Chips grades a final exam by starting with a score of 200 points and subtracting 5 points for each incorrect answer. If x represents the number of incorrect answers and $s(x)$ is the student's score on the exam, $s(x) = 200 - 5x$.

   a. What score would a student receive if he or she missed 7 questions?

   b. Should a student who incorrectly answered 11 questions receive a score of 145?

   c. What score will a student who correctly answered all the questions receive?

   d. What limits apply to the domain of this equation for scoring purposes?

61. Itsu is measuring the borders around equilateral triangles for a science project. He finds that a triangle with a side of 2 inches has a border of 6 inches, one with a side of 3.5 inches has a border of 10.5 inches, and one with a side of 10.5 inches has a border of 31.5 inches.

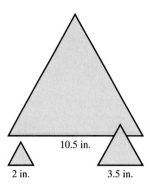

10.5 in.

2 in.   3.5 in.

a. Let x be the length of a side of the equilateral triangle, and y be the length of the border around the triangle. Write three ordered pairs from the information given.

b. Graph a linear representation of the information.

c. Predict what the border would be for an equilateral triangle with a side of 4 inches.

d. Is it reasonable to assume that the relation represented by the graph would work for any equilateral triangle? Explain your answer.

62. Carla measured the perimeters of several rectangles, all of which had the same width but differing lengths. The perimeter of a rectangle with a length of 15 cm was 50 cm. Another with a length of 25 cm had a perimeter of 70 cm. A third with a length of 10 cm had a perimeter of 40 cm.

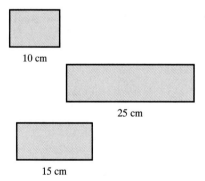

10 cm

25 cm

15 cm

a. Let x be the length of the rectangle, and let y be the perimeter. Write three ordered pairs from the information given.

b. Graph a linear representation of the information.

c. Using the graph, what would the perimeter be for a rectangle with the same width and with a length of 20 cm?

d. Would this relation hold for all rectangles that had the same width and varying lengths? Explain your answer.

63. Toasty Toasters determines that the fixed cost of manufacturing toasters is $250.00 per day and the variable cost of manufacturing is $3.75 per toaster. If $D(x)$ is the daily cost of manufacturing x toasters, then $D(x) = 3.75x + 250$.

a. What would be the cost of manufacturing 20 toasters per day?

b. What would be the cost of manufacturing 30 toasters per day?

c. Is it true that the cost of manufacturing 25 toasters per day would be less than $350.00?

d. Construct a table of values showing the cost of manufacturing x toasters per day, where x begins at 0 and increases up to 50 in increments of 5 toasters per day.

64. Appalachian Crafts agrees to pay Anne $300 per month to provide pottery exclusively to their shop for sale, and further agrees to pay her $25 for each item sold. If $P(x)$ represents the amount paid to Anne for a month, and x represents the number of pieces of art sold, $P(x) = 25x + 300$.

a. How much will Anne earn if the shop sells 12 items in a month?

b. What will Anne earn in a month when 5 items sell?

c. If the shop sells 8 items, will Anne earn $500?

d. Construct a table of values to show Anne's monthly earnings for selling x items in the shop, where x begins at 0 and increases up to 20 in increments of 2 items.

65. The cost of producing items is related to the number of items produced, as shown in the following graph. Find three ordered pairs from the graph and explain the meaning of the numbers.

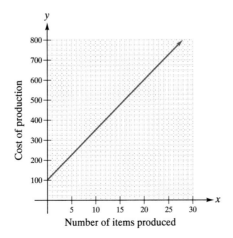

66. The outstanding balance of a loan is related to the number of monthly payments, as shown in the following graph. Determine three ordered pairs from the graph. Explain what the numbers mean.

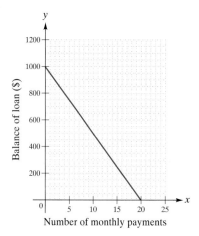

![Graph with y-axis labeled "Balance of loan ($)" ranging from 0 to 1200 in increments of 200, and x-axis labeled "Number of monthly payments" ranging from 0 to 25 in increments of 5. A line decreases from about (0, 1000) to (20, 0).]

Experiencing Algebra the Calculator Way

Use your calculator to determine whether each ordered pair is a solution of the given equation.

1. $y = 6.871x - 35.711249$; (4.719, 3.287)

2. $1.05x + 1.45y = -23.75$; (25, 50)

3. $132x - 297y = 1526$; $\left(\dfrac{17}{33}, -4\dfrac{10}{11}\right)$

Use your calculator to complete the table of values for each equation.

4. $y = 3.721x - 1.857$

x	y
1.5	
1.6	
1.7	
1.8	
1.9	
2.0	

5. $y = \dfrac{13}{28}x - 5$

x	y
0	
7	
14	
21	
28	
35	

In exercises 6–7, graph each equation. Then use the TRACE *key to complete the ordered-pairs list of solutions, rounding the coordinates to two decimal places.*

6. $y = \sqrt{3}\,x - \sqrt{2}$
(0, ___) (2, ___) (4, ___) (6, ___) (8, ___)

7. $y = \pi r^2 x$, where $r = 0.25$ inches is the radius of a cylinder with height of x inches and volume of y cubic inches.
(1, ___) (2, ___) (3, ___) (4, ___) (5, ___)

8. An insurance company charges $9.64 per $1000 of life insurance coverage for a male who takes out a policy at age 21. If x represents the number of $1000 increments of insurance the male purchases, and y is the total cost of the premium, construct a table of values showing the cost of purchasing x units of insurance, where x begins at 5 units and increases to 100 units in increments of 5 units.

Experiencing Algebra the Group Way

In this section, you learned to graph a linear equation in two variables by first constructing a table of values, plotting the coordinate pairs from the table, and connecting the points to obtain the graph. When using this approach, it is easier to plot the points if you can use points that have integer coordinate values. By avoiding values that are fractions, mixed numbers, or decimals, you will be able to plot points more accurately. You should practice selecting values for the x-coordinate that will yield integer values for the y-coordinate. Have your group discuss each of the linear equations presented here, and describe how you would select values for x that result in integer values for y. Once the group has determined how to do this, have each member generate a table of values that has three coordinate pairs. Compare your results and make sure that every member of the group has been able to obtain the pairs.

Warning: You may not be able to find a way to obtain integer pairs for every equation listed here.

1. $y = \dfrac{2}{5}x + 3$ **2.** $y = -\dfrac{3}{4}x + 6$ **3.** $3x - 2y = 8$ **4.** $y = 0.3x - 1$

5. $x + 4y = 7$ **6.** $0.25x - y = 3$ **7.** $3x + 9y = 4$ **8.** $x - 7y = 5$

Are there any equations in this set where it might be better to choose values for y and then solve for x? Will you still be able to obtain a table of values if you do this? Is there any way that you can use your calculator to help you find values that are integer pairs? Is there any equation for which it is not easy to find integer pairs, maybe even impossible?

Experiencing Algebra the Write Way

1. The standard form for a linear equation in two variables is

$$ax + by = c,$$

where a, b, and c are real numbers and a and b are not both equal to 0. Give examples in which a or b are equal to 0. Then explain why the equation cannot have a and b both equal to 0.

2. It is important that you fully understand the relationship between the solutions of a linear equation in two variables and the graph of the linear equation. Explain what a graph represents with respect to a linear equation in two variables. Explain what a graph can tell you about a linear equation in two variables. Exactly what is the purpose of graphing the linear equation in two variables?

6.2   Graphing Using the Intercept Method

Objectives

1   Determine the y-intercept and x-intercept of a graph.

2   Discover linear equations in two variables whose graphs have only one intercept.

3   Graph linear equations in two variables using the intercept method.

4   Model real-world situations using graphs.

Application

In 1974, an SR-71 Blackbird jet plane was flown from New York City to London in 1 hour and 55 minutes, the fastest transatlantic flight ever. If we let y represent the plane's distance from London, then an equation representing the plane's motion is $y = 3462 - 1807t$, where t is the time in hours in flight. Graph the equation and interpret the intercepts of the graph.

After completing this section, we will discuss this application further. See page 422.

---

1 Determining the *y*-Intercept and *x*-Intercept of a Graph

Special solutions of a linear equation in two variables are the *y*-intercept and *x*-intercept of its graph. Remember that we discussed these points in Chapter 4. The *y*-intercept is the point where a graph intersects or crosses the *y*-axis. The *x*-coordinate of this point is 0. Similarly, the *x*-intercept is the point where a graph intersects or crosses the *x*-axis. The *y*-coordinate of this point is 0.

To determine the *y*-intercept of a graph, determine the point where the graph intersects the *y*-axis. To determine the *x*-intercept of a graph, determine the point where the graph intersects the *x*-axis.

To determine the *y*-intercept of a graph on your calculator:

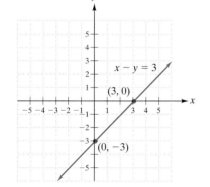

- Use a default screen; the *y*-intercept is always given as the first traced point (the point with an *x*-coordinate of 0).
- Alternatively, use Value under the CALC function and ask for the *x*-value of 0.

To determine the *x*-intercept of a graph on your calculator:

- Trace the graph to find the *x*-intercept (the point with a *y*-coordinate of 0).
- Alternatively, use Zero under the CALC function.

For example, label the *y*-intercept and *x*-intercept of the linear equation $x - y = 3$, graphed in the figure to the left.

On your calculator, the intercepts are the same.

$(-47, 47, -31, 31)$

$(-47, 47, -31, 31)$

EXAMPLE 1   Determine the *y*-intercept and *x*-intercept of each graph.

a.

b.

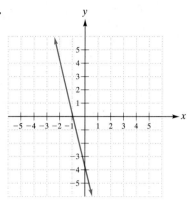

Solution

The *x*-intercept and *y*-intercept are labeled in the figures.

a.

b.

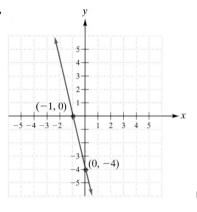

■

EXAMPLE 2   Graph each equation on your calculator integer screen and determine the *y*-intercept and *x*-intercept.

a. $y = 2x - 4$ **b.** $-3x + 2y = 10$

Calculator Solution

a. The *y*-intercept and *x*-intercept of the graph are shown in Figures 6.10a and 6.10b, respectively.

TECHNOLOGY

Y1 = 2x − 4

(−47, 47, −31, 31)

Figure 6.10a

Y1 = 2x − 4

(−47, 47, −31, 31)

Figure 6.10b

For Figures 6.10a and 6.10b

Use the right and left arrows to find the intercepts.

b. Solve for y.

$$-3x + 2y = 10$$

$$-3x + 2y + 3x = 10 + 3x$$

$$2y = 10 + 3x$$

$$\frac{2y}{2} = \frac{10 + 3x}{2}$$

$$y = 5 + \frac{3}{2}x$$

$$y = \frac{3}{2}x + 5$$

The y-intercept and x-intercept of the graph are shown in Figures 6.11a and 6.11b, respectively. ∎

TECHNOLOGY

$Y1 = \frac{3}{2}x + 5$ $Y1 = \frac{3}{2}x + 5$

$(-47, 47, -31, 31)$ $(-47, 47, -31, 31)$

Figure 6.11a   Figure 6.11b

For Figures 6.11a and 6.11b

ZOOM	6	ZOOM	8	ENTER	Y=
(	3	÷	2	)	X, T, θ, n	+	5
GRAPH	TRACE

Choose Zero under the CALC function to find the x-intercept.

2nd   CALC   2   Move the cursor to the left of the x-intercept.

ENTER   Move the cursor to the right of the x-intercept.

ENTER   Enter a guess.   ENTER

It is important to remember that the y-coordinate of the x-intercept is always 0 (because it is on the x-axis). Also, the x-coordinate of the y-intercept is always 0 (because it is on the y-axis).

To determine algebraically the y-intercept of a graph from its linear equation:

- The x-coordinate is always 0.
- The y-coordinate is found by substituting 0 for x and solving for y.

To determine algebraically the x-intercept of a graph from its linear equation:

- The y-coordinate is always 0.
- The x-coordinate is found by substituting 0 for y and solving for x.

For example, given the linear equation in two variables $x - y = 3$, find the y-intercept and the x-intercept algebraically.

The graph's y-intercept is (0, ____). To determine the y-coordinate, we substitute $x = 0$ in the equation.

$$x - y = 3$$
$$0 - y = 3$$
$$-y = 3$$
$$\frac{-y}{-1} = \frac{3}{-1}$$
$$y = -3$$

Therefore, the y-coordinate is -3. The y-intercept is $(0, -3)$.

The graph's x-intercept is (____, 0). To determine the x-coordinate, we substitute $y = 0$ in the equation.

$$x - y = 3$$
$$x - 0 = 3$$
$$x = 3$$

Therefore, the x-coordinate is 3. The x-intercept is $(3, 0)$.

There is another way to determine the graph's y-intercept from its linear equation. To see what this method is, complete the following set of exercises on your calculator.

DISCOVERY 1

y-intercepts

Graph each linear equation and label the y-intercept.

1. $y = x - 5$ **2.** $y = x + 5$

3. $y = x - 10$ **4.** $y = x + 10$

Write a rule to determine the y-coordinate of the y-intercept of a graph from its linear equation.

The y-coordinate of the y-intercept of the graph is the same as the constant term in the equation when the equation is solved for y.

To determine algebraically the y-intercept of a graph from its linear equation:

- Solve the equation for y.
- The constant term is the y-coordinate of the y-intercept.

Remember, the x-coordinate is 0.

For example, determine the y-intercept of the graph of the linear equation $x - y = 3$.

Solve for y and obtain $y = x - 3$. The constant term is -3, so the y-coordinate of the y-intercept is -3. The y-intercept is $(0, -3)$.

EXAMPLE 3   Determine algebraically the x-intercept and y-intercept of the graph for the linear equation $2x + y = 5$.

Solution

To determine the x-coordinate of the x-intercept, substitute 0 for y in the equation and solve for x.

$$2x + y = 5$$
$$2x + 0 = 5$$

$$2x = 5$$

$$\frac{2x}{2} = \frac{5}{2}$$

$$x = \frac{5}{2}$$

The x-intercept is $\left(\frac{5}{2}, 0\right)$.

To determine the y-coordinate of the y-intercept, substitute 0 for x in the equation and solve for y.

$$2x + y = 5$$
$$2(0) + y = 5$$
$$y = 5$$

The y intercept is $(0, 5)$.

The alternative way to determine the y-intercept is to solve the equation for y.

$$2x + y = 5$$
$$2x + y - 2x = 5 - 2x$$
$$y = 5 - 2x$$
$$y = -2x + 5$$

The y-coordinate of the y-intercept is 5. The y-intercept is $(0, 5)$. ∎

Experiencing Algebra the Checkup Way

Determine the x-intercept and y-intercept of each graph.

1.

2.

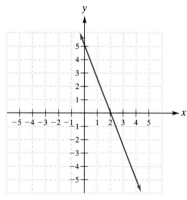

Graph each equation on your calculator integer screen and determine the x-intercept and y-intercept.

3. $y = -x + 1$ **4.** $2x + y = 5$

Determine algebraically the x-intercept and y-intercept of the graph for each equation.

5. $6x + y = 12$ **6.** $y = 5x + 11$

In exercises 7–8, solve for y and state the y-intercept for each equation.

7. $7x - y = 15$ **8.** $4x + 3y = 24$

9. Describe how you would determine the x-intercept and y-intercept of a graph of a linear equation in two variables from its graph. Then describe how you would determine these two points algebraically.

2 Linear Graphs with One Intercept

The graphs of most linear equations in two variables have two distinct points as the x-intercept and the y-intercept. However, some graphs may have the x-intercept and the y-intercept at the same point. Others may have an x-intercept or a y-intercept but not both. Let's see what some of these graphs look like. Complete the following set of exercises on your calculator.

DISCOVERY 2

Graphs Whose x-Intercept and y-Intercept Are the Same Point
Graph the following linear equations in two variables and label the x-intercept and y-intercept.

1. $x + y = 0$ **2.** $x + y = 5$
3. $-2x + 3y = 0$ **4.** $-2x + 3y = -10$

Write a rule to determine from an equation when its corresponding graph has one point that is both the x-intercept and y-intercept.

First, note that the equations are in standard form, $ax + by = c$. The equations on the left have c equal to 0. The equations on the right have c equal to a constant other than 0. We see that the graphs of the equations on the left have the same point for the x-intercept and the y-intercept. We see that the graphs of the equations on the right have two different points, one for the x-intercept and one for the y-intercept. The graph of a linear equation in two variables written in standard form has the same point for the x-intercept and y-intercept if the constant term equals 0. The intercept is the origin, $(0, 0)$.

In standard form, $ax + by = c$, when $a = 0$, we have a linear equation in two variables of the form $by = c$. An example of such an equation is $2y = 8$.

Set up a table of values for $2y = 8$.

First, solve the equation for y.

$$2y = 8$$
$$\frac{2y}{2} = \frac{8}{2}$$
$$y = 4$$

Since there is no x-term in the equation to substitute values into, we will always obtain $y = 4$ for every x-value.

x	$y = 4$	y
0	$y = 4$	4
1	$y = 4$	4
2	$y = 4$	4

A graph corresponding to the table is shown.
There is only one intercept, the y-intercept, $(0, 4)$. The line is horizontal.

In standard form, $ax + by = c$, when $b = 0$, we have a linear equation in two variables of the form $ax = c$. An example of such an equation is $2x = -12$.

Set up a table of values for $2x = -12$.

First, we cannot solve the equation for y. Therefore, we solve the equation for x.

$$2x = -12$$

$$\frac{2x}{2} = \frac{-12}{2}$$

$$x = -6$$

Now if we substitute values for x, other than -6, the result will be a false statement. Therefore, to obtain ordered pairs, we substitute values for y. Since there is no y-term in the equation to substitute values into, we will always obtain $x = -6$ for each y-value.

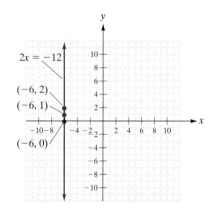

x	$x = -6$	y
-6	$x = -6$	0
-6	$x = -6$	1
-6	$x = -6$	2

A graph corresponding to the table is shown.

There is only one intercept, the x-intercept, $(-6, 0)$. The line is vertical. This relation is not a function. In fact, a vertical line is the only case in which a linear equation in two variables is not a function. These equations cannot be graphed on a calculator using the $\boxed{\text{Y=}}$ menu.

> *Graphs with One Intercept*
> The graph of a linear equation in two variables has one point for an intercept if the equation written in standard form, $ax + by = c$, has either a, b, or c equal to 0.
>
> - If only $a = 0$, the graph $by = c$ is a horizontal line with a y-intercept of $\left(0, \frac{c}{b}\right)$.
> - If only $b = 0$, the graph $ax = c$ is a vertical line with a x-intercept of $\left(\frac{c}{a}, 0\right)$.
> - If only $c = 0$, the graph $ax + by = 0$ has one intercept at the origin, $(0, 0)$.

EXAMPLE 4 Determine the intercept of the graph for each linear equation in two variables. Then graph to check.

    a. $y = 3$ **b.** $x = y$ **c.** $2x = 6$

Solution

a. In standard form, the equation is $0x + y = 3$. Since $a = 0$ and $\frac{c}{b} = \frac{3}{1} = 3$, the y-intercept is $(0, 3)$.

b. In standard form, the equation is $x - y = 0$. Since $c = 0$, then the x-intercept and the y-intercept are both the origin, $(0, 0)$.

c. In standard form, the equation is $2x + 0y = 6$. Since $b = 0$ and $\frac{c}{a} = \frac{6}{2} = 3$, the x-intercept is $(3, 0)$.

Check your results by graphing the equation.

a.

b.

c.

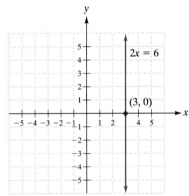

■

Experiencing Algebra the Checkup Way

In exercises 1–6, determine the intercepts of the graph for each linear equation. Then graph to check.

1. $\frac{1}{2}x = 8$

2. $2x + 4y = 0$

3. $3x = 6y$

4. $y = -1$

5. $5y = 3$

6. $1.7x - 2.55 = 0$

7. When will the graph of a linear equation have only an x-intercept?

8. When will the graph of a linear equation have only a y-intercept?

9. When will the x-intercept and the y-intercept of the graph of a linear equation be at the same point?

---

3 Graphing Linear Equations in Two Variables Using the Intercept Method

Now we are ready to graph a linear equation in two variables using the intercept method. We can only use this method if the graph has two distinct points as the x-intercept and y-intercept. In other words, the equation written in standard form must not have a, b, or c equal to 0.

The intercept method of graphing is to determine the two intercepts and connect them with a straight line.

To graph a linear equation in two variables using the intercept method:

- Determine the x-intercept.
- Determine the y-intercept.
- Plot the intercepts and label their coordinates.
- Connect the intercepts with a straight line.
- Check the graph by locating a third point on the graph and determine that its coordinates are a solution of the equation.

For example, graph the linear equation in two variables $x - y = 3$ using the intercept method.

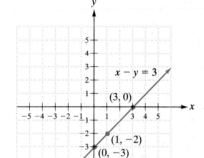

Graph the two intercepts found for the equation, $(3, 0)$ and $(0, -3)$.

To check the graph, determine a point on the graph of the line and check to see if it is a solution of the equation. Let's check the point $(1, -2)$.

$$
\begin{array}{c|c}
x - \quad y \ = 3 \\
\hline
1 - (-2) & 3 \\
1 + \quad 2 \\
\quad 3
\end{array}
$$

Since $3 = 3$, $(1, -2)$ is a solution. The graph checks.

EXAMPLE 5 Graph the linear equation $3x + 4y = 5$ using the intercept method.

Solution

Determine the y-intercept.

Solve for y.

$$3x + 4y = 5$$
$$3x + 4y - 3x = 5 - 3x$$
$$4y = 5 - 3x$$
$$\frac{4y}{4} = \frac{5 - 3x}{4}$$
$$y = \frac{5}{4} - \frac{3x}{4}$$
$$y = -\frac{3}{4}x + \frac{5}{4}$$

An alternative method is to substitute 0 for x and solve for y.

$$3(0) + 4y = 5$$
$$4y = 5$$
$$\frac{4y}{4} = \frac{5}{4}$$
$$y = \frac{5}{4}$$

The y-coordinate is the constant $\frac{5}{4}$. The x-coordinate is 0. The y-intercept is $\left(0, \frac{5}{4}\right)$.

Determine the x-intercept.

Substitute 0 for y and solve for x.

$$3x + 4(0) = 5$$

$$3x = 5$$

$$\frac{3x}{3} = \frac{5}{3}$$

$$x = \frac{5}{3}$$

The x-intercept is $\left(\frac{5}{3}, 0\right)$.

Graph the two intercepts and connect the points with a straight line.

 Helping Hand When the intercepts are not integers, it is difficult to graph the intercepts accurately.

Check the graph by checking a point on the line. One of the integer ordered pairs located on the graph is $(3, -1)$.

$$\begin{array}{r|c} 3x + 4y & = 5 \\ \hline 3(3) + 4(-1) & 5 \\ 9 + (-4) & \\ 5 & \end{array}$$

Since $5 = 5$, $(3, -1)$ is a solution. The graph checks. ∎

Experiencing Algebra the Checkup Way

In exercises 1–2, graph each equation using using the intercept method. Check your graphs using a third point. Label the intercepts and third point on each graph.

1. $2x - 4y = 8$ **2.** $2x + 5y = 7$

3. How would you graph a linear equation using the intercept method?

4 Modeling the Real World   Using the intercept method to graph an equation is often simpler than other methods because you can find the intercepts by just substituting 0 for the variables in the equation. When the equation is based on a real-world relationship, you may get an extra bonus because the intercepts may be significant points themselves. For example, if your graph shows a relationship between distance and time, then the y-intercept occurs where time (the x-coordinate) is 0; that is, the starting distance. The x-intercept (if there is one) occurs where distance (the y-coordinate) is 0. It is usually worthwhile to find the intercepts of a real-world graph and see what information they can give you.

EXAMPLE 6

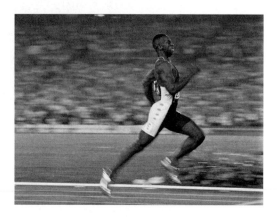

The 1996 Olympic record for the men's 200-meter run was set in Atlanta by Michael Johnson. Let y represent the distance (in meters) the runner is from the starting point, and let t represent the time (in seconds) from the starting point. An equation representing the distance from the starting point is $y = 10.35x$. Graph the equation and interpret the intercepts of the graph.

Solution

We cannot graph this equation by the intercept method because the graph does not have two distinct intercepts. The graph has one intercept, the origin. We know this because the equation solved for y does not have a constant term. We will need to complete a table of values in order to determine ordered pairs to plot for the graph.

x	$y = 10.35x$	y
5	$y = 10.35(5)$ $y = 51.75$	51.75
10	$y = 10.35(10)$ $y = 103.5$	103.5
15	$y = 10.35(15)$ $y = 155.25$	155.25

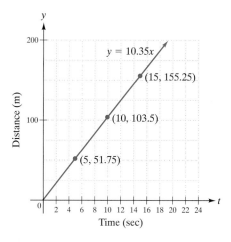

The graph intercepts the origin. The coordinates of the origin, $(0, 0)$, means that at a time of 0 seconds, the runner is 0 meters from the starting point. ∎

Application

In 1974, an SR-71 Blackbird jet plane was flown from New York City to London in 1 hour and 55 minutes, the fastest transatlantic flight ever. If we let y represent the plane's distance from London, then an equation representing the plane's motion is $y = 3462 - 1807t$, where t is the time (in hours) in flight. Graph the equation and interpret the intercepts of the graph.

Discussion

Let t = time (in hours) in flight

y = plane's distance (in miles) from London

The equation $y = 3462 - 1807t$ is solved for y. The constant term 3462 is the y-coordinate of the y-intercept. The y-intercept is $(0, 3462)$.

We determine the t-intercept by substituting 0 for y and solving for t.

$$0 = 3462 - 1807t$$

$$1807t = 3462$$

$$\frac{1807t}{1807} = \frac{3462}{1807}$$

$$t \approx 1.92$$

The t-intercept is approximately $(1.92, 0)$.

Graph the two intercepts and connect the points with a straight line.

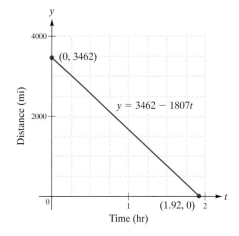

The coordinates of the y-intercept $(0, 3462)$, mean that at a time of 0 hours (before the plane begins flight), the plane is 3462 miles from London. This is the distance from New York City to London.

The coordinates of the t-intercept, approximately $(1.92, 0)$, mean that at a time of approximately 1.92 hours, the plane will be 0 miles from London. In other words, the plane will arrive in London in approximately 1.92 hours. ∎

Experiencing Algebra the Checkup Way

A butane gas tank is used in a metal shop as a fuel supply. The tank has a capacity of 6 gallons. The gas is used at a rate of $\frac{1}{4}$ gallon per hour. Let $g(x)$ = the number of gallons of butane remaining in the tank, where x is the number of hours that the tank has been used as a fuel supply. Then $g(x) = 6 - \frac{1}{4}x$. From the equation, find the intercepts for a graph of the equation. Interpret what each intercept means. Graph the equation by the intercept method. From the graph, determine how much butane remains in the tank after 8 hours of use.

PROBLEM SET 6.2

Experiencing Algebra the Exercise Way

Determine the x-intercept and y-intercept of each graph.

1.

2.

3.

4.

5.

6.

7.

8.

9.

10.

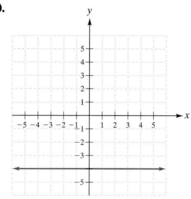

Graph each equation on your calculator integer screen and find the intercepts.

11. $y = 5x - 24$

12. $y = -4x + 21$

13. $y = 3x + 18$

14. $y = -6x - 33$

15. $5x + 4y = 30$

16. $8x + 5y = 32$

17. $5x - 7y = 28$

18. $3x - y = 15$

19. $-2x - 3y = 10$

20. $-x - 8y = 16$

Determine algebraically the x-intercept and y-intercept of the graph for each linear equation.

21. $3x + 5y = 12$

22. $7x + 9y = 63$

23. $4x - 7y = 14$

24. $x - y = 31$

25. $-2x - 9y = 27$

26. $-12x - 8y = 36$

27. $6x + 9y - 36 = 0$

28. $5x + 3y + 45 = 0$

29. $3x + 7y = 0$

30. $16x + 3y = 0$

31. $6x - 8 = 2x + 32$

32. $3x - 12 = x - 2$

33. $y = 3y - 22$

34. $6y = y - 25$

Solve each linear equation for y to determine the y-intercept.

35. $12x - y = 24$

36. $x + 9y = 18$

37. $y = 5(x - 3)$

38. $y = 3(x - 7) + 5$

39. $5x - 15y = 0$

40. $14x = 42y$

41. $3y = 12y + 18$

42. $18 - 5y = y$

43. $y = 0$

44. $3(y + 7) - 4 = 17$

45. $-17.6x + 2.2y = 19.8$

46. $12.6x - 6.3y = 50.4$

47. $x = 12y$

48. $y = -0.05x$

Graph each equation using the intercept method. Check your graphs using a third point. Label the intercepts and third point on each graph.

49. $3x + 5y = 30$ **50.** $x + 3y = 33$ **51.** $4x - 3y = 24$ **52.** $5x - 7y = 70$

53. $x - y = 9$ **54.** $-x + y = 9$ **55.** $-x - y = 9$ **56.** $x + y = 9$

57. $3x - 7y = -14$ **58.** $8x - 5y = 24$ **59.** $y = 6.1x - 23.18$ **60.** $y = 2.9x + 24.94$

61. $y = \dfrac{5}{3}x + 10$ **62.** $y = -\dfrac{5}{3}x - 15$

Write a linear equation in two variables to represent each situation. Determine the intercepts of the graph of the equation. Interpret what the intercepts represent. Graph the equation, and from the graph, answer the question.

63. A car is traveling at a constant speed of 40 miles per hour and is 200 miles from its destination. Let y be the distance from the destination, and let x be the number of hours of travel. Determine how far from the destination the car will be after 2.5 hours of travel.

64. Joel owed his father $370 and agreed to pay him $20 a week until the loan was repaid. Let y be the amount of money Joel still owed, and let x be the number of weeks he has made payment. Determine how much is still owed if Joel has made 11 weekly payments.

65. A water tank holds 150 gallons of water. The water is being drained from the tank at a rate of 4 gallons per minute. Let y represent the number of gallons of water remaining in the tank after x minutes spent in draining the tank. Determine how much water remains in the tank after 20 minutes of draining.

66. A storage tank has 50 gallons of liquid in it. More liquid is being pumped into the tank at the rate of 2 gallons per hour. Liquid is being drained out of the tank at the rate of 5 gallons per hour. Let y represent the number of gallons of liquid in the tank after x hours. Determine how much liquid remains in the tank after 8 hours.

67. The graph represents the variable dollar cost of producing a given number of units in an assembly plant. From the graph, determine the intercepts and interpret what they represent. What will be the cost of producing 50 units? What will be the cost of producing 75 units?

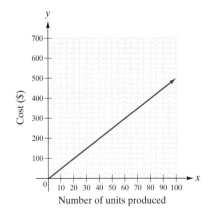

68. The graph represents the net profit earned by a lawn care business as a function of the number of lawns being cared for. (Net profit represents what the owner of the business clears after paying expenses such as labor, material, and so on from the revenues the business collects.) From the graph, determine the intercepts and interpret what they represent. How much will be earned in net profits for caring for 25 lawns? How much will be earned in net profits for caring for 40 lawns?

 ## Experiencing Algebra the Calculator Way

In exercises 1–4, use your calculator to graph each linear equation in two variables and determine the intercepts. (Hint: You should convert the equations to x and y variables before graphing on the calculator.)

1. $y = \dfrac{45}{88}x - 15$ **2.** $y = -2.56x + 33.71$ **3.** $F = \dfrac{9}{5}C + 32$ **4.** $C = \dfrac{5}{9}(F - 32)$

5. In exercises 3 and 4, interpret what the intercepts mean.

 ## Experiencing Algebra the Group Way

This exercise is intended to help you see the value of alternative uses of your calculator to solve a problem, and also its limitations when your algebra skills will be required. Discuss the problem in your group and work together to solve it.

An investment of $500 is made into an account paying 0.5% simple interest per month, for *x* months. Let *y* be the amount in the account after x months.

1. Write a linear equation in two variables to show the amount in the account after *x* months.

2. Without graphing, find the intercepts for the graph of the linear equation.

3. What does the *y*-intercept represent?

4. Does the *x*-intercept have any meaning in this problem?

5. Starting with the integer screen, graph the equation on your calculator. In order to see the line, repeatedly use the | ZOOM | | 3 | keys. Can you trace along the line for integer values of *x*?

6. How can you get your calculator to determine the amount of money after 8 months if you cannot tell from this graph? (Would a table of values help?)

7. Experiment with changing the window to accommodate the numbers you would expect. (For example, set the window to (0, 94, 10, 0, 620, 10, 1). Can you determine how this window was selected, starting with the integer settings? Explain to your group.)

Share what you have discovered with the class.

Experiencing Algebra the Write Way

In this section, you were encouraged to use a third point to check graphs that you had constructed using the intercept method. Think about the geometry associated with drawing a straight line. How many points does it take to determine the location of a straight line in a coordinate system? Then write a short paragraph to explain in your own words why using a third point can help you check to see that you have correctly graphed the linear equation in two variables.

6.3 Graphing Using the Slope-Intercept Method

Objectives

1 Determine the slope of a line from its graph.

2 Determine the slope of a line given two points on the line.

3 Determine the slope of a line from its linear equation in two variables.

4 Graph linear equations in two variables using the slope-intercept method.

5 Determine the average rate of change given real-world data. Model real-world situations using graphs.

Application

David rode his bicycle to Green Acres Picnic Area, a distance of 20 miles. He left his house at 9:00 A.M. and arrived at the picnic site at 11:00 A.M. David's wife, Mary, took the car (with all the food), leaving the house at 10:30 A.M. and arriving at the picnic spot at 11:10 A.M. Determine the average rate of change of distance with respect to time for David and Mary.

After completing this section, we will discuss this application further. See page 444.

1 Determining the Slope of a Line from Its Graph

If we view the graphs of linear equations, they may appear to rise or fall from left to right. They may be horizontal or vertical. They may be more steep or less steep.

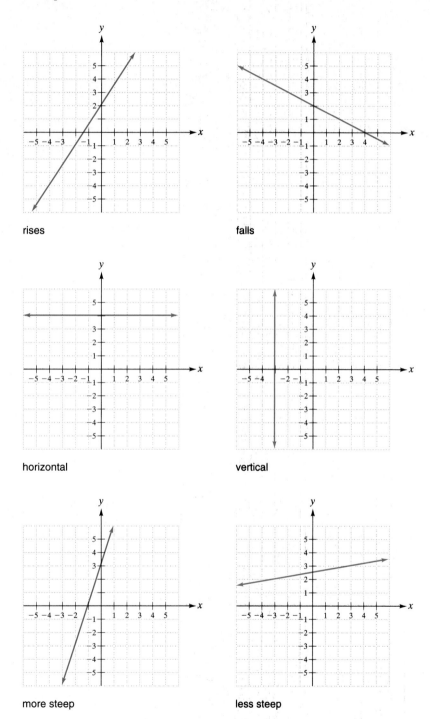

rises

falls

horizontal

vertical

more steep

less steep

We describe the graph of a line by its steepness, which we call the slope of a line. We calculate this slope by determining the change in vertical distance

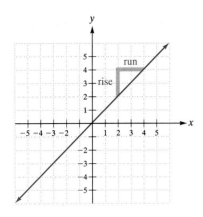

of the line (called the **rise**) that corresponds to a change in horizontal distance of the line (called the **run**). The **slope** of a line is defined as the ratio of the amount of rise to the amount of run.

> *Slope of a Line*
> The slope of a line is the ratio of the amount of rise to the amount of run, $\frac{\text{amount of rise}}{\text{amount of run}}$.

To determine the slope of a line graphically:

- Locate two points on the graph whose coordinates are integers.
- Draw two legs needed to complete a right triangle with the given ordered pairs as vertices.
- Determine the length of the two legs drawn (one leg is the rise and the other is the run).
- Write a ratio of the rise to run, $\frac{\text{rise}}{\text{run}}$.

For example, determine graphically the slope of the given line.

Two possible integer ordered pairs are located; the triangle legs drawn; and the leg lengths determined. The slope is $\frac{\text{rise}}{\text{run}} = \frac{2}{5}$.

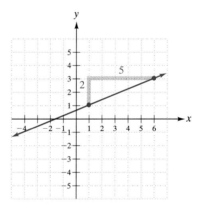

Note: The right triangle could have been drawn differently but would result in the same slope. Also, the slope of the line remains the same for any set of ordered pairs located on the line, including noninteger ones.

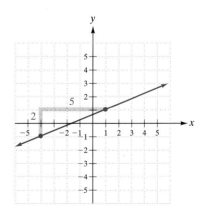

EXAMPLE 1   Determine graphically the slope of each line.

a.

b.

c.

d.

Solution

a.

b.

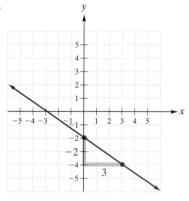

The slope is $\frac{3}{1} = 3$.   The slope is $\frac{-2}{3}$.

No right triangles can be drawn for Examples 1c and 1d.

c. The slope is $\frac{\text{any number}}{0}$ or undefined.

d. The slope is $\frac{0}{\text{any number}}$ or 0. ■

Example 1 shows us that different lines can have slopes that are positive, negative, 0, or undefined. Let's take a closer look at these different slopes. Complete the following set of exercises to discover different types of slopes.

DISCOVERY 3

Types of Slopes
Determine the slopes for the following graphs.

1.

2.

3.

4.

5.

6.

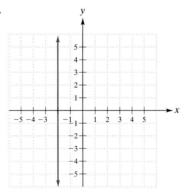

Choose the correct answer.

7. The slopes in exercises 1 and 2 have a *positive/negative* value. Viewing the graphs from left to right, they both *rise/fall*.

8. The slopes in exercises 3 and 4 have a *positive/negative* value. Viewing the graphs from left to right, they both *rise/fall*.

9. The slope in exercise 5 is *0/undefined*. The graph is a *vertical/horizontal* line.

10. The slope in exercise 6 is *0/undefined*. The graph is a *vertical/horizontal* line.

11. In observing the absolute value of the slope, we see that the larger the absolute value, the *more/less* steep the graph.

A graph with a positive slope rises from left to right. A graph with a negative slope falls from left to right. A horizontal line has a slope of 0. A vertical line has an undefined slope. The larger the absolute value of the slope, the steeper the graph of the line.

EXAMPLE 2 Determine by inspection whether each graph has a positive, negative, zero, or undefined slope.

a.

b.

c.

d.

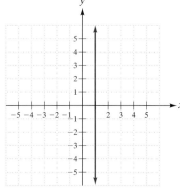

Solution

a. positive (line rises)

b. zero (horizontal line)

c. negative (line falls)

d. undefined (vertical line) ∎

Slope has many applications. One real-world application is the **grade** of a road or a measure of how steep a road is. We usually represent a grade as a percent. For example, a 4% grade means that for every vertical distance of 100 feet, the road drops or rises 4 feet. Note that we do not use a positive or a negative percent because we do not know the orientation of the person viewing the road.

100 ft

EXAMPLE 3 Off-road vehicles for a certain branch of the armed services must be able to drive on terrain rising 30 feet vertically over a horizontal distance of 50 feet. Find the grade of the terrain.

Solution

The grade of the terrain is the slope written as a percent.

$$m = \frac{\text{rise}}{\text{run}} = \frac{30}{50} = 0.6 = 60\%$$

The grade of the terrain for an off-road vehicle is 60%. ■

Experiencing Algebra the Checkup Way

In exercises 1–4, determine by inspection whether the line in each graph has a positive, negative, zero, or undefined slope. Then determine graphically the slope.

1.

2.

3.

4.

5. A road rises 54 feet vertically over a horizontal distance of 1200 feet. What is the grade of the road?

6. Explain how the slope of the line of a linear equation can be used to describe its graph.

---

2 Determining the Slope of a Line Given Two Points on the Line

The slope of a line is a very important characteristic of the linear equation represented by that line. In fact, there are times when we might want to determine the slope of a line even when the graph is not drawn for us. For example, suppose we know only two points on a line. We could plot the points, draw the graph, and then determine the slope. But sometimes it's easier to find the slope without drawing the graph. To see how to do this, complete the following set of exercises.

DISCOVERY 4

Slope Formula

1. Locate and label the points (1, 3) and (5, 4) on a graph.
   Draw a line to connect the points.
   Draw the legs of a right triangle needed to determine the slope and label each length.
2. The rise of the graph is ____.
3. The run of the graph is ____.
4. The difference in the y-coordinates of the ordered pairs is $4 - 3 =$ ____.
5. The difference in the x-coordinates of the ordered pairs is $5 - 1 =$ ____.
6. The slope of the graph is ____.

Write a rule to determine the slope of a graph from the coordinates of two ordered pairs.

The rise of the graph and the difference of the y-coordinates of the ordered pairs are the same. The run of the graph and the difference of the x-coordinates of the ordered pairs are the same.

Before we write a formula for the slope of a graph, we need to define some notation. The traditional symbol for slope is m. To label the coordinates of the two ordered pairs, we use subscripts to distinguish the coordinates of the different points. For example, (x_1, y_1) and (x_2, y_2) distinguish two different ordered pairs.

> *Slope of a Line through Two Given Points*
> Given two ordered pairs, (x_1, y_1) and (x_2, y_2),
>
> $$m = \frac{\text{rise}}{\text{run}} = \frac{\text{difference in } y\text{-coordinates}}{\text{difference in } x\text{-coordinates}} = \frac{y_2 - y_1}{x_2 - x_1}$$

Helping Hand It is very important to subtract both coordinates of the first point from both coordinates of the second point. Do not mix up the order of coordinates during the subtraction.

For example, determine numerically the slope of a line containing the ordered pairs (1, 3) and (5, 4).

Let $(x_1, y_1) = (1, 3)$ and $(x_2, y_2) = (5, 4)$.
Therefore, $x_1 = 1, y_1 = 3, x_2 = 5,$ and $y_2 = 4$.

$$m = \frac{y_2 - y_1}{x_2 - x_1}$$

$$m = \frac{4 - 3}{5 - 1}$$

$$m = \frac{1}{4}$$

Helping Hand The order of labeling the points does not matter. The results would be the same if $(x_1, y_1) = (5, 4)$ and $(x_2, y_2) = (1, 3)$:

$$m = \frac{y_2 - y_1}{x_2 - x_1}$$

$$m = \frac{3 - 4}{1 - 5}$$

$$m = \frac{-1}{-4}$$

$$m = \frac{1}{4}$$

EXAMPLE 4 Determine numerically the slope of a line containing the given points.

    a. $(-6, 2)$ and $(-3, 5)$ **b.** $(9, 2)$ and $(9, -1)$ **c.** $(3, -4)$ and $(2, -4)$

Solution

a. $x_1 = -6, y_1 = 2$ **b.** $x_1 = 9, y_1 = 2$ **c.** $x_1 = 3, y_1 = -4$

    $x_2 = -3, y_2 = 5$ $x_2 = 9, y_2 = -1$ $x_2 = 2, y_2 = -4$

$$m = \frac{y_2 - y_1}{x_2 - x_1} \qquad m = \frac{y_2 - y_1}{x_2 - x_1} \qquad m = \frac{y_2 - y_1}{x_2 - x_1}$$

$$m = \frac{5 - 2}{-3 - (-6)} \qquad m = \frac{-1 - 2}{9 - 9} \qquad m = \frac{-4 - (-4)}{2 - 3}$$

$$m = \frac{3}{3} \qquad m = \frac{-3}{0} \qquad m = \frac{0}{-1}$$

$$m = 1 \qquad m \text{ is undefined} \qquad m = 0 \qquad \blacksquare$$

 Experiencing Algebra the Checkup Way

In exercises 1–4, determine numerically the slope of the line containing the given points.

1. $(-3, -2)$ and $(1, 4)$ **2.** $(4, 2)$ and $(-1, 2)$ **3.** $(2, 1)$ and $(2, -4)$ **4.** $(-3, 4)$ and $(3, -4)$

3 Determining the Slope of a Line from Its Linear Equation We may also need to determine the slope of a line when a graph is not given and only its linear equation is known. Even though we could graph the line from the equation and then determine the slope, it is easier to determine the slope algebraically without drawing the graph. Complete the following discovery to see how to find the slope from the known equation.

DISCOVERY 5 **Determining Slope from a Linear Equation**

1. Graph the given linear equations in two variables. Label two integer coordinate points.

   a. $y = 2x + 4$ **b.** $y = -2x$ **c.** $y = \frac{1}{2}x - 5$

2. Determine the slope of each line.
   a. $m =$ ____   **b.** $m =$ ____   **c.** $m =$ ____

3. Determine the coefficient of the x-term for each equation.
   a.   **b.**   **c.**

Write a rule to determine the slope of the graph from a linear equation in two variables.

The slope of each graph is the same as the coefficient of the x-term in the linear equation when it is solved for y.

> *Slope of a Line Given a Linear Equation*
> Given a linear equation in two variables solved for the dependent variable y, the slope of the line of the equation is the coefficient of the independent variable x.

To determine the slope of a line from its linear equation:

- Solve the equation for y.
- The coefficient of the x-term is the slope of the graph.

For example, determine the slope of the line for the linear equation in two variables, $-2x + 3y = 5$.

Solve for y.

$$-2x + 3y + 2x = 5 + 2x$$
$$3y = 5 + 2x$$
$$3y = 2x + 5$$
$$\frac{3y}{3} = \frac{2x + 5}{3}$$
$$y = \frac{2}{3}x + \frac{5}{3}$$

The slope of the graph is the coefficient of the x-term, or $\frac{2}{3}$.

> *Two Special Cases of the Slope of a Line Given a Linear Equation*
> Given a linear equation in two variables of the form $x = c$, the graph is a vertical line with an undefined slope.
>   Given a linear equation in two variables of the form $y = c$, the graph is a horizontal line with a zero slope.

 Helping Hand A slope of 0 and an undefined slope are not the same.

EXAMPLE 5 Determine by inspection the slope of the line for the given linear equation.

a. $f(x) = -3x + 7$ **b.** $6y = 19$ **c.** $x - 4 = 10$

Solution

a. The coefficient of the x-term is -3. Therefore, $m = -3$.
b. Solve for y.

$$\frac{6y}{6} = \frac{19}{6}$$

$$y = \frac{19}{6} \quad \text{or} \quad y = 0x + \frac{19}{6}$$

The coefficient of the x term is 0. Therefore, $m = 0$.
c. Solve for x because there are no y's.

$$x - 4 = 10$$
$$x - 4 + 4 = 10 + 4$$
$$x = 14$$

Therefore, m is undefined because $x = 14$ is a vertical line. ∎

Experiencing Algebra the Checkup Way

In exercises 1–4, determine the slope of the line for each linear equation by inspection.

1. $t(x) = -\dfrac{7}{11}x + 13$ **2.** $8x + 3y = 12$ **3.** $2y - 5 = 3y + 1$ **4.** $4x - 3 = x + 6$

5. How can you determine the slope of the line for a linear equation by inspecting the equation?

---

4 Graphing Linear Equations Using the Slope-Intercept Method

We said earlier that the slope of a line is an important characteristic of a linear equation. One reason for its importance is that if you know the slope of a line, you can graph the line even if you know only one point on that line, instead of two.

To graph a line when you know a point on the line and its slope:

- Plot the known point and label its coordinates.
- Count the rise and run from the located point. For a positive rise, count upward; for a negative rise, count downward. For a positive run, count to the right; for a negative run, count to the left.
- Place a second point where the next ordered pair is located. Label the coordinates of the point.
- Draw a straight line connecting the two points.

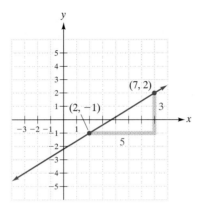

For example, graph a line that contains the point $(2, -1)$ and has a slope of $\frac{3}{5}$.

Plot the point $(2, -1)$. Locate a second point by counting the slope (rise of 3 and run of 5). Draw a straight line connecting the two points.

Helping Hand The slope can be counted using different triangles, as shown.

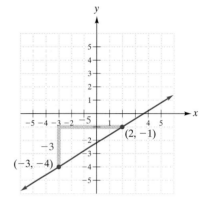

Remember that $\frac{-3}{-5} = \frac{3}{5}$.

EXAMPLE 6 Graph a line that contains the given point and has the given slope. Label two points.

a. $(5, 1); m = -2$ **b.** $(3, 4); m = 0$

c. $(-5, -2); m$ is undefined

Solution

Locate the point given and count the rise and run.

a.

b.

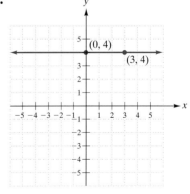

Note: The line is horizontal because $m = 0$.

c.

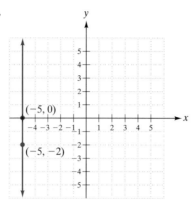

Note: The line is vertical because m is undefined. ∎

We have determined that if a linear equation in two variables is solved for y, the slope of its graph is the coefficient of the x-term. The constant term is the y-coordinate of the y-intercept. Therefore, we have a linear equation in two variables in what we call the **slope-intercept form**.

> *Slope-Intercept Form for a Linear Equation in Two Variables*
> The slope-intercept form for a linear equation in two variables is
>
> $$y = mx + b,$$
>
> where m is the slope of its graphed line and b is the y-coordinate of the y-intercept of the graph.

We have enough information from the slope-intercept equation to graph a line.
To graph a linear equation in two variables using the slope-intercept method:

- Solve the equation for y.
- Determine the slope and y-coordinate of the y-intercept from the equation.
- Plot the y-intercept and label its coordinates.
- Locate the next point on the line by counting the slope (rise and run). Label its coordinates.
- Draw a straight line through the two points.

For example, graph the linear equation in two variables $3x + y = -1$.

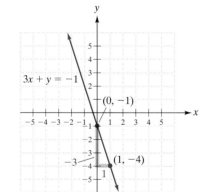

First, solve for y.

$$3x + y = -1$$
$$3x + y - 3x = -1 - 3x$$
$$y = -1 - 3x$$
$$y = -3x - 1$$

Therefore, $m = -3$ and $b = -1$.
The y-intercept is $(0, -1)$ and the slope is -3 or $\frac{-3}{1}$.
Locate the y-intercept and count the slope. Label the coordinates of both points. Draw a straight line through the two points.

EXAMPLE 7   Graph the given linear equation using the slope-intercept method. Check by graphing on your calculator.

    a. $b(x) = -3x + 7$ **b.** $3x + 4y = 1$ **c.** $6y = 19$

Solution

a. $b(x) = -3x + 7$

b. Solve for y.

$$y = -\frac{3}{4}x + \frac{1}{4}$$

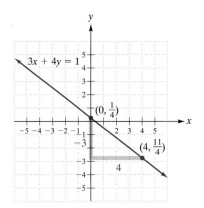

c. Solve for y.

$$y = \frac{19}{6} \quad \text{or} \quad y = 0x + \frac{19}{6}.$$

The line is horizontal because the slope is zero.

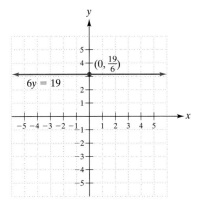

Solve each equation for y and enter into your calculator to check, as in previous examples.

a.   Y1 = $-3x + 7$

$(-47, 47, -31, 31)$

b.   Y1 = $-\frac{3}{4}x + \frac{1}{4}$

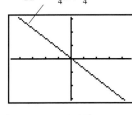

$(-47, 47, -31, 31)$

c.

$$Y1 = \frac{19}{6}$$

$(-47, 47, -31, 31)$

■

 Experiencing Algebra the Checkup Way

Graph a line that contains the given point and has the given slope.

1. $(-4, -3)$; $m = \dfrac{2}{3}$ **2.** $(-2, 4)$; $m = -1$ **3.** $(6, 0)$; m is undefined   **4.** $(3, 6)$; $m = 0$

Graph exercises 5–7 using the slope-intercept method. Check by graphing on your calculator.

5. $v(x) = \dfrac{4}{3}x - 2$ **6.** $5x + 2y = 3$ **7.** $6y = 2y + 7$

8. How is it possible to graph the line for a linear equation if you only know one point that it passes through and the slope of the line?

---

5 Modeling the Real World

When we use a linear equation to represent a real-world situation, the slope can be a very interesting, as well as important, quantity. A common situation occurs when the independent variable represents time. In this case, the slope tells us how the dependent variable changes over a period of time. We call this the **average rate of change** of the dependent variable. From the average rate of change, we can sometimes predict what value a quantity will have in the future, or what value it had in the past—though as we saw earlier, once the equation stops being linear, we have to change our idea of slope.

EXAMPLE 8
According to the National Association of Realtors, in 1989 the median price of an existing home was $93,100. In 1993, the median price of an existing home was $106,100.

a. Find the average rate of change per year in the median cost of existing homes from 1989 to 1993.
b. Let y = median cost of an existing home
  x = number of years after 1989
  Write an equation to find the median cost of a home (y) in terms of the number of years after 1989 (x).
c. Graph the equation using the slope-intercept method.
d. Graph the equation on a calculator using the window (0, 9.4, 1, 0, 124000, 10000, 1)

1989

FOR SALE
$93,100

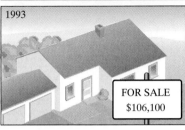

1993

FOR SALE
$106,100

e. Given the complete table of information shown, did the equation provide a good estimate of the median cost of a 1991 home?

Year	Median Price of an Existing Home
1989	93,100
1990	97,500
1991	99,700
1992	100,900
1993	106,100

f. Predict the 1994 median cost of a home from your calculator graph.

Solution

a. The average rate of change per year in the median cost of existing homes from 1989 to 1993 is

$$\frac{\text{difference in cost}}{\text{difference in years}} = \frac{106,100 - 93,100}{1993 - 1989} = \frac{13,000}{4} = 3250$$

The average rate of change per year in the median cost of a home was $3250 between 1989 and 1993.

b. The median cost of a home (y) equals the median cost of a home in 1989 (93,100) plus the average rate of change per year (3250) times the number of years (x).

$$y = 93,100 + 3250x \quad \text{or} \quad y = 3250x + 93,100$$

Note: The average rate of change per year is the slope of the linear graph.

c.

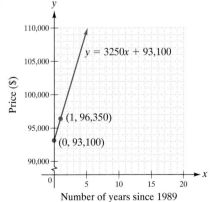

Price ($)

$y = 3250x + 93,100$

110,000

105,000

100,000

(1, 96,350)

95,000

(0, 93,100)

90,000

0   5   10   15   20 x

Number of years since 1989

d.

Y1 = 3250x + 93100

(0, 9.4, 0, 124000)

e. Since 1991 is 2 years after 1989, on the graph 1991 would be represented by $x = 2$. Therefore, the ordered pair (2, 99,600) is found on the traced graph.

$Y1 = 3250x + 93100$

(0, 9.4, 0, 124000)

The true cost was $99,700. Yes, this is a good estimate.

f. The year 1994 is represented as $x = 5$. The corresponding ordered pair (5, 109,350), is found on the traced graph.

$Y1 = 3250x + 93100$

(0, 9.4, 0, 124000)

Therefore, the estimated median cost of a home in 1994 is $109,350. ∎

Application

David rode his bicycle to Green Acres Picnic Area, a distance of 20 miles. He left his house at 9:00 A.M. and arrived at the picnic site at 11:00 A.M. David's wife, Mary, took the car (with all the food), leaving the house at 10:30 A.M. and arriving at the picnic spot at 11:10 A.M. Determine the average rate of change of distance with respect to time for David and Mary.

Discussion

$$\text{average rate of change} = \frac{\text{distance traveled}}{\text{time traveled}}$$

David traveled 20 miles in 2 hours. His average rate of change of distance with respect to time (speed) is

$$\frac{20}{2} = 10$$

David traveled an average of 10 miles per hour.

Mary traveled 20 miles in 40 minutes or $\frac{40}{60} = \frac{2}{3}$ hours. Her average rate of change of distance with respect to time (speed) is

$$\frac{20}{\frac{2}{3}} = 20 \div \frac{2}{3} = 20 \cdot \frac{3}{2} = 30$$

Mary traveled an average of 30 miles per hour.

Helping Hand The average rates of change are the average speeds. ∎

Experiencing Algebra the Checkup Way

1. The number of corporate bond listings on the American Stock Exchange (Amex) in 1970 was 169. In 1990, it had risen to 260 listings.

   a. Assuming a linear relationship, find the average rate of change per year in the number of corporate bond listings.

   b. Write a linear equation to find the number of corporate listings in terms of the number of years after 1970.

   c. Graph the equation on your calculator using a screen of (0, 37.6, 4, 0, 310, 50, 1).

   d. From the graph, estimate the number of corporate listings in 1980. The actual number is 225. How well did your graph estimate this number?

   e. What would the equation estimate for the number of corporate listings in the year 2000?

2. A scuba diver is 100 feet below the surface of the water. She must gradually come to the surface. After 5 minutes, she is 50 feet from the surface. Determine her average rate of ascent.

PROBLEM SET 6.3

 Experiencing Algebra the Exercise Way

First determine by inspection whether each graph has a positive, negative, zero, or undefined slope. Then determine graphically the slope of the line.

1.

2.

3.

4.

5.

6.

7.

8.

Determine numerically the slope of the line containing the given points.

9. $(-7, -2)$ and $(5, 6)$ **10.** $(3, -1)$ and $(-2, 8)$ **11.** $(-12, -9)$ and $(4, -9)$ **12.** $(-8, 9)$ and $(-8, -5)$

13. $(0, 3)$ and $(0, 8)$ **14.** $(1, -6)$ and $(8, 9)$ **15.** $(6, -4)$ and $(7, -6)$ **16.** $(-5, 0)$ and $(7, 0)$

17. $(0, 4)$ and $(5, 0)$ **18.** $(-3, 0)$ and $(0, 5)$ **19.** $(11.5, -9.2)$ and $(6.9, 18.4)$

20. $(-3.8, 1.9)$ and $(5.7, 5.7)$ **21.** $\left(\frac{1}{2}, \frac{3}{4}\right)$ and $\left(-\frac{1}{2}, -\frac{5}{6}\right)$ **22.** $\left(-\frac{3}{7}, \frac{1}{4}\right)$ and $\left(\frac{5}{14}, -\frac{7}{8}\right)$

Determine by inspection the slope and the y-intercept of the line for each equation, if possible.

23. $y = 21x + 15$ **24.** $y = -19x + 28$ **25.** $y = \frac{11}{15}x - \frac{21}{25}$ **26.** $y = -\frac{5}{9}x + \frac{17}{18}$

27. $y = 5.95x - 2.01$ **28.** $y = 14.8 - 3.6x$ **29.** $y = 85,600 - 1255x$ **30.** $y = 45x + 1250$

31. $16x - 4y = 64$ **32.** $24x + 3y = 39$ **33.** $7y + 18 = 2(y + 6) - 4$ **34.** $12(y + 2) = 5(2y - 4)$

35. $7.83x - 2.61y = 10.44$ **36.** $13.93x + 5.97y = 11.94$ **37.** $\frac{3}{2}x - \frac{3}{5}y = \frac{21}{10}$ **38.** $-\frac{5}{3}x + \frac{5}{4}y = \frac{25}{12}$

39. $x = -4\frac{7}{8}$ **40.** $\frac{5}{9}x = -15$

Graph a line that contains the given point and has the given slope.

41. $(8, 3); m = \dfrac{4}{7}$

42. $(-7, -6); m = \dfrac{5}{6}$

43. $(-10, 4); m = -\dfrac{5}{9}$

44. $(9, -10); m = -\dfrac{4}{5}$

45. $(5, 7);$ and $m = 4$

46. $(-8, 7);$ and $m = -6$

47. $(0, 9);$ and $m = 0$

48. $(0, 9); m$ is undefined

49. $(9, 0); m$ is undefined

50. $(9, 0); m = 0$

Graph exercises 51–62 using the slope-intercept method. Check by graphing on your calculator.

51. $y = \dfrac{5}{3}x - 4$

52. $y = -\dfrac{3}{4}x + 6$

53. $16x - 8y = 40$

54. $-21x + 7y = -35$

55. $7x + 2y = -16$

56. $9x - 4y = 24$

57. $14y + 21 = 6y + 5$

58. $31y - 19 = 26y + 6$

59. $5y = 150x + 350$

60. $6y = 300x - 360$

61. $f(x) = 0.3x - 1.2$

62. $m(x) = -0.8x + 2.7$

63. A car dealer advertises that its off-the-road vehicles can drive on terrain rising 56 feet vertically over a horizontal distance of 160 feet. Find the grade of the advertised terrain.

64. A motor bike drives on a terrain rising 31 feet vertically over a horizontal distance of 124 feet. What is the grade of the terrain?

The pitch of a roof is really the measure of the steepness of the roof. Often the pitch is reported as a fraction whose denominator is 12. A roof which rises 3.6 inches over a horizontal distance of 12 inches is said to have a pitch of 0.30 or 30%.

65. What is the pitch of a roof that rises 3.3 inches over a horizontal distance of 12 inches?

66. Find the pitch of a roof that rises 5 inches over a horizontal distance of 12 inches.

67. Candy and Chad paddled their canoe down a river in the mountains. They left at 9:15 in the morning and arrived at a picnic area beside the river at 10:45 that morning. They had traveled a distance of 10.5 miles. What was their average speed for the canoe trip? Write an equation for the distance traveled if they canoed for x hours at this same speed. Graph the equation using the slope-intercept method. Use the graph to determine the distance they would canoe if they maintained this average rate of travel for 2.5 hours.

68. Hans drove a distance of 240 kilometers in 2.5 hours. What was his average speed for the trip? Write an equation for the distance he would travel if he maintained this speed for x hours. Graph the equation using the slope-intercept method. Use the graph to determine the distance he would travel if he drove at this average rate of travel for 4 hours.

69. The following table partially lists the total points given by sportswriters and broadcasters in the final regular-season Associated Press poll of men's college basketball teams for the 1991–1992 regular season.

Rank	College	Points	x, Rank Minus 1	y, Predicted Points
1	Duke	1624		
2	Kansas	1543		
3	Ohio State	1461		
4	UCLA	1390		
5	Indiana	1266		
6	Kentucky	1242		
7	UNLV	1182		
8	USC	1164		
9	Arkansas	1081		
10	Arizona	1045		

a. Find the average rate of change in total points with respect to rank between the 1st-ranked team and the 10th-ranked team.

b. Let y = total points and x = rank minus 1 (so that x will vary between 0 and 9). Write an equation to find the total points, y, in terms of x.

c. Graph the equation on your calculator using the window (0, 9.4, 1, 0, 3100, 500, 1).

d. Trace on the graph or use the TABLE feature of the calculator to predict the number of points for each ranking. Was the equation a good predictor of the points given by the poll? Explain.

70.

The following table partially lists the total points given by sportswriters and broadcasters in the final regular-season Associated Press poll of women's college basketball teams at the end of the 1991–1992 regular season.

Rank	College	Points	*x,* Rank Minus 1	*y,* Predicted Points
1	Virginia	1745		
2	Tennessee	1685		
3	Stanford	1561		
4	S.F. Austin State	1490		
5	Mississippi	1441		
6	Miami-Fl	1384		
7	Iowa	1381		
8	Maryland	1271		
9	Penn State	1185		
10	SW Missouri State	1054		

a. Find the average rate of change in total points with respect to rank between the 1st-ranked team and the 10th-ranked team.

b. Let y = total points and x = rank minus 1. Write an equation to find the total points, y, in terms of x.

c. Graph the equation on your calculator using the window (0, 9.4, 1, 0, 3100, 500, 1).

d. Use the TRACE feature or the TABLE feature of the calculator to find the predicted number of points for each rank. Was the equation a good predictor of the points given by the poll?

71. In the study of statistics, much attention is given to developing linear relationships between two variables. As an example, consider the following ordered pairs, in which the first coordinate is the number of push-ups that can be done by randomly selected students in a physical fitness course, and the second coordinate is the number of sit-ups the same student can do.

(27, 30)   (22, 26)   (15, 25)   (35, 42)   (30, 38)
(52, 40)   (35, 32)   (55, 54)   (40, 50)   (40, 43)

Using statistical methods, the best equation to represent the data is

$y = 14.9 + 0.66x,$

where x is the number of push-ups a student can do and y is the number of sit-ups the same student can do.

a. Graph the equation on your calculator using the window (0, 94, 10, 0, 62, 10, 1).

b. Use the equation to predict the number of sit-ups, y, a student can do if he can do 15 push-ups. How far off was the prediction from the actual value?

c. Construct a table of values to predict the number of sit-ups for each of the recorded values for the number of push-ups. In the table, set the first column to the number of push-ups (x), the second column to the actual recorded value, the third column to the predicted value (y), and the fourth column to be the difference between the recorded and predicted values of y. This table should help you decide whether or not the equation is a good predictor.

72. The following data illustrate another statistically developed linear relationship between a woman's height (to the nearest inch) and her weight (to the nearest 5 pounds).

Height	65	65	62	67	69	65	61	67
Weight	105	125	110	120	140	135	95	130

Using statistical methods, the best equation to represent the data is

$$y = -186.5 + 4.71x,$$

where x is the woman's height and y is her weight.

a. Graph the equation on your calculator using the window $(0, 94, 10, -310, 310, 100, 1)$.

b. How well does the equation predict the weight of a woman who is 67 inches tall? How far off was the prediction from the recorded values?

c. Add a third line to the table to enter the predicted weights, y, for each woman. Then add a fourth line to enter the difference between the recorded and the predicted values of y. Does the table help you decide whether or not the equation is a good predictor of weight, based upon height of women?

In business applications, supply and demand functions are often used to study the economics associated with marketing products. The studies associate the price at which you sell a product with the available supply or demanded quantity of the product. (For example, when VCRs first were placed on the market, supply was low, causing the price to be high, and the demand was low. Later, the supply increased, the price decreased, and demand rose.) Exercises 73 and 74 deal with supply and demand functions.

73. Suppose the daily demand, $D(p)$, for a product is given by

$$D(p) = 80 - \frac{4}{5}p,$$

where $D(p)$ is the quantity demanded each day by consumers when the price is p dollars per item.

a. Graph the equation using the slope-intercept method.

b. Use the graph to determine what the demand for the product will be when the price is $10 per item; $20 per item; $40 per item; $64 per item.

c. Explain in general what is happening with the demand for the product as the price increases.

d. Are there any practical limits on the price per item, p, for this equation, that would result in an unreasonable price? Explain.

74. Suppose the daily supply, $S(p)$, of a product is given by

$$S(p) = \frac{5}{8}p,$$

where $S(p)$ is the quantity supplied each day when the price is p dollars per item.

a. Graph the equation using the slope-intercept method.

b. What will the daily supply be if the price is $10 per item; $20 per item; $40 per item; $64 per item?

c. Explain in general what is happening with the supply for the product as the price increases.

d. Are there any practical limits on the price per item for this equation? Explain.

Experiencing Algebra the Calculator Way

For each exercise, use your calculator to graph the three equations on the same coordinate system, using an integer window.

1. a. $y = 4x$ **b.** $y = 2x$ **c.** $y = \dfrac{1}{2}x$

     $m =$ ____ $m =$ ____ $m =$ ____

     $b =$ ____ $b =$ ____ $b =$ ____

     In all three equations, what is the same? What is different? What effect does this have on the graphs?

2. a. $y = -4x$ **b.** $y = -2x$ **c.** $y = -\dfrac{1}{2}x$

     $m =$ ____ $m =$ ____ $m =$ ____

     $b =$ ____ $b =$ ____ $b =$ ____

     In all three equations, what is the same? What is different? What effect does this have on the graphs?

3. a. $y = 4x + 9$ **b.** $y = 4x$ **c.** $y = 4x - 9$

     $m =$ ____ $m =$ ____ $m =$ ____

     $b =$ ____ $b =$ ____ $b =$ ____

     In all three equations, what is the same? What is different? What effect does this have on the graphs?

4. a. $y = -4x + 9$ **b.** $y = -4x$ **c.** $y = -4x - 9$

     $m =$ ____ $m =$ ____ $m =$ ____

     $b =$ ____ $b =$ ____ $b =$ ____

     In all three equations, what is the same? What is different? What effect does this have on the graphs?

Experiencing Algebra the Group Way

1. Have each member of the group complete the following table without graphing. (Remember to first solve the equation for y to obtain the slope-intercept form.) Then check your conclusions by graphing each equation.

Equation	m	b	Graph's Inclination ↗ or ↘	Graph's y-Intercept
$y = 3x + 6$				
$y = -2x + 7$				
$y = -x - 3$				
$y = 4x - 1$				
$5x - 3y = 9$				
$4x + 5y = 10$				
$y = \dfrac{7}{8}x - \dfrac{3}{4}$				
$y = -1.7x + 3.2$				

Discuss what effect m has on the graph of a linear equation in two variables.
Discuss what effect b has on the graph of a linear equation in two variables.

2. You have learned three methods for graphing a linear equation in two variables: using a table of values of coordinate pairs, using the intercept method, and using the slope-intercept method. Assign each member of the group one of the three methods to graph each of the given linear equations (if possible). After each member has graphed the equations using his or her assigned method, share your results and decide which is the best method for each equation, and explain why.

a. $x + 2y = 4$ **b.** $y = -x + 3$ **c.** $3x + 5y = -15$ **d.** $y = \dfrac{2}{3}x - 1$

e. $7x + y = 18$ **f.** $y = 2.5x + 4.5$ **g.** $3y = 2y - 3$ **h.** $5x - 7 = 3x + 1$

Experiencing Algebra the Write Way

1. Explain how to determine the slope of a line if a graph is given.
2. Explain how to determine the slope of a line if an equation is given.
3. Explain the importance of m and b in determining the graph of a line when its equation is in the form $y = mx + b$.

6.4 Coinciding, Parallel, and Perpendicular Lines

Objectives

1 Determine whether two linear graphs are coinciding by inspecting their corresponding equations.

2 Determine whether two linear graphs are parallel by inspecting their corresponding equations.

3 Determine whether two linear graphs are intersecting or intersecting and perpendicular by inspecting their corresponding equations.

4 Determine from real-world data whether two linear graphs are coinciding, parallel, intersecting, or intersecting and perpendicular.

Application

Black Bart's Gang robbed the bank at Dry Gulch and rode out of town, heading for the state line 50 miles away. Heavy saddlebags, filled with gold, slowed the horses to 20 miles per hour. Marshal Bozik organized a posse and rode after Black Bart, leaving Dry Gulch a half-hour behind the gang, but riding 30 miles per hour. Can Marshal Bozik's posse catch Black Bart before reaching the state line?

After completing this section, we will discuss this application further. See page 462.

From previous graphing, we know that the graphs of two lines may have one of three different relationships. Two **coinciding** lines have all points in common. Two **parallel** lines have no points in common. Two **intersecting** lines have one common point. In this section, we will see how the concept of slope enables us to tell which of these three cases we have, just from analyzing the equations of the lines.

1   Determining Coinciding Lines

Let's first look at the characteristics of coinciding lines. Complete the following set of exercises on your calculator to determine whether the two linear equations graph as coinciding lines.

DISCOVERY 6

Coinciding Lines

1. Graph the given pairs of linear equations.
   a. $-2x + y = 1$ b. $x - 2y = 3$ c. $-3x - y = 5$
      $y = 2x + 1$ $2x - 4y = 6$ $3x + y = -5$

2. Determine the slope and y-coordinate of the y-intercept for each graph.
   a. $-2x + y = 1$ b. $x - 2y = 3$ c. $-3x - y = 5$
      $m =$ ____ $m =$ ____ $m =$ ____
      $b =$ ____ $b =$ ____ $b =$ ____
      $y = 2x + 1$ $2x - 4y = 6$ $3x + y = -5$
      $m =$ ____ $m =$ ____ $m =$ ____
      $b =$ ____ $b =$ ____ $b =$ ____

   Choose the correct answers:

3. The lines graphed are *coinciding/parallel/intersecting/intersecting and perpendicular.*
4. The slopes, m, in each pair of linear equations are *equal/not equal.*
5. The y-coordinates of the y-intercepts, b, in each pair of linear equations are *equal/not equal.*

Write a rule to determine that the graphs of two linear equations are coinciding.

Each pair of lines graphed are coinciding. Also, the slopes in each pair are equal and the y-coordinates of the y-intercepts in each pair are equal.

> *Coinciding Lines*
> The graphs of two linear equations are coinciding if the graphs have equal slopes, m, and equal y-coordinates of the y-intercepts, b.

To determine whether two nonvertical lines are coinciding by inspecting their equations:

- Solve both equations for y.
- Determine the slope, m, and y-coordinate of the y-intercept, b, for each equation.

Nonvertical coinciding lines have equal slopes (m) and equal y-coordinates of the y-intercepts (b).

To determine whether two vertical lines are coinciding by inspecting their equations:

- Solve both equations for x.

Vertical coinciding lines have the same constant term.

 Helping Hand Coinciding lines are the same line, so they must have the same slope and y-intercept.

EXAMPLE 1 Determine by inspection whether the graphs of the given pairs of linear equations are coinciding.

a. $y = 2x + 4$
$\quad y = 2x - 4$

b. $3x - y = 2$
$\quad -3x + y = -2$

c. $3x = 15$
$\quad x = 5$

d. $y = 5$
$\quad x = 5$

Solution

a. $\quad y = 2x + 4 \quad m = 2 \quad b = 4$
$\qquad y = 2x - 4 \quad m = 2 \quad b = -4$

The lines are not coinciding because the y-coordinates of the y-intercepts (b) are not equal: $4 \neq -4$.

b. Solve both equations for y.

$\quad y = 3x - 2 \quad m = 3 \quad b = -2$
$\quad y = 3x - 2 \quad m = 3 \quad b = -2$

The lines are coinciding because the slopes (m) are equal and the y-coordinates of the y-intercepts (b) are equal.

c. Solve both equations for x.

$\quad x = 5$
$\quad x = 5$

The vertical lines are coinciding because the constant terms are equal: $5 = 5$.

d. $\quad y = 5 \quad$ Horizontal line with $m = 0$
$\qquad x = 5 \quad$ Vertical line with m undefined

The lines are not coinciding because the slopes are not equal: 0 and undefined are not the same.

Calculator Check

Graph the two lines on your calculator to check. *Note:* Since the coinciding lines are the same, use the up and down arrows while tracing to determine that more than one line is graphed. The equation for the traced line is displayed on the screen.

A check of Example 1b is shown.

Note: The ordered pair $(0, -2)$ is located on the graphs of both equations; therefore, the graphs coincide.

$(-47, 47, -31, 31)$ $(-47, 47, -31, 31)$ ∎

 Experiencing Algebra the Checkup Way

In exercises 1–4, determine by inspection whether the graphs of the given pairs of linear equations are coinciding.

1. $3x - y = -11$ **2.** $4y = 16$ **3.** $5x - y = 7$ **4.** $4y - 2 = 6$
$3(x - y) = -2y - 11$ $2y - 8 = 8 - 2y$ $5x + y = -7$ $x = 2$

5. What does it mean to say that the graphs of two linear equations result in coinciding lines?

6. How can you tell that the graphs of two linear equations will be coinciding lines by simply inspecting the two equations?

---

2 Determining Parallel Lines

Now let's take a look at the characteristics of two parallel lines. Complete the following set of exercises on your calculator to determine whether the two linear equations graph as parallel lines.

DISCOVERY 7

Parallel Lines

1. Graph the given pairs of linear equations.

     a. $-2x + y = 1$ **b.** $x - 2y = 3$ **c.** $-3x - y = 5$
        $y = 2x + 10$ $2x - 4y = -12$ $3x + y = 5$

2. Determine the slope and y-coordinate of the y-intercept for each graph.

     a. $-2x + y = 1$ **b.** $x - 2y = 3$ **c.** $-3x - y = 5$
        $m = \underline{\quad}$ $m = \underline{\quad}$ $m = \underline{\quad}$
        $b = \underline{\quad}$ $b = \underline{\quad}$ $b = \underline{\quad}$
        $y = 2x + 10$ $2x - 4y = -12$ $3x + y = 5$
        $m = \underline{\quad}$ $m = \underline{\quad}$ $m = \underline{\quad}$
        $b = \underline{\quad}$ $b = \underline{\quad}$ $b = \underline{\quad}$

Choose the correct answers:

3. The lines graphed are *coinciding/parallel/intersecting/intersecting and perpendicular.*

4. The slopes, m, in each pair of linear equations in two variables are *equal/not equal.*

5. The y-coordinates of the y-intercepts, b, in each pair of linear equations in two variables are *equal/not equal.*

Write a rule to determine that the graphs of two linear equations in two variables are parallel.

Each pair of lines graphed are parallel. Also, the slopes in each pair are equal. The y-coordinates of the y-intercepts in each pair are not equal.

> *Parallel Lines*
> The graphs of two linear equations are parallel if the graphs have equal slopes, m, and unequal y-coordinates of the y-intercepts, b.

To determine whether two nonvertical lines are parallel by inspecting their equations:

- Solve the equations for y.
- Determine the slope, m, and y-coordinate of the y-intercept, b, for each equation.

Nonvertical parallel lines have equal slopes (m) and unequal y-coordinates of the y-intercepts (b).

To determine whether two vertical lines are parallel by inspecting their equations:

- Solve the equations for x.

Vertical parallel lines have different constant terms.

 Helping Hand Parallel lines never intersect, so they must have a different y-intercept (or x-intercept for vertical lines) and the same slope.

EXAMPLE 2   Determine by inspection whether the graphs of the given pairs of linear equations are parallel.

a. $y = 2x + 4$ **b.** $3x - 2y = 6$ **c.** $x = 5$
  $y = 2x - 4$ $6x - 4y = 6$ $2x - 3 = 1$

d. $y = 5$
  $x = 5$

Solution

a. $y = 2x + 4$ $m = 2$ $b = 4$

  $y = 2x - 4$ $m = 2$ $b = -4$

The lines are parallel because the slopes (m) are equal and the y-coordinates of the y-intercepts (b) are not equal.

b. Solve the equations for y.

$$y = \frac{3}{2}x - 3 \quad m = \tfrac{3}{2} \quad b = -3$$

$$y = \frac{3}{2}x - \frac{3}{2} \quad m = \tfrac{3}{2} \quad b = -\tfrac{3}{2}$$

The lines are parallel because the slopes (m) are equal and the y-coordinates of the y-intercepts (b) are not equal.

c. Solve the equations for x.

  $x = 5$

  $x = 2$

The vertical lines are parallel because the constant terms are not equal.

d. $y = 5$ Horizontal line with $m = 0$

  $x = 5$ Vertical line with m undefined

The lines are not parallel because the slopes are not equal: 0 and undefined are not the same.

Graph the two lines on your calculator to check. Use the up and down arrows to move between the lines while tracing. The lines are parallel if for each x-coordinate the differences in the corresponding y-coordinates remain the same. ■

Experiencing Algebra the Checkup Way

In exercises 1–4, determine by inspection whether the graphs of the given pairs of linear equations are parallel.

1. $2y = 9$
$y + 12 = 3 - y$

2. $3x + y = 7$
$3x - y = -7$

3. $7x - 3y = -6$
$7x - 3y = 15$

4. $-3x = 18$
$x - 4 = 4 - x$

5. What does it mean to say that the graphs of two linear equations result in parallel lines?

6. How can you tell that the graphs of two linear equations will result in parallel lines by inspecting the two equations?

---

3 Determining Intersecting and Perpendicular Lines

The next "Discovery" exercise explores the characteristics of intersecting lines. Complete the following set of exercises on your calculator to determine whether the two linear equations graph as intersecting lines.

DISCOVERY 8

Intersecting Lines

1. Graph the given pairs of linear equations.

  a. $-2x + y = 1$ **b.** $x - 2y = 3$ **c.** $-3x - y = 5$
       $y = 3x + 10$ $4x - 4y = -12$ $-3x + y = -5$

2. Determine the slope and y-coordinate of the y-intercept for each graph.

  a. $-2x + y = 1$ **b.** $x - 2y = 3$ **c.** $-3x - y = 5$
      $m = \underline{\quad}$ $m = \underline{\quad}$ $m = \underline{\quad}$
      $b = \underline{\quad}$ $b = \underline{\quad}$ $b = \underline{\quad}$
      $y = 3x + 10$ $4x - 4y = -12$ $-3x + y = -5$
      $m = \underline{\quad}$ $m = \underline{\quad}$ $m = \underline{\quad}$
      $b = \underline{\quad}$ $b = \underline{\quad}$ $b = \underline{\quad}$

Choose the correct answers:

3. The lines graphed are *coinciding/parallel/intersecting/intersecting and perpendicular.*

4. The slopes, m, in each pair of linear equations in two variables are *equal/not equal.*

Write a rule to determine that the graphs of two linear equations in two variables are intersecting.

Each pair of lines graphed are intersecting. Also, the slopes in each pair are unequal.

> *Intersecting Lines*
> The graphs of two linear equations are intersecting if the graphs have unequal slopes, m.

Perpendicular lines are a special case of intersecting lines. Two intersecting lines that form four right angles are called **perpendicular** lines. Complete the following set of exercises on your calculator to investigate this special case of intersecting lines.

D I S C O V E R Y 9

Perpendicular Lines

1. Graph the given pairs of linear equations.

    a. $-2x + 3y = 3$ **b.** $x - 2y = 3$ **c.** $-3x - y = 5$

      $y = -\dfrac{3}{2}x - 2$ $-8x - 4y = -12$ $-x + 3y = -15$

2. Determine the slope and y-coordinate of the y-intercept for each graph.

    a. $-2x + 3y = 3$ **b.** $x - 2y = 3$ **c.** $-3x - y = 5$

      $m = \underline{\quad}$ $m = \underline{\quad}$ $m = \underline{\quad}$

      $b = \underline{\quad}$ $b = \underline{\quad}$ $b = \underline{\quad}$

      $y = -\dfrac{3}{2}x - 2$ $-8x - 4y = -12$ $-x + 3y = -15$

      $m = \underline{\quad}$ $m = \underline{\quad}$ $m = \underline{\quad}$

      $b = \underline{\quad}$ $b = \underline{\quad}$ $b = \underline{\quad}$

Choose the correct answers:

3. The lines graphed are *coinciding/parallel/intersecting/intersecting and perpendicular.*

4. The slopes, m, in each pair of linear equations in two variables are *equal/not equal.*

5. The two slopes, m, in each pair of linear equations in two variables are reciprocals and have the *same/opposite* sign.

Write a rule to determine that the graphs of two linear equations in two variables are intersecting and perpendicular.

Each pair of lines graphed are intersecting and perpendicular. The slopes are opposite reciprocals of each other.

> *Intersecting and Perpendicular Lines*
> The graphs of two linear equations are intersecting and perpendicular if the graphs have slopes, m, that are opposite reciprocals of each other.

To determine whether two nonvertical lines are intersecting or intersecting and perpendicular by inspecting their equations:

- Solve the equations for y.
- Determine the slope, m, and y-coordinate of the y-intercept, b, for each equation.

Intersecting lines have unequal slopes (m). Nonvertical intersecting and perpendicular lines have slopes (m) that are opposite reciprocals of each other.

Helping Hand The product of the slopes of nonvertical perpendicular lines is -1. For example, $m = \frac{2}{3}$ and $m = \frac{-3}{2}$ are slopes of perpendicular lines and $\left(\frac{2}{3}\right)\left(\frac{-3}{2}\right) = -1$. This can be used as a test for perpendicular lines.

A special case of perpendicular lines is when one line is vertical ($x = c$) and the other line is horizontal ($y = d$).

EXAMPLE 3   Determine by inspection whether the graphs of the given pairs of linear equations are intersecting at one point, intersecting and perpendicular, or neither.

a. $y = 2x + 4$
$-y = -2x - 4$

b. $2x - y = 6$
$2x + y = 6$

c. $2x + 3y = 1$
$3x - 2y = 1$

d. $x = 5$
$3x + 4 = 7$

e. $y = 5$
$x = 5$

Solution

a. Solve the equations for y.

$$y = 2x + 4 \qquad m = 2$$
$$y = 2x + 4 \qquad m = 2$$

The lines are not intersecting because the slopes (m) are equal.

b. Solve the equations for y.

$$y = 2x - 6 \qquad m = 2$$
$$y = -2x + 6 \qquad m = -2$$

The lines are intersecting at one point because the slopes (m) are not equal: $2 \neq -2$. However, even though the slopes have opposite signs, the slopes are not reciprocals of each other; therefore, the lines are not perpendicular.

c. Solve the equations for y.

$$y = -\frac{2}{3}x + \frac{1}{3} \qquad m = -\tfrac{2}{3}$$

$$y = \frac{3}{2}x - \frac{1}{2} \qquad m = \tfrac{3}{2}$$

The lines are intersecting and perpendicular because the slopes (m) are opposite reciprocals of each other: $-\frac{2}{3}$ and $\frac{3}{2}$. The product of the slopes is -1.

d. The lines are not intersecting because both are vertical lines.

e. The lines are intersecting and perpendicular because one line is vertical and the other is horizontal.

Graph the two lines on your calculator to check. *Note:* An integer or decimal screen (square screen) is necessary to determine by inspection perpendicular lines. Other screens may skew the picture. For example, the check for Example 3c is shown on an integer screen and on the standard screen.

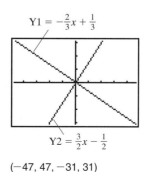

Y1 $= -\frac{2}{3}x + \frac{1}{3}$

Y2 $= \frac{3}{2}x - \frac{1}{2}$

$(-47, 47, -31, 31)$

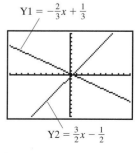

Y1 $= -\frac{2}{3}x + \frac{1}{3}$

Y2 $= \frac{3}{2}x - \frac{1}{2}$

$(-10, 10, -10, 10)$

■

All of the relationships we have just completed are summarized below.

> *Determining the Relationship between Two Lines from the Linear Equations in Two Variables*
>
> Two linear equations written in slope-intercept form, $y = mx + b$, have graphs that are
>
> - **Coinciding lines** if the equations have equal slopes (m) and equal y-coordinates of the y-intercepts (b).
> - **Parallel lines** if the equations have equal slopes (m) and nonequal y-coordinates of the y-intercepts (b).
> - **Intersecting lines** if the equations have nonequal slopes (m).
> - **Intersecting and perpendicular lines** if the equations have slopes (m) that are opposite reciprocals of each other.
>
> Two linear equations written in the form $x = a$ have graphs that are
>
> - **Coinciding lines** if they have the same constant term.
> - **Parallel lines** if the equations have different constant terms.
>
> A special case of intersecting and perpendicular lines is when one line is vertical ($x = a$) and the other line is horizontal ($y = b$).

Experiencing Algebra the Checkup Way

In exercises 1–4, determine by inspection whether the graphs of the given pairs of linear equations are intersecting at one point, intersecting and perpendicular, or neither.

1. $4x - 5y = 10$
$5x + 4y = 4$

2. $2x - 3y = 9$
$2x - 3y = -9$

3. $5x - y = -1$
$3x + 2y = -4$

4. $2y = 14$
$y + 3 = 0$

5. What is meant by intersecting lines when two linear equations are graphed?

6. What is meant by perpendicular lines when two linear equations are graphed?

7. How can you tell that the graphs of two linear equations will result in intersecting lines by inspecting the equations?

8. How can you tell that the graphs of two linear equations will result in perpendicular lines by inspecting the equations?

---

4 Modeling the Real World

How useful is it to know that two graph lines are coinciding, parallel, or intersecting? If the lines represent equations based on real-world situations, this knowledge can be very useful. For example, economists often graph sales revenue and production costs on the same coordinate system. If the two lines intersect, the point of intersection is called the **break-even point**. The values of the coordinates of this point correspond to how much money you have to make in sales in order to equal the money you spend in production costs. If the two lines don't intersect, it may mean you can never earn back in sales the money you spent as costs. This is certainly an important thing to know. In other situations, the point of intersection of two lines may correspond to when one moving object is going to catch up to another. Even without knowing just where the point of intersection is, it's often useful to know from the equations whether there is a point of intersection at all.

EXAMPLE 4   Amy sells wooden Christmas ornaments at a fair booth. The paint costs $0.89 per ornament, the ribbon costs $0.11 per ornament, and the unpainted ornaments cost $0.50 each. The fair charges $25.00 to set up a booth.

a. Write an equation for the total cost (y) in terms of x ornaments.
b. Last year Amy sold the ornaments for $1.50 each. If she plans to sell the ornaments at the same price this year, write an equation for the total revenue (y) in terms of x ornaments.
c. Will there be a break-even point (intersection of the two graphs in parts (a) and (b)? Explain.
d. Write an equation for the total revenue (y) in terms of x ornaments if Amy decides to sell the ornaments for $2.00. Will there be a break-even point? Explain.
e. Graph the equations on your calculator using the window (0, 100, 10, 0, 250, 10, 1). Determine the break-even point. Interpret your answer.

Solution

a. The cost per ornament will be $1.50:

$$0.89 + 0.11 + 0.50 = 1.50$$

The total cost will be $1.50 per ornament plus the booth cost of $25.00.
Let y = total cost
   x = number of ornaments

$$y = 1.50x + 25.00$$

b. The total revenue will be $1.50 per ornament.
Let y = total revenue
   x = number of ornaments

$$y = 1.50x$$

c. Using the equations $y = 1.50x + 25.00$ and $y = 1.50x$, we see that the linear equations have equal slopes: $1.50 = 1.50$. They also have unequal y-coordinates of the y-intercepts: $25.00 \neq 0$. Therefore, the lines are parallel and do not intersect for a break-even point.

d. The total revenue will be $2.00 per ornament.
Let y = total revenue
   x = number of ornaments

$$y = 2.00x$$

Using the equations, $y = 1.50x + 25.00$ and $y = 2.00x$, we see that the linear equations have unequal slopes: $1.50 \neq 2.00$. The lines will intersect at one point, the break-even point.

e.
$$Y1 = 1.50x + 25.00$$
$$Y2 = 2.00x$$

(0, 100, 0, 250)

The intersection is (50, 100). Amy will break even and begin to make a profit if she sells 50 ornaments for $100. ∎

Application

Black Bart's Gang robbed the bank at Dry Gulch and rode out of town, heading for the state line 50 miles away. Heavy saddlebags, filled with gold, slowed the horses to 20 miles per hour. Marshal Bozik organized a posse and rode after Black Bart, leaving Dry Gulch a half-hour behind the gang, but riding 30 miles per hour. Can Marshal Bozik's posse catch Black Bart before reaching the state line?

Discussion

Let t = the time (in hours) that Black Bart's Gang traveled
Let $B(t)$ = the distance (in miles) Black Bart's Gang traveled

$$B(t) = 20t \quad \text{Distance} = \text{rate} \cdot \text{time}$$

Let $M(t)$ = the distance (in miles) Marshal Bozik's posse traveled
$t - \frac{1}{2}$ = the time (in hours) that Marshal Bozik's posse traveled

$$M(t) = 30\left(t - \frac{1}{2}\right) \quad \text{Distance} = \text{rate} \cdot \text{time}$$
$$M(t) = 30t - 15$$

$$Y2 = 30x - 15$$
$$Y1 = 20x$$

(0, 5, 0, 50)

The graphs of the two distance functions $B(t)$ and $M(t)$ will intersect because the slopes of the graphs, 20 and 30, are not equal.

Graph the two functions and determine the point of intersection.

The two linear graphs intersect at (1.5, 30).

Marshal Bozik's posse will catch Black Bart's Gang 30 miles from Dry Gulch and before they reach the state line, 1.5 hours after the gang left town. ∎

Experiencing Algebra the Checkup Way

Tim has a lawn care business. He spends an average of $8.50 per lawn for fertilizer and spends an average of $6.50 per lawn for labor to spread the fertilizer. He paid $85 for the spreader.

1. Write an equation for the total cost, y, of providing this service for x lawns.

2. Tim charges $20 per lawn for the service. Write an equation for the total revenue, y, from providing this service for x lawns.

3. Will there be a break-even point? Explain.

4. Write an equation for the total revenue, y, from providing this service for x lawns if Tim charges $15 per lawn. Will there be a break-even point? Explain.

5. Graph the equations from exercises 1 and 2, using a calculator window of (0, 47, 5, 0, 620, 100, 1). Determine the break-even point. Interpret your answer.

PROBLEM SET 6.4

Experiencing Algebra the Exercise Way

In exercises 1–26, determine by inspection whether the graphs of the given pairs of linear equations are (a) coinciding lines, (b) parallel lines, (c) only intersecting lines, or (d) both intersecting and perpendicular lines. Check by graphing.

1. $3x - 2y = 5(y + 7)$
$7x = 3(1 - y)$

2. $4x + 5 = 0$
$2(y - 1) = 6 - y$

3. $x = 4(y - 3)$
$x = 4(y + 5)$

4. $x - 6 = 0$
$x + 6 = 0$

5. $4x - y = 6$
$2x - y + 3 = 0$

6. $x + y = 0$
$x + 4y = 8$

7. $x = 2(y - 7)$
$y = \frac{1}{2}x + 7$

8. $2x - 5 = x + 5$
$x - 6 = 4$

9. $5x + y = -6$
$3x + y = 0$

10. $y = 3x - 4$
$2x = 3y + 6$

11. $4x + y = 8$
$4x + y + 2 = 0$

12. $y = 4x - 5$
$y + 1 = 4(x - 1)$

13. $y - 5 = 0$
$2x + 6 = x + 9$

14. $5x + y = 3$
$x = 5y$

15. $2y - 3 = 13$
$y + 1 = 4$

16. $x = -6$
$x + 3y = 3$

17. $x + 3 = 0$
$x - 5 = 0$

18. $14x - 2y = -1$
$7x - y = 6$

19. $2x - 9 = 0$
$x - 4 = 5 - x$

20. $y = 1$
$3(y + 3) = 2(y + 4)$

21. $3(y - 3) = 1$
$5y = 10 + 2y$

22. $y + 4 = 0$
$2x - 5y = 15$

23. $x = 2$
$y = 2x - 1$

24. $x + y = 9$
$y = -(x + 3)$

25. $y - 3 = 0$
$2x + 3y = 0$

26. $y + 3 = 0$
$y + 6 = 0$

27. Brook can buy candy bars at wholesale for 15 cents each. He wants to resell them in his dormitory to earn some spending money. He hires his roommate Eric to sell for him, paying Eric $2.50 per day, plus 10 cents per candy bar sold. The dorm's resident advisor charges Brook $1.00 a day for permission to sell the candy at the dorm.

  a. Write an equation for the total cost (y) in terms of x candy bars sold by Eric in one day.

  b. Write an equation for the total revenue (y) in terms of x candy bars sold when Eric sells the candy bars for 25 cents each.

  c. Find the break-even point, if there is one, when Brook will start making a profit for each day Eric sells candy for him.

  d. Write an equation for the total revenue (y) in terms of x candy bars sold when Eric sells the candy bars for three for a dollar.

  e. Find the break-even point, if there is one, when Brook will start making a profit for each day Eric sells candy for him at this price.

  f. What will be the break-even point if Brook sells his own candy bars for 25 cents each?

  g. What will be the break-even point if Brook sells his own candy bars for three for a dollar?

  h. What do you think Brook should do?

28. Joe wants to start a business selling restored antique radios. He can rent a counter in the local antiques mall for $200 per month. Miscellaneous costs average to $85 per month. From his past bookkeeping records, he figures that he has purchased antique radios for an average of $70 each. He figures that his labor and parts to restore them average to $130 each. (For the calculator graphs, use a window of (0, 20, 1, 0, 2000, 100, 1).)

$250

a. Write a cost function for the total cost (y) of setting up shop to restore and sell x radios in a given month.

b. Write an equation for the total revenue (y) received if Joe sells x radios at $200 each.

c. Find the break-even point, if there is one, when Joe will start making a profit each month.

d. Write an equation for the total revenue if Joe sells his radios at $300 each.

e. Find the break-even point, if there is one, when Joe will start making a profit each month at this price.

f. What will be the break-even point if Joe sells his radios for $250, reduces his counter rental to $125 per month by moving, and decreases his miscellaneous costs to $50 per month?

g. What do you think Joe should do?

29. Laurie can rent a car for $35.00 per day plus $0.25 per mile from Krazy Kar Rental, or she can rent a car for $60.00 per day with unlimited miles from Rational Car Rental. Write equations to represent her cost for one day of rental from each company, if she drives the car x miles. Inspect the equations to determine whether their graphs will intersect. Explain. If the graphs do intersect, graph and find the intersection point and interpret what it represents.

30. Jim can rent a stump grinder for a day for a flat fee of $65 from Rent All Inc., or he can rent a grinder for a fee of $15 plus $10 per hour from Best Rental. Write equations to represent his cost for one day of rental from each company, if he rents the grinder for x hours. Will the graphs of the equations intersect? Explain. If they do, graph and find the intersection point. Explain what the point represents.

31. Kate has a choice to make. As a Christmas present, her grandfather offers to give her each year an amount of money equal to $50 plus twice her age, or she can receive a fixed amount of $75 each year. Write two equations to represent the amounts of money she will receive when she is x years old. Given that she is 8 years old, write a third equation to represent her age. Will the graph of this equation intersect the graphs of the other two equations? Explain. Will it be perpendicular to either of the first two equations' graphs? What do the intersection points of the three graphs represent?

32. A newspaper accepts classified ads under two payment plans. The first plan charges $0.26 per word for the ad. The second plan charges a fee of $8.00 plus $0.02 per word. Write two equations to represent the cost of placing an ad of x words under each plan. Given that your ad contains 30 words, write a third equation to represent the length of your ad. Will the graph of this equation intersect the graphs of the first two equations? Explain. Will it be perpendicular to either of the first two equations' graphs? Interpret the intersection points.

33. Football superstar Archie receives a pass at the 50-yard line. He races in for a touchdown at a speed of 10 feet per second. Write an equation for the distance he will travel in x seconds. Defensive superstar Speedie is behind the 50-yard line. He races to catch Archie at a speed of 15 feet per second, and crosses the 50-yard line 4 seconds after Archie. Write an equation for the distance he will travel beyond the 50-yard line. Use the equations to determine whether Speedie will catch Archie before he reaches the end zone, which is 150 feet away.

34. In the Great Automobile Race of 1895, Villainous Victor left the starting line in Paris at 12 noon, and averaged 18 miles per hour with his automobile. Trueheart Tom left the starting line 45 minutes later, because of startup problems, but he was able to average 21.5 miles per hour with his gasoline-powered carriage. Write equations to determine the distance each man traveled, where x is the number of hours since 12 noon. Use the equations to determine at what distance Tom will overtake Victor, assuming neither has car trouble in the race.

 Experiencing Algebra the Calculator Way

Let's explore settings of the window for graphing a linear equation in two variables.

1. Clear out any equations in the ⃞ Y= ⃞ key. Use the ⃞ ZOOM ⃞ key to set the coordinate system to the Standard setting. What are the window settings for this choice?

Xmin =

Xmax =

Xscl =

Ymin =

Ymax =

Yscl =

2. Set the coordinate system to the Integer setting. What are the window settings for this choice?

Xmin =

Xmax =

Xscl =

Ymin =

Ymax =

Yscl =

3. Reset the Integer setting by adding 47 to the x limits and 31 to the y limits.

Xmin =

Xmax =

Xscl =

Ymin =

Ymax =

Yscl =

Use the left and right arrow keys to move the cursor. Do you see that you have been able to reset the coordinate system and still maintain integer pairs for x and y?

4. Repeat step 2, and then reset the Integer setting by multiplying each setting by 10.

Xmin =

Xmax =

Xscl =

Ymin =

Ymax =

Yscl =

Move left and right. Are the x- and y-values still integer pairs?

Are you beginning to see how you can adjust the window to be any domain and range that is appropriate for your needs while still maintaining integer pairs? Experiment with other settings. Remember that you can always go back to ZOOM 6 ZOOM 8 ENTER to get back to your familiar settings.

Experiencing Algebra the Group Way

Assume that you intend to graph two linear equations, given by

$$y = m_1 + b_1 x \quad \text{and} \quad y = m_2 + b_2 x.$$

Before graphing the equations, you study them to compare the values of their slopes and the y-coordinates of their y-intercepts. In your group, discuss what these values can indicate to you, and then complete the following matching exercise. Match the conditions with the proper outcome for the graphs of two lines.

____**1.** Nonvertical coinciding   **a.** $m_1 = m_2, b_1 \neq b_2$

____**2.** Vertical coinciding   **b.** $m_1 \cdot m_2 = -1$ or $m_2 = -\dfrac{1}{m_1}$

____**3.** Nonvertical parallel   **c.** $m_1 = m_2, b_1 = b_2$

____**4.** Vertical parallel   **d.** $m_1 \neq m_2$

____**5.** Intersecting   **e.** $x = c, y = d$

____**6.** Nonvertical perpendicular   **f.** $x = c, x = d, c = d$

____**7.** Special perpendicular   **g.** $x = c, x = d, c \neq d$

Use the techniques in "Experiencing Algebra the Calculator Way" to experiment with setting the windows for a calculator graph to analyze the following break-even exercises. Determine which pairs of equations will result in intersecting graphs, which will be parallel, which will be perpendicular, and which will be coinciding. For graphs that intersect, find the point of intersection.

8. Cost function: $y = 300x + 450$
Revenue function: $y = 375x$

9. Cost function: $y = 1250 + 725x$
Revenue function: $y = 725x$

10. Cost function: $y = 1800$
Revenue function: $y = 125x$

Experiencing Algebra the Write Way

For one of the "Experiencing Algebra the Group Way" exercises, write a story to go along with the equations that would make sense to you. Imagine a situation in which someone is selling a product and experiences some costs with acquiring or producing the items for sale. You may want to refer to a business textbook in the library for ideas to help you come up with a story.

6.5   Writing Linear Equations from Given Data

Objectives

1   Write a linear equation in two variables given the *y*-intercept and slope of its graph.

2   Write a linear equation in two variables given the slope of its graph and the coordinates of a point through which its graph passes.

3   Write a linear equation in two variables given the coordinates of two points through which its graph passes.

4   Write a linear equation in two variables given the coordinates of a point through which its graph passes and a description of the line in terms of a second equation.

5   Model real-world situations using linear equations in two variables.

Application

Astronomers discovered the comet Hale-Farewell traveling straight toward the planet Jupiter. They measured its speed as 20,000 km/hr and its position as 3.0×10^7 km from Jupiter. Assuming the comet continues on its course in a straight line at the same speed, write an equation for its motion and determine when it will hit Jupiter.

After completing this section, we will discuss this application further. See page 479.

So far, we have determined graphs for linear equations in two variables. However, suppose we are given information about a graph and need to determine its corresponding equation. Now, we will see how to determine an equation from information given about its graph.

1   Writing a Linear Equation Given a Slope and *y*-Intercept

We already know the slope-intercept form of a linear equation, $y = mx + b$. Therefore, if we are given the slope, m, and the *y*-coordinate of the *y*-intercept, b, of a line, we can use this form to write an equation.

For example, write a linear equation in two variables for a line that has a slope of $\frac{1}{2}$ and a *y*-intercept of $(0, 3)$.

$m = \frac{1}{2}$ and $b = 3$ (*y*-coordinate of the *y*-intercept).

Using the slope-intercept form of a linear equation, $y = mx + b$,

$$y = \frac{1}{2}x + 3 \qquad \text{Substitute values for } m \text{ and } b.$$

The slope and *y*-intercept may also be determined from a linear graph. Therefore, we can write an equation if we are given a linear graph.

To write a linear equation in two variables from a given nonvertical graph:

- Determine the y-coordinate of the y-intercept (b).
- Determine the slope of the line (m) by counting the rise and the run between two integer coordinate points.
- Write a linear equation in two variables by substituting the values for m and b into the slope-intercept form of the equation, $y = mx + b$.

To write a linear equation in two variables from a given vertical graph, write an equation in the form $x = c$, where c is the x-coordinate of the x-intercept of the graph.

For example, write a linear equation for the following graph.

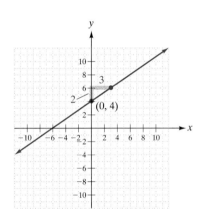

On the graph, label the y-intercept and draw the legs of a right triangle, using two integer coordinate points on the line as vertices.

The y-coordinate of the y-intercept (b) is 4. The slope (m) is $\frac{2}{3}$.

The equation is

$$y = mx + b$$

$$y = \frac{2}{3}x + 4$$

EXAMPLE 1 Write a linear equation in two variables for the given graph or information.

a.

b.

c.

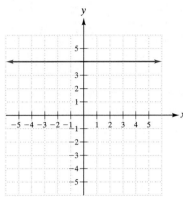

d. $m = 1; b = 0$ **e.** $m = 0; b = 3$

Solution

The graphs are labeled with the information needed to write an equation.

a.

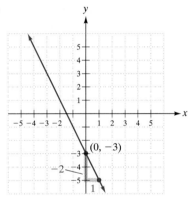

$m = -2 \quad b = -3$

$y = mx + b$

$y = -2x - 3$

b.

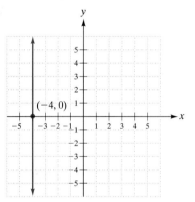

Vertical line with

$c = -4$

$x = -4$

c.

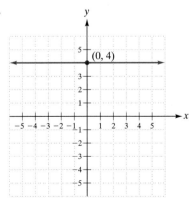

$m = 0 \quad b = 4$

$y = mx + b$

$y = 0x + 4$

$y = 4$

d. $y = mx + b$
$y = 1x + 0$
$y = x$

e. $y = mx + b$
$y = 0x + 3$
$y = 3$ ■

Experiencing Algebra the Checkup Way

In exercises 1–6, write a linear equation in two variables for the given graph or information.

1.

2.

3.

4.

5. $m = 4; b = -1$

6. $m = -\frac{2}{5}; b = 3.2$

7. Explain how you can write the equation of a line if you are given information about its slope and its *y*-intercept.

---

2 Writing a Linear Equation for a Given Point and Slope

Sometimes we know the slope of a line and the coordinates of a point through which the line passes (x_1, y_1) and want to write a linear equation in two variables for the line. To do so, we need a form for a linear equation in two variables that involves slope and the coordinates of a point.

To write such a form for a linear equation in two variables, we will use a revised form of the slope formula, $m = \frac{y_2 - y_1}{x_2 - x_1}$. Instead of having the formula use two points on the line, we will use the variables x and y and use only the coordinates of one point, (x_1, y_1):

$$m = \frac{y_2 - y_1}{x_2 - x_1}$$

$$m = \frac{y - y_1}{x - x_1}$$

Use *x* and *y* instead of x_2 and y_2.

$$m(x - x_1) = \frac{y - y_1}{x - x_1}(x - x_1) \qquad \text{Multiply both sides by } (x - x_1).$$

$$m(x - x_1) = y - y_1 \qquad \text{Simplify.}$$

$$y - y_1 = m(x - x_1) \qquad \text{Write an equivalent equation.}$$

This form of a linear equation in two variables is called the **point-slope form**.

> *Point-Slope Form for a Linear Equation in Two Variables*
> The point-slope form for a linear equation in two variables is $y - y_1 = m(x - x_1)$, where m is the slope of the line and (x_1, y_1) are coordinates of a point located on the line.

We can use this point-slope form to write a linear equation in two variables given the slope of a line and a point through which the line passes. For example, write a linear equation in two variables for the line that has a slope of 5 and passes through the point (2, 1).

Let $m = 5$, $x_1 = 2$, and $y_1 = 1$. Substitute values for m, x_1, and y_1 for the variables in the point-slope form for an equation and solve for y.

$$y - y_1 = m(x - x_1) \qquad \text{Point-slope form}$$

$$y - 1 = 5(x - 2) \qquad \text{Substitute values.}$$

$$y - 1 = 5x - 10$$

$$y = 5x - 9$$

We need to check our equation. Since the equation is in slope-intercept form, $y = mx + b$, we can see that the slope is 5.

$$y = mx + b$$

$$y = 5x - 9$$

Y1 = 5x − 9

(−47, 47, −31, 31)

Figure 6.12

Graph the equation on your calculator to check that the line passes through the point (2, 1), as shown in Figure 6.12.

EXAMPLE 2 Write a linear equation in two variables for a line with a slope of $\frac{1}{2}$ and containing the point $(-3, 2)$.

Solution

Use the point-slope form for a linear equation. Let $m = \frac{1}{2}$, $x_1 = -3$, and $y_1 = 2$.

$$y - y_1 = m(x - x_1)$$

$$y - 2 = \frac{1}{2}\big[x - (-3)\big]$$

$$y - 2 = \frac{1}{2}(x + 3)$$

$$y - 2 = \frac{1}{2}x + \frac{3}{2}$$

$$y = \frac{1}{2}x + \frac{3}{2} + 2$$

$$y = \frac{1}{2}x + \frac{7}{2}$$

First, examine the equation to check the slope. Second, graph the equation on your calculator to determine that the given point is on the line.

$$y = mx + b$$

$$y = \frac{1}{2}x + \frac{7}{2}$$

By examination, the slope is $\frac{1}{2}$. ∎

$(-47, 47, -31, 31)$

 Experiencing Algebra the Checkup Way

In exercises 1–2, write a linear equation in two variables for a line with the given slope and containing the given ordered pair. Graph the equation to check.

1. $m = 2; (-1, 1)$ **2.** $m = \frac{3}{4}; (2, -3)$

3. If you are given the slope of a line and a point that lies on a line, how can you determine the equation of the line?

---

3   Writing a Linear Equation for Two Given Points

If we know two ordered pairs (x_1, y_1) and (x_2, y_2) on a line and want to write a linear equation in two variables for the line, we must first determine the slope of the line and then use the point-slope form for a linear equation.

To write a linear equation in two variables given two data points:

• Determine the slope of the line (m) using the slope formula.
• Write a linear equation in two variables by substituting the values for m and (x_1, y_1) into the point-slope form of the equation, $y - y_1 = m(x - x_1)$.

For example, write a linear equation in two variables for the line that contains the two points $(1, 3)$ and $(2, 7)$.

First, determine the slope of the line.
Let $x_1 = 1, y_1 = 3, x_2 = 2$, and $y_2 = 7$.

$$m = \frac{y_2 - y_1}{x_2 - x_1}$$

$$m = \frac{7 - 3}{2 - 1}$$

$$m = \frac{4}{1}$$

$$m = 4$$

Now substitute into the point-slope form one of the given ordered pairs, $(1, 3)$, and the slope, 4.

$$y - y_1 = m(x - x_1)$$

$$y - 3 = 4(x - 1)$$ $(x_1, y_1) = (1, 3)$ $m = 4$

$$y - 3 = 4x - 4$$
$$y = 4x - 1$$

It does not matter which ordered-pair coordinates are used. The results are the same.

$$y - y_1 = m(x - x_1)$$
$$y - 7 = 4(x - 2) \qquad (x_1, y_1) = (2, 7) \quad m = 4$$
$$y - 7 = 4x - 8$$
$$y = 4x - 1$$

Graph this equation on your calculator to check that the line contains both points. Enter the equation in Y1, graph, and trace the graph to locate the given points.

$(-47, 47, -31, 31)$

$(-47, 47, -31, 31)$

EXAMPLE 3   Write a linear equation in two variables for a line containing the given ordered pairs. Graph the equation on your calculator to check.

a. $(0, 2)$ and $(4, 5)$ **b.** $(3, 0)$ and $(4, 5)$
c. $(-1, 5)$ and $(-1, -2)$ **d.** $(-1, 4)$ and $(2, 4)$

Solution

a. Determine the slope from the two given points.
Let $x_1 = 0$, $y_1 = 2$, $x_2 = 4$, and $y_2 = 5$.

$$m = \frac{y_2 - y_1}{x_2 - x_1}$$

$$m = \frac{5 - 2}{4 - 0}$$

$$m = \frac{3}{4}$$

The point $(0, 2)$ is the y-intercept. Use the slope-intercept form.

$$y = mx + b$$

$$y = \frac{3}{4}x + 2$$

b. Determine the slope from the two given points.
Let $x_1 = 3$, $y_1 = 0$, $x_2 = 4$, and $y_2 = 5$.

$$m = \frac{y_2 - y_1}{x_2 - x_1}$$

$$m = \frac{5 - 0}{4 - 3}$$

$$m = \frac{5}{1}$$

$$m = 5$$

Use the point-slope form. We will use $(3, 0)$ as the point. Therefore $x_1 = 3$ and $y_1 = 0$.

$$y - y_1 = m(x - x_1)$$
$$y - 0 = 5(x - 3)$$
$$y - 0 = 5x - 15$$
$$y = 5x - 15$$

c. Determine the slope from the two given points.
Let $x_1 = -1$, $y_1 = 5$, $x_2 = -1$, and $y_2 = -2$.

$$m = \frac{y_2 - y_1}{x_2 - x_1}$$

$$m = \frac{-2 - 5}{-1 - (-1)}$$

$$m = \frac{-7}{0}$$

m is undefined.

The line is a vertical line. The constant term of the equation is -1 because both ordered pairs have an x-coordinate of -1. The equation is $x = -1$.

d. Determine the slope from the two given points.
Let $x_1 = -1$, $y_1 = 4$, $x_2 = 2$, and $y_2 = 4$.

$$m = \frac{y_2 - y_1}{x_2 - x_1}$$

$$m = \frac{4 - 4}{2 - (-1)}$$

$$m = \frac{0}{3}$$

$$m = 0$$

The line is a horizontal line. The constant term is 4 because both ordered pairs have a y-coordinate of 4. The equation is $y = 4$.

If we had not noticed the line was horizontal, we could have written the equation using the point-slope form. Use $(2, 4)$ as the point.

$$y - y_1 = m(x - x_1)$$
$$y - 4 = 0(x - 2)$$
$$y - 4 = 0x - 0$$
$$y - 4 = 0$$
$$y = 4$$

To check the equation on your calculator to determine that the given points are on the line graphed, enter the equation in Y1, graph the line, and trace the graph to locate the points. The line in Example 3c is a vertical line and cannot be graphed on your calculator.

a.

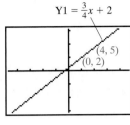

$(-47, 47, -31, 31)$

b.

$(-47, 47, -31, 31)$

d.

$(-47, 47, -31, 31)$

■

✓ Experiencing Algebra the Checkup Way

In exercises 1–4, write a linear equation in two variables for a line containing the given ordered pairs. Graph the equation to check.

1. $(2, 3)$ and $(-1, 1)$

2. $(-1, 3)$ and $(0, -1)$

3. $\left(-2, \dfrac{3}{2}\right)$ and $\left(4, \dfrac{3}{2}\right)$

4. $\left(-\dfrac{5}{2}, \dfrac{9}{2}\right)$ and $\left(-\dfrac{5}{2}, 2\right)$

5. If you are given two points that lie on a line, how can you determine the slope of the line? How can you determine the equation of the line that contains the given points?

---

4   Writing a Linear Equation for a Graph Described by a Second Equation

In some situations we need to write a linear equation in two variables when its graph is described in terms of a second equation. The details may vary from case to case, but the procedure always boils down to finding the slope and a point on the line.

EXAMPLE 4

Write a linear equation in two variables for a line determined by the given information. Graph the equation on your calculator to check.

a. A line passes through the point $(2, -1)$ and has the same slope as the graph of the line for $y = 3x + 4$.

b. A line passes through the point $(-1, -3)$ and is parallel to the graph of the line for $2x + 3y = -2$.

c. A line passes through the point $(3, 5)$ and is perpendicular to the graph of the line for $x - 2y = 1$.

Solution

a. The slope of the given equation, $y = 3x + 4$, is 3 because 3 is the coefficient of the x-term.

Use the point-slope form with $m = 3$, $x_1 = 2$, and $y_1 = -1$.

$$y - y_1 = m(x - x_1)$$
$$y - (-1) = 3(x - 2)$$
$$y + 1 = 3x - 6$$
$$y = 3x - 7$$

b. Parallel lines have equal slopes. The slope of the given line is found by solving the equation for y to obtain the slope-intercept form, $y = mx + b$.

$$2x + 3y = -2$$
$$2x + 3y - 2x = -2 - 2x$$
$$3y = -2 - 2x$$
$$3y = -2x - 2$$
$$\frac{3y}{3} = \frac{-2x - 2}{3}$$
$$y = -\frac{2}{3}x - \frac{2}{3}$$

The slope of the given line is $\frac{-2}{3}$. A parallel line will have the same slope. Use the point-slope form with $\frac{-2}{3}$ as the slope and $(-1, -3)$ as the point.

$$y - y_1 = m(x - x_1)$$
$$y - (-3) = -\frac{2}{3}[x - (-1)]$$
$$y + 3 = -\frac{2}{3}(x + 1)$$
$$y + 3 = -\frac{2}{3}x - \frac{2}{3}$$
$$y + 3 - 3 = -\frac{2}{3}x - \frac{2}{3} - 3$$
$$y = -\frac{2}{3}x - \frac{2}{3} - \frac{9}{3}$$
$$y = -\frac{2}{3}x - \frac{11}{3}$$

c. Perpendicular lines have opposite reciprocal slopes. The slope of the given line is found by solving the equation for y to obtain the slope-intercept form, $y = mx + b$.

$$x - 2y = 1$$
$$x - 2y - x = 1 - x$$
$$-2y = 1 - x$$
$$\frac{-2y}{-2} = \frac{1 - x}{-2}$$
$$y = \frac{-1}{2} + \frac{1}{2}x$$
$$y = \frac{1}{2}x - \frac{1}{2}$$

The slope of the given line is $\frac{1}{2}$. The slope of a line perpendicular to this given line is -2 $\left(\text{opposite reciprocal of } \frac{1}{2}\right)$.

Use the point-slope form. Use -2 as the slope and $(3, 5)$ as the point.

$$y - y_1 = m(x - x_1)$$
$$y - (5) = -2(x - 3)$$
$$y - 5 = -2x + 6$$
$$y - 5 + 5 = -2x + 6 + 5$$
$$y = -2x + 11$$

Check the equation on your calculator to determine that the given points are on the line graphed. Enter the equation in Y1, graph the line, and trace the graph to locate the point given and inspect for other conditions given, as shown in Figures 6.13a, 6.13b, and 6.13c. ∎

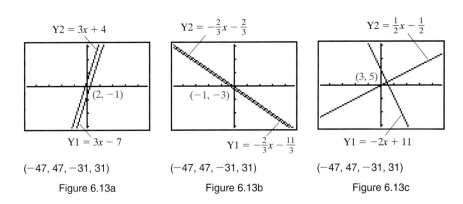

Y2 = 3x + 4	Y2 = $-\frac{2}{3}x - \frac{2}{3}$	Y2 = $\frac{1}{2}x - \frac{1}{2}$
(2, −1)	(−1, −3)	(3, 5)
Y1 = 3x − 7	Y1 = $-\frac{2}{3}x - \frac{11}{3}$	Y1 = −2x + 11
(−47, 47, −31, 31)	(−47, 47, −31, 31)	(−47, 47, −31, 31)
Figure 6.13a	Figure 6.13b	Figure 6.13c

 Experiencing Algebra the Checkup Way

In exercises 1–3, write a linear equation in two variables for a line determined by the given information. Graph the equation on your calculator to check.

1. A line passes through the point $(-1, -2)$ and has the same slope as the line for $y = x + 1$.

2. A line passes through the point $(3, 2)$ and is parallel to the graph of the line for $3x + 2y = 3$.

3. A line passes through the point $(1, -1)$ and is perpendicular to the graph of the line for $2x - 5y = 15$.

4. If you must find the equation of a line that is parallel to the graph of another equation, how can you find the slope to use for your equation?

5. If you must find the equation of a line that is perpendicular to the graph of another equation, how can you find the slope to use for your equation?

5 Modeling the Real World

Many real-world situations involve complicated relationships, described by equations that are difficult to solve. But often you can use a linear equation in two variables to approximate a solution. All you need to graph the linear equation is a point on the line and the slope of the line; then you can use the graph to find an approximate solution to your original problem. This is usually a lot easier to do than solving a more complicated equation, and often the approximate solution is pretty close to the actual solution.

EXAMPLE 5 According to the National Safety Council, accidental deaths have decreased at a rate of 1000 deaths per year since 1990. In 1992, approximately 19,500 deaths were reported to be accidental.

a. Write an equation to determine the number of accidental deaths (y) in terms of x years after 1990.

b. Use the equation to determine the number of accidental deaths in 1990. According to the information given in the report, this number was 21,500. Compare your answer and explain whether this equation is a good representation of the data given.

c. Using the equation, predict the number of accidental deaths expected in 2000.

Solution

a. The slope of the line is the average rate of change, -1000. Since 1992 is 2 years after 1990, we have a data point of $(2, 19{,}500)$.

Use the point-slope form to write an equation.

$$y - y_1 = m(x - x_1)$$
$$y - 19{,}500 = -1000(x - 2)$$
$$y - 19{,}500 = -1000x + 2000$$
$$y = -1000x + 21{,}500$$

b. Substitute $x = 0$ for the year 1990.

$$y = -1000x + 21{,}500$$
$$y = -1000(0) + 21{,}500$$
$$y = 21{,}500$$

There were 21,500 accidental deaths in 1990. This is the same value given in the report. It appears that the equation is a good representation of this data.

c. Substitute $x = 10$ for the year 2000.

$$y = -1000x + 21{,}500$$
$$y = -1000(10) + 21{,}500$$
$$y = -10{,}000 + 21{,}500$$
$$y = 11{,}500$$

The equation predicts 11,500 accidental deaths in 2000. ∎

EXAMPLE 6 Many formulas are found by writing equations to fit given data points. An example of this is the temperature conversion formulas. Two known reference points on the Celsius and Fahrenheit temperature scales are the freezing and boiling points of water. Water freezes at 0 degrees Celsius and 32 degrees Fahrenheit. Water boils at 100 degrees Celsius and 212 degrees Fahrenheit.

a. Write a formula (equation) for the Fahrenheit temperature (F) in terms of the Celsius temperature (C).

b. Using the formula, determine the temperature in degrees Fahrenheit if the temperature is 20 degrees Celsius.

Solution

a. The two data points (C, F) are $(0, 32)$ and $(100, 212)$. First, determine the slope.

$$m = \frac{F_2 - F_1}{C_2 - C_1}$$

$$m = \frac{212 - 32}{100 - 0}$$

$$m = \frac{180}{100}$$

$$m = \frac{9}{5}$$

Use the point-slope form to write an equation. We write the equation in terms of C and F instead of x and y.

$$F - F_1 = m(C - C_1)$$

$$F - 32 = \frac{9}{5}(C - 0)$$

$$F - 32 = \frac{9}{5}C - 0$$

$$F = \frac{9}{5}C + 32$$

b. Substitute 20 for C in the equation just determined.

$$F = \frac{9}{5}C + 32$$

$$F = \frac{9}{5}(20) + 32$$

$$F = 36 + 32$$

$$F = 68$$

The temperature is 68 degrees Fahrenheit when the Celsius reading is 20 degrees. ∎

Application Astronomers discovered the comet Hale-Farewell traveling straight toward the planet Jupiter. They measured its speed as 20,000 km/hr and its position as 3.0×10^7 km from Jupiter. Assuming the comet continues on its course in a straight line at the same speed, write an equation for its motion and determine when it will hit Jupiter.

Discussion

Let $x =$ the travel time (in hours) of the comet
  $y =$ the distance (in kilometers) the comet is from Jupiter

The average rate of change is decreasing at a rate of 20,000 km/hr (the speed). Therefore, $m = -20{,}000$ or -2.0×10^4.
  At the time of 0 hours, the comet's distance from Jupiter is 3.0×10^7 km. This gives us a data point of $(0, 3.0 \times 10^7)$. Therefore, $b = 3.0 \times 10^7$.

$$y = mx + b \qquad \text{Slope-intercept form}$$

$$y = (-2.0 \times 10^4)x + (3.0 \times 10^7) \qquad \text{Substitute values for } m \text{ and } b.$$

The comet will hit Jupiter when $y = 0$ because its distance from Jupiter, y, is 0 km. Therefore, substitute 0 for y and solve for x. (This point is the x-intercept.)

$$y = (-2.0 \times 10^4)x + (3.0 \times 10^7)$$
$$0 = (-2.0 \times 10^4)x + (3.0 \times 10^7)$$
$$0 + (2.0 \times 10^4)x = (-2.0 \times 10^4)x + (3.0 \times 10^7) + (2.0 \times 10^4)$$
$$(2.0 \times 10^4)x = (3.0 \times 10^7)$$
$$\frac{(2.0 \times 10^4)x}{2.0 \times 10^4} = \frac{3.0 \times 10^7}{2.0 \times 10^4}$$
$$x = 1.5 \times 10^3$$
$$x = 1500$$

The comet will hit Jupiter in 1500 hours.

Comet P/Shoemaker-Levy 9 (1993e)

"String of Pearls"

600,000 MILES	100,000 MILES	40,000 MILES
Ground Based	HST View	HST View
Wide Angle View	Region Containing the Nuclei	Closeup Near Brightest Nucleus

Astronomers actually did a calculation like this for Comet Shoemaker-Levy, which slammed into Jupiter on July 16, 1994. Of course, the actual calculation was more complicated because the comet wasn't moving at a constant speed or in a straight line, but even so, astronomers were able to pinpoint the time of collision to within minutes for each part of the "string-of-pearls" comet. For example, on July 12, a table of anticipated collision times was published in the *New York Times*. The predicted time for the largest piece, Fragment G, was 3:24 A.M. Eastern Time. On July 19, the *New York Times* reported that the time of impact for Fragment G was 3:28 A.M. Eastern Time, only 4 minutes off the predicted time. ∎

Experiencing Algebra the Checkup Way

1. In 1992, the accidental death rate was 32.5 deaths per 100,000 population. In 1912, the rate was 82.5 per 100,000 population. Let x represent the number of years since 1900, and let y represent the accidental death rate per 100,000 population.

a. Using the two points (12, 82.5) and (92, 32.5), find the slope of the line connecting these two points.

b. Write an equation to determine the number of accidental deaths per 100,000 population after 1900. Graph the equation using a window of (0, 94, 10, 0, 124, 20, 1).

c. Use the equation to predict the number of accidental deaths per 100,000 population in 1991. The actual number recorded was 34.6 deaths per 100,000 population. Was your prediction close?

d. What would this equation predict as the rate of accidental deaths for 1999?

2. If we reverse the variables in the temperature example (Example 5), the two data points (F, C) will become (32, 0) and (212, 100).

a. Determine the new slope of the relation between F and C.

b. Use the point-slope form to write a new equation for C in terms of F.

c. Using the formula, find the Celsius temperature if the temperature is 75 degrees Fahrenheit.

PROBLEM SET 6.5

Experiencing Algebra the Exercise Way

Write a linear equation for each graph.

1.

2.

3.

4.

$(4\frac{1}{2}, 0)$

5.

6.

$(0, 3\frac{1}{3})$

7.

$(0, -\frac{3}{2})$

8.

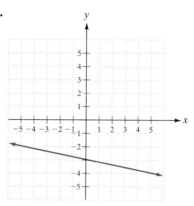

Write a linear equation for the given information.

9. $m = -\dfrac{2}{5}, b = 4$

10. $m = -\dfrac{1}{7}, b = -9$

11. $m = \dfrac{5}{9}, b = 0$

12. $m = \dfrac{1}{7}, b = -1$

13. $m = 4, b = -\dfrac{3}{4}$

14. $m = 11, b = \dfrac{1}{2}$

15. $m = -4.1, b = 0.5$

16. $m = -6.2, b = -2.2$

17. $m = 0, b = -33$

18. $m = -4, b = 0$

Write a linear equation in two variables for a line with the given slope and containing the given ordered pair. Graph the equation to check.

19. $m = \dfrac{2}{3}, (3, -3)$

20. $m = -2, (4, 0)$

21. $m = -3, (0, 4)$

22. $m = \dfrac{4}{3}, (-6, -3)$

23. $m = -1.7, (3, -1.5)$

24. $m = 1.4, (1.5, -1.2)$

Write a linear equation for a line containing the given ordered pairs. Graph the equation to check.

25. $(-1, 1)$ and $(1, -2)$

26. $(8, 6)$ and $(1, 6)$

27. $(-1, -2)$ and $(-1, 5)$

28. $(1, 6)$ and $(2, 1)$

29. $(-1, 1)$ and $(-2, -1)$

30. $(-3, 2)$ and $(4, 4)$

31. $(-2, 2)$ and $(4, 2)$

32. $(2, 9)$ and $(2, 1)$

33. $\left(4\dfrac{1}{2}, 5\dfrac{1}{4}\right)$ and $(1, 4)$

34. $\left(-2, -1\dfrac{1}{3}\right)$ and $\left(2\dfrac{1}{2}, 1\right)$

35. $\left(-1\dfrac{1}{3}, 2\right)$ and $(0, 0)$

36. $\left(2\dfrac{1}{2}, 5\dfrac{1}{2}\right)$ and $\left(3\dfrac{1}{2}, 1\right)$

37. $(0.5, 0)$ and $(-0.8, 4.2)$

38. $(-4, -1)$ and $(-5.1, -4.5)$

39. $(2.4, 2.8)$ and $(-2.6, -2.2)$

40. $(1, 6)$ and $(1.5, -3.5)$

In exercises 41–48, write a linear equation for a line determined by the given information. Graph the equation to check.

41. A line passes through the point $(8, 7)$ and has the same slope as the line for $3x - 8y = 32$.

42. A line passes through the point $(0, 0)$ and has the same slope as the line for $5x + 3y = 15$.

43. A line passes through the point $\left(\frac{4}{9}, -\frac{5}{6}\right)$ and is parallel to the graph for $y = 3x - 10$.

44. A line, parallel to the graph for $y = -0.8x + 2.4$, passes through the point $(9, -3)$.

45. A line passes through the point $(3.6, 5.8)$ and is perpendicular to the line for $y = 3x + 12$.

46. A line passes through the point $(-3.6, 1.8)$ and is perpendicular to the graph for $y = -6x$.

47. A line passes through the point $(15, -30)$ and is perpendicular to the graph for $y = 5x - 1$.

48. A line passes through the point $(0, 0)$ and is perpendicular to the graph for $y = \frac{5}{7}x + 6$.

49. According to the Statistical Abstract of the United States, in 1965, 42.4 percent of adults (18 years and older) were smokers. In 1990, this percentage dropped to 25.5 percent. Let x represent the number of years after 1965, and let y represent the percent of adult smokers.

    a. Using the points $(0, 42.4)$ and $(25, 25.5)$, find the slope of the line connecting these two points.

    b. Write an equation to predict the percentage of adults who are smokers x years after 1965. Graph the equation.

    c. What would you predict the percentage to be of adults who smoked in 1988? The reported percentage was 28.1 percent. Is your prediction close?

    d. What does the equation predict for the percentage of adults who smoke in the year 2005?

    e. In what year would the predicted percentage become close to 0? Is this a realistic prediction? Explain.

50. The Statistical Abstract of the United States stated that in 1965, 51.9 percent of adult males were smokers. In 1990, this percentage dropped to 28.4 percent. Let x represent the years after 1965, and let y represent the percentage of adult male smokers.

    a. Find the slope of the line connecting the two points $(0, 51.9)$ and $(25, 28.4)$.

    b. Write an equation to predict the percentage of adult males who are smokers x years after 1965, and graph the equation.

    c. Predict the percentage of adult males who smoked in 1985. Compare this to the reported percentage of 32.6%. Did the equation do well to predict this value?

    d. What does the equation predict will be the percentage of adult male smokers in the year 2005?

    e. In what year would the percentage become close to 0? Is this a realistic prediction? Explain.

51. In scientific work, the Kelvin temperature scale measures temperatures from absolute zero, which is the lowest possible temperature. Temperatures on this scale have a linear relationship with the Celsius scale. Given the points (C, K) of $(0, 273)$ and $(-10, 263)$, use the slope-intercept form to write the relationship between the two scales. What Kelvin temperature corresponds to 100°C?

52. The Rankine temperature scale is used in engineering practice. Temperatures on this scale have a linear relationship with the Fahrenheit scale. Given the points (F, R) of $(32, 492)$ and $(180, 640)$, use the point-slope form to determine the relationship between the two scales. What Rankine temperature corresponds to 75°F?

The tables in exercises 53 and 54 were reported to be generated from linear equations. Use the data in the tables to find the equations, and then verify the data points.

53.

x	1.2	1.6	2.0	2.4	2.8
y	15.92	16.96	18.00	19.04	20.08

54.

x	1.0	1.5	2.0	2.5	3.0
y	17.8	15.9	14.0	12.1	10.2

55. A consumer article reported that a car weighing 2500 pounds averages 40 miles per gallon of gasoline, while a car weighing 3500 pounds averages 35 miles per gallon. Write a linear equation relating the gas mileage (y) to the weight of the car (x).

56. A consumer article reported that a car weighing 5000 pounds averages 15 miles per gallon of gasoline, while a car weighing 4500 pounds averages 19 miles per gallon. Write a linear equation relating the gas mileage to the weight of the car. How does this compare with the result for exercise 55? Can you explain any differences?

57. In one city, a company ran radio advertisements 6 times per week and had sales of 5000 units. In another city, they ran the radio advertisements 15 times per week and had sales of 14,000 units. Write a linear equation that relates sales (y) to the number of times the advertisements were run each week (x). What would you predict the sales would be if the advertisements were run 10 times per week?

58. A study of aging found that people who were 65 years old tended to live an additional 16.5 years on the average. Persons who were 79 years old tended to live an average of 8.4 years longer. Write a linear equation that relates the average additional years of life (y) to a person's age (x). What would you predict is the remaining life span for a 70-year-old person?

59. At New Futures Community College, enrollment has increased at a rate of 120 students per year. In 1990, the enrollment of the college was 5470 students. Write a linear equation to determine the enrollment of the college x years after 1990. Use the equation to determine the enrollment of the college in 1996. If the actual enrollment in 1996 was 6225, did the equation provide a good estimate of this number? If the increase continues, use the equation to predict what the enrollment should be in the year 2000.

60. At New Endeavors Computer Systems, business has been declining at a rate of $250,000 per year. The company's business total for 1993 was $4,375,000. Write a linear equation to determine the amount of business the company has x years after 1990. Use the equation to determine the amount of business in 1990. How does this compare with the actual amount of $5,065,000? If the decline continues, use the equation to predict what the amount of business will be in the year 2000.

 Experiencing Algebra the Calculator Way

Graphing calculators have statistical procedures that can be used to find the equation of a line passing through two points. While this is not the intent of the procedures, they can be used to write such an equation. As an example, suppose you wish to find the equation of the line that passes through the points (3, 55) and (1, 10).

a. Clear any data from the lists L1 and L2, which is where the coordinate pairs will be stored:

| STAT | 4 | 2nd | L1 | , | 2nd | L2 | ENTER |

```
ClrList L₁,L₂
            Done
```

b. Store the coordinate pairs in your calculator, using L1 for the x-coordinate and L2 for the y-coordinate:

| STAT | 1 |

Use the arrow keys to move to the L1 column.

c. Calculate the "linear regression," which will provide the equation:

| STAT | ▶ | 4 | 2nd | L1 | , | 2nd | L2 | ENTER |

```
LinReg(ax+b) L1,
L2
```

This instruction directs the calculator to find the *x*-coordinates in list L1 and the *y*-coordinates in list L2 and to find the equation. When the ENTER command is keyed, the calculator displays the result.

```
LinReg
y=ax+b
a=22.5
b=-12.5
```

d. The equation for the line passing through the two points is given by

$$y = 22.5x - 12.5$$

Use this method to find the equations of the lines passing through the following pairs of points. Check the solutions by graphing or by substituting the coordinate pairs into the equations.

1. $(12, 925)$ and $(72, 4225)$ **2.** $(16, -351)$ and $(40, 417)$ **3.** $(0, 6.4)$ and $(36.4, 103.59)$

4. $\left(1, \dfrac{17}{4}\right)$ and $\left(3, \dfrac{57}{4}\right)$ **5.** $(-5, 21)$ and $(-9, 7)$ **6.** $(16, -2)$ and $(7, 4)$

Experiencing Algebra the Group Way

Each member of the group should complete exercises 1 and 2. Discuss the best methods for finding the equations and for completing the tables. After you have shared your ideas, take the best of these and individually complete exercise 3.

1. It costs $75 to rent a car for one day and travel 100 miles. It costs $65 to rent the same car for one day and travel 50 miles. Write a linear equation to fit the data given. Use the linear equation to complete the following table to be used by clerks at the rental company.

Number of Miles	Cost
10	
20	
30	
40	
50	$65.00
60	
70	
80	
90	
100	$75.00

2. A garden tiller costs $66.00 to rent for 8 hours and $49.50 to rent for 5 hours. Write a linear equation to fit the data given. Use the linear equation to complete the following table to be used by clerks at the rental company.

Number of Hours	Cost
1	
2	
3	
4	
5	$49.50
6	
7	
8	$66.00
9	
10	

3. Search for a reference containing data that might be used to establish a linear relationship. You might look in popular news sources such as *USA Today*, *Newsweek*, *Time*, and *Money* magazine, or in textbooks devoted to the study of business, science, and so on. Record the exact data as they are presented. From the data, select two extreme points that could be used to find a linear equation in two variables using the point-slope form. Then select an intermediate point in the data and check to see how well your equation predicts the point. Finally, select a point outside the data and see if you can use your equation to predict what will happen there.

Experiencing Algebra the Write Way

In the examples and exercises in this section, you have seen several applications in which a linear equation has been derived to fit a pair of points observed in a set of data. Then the linear equation was used to estimate values for the dependent variable for other choices of the independent variable. Think of when this might be an appropriate method to follow to predict values of *y* for given values of *x*. Then think of situations where using such a linear equation might not be appropriate. Also think of limitations that you might want to place on using such a linear model. Write a short summary of precautions that you might want to take when using these methods. Be as specific as you can in describing problems that might occur.

CHAPTER 6 | Summary

After completing this chapter, you should be able to define in your own words the following key terms and rules.

Terms
linear equation in two variables
linear function
solution
rise
run
slope
grade
slope-intercept form
average rate of change
coinciding
parallel

intersecting
perpendicular
break-even point
point-slope form

Rules
Standard form for a linear equation in two variables
Solution of a linear equation in two variables
Graphs with one intercept
Slope of a line

Slope of a line through two given points
Slope of a line given a linear equation
Two special cases of the slope of a line given a linear equation
Slope-intercept form for a linear equation in two variables
Coinciding lines
Parallel lines
Intersecting lines
Intersecting and perpendicular lines
Point-slope form for a linear equation in two variables

CHAPTER 6 | Review

Reflections

1. Consider first a linear equation in one variable, $ax + b = c$, and then a linear equation in two variables, $ax + by = c$. How do the solutions for the two types of equations differ?

2. How can you determine algebraically the *x*-intercept and the *y*-intercept of the graph of a linear equation?

3. If the graph of a linear equation is a horizontal line, what can you say about its intercepts? If the graph of a linear equation is a vertical line, what can you say about its intercepts?

4. Explain how to graph a linear equation in two variables using the intercept method.

5. What does the slope of a line measure? How can you determine the slope of a line?

6. Describe what the graph of a linear equation in two variables will look like if
   a. the slope of the line is positive,
   b. the slope of the line is negative,
   c. the slope of the line is 0,
   d. the slope of the line is undefined.

7. How would you graph a linear equation in two variables using the slope-intercept method?

8. What can you say about the slopes of two lines if
   a. the lines are parallel,
   b. the lines are intersecting,
   c. the lines are perpendicular,
   d. the lines are coinciding?

9. How can you write an equation for a line if it is described by
   a. its slope and *y*-intercept, **b.** its slope and a point on the line,
   c. two points on the line?

6.1

Identify each equation as linear or nonlinear. Express each linear equation in standard form.

1. $y = 0.6x + 2.3$ **2.** $y = 4x^2 - 2$ **3.** $3x - 6y + 12 = 0$
4. $5x - 3y + 7 = x - y + 9$ **5.** $3x^2 + y = 1$ **6.** $5y - 12 = 7 - y$

Determine whether each ordered pair is a solution for the given equation.

7. $f(x) = 10x - 42; (4, -2)$ **8.** $3x - 2y = 6; (1, -1)$
9. $\dfrac{3}{5}x - \dfrac{8}{9}y = 1; (15, 18)$ **10.** $45x - 14y = 31; \left(\dfrac{5}{12}, -\dfrac{7}{8}\right)$

Determine three solutions for each equation using a table of values.

11. $12x + 6y = 48$ **12.** $y = \dfrac{8}{13}x - 7$ **13.** $y = -9$

Graph the equation. Determine three solutions from the graph.

14. $9x - y = 12$ **15.** $y = -\dfrac{4}{3}x + 2$
16. $5y - 2 = y - 10$ **17.** $2x + 16 = x + 18$

18. Noriko translates Japanese texts into English as a consultant to a firm that does business in Japan. She is paid $85 to translate 10 pages of text on one job, and $160 to translate 20 pages of text on another job.
    a. Let *x* represent the number of pages translated on a particular job, and let *y* represent her pay for the job. Graph a representation of the information.
    b. Assume the information is from a linear relation, and connect the points. From the graph, how much will Noriko receive for a job that is 30 pages long?

19. Lloyd is hired at a hair salon at $20 per day plus $9 for each haircut. Let *x* represent the number of haircuts per day, and let *y* represent Lloyd's total daily earnings. Then $y = 20 + 9x$.

    a. How much would Lloyd earn if he cut the hair of 10 people in a day?
    b. Should Lloyd be paid $145 for cutting hair for 15 people in a day?
    c. If Lloyd had a day with no customers, how much would he earn?

6.2

Determine the x-intercept and the y-intercept of each graph of each linear equation. Check using your calculator.

20. $8x + 12y = -24$ **21.** $y = \dfrac{2}{5}x + 4$

Solve each equation for y to determine the y-intercept.

22. $9x - 3y = -12$ **23.** $6x + 2y = x$

Graph each equation using the intercept method. Label the points.

24. $7x + 11y = 77$ **25.** $-x - y = 2$ **26.** $7.4x + 14.8y = 29.6$

27. Kari was awarded a scholarship for a year of college. The amount awarded was $5200 to be paid out as $100 weekly. Let x represent the number of weeks payment has been made, and let y represent the balance of the scholarship account.

   a. Write a linear equation in two variables for the balance of the account after x weeks of payments.

   b. Without graphing, determine the intercepts for a graph of the equation. Interpret what the intercepts represent.

   c. Graph the equation using the intercept method.

   d. From the graph, determine how much money remains in the account after 32 weeks of payments.

28. A slot machine requires $1.00 in quarters for each play. It pays off a jackpot of $50.00 every 100 plays, on the average, so that the average payoff per play is $0.50. Bryon has $50.00 to play. Let x represent the number of times he plays the machine, and let y represent the amount of money he has remaining, assuming he wins an average of $0.50 per play.

   a. Write a linear equation in two variables for the balance of money Bryon has after x plays.

   b. Without graphing, determine the intercepts for a graph of the equation. Interpret what the intercepts represent.

   c. Graph the equation using the intercept method.

   d. From the graph, determine how much money Bryon has after playing the machine 60 times.

6.3

Determine graphically the slope of each line.

29.

30.

31.

32.

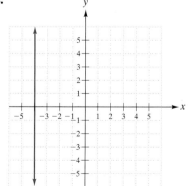

Determine numerically the slope of the line containing the given points.

33. $(-5, -3)$ and $(1, 0)$ **34.** $(-7, 7)$ and $(-4, 2)$ **35.** $(4, -3)$ and $(10, -3)$ **36.** $(4, -3)$ and $(4, 3)$

Determine by inspection the slope and the y-intercept of the line for the given equation.

37. $y = 23x - 51$ **38.** $y = -3.05x + 2.97$

39. $6x + 5y = 12$ **40.** $4(y - 2) = 3(2y - 1) + 4$

Graph a line that contains the given point and has the given slope.

41. $(-2, 3); m = \dfrac{5}{9}$ **42.** $(3, -2); m = 3$

43. $(-2, -2); m = 0$ **44.** $(-2, -2); m$ is undefined.

Graph each equation using the slope-intercept method. Label the points.

45. $y = -\dfrac{5}{3}x + 2$ **46.** $3x + 2y = 12$ **47.** $m(x) = \dfrac{5}{8}x$ **48.** $y = -4$

49. Kristi decided to see if the amount of time studying for an algebra test really made a difference. She asked 10 of her classmates to record the amount of time they spent studying for the last exam. The study time and the exam grades are recorded below.

Hours	2	3	4	2	2.5	1	0	3.5	2.5	3.5
Grade	82	98	100	80	92	74	62	100	88	94

  a. Use the lowest time and the highest time to find the slope of the line connecting the two coordinate pairs, where x is the hours studied and y is the grade.

  b. Write an equation to predict a student's grade on the exam in terms of the hours studied.

  c. Graph the equation using a window of $(0, 9.4, 1, 0, 110, 10, 1)$. Did the equation predict closely the grade earned by the student who studied 3 hours? How about the two students who studied 2 hours?

  d. What grade would you predict for a student who studied 1.5 hours?

6.4

Determine by inspection whether the graphs of each pair of equations are coinciding lines, parallel lines, only intersecting lines, or both intersecting and perpendicular lines. Check by graphing.

50. $y = 2x + 6$
$3y - x = 15$

51. $2y - 2x = y + 3x + 2$
$5x - y = -2$

52. $4x - 20 = 0$
$2x + 3 = x + 4$

53. $2x + y = 4$
$y = -2(x + 2)$

54. $3(y + 2) = 2(y + 4)$
$2(x - 2) = 0$

55. $5y - 4(y + 3) = -10$
$y - 1 = -2(x - 1)$

56. $2x - 3y = -9$
$3x + 2y = 6$

57. $y = x + 7$
$y = -x + 7$

58. J. R. decides to go into business buying and selling used graphing calculators to students. He spends $25 having posters printed to hang on student bulletin boards and pays $35 to place an ad in the student newspaper. He will buy used calculators at $30 each. Since he is too busy to sell the calculators, he pays Brandon a flat fee of $25 to help him, with the promise of paying him $5 for each calculator he sells.

  a. Let x represent the number of calculators bought and resold, and let y represent the cost of selling calculators. Write a linear equation for the total cost of selling x calculators.

  b. If Brandon sells the calculators at $35 each, write a linear equation for the total revenue of selling x calculators.

  c. Graph the two equations and find the break-even point, if there is one, where the revenue equals the cost for selling x calculators.

d. If Brandon sells the calculators at $60 each, write a new linear equation for the total revenue of selling x calculators.

e. Graph the original cost function and the new revenue function and determine the new break-even point, if there is one.

f. What would you recommend that J. R. do?

6.5
59. Write a linear equation for the graph.

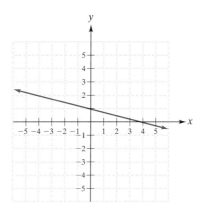

Write an equation for a line that satisfies each of the following conditions.

60. The line has a y-intercept of $(0, 3)$ and a slope of -2.
61. The line passes through $(0, -2)$ with a slope of $\frac{3}{5}$.
62. The line is horizontal with a y-intercept of $(0, -3.5)$.
63. The line is vertical with an x-intercept of $(2.6, 0)$.
64. The line has a slope of -5 and passes through $(2, -3)$.
65. The line passes through the points $(9, 5)$ and $(-2, 2)$.
66. The line passes through $(4, 6)$ and has a slope of $\frac{1}{3}$.
67. The line passes through $(1, 1)$ and is parallel to the graph for $y = 4x + 5$.
68. The line passes through $(2, 4)$ and is perpendicular to the graph for $y = 2x - 1$.
69. Holly Carton researched the sales of her latest record for the 10 weeks after its release. She found the sales (measured in thousands of records sold) for each week to be given by the following table.

Week	1	2	3	4	5	6	7	8	9	10
Records Sold	12	15	19	26	28	29	30	30	29	28

a. Use the information for week 2 and week 8 to find a linear equation relating sales to the number of weeks since release. The two coordinate pairs would be $(2, 15)$ and $(8, 30)$.

b. What would the equation predict sales to be for week 5? Is this close to the actual figure of 28?

CHAPTER 6 | **Mixed Review**

Graph each linear equation using a table of values. Label the points.

1. $3(y - 5) = y + 7$ **2.** $14x + 7y = 7$ **3.** $y = -\dfrac{7}{5}x - 10$

Graph a line containing the given point with the given slope.

4. $(2, 6)$; $m = 0$

5. $(2, 6)$; m is undefined

6. $(1, -4)$; $m = -2$

7. $(0, 3)$; $m = \dfrac{2}{7}$

Graph each equation using the slope-intercept method. Label the points.

8. $y = \dfrac{-3}{8} x$

9. $y = 7$

10. $5x - 4y = 12$

Graph each equation using the intercept method. Label the points.

11. $15.5x + 21.7y = 108.5$

12. $12x - 24y = -48$

13. $-x + y = -6$

Determine by inspection whether the graphs of each pair of linear equations are coinciding lines, parallel lines, only intersecting lines, or both intersecting and perpendicular lines.

14. $2x - 3 = 1$
$4x - 3y = 6$

15. $5x - 4y = 8$
$4x - 5y = -15$

16. $y = 5(x - 1)$
$2(x - 1) = 7x - y + 3$

17. $5(x + 1) = 15$
$3y + 1 = 10$

18. $y = -2x + 3$
$2(x + y) = y + 3$

19. $y = x + 3$
$y = -x - 4$

20. $5y = 20$
$2(y + 3) = -2$

Determine three solutions for each equation using a table of values.

21. $y = 8$

22. $8x - 9y = -72$

23. $t(x) = \dfrac{9}{11} x - 8$

Identify each equation as linear or nonlinear. Express each linear equation in standard form.

24. $y = x$

25. $y = 2x^2 - 8$

26. $y = 1.3x - 0.5$

27. $y = 15x$

28. $8y - 5x = 21$

29. $2x + 3y - 1 = y^2 + x$

Determine whether each ordered pair is a solution for the given linear equation.

30. $\dfrac{2}{3} x + \dfrac{3}{4} y = 2$; $(12, -8)$

31. $22x - 5y = 17$; $\left(\dfrac{7}{12}, -\dfrac{5}{6} \right)$

32. $u(x) = -8x + 2$; $(2, -14)$

33. $7x + 8y = 8$; $(0, -3)$

34. $x = -8$; $(-8, -2)$

35. $v(x) = 12$; $(12, -2)$

Determine by inspection the slope and the y-intercept of the line for each linear equation.

36. $x + 4(x - 2) = 2$

37. $x - 3(y + 2) = 4(x + 1) - y$

38. $12x - 4y = 8$

39. $2y - 6 = 4(y - 2) + 2$

40. $y = 13x - 15$

41. $y = -5.03x + 7.92$

Determine numerically the slope of the line containing the given points.

42. $(5, 5)$ and $(8, 5)$

43. $(-3, -3)$ and $(-3, 3)$

44. $(-4, 4)$ and $(-1, -5)$

45. $\left(-\dfrac{2}{5}, \dfrac{4}{7} \right)$ and $\left(-\dfrac{4}{7}, \dfrac{1}{5} \right)$

In exercises 46–54, write an equation for a line that satisfies the following conditions.

46. The line contains the points $(4, -2)$ and $(5, 2)$.

47. The line passes through $(-1, -1)$ and has a slope of $-\frac{1}{4}$.

48. The line passes through $(0, 5)$ with a slope of $-\frac{2}{3}$.

49. The line is vertical with an x-intercept of $(4.1, 0)$.

50. The line passes through $(-2, -2)$ and is parallel to the line for $y = -3x + 6$.

51. The line is horizontal with a y-intercept of $(0, 8)$.

52. The line has a slope of 4 and passes through the point $(1.2, 8)$.

53. The line has a y-intercept of $(0, -2)$ and a slope of 3.

54. The line passes through $(0, 2)$ and is perpendicular to the line for $y = \frac{-1}{2}x - 1$.

55. Ms. Burwell wanted to study the relation between her students' pre-final averages and their scores on the final exam. She took a sample of eight students from her class and recorded the following scores.

Pre-Final	76	94	79	80	87	91	50	72
Final	68	99	81	78	88	86	57	67

    a. Use the information from the lowest pre-final and the highest pre-final scores to find a linear equation relating final (y) to pre-final (x) scores. The two coordinate pairs would be $(50, 57)$ and $(94, 99)$.

    b. What would the equation predict the final score to be for a student whose pre-final score was 80? Is this close to the actual final score for the student who had a pre-final score of 80?

56. Frank earned school money as a freelance umpire for intramural baseball games. He was paid \$24 for a game that lasted 7 innings. For another game that went 9 innings, he was paid \$28. Denote his pay as y and the number of innings he worked as x.

    a. Graph these two coordinate pairs.

    b. Assume the information is from a linear relation, and connect the points. How much would Frank receive for a game that lasted 8 innings? How much for a game that lasted 10 innings?

57. A storage tank contains 180 gallons of liquid. At the start of a production run, liquid is being added to the tank at a rate of 10 gallons per hour. At the same time, liquid is being drained from the tank and bottled at the rate of 15 gallons per hour. Let y represent the amount of liquid in the tank, and let x represent the number of hours of production.

    a. Write a linear equation in two variables for the amount of liquid in the tank after x hours of production.

    b. Without graphing, determine the intercepts for a graph of the equation. Interpret what the intercepts represent.

    c. Graph the equation using the intercept method.

    d. From the graph, determine how much liquid remains in the tank after 16 hours of production.

58. A sports trainer charges his clients \$15 per visit plus \$25 per hour to come to their homes and conduct fitness training sessions.

    a. Let x represent the number of hours for the training session, and let y represent the total charge for the session. Write an equation to represent his total charge for a session.

    b. How much would the trainer earn if he trained for 2 hours?

    c. How much would he earn for a session that lasted $1\frac{1}{2}$ hours?

59. Shannon set up a business to sell hair bows at a kiosk in the mall during the holiday season. The cost of renting the kiosk is \$75.00 per week. She had to purchase materials and supplies, which cost \$150.00. In addition, the materials used to make each hair bow cost her \$0.75 each.

    a. Write a linear equation to determine her total cost, $c(x)$, in terms of the number of hair bows, x, she makes and sells during the week.

    b. If she sells the hair bows for \$2.00 each, write a linear equation to represent her revenue, $r(x)$, for selling x bows during the week.

    c. Graph the two equations and find the break-even point, if there is one, where revenue equals cost.

    d. Will she make a profit if she sells 150 hair bows during the week? What if she sells 200 hair bows? What is the minimum number of hair bows she must sell to avoid a loss?

60. National Motors Incorporated advertises that their all-terrain vehicle, the Conqueror, can climb a hill which rises 60 feet vertically over a horizontal distance of 125 feet. Find the grade of the hill.

CHAPTER 6	Test

Test-Taking Tips

Rehearse for a test just as you would rehearse for a speech in speech class. By this, we mean practice, practice, practice. If you have practice tests available, you should always study them. Aim for 100% understanding. If you don't understand an exercise, get help immediately. Start this practice at least a week before the test, and work on it each day for a reasonable length of time. If you find you are weak on certain topics, find similar exercises to practice. Make index card notes summarizing examples that you can review each day. These are like the flash cards that helped you when you were a youngster. Rehearsing moves information from your short-term memory to your long-term memory. It is the only way you can achieve the kind of recall you will need to reach your goal of 100% mastery. Remember, if you don't set this goal, you have no incentive to reach it!

Determine whether each ordered pair is a solution of the given linear equation.

1. $7x = 8(y - 3); (8, 10)$ **2.** $x - 8y = 16; (-8, -2)$

Identify each equation as linear or nonlinear.

3. $5x - 7y = 2(x + 1) - 3$ **4.** $y = \dfrac{11}{12}x - 5$ **5.** $y^2 - 16 = 0$ **6.** $7x + 2y = 3x^2 + 3$

Graph the equation using a table of values. Label the points.

7. $2x - 8y = 0$

Graph using the intercept method. Label the points.

8. $12x + 15y = 60$

Graph using the slope-intercept method. Label the points.

9. $g(x) = 3x - 5$

Determine the slope of the line containing the two points.

10. $(0, -1)$ and $(-1, -1)$ **11.** $(4.8, 0.6)$ and $(-1.5, 2.4)$ **12.** $(-3, -4)$ and $(1, 0)$ **13.** $(-2, 2)$ and $(-2, 8)$

Determine whether the graphs of each pair of equations are coinciding lines, parallel lines, only intersecting lines, or both intersecting and perpendicular lines.

14. $y = -8x + 1$
$y = x - 8$

15. $9(y - 2) + 2x = 7x$
$4x = 9(y + 4) - x$

16. $3x - y = 2$
$y - x = 2(x - 1)$

17. $5y - 2 = 3y + 2$
$3x = 2(x + 2)$

Determine the slope and the y-intercept of the graph of each linear equation.

18. $4y = 3x + 12$ **19.** $7x + 7y = 21$

Write an equation for a line that satisfies each of the following conditions.

20. A line passes through (2, 1) and is perpendicular to the graph for $y = \frac{3}{5}x$.

21. A line passes through (0, 7) with a slope of 9.

22. A line passes through (−1, 2) with a slope of 6.

23. A line passes through (2, 3) and (−4, 1).

24. Marty is paying off a $1450 loan at the rate of $150 per month. Write a linear equation for his balance, *y*, in terms of the number of payments, *x*, he has made. Graph the equation. Find the first value of *x* for which his loan drops below $1000. Explain what this value represents.

25 What is the difference between graphing a linear equation by the intercept method and graphing it by the slope-intercept method?

7

Systems of Linear Equations in Two Variables

Now we have seen several methods for solving linear equations in two variables. But many situations in mathematics require more than one equation to describe the relation between two variables. In this chapter we examine the methods for solving systems of linear equations in two variables. We will confine ourselves to systems of two equations, though the same methods can be used for systems of three, four, or more linear equations. These methods provide graphical solutions and algebraic solutions, just as for single linear equations. Under the category of algebraic solutions, we will study two methods: substitution and elimination. Then we will apply these methods to solving several types of real-world problems.

One of the real-world problems we've all encountered is how to go about saving money. It seems as if there are dozens of different kinds of savings accounts available today, offering different interest rates, different minimum amounts of deposit, and different minimum times for maintaining a balance. In this chapter we will look at some of these different types of accounts and use systems of linear equations in two variables to see how we can plan investments to achieve particular financial goals. We do not expect this course to make you wealthy, unfortunately; but the material in this chapter will help you understand how to arrive at solutions to more complex mathematical problems.

7.1 Solving Systems of Equations Graphically

Objectives

1 Determine whether a given ordered pair is a solution of a system of linear equations.

2 Solve systems of linear equations graphically.

3 Model real-world situations using systems of linear equations and solve graphically.

Application

Gil Bates, Chairman of MuchoSoft Corp., finds some loose change in his pocket totaling $20,000. He decides to invest it. He finds that the annual interest rate on a regular savings account is 2.75%. However, he can get a sterling account with an annual interest rate of 4% if he keeps a minimum balance of $2500. Gil wants to earn $750 in simple interest for 1 year, and he wants to keep at least $2000 in a regular account so he can access it easily. How much money should Gil deposit in each account in order to meet his goals?

After completing this section, we will discuss this application further. See page 507.

---

1 Determining a Solution of a System of Linear Equations

In Chapter 6 we discussed how to solve a linear equation in two variables. But it often happens that the relationships in a situation are described by more than one equation at a time. What do we do then? How do we solve several equations at one time? The first step is to define the situation mathematically.

> *System of Linear Equations in Two Variables*
> A system of linear equations is a set of more than one linear equation that is to be solved at the same time.

For example, a system of linear equations in two variables may be

$$2x - y = 4$$
$$x + y = 2.$$

To determine a solution of a system of linear equations in two variables, we need to find an ordered pair that satisfies *all* equations in the system—that is, when the ordered-pair coordinates are substituted into all equations, the resulting equations are true.

> *Solution of a System of Linear Equations*
> An ordered pair is a solution of a system of linear equations if it is a solution of every equation in the system.

To determine that an ordered pair is a solution of a system of linear equations in two variables, substitute the coordinates of the ordered pair into each equation. If all the resulting equations are true, then the ordered pair is a solution of the system.

To determine on your calculator that an ordered pair is a solution of a system of linear equations in two variables:

- Store the values of the ordered-pair coordinates for the variables.
- Enter the first equation.
- Enter the second equation.

The result should be 1 (true) for both equations.

Remember that a result of 0 for false should be rechecked, because some calculators may have rounded in the calculations and give a false answer for a true equation. To do this, enter both sides of the equation separately and check for equal values. For example, determine that $(2, 0)$ is a solution of the system

$$2x - y = 4$$

$$x + y = 2.$$

Substitute the values for the coordinates.

$$\begin{array}{c|c} 2x \;-\; y \;=\; 4 \\ \hline 2(2) \;-\; (0) & 4 \\ 4 \;+\; 0 \\ 4 \end{array} \qquad \begin{array}{c|c} x \;+\; y \;=\; 2 \\ \hline 2 \;+\; (0) & 2 \\ 2 \end{array}$$

The solution is $(2, 0)$ because it satisfies both equations.

On your calculator, the solution is determined by storing 2 for x and 0 for y and evaluating both equations. The solution is $(2, 0)$ because it satisfies both equations, as shown in Figure 7.1.

TECHNOLOGY

Figure 7.1

For Figure 7.1
Store values for x and y.

| 2 | STO▶ | X, T, θ, n | ALPHA | : | 0 | STO▶ | ALPHA | Y |
| ALPHA | : |

Enter the first equation.

| 2 | X, T, θ, n | − | ALPHA | Y | 2nd | TEST | 1 | 4 | ENTER |

Enter the second equation.

| X, T, θ, n | + | ALPHA | Y | 2nd | TEST | 1 | 2 | ENTER |

EXAMPLE 1   Determine whether each ordered pair is a solution of the given system of linear equations.

a. $(-2, 1)$; $-2x - 3y = 1$
$x + 3y = 1$

b. $(5, -3)$; $2y = -6$
$-x - 2y = 1$

c. $(-3, -2)$; $x = -3$
$y = 2$

Solution

Substitute the values for the coordinates.

a.

$$\begin{array}{c|c} -2x \quad - \quad 3y \ = 1 \\ \hline -2(-2) - 3(1) & 1 \\ 4 \quad - \quad 3 \\ 1 \end{array} \qquad \begin{array}{c|c} x \quad + \quad 3y \ = 1 \\ \hline (-2) + 3(1) & 1 \\ -2 \ + \ 3 \\ 1 \end{array}$$

Both equations are true. Therefore, $(-2, 1)$ is a solution of the system.

b.

$$\begin{array}{c|c} 2y \quad = -6 \\ \hline 2(-3) & -6 \\ -6 \end{array} \qquad \begin{array}{c|c} -x \quad - \quad 2y \ = 1 \\ \hline -(5) - 2(-3) & 1 \\ -5 \ + \ 6 \\ 1 \end{array}$$

Both equations are true. Therefore, $(5, -3)$ is a solution of the system.

c.

$$\begin{array}{c|c} x \ = -3 \\ \hline -3 & -3 \end{array} \qquad \begin{array}{c|c} y \ = 2 \\ \hline -2 & 2 \end{array}$$

The second equation is false because $-2 \neq 2$. Therefore, $(-3, -2)$ is not a solution of the system.

Check your results on your calculator. In part a, both equations are true. Therefore, $(-2, 1)$ is a solution of the system.

In part b, both equations are true. Therefore, $(5, -3)$ is a solution of the system.

In part c, the second equation is false. Therefore, $(-3, -2)$ is not a solution of the system.

a.
```
-2→X:1→Y: -2X-3Y=
1
               1
X+3Y=1
               1
```

b.
```
5→X: -3→Y:2Y= -6
               1
-X-2Y=1
               1
```

c.
```
-3→X: -2→Y:X= -3
               1
Y=2
               0
```

■

![checkmark] **Experiencing Algebra the Checkup Way**

In exercises 1–4, determine whether each ordered pair is a solution of the given system of linear equations.

1. $(3, -2); x - 2y = 7$
$3x + y = 7$

2. $(3, 1); 2x - 3y = 3$
$x + 2y = 6$

3. $(-2, 1); x + 5 = 4$
$3y - 1 = 2$

4. $(5, 0); y = 3x - 15$
$x - 5 = 0$

5. How does the solution of a system of linear equations differ from the solution of a single linear equation?

6. What must be true of a coordinate pair in order for it to be a solution of a system of linear equations?

2 Solving Systems of Linear Equations Graphically

We know that we can represent the solutions of a linear equation in two variables by graphing. Therefore, if we graph all the linear equations in a system, we should be able to determine the solution of the system. Let's see how it works. Complete the following set of exercises on your calculator.

DISCOVERY 1

System of Linear Equations with One Solution

Solve the given system of linear equations by graphing both equations on the same integer screen.

$$y = 2x + 1$$
$$y = 4x - 3$$

1. The point of intersection is _____.
2. Substitute the coordinates of the intersection point into both equations of the system. The solution of the system is _____.

Write a rule to solve a system of linear equations graphically.

The coordinates of the point of intersection of the graphs are an ordered-pair solution of the system.

> *Solving a System of Linear Equations Graphically*
> To solve a system of linear equations graphically, graph the equations on the same coordinate plane. The coordinates of the point of intersection are the ordered-pair solution.

To solve a system of linear equations graphically on your calculator:

- Store the equations in Y1 and Y2 and graph. (If more than two equations are in the system, continue this pattern.)
- Determine the intersection. Trace the first graph using the right and left arrow to move along the graph to the point of intersection. The up and down arrow will move to the other graphs. If the coordinates displayed at the bottom of the screen do not change when moving between the graphs, we have located the point of intersection.
- Intersect under the CALC function will determine the intersection if it cannot be located by tracing or if you want to check the answer found by tracing. The calculator will display the coordinates of the intersection on the bottom of the screen.

The point of intersection is the ordered-pair solution of the system.

Helping Hand Remember that equations of the form $x = c$ can't be graphed on a calculator. (They are vertical lines.) If a system contains such an equation, we will not be able to solve it on a calculator.

For example, solve the following system of equations graphically:

$$2x - y = 4$$
$$x + y = 2.$$

Graph both equations of the system on the same coordinate plane.

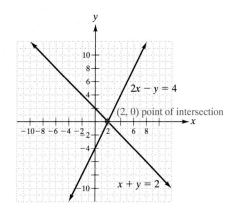

The solution is the coordinates of the intersection $(2, 0)$.

To solve on your calculator, first solve the equations for y.

$$y = 2x - 4$$
$$y = -x + 2$$

Enter the equations in Y1 and Y2, graph, and locate the point of intersection. The solution is $(2, 0)$, as shown in Figure 7.2.

TECHNOLOGY

Y1 = 2x − 4

X=2   Y=0

Y2 = −x + 2

$(-47, 47, -31, 31)$

Figure 7.2

For Figure 7.2
Enter the equations in Y1 and Y2.

| Y= | 2 | X, T, θ, n | − | 4 | ENTER | (−) | X, T, θ, n | + | 2 |

Graph.

| GRAPH |

Trace to find the point of intersection.

Use | TRACE | followed by the right and left arrow keys to locate the intersection on the first graph. Use the up and down arrow keys to confirm that the point is on the other graph.

EXAMPLE 2 Solve each system of linear equations graphically.

a. $-2x - 3y = 1$
  $x + 3y = 1$

b. $2y = -6$
  $-x - 2y = 1$

c. $x = -3$
  $y = 2$

Graphic Solution

Graph both equations of the system on the same coordinate plane.

a.

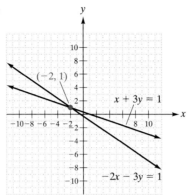

The solution is $(-2, 1)$.

b.

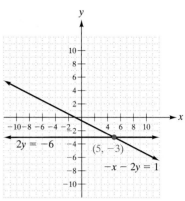

The solution is $(5, -3)$.

c.

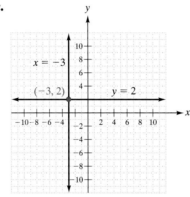

The solution is $(-3, 2)$.

Calculator Graphic Solution

Solve each equation for y and graph.

a. $Y1 = -\frac{2}{3}x - \frac{1}{3}$ $Y2 = -\frac{1}{3}x + \frac{1}{3}$
The solution is $(-2, 1)$ as shown to the left.

b. $Y1 = -3$ $Y2 = -\frac{1}{2}x - \frac{1}{2}$
The solution is $(5, -3)$ as shown to the left.

c. The system contains a vertical line graph, $x = -3$. The calculator is not appropriate for this system. ∎

All of the systems in Example 2 had one solution. We call a system with at least one solution a **consistent** system. A system with no solution is called an **inconsistent** system.

In Chapter 6, we determined that two linear graphs can be parallel or coinciding, as well as intersect in one point. We call equations whose graphs coincide **dependent**. We call equations whose graphs do not coincide **independent**.

All of the systems we solved in Example 2 are consistent and the equations are independent. Now let's look at inconsistent systems and systems

$Y1 = -\frac{2}{3}x - \frac{1}{3}$

$Y2 = -\frac{1}{3}x + \frac{1}{3}$

$(-47, 47, -31, 31)$

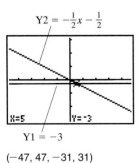

$Y2 = -\frac{1}{2}x - \frac{1}{2}$

$Y1 = -3$

$(-47, 47, -31, 31)$

with equations that are dependent. Complete the following sets of exercises on your calculator.

DISCOVERY 2

Inconsistent System of Linear Equations

Solve the given system of linear equations by graphing both equations on the same integer screen.

$$-2x + y = 1$$
$$-4x + 2y = 10$$

Write a rule to determine, by graphing, that a system of linear equations is inconsistent or that it has no solution.

The two graphs are parallel and do not intersect. Since the graphs do not intersect, there is no ordered-pair solution of the system. The system is inconsistent.

We saw in Chapter 6 that two equations graph as parallel lines if their slopes (m) are the same and the y-coordinates of the y-intercepts (b) are different. If the equations in the system are both solved for y (slope-intercept form), the system has no solution if the equations have the same slope (m) and different y-coordinates of the y-intercepts (b). Therefore, it is not necessary to actually graph the equations to determine that there is no solution.

DISCOVERY 3

System of Dependent Linear Equations

Solve the given system of linear equations by graphing both equations on the same integer screen.

$$-3x - y = -2$$
$$y = -3x + 2$$

Write a rule to determine, by graphing, that a system of linear equations consists of dependent equations or that it has an infinite number of solutions.

The two graphs are coinciding. Since the graphs coincide at all points on the graphs of the lines, all ordered pairs that satisfy one equation also satisfy the second equation in the system. The number of solutions is infinite. In order to represent all these solutions, we need to determine all ordered pairs (x, y) that satisfy one of the linear equations. Since both equations in the system are the same, the solutions are the ordered pairs that satisfy either equation. The equations in this system are dependent.

We also saw in Chapter 6 that two equations graph as coinciding lines if they have the same slope (m) and the same y-coordinates of the y-intercept (b). If the equations in the system are both solved for y (slope-intercept form), the system has an infinite number of solutions if the equations have the same slope (m) and the same y-coordinates of the y-intercept (b). Therefore, it is not necessary to actually graph the equations to determine that there are an infinite number of solutions.

EXAMPLE 3 Determine if the given systems of linear equations have no solution or infinitely many solutions. If the system has an infinite number of solutions, describe the solutions.

a. $y = -x - 3$
$y = -x + 2$

b. $y = \dfrac{2}{3}x - \dfrac{1}{3}$
$3y = 2x - 1$

c. $x = -7$
$2x = -2$

d. $y = 5$
$2y - 10 = 0$

Solution

a. The slopes are equal $(-1 = -1)$, and the y-coordinates of the y-intercepts are different $(-3 \neq 2)$. The graphs will be parallel. There is no solution of the system.

b. Solve the second equation for y: $y = \frac{2}{3}x - \frac{1}{3}$. The slopes are equal $\left(\frac{2}{3} = \frac{2}{3}\right)$, and the y-coordinates of the y-intercepts are equal $\left(-\frac{1}{3} = -\frac{1}{3}\right)$. The graphs will be coinciding. There are an infinite number of solutions of the system. The solutions are all ordered pairs (x, y) that satisfy $y = \frac{2}{3}x - \frac{1}{3}$.

c. The equations will graph vertical lines (equal undefined slopes) with different x-coordinates of the x-intercepts $(-7 \neq -1)$. The graphs will be parallel. There is no solution of the system.

d. Solve the second equation for y: $y = 5$. The equations will graph horizontal lines (equal slopes of $0 = 0$) and equal y-coordinates of y-intercepts, $(5 = 5)$. The graphs will be coinciding. There are an infinite number of solutions of the system. The solutions are all ordered pairs (x, y) that satisfy $y = 5$.

Use your calculator to check your results. Solve the equations for y, if necessary, and graph both equations of the system on the same window. In part a, the graphs are parallel. There is no solution of the system. In part b, the graphs are coinciding. There are an infinite number of solutions of the system. The solutions are all ordered pairs (x, y) that satisfy $y = \frac{2}{3}x - \frac{1}{3}$. In part c, the system contains two vertical lines. The calculator is not appropriate for this system. In part d, the graphs are coinciding. There are an infinite number of solutions of the system. The solutions are all ordered pairs (x, y) that satisfy $y = 5$.

a.

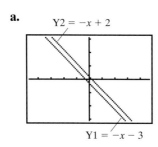

Y2 $= -x + 2$

Y1 $= -x - 3$

$(-47, 47, -31, 31)$

b.

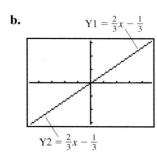

Y1 $= \frac{2}{3}x - \frac{1}{3}$

Y2 $= \frac{2}{3}x - \frac{1}{3}$

$(-47, 47, -31, 31)$

d.

Y1 = 5

Y2 = 5

$(-47, 47, -31, 31)$

Graphical Solutions of a System of Linear Equations
When solving a system of linear equations in two variables graphically, one of three possibilities will occur.

1. **The equations have different slopes (m).**
   The graphs intersect.

   One solution exists—the ordered-pair intersection.

   The system is consistent.

   The equations are independent.

2. **The equations have the same slope (m) and different y-coordinates of the y-intercepts (b). The graphs are parallel.**

   No solution exists.

   The system is inconsistent.

   The equations are independent.

3. **The equations have the same slope (m) and the same y-coordinates of the y-intercept (b). The graphs coincide.**

   An infinite number of solutions exist. The solutions are all ordered pairs (x, y) that satisfy either equation of the system.

   The system is consistent.

   The equations are dependent.

 Experiencing Algebra the Checkup Way

Solve each system of equations graphically. Check your solution.

1. $y = -3x + 4$
$x + y = 2$

2. $y = -2x + 3$
$x = 4$

3. $y + 3 = 0$
$x + 7 = 5$

In exercises 4–6, determine whether each system of equations has no solution or infinitely many solutions. If the system has an infinite number of solutions, describe the solutions.

4. $3y = x + 6$
$x - 3y = 9$

5. $y = 2x + 3$
$y - x + 1 = x + 4$

6. $y = -3$
$y + 4 = 7$

7. When solving a system of linear equations, describe the three outcomes that could occur. If solving graphically, explain what you would look for in the graphs for each of the three outcomes.

8. What is meant by a dependent system of linear equations; an independent system; a consistent system; an inconsistent system?

3 Modeling the Real World

There are two common situations in which graphing two linear equations in two variables at the same time is very helpful. The first situation is to compare two different relationships. For example, you might be offered two different car rental plans. Which one should you choose? You could graph the two equations describing the plans and find where they intersect. Beyond that point, one graph is higher than the other, meaning it will cost more. If you need to rent the car for longer than the time corresponding to the intersection point, you want to choose the plan whose graph is lower beyond that time.

The other situation occurs when the two variables in an equation are related in more than one way. For example, you can design many different rectangular rooms that will have the same perimeter. If the perimeter is 42 feet, the sides of the room could be 10 feet by 11 feet, or 8 feet by 13 feet, or many other dimensions. But if you have to make the length of the room equal twice the width of the room, then only one pair of dimensions will work. (Can you guess what the dimensions are? Take a look at Example 5.)

EXAMPLE 4

Brenda wants to rent a car at the airport for one day. The Rent Thataway rental company has two rental plans. Plan A is $33.95 per day and $0.20 per mile. Plan B is $41.95 per day and $0.10 per mile.

a. Write a system of two linear equations in two variables for the cost of car rental for one day, $C(x)$, in terms of x miles.
b. Determine on your calculator, using the window (0, 141, 10, 0, 124, 10, 1), a solution of the system of equations.
c. Interpret the solution in terms of the cost of renting a car.
d. If Brenda plans to travel less than 75 miles, which plan should she choose?
e. If Brenda plans to travel more than 150 miles, which plan should she choose?

Solution

a. Let $C(x)$ = cost of car rental for one day
        x = number of miles driven in one day

$$C(x) = 0.20x + 33.95 \text{ for Plan A}$$
$$C(x) = 0.10x + 41.95 \text{ for Plan B}$$

b. Y2 = 0.10x + 41.95

Y1 = 0.20x + 33.95

Intersection
X=80   Y=49.95

(0, 141, 0, 124)

The solution is (80, 49.95).

c. The cost of rental on both plans will be the same, $49.95, when traveling 80 miles.

d. The graph for Plan A is below the graph for Plan B when x is less than 80 miles. Therefore, the cost of Plan A is less than the cost of Plan B when traveling less than 80 miles. Brenda should choose Plan A if she will be traveling less than 75 miles.

e. The graph of Plan B is below the graph of Plan A when x is greater than 80 miles. Therefore, the cost of Plan B is less than the cost of Plan A when traveling more than 80 miles. Brenda should choose Plan B if she will be traveling more than 150 miles. ∎

EXAMPLE 5 Leopoldo has 42 feet of baseboard. He plans to use all of the baseboard in his new office. He would like to build the rectangular room such that the length of the room is twice the width. Find the dimensions that Leopoldo should use for his new office if the door opening is 2 feet.

Solution

Let W = width of the room

$\quad\quad L$ = length of the room

Since Leopoldo has 42 feet of baseboard and the door opening is 2 feet, we know the perimeter of the room, $P = 42 + 2 = 44$ feet. We also know a formula for the perimeter of a rectangle, $P = 2L + 2W$. If we substitute 44 for P in the formula, we obtain one equation.

$$P = 2L + 2W$$
$$44 = 2L + 2W$$

Since the room's length is to be twice the room's width, a second equation is

$$L = 2W.$$

To solve graphically the system of equations

$$44 = 2L + 2W$$
$$L = 2W,$$

Y2 = 2x (or L = 2W)

Intersection
X=7.3333333 Y=14.666667

Y1 = 22 − x (or 44 = 2L + 2W)

(−47, 47, −31, 31)

we graph both equations on the same coordinate system.

The solution is $\left(7\frac{1}{3}, 14\frac{2}{3}\right)$.

Leopoldo should build the office $7\frac{1}{3}$ feet by $14\frac{2}{3}$ feet. ∎

Application

Gil Bates, Chairman of MuchoSoft Corp., finds some loose change in his pocket totaling $20,000. He decides to invest it. He finds that the annual interest rate on a regular savings account is 2.75%. However, he can get a sterling account with an annual interest rate of 4% if he keeps a minimum balance of $2500. Gil wants to earn $750 in simple interest for 1 year, and he wants to keep at least $2000 in a regular account so he can access it easily. How much money should Gil deposit in each account in order to meet his goals?

Discussion

Let $x =$ amount in regular savings account
$y =$ amount in sterling account

The sum of the amount in each account is 20,000.

(1) $x + y = 20{,}000$

Simple interest for one year is determined by the product of the annual interest rate and the amount in the account. Therefore,

$0.0275x =$ amount of interest for the regular savings account

$0.04y =$ amount of interest for the sterling savings account

The sum of the two interests is $750.

(2) $0.0275x + 0.04y = 750$

Solve each equation for y and graph.

(1) $y = 20{,}000 - x$

(2) $y = 18{,}750 - 0.6875x$

The intersection point (4000, 16,000) indicates that $4000 (more than the minimum of $2,000) must be deposited in the regular account and $16,000 (at least $2,500) must be deposited in the sterling account. ∎

Y2 = 18750 − 0.6875x
Y1 = 20000 − x
Intersection X=4000 Y=16000
(0, 9400, 0, 31000)

 Experiencing Algebra the Checkup Way

1. Deanna sets up a bakery in her home to bake German chocolate cakes to sell to local restaurants. She spent $255.00 on supplies such as pans, trays, storage, etc. She estimates that each cake she sells will cost her $2.50 to produce. She will sell the cakes to the restaurants for $20.00 each.

   a. Write a system of equations consisting of two linear equations in two variables for the cost, $C(x)$, of producing x cakes and for the revenue, $R(x)$, for selling x cakes.

   b. Determine a solution of the system of equations using your calculator with a window of (0, 94, 10, 0, 620, 100, 1).

   c. Interpret the solution in terms of the number of cakes she sells.

   d. How many cakes can she sell and lose money on the venture?

   e. How many cakes can she sell and make a profit on the venture?

2. Nola's rectangular vegetable garden is surrounded by 64 feet of fencing. Next year she will enlarge the garden by doubling the width and increasing the length by 15 feet. She will need 118 feet of fencing to surround the larger garden. Write a system of equations and solve them to find the dimensions of her current garden and her future garden.

PROBLEM SET 7.1

Experiencing Algebra the Exercise Way

Determine whether each ordered pair is a solution of the given system of linear equations.

1. $(3, 4)$; $y = x + 1$

$2y = x + 5$

2. $(-1, -6)$; $y = 3x - 3$

$y + 6 = 0$

3. $\left(\dfrac{4}{5}, \dfrac{6}{5}\right)$; $p(x) = \dfrac{1}{4}x + 1$

$q(x) = \dfrac{1}{2}x + \dfrac{4}{5}$

4. $\left(7, \dfrac{2}{5}\right)$; $y = \dfrac{1}{7}x - \dfrac{3}{5}$

$7y = x + \dfrac{28}{5}$

5. $(0.3, 2.1)$; $3y = x + 6$

$10y = 25$

6. $(0.8, 0.5)$; $y = 2x - 1$

$10y = 10x - 2$

7. $\left(\dfrac{2}{3}, \dfrac{5}{7}\right)$; $7y + 2 = 7$

$5y + 3 = 0$

8. $\left(\dfrac{1}{8}, \dfrac{1}{8}\right)$; $y = x$

$8y = 1$

9. $(5, -2)$; $2y = -x$

$x = 5$

10. $(-4, -8)$; $y = -2x$

$x = -4$

Solve each system of linear equations graphically. If the system has infinitely many solutions, describe the solutions.

11. $2x + 3y = -6$
   $x - 4y = 8$

12. $-2x - 6y = -6$
   $x + 3y = 3$

13. $a + b = 4$
   $a - 2b = 7$

14. $5x - 3y = 15$
   $4x + y = 12$

15. $x + 2y = 6$
   $x + 2y = 2$

16. $2p + 4q = 8$
   $3p + q = -8$

17. $x - y = -1$
   $3x - 3y = -3$

18. $2x - 3y = -6$
   $-2x + 3y = -6$

19. $y = \dfrac{1}{2}x + 3$
   $y = -\dfrac{3}{2}x - 1$

20. $y = \dfrac{3}{4}x + 1$
   $y = -\dfrac{2}{3}x + 1$

21. $f(x) = 3x - 1$
   $g(x) = -2x + 4$

22. $y = -\dfrac{2}{3}x - 2$
   $6y = -4x - 12$

23. $F(x) = 2x + 2$
   $G(x) = 2x - 3$

24. $h(x) = 3x - 6$
   $k(x) = -5x + 2$

25. $y = \dfrac{1}{2}x + 2$
   $6y = 3x + 12$

26. $F(x) = -3x + 2$
   $G(x) = -3x$

27. $3x + 2y = 12$
   $y - 2 = 1$

28. $x + 4 = 0$
   $3x + 2 = -4$

29. $3y - 2 = 2y + 2$
   $x - 1 = 0$

30. $-x + 2y = 4$
   $3x - 2 = 4$

31. $y - 1 = 0$
   $y + 3 = 0$

32. $5x + 10 = -5$
   $2y + 7 = 5$

33. $y = 3x - 5$
   $x = 4 - 2y$

34. $y = -2x + 3$
   $3x = 2y + 8$

35. $y = x - 7$
   $x = y + 7$

36. $y = \dfrac{1}{2}x + 3$
   $x + 2y = 6$

37. $a(x) = 1 + 4x$
   $b(x) = 4x - 2$

38. $c(x) = -2x - 4$
   $d(x) = 6 - 2x$

39. Ahmet needs to rent a moving van. Turtle Rental will rent him a van for \$39.95 plus \$0.25 per mile for every mile over 150 miles. Snail Rental will rent him a similar van for \$79.95 plus \$0.15 per mile for every mile over 200 miles.

   a. Write a system of linear equations in two variables, relating the cost of rental, y, in terms of the miles, x, driven. (*Hint:* In the equations, multiply the mileage charge times $x - 150$ for the first equation, and times $x - 200$ for the second equation.)

   b. Using a window of $(0, 940, 100, 0, 620, 100, 1)$, determine a solution of the system on your calculator.

   c. Interpret the solution in terms of which rental option would be better for Ahmet.

   d. If Ahmet plans a short move of less than 300 miles, which firm should he rent from?

   e. If he plans a longer move of 600 miles or more, which firm should he rent from?

40. In exercise 39, Ahmet had to choose between two rental plans. Rework the exercise assuming that Turtle Rental will rent a truck for $49.95 plus $0.30 per mile, and that Snail Rental will rent a truck for $19.95 plus $0.40 per mile.

41. An advertising firm needs to decide whether to use bulk-rate or first-class mailing in one of its promotions. To use bulk-rate mailing, they must buy a permit that costs $75 and then pay 22.6 cents per piece of mail. If they use first-class mailing, they will pay 32.0 cents per piece of mail.

   a. Write a system of linear equations in two variables to represent the cost, y, of mailing x pieces of mail under each option.

   b. Graph the system on your calculator using a window of (0, 940, 100, 0, 620, 100, 1). Determine the solution of the system of equations.

   c. When will it be more cost-effective to use the bulk-rate mailing? Explain your answer.

   d. When will it be more cost-effective to use the first-class mailing? Explain your answer.

42. A dinner coupon book sells for $50.00. With the book, you save $4.00 on each dinner purchased. The average cost of the dinners is $17.50.

   a. Write a system of linear equations in two variables to represent the total cost, y, of purchasing x dinners with or without the coupon book.

   b. Solve the system of equations.

   c. When will it be beneficial to purchase the coupon book?

   d. When will it be more cost-effective not to purchase the coupon book? Explain.

43. Kelly spends a total of $500 per month for rent and car payments. Her rent payment is three times as large as her car payment. Write a system of equations to represent these facts, with x representing the car payment and y representing the rent payment. Solve the system. Explain.

44. Jim is designing an apartment complex for a client. The client wants the complex to generate exactly $7800 per month to be fiscally sound. The complex will have one-bedroom apartments renting for $330 and two-bedroom apartments renting for $450. The complex will have 20 units. Write a system of equations to represent this situation. Solve the system to determine how many of each size apartment should be built.

45. Jenny works 40 hours per week at two part-time jobs. One job pays $7.00 per hour and the other pays $8.20 per hour. She wishes to earn exactly $298 to meet her budgeted expenses. Use a system of equations to find how many hours Jenny should work on each job to meet her budget.

46. Hugh earned $316 per week, working part-time at two jobs. One job paid $3.00 more per hour than the other job. Hugh worked 18 hours per week at the lower-paying job and 22 hours per week at the higher-paying job. Use a system of equations to find the hourly wage Hugh earned for each job.

47. The Shriners added an assembly room to their temple for gatherings. The room was rectangular, with a length that was 25 feet less than twice the width. The perimeter of the room was 550 feet. Write and solve a system of equations to find the dimensions of the room.

48. The Knights of Columbus expanded their council home by adding an assembly hall. The width of the hall was 5 feet more than half the length. The perimeter of the hall was 310 feet. Write and solve a system of equations to find the dimensions of the room.

49. Reba had one more than twice as many Top Ten records as Shania. Together they had 22 Top Ten records. Write and solve a system of equations to find how many Top Ten records each had.

50. An heirloom tea set had 21 pieces consisting of saucers and cups. There were 5 more saucers than cups. Write and solve a system of equations to determine how many cups and saucers were in the set.

Experiencing Algebra the Calculator Way

Use your calculator to graphically solve each system of linear equations. Round your answers to the nearest hundredth.

1. $y = 2.4x + 1.2$
$y = -1.3x - 2.7$

2. $y = 0.4x - 8.3$
$y = 2.2x + 2.4$

3. $h(x) = 13.7x$
$k(x) = -115.3$

4. $12y + 8x = 36$
$18x - 15y = 45$

5. $15x - 3y = 12$
$y = 5x - 20$

6. $7x + 21y = 49$
$y = \dfrac{-x + 7}{3}$

7. $F(x) = 45x + 705$
$G(x) = -35x + 155$

8. $y = 35x + 25$
$y = 575$

9. $y = 100x + 6000$
$y = 300x$

Experiencing Algebra the Group Way

In several of the application exercises in this section, and in the application examples, graphing windows were suggested for you to use. Study these windows in comparison to the window for an integer setting. Can you see how you would use the integer setting to move to another window that would still yield x-values on a trace that are integers or decimals? Pick a particular window from those suggested, and explain how each of the settings is changed from that of the integer setting. You should try to understand the pattern, since it will help you decide on window settings for other problems you may encounter. If you understand how these settings were determined, explain to your group what you perceive.

Experiencing Algebra the Write Way

1. In this section, the following statement was made: "we can represent the solutions of a linear equation in two variables by graphing." Explain what this statement means. In your explanation, discuss the relationship between ordered-pair solutions of a linear equation in two variables, and points on the line of the graph of the equation. Explain why the graph is the best way to indicate solutions of such an equation.

2. In the exercises in this section, sometimes it would be best to use the intercept method to graph the system of equations; other times it would be best to use the slope-intercept method; and in some cases it might be best to use the table-of-values method or the method for horizontal and vertical lines. First, recall what each of these methods requires. Then look at the equations given in the exercises for each suggestion, and see if you can tell why a particular method would be best. Write a short paragraph explaining how the form of the equation might lead you to use a particular method; that is, try to identify the clues in the equation forms that suggest a particular method.

7.2 Solving Systems of Equations Using Substitution

Objectives

1 Solve systems of linear equations using substitution.

2 Model real-world situations using systems of linear equations and solve by substitution.

Application

Gil Bates's friend Mitch has $100,000 to invest. He likes the sterling account Gil told him about, which gives 4% interest with a minimum $2500 balance. However, Mitch finds out about a 12-month certificate account that offers 5%

interest. (The money deposited cannot be withdrawn for 12 months.) Mitch wants to obtain $4400 in simple interest after 1 year, and he wants to keep at least half of his investment in the sterling account for easy access. How much should he invest in each account to achieve this?

After completing this section, we will discuss this application further. See page 520.

1 Solving Systems of Linear Equations Using Substitution

Sometimes an ordered-pair solution of a system of linear equations may not have integer coordinates. Graphically solving these systems without a calculator will be difficult. (See "Experiencing Algebra the Calculator Way" in the previous section.) Therefore, algebraic methods are needed. One such method is the **substitution method**.

To understand the substitution method, let's review the process of substitution. We have evaluated equations when we know values for the variables by substituting the value for the variable and simplifying the equation. Let's apply this idea to a system of equations.

Solve the system $4x + y = 2$
$$x = 3.$$

Using substitution, substitute 3 for x in the first equation.

$$4x + y = 2$$
$$4(3) + y = 2 \quad \text{Substitute 3 for } x.$$
$$12 + y = 2 \quad \text{Simplify.}$$

Solve for the variable y.

$$12 + y - 12 = 2 - 12 \quad \text{Subtract 12 from both sides.}$$
$$y = -10 \quad \text{Simplify.}$$

The solution must have $x = 3$ and $y = -10$ as coordinate values. The ordered-pair solution is $(3, -10)$.

A more complicated example occurs when x equals an expression instead of a number. For example, solve the system $4x + y = 2$
$$x = y + 3.$$

Since $x = y + 3$, substitute $(y + 3)$ for x in the first equation.

 Helping Hand Be careful to include parentheses around the expression being substituted.

$$4x + y = 2$$
$$4(y + 3) + y = 2 \quad \text{Substitute } y + 3 \text{ for } x.$$
$$4y + 12 + y = 2 \quad \text{Distribute 4.}$$
$$5y + 12 = 2 \quad \text{Simplify.}$$

Solve for the variable y.

$$5y + 12 - 12 = 2 - 12 \quad \text{Subtract 12 from both sides.}$$
$$5y = -10 \quad \text{Simplify.}$$
$$\frac{5y}{5} = \frac{-10}{5} \quad \text{Divide both sides by 5.}$$
$$y = -2 \quad \text{Simplify.}$$

To determine the x-coordinate, substitute -2 for y in the second equation of the system and solve for x.

$x = y + 3$

$x = -2 + 3$ Substitute -2 for y.

$x = 1$ Simplify.

The solution is $(1, -2)$.

An even more complicated example is the following:

Solve the system $4x + y = 2$
 $x - 2y = 3.$

First, we must solve one of the equations for a variable. If we solve the second equation for x, we obtain $x = 2y + 3$. Using substitution, we substitute $(2y + 3)$ for x in the first equation, $4x + y = 2$.

$4x + y = 2$

$4(2y + 3) + y = 2$ Substitute $2y + 3$ for x.

$8y + 12 + y = 2$ Distribute 4.

$9y + 12 = 2$ Simplify.

Solve for y.

$9y + 12 - 12 = 2 - 12$ Subtract 12 from both sides.

$9y = -10$ Simplify.

$\dfrac{9y}{9} = -\dfrac{10}{9}$ Divide both sides by 9.

$y = -\dfrac{10}{9}$ Simplify.

Next, substitute $-\frac{10}{9}$ for y in the second equation of the system and solve for x.

$x - 2y = 3$

$x - 2\left(-\dfrac{10}{9}\right) = 3$ Substitute $-\frac{10}{9}$ for y.

$x + \dfrac{20}{9} = 3$ Simplify.

$x + \dfrac{20}{9} - \dfrac{20}{9} = 3 - \dfrac{20}{9}$ Subtract $\frac{20}{9}$ from both sides.

$x = \dfrac{27}{9} - \dfrac{20}{9}$ Simplify.

$x = \dfrac{7}{9}$ Simplify.

The solution is $\left(\frac{7}{9}, -\frac{10}{9}\right)$.

*Solving a System of Linear Equations
in Two Variables Using Substitution*
To solve a system of linear equations in two variables using substitution:

- Solve one of the equations for a variable (preferably choose a variable with a numerical coefficient of 1).

- Substitute the expression found in the first step in the other equation of the system.
- Solve the resulting equation for the second variable.
- Substitute the value obtained for the second variable into one of the original equations.
- Solve for the remaining variable.

The ordered-pair solution is determined by the values obtained when solving for each individual variable.

 Helping Hand Remember to check your solutions by substituting the solution in the original equations.

EXAMPLE 1 Solve each system of linear equations in two variables using substitution. Check the solution.

  a. $3x + y = 2$ **b.** $2y = -6$ **c.** $-2x - 3y = 1$
  $\quad x = 1$ $\quad -x - 2y = 1$ $\quad x + 3y = 1$

Algebraic Solution

a. Since the second equation, $x = 1$, is already solved for the variable x, substitute 1 for x in the first equation.

$$3x + y = 2$$
$$3(1) + y = 2 \quad \text{Substitute 1 for } x.$$
$$3 + y = 2 \quad \text{Simplify.}$$

Solve for y.

$$3 + y - 3 = 2 - 3 \quad \text{Subtract 3 from both sides.}$$
$$y = -1 \quad \text{Simplify.}$$

The solution is $(1, -1)$.

To check on your calculator, store the values for the variables and enter both equations.

The results are 1 for true. (The second check was not needed due to the fact this equation was obviously true.)

b. Solve the first equation for y: $y = -3$.
Substitute -3 for y in the second equation.

$$-x - 2y = 1$$
$$-x - 2(-3) = 1 \quad \text{Substitute } -3 \text{ for } y.$$
$$-x + 6 = 1 \quad \text{Simplify.}$$

Solve for x.

$$-x + 6 - 6 = 1 - 6 \quad \text{Subtract 6 from both sides.}$$
$$-x = -5 \quad \text{Simplify.}$$
$$\frac{-x}{-1} = \frac{-5}{-1} \quad \text{Divide both sides by } -1.$$
$$x = 5 \quad \text{Simplify.}$$

The solution is $(5, -3)$.

Check by substituting the solution back into the original equations.

$$\frac{2y = -6}{2(-3) \mid -6}$$
$$-6 \mid$$

$$\frac{-x - 2y = 1}{-(5) - 2(-3) \mid 1}$$
$$-5 + 6$$
$$1 \mid$$

The solution checks in both equations.

c. Solve the second equation for x: $x = -3y + 1$.

Helping Hand It is easier to solve an equation for the variable that has a coefficient of 1.

Substitute the expression $(-3y + 1)$ for x in the first equation.

$$-2x - 3y = 1$$
$$-2(-3y + 1) - 3y = 1 \qquad \text{Substitute } (-3y + 1) \text{ for } x.$$
$$6y - 2 - 3y = 1 \qquad \text{Distribute } -2.$$
$$3y - 2 = 1 \qquad \text{Simplify.}$$

Solve for y.

$$3y - 2 + 2 = 1 + 2 \qquad \text{Add 2 to both sides.}$$
$$3y = 3 \qquad \text{Simplify.}$$
$$\frac{3y}{3} = \frac{3}{3} \qquad \text{Divide both sides by 3.}$$
$$y = 1 \qquad \text{Simplify.}$$

Substitute 1 for y in one of the original equations.

$$x + 3y = 1$$
$$x + 3(1) = 1 \qquad \text{Substitute 1 for } y.$$
$$x + 3 = 1 \qquad \text{Simplify.}$$
$$x = -2 \qquad \text{Solve for } x$$

The solution is $(-2, 1)$.
The check is left to you. ∎

Each of the systems in Example 1 had one solution. However, we know from the previous section that a system may have no solution or an infinite number of solutions. Let's try substitution on these kinds of systems. Complete the following sets of exercises.

DISCOVERY 4

Inconsistent System of Linear Equations
Solve the given system of linear equations using substitution.

$$-2x + y = 1$$
$$-4x + 2y = 3$$

Write a rule to determine, using the substitution method, that a system of linear equations is inconsistent or that it has no solution.

A system has no solution if, after substitution, the resulting equation is a contradiction—that is, the resulting equation does not contain a variable and it is false.

DISCOVERY 5

System of Dependent Linear Equations
Solve the given system of linear equations using substitution.

$$-3x - y = -2$$
$$y = -3x + 2$$

Write a rule to determine, using the substitution method, that a system of linear equations has dependent equations or that it has an infinite number of solutions.

A system has an infinite number of solutions if, after substitution, the resulting equation is an identity—that is, the resulting equation does not contain a variable and it is true.

EXAMPLE 2 Determine, using substitution, whether each system of equations has no solution or infinitely many solutions. If the system has an infinite number of solutions, describe the solutions. Check by solving graphically.

a. $y = -x - 3$

$\quad\ y = -x + 2$

b. $y = \dfrac{2}{3}x - \dfrac{1}{3}$

$\quad\ 3y = 2x - 1$

Algebraic Solution

a. Since the first equation is solved for y, substitute the expression $(-x - 3)$ for y in the second equation.

$$y = -x + 2$$
$$-x - 3 = -x + 2 \quad \text{Substitute } (-x - 3) \text{ for } y.$$

Solve for x.

$$-x - 3 + x = -x + 2 + x \quad \text{Add } x \text{ to both sides.}$$
$$-3 = 2 \quad\quad\quad\quad\quad \text{Simplify.}$$

The result is a contradiction. There is no solution of the system.

Checking by solving graphically results in the graphs of two parallel lines.

b. Since the first equation is solved for y, substitute the expression $\left(\frac{2}{3}x - \frac{1}{3}\right)$ for y in the second equation.

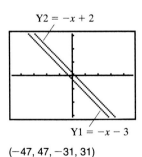

Y2 = −x + 2

Y1 = −x − 3

(−47, 47, −31, 31)

$$3y = 2x - 1$$

$$3\left(\frac{2}{3}x - \frac{1}{3}\right) = 2x - 1 \qquad \text{Substitute } \left(\frac{2}{3}x - \frac{1}{3}\right) \text{ for } y.$$

$$2x - 1 = 2x - 1 \qquad \text{Distribute 3.}$$

Solve for x.

$$2x - 1 - 2x = 2x - 1 - 2x \qquad \text{Subtract } 2x \text{ from both sides.}$$

$$-1 = -1 \qquad \text{Simplify.}$$

The result is an identity. There are an infinite number of solutions. The solutions are all ordered pairs (x, y) that satisfy $y = \frac{2}{3}x - \frac{1}{3}$.

Checking by solving graphically results in the graphs of two coinciding lines. ∎

Y1 $= \frac{2}{3}x - \frac{1}{3}$

Y2 $= \frac{2}{3}x - \frac{1}{3}$

$(-47, 47, -31, 31)$

The following table summarizes the process of algebraically solving a system of linear equations using substitution.

Solutions of a System of Linear Equations Using Substitution
When solving a system of linear equations in two variables using substitution, one of three possibilities will occur.

1. **A value for both variables will be determined.**

   One solution exists—the ordered-pair coordinates.

   The system is consistent.

   The equations are independent.

2. **The substitution will result in a contradiction.**

   No solution exists.

   The system is inconsistent.

   The equations are independent.

3. **The substitution will result in an identity.**

   An infinite number of solutions exist. The solutions are all ordered pairs (x, y) that satisfy either equation of the system.

   The system is consistent.

   The equations are dependent.

 Experiencing Algebra the Checkup Way

Solve each system of linear equations in two variables using substitution. Check your solution.

1. $4x - 2y = 6$
   $y = -1$

2. $2x - y = 5$
   $4x = 1$

3. $-x + 5y = -12$
   $2x + y = -2$

In exercises 4–5, determine by substitution whether each system of equations has no solution or infinitely many solutions. If the system has an infinite number of solutions, describe the solutions.

4. $10x - 2y = 6$

   $y = 5x - 3$

5. $y = \dfrac{1}{2}x - 7$

   $2y = x + 6$

6. When solving a system of linear equations using the substitution method, describe what happens when the system has one ordered pair as a solution; what happens when the system has many ordered pairs as the solution; and what happens when the system has no solution.

---

2 Modeling the Real World

The substitution method for solving a system of linear equations works best when one of the equations is relatively easy to solve for one variable. This often happens in geometry problems, where you can frequently solve a geometric formula for a side of a rectangle or the radius of a circle in terms of other variables and numbers.

EXAMPLE 3 Reza is building a fence around an archery field. He purchased 175 feet of fencing and a 5-foot gate. He plans to construct a rectangular area using all of the materials purchased. He wants the length to be 10 feet more than the width.

a. Write a system of equations to describe the dimensions of the field.
b. Find the possible dimensions for the field.

Algebraic Solution

The formula for the perimeter of a rectangle is $P = 2L + 2W$, where L is the length measurement and W is the width measurement. Reza has 175 feet of fencing and a 5-foot gate, for a total of 180 feet. Therefore, the field has a perimeter of 180 feet. An equation for the perimeter is

$$P = 2L + 2W$$
$$180 = 2L + 2W. \quad \text{Substitute 180 for } P.$$

The length is 10 feet more than the width, or

$$L = W + 10.$$

a. A system of equations is

(1) $180 = 2L + 2W$
(2) $L = W + 10.$

b. Use substitution to solve the system of equations.

(1) $180 = 2L + 2W$
$180 = 2(W + 10) + 2W$ Substitute $(W + 10)$ for L.
$180 = 2W + 20 + 2W$ Distribute 2.
$180 = 4W + 20$ Simplify.

Solve for W.

$$180 - 20 = 4W + 20 - 20 \qquad \text{Subtract 20 from both sides.}$$
$$160 = 4W \qquad\qquad\quad \text{Simplify.}$$
$$\frac{160}{4} = \frac{4W}{4} \qquad\qquad\quad \text{Divide both sides by 4.}$$
$$40 = W \qquad\qquad\qquad \text{Simplify.}$$

Substitute 40 for W in the second equation and solve for L.

(2) $L = W + 10$

$L = 40 + 10 \qquad$ Substitute 40 for W.

$L = 50 \qquad\qquad$ Simplify.

The solution is (50, 40).
   Check the solution against the given facts in the problem.
   The dimensions of the archery field are 50 feet by 40 feet. ∎

Recall from Chapter 3 that in geometry we define complementary angles to be two angles whose measures sum to 90 degrees. Also, supplementary angles have a sum of angle measurements of 180 degrees.

EXAMPLE 4   If two angles are complementary and one angle is twice the second, find the measures of the angles.

Algebraic Solution

Let $x =$ the measure of the first angle
   $y =$ the measure of the complementary angle

Since the sum of the angle measurements is 90 degrees, we write the following equation:

$$x + y = 90$$

One angle is twice the other:

$$x = 2y$$

The system to be solved is

(1) $x + y = 90$
(2) $x = 2y$

We substitute $2y$ for x in the first equation.

(1) $x + y = 90$

$2y + y = 90 \qquad$ Substitute $2y$ for x.

$3y = 90 \qquad$ Simplify.

Solve for y.

$$\frac{3y}{3} = \frac{90}{3} \qquad \text{Divide both sides by 3.}$$

$$y = 30 \qquad \text{Simplify.}$$

Substitute 30 for y in the second equation.

(2) $x = 2y$

$x = 2(30)$ Substitute 30 for y.

$x = 60$ Simplify.

The check is left to you.

The complementary angles have measures of 30 degrees and 60 degrees.

■

Application

Gil Bates's friend Mitch has $100,000 to invest. He likes the sterling account Gil told him about, which gives 4% interest with a minimum $2500 balance. However, Mitch finds out about a 12-month certificate account that offers 5% interest. (The money deposited cannot be withdrawn for 12 months.) Mitch wants to obtain $4400 in simple interest after 1 year, and he wants to keep at least half of his investment in the sterling account for easy access. How much should he invest in each account to achieve this?

Discussion

Let x = the amount deposited at 4% interest rate
     y = the amount deposited at 5% interest rate

The total amount deposited is 100,000.

$x + y = 100,000$

Simple interest for 1 year is determined by the product of the annual interest rate and the amount in the account. Therefore,

$0.04x$ = amount of interest for the sterling account

$0.05y$ = amount of interest for the 12-month certificate

The sum of the two interests is $4400.

$0.04x + 0.05y = 4400$

Therefore, the system of equations is

(1) $x + y = 100,000$
(2) $0.04x + 0.05y = 4400$.

Solve the first equation, $x + y = 100,000$, for x or y. We will solve for x.

(1) $x = 100,000 - y$

Substitute in the second equation.

(2) $0.04(100,000 - y) + 0.05y = 4400$

$4000 - 0.04y + 0.05y = 4400$

$4000 + 0.01y = 4400$

$4000 + 0.01y - 4000 = 4400 - 4000$

$0.01y = 400$

$\dfrac{0.01y}{0.01} = \dfrac{400}{0.01}$

$y = 40,000$

Substitute in the first equation and solve for x.

$$(1) \qquad x + y = 100{,}000$$
$$x + 40{,}000 = 100{,}000$$
$$x = 60{,}000$$

$60,000 (at least $50,000 or half of the deposit) must be deposited in the sterling account (4%) and $40,000 must be deposited in the certificate account (5%). ∎

Experiencing Algebra the Checkup Way

1. Monroe designed a rose garden for his wife Mary. He measured out a square plot of ground with a perimeter of 46 feet. He put a brick walkway around the garden, which created an enlarged square whose sides were each two feet longer than the original square's sides.

   a. Write a system of linear equations to describe the garden and the walkway.

   b. Find the dimensions of the garden and outside dimensions of the walkway.

   c. Find the outside perimeter of the walkway.

2. Two angles are supplementary. The larger angle measures 15 degrees more than twice the smaller angle. Find the measures of the two angles.

PROBLEM SET 7.2

Experiencing Algebra the Exercise Way

Solve each system of linear equations using substitution. Check the solution. If a system has an infinite number of solutions, describe the solutions.

1. $x - 2y = 26$
$5x + 10y = -10$

2. $2x - 3y = 5$
$2y + 6 = 8$

3. $y = 3x - 15$
$x - 5 = 0$

4. $3x + 5y = 15$
$4x - 2y = 7$

5. $x - 5y = 20$
$2y + 3 = -7$

6. $y = -4x + 3$
$5(x - 1) = 0$

7. $3y = x + 6$
$x - 3y = 9$

8. $y = 2x + 3$
$y - x + 1 = x + 4$

9. $y = x - 3$
$2x - y = 19$

10. $y = -3x + 4$
$5x - 5y = 20$

11. $y = x + 1$
$5x - 10y = 3$

12. $y = 3x - 3$
$5(y - 5) = 20$

13. $4y = x + 4$

$5y = 2x + 11$

14. $y = \dfrac{1}{7}x - \dfrac{3}{5}$

$7y = x + \dfrac{28}{5}$

15. $3y = x + 6$

$10y = 25$

16. $y = 2x - 1$

$y = x - 4$

17. $y = -3x + 2$
    $2y + 2x = 2 + y - x$

18. $y = -x - 3$
    $2x + y = 1$

19. $2x + y = -3$
    $y = -0.5x + 3$

20. $2x + 3y = -6$
    $x - 4y = 8$

21. $5x - 3y = -13$
    $4x + y = 27$

22. $x + y = 4$
    $x - 2y = 7$

23. $x + 2y = -28$
    $3x + y = -9$

24. $x + 2y = 6$
    $x + 2y = 2$

25. $x - y = -1$
    $3x - 3y = -3$

26. $-2x - 6y = -6$
    $x + 3y = 3$

27. $y = 3x - 1$
    $2x + y = 4$

28. $y = 3x - 6$
    $5x + y = 2$

29. $y = \dfrac{1}{2}x + 3$
    $3x + 2y = -2$

30. $y = \dfrac{3}{4}x + 1$
    $2x + 3y = 37$

31. $y = \dfrac{1}{2}x + 2$
    $6y = 3x + 12$

32. $x = -\dfrac{3}{2}y - 3$
    $4x + 6y = -12$

33. $y = 2x + 2$
    $2x - y = 3$

34. $3x + y = 2$
    $y = -3x$

35. $3x + 2y = 12$
    $y - 2 = 1$

36. $x - 2y = -4$
    $3x - 2 = 4$

37. $3x - y = 5$
    $x + 2y = 4$

38. $3x - 2y = 8$
    $y = -2x + 3$

39. $y = x - 7$
    $x = y + 7$

40. $2y = x + 3$
    $x + 2y = 6$

41. $y = 1 + 4x$
    $4x - y = 2$

42. $y = -2x - 4$
    $2x + y = 6$

43. $5x + 7y = 35$
    $2x - 5y = 53$

44. $2x - 5y = 8$
    $3x + 4y = 35$

Write a system of equations for each situation and solve.

45. The dance floor in Liza's rehearsal hall is rectangular, with a perimeter of 146 feet. The length of the dance floor is 11 feet less than twice the width. Find the dimensions of the floor.

46. The rectangular rooftop of the Ritz Parton Hotel has a perimeter of 2100 feet. The length is 50 feet more than three times the width. Find the dimensions of the roof.

47. Two angles are complementary. The larger angle measures 10 degrees less than four times the smaller angle. Find the measures of the angles.

48. Two angles are supplementary. The difference of their measures is 40 degrees. Find the measures of the angles.

49. Two angles of a triangle measure the same. The third angle measures 20 degrees more than the sum of the other two angles. How much does each angle measure?

50. Two angles of a triangle are the same size. The third angle is 15 degrees larger than each of the other two. What is the size of each angle?

51. The radius of a large circle is 5 inches more than twice the radius of a smaller circle. The larger circle has a circumference of 283 inches. Find the radius of the smaller circle and the radius of the larger circle, to the nearest inch.

52. A large circle has a circumference of 163 cm. Its radius is 10 cm less than three times the radius of a smaller circle. What is the radius of each circle, to the nearest cm?

53. Princess Fiona needed to borrow $100,000 for a short-term loan. No one loan company would give her the total amount, so she borrowed part of the amount from one company at 7% simple interest and the rest from another company at 6% simple interest. The total interest on the loans was $6450. How much did she borrow at each interest rate?

54. D. J. deposited $1500 into one savings account and $1200 into another savings account. The two accounts earned $117.90 in simple interest after 1 year. The $1200 investment paid 0.3% more in simple interest than did the $1500 investment. What were the two interest rates for the investments?

55. Mr. McDonald had 15 acres of farmland, some of which he planted in corn and the rest in soybeans. The number of acres planted in corn was equivalent to 25 acres of farmland less the number of acres planted in soybeans. How many acres were planted in each crop?

56. A field has 12 acres of farmland, part of which is planted in wheat and the rest in alfalfa. The number of acres of wheat equals one-half the difference of a 24-acre field less twice the acreage of the alfalfa. How many acres are planted in each crop?

57. The total receipts of the United States for 1996 were reported to be 1.4155×10^{12} dollars. Some of these receipts were from individual income taxes and the rest were from other sources, such as corporate income taxes, social security taxes, excise taxes, and miscellaneous taxes. The receipts from other sources were 1.687×10^{11} dollars more than the receipts from individual income taxes. Determine how much was received from individual income taxes and how much was received from other sources.

58. Helium atoms have a much smaller diameter than cesium atoms. The arithmetic average of the two diameters is 2.75×10^{-10} m. The difference in size of the two diameters is 4.5×10^{-10} m. Determine the two diameters.

Experiencing Algebra the Calculator Way

Use the substitution method to solve each system, and use your calculator to help you with the arithmetic.

1. $15.8x + y = 2655.10$

$18.4x + 73.2y = 19361.22$

2. $x + \dfrac{9}{17}y = \dfrac{137}{170}$

$\dfrac{3}{8}x + \dfrac{7}{16}y = \dfrac{2303}{5280}$

Use your calculator to check the solution of each system of equations.

3. $(0.0983, -1.0768);\ 4.055x - 8.752y = 9.8277601$
$\qquad\qquad\qquad\quad -5.385x - 0.405y = -0.0932415$

4. $(-2897.65, 1725.85);\ 0.408a + 0.526b = -274.4441$
$\qquad\qquad\qquad\qquad\quad 0.005a - 0.802b = -1398.720$

5. $\left(\dfrac{13}{35}, -\dfrac{17}{55}\right);\ \dfrac{7}{39}m + \dfrac{5}{34}n = \dfrac{7}{330}$
$\qquad\qquad\qquad\ \dfrac{5}{42}m - \dfrac{11}{85}n = \dfrac{169}{7350}$

6. $\left(-\dfrac{78}{85}, \dfrac{28}{51}\right);\ \dfrac{34}{65}p + \dfrac{51}{56}q = -\dfrac{16}{325}$
$\qquad\qquad\qquad\ \dfrac{35}{66}p - \dfrac{18}{49}q = -\dfrac{53}{77}$

Experiencing Algebra the Group Way

You have learned two methods to solve systems of equations: the graphical method and the substitution method. Divide your group into two units, and have one unit use the graphical method to solve the following systems, and have the other unit use the substitution method to solve the systems. After you have found the solutions, share your work. Decide which method was easier to use to solve each system. List your reasons for your decision.

1. $y = 0.0803x + 1.0507$
$\quad y = -0.8532x + 1.9842$

2. $y = 85x + 300$
$\quad 450x - y = 286{,}225$

Experiencing Algebra the Write Way

Study the examples presented in "Modeling the Real World." Describe the steps followed in solving a problem, analyzing the steps followed in the examples. Be as specific as you can. Concentrate on the clues in the description of the problem that enable you to convert the information to a mathematical model you can solve. (The term *model* means the system of linear equations with the explanations that accompanies them.)

7.3 Solving Systems of Equations Using Elimination

Objectives
1 Solve systems of linear equations using elimination.
2 Model real-world situations using systems of equations and solve by elimination.

Application

Basketball star Coleman Hill has signed a contract that gives him a bonus of $100,000. His agent recommends that Coleman invest some of this bonus in a 24-month certificate of deposit earning a simple-interest rate of 5.5% annually. However, the agent suggests that Coleman keep at least half of his bonus in a regular savings account earning an annual interest rate of 3%, where he can access his money at any time. Coleman knows that he needs to earn $8250 in interest over 2 years so that he can buy the next 2 years' worth of new basketball shoes. How much should he invest in each account to earn that much interest?

After completing this section, we will discuss this application further. See page 533.

---

1 Solving Systems of Linear Equations Using Elimination

Sometimes neither equation in a system can be solved for one variable simply. Therefore, a second algebraic method is needed. We call this second method for solving a system of linear equations the **elimination method**.

In order to understand the elimination method, we will review the addition property of equations. This property states that we may add equivalent expressions to both sides of an equation and the result is an equivalent equation—that is,

> If $a = b$ and $c = d$, then $a + c = b + d$ for any expressions a, b, c, and d.

Remember that in Chapter 5 we illustrated why this is true with a balanced scale representing the equation. Now we begin with two equations (balanced scales).

We will apply this property to a system of equations to obtain a new equation that has one variable eliminated.

If $a = b$

and $c = d$

then $a + c = b + d$

Solve the system $2x - y = 8$
$\qquad\qquad\quad y = 4.$

Using the addition property of equations,

If $2x - y = 8$ and $y = 4$, then $2x - y + y = 8 + 4.$

If $\ a\ = b$ and $c = d$, then $\ a\ + c = b + d.$

We add to each member of the first equation the corresponding member of the second equation. In other words, we add y to the left side of the first equation, $2x - y$, and 4 to the right side of the first equation, 8.

$$
\begin{aligned}
2x - y &= 8 \\
y &\quad 4 \qquad \text{Add corresponding members of the equations.} \\
\hline
2x &= 12 \qquad \text{Simplify.}
\end{aligned}
$$

$$\frac{2x}{2} = \frac{12}{2} \qquad \text{Divide both sides by 2.}$$

$$x = 6 \qquad \text{Simplify.}$$

Since $y = 4$, the solution of the system is $(6, 4)$.

This process works very nicely if one of the variables is eliminated when we apply the addition property. However, in many cases we will need to write equivalent equations for the system before we apply the addition property. For example, solve the system $2x - y = -1$
$\qquad\qquad\qquad\qquad\qquad 4x - y = 3.$

If we add $4x - y$ to the expression on the left side of the first equation, $2x - y$, we obtain $6x - 2y$. No variable is eliminated. However, we should see that if the y-term is positive in one expression and negative in the other expression, the y-variable would have been eliminated. In order to do this, we need to multiply one of the variable expressions by -1 to change the sign of y. To do this, we apply the multiplication property of equations and multiply *both* sides of the equation by the same value, -1.

(1) $2x - y = -1$
(2) $4x - y = 3$

(1) $2x - y = -1$
(2) $-1(4x - y) = -1(3)$ $\quad$ Multiply both sides by -1.

Helping Hand Even though the second equation is the only equation changed in this process, rewrite the entire system each time an equation changes. This helps you keep track of what the system presently looks like.

$$
\begin{aligned}
(1)\quad 2x - y &= -1 \\
(2)\quad -4x + y &= -3 \\
\hline
-2x &= -4 \qquad \text{Add corresponding members of the equation.}
\end{aligned}
$$

$$\frac{-2x}{-2} = \frac{-4}{-2} \qquad \text{Divide both sides by } -2.$$

$$x = 2 \qquad \text{Simplify.}$$

Substitute 2 for x in the first equation to find the y-value of the solution.

$$(1) \quad 2x - y = -1$$
$$2(2) - y = -1 \qquad \text{Substitute 2 for } x.$$
$$4 - y = -1 \qquad \text{Simplify.}$$
$$4 - y - 4 = -1 - 4 \qquad \text{Subtract 4 from both sides.}$$
$$-y = -5 \qquad \text{Simplify.}$$
$$\frac{-y}{-1} = \frac{-5}{-1} \qquad \text{Divide both sides by } -1.$$
$$y = 5 \qquad \text{Simplify.}$$

The solution of the system is $(2, 5)$.

In some cases, we will need to rewrite both equations in the system before applying the addition property to eliminate a variable. For example, solve the system $2x + 3y = 5$
$ 3x + 2y = -5.$

We see that no variable is eliminated if we apply the addition property of equations. Also, the x-variable will not be eliminated if we multiply either expression by an integer. The same is true for the y-variable. However, the least common multiple for the coefficients of the variables could be found and then used to determine a number needed to multiply each equation in the system. For example, if we want to eliminate the x-variable in the system, we determine the least common multiple, 6, for the x-coefficients, 2 and 3. To eliminate the x-variable, we want one expression to have 6 and the other expression to have -6 as the x-coefficients. One way to accomplish this is by multiplying the members of the first equation by 3 and the members of the second equation by -2.

$(1) \; 2x + 3y = 5$

$(2) \; 3x + 2y = -5$

$(1) \; 3(2x + 3y) = 3(5)$ $\qquad$ Multiply both sides by 3.

$(2) \; -2(3x + 2y) = -2(-5)$ $\qquad$ Multiply both sides by -2.

$$
\begin{array}{rl}
(1) & 6x + 9y = 15 \\
(2) & \underline{-6x - 4y = 10} \\
& 5y = 25
\end{array}
$$
$\qquad$ Add corresponding members of the equation.

$$\frac{5y}{5} = \frac{25}{5} \qquad \text{Divide both sides by 5.}$$
$$y = 5 \qquad \text{Simplify.}$$

Substitute 5 for y in the first equation to find the x-value of the solution.

$$(1) \quad 2x + 3y = 5$$
$$2x + 3(5) = 5 \qquad \text{Substitute 5 for } y.$$
$$2x + 15 = 5 \qquad \text{Simplify.}$$
$$2x + 15 - 15 = 5 - 15 \qquad \text{Subtract 15 from both sides.}$$
$$2x = -10 \qquad \text{Simplify.}$$

$$\frac{2x}{2} = \frac{-10}{2} \qquad \text{Divide both sides by 2.}$$

$$x = -5 \qquad \text{Simplify.}$$

The solution of the system is $(-5, 5)$.

> *Solving a System of Linear Equations in Two Variables Using Elimination*
>
> To solve a system of linear equations in two variables using elimination:
>
> - Write both equations in standard form.
> - Determine the least common multiple for the coefficients of the variable to be eliminated.
> - Determine the number(s) to multiply the members of the equation(s), if necessary, to obtain coefficients with the least common multiple and opposite signs.
> - Add the expressions in the second equation to the corresponding expressions in the first equation, eliminating one of the variables.
> - Solve the resulting equation for the remaining variable.
> - Substitute the value obtained in one of the original equations and solve for the other variable.
>
> The ordered-pair solution is determined by the values obtained when solving for each individual variable.

EXAMPLE 1 Solve each system of linear equations in two variables using elimination. Check the solution by substituting into the original equations.

a. $3x + 2y = 2$
$-3x + 2y = 6$

b. $2x = -3y + 1$
$x + 2y = -1$

c. $3x + 2y = 1$

$2x - 5y = -2$

d. $\dfrac{1}{2}x + \dfrac{2}{3}y = 1$

$\dfrac{1}{4}x - \dfrac{1}{5}y = -\dfrac{1}{10}$

Algebraic Solution

a. $(1) \quad 3x + 2y = 2$
$(2) \quad \underline{-3x + 2y = 6}$
$\qquad\qquad\;\; 4y = 8 \qquad \text{Add corresponding members of the equations.}$

$$\frac{4y}{4} = \frac{8}{4} \qquad \text{Divide both sides by 4.}$$

$$y = 2 \qquad \text{Simplify.}$$

Substitute 2 for y in the first equation to find the x-value of the solution.

$(1) \qquad 3x + 2y = 2$
$\qquad\;\; 3x + 2(2) = 2 \qquad \text{Substitute 2 for } y.$
$\qquad\qquad 3x + 4 = 2 \qquad \text{Simplify.}$
$\quad\; 3x + 4 - 4 = 2 - 4 \qquad \text{Subtract 4 from both sides of the equation.}$
$\qquad\qquad\quad\; 3x = -2 \qquad \text{Simplify.}$

$$\frac{3x}{3} = \frac{-2}{3} \qquad \text{Divide both sides by 3.}$$

$$x = -\frac{2}{3} \qquad \text{Simplify.}$$

The solution of the system is $\left(-\frac{2}{3}, 2\right)$.
   Check by substituting the solution into the original equations.

$3x \ + \ 2y \ = 2$		$-3x \ + \ 2y \ = 6$	
$3\left(-\dfrac{2}{3}\right) + 2(2)$	2	$-3\left(-\dfrac{2}{3}\right) + 2(2)$	6
$-2 + \ 4$		$-2 + \ 4$	
2		6	

The solution checks in both equations.
   To check on your calculator, store the values for the variables and enter both equations.

b. (1) $2x = -3y + 1$

(2) $x + 2y = -1$

Write the first equation in standard form.

$$2x + 3y = -3y + 1 + 3y \qquad \text{Add } 3y \text{ to both sides of the equation.}$$
$$2x + 3y = 1 \qquad\qquad\qquad \text{Simplify.}$$

The system with equations in standard form is as follows:

(1) $2x + 3y = 1$

(2) $x + 2y = -1$

(1) $2x + 3y = 1$

(2) $-2(x + 2y) = -2(-1)$ Multiply both sides by −2.

$$
\begin{aligned}
(1) \quad & 2x + 3y = 1 \\
(2) \quad & \underline{-2x - 4y = 2} \\
& \quad\quad -y = 3 \qquad \text{Add corresponding members of the equations.}
\end{aligned}
$$

$$\frac{-y}{-1} = \frac{3}{-1} \qquad \text{Divide both sides by } -1.$$

$$y = -3 \qquad \text{Simplify.}$$

Substitute -3 for y in the second equation to find the x-value of the solution.

$$
\begin{aligned}
(2) \quad & x + 2y = -1 \\
& x + 2(-3) = -1 \qquad \text{Substitute } -3 \text{ for } y. \\
& x - 6 = -1 \qquad\quad\; \text{Simplify.} \\
& x - 6 + 6 = -1 + 6 \quad \text{Add 6 to both sides.} \\
& x = 5 \qquad\qquad\quad \text{Simplify.}
\end{aligned}
$$

The solution of the system is $(5, -3)$.
   The check is left to you.

c. (1) $3x + 2y = 1$

(2) $2x - 5y = -2$

The least common multiple of the x-coefficients is 6. Therefore, the members of the first equation must be multiplied by 2 and the members of the second equation by -3 to obtain the x-coefficients of 6 and -6.

(1) $2(3x + 2y) = 2(1)$ Multiply both sides by 2.

(2) $-3(2x - 5y) = -3(-2)$ Multiply both sides by -3.

$$\begin{aligned}(1) \quad\quad 6x + 4y &= 2 \\ (2) \quad -6x + 15y &= 6 \\ \hline 19y &= 8 \end{aligned}$$ Add corresponding members of the equations.

$$\frac{19y}{19} = \frac{8}{19}$$ Divide both sides by 19.

$$y = \frac{8}{19}$$ Simplify.

Substitute $\frac{8}{19}$ for y in the first equation to find the x-value of the solution.

(1) $3x + 2y = 1$

$$3x + 2\left(\frac{8}{19}\right) = 1$$ Substitute $\frac{8}{19}$ for y.

$$3x + \frac{16}{19} = 1$$ Simplify.

$$3x + \frac{16}{19} - \frac{16}{19} = 1 - \frac{16}{19}$$ Subtract $\frac{16}{19}$ from both sides.

$$3x = \frac{3}{19}$$ Simplify.

$$3x\left(\frac{1}{3}\right) = \left(\frac{3}{19}\right)\left(\frac{1}{3}\right)$$ Multiply both sides by $\frac{1}{3}$.

$$x = \frac{1}{19}$$ Simplify.

The solution of the system is $\left(\frac{1}{19}, \frac{8}{19}\right)$.

The check is left to you.

d. (1) $\dfrac{1}{2}x + \dfrac{2}{3}y = 1$

(2) $\dfrac{1}{4}x - \dfrac{1}{5}y = -\dfrac{1}{10}$

Eliminate the fractions in the system of equations by multiplying the members of each equation by the least common multiple of the denominators in the equation.

(1) $6\left(\dfrac{1}{2}x + \dfrac{2}{3}y\right) = 6(1)$ Multiply by the LCD of 2 and 3.

(2) $20\left(\dfrac{1}{4}x - \dfrac{1}{5}y\right) = 20\left(-\dfrac{1}{10}\right)$ Multiply by the LCD of 4, 5, and 10.

$$(1)\ 3x + 4y = 6$$
$$(2)\ \underline{5x - 4y = -2}$$
$$8x = 4$$

Add corresponding members of the equations.

$$\frac{8x}{8} = \frac{4}{8}$$

Divide both sides by 8.

$$x = \frac{1}{2}$$

Simplify.

Substitute $\frac{1}{2}$ for x in the first equation to find the y-value of the solution.

$$(1) \qquad \frac{1}{2}x + \frac{2}{3}y = 1$$

$$\frac{1}{2}\left(\frac{1}{2}\right) + \frac{2}{3}y = 1$$

Substitute $\frac{1}{2}$ for x.

$$\frac{1}{4} + \frac{2}{3}y = 1$$

Simplify.

$$\frac{1}{4} + \frac{2}{3}y - \frac{1}{4} = 1 - \frac{1}{4}$$

Subtract $\frac{1}{4}$ from both sides.

$$\frac{2}{3}y = \frac{3}{4}$$

Simplify.

$$\frac{3}{2}\left(\frac{2}{3}y\right) = \frac{3}{2}\left(\frac{3}{4}\right)$$

Multiply both sides by $\frac{3}{2}$.

$$y = \frac{9}{8}$$

Simplify.

The solution of the system is $\left(\frac{1}{2}, \frac{9}{8}\right)$.
The check is left to you. ∎

As we have seen in the other sections of this chapter, a system may have no solution or an infinite number of solutions. Let's see what happens when we apply elimination to systems of these types. Complete the following sets of exercises.

D I S C O V E R Y   6

Inconsistent System of Linear Equations

Solve the given system of linear equations using elimination.

$$-2x + y = 1$$
$$-4x + 2y = 3$$

Write a rule to determine, using the elimination method, that a system of linear equations is inconsistent or that it has no solution.

A system has no solution if, after elimination, the resulting equation is a contradiction—that is, the resulting equation does not contain a variable and it is false.

DISCOVERY 7

System of Dependent Linear Equations

Solve the given system of linear equations using elimination.

$$-3x - y = -2$$
$$y = -3x + 2$$

Write a rule to determine, using the elimination method, that a system of linear equations has dependent equations or there are an infinite number of solutions.

A system has an infinite number of solutions if, after elimination, the resulting equation is an identity—that is, the resulting equation does not contain a variable and it is true.

EXAMPLE 2   Solve each system of equations using elimination. If the system has an infinite number of possibilities, describe the solutions.

a. $x + y = -3$ **b.** $y = \dfrac{2}{3}x - \dfrac{1}{3}$

 $x + y = 2$ $3y = 2x - 1$

Algebraic Solution

a. (1) $x + y = -3$

 (2) $x + y = 2$

 (1) $-1(x + y) = -1(-3)$ Multiply both sides of the first equation by −1.

 (2) $x + y = 2$

 (1) $-x - y = 3$

 (2) $\underline{x + y = 2}$

$0 = 5$ Add corresponding members of the equations.

The result is a contradiction. There is no solution of the system.

b. (1) $y = \dfrac{2}{3}x - \dfrac{1}{3}$

 (2) $3y = 2x - 1$

Write the first equation in standard form.

$$3(y) = 3\left(\frac{2}{3}x - \frac{1}{3}\right)$$ Multiply by the LCD of 3 to clear the fractions.

$$3y = 2x - 1$$ Simplify.

$$3y - 2x = 2x - 1 - 2x$$ Subtract 2x from both sides.

$$-2x + 3y = -1$$ Simplify and rearrange.

Write the second equation in standard form.

$$3y - 2x = 2x - 1 - 2x$$ Subtract 2x from both sides.

$$-2x + 3y = -1$$ Simplify and rearrange.

The system in standard form is as follows:

(1) $-2x + 3y = -1$

(2) $-2x + 3y = -1$

(1) $-1(-2x + 3y) = -1(-1)$ Multiply both sides of the first equation by -1.

(2) $-2x + 3y = -1$

(1) $2x - 3y = 1$

(2) $\underline{-2x + 3y = -1}$

$\qquad\qquad 0 = 0$ Add corresponding members of the equations.

The result is an identity. The solutions are all ordered pairs (x, y) that satisfy $y = \frac{2}{3}x - \frac{1}{3}$.

The check is left to you. ∎

The following table summarizes the process of algebraically solving a system of linear equations using elimination.

Solutions of a System of Linear Equations Using Elimination
When solving a system of linear equations in two variables, one of three possibilities will occur.

1. **A value for both variables will be determined.**

   One solution exists—(the ordered-pair coordinates.)

   The system is consistent.

   The equations are independent.

2. **The elimination will result in a contradiction.**

   No solution exists.

   The system is inconsistent.

   The equations are independent.

3. **The elimination will result in an identity.**

   An infinite number of solutions exist. The solutions are all ordered pairs (x, y) that satisfy either equation of the system.

   The system is consistent.

   The equations are dependent.

✓ **Experiencing Algebra the Checkup Way**

Solve each system of equations using the elimination method. Check the solution.

1. $x + y = 10$

$\quad x - y = 2$

2. $x = 5y + 32$

$\quad 2x + y = -2$

3. $4x + 7y = -3$

$\quad 7x - 2y = 9$

4. $\dfrac{1}{2}x + \dfrac{5}{8}y = \dfrac{9}{8}$

$\quad \dfrac{2}{5}x - \dfrac{1}{2}y = -\dfrac{7}{10}$

In exercises 5–6, solve each system of equations using the elimination method. If the system has an infinite number of solutions, describe the solutions.

5. $x + 2y = 6$

$\quad 3x = 20 - 6y$

6. $y = 5x + 12$

$\quad 7x + 24 = 2y - 3x$

7. You now know three methods to solve a system of linear equations in two variables: the graphical method, the substitution method, and the elimination method. Write a short explanation of how you would apply each of these methods to obtain the solution to a system of linear equations.

---

2 Modeling the Real World

When two equations are needed to describe the relationship between two variables, we sometimes say that the system consists of **simultaneous equations**, since they both apply at the same time. The method of elimination is probably the most common way of solving simultaneous equations, unless we can get one equation into a simple enough form so that substitution can be used. In fact, elimination is the underlying method for more complicated techniques that we can use to solve systems of three, four, or more simultaneous equations. However, we'll stick to systems of two linear equations in this text.

EXAMPLE 3

Melinda's class charged admission of $2.50 for adults and $1.25 for students to its play. Melinda counted 10 chairs remaining empty in the auditorium, which holds 500. If the amount collected was $1013.75, how many adults and students attended?

"CLASS PLAY"
$1.25 students
$2.50 adults

Algebraic Solution

Let a = number of adults attending
c = number of students attending

(1) $a + c = 490$ — The number attending was 500 − 10 or 490.

(2) $2.50a + 1.25c = 1013.75$ — The cost is the sum of the amount collected for adults, $2.50a$, and the amount collected for students, $1.25c$.

(1) $-1.25(a + c) = -1.25(490)$ — Multiply both sides by −1.25.

(2) $2.50a + 1.25c = 1013.75$

(1) $-1.25a - 1.25c = -612.50$

(2) $\underline{2.50a + 1.25c = 1013.75}$

$1.25a \qquad = 401.25$ — Add corresponding members of the equations.

$\dfrac{1.25a}{1.25} = \dfrac{401.25}{1.25}$ — Divide both sides by 1.25.

$a = 321$ — Simplify.

Substitute 321 for a in the first equation to find the c-value of the solution.

(1) $a + c = 490$

$321 + c = 490$ — Substitute 321 for a.

$321 + c - 321 = 490 - 321$ — Subtract 321 from both sides of the equation.

$c = 169$ — Simplify.

The check is left to you.
There were 321 adults and 169 students attending the play. ∎

Application

Basketball star Coleman Hill has signed a contract that gives him a bonus of $100,000. His agent recommends that Coleman invest some of this bonus in a 24-month certificate of deposit earning a simple-interest rate of 5.5% annually. However, the agent suggests that Coleman keep at least half of his bonus in a regular savings account earning an annual interest rate of 3%, where he can access his money at any time. Coleman knows that he needs to earn $8250 in interest over 2 years so that he can buy the next 2 years' worth of new basketball shoes. How much should he invest in each account to earn that much interest?

Discussion

Let $x =$ the amount deposited at a 3% interest rate
$\quad y =$ the amount deposited at a 5.5% interest rate

The total amount deposited is 100,000.

(1)　$x + y = 100{,}000$

Simple interest is determined by the product of the amount in the account, the annual interest rate, and the number of years invested. Therefore, the amount of simple interest for the regular account is

$$(0.03)(x)(2) = 0.06x.$$

The amount of simple interest for the 24-month certificate is

$$(0.055)(y)(2) = 0.11y.$$

The sum of the two interest amounts is $8250.

(2)　$0.06x + 0.11y = 8250$

Algebraically solve the system by elimination.

(1)　$x + y = 100{,}000$
(2)　$0.06x + 0.11y = 8250$

(1)　$-0.06x - 0.06y = -6000$　　Multiply both sides of the first equation by −0.06.
(2)　$\underline{0.06x + 0.11y = 8250}$
$\qquad\qquad\qquad 0.05y = 2250$　　Add corresponding members of the equations.
$\qquad\qquad\qquad\quad y = 45{,}000$　　Divide both sides of the equation by 0.05 and simplify.

(1)　　　$x + y = 100{,}000$
$\qquad\quad x + 45{,}000 = 100{,}000$　　Substitute 45,000 for y.
$\qquad\qquad\qquad y = 55{,}000$

Therefore, Coleman should deposit $55,000 (at least $50,000 or half of the deposit) in the regular account and $45,000 in the certificate account. ∎

Experiencing Algebra the Checkup Way

The Pocahontas circle of the Indian Maidens sold cans of nuts as a fund-raiser. They sold 262 cans. Cashews sold for $6.50 per can and peanuts for $4.00 per can. The proceeds from the sale were $1240.50. They lost their tally of how many cans of each were sold. Write and solve a system of equations to help them determine how many of each they sold.

PROBLEM SET 7.3

Experiencing Algebra the Exercise Way

Solve each system of equations using the elimination method. Check your solution.

1. $2x - y = -6$
   $5x + y = -8$

2. $5x + y = 8$
   $3x - y = 16$

3. $x + 7y = 19$
   $2y = x - 1$

4. $x + 9y = -12$
   $-x + 8y = -5$

5. $5x + y = -24$
   $3x - 2y = 9$

6. $4x - 3y = 26$
   $2x + y = 18$

7. $x + 3y = 2$
   $x + 5y = -2$

8. $x + 8y = 37$
   $x + 11y = 52$

9. $2x + 7y = 29$
   $4x + 3y = 25$

10. $5x + 11y = -27$
   $10x + 13y = -36$

11. $3x - 5y = 66$
   $4x + 3y = 1$

12. $2x + 7y = 33$
   $3x - 4y = -52$

13. $2x + 9y = 102$
   $5x - 11y = -147$

14. $11x + 5y = 133$
   $15x + 4y = 187$

15. $40x = 23 + 10y$
   $50x + 10y = 94$

16. $15x + 10y = -2$
   $5x = 10y + 18$

17. $5x + 40y = 77$
   $5x + 15y = 17$

18. $4x + 2y = 15$
   $-6x + 2y = -30$

19. $10x - 4y = 28$
   $5x + 4y = 35$

20. $2x + y = -7$
   $3x - y = -2$

21. $2x + 8y = 29$

   $13y = 3x + 39$

22. $5x + 15y = -10$

   $19y = 7x + 42$

23. $\dfrac{1}{4}x + \dfrac{1}{3}y = \dfrac{5}{12}$

   $\dfrac{1}{4}x = \dfrac{1}{3}y - \dfrac{1}{12}$

24. $\dfrac{2}{3}x + \dfrac{3}{5}y = \dfrac{9}{10}$

   $\dfrac{2}{3}x = \dfrac{3}{5}y - \dfrac{1}{10}$

25. $\dfrac{1}{3}x + \dfrac{1}{2}y = -\dfrac{1}{4}$

   $\dfrac{1}{6}x - \dfrac{5}{6}y = \dfrac{11}{16}$

26. $\dfrac{3}{7}x + \dfrac{4}{5}y = -\dfrac{1}{6}$

   $\dfrac{3}{7}x - \dfrac{8}{15}y = \dfrac{2}{3}$

27. $y = \dfrac{3}{2}x - 9$

   $\dfrac{1}{6}x - \dfrac{1}{9}y = 1$

28. $y = \dfrac{6}{5}x + 2$

   $\dfrac{3}{5}x - \dfrac{1}{2}y = -1$

29. $\dfrac{4}{5}x - \dfrac{3}{5}y = -1$

   $\dfrac{3}{2}x - \dfrac{9}{8}y = 1$

30. $\dfrac{1}{12}x - \dfrac{1}{8}y = -1$

   $\dfrac{1}{3}x - \dfrac{1}{2}y = 1$

31. $x - 20y = 70$

   $3x + 10y = 70$

32. $x + 35y = 300$

   $4x + 15y = 200$

33. $3x + y = 40$
   $x + y = 20$

34. $x + 4y = 0$
   $x + 7y = -30$

35. $x - y = 300$
   $2x - y = -100$

36. $x + y = 300$
   $x + 3y = 1400$

37. $10x - 10y = 22$
   $y = 2x - 11$

38. $5x + 5y = 10$
   $y = 9x - 41$

39. $3.2x + 4.2y = 368$
   $4.4x - 2.1y = 128$

40. $1.4x + 2.4y = 225$
   $3.4x - 1.6y = 123$

41. $0.05x + 0.10y = 0.75$
   $x + y = 11$

42. $0.25x + 0.50y = 5.75$
   $x + y = 14$

43. $0.3x + 0.45y = 43.5$
   $x + y = 110$

44. $0.55x + 0.25y = 49$
   $x + y = 100$

45. $12.50x + 6.50y = 1780$
   $x + y = 200$

46. $7.95x + 2.25y = 914.70$
   $x + y = 214$

Write a system of equations for each application and solve using the elimination method.

47. At Centennial High School's football game, the gate indicated that 683 persons entered. Students were charged $1.50 admission while the others were charged $5.00 admission. The total receipts at the game were $2645.00. The principal wanted to know how many students attended the game, but unfortunately the count was not recorded. Can you find the answer for the principal?

48. A church sponsored a bus trip to attend the play *Godspell* at the summer stock theater in a nearby town. Senior citizens were charged $30.00 for the trip, including all expenses, while others were charged $45.00. A total of 56 people took the trip and paid $2190 for the privilege. How many seniors and how many others took the trip?

49. To raise money for a scholarship fund, the faculty and staff at the Community College for Mathematics decided to print a cookbook and a calendar. They sold 50 more cookbooks than calendars, and raised $3462.50, selling the cookbooks for $8.50 each and the calendars for $5.00 each. How many of each were sold?

50. For a luncheon, Karlene ordered a tray of ham and cheese from the local deli. The deli advertised the tray as having a weight of 5.5 pounds total. The ham sold for $6.00 per pound, and the cheese sold for $4.00 per pound. The total charge for the tray was $29.50. Karlene wanted to know how much ham and how much cheese they sold her. Can you help her?

51. Zelda has inherited $16,500, which she would like to invest. She has an opportunity to invest part of the money in a simple-interest savings account paying 5% per year, and the rest in a certificate of deposit paying 7.25% per year. If she wishes to earn $1000 for a vacation next year, and also wants to keep some money in the savings account in case she needs it sooner, how much should she invest in each account?

52. In exercise 51, Zelda planned to invest her inheritance. However, she learns that she must pay taxes on the inheritance, and will have only $11,000 to invest. She decides to invest the money to earn $600 instead for a vacation. How much should she now invest in each account?

53. The number of adults and children at Midtown Nursery's school play totaled 385. Adults were charged $2 admission, and by mistake, the children were also charged $2 each. The receipts for the play amounted to $770. How many adults and how many children attended the play?

54. Mama Mia's Restaurant offers two lists of items on its menu. The first list contains items all at one price and the second list contains items all at a second price. If a patron selects one item from each list, the price for the meal is $8.95. If a patron selects two items from each list, the price for the meal is $13.95. Find the price of an item from the first list and the price of an item from the second list.

55. Corinna jogs around a rectangular field that has a perimeter of 620 yards. When she jogs around an alternate field that has the same width but is 90 yards longer, she jogs a distance of 800 yards. What are the dimensions of the smaller field?

56. Evan can use either of two circular tracks at the gym for his jogging. The radius of one track is 10 yards larger than the second track. The circumference of the larger track is 20π yards more than the circumference of the smaller track. What is the radius of each track?

57. A triangle has two angles that are equal in size. The third angle equals 90 degrees minus the sum of the measures of the other two angles. What is the size of each angle?

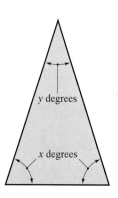

58. Two angles are supplementary. One angle is 30 degrees larger than the other. How large is each angle?

59. The distance from the Sun to the red planet Mars is approximately 4.864×10^7 miles greater than the distance of the Earth from the Sun. The average of the distances from the Sun for the two planets is 1.1728×10^8 miles. Find the approximate distances of the two planets from the Sun.

60. The planet Mercury is approximately 3.6302×10^9 miles closer to the Sun than the planet Pluto. The average distance from the Sun for the two planets is approximately 1.851×10^9 miles. What are the approximate distances of these planets from the Sun?

 ## Experiencing Algebra the Calculator Way

The elimination method is basically a paper-and-pencil method, but the calculator can assist with the arithmetic. Use your calculator to help solve the following systems using the elimination method and to check your solutions.

1. $2578x - 4823y = 299{,}758$
$7395x + 4823y = 3{,}210{,}738$

2. $487x + 182y = 51{,}567$
$976x + 364y = 103{,}280$

3. $4.376x - 2.659y = 4.479378$
$-2.188x - 5.033y = 19.787286$

4. $5882x + 0.473y = 2764.366$

$2750x - y = -4508$

5. $\dfrac{27}{85}x + y = -\dfrac{37}{95}$

$x + \dfrac{57}{82}y = \dfrac{7}{72}$

6. $\dfrac{5}{17}x - \dfrac{4}{19}y = \dfrac{421}{1615}$

$\dfrac{8}{19}x + \dfrac{11}{17}y = -\dfrac{2}{323}$

 ## Experiencing Algebra the Group Way

A. A variation of the elimination method, called the *method of alternates*, can be used to obtain opposite coefficients. Consider the system

(1) $6x - 7y = -21$
(2) $15x - 11y = 6.$

Rather than find the least common multiple of 6 and 15, multiply the members of each equation by the coefficient of x in the alternate equation, yielding

(1) $15(6x - 7y) = 15(-21)$ $\rightarrow$ $90x - 105y = -315$
(2) $6(15x - 11y) = 6(6)$ $\rightarrow$ $90x - 66y = 36$

Then multiply the members of the second equation by -1 and add.

(1) $\quad 90x - 105y = -315$
(2) $\underline{-90x + 66y = -36}$
$\qquad\qquad -39y = -351,$ yielding $y = 9.$

By substitution into one of original equations, $x = 7.$

    Divide your group into two units. One unit will use the method of alternates, and the other unit will find the least common multiple, to solve the following systems of equations. See which group finishes first. Discuss which method seems to be the best and why.

1. $6x + 35y = -52$
$9x - 14y = 55$

2. $12x - 35y = 81$
$15x - 28y = 54$

3. $21a + 10b = -88$
$14a + 15b = 8$

4. $33x + 7y = -3.1$
$6x + 13y = -33.4$

5. $10x + 21y = 19$
$14x - 9y = 1$

6. $8x - 9y = 8$
$12x + 21y = -11$

B. To be sure you understand all three methods for solving a system of linear equations in two variables, divide your group into three units. Assign each unit one of the three methods for solving systems of equations. Then have each unit solve the following systems using the assigned method. After each unit has completed the work, discuss which method appears to be the best for each system.

1. $3x + y = 62$
$5x + 19y = 203$

2. $14x - 3y = -240$
$5x + 3y = -45$

3. $y = 2x - 69$
$y = x - 17$

Experiencing Algebra the Write Way

When using the elimination method, you should look for certain characteristics in the coefficients in order to eliminate a variable in the simplest way. Try to construct a list of what you would look for in the coefficients when attempting to solve by elimination. For each characteristic, either find an example in the text exercises or construct one of your own. Use the example to illustrate the characteristic you listed. Write a short paragraph describing what you have discovered.

7.4 More Real-World Models

Objectives

1 Model real-world situations involving distance traveled.

2 Model real-world situations involving mixtures and collections.

Application

You have just won $50,000 in a sweepstakes and you want to invest your winnings right away. You want to earn $2125 in interest each year to pay for more sweepstakes entries. Your financial consultant suggests that you put half of your investment, $25,000, in a 12-month certificate of deposit earning 5% interest. Then you can place part of your investment in a sterling account earning 4% annual interest on a minimum balance of $2500. The final portion of your investment should go into a regular savings account earning 2.75% annual interest. How much do you need to place in each of these accounts in order to earn the interest you want?

After completing this section, we will discuss this application further. See page 546.

We have now discussed three methods for solving a system of linear equations in two variables: a system can be solved graphically, algebraically by substitution, or algebraically by elimination. We have also solved real-world models with each of these methods. However, several other types of models can be solved with these methods.

In this section we discuss other applications involving systems of linear equations. Once a system of linear equations model is written for the problem, it may be solved with any of the methods we have presented.

Let's review the method we have been using to answer a question about a real-world model.

> *Modeling Real-World Situations*
> To model a real-world situation:
>
> - Read and understand the problem.
> - Define variables for the unknown quantities and define other quantities in terms of the defined variables.
> - Write equations with the information given.

- Solve the system either graphically or algebraically.
- Check the solution.
- Write an answer for the question asked, in a complete sentence.

---

1 Solving Distance-Traveled Models

We have used the formula for distance traveled in previous chapters. Remember, the distance traveled, d, is equal to the rate of motion, r, times the time traveled, t.

$$d = rt$$

We may be given information about more than one situation involving distance traveled. In such a case, we need to solve a system of equations in two variables.

EXAMPLE 1 Romeo and Juliet live 680 miles apart. They plan to meet each other at a designated location between their homes. Juliet is planning to drive her sports car at an average speed of 65 mph. However, Romeo is driving his pickup truck and towing a boat, so he plans on driving an average of 45 mph. If they both plan to leave at the same time, how many miles from Juliet's home should they plan to meet?

Algebraic Solution

A picture of the trip may help us to determine the equations.

Let d = number of miles from Juliet's home to the meeting place
$680 - d$ = number of miles from Romeo's home to the meeting place
     t = time traveled (both drivers travel the same time)

Using the distance traveled formula, $d = rt$, for each trip, we write the following equations:

$$d = rt$$
(1) Juliet: $d = 65t$
(2) Romeo: $680 - d = 45t$

We will use substitution to solve this system, since the first equation, $d = 65t$, is already solved for d. Substitute $65t$ for d in the second equation and solve for t.

(2) $680 - d = 45t$	
$680 - 65t = 45t$	Substitute 65t for d.
$680 - 65t + 65t = 45t + 65t$	Add 65t to both sides.
$680 = 110t$	Simplify.
$\dfrac{680}{110} = \dfrac{110t}{110}$	Divide both sides by 110.
$6.182 \approx t$	Simplify.

To find the distance from Juliet's home, d, substitute 6.182 for t in the first equation.

(1) $d = 65t$

    $d \approx 65(6.182)$ Substitute 6.182 for t.

    $d \approx 401.830$ Simplify.

To check the solution, substitute the solution in both of the original equations.

d	$=$	$65t$
401.830		65(6.182)
		401.830

$680 -$	d	$=$	$45t$
$680 -$	401.830		45(6.182)
	278.170		278.190

Remember, we rounded our answer for t. Therefore, the numbers will not check exactly.

The designated location for the meeting place should be about 401.8 miles from Juliet's home.

Graphic Solution

The equations must be rewritten in x and y.

    $y = 65x$

    $680 - y = 45x$

Solve the equations for y.

    $y = 65x$

    $y = -45x + 680$

Y1 = 65x
Y2 = −45x + 680

Intersection
X=6.1818182 Y=401.81818

(0, 20, 0, 1000)

A calculator graph for the solution, (6.182, 401.818), is shown on a window of (0, 20, 10, 0, 1000, 100, 1) using the CALC function to determine the exact intersection. The difference is due to rounding.

The designated location for the meeting place should be about 401.8 miles from Juliet's home. ∎

EXAMPLE 2   Simon and his family spent their vacation camping on the Tennessee River. The family traveled upstream 714 miles for 3 days, spending 21 hours traveling on the river. The return trip of 3 days took 17 hours of river travel. Determine the average speed of the boat in still water and the average current speed.

Algebraic Solution

A picture of the trip may help us determine the equations we need to describe this situation.

upstream travel   downstream travel

Let x = speed of the boat in still water
y = speed of the current

The speed traveled upstream, against the current, is the speed of the boat, x, less the speed of the current, y.

$x - y$ = speed of the boat against the current (upstream)

The speed traveled downstream, with the current, is the speed of the boat, x, plus the speed of the current, y.

$x + y$ = speed of the boat with the current (downstream)

Helping Hand If an object is traveling in the direction of an additional force, add the rates of motion. If an object is traveling in the opposite direction of an additional force, subtract the rates of motion.

Using the distance-traveled formula, $d = rt$, for each trip, we write the following equations:

(1) $714 = (x - y)21$

(2) $714 = (x + y)17$

(1) $714 = 21x - 21y$ Simplify.

(2) $714 = 17x + 17y$ Simplify.

We will use elimination to solve this system, since both equations are in standard form. The LCM of the coefficients of y is 357. Multiply both members of the first equation by 17 and both members of the second equation by 21.

(1) $17(714) = 17(21x - 21y)$ Multiply both sides by 17.

(2) $21(714) = 21(17x + 17y)$ Multiply both sides by 21.

(1) $12138 = 357x - 357y$

(2) $\underline{14994 = 357x + 357y}$

$27132 = 714x$ Add corresponding members of the equations.

$\dfrac{27132}{714} = \dfrac{714x}{714}$ Divide both sides by 714.

$38 = x$ Simplify.

Substitute 38 for x in the first equation and solve for y.

(1)
$$714 = 21x - 21y$$
$$714 = 21(38) - 21y \quad \text{Substitute 38 for } x.$$
$$714 = 798 - 21y \quad \text{Simplify.}$$
$$714 - 798 = 798 - 21y - 798 \quad \text{Subtract 798 from both sides.}$$
$$-84 = -21y \quad \text{Simplify.}$$
$$\frac{-84}{-21} = \frac{-21y}{-21} \quad \text{Divide both sides by } -21.$$
$$4 = y \quad \text{Simplify.}$$

```
38→X:4→Y:714=(X-
Y)21
                    1
714=(X+Y)17
                    1
```

Check your solution on your calculator.

Simon's boat traveled at an average speed of 38 mph. The river current was an average of 4 mph. ∎

✓ Experiencing Algebra the Checkup Way

Write and solve a system of equations for each exercise.

1. Patty left her house to attend her cousin's wedding, traveling up the interstate at 55 miles per hour. After she had been gone for half an hour, her father realized she had forgotten to take her bridal-party dress. He immediately left to overtake her. If he drives at the legal speed of 65 miles per hour, how long will it be until he overtakes her on the interstate?

2. Two Girl Scouts took a canoe trip up a stream. They paddled for 4 hours against the stream's current and reached their destination, which was 16 miles from their starting point. After resting for a while, they made the return trip in 2 hours. How fast were the girls able to paddle in still water, and what was the speed of the stream's current?

---

2 Solving Mixture and Collection Models

Previously we solved mixture and collection problems using a linear equation in one variable. A second method is to use a system of linear equations in two variables. The general method is to set up one equation expressing the amount of each component in the mixture and a second equation that relates the amounts of each component to one another, according to the statement of the problem.

EXAMPLE 3 Susan works in a candy store that stocks two popular Halloween candies. Candy corn sells for $1.25 per pound and candy witches sell for $2.50 per pound. She mixes 2 pounds of candy corn for every pound of candy witches. A customer wants to buy $25.00 worth of the mixture. How many pounds of each must Susan use in the mixture?

Algebraic Solution

Let c = number of pounds of candy corn
     w = number of pounds of candy witches

Helping Hand It is convenient to use variable names that will make it easy to remember which variable represents each unknown quantity. In this example, we chose c for corn and w for witches.

Since the mixture contains 2 pounds of candy corn to 1 pound of candy witches, the number of pounds of candy corn, c, equals 2 times the number of pounds of candy witches, w.

$$c = 2w$$

The cost of the mixture will be 1.25 times the number of pounds of candy corn, c, plus 2.50 times the number of pounds of candy witches, w. This will equal the cost of 25.00.

$$1.25c + 2.50w = 25.00$$

The system of equations to be solved is

(1) $c = 2w$

(2) $1.25c + 2.50w = 25.00$

We will use substitution to solve this system because the first equation is already solved for variable c. Substitute $2w$ for c in the second equation and solve for w.

$$(2) \qquad 1.25c + 2.50w = 25.00$$

$$1.25(2w) + 2.50w = 25.00 \qquad \text{Substitute } 2w \text{ for } c.$$

$$2.50w + 2.50w = 25.00 \qquad \text{Simplify.}$$

$$5.00w = 25.00 \qquad \text{Simplify.}$$

$$\frac{5.00w}{5.00} = \frac{25.00}{5.00} \qquad \text{Divide both sides by 5.00.}$$

$$w = 5 \qquad \text{Simplify.}$$

Substitute 5 for w in the first equation and solve for c.

$$(1) \quad c = 2w$$

$$c = 2(5) \qquad \text{Substitute 5 for } w.$$

$$c = 10 \qquad \text{Simplify.}$$

To check the solution, substitute the solution in both of the original equations.

c	$=$	$2w$
10		2(5)
		10

$1.25c + 2.50w$	$= 25.00$
$1.25(10) + 2.50(5)$	25.00
$12.50 + 12.50$	
25.00	

The solution checks.

Susan will need to mix 10 pounds of candy corn with 5 pounds of candy witches in order to sell the mixture for $25.00. ∎

EXAMPLE 4 Su Yung has a collection of 15 antique coins, consisting of nickels and dimes. The face value of the coins is $1.10. How many of each denomination does she have?

Algebraic Solution

Let n = number of nickels
d = number of dimes

Since there is a total of 15 coins, we add the number of nickels, n, and the number of dimes, d.

$$n + d = 15$$

The value of the nickels is 0.05 times the number of nickels, n or $0.05n$. The value of the dimes is 0.10 times the number of dimes, d, or $0.10d$. The value of the collection, 1.10, is equal to the sum of the value of the coins.

$$0.05n + 0.10d = 1.10$$

To eliminate the decimals in the equation, multiply both sides of the equation by 100, the LCM of the decimal place values.

$$100(0.05n + 0.10d) = 100(1.10)$$
$$5n + 10d = 110$$

The system to be solved is

(1) $n + d = 15$
(2) $5n + 10d = 110$

We will use elimination to solve the system, since both equations are written in standard form. To eliminate the variable n, we will multiply both sides of the first equation by -5.

(1) $-5(n + d) = -5(15)$ Multiply both sides by -5.
(2) $5n + 10d = 110$

(1) $-5n - 5d = -75$
(2) $\underline{5n + 10d = 110}$ Add corresponding members of the equations.
$\qquad\quad 5d = 35$

$$\frac{5d}{5} = \frac{35}{5} \qquad \text{Divide both sides by 5.}$$

$$d = 7 \qquad \text{Simplify.}$$

Substitute 7 for d in the first equation and solve for n.

(1) $\qquad n + d = 15$
$\qquad\qquad n + 7 = 15$ Substitute 7 for d.
$\qquad n + 7 - 7 = 15 - 7$ Subtract 7 from both sides.
$\qquad\qquad\quad n = 8$ Simplify.

To check the solution, substitute the solution in both of the original equations.

$$\begin{array}{r|l} n + d = 15 \\ \hline 8 + 7 & 15 \\ 15 & \end{array} \qquad\qquad \begin{array}{r|l} 5n + 10d = 110 \\ \hline 5(8) + 10(7) & 110 \\ 40 + 70 & \\ 110 & \end{array}$$

The solution checks.
  Su Yung has 8 nickels and 7 dimes. ■

EXAMPLE 5   Dr. Joe Ben has a solution of 25% glucose. He needs 2 liters of a solution of 5% glucose. How many liters of the 25% solution and sterile water must he mix?

Algebraic Solution

Let g = number of liters of 25% glucose solution
      w = number of liters of sterile water

Since 2 liters of 5% glucose solution are needed, we will add the number of liters of the 25% glucose solution, g, and the number of liters of the sterile water, w.

$$g + w = 2$$

The amount of glucose in the 25% glucose solution will be 25% of the number of liters, g, or $0.25g$. The amount of glucose in the sterile water (0% glucose) will be 0% of the number of liters, w, or $0w$. The amount of glucose in the 5% glucose solution will be 5% of the number of liters, 2, or $0.05(2)$.

$$0.25g + 0w = 0.05(2)$$
$$0.25g = 0.1$$

To eliminate the decimals in the equation we will multiply both sides of the equation by 100, the LCM of the decimal place values.

$$100(0.25g) = 100(0.1)$$
$$25g = 10$$

The system to be solved is

(1) $g + w = 2$
(2) $25g = 10$

We use substitution and solve the second equation for g.

(2) $25g = 10$

$$\frac{25g}{25} = \frac{10}{25} \qquad \text{Divide both sides by 25.}$$

$$g = 0.4 \qquad \text{Simplify.}$$

Substitute 0.4 for g in the first equation and solve for w.

(1) $g + w = 2$
                 $0.4 + w = 2$ Substitute 0.4 for g.
         $0.4 + w - 0.4 = 2 - 0.4$ Subtract 0.4 from both sides.
                      $w = 1.6$ Simplify.

To check the solution, substitute the solution in both of the original equations.

g	+	w	= 2
0.4	+	1.6	2
		2	

$25g$	= 10
25(0.4)	10
10	

The solution checks.

   Dr. Joe Ben will need to mix 0.4 liters of the 25% glucose solution and 1.6 liters of sterile water to obtain 2 liters of a 5% glucose solution.   ∎

Application

You have just won $50,000 in a sweepstakes and you want to invest your winnings right away. You want to earn $2125 in interest each year to pay for more sweepstakes entries. Your financial consultant suggests that you put half of your investment, $25,000, in a 12-month certificate of deposit earning 5% interest. Then you can place part of your investment in a sterling account earning 4% annual interest on a minimum balance of $2500. The final portion of your investment should go into a regular savings account earning 2.75% annual interest. How much do you need to place in each of these accounts in order to earn the interest you want?

Discussion

Let x = amount invested at a 2.75% interest rate
   y = amount invested at a 4% interest rate

The amount invested at the 2.75% and 4% interest rates equals the amount invested in the certificate account, $25,000.

$$x + y = 25,000$$

The interest amount of $2125 is the total of the amount of interest at each rate: $0.0275x$, $0.04y$, and $0.05(25,000)$ or 1250.

$$0.0275x + 0.04y + 1250 = 2125$$
$$0.0275x + 0.04y = 875$$

To eliminate the decimals in the equation, multiply both sides of the equation by 10,000, the LCM of the decimal place values.

$$275x + 400y = 8,750,000$$

The system to be solved is:

(1) $x + y = 25,000$
(2) $275x + 400y = 8,750,000$

We will use the substitution method and solve the first equation for x.

(1) $x = 25,000 - y$

Substitute $(25,000 - y)$ for x in the second equation and solve for y.

(2) $275x + 400y = 8,750,000$
$275(25,000 - y) + 400y = 8,750,000$ Substitute $(25,000 - y)$ for x.
$6,875,000 - 275y + 400y = 8,750,000$ Simplify.
$6,875,000 + 125y = 8,750,000$ Simplify.
$125y = 1,875,000$ Subtract 6,875,000 from both sides.
$y = 15,000$ Divide both sides by 125.

Substitute 15,000 for y in the equation solved for x.

(1) $x = 25,000 - 15,000$
      $x = 10,000$

The check is left for you.

  You must deposit $10,000 in the regular account and $15,000 (at least $2,500) in the sterling account, in addition to the $25,000 in the certificate account. ∎

✔ Experiencing Algebra the Checkup Way

Write and solve a system of equations for each mixture and collection exercise.

1. Brian is mixing two types of grass seed to sell as a blend. He must mix x pounds of coarse fescue with y pounds of Kentucky bluegrass to make 100 pounds of mix. The coarse fescue sells for $0.75 per pound, while the bluegrass sells for $1.25 per pound. He wants to sell the mix for $1.00 a pound. How much of each should he mix?

2. Rosita had been saving coins to buy Christmas gifts for the family. She had just counted the coins and told her parents there was a total of 498 coins, consisting of 120 nickels and the rest a mix of dimes and quarters. She proudly told them that the coins totaled $63.75. While the family was out, a burglar entered the house and stole some items, including Rosita's coin collection. The family felt that Rosita was too young to deal with this, so they decided to replace the coins in exactly the same mix. How many dimes and quarters did they need to add to the 120 nickels to restore Rosita's collection?

3. Dr. Joe Ben needs to mix a 25% glucose solution with a 5% glucose solution to make a new solution that is 10% glucose. If he wants to have 1 liter of the 10% glucose solution, how many liters of the other two should he mix?

PROBLEM SET 7.4

Experiencing Algebra the Exercise Way

Write and solve a system of equations for each application.

1. A grocer wishes to mix peanuts, which sell for $0.90 per pound, with candy, which sells for $1.50 per pound. She wishes to have 30 pounds of mix and will sell it at $1.25 per pound. How much of each should she mix?

2. Collector's Corner wants to mix some 25-cent pogs with some 10-cent pogs and allow customers to buy the mix at 15 cents per pog. How many 10-cent pogs should be mixed with 100 of the 25-cent pogs in order to come out even on the costs? How many pogs will be in the mix?

3. Radio station WALG runs a contest to see whether listeners can guess the makeup of a stack of $5 and $10 bills. They announce that the stack contains 65 bills and is worth $365. The first listener who calls in with the correct number of each wins the money. Can you quickly determine the correct mix?

4. Tillie, the teller at the bank, has a stack of 35 bills. Some are $20 bills and the rest are $50 bills. If the value of the bills is $1300, how many of each does she have?

5. Concentrate for a fruit punch is to be mixed with spring water to make a drink for a reception. The concentrate is 65% fruit juice and is to be mixed with the water to make a drink that is 35% fruit juice. If the reception needs 130 gallons of punch, how many gallons of concentrate need to be mixed with how many gallons of water?

6. A car mechanic tests the antifreeze in your car and finds it is 35% antifreeze. How much antifreeze should be drained and replaced with pure antifreeze in order to bring the car up to 5 gallons of 50% antifreeze? (Round your answer to the nearest tenth of a gallon.)

7. A plane flew for 3 hours with a tail wind to reach its destination 450 miles away. The return trip with the same speed head wind took 5 hours. How fast could the plane fly with no wind, and what was the speed of the wind? (*Note:* A tail wind increases a plane's speed by applying force in the direction of travel, while a head wind decreases a plane's speed by applying force against the direction of travel.)

Tail Wind

Head Wind

8. Ronnie won a light-plane rally by completing the flight in 4 hours. The next year, he was able to increase his speed by 40 miles per hour, and won the race over the same distance in 3 hours. How fast did he fly the first time? What was the distance of the race?

9. The first screening of the latest movie sequel, *Cretaceous Park: The Found World*, had a box office of $3937.50 at the local theater. Adults paid $7.50 and children paid $4.50 per ticket. The number of admissions was 625. How many of these were adults and how many were children?

10. The blockbuster movie, *Car Wars, Part 12: The Princess Drives Back*, opened at the local theater. Adults paid $10.00 and children paid $5.50 per ticket for this show. There were twice as many children as adults at the show, and the box office receipts were $5355.00. How many adults and how many children attended the showing?

11. A gardener has a solution that is 70% weed killer. He wants to mix this with another solution that is 40% weed killer, to make 5 pints of a solution that will be 50% weed killer. How many pints of each should he mix?

12. Al Falfa, a milk farmer, wants to mix milk that is 4.3% butterfat with skim milk that has no butterfat, in order to make milk that is 2% butterfat. How much of each should he mix to make 200 gallons of the 2% butterfat milk? (Round your answer to the nearest gallon.)

13. Gary's Gourmet Coffee Shop mixes French vanilla coffee, which sells for $9.50 per pound, with hazelnut coffee, which sells for $7.00 per pound. The mix, called Croissant blend, sells for $8.50 per pound. If Gary wishes to make 20 pounds of the blend, how many pounds of each should he use?

14. LaToyia's Tea Shop blended orange spice tea, which sold for $3.50 per pound, with lemon honey tea, which sold for $7.50 per pound. The blend, sold as Spicy Citrus, amounted to 10 pounds of tea, which sold for $5.00 per pound. How much of each flavor was used to make the blend?

15. In order to reduce her risk, Catherine split her investment in two mutual funds between one that paid 8.5% simple interest annually, and another that paid 7% simple interest annually. She had

$10,000 to invest, and at the end of the year she received a total of $752.50 in interest. How much did she invest in each fund?

16. Ali received two student loans for school totaling $10,000. He borrowed the maximum allowed at 7% and the remainder at 8.25%, both at simple interest for a year. At the end of the first year, he owed $725 in interest. How much did he borrow at each interest rate?

17. After Kenny's car broke down, he started walking home. Dolly came by and picked him up. The time he walked was twice as long as the time he rode with Dolly. He was walking at an average rate of 3 miles per hour, and Dolly drove at an average rate of 60 miles per hour. If the total distance to his home was 11 miles when he started walking, how much time did he spend walking and how much time riding?

18. On an outing, a troop of mountain scouts canoed at 12 miles per hour for the first leg of their trip. Then they hiked at 3 miles per hour to reach their destination. It took as many hours for the canoe trip as it did for the hike. If the total distance traveled was 30 miles, find the time they spent canoeing and hiking, and find the distance they covered by canoe.

19. Marian budgeted $250 to buy landscaping plants for her home. She needed 30 plants. If azaleas sell for $5 each and rhododendrons sell for $12 each, how many of each can Marian buy with her budget?

20. Sharon went to the local burger palace to buy burgers and hot dogs for a class picnic. She needed to buy 50 sandwiches for the class with the $95.00 she collected. If hot dogs sell for $1.00 each and burgers sell for $2.50 each, how many of each should she order?

21. Cher works part-time as a waitress in one restaurant and part-time as a cook in another restaurant. In one week, she worked 15 hours waitressing and 20 hours as a cook and earned $320. In another week, she worked 18 hours waitressing and 24 hours cooking, and earned $384. What is her hourly wage on each job?

22. A sale at Denney's Department Store attracted a throng of customers. One customer bought two shirts and four blouses and paid $132 for the purchase. Another customer bought three shirts and six blouses from the same counters and paid $180 for the purchase. What were the sale prices of the shirts and blouses?

 Experiencing Algebra the Calculator Way

1. Shine-Bright Company produces lamps. Retailers purchase the lamps for $25.00 each. The fixed cost of renting the building, utilities, and overhead is $1500.00 per month. The production cost is $10.00 per lamp. Follow the steps listed to find the break-even point (the number of lamps that must be produced and sold in order to break even with costs).

   a. Write a revenue equation (the amount of money, $R(x)$, taken in monthly by selling x lamps).

   b. Write the cost equation (the amount of money, $C(x)$, spent monthly producing x lamps).

   c. Graph the system of equations using a window of (0, 200, 10, 0, 6000, 1000, 1).

   d. Identify the break-even point by finding the intersection of the two graphs.

   e. Check your solution to see that it is in fact the break-even point in terms of the number of lamps produced and sold, where cost of production equals revenue from sales.

2. Woodchuck Company produces tables. Retailers purchase the tables for $45 each. The fixed cost of renting the building, utilities, and overhead is $2500 per month. The production cost of a table is $25 per table. Find the break-even point using the same steps outlined in exercise 1.

3. Sow's Ear, Inc., produces purses. Retailers buy the purses for $32.49 each. The fixed cost is $1256.00 per month. The cost of producing each purse is $15.89. Find the break-even point.

Experiencing Algebra the Group Way

A. Each member of the group should select an algebraic method, either the elimination method or the substitution method, to solve the three application exercises described in "Experiencing Algebra the Calculator Way." Use your calculator to assist with the arithmetic calculations. After solving the three exercises, discuss which method seemed to be the easier way to work the problem. Try to list reasons for your preferences. Discuss the merits of the methods in relation to these applications.

B. Another application of systems of linear equations is the classic age problem. Work as a group to write and solve a system of equations for each situation.

1. Stella is 4 years younger than three times her son's age. Five years ago, Stella was 1 year younger than four times her son's age. How old are Stella and her son now?

2. Gulen was daydreaming about her daughter Cecilia. In thinking about their ages, she realized that in 6 years she would be five times as old as Cecilia. In 13 years, she would be three times as old as Cecilia. Can you tell how old Gulen and Cecilia are now?

3. Joe wants to take early retirement in 10 years, when he will be twice as old as his son Paul. Joe is now 25 years older than Paul. How old is Joe now, and how old will he be when he retires?

4. Jenny and Katie bet Susan that she can't solve the riddle about their ages. Jenny is 2 years younger than Katie. In 5 years, Katie will be 10% older than Jenny. Help Susan find their ages now.

5. Egan was researching her family history for a school project. In a box of mementos, she found a birthday card from her grandmother to her mom. The card was dated 1965 and the note inside said, "Congratulations, Mary, you are now $\frac{1}{3}$ as old as I am." She found a second card, dated 1977, also from her grandmother to her mother, which read, "Congratulations, Mary, you are now $\frac{1}{2}$ as old as I am!" When Egan asked her mom how old she was on these two birthdays, her mom (a math teacher) told her to figure it out for herself. How old were her mom and her grandmother in these two years?

6. An antiques dealer found an old dresser and bed with a note attached. The note said that in 1902, the combined age of the bed and dresser was 148 years. It also said that in 4 more years, the dresser would be twice as old as the bed. How old were the two pieces of furniture in 1902?

7. Katie's friend wants to know Katie's age. Since Katie's mom is a math teacher, Katie decides to give the answer in a math riddle. She gives her friend the following information. Katie's mom, Brenda, is eight times as old as Katie. In 10 years, Brenda will be three times as old as Katie. How old are they both now?

8. The tie-breaker question in a math contest was an age problem: Fric is three times as old as Frac. In 5 years, Fric's age will be 2 years more than twice Frac's age. How old are they now?

Experiencing Algebra the Write Way

1. Many of the application exercises presented in this section have become classic algebra problems. You will find variations of them in most algebra textbooks. Some students object to these as being contrived and not very practical. For example, students often state that age problems have no practical significance, and one sometimes sees cartoons that joke about distance-traveled problems. Write a short paragraph describing how you feel about these applications. Do you feel they are worthwhile, and if so, why? Do you think they are contrived? Can you suggest better applications?

2. Many texts use a system-of-equations approach to solve application problems. Search the library for a textbook that uses this technique in an application. You might want to search in business texts, industrial engineering texts, applied mathematics texts, etc. Sometimes a search of the index will identify an application of systems of linear equations. As the application becomes more complex, more sophisticated techniques for solution are applied. Avoid these examples for now. When

you find a suitable application, make a copy of the example and note the call number of the text and the publishing information. Then prepare a short writeup describing the application and noting the methods involved in the solution. Attach your copy of the example and the reference information on the text to your writeup before submitting it to your instructor.

CHAPTER 7	Summary

After completing this chapter, you should be able to define in your own words the following key terms, definitions, and rules.

Terms
consistent
inconsistent
dependent
independent
substitution method
elimination method
simultaneous equations

Definitions
System of linear equations in two
  variables
Solution of a system of linear equations

Rules
Solving a system of linear equations
  graphically

Solving a system of linear equations in
  two variables using substitution
Solving a system of linear equations in
  two variables using elimination
Modeling real-world situations

CHAPTER 7	Review

Reflections

1. Explain the difference between a solution of a linear equation in two variables and a solution of a system of linear equations in two variables.

2. Describe the method of solving a system of linear equations graphically.

3. What do we mean by an inconsistent system of linear equations?

4. What do we mean by a system of dependent linear equations?

5. What can you say about the solutions to a consistent system of independent linear equations?

6. How do you solve a system of linear equations using the substitution method?

7. How do you solve a system of linear equations using the elimination method?

8. When solving a system of linear equations algebraically, how do you know that there is no solution? How do you know that there are many solutions?

7.1

Determine whether each ordered pair is a solution for the given system of linear equations.

1. $(2, -4)$; $3x + 2y = -2$
   $4x - 3y = 20$

2. $\left(\dfrac{17}{7}, \dfrac{8}{7}\right)$; $2x + y = 6$
   $-x + 3y = 1$

3. $(0.25, -0.45)$; $4x - 5y = 3$
   $8x + 5y = 0$

4. $(7, -2)$; $x + 3y = 13$
   $x - y = 5$

5. $\left(\dfrac{2}{3}, \dfrac{2}{3}\right)$; $3x + 6y = -2$
   $6x - 3y = 6$

6. $(1.5, -2.4)$; $6x + 5y = -3$
   $2x - 10y = 27$

7. $(4, 2)$; $2(x - 3) = 2$
   $3(y + 1) = -3$

8. $(-3, 5)$; $x + 5 = 2$
   $2y - 3 = 7$

Solve each system of equations graphically.

9. $2x + y = 17$
   $y = 3x - 18$

10. $3(x + 2) + 1 = -5$
    $2x - y = -10$

11. $x + 6 = 4$
    $2(y + 2) = y + 3$

12. $x - 2y = 11$
    $2x + 3y = -6$

13. $y = 2(x + 2)$
    $2x - y = 5$

14. $y = \dfrac{3}{2}x - 6$
    $3x - 2y = 12$

15. $y = 3x - 6$
    $y = -3$

16. $2y - 3 = 1$
    $5(y - 4) = 10$

17. $2x - 11 = 3$
$14 - 2x = x - 7$

18. $y - 1 = 4$
$3y - 2 = 13$

19. $2x + 3y = 6$
$x + y = 1$

20. $f(x) = 2x - 15$
$g(x) = -3x + 10$

21. $y = 2x + 1$
$x = 2y + 7$

22. $2y + 6 = 3y + 5$
$2(x - 3) + 1 = 5$

Write a system of linear equations to represent each situation and solve graphically.

23. A survey of 500 voters revealed that 120 people considered themselves Independents. Of the remaining people surveyed, there were 40 more Republicans than Democrats. However, the survey failed to report how many of each there were. How many more Democrats than Independents were surveyed?

24. The perimeter of a rectangular bath towel is 116.6 inches. A second bath towel has a width that is 4.7 inches larger, and a length that is 2.9 inches shorter. The perimeter of the second bath towel is 120.2 inches. Find the dimensions of each towel.

7.2

Solve each system of linear equations using substitution.

25. $8y = 5$
$4x + 8y = 2$

26. $10x - 5y = -14$
$5x - 1 = 0$

27. $4x - y = 5$
$y = 4x + 3$

28. $x - 2y = 71$
$3x - 7y = 275$

29. $2x + 3y = -69$
$2x - 4y = 218$

30. $3(x + 2) - y = -1$
$y = 3x + 7$

31. $x + 8y = 5$
$12x + y = 10$

32. $5x - 3y = 406$
$2x - y = 327$

33. $y = \dfrac{1}{3}x - 4$
$x - 5y = 0$

34. $y = \dfrac{1}{2}x + 7$
$y = -\dfrac{3}{5}x - 4$

35. $3x - y = 10$
$2x - 6y = 26$

36. $x = 160y$
$3x - 440y = 30$

Write a system of linear equations to represent each situation and solve using substitution.

37. Two angles are complementary. The second angle is 12 degrees more than twice the first angle. What is the difference in the measures of the two angles?

38. A machinist has to make a rectangular metal plate meeting the following requirements: The length is to be 2.5 cm less than three times the width, and the perimeter is to be 31.8 cm. What will be the area of the rectangular metal plate?

39. Demi invested her salary from her last blockbuster movie in two simple-interest funds. Her salary was $10,000,000. One fund paid 4.5% simple interest and the other fund paid 6% simple interest. At the end of the year, she received a total of $487,500 in interest payments. How much did she invest in each fund?

7.3

Solve each system of equations using the elimination method.

40. $5x + 3y = -10$
$5x - 3y = 80$

41. $x = 18 - 2y$
$3x + 2y = 30$

42. $\dfrac{1}{2}x + \dfrac{1}{3}y = 3$
$\dfrac{1}{4}x - \dfrac{2}{5}y = -7$

43. $5x + 10y = -55$
$2x - 3y = 6$

44. $2x = 3y + 1$
$15y = 10x + 5$

45. $5x + 7y = 21$
$3x - 2y = 13$

46. $3x + y = 20$
$y = \dfrac{2}{3}x + \dfrac{16}{3}$

47. $7(y - 1) = 5x$
$y = \dfrac{5}{7}x + 1$

48. $3x - 3y = 4$
$9x + 9y = -2$

49. $3x - y = 0$
$2x + 2y = 7$

50. $0.25x + 0.3y = 4$
$0.5x - 0.2y = 4$

51. $0.2x + 0.1y = 5$
$0.02x - 0.01y = 13.5$

Write a system of equations to represent each situation and solve using the elimination method.

52. One alloy contains 25% copper and another contains 30% copper. The two alloys are combined to form 100 pounds of an alloy that contains 27% copper. How much of each alloy should be used in the process?

53. A realtor is refurbishing a building to hold 40 offices. She will rent small offices for $250 per month and larger offices for $400 per month. She wants to collect exactly $12,700 per month in order to recover her investment with a reasonable profit. Which will she have more of — the small offices or the large offices? How many of each will she have?

54. The mass of the Earth is approximately 5.328×10^{24} kg greater than the mass of the planet Mars. The average mass of the two planets is approximately 3.306×10^{24} kg. Find the mass of both planets.

7.4

Write and solve a system of linear equations for each situation.

55. A manufacturing plant receives the same component from two suppliers. Supplier A can provide the component at $25 each, while Supplier B can provide the component at $35 each. Under ideal conditions, the plant would buy all of the components from Supplier A. But the plant manager recognizes that it should do business with both suppliers in order to ensure a supply of the components and to promote competition. The budget allows $5500 per month for the component and the plant needs 200 components each month. How many components should the plant order from each supplier in order to satisfy the budget limitation?

56. A plant-food manufacturer wants to blend a fertilizer that is 10% nitrogen with another that is 5% nitrogen to obtain a blend that is 8% nitrogen. If he wants to make 150 pounds of the blend, how many pounds of each should he use?

57. A food-processing plant is producing frozen vegetables consisting of a mixture of broccoli and cauliflower. The plant will sell the mixture for 69 cents per pound. They sell the broccoli separately for 49 cents a pound and the cauliflower for 99 cents per pound. If they wish to produce 200 pounds of the mixture, how many pounds of each vegetable should be mixed?

58. A trucking company had to send a truck on a delivery 600 miles away. Part of the route was on an interstate where the driver drove at 65 mph. The rest was on rural highways where his speed was 45 mph. If the driver made the trip in 10 hours, how many miles did he drive on the interstate? (*Hint:* If x = hours of interstate driving, then $10 - x$ = hours of highway driving. Likewise, if y = interstate miles, then $600 - y$ = highway miles.)

59. In Olympic competition, a kayak racer had a winning time of 3:37.26, which equals 217.26 seconds over the course. The runner-up had a time of 3:37.50, which equals 217.50 seconds over the same course. If the speed of the winning racer was 1.603 meters per second (mps) in still water, and that of the runner up was 1.598 mps in still water, find the speed of the current and the distance of the race.

60. A company has setup costs for a production run of $400.00. Each item costs $5.00 to produce. The items sell for $8.50 each. Write a cost and revenue function for this situation, and find the break-even point. Interpret the break-even point in terms of its impact on the company's production strategy.

61. Dave can lease a car from company A for $150.00 per week plus $0.25 per mile. He can lease the same car from company B for $175.00 per week plus $0.20 per mile. How many miles must he drive in the week in order for the company B car to be more economical?

| CHAPTER 7 ' | **Mixed Review** |

Solve each system of equations using the elimination method.

1. $y = \frac{4}{7}x + 2$

$x - 3y = 4$

2. $y = \frac{4}{5}x - 6$

$5y + 2 = 4(x - 7)$

3. $1.25x + 3.5y = -25$

$4.5x + 2.8y = 8$

4. $0.55x - 0.68y = 48$

$-0.51x + 0.68y = 0$

5. $8x + 2y = -6$

$6x - 2y = -78$

6. $2x + 8y = -12$

$y = 2x + 3$

7. $3x + y = 4$

$12x + 4y = 9$

8. $3x - 5y = 11$

$4x + 2y = 13$

9. $\frac{1}{3}x - \frac{2}{5}y = 10$

$\frac{1}{2}x + \frac{4}{5}y = -13$

10. $4x + 8y = 68$

$5x - 3y = -6$

11. $2x + y = 0$

$x + 4y = 3$

12. $5x + 3y = 9$

$x - y = 6$

Solve each system of linear equations graphically.

13. $2y + 2 = y$

$y = -x + 1$

14. $2x + 3 = x$

$2x = 5$

15. $y = 2x + 10$

$3x + y = -10$

16. $2(x - 1) - 4 = 0$

$2x + y = 3$

17. $x + y = 9 - x$

$2x + y = 5$

18. $y = -4x - 3$

$4x + 2y = y - 3$

19. $3x + 4 = 2x$

$x + 7 = 3$

20. $3y + 7 = 2y + 5$

$y + 9 = 7$

21. $3(x - 3) - 1 = 8$

$3y - 10 = 15 - 2y$

22. $y = 3x + 7$

$x - y = -1$

23. $x - 5y = 15$

$x + 5y = -5$

24. $f(x) = -4x - 6$

$g(x) = 3x + 8$

25. $y = x$

$x = 2 - y$

26. $x + 9 = 3$

$3y = 2y - 1$

Solve each system of linear equations using substitution.

27. $y = \frac{5}{11}x - 43$

$x + 2y = -2$

28. $y = \frac{3}{4}x + 14$

$y = -\frac{2}{3}x - 3$

29. $2x + 3y = 53$

$2x - 4y = -248$

30. $y = 4x - 7$

$2y + 12 = 4x + y + 5$

31. $y = -5x$

$x - y = 1$

32. $5x - 10y = 21$

$5x = -3$

33. $x + 7y = 3$

$4x + y = 9$

34. $5x + 6y = 669$

$x - 2y = 1705$

35. $x - y = 5$

$6x + 2y = 9$

36. $x = 324y$

$3x - 810y = 90$

37. $y = -2x + 7$

$2x + y = 0$

38. $2x - y = 60$

$5x - 3y = 60$

Determine whether each ordered pair is a solution for the given system of linear equations.

39. $\left(\frac{5}{6}, -\frac{1}{6}\right)$; $4x + 2y = 3$

$x - y = -1$

40. $(-1.6, 3.8)$; $3x + y = -1$

$5x + 5y = 11$

41. $(-4, 2)$; $5x + 7y = -6$

$2x - 7y = -22$

42. $\left(\frac{13}{9}, -\frac{4}{9}\right)$; $x + y = 1$

$8x - y = 12$

43. $(3, -2)$; $2x - 1 = 5$

$3y + 5 = 2$

44. $(-5, -3)$; $x + 10 = 5$

$3y + 11 = 2$

45. $(-0.44, 1.22)$; $x + 2y = 2$

$2x + 4y = 5$

46. $(-2, -3)$; $2x + 5y = -19$

$3x - 7y = 10$

Write and solve a system of linear equations for each situation.

47. An alloy containing 15% brass is to be combined with an alloy containing 35% brass to form an alloy containing 27% brass. How much of each alloy should be combined to make 200 pounds of the 27% brass alloy? How much more of the 35% alloy will be used than of the 15% alloy?

48. A landlord has 8 one-bedroom apartments and 12 two-bedroom apartments to rent. She wants the two-bedroom apartments to rent for $150 more than the one-bedroom apartments. She wants the total monthly rental income to be $7300. She must determine how much to charge as the monthly rental for each type of apartment. How much will she receive in total rentals each month for all the one-bedroom apartments? How much will she receive in total rentals each month for all the two-bedroom apartments?

49. Two angles are supplementary. The second angle must measure 10 degrees more than the first angle. What does the smaller angle measure?

50. A sculptor has a 100-inch iron rod that must be formed into two squares. The second square must have a side that is 5 inches more than the first square's side. What will be the area of each of the squares formed?

51. A survey of 700 people was conducted. Forty percent of the men surveyed supported the issue at question, while 70 percent of the women favored it. A total of 400 people favored the issue. How many more women than men were surveyed?

52. Two angles are supplementary. One angle measures 12 degrees more than three times the other angle. Find the measures of the angles.

53. A chemist wants to mix a solution containing 15% sulfuric acid with a solution containing 25% sulfuric acid to make 30 cc of a mixture that is 21% sulfuric acid. How much of each concentration should she use?

54. A cardiac patient is put on an exercise program of walking and jogging. He reports to his doctor that one day he walked for 30 minutes and jogged for 20 minutes and covered a distance of 3.5 miles. The next day he walked for 40 minutes and jogged for 20 minutes and covered a distance of 4 miles. Assuming that his rates of walking and jogging are the same each day, determine how fast he walked and how fast he jogged, in miles per hour. (*Note:* Convert the times to hours before solving the exercise.)

55. A coffee shop blends gourmet coffee, which sells for $8.50 per pound, with gourmet Dutch chocolate, which sells for $12.50 per pound. They make a mocha blend that sells for $9.50 per pound. How much of each should be mixed to make 50 pounds of the blend?

56. Nikki has been offered two part-time jobs while she attends college. One job pays $10.75 per hour and requires her to work on a production line. The other pays $6.50 per hour as a night clerk and allows her to spend her time studying. She can work a total of 20 hours per week without affecting her studies. She wants to earn exactly $181.00 per week to pay for room and board. How many hours should she work on each job to meet her requirements?

57. When planes fly west to California, they often encounter head winds; while flying east, they encounter tail winds. If a plane flies at 400 mph with no wind, and the prevailing winds are 40 mph west to east, what would be the distance traveled, given that the return trip east was 1 hour shorter in duration than the trip west?

58. U Rent It will lease a moving van for $39.95 plus $0.15 per mile. Budget Haul It will lease the same type of van for $19.95 plus $0.22 per mile. How many miles must you drive in order for the U Rent It deal to be the less costly choice?

59. A shopkeeper has fixed costs of $75.00 per day and material costs of $2.50 per item produced and sold. The items sell for $6.50 each. How many items must the shopkeeper produce and sell each day in order not to lose money?

CHAPTER 7 | **Test**

Test-Taking Tips

Having the right attitude can make the difference between successfully completing a test or not. Students who say "I've always hated mathematics" or "I've never been good at math" often defeat themselves before they start. Start thinking about ways in which you can overcome "math inability." Pay attention to detail. Don't rush through the arithmetic calculations. Check your addition and subtraction. When allowed, repeat the calculation on your calculator. Develop a persistent, "don't quit" attitude. Tell yourself that you won't stop working on the test until the time is up. If you are stuck on a problem, start writing on paper what you know. Sometimes the act of writing will unleash thoughts in your mind that will help you solve a problem. Take pleasure in the math exercises you *can* do. This alone may improve your attitude, build up your confidence, and cause you to think more clearly on the test.

---

1. Determine whether each ordered pair is a solution of the given system of equations.

$(22.8, -64.3);$ $y = -3.5x + 15.5$
$$15x + 10y = -301$$

Solve each system of equations graphically.

2. $2y - 8 = 0$

   $y = 4$

3. $y = \dfrac{1}{2}x + 3$

   $y = \dfrac{1}{2}x - 5$

4. $y = 5x - 9$

   $4x + 8y = 16$

Solve each system of equations using the substitution method.

5. $x + 2y = 6$
   $5x - 11y = -54$

6. $3x + 6y = 12$
   $x + 2y = -5$

7. $x + 6y = -2$
   $x - 2y = 1$

Solve each system of equations using the elimination method.

8. $3x + 7y = 11$
   $6x + 14y = 2$

9. $2x + 9y = 16$
   $5y = 8 - x$

10. $5x + 3y = 11$
    $2x + 5y = 7$

In exercises 11–16, write and solve a system of equations for the information given.

11. A factory has a setup cost of $5500 and a cost per item of $65 each to produce. The items sell for $125 each. This yields a cost function of $C(x) = 5500 + 65x$ and a revenue function of $R(x) = 125x$. Find the break-even point for this production process, and interpret what it represents.

12. It took Kenny 3 hours to pedal a tandem bicycle built for two to where Dolly was waiting. Dolly's pedaling increased their speed by 4 mph and the return trip took them only 2 hours. How fast could Kenny pedal alone, and how far did he have to go to find Dolly?

13. A high-speed computer takes 58 nanoseconds (ns) to perform 6 additions and 8 multiplication operations. It takes 55 nanoseconds to perform 10 additions and 5 multiplications. How many nanoseconds does the computer take to perform one addition? How many nanoseconds for one multiplication?

14. A candy shop owner is mixing chocolate-covered raisins selling at $1.25 per pound with chocolate-covered peanuts, which sell for $2.00 per pound. He makes a mix to sell at $1.50 per pound. How many pounds of each should he mix in order to make 30 pounds of the mix?

15. Mel is placing a triangular flower garden in one corner of his yard. The corner angle will be 90 degrees. The other two angles will be complementary, and he wants one of these angles to be twice as large as the other. How large will each angle be?

16. A chemist needs 100 cc of a 30% nitric acid solution. She has a 50% solution and a 10% solution in stock. How many cc of each must she mix in order to make the required solution?

17. When solving a system of linear equations, one of three outcomes can occur. List the three outcomes, and explain how you would identify them if you were solving the system of equations using the graphical method.

8

Inequalities

I n the last few chapters we have studied several ways to solve equations. But sometimes it is useful to work with relations in which one quantity is not necessarily equal to some other quantity. Instead, it can be helpful to know that an algebraic expression is simply less than or greater than some other one.

In this chapter we will examine linear inequalities and methods of solving them. We will discuss linear inequalities in one variable and in two variables, and systems of linear inequalities in two variables. We will see that the same methods used for solving equations—numeric, graphic, and algebraic—work for solving inequalities as well.

Linear inequalities are important in many areas of practical mathematics. For example, keeping within a budget is a familiar and important application of inequalities, both in large businesses and in our personal lives. We will look at several ways of describing costs and budgets in this chapter and show how to solve some kinds of budgetary problems.

8.1   Introduction to Linear Inequalities

Objectives   1   Identify linear inequalities in one variable.

2   Represent linear inequalities as graphs on a number line.

3   Represent linear inequalities using interval notation.

4   Model real-world situations using linear inequalities.

Application

United Parcel Service (UPS) air pricing for a 6-pound package is $22.75 per package for Next Day Air delivery.[1] With 24-hour notice, there is a flat fee of $5.00 for package pickup. Write a linear inequality in one variable to determine the possible number of packages that your company can ship this way and still stay within its budget of $500.00 per day.

After completing this section, we will discuss this application further. See page 567.

1   Linear Inequalities in One Variable
In this chapter we will be solving inequalities of various forms. In this section we will solve linear inequalities in one variable. A **linear inequality in one variable** (sometimes shortened to **linear inequality**) is written by replacing the equal symbol in a linear equation in one variable with an order symbol. The **order symbols** are "greater than" ($>$), "less than" ($<$), "greater than or equal to" ($\geq$), and "less than or equal to" ($\leq$).

> *Standard Form for a Linear Inequality in One Variable*
> A linear inequality in one variable is an inequality in standard form that can be written in one of the following ways:
>
> $$ax + b < 0$$
> $$ax + b > 0$$
> $$ax + b \geq 0$$
> $$ax + b \leq 0$$
>
> where a and b are real numbers and $a \neq 0$.

[1] "United Parcel Service," *The 1995 Information Please Business Almanac and Sourcebook.* Copyright 1994, Seth Godin Productions, Inc.

For example,

$ax + b < 0$

1. $2x + 5 < 0$

2. $2x - 5 < 6$

3. $x + 2 + 3(x - 4) < 3x - 8$

The first inequality is in the exact form $ax + b < 0$. The other inequalities can be written in this form with algebraic manipulations that we will learn later in this section.

Note that in a linear inequality, the variable is raised to the first power. An example of a nonlinear inequality, which we will solve later in this text, is $2x^2 - 4 < 0$.

Until we learn algebraic manipulations for inequalities, we will identify a linear inequality in one variable, x, as an inequality consisting of two expressions. Each of these expressions can be simplified to the form $ax + b$, where $a \neq 0$ in at least one of the expressions and the coefficient a is not the same in each expression. Using the previous linear examples,

$$ax + b \qquad ax + b$$

1. $\qquad 2x + 5 < 0x + 0$

2. $2x + (-5) < 0x + 6$

3. $4x + (-10) < 3x + (-8)$

EXAMPLE 1 Identify each inequality as linear or nonlinear.

a. $5x + (x - 2) > 3(x - 2)$ **b.** $x + 5 < x^3 - 2x$

c. $\sqrt[4]{x + 2} \geq 3x - 7$

Solution

a. Linear, because the inequality simplifies to $6x + (-2) > 3x + (-6)$.
b. Nonlinear, because the variable x has an exponent of 3.
c. Nonlinear, because the radical expression contains a variable. ∎

 Experiencing Algebra the Checkup Way

In exercises 1–5, identify each inequality as linear or nonlinear.

1. $4x + 3 \geq 11$ **2.** $6x - (3x + 2) < 4(x - 1)$ **3.** $x^2 + 3x < 2x - 5$

4. $\sqrt[3]{x} + 3 \leq 5x + 1$ **5.** $\dfrac{1}{x} + 3x \geq 2x - 1$

6. What is the difference between a linear equation in one variable and a linear inequality in one variable?

7. How can you decide whether an inequality in one variable is a linear inequality?

2   Representing Linear Inequalities on a Number Line

In section 1.1 we discussed order relations involving rational numbers. These numeric inequalities were all true statements. However, just as numeric equations may be true or false, numeric inequalities may also be true or false. For example,

$1 < 5$ is a true inequality because 1 is less than 5.

$-6 > 7$ is a false inequality because -6 is less than 7, not greater than 7.

$-1 \geq -1$ is a true inequality because -1 is equal to -1.

Remember, the calculator will test these inequalities and display a 1 for true and 0 for false. For example, test these inequalities on your calculator, as shown in Figure 8.1.

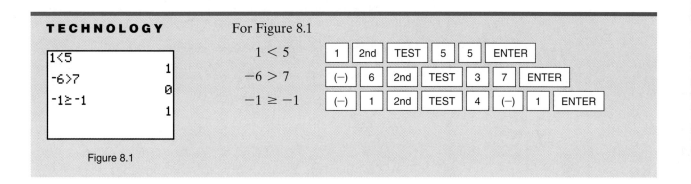

TECHNOLOGY

For Figure 8.1

$1 < 5$ — | 1 | 2nd | TEST | 5 | 5 | ENTER |

$-6 > 7$ — | (−) | 6 | 2nd | TEST | 3 | 7 | ENTER |

$-1 \geq -1$ — | (−) | 1 | 2nd | TEST | 4 | (−) | 1 | ENTER |

Figure 8.1

Linear inequalities that include variables may be true or false, depending on the value of the variable being substituted. A solution of a linear inequality is a number that will make the inequality true. For example,

$x < 5$ is a linear inequality.

There are many possible solutions of this inequality.

4 is a solution because $4 < 5$.

3 is a solution because $3 < 5$.

$4\frac{1}{2}$ is a solution because $4\frac{1}{2} < 5$.

4.75 is a solution because $4.75 < 5$.

In fact, it is impossible to name all the solutions because there are an infinite number of numbers less than 5. Therefore, we say we have a set of solutions. A solution set is a set of all possible solutions.

We can represent a solution set as a graph on a number line. For example, graph on a number line the solution set of $x < 5$.

Since we want to represent all numbers less than 5, we say that 5 is the **upper bound** of the solution set. We will graph 5 with an open dot because 5 itself is not a solution. All numbers less than 5 are graphed to the left of 5 on the number line.

Note: Given the inequality $x > 5$, we say that 5 is the **lower bound** because we want to represent all numbers greater than 5.

Number Line Notation
To graph the solution set of a linear inequality in the form $x < c$, $x > c, x \leq c$, or $x \geq c$ on a number line:

1. Plot the upper or lower bound, c, of the inequality on the number line.

- Use an open dot if the bound is not included in the solution.
- Use a closed dot if the bound is a solution.

2. Complete the graph using a solid line.

- Cover all points to the left of the upper bound for a "less than" or "less than or equal to" inequality.
- Cover all points to the right of the lower bound for a "greater than" or "greater than or equal to" inequality.

To graph the solution set of a linear inequality in the form $x < c$, $x > c$, $x \leq c$, or $x \geq c$ on a number line on your calculator:

- Set the screen to integer coordinates. If this is hard to read, change the y-values to -3.1, 3.1, 10.
- Define Y1 to be the inequality.

The calculator will test the inequality for x-values and graph an ordered pair $(x, 1)$ for true and $(x, 0)$ for false.

- Trace and use the arrow keys to display the coordinates graphed. The x-coordinate is a solution and is graphed on the number line if the y-coordinate is 1.

Helping Hand Be careful when interpreting this representation. If the bound is not included in the solution set, it is difficult to determine its value.

For example, on your calculator, graph on a number line the solution set of $x < 5$, as shown in Figure 8.2.

TECHNOLOGY

Y1 = x < 5
(−47, 47, −3.1, 3.1)

Figure 8.2

For Figure 8.2
Set the screen for the number line.

Enter the inequality in Y1.

| Y= | X, T, θ, n | 2nd | TEST | 5 | 5 |

Graph the number line.

| GRAPH |

| TRACE | and use the arrow keys to determine the graph with y-coordinates equal to 1. Notice that y is 0 when x is 5 because 5 is not a solution of the inequality.

EXAMPLE 2   Graph on a number line the solution set of $x \geq 5$.

Solution

Since we want to represent all numbers greater than or equal to 5, we say that 5 is the lower bound of the solution set. We will graph 5 with a closed dot because it is a solution. All numbers greater than 5 are graphed to the right of 5 on the number line.

Y1 = x ≥ 5
(−47, 47, −3.1, 3.1)

Check the graph of the solution set on your calculator. Notice that y is 1 when x is 5 because 5 is a solution of the inequality. ∎

EXAMPLE 3   Graph on a number line the solution set of $-2 < x \leq 3$.

Solution

This inequality is a special case of a linear inequality.

Since we want to represent all numbers between −2 and 3, including 3, we will graph the lower bound, −2, with an open dot because it is not a solution and the upper bound, 3, with a closed dot because it is a solution. All numbers between −2 and 3 are also graphed.

To check the graph of the solution set, partition the inequality into two inequalities, and place each in parentheses when storing in Y1. The calculator will multiply 0's and 1's to define the true region. For example, to graph $-2 < x \le 3$, the two partitions are $-2 < x$ and $x \le 3$.

TECHNOLOGY

Y1 = $(-2 < x)(x \le 3)$
$(-47, 47, -3.1, 3.1)$

Figure 8.3

For Figure 8.3
Set the screen for the number line.

| ZOOM | 6 | ZOOM | 8 | ENTER | WINDOW | ▼ | ▼ | ▼ | (−) |

| 3 | . | 1 | ▼ | 3 | . | 1 | ▼ | 1 | 0 |

Enter the inequalities in Y1.

| Y= | (| (−) | 2 | 2nd | TEST | 5 | X, T, θ, n |) | (| X, T, θ, n |

| 2nd | TEST | 6 | 3 |) |

Graph the number line.

| GRAPH |

| TRACE | and use the arrow keys to determine the graph with y-coordinates equal to 1.

✓ Experiencing Algebra the Checkup Way

In exercises 1–3, graph the solution set of each inequality on a number line.

1. $x > -2$ **2.** $x \le 3$ **3.** $1 \le x < 5$

4. When graphing a linear inequality on a number line, how can you indicate whether or not the boundary point is included in the solution?

3 Representing Linear Inequalities in Interval Notation

A solution set of a linear inequality can also be written in interval notation. **Interval notation** consists of two numbers or symbols representing the lower and upper bounds, if they exist, enclosed in either parentheses or brackets, indicating whether the bound is included in the set or not. If no lower bound exists, we use the symbol $-\infty$ (**negative infinity**) in its place. If no upper bound exists, we use the symbol ∞ (**infinity**) in its place. If the bound is included in the solution, it is enclosed in a bracket. (This corresponds to a closed dot on a number line.) If the bound is not included in the set, it is enclosed in a parenthesis. (This corresponds to an open dot on a number line.) The symbols $-\infty$ and ∞ are not numbers, but indicate that the set continues without bound. Therefore, the symbols $-\infty$ and ∞ are always enclosed in parentheses.

Helping Hand The interval notation to represent a solution set of all real numbers is $(-\infty, \infty)$.

For example, write in interval notation the solution set of $x < 5$.

The solution set includes all numbers less than 5. The upper bound is 5. There is no lower bound, so $-\infty$ will be used in its place. The symbol $-\infty$ must be enclosed in a parenthesis. The upper bound, 5, is not included in the solution set, so it is also enclosed in a parenthesis.

lower bound, upper bound

> *Interval Notation*
> To write the solution set of a linear inequality in the form $x < c, x > c,$ $x \leq c,$ or $x \geq c$ using interval notation:
>
> - Determine the bounds for the solutions, if they exist. Write the bounds in increasing order separated by a comma. If no lower bound exists, use the symbol $-\infty$ in its place. If no upper bound exists, use the symbol ∞ in its place.
>
> - Enclose each bound of the inequality in a parenthesis or bracket. A parenthesis is used to denote that the lower or upper bound is not included in the solution set. A bracket is used to denote that the lower or upper bound is included in the solution set.
>
> Remember, the symbols $-\infty$ and ∞ are not numbers and are enclosed in a parenthesis.

EXAMPLE 4   Write in interval notation the solution set of $x \geq 5$.

Solution

The solution set includes all numbers greater than or equal to 5. The lower bound is 5. There is no upper bound, so ∞ will be used in its place. The symbol ∞ must be enclosed in a parenthesis. The lower bound, 5, is included in the solution set, so it is enclosed in a bracket.
   The solution set is $[5, \infty)$. ∎

EXAMPLE 5   Write in interval notation the solution set of $-2 < x \leq 3$.

Solution

This inequality is a special case of a linear inequality. The solution set includes all numbers between -2 and 3, including 3. The lower bound is -2. The upper bound is 3. The lower bound, -2, is not included in the solution set, so it is enclosed in a parenthesis. The upper bound, 3, is included in the solution set, so it is enclosed with a bracket.
   The solution set is $(-2, 3]$. ∎

The following table summarizes what we have learned in this section by describing some of the most common inequalities you may encounter.

Inequality	Number Line	Interval Notation
$x < a$		$(-\infty, a)$
$x \leq a$		$(-\infty, a]$
$x > a$		(a, ∞)
$x \geq a$		$[a, \infty)$
$a < x < b$		(a, b)
$a \leq x \leq b$		$[a, b]$

EXAMPLE 6   Complete the following table.

Inequality	Number Line	Interval Notation
$x > 5$		
		$[-3, \infty)$
$-3 \leq x < 0$		

Solution

Inequality	Number Line	Interval Notation
$x > 5$		$(5, \infty)$
$x \leq -1$		$(-\infty, -1]$
$x \geq -3$		$[-3, \infty)$
$-3 \leq x < 0$		$[-3, 0)$

Experiencing Algebra the Checkup Way

Write the solution set for each inequality in interval notation.

1. $x > -2$ **2.** $x \leq 3$ **3.** $1 \leq x < 5$

Complete the following table.

	Inequality	Number Line	Interval Notation
4.	$x > -3$		
5.			
6.			$[-4, 1)$

7. When writing the solution to a linear inequality using interval notation, what is the interpretation of a bound that is enclosed with a parenthesis, and what is the interpretation of a bound that is enclosed with a bracket?

8. When using interval notation, how can you indicate that there is no lower bound or no upper bound on the solution set of a linear inequality?

---

4 Modeling the Real World

Inequalities are very useful kinds of relations in real-world situations. They're especially helpful if you have to calculate quantities that must be more or less than a given value, such as calculating what you can spend within a given budget. Sometimes you might want to determine quantities that are between two given values, such as how many guests you can invite to a dinner that costs between $100 and $150. In these situations as well, inequalities are the kind of mathematics you need.

EXAMPLE 7

Qu is purchasing begonia tubers for her garden from a mail-order catalog. The special offer reads, "Buy 12 tubers of one color for $9.65. Free shipping on orders over $30.00." Write a linear inequality to determine the number of different colors Qu can purchase and receive free shipping and still stay within her budget of $50.00.

Solution

Let x = number of colors Qu can order

The cost is $9.65 per color ordered ($9.65x$). The lower bound is $30.00 and the upper bound is $50.00. The lower bound is not included because she must spend over $30.00. The upper bound is included, as this is the most she can spend.

$$30.00 < 9.65x \leq 50.00$$ ∎

Application

United Parcel Service (UPS) air pricing for a 6-pound package is $22.75 per package for Next Day Air delivery.[1] With 24-hour notice, there is a flat fee of $5.00 for package pickup. Write a linear inequality in one variable to

[1] "United Parcel Service," *The 1995 Information Please Business Almanac and Sourcebook.* Copyright 1994 Seth Godin Productions, Inc.

determine the possible number of packages that your company can ship this way and still stay within its budget of $500.00 per day.

Discussion

Let $x =$ the number of packages shipped

The shipping cost is $22.75 per package, or $22.75x$.
The total cost is the $5.00 pickup fee added to the shipping cost, or $22.75x + 5.00$.
We want this total cost to be less than $500.00, so we have the inequality:

$$22.75x + 5.00 \leq 500.00$$

We will see in the next section how to solve this kind of inequality, which gives us an answer of at most 21 packages shipped per day. If this is not close to the number of packages your company usually ships, on average, then you know you need to change your method of shipping or be prepared to change your budget. ∎

Experiencing Algebra the Checkup Way

Joseph joined a music compact disc club. The club offered a sale in which he could purchase compact discs for $6.99 each, plus a one-time charge of $5.99 for shipping and handling his order. Write a linear inequality in one variable to determine the possible number of CDs Joseph can order if he can spend no more than $50.00.

PROBLEM SET 8.1

Experiencing Algebra the Exercise Way

Identify each inequality as linear or nonlinear.

1. $3(x + 1) > -(5x - 4)$

2. $x + 3 > 2(4x - 1) + 6(x + 2)$

3. $4x^2 + 1 < 3x + 2$

4. $\sqrt[3]{x} + 1 \geq x - 1$

5. $\frac{5}{7}(a + 2) \geq \frac{3}{7}a + \frac{2}{3}$

6. $\frac{2}{3}(b - 6) \leq \frac{1}{3}b - \frac{2}{3}$

7. $0.6x + 2.7 \leq 5.2 - 1.9x$

8. $4d - 7 > -4$

9. $x + 4(x - 8) > 2(3x + 1)$

10. $4x^3 - 1 > 2x^2 - 5$

11. $\sqrt{2x - 7} \leq x + 3$

12. $\frac{3}{y} - y < 2$

13. $\frac{5}{x} + 2x > 0$

14. $2(x - 1) < -3(x - 2)$

15. $2p + 6 < 0$

16. $0.8z - 1.3 \leq 4.7 - 2.6z$

Graph the solution set of each inequality on the number line. Then write the solution set in interval notation.

17. $x \geq 6$

18. $x \leq 9$

19. $z < 12$

20. $c > -7$

21. $b > -\frac{13}{5}$

22. $x < 3\frac{5}{6}$

23. $x \leq 4\frac{2}{3}$

24. $k \geq \frac{16}{3}$

25. $P \leq 12.59$

26. $x \geq 5.1$

27. $q > -6.7$

28. $R < 45.65$

29. $5 < x < 13$

30. $-2 < x < -1$

31. $2 < x < 8$

32. $3 \leq w \leq 6$

33. $-4 < d \le 0$ **34.** $0 \le g < 5$ **35.** $-1 \le m < 6$ **36.** $7 \ge x > 2$

37. $2 \le t \le 7$ **38.** $15 \le j \le 30$ **39.** $\dfrac{2}{5} < s \le 3\dfrac{1}{3}$ **40.** $-1\dfrac{3}{4} \le a \le \dfrac{2}{3}$

41. $-2.5 \le q < 3.5$ **42.** $-6.5 < y < -1.5$ **43.** $\dfrac{4}{5} \le x \le 4.5$ **44.** $-2.5 < x < \dfrac{2}{5}$

45. Complete the following table.

	Inequality	Number Line	Interval Notation
a.	$x < 4.5$		
b.		filled point at 3 on a line from -9 to 9	
c.			$(-\infty, -2)$
d.	$z \ge 5.7$		
e.		open point at -7 on a line from -9 to 9	
f.			$(2, \infty)$
g.	$2 < y < 8$		
h.		filled point at -3 and open point at 5 on a line from -9 to 9	
i.			$[0, 9]$

46. Complete the following table.

	Inequality	Number Line	Interval Notation
a.			$(-\infty, -9)$
b.		filled point at 5 on a line from -9 to 9	
c.	$a < \dfrac{1}{2}$		
d.			$[0, \infty)$
e.		open point at -4 on a line from -9 to 9	
f.	$b > 2.7$		
g.			$(4, 11)$
h.		filled point at 1 and open point at 5 on a line from -9 to 9	
i.	$-5 \le c \le -1$		

Write a linear inequality in one variable to represent each situation described. Do not attempt to solve the inequality.

47. A car rental firm leases a car for $39.95 plus $0.20 per mile. If your cost of rental is not to exceed $150.00, how many miles can you drive the car?

48. The cost of a production run at a factory is the sum of a setup cost of $300 plus a labor and materials cost of $22 per item produced. What is the number of items that can be produced if the production cost is to be less than $1000?

49. Pete is paid a weekly salary of $450 plus 5% commission on his weekly sales. What must his sales be if he wishes his weekly pay to be more than $800?

50. Josephine pays a weekly rental of $125 for a booth at the local mall. She sells handcrafted baskets there for a price of $15 each. What must be the number of items sold in order for her to realize a 2 of at least $250 per week?

51. Sally is planning a shower for her best friend. She has reserved a party room at Le Chien Restaurant, which will charge her $25 for the room and $12.50 per person for lunch. How many people can she invite to the shower if she wishes to spend between $150 and $200 at the restaurant?

52. The local high school is staging *Romeo and Juliet* as a Valentine's Day event. They have spent $350.00 for costumes, props, and so on for the play. They are charging $4.50 per person for admission. How many tickets must they sell in order to realize a profit between $200.00 and $500.00?

Experiencing Algebra the Calculator Way

If you have a calculator with split-screen capability, it is often helpful to use the split screen to view the inequality at the same time that you are viewing its graph. As an example, suppose you wish to graph the inequality $x > -3$. The steps to view this inequality and its graph simultaneously follow.

| MODE | ▼ | ▼ | ▼ | ▼ | ▼ | ▼ | ▼ | ► | ENTER | 2nd | QUIT |

The calculator should exhibit a split screen with the coordinate system above and the home screen below. Now you can enter the instructions to graph the inequality.

| ZOOM | 6 | ZOOM | 8 | ENTER | WINDOW | ▼ | ▼ | ▼ | (−) | 1 | . | 5 |

| ▼ | 1 | . | 5 | ▼ | 1 | ENTER |

| 2nd | QUIT | Y= | X, T, θ, n | 2nd | TEST | 3 | (−) | 3 | GRAPH |

The graph of the inequality is displayed above, and the inequality is displayed below.

Use the split screen to view the graphs of the following inequalities. Trace to view the bounds.

1. $x < -2$ **2.** $x > -2$ **3.** $x \leq -2$ **4.** $x \geq -2$

Change the window to decimal scale by entering | ZOOM | 4 | *and view the following graphs.*

5. $-2.5 \leq x \leq 2.5$ **6.** $-2.5 \leq x < 2.5$ **7.** $-2.5 < x < 2.5$

When you wish to return to a full screen, simply use the | MODE | key, move the cursor down to Full, and press | ENTER | . When you quit the MODE function you will be back to full screen.

Experiencing Algebra the Group Way

In your group, consider the following list of phrases that imply an order relation. Discuss and agree on the correct order relation symbol that applies to each phrase.

____ **1.** At least   ____ **2.** At most   ____ **3.** No more than

____ **4.** No greater than   ____ **5.** Larger than   ____ **6.** Smaller than

____ **7.** Not to exceed   ____ **8.** Below   ____ **9.** Above

____ **10.** Greater than   ____ **11.** Greater than or equal to   ____ **12.** Less than

____ **13.** Less than or equal to   ____ **14.** No fewer than   ____ **15.** No less than

____ **16.** No smaller than   ____ **17.** A maximum of   ____ **18.** A minimum of

____ **19.** Up to   ____ **20.** Down to

After completing the list, have members of the group suggest at least one additional phrase that matches each of the following order relations.

21. $<$ _____   **22.** $>$ _____

23. $\leq$ _____   **24.** $\geq$ _____

Experiencing Algebra the Write Way

Use the phrases in "Experiencing Algebra the Group Way" to write a real-world application that involves an inequality relation. Write a complete narrative describing the problem. Then write the linear inequality in one variable that represents the application you described.

8.2 Linear Inequalities in One Variable

Objectives
1 Solve linear inequalities in one variable numerically.

2 Solve linear inequalities in one variable graphically.

3 Solve linear inequalities in one variable algebraically.

4 Model real-world situations using linear inequalities in one variable and solve.

Application

You are trying to establish a budget for your company's contribution to employee health care. One plan offers health care with a company contribution of $124.95 per employee and an annual fixed charge of $3000 for the company. If you want to keep your total health care cost below $10,000 per year, how many employees can be covered by this plan?

After completing this section, we will discuss this application further. See page 587.

1 Solving Linear Inequalities Numerically

In previous chapters we determined whether a number was a solution of an equation by substituting the number for the variable and evaluating the two resulting expressions. If the expressions were equivalent, then the number substituted was called the solution.

We determine a solution of a linear inequality by using the same method of substituting and evaluating. However, we need to determine whether the resulting inequality is true. For example, given $2x + 3 \leq x + 5$, determine whether 3 is a solution.

$$
\begin{array}{c|c}
\multicolumn{2}{c}{2x + 3 \leq x + 5} \\
\hline
2(3) + 3 & 3 + 5 \\
6 + 3 & 8 \\
9 &
\end{array}
$$

Therefore, 3 is not a solution because the resulting inequality, $9 \leq 8$, is not true.

To find a solution of this inequality, $2x + 3 \leq x + 5$, we continue to substitute values for x until we find a number that results in a true inequality. To do this, it is convenient to use a table, as we did when solving equations numerically.

Solving a Linear Inequality in One Variable Numerically
To solve a linear inequality numerically:
Set up an extended table of values.

- The first column is labeled with the name of the independent variable.

- The second column is labeled with the expression on the left side of the inequality.

- The third column is labeled with the expression on the right side of the inequality.

Complete the table.

- Substitute values for the independent variable.

- Evaluate the second and third columns.

- Continue until the values for the two expressions (the numbers in the second and third columns) result in a true inequality.

The values for the independent variable (the numbers in the first column) used to determine a true inequality are solutions of the inequality.

Helping Hand Not all solutions may be found by this method. We are limited to those numbers substituted for the independent variable.

For example, solve numerically $2x + 3 \leq x + 5$ for integer solutions.

A sample table to determine the integer solutions follows.

x	$2x + 3$	$x + 5$	
3	2(3) + 3 6 + 3 9	3 + 5 8	$9 \nleq 8$
2	2(2) + 3 4 + 3 7	2 + 5 7	$7 \leq 7$
1	2(1) + 3 2 + 3 5	1 + 5 6	$5 \leq 6$
0	2(0) + 3 0 + 3 3	0 + 5 5	$3 \leq 5$

According to the table, when 2 is substituted for the variable x, the resulting inequality is true ($7 \leq 7$). Therefore, 2 is a solution of the linear inequality $2x + 3 \leq x + 5$. When 1 is substituted for x, the resulting inequality is true ($5 \leq 6$). Therefore, 1 is a solution of the linear inequality $2x + 3 \leq x + 5$. Also, when 0 is substituted for the variable, the resulting inequality is true ($3 \leq 5$). Therefore, 0 is a solution of the linear inequality $2x + 3 \leq x + 5$. If the table is extended further, more integer solutions will be found. In fact, all integers completing this pattern will result in true inequalities. Therefore, we know that all integers 2 and less than 2 will be solutions of the inequality.

This table results in only integer solutions and does not result in all solutions. We could have included noninteger solutions, but it would still be impossible to include all of these.

To solve a linear inequality numerically on your calculator:

- Rename the independent variable as x.

Set up the table.

- Set up the first column for the independent variable by setting a minimum value and increments. Since we do not know the solution, we may want to set a minimum number of 0. We will probably want to use increments of 1 for integer values. Then set the calculator to automatically perform the evaluations.
- Set up the second column of the table to be the expression on the left side by entering the leftmost expression of the inequality in Y1.
- Set up the third column of the table to be the expression on the right side by entering the rightmost expression of the inequality in Y2.

View the table.

- Move beyond the screen to view additional rows by using the up and down arrows.

The solutions are the x-values that determine a true inequality.

For example, solve numerically $2x + 3 \leq x + 5$ for integer solutions on your calculator.

The resulting table is a different ordering of the same table completed without the calculator. Therefore, the solutions of the inequality are all integers 2 and less than 2, as shown in Figures 8.4a, 8.4b, and 8.4c.

TECHNOLOGY

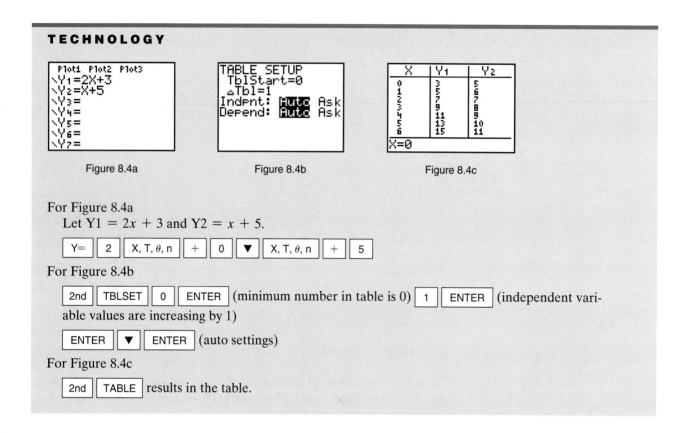

Figure 8.4a   Figure 8.4b   Figure 8.4c

For Figure 8.4a
Let Y1 = $2x + 3$ and Y2 = $x + 5$.

| Y= | 2 | X, T, θ, n | + | 0 | ▼ | X, T, θ, n | + | 5 |

For Figure 8.4b

| 2nd | TBLSET | 0 | ENTER | (minimum number in table is 0) | 1 | ENTER | (independent variable values are increasing by 1)

| ENTER | ▼ | ENTER | (auto settings)

For Figure 8.4c

| 2nd | TABLE | results in the table.

This method does not result in all solutions—only integer solutions. However, this visualization may be used to check other methods.

 Experiencing Algebra the Checkup Way

In exercises 1–2, solve numerically for integer solutions. Check each solution on your calculator.

1. $2x - 5 < 4x - 3$ **2.** $5z + 2 > 3z$

3. Explain how to solve a linear inequality numerically.

4. What are the limitations of solving a linear inequality numerically?

2 Solving Linear Inequalities Graphically   A second and more inclusive method to determine a solution set of a linear inequality is to graph two functions. The functions to be graphed are written by using the expression on the left side of the inequality as a rule for the first function and the expression on the right side as a rule for the second function. For the inequality $2x + 3 \le x + 5$, we write the two functions $y_1 = 2x + 3$ and $y_2 = x + 5$. We then determine the solutions of the inequality $y_1 \le y_2$. Let's explore this method on the graphing calculator. Complete the following set of exercises on your calculator.

DISCOVERY 1

Graphical Solutions of a "Less Than" Linear Inequality in One Variable

To determine the solutions of the inequality $2x + 3 \le x + 5$, graph the functions Y1 $= 2x + 3$ and Y2 $= x + 5$. Sketch the graphs. Label the point of intersection of the graphs.

1. The intersection of the two graphs is _____.
2. The solution that corresponds to the equality is _____.
3. To solve a "less than" inequality, Y1 < Y2, locate the portion of the Y1 graph <u>above/below</u> the Y2 graph. When tracing the graph of Y1, this is to the <u>left/right</u> of the intersection. The x-coordinates of the points in this direction are <u>less than/greater than</u> the x-coordinate of the point of intersection.
4. Combining the solutions found for the equality and the "less than," we determine that the solution set is _____.

The solution set of the inequality $2x + 3 \le x + 5$ consists of the x-coordinate of the point of intersection and the x-coordinates of the points to the left of the intersection. Written as an inequality, the solutions are all x that satisfy $x \le 2$.

Correspondingly, we can solve the inequality $2x + 3 \ge x + 5$ graphically. Complete the following set of exercises on your calculator.

DISCOVERY 2

Graphical Solutions of a "Greater Than" Linear Inequality in One Variable

To determine the solution of the inequality $2x + 3 \ge x + 5$, graph the functions Y1 $= 2x + 3$ and Y2 $= x + 5$. Sketch the graph. Label the point of intersection of the graphs.

1. The intersection of the two graphs is _____.
2. The solution that corresponds to the equality is _____.
3. To solve a "greater than" inequality, Y1 > Y2, locate the portion of the Y1 graph <u>above/below</u> the Y2 graph. When tracing the graph of Y1, this is to the <u>left/right</u> of the intersection. The x-coordinates of the points in this direction are <u>less than/greater than</u> the x-coordinate of the point of intersection.
4. Combining the solutions found for the equality and the "greater than," we determine that the solution set is _____.

The solution set of the inequality $2x + 3 \ge x + 5$ consists of the x-coordinate of the point of intersection and the x-coordinates of the points to the right of the intersection. Written as an inequality, the solution set is all x that satisfy $x \ge 2$.

Solving a Linear Inequality in One Variable Graphically
To solve a linear inequality graphically:

- Write two functions, y_1 and y_2, using the expressions on the left and right sides of the inequality, respectively.
- Graph both functions on the same coordinate plane.
- Determine the intersection, if it exists, of the y_1 and y_2 graphs.
- Locate the portion of the y_1 graph below the y_2 graph if the inequality is "less than." Locate the portion of the y_1 graph above the y_2 graph if the inequality is "greater than."
- Determine the x-coordinates for this portion of the graph.
  - If the portion is to the left of the intersection, then x is less than the x-coordinate of the intersection.
  - If the portion is to the right of the intersection, then x is greater than the x-coordinate of the intersection.

The solution set includes either x-values less than or x-values greater than the x-coordinate of the point of intersection. The solution set also includes the x-coordinate of the point of intersection if the inequality includes equality.

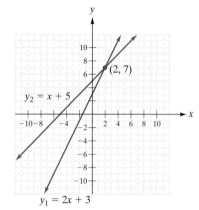

$y_2 = x + 5$

$y_1 = 2x + 3$

For example, solve graphically $2x + 3 > x + 5$.

Graph $y_1 = 2x + 3$ and $y_2 = x + 5$.
The intersection of the lines is $(2, 7)$. We do not include the x-coordinate of the intersection in the solution because the inequality does not include equality.
The inequality is "greater than," so we determine the graph of y_1 to be above the graph of y_2 to the right of the point of intersection. This is interpreted as an inequality: x is greater than the x-coordinate of the intersection, 2.
The solution set is all x that satisfy $x > 2$.

To solve a linear inequality graphically on your calculator:

- Rename the independent variable as x.
- Set the screen to the desired setting.
- Enter the expression on the left side of the inequality in Y1.
- Enter the expression on the right side of the inequality in Y2.
- Graph.
- Find the point of intersection.
- Locate the portion of the Y1 graph below the Y2 graph if the inequality is "less than." Locate the portion of the Y1 graph above the Y2 graph if the inequality is "greater than."
- Determine the x-coordinates for this portion of the graph.
  - If the portion is to the left of the intersection, then x is less than the x-coordinate of the intersection.

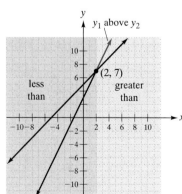

y_1 above y_2

less than

greater than

- If the portion is to the right of the intersection, then x is greater than the x-coordinate of the intersection.

For example, solve graphically $2x + 3 > x + 5$ on your calculator.

See Figure 8.5.

The intersection of the graph is $(2, 7)$. We do not include the x-coordinate of the intersection in the solution because the inequality does not include equality. The inequality is "greater than," so we determine the graph of Y1 to be above the graph of Y2 to the right of the point of intersection. The solution set consists of the x-values greater than the x-coordinate of the intersection, 2, or all x that satisfy $x > 2$.

TECHNOLOGY

Y1 = 2x + 3

X=2 Y=7

Y2 = x + 5

(−47, 47, −31, 31)

Figure 8.5

For Figure 8.5

Set the screen to the desired setting (integer screen).

| ZOOM | 6 | ZOOM | 8 | ENTER |

Enter Y1 and Y2.

| Y= | 2 | X, T, θ, n | + | 3 | ▼ | X, T, θ, n | + | 5 |

Graph.

| GRAPH |

Find the intersection.

| TRACE | Use arrows to find the intersection.

EXAMPLE 1 Solve graphically. Represent the solution in the notation specified.

a. $x - 3 < 2x - 2$; inequality notation
b. $3a + 5 > 2a$; interval notation
c. $6x - (4x + 3) \leq 7 - 3x$; number line

Calculator/Graphic Solution

a.

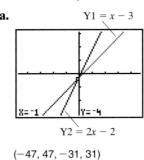

Y1 = x − 3

X=-1 Y=-4

Y2 = 2x − 2

(−47, 47, −31, 31)

The intersection of the graphs is $(-1, -4)$. The inequality is "less than," so we locate the portion of the graph of Y1 that is below the graph of Y2. These points are to the right of the point of intersection where x is greater than -1. The solution does not include the x-coordinate of the point of intersection because the inequality does not include equality. The solution set is all x that satisfy $x > -1$.

b.

Y1 = 3x + 5

Y2 = 2x

$(-47, 47, -31, 31)$

The intersection of the graphs is $(-5, -10)$. The inequality is "greater than," so we locate the portion of the graph of Y1 that is above the graph of Y2. These points are to the right of the point of intersection where a is greater than -5. The solution does not include the x-coordinate of the point of intersection because the inequality does not include equality. The solution set is all a that satisfy $a > -5$ or $(-5, \infty)$.

c.

Y2 = 7 − 3x

Y1 = 6x − (4x + 3)

$(-47, 47, -31, 31)$

The intersection of the graphs is $(2, 1)$. The inequality is "less than," so we locate the portion of the graph of Y1 that is below the graph of Y2. These points are to the left of the point of intersection where x is less than 2. The solution includes the x-coordinate of the point of intersection because the inequality includes equality. The solution set is all x that satisfy $x \le 2$. A number line representation is shown.

EXAMPLE 2 $(5x + 4) - 2(3x + 1) \ge 2(x - 7)$ does not have an integer-value intersection. Use the Intersect function on your calculator to find the approximate intersection and determine the solution set.

Calculator/Graphic Solution

Trace will not locate the intersection. Use Intersect under the CALC function, as shown in Figure 8.6.

The intersection of the two graphs is approximately $(5.33, -3.33)$. The Y1 graph is above the Y2 graph to the left of the point of intersection. The solution includes the x-coordinate of the intersection point. The solution set is all x that satisfy $x \leq 5.33$. ∎

TECHNOLOGY

Y1 = (5x + 4) − 2(3x + 1)

Y2 = 2(x − 7)

Intersection
X=5.3333333 Y=-3.333333

(−47, 47, −31, 31)

Figure 8.6

For Figure 8.6

Set the screen to the desired setting (integer screen).

| ZOOM | 6 | ZOOM | 8 | ENTER |

Enter Y1 and Y2.

| Y= | (| 5 | X, T, θ, n | + | 4 |) | − | 2 | (| 3 | X, T, θ, n |

| + | 1 |) |

| ▼ | 2 | (| X, T, θ, n | − | 7 |) |

Graph.

| GRAPH |

Use Intersect under the CALC function to find the intersection.

| 2nd | CALC | 5 | ENTER | ENTER | ENTER |

Remember from Chapter 5 that linear equations may have no solution or may have all-real-number solutions. The same is true for linear inequalities. Graphically solving linear inequalities can result in these possibilities. You can see what we mean in the following "Discovery" boxes. Complete the following sets of exercises on your calculator.

DISCOVERY 3

Graphical Solutions of Linear Inequalities with No Solution
Solve graphically the linear inequality $2x + 5 > 2x + 10$.
    Write a rule to determine from its graph that there is no solution of a linear inequality.

The graphs for the two functions do not intersect. The graph of Y1 is always below the graph of Y2. There are no points in which the graph of Y1 is above the graph of Y2. Therefore, there is no solution.

DISCOVERY 4

Graphical Solutions of Linear Inequalities with All-Real-Number Solutions
Solve graphically the linear inequality $2x + 5 < 2x + 10$.
    Write a rule to determine from its graph that the solution of a linear inequality is the set of all real numbers.

The two functions do not intersect. The graph of Y1 is always below the graph of Y2. All points on the graph of Y1 are below the graph of Y2. Therefore, the solution set is all *x*-coordinates of the points on the line, or all real numbers.

EXAMPLE 3 Solve graphically.

a. $4(x - 2) < 4x + 10$ **b.** $3x + 4 \geq 2x + (x + 10)$

c. $2a + 12 \leq 2(a + 3) + 6$

Calculator/Graphic Solution

a.

$Y2 = 4x + 10$

$Y1 = 4(x - 2)$

$(-47, 47, -31, 31)$

The graphs are parallel and the graph of Y1 is always below the graph of Y2. Since the inequality is "less than," all of the Y1 graph will determine solutions of the inequality. The solution set is all real numbers.

b.

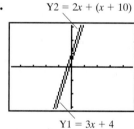

$Y2 = 2x + (x + 10)$

$Y1 = 3x + 4$

$(-47, 47, -31, 31)$

The graphs are parallel and the graph of Y1 is always below the graph of Y2. Since the inequality is "greater than" and the Y1 graph will not have any points above the Y2 graph, there is no solution of the inequality.

c. Change the variables to *x*.

$Y1 = 2x + 12$

$Y2 = 2(x + 3) + 6$

$(-47, 47, -31, 31)$

The graphs are the same line. Since the inequality includes an equal symbol, all ordered pairs on the line will determine solutions of the inequality. The solution set is all real numbers. ∎

Graphical Solutions of Linear Inequalities in One Variable
When solving a linear inequality graphically where Y1 equals the expression on the left side of the inequality and Y2 equals the expression on the right side of the inequality, one of three possibilities will occur:

1. A solution set exists.

2. No solution exists.
   This occurs for the following conditions:
   Y1 < Y2 and the graph of Y1 is the same as Y2 or always above Y2.
   Y1 > Y2 and the graph of Y1 is the same as Y2 or always below Y2.
   Y1 ≤ Y2 and the graph of Y1 is always above Y2.
   Y1 ≥ Y2 and the graph of Y1 is always below Y2.

3. A solution set of all real numbers exists.
   This occurs for the following conditions:
   Y1 < Y2 and the graph of Y1 is always below Y2.
   Y1 > Y2 and the graph of Y1 is always above Y2.
   Y1 ≤ Y2 and the graph of Y1 is the same as Y2 or always below Y2.
   Y1 ≥ Y2 and the graph of Y1 is the same as Y2 or always above Y2.

 Experiencing Algebra the Checkup Way

Solve graphically and represent the solution in the notation specified.

1. $2x - 5 > 4x - 3$; inequality notation
2. $5z + 2 \leq 3z$; number line
3. $4(x + 2) - 3(x + 3) < 7 - 3x$; interval notation

Use the Intersect function on your calculator to find the exact intersection and determine the solution set.

4. $3(2x - 1) - (2x + 4) < 2(x - 2) + 2$

In exercises 5–7, solve graphically to determine whether there is no solution or the solution set is all real numbers.

5. $3(x + 2) - 4(2x + 1) > 3(2 - x) + 2(1 - x)$
6. $3x - (2x + 5) \geq \dfrac{1}{2}(2x + 4) - 7$

7. $\dfrac{1}{2}x + 2 > 0.5x - 1$

8. Explain how you would solve a linear inequality graphically.

9. How would you know from the graphic solution that the solution set is a part of the number line?

10. How would you know from the graphic solution that the solution set is the entire number line or that there is no solution?

3 Solving Linear Inequalities Algebraically

In order to solve a linear equation algebraically, we used the addition and multiplication properties of equations (section 5.2). In order to solve a linear inequality algebraically, we will need to know similar properties of inequalities. First, let's see if an addition property of inequalities exists. Complete the following set of exercises.

D I S C O V E R Y   5

Addition (Subtraction) Property of Inequalities

1. Given the inequality $10 < 12$, add 2 to both expressions.

$$\frac{10 < 12}{\begin{array}{c|c} 10 + 2 & 12 + 2 \\ 12 & 14 \end{array}}$$

2. Given the inequality $10 < 12$, add -2 to both expressions.

$$\frac{10 < 12}{}$$

3. Given the inequality $10 < 12$, subtract 2 from both expressions.

$$\frac{10 < 12}{}$$

4. Given the inequality $10 < 12$, subtract -2 from both expressions.

$$\frac{10 < 12}{}$$

Write a rule for the addition property of inequalities.

In each of the preceding exercises, we began with a true inequality and added (or subtracted) the same number to (or from) both expressions. The result remained a true inequality. We see that if a number is added to (or subtracted from) both expressions in an inequality, the result is a true inequality.

Addition Property of Inequalities
Given expressions a, b, and c,

  if $a < b$, then $a + c < b + c$.
  if $a > b$, then $a + c > b + c$.
  if $a \leq b$, then $a + c \leq b + c$.
  if $a \geq b$, then $a + c \geq b + c$.

This property holds true for subtraction as well, because subtraction is defined as adding the opposite of a number.

Now let's consider a property of inequalities involving multiplication. Complete the following set of exercises.

D I S C O V E R Y   6

Multiplication (Division) Property of Inequalities

1. Given the inequality $10 < 12$, multiply both expressions by 2.

$$\frac{10 < 12}{\begin{array}{c|c} 10 \cdot 2 & 12 \cdot 2 \\ 20 & 24 \end{array}}$$

Continued

2. Given the inequality $10 < 12$, multiply both expressions by -2.

$$10 < 12$$

3. Given the inequality $10 < 12$, divide both expressions by 2.

$$10 < 12$$

4. Given the inequality $10 < 12$, divide both expressions by -2.

$$10 < 12$$

Write a rule for the multiplication (division) property of inequalities.

In each of the preceding exercises, we began with a true inequality and multiplied (or divided) both expressions by the same number. When a positive number was used, the result was a true inequality. When a negative number was used, the result was a false inequality. To make the false inequality true, the inequality symbol must be reversed from "less than" to "greater than" or vice versa.

> *Multiplication Property of Inequalities*
> Given expressions a, b, and c with $c > 0$,
>
> if $a < b$, then $ac < bc$.
> if $a > b$, then $ac > bc$.
> if $a \leq b$, then $ac \leq bc$.
> if $a \geq b$, then $ac \geq bc$.
>
> Given expressions a, b, and c, with $c < 0$,
>
> if $a < b$, then $ac > bc$
> if $a > b$, then $ac < bc$.
> if $a \leq b$, then $ac \geq bc$
> if $a \geq b$, then $ac \leq bc$.

This property holds true for division as well, because division is defined as multiplying by the reciprocal of a number.

We are now ready to solve linear inequalities algebraically. To do this, we will need to apply a combination of the properties of inequalities. Since there are several different possible ways to solve linear inequalities, we will set up a few rules so that at least in the beginning we are doing the same steps. When we become more sure of ourselves, we may do these steps in different orders and obtain the same results in the end.

> *Solving a Linear Inequality in One Variable Algebraically*
> To solve a linear inequality using a combination of properties of inequalities:
> - Simplify both expressions in the inequality (preferably without fractions).
> - Isolate the variable in one expression of the inequality (preferably the expression on the left side) by using the addition property of inequalities.
> - Use the addition property of inequalities to isolate the constants in the other expression (preferably the expression on the right side).
> - Use the multiplication property of inequalities to reduce the coefficient of the variable to 1.
>
> Remember to reverse the inequality symbol if a negative number is being used to multiply (or divide) both sides of the inequality.

For example, solve $2x + 3 > 7$.

$$2x + 3 > 7$$
$$2x + 3 - 3 > 7 - 3 \quad \text{Subtract 3 from both sides.}$$
$$2x > 4 \quad \text{Simplify.}$$
$$\frac{2x}{2} > \frac{4}{2} \quad \text{Divide both sides by 2.}$$
$$x > 2$$

The solutions are all x that satisfy $x > 2$.

EXAMPLE 4 Solve. Represent the solution set in the notation given.

a. $2x - 3 < 7$; inequality notation

b. $5x + 4 \geq 6x - 16$; number line

c. $\frac{3}{8}\left(x + \frac{1}{4}\right) > \frac{5}{6}x + 2$; interval notation

Algebraic Solution

a.
$$2x - 3 < 7$$
$$2x - 3 + 3 < 7 + 3 \quad \text{Add 3 to both sides.}$$
$$2x < 10 \quad \text{Simplify.}$$
$$\frac{2x}{2} < \frac{10}{2} \quad \text{Divide both sides by 2.}$$
$$x < 5 \quad \text{Simplify.}$$

The solutions are all x that satisfy $x < 5$.

b.
$$5x + 4 \geq 6x - 16$$
$$5x + 4 - 6x \geq 6x - 16 - 6x \quad \text{Subtract 6x from both sides.}$$
$$-x + 4 \geq -16 \quad \text{Simplify.}$$
$$-x + 4 - 4 \geq -16 - 4 \quad \text{Subtract 4 from both sides.}$$
$$-x \geq -20 \quad \text{Simplify.}$$
$$\frac{-x}{-1} \leq \frac{-20}{-1} \quad \text{Divide both sides by −1 (the coefficient of x). Remember to reverse the inequality symbol.}$$
$$x \leq 20 \quad \text{Simplify.}$$

A number line representation is shown.

c.
$$\frac{3}{8}\left(x + \frac{1}{4}\right) > \frac{5}{6}x + 2$$

$$\frac{3}{8}x + \frac{3}{32} > \frac{5}{6}x + 2 \qquad \text{Distribute.}$$

$$96\left(\frac{3}{8}x + \frac{3}{32}\right) > 96\left(\frac{5}{6}x + 2\right) \qquad \begin{array}{l}\text{Multiply both sides by 96, the}\\ \text{LCD of 8, 32, and 6.}\end{array}$$

$$96\left(\frac{3}{8}x\right) + 96\left(\frac{3}{32}\right) > 96\left(\frac{5}{6}x\right) + 96(2) \qquad \text{Distribute.}$$

$$36x + 9 > 80x + 192 \qquad \text{Simplify.}$$

$$36x + 9 - 80x > 80x + 192 - 80x \qquad \text{Subtract } 80x \text{ from both sides.}$$

$$-44x + 9 > 192 \qquad \text{Simplify.}$$

$$-44x + 9 - 9 > 192 - 9 \qquad \text{Subtract 9 from both sides.}$$

$$-44x > 183 \qquad \text{Simplify.}$$

$$\frac{-44x}{-44} < \frac{183}{-44} \qquad \begin{array}{l}\text{Divide both sides by } -44.\\ \text{Remember to reverse the}\\ \text{inequality symbol.}\end{array}$$

$$x < \frac{-183}{44} \qquad \text{Simplify.}$$

The solution set is $\left(-\infty, \frac{-183}{44}\right)$. ∎

As we discussed earlier, linear inequalities may have no solution or all-real-number solutions. Let's see what happens when we solve such inequalities algebraically. Complete the following set of exercises.

D I S C O V E R Y   7

Algebraic Solutions of Linear Inequalities with No Solution
Solve algebraically the previous graphical example of a linear inequality with no solution, $2x + 5 > 2x + 10$.
    Write a rule to determine that there is no solution of a linear inequality when solving algebraically.

When we attempt to isolate the variable to one expression, the variable is deleted. The resulting inequality is a contradiction. Therefore, there is no solution.

D I S C O V E R Y   8

**Algebraic Solutions of Linear Inequalities
with All-Real-Number Solutions**
Solve algebraically the previous graphical example of a linear inequality with a solution of all real numbers, $2x + 5 < 2x + 10$.
    Write a rule to determine that the solution of a linear inequality is the set of all real numbers when solving algebraically.

When we attempt to isolate the variable to one expression, the variable is deleted. The resulting inequality is an identity. Therefore, the solution set is all real numbers.

EXAMPLE 5 Solve algebraically.

  a. $4(x + 2) < 4x - 10$ **b.** $3x + 4 \leq 2x + (x + 4)$

Algebraic Solution

a. $\quad 4(x + 2) < 4x - 10$

$\qquad\quad 4x + 8 < 4x - 10$ Distribute 4.

$\quad 4x + 8 - 4x < 4x - 10 - 4x$ Subtract 4x from both sides.

$\qquad\qquad\quad 8 < -10$ Simplify.

Since this is a false inequality (contradiction), there is no solution.

b. $\qquad 3x + 4 \leq 2x + (x + 4)$

$\qquad\quad 3x + 4 \leq 2x + x + 4$ Remove parentheses.

$\qquad\quad 3x + 4 \leq 3x + 4$ Simplify.

$\quad 3x + 4 - 3x \leq 3x + 4 - 3x$ Subtract 3x from both sides.

$\qquad\qquad\quad 4 \leq 4$ Simplify.

Since this is a true inequality (identity), the solution set is all real numbers.

∎

> *Algebraic Solutions of Linear Inequalities in One Variable*
> When solving a linear inequality algebraically, one of three possibilities will occur:
>
> **1. A solution set exists.**
>
> **2. No solution exists.**
>   The solving process results in a contradiction.
>
> **3. A solution set exists and it is the set of all real numbers.**
>   The solving process results in an identity.

✓ **Experiencing Algebra the Checkup Way**

Solve exercises 1–5 algebraically. Represent the solution in the notation specified.

1. $5x - 8 > 2$; interval notation

2. $3z + 7 \leq 7z - 5$; inequality notation

3. $\dfrac{2}{3}\left(x - \dfrac{1}{5}\right) < \dfrac{1}{4}x + 3$; number line

4. $3(x + 2) - 4(2x + 1) > 3(2 - x) + 2(1 - x)$; inequality notation

5. $3x - (2x + 5) \geq \dfrac{1}{2}(2x + 4) - 7$; interval notation

6. When solving a linear inequality algebraically, which property should be used first to isolate the variable to one side of the inequality?

7. How would you know there is no solution of a linear inequality when you solve it algebraically?

8. How would you know that the solution set of a linear inequality is the set of all real numbers when you solve it algebraically?

4 Modeling the Real World

In real-world situations, the terms *less than or equal to* and *greater than or equal to* may be expressed in a variety of ways. For example, two expressions used frequently are *at least* (greater than or equal to) and *at most* (less than or equal to). Situations involving these terms, or phrases like them, can be analyzed as inequalities and then solved graphically or algebraically as we have described. The same rules apply about including a solution point if the relation includes equality and about reversing the direction of an inequality if you need to multiply or divide by a negative number.

EXAMPLE 6

Eata wants to make an A in her algebra class. The grading scale states that the range for an A is 94–100. Her first four test grades were 93, 100, 88, and 97. Determine the range of grades she must score on her last test in order to make an A.

Algebraic Solution

Let x = fifth test grade

The average of the test grades must be at least (greater than or equal to) 94 in order to make an A.

$$\frac{93 + 100 + 88 + 97 + x}{5} \geq 94$$

$$\frac{378 + x}{5} \geq 94 \qquad \text{Simplify.}$$

$$5\left(\frac{378 + x}{5}\right) \geq 5(94) \qquad \text{Multiply by 5.}$$

$$378 + x \geq 470 \qquad \text{Simplify.}$$

$$378 + x - 378 \geq 470 - 378 \qquad \text{Subtract 378.}$$

$$x \geq 92 \qquad \text{Simplify.}$$

Eata must score at least 92 on her fifth test in order to make an A.

Calculator/Graphic Solution

Let x = fifth test grade

The average of the test grades must be greater than or equal to 94 in order to make an A.

$$\frac{93 + 100 + 88 + 97 + x}{5} \geq 94$$

The intersection is $(92, 94)$ as shown to the left. The inequality is "greater than or equal to." The portion of the graph of Y1 above Y2 is to the right of the intersection where x is greater than 92. The solution includes the x-coordinate of the intersection. The solutions are all x that satisfy $x \geq 92$. Eata must score at least 92 on her fifth test in order to make an A. ∎

$Y1 = \dfrac{93 + 100 + 88 + 97 + x}{5}$

$Y2 = 94$

(0, 200, 0, 200)

Application

You are trying to establish a budget for your company's contribution to employee health care. One plan offers health care with a company contribution of $124.95 per employee and an annual fixed charge of $3000 for the company. If you want to keep your total health care cost below $10,000 per year, how many employees can be covered by this plan?

Discussion

Let x = number of employees that can be covered by the health plan

The company pays \$124.95 per employee covered, or 124.95x.

The total cost of the plan is 124.95x plus the annual charge of \$3000, or 124.95x + 3000.

The total cost must be below \$10,000. Therefore, we have the following inequality:

$$124.95x + 3000 < 10,000$$
$$124.95x + 3000 - 3000 < 10,000 - 3000 \qquad \text{Subtract 3000 from both sides.}$$
$$124.95x < 7000 \qquad \text{Simplify.}$$
$$\frac{124.95x}{124.95} < \frac{7000}{124.95} \qquad \text{Divide both sides by 124.95.}$$
$$x < 56.02 \qquad \text{Simplify (round answer).}$$

 Helping Hand It is impossible to have a fractional part of a person.

The company can cover 56 or fewer employees and keep its cost below \$10,000 annually. ■

 ## Experiencing Algebra the Checkup Way

Maria has earned \$1275 so far during the school year. She has a part-time job that pays her \$7.50 per hour. In order to keep her scholarship, she can earn at most \$3000 during the school year. How many hours can she work and still maintain her scholarship?

PROBLEM SET 8.2

 ## Experiencing Algebra the Exercise Way

Solve numerically for integer solutions.

1. $6(x - 12) < 3x$ **2.** $3x + 6 > 0$ **3.** $3(x + 5) + 3 > 3x + 18$

4. $x + 5 > 2(x - 1) - (x - 1)$ **5.** $3x + 3 > x + 2$ **6.** $3x + 5 < 2x - 1$

7. $2(4x + 2) + 2x - 7 < 2(5x + 4)$ **8.** $a + 3(a + 2) < 6(a + 1) - 2a$

Solve graphically, and represent the solution in inequality notation.

9. $\frac{2}{3}x - \frac{2}{3} \geq -\frac{3}{4}x - \frac{7}{2}$ **10.** $\frac{1}{4}x - \frac{5}{2} \leq -\frac{1}{2}x - 1$

11. $2(x + 3) - (x - 1) > 8 - (x + 9)$ **12.** $3(x - 2) - (x - 5) > 7 - (x + 2)$

13. $0.4x - 3.2 \leq -0.6x - 0.2$ **14.** $0.2(2x + 1) \geq -0.2(x - 7)$

15. $2(x + 1) > 3(x - 1) - x$ **16.** $5 - (2x + 5) > 2(2x - 1) - 2(3x + 1)$

17. $x - (3x + 1) > -x - (x + 1)$ **18.** $3(x - 1) - 5x > 2(1 - x)$

Solve algebraically. Represent the solution in interval notation.

19. $4x + 12 > 0$

20. $5x - 40 < 25$

21. $6x - 8 < -32$

22. $-x - 27 > 11$

23. $-3x + 12 \geq 12$

24. $36 \geq 5x + 8$

25. $-7x - 12 < -26$

26. $-3x + 11 < -10$

27. $15.17 < 5.9x - 4.3$

28. $-4.22c - 0.4 < -21.5$

29. $6.1 > -0.55a + 6.1$

30. $3.05y + 0.09 > 31.2$

31. $2.07z + 4.12 \geq 16.54$

32. $8.2b - 1.9 \leq 51.7$

33. $-9.2b - 4.3 \leq 70.6$

34. $-6.3p + 1.5 \geq -4.8$

35. $-\dfrac{5}{9}b + \dfrac{11}{12} < \dfrac{23}{36}$

36. $-\dfrac{4}{7}z + \dfrac{3}{14} > \dfrac{5}{14}$

37. $156z - 210 > 47z + 662$

38. $728a + 958 < 116a - 878$

39. $-1.05x - 15.41 < 2.55x - 47.09$

40. $21.1x + 0.46 > 10.9x + 0.46$

41. $11x + \dfrac{1}{4} \leq 2x + \dfrac{7}{36}$

42. $5p + \dfrac{3}{8} \geq 3p - \dfrac{3}{8}$

43. $\dfrac{2}{5}b - 12 < \dfrac{2}{3}b + 20$

44. $\dfrac{7}{9}x - 15 > \dfrac{4}{9}x - 37$

45. $4x - (3x + 5) < x - 5$

46. $7x + 4 > 3x + 2(2x + 2)$

47. $4x - (3x + 5) \leq x - 5$

48. $7x + 4 \geq 3x + 2(2x + 2)$

49. $0.05x + 10.5 < 0.15x - 0.25$

50. $0.01x + 0.11 > 0.47 - 0.09x$

Write a linear inequality to represent each application and solve.

51. Lee is trying to earn a B in his algebra class. To do so, he must have an average of no less than 87 points. He has scored 73, 97, 82, 89, 95 on his first five tests. What range of scores on his last test will earn at least a B?

52. Beckie types student papers for a fee. If her earnings were $38, $62, $56, and $42 for the first four weeks of the term, how much must she earn for the fifth week of the term in order to average more than $50 per week?

53. Luigi is retired but has a part-time job. He will lose some of his retirement benefits if he earns more than $7500 per year. He makes $9.75 per hour at his part-time job. If he has already earned $5200 this year, how many hours can he work without losing benefits?

54. Bobby rents a stump grinder for $22.00 plus $3.50 per hour. How many hours can he use the grinder and spend no more than $55.00?

55. Elevators must post a weight limit, usually a maximum of 2000 pounds. If the average person weighs 165 pounds, how many can safely ride the elevator?

56. Judy has $120.00 to spend on clothing. She buys a slack suit for $87.50. She would like to buy some sweaters that sell for $12.50 each. How many sweaters can she buy and stay within her budget?

57. Orpha's diet allows her no more than 1200 calories per day. Her lunch allowance is 150 calories more than her breakfast allowance. Her dinner allowance is 50 calories more than twice her breakfast allowance. How many calories can she have for breakfast? How many calories can she have for lunch? How many for dinner?

58. Tommy and Shawn agree to do volunteer work through their school program. Shawn agrees to work 10 hours less than twice the time that Tommy will work. Together they must volunteer no less than 110 hours. How many hours must Tommy work? How many hours must Shawn work?

59. Angie has invited 120 people to her wedding reception. It will cost her $6.50 to serve a vegetarian plate and $8.50 to serve a meat entrée plate. If she plans to spend no more than $950 for the dinner, use an inequality to state the number of meat entrée plates she can order.

60. Hervis leases cars for $25.00 a day and $0.22 per mile. Artz leases cars for $15.00 per day and $0.35 per mile. If you rent a car from Artz, how many miles can you drive per day and still spend less than Hervis would charge?

61. Mike wants to enclose a rectangular garden by using a barn as one of the lengths, with fencing for the other three sides. He wants the length to be 30 feet more than $\frac{3}{4}$ of the width. He has a maximum of 185 feet of fencing and a gate that is 4 feet wide. Find the possible widths for the garden.

62. A rectangular swimming pool is to have a perimeter that does not exceed 240 feet. If the length is to be 15 feet more than twice the width, what widths would satisfy this condition?

63. Peggy has a choice of two pay plans as a salesperson in a furniture store. Plan A pays her a weekly salary of $300 plus a commission of 5% of all sales in excess of $1000 (that is, if x is her weekly sales, the commission is 5% of $x - 1000$). Plan B pays her a weekly salary of $500 plus a commission of 5% of all sales in excess of $2000. For what values of sales will plan A pay Peggy more than plan B?

64. Allen went shopping for clothes. At one store, he saw sweaters selling for $37 each and a winter coat for $125. At another store he saw dress shirts selling for $25 with matching ties selling for $12, and a suit for $175. Suppose he must choose between buying the coat and x sweaters or buying the suit and x shirts with matching ties. For how many sweaters will the cost of the sweaters and coat be a smaller total than the cost of the suit and shirts with matching ties?

65. The total expenditures (federal, state and local) for social welfare can be estimated by the linear function

$$c(n) = (4.73 \times 10^{10})n + (7.66 \times 10^{10}),$$

where n is the number of years since 1970 and $c(n)$ is the total cost in dollars for the year $1970 + n$. Use this function to determine the years in which total expenditures exceeded one trillion dollars ($\$1 \times 10^{12}$).

66. Federal expenditures for social welfare can be estimated by the linear function

$$c(n) = (2.803 \times 10^{10})n + (4.447 \times 10^{10}),$$

where n is the number of years since 1970 and $c(n)$ is the total federal cost in dollars for the year $1970 + n$. Use the function to determine the years in which federal expenditures exceeded $500 billion ($\$5 \times 10^{11}$).

 ## Experiencing Algebra the Calculator Way

Another way to use your calculator to graphically solve an inequality is to store the expression on the right in Y1 and the expression on the left in Y2, and then graph Y3 = Y1 − Y2 to determine the solution set. If you seek values of x that make Y1 < Y2 (or equivalently, Y1 − Y2 < 0) find the interval where Y3 is below the x-axis (Y3 < 0). If you seek values of x that make Y1 > Y2, find the interval where Y3 is above the x-axis.

For example, use your calculator to solve $2x + 3 > x + 5$ graphically.

- Set the screen to the desired window.
- Enter the expression on the left side of the inequality in Y1.

| Y= | 2 | X, T, θ, n | + | 3 |

- Enter the expression on the right side of the inequality in Y2.

  | ▼ | X, T, θ, n | + | 5 |

- Set Y3 equal to Y1 $-$ Y2.

  | ▼ | VARS | ▶ | 1 | 1 | $-$ | VARS | ▶ | 1 | 2 |

- Turn off Y1 and Y2.

  | ◀ | ◀ | ◀ | ◀ | ▲ | ENTER | ▲ | ENTER | 2nd | QUIT |

- Graph Y3.

  | GRAPH |

Since we want Y1 $>$ Y2, find where Y3 is above the *x*-axis. This occurs where $x > 2$, which can be determined by using the | TRACE | key or by using the | 2nd | | CALC | | 2 | keys to find the "zero" of the graph (that is, the point at which the graph crosses the *x*-axis).

Try this approach on some of the exercises in this section. You must still decide whether to include the bound in your solution set.

Experiencing Algebra the Group Way

Divide your group into three units. Then assign each unit one method to solve the following inequalities: numerically, graphically, or algebraically. After the units have attempted to solve the exercises, discuss which method seemed best for each. Give reasons for your choice.

1. $3x + 4 < x + 12$

2. $\dfrac{1}{2}x - \dfrac{1}{4} \geq \dfrac{1}{8}x + \dfrac{7}{12}$

3. $125x + 30 > 75x - 190$

4. $3.6x - 1.47 < 5.9x - 6.53$

5. $7x + 11 \leq 3(x + 5) + 4(x - 2)$

6. $\dfrac{4}{5}\left(x + \dfrac{1}{8}\right) > \dfrac{2}{3}\left(x - \dfrac{1}{4}\right) + \dfrac{2}{15}(x - 3)$

7. $0.8(x + 4.5) \leq \dfrac{4}{5}x + 3\dfrac{3}{5}$

8. $\dfrac{1}{5}(x + 16) < 0.2x + 3.2$

Experiencing Algebra the Write Way

Consider exercises 61–64 in "Experiencing Algebra the Exercise Way." The inequality symbol determines the type of solution. Explain why this is so.

8.3 Linear Inequalities in Two Variables

Objectives
1 Identify linear inequalities in two variables.
2 Solve linear inequalities in two variables numerically.
3 Graph linear inequalities in two variables.
4 Graph the two special cases of linear inequalities in two variables.
5 Model real-world situations using linear inequalities in two variables.

Application

Your company publishes *Guides to the Internet*, available on three floppy disks or one CD-ROM. You can package the three-disk version for $0.09 per set, or package the CD-ROM for $0.14. You want to spend no more than $500 per day on packaging. Determine the possible combinations of each version of the guide you can package within this budget.

After completing this section, we will discuss this application further. See page 603.

1 Linear Inequalities in Two Variables

In this section we will be solving linear inequalities in two variables. Before we begin, we need to identify a linear inequality in two variables. A **linear inequality in two variables** is written by replacing the equal symbol in a linear equation in two variables with an order symbol.

> *Standard Form for a Linear Inequality in Two Variables*
> A linear inequality in two variables is an inequality that can be written in one of the following forms:
>
> $$ax + by < c$$
> $$ax + by > c$$
> $$ax + by \leq c$$
> $$ax + by \geq c$$
>
> where a, b, and c are real numbers and a and b are not both equal to 0.

For example,

Standard form: $ax + by < c$

1. $2x + 5y < 0$ $a = 2$ $b = 5$ $c = 0$
2. $3x - y < 12$ $a = 3$ $b = -1$ $c = 12$
3. $2x < 8$ $a = 2$ $b = 0$ $c = 8$
4. $3y < -9$ $a = 0$ $b = 3$ $c = -9$

Each of these inequalities is in standard form. Note that each of the variables, x and y, is raised to the first power. This *must* be the case for a linear inequality in two variables.

However, the inequality $y < 5x + 7$ is also a linear inequality in two variables because we can use the properties of inequalities to rearrange it into standard form. For example,

$$y < 5x + 7$$
$$y - 5x < 5x + 7 - 5x \quad \text{Subtract 5x from both sides.}$$
$$y - 5x < 7 \quad \text{Simplify.}$$
$$-5x + y < 7 \quad \text{Rearrange the left side.}$$

EXAMPLE 1   Identify each inequality as linear or nonlinear. Express each linear inequality in standard form and determine values for a, b, and c.

a. $2x^2 + 3y > 4$ **b.** $y \geq -3x$ **c.** $x \leq 0$

Solution

a. Nonlinear, because the x-term is squared.
b. Linear
 In standard form,

$$y \geq -3x$$
$$y + 3x \geq -3x + 3x$$
$$y + 3x \geq 0$$
$$3x + y \geq 0$$

 Therefore, $a = 3$, $b = 1$, and $c = 0$.
c. Linear
 It is written in standard form, $x \leq 0$.
 Therefore, $a = 1$, $b = 0$, and $c = 0$. ∎

Experiencing Algebra the Checkup Way

Identify each inequality as linear or nonlinear. Express each linear inequality in standard form and determine values for a, b, and c.

1. $y > 7x - 10$

2. $\dfrac{1}{3}x < y + 4$

3. $2x + 4 > 5y^2 - 3$

4. $5x + 2y < x + y + 10$

5. $3x - 4xy - 6y < 12$

6. $y < -\dfrac{3}{x} + 7$

2 Solving Linear Inequalities Numerically   To solve a linear inequality in two variables, we will perform the same procedure as we have used in previous sections. That is, we will substitute the values for the two variables into the inequality and determine whether the inequality is true. A solution of a linear inequality in two variables is an ordered pair that produces a true statement (satisfies the inequality). For example, in solving $y \leq x + 5$ we can obtain many possible solutions.

$(4, 9)$ is a solution because when $x = 4$ and $y = 9$ the inequality results in $9 \leq 9$.
$(5, 7)$ is a solution because when $x = 5$ and $y = 7$ the inequality results in $7 \leq 10$.

$(0.5, 3)$ is a solution because when $x = 0.5$ and $y = 3$ the inequality results in $3 \leq 5.5$.

To solve the linear inequality numerically, we begin the same way we have completed all other numeric solutions, by completing a table of values. For example, in solving $y \leq x + 5$,

x	$y \leq x + 5$	y	
-3	$y \leq -3 + 5$ $y \leq 2$	$y \leq 2$	This means when $x = -3$ we have values for y less than or equal to 2.
-2	$y \leq -2 + 5$ $y \leq 3$	$y \leq 3$	This means when $x = -2$ we have values for y less than or equal to 3.
-1	$y \leq -1 + 5$ $y \leq 4$	$y \leq 4$	This means when $x = -1$ we have values for y less than or equal to 4.
0	$y \leq 0 + 5$ $y \leq 5$	$y \leq 5$	This means when $x = 0$ we have values for y less than or equal to 5.
1	$y \leq 1 + 5$ $y \leq 6$	$y \leq 6$	This means when $x = 1$ we have values for y less than or equal to 6.
2	$y \leq 2 + 5$ $y \leq 7$	$y \leq 7$	This means when $x = 2$ we have values for y less than or equal to 7.

We can see that the number of solutions is infinite. A table of values is not an adequate method to find all the solutions. Therefore, we will not complete any examples using the numeric method.

Experiencing Algebra the Checkup Way

1. What do we mean by the solution of a linear inequality in two variables?
2. If you wanted to list some solutions of a linear inequality in two variables, how would a table of values help to do this?
3. Why is a table of values not a suitable way to indicate all solutions of a linear inequality in two variables?

3 Graphing Linear Inequalities

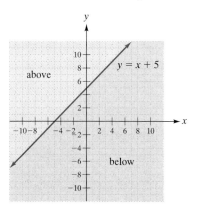

We used a rectangular coordinate system and graphical methods to illustrate the solutions of linear equations in two variables because the number of solutions was infinite and they could not be listed numerically. We will do the same for linear inequalities in two variables.

To graph an inequality means to create an illustration that represents its solutions.

1. Every solution of an inequality can be represented by a point on its graph.
2. Every point on a graph represents a solution of its inequality.

The graph of an equation partitions the coordinate plane into three regions: (1) the coordinate pairs that lie on the line; (2) the coordinate pairs above the line; and (3) the coordinate pairs below the line. For example, see the graph of the equation $y = x + 5$ at the left.

If we graph the solutions of $y \leq x + 5$ from the table of values found in the previous section, we obtain a series of vertical-line solutions of the inequality. Each line starts at a boundary point on the line for $y = x + 5$ and extends below the line for $y = x + 5$.

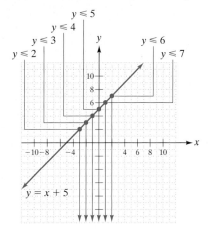

To illustrate the solutions of $y \leq x + 5$, we graph the line for $y = x + 5$ and shade all points below the line.

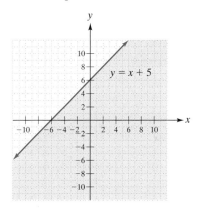

While this method illustrates why we shade a region on one side of the boundary line, it is not the easiest way to graph an inequality. To discover a more straightforward method to graph a "less than or equal to" inequality, complete the following set of exercises.

DISCOVERY 9

Graphing a "Less Than or Equal To" Linear Inequality in Two Variables

Graph the line determined by the equation $y = 2x + 4$.

1. Trace to determine the coordinates of points on the line.
   a. List two of these ordered pairs. _____ _____
   b. Are the ordered pairs solutions of the inequality $y \leq 2x + 4$?
2. Clear the trace and use the free-moving cursor (arrow keys) to determine ordered pairs above the line.
   a. List two of these ordered pairs. _____ _____
   b. Are the ordered pairs solutions of the inequality $y \leq 2x + 4$?
   Continued

3. Now use the free-moving cursor (arrow keys) to determine ordered pairs below the line.
   a. List two of these ordered pairs. _____ _____
   b. Are the ordered pairs solutions of the inequality $y \le 2x + 4$?

Write in your own words the rule for graphing a "less than or equal to" linear inequality.

First, we see that the inequality is solved for y. The ordered pairs on the graphed line are solutions of the equation and the "equal to" part of the inequality. We use a solid line to indicate that the ordered-pairs on the line are included in the solution. (This is comparable to using a solid dot on a number line for a linear inequality in one variable.) Second, we see that the ordered-pair solutions of the "less than" portion of the inequality are found in the region below the graphed line. We shade this region to indicate that they are included in the solution.

To discover a method for graphing an inequality that does not include equality, complete the following set of exercises.

D I S C O V E R Y   1 0

Graphing a "Greater Than" Linear Inequality in Two Variables
Graph the line determined by the equation $y = 2x + 4$.

1. Trace to determine the coordinates of points on the line.
   a. List two of these ordered pairs. _____ _____
   b. Are the ordered pairs solutions of the inequality $y > 2x + 4$?
2. Clear the trace and use the free-moving cursor (arrow keys) to determine ordered pairs above the line.
   a. List two of these ordered pairs. _____ _____
   b. Are the ordered pairs solutions of the inequality $y > 2x + 4$?
3. Now use the free-moving cursor (arrow keys) to determine ordered pairs below the line.
   a. List two of these ordered pairs. _____ _____
   b. Are the ordered pairs solutions of the inequality $y > 2x + 4$?

Write in your own words the rule for graphing a "greater than" linear inequality.

First, we see that the inequality is solved for y. The ordered pairs on the graphed line are solutions of the equation, but not solutions of the inequality. We use a dashed line to indicate that they are not included in the solution. (This is comparable to using an open dot on a number line for a linear inequality in one variable.) We also see that the ordered-pair solutions of the "greater than" portion of the inequality are found in the region above the graphed line. We shade this region to indicate that they are included in the solution.

Graphing a Linear Inequality in Two Variables with a y-Term
To graph a linear inequality in two variables:

- Solve the inequality for y (for example, $y < ax + $ b).
- Graph the boundary line determined by the related equation $y = ax + b$.
  - Use a solid line when the inequality includes equality.
  - Use a dashed line when the inequality does not include equality.
- Shade the correct portion of the coordinate plane determined by the inequality solved for y.
  - Shade below the line for a "less than" inequality.
  - Shade above the line for a "greater than" inequality.
- Check for the correct shading by choosing a test point in the shaded region determine whether it is a solution of the inequality.

For example, graph $x - y < -5$.

First, solve the inequality for y.

$$x - y < -5$$
$$x - y - x < -5 - x$$
$$-y < -x - 5$$
$$\frac{-y}{-1} > \frac{-x - 5}{-1} \qquad \text{Reverse the inequality when dividing by a negative number.}$$
$$y > x + 5$$

Graph the boundary line determined by $y = x + 5$. This boundary is a dashed line because there is no equality in the inequality. Since the inequality is "greater than," the boundary line is a lower boundary, so we shade above the boundary. (Remember, after solving for y we have a "greater than" inequality.)

Check a point in the shaded portion. A sample ordered pair is $(-6, 5)$. Substituting this possible solution in the original inequality results in

$$\frac{\begin{array}{ccc} x & - & y \\ (-6) & - & 5 \\ & -11 \end{array}}{} \quad \begin{array}{c} < -5 \\ -5 \\ \hline \end{array}$$

The sample ordered pair is a solution.

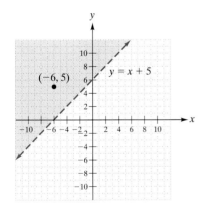

To graph a linear inequality in two variables on a calculator, we need to do similar steps to those we do by hand.

To graph a linear inequality in two variables on your calculator:

- Solve the inequality for y.
- Enter the boundary equation in Y1.
- Determine the type of inequality from the inequality solved for y.

- Shade the coordinate plane determined by the inequality solved for y.
  - For a "less than" inequality, shade below the boundary line.
  - For a "greater than" inequality, shade above the boundary line.

 Helping Hand The calculator does not graph dashed lines. It includes the boundary in the graph. It will be up to you not to include it in your graph.

For example, graph $x - y < -5$ on your calculator.

First, solve the inequality for y: $y > x + 5$.
Enter the boundary equation $y = x + 5$ in Y1.
Since the inequality is "greater than," shade above the boundary line, as shown in Figure 8.7.

T E C H N O L O G Y

Y1 = x + 5

(−47, 47, −31, 31)

Figure 8.7

For Figure 8.7
Enter the boundary equation $y = x + 5$ in Y1.

Shade above the boundary line.

Move to the left of Y1.

| ◄ | ◄ | ◄ | ◄ | ◄ |

Choose the "shade above" option. The calculator will display a blinking triangle above a diagonal.

| ENTER | ENTER |

Graph.

| GRAPH |

 Helping Hand After entering the boundary equation, to shade above press Enter twice; to shade below press Enter three times.

EXAMPLE 2 Graph $6x + 2y \leq -10$.

Solution

Solve the inequality for y.

$$6x + 2y \leq -10$$

$$6x + 2y - 6x \leq -10 - 6x$$

$$2y \leq -6x - 10$$

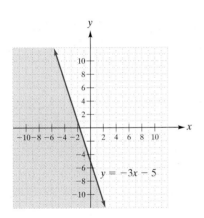

$$\frac{2y}{2} \le \frac{-6x - 10}{2}$$

$$y \le -3x - 5$$

The boundary line is the graph for the equation $y = -3x - 5$. This boundary is a solid line because the inequality includes equality. The boundary line is an upper boundary for a "less than" inequality, so shade below the boundary.

Check a point in the shaded region.

Calculator Solution

Solve for y: $y \le -3x - 5$.

$$Y1 = -3x - 5$$

Since the inequality is a "less than," we want to shade below the boundary line, as shown in Figure 8.8. ∎

TECHNOLOGY

Y1 = -3x - 5

(−47, 47, −31, 31)

Figure 8.8

For Figure 8.8
Enter the boundary line $y = -3x - 5$ in Y1.

Shade below the boundary line.

Move to the left of Y1.

◄	◄	◄	◄	◄	◄	◄

Choose the "shade below" option. (The calculator will display a blinking triangle below a diagonal.)

ENTER	ENTER	ENTER

Graph.

GRAPH

✓ Experiencing Algebra the Checkup Way

Graph exercises 1–4. Check each solution on your calculator.

1. $2x + y < 4$

2. $3x - 2y > 6$

3. $y \le -3x + 7$

4. $y \ge \frac{2}{3}x - 4$

5. When graphing a linear inequality in two variables, what is the meaning of using a dashed boundary line?

6. When graphing a linear inequality in two variables, what is the meaning of using a solid boundary line?

7. After graphing a linear inequality in two variables, how can you check that you shaded the proper region of the graph?

4 Graphing Special Cases of Linear Inequalities

The special cases of linear equations in two variables were the cases when $y = c$ or $x = c$ (section 6.2). Let's graph inequalities related to each of these cases; that is, given the linear inequality $ax + by < c$ when either $a = 0$ or $b = 0$ but not both.

EXAMPLE 3 Graph $y < 5$.

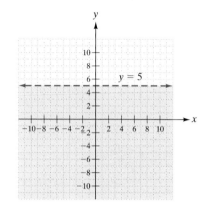

Solution

Graph the boundary line, $y = 5$, with a dashed line. This is a horizontal line. Shade the "less than" portion of the coordinate plane, which is below the upper boundary. Check a point.

Calculator Solution

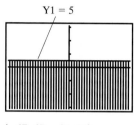

Y1 = 5

$(-47, 47, -31, 31)$ ■

Inequalities with only a y-variable are graphed in the same manner as all other previous inequalities. However, the graph of an inequality not containing a y-variable must be determined in a different manner. To graph an inequality not containing a y-variable, complete the following set of exercises.

DISCOVERY 11

Graphing a Linear Inequality in Two Variables with No *y*-Term
Graph the line determined by the equation $x = 9$.

1. List two ordered pairs on the graph. _____ _____
   Determine whether the ordered pairs are solutions of the following inequalities:
   a. $x \leq 9$ **b.** $x < 9$ **c.** $x \geq 9$ **d.** $x > 9$

2. Determine ordered pairs to the left of the line. List two of these ordered pairs. _____ _____
   Determine whether the ordered pairs are solutions of the following inequalities:
   a. $x \leq 9$ **b.** $x < 9$ **c.** $x \geq 9$ **d.** $x > 9$

3. Determine ordered pairs to the right of the line. List two of these ordered pairs. _____ _____
   Determine whether the ordered pairs are solutions of the following inequalities:
   a. $x \leq 9$ **b.** $x < 9$ **c.** $x \geq 9$ **d.** $x > 9$

Write in your own words the rule for graphing a linear inequality with no y-term.

First, we see that the inequality does not contain a y-term. The ordered pairs on the graphed line are solutions of the equality portion of the inequality. The line divides the coordinate plane into two parts. Ordered-pair solutions of "less than" inequalities are located in the region to the left of the graphed line (right boundary). Ordered-pair solutions of "greater than" inequalities are located to the right of the graphed line (left boundary).

> *Graphing a Linear Inequality in Two Variables with No y-Term*
> To graph a linear inequality in two variables with no y-term:
>
> - Solve for x.
> - Graph a vertical boundary line for the equation $x = c$.
>   - Use a solid line if the inequality includes equality.
>   - Use a dashed line if it does not include equality.
> - Shade the correct portion of the coordinate plane determined by the inequality solved for x.
>   - Shade to the left of the boundary for a "less than" inequality.
>   - Shade to the right of the boundary for a "greater than" inequality.
> - Check for the correct shading by choosing a test point in the shaded region to determine whether it is a solution of the inequality.

Since an inequality with no y-variable (such as $ax < 0$ or $ax > 0$) does not have a related function, we cannot use our previous calculator method to graph. (See "Experiencing Algebra the Calculator Way" at the end of this section for the calculator method.)

EXAMPLE 4   Graph $x - 3 < 8$.

Solution

Solve for x.

$$x - 3 < 8$$
$$x - 3 + 3 < 8 + 3$$
$$x < 11$$

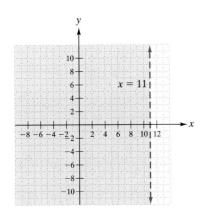

Graph the boundary line $x = 11$ as a dashed line because $x < 11$ has no equality. This is a vertical line. Shade to the left of the boundary because the inequality is "less than."

Since $x = 11$ is not a function, we will choose not to use the calculator to graph the inequality. ∎

✓   **Experiencing Algebra the Checkup Way**

Graph exercises 1–4.

1. $2y \leq 3$ **2.** $3x - 2 < 3$ **3.** $y + 3 > 8$ **4.** $5 - 2x \leq 9$

5. What must be true for a linear inequality in two variables if its graph has a vertical boundary line?

6. What must be true for a linear inequality in two variables if its graph has a horizontal boundary line?

5 Modeling the Real World

Many situations in the real world involve ranges of values rather than specific numbers. For example, in business, you want sales income to be greater than cost, regardless of the actual numbers. You want to spend less than your budget, whatever the budget is, and you want to produce as many items as you can, whatever that number is. Graphing inequalities can give you a picture of these ranges of values, so you can see whether you're close to your budget or you still have room to spend. As in most real-world situations, remember to check the domain of your variables, so you don't graph negative values of items or time, for example.

EXAMPLE 5

Shanda is a temporary worker for Make or Break Manufacturing Co. She works at most an 8-hour shift with a 30-minute break. (On slow days, she may work shorter hours.) Shanda has been trained to work on two different assembly lines. She may be assigned one or both during her shift. One assembly-line job requires 20 minutes per item. The other job requires 10 minutes per item.

a. Write a linear inequality in two variables needed to determine the numbers of items Shanda can complete during one shift.
b. Graph the inequality. Only positive coordinates found in the first quadrant would make sense in this situation. Why?
c. Determine from the graph two possible combinations of 20-minute and 10-minute items Shanda can produce during one shift.

Solution

a. Let x = number of items assembled in 20 minutes
y = number of items assembled in 10 minutes

The time required to assemble the 20-minute items is $20x$.
The time required to assemble the 10-minute items is $10y$.
The total time required for both items is the sum $20x + 10y$. This sum is at most ($\leq$) 480 minutes (8 hours $\times$ 60 minutes per hour) minus the 30-minute break, or a total of 450 minutes.

$$20x + 10y \leq 450$$

b. First, solve the inequality for y.

$$20x + 10y - 20x \leq 450 - 20x$$
$$10y \leq -20x + 450$$
$$\frac{10y}{10} \leq \frac{-20x + 450}{10}$$
$$y \leq -2x + 45$$

Only positive values for x and y make sense because Shanda cannot assemble a negative number of items.

Graph the boundary line, $y = -2x + 45$. This boundary is included as a solid line in the solution and is an upper boundary. Therefore, the region below the line is shaded.

On your calculator, use a window of (0, 47, 10, 0, 62, 10, 1) to view the first quadrant.

Y1 = $-2x + 45$

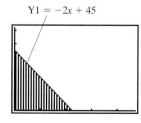

(0, 47, 0, 62)

c.

Y1 = −2x + 45

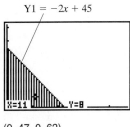

(0, 47, 0, 62)

Y1 = −2x + 45

(0, 47, 0, 62)

Shanda can produce any combination of 20-minute and 10-minute items determined by the ordered pairs found in the shaded region. For example, $(4, 25)$ and $(11, 8)$ are two ordered pairs in the shaded region.

The ordered pair $(4, 25)$ means that Shanda can produce four 20-minute items and twenty-five 10-minute items during one shift.

The ordered pair $(11, 8)$ means that Shanda can produce eleven 20-minute items and eight 10-minute items during one shift. ∎

Application

Your company publishes *Guides to the Internet*, available on three floppy disks or one CD-ROM. You can package the three-disk version for $0.09 per set, or package the CD-ROM for $0.14. You want to spend no more than $500 per day on packaging. Determine the possible combinations of each version of the guide you can package within this budget.

Discussion

Let $x =$ the number of three-disk packages
$y =$ the number of CD-ROM packages

The cost of packaging the three-disk version is $0.09 per package, or $0.09x$. The cost of packaging the CD-ROM is $0.14 per package, or $0.14y$. The total cost, $0.09x + 0.14y$, should be no more than ($\leq$) $500. Therefore, we have the inequality

$$0.09x + 0.14y \leq 500.$$

Solve the inequality for y.

$$0.09x + 0.14y \leq 500$$
$$0.09x + 0.14y - 0.09x \leq 500 - 0.09x$$
$$0.14y \leq -0.09x + 500$$
$$\frac{0.14y}{0.14} \leq \frac{-0.09x + 500}{0.14}$$
$$y \leq -0.64x + 3571.43 \quad \text{Round to the nearest hundredth.}$$

Y1 = −0.64x + 3571.43

(0, 9400, 0, 6200)

Graph the inequality.

The ordered pairs in the shaded region represent the possible combination of packages that can be packaged and stay within the budget. For example, $(1700, 1800)$ is found in the shaded region. Therefore, 1700 three-disk versions and 1800 CD-ROM versions can be packaged and stay within the budget of no more than $500. ∎

Experiencing Algebra the Checkup Way

1. Lana was approved for a student loan of no more than $1500 per semester. She figures that she can afford to pay back the loan at the rate of $60 per week. Her parents will contribute $125 occasionally to help her pay back the loan.

   a. Describe Lana's payment plan using a linear inequality in two variables, where x represents the number of weekly payments Lana makes and y represents the number of occasional payments her parents make on the loan.

   b. Graph the inequality in the first quadrant.

   c. Would a loan where Lana makes 9 weekly payments and her parents make 6 occasional payments be within the approved loan limit?

   d. Would a loan where Lana makes 18 weekly payments and her parents make 5 occasional payments be within the approved loan limit?

2. Sureworks Software Company markets two different software packages. One package is a word-processing package that sells for $225. The other package is a spreadsheet package that sells for $75. The company wants daily sales of the two packages to be at least $3600 in the test market. Write a linear inequality to represent this situation. Graph the inequality. List three different combinations of sales of the two packages that would meet the company's goal.

PROBLEM SET 8.3

Experiencing Algebra the Exercise Way

Identify each inequality as linear or nonlinear. Express each linear inequality in standard form and determine values for a, b, and c.

1. $2x + 1.7y > x - 4.6$ **2.** $y < \sqrt{x - 4} + 9$ **3.** $y < x^2 + 2x - 3$ **4.** $-5x + 10y \geq 15$

5. $y > \sqrt{x} + 9$ **6.** $y > x^3 - 27$ **7.** $\dfrac{x}{2} - \dfrac{y}{6} > \dfrac{1}{12}$ **8.** $y \geq -\dfrac{3}{4}x^2 + \dfrac{5}{8}$

9. $4x + 16 \leq y$ **10.** $3.5y < 4.2x - 2.8$ **11.** $y \leq -\dfrac{2}{5}x + \dfrac{7}{15}$ **12.** $\dfrac{x}{6} + \dfrac{y}{3} < 2$

Graph.

13. $2x + y < 3$ **14.** $5x - y < 6$ **15.** $5x - 3y \geq 6$

16. $8x + 7y \geq 14$ **17.** $y < -\dfrac{3}{4}x + 4$ **18.** $y < \dfrac{5}{6}x - 3$

19. $y \geq 2.8x - 1.6$ **20.** $y \geq 4.7 - 1.9x$ **21.** $2y > 3x - 5$

22. $5y > 3x - 2$ **23.** $3x + y - 4 \leq x + 2y - 3$ **24.** $7x - 2y + 8 \leq 5x - 3y + 1$

25. $5y > -20$ **26.** $3y + 7 > 25$ **27.** $3x + 6 \leq 9$

28. $2x - 4 \leq 6$ **29.** $3x + 5y \geq 12$ **30.** $7x + 9y \geq 63$

31. $-x - y < 7$ **32.** $x - y > 3$ **33.** $-3x - 9y > 27$

34. $-12x - 9y > 36$ **35.** $\dfrac{x}{8} + \dfrac{y}{3} \leq 1$ **36.** $\dfrac{x}{9} - \dfrac{y}{6} \leq 1$

37. $-\dfrac{4}{7}x + \dfrac{2}{3}y \geq \dfrac{10}{21}$ **38.** $\dfrac{3}{4}x - \dfrac{5}{6}y \geq \dfrac{13}{24}$ **39.** $1.8x - 3.2y > 0$

40. $58.2x + 19.4y > 0$ **41.** $4.6y < 3.5y + 5.94$ **42.** $8.1y + 16.2 < 72.9y$

43. $x - y > 9$ **44.** $-x + y > 9$ **45.** $-x - y > 9$

46. $x + y > 9$ **47.** $y \le x$ **48.** $y \ge -x$

Write and graph a linear inequality in two variables to represent each situation and answer the questions.

49. A Christmas shop sells village pieces for $25.00 each and angel ornaments for $12.00 each. Rita was given a limit of no more than $225.00 to spend to buy decorations for the reception area of her office. What combinations can she buy and stay within the limit imposed? Would she be within the budget if she bought four village pieces and seven angel ornaments? What if she bought seven village pieces and nine angel ornaments?

50. The sale of coupon booklets netted the sixth-grade class $240. The money is to be used to buy books and videos for the class library. If the books sell for $12 each and the videos sell for $18 each, what combinations would be within the amount available? Would they be able to buy 7 books and 6 videos? Would they be able to buy 12 books and 8 videos?

51. Barbara bought 220 feet of wallpaper border on sale. What are the limits on the dimensions of a rectangular room if she wants to run the border around the top of the walls? Would she have enough for a 70-by-60-foot room? Would she have enough for a 40-by-60-foot room?

52. In exercise 51, the rooms Barbara will decorate have 10-foot ceilings. She also bought enough rolls of wallpaper to cover 2400 square feet of wall space. What are the limits on a rectangular room if she wants to paper all four walls, with no allowances for windows or doors? Does she have enough for a 70-by-60-foot room? Does she have enough for a 40-by-50-foot room?

53. Pablo will be paid $15 per day for demonstrating crafts, plus $12 for each item he sells at a crafts fair. What combinations will allow the artist to earn at least $400? If he works three days and sells 20 items, will he earn at least $400? If he works five days and sells 30 items, will he earn the minimum?

54. Jason is renting a chain saw for $15 per day. He will charge $10 for each tree he cuts down in his neighbors' yards. What combinations of days and trees will allow him to earn at least $75 for the venture? If he cuts 16 trees in three days, will he make his goal of at least $75? What if he does 10 trees in four days?

55. At a school fund-raiser, adults were charged $4.50 each and children were charged $2.00 to attend a chili supper. If the school wished to raise at least $250.00, what combinations of ticket sales would assure this? Would 40 adult and 25 children tickets be enough in sales to make the goal? Would 42 adult and 45 children ticket sales be enough?

56. An elevator has a load limit of 2000 pounds. If the average adult weighs 160 pounds and the average child weighs 65 pounds, what combinations would be safe to ride the elevator? Would a group with 5 teachers and 15 children be safe on the elevator? How about a group with 10 teachers and 12 children?

Experiencing Algebra the Calculator Way

A. Graphing a Linear Inequality Using the Shade Command

There is another method for graphing a linear inequality using the calculator. It involves a command called "Shade." To graph a linear inequality in two variables on the calculator using the Shade command, we still must do similar steps as those we do by hand. First, we must solve the inequality for y. Enter the boundary equation, $y = ax + b$, into the calculator in Y1. Determine the type of inequality (less than or greater than) from the inequality solved for y. Then use the shade command in the calculator; Shade (lower boundary, upper boundary). To graph solutions of a "less than" inequality, we want to shade below a line. Therefore, we will use the bottom of the screen (Ymin) for the lower boundary and the boundary line stored in Y1 for the upper boundary. To graph solutions of a "greater than" inequality, we want to shade above a line. Therefore, the boundary line stored in Y1 is the lower boundary and the top of the screen (Ymax) is the upper boundary.

To graph a linear inequality in two variables on your calculator, complete the following steps:

- Solve the inequality for y.

- Enter the boundary equation in Y1.

- Shade the inequality solved for y.

  - For a "less than" inequality, enter Shade (Ymin, Y1).

  - For a "greater than" inequality, enter Shade (Y1, Ymax).

- Clear the screen before entering a new inequality.

| 2nd | DRAW | 1 |

As an example, use the Shade command to graph $x - y < -5$.

First, solve the inequality for y: $y > x + 5$.
Enter the boundary equation $y = x + 5$ in Y1.

| Y= | X, T, θ, n | + | 5 |

Since the inequality is "greater than," we want to display Shade (Y1, Ymax).

| 2nd | DRAW | 7 | VARS | ▶ | 1 | 1 | , | VARS | 1 | 5 |) | ENTER |

$Y1 = x + 5$

$(-47, 47, -31, 31)$

As another example, graph $6x + 2y \le -10$.

Solve the inequality for y: $y \le -3x - 5$.
The boundary line is the graph for the equation $y = -3x - 5$.

Since the inequality is "less than," we want to display Shade (Ymin, Y1).

2nd | DRAW | 7 | VARS | 1 | 4 | , | VARS | ▶ | 1 | 1 |) | ENTER

Y1 = −3x − 5

(−47, 47, −31, 31)

Select a few exercises from "Experiencing Algebra the Exercise Way," write the Shade command for each, and use the Shade command to graph the inequalities.

Graphing linear inequalities on your calculator using the Shade command requires a knowledge of the solution set and recall of the Shade command. The Shade command will not just "give" you the graph. The method is not as easy as the method presented in the text of this section. However, knowledge of the Shade command can be helpful when the boundary line of the inequality is a vertical line. This procedure is explained next.

B. Graphing a Linear Inequality Having a Vertical Boundary Line

The text stated that the calculator would not be used to graph an inequality of the form $ax < c$, since $ax = c$ is not a function. Actually, the calculator does contain a variation of the Shade instruction to graph this type of inequality. To graph $x < c$ or other such linear inequalities that have no y-variable, we will use Shade (lower boundary, upper boundary, left boundary, right boundary). Use the default arguments, Ymin and Ymax, for the lower and upper boundaries.

For a "less than" inequality, $x < c$, use Shade (Ymin, Ymax, Xmin, c.). Enter the shade command as follows:

2nd | DRAW | 7 | VARS | 1 | 4 | , | VARS | 1 | 5 | , | VARS | 1 | 1 | ,
the value c) | ENTER .

For a "greater than" inequality, $x > c$, use Shade (Ymin, Ymax, c, Xmax). Enter the Shade command as follows:

2nd | DRAW | 7 | VARS | 1 | 4 | , | VARS | 1 | 5 | , | *the value c* , | VARS
1 | 2 |) | ENTER .

To clear the shade, enter 2nd | DRAW | 1 .

As an example of this method, graph $x - 3 < 8$.

$$x - 3 + 3 < 8 + 3$$
$$x < 11$$

Since the inequality is "less than" and $c = 11$, we want to use Shade (Ymin, Ymax, Xmin, 11).

| 2nd | DRAW | 7 | VARS | 1 | 4 | , | VARS | 1 | 5 | , | VARS | 1 | 1 | , |

| 1 | 1 |) | ENTER | .

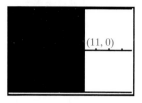

$(-47, 47, -31, 31)$

Write the Shade instruction to graph each inequality. Use your calculator to graph.

1. $6x - 8 < 2x + 32$ **2.** $3(x - 4) < x - 2$ **3.** $5x > 14$

4. $2x - 3.6 \geq 1.8$ **5.** $x \leq \pi$ **6.** $x + \sqrt{2} \leq 3$

Experiencing Algebra the Group Way

In this section you have learned how to graph a linear inequality in two variables using two methods: with a pencil and paper, or with your calculator. It would be helpful to summarize what you have learned. As a group, work together to complete the following table. Keep it as a reference to help you remember details in graphing these linear inequalities.

Inequality	Boundary	Line	Shading
$y < ax + b$	$y = ax + b$		
$y \leq ax + b$			below
$y > ax + b$		dashed	
$y \geq ax + b$			
$y < c$	$y = c$		
$y \leq c$		solid	
$y > c$			above
$y \geq c$			
$x < c$		dashed	
$x \leq c$			left
$x > c$	$x = c$		
$x \geq c$			

Experiencing Algebra the Write Way

Describe the difference between a linear equation in two variables and a linear inequality in two variables. Explain how the two differ in terms of their solutions, using a coordinate system as part of the explanation. Discuss how application problems might give rise to each type of mathematical statement, using key words that would yield either an equation or an inequality.

8.4   Systems of Linear Inequalities in Two Variables

Objectives

1   Graph systems of linear inequalities in two variables.
2   Graph systems of linear inequalities in two variables using a calculator.
3   Graph special cases of systems of linear inequalities in two variables.
4   Model real-world situations using systems of linear inequalities.

Application

Your company's sales goal for the *Guide to the Internet* works out to a total of $750 per day for all versions. The CD-ROM version sells for $20.75 net and the set of three floppy disks sells for $24.00 net. Determine the possible combinations of sales of each version that will meet your sales goal.

After completing this section, we will discuss this application further. See page 619.

1   Graphing Systems of Linear Inequalities in Two Variables

We have determined solutions of one linear equation in two variables. But sometimes we may need to know the solution of more than one inequality at a time. A **system of linear inequalities in two variables** consists of two or more linear inequalities in two variables. For example, $x + y < 30$ and $2x - 5y > 40$ is a system of linear inequalities. We usually write this system without the word *and*:

$$x + y < 30$$
$$2x - 5y > 40$$

A solution of a system of inequalities is an ordered pair that makes both inequalities true. We have learned to graphically illustrate the solution set of one linear inequality in two variables using shaded regions. To solve a system of inequalities, we will need to graph each inequality individually and then determine the ordered pairs that make both inequalities true at the same time. These ordered pairs lie in the overlap of the shaded regions.

Graphing a System of Linear Inequalities in Two Variables
To graph the solution of a system of linear inequalities in two variables:

- Graph each inequality individually on the same rectangular coordinate plane.
- Determine all intersections of the boundary lines.
- Determine the region of the coordinate plane that contains solutions of all inequalities (the overlapping shaded regions).
- Check a point in the overlap region to determine whether it is a solution.

EXAMPLE 1   Graph the following system of linear inequalities in two variables.

$$2x - y < 7$$
$$-x + y \geq 2$$

Solution

a. First, solve each inequality for y.

$$2x - y < 7 \qquad \text{and} \qquad -x + y \geq 2$$
$$y > 2x - 7 \qquad\qquad\qquad y \geq x + 2$$

a.

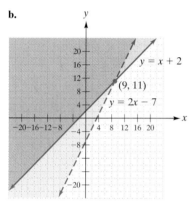

Graph the boundary lines for each inequality. The first inequality has a dashed boundary line (no equality) and the second inequality has a solid boundary line to include the points on the line in the solution set (includes equality).

Determine the intersection of the boundary lines algebraically by solving the related system of equations.

(1) $2x - y = 7$

(2) $-x + y = 2$

By elimination, we obtain

$$x = 9.$$

By substitution, we obtain

(1) $-x + y = 2$

$$-(9) + y = 2$$
$$-9 + y = 2$$
$$-9 + y + 9 = 2 + 9$$
$$y = 11.$$

The intersection of the boundaries is $(9, 11)$.

b.

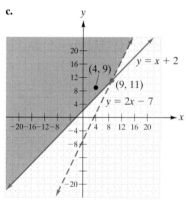

b. Shade above both boundaries, because each inequality when solved for y was a "greater than" inequality.

The overlap of the shaded regions and the included boundary line shown contains the ordered-pair solutions of the system.

c.

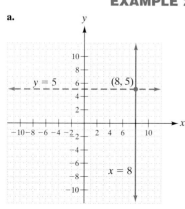

c. Check a point in the shaded portion. One such point is $(4, 9)$. Check to see whether it is a solution of both inequalities of the system.

$$\begin{array}{c|c} 2x - y < 7 \\ \hline 2(4) - 9 & 7 \\ 8 - 9 & \\ -1 & \end{array} \qquad \text{and} \qquad \begin{array}{c|c} -x + y \ge 2 \\ \hline -(4) + 9 & 2 \\ -4 + 9 & \\ 5 & \end{array}$$

The check point $(4, 9)$ is a solution. ∎

If the system of linear inequalities has inequalities with one variable missing, the procedure outlined in Example 1 still applies.

EXAMPLE 2 Graph the following system of linear inequalities in two variables.

$$y < 5$$
$$x + 4 \ge 12$$

Solution

a. Solve the first inequality for y: $y < 5$.

The second inequality does not contain a y and should be solved for x.

$$x + 4 \ge 12$$
$$x + 4 - 4 \ge 12 - 4$$
$$x \ge 8$$

b.

c.

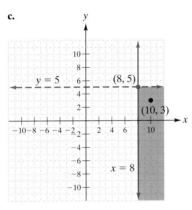

Graph the boundary lines for each inequality. The first line is dashed and the second is solid.

Determine the intersection of the boundary lines algebraically by solving the related system of equations.

$$y = 5$$
$$x = 8$$

The intersection is the ordered pair $(8, 5)$.

b. Shade below the line $y = 5$ for "less than" and shade to the right of the line $x = 8$ for "greater than."

The overlap of both shaded regions and the included boundary line shown contains the ordered-pair solutions of the system.

c. Check a point in the shaded portion. One such point is $(10, 3)$. Check to see whether it is a solution of both inequalities of the system.

$$\begin{array}{c|c} y < 5 \\ \hline 3 & 5 \end{array} \qquad \text{and} \qquad \begin{array}{c|c} x + 4 \geq 12 \\ \hline 10 + 4 & 12 \\ 14 & \end{array}$$

The check point $(10, 3)$ is a solution. ∎

Systems of linear inequalities may involve more than two inequalities. A solution of such a system is still an ordered pair that makes all the inequalities true. We graphically illustrate the solutions of the system in the same manner as with two inequalities. That is, we graph all the inequalities on the same coordinate system and determine the overlap shading of the graphs.

This overlap shading may be hard to determine. It may be easier to graph the boundary lines, then choose a point in each of the regions of the coordinate plane and check to see whether it satisfies all inequalities in the system.

EXAMPLE 3 Graph the following system of linear inequalities in two variables.

$$x + y \leq 10$$
$$y \leq 4$$
$$y \geq 0$$
$$x \geq 0$$

Solution

a. Solve the first inequality for y.

$$y \leq -x + 10$$

Graph the boundary lines for the inequalities. All the boundaries are solid lines because all the inequalities include equality.

Determine the intersections.

b. Shade the regions for each inequality and determine the overlapping shaded region.

a.

$y \leq -x + 10$

$y \leq 4$

$y \geq 0$

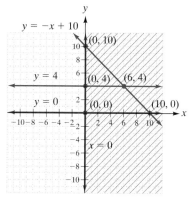

$x \geq 0$

The overlap of all shaded regions and the included boundary lines shown contains the ordered-pair solutions of the system. Because it is so difficult to see the overlap shading when more than two areas are shaded, it is often advisable to graph only the overlap region, as shown in Figure 8.9.

b.

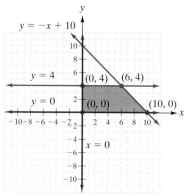

Figure 8.9

c. Alternatively, instead of shading, pick a check point in each of the regions defined by the boundaries in the first quadrant. Test to determine which of these points makes the entire system of inequalities true. Then shade the region that contains this point.

c.

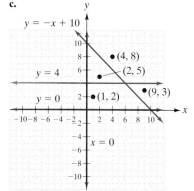

A point in each region is labeled on the graph. Substitute the coordinates of each point into all the inequalities. The ordered pair $(1, 2)$ satisfies all the inequalities. Therefore, shade the region in the first quadrant where it is located. The result is the same as Figure 8.9. ∎

Experiencing Algebra the Checkup Way

In exercises 1–5, graph each system of linear inequalities.

1. $3x + 5y < 15$
  $2x - y < 3$

2. $3x - 5y \leq 5$
  $2y + 3 > 7$

3. $y \geq -4x + 3$
  $x \geq 1$

4. $y + 3 < 0$
  $x + 7 > 5$

5. $x + y < 5$
  $y > x + 1$
  $x \geq 0$
  $y \geq 0$

6. What is the difference between finding the solutions of a linear inequality in two variables and finding the solutions of a system of linear inequalities in two variables?

7. Explain how you would solve a system of linear inequalities graphically.

---

2 Graphing Systems of Linear Inequalities Using a Calculator

To graph a system of linear inequalities in two variables on a calculator, we do the same steps as we do by hand.

To graph a system of linear inequalities in two variables, when both inequalities contain a *y*-term, on your calculator:

- Solve the inequalities for *y*.
- Enter the algebraic expressions in Y1 and Y2.
- Determine the intersection of the boundaries by tracing or using Intersect under the CALC function.
- Shade the coordinate plane determined by the inequality solved for *y*.
  - For a "less than" inequality, shade below the boundary line.
  - For a "greater than" inequality, shade above the boundary line.
  - The second inequality should be entered in the same way as the first.

Helping Hand The calculator does not graph dashed lines. It includes the boundary in the graph. It will be up to you not to include it in your graph.

EXAMPLE 4 Use your calculator to graph the following system of linear inequalities in two variables.

$$2x - y < 7$$
$$-x + y \geq 2$$

Solution

Solve the inequalities for *y*.

$$y > 2x - 7$$
$$y \geq x + 2.$$

Enter the boundaries, graph, and determine the intersection of the lines. Let Y1 $= 2x - 7$ and Y2 $= x + 2$, as shown in Figure 8.10.

Shade above the Y1 graph for a "greater than" inequality. Shade above the Y2 graph for a "greater than or equal to" inequality. The solution set consists of the ordered pairs in the portion of the graph that is shaded twice, as shown in Figure 8.11. ■

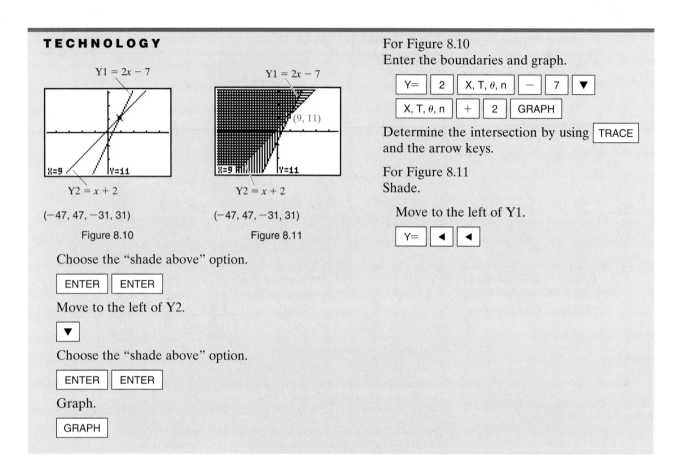

TECHNOLOGY

Y1 = 2x − 7

Y2 = x + 2

(−47, 47, −31, 31)

Figure 8.10

Y1 = 2x − 7

(9, 11)

Y2 = x + 2

(−47, 47, −31, 31)

Figure 8.11

Choose the "shade above" option.

ENTER   ENTER

Move to the left of Y2.

▼

Choose the "shade above" option.

ENTER   ENTER

Graph.

GRAPH

For Figure 8.10
Enter the boundaries and graph.

Y=   2   X, T, θ, n   −   7   ▼
X, T, θ, n   +   2   GRAPH

Determine the intersection by using TRACE and the arrow keys.

For Figure 8.11
Shade.

Move to the left of Y1.

Y=   ◄   ◄

Solving a system of linear inequalities in two variables when one or more inequalities do not contain a y-term is more complicated on the calculator. Since the boundary for this type of inequality is not a function, we will not present the calculator procedure here. (See "Experiencing Algebra the Calculator Way" at the end of this section for instructions.)

When a system of linear inequalities has more than two inequalities, shade the correct portion of the coordinate plane for each inequality that has a boundary line consisting of a function.

EXAMPLE 5   Use your calculator to graph the following system of linear inequalities in two variables.

$$x + y \leq 10$$
$$y \leq 4$$
$$y \geq 0$$
$$x \geq 0$$

Calculator Solution

We will need to use a close view for this system.

$$(-14.1, 14.1, 1, -12.4, 12.4, 1, 1)$$

Enter the boundaries for the first three inequalities, which contain a y-variable.

$$Y1 = -x + 10$$

$$Y2 = 4$$

$$Y3 = 0$$

Because the fourth inequality's boundary, $x = 0$, is not a function, do not graph it. But remember to include it when describing the solution set of the system of inequalities, that is, include the y-axis and all points to its right.

Determine the intersections by tracing. Shade below Y1 and Y2 for a "less than or equal to" inequality. Shade above Y3 for a "greater than or equal to" inequality.

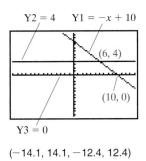

Y2 = 4   Y1 = −x + 10

(6, 4)

(10, 0)

Y3 = 0

$(-14.1, 14.1, -12.4, 12.4)$

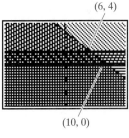

(6, 4)

(10, 0)

$(-14.1, 14.1, -12.4, 12.4)$

Note: The shaded figure is very difficult to see.

The solution set consists of the ordered pairs in the portion of the graph that is shaded three times and also on the y-axis or to the right of the y-axis (because $x \geq 0$). ∎

Experiencing Algebra the Checkup Way

Graph each system of linear inequalities using your calculator.

1. $y \leq x - 3$

$2x - y \geq -1$

2. $y > -3x + 4$

$x + y > 2$

3. $y \leq \dfrac{2}{3}x + 1$

$y \leq -\dfrac{3}{4}x + 5$

$x \geq 0$

$y \geq 0$

3 Some Special Cases   When graphing a system of linear inequalities, some special cases can occur. Some of these cases are as follows:

- Parallel boundary lines with shading occurring within the parallel lines.
- Parallel boundary lines with shadings occurring on correspondingly the same side of the boundary lines (indicating that solutions of the system occur in the overlap region of the shadings).
- Parallel boundary lines with shadings occurring outside and on opposite sides of the parallel lines (indicating no overlap and no solution of the system).
- Coinciding boundary lines with shading occurring on the same side of the line.
- Coinciding boundary lines with shading occurring on different sides of the boundary line (indicating that solutions of the system occur on the line only if it is a solid line for all inequalities).

EXAMPLE 6   Graph each system of linear inequalities in two variables. Describe the solution of the system.

a. $x + y \leq 3$ 　　　　**b.** $y \leq 3$ 　　　　**c.** $x + 2y \geq 4$
　　$x + y \geq -2$ 　　　　　　$y < 1$ 　　　　　　$x + 2y < 0$

d. $x - 3y \geq 3$ 　　　　**e.** $y < -\dfrac{1}{4}x + 1$

　　$x \geq 3(y + 1)$ 　　　　　　$x + 4y > 4$

Solution

a.

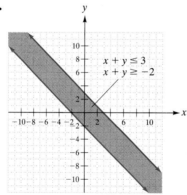

The solution is all ordered pairs contained in the shaded region and on the two boundary lines.

b.

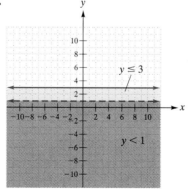

The solution is all ordered pairs contained in the shaded region below the boundary line $y = 1$.

c.

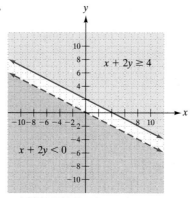

There are no ordered pairs that satisfy this system of linear inequalities.

d.

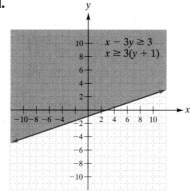

The solution is all ordered pairs contained in the shaded region and on the boundary line.

e.

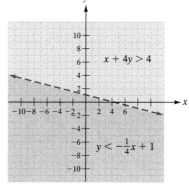

There are no ordered pairs that satisfy this system of linear inequalities. ∎

Experiencing Algebra the Checkup Way

Graph each system of linear inequalities in two variables. Describe the solution set of the system.

1. $3y < x + 6$
$x - 3y \leq 9$

2. $y \leq 2x + 3$
$y - x + 1 \geq x + 4$

3. $y \leq 2x + 1$
$y \geq 2x + 3$

4. $y \leq \dfrac{1}{2}x - 4$
$2y + 3 < x - 5$

5. $x > -1$
$x \geq 1$

---

4 Modeling the Real World

We have seen that systems of inequalities often have many solutions, even an infinite number of solutions. In many real-world situations we need to restrict the number of solutions to those that make sense, such as restricting solutions to positive values for time. We can do this by adding another inequality to the system, called a **constraint** on the variables. For example, we can add the inequality $t > 0$ to a system involving the variable t for time, so the solutions will include only positive values for t. We may want to add constraints to a system of inequalities to restrict the set of solutions to certain values. For instance, we may want to search a database for unmarried males whose age is over 21 and less than 30, and add a constraint that their annual income exceed $100,000. Mathematically, we treat the constraint inequality as just another inequality in the system.

EXAMPLE 7

Donzietta and Kathy make dolls to sell. Donzietta cuts out the patterns and sews and stuffs each doll. This requires 2 hours of work for a rag doll and 6 hours of work for a sculptured doll. Kathy finishes the features and hair of each doll. This requires 3 hours for a rag doll and 2 hours for a sculptured doll. Donzietta plans to work at most 40 hours a week and Kathy at most 32 hours a week.

a. Determine the constraints of producing the dolls for a week.
b. Graph the system of linear inequalities and determine two possible combinations that satisfy the system.

Solution

a. Let x = number of rag dolls produced per week
y = number of sculptured dolls produced per week

An inequality for Donzietta's contribution is

$2x + 6y \leq 40$.

An inequality for Kathy's contribution is

$3x + 2y \leq 32$.

Constraints not stated in the exercise would be that the number of dolls of each kind may not be a negative number.

$x \geq 0$
$y \geq 0$

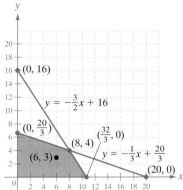

Solve each inequality for y.

$$y \leq -\frac{1}{3}x + \frac{20}{3}$$

$$y \leq -\frac{3}{2}x + 16$$

$$y \geq 0$$

The last constraint is solved for x.

$$x \geq 0$$

Graph the boundaries with solid lines for equality and determine the intersections.

    Shade each portion of the graph.

    For $y \leq -\frac{1}{3}x + \frac{20}{3}$, shade below the boundary line.

    For $y \leq -\frac{3}{2}x + 16$, shade below the boundary line.

    For $y \geq 0$, shade above the boundary line.

    For $x \geq 0$, shade to the right of the boundary line.

b. The solution set consists of all the ordered pairs contained on the boundary lines and in the overlap of the shaded regions. Two possible ordered-pair solutions are $(6, 3)$ and $(8, 4)$.

    $(6, 3)$ means six rag dolls and three sculptured dolls can be produced.

    $(8, 4)$ means eight rag dolls and four sculptured dolls can be produced. ■

Application

Your company's sales goal for the *Guide to the Internet* works out to a total of $750 per day for all versions. The CD-ROM version sells for $20.75 net and the set of three floppy disks sells for $24.00 net. Determine the possible combinations of sales of each version that will meet your sales goal.

Discussion

Let $x =$ the number of three-disk versions sold
     $y =$ the number of CD-ROM versions sold

The sales from the three-disk version is $24.00x$. The sales from the CD-ROM version is $20.75y$. The total sales is $24.00x + 20.75y$.

    The sales goal is $750. Therefore, the total sales must be greater than or equal to 750.

    An inequality for this relationship is

$$24.00x + 20.75y \geq 750.$$

Also, the number of three-disk versions must not be negative.

$$x \geq 0$$

The number of CD-ROM versions also must not be negative.

$$y \geq 0$$

A graph for the system is shown.

    The solutions are the ordered pairs contained on the boundary lines and in the overlap of the shaded regions in the first quadrant. One possible solution is $(12, 13)$, interpreted as sales of 12 three-disk versions and 13 CD-ROM versions. ■

$(0, 47, 0, 62)$

Experiencing Algebra the Checkup Way

1. Donzietta and Kathy decide to streamline their doll-making operation. They purchase kits that shorten the time required to produce the dolls they make. Donzietta can use precut patterns so that she now spends 1.5 hours of work for each rag doll and 4 hours of work for each sculptured doll. Kathy uses doll heads that already have been prefinished, so she can now finish a rag doll in 1.5 hours and a sculptured doll in 1 hour. Donzietta changes her plans to work no more than 30 hours per week and Kathy changes hers to work no more than 24 hours per week. Determine the new constraints for producing dolls for a week. Graph the system of linear inequalities and determine two possible combinations that satisfy the system.

2. An entrepreneur stages an amateur show to raise money. The theater holds at most 150 people. If he charges each adult $3.00 and each child $2.00, what combinations of ticket sales will result in returns of at least $250.00? Will sales of 60 adult tickets and 60 child tickets meet his criteria? What about sales of 80 adult tickets and 90 child tickets? How about 30 adult tickets and 40 child tickets?

PROBLEM SET 8.4

Experiencing Algebra the Exercise Way

Graph each system of linear inequalities. Label the points of intersection.

1. $5x - 3y > 15$
$4x + y > 12$

2. $2x + 3y > -6$
$x - 4y < 8$

3. $2x + 4y \geq 8$
$3x + y \leq -8$

4. $x + y \leq 4$
$x - 2y \leq 7$

5. $y > 3x - 1$
$y > -2x + 4$

6. $y > 3x - 6$
$y > -5x + 2$

7. $y < \frac{3}{4}x + 1$
$y < -\frac{2}{3}x + 1$

8. $y < \frac{1}{2}x + 3$
$y < -\frac{3}{2}x - 1$

9. $3x + 2y < 12$
$y - 2 < 1$

10. $-x + 2y > 4$
$3x - 2 < 4$

11. $3y - 2 > 2y + 2$
$x - 1 < 0$

12. $5x + 10 < -5$
$2y + 7 > 5$

13. $y \leq 3x - 5$
$x > 4 - 2y$

14. $y \geq -2x + 3$
$3x \leq 2y + 8$

15. $y \leq \frac{1}{2}x + 3$
$x + 2y < 6$

16. $y > x + 1$
$x + y < 1$

17. $y \leq 10 - x$
$2y > x + 6$
$y > 0$
$x < 3$

18. $y > \frac{1}{2}x$
$y \leq -2x + 8$
$y \geq 0$
$y \leq 4$
$x \geq 0$

Graph each system of linear inequalities using your calculator. Determine the points of intersection.

19. $x - 2y > 7$
$5x + 10y < -3$

20. $2x - 3y < 5$
$2y + 6 > 8$

21. $3x - 5y \geq 5$
$10y + 15 > 2$

22. $3x + 5y \geq 15$
$4x - 2y > 7$

23. $y \geq x - 3$
$10x - 5y \geq 14$

24. $y \geq -3x + 4$
$5x - 5y \geq 2$

25. $2x + 9y < 102$
$5x - 11y < -147$

26. $11x + 5y < 133$
$15x + 4y > 187$

27. $3.2x + 4.2y > 368$
$4.4x - 2.1y > 128$

28. $1.4x + 2.4y > 225$
$3.4x - 1.6y > 123$

29. $0.05x + 0.10y < 0.75$
$x + y > 11$

30. $0.25x + 0.50y < 5.75$
$x + y > 14$

Graph the following special cases of systems of linear inequalities. Describe the solution set of each system.

31. $2x - 3y > -6$
  $-2x + 3y > -6$

32. $x + 2y < 6$
  $x + 2y > 2$

33. $y > -3x + 2$
  $y \le -3x$

34. $y > 2x + 2$
  $y \le 2x - 3$

35. $x + 4 > 0$
  $3x + 2 < -4$

36. $y - 1 < 0$
  $y + 3 > 0$

37. $y < 4 - 2x$
  $2x + y \le -1$

38. $y < x - 7$
  $x > y + 9$

39. $3y \le x + 6$
  $3y - x \ge 6$

40. $y < 2x + 3$
  $y - x + 4 > x + 7$

41. $y < 7$
  $2y - 3 \le y + 4$

42. $y \ge 3x + 4$
  $3x + 5 \le y + 1$

Use the steps for solving application problems (see section 7.4) to develop a system of linear inequalities to represent each situation. Graph the system. Determine one possible solution from the solution set.

43. A contractor is staking out an area for a rectangular patio. The perimeter of the patio must be no more than 100 feet. The length must be at least 10 feet more than the width. What are the possible dimensions for the patio?

44. After seeing the design for the patio in exercise 43, the customer decides that while the perimeter still should be no more than 100 feet, the length should be at least twice the width. What are the new possible dimensions for the patio?

45. One investment pays 6% simple interest for a year, while another pays 8% simple interest for a year. If you have no more than $3000 to invest, how much can you invest at each rate in order to earn at least $200 in interest for the year?

46. If you have up to $5000 to invest, part at 6% and part at 8% simple interest for a year, how much can you invest at each rate to earn at least $350 in interest?

47. Hans has two part-time jobs. Because of school, he is limited to work no more than 20 hours per week. He earns $6.50 per hour on the first job and $8.25 on the second job. For what combination of work hours will he earn at least $150.00 per week? Will he earn at least $150.00 if he works 7 hours on the first job and 10 hours on the second job? How about if he works 5 hours on the first job and 15 hours on the second job?

48. Happy Harry's charges $20 per hour to rent its party room and $5 per guest for snacks and beverages. The minimum number of hours of rental is 1.5 hours. For what combination of the number of guests and the number of hours of rental will the cost be no more than $150? Will 15 guests and a 2-hour rental meet the requirements? How about 25 guests and 2.5 hours of rental?

49. Rosie sells two different entrées at her restaurant. Lasagna costs $1.75 per serving to prepare. Veal parmigiana costs $2.25 per serving to prepare. Past experience indicates that she must prepare at least 50 servings of the lasagna and 25 servings of the veal parmigiana each day. If she wants her cost of preparing the entrées to be no more than $200 per day, what combinations of the number of each entrée will do? If she prepares 60 servings of lasagna and 35 servings of veal parmigiana, will the cost be in the permissible range? What if she prepares 60 servings of lasagna and 50 servings of veal parmigiana?

50. Math Academy wants to consider contracting out its copying operations. They can pay $0.05 per page to copy the manuscript at the local copy center if they contract for more than 25,000 pages. They can purchase a copy machine for a minimum of $1399, after which it would cost them $0.01 per page to copy at the academy. For what combination of machine cost and number of copies will it be cheaper to buy the machine and copy in-house? Will it be cheaper to copy in-house if 30,000 copies are needed and the cost of a machine is $1500? What if the academy needs 40,000 copies and the machine cost is $1400?

 Experiencing Algebra the Calculator Way

A. Graphing a System of Linear Inequalities Using the Shade Command

Just as we used the Shade command to graph a single linear inequality on the calculator, we can also use the command to graph a system of linear inequalities. First, we graph the boundaries and determine the intersections. Next, we shade the correct portion of the coordinate plane. Remember, the calculator's Shade command asks for several inputs. We will need to use additional inputs that we did not use when graphing one inequality. The calculator's Shade command in expanded form appears as follows: Shade(lower boundary, upper boundary, left boundary, right boundary, pattern, resolution). We have previously used the lower and upper boundaries as boundaries for *y*. The left and right boundaries are for *x*, and the screen boundaries are Xmin and Xmax. "Pattern" is specified as an integer between 1 and 4, inclusive. The patterns we will use most often are 1 for vertical and 2 for horizontal. "Resolution" sets the shading and is specified as an integer between 1 and 8, inclusive. Its default value is 1, where all pixels are shaded; a 2 shades every second pixel; a 3 shades every third pixel, and so forth. The different shading resolutions allow us to distinguish between the different shaded portions on the screen when more than one Shade command is performed. Prime numbers (2, 3, 5, 7) work best for resolution settings.

A combination of different patterns and resolutions enables us to see the different shadings and the intersections. For two inequalities, use pattern 1, resolution 2 for the first inequality and pattern 2, resolution 2 for the second inequality. If more than two inequalities are in the system, you may choose other combinations for each.

Use the following steps to graph a system of linear inequalities in two variables using the Shade command on your calculator.

- Solve the inequalities for *y*.
- Enter the algebraic expressions in Y1 and Y2.
- Determine the intersection of the boundaries by tracing or using Intersect under the CALC function.
- Shade the first inequality solved for *y*.
  - For a "less than" inequality,
    Shade (Ymin, Y1, Xmin, Xmax, 1, 2).

| 2nd | DRAW | 7 | VARS | 1 | 4 | , | VARS | ▶ | 1 | 1 | , | VARS | 1 | 1 |

| , | VARS | 1 | 2 | , | 1 | , | 2 |) | ENTER |

  - For a "greater than" inequality,
    Shade (Y1, Ymax, Xmin, Xmax, 1, 2).

| 2nd | DRAW | 7 | VARS | ▶ | 1 | 1 | , | VARS | 1 | 5 | , | VARS | 1 | 1 |

| , | VARS | 1 | 2 | , | 1 | , | 2 |) | ENTER |

- The second inequality should be entered in the same way as the first except using a horizontal pattern (2) and using Y2 instead of Y1.
  - A "less than" Shade command is
    Shade (Ymin, Y2, Xmin, Xmax, 2, 2)

- A "greater than" Shade command is
  Shade (Y2, Ymax, Xmin, Xmax, 2, 2).

• Clear the screen before entering a new system.

| 2nd | DRAW | 1 | .

As an example, use the Shade command of your calculator to graph the following system of linear inequalities in two variables:

$$2x - y < 7$$
$$-x + y \geq 2$$

Solve the inequalities for y: $y > 2x - 7$ and $y \geq x + 2$.
   Enter the boundaries, graph, and trace to determine the intersection of the lines.

| Y= | 2 | X, T, θ, n | − | 7 | ▼ | X, T, θ, n | + | 2 | GRAPH |

Y1 = 2x − 7

Y2 = x + 2

$(-47, 47, -31, 31)$

Enter the Shade commands.

   Shade (Y1, Ymax, Xmin, Xmax, 1, 2)

   Shade (Y2, Ymax, Xmin, Xmax, 2, 2)

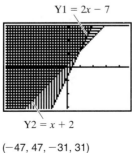

Y1 = 2x − 7

Y2 = x + 2

$(-47, 47, -31, 31)$

The solution set consists of the ordered pairs in the portion of the graph that is shaded twice.

Chapter 8 Inequalities

Once again, the use of the Shade command is not as simple as the method suggested earlier in this section, but it is helpful in situations where there are vertical boundary lines. This situation is described next.

B. Graphing a System of Linear Inequalities with Vertical Boundary Lines

With the shade command, it is possible to graph a system of linear inequalities in two variables on the calculator, when at least one inequality has no y-term.

- Solve the inequality that does not contain a y-term for x. The result will be an inequality with an x-term and a constant term, c.

- For a "less than" inequality, shade the correct portion of the graph with the Shade command.

  Shade (Ymin, Ymax, Xmin, c, 1, 2).

  | 2nd | DRAW | 7 | VARS | 1 | 4 | , | VARS | 1 | 5 | , | VARS | 1 | 1 | , |

  the constant term c | , | 1 | , | 2 |) | ENTER |

- For a "greater than" inequality, shade the correct portion of the graph with the Shade command.

  Shade (Ymin, Ymax, c, Xmax, 1, 2)

  | 2nd | DRAW | 7 | VARS | 1 | 4 | , | VARS | 1 | 5 | , |

  the constant term c | , | VARS | 1 | 2 | , | 1 | , | 2 |) | ENTER |

- Repeat the previous steps if the second inequality does not contain a y-term, replacing the pattern with the number 2.

- If the second inequality contains a y-term, use the steps in Part A for the second inequality.

- To clear the shade, enter | 2nd | DRAW | 1 | .

The intersections may not be calculated using these steps.

As an example, graph

$$y < 5$$
$$x + 4 \geq 12.$$

On your calculator, use the inequalities solved for y and x, $y < 5$ and $x \geq 8$.
Enter the boundary for the inequality containing y.

| Y= | 5 |

Enter the Shade commands:
For $y < 5$, enter Shade (Ymin, Y1, Xmin, Xmax, 1, 2)

| 2nd | DRAW | 7 | VARS | 1 | 4 | , | VARS | ▶ | 1 | 1 | , | VARS | 1 | 1 |

| , | VARS | 1 | 2 | , | 1 | , | 2 |) | ENTER |

For $x \geq 8$, enter Shade (Ymin, Ymax, 8, Xmax, 2, 2)

| 2nd | DRAW | 7 | VARS | 1 | 4 | , | VARS | 1 | 5 | , | 8 | , | VARS | 1 |

| 2 | , | 2 | , | 2 |) | ENTER |

Y1 = 5

$(-47, 47, -31, 31)$

The solution set is the ordered pairs in the region of the graph that is shaded twice. The intersection of the two lines is (8, 4), which is discerned from your knowledge of vertical and horizontal lines. It cannot be determined using the CALC function.

Use these methods to graph the following systems on your calculator.

1. $3x + 4y > 12$
$2x + 5 < x + 7$

2. $x - 4y \geq 8$
$3x - 1 \leq x - 4$

3. $x > 3$
$x - 3 < 2$

4. $2x + 3 > x$
$4y + 3 \geq -5$

5. $4x - 7 < 4$
$3x - 9 \leq 2 - x$

6. $3x + 4 \leq 2x + 5$
$5x - 9 \geq 4(x - 2)$

Experiencing Algebra the Group Way

When graphing a system of linear inequalities on your calculator, the choice of an appropriate window is key to being able to see the graph. The window should be large enough to show the intercepts. If any of the inequalities limit the solution space to the first quadrant, the minimum values for x and y should be chosen accordingly. As an example, graph the following system on your calculator using the window indicated.

1. $5.8x + y > 1055.10$
$18.4x + 73.2y < 19,361.22$
$x \geq 0$
$y \geq 0$
Window: (0, 1000, 100, 0, 1200, 100, 1)

In your group, first discuss the choice of window suggested for exercise 1. Decide whether you would graph the third and fourth inequalities. If not, give reasons. After you understand why these choices were made, discuss what you would choose as a suitable window for exercise 2, and which inequalities you would graph. Then graph the system and describe the solution set.

2. $487x + 182y < 51,567$
$182x + 487y < 103,280$
$x \geq 0$
$y \geq 0$

Experiencing Algebra the Write Way

Systems of linear inequalities are used extensively in solving real-world problems called linear programming applications. These applications seek to minimize or maximize a function, with constraints expressed as linear inequalities. These are very interesting applications. Search in the library for a text on algebra or precalculus that presents examples of linear programming. Prepare a short summary of one such example. Try to use your calculator to help you reproduce the solution set for the example. Be sure to reference the text in which you find the example.

CHAPTER 8	**Summary**

After completing this chapter, you should be able to define in your own words the following key terms, definitions, properties, and rules.

Terms
linear inequality in one variable
order symbols
upper bound
lower bound
interval notation
negative infinity
infinity
linear inequality in two
   variables
system of linear inequalities in two
   variables
constraint

Definitions
Standard form for a linear inequality in
   one variable
Standard form for a linear inequality in
   two variables

Properties
Addition property of inequalities
Multiplication property of inequalities

Rules
Number line notation
Interval notation

Solving a linear inequality in one
   variable numerically
Solving a linear inequality in one
   variable graphically
Solving a linear inequality in one
   variable algebraically
Graphing a linear inequality in two
   variables with a y-term
Graphing a linear inequality in two
   variables with no y-term
Graphing a system of linear
   inequalities in two variables

CHAPTER 8	**Review**

Reflections

1. What is the difference between a linear equation in one variable and a linear inequality in one variable?

2. The solution to a linear inequality can be expressed in interval notation or graphed on the number line. Describe each of these representations.

3. What is the addition property of inequalities? Are there any special considerations when using this property?

4. What is the multiplication property of inequalities? Are there any special considerations when using this property?

5. When algebraically solving a linear inequality in one variable, how can you tell that there is no solution? How can you tell that the solution set consists of all real numbers?

6. How does the solution of a linear inequality in two variables differ from the solution of a linear inequality in one variable?

7. How can you graphically show the solution set of a system of linear inequalities in two variables?

8.1

Identify each inequality as linear or nonlinear.

1. $3x^2 - 2x + 1 < 0$
2. $5x - 4 > x + 7$
3. $\frac{2}{3}x + \frac{4}{5} \leq \frac{7}{15}$

4. $\sqrt{x} - 3 \geq 6$
5. $x - 3 \geq 6$
6. $\frac{1}{x} - 3x \geq 6$

7. $1.5z - 12.6 < 14.7z$
8. $3(a + 2) < 15a - (2a + 1)$

Graph each inequality on a number line. Then write the solution set in interval notation.

9. $x < 3$
10. $x > -2$
11. $x \leq -5$

12. $x \geq -3.5$
13. $-2 < a < 4$
14. $-1 < b \leq 0$

15. $3 \leq c \leq 5.5$
16. $2\frac{1}{2} < d < 8$
17. $-2.3 \leq f \leq -1\frac{1}{3}$

Write a linear inequality in one variable to represent each situation. Do not solve the inequality.

18. One copy machine can make 30 copies per minute, while another machine can make 25 copies per minute. If both machines are used to make copies, how long will it take to make at least 300 copies of a one-page flyer?

19. In designing a roadway, a civil engineer uses the following rules of thumb. The pavement will cost twice the amount of the base material. The sidewalk will cost one-fourth the amount of the pavement. What will the cost of the base material be if the cost of the roadway must be below $200,000?

20. A political campaign manager is deciding whether to use bulk-rate or first-class mailing. The bulk-rate permit costs $60 and the bulk mailing rate is 18 cents per piece. For what number of mailings will the bulk-rate cost be cheaper than the first-class mailing cost of 32 cents per piece?

8.2

Solve each inequality numerically for integer solutions.

21. $4x + 7 < 2x - 5$ **22.** $2.4x - 9.6 > 4.8$ **23.** $\dfrac{3}{5}x - \dfrac{7}{10} \le \dfrac{1}{5}x + \dfrac{1}{2}$ **24.** $\dfrac{1}{2}x - 2 \ge -\dfrac{1}{3}x - \dfrac{11}{3}$

Solve each inequality graphically and represent the solution in all three forms: inequality notation, interval notation, and number line notation.

25. $2x - 2 > -x + 4$ **26.** $1.2x + 0.72 \le -2.1x + 8.64$

27. $(x + 6) - 3(x + 1) < (2x + 5) - 2(2x + 3)$ **28.** $(x + 3) + (x + 1) \ge 3(x + 1) - (x - 1)$

Solve each inequality algebraically. Represent the solution in interval notation.

29. $412 + x > 671$ **30.** $y - \dfrac{7}{13} < \dfrac{11}{39}$ **31.** $3x + 7 < 4x + 21$

32. $14 + 2x < 2x$ **33.** $8.7x + 4.33 \le -2.4x - 33.41$ **34.** $6.8z - 9.52 \ge 0$

35. $2(x + 5) - (x + 6) < 2(x + 2)$ **36.** $3(x - 4) + 2(x + 1) > 5x + 10$

Write and solve an inequality to represent each situation.

37. Your company has placed a limit on car rentals of no more than $150.00 per trip. If the rental agency charges a flat fee of $49.95 plus $0.18 per mile driven, what range of miles will keep you within budget?

38. Ali must average sales of more than $1500 per month in order to receive his 6-month commission. For the first 5 months his sales were $2100, $1300, $1650, $1250, and $1725. What should his sales be in the sixth month in order for him to receive his commission?

39. A rectangular flower bed must have a perimeter of no more than 40 feet. If the length must be 4 feet more than the width, what widths would be within the limits?

8.3

Identify each inequality as linear or nonlinear. Express each linear inequality in standard form and determine values for a, b, and c.

40. $x + 2y < 12$ **41.** $y < \dfrac{2}{3}x + \dfrac{5}{9}$ **42.** $x^2 + y^2 \ge 1$

43. $0.3x + 2.9 > 1.4y$ **44.** $y \ge \sqrt{x} - 1.44$ **45.** $y < x^2 + 9$

Graph each linear inequality in two variables.

46. $12x + 6y < 48$ **47.** $y > \dfrac{3}{5}x - 6$ **48.** $4y \le x + 12$ **49.** $y + 9 \ge 12$

50. $5y - 2 < y - 10$ **51.** $2x + 16 > x + 18$ **52.** $8x - 12y > 24$ **53.** $4.4x + 1.1y \ge 12.1$

54. $7.4x - 14.8y \le 29.6$ **55.** $\dfrac{x}{12} + \dfrac{y}{8} > -\dfrac{5}{4}$ **56.** $-x - y < 2$ **57.** $y > -9x + 6$

Write and graph a linear inequality in two variables to represent each situation. Determine from the graph two possible solutions.

58. Oksana has at most $85 to spend on plants for her flower garden. She can buy rhododendrons at $4 a pot and azaleas at $6 a pot. What are the possible combinations of plants she can buy and not go over her budget?

59. Rosa gained 5 points for every homework exercise she correctly solved and lost 3 points for every exercise incorrectly solved or skipped. What combinations would allow her to score at least 80 points on her homework assignment?

8.4

Graph each system of linear inequalities. Label points of intersection.

60. $2x + y > 10$
$y < 3x - 5$

61. $3(x + 2) + 1 > -5$
$2x - y < -8$

62. $x + 6 < 4$
$2(y + 2) > y + 3$

63. $x - 2y \geq 12$
$2x + 3y < -6$

64. $y \geq 2(x + 2)$
$2x - y \geq 5$

65. $y > \frac{3}{2}x - 6$
$3x - 2y > 12$

66. $y < 3x - 6$
$y < -3$

67. $2y - 3 > 1$
$5(y - 4) > 10$

68. $2x - 11 < 3$
$14 - 2x > x - 7$

69. $y - 1 < 4$
$3y - 2 < 13$

70. $2x + 3y \leq 6$
$x + y \leq 1$

71. $y < 2x - 15$
$y > -3x + 10$

72. $y > 2x + 1$

$x > 2y + 7$

73. $2y + 6 \leq 3y + 5$

$2(x - 3) + 1 > 5$

74. $y < 6 - x$

$y < 2x + 1$
$x \geq 0$
$y \geq 0$

75. $y < 25 - \frac{1}{4}x$

$y < \frac{2}{3}x + 5$
$x \geq 0$
$y \geq 0$

Write a system of linear inequalities in two variables to represent each situation and graph. Determine one possible solution from the graph.

76. Oksana has at most $85 to purchase potted rhododendrons at $4 each and azaleas at $6 each. She needs at least four more rhododendron plants than azaleas. What possible combinations will meet both criteria?

77. If you have $4000 to invest, part at 5% and part at 6% simple interest for a year, how much can you invest at each to earn at least $225?

CHAPTER 8 | **Mixed Review**

Graph each inequality on a number line. Write equivalent interval notation for the inequality.

1. $x < -2$

2. $x > 7$

3. $-1 < x < 3$

4. $x \geq 2.6$

5. $x \leq 3\frac{2}{3}$

6. $-2.4 < x \leq 4\frac{1}{3}$

Solve numerically for integer solutions.

7. $5x + 3 < 2x - 9$

8. $5.6x - 15.3 > 1.3x + 19.1$

9. $\frac{1}{6}x + \frac{23}{3} \leq \frac{13}{6} - \frac{5}{3}x$

10. $\frac{3}{7}x + \frac{9}{5} \geq \frac{4}{5}x - \frac{17}{5}$

Solve each inequality. Represent the solution in all three forms: inequality notation, interval notation, and number line notation.

11. $5x - 13 > 3(1 - x)$

12. $2.1x + 31.71 \leq 8.19 - 3.5x$

13. $3(x - 1) + (x - 1) < 2(x - 1) + 2x - 1$

14. $4(x + 2) - 3(x - 5) \leq 5x + 8 - 4(x + 3)$

Solve each inequality. Represent the solution in interval notation form.

15. $173 - x < 359$

16. $z - \frac{4}{17} > \frac{15}{34}$

17. $5x + 4 > 3x + 18$

18. $8x < 8x - 16$

19. $3.5x + 19.88 \geq -1.9x + 4.76$

20. $2.6y + 9.62 \leq 0$

21. $3(x + 3) < 4(x + 1) - 2(x - 2)$

22. $3(x - 3) + 2(x + 2) < 5x + 7$

Graph each system of linear inequalities. Label points of intersection.

23. $2y + 2 > y$
$y < -x + 1$

24. $2x + 3 > x$
$2x < 6$

25. $y \geq 2x - 8$
$3x + y < 8$

26. $2(x - 1) - 4 > 0$
$2x + y \leq 3$

27. $x + y < 9 - x$
$2x + y > 5$

28. $y < -4x - 3$
$4x + 2y < y - 3$

29. $3x + 4 \geq 2x$
$x + 7 \leq 3$

30. $3y + 7 > 2y + 5$
$y + 9 < 7$

31. $3(x - 3) - 1 > 8$
$3y - 10 < 15 - 2y$

32. $y < 3x + 7$
$x - y > -1$

33. $x - 5y \leq 15$
$x + 5y \leq -5$

34. $y < -4x + 6$
$y > 3x - 8$

35. $y > x$

$x > 2 - y$

36. $x + 9 \leq 3$

$3y > 2y - 1$

37. $y < -2x + 7$

$y < 2x$

$x \geq 0$

$y \geq 0$

38. $y > \frac{3}{4}x - 4$

$y > -\frac{2}{3}x + 3$

$x \geq 0$

$y \geq 0$

Graph each linear inequality in two variables.

39. $9x - 5y < 45$

40. $y > \frac{4}{3}x - 5$

41. $3y \leq 2x + 9$

42. $y + 13 \geq 8$

43. $-2y - 6 < y - 11$

44. $x - 13 > 3x + 19$

45. $x - 7y > 21$

46. $2.7x + 5.4y \geq 16.2$

47. $4.8x - 1.8y \leq 14.4$

48. $\frac{x}{12} + \frac{y}{9} > -\frac{1}{3}$

49. $x - y < 7$

50. $y > -5x + 7$

Write a system of linear inequalities in two variables to represent each situation and graph. Determine one possible solution from the graph.

51. Farmer McGregor plants oats and wheat on his farm. For conservation purposes, he plants at least twice as many acres of wheat as oats. He can handle up to a total of 540 acres of planting. What combinations of plantings can he consider?

52. A realtor has three efficiency apartments and five regular apartments to rent. The regular apartments will rent for at least $75 more than the efficiency apartments. If the realtor would like to gross $6000 per month, what combination of rental rates will meet his wishes?

Write and solve a linear inequality in one variable to represent each situation. State one possible solution from the solution set.

53. The setup cost for producing gourmet packs of coffee is $255.00. The materials cost $2.50 per pack. The packs will be sold for $12.50 each. How many packs must be sold in order to begin to make a profit?

54. Catherine wants to keep her average telephone bill below $42. Her first five months had bills of $45, $36, $52, $48, and $31. What are the limits on her bill for the sixth month?

55. The width of a rectangular street sign has been set at 18 inches. What must the length be if the area of the sign must be more than 600 square inches?

Write and graph a linear inequality in two variables to represent each situation. Determine one possible solution from the graph.

56. A soccer team needs to earn at least 25 points during the season to make the finals playoff. If they earn three points for each win, one point for each tie, and no points for a loss, what combinations of wins and ties will land them in the playoffs?

57. What combinations of a 25% alcohol solution and a 40% alcohol solution would yield a mixture with no more than 30% alcohol? (*Note:* let x = number of liters of the 25% solution, y = number of liters of the 40% solution, and $x + y$ = number of liters of the mixture.)

CHAPTER 8 | **Test**

Test-Taking Tips

When attempting to solve a problem on a test, it is helpful to follow some routine procedures. Practice these on your homework so that you will be comfortable using them during a test.

- Write down key information about the problem.
- Identify what you need to solve for.
- List any formulas or rules you may need for the solution.
- Numerically estimate the answer using rounded numbers.
- Imagine the same problem with simpler numbers.
- If time permits, solve the problem two different ways as a check (for example, algebraically and graphically).
- Always check your work.

Identify each inequality as linear or nonlinear.

1. $2x - 3y > x + 8$ **2.** $4x^2 + 2x < x - 9$ **3.** $5(x - 3) \geq 4 - (x + 1)$ **4.** $\frac{1}{2}x - 4 \geq y + \frac{3}{8}$

Solve each inequality and represent the solution using the number line and interval notation.

5. $7(x + 2) - 3(x + 1) > 4(x + 8)$ **6.** $5x + 9 < 2x - 3$

7. $\frac{4}{5}(x - 10) < \frac{1}{5}(4x + 5) + 1$ **8.** $5a - 7 \geq 8a + 1$

Graph each linear inequality in two variables.

9. $y < -2x + 5$ **10.** $x + 3 > 2x - 1$

Graph each system of linear inequalities in two variables. Label points of intersection.

11. $x - y > 4$
$x + 2y > 4$

12. $y \geq 4x - 5$
$y > -3x + 4$

13. $y < 2x + 6$
$y < 2x - 1$

14. $3y - 1 > 2$
$x - 3 \leq -5$

Write and solve a linear inequality in one variable to represent the following application. Determine one possible solution from the solution set.

15. The average of three exams must be at least an 80 to pass a course. If the first exam score was 83 and the second exam score was 72, what are the possible scores on the third exam to pass the course?

Write and graph a linear inequality in two variables to represent the following application. Determine one possible solution from the solution set.

16. A Cub Scout earns 5 points for every good deed and 2 points for every activity sheet completed. If a scout must earn at least 20 points in order to receive a medal, what combinations of good deeds and activity sheets will suffice?

Write and graph a system of linear inequalities to represent the application in exercise 17. Determine one possible solution from the solution set.

17. If you have at most $6000 to invest, part at 4% simple interest and part at 8% simple interest, what investment strategies will assure you of earning at least $400 in interest for a year?

18. What do we mean by the solution of a system of linear inequalities in two variables?

CHAPTERS 1–8 | Cumulative Review

Evaluate.

1. $-(-9)$

2. $-|-9|$

3. $\sqrt[3]{-\dfrac{27}{64}}$

4. $\left(\dfrac{-3}{8}\right)^{-2}$

5. $\left(-\dfrac{9}{14}\right)\left(\dfrac{7}{3}\right)$

6. $-\dfrac{3}{8} \div \left(-1\dfrac{2}{3}\right)$

7. $12(-3) \div (-6)(2) \div (-2)$

8. $40 + 16 \div 8 - \sqrt{3^2 + 7 \cdot 5} + 5$

9. $\dfrac{2(5^2 - 10) + 4^2 - 1}{8^2 - 2(32)}$

Simplify.

10. $6x - 2(4x - 1)$

11. $4[2(x - 3) + 1] - [5(2x - 4) - 6]$

Consider the relation $y = 2x^2 - 3$.

12. Graph the relation.

13. What is the domain of the relation? The range?

14. Is the relation a function? Justify your answer.

15. Determine the relative minima and the relative maxima.

16. Determine the x-values for which the relation is increasing and decreasing.

17. Determine the x-intercept and the y-intercept.

Solve.

18. $7x - 3 = 5$

19. $(x + 3) - 2(3x + 4) = 5$

20. $1.2(x + 3) - 4(0.3x + 0.15) = 3$

21. $|2x + 6| = 10$

22. $5|x| + 8 = 8$

Solve. Represent the solution as an inequality, using interval notation, and as a graph on a number line.

23. $5x + 4 > x - 8$

24. $-12x + 4 \geq -2x + 8$

25. $4(x + 3) - 3(x - 2) \leq x - 5$

Graph. Label enough points to determine the graph.

26. $f(x) = -3x + 4$

27. $6x + 3y = 9$

28. $2x + 3 = 11$

29. $3y - 2 = 5$ **30.** $y < 4x - 3$

Determine if the graphs of the pair of equations are coinciding lines, parallel lines, only intersecting lines, or both intersecting and perpendicular.

31. $2x + 3y = 21$
$3x - 2y = 2$

Solve the system of equations.

32. $y = 3x + 4$
$y = 2x - 5$

33. $4x + 2y = 8$
$y = -2x + 4$

Graph the system of inequalities. Determine one possible solution from the graph.

34. $y \geq -x$
$y < 2x + 4$

Determine the slope of a line that satisfies the following conditions.

35. Passes through $(-2, 3)$ and $(-1, -2)$ **36.** Passes through $(6, -5)$ and $(6, 3)$

37. $y = 2x + 3$ **38.** $y = 1.4$

Write an equation for a line that satisfies the following conditions.

39. Passes through $(2, -3)$ and $(-1, -2)$

40. Passes through $(5, 4)$ and is parallel to the graph of $2x + 3y = 1$.

Write in scientific notation.

41. 5,340,000

Write exercise 42 and 43 in standard notation.

42. 1.2×10^{-4} **43.** $-4.783\text{E-}5$

44. Solve for L: $P = 2L + 2W$ **45.** Given $f(x) = x^2 + 2x - 1$, find $f(-3)$.

46. An investment plan offers 11% simple interest on an investment. How much should Lance invest in order to receive $2775 at the end of one year?

47. Two angles are complementary. The larger angle measures 25 degrees more than twice the smaller angle. Find the measures of the two angles.

48. Michael's Coffee Shop sells a special blend called Mike's Favorite. For the blend, Michael mixes Hazelnut Coffee, which sells for $7.50 per pound, with Cinnamon Coffee, which sells for $6.75 per pound. How much of each flavor must he use to create 10 pounds of the Mike's Favorite blend if he sells it for $7.00?

49. April scored 82, 88, 80, and 95 on the first four tests in her Algebra class. There is one more test in the class. In order to earn a B, she must have a test average of at least 85. Determine the score she must earn on the last test in order to earn a B for the semester.

50. Reliable Rentals is running a special. The cost of renting a chain saw is $35 per day plus $1.50 per hour. Write a cost function to represent the cost of renting the chain saw for one day for x hours. What is the cost of renting the chain saw for 12 hours?

Polynomial Functions

9

I n this chapter, we return to the idea of functions that we first discussed in Chapter 4. We examine a particular family of functions, referred to as polynomials, starting in this chapter and continuing for the next few chapters. Polynomials are worth special study because of their importance in so many areas of our daily lives, from calculating costs for repairing or selling homes and stores, to determining sales and profits for business items. Even how high we can throw a ball in the air depends on a polynomial function.

The motion of an object dropped from a height or thrown into the air is determined by the Earth's gravity. The motion is described by a kind of polynomial function called a quadratic function, which we will discuss in this chapter. We will present several different functions in this chapter that model the motion of a falling object in typical situations. The fact that the motion of an object due to gravity could be described by a polynomial equation was one of the great scientific and mathematical discoveries of the 17th century, and led directly to our present understanding of planetary motion and space travel.

9.1 Introduction to Polynomials

Objectives
1 Identify polynomials.
2 Identify the terms of polynomials and classify polynomials by the number of terms.
3 Identify the degree of terms of polynomials and classify polynomials by degree.
4 Write polynomials in one variable in descending and ascending order.
5 Evaluate polynomials.
6 Model real-world situations using polynomial expressions.

Application

An emergency medical supply package is dropped from a helicopter at an altitude of 1000 feet.

A polynomial that describes the distance (in feet) above ground of the supply package t seconds after release is given by $1000 - 16t^2$. Determine the distance of the package from the ground 5 seconds after release.

After completing this section, we will discuss this application further. See page 641.

1000 ft

?

1 Identifying Polynomials

In Chapter 3 we introduced algebraic expressions. An **algebraic expression** is an expression that contains variables. For example, $6x^2 - 5x + 3x + 7$ is an algebraic expression.

The **terms** of an algebraic expression are its addends. There are two types of terms: constant and variable. A **constant term** represents only one number. A **variable term** represents different numbers. In the algebraic expression $6x^2 - 5x + 3x + 7$, the variable terms are $6x^2, -5x$, and $3x$. The constant term is 7.

A **numerical coefficient (coefficient)** is the numerical factor of a term. In the expression $6x^2 - 5x + 3x + 7$, the coefficients of the terms are 6, -5, 3, and 7.

Terms are considered to be **like terms** if they are both constants or if both are variable terms that contain the same variables with the same exponents. We **collect like terms** in order to simplify an algebraic expression. This means that we add the coefficients of the like terms, keeping the variable part. In the expression $6x^2 - 5x + 3x + 7$, the like terms, $-5x$ and $3x$, combine to $-2x$. Therefore, $6x^2 - 5x + 3x + 7 = 6x^2 - 2x + 7$.

In this chapter, we consider algebraic expressions called monomials. A **monomial** is either a constant term or a variable term consisting of one or more variable factors, each having a nonnegative integer exponent. Examples of monomials are:

2	A constant term.
$-3x$	A variable term with a coefficient of -3 and the variable, x, having an exponent of 1.
$4x^2$	A variable term with a coefficient of 4 and the variable, x, having an exponent of 2.
$-5x^2y^3z$	A variable term with a coefficient of -5 and three variables x, y, and z, having exponents of 2, 3, and 1, respectively.

Algebraic expressions are not monomials if they have a variable raised to a power other than a nonnegative integer. These include expressions with a variable in the denominator of a fraction and expressions with a variable in the radicand of a radical expression. We will explain why this is so later in this text. For example, $x^{2/3}$, x^{-5}, $\frac{3}{x^2}$ and $-25\sqrt{4x}$ are not monomials.

A **polynomial** is a monomial or a sum of monomials. Some examples are:

x^3y	A monomial.
$x + 2$	The sum of two monomials: x and 2.
$-7x^2 - 4x$	The sum of two monomials: $-7x^2$ and $-4x$.
$\dfrac{1}{3}a + 9b^2 - a^3b$	The sum of three monomials: $\dfrac{1}{3}a$, $9b^2$, and $-a^3b$.

EXAMPLE 1   Determine whether each expression is a polynomial.

a. $\dfrac{2}{3}x^2 + \sqrt{5}xy^3$ **b.** $\dfrac{1}{x^2} - 4\sqrt{xy}$

Solution

a. $\frac{2}{3}x^2 + \sqrt{5}xy^3$ is a polynomial because the two terms, $\frac{2}{3}x^2$ and $\sqrt{5}xy^3$, are monomials, each consisting of a coefficient and variables with nonnegative integer exponents.

b. $\frac{1}{x^2} - 4\sqrt{xy}$ is not a polynomial because the first term, $\frac{1}{x^2}$, and the second term, $-4\sqrt{xy}$, are not monomials. The first term has a variable in the denominator of a fraction and the second term has a variable in a radicand. ∎

✓ Experiencing Algebra the Checkup Way

In exercises 1–6, determine whether each expression is a polynomial.

1. $3xy^4$ **2.** $\dfrac{2}{3}x - 3x^2$ **3.** $\dfrac{2}{x} - 5$

4. $3x^{-2} + 4x$ **5.** $\sqrt{3x} + 2$ **6.** $3\sqrt{x} + 2$

7. Explain the difference between the terms of an algebraic expression and the factors of a term.

8. All monomials are polynomials but not all polynomials are monomials. Explain what this statement means.

9. A polynomial can be simplified by collecting its like terms. What are like terms?

2 Classifying Polynomials by Number of Terms

We can classify a polynomial by the number of its terms. A polynomial with one term is called a monomial. A polynomial with two terms is a **binomial**, a polynomial with three terms is a **trinomial**. We usually refer to a polynomial with more than three terms simply as a polynomial. Before we determine the classification, we must first simplify the polynomial by collecting like terms. For example, classify the polynomial $2x + 5y + 7x - 8y - x$ by the number of its terms.

> First, simplify it to $8x - 3y$. The simplified polynomial has two terms, $8x$ and $-3y$; it is a binomial.

EXAMPLE 2 Classify each polynomial as a monomial, a binomial, a trinomial, or a polynomial.

a. $6a^2 + 5b^2 + 4ab - a^2 - 2ab + c^2$

b. $-x^2 + 2xy - 3x + x^2 - y^3$

Solution

First, simplify each polynomial by collecting like terms.

a. $6a^2 + 5b^2 + 4ab - a^2 - 2ab + c^2 = 5a^2 + 5b^2 + 2ab + c^2$

There are four terms: $5a^2, 5b^2, 2ab,$ and c^2.
The expression is a polynomial.

b. $-x^2 + 2xy - 3x + x^2 - y^3 = 2xy - 3x - y^3$ Note: $-x^2 + x^2 = 0x^2$ or 0

There are three terms: $2xy, -3x,$ and $-y^3$.
The expression is a trinomial. ∎

Experiencing Algebra the Checkup Way

In exercises 1–4, classify each expression as a monomial, a binomial, a trinomial, or a polynomial.

1. $6b^3 + 4b^2c - 3bc^2 - c^3$

2. $3x - 5 + 7x + 12$

3. $5p^2 - 3p + 12 - 5p + 7$

4. xyz

5. How can you tell whether a polynomial is a monomial, a binomial, or a trinomial?

3 Classifying Polynomials by Degree

The **degree of a term** is the sum of the exponents of its variable factors. The **degree of a polynomial** is the largest degree of its variable terms. Remember to simplify the polynomial before determining its degree. For example, determine the degree of the polynomial $2xy - 3x - x^3 + 4$.

> The term $2xy$ has a degree of 2 because the exponent of x is 1 and the exponent of y is 1, and $1 + 1 = 2$.
>
> The term $-3x$ has a degree of 1 because the exponent of x is 1.
>
> The term $-x^3$ has a degree of 3 because the exponent of x is 3.
>
> The constant term 4 can be written as $4x^0$ because any nonzero number raised to the power of 0 equals 1. Therefore, the constant term 4 has a degree 0.

The terms have degrees of 2, 1, 3, and 0. The polynomial has a degree of 3, the largest degree of any of its terms.

EXAMPLE 3 Determine the degree of each term of each polynomial and then determine the degree of the polynomial.

a. $6x^2 + 5x^2 y^3 - 7x^2$ **b.** $-5x + 6 + 7x - 2x$ **c.** $9x^2 y^3 z^4$

Solution

First, simplify each polynomial by collecting like terms.

a. $6x^2 + 5x^2 y^3 - 7x^2 = -x^2 + 5x^2 y^3$

The terms are $-x^2$, with a degree of 2, and $5x^2 y^3$, with a degree of $2 + 3$, or 5. The degree of the polynomial is 5, the largest degree of any of its terms.

b. $-5x + 6 + 7x - 2x = 6$

The constant term, 6 or $6x^0$, has a degree of 0.
The degree of the polynomial is 0.

c. $9x^2 y^3 z^4$ will not simplify. It is a monomial.

The one term has a degree of $2 + 3 + 4$, or 9.
The degree of the polynomial is 9. ∎

Experiencing Algebra the Checkup Way

In exercises 1–3, determine the degree of each term of the polynomial and then determine the degree of the polynomial.

1. $6x^2 - 3xy^3 + 5y^3$ **2.** $5x + 3x^3 - 2x^2 - 3x^3 + 1$ **3.** $-5x^5 y^2 z^3 + 2x^2 y^3 z^4$

4. What is the difference between the degree of a term of a polynomial and the degree of the polynomial?

---

4 Writing Polynomials in Descending and Ascending Order

The conventional way to write a polynomial in one variable is to write the terms in order of descending degrees. That is, a polynomial in one variable in **descending order** is written with decreasing values of its variable exponents. Remember that a constant term has a degree of 0 and is always written as the last term. The polynomial $4x^3 - 2x^7 + x^2 - 8$, written in descending order, is $-2x^7 + 4x^3 + x^2 - 8$.

Sometimes it may be desirable to write a polynomial in one variable in ascending order. A polynomial in one variable in **ascending order** is written with increasing values of its variable exponents. The polynomial $4x^3 - 2x^7 + x^2 - 8$, written in ascending order, is $-8 + x^2 + 4x^3 - 2x^7$.

EXAMPLE 4 Complete the following table by writing each polynomial in descending and ascending order.

Polynomial	Descending Order	Ascending Order
$6x^2 + 8x - 7x^4$		
$5 - x^4 + x$		

Solution

Polynomial	Descending Order	Ascending Order
$6x^2 + 8x - 7x^4$	$-7x^4 + 6x^2 + 8x$	$8x + 6x^2 - 7x^4$
$5 - x^4 + x$	$-x^4 + x + 5$	$5 + x - x^4$

■

Experiencing Algebra the Checkup Way

Complete the following table by writing each polynomial in descending and ascending order.

	Polynomial	Descending Order	Ascending Order
1.	$3 + 2x^3 - 5x - x^2$		
2.	$12 + y$		

5 Evaluating Polynomials

A polynomial, like an algebraic expression, represents different values depending on the value(s) of its variable(s).

To determine a value for a polynomial, we substitute a value for each variable. We then determine the value of the resulting numeric expression. This process is called **evaluating** the polynomial.

To evaluate a polynomial on your calculator:

- Store the values for each of the variables.
- Enter the polynomial.

EXAMPLE 5 Evaluate $x^2 + 2xy - 7y^2$

a. for $x = 2$ and $y = -1$. **b.** for $x = \dfrac{3}{4}$ and $y = \dfrac{1}{2}$.

Solution

a. $x^2 + 2xy - 7y^2 = (2)^2 + 2(2)(-1) - 7(-1)^2$ Substitute 2 for x and -1 for y.
$$= 4 + 4(-1) - 7(1)$$
$$= 4 - 4 - 7$$
$$= -7$$

b. $x^2 + 2xy - 7y^2 = \left(\dfrac{3}{4}\right)^2 + 2\left(\dfrac{3}{4}\right)\left(\dfrac{1}{2}\right) - 7\left(\dfrac{1}{2}\right)^2$ Substitute $\frac{3}{4}$ for x and $\frac{1}{2}$

$$= \dfrac{9}{16} + \dfrac{3}{4} - \dfrac{7}{4}$$

$$= \dfrac{9}{16} + \dfrac{12}{16} - \dfrac{28}{16}$$

$$= -\dfrac{7}{16}$$

The calculator solutions are shown in Figure 9.1.   ■

TECHNOLOGY

```
2→X: -1→Y:X²+2XY-
7Y²
                  -7
3/4→X:1/2→Y:X²+2
XY-7Y²▶Frac
              -7/16
```

Figure 9.1

For Figure 9.1
Store the value for the variable x.

| 2 | STO▶ | X, T, θ, n |

Enter a new line.

| ALPHA | : |

Store the value for the variable y.

| (−) | 1 | STO▶ | ALPHA | Y |

Enter a new line.

| ALPHA | : |

Enter the polynomial.

| X, T, θ, n | x² | + | 2 | X, T, θ, n | ALPHA | Y | − | 7 | ALPHA | Y | x² | ENTER |

Recall the last entry.

| 2nd | ENTRY |

Change 2 to $\frac{3}{4}$.

First delete the 2. Use the arrow keys to move on top of the stored 2, then enter | DEL |. Next, reenter $\frac{3}{4}$:

| 2nd | INS | 3 | ÷ | 4 | .

Change the −1 to $\frac{1}{2}$.

First delete the negative sign. Use the arrow keys to move on top of (−), then enter | DEL |. Next, insert the remainder of the fraction. Move on top of the second store symbol, then enter | 2nd | INS | ÷ | 2 |.

Evaluate the results as a fraction.
Move to the end of the entry.

| MATH | 1 | ENTER |

Experiencing Algebra the Checkup Way

1. Evaluate $2a^2 - 5ab - 9b^2$ for the given values.

   a. $a = -8$ and $b = 2$ **b.** $a = 4$ and $b = -3$

2. Evaluate $5x^3 - 55x^2 + 90x - 246$ for the given values.

   a. $x = 1.4$ **b.** $x = -\dfrac{4}{5}$

---

6 Modeling the Real World

Many real-life situations can be described by polynomials, including many geometric problems, business situations, and scientific relationships. Many other relationships can be approximated by polynomials, which sometimes makes them easier to work with.

EXAMPLE 6

A rectangular swimming pool is to be enclosed by a fence. The fenced area is a square.

a. Write a polynomial for the fenced area that is not covered by the pool.
b. If the pool is 25 feet by 15 feet, and the fence measures 30 feet on a side, determine the fenced area that is not covered by the pool.

Solution

a.

Let L = length of the pool (in feet)
     W = width of the pool (in feet)
     s = length of the side of the fence (in feet)

Fenced area: The area of a square is determined by the product of the two sides, $s \cdot s$ or s^2.

Pool area: The area of a rectangle is determined by the product of the length times the width, LW.

The fenced area not covered by the pool is the difference of the fenced area minus the pool area, or $\left(s^2 - LW\right)$ square feet.

b. $L = 25$ feet, $W = 15$ feet, and $s = 30$ feet

$$s^2 - LW = (30)^2 - (25)(15) \quad \text{Substitute.}$$
$$= 900 - 375$$
$$= 525$$

The fenced area not covered by the pool is 525 square feet. ∎

EXAMPLE 7   Jana decorates sweatshirts for Christy's Crafts in the mall. She is paid $15.00 per sweatshirt and $7.50 per delivery trip. She buys her supplies every delivery trip. She pays $5.41 per sweatshirt, $1.57 for the paint per sweatshirt, and $6.00 in gasoline for each trip.

a. Write a polynomial to represent Jana's revenue.
b. Write a polynomial to represent Jana's cost.
c. If Jana produces 12 sweatshirts and makes one trip to the mall, what is her revenue and cost?

Solution

Let x = the number of sweatshirts
    y = the number of trips to the mall

a. Jana's revenue is $15.00 per sweatshirt and $7.50 per trip, or

$$15.00x + 7.50y.$$

b. Jana's cost is $5.41 per sweatshirt plus $1.57 per sweatshirt (paint) and $6.00 per trip, or

$$5.41x + 1.57x + 6.00y = 6.98x + 6.00y$$

c. Evaluate the polynomials representing revenue and cost for $x = 12$ and $y = 1$.

$$\text{Revenue: } 15.00x + 7.50y = 15.00(12) + 7.50(1)$$
$$= 187.50$$
Jana's revenue is $187.50.

$$\text{Cost: } \quad 6.98x + 6.00y = 6.98(12) + 6.00(1)$$
$$= 89.76$$
Jana's cost is $89.76. ∎

Application   An emergency medical supply package is to be dropped from a helicopter at an altitude of 1000 feet.
    A polynomial that describes the distance (in feet) above ground of the supply package t seconds after release is given by $1000 - 16t^2$. Determine the distance of the package from the ground 5 seconds after release.

1000 ft

?

Discussion

Since t is the time (in seconds) after release, and the position (in feet) is given by $1000 - 16t^2$, we evaluate the polynomial for $t = 5$.

$$1000 - 16t^2 = 1000 - 16(5)^2 = 1000 - 16(25) = 1000 - 400 = 600$$

The package will be 600 feet above the ground 5 seconds after release. ∎

Experiencing Algebra the Checkup Way

1. A cabin with a square-shaped base is built upon a rectangular lot.

   a. Write a polynomial for the area of the lot that is not covered by the cabin.

   b. If the base of the cabin measures 35 feet on a side, and the lot measures 150 feet by 200 feet, determine the area of the lot that is not covered by the cabin.

2. Mike builds folding tables and birdhouses to sell at a flea market. He can sell the tables for $12 each and the birdhouses for $15 each. The flea market charges him $35.00 each week to rent a booth. He spends $4.25 on materials for each table and $5.85 on materials for each birdhouse. His miscellaneous expenses (travel, packing bags, and so on) cost him $12 each week.

   a. Write a polynomial to represent the revenue Mike earns in a week.

   b. Write a polynomial to represent his cost for a week.

   c. What will be his revenue and cost if he makes and sells 22 tables and 19 birdhouses in a week? What will be his net return (revenue minus cost)?

PROBLEM SET 9.1

 Experiencing Algebra the Exercise Way

Determine whether each expression is a polynomial.

1. $2a + 5$

2. $y^{1/3} + y - 1$

3. $x^2 - 3x + 2$

4. $2z^{-2} - 3z^{-1} + 4$

5. $x^{1/2} - 6x - 7$

6. $a^2 + 4a - 17$

7. $5x^2 + 12xy + 2y^2$

8. $\sqrt{b^2 - 4ac}$

9. $\sqrt{5}x - \sqrt{3}y$

10. $2.44x^2 - 1.05x - 15.7$

11. $5\sqrt{x} - 3\sqrt{y}$

12. $\frac{3}{4}x^2 + \frac{5}{8}x - \frac{9}{16}$

13. $\frac{3}{5}x^3 - \frac{2}{3}x^2 + 4x - \frac{7}{10}$

14. $\frac{1}{a} + a + 1$

15. $\frac{4}{x^2} + \frac{1}{x} - \frac{5}{7}$

16. $0.8x - 2.3$

17. $a^{-2} + 17a^{-1} + 13$

18. $\sqrt{6r} + 5$

19. $0.07b^2 - 2.6b + 13.908$

20. $4p^2 - 6pq + q^2$

Classify each expression as a monomial, a binomial, a trinomial, or a polynomial.

21. $3a + 4b - 5c$

22. $3x^3 - 2x^2y + 5xy^2 + 6y^3$

23. $2z^2$

24. $2 - 4b + 7$

25. $x - y$

26. $\frac{1}{7}x + \frac{2}{7}y + \frac{3}{7}z$

27. $4p^4 - 2p^3 + 11p - 57$

28. $b - 2b + 3b - 4b + 5b$

29. $6x^2 - 12 + 8x - 5x^2 + x - 17$

30. $-14x^3$

31. $3b - 4 + 7b$

32. $p + q$

33. $x + 2x + 3x + 4x + 5x$

34. $2a^2 - 6 + a + a^2 - 16a + 6$

35. $\frac{1}{2}x + \frac{2}{3}y - \frac{3}{4}z$

36. $b^2 - 4ac$

Determine the degree of each term of each polynomial and then the degree of the polynomial.

37. $2 - 15c$

38. $-3{,}298{,}175$

39. 123

40. $8x^4 + 5x^3 y^3 - y^4$

41. $5 + 5x - 4x - x$

42. $b^2 - 4ac$

43. $7x^5 + 2x^2 y^2 - 12$

44. $5a + 7$

45. $\pi r^2 + 2\pi rh$

46. $5a^5 bc^3 + 6abc^4 + 3ab^2 c^2$

47. $4x^2 yz^{12} - 8xy^2 z^9 + 3x^3 y^3 z$

48. $6y^2 + 3y - y + y^2 - 2y$

Write each polynomial in descending order.

49. $5 - 2a + 3a^2 + a^3$

50. $4a^9 - 17 + 3a^3 - 2a^6$

51. $\dfrac{3}{5}x + \dfrac{4}{5}x^3 - \dfrac{7}{15}x - \dfrac{8}{15}x^4$

52. $p^2 - p^5 + p^3 - p^4 - p - 1$

53. $0.1x^3 - 1.72 + 4.6x^2 + 3.06x^4$

54. $7x + 5x^3 + 9x^5 + 15x^7 + 23x^9 + 33$

In exercises 55–60, write each polynomial in ascending order.

55. $7b^2 - 6b^3 + 11 - 2b$

56. $x^2 - 8x^6 + 6x^5 - 4x^3 + x^4$

57. $\dfrac{2}{7}x + \dfrac{1}{7}x^5 - \dfrac{3}{14}x - \dfrac{5}{14}x^3$

58. $q^2 - q^5 + q^3 - q^4 - q - 1$

59. $0.5x^7 - 2.77 + 3.2x^3 + 9.76x^5$

60. $x^5 - 4x^4 - 2x^3 + 4x^2 - 2x + 4$

61. Evaluate $3x^2 - 4x + 1$ for the given values.

    a. $x = 4$ **b.** $x = -2$ **c.** $x = 0$

62. Evaluate $3x^3 + 2x^2 + x + 1$ for the given values.

    a. $x = 2$ **b.** $x = -1$ **c.** $x = 0$

63. Evaluate $x^2 + 4xy + y^2$ for the given values.

    a. $x = 2, y = 3$ **b.** $x = -2, y = -3$ **c.** $x = 0, y = 0$

64. Evaluate $a^3 + a^2 b + ab^2 + b^3$ for the given values.

    a. $a = 2, b = 1$ **b.** $a = -1, b = -2$ **c.** $a = 0, b = 3$

65. Evaluate $1.3m^3 - 2.5m^2 + 3.7m - 4.9$ for the given values.

    a. $m = 1$ **b.** $m = 2.5$ **c.** $m = -1.5$

66. Evaluate $0.6z^2 + 3.7z - 5.8$ for the given values.

    a. $z = 2$ **b.** $z = 4.3$ **c.** $z = -2.5$

67. Evaluate $\dfrac{2}{3}x^2 - x - 3$ for the given values.

    a. $x = -\dfrac{3}{2}$ **b.** $x = \dfrac{1}{4}$ **c.** $x = 3$

68. Evaluate $\dfrac{3}{4}x^2 - \dfrac{3}{2}x - \dfrac{4}{3}$ for the given values.

    a. $x = \dfrac{2}{3}$ **b.** $x = -\dfrac{2}{3}$ **c.** $x = 8$

Geometric formulas were introduced in Chapter 3 and are summarized on the inside book cover. The following exercises refer to these formulas.

69. Write a polynomial for the perimeter of a triangle whose second side is twice as long as the first side, and whose third side is 1 inch longer than the first side. What is the perimeter if the first side measures 8 inches?

70. Write a polynomial for the surface area of a cylinder with a height equal to the radius of its base. What is the surface area of the cylinder if the radius of the base measures 4 inches?

71. Write a polynomial for the surface area of a rectangular solid whose width and length are equal and whose height is 3 meters. What is the surface area of the solid if the width measures 1.5 meters?

72. Write a polynomial for the surface area of a rectangular solid whose width is 5 inches, whose length is 10 inches, and whose height is h inches. What is the surface area if the height is $3\frac{1}{2}$ inches?

73. Write a polynomial for the total area of the three geometric shapes shown in Figure 9.2. Shape A is a square and shapes B and C are rectangles.

Figure 9.2

74. Write a polynomial for the total area of the three geometric shapes shown in Figure 9.3. Shape A is a right triangle and shapes B and C are squares.

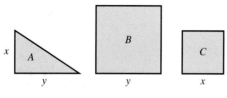

Figure 9.3

75. A rectangular patio measuring 15 feet by 20 feet is placed in a rectangular yard. Write a polynomial for the area of the yard not covered by the patio. What is the area of the yard not covered by the patio if the yard measures 75 feet by 120 feet?

76. A circular swimming pool is placed in a rectangular yard. Write a polynomial for the area of the yard not covered by the pool. What is the area of the yard not covered by the pool if the yard measures 25 meters by 35 meters and the pool has a radius of 4.5 meters?

77. Write a polynomial to represent the square of the length of the hypotenuse of a right triangle whose legs measure x feet and y feet, respectively. What is the square of the length of the hypotenuse if the legs measure 4 feet and 7 feet? What is the length of the hypotenuse?

78. Write a polynomial to represent the square of the length of one leg of a right triangle whose hypotenuse measures x feet and whose other leg measures y feet long. What is the square of the length of the leg of the right triangle if the hypotenuse measures 10 feet and the other leg measures 6 feet? What is the length of the leg?

79. Write a polynomial to represent the cost of replacing a square patio if the replacement cost is $12 per square foot. What will be the cost of replacing a square patio measuring 12 feet on a side?

80. Write a polynomial to represent the cost of replacing a circular patio if the replacement cost is $12 per square foot. What will be the cost of replacing a circular patio with a radius of 12 feet?

81. A contractor charges a flat fee of $200.00 plus $12.00 per square foot to build a deck for an existing house. The contractor incurs setup costs of $75.00 plus $2.75 per square foot for materials for the project.

    a. Write a polynomial to represent the revenue for building a square deck.

    b. Write a polynomial to represent the cost for building the deck.

    c. What will be the revenue and cost for a deck measuring 15 feet on a side? What will be the net return (revenue minus cost) for building this deck?

82. A contractor charges a flat fee of $350.00 plus $15.00 per square foot to build a deck for an existing house. The contractor incurs setup costs of $100.00 plus $5.25 per square foot for materials for the project.

    a. Write a polynomial to represent the revenue for building a rectangular deck.

    b. Write a polynomial to represent the cost for building the deck.

    c. What will be the revenue and cost for a deck measuring 15 feet by 18 feet?

Experiencing Algebra the Calculator Way

If you are evaluating a polynomial for several values, it is sometimes helpful to use the List feature of the calculator. As an example, suppose you wish to evaluate the polynomial $0.2x^3 - 1.2x + 6.4$ when x equals the values in the list {0, 1, 2, 3, 4, 5}. We would store these values in a list, and then enter the polynomial using the list symbol in place of the variable. The keystrokes to do this follow.

| 2nd | { | 0 | , | 1 | , | 2 | , | 3 | , | 4 | , | 5 | 2nd | } | STO▶ | 2nd |

| L1 | ALPHA | : | 0 | . | 2 | 2nd | L1 | ^ | 3 | − | 1 | . | 2 | 2nd | L1 | + |

| 6 | . | 4 | ENTER |

Read the results using the arrow keys to move from left to right. The calculator returns the list {6.4, 5.4, 5.6, 8.2, 14.4, 25.4}, which represents the result of evaluating the polynomial for the list of x-values. You could also have used the TABLE feature of the calculator to do this. However, the list feature is more flexible when you have several variables, as the next example illustrates.

    Evaluate $a^2 + 2ab - 3b^2$ when a and b equal the pairs of values in the list {(2,6),(3,7),(4,8)}, where a is the first value of the pair and b is the second value of the pair. Store the a values in L1, the b values in L2, maintaining the order of the pairs, and replace a and b by their list notations when entering the expression. The keystrokes follow.

| 2nd | { | 2 | , | 3 | , | 4 | 2nd | } | STO▶ | 2nd | L1 | ALPHA | : |

| 2nd | { | 6 | , | 7 | , | 8 | 2nd | } | STO▶ | 2nd | L2 | ALPHA | : |

| 2nd | L1 | x² | + | 2 | 2nd | L1 | 2nd | L2 | − | 3 | 2nd | L2 | x² | ENTER |

The calculator returns the list {-80, -96, -112} as the results of the evaluation.
    Use this method to evaluate the following polynomials for the given values.

    1. $3x^3 - 8x^2 + 9x - 12$ when $x = \{-3, -1, 1, 3\}$

    2. $4a^3 + 2a^2b + 2ab^2 + b^3$ for $\{(-5, 2), (-3, 0), (-1, -2)\}$

    3. $\dfrac{1}{2}x^2 + \dfrac{3}{5}xy - \dfrac{1}{4}y^3$ for the (x, y) pairs $\left(\dfrac{1}{2}, \dfrac{2}{5}\right), \left(\dfrac{1}{4}, \dfrac{3}{5}\right), \left(-\dfrac{1}{2}, 5\right), \left(0, \dfrac{2}{5}\right)$

Experiencing Algebra the Group Way

Polynomials are one form of a mathematical model often developed to simulate real-world situations. In many cases, the model is intended to predict what may happen over a range of values close to those used to develop the model. Alternatively, the model may be used to determine a value within the range of those used to develop the model.

    A statistical study related the average salary of individuals to their years of experience, x. The "best" polynomial was determined to be

$$19.9801 + 3.2152x - 0.0643x^2,$$

where the salary is measured in thousands of dollars. The data used for the study ranged from 1 to 30 years of experience.

In your group, discuss how you would most efficiently use your calculator to evaluate this polynomial for different values of x. Then have each member of the group separately answer the following questions and write out your results to compare with the group.

1. Use the polynomial to estimate what the average salary would be for a person with 10 years of experience.

2. Estimate the dollar increase in average salary for a person with 20 years of experience over that for a person with 10 years of experience.

3. Find the percentage increase in the average salary of a person with 25 years experience over that of a person with 10 years experience.

4. Estimate the average salary of a person with 35 years experience. This goes beyond the range of the original study that yielded the polynomial. Does the value obtained seem reasonable?

5. Determine the average salaries of people with 0, 5, 10, 15, 20, 25, 30, and 35 years experience. For which of these values is the average salary a maximum? Does it make sense that the maximum does not occur for the largest number of years of experience? Can you give reasons to support this mathematical model when this is so?

Compare the results of your calculations in your group. Did you all reach the same conclusions in your analysis of your results?

Experiencing Algebra the Write Way

As you begin the study of polynomials, you will be expanding your knowledge of mathematical models. This would be a good time for you to reflect on your feelings toward the study of mathematics. Prepare a short essay describing your experiences to date in the study of mathematics. If this study has been a struggle, try to list reasons. Do you have personal situations that compete with your studies for your attention? Does your work situation make it difficult to find study time? Have you had a bad past experience in the study of mathematics? Do you have a study group that you can use to help you? Have you developed a negative attitude toward mathematics? If so, can you understand where this attitude originated?

After you have described your current attitudes and situation, reflect on what you can do to make your further study of mathematics a success. What can you do to develop a more positive attitude? What can you do to ensure adequate study time? What can you do to obtain the help you may need with your studies? Try to list a strategy to which you can refer periodically through your studies to keep you on a positive track.

9.2 Polynomial Functions and Their Graphs

Objectives
1 Create tables of values for polynomial relations.
2 Graph polynomial relations using sets of ordered pairs.
3 Determine ranges for polynomial relations.
4 Evaluate polynomial functions.
5 Model real-world situations using polynomial functions.

Application

In his latest movie, Arnold fires a dummy bullet at a helicopter directly above him. The bullet leaves the gun with an initial velocity of 246 feet per second at a height of 5 feet above the ground.

The position function for the bullet is $s(t) = -16t^2 + 246t + 5$, where $s(t)$ is the height above ground level (in feet) and t is the time (in seconds) after the bullet was shot from the gun. Determine the range of the function.

After completing this section, we will discuss this application further. See page 659.

1 Creating Tables of Values

In previous chapters of this text, we developed the concept of a relation. A **relation** is a set of ordered pairs. A relation can be written in equation form. The equation then relates a value for an independent variable with a value for a dependent variable. For example, $y = 3x + 2$ relates a value for the independent variable x to a value for the dependent variable y.

A **polynomial relation** equates a polynomial expression in one independent variable to a dependent variable.

> *Polynomial Relation*
> A polynomial relation is a relation that can be written in the form
> $$y = a_n x^n + a_{n-1} x^{n-1} + a_{n-2} x^{n-2} + \cdots + a_1 x^1 + a_0$$
> where n is the degree of the polynomial; $a_0, a_1, a_2, \ldots, a_n$ are real numbers; and $a_n \neq 0$.

By this definition, all linear equations, $y = ax + b$, are polynomial relations.

Another example of a polynomial relation is $y = x^2 + 2x + 7$. The polynomial $x^2 + 2x + 7$, with the independent variable x, equals the dependent variable y.

A set of all possible values for the independent variable is called the **domain** of the relation. The domain of the relation $y = x^2 + 2x + 7$ is all real numbers.

We can determine an ordered-pair solution of this relation by substituting a value for the independent variable from its domain and obtaining a value for the dependent variable. The corresponding values represent an ordered pair solution. For example,

$$\text{if } x = 2, \text{ then } y = x^2 + 2x + 7$$
$$y = (2)^2 + 2(2) + 7$$
$$y = 4 + 4 + 7$$
$$y = 15.$$

An ordered-pair solution of the relation is $(2, 15)$.

An infinite number of solutions may be found by this method. We have previously organized this procedure in a table of values. (See sections 4.1 and 6.1.) A **table of values** is a table with a column for the independent variable and a column for the dependent variable. We may want to add a third column between these to show our work.

To complete a table of values:

- Enter a number from the domain in the first column.
- Substitute this value for the independent variable in the second column.
- Evaluate the expression and enter this result in the third column.

To construct a table of values on your calculator:

- Rename the independent variable as x and the dependent variable as y and enter the equation in Y1.
- Set the calculator to generate the table by entering a minimum value, amount of increments being added to the minimum number, and setting the calculator to automatically perform the evaluations.

An alternative method is to set up the calculator to ask for the x-values.

- Ignore the minimum value and increments. Set the calculator to ask for the x-values and to automatically perform the evaluations.
- Enter values for x.

For example, a table of values for $y = x^2 + 2x + 7$, using elements from its domain, $-3, -2, -1, 0, 1$, and 2, for x follows.

x	$y = x^2 + 2x + 7$	y
-3	$y = (-3)^2 + 2(-3) + 7$ $y = 9 + (-6) + 7$ $y = 10$	10
-2	$y = (-2)^2 + 2(-2) + 7$ $y = 4 + (-4) + 7$ $y = 7$	7
-1	$y = (-1)^2 + 2(-1) + 7$ $y = 1 + (-2) + 7$ $y = 6$	6
0	$y = (0)^2 + 2(0) + 7$ $y = 0 + 0 + 7$ $y = 7$	7
1	$y = (1)^2 + 2(1) + 7$ $y = 1 + 2 + 7$ $y = 10$	10
2	$y = (2)^2 + 2(2) + 7$ $y = 4 + 4 + 7$ $y = 15$	15

Two calculator versions of the table are shown in Figure 9.4a and Figure 9.4b.

The ordered pairs found in the table, $(-3, 10), (-2, 7), (-1, 6), (0, 7), (1, 10)$, and $(2, 15)$, are integer solutions of the relation $y = x^2 + 2x + 7$.

TECHNOLOGY

X	Y1	
-3	10	
-2	7	
-1	6	
0	7	
1	10	
2	15	
3	22	

X=-3

Figure 9.4a

X	Y1	
-3	10	
-2	7	
-1	6	
0	7	
1	10	
2	15	

X=

Figure 9.4b

For Figure 9.4a
Use the Auto mode of TBLSET to generate the table.
Enter the equation in Y1.

| Y= | X, T, θ, n | x² | + | 2 | X, T, θ, n | + | 7 |

Set up the table with a minimum of −3 and increments of 1.

| 2nd | TBLSET | (−) | 3 | ENTER | 1 | ENTER | ENTER | ▼ | ENTER |

View the table.

| 2nd | TABLE |

For Figure 9.4b
An alternative method is to use the Ask mode of TBLSET.
Enter the equation in Y1.

| Y= | X, T, θ, n | x² | + | 2 | X, T, θ, n | + | 7 |

Set up the table to ask for *x*-values.

| 2nd | TBLSET | ▼ | ▼ | ▶ | ENTER |

View the table.

| 2nd | TABLE |

Enter the *x*-values.

| (−) | 3 | ENTER | (−) | 2 | ENTER | (−) | 1 | ENTER | 0 | ENTER | 1 | ENTER | 2 | ENTER |

EXAMPLE 1   Create a table of values of possible integer solutions of the polynomial relation $y = -2x^3 + 8x - 5$.

Solution

The domain of $y = -2x^3 + 8x - 5$ is all real numbers. To determine a table of values, we will use $x = -3, -2, -1, 0, 1, 2,$ and 3.

x	$y = -2x^3 + 8x - 5$	y
−3	$y = -2(-3)^3 + 8(-3) - 5$ $y = 54 + (-24) - 5$ $y = 25$	25
−2	$y = -2(-2)^3 + 8(-2) - 5$ $y = 16 + (-16) - 5$ $y = -5$	−5
−1	$y = -2(-1)^3 + 8(-1) - 5$ $y = 2 + (-8) - 5$ $y = -11$	−11
0	$y = -2(0)^3 + 8(0) - 5$ $y = 0 + 0 - 5$ $y = -5$	−5
1	$y = -2(1)^3 + 8(1) - 5$ $y = -2 + 8 - 5$ $y = 1$	1
2	$y = -2(2)^3 + 8(2) - 5$ $y = -16 + 16 - 5$ $y = -5$	−5
3	$y = -2(3)^3 + 8(3) - 5$ $y = -54 + 24 - 5$ $y = -35$	−35

Figure 9.5

The domain is all real numbers. A table of values for the relation is shown in Figure 9.5.

![checkmark] **Experiencing Algebra the Checkup Way**

1. Create a table of values with six possible integer solutions of the polynomial relation $y = x^3 + 2x^2 - 5x - 6$.

2. Consider the polynomial relation in exercise 1.

   a. Which is the independent variable?

   b. Which is the dependent variable?

   c. What is the domain of the relation?

---

2 Graphing Polynomial Relations

Polynomial relations have an infinite number of possible ordered-pair solutions. In order to illustrate these solutions, we use a **graph**.

To graph a polynomial relation means to create an illustration that represents its solutions. It is true that:

1. Every solution of a polynomial relation can be represented by a point on its graph; and
2. Every point on a graph represents a solution of its polynomial relation.

To graph a polynomial relation using ordered pairs:

- Graph ordered-pair solutions found in a table of values.
- Identify a pattern and complete the pattern.
- Label the coordinates of the points graphed.

To graph a polynomial relation on your calculator:

- Select a viewing screen, such as the integer window.
- Enter the equation in Y1.
- Graph.

For example, graph the relation $y = x^2 + 2x + 7$.

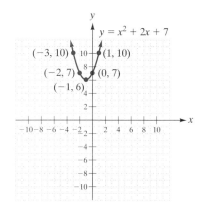

Graph the ordered pairs, $(-3, 10)$, $(-2, 7)$, $(-1, 6)$, $(0, 7)$, and $(1, 10)$, found in the previous table of values and connect the points with a smooth curve.

A calculator graph is shown in Figure 9.6.

TECHNOLOGY

$Y1 = x^2 + 2x + 7$

$(-47, 47, -31, 31)$

Figure 9.6

For Figure 9.6
Select the integer window.

| ZOOM | 6 | ZOOM | 8 | ENTER |

Enter the equation in Y1.

| Y= | X, T, θ, n | x² | + | 2 | X, T, θ, n | + | 7 |

Graph.

| GRAPH |

EXAMPLE 2   Graph the polynomial relation $y = x^3 + x^2 + 6$.

Solution

The domain of $y = x^3 + x^2 + 6$ is all real numbers. To determine a table of values, we will use $x = -3, -2, -1, 0, 1, 2,$ and 3.

x	$y = x^3 + x^2 + 6$	y
-3	$y = (-3)^3 + (-3)^2 + 6$ $y = -27 + 9 + 6$ $y = -12$	-12
-2	$y = (-2)^3 + (-2)^2 + 6$ $y = -8 + 4 + 6$ $y = 2$	2
-1	$y = (-1)^3 + (-1)^2 + 6$ $y = -1 + 1 + 6$ $y = 6$	6
0	$y = (0)^3 + (0)^2 + 6$ $y = 0 + 0 + 6$ $y = 6$	6
1	$y = (1)^3 + (1)^2 + 6$ $y = 1 + 1 + 6$ $y = 8$	8
2	$y = (2)^3 + (2)^2 + 6$ $y = 8 + 4 + 6$ $y = 18$	18
3	$y = (3)^3 + (3)^2 + 6$ $y = 27 + 9 + 6$ $y = 42$	42

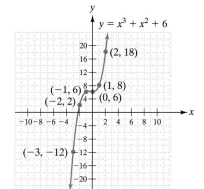

On a coordinate plane, graph the ordered pairs and connect with a smooth curve.

Calculator Solution

Two calculator graphs in different windows are shown in Figures 9.7a and 9.7b. ∎

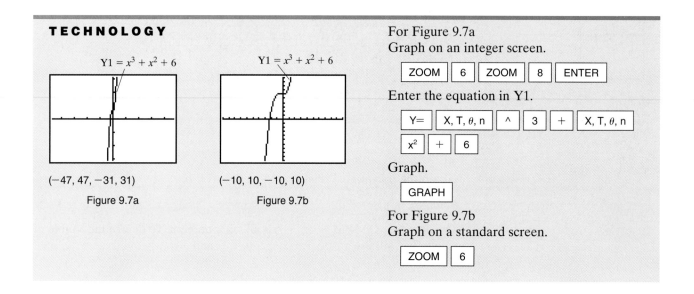

TECHNOLOGY

$Y1 = x^3 + x^2 + 6$

$Y1 = x^3 + x^2 + 6$

$(-47, 47, -31, 31)$

Figure 9.7a

$(-10, 10, -10, 10)$

Figure 9.7b

For Figure 9.7a
Graph on an integer screen.

| ZOOM | 6 | ZOOM | 8 | ENTER |

Enter the equation in Y1.

| Y= | X, T, θ, n | ^ | 3 | + | X, T, θ, n |

| x² | + | 6 |

Graph.

| GRAPH |

For Figure 9.7b
Graph on a standard screen.

| ZOOM | 6 |

 Experiencing Algebra the Checkup Way

1. Graph $y = x^3 + 2x^2 - 5x - 6$. (*Note:* This is the same relation used to construct a table of values in the preceding "Experiencing Algebra the Checkup Way.")
2. What are some advantages of representing a polynomial relation using a graph rather than a table?
3. When the domain of a polynomial relation is all real numbers, is it possible to graphically show all solutions? Explain.

3 Determining Ranges for Polynomial Relations

The set of all possible values for the dependent variable of a polynomial relation is called the **range** of the relation. To determine the range, we need to consider the relation for all values in its domain. If the domain is infinite, a more effective method to determine the range is to view the graph of the relation.

To determine the range of a polynomial relation from its graph, write a set of the values of the dependent variable (y-coordinates) used in the graph. That is, the range lies between the **absolute minimum** of the relation (smallest value of y) and the **absolute maximum** of the relation (largest value of y), if they exist.

The range is all real numbers if the y-coordinates have no absolute minimum value and no absolute maximum value. If the y-coordinates have no absolute maximum value, the range is the set of all real numbers greater than or equal to the absolute minimum value of the y-coordinates. If the y-coordinates have no absolute minimum value, the range is the set of all real numbers less than or equal to the absolute maximum value of the y-coordinates.

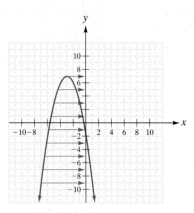

The range is all real numbers.

The range is all real numbers greater than or equal to 3.

The range is all real numbers less than or equal to 7.

For example, determine the range of the relation $y = x^2 + 2x + 7$ from its graph.

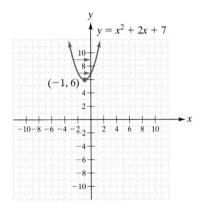

The range of the relation $y = x^2 + 2x + 7$ is all real numbers greater than or equal to 6 because there is no absolute maximum value for the y-coordinates, and 6 is the absolute minimum value of the y-coordinates on the graph of the solutions.

To determine the range of a polynomial relation from a calculator graph:

- Trace the graph to determine the y-coordinates of the points. Note the absolute minimum and the absolute maximum.
- Use the CALC function to determine the absolute minimum if it cannot be determined by tracing.
- Use the CALC function to determine the absolute maximum if it cannot be determined by tracing.

The range is defined using these values, as previously.

For example, on your calculator, determine the range of the relation $y = x^2 + 2x + 7$ from its graph.

As shown in Figure 9.8a and Figure 9.8b, the range is the same as earlier; that is, all real numbers greater than or equal to 6.

EXAMPLE 3   Graphically determine the range of each relation.

a. $y = -2x^3 + 5x - 1$ **b.** $y = -x^4 + x - 5$

Calculator Solution

Graph each relation.

a.   Y1 $= -2x^3 + 5x - 1$

(−10, 10, −10, 10)

TECHNOLOGY

$(-47, 47, -31, 31)$

Figure 9.8a

Figure 9.8b

For Figure 9.8a
Graph on an integer screen.

Enter the polynomial in Y1.

| Y= | X, T, θ, n | x² | + | 2 | X, T, θ, n |

| + | 7 |

Trace the graph to determine the
y-coordinates.

| TRACE | and use the arrow keys.

The absolute minimum value of the y-coordinates is 6.

For Figure 9.8b
Check your results by choosing minimum under the CALC function.

| 2nd | CALC | 3 |

Move to the left of the minimum value.

| ENTER |

Move to the right of the minimum value.

| ENTER |

Move close to the minimum value.

| ENTER |

The absolute minimum value of the y-coordinate is 6.

The y-coordinates have no absolute maximum or absolute minimum value. The range is all real numbers.

b.

$(-10, 10, -10, 10)$

The y-coordinates have an absolute maximum value at approximately -4.53. There is no absolute minimum value. The range is all real numbers less than or equal to -4.53. ∎

✓ Experiencing Algebra the Checkup Way

In exercises 1–4, graphically determine the range of each relation.

1. $y = x^3 + 2x^2 - 5x - 6$

2. $y = 8 + 2x - x^2$

3. $y = x^5 - 5x^3 + 4x$

4. $y = x^4 + x^3 - 7x^2 - x + 6$

5. What is the difference between the range of a polynomial relation and the domain of a polynomial relation?

6. If a polynomial relation has an absolute minimum value, what will be true about its range?

7. If a polynomial relation has an absolute maximum value, what will be true about its range?

4 Evaluating Polynomial Functions

Recall from Chapter 4 that a function is a special type of relation. A **function** relates every element in its domain with only one element in its range. To determine graphically whether a relation is a function, we use the vertical line test.

> *Vertical Line Test*
> If a vertical line can be drawn such that it intersects the graph of a relation more than once, the graph does not represent a function. If it is not possible to draw such a vertical line, then the graph represents a function.

Remember that the vertical line test works because a function can have only one y-value for every x-value. Any graph that crosses a vertical line more than once must be a relation, not a function.

Are all polynomial relations also functions? To find out, complete the following set of exercises.

DISCOVERY 1

Graphs of Polynomial Functions
Graph each polynomial relation. Draw a vertical line through more than one point on the graph, if possible.

1. $y = x$ **2.** $y = x^2$ **3.** $y = x^3$ **4.** $y = x^4$

It is not possible to draw a vertical line through more than one point on the graphs of these polynomial relations. Therefore, these polynomial relations are *all* functions. In fact, *all* polynomial relations are functions.

To write a function, we use **function notation**. We replace the dependent variable with the name of the function and put the name of the independent variable in parentheses.

> *Polynomial Function*
> A polynomial function f is a function that can be written in the form
>
> $$f(x) = a_n x^n + a_{n-1} x^{n-1} + a_{n-2} x^{n-2} + \cdots + a_1 x^1 + a_0$$
>
> where n is the degree of the polynomial; $a_0, a_1, a_2, \ldots, a_n$ are real numbers; and $a_n \neq 0$.

Helping Hand Remember from Chapter 4 that $f(x)$ does *not* mean f times x.

For example, the relation $y = x^2 + 2x + 7$ may be written as the function $f(x) = x^2 + 2x + 7$. We read this as "f of x equals x squared plus 2 times x plus 7."

We may need to evaluate a function for a given value. We use function notation to write this by replacing the independent variable with the given value. For example, "evaluate $f(x) = x^2 + 2x + 7$ for $x = 2$" is written "evaluate $f(2)$ given $f(x) = x^2 + 2x + 7$."

To evaluate a function for a value:

- Substitute the value for the independent variable.
- Evaluate the resulting numeric expression.

To evaluate a function for a value on your calculator:

- Rewrite the function notation into an equation form in terms of x, if needed.
- Enter the equation for Y1.
- Return to the home screen.
- Evaluate Y1 for the value.

For example, evaluate $f(2)$ given $f(x) = x^2 + 2x + 7$.

$$f(x) = x^2 + 2x + 7 \qquad \text{Given function}$$
$$f(2) = (2)^2 + 2(2) + 7 \qquad \text{Substitute 2 for } x.$$
$$f(2) = 4 + 4 + 7 \qquad \text{Simplify.}$$
$$f(2) = 15$$

A calculator solution is shown in Figure 9.9.

TECHNOLOGY

Y1(2)
                    15

Figure 9.9

For Figure 9.9
Enter the equation in Y1.

| Y= | X, T, θ, n | x² | + | 2 | X, T, θ, n | + | 7 |

Return to the home screen.

| 2nd | QUIT |

Evaluate Y1 for $x = 2$.

| VARS | ▶ | 1 | 1 | (| 2 |) | ENTER |

EXAMPLE 4 Evaluate the function $g(x) = x^3 - x^2 + 5x - 6$ at the given values.

a. $g(4)$ **b.** $g(-4)$

Solution

a. $g(4) = (4)^3 - (4)^2 + 5(4) - 6$
$g(4) = 64 - 16 + 20 - 6$
$g(4) = 62$

b. $g(-4) = (-4)^3 - (-4)^2 + 5(-4) - 6$
$g(-4) = -64 - 16 - 20 - 6$
$g(-4) = -106$

The calculator solutions are shown in Figure 9.10. ∎

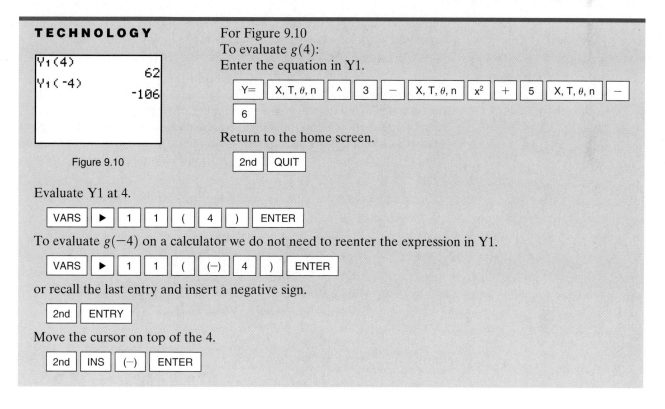

TECHNOLOGY

Figure 9.10

For Figure 9.10
To evaluate $g(4)$:
Enter the equation in Y1.

Return to the home screen.

Evaluate Y1 at 4.

To evaluate $g(-4)$ on a calculator we do not need to reenter the expression in Y1.

or recall the last entry and insert a negative sign.

Move the cursor on top of the 4.

EXAMPLE 5   Given the function $g(x) = x^3 + 50x^2 + 100$, evaluate $g(4000)$ on your calculator.

Solution

$g(4000) \approx 6.48 \times 10^{10}$ or approximately 64,800,000,000.   ■

$Y1 = x^3 + 50x^2 + 100$

 Experiencing Algebra the Checkup Way

1. Evaluate $h(x) = 2x^3 - x^2 - 27x + 36$ at the given values.

   a. $h(0)$ **b.** $h(-1)$ **c.** $h(1)$ **d.** $h(3)$ **e.** $h(-4)$ **f.** $h\left(\dfrac{3}{2}\right)$ **g.** $h(0.1)$

2. When evaluating a polynomial function, is it important to know the rules for order of operations? Explain.

5 Modeling the Real World   Often, certain values of a polynomial function have special importance for real-world situations. For example, the absolute maximum value of the polynomial function describing the path of a ball thrown into the air tells how high the ball goes before falling back to earth. If the velocity of an object, such as a rocket, is described by a polynomial function, then any time the function has a value of 0 represents a time when the object is changing direction, from positive to negative or from negative to positive. Graphs of such polynomial functions are often useful for seeing where these special values occur and approximately what the values of the variables are.

EXAMPLE 6 George makes wooden duck decoys and sells them for $10.00. However, to reduce his inventory before winter, George plans to give a discount of $0.50 for each decoy purchased. If x is the number of decoys a person purchases, then the discount is $0.50 for each decoy purchased, or $0.50x$. The purchase price is $10.00 minus the discount, or $10.00 - 0.50x$. The amount of revenue $R(x)$ is the purchase price, $10.00 - 0.50x$, times the number of decoys purchased (x):

$$R(x) = (10.00 - 0.50x)x, \text{ which becomes } R(x) = 10.00x - 0.50x^2$$

a. Determine the amount of revenue if George sells 5 decoys, 10 decoys, or 20 decoys.
b. What is the range of the revenue function?
c. What does this range tell us about George's discount plan?

Solution

a. $R(5) = 10.00(5) - 0.50(5)^2$
$R(5) = 50.00 - 0.50(25)$
$R(5) = 50.00 - 12.50$
$R(5) = 37.50$

If George sells 5 decoys, his revenue is $37.50.

$R(10) = 10.00(10) - 0.50(10)^2$
$R(10) = 50.00$

If George sells 10 decoys, his revenue is $50.00.

$R(20) = 10.00(20) - 0.50(20)^2$
$R(20) = 0.00$

If George sells 20 decoys, his revenue is $0.00.

b.

(0, 47, 0, 93)

The range is all real numbers less than or equal to 50.00.

c. This range shows us that if George gives this discount, his largest revenue would be $50.00. (According to part (*b*), this occurs when he sells 10 decoys.) If George does not limit this discount, he would have a revenue of 0 (20 decoys sold) or a negative revenue (more than 20 decoys sold), which is not a good thing to have. If George wants a more accurate picture of how his discount plan affects his possible profits, he should take into account the cost of manufacturing the decoys and the cost of selling them. ■

Application

In his latest movie, Arnold fires a dummy bullet at a helicopter directly above him. The bullet leaves the gun with an initial velocity of 246 feet per second at a height of 5 feet above the ground.

The position function for the bullet is $s(t) = -16t^2 + 246t + 5$, where $s(t)$ is the height above ground level (in feet) and t is the time (in seconds) after the bullet was shot from the gun. Determine the range of the function.

Discussion

Let $Y1 = -16x^2 + 246x + 5$.

(0, 47, 0, 1240)

The range of the function (the bullet) is all positive real numbers less than or equal to 950.5625 (feet).

The helicopter should remain at a height greater than this range. ■

✓ Experiencing Algebra the Checkup Way

Consenting Consultants, Inc., offers training to a major manufacturer. They charge $150 - 4x$ *dollars per person, where x is the number of people attending the training. (Note that CCI is offering a discount depending upon the number of people who attend.) The revenue CCI collects is given by the function*

$$R(x) = 150x - 4x^2.$$

1. Determine the amount of revenue CCI will realize if 5 people attend the training; if 10 attend; if 15 attend; if 20 attend; if 25 attend; if 30 attend; if 35 attend; if 40 attend.
2. What is the range of the revenue function?
3. Interpret the range in terms of the discount being offered.

PROBLEM SET 9.2

 ### Experiencing Algebra the Exercise Way

Create a table of values of five possible integer solutions of each polynomial relation.

1. $y = x^3 + 2x^2 - 5x - 6$ **2.** $y = x^3 - 2x^2 - 5x + 6$ **3.** $y = x^2 + 4x + 1$ **4.** $y = x^2 - 4x + 1$

Graphically determine the range of each relation.

5. $y = 2x - 5$ **6.** $y = -3x + 2$ **7.** $y = -x^2 + 6x - 4$

8. $y = -2x^2 - 8x + 1$ **9.** $y = 2x^2 - 8x + 3$ **10.** $y = x^2 - 4x - 3$

11. $y = x^3 + 3x^2 - 10x - 24$ **12.** $y = x^3 - 7x + 6$ **13.** $y = -x^4 - x^3 + 11x^2 + 9x - 18$

14. $y = x^4 + x^3 - 6x^2 - 4x + 8$

Evaluate the function $f(x) = -2x^3 + x^2 - 5x + 8$ at the given values.

15. $f(-2)$ **16.** $f(-1)$ **17.** $f(2)$ **18.** $f(3)$

Evaluate the function $g(x) = 2.7x^3 - 1.5x^2 + 3.5x - 6.7$ at the given values.

19. $g(-1.7)$ **20.** $g(-1.9)$ **21.** $g(2564.5)$ **22.** $g(3079.8)$

23. $g(1.5)$ **24.** $g(1.8)$ **25.** $g(1.1995)$ **26.** $g(0)$

Evaluate the function $h(x) = \frac{1}{2}x^3 - \frac{3}{4}x^2 + \frac{3}{8}x - \frac{5}{8}$ at the given values. Express your results in fraction notation.

27. $h\left(-\dfrac{3}{2}\right)$ **28.** $h\left(-\dfrac{1}{2}\right)$ **29.** $h\left(\dfrac{5}{2}\right)$ **30.** $h\left(\dfrac{7}{2}\right)$

31. In order to encourage multiple purchases, Dave's Wholesale Jewelers sells watches at a price that is a function of the number of watches ordered. For x watches ordered, the price will be $150 - 5x$ dollars per watch. Thus, one watch costs \$145, two watches cost \$140 each, and so forth. The revenue function for an order of x watches is

$$R(x) = 150x - 5x^2$$

   a. Determine the revenue if 5 watches are ordered; if 10 watches are ordered; if 15 watches are ordered; if 20 watches are ordered; if 25 watches are ordered; if 30 are watches ordered.

   b. Find the range of the revenue function.

   c. Interpret the range in terms of the discount offered.

32. Honest Al rents space at his merchandise mart and offers sliding scale rates for multi-month rentals. His rate is $300 - 5x$ dollars per month for x months of rental. Thus the rate for one month's rental is \$295, the rate for two months' rental is \$290 per month, the rate for three months' rental is \$285 per month, and so forth. The total cost for renting the space for x months is

$$C(x) = 300x - 5x^2$$

   a. Determine the cost of renting space for 10 months; for 20 months; for 30 months; for 40 months; for 50 months; for 60 months.

   b. Determine the range of the cost function.

   c. Interpret the cost function in terms of the discount offered.

33. A statistical study collected data on the length of a Medicare patient's hospital stay and the patient's age. For female patients, a function that relates the length of stay, $S(x)$, to the patient's age, x, is given by

$$S(x) = -0.011x^2 + 1.91x - 72.54$$

Use this function to estimate a patient's length of stay, given the following ages.

Age (x)	63	65	70	75	80	85
Days $(S(x))$						

   a. The actual data included an 85-year-old woman who had a hospital stay of 8 days. How well did the function predict this stay?

   b. One 70-year-old woman had a stay of 9 days, and another 70-year-old woman had a stay of 6 days. Did the function predict these stays closely?

   c. If you don't think the function predicts well, can you explain why it doesn't?

34. A term life insurance policy lists the following annual premiums for male nonsmokers as a function of their ages.

Age	35	40	45	50	55	60	65	70
Premium	$385	$505	$770	$1165	$1700	$2645	$4355	$8285

Statistical methods calculate a third-degree polynomial function for this table as

$$P(x) = 0.43x^3 - 58.08x^2 + 2629.48x - 39096,$$

where $P(x)$ is the premium and x is the age. Use this function to estimate the premiums for the following values of x shown in the table.

Age (x)	35	40	45	50	55	60	65	70
Premium $(P(x))$								

a. How well does the function predict the actual premium for a male who is 35 years old?

b. Did the function predict the premium closely for a 70 year-old male?

c. If you don't think the function closely predicts the actual premiums, can you offer a reason why?

35. For the Labor Day picnic, an expert pyrotechnician shoots a fireworks rocket from ground level with an initial velocity of 270 feet per second. The position function for the rocket, in feet above ground level, is $s(t) = -16t^2 + 270t$, where t is the time in seconds after the rocket is launched and $0 < t < 8$. State the domain and interpret it. Find the range of the function and interpret it.

36. At the Fourth of July celebration, a professional pyrotechnics expert shoots a rocket straight up from the top of a 20 foot tower. The rocket's initial velocity is 300 feet per second. The position function for the rocket, in feet above ground level, is $s(t) = -16t^2 + 300t + 20$, where t is the time in seconds after the rocket is launched and $0 < t < 10$. State the domain and interpret it. Find the range of the function and interpret it.

Experiencing Algebra the Calculator Way

In statistical research, polynomials are often used to estimate relationships between variables. As an example, a sales manager collects data to relate each salesperson's yearly sales, $S(x)$, to the number of years, x, the salesperson spends in the same territory. The function he develops from the data is given by

$$S(x) = -144{,}100 + 354{,}050x - 52{,}176x^2$$

1. What is the domain of the function?   2. What is the range of the function?

3. One of the salespeople has been in the same territory for 4.4 years. Her actual sales were $402,000. Use the polynomial function to estimate her sales and compare to the actual value.

4. Complete the table to compare actual sales to predicted sales from the function.

Years (x)	Actual Sales	Predicted Sales ($S(x)$)	Difference: Actual − Predicted Sales
0.8	$102,000		
1.1	$195,000		
1.4	$265,000		
1.5	$237,000		
2.2	$345,000		
3.0	$533,000		
3.6	$473,000		
4.4	$402,000		
4.5	$298,000		
5.5	$263,000		

After studying the differences between actual and predicted sales, do you think the function is a good mathematical model for the sales manager to use? Explain.

Experiencing Algebra the Group Way

Each member of the group should graph the following polynomial functions with a calculator. In order to view the graph easily, use the decimal viewing window. Then draw a sketch of each graph, labeling the intercepts.

1. $y = x$ **2.** $y = x^2 + x$ **3.** $y = x^3 - x$

4. $y = x^4 + 2x^3 - x^2 - 2x$ **5.** $y = x^5 - 5x^3 + 4x$

Each member of the group should determine the degree of each polynomial.

After completing these tasks, the group should discuss and compare the graphs. Agree on how many times each graph changes direction, either moving up from left to right, or moving down from left to right. Compare this number with the degree of the polynomial graphed. Complete the following table.

Polynomial	Degree of Polynomial	Number of Changes in Direction
$y = x$		
$y = x^2 + x$		
$y = x^3 - x$		
$y = x^4 + 2x^3 - x^2 - 2x$		
$y = x^5 - 5x^3 + 4x$		

Discuss the apparent relationship between the degree of the polynomial and the number of times the graph changes direction.

Next, notice which graphs have tails that extend in opposite directions, and which graphs have tails that extend in the same direction. Discuss and compare this feature with the degree of the polynomials. Do you see a relationship?

Also notice that when the tails extend in opposite directions, there is at least one value of x that will make the polynomial evaluate to 0. Discuss why this is so.

The degree of the polynomial in a polynomial function can be a useful feature to study in order to understand what the function's graph will look like. Have one member of your group share your findings with the class.

Experiencing Algebra the Write Way

In this section, several examples or exercises mention statistics as an area of mathematics that often uses polynomials in order to explain the relationship between pairs of observations in actual data collected from an application. In the library, browse some statistics texts to find another example where this is done. (*Note:* In the statistics texts, you will find this done under a method called regression analysis.) Don't try to understand the description of how the relation is developed; just take note of the example presented.

Write a short paragraph describing the independent variable and the dependent variable being studied in the example. Also present the relation developed. Experiment with the relation to see if you can substitute values for the independent variable to estimate what the value will be for the dependent variable. Explain what this example means to you. Footnote the text in which you found the example and provide the library call number for the text.

9.3   Quadratic Functions and Their Graphs

Objectives

1 Identify quadratic functions.

2 Understand the effects of the coefficients of a quadratic function on its graph.

3 Graph quadratic functions.

4 Model real-world situations using graphs of quadratic functions.

Application

A signal flare is shot upward from a cliff 100 meters high. If the initial velocity of the flare was 91.2 meters per second, a position function for the flare is $s(t) = -4.9t^2 + 91.2t + 100$, where $s(t)$ is measured in meters and time, t, is measured in seconds.

Determine the signal flare's maximum height in meters.

After completing this section, we will discuss this application further. See page 675.

? m

100 m

1 Identifying Quadratic Functions

In this section, we discuss a special case of a polynomial function, called a quadratic function. A *quadratic function* is a polynomial function with a degree of 2.

> *Standard Form for a Quadratic Function*
> A quadratic function can be written in the standard form
>
> $$y = ax^2 + bx + c, \text{ where } a \neq 0$$
> $$\text{or } f(x) = ax^2 + bx + c, \text{ where } a \neq 0.$$

For example,

Standard form: $y = ax^2 + bx + c$

1. $y = 2x^2 + 3x - 4$ $a = 2, b = 3,$ and $c = -4$
2. $y = x^2 - 2x$ $a = 1, b = -2,$ and $c = 0$
3. $y = -3x^2 + 5$ $a = -3, b = 0,$ and $c = 5$
4. $y = x^2$ $a = 1, b = 0,$ and $c = 0$

The coefficients are identified next to each function. Remember, $a \neq 0$. If $a = 0$, we no longer have a quadratic function. We would then have a linear function of the form $y = bx + c$.

EXAMPLE 1   Identify each function as quadratic or nonquadratic.

   a. $y = x^3 + x^2 - 6x$ **b.** $h(x) = 2x - x^2$ **c.** $y = \dfrac{6}{x^2} + 2x - 7$

Solution

   a. $y = x^3 + x^2 - 6x$ is not a quadratic function because $x^3 + x^2 - 6x$ is a third-degree polynomial (x is cubed).

   b. $h(x) = 2x - x^2$ is a quadratic function because it can be rearranged into standard form, $h(x) = -x^2 + 2x + 0$.

   c. $y = \dfrac{6}{x^2} + 2x - 7$ is not a quadratic function because $\dfrac{6}{x^2} + 2x - 7$ is not a polynomial (the squared variable term is in the denominator of a fraction). ∎

✓ Experiencing Algebra the Checkup Way

In exercises 1–6, identify each function as quadratic or nonquadratic.

1. $y = -2x^2 + 9x - 125$ 2. $y = 8x^2 - 12$ 3. $h(x) = 5x - 13$

4. $f(x) = 3 - 9x - 7x^2$ 5. $y = x^3 + x^2 - x$ 6. $y = -\dfrac{3}{x^2} - 4$

7. What is meant by the standard form of a quadratic function?

8. What must be true about the coefficient of the quadratic term of a quadratic function? Why is this so?

---

2 Understanding the Effects of the Coefficients

Just as the coefficients m and b of a linear function $y = mx + b$ affect its graph, the values of the coefficients a, b, and c in the standard form of a quadratic function, $y = ax^2 + bx + c$, affect its graph.

All quadratic functions have a U-shaped graph called a **parabola**.

 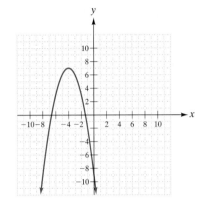

The term ax^2 in the function is called the **quadratic term**. To determine what effect the coefficient a has on the parabola, complete the following set of exercises.

DISCOVERY 2

Effect of the Coefficient a on a Quadratic Graph

Sketch the graphs of the following quadratic functions of the form $y = ax^2$, where $b = c = 0$, on the same coordinate plane. Use the decimal window.

1. $y = 0.2x^2$ **2.** $y = x^2$ **3.** $y = 2x^2$

4. $y = -0.2x^2$ **5.** $y = -x^2$ **6.** $y = -2x^2$

Complete the following sentences by choosing the correct words.

7. In exercises 1–3, a is a *positive/negative* number. All graphs open *upward/downward*.

8. In exercises 4–6, a is a *positive/negative* number. All graphs open *upward/downward*.

9. In exercises 3 and 6, the absolute value of a is greater than 1. The shape of the parabola is *wider/narrower* than the graphs in exercises 2 and 5, where $a = 1$ or -1.

10. In exercises 1 and 4, the absolute value of a is less than 1. The shape of the parabola is *wider/narrower* than the graphs in exercises 2 and 5, where $a = 1$ or -1.

The coefficient a of the quadratic term affects the form of the parabola graphed. If the coefficient is positive, the graph opens upward. We say the graph is **concave upward**. If the coefficient is negative, the graph opens downward, or is **concave downward**.

Concave upward

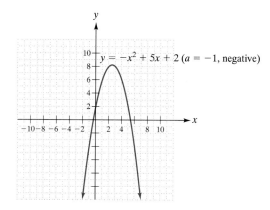

Concave downward

If the absolute value of the coefficient is greater than 1, the graph is narrower than the graph when the coefficient is 1. If the absolute value of the coefficient is less than 1, the graph is wider than the graph when the coefficient is 1.

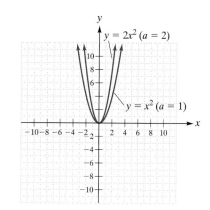

Remember from Chapter 4 that a function value is called a **relative maximum** if it is larger than the function values of its neighboring points. The largest relative maximum is called the *absolute maximum*. If a parabola is concave downward, its quadratic function will have an absolute maximum equal to the function value of the highest point of the parabola.

A function value is called a **relative minimum** if it is smaller than the function values of its neighboring points. The smallest relative minimum is called the *absolute minimum*. If a parabola is concave upward, its quadratic function will have an absolute minimum equal to the function value of the lowest point of the parabola.

The highest point on a concave-down parabola or the lowest point on a concave-up parabola is called the **vertex** of the parabola.

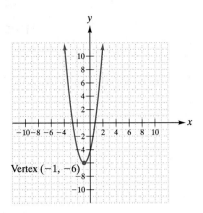

Concave upward
Absolute minimum of −6

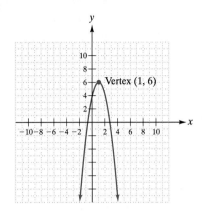

Concave downward
Absolute maximum of 6

The coefficients a and b determine the x-coordinate of the vertex. A formula for this is

$$x = \frac{-b}{2a}.$$

We use this x-coordinate to find the y-coordinate of the vertex, which is either the absolute maximum or the absolute minimum of the quadratic function.

To determine the vertex of a quadratic function $y = ax^2 + bx + c$:

- Use the formula for the x-coordinate of the vertex of a quadratic function, which is $x = \frac{-b}{2a}$.
- Find the y-coordinate of the vertex by substituting the x-coordinate value in the original function and solving for y.

To determine the vertex of a quadratic function on your calculator:

- Enter the function in Y1.
- Graph the function.
- Trace the graph to determine its highest or lowest point.
- Use the CALC function to determine the minimum or maximum if it cannot be found by tracing.

Helping Hand The calculator may display the approximate vertex, so it may not be exact.

For example, given the quadratic function $y = 2x^2 + 4x + 3$, determine the coordinates of the vertex of its graph.

To determine the x-coordinate of the vertex, use the formula

$$x = \frac{-b}{2a}$$

$$x = \frac{-(4)}{2(2)} \quad a = 2, b = 4$$

$$x = -1$$

To determine the y-coordinate of the vertex, substitute the x-coordinate value into the function and solve for y.

$$y = 2x^2 + 4x + 3$$
$$y = 2(-1)^2 + 4(-1) + 3$$
$$y = 2 - 4 + 3$$
$$y = 1$$

The vertex is $(-1, 1)$.

To determine the vertex on your calculator, see Figures 9.11a and 9.11b.

TECHNOLOGY

Y1 = 2x² + 4x + 3

X=-1   Y=1

(−4.7, 4.7, −3.1, 3.1)

Figure 9.11a

Y1 = 2x² + 4x + 3

Minimum
X=-1.000007 Y=1

(−4.7, 4.7, −3.1, 3.1)

Figure 9.11b

For Figure 9.11a
Enter the function in Y1.

| Y= | 2 | X, T, θ, n | x² | + | 4 |

| X, T, θ, n | + | 3 |

Graph on a decimal screen.

| ZOOM | 4 |

Trace.

| TRACE |

For Figure 9.11b
To determine the vertex with the CALC function, enter | 2nd | CALC | 3 |
Move to the left of the vertex.

| ENTER |

Move to the right of the vertex.

| ENTER |

Move close to the vertex.

| ENTER |

The result gives the approximate coordinates of the vertex.

Another feature of a quadratic function's graph is its symmetry. To visualize the meaning of symmetry, complete the following set of exercises on your calculator.

DISCOVERY 3

Symmetric Graph

1. Consider the graph of $y = x^2$. The vertex of the graph is $(0, 0)$. Complete the table of values for the three integer x-values on either side of $x = 0$, the x-coordinate of the vertex.

x	y	
-3		
-2		
-1		
0	0	← vertex
1		
2		
3		

2. Graph the function, using the table of values. Label all points graphed.

Compare the y-values for the x-values equidistant from $x = 0$.

3. If $x = 1$ or $x = -1$, then $y =$ _____.
4. If $x = 2$ or $x = -2$, then $y =$ _____.
5. If $x = 3$ or $x = -3$, then $y =$ _____.

The graph of $y = x^2$ is a parabola symmetric with respect to the y-axis, or to the line graphed by the equation $x = 0$. The y-values that correspond to the x-values equidistant from $x = 0$ are equal. Therefore, if the graph is folded together along the line $x = 0$, the two sides will coincide. We call the vertical line through the vertex the **axis of symmetry** of the parabola.

The constant term c of the quadratic function also affects the graph. To determine the effect of the constant term c, complete the following set of exercises on your calculator.

DISCOVERY 4

Effect of the Coefficient c on a Quadratic Graph

Sketch the graph of the following quadratic functions of the form $y = ax^2 + c$, where $b = 0$, on the same coordinate plane. Use the decimal window and label the y-intercept of each graph.

$$y = 2x^2 \qquad y = 2x^2 + 1 \qquad y = 2x^2 - 3$$

1. Write a rule to determine the y-coordinate of the y-intercept of a parabola from its equation.
2. Check your rule for $y = 2x^2 + 3x - 1$.

The y-coordinate of the y-intercept is the constant term. (This is the same as when we were graphing linear equations.) We can determine the y-intercept algebraically in the same manner as we did for a linear equation—that is, substitute 0 for x and solve for y.

For example, given $y = 2x^2 + 3x - 1$, substitute 0 for x.

$$y = 2x^2 + 3x - 1$$
$$y = 2(0)^2 + 3(0) - 1$$
$$y = 0 + 0 - 1$$
$$y = -1$$

The y-coordinate of the y-intercept is -1, the constant term of the function.

Summary of the Effects of the Coefficients of a Quadratic Function on Its Graph

The coefficients of a quadratic function written in standard form, $y = ax^2 + bx + c$, affect its graph.

Coefficient a:
If $a > 0$ (positive), then the graph is concave upward.
If $a < 0$ (negative), then the graph is concave downward.

Absolute value of a:
If $|a| > 1$, then the graph is narrower than when $a = 1$.
If $|a| < 1$, then the graph is wider than when $a = 1$.

Coefficient c:
The coefficient c is the y-coordinate of the y-intercept of the graph.

The x-coordinate of the vertex is $\frac{-b}{2a}$.
The axis of symmetry is the line graphed by $x = \frac{-b}{2a}$.

EXAMPLE 2 Complete the following table.

	Coefficients			Properties of Graph			
Function	a	b	c	Wide/Narrow	Concave Upward/Downward	Vertex	Axis of Symmetry
$y = 3x^2 + 6$							
$y = -0.5x^2 - 2$							
$y = -2x^2 + 6x - 1$							
$y = \frac{1}{4}x^2 - x + 2$							

Solution

	Coefficients			Properties of Graph			
Function	a	b	c	Wide/Narrow	Concave Upward/Downward	Vertex	Axis of Symmetry
$y = 3x^2 + 6$	3	0	6	narrow	upward	$(0, 6)$	$x = 0$
$y = -0.5x^2 - 2$	-0.5	0	-2	wide	downward	$(0, -2)$	$x = 0$
$y = -2x^2 + 6x - 1$	-2	6	-1	narrow	downward	$\left(\frac{3}{2}, \frac{7}{2}\right)$	$x = \frac{3}{2}$
$y = \frac{1}{4}x^2 - x + 2$	$\frac{1}{4}$	-1	2	wide	upward	$(2, 1)$	$x = 2$

■

Experiencing Algebra the Checkup Way

Complete the following table. Check your work by viewing the graphs on your calculator.

	Function	Coefficients			Properties of Graph			
		a	b	c	Wide/Narrow	Concave Upward/Downward	Vertex	Axis of Symmetry
1.	$y = -3x^2 + 2$							
2.	$y = 4x^2 - 8x + 5$							
3.	$y = 0.25x^2 + x - 2$							
4.	$y = \dfrac{2}{3}x^2 + x$							

5. When graphing the quadratic function $y = ax^2 + bx + c$, how is the concavity (upward or downward) determined by the coefficients?

6. When graphing a quadratic function, how is the location of the vertex determined by the coefficients?

7. When graphing the quadratic function, how does the constant term affect the graph?

---

3 Graphing Quadratic Functions

When we graphed linear functions, we needed two points to determine the linear pattern. However, quadratic functions do not have a linear pattern, so we will need more than two solutions to determine a pattern.

To graph a quadratic function:

- Determine the coordinates of the vertex by finding the x-coordinate from the formula $x = \frac{-b}{2a}$, substituting the x-coordinate into the original quadratic function, and solving for y to determine the y-coordinate.
- Determine a table of values by choosing at least two x-values greater than the x-coordinate of the vertex and two corresponding x-values less than the x-coordinate of the vertex.
- Graph the function by plotting the vertex and the set of ordered pairs from the table of values and connecting the points with a smooth curve.

 Helping Hand It is often useful to graph the axis of symmetry.

To graph a quadratic function on your calculator:

- Enter the function in Y1.
- Graph.

To determine individual solutions, trace the graph.

For example, graph the quadratic function $y = x^2 + 3x + 1$.

The coefficients are $a = 1$, $b = 3$, and $c = 1$.
First, determine the coordinates of the vertex.
The x-coordinate is found by the formula

$$x = \frac{-b}{2a}$$

$$x = \frac{-3}{2(1)}$$

$$x = -\frac{3}{2}.$$

Determine the y-coordinate of the vertex by substituting the x-coordinate value in the function and solving for y.

$$y = x^2 + 3x + 1$$

$$y = \left(-\frac{3}{2}\right)^2 + 3\left(-\frac{3}{2}\right) + 1$$

$$y = -\frac{5}{4}$$

The vertex is $\left(-\frac{3}{2}, -\frac{5}{4}\right)$.
The axis of symmetry is the line $x = -\frac{3}{2}$.
Complete a table of values by choosing two x-values less than $-\frac{3}{2}$, such as -2 and -3, and two x-values greater than $-\frac{3}{2}$, such as -1 and 0.

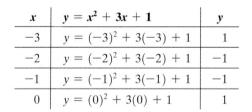

x	$y = x^2 + 3x + 1$	y
-3	$y = (-3)^2 + 3(-3) + 1$	1
-2	$y = (-2)^2 + 3(-2) + 1$	-1
-1	$y = (-1)^2 + 3(-1) + 1$	-1
0	$y = (0)^2 + 3(0) + 1$	1

Plot the vertex and the ordered pairs found in the table of values. Connect the points with a smooth curve and graph the axis of symmetry.

On your calculator, enter the function in Y1 and graph on an integer screen as shown in Figure 9.12a.

The decimal screen provides a better picture. See Figure 9.12b.

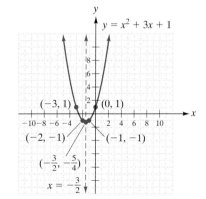

EXAMPLE 3 Graph the quadratic function $s(x) = -x^2 + 2x + 1$. Label the vertex. Draw and label the axis of symmetry.

Solution

Given $s(x) = -x^2 + 2x + 1$, we know that $a = -1$, $b = 2$, and $c = 1$.
Determine the coordinates of the vertex.

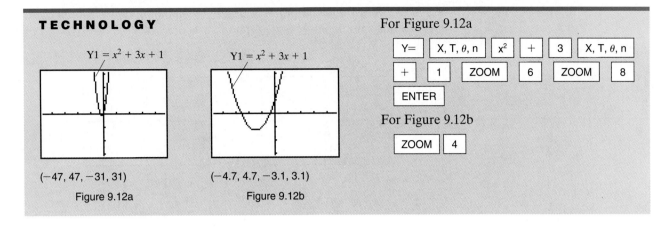

TECHNOLOGY

$Y1 = x^2 + 3x + 1$

$(-47, 47, -31, 31)$

Figure 9.12a

$Y1 = x^2 + 3x + 1$

$(-4.7, 4.7, -3.1, 3.1)$

Figure 9.12b

For Figure 9.12a

| Y= | X, T, θ, n | x^2 | + | 3 | X, T, θ, n |
| + | 1 | ZOOM | 6 | ZOOM | 8 |

| ENTER |

For Figure 9.12b

| ZOOM | 4 |

Use the formula $x = \dfrac{-b}{2a}$

$$x = \dfrac{-2}{2(-1)}$$

$$x = 1.$$

Substitute 1 for x in the function.

$$s(1) = -(1)^2 + 2(1) + 1$$
$$s(1) = -1 + 2 + 1$$
$$s(1) = 2$$

The vertex is $(1, 2)$.

  The axis of symmetry is the line $x = 1$.

  Set up a table of values using x-values less than and greater than the x-coordinate of the vertex, 1.

x	$s(x) = -x^2 + 2x + 1$	$s(x)$
-1	$s(-1) = -(-1)^2 + 2(-1) + 1$ $s(-1) = -1 - 2 + 1$ $s(-1) = -2$	-2
0	$s(0) = -(0)^2 + 2(0) + 1$ $s(0) = -0 + 0 + 1$ $s(0) = 1$	1
2	$s(2) = -(2)^2 + 2(2) + 1$ $s(2) = -4 + 4 + 1$ $s(2) = 1$	1
3	$s(3) = -(3)^2 + 2(3) + 1$ $s(3) = -9 + 6 + 1$ $s(3) = -2$	-2

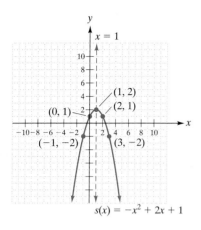

$$s(x) = -x^2 + 2x + 1$$

Graph the vertex and the points found in the table of values. Connect the points with a smooth curve and graph the axis of symmetry.

Calculator Solution

Y1 = $-x^2 + 2x + 1$

$(-47, 47, -31, 31)$

Y1 = $-x^2 + 2x + 1$

$(-4.7, 4.7, -3.1, 3.1)$

The decimal screen provides a better picture.

Trace the graph to check the points found in the table of values. ∎

✓ Experiencing Algebra the Checkup Way

Graph each quadratic function in exercises 1–2. Label the vertex. Draw and label the axis of symmetry.

1. $A(x) = 2x^2 - x - 6$ 2. $y = -x^2 + 12x - 26$

3. When graphing a quadratic function, why is it recommended that you first find the location of the vertex?

4. After graphing a quadratic function, how can you use the coefficients of the quadratic polynomial to check that your graph is correct?

---

4 Modeling the Real World

Quadratic functions model many real-world applications, as we've seen earlier in this chapter. We can use the methods in this section to find the maximum or minimum values of a quadratic function, which is often useful and important information. For example, we can use a quadratic function to determine the area of a rectangle for various lengths and widths. The absolute maximum of the function corresponds to the maximum area of the rectangle.

EXAMPLE 4

Jerome is planning to add a new family room to his home. The maximum length he can fit is 24 feet. He plans to subtract 1 foot from the maximum length for every foot he adds to the width. If x is the width of the room in feet, then the length is $(24 - x)$ feet. An area function, $A(x)$, for the family room is determined by multiplying the length times the width and is measured in square feet.

$$A(x) = (24 - x)x \quad \text{or} \quad A(x) = 24x - x^2$$

Determine the maximum area for the family room. What are the dimensions for this maximum area?

Solution

Let Y1 = $(24 - x)x$ or
  Y1 = $24x - x^2$.

Y1 = $24x - x^2$

$(0, 47, 0, 310)$

Graph the quadratic function and determine its absolute maximum.

The vertex of the graph is (12, 144). The absolute maximum of the function is 144. Therefore, the maximum area is 144 square feet. Since $x = 12$ (width) and $24 - x = 12$ (length), the dimensions that give the maximum area are 12 feet by 12 feet. ∎

Application

A signal flare is shot upward from a cliff 100 meters high. If the initial velocity of the flare was 91.2 meters per second, a position function for the flare is $s(t) = -4.9t^2 + 91.2t + 100$, where $s(t)$ is measured in meters and time, t, is measured in seconds. Determine the signal flare's maximum height in meters.

Discussion

Let $Y1 = -4.9x^2 + 91.2x + 100$.

$Y1 = -4.9x^2 + 91.2x + 100$

Maximum
X=9.3061235 Y=524.35918

(0, 47, 0, 620)

The vertex of the graph is approximately $(9.31, 524.36)$. Therefore, the maximum height of the signal flare is 524.36 meters at approximately 9.31 seconds.

✓ Experiencing Algebra the Checkup Way

1. If a water balloon is tossed upward with an initial velocity of 14 meters per second from a window that is 70 meters above the ground, the position formula representing its height at time t is given by $s(t) = -4.9t^2 + 14t + 70$. Graph the function. Find the maximum height the balloon will reach. From the graph, determine the time at which the balloon will return to the ground, to the nearest second.

2. A farmer wishes to enclose a plot of land for a garden. He has 400 feet of fencing, including a gate, to use for the garden. The garden will be rectangular. If x is the width of the garden in feet, the length will be $200 - x$ feet, and the area will be $A(x) = 200x - x^2$ square feet. Graph the function for the area of the garden. For what value of x will the area of the garden be maximized? What will the maximum area of the garden be?

PROBLEM SET 9.3

Experiencing Algebra the Exercise Way

Identify each function as quadratic or nonquadratic.

1. $y = 1 - x - x^2 - x^3$

2. $g(x) = 1.3x^2 - 4.7$

3. $f(x) = 8x + 11$

4. $y = x + 2x^2 - 9$

5. $g(x) = 0.5x^2 + 2.6x - 8.4$

6. $y = 8x^2$

7. $y = -2x^2 - 5x - 7$

8. $r(x) = \dfrac{1}{x^2} - 3$

9. $a = \pi r^2$

10. $s = 4\pi r^2$

11. $S = 6e^2$

12. $y = 3x^3 + 2x - 5$

13. $y = \dfrac{7}{x^2} + 3x - 12$

14. $A(x) = \dfrac{1}{2}x^2$

15. $y = 2x^2 - 2x + 5$

16. $f(x) = 6 - 4x$

Complete the following table. Check your work on your calculator.

	Function	Coefficients			Properties of Graph			
		a	**b**	**c**	**Wide/Narrow**	**Concave Upward/Downward**	**Vertex**	**Axis of Symmetry**
17.	$y = -5x^2 + 10x + 1$							
18.	$y = 6x^2 - 6x - 5$							
19.	$y = 0.6x^2 + 6x - 2$							
20.	$y = -x^2 + 6x - 2$							
21.	$y = 2x^2 + 3x + 5$							
22.	$y = -3x^2 + 6x - 5$							
23.	$y = -\dfrac{1}{4}x^2 + x - 3$							
24.	$y = \dfrac{1}{3}x^2 + 2x - 1$							
25.	$f(x) = x^2 + 8x + 1$							
26.	$y = -0.4x^2 + 2.4x - 1.1$							

Graph each quadratic function in exercises 27–42. Label the vertex. Draw and label the axis of symmetry.

27. $f(x) = 2x^2 + 5x - 7$ **28.** $y = 2x^2 + 6x - 5$ **29.** $y = \dfrac{1}{6}x^2 + 3x + 12$ **30.** $y = \dfrac{3}{4}x^2 - 6x + 7$

31. $h(x) = 14 + 5x - x^2$ **32.** $f(x) = 11 - 4x + x^2$ **33.** $y = -2x^2 + 8x - 3$ **34.** $y = -3x^2 + 6x + 1$

35. $g(x) = 0.8x^2 - 1.2x$ **36.** $h(x) = 1.2x^2 + 3.6x$ **37.** $y = 0.4x^2$ **38.** $y = -0.7x^2$

39. $y = 3x^2 - 3$ **40.** $y = -6x^2 + 3$ **41.** $f(x) = -0.5x^2 + 3x$ **42.** $g(x) = -0.2x^2 + 4x$

43. Eve threw an apple upward with a speed of 12 feet per second from a height of 24 feet. The position function for the apple is given by $s(t) = -16t^2 + 12t + 24$. Graph the function. Find the maximum height the apple will reach. From the graph, determine the time at which the apple will hit the ground beside Adam, to the nearest tenth of a second.

44. A football is kicked upward at 80 feet per second from ground level. The position function for the football is given by $s(t) = -16t^2 + 80t$. Graph the function. Determine the coordinates of the vertex of the graph. Interpret these values. How long will it take for the football to return to the ground?

45. Gramps is building Granny a cottage. He wants the foundation to be 280 feet around, but isn't sure what width and length to build. If the width of the foundation is x feet, the area of the foundation is given by $A(x) = 140x - x^2$. Graph the function. Find the vertex. Explain what the coordinates of the vertex indicate.

46. Farmer Jones plans to build a small animal pen next to his barn. The pen will be rectangular, with one side formed by the barn. The other three sides will be constructed from 120 feet of fencing. The area of the pen is given by the quadratic function $A(x) = 120x - 2x^2$. Graph the function. Find the vertex. Explain the meaning of the coordinates of the vertex.

47. The base of a right triangle measures 20 inches less twice the measure of its height. The square of the hypotenuse of the triangle is given by $s(x) = 5x^2 - 80x + 400$, where x is the height of the triangle in inches. Graph the function. For what value of the height will the square of the hypotenuse be minimized? What will be the minimum value of the square of the hypotenuse?

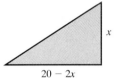

48. The length of a rectangular billboard is 10 feet more than its width. If the width is denoted by x, the area of the billboard will be given by $A(x) = x^2 + 10x$. Graph the function. Find the vertex. Does the vertex have any physical meaning?

49. Suppose the price of collectible dolls is set to encourage customers to buy more than one. The price is given by the expression $46 - x$. Thus if you buy one doll, the price is $45; if you buy two dolls, the price is $44, and so forth. If x dolls are purchased, the total revenue for the dolls will be $R(x) = 46x - x^2$. Graph the function. For what value of x will the revenue function be maximized? What is the maximum revenue?

50. The cost of producing bicycles includes a setup cost of $200 plus a variable cost that is a function of the number of bicycles produced. The cost is $25 - 0.50x$ per bicycle, where x is the number of bicycles produced on a run. The total cost for a run of x bicycles is given by the cost function

$$C(x) = 200 + 25x - 0.5x^2.$$

Graph the function. For what value of x will the cost function be maximized? What is the meaning of this value?

Experiencing Algebra the Calculator Way

Sometimes it is desirable to view two screens on your calculator at the same time. For example, suppose you wish to study the impact of various coefficients in quadratic functions by graphing several on the same coordinate plane. At the same time, you want to view the functions along with the graphs. To do so, first split the screen as follows.

Enter ⎣MODE⎦ . Arrow down to the option "Full Horiz G-T."

Arrow over to "Horiz."

Press ⎣ENTER⎦ ⎣2nd⎦ ⎣QUIT⎦ .

The top half of the screen will display graphs and the bottom half of the screen will be the home screen, where you can key instructions in the same manner as with a full screen.

Graph the following combinations of quadratic functions using the split screen and a decimal window setting (ZOOM 4).

1. $y_1 = x^2 - 2x$ $y_2 = x^2$ $y_3 = x^2 + 2x$

    This will show how the graphs of the functions are affected by the coefficients a and b.

2. $y_1 = x^2 - 1$ $y_2 = x^2$ $y_3 = x^2 + 1$

    This will show how the graphs of the functions are affected by the coefficient c.

The bottom half of the screen continues to be available for use, as if you did not have a split screen. This is a handy feature when graphing several functions together. Unfortunately, sometimes the graphs are so compressed that they become difficult to read. You can experiment with changing the window settings to adjust for this. When you are through with the split screen, you can return to a full screen:

Enter ⎣MODE⎦ . Arrow down to the option "Full Horiz G-T."

Press ⎣ENTER⎦ ⎣2nd⎦ ⎣QUIT⎦ .

Use the split screen to examine the following sets of quadratic functions.

3. $y_1 = 0.3x^2$ $y_2 = x^2$ $y_3 = 3x^2$

4. $y_1 = -3x^2$ $y_2 = 3x^2$

5. $y_1 = 3x^2$ $y_2 = 3x^2 + 1$ $y_3 = 3x^2 - 2$

6. $y_1 = x^2 + 1$ $y_2 = x^2 + 2x + 1$ $y_3 = x^2 - 2x + 1$

From your examination, describe how the coefficients of the quadratic functions affect the graphs.

Experiencing Algebra the Group Way

Another way to write a quadratic function is to write it in the form

$$y = a(x - h)^2 + k.$$

This form has some interesting features, which will become apparent as you graph. Each member of the group should graph the following functions. In each case, label the vertex.

1. $y = 2(x - 2)^2 + 3$ **2.** $y = (x - 1)^2 + 3$ **3.** $y = 0.2(x - 2)^2 - 5$ **4.** $y = -2(x - 1)^2 - 5$

In your group, discuss these results. What do you notice about the graphs for exercises 1–4? Compare the coordinates of the vertex of each graph with the values of h and k in the function. Can you tell what the vertex will be for each of the graphs of the following functions, without graphing first? Verify your coordinates for the vertices by graphing.

5. $y = (x + 1)^2 + 4$ **6.** $y = (x - 3)^2 + 2$ **7.** $y = (x - 1)^2$ **8.** $y = x^2 - 3$

State where the vertex will be when the quadratic function is written as $y = a(x - h)^2 + k$. Later, you will learn how to take a quadratic function and transform it into this form by completing the square. This form is called the vertex form of a quadratic function. Have one member of your group present your findings to the class.

Experiencing Algebra the Write Way

In this section, you discovered how the graph of a quadratic function is affected by the coefficients of the terms. You also saw that certain points can be helpful in sketching the graph. In your own words, write a step-by-step procedure that you think would be useful in drawing graphs of quadratic functions. List all of the possible helpful features of the graph and place them in the order in which you would use them to sketch the graph. Illustrate your list with an example of a quadratic function for which you sketch the graph.

9.4 Writing Quadratic Functions

Objectives

1 Write quadratic functions given the *y*-intercept and the two *x*-intercepts.

2 Write quadratic functions given three data points.

3 Model real-world situations using quadratic functions determined from data and use the functions to make predictions.

Application

On the Moon, the gravitational force is less than on the Earth. A supply package is dropped from a space ship 1000 meters above the Moon's surface. After 5 seconds, the package is 980 meters above the ground. After 10 seconds, the package is 920 meters above the ground. Determine a position function for the distance of the package above the Moon's surface at any time *t*.

After completing this section, we will discuss this application further. See page 687.

1000 m

1 Writing Quadratic Functions Given Three Intercepts

We have graphed quadratic functions from the equation of the function. However, we may be given information in the form of a graph or data points and need to determine the equation of the function graphed.

We need at least two points to graph a linear function. For a quadratic function, we need at least three points.

The standard form of a quadratic function is the equation $y = ax^2 + bx + c$. If we know a point on the graph, we know that substituting its coordinates into the equation will result in a true statement. Therefore, if we know three points on the graph, we will know three true equations. We can use these equations to determine the values for a, b, and c.

Writing Quadratic Functions Using the y-Intercept and the Two x-Intercepts
To write a quadratic function given the y-intercept and the two x-intercepts:

- Write three equations by substituting the data points into the standard form of the quadratic function.
- Simplify the three equations.
- Substitute the value determined for c into the other two equations.
- Solve the resulting system of two equations and two unknowns.
- Substitute the values found for a, b, and c into the standard form of the quadratic function.

For example, write a quadratic function for the following graph:

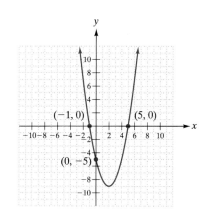

The three intercepts on the graph are $(-1, 0)$, $(5, 0)$, and $(0, -5)$. This will result in three equations:

$$y = ax^2 + bx + c \qquad \text{Standard form}$$

(1) $\quad 0 = a(-1)^2 + b(-1) + c \qquad$ Substitute $(-1, 0)$.
(2) $\quad 0 = a(5)^2 + b(5) + c \qquad$ Substitute $(5, 0)$.
(3) $\quad -5 = a(0)^2 + b(0) + c \qquad$ Substitute $(0, -5)$.

Simplify each equation.

(1) $\quad 0 = a - b + c$
(2) $\quad 0 = 25a + 5b + c$
(3) $\quad -5 = c$

Substitute -5 for c in the simplified equations (1) and (2).

(1) $\quad 0 = a - b + (-5)$
(2) $\quad 0 = 25a + 5b + (-5)$

Simplify the equations.

(1) $\quad a - b = 5$
(2) $\quad 25a + 5b = 5$

Solve the remaining system of linear equations. We will use the elimination method in the example.

(1) $\quad 5a - 5b = 25 \qquad$ Multiply both expressions by 5.
(2) $\quad \underline{25a + 5b = 5}$
$\qquad\quad 30a = 30$
$\qquad\qquad\quad a = 1$

(1) $a - b = 5$ Substitute 1 for a in equation (1).

$1 - b = 5$

$-b = 4$

$b = -4$

Therefore, $a = 1$, $b = -4$, and $c = -5$. Substitute these values in the standard form of the quadratic function.

$y = ax^2 + bx + c$

$y = (1)x^2 + (-4)x + (-5)$

$y = x^2 - 4x - 5$

Graph the function and check to see that the graph goes through the three given points.

Y1 = $x^2 - 4x - 5$

$(5, 0)$

$(-1, 0)$

$(0, -5)$

$(-47, 47, -31, 31)$

EXAMPLE 1 Write a quadratic function whose graph will pass through $(0, 2)$, $\left(\frac{3}{2}, 0\right)$, and $(-2, 0)$.

Solution

This will result in three equations:

$y = ax^2 + bx + c$ Standard form

(1) $2 = a(0)^2 + b(0) + c$ Substitute $(0, 2)$.

(2) $0 = a\left(\frac{3}{2}\right)^2 + b\left(\frac{3}{2}\right) + c$ Sustitute $\left(\frac{3}{2}, 0\right)$

(3) $0 = a(-2)^2 + b(-2) + c$ Substitute $(-2, 0)$.

Simplify each equation.

(1) $2 = c$

(2) $0 = \frac{9}{4}a + \frac{3}{2}b + c$

(3) $0 = 4a - 2b + c$

Clear the fractions in equation 2 by multiplying both expressions by the LCD of the fractions, 4.

(1) $2 = c$

(2) $0 = 9a + 6b + 4c$

(3) $0 = 4a - 2b + c$

Substitute 2 for c in the simplified equations (2) and (3).

(2) $0 = 9a + 6b + 4(2)$

(3) $0 = 4a - 2b + 2$

Simplify the equations.

(2) $9a + 6b = -8$

(3) $4a - 2b = -2$

Solve the remaining system of linear equations. We will use the elimination method in the example.

(2) $9a + 6b = -8$

(3) $\dfrac{12a - 6b = -6}{21a \qquad = -14}$ Multiply both expressions by 3.

$$a = -\frac{2}{3}$$

(3) $4a - 2b = -2$ Substitute $-\frac{2}{3}$ for a in equation (3).

$$4\left(-\frac{2}{3}\right) - 2b = -2$$

$$-\frac{8}{3} - 2b = -2$$

$$-2b = \frac{2}{3}$$

$$b = -\frac{1}{3}$$

Therefore, $a = -\frac{2}{3}$, $b = -\frac{1}{3}$, and $c = 2$. Substitute these values in the standard form of the quadratic function.

$$y = ax^2 + bx + c$$

$$y = \left(-\frac{2}{3}\right)x^2 + \left(-\frac{1}{3}\right)x + 2$$

$$y = -\frac{2}{3}x^2 - \frac{1}{3}x + 2$$

Y1 $= -\frac{2}{3}x^2 - \frac{1}{3}x + 2$

$(-47, 47, -31, 31)$

Graph the function and check to see that the graph passes through the three given points. ∎

Experiencing Algebra the Checkup Way

In exercises 1–2, write a quadratic function that has the given intercepts. Graph the function and check the points.

1. $(0, 2)$, $(1, 0)$, and $(-3, 0)$ 2. $(0, -1)$, $(-4, 0)$ and $\left(\dfrac{1}{3}, 0\right)$

3. In this section, you learned how to find the equation of a quadratic function when you know its y-intercept and its two x-intercepts. Will a quadratic function always have a y-intercept? Explain.

4. Will a quadratic function always have two x-intercepts? Explain.

---

2 Writing Quadratic Functions Given Three Points

If we do not know the y-intercept, it is more difficult to write a quadratic function given three data points.

> *Writing Quadratic Functions Using Three Data Points*
> To write a quadratic function given three data points:
>
> • Write three equations by substituting the data points into the standard form of the quadratic function.
>
> • Simplify the three equations.

- Determine two systems containing two equations each. One such choice is the first and second equation and the second and third equation.

- Eliminate the same variable in each system.

- Determine a new system containing the resulting equations.

- Solve the new system.

- Substitute the values found for a, b, and c into the standard form of the quadratic function.

For example, write a quadratic function for a graph that will pass through $(1, 9)$, $(2, 16)$, and $(3, 25)$.

This will result in the three equations:

$$y = ax^2 + bx + c$$

(1) $\quad 9 = a(1)^2 + b(1) + c$ Substitute (1, 9).

(2) $\quad 16 = a(2)^2 + b(2) + c$ Substitute (2, 16).

(3) $\quad 25 = a(3)^2 + b(3) + c$ Substitute (3, 25).

Simplify each equation.

(1) $\quad 9 = a + b + c$

(2) $\quad 16 = 4a + 2b + c$

(3) $\quad 25 = 9a + 3b + c$

Since we do not have a value for any variable, we will need to make two systems with two equations in each and eliminate the same variable in each system. We will pair equations 1 and 2 for one system and equations 2 and 3 for the other system. We will eliminate c in both systems.

First system:

(1) $\quad 9 = a + b + c$

(2) $\quad 16 = 4a + 2b + c$

(1) $\quad -9 = -a - b - c$ Multiply both expressions by -1.

(2) $\quad \underline{16 = 4a + 2b + c}$

(4) $\quad 7 = 3a + b$

Second system:

(2) $\quad 16 = 4a + 2b + c$

(3) $\quad 25 = 9a + 3b + c$

(2) $\quad -16 = -4a - 2b - c$ Multiply both expressions by -1.

(3) $\quad \underline{25 = 9a + 3b + c}$

(5) $\quad 9 = 5a + b$

Write a new system containing the two equations in a and b. Solve the system.

New system:

(4) $7 = 3a + b$

(5) $9 = 5a + b$

(4) $-7 = -3a - b$ Multiply both expressions by −1.

(5) $\underline{9 = 5a + b}$

$\quad 2 = 2a$

$\quad 1 = a$

Substitute 1 for a in an equation from the new system. Let's use equation (4), and solve for b.

(4) $7 = 3a + b$

$\ 7 = 3(1) + b$

$\ 4 = b$

Substitute a and b in an original simplified equation. Let's use equation (1).

$9 = a + b + c$

$9 = 1 + 4 + c$

$4 = c$

Therefore, $a = 1$, $b = 4$, and $c = 4$. Substitute these values in the standard form of the function.

$y = ax^2 + bx + c$

$y = (1)x^2 + (4)x + (4)$

$y = x^2 + 4x + 4$

Graph the function and check to see that the graph passes through the three given points.

Y1 = x^2 + 4x + 4

(3, 25)
(2, 16)
(1, 9)

(−47, 47, −31, 31)

EXAMPLE 2 Write a function $h(x)$ for a graph that passes through $(-3, -21)$, $(1, -5)$, and $(2, 6)$.

Solution

This will result in the three equations:

$\ h(x) = ax^2 + bx + c$ Standard form

(1) $-21 = a(-3)^2 + b(-3) + c$ Substitute (−3, −21).

(2) ${-5} = a(1)^2 + b(1) + c$ Substitute (1, −5).

(3) $6 = a(2)^2 + b(2) + c$ Substitute (2, 6).

Simplify each equation.

(1) $-21 = 9a - 3b + c$

(2) ${-5} = a + b + c$

(3) $6 = 4a + 2b + c$

Since we do not have a value for any variable, we will need to make two systems with two equations in each and eliminate the same variable in each system. We will pair equations 1 and 2 for one system and equations 2 and 3 for the other system. We will eliminate c in both systems.

First system:

(1) $-21 = 9a - 3b + c$

(2) $-5 = a + b + c$

(1) $21 = -9a + 3b - c$ Multiply both expressions by -1.

(2) $\underline{-5 = \quad a + \quad b + c}$

(4) $16 = -8a + 4b$

Second system:

(2) $-5 = a + b + c$

(3) $6 = 4a + 2b + c$

(2) $5 = -a - b - c$ Multiply both expressions by -1.

(3) $\underline{6 = 4a + 2b + c}$

(5) $11 = 3a + b$

Write a new system containing the two equations in a and b. Solve the system.

   New system:

(4) $16 = -8a + 4b$

(5) $11 = 3a + b$

(4) $16 = -8a + 4b$

(5) $\underline{-44 = -12a - 4b}$ Multiply both expressions by -4.

    $-28 = -20a$

    $\dfrac{7}{5} = a$

Substitute $\frac{7}{5}$ for a in an equation from the new system. Let's use equation 5 and solve for b.

(5) $11 = 3a + b$

    $11 = 3\left(\dfrac{7}{5}\right) + b$

    $\dfrac{34}{5} = b$

Substitute a and b in an original simplified equation. Let's use equation 2.

    $-5 = a + b + c$

    $-5 = \dfrac{7}{5} + \dfrac{34}{5} + c$

    $-\dfrac{66}{5} = c$

Therefore, $a = \frac{7}{5}$, $b = \frac{34}{5}$, and $c = -\frac{66}{5}$. Substitute these values in the standard form of the function.

    $h(x) = ax^2 + bx + c$

    $h(x) = \left(\dfrac{7}{5}\right)x^2 + \left(\dfrac{34}{5}\right)x + \left(-\dfrac{66}{5}\right)$

    $h(x) = \dfrac{7}{5}x^2 + \dfrac{34}{5}x - \dfrac{66}{5}$

$$Y1 = \tfrac{7}{5}x^2 + \tfrac{34}{5}x - \tfrac{66}{5}$$

(2, 6)
(1, −5)
(−3, −21)

$(-47, 47, -31, 31)$

Graph the function and check to see that the graph passes through the three given points. ∎

 Experiencing Algebra the Checkup Way

In exercises 1–2, write a quadratic function for a graph that passes through the points specified. Graph the function and check the given points.

1. $(1, -4), (2, 0), (-2, -4)$

2. $(2, 2), (-2, -2), (4, 10)$

3. When you obtain the three equations by substituting the three given points in the quadratic function, must you use the elimination method to solve the system of equations that results? Are there other methods that can be used to solve the system? Explain.

---

3 Modeling the Real World

We've just seen how to write a quadratic function given three data points. So what? What's the big deal? The point to realize is that in the real world, you aren't usually given a function all ready for you to graph and analyze. More often than not, you're given some data—observations, computer printouts, whatever—and you need to determine the function that fits these data. Why bother? Aha—that is part of the power of mathematics. Because once you have the function that fits the data, you can use it to predict other pairs of data. As long as the conditions for your model don't change, you can determine new data based on the function you derived from the given data. It's like getting something for nothing—nothing except some work with algebra.

EXAMPLE 3

Your laboratory partner projects a stone upward from a cliff of a height of 250 feet. After 1 second the stone is 324 feet above the base of the cliff and after 2 seconds the stone is 366 feet above the base of the cliff.

a. Write a quadratic function for the height of the stone.
b. Graph the function.
c. Use the graph to predict the length of time required for the stone to hit the ground at the base of the cliff.
d. Use the graph to predict the maximum height of the stone.

Solution

a. Let $t = $ the time in seconds

We need to determine the position function, $s(t)$. We have three data points: (0, 250), (1, 324), and (2, 366).

$$s(t) = at^2 + bt + c \qquad \text{Standard form}$$

(1) $250 = a(0)^2 + b(0) + c$ Substitute (0, 250).

(2) $324 = a(1)^2 + b(1) + c$ Substitute (1, 324).

(3) $366 = a(2)^2 + b(2) + c$ Substitute (2, 366).

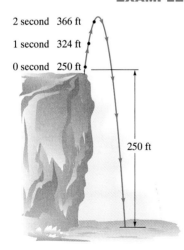

2 second 366 ft
1 second 324 ft
0 second 250 ft

250 ft

Simplify each equation.

(1) $250 = c$

(2) $324 = a + b + c$

(3) $366 = 4a + 2b + c$

Since we know $c = 250$, we substitute 250 for c in the simplified equations 2 and 3.

(2) $324 = a + b + 250$

(3) $366 = 4a + 2b + 250$

Simplify the equations.

(2) $a + b = 74$

(3) $2a + b = 58$

Solve the remaining system of linear equations. We will use the elimination method in the example.

(2) $-a - b = -74$ Multiply both expressions by −1.

(3) $\underline{2a + b = 58}$

$a = -16$

$a = -16$

(2) $a + b = 74$ Substitute −16 for a in equation 2.

$-16 + b = 74$

$b = 90$

Therefore, $a = -16$, $b = 90$, and $c = 250$. Substitute these values in the standard form of the quadratic function.

$$s(t) = at^2 + bt + c$$
$$s(t) = -16t^2 + 90t + 250$$

c. $Y1 = -16x^2 + 90x + 250$

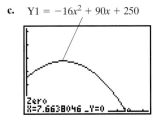

(0, 9.4, 0, 620)

d. $Y1 = -16x^2 + 90x + 250$

(0, 9.4, 0, 620)

b. $Y1 = -16x^2 + 90x + 250$

(0, 9.4, 0, 620)

c. Trace the graph to determine when the stone's position is 0 feet above the ground, or $s(t) = 0$.

The stone will hit the ground in approximately 7.66 seconds.

d. Trace the graph to determine the absolute maximum of the function, or the function value of the vertex.

The stone will reach a maximum height of approximately 376.56 feet.

■

Application

On the Moon, the gravitational force is less than on the Earth. A supply package is dropped from a space ship 1000 meters above the Moon's surface.

1000 m

After 5 seconds, the package is 980 meters above ground. After 10 seconds, the package is 920 meters above the ground. Determine a position function for the distance of the package above the Moon's surface at any time t.

Discussion

Let $\quad t =$ time in seconds after release
$\quad\quad s(t) =$ position of package in meters above ground

The data points for the position function are $(0, 1000)$, $(5, 980)$, and $(10, 920)$.

$$s(t) = at^2 + bt + c$$

(1) $\quad 1000 = a(0)^2 + b(0) + c$
(2) $\quad 980 = a(5)^2 + b(5) + c$
(3) $\quad 920 = a(10)^2 + b(10) + c$

Simplify each equation.

(1) $\quad 1000 = c$
(2) $\quad\;\; 980 = 25a + 5b + c$
(3) $\quad\;\; 920 = 100a + 10b + c$

Substitute 1000 for c in the simplified equations 2 and 3.

(2) $\quad 980 = 25a + 5b + 1000$
(3) $\quad 920 = 100a + 10b + 1000$

Simplify the equations.

(2) $\quad 25a + 5b = -20$
(3) $\quad 100a + 10b = -80$

Solve the remaining system of linear equations. We will use the elimination method in the example.

(2) $\quad -100a - \;\;\; 20b = 80$ $\qquad$ Multiply both expressions by -4.
(3) $\quad\underline{\;\;\;\; 100a + \;\;\; 10b = -80}$
$\qquad\qquad\qquad -10b = 0$
$\qquad\qquad\qquad\quad\;\; b = 0$

(2) $\quad 25a + 5(0) = -20$ $\qquad$ Substitute 0 for b in equation 2.
$\qquad\qquad\; 25a = -20$
$\qquad\qquad\quad\; a = -0.8$

Therefore, $a = -0.8$, $b = 0$, and $c = 1000$. Substitute these values in the standard form of the quadratic function.

$$s(t) = at^2 + bt + c$$
$$\quad\; = -0.8t^2 + 1000$$ ∎

Y1 $= -0.8x^2 + 1000$

$(0, 1000)$ $\;\;(5, 980)$
$\qquad\qquad(10, 920)$

$(-47, 47, 0, 1550)$

 Experiencing Algebra the Checkup Way

A message in an attache case is thrown downward from a plane that is 1500 feet above the water. After 1 second, the case is 1454 feet above the water and after 2 seconds, it is 1376 feet above the water. Write a quadratic position function for the distance the case is above the water after t seconds. How long will it take the case to reach the water?

PROBLEM SET 9.4

Experiencing Algebra the Exercise Way

Write the quadratic function for the graph that passes through the given x-intercepts and y-intercept. Graph the function and check the given points.

1. $(2, 0), (-4, 0), (0, -8)$ **2.** $(3, 0), (-1, 0), (0, 3)$ **3.** $(-4, 0), \left(\frac{1}{2}, 0\right), (0, -4)$ **4.** $(-1, 0), \left(\frac{2}{3}, 0\right), (0, -2)$

5. $(0, 3), (3, 0), (-3, 0)$ **6.** $(0, 1), (4, 0), (-4, 0)$ **7.** $(0, -4), (2, 0), (-4, 0)$ **8.** $(0, -2), (3, 0), (-2, 0)$

9. $\left(0, \frac{2}{3}\right), (-2, 0), (2, 0)$ **10.** $\left(0, \frac{1}{4}\right), (1, 0), (-2, 0)$ **11.** $(0, -2), \left(\frac{1}{2}, 0\right), \left(\frac{9}{2}, 0\right)$ **12.** $(0, 1), \left(\frac{1}{3}, 0\right), \left(\frac{-2}{3}, 0\right)$

Write a quadratic function for a graph that passes through the points specified. Graph the function and check the given points.

13. $(2, -15), (-2, -7), (-4, 9)$ **14.** $(2, -8), (4, 10), (-5, -8)$ **15.** $(1, -10), (-2, 5), (2, -7)$

16. $(-1, 10), (1, -12), (3, -10)$ **17.** $(3, 2), (-3, 14), (6, 5)$ **18.** $(2, 1), (-2, -3), (-4, 4)$

19. $(-1, -2), (1, 6), (4, 3)$ **20.** $(2, -3), (-2, 5), (1, 2)$ **21.** $(-1, -3), (-2, -5), (1, -11)$

22. $(2, -3), (-2, -15), (6, -7)$ **23.** $(-2, 4), \left(-3, \frac{5}{2}\right), \left(-1, \frac{13}{2}\right)$ **24.** $\left(5, \frac{13}{3}\right), (6, 4), (3, 7)$

In exercises 25–30, solve using the position function, $s(t) = at^2 + bt + c$. Round your answers to the nearest tenth of a second.

25. A tennis ball is thrown upward from a height of 150 feet. After 1 second, it is 146 feet above the ground; after 2 seconds, it is 110 feet above the ground. Write the position function for the ball. How long will it take for the ball to reach the ground?

26. A custard pie is thrown upward from a height of 220 feet. After 1 second, the pie is 222 feet above the ground. After 3 seconds, it is 130 feet above the ground. Write a position function for the pie. How many seconds will it take to reach the ground?

27. A movie stunt dummy is dropped from a height of 400 feet. After 2 seconds it is 336 feet above the ground. After 4 seconds, it is 144 feet above the ground. Write the position function for the dummy. How many seconds will it take to fall to the ground?

400 ft

28. A child drops a Beanie Baby from a height of 600 feet. After 2 seconds it is 536 feet above the ground. After 3 seconds, it is 456 feet above the ground. Write the position function for the toy. How many seconds will it take to fall to the ground?

29. An empty fuel cylinder is dropped from a lunar module 2000 feet above the surface of the Moon. After 10 seconds, the cylinder is 1730 feet above the lunar surface. After 20 seconds, it is 920 feet above the lunar surface. Determine the position function for the distance of the cylinder above the surface at any time. After how many seconds will the cylinder touch the surface?

30. A probe is ejected upward from a lunar module 3000 feet above the surface of the Moon. After 10 seconds, the probe is 2980 feet above the lunar surface. After 20 seconds, it is 2420 feet above the lunar surface. Determine the position function for the distance of the probe above the surface at any time. How many seconds will it take for the probe to reach the lunar surface?

31. In 1980, dry natural gas production in North America was 23.06 trillion cubic feet. In 1985, the production dropped to 20.39 trillion cubic feet, and in 1992, it rose to 23.20 trillion cubic feet. If x represents the number of years since 1980, these data points become (0, 23.06), (5, 20.39), and (12, 23.20). Write the quadratic function whose graph contains these points. What would this function predict the natural gas production to be for the year 2000? Do you think it is reasonable to assume that production would continue to increase as this function indicates? Explain your answer.

32. In 1980, dry natural gas production worldwide was 53.11 trillion cubic feet. In 1985, the production rose to 61.78 trillion cubic feet, and in 1992, it rose to 75.00 trillion cubic feet. If x represents the number of years since 1980, these data points become (0, 53.11), (5, 61.78), and (12, 75.00). Write the quadratic function whose graph contains these points. What would the function predict the production to be for 1997? Do you think this is a reasonable way to predict production? Explain your answer.

33. The *Chicago Tribune*[1] reported that there were 738 McDonald's franchises in the United States in 1965. In 1975, the number of franchises grew to 3352, and in 1985, the number of franchises was 6972. Write a quadratic function whose graph contains these points. Explain how you define the independent variable, x. Use the function to predict the number of franchises in 1995. How close is your prediction to the actual number of franchises, which was reported to be 10,953? Do you think the function is a good predictor? Explain your answer.

34. An article in the *Chicago Tribune* noted that the African country of Zimbabwe is a prosperous country that has experienced a population explosion.[2] The population, in millions, was 2.7 in 1950, 5.3 in 1970, and 7.1 in 1980. Write a quadratic function whose graph contains these points. Use the function to predict the population, in millions, for 1990. How does your prediction compare to the actual number of 9.9 reported in the article? Is the function a good predictor? Explain your answer.

35. Cal's Contracting Service offers to build various-size rectangular patios for its customers. One patio with a width of 5 yards is advertised to cover 75 square yards. Another with a width of 10 yards covers 100 square yards. A third with a width of 8 yards covers 96 square yards. Write three coordinate pairs, where the independent variable is the width of the patio and the dependent variable is the area of the patio.

   a. Determine the quadratic function that has these pairs as solutions.

   b. Graph the function.

   c. Determine the vertex of the graph and interpret its meaning.

36. Triangular sailcloths are sold in various sizes. A cloth with a height of 4 feet covers an area of 32 square feet. Another with a height of 8 feet covers an area of 96 square feet. A third with a height of 12 feet covers an area of 192 square feet. Write three coordinate pairs, where the independent variable is the height of the cloth and the dependent variable is the area of the cloth.

[1] *Chicago Tribune*, January 21, 1996, sec. 1, pp. 1, 7.
[2] *Chicago Tribune*, January 30, 1996, sec. 1, p. 8.

a. Determine the quadratic function that has these pairs as solutions.

   b. Graph the function.

   c. Determine the domain of the function and interpret its meaning.

 ## Experiencing Algebra the Calculator Way

In the study of statistics, a technique is used to "fit" coordinate pairs to a function. The technique is called regression analysis. While it is intended to statistically analyze data, it can be used to find the quadratic function that passes through three points in the coordinate plane. Many calculators include this feature. We will illustrate the keystrokes needed to apply this technique. As an example, suppose we wish to find the quadratic function that passes through the points $(-2, 42)$, $(1, -9)$, and $(3, 57)$.

- Clear the lists where the three data points will be stored:

  [STAT] [4] [2nd] [L1] [,] [2nd] [L2] [ENTER] . The calculator will respond "Done."

- Enter the coordinate pairs in L1 for x, and L2 for y:

  [STAT] [1] . Key the values of x into L1, pressing [ENTER] after each one. Then move the cursor to L2 with the [▶] key. Key the values of y into L2, pressing [ENTER] after each one. Be sure the x and y values are correctly paired in the two columns. Then exit with [2nd] [QUIT] .

- Now you are ready to calculate the function:

  [STAT] [▶] [5] [2nd] [L1] [,] [2nd] [L2] [ENTER] . The calculator displays:

  QuadReg
  $y = ax^2 + bx + c$
  $a = 10$
  $b = -7$
  $c = -12$

- You have obtained the quadratic function

  $y = 10x^2 - 7x - 12.$

  If you graph this function, you will see that its graph does indeed pass through the three points specified.

Follow this procedure to determine the quadratic function that passes through the following points.

1. $(5, 15.8)$, $(15, 130.8)$, $(25, 353.8)$ **2.** $(1, 767)$, $(2, 1526)$, $(4, 3344)$ **3.** $(-2, 53)$, $(-1, -66)$, $(2, 297)$

You may wish to go back and use this method to rework some of the exercises in this section that asked you to determine a quadratic function, given three coordinate pairs.

Experiencing Algebra the Group Way

Many models used in mathematics are functions. Some are linear functions; others are nonlinear. Data gathered from a real-world situation can be used to write mathematical functions to represent the situation. Consider the following data, which come from a production and sales situation. Work together in your group to carry out the development of the mathematical models suggested here.

Number of Items Produced and Sold	5	30	35	40
Cost of production	$155		$335	$365
Revenue from sales	$450	$1200	$1050	
Profit				

1. Make ordered pairs of the data, using the number of items produced and sold as the independent variable, and the cost of production as the dependent variable. Plot the data. Does the graph look linear? If so, write a linear function of the form $C(x) = mx + b$ for the relation.

2. Make another set of ordered pairs of data, using the same independent variable, but using revenue from sales as the dependent variable. Plot these data. Does the graph look like a quadratic function? If so, write a quadratic function of the form $R(x) = ax^2 + bx + c$ for the relation.

3. Use the functions to fill in the missing data in the preceding table for cost of production and revenue. Then complete the last line of the table by calculating profit as revenue minus cost of production.

4. Make a third set of ordered pairs of data, using the same independent variable, but using profit as the dependent variable. Graph these data pairs. Does the relation appear to be a quadratic function? If so, use three of the data pairs to write a quadratic function to represent this relation. Check the relation to see whether the fourth data pair satisfies the function.

5. For the profit function, find the values of x that make the profit function 0 or less. Discuss what these points represent.

6. For the profit function, find the coordinates of the vertex. Discuss what these values represent.

This is an example of using mathematical models to represent data. Other techniques may be studied to find the "best fit" of a function for a set of data. Once a function has been obtained, it can be used to explain relationships and to answer questions about a relationship. It is a very powerful technique for understanding data. Discuss what this example means to you as a meaningful use of mathematics.

Experiencing Algebra the Write Way

In this section, it was stated that you need two coordinate pairs to determine a linear relationship between two variables, and you need three coordinate pairs to determine a quadratic relationship between two variables. Discuss why this is so. Then consider what would happen if you had more than two coordinate pairs and wished to establish a linear relationship. Also discuss what would happen if you had more than three coordinate pairs and wished to establish a quadratic relationship. What problems could you encounter in each case? How would you deal with these?

| CHAPTER 9 | **Summary** |

After completing this chapter, you should be able to define in your own words the following key terms, definitions, and rules.

Terms
algebraic expression
terms
constant term
variable term
numerical coefficient
coefficient
like terms
collect like terms
monomial
polynomial
binomial
trinomial
degree of a term
degree of a polynomial
descending order
ascending order

evaluating
relation
polynomial relation
domain
table of values
graph
range
absolute minimum
absolute maximum
function
function notation
quadratic function
parabola
quadratic term
concave upward
concave downward
relative maximum

relative minimum
vertex
axis of symmetry

Definitions
Polynomial relation
Polynomial function
Standard form for a quadratic
function

Rules
Vertical line test
Writing quadratic functions using the
y-intercept and the two
x-intercepts
Writing quadratic functions using three
data points

| CHAPTER 9 | **Review** |

Reflections

1. In this chapter, you studied polynomial expressions and polynomial functions (or equations). Explain the difference between these two terms.

2. What is the difference between the degree of a polynomial expression and the degree of a term of a polynomial expression?

3. What is the difference between simplifying a polynomial expression and evaluating a polynomial expression?

4. Explain how the graph of a quadratic function differs from the graph of a linear function.

5. Given a graph, describe the difference between a parabola that is concave upward and one that is concave downward. Given an equation, explain when the graph of the parabola is concave upward and when it is concave downward.

6. The graph of a polynomial function may have relative maxima and an absolute maximum. Alternatively, the graph may have relative minima and an absolute minimum. Explain the differences in these terms.

7. In the graph of a quadratic function, what is the relationship between the vertex of the parabola and the axis of symmetry?

8. In order to determine the equation of a line from information about points that lie on the graph, you must have two coordinate pairs. In order to determine the equation of a parabola from information about points that lie on the graph, you must have three coordinate pairs. Can you explain why you need an additional coordinate pair?

9.1
Determine whether each expression is a polynomial. For those that are polynomials, classify them as monomials, binomials, trinomials, or polynomials.

1. x

2. $5x - 3$

3. $\sqrt{x} + 2$

4. $3x^3 - 4x^2 + x - 1$

5. $\dfrac{3}{a} - 2a + 1$

6. $3a^4 - 2a^2 + 5$

Determine the degree of each term of each polynomial and then the degree of the polynomial.

7. $5x + 3x^3 - 2$

8. $2x^2y + 3xy - 5$

9. $x + 9$

10. $0.5a - 3.1a^2 + 9.6a + 3.1a^2$

11. $12x^2 + 30x + 3$

Write each polynomial in descending order.

12. $5y^2 + 11y^4 + 12 - 6y + 9y^3$

13. $5 - p$

14. $\frac{1}{4}z^4 + \frac{1}{2}z^2 + z + \frac{1}{3}z^3 + 1$

15. $0.6b - 2.3b^5 + 1.8 - 9.1b^3$

Evaluate $2x^3 + 11x^2 - 21x - 90$ for the given values.

16. $x = 3$

17. $x = 0$

18. $x = 1$

19. $x = -6$

20. $x = -\dfrac{5}{2}$

In exercises 21–26, evaluate $a^3 + 2a^2b - 3ab^2 - b^3$ for the given values.

21. $a = 0, b = 1$

22. $a = -1, b = 0$

23. $a = 0, b = 0$

24. $a = 1, b = 1$

25. $a = -1, b = 1$

26. $a = -1, b = -1$

27. Write a polynomial for the perimeter of a rectangle whose length is numerically equal to the square of its width. What is the perimeter if the rectangle has a width of 7 yards?

28. Write a polynomial for the perimeter of a triangle whose second side is three times as long as the first side and whose third side is numerically equal to 1 inch more than the square of the first side. What is the perimeter if the triangle's first side measures 4 inches?

29. Write a polynomial for the total area of the figures shown.

30. Write a polynomial for the shaded area shown.

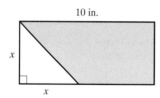

31. A triangular flower garden with a height of x feet and a base of y feet is placed in the center of a square lawn that measures z feet on a side. Write a polynomial for the area of the lawn not covered by the garden. What is this area if the triangle has a height of 6 feet and a base of 10 feet, and the lawn measures 80 feet on a side?

32. A contractor charges a flat fee of $500 plus $40 per square foot to build an addition onto an existing home. The contractor incurs setup costs of $275 plus a materials cost of $12 per square foot.

   a. Write a polynomial to represent the charge for a room.

   b. Write a polynomial to represent the cost to the contractor to build the room.

   c. What are the revenue and cost for building a room that is 15 feet wide and 25 feet long? What would be the net return for taking on this job?

9.2

33. Create a table of values for the polynomial relation, $y = x^3 - x^2 - 6x$, where x is an integer between -4 and 4.

Graphically determine the range of each function.

34. $y = -3x + 5$

35. $y = 2x^2 - 2x - 12$

36. $y = x^3 + 2x^2 - 5x - 6$

37. $y = x^4 + 2x^3 - 5x^2 - 6x$

In exercises 38–42, evaluate the function $f(x) = 3x^3 - x^2 + 2x - 4$ at the given values.

38. $f(-2)$

39. $f(0)$

40. $f(2)$

41. $f\left(-\dfrac{1}{2}\right)$

42. $f(1.7)$

43. Tony's Tees will discount the price of a T-shirt depending on the number purchased. If a person purchases x shirts, the price per shirt will be $(12 - 0.50x)$ dollars. Tony pays $4 per shirt.

    a. If x shirts are sold, the revenue function for the sale is $R(x) = 12x - 0.50x^2$. Determine the revenue if 5 shirts are sold; if 10 shirts are sold; if 15 shirts are sold; if 20 shirts are sold; if 25 shirts are sold. What does this tell you about limits that should be placed on the price per shirt?

    b. If x shirts are sold, the total cost to Tony of these shirts is $C(x) = 4x$. What is the cost to Tony of 5 shirts; 10 shirts; 15 shirts; 20 shirts?

    c. Use the results from parts (a) and (b) to determine how much profit will be made from a sale of 5 shirts; 10 shirts; 15 shirts; 20 shirts.

    d. What would you tell Tony to do in terms of limiting the price per shirt?

44. A statistical study related the cost of milk production, y, with the number of gallons produced, x. The relation developed was

$$y = 15{,}800 + 2.2x - 0.001x^2.$$

where x is measured in gallons and y is measured in dollars. Use the relation to estimate the cost for the following number of gallons produced.

Gallons (x)	900	1000	1100	1200	1300	1400
Cost (y)						

What does this relation tell you about the cost of production? If you were the owner of the dairy farm, can you suggest a strategy to contain your cost of production, based upon what this table shows?

9.3

Identify each equation as quadratic or nonquadratic.

45. $y = x^2 + x + 1$

46. $y = x^3 - x - 1$

47. $y = \dfrac{5}{x^2} + x + 1$

48. $y = x^2 + 4x + 4$

Complete the table. Check using the calculator.

	Function	Coefficients			Properties of Graph			
		a	*b*	*c*	Wide/Narrow	Concave Upward/Downward	Vertex	Axis of Symmetry
49.	$y = -\dfrac{1}{4}x^2 + \dfrac{1}{2}x + 1$							
50.	$f(x) = -2x^2 + 4x$							
51.	$g(x) = \dfrac{1}{3}x^2 + x$							
52.	$y = 3x^2 - 3x + 1$							

In exercises 53–55, graph each quadratic function. Label the vertex. Draw and label the axis of symmetry.

53. $f(x) = x^2 + 2x - 8$ **54.** $y = -\dfrac{1}{2}x^2 + x - 2$ **55.** $h(x) = 2x^2 - 8$

56. The length of a patio measures 8 feet more than its width. If the width of the patio is denoted by w, its area is given by the function $A(w) = w^2 + 8w$. Graph the function and find its vertex. Does the vertex have any physical meaning?

57. A bridal photographer sets the price of 8-by-10-inch wedding photos by the number of photos ordered. If the bride orders x photos, the price will be $(30 - 0.50x)$ dollars for each photo ordered, and the total revenue will be $R(x) = 30x - 0.50x^2$ dollars for the sale. Graph the function and find its vertex. Explain what this vertex represents.

58. An egg is thrown upward with a velocity of 60 feet per second from a height of 120 feet. The position function for the egg is given by $s(t) = -16t^2 + 60t + 120$. Determine the vertex of the function and interpret the values. How long will it take the egg to reach the ground?

9.4

In exercises 59–61, write the quadratic function for the graph that passes through the given three points. Check by graphing.

59. $(8, 0), (-3, 0), (0, -24)$ **60.** $(0, 5), (5, 0), \left(-\dfrac{1}{2}, 0\right)$ **61.** $(2, -4), (4, -6), (7, 6)$

62. Use the position function, $s(t) = at^2 + bt + c$, to solve the following application. A hammer is thrown upward from a height of 160 feet. After 1 second, it is 176 feet above the ground. After two seconds, it is 160 feet above the ground. Write the position function for the falling hammer. To the nearest tenth of a second, how long will it take the hammer to reach the ground?

63. In 1910, the number of people age 65 and over in the United States was 4.0 million. In 1950, the number had grown to 12.4 million. In 1990, the number was 31.2 million. Write a quadratic function that relates the number of people age 65 and over to the number of years since 1900. The actual numbers of people age 65 and over were 25.5 million in 1980, 20.1 million in 1970, and 16.7 million in 1960. How well does your quadratic function predict these values? Would you conclude that a quadratic function is a good model to use for these data? What would you predict the number of people age 65 and over to be in the year 2000?

CHAPTER 9	**Mixed Review**

Evaluate $2x^3 - 3x^2 - 29x - 30$ for the given values.

1. $x = 5$ **2.** $x = 0$ **3.** $x = 1$

4. $x = -2$ **5.** $x = -\dfrac{3}{2}$

Evaluate $2a^3 + 4a^2b - 2ab^2 + b^3$ for the given values.

6. $a = -1, b = 0$ **7.** $a = 1, b = 1$ **8.** $a = -1, b = 1$ **9.** $a = -1, b = -1$

10. Classify each expression as a monomial, a binomial, a trinomial, or polynomial. Determine the degree of each term and the degree of the polynomial. Write the polynomial in descending order.
   a. $5 + 3x^2$ **b.** $15a^2 - 5a^3 + 4 + a$ **c.** $5x^4 + x - 2 + x^5 - 3x^2$

11. Classify each expression as a monomial, a binomial, a trinomial, or polynomial. Determine the degree of each term and the degree of the polynomial.
   a. $7b + 3b^2 - 4 + 6b$ **b.** $3x^2y - 4xy + 3xy^2 + 5 - 4x^2y^2$ **c.** $4xyz - 2 + 3xyz - 5 - xyz + 7$

In exercises 12–16, evaluate the function $f(x) = 2x^3 - 3x^2 - 23x + 12$ at the given values.

12. $f(-3)$ **13.** $f(0)$ **14.** $f(4)$

15. $f\left(\dfrac{1}{2}\right)$ **16.** $f(2.2)$

17. Construct a table of values for the polynomial relation $y = 2x^3 + 2x^2 - 12x$, where x is an integer between -4 and 4.

Graphically determine the range of each function.

18. $y = 4x - 2$ **19.** $y = 3x^2 + 3x - 6$
20. $y = x^3 - 3x^2 - 13x + 15$ **21.** $y = x^4 - 3x^3 - 13x^2 + 15x$

Graph each quadratic function, labeling the vertex and drawing the axis of symmetry.

22. $f(x) = 2x^2 + 7x - 4$ **23.** $y = \dfrac{1}{4}x^2 - x + 3$ **24.** $h(x) = -x^2 + 9$

Complete the table. Check using your calculator.

	Function	Coefficients			Properties of Graph			
		a	b	c	Wide/Narrow	Concave Upward/Downward	Vertex	Axis of Symmetry
25.	$y = \dfrac{1}{3}x^2 + \dfrac{2}{3}x + 1$							
26.	$f(x) = -3x^2 + 6x$							
27.	$y = -\dfrac{1}{4}x^2 + x + 3$							
28.	$g(x) = 2x^2 + 4x - 6$							

In exercises 29–31, write the quadratic function for the graph that passes through the given three points. Check by graphing.

29. $(-2, 12), (-4, 8), (-7, 17)$ **30.** $(9, 0), (-4, 0), (0, -36)$ **31.** $(0, -12), (3, 0), \left(-\dfrac{4}{3}, 0\right)$

32. Write a polynomial for the perimeter of a rectangle whose length has a numerical value that is 5 units more than the cube of the numerical value for its width. What is the perimeter if the width of the rectangle is 3 feet?

33. Write a polynomial for the perimeter of a triangle whose second side has a numerical value that is 3 units less than twice the numerical value of its first side, and whose third side has a numerical value that is 7 units less than the square of the numerical value of its first side. What is the perimeter if the first side of the triangle measures 10 centimeters?

34. Write a polynomial for the total area of the figures shown.

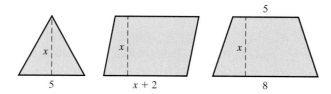

35. Write a polynomial for the shaded area shown.

36. A circular pool with a radius of z feet is placed in a rectangular yard with a length of x feet and a width of y feet. Write a polynomial for the area of the yard not covered by the pool. What does this area measure if the pool has a radius of 8 feet and the yard measures 50 feet by 80 feet?

37. Kitchen floor tiles measure 1 foot on a side and sell for $1.50 each. A contractor offers to retile the kitchen floor for a payment of $800. The floor is rectangular.

   a. Write a polynomial to represent the cost to the contractor for the materials.

   b. Write a polynomial to represent the net return (payment minus cost) that the contractor will realize on the job.

   c. What will be the net return for a kitchen whose width is 10 feet and whose length is 15 feet?

38. A reward system for grades has been designed to be progressive. Pop will pay his child for a report card with no failing grades according to the number of A's earned. If the child earns x grades of A, Pop will pay the child $10 + 2x$ dollars for each A. Thus the total amount Pop will pay the child is $P(x) = 10x + 2x^2$.

   a. Set up a table of possible values to show how much the child can earn for his report card, given that he is enrolled in seven classes.

   b. Interpret the table. What can you say about the payments in relation to the number of A's?

39. A director of a business school graduate program wanted to relate a student's grade point average (GPA) in the school's master of business administration (MBA) program with the student's GPA in undergraduate school and the student's score on the standardized test given to business school applicants (GMAT). He developed the mathematical model

$$y = -0.25 + 0.5x + 0.0082z - 0.0000081z^2,$$

where

y is the student's GPA in the MBA program,
x is the student's GPA in undergraduate school, and
z is the student's score on the GMAT.

a. Using this model, what would you predict a student's GPA to be if her undergraduate GPA was 3.71 and her GMAT score was 750?

b. Assume a student has an undergraduate GPA of 3.50. Complete the following table to relate his GPA in the MBA program to his GMAT score.

GMAT score (z)	500	550	600	650	700	750
GPA in MBA (y)						

c. This table should surprise you. What does it say about the relationship between the entrance exam score (GMAT) and the student's performance in graduate school?

40. A supply package is dropped from a lunar module hovering at 1500 meters above the surface. The position function for the package is $s(t) = -0.8t^2 + 1500$, where t is the number of seconds since the drop. Graph the function. How many seconds will it take for the object to reach the ground?

41. In 1920, the divorce rate per 1000 population was 1.6; in 1940, the divorce rate was 2.0; and in 1970, the divorce rate was 3.5. Write a quadratic function to use as a mathematical model that relates the divorce rate to the number of years since 1900. In 1930, the actual divorce rate was 1.6 and in 1990 it was 4.7. How well does your function predict these values? Would you conclude that the function is a good mathematical model to use to explain the relation between the divorce rate and time? What does the model predict the divorce rate will be for the year 2000?

CHAPTER 9 | **Test**

Test-Taking Tips

When reviewing material for a test, it is important to read carefully and deliberately. Do not read your mathematics text the same way that you read a history book, a novel, or a newspaper. You must read a mathematics text slowly, absorbing each and every word. You may have to reread the material several times until it begins to make sense. Each word or symbol is important because mathematics texts have many thoughts condensed into a few statements.

Do not try to memorize illustrative examples. You will be overwhelmed with memorization, and the further you go, the more difficult this will be. Much of mathematics is based upon a few fundamental principles (for example, the distributive property) and definitions (for example, *integers*). Concentrate on these principles and definitions and commit them to memory. Try to see how each example is just a reapplication of these principles and definitions, and you won't have to memorize the examples.

Classify each expression as a monomial, a binomial, a trinomial, or a polynomial.

1. $123x^2 y^3 z$

2. $3a^3 + 5a^2 b + 7ab^2 + 9b^3$

3. $2 - c$

Determine the degree of each polynomial.

4. $13 - 3x^3 + 6x - 0.5x^5 + 1.7x^2 - x^4$

5. $5x^2 y^3 + 3xy^2 - y + 17$

Write the polynomial in descending order.

6. $15 + 3x^4 - 7x + x^5 + 9x^2 + 21x$

Write the polynomial in ascending order.

7. $a - \dfrac{2}{3}a^3 - \dfrac{5}{6}a^2 - \dfrac{4}{9}$

Evaluate $a^2 + 3ab^3 - 7b^2 - b - 6$ for the given values.

8. $a = 0, b = 3$ **9.** $a = -2, b = 0$ **10.** $a = 2, b = -3$

11. Carpeting for a living room sells for \$16.50 per square yard, with an installation charge of \$75.00. Write a polynomial for the total cost of carpeting a rectangular room. What will the cost be for a room that measures 15 feet by 22 feet, which is 5 yards by $7\frac{1}{3}$ yards?

Given $g(x) = 3x^2 + 7x - 6$, find

12. $g(-3)$.   **13.** $g(0)$.   **14.** $g(1)$.

Consider the relation $y = \dfrac{1}{2}x^2 - 2x - 6$.

15. Graph the relation.   **16.** Find the vertex.   **17.** Graphically determine the range of the relation.

18. Is this relation a function? Justify your answer.

Complete the following table.

	Function	Coefficients			Properties of Graph			
		a	b	c	Wide/Narrow	Concave Upward/Downward	Vertex	Axis of Symmetry
19.	$y = \dfrac{1}{2}x^2 + 2x + 3$							
20.	$y = 3x^2 - 3x + \dfrac{1}{4}$							

In exercises 21–22, write the quadratic function for the graph that passes through the given points.

21. $(0, 8), (2, 0), (4, 0)$ **22.** $(-1, 6), (1, 4), (2, 9)$

23. Define what is meant by the term *quadratic function*. Describe the special features of such a function. Explain how you would sketch the graph of such a function.

Working with Polynomial Expressions

W e've seen how to write and evaluate polynomials and how to graph them; our next step is to learn how to work with them. We will look at how to add, subtract, multiply, and divide polynomials. In addition, we will study methods of factoring a polynomial; that is, breaking it down into its simpler component factors. This will turn out to be very important for simplifying complicated polynomial expressions and making them easier to work with when solving polynomial equations and inequalities and dealing with rational expressions.

Geometric figures often involve areas and volumes that can be described by polynomial expressions. Designers and architects must work with these expressions as they draw plans for efficient use of space in a home, office, or manufacturing plant. Engineers and construction workers also use these polynomials as a check on the dimensions written on the plans and materials lists. We will describe some of these applications of working with polynomials in each section of this chapter.

10.1 Rules for Exponents

Objectives   1 Rewrite exponential expressions using the definitions for exponential expressions.

2 Simplify exponential expressions using the product rule.

3 Simplify exponential expressions using the quotient rule.

4 Simplify exponential expressions using the power-to-a-power rule.

5 Simplify exponential expressions using the product-to-a-power or quotient-to-a-power rule.

6 Model real-world situations using exponential expressions.

Application   Determine the area of a square mail room with sides of length s feet. A publishing company is expanding into new offices, and the new mail room will still be a square, but with sides of length $2s$. Determine the area of the new mail room and compare it to the area of the original mail room.

After completing this section, we will discuss this application further. See page 710.

---

1 Defining Exponential Expressions

We have discussed numeric exponential expressions in previous chapters. An **exponential expression** is an expression that has a **base** and an **exponent**. An example of a numeric exponential expression is 4^3. The base is 4 and the exponent is 3. We evaluate this expression by writing it in **expanded form** and using repeated multiplication. The base is repeated as a factor for the number of times represented by the exponent. That is, $4^3 = 4 \cdot 4 \cdot 4 = 64$.

In Chapter 2, we defined an exponential expression with a nonzero base and a zero exponent as equal to 1. That is, $4^0 = 1$.

Remember, 0^0 is indeterminate. We will explain why this is true later in this chapter.

It is not conventional to write an exponent of 1, though we might do this in an intermediate step in solving a problem. 4^1 is written as 4.

To evaluate an exponential expression with a nonzero base raised to a negative exponent, rewrite it as an exponential expression with the reciprocal of the base and the opposite value of the exponent (a positive number). For example,

$$4^{-3} = \left(\frac{4}{1}\right)^{-3} = \left(\frac{1}{4}\right)^{3} = \frac{1}{4} \cdot \frac{1}{4} \cdot \frac{1}{4} = \frac{1}{4^3} = \frac{1}{64}.$$

$$\frac{1}{4^{-3}} = \frac{1}{\left(\frac{4}{1}\right)^{-3}} = \frac{1}{\left(\frac{1}{4}\right)^{3}} = \frac{1}{\frac{1}{4} \cdot \frac{1}{4} \cdot \frac{1}{4}} = \frac{1}{\frac{1}{4^3}} = 1 \div \frac{1}{4^3} = 1 \cdot \frac{4^3}{1} = 4^3 = 64$$

Remember that 0 raised to a negative exponent is undefined. For example, $0^{-2} = \left(\frac{0}{1}\right)^{-2} = \left(\frac{1}{0}\right)^{2}$, which is undefined.

We define variable exponential expressions in the same manner as numeric exponential expressions.

> *Integer Exponents*
> For any base a and nonnegative integer exponent n,
>
> $$a^n = a \cdot a \cdot a \cdot \ldots \cdot a. \quad \text{n factors}$$
>
> $$a^1 = a.$$
>
> $$a^0 = 1, \text{where } a \neq 0.$$
>
> $$a^{-n} = \frac{1}{a^n}, \text{where } a \neq 0.$$
>
> $$\frac{1}{a^{-n}} = a^n, \text{where } a \neq 0.$$
>
> The base a may be a constant, a variable, or an expression.

For example,

$$x^4 = x \cdot x \cdot x \cdot x$$
$$x^1 = x$$

For all $x \neq 0$,

$$x^0 = 1$$

$$x^{-4} = \left(\frac{x}{1}\right)^{-4} = \left(\frac{1}{x}\right)^4 = \frac{1}{x^4}$$

$$\frac{1}{x^{-4}} = \frac{1}{\left(\frac{1}{x}\right)^4} = \frac{1}{\frac{1}{x} \cdot \frac{1}{x} \cdot \frac{1}{x} \cdot \frac{1}{x}} = \frac{1}{\frac{1}{x^4}} = 1 \div \frac{1}{x^4} = 1 \cdot \frac{x^4}{1} = x^4$$

 Helping Hand As long as only *factors* are involved, a base with a negative exponent in the numerator is placed in the denominator with a positive exponent. Also, a base with a negative exponent in the denominator is placed in the numerator with a positive exponent.

In this text, we will assume that variables represent nonzero values so that the given expressions are defined.

EXAMPLE 1   Write in expanded form.

   a. $a^3 b^2$ **b.** $(x + 2)^2$ **c.** mn^0

   Solution

   a. $a^3 b^2 = a \cdot a \cdot a \cdot b \cdot b$ **b.** $(x + 2)^2 = (x + 2)(x + 2)$
   c. $mn^0 = m \cdot 1 = m$ Remember, $n^0 = 1$. ∎

EXAMPLE 2   Write with positive exponents.

   a. $\dfrac{x^{-2}}{y^{-3}}$ **b.** $\dfrac{x^3 y^{-1}}{3^{-2} z^2}$

Solution

a. $\dfrac{x^{-2}}{y^{-3}} = \dfrac{y^3}{x^2}$

Move the factor x^{-2} from the numerator into the denominator as the factor x^2.
Move the factor y^{-3} from the denominator into the numerator as the factor y^3.

b. $\dfrac{x^3 y^{-1}}{3^{-2} z^2} = \dfrac{3^2 x^3}{y z^2}$

Move the factor y^{-1} from the numerator into the denominator as the factor y.

$\ = \dfrac{9x^3}{y z^2}$

Move the factor 3^{-2} from the denominator into the numerator as 3^2.
Evaluate 3^2. ∎

Experiencing Algebra the Checkup Way

Write in expanded form.

1. $3^2 x^3$ **2.** $(-2x)^3$ **3.** $(a - b)^4$ **4.** $p^0 q^4$

In exercises 5–9, write each expression with positive exponents.

5. x^{-4} **6.** $\dfrac{1}{y^{-2}}$ **7.** $\dfrac{x^{-4}}{y^{-2}}$ **8.** $\dfrac{5^{-2} a^4}{2^{-3} b^{-3}}$ **9.** $p^{-5} q^5$

10. Explain the difference between the terms *expanded form* and *exponential expression*.

---

2 The Product Rule   In order to perform multiplication involving exponential expressions, we need to discover a few rules. Use your calculator to complete the following set of exercises to determine a rule for multiplication of exponential expressions with the same base.

DISCOVERY 1

Multiplication of Exponential Expressions with the Same Base
Evaluate each expression and compare the results obtained in the first column to the corresponding results in the second column.

1. a. $4^3 \cdot 4^2 =$ ____   **b.** $4^5 =$ ____
2. a. $(-2)^4 \cdot (-2)^2 =$ ____   **b.** $(-2)^6 =$ ____
3. a. $\left(\dfrac{3}{4}\right)^2 \cdot \left(\dfrac{3}{4}\right) =$ ____   **b.** $\left(\dfrac{3}{4}\right)^3 =$ ____

Write a rule for multiplication of two exponential expressions with the same base.

4. Use the rule to simplify $x^4 \cdot x^3 =$ ____ .

In the first column, the base of each factor is the same. In the second column, the base is the same as the bases of the factors in the first column and the exponent is the sum of the factors' exponents. Therefore, to multiply exponential expressions with like bases, add the exponents.

Using this rule, the product of $x^4 \cdot x^3$ is x^{4+3} or x^7. We can illustrate this rule by rewriting each expression as a product of its factors and simplifying.

$$x^4 \cdot x^3 = (x \cdot x \cdot x \cdot x) \cdot (x \cdot x \cdot x)$$
$$= x \cdot x \cdot x \cdot x \cdot x \cdot x \cdot x$$
$$= x^7$$

> *Product Rule for Exponents*
> For any base a and integer exponents m and n,
>
> $$a^m \cdot a^n = a^{m+n}.$$
>
> The base a may be a constant, a variable, or an expression.

EXAMPLE 3 Multiply.

a. $x^3 \cdot x^{-2}$ **b.** $(a + b)^4(a + b)$

Solution

a. $x^3 \cdot x^{-2} = x^{3+(-2)} = x^1 = x$
b. $(a + b)^4(a + b) = (a + b)^{4+1} = (a + b)^5$ ∎

Experiencing Algebra the Checkup Way

Multiply exercises 1–3. Express your results using positive exponents.

1. $a^3 \cdot a^6$ **2.** $z^{-6} \cdot z^3$ **3.** $(x + y)(x + y)^7$

4. What is the difference between $x^2 \cdot x^3$ and $x^2 + x^3$? Which of these expressions can be simplified using the product rule?

---

3 The Quotient Rule   Before we begin to discuss division of polynomials, we must first discover rules of exponents involving division. Use your calculator to complete the following set of exercises to determine a rule for division of exponential expressions with the same base.

D I S C O V E R Y 2   **Division of Exponential Expressions with the Same Base**
    Evaluate each expression and compare the results obtained in the first column to the corresponding results in the second column.

1. a. $\dfrac{4^5}{4^2} =$ ____   **b.** $4^3 =$ ____

2. a. $\dfrac{(-2)^4}{(-2)^2} =$ ____   **b.** $(-2)^2 =$ ____

3. a. $\dfrac{\left(\dfrac{3}{4}\right)^3}{\left(\dfrac{3}{4}\right)} =$ ____   **b.** $\left(\dfrac{3}{4}\right)^2 =$ ____

4. a. $\dfrac{0^5}{0^5} =$ ____   **b.** $0^0 =$ ____

Continued

Write a rule for division of two exponential expressions with the same base.

5. Use the rule to simplify $\dfrac{x^7}{x^3} = $ ____.

In the first column, the bases of the divisor and dividend are the same. In the second column, the base is the same as the bases of the divisor and dividend and the exponent is the difference of the exponents in the quotient. Therefore, to divide exponential expressions with like bases, subtract the exponent in the denominator from the exponent in the numerator.

Using this rule, the quotient of $\dfrac{x^7}{x^3}$ is x^{7-3} or x^4. We can illustrate this rule by rewriting each expression as a product of its factors and simplifying.

$$\frac{x^7}{x^3} = \frac{x \cdot x \cdot x \cdot x \cdot x \cdot x \cdot x}{x \cdot x \cdot x}$$
$$= x \cdot x \cdot x \cdot x$$
$$= x^4$$

Note: In the discovery, we evaluated $\frac{0^5}{0^5} = \frac{0}{0}$, which we determined to be indeterminate in Chapter 1. However, using this rule $\frac{0^5}{0^5} = 0^{5-5} = 0^0$. Therefore, it follows that 0^0 is indeterminate.

Quotient Rule for Exponents
For any nonzero base a and integer exponents m and n,

$$\frac{a^m}{a^n} = a^{m-n}.$$

The base a may be a constant, a variable, or an expression.

EXAMPLE 4 Divide. Express your answers using positive exponents.

a. $\dfrac{x^3}{x^{-2}}$ **b.** $\dfrac{(a+b)^4}{(a+b)}$

Solution

a. $\dfrac{x^3}{x^{-2}} = x^{3-(-2)} = x^5$ **b.** $\dfrac{(a+b)^4}{(a+b)} = (a+b)^{4-1} = (a+b)^3$ ∎

Experiencing Algebra the Checkup Way

Divide exercises 1–4. Express your answers using positive exponents.

1. $\dfrac{a^{12}}{a^8}$ **2.** $\dfrac{b^7}{b^{-2}}$ **3.** $\dfrac{c^4}{c^9}$ **4.** $\dfrac{(x+5)^6}{(x+5)^4}$

5. What is the difference between $\dfrac{x^5}{x^2}$ and $x^5 - x^2$? Which can be simplified using the quotient rule for exponents?

4   The Power-to-a-Power Rule   Sometimes, we may need to simplify an exponential expression raised to a power. Use your calculator to complete the following set of exercises to determine a rule for an exponential expression raised to a power.

DISCOVERY 3

Exponential Expressions Raised to a Power

Evaluate each expression and compare the results obtained in the first column to the corresponding results in the second column.

1. a. $\left(4^3\right)^2 =$ _____   **b.** $4^6 =$ _____

2. a. $\left[(-2)^2\right]^4 =$ _____   **b.** $(-2)^8 =$ _____

3. a. $\left[\left(\dfrac{3}{4}\right)^2\right]^3 =$ _____   **b.** $\left(\dfrac{3}{4}\right)^6 =$ _____

Write a rule for raising an exponential expression to a power.

4. Use the rule to simplify $\left(x^4\right)^3 =$ _____ .

In the second column, the base is the same as the base in the first column and the exponent is the product of the exponents in the first column. Therefore, to raise an exponential expression to a power, multiply the exponents.

With this rule, $\left(x^4\right)^3$ is $x^{4\cdot3}$ or x^{12}. We can illustrate this rule by rewriting the expression as a product of its factors and simplifying.

$$\left(x^4\right)^3 = (x \cdot x \cdot x \cdot x)^3$$
$$= (x \cdot x \cdot x \cdot x) \cdot (x \cdot x \cdot x \cdot x) \cdot (x \cdot x \cdot x \cdot x)$$
$$= x \cdot x \cdot x \cdot x \cdot x \cdot x \cdot x \cdot x \cdot x \cdot x \cdot x \cdot x$$
$$= x^{12}$$

> *Power-to-a-Power Rule for Exponents*
> For any base a and integer exponents m and n,
> $$\left(a^m\right)^n = a^{mn}.$$
> The base a may be a constant, a variable, or an expression.

EXAMPLE 5   Simplify, using the power-to-a-power rule for exponents.

a. $\left(c^5\right)^2$ **b.** $\left(y^{-2}\right)^{-3}$

Solution

a. $\left(c^5\right)^2 = c^{5\cdot2} = c^{10}$ **b.** $\left(y^{-2}\right)^{-3} = y^{(-2)\cdot(-3)} = y^6$ ∎

 Experiencing Algebra the Checkup Way

In exercises 1–3, simplify using the power-to-a-power rule for exponents. Express your results using positive exponents.

1. $\left(x^3\right)^4$ **2.** $\left(y^5\right)^{-2}$ **3.** $\left(z^{-2}\right)^{-6}$

4. What is the difference between $\left(x^5\right)^2$ and $x^5 \cdot x^2$? Which can be simplified using the power to a power rule? How can the other expression be simplified?

5 The Product-to-a-Power or Quotient-to-a-Power Rule

We also need rules to simplify a product or a quotient raised to a power. Use your calculator to complete the following set of exercises to determine a rule for a product raised to a power.

DISCOVERY 4

Products Raised to a Power

Evaluate each expression and compare the results obtained in the first column to the corresponding results in the second column.

1. a. $(4 \cdot 2)^3 = $ ____   **b.** $4^3 \cdot 2^3 = $ ____

2. a. $(-2 \cdot 3)^2 = $ ____   **b.** $(-2)^2 \cdot 3^2 = $ ____

3. a. $\left(\dfrac{3}{4} \cdot \dfrac{2}{5}\right)^3 = $ ____   **b.** $\left(\dfrac{3}{4}\right)^3 \cdot \left(\dfrac{2}{5}\right)^3 = $ ____

Write a rule for a product raised to a power.

4. Use the rule to simplify $(xy)^4 = $ ____ .

In the first column, we determine a product and then raise the product to a power. In the second column, we raise each factor to a power and then multiply the result. Therefore, raising a product to a power is equivalent to the product of the factors raised to a power.

Applying this rule, $(xy)^4 = x^4 y^4$. We can illustrate this rule by rewriting the exponential expression as its factors, rearranging the factors using the commutative and associative properties, and simplifying.

$$(xy)^4 = (xy)(xy)(xy)(xy)$$
$$= x \cdot y \cdot x \cdot y \cdot x \cdot y \cdot x \cdot y$$
$$= x \cdot x \cdot x \cdot x \cdot y \cdot y \cdot y \cdot y$$
$$= x^4 y^4$$

The result for a quotient raised to a power is determined in a similar way. For example,

$$\left(\frac{x}{y}\right)^4 = \left(\frac{x}{y}\right)\left(\frac{x}{y}\right)\left(\frac{x}{y}\right)\left(\frac{x}{y}\right) = \frac{x^4}{y^4}$$

Product-to-a-Power and Quotient-to-a-Power Rules
For any factors a and b and integer exponent m,

$$(ab)^m = a^m b^m.$$

For any dividend a, nonzero divisor b, and integer exponent m,

$$\left(\frac{a}{b}\right)^m = \frac{a^m}{b^m}.$$

The elements a and b may be constants, variables, or expressions.

If the exponent is negative and we apply this rule to a quotient, we obtain

$$\left(\frac{x}{y}\right)^{-4} = \frac{x^{-4}}{y^{-4}} = \frac{y^4}{x^4}.$$

The result is the reciprocal of the quotient raised to the positive power. We will write a special rule for this case.

> *Quotient-to-a-Negative-Power Rule*
> For any nonzero dividend and divisor a and b and integer exponent $m > 0$,
> $$\left(\frac{a}{b}\right)^{-m} = \left(\frac{b}{a}\right)^{m} = \frac{b^m}{a^m}.$$
> The elements a and b may be constants, variables, or expressions.

EXAMPLE 6   Simplify. Express all answers using positive exponents.

a. $(2x)^4$ **b.** $\left(\dfrac{5y}{z}\right)^3$ **c.** $\left(\dfrac{-3a}{b}\right)^{-2}$

Solution

a. $(2x)^4 = 2^4 x^4 = 16x^4$ Product-to-a-power rule

b. $\left(\dfrac{5y}{z}\right)^3 = \dfrac{5^3 y^3}{z^3} = \dfrac{125y^3}{z^3}$ Quotient-to-a-power rule

c. $\left(\dfrac{-3a}{b}\right)^{-2} = \left(\dfrac{b}{-3a}\right)^{2}$ Quotient-to-a-negative-power rule

$= \dfrac{b^2}{(-3)^2 a^2}$ Quotient-to-a-power rule

$= \dfrac{b^2}{9a^2}$ ∎

Experiencing Algebra the Checkup Way

Simplify exercises 1–5. Express your results using positive exponents.

1. $(-2a)^6$ **2.** $\left(\dfrac{x}{y}\right)^{-9}$ **3.** $(ab)^{18}$ **4.** $\left(\dfrac{-4xy}{z}\right)^3$ **5.** $\left(\dfrac{-2p}{q}\right)^{-4}$

6. What is the difference between $2x^3$ and $(2x)^3$? For which expression can you use the product-to-a-power rule to simplify?

---

6 Modeling the Real World   Exponential expressions occur frequently in all kinds of real-world situations. As always, you must remember to include the units of real quantities in your calculations—that is, raising the quantity 3 feet to the third power does not give you 27 feet, but 27 cubic feet $\left(\text{ft}^3\right)$.

EXAMPLE 7   To allow his puppy to exercise without running away, Ricardo chains him to a stake in an open area of his backyard.

a. Determine the area in which the puppy may exercise if the chain is x meters long.

b. When the puppy is fully grown, it will need a larger area to exercise. If Ricardo replaces the chain with a new chain that is four times the original length, determine the new extended exercise area.

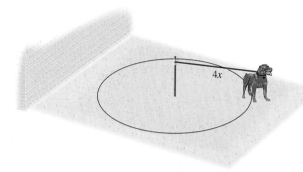

c. If the original chain is 3 meters, determine the original area and the extended area.

Solution

a. Let x = original chain length in meters
The area is a circle with a radius of x meters or πx^2 square meters.
b. Let $4x$ = new chain length in meters
The area is a circle with a radius of $4x$ meters.
$$\pi(4x)^2 = \pi(16x^2) \text{ or } 16\pi x^2 \text{ square meters.}$$
c. If x = 3 meters, then the original area is
$\pi x^2 = \pi(3)^2 = \pi(9) = 9\pi$ square meters, or approximately 28.3 square meters.
The new area is $16\pi x^2 = 16\pi(3)^2 = 16\pi(9) = 144\pi$ square meters or approximately 452.4 square meters. ∎

Application

Determine the area of a square mail room with sides of length s feet. A publishing company is expanding into new offices, and the new mail room will still be a square, but with sides of length $2s$. Determine the area of the new mail room and compare it to the area of the original mail room.

Discussion

Let s = length of the side of the original mail room
Area is found by squaring the length of the side of a square. The original mail room is s^2 square feet.

Let $2s = $ length of the side of the new mailroom
Area is found by squaring the length of the side of a square. The new mailroom is $(2s)^2 = 2^2 s^2 = 4s^2$ square feet.
Since the new mailroom is $4s^2$ and the original mailroom is s^2, the new room is 4 times the area of the original room. ∎

Experiencing Algebra the Checkup Way

A box has the shape of a cube, with each side measuring x inches. Determine the volume of the box. If another box is to be made with each side measuring $\frac{1}{2}$ of the length of the original box, determine the volume of the new box. Compare the volume of the original box with that of the new box. What are the two volumes if the first box has a side measuring 1.5 meters on a side?

PROBLEM SET 10.1

Experiencing Algebra the Exercise Way

Write in expanded form.

1. $4^3 a^2$ **2.** $-3b^3$ **3.** $(-3x)^4$ **4.** $(-4c)^3$

5. $a^3 b^0 c^5$ **6.** $x^2 y z^0$ **7.** $\left(\dfrac{3x}{4}\right)^3$ **8.** $\left(\dfrac{2}{3}\right)^2 \cdot x^3$

9. $5(x + y)^2$ **10.** $-4(p - q)^2$

Write with positive exponents.

11. p^{-3} **12.** q^{-2} **13.** $\dfrac{1}{q^{-5}}$ **14.** $\dfrac{2}{p^{-3}}$

15. $\dfrac{p^{-3}}{q^{-5}}$ **16.** $\dfrac{2q^{-2}}{p^{-3}}$ **17.** $p^{-3} q^5$ **18.** $p^3 q^{-2}$

19. $\dfrac{4^3 m^{-2}}{3^4 n^{-3}}$ **20.** $\dfrac{2^5 x^{-3}}{5^2 y^{-4}}$ **21.** $\dfrac{4^{-3} m^{-2}}{3^{-4} n^{-3}}$ **22.** $\dfrac{2^{-5} x^{-3}}{5^{-2} y^{-4}}$

23. $\dfrac{-4(m - n)^{-1}}{5(m + n)^{-2}}$ **24.** $\dfrac{5(a + b)^{-2}}{7(a - b)^{-3}}$ **25.** $\dfrac{4^{-1}(m - n)}{5^{-1}(m + n)^2}$ **26.** $\dfrac{-5(a + b)^2}{7^{-1}(a - b)^3}$

27. $a^{-3} + 2a^{-2} - 3a^{-1} + 4a^0$ **28.** $x^{-3} + x^{-2} - x^{-1}$

Multiply. Express your results with positive exponents.

29. $x^5 \cdot x^8$ **30.** $a^9 \cdot a^{14}$ **31.** $y^{-5} \cdot y^{13}$ **32.** $b^{-7} \cdot b^{23}$

33. $z^{-9} \cdot z^4$ **34.** $c^{-12} \cdot c^4$ **35.** $p^{-2} \cdot p^{-7}$ **36.** $d^{-4} \cdot d^{-7}$

37. $(x + y)^4 (x + y)^{-4}$ **38.** $(x - y)^5 (x - y)^{-5}$ **39.** $(x + 3)^2 (x + 3)$ **40.** $(x + 9)^{12}(x + 9)$

Divide. Express your answers using positive exponents.

41. $\dfrac{p^{11}}{p^6}$ **42.** $\dfrac{a^5}{a}$ **43.** $\dfrac{y^{-4}}{y^{-5}}$ **44.** $\dfrac{x^{-8}}{x^{-12}}$

45. $\dfrac{b^6}{b^8}$ **46.** $\dfrac{t^{11}}{t^{14}}$ **47.** $\dfrac{(2x - 3)^8}{(2x - 3)^3}$ **48.** $\dfrac{(4x + 7)^9}{(4x + 7)^2}$

49. $\dfrac{(p + q)^2}{(p + q)^{-1}}$ **50.** $\dfrac{(xy + 2)^4}{(xy + 2)^{-2}}$ **51.** $\dfrac{(4 - x)^{-3}}{(4 - x)^2}$ **52.** $\dfrac{(15 - 3t)^{-7}}{(15 - 3t)}$

53. $\dfrac{(z-5)^{-4}}{(z-5)^{-1}}$

54. $\dfrac{(r+s)^{-6}}{(r+s)^{-3}}$

Simplify exercises 55–84. Express your results with positive exponents.

55. $\left(a^5\right)^6$

56. $\left(m^7\right)^4$

57. $\left(c^{-4}\right)^{-2}$

58. $\left(p^{-3}\right)^{-2}$

59. $\left[(x+y)^3\right]^2$

60. $\left[(a+2b)^4\right]^3$

61. $\left[(a-b)^4\right]^{-1}$

62. $\left[(c-3d)^5\right]^{-1}$

63. $\left(x^2\right)^0$

64. $\left(x^0\right)^3$

65. $(5m)^4$

66. $(3k)^4$

67. $\left(\dfrac{b}{d}\right)^4$

68. $\left(\dfrac{m}{n}\right)^5$

69. $(pq)^{21}$

70. $(xyz)^9$

71. $\left(\dfrac{3b}{c}\right)^4$

72. $\left(\dfrac{5y}{z}\right)^3$

73. $(-2c)^6$

74. $(-2c)^4$

75. $\left(\dfrac{4x}{y}\right)^{-3}$

76. $\left(\dfrac{3a}{b}\right)^{-5}$

77. $\left(\dfrac{-3p}{q}\right)^{-4}$

78. $\left(\dfrac{-5c}{d}\right)^{-2}$

79. $\left(p^5q^7\right)^3$

80. $\left(k^4m^6\right)^2$

81. $\left[(2a)^2\right]^5$

82. $\left[(-3t)^2\right]^2$

83. $\left[\left(\dfrac{x}{2y}\right)^2\right]^3$

84. $\left[\left(\dfrac{3z}{w}\right)^2\right]^3$

85. A child's square play area is enlarged by increasing each side by a factor of 5 (that is, each side is multiplied by 5). Write exponential expressions for the areas of the original play area and the enlarged play area. Compare the areas of the two squares. What are the two areas if the original area had a side of 6 feet?

86. A department store's square display area is enlarged by increasing each side by a factor of 2.6. Write exponential expressions for the areas of the original and the enlarged display areas. Compare the two areas. What are the two areas if the original area had a side of 12 feet?

87. A storage bin in the shape of a cube is enlarged by increasing each side by a factor of 4. Write exponential expressions for the volume of the original bin and the enlarged bin. Compare the volumes of the two bins. What are the two volumes if the original bin had a side of 1.5 feet?

88. A block of ice with the shape of a cube begins to melt. Its size is decreased so that each side is 0.8 of its original length. Write exponential expressions for the volumes of the original cube of ice and the smaller cube of ice. Compare the volumes of the two cubes of ice. What are the two volumes if the larger cube of ice measured 22 inches on a side?

 Experiencing Algebra the Calculator Way

The calculator can be used to check for equivalence of simplified exponential expressions, if the expressions involve a single variable. To do so, first store the original exponential expression in Y1 and the simplified exponential expression in Y2. Then graph the expressions one at a time, comparing the graphs. Finally, graph the expressions at the same time and use the TRACE command to verify that the two graphs are identical. If they are, you should be able to move from one graph to the other, and note that the *y*-coordinates of the points traced are identical. The steps are outlined next.

Is $\left(\dfrac{3}{5}x^3\right)^2 = \dfrac{9}{25}x^6$?

a. Set the screen to a decimal window.

b. Enter the first expression in Y1.

c. Graph the first expression.

d. Turn off the first graph. Enter the second expression in Y2.

e. Graph the second expression.

f. The two graphs should be the same. Turn the Y1 graph on to look at both graphs simultaneously.

g. Trace the two graphs to determine equivalence, using the arrow keys to move along both graphs.

This method is dependent upon being able to find a good viewing rectangle for your window. You may have to experiment with several choices to find the window.

While it may not give you as complete a comparison of the two expressions, you may also wish to view a table of values for the two. Again, store the original expression in Y1 and the simplified expression in Y2. Set the table to generate values for the independent variable automatically, using appropriate increments. If the table yields corresponding values for Y1 and Y2 that are equal, it suggests that the two expressions are equivalent.

Use the same steps to check for equivalence of the following expressions.

1. $x^3 \cdot x^2 = x^6$ **2.** $x^3 \cdot x^2 = x^5$ **3.** $\dfrac{x^3}{x^{-2}} = x^5$

4. $\dfrac{x^3}{x^{-2}} = x$ **5.** $\dfrac{x^3}{x^2} = x^5$ **6.** $\dfrac{x^3}{x^2} = x$

 ## Experiencing Algebra the Group Way

Sometimes a combination of the rules of exponents can be used to simplify an expression. For example, we can simplify the following expression as shown:

$$\left[\left(\dfrac{-2x}{3y}\right)^2\right]^3 = \left(\dfrac{-2x}{3y}\right)^6 = \dfrac{(-2x)^6}{(3y)^6} = \dfrac{(-2)^6 x^6}{3^6 y^6} = \dfrac{64x^6}{729y^6}$$

In your group, discuss which rule of exponents was used to move from the first exponential expression to each subsequent exponential expression. Then discuss whether this is the only sequence of steps that could be used to simplify this expression. If your group believes another sequence can be used, attempt to simplify using it, and see if you obtain the same result. Save your work so that you can present it to the class.

Next, have each member of the group simplify the following expressions. After doing so, compare your answers. If you disagree on an answer, explain your steps so that the group can decide which answer is correct. Also, see how many different ways were used to obtain the result.

1. $\left[\left(\dfrac{x}{y}\right)^3\right]^3$ **2.** $\left[(2a)^6\right]^2$ **3.** $\left[(-x)^5\right]^3$

4. $\left[(ab)^9\right]^2$ **5.** $\left(x^2 y^3\right)^5$ **6.** $\left(2a^5 b^{-2} c\right)^3$

Experiencing Algebra the Write Way

The rules of exponents sometimes yield results that may run contrary to your intuition. To help you deal with this, briefly explain why the following statements are true, and illustrate each with an example.

1. A positive number raised to a negative power results in a positive number.

2. A negative number raised to an even power results in a positive number.

3. A negative number raised to an odd power results in a negative number.

4. When two exponential expressions have the same base, but different exponents, you may properly write their product as the base to the sum of the exponents.

5. When two exponential expressions have different bases, but the same exponent, you may *not* properly write their product as the product of the bases to the sum of the exponents.

10.2 Polynomial Operations

Objectives

1 Add and subtract polynomials.

2 Multiply polynomials by monomials.

3 Divide polynomials by monomials.

4 Model real-world situations using polynomials.

Application

The building committee members for the recreation department agreed that an ideal concession area should be square. The concession stand will also be used for storage and restrooms, so an additional 8 feet will be added to one side of the building. They submitted the following sketch of a proposed concession stand.

Determine a polynomial for the area of the building. Evaluate the polynomial when the concession area is 12 feet on a side; 20 feet on a side.

After completing this section, we will discuss this application further. See page 720.

side

side

concession
area

8 ft

restroom   storage   restroom

In previous chapters, we performed operations on algebraic expressions. In this section, we review these methods and expand them to more difficult examples.

1 Adding and Subtracting Polynomials

To add two algebraic expressions, we removed the parentheses and collected like terms. To subtract algebraic expressions, we removed the parentheses by taking the opposite of the subtrahend, added it to the minuend, and collected like terms. We will do the same for polynomials.

Addition and Subtraction of Polynomials
To add polynomials enclosed in a set of parentheses:

- Remove the parentheses.
- Collect like terms.

To subtract polynomials enclosed in a set of parentheses:

- Remove the parentheses, remembering to take the opposite of the terms within the subtrahend.
- Collect like terms.

For example, add the polynomials $\left(2x^3 - 3x^2 + x - 5\right)$ and $\left(5x^3 - 3x^2 + 7\right)$.

$$\left(2x^3 - 3x^2 + x - 5\right) + \left(5x^3 - 3x^2 + 7\right)$$

$= 2x^3 - 3x^2 + x - 5 + 5x^3 - 3x^2 + 7$ Remove the parentheses.

$= 7x^3 - 6x^2 + x + 2$ Collect like terms.

Sometimes it is easier to see the like terms if we align the polynomials in columns with like terms aligned. We can write missing addends with a coefficient of 0 to keep the columns complete.

$$\begin{array}{r} 2x^3 - 3x^2 + x - 5 \\ + \left(5x^3 - 3x^2 + 0x + 7\right) \\ \hline 7x^3 - 6x^2 + x + 2 \end{array}$$

For another example, subtract the polynomial $\left(5x^3 - 3x^2 + 7\right)$ from the polynomial $\left(2x^3 - 3x^2 + x - 5\right)$.

$$\left(2x^3 - 3x^2 + x - 5\right) - \left(5x^3 - 3x^2 + 7\right)$$

$= 2x^3 - 3x^2 + x - 5 - 5x^3 + 3x^2 - 7$ Remove the parentheses. (Take the opposite of the subtrahend.)

$= -3x^3 + x - 12$ Collect like terms.

To use column subtraction, align like terms. However, remember to take the opposite of the subtrahend before adding.

$$\begin{array}{r} 2x^3 - 3x^2 + x - 5 \\ - \left(5x^3 - 3x^2 + 0x + 7\right) \end{array} \quad \text{or} \quad \begin{array}{r} 2x^3 - 3x^2 + x - 5 \\ -5x^3 + 3x^2 - 0x - 7 \\ \hline -3x^3 + x - 12 \end{array} \quad \begin{array}{l} \text{Change} \\ \text{signs.} \end{array}$$

EXAMPLE 1   Add or subtract each set of polynomials.

a. $\left(6x^2y + 4x^2 - xy^2 + xy\right) + \left(5xy + 6x^2 - x^2y^3\right)$

b. $\left(6x^2y + 4x^2 - xy^2 + xy\right) - \left(5xy + 6x^2 - x^2y^3\right)$

Solution

a. $\left(6x^2y + 4x^2 - xy^2 + xy\right) + \left(5xy + 6x^2 - x^2y^3\right)$

$= 6x^2y + 4x^2 - xy^2 + xy + 5xy + 6x^2 - x^2y^3$ Remove the parentheses.

$= 6x^2y - x^2y^3 - xy^2 + 6xy + 10x^2$ Collect like terms.

Aligned in columns:

$$\begin{array}{r} 6x^2y + 4x^2 - xy^2 + xy \\ + (6x^2 + 5xy - x^2y^3) \\ \hline 6x^2y + 10x^2 - xy^2 + 6xy - x^2y^3 \end{array} \quad \text{Align like terms.}$$

b. $\left(6x^2y + 4x^2 - xy^2 + xy\right) - \left(5xy + 6x^2 - x^2y^3\right)$

$= 6x^2y + 4x^2 - xy^2 + xy - 5xy - 6x^2 + x^2y^3$ Take the opposite of the subtrahend.

$= 6x^2y - 2x^2 + x^2y^3 - xy^2 - 4xy$ Collect like terms.

Aligned in columns:

$$6x^2y + 4x^2 - xy^2 + xy$$
$$-(\qquad 6x^2 \qquad + 5xy - x^2y^3) \quad \text{or}$$

$$\begin{aligned}6x^2y + 4x^2 - xy^2 + xy\\ - 6x^2 \qquad\qquad - 5xy + x^2y^3\\ \hline 6x^2y - 2x^2 - xy^2 - 4xy + x^2y^3\end{aligned}$$ ∎

Experiencing Algebra The Checkup Way

Add as indicated.

1. Add $(3x^3 + 2x^2 - 5x + 7)$ and $(5x^3 - 5x^2 + 2 + 4x)$.
2. $(3x^3 + 2x^2y - 4xy^2 + y^3) + (4y^3 - 3xy^2 - 3x^2y + 4x^3)$

Subtract exercises 3–4 as indicated.

3. Subtract $(5a^2 - 2 + 6a)$ from $(6a + 13 - 2a^2 + a^3)$.
4. $(4a^4 + 3a^3b - 7a^2b^2 + 9ab^3 - 3b^4) - (2a^2b^2 + 4ab^3 - 5b^4)$
5. When subtracting polynomials, which polynomial is the subtrahend, and why must you take the opposite of each term of the subtrahend when removing its parentheses? Why do you not have to do this operation when adding two polynomials?

2 Multiplying with Monomials

We are ready to begin multiplication of polynomials. We start by multiplying two monomials. Remember that we multiplied algebraic expressions with one term by using the commutative and associative properties to rearrange the factors. Now, we also use the rules for exponents to help simplify the products. For example,

$$\begin{aligned}(5x^2y)(-3xy) &= 5\cdot x^2\cdot y\cdot -3\cdot x\cdot y\\ &= 5\cdot -3\cdot x^2\cdot x\cdot y\cdot y\\ &= -15\cdot x^{2+1}\cdot y^{1+1} \qquad \text{Product rule}\\ &= -15x^3y^2\end{aligned}$$

We have also multiplied expressions when one factor had more than one term, using the distributive law. We do the same when multiplying a monomial and a polynomial. For example,

$$\begin{aligned}2x^2(x - y + 2z) &= 2x^2\cdot x - 2x^2\cdot y + 2x^2\cdot 2z \qquad \text{Distribute } 2x^2.\\ &= 2x^3 - 2x^2y + 4x^2z \qquad \text{Product rule}\end{aligned}$$

If we multiply in column form, we write the following.

$$\begin{aligned}x - y + \quad 2z\\ 2x^2\\ \hline 2x^3 - \quad 2x^2y + 4x^2z\end{aligned}$$

> *Products with a Monomial Factor*
> To multiply a monomial by a monomial, use the commutative and associative properties to rearrange factors. Simplify using the rules of exponents.
> To multiply a polynomial with more than one term by a monomial, use the distributive law. Simplify using the rules of exponents.

EXAMPLE 2   Multiply. Express your answers with positive exponents.

a. $(-8xy^2)(3x^{-1}y^{-3})$ b. $2x^2(x + 3y - 5xy)$

Solution

a. $(-8xy^2)(3x^{-1}y^{-3}) = -8 \cdot 3x^{1+(-1)}y^{2+(-3)}$ Product rule

$= -24x^0y^{-1}$ Simplify.

$= -24(1)\left(\dfrac{1}{y}\right)$ $x^0 = 1$ and $y^{-1} = \frac{1}{y}$

$= \dfrac{-24}{y}$

b. $2x^2(x + 3y - 5xy) = 2x^2 \cdot x + 2x^2 \cdot 3y + 2x^2 \cdot (-5xy)$ Distribute $2x^2$.

$= 2x^{2+1} + 6x^2y - 10x^{2+1}y$ Product rule

$= 2x^3 + 6x^2y - 10x^3y$ Simplify. ■

Experiencing Algebra the Checkup Way

In exercises 1–2, multiply. Express your answers with positive exponents.

1. $5a^2b^4 \cdot (-5a^3b^{-4}c)$ 2. $-4m^3(m^2n - 5mn^2 + n^3)$

3. When multiplying two polynomials, when would you use only the commutative and associative laws? For what type of polynomial multiplication would you need to use the distributive law?

---

3 Dividing with Monomials   We have already divided algebraic expressions by a single-term expression. To divide two monomials, we use the commutative and associative properties to rearrange the factors. We also use the rules for exponents to help simplify the quotient. *We will assume that variables represent nonzero values so that the expressions are defined.* For example,

$$\dfrac{6x^5y^4z}{-2xy^2z} = \dfrac{6}{-2} \cdot \dfrac{x^5}{x} \cdot \dfrac{y^4}{y^2} \cdot \dfrac{z}{z}$$

$$= -3 \cdot x^{5-1} \cdot y^{4-2} \cdot z^{1-1}$$ Quotient rule

$$= -3x^4y^2z^0$$ Remember, $z^0 = 1$.

$$= -3x^4y^2$$

In order to divide a polynomial of more than one term by a monomial, we use the distributive law, as we did with algebraic expressions. For example,

$$\dfrac{4x^2y^3z - 2xy^2z}{2xyz} = \dfrac{4x^2y^3z}{2xyz} - \dfrac{2xy^2z}{2xyz}$$

$$= \dfrac{4}{2} \cdot \dfrac{x^2}{x} \cdot \dfrac{y^3}{y} \cdot \dfrac{z}{z} - \dfrac{2}{2} \cdot \dfrac{x}{x} \cdot \dfrac{y^2}{y} \cdot \dfrac{z}{z}$$

$$= 2x^{2-1}y^{3-1}z^{1-1} - 1x^{1-1}y^{2-1}z^{1-1}$$ Quotient rule

$$= 2x^1y^2z^0 - 1x^0y^1z^0$$

$$= 2xy^2 - y$$

> *Quotients with a Monomial Divisor*
> To divide a monomial by a monomial, use the commutative and associative properties to rearrange factors. Simplify using the rules of exponents.
>   To divide a polynomial with more than one term by a monomial, use the distributive law. Simplify using the rules of exponents.

EXAMPLE 3 Divide. Express your answers with positive exponents.

a. $\dfrac{36a^5 b^{-2}}{5a^3 b}$ **b.** $\dfrac{\left(2x^2 y\right)^5}{4x^{-2} y}$ **c.** $\dfrac{2a^2 + 6a^2 b - 4b^2}{2a}$

Solution

a. $\dfrac{36a^5 b^{-2}}{5a^3 b} = \dfrac{36}{5} \cdot \dfrac{a^5}{a^3} \cdot \dfrac{b^{-2}}{b}$ Rearrange factors.

$= \dfrac{36}{5} \cdot a^{5-3} \cdot b^{-2-1}$ Quotient rule

$= \dfrac{36}{5} \cdot a^2 \cdot b^{-3}$ Simplify.

$= \dfrac{36}{5} \cdot a^2 \cdot \dfrac{1}{b^3}$ Write with a positive exponent.

$= \dfrac{36a^2}{5b^3}$ Simplify.

b. $\dfrac{\left(2x^2 y\right)^5}{4x^{-2} y} = \dfrac{2^5 x^{2 \cdot 5} y^5}{4x^{-2} y}$ Power-to-a-power rule

$= \dfrac{32x^{10} y^5}{4x^{-2} y}$ Simplify.

$= \dfrac{32}{4} \cdot \dfrac{x^{10}}{x^{-2}} \cdot \dfrac{y^5}{y}$ Rearrange factors.

$= 8x^{12} y^4$ Quotient rule. Simplify.

c. $\dfrac{2a^2 + 6a^2 b - 4b^2}{2a} = \dfrac{2a^2}{2a} + \dfrac{6a^2 b}{2a} - \dfrac{4b^2}{2a}$ Distribute 2a.

$= 1a^{2-1} + 3a^{2-1}b - 2a^{-1}b^2$ Rules of exponents

$= a + 3ab - \dfrac{2b^2}{a}$ Simplify. ∎

✓ Experiencing Algebra the Checkup Way

In exercises 1–4, divide. Express your answers with positive exponents.

1. $\dfrac{27a^2 b^5 c^{-2}}{9a^4 b^2 c^{-3}}$ **2.** $\dfrac{\left(3xy^2\right)^3}{18\left(x^{-1} y^2\right)^{-1}}$ **3.** $\dfrac{(2a)^3}{(2a)^5}$

4. $\dfrac{12x^3 + 6x^2 y - 9xy^2 - 2y^3}{4x^2 y}$

5. When dividing a polynomial by a monomial, when would you need to use the distributive law?

4 Modeling the Real World

We've already mentioned that polynomial functions and exponential expressions are both very common in modeling real-world situations. Therefore, performing mathematical operations with these expressions becomes an important part of working with applications of mathematics. Any operation you can do with numbers, you can also do with polynomials. The only difference is that polynomials don't reduce to simple terms quite as easily as real numbers do.

EXAMPLE 4

Alfredo Travel Company offers a spring tour of Lutz's Gardens. The cost is $99.95 per package. A reduction of $1.00 per purchased package is given for groups. The bus expenses are estimated to be $105.00, the driver is paid $300.00, and the tickets to the gardens are $19.95 per person. The bus can carry up to 30 people.

a. Determine a cost function, $C(x)$.
b. Determine a revenue function, $R(x)$.
c. Determine a profit function, $P(x)$.
d. Determine an average profit (profit per package) function, $A(x)$.
e. If 23 members of Springfield Garden Club purchase a tour package, what is the profit per package for Alfredo Travel Company?

Solution

Let x = the number of tour packages purchased

a. The total cost is $105.00 plus $300.00 (that is, $405.00) plus $19.95 per ticket (number of tour packages purchased).

$$C(x) = 19.95x + 405$$

b. The reduction in the package is $1.00 times the number of packages purchased, or $1.00x$. The cost of the package is $99.95 minus the reduction, or $(99.95 - 1.00x)$. The revenue is the cost of the package times the number of packages purchased, or $(99.95 - 1.00x)x$.

$$R(x) = (99.95 - 1.00x)x$$
$$R(x) = 99.95x - x^2$$

c. The profit is the revenue minus the cost.

$$P(x) = (99.95x - x^2) - (19.95x + 405)$$
$$P(x) = 99.95x - x^2 - 19.95x - 405$$
$$P(x) = -x^2 + 80x - 405$$

d. The average profit (profit per package) is determined by dividing the profit by the number of packages purchased.

$$A(x) = \frac{-x^2 + 80x - 405}{x}$$

e. If $x = 23$, then find $A(23)$.

$$A(23) = \frac{-(23)^2 + 80(23) - 405}{23}$$

$$A(23) \approx 39.39$$

The average profit for Alfredo Travel Company is $39.39 per package if 23 packages are purchased. ∎

Application

The building committee members for the recreation department agreed that an ideal concession area should be square. The concession stand will also be used for storage and restrooms, so an additional 8 feet will be added to one side of the building. They submitted the following sketch of a proposed concession stand.

Determine a polynomial for the area of the building. Evaluate the polynomial when the concession area is 12 feet on a side; 20 feet on a side.

Discussion

The concession area is a square.
Let s = the length of one side of the concession area

Therefore,
s = the length of one side of the building
$s + 8$ = the length of the other side of the building

The area of the building is the product of the lengths of the two sides of the building.

$$s(s + 8) = s^2 + 8s$$

The area is $(s^2 + 8s)$ square feet.
For $s = 12$, the area is

$$s^2 + 8s = (12)^2 + 8(12) = 144 + 96 = 240 \text{ square feet.}$$

For $s = 20$, the area is

$$s^2 + 8s = (20)^2 + 8(20) = 400 + 160 = 560 \text{ square feet.} \blacksquare$$

Experiencing Algebra the Checkup Way

1. Sybil sells box lunches from a booth in the town square. She pays $15.00 per day to use the booth, and her box lunches cost $1.25 each to prepare. She sells the box lunches for $4.50 each.

   a. Determine a daily cost function, $C(x)$.

   b. Determine a daily revenue function, $R(x)$.

   c. Determine a daily profit function, $P(x)$.

   d. Determine a function for the daily profit per lunch sold, $A(x)$.

   e. If Sybil sells 60 box lunches each day, what is her average profit for each?

2. Bridgette works at home. She wants to build an office attached to her garage. The office will have a square floor plan with a storage area for files and documents built on one side of the office. The storage area will have a depth of 2 yards, which will be space subtracted from the office. Bridgette plans to carpet the office, but not the storage space. Determine a polynomial for the area of the office less the storage space. Set up a table to determine the area of the carpeted office as the side of the square office varies from 6 yards to 8 yards in increments of 0.5 yards. For each of these areas, what will be the cost of carpeting the office if the carpeting costs $21 per square yard to purchase and install? What size office should Bridgette build if she wants the carpeting cost to be less than $750?

PROBLEM SET 10.2

Experiencing Algebra the Exercise Way

Add the polynomials.

1.
$$9x^2 - 17x + 31$$
$$2x^4 \quad\quad + 3x^2 \quad\quad + 12$$
$$5x^3 \quad\quad - 17x + 11$$
$$\overline{2x^4 + 4x^3 - 7x^2 - 8x - 26}$$

2.
$$b^3 + 2b^2 + 5b$$
$$4b^2 - b + 2$$
$$b^3 \quad\quad - 12b + 6$$
$$\overline{3b^3 - 6b^2 + 8b - 12}$$

3. $\left(5x^4 + 6x + 3x^3 - 2x^2 - 12\right) + \left(4x^4 + 21 - 8x^2 - 9x\right)$

4. $\left(-z^3 + z + z^2 + 1\right) + \left(2z^3 + 5 + 4z\right)$

5. Add $\left(5x^2y - 3xy^2 + 6y^3\right)$ and $\left(15x^3 - 8x^2y + 3xy^2\right)$.

6. Add $\left(3a^3 + 5a^2b - 2ab^2 + 6b^3\right)$ and $\left(b^3 + ab^2 + a^2b + a^3\right)$.

7. Add $\left(6 - 7a^3 + 3a^2 - 5a\right), \left(6a + 8a^3 + 2\right)$, and $\left(5a^2 - 8a - 9\right)$.

8. Add $\left(x + 5 + x^2\right), \left(2x^2 - 4x\right)$, and $(3x + 7)$.

9. $\left(\dfrac{2}{3}y^4 + \dfrac{1}{6}y^3 + 3y^2 - \dfrac{1}{3}y + \dfrac{5}{9}\right) + \left(\dfrac{7}{3}y^3 - \dfrac{8}{9}y^2 + \dfrac{5}{6}y - 3\right)$

10. $\left(\dfrac{5}{6}x^3 + \dfrac{17}{24} - \dfrac{1}{2}x^2 - \dfrac{3}{4}x\right) + \left(\dfrac{7}{8} + \dfrac{1}{4}x^3 - \dfrac{1}{6}x^2 + \dfrac{1}{2}x\right)$

11. $\left(12.07x^3 + 8.6x^2 - 3.19x + 14\right) + \left(6.7x^3 - 9.83x^2 + 7x - 4.265\right)$

12. $\left(5.1y^2 - 3.6y + 0.8y^3 - 3.7\right) + \left(4 - 0.8y - 0.1y^3 + 1.1y^2\right)$

13. Add $\left(4756a^3 - 3219a^2 - 1816a + 2083\right)$ and $\left(361a^3 + 54217a^2 + 12\right)$.

14. Add $\left(509b - 471b^3 + 211 + 54b^2\right)$ and $\left(471b^3 - 509b - 4b^2 - 11\right)$.

15. $(3a + 4b) + (5c + 6d)$

16. $(5x + 7y) + (-6y + 11z)$

Subtract the polynomials as indicated.

17. $\left(5z^3 + 27z^2 - 35z + 42\right) - \left(3z^3 + 16z - 72\right)$

18. $\left(a^3 - 5a^2 - 4a + 10\right) - \left(a^3 - 2a^2 + a - 5\right)$

19. $\left(a^5 - 9\right) - \left(a^5 - a^4 + a^3 - a^2 + a - 9\right)$

20. $\left(b^9 + b^7 + b^5 + b^3 + b + 15\right) - \left(b^9 + 15\right)$

21. Subtract $\left(12x + 7 + 9x^2\right)$ from $\left(16x^2 - 32 + 9x\right)$.

22. Subtract $\left(11y^3 + 3 + y^2 - 6y\right)$ from $\left(6y^3 - 8 + 2y + y^2\right)$.

23. $\left(13a^3 - 6a^2 + 11\right)$ minus $\left(12a - 3 + 18a^3\right)$

24. $\left(15 + 3x + 6x^3\right)$ minus $\left(5x^3 + 2x^2 + 6\right)$

25. $\left(42x^3 + 17x^2y + 3xy^2 + 23y^3\right)$ less $\left(47x^2y + 12y^3\right)$

26. $\left(51p^3 + 18p^2q - 7pq^2 + 41q^3\right)$ less $\left(9pq^2 - 8p^2q - 10\right)$

27. $(4a + 7c)$ decreased by $(2b + 6d)$

28. $(12x + 17y)$ decreased by $(12y - 8z)$

29. $\left(\dfrac{5}{7}x^2 + \dfrac{8}{21}x - \dfrac{11}{14}\right) - \left(\dfrac{1}{2}x^2 + \dfrac{5}{6}x + \dfrac{19}{42}\right)$

30. $\left(\dfrac{2}{3}x^3 - \dfrac{17}{24}x + \dfrac{5}{8}x^2\right) - \left(\dfrac{3}{8}x^3 + \dfrac{1}{6}x^2 - \dfrac{11}{24}x + \dfrac{1}{3}\right)$

31. Subtract $\left(12.2x^3 - 0.1x^2y + 0.78xy^2 + 13.07y^3\right)$ from $\left(21.2x^3 + 0.9x^2y - 13.22xy^2 + 81.07y^3\right)$.

32. Subtract $\left(4.6x^2 + 9.3xy + 17.02y^2\right)$ from $\left(7.08x^2 - 3.21xy + 8.27y^2\right)$.

33. $\left(5062z^2 - 106z + 8295\right)$ minus $\left(379z^2 + 4297z + 1108\right)$

34. $\left(476b^3 + 178b^2 - 471b + 972\right)$ minus $\left(562b^3 + 873b - 619\right)$

Multiply. Express your results with only positive exponents.

35. $-6p^3q \cdot 7p^{-3}q^{-4}$

36. $13x^3y \cdot 3x^{-2}y^2$

37. $\left(1.4x^2\right) \cdot \left(4.3x^3y^{-2}\right)$

38. $(5.7yz) \cdot (2.7y^2 z^{-1})$

39. $\left(\dfrac{3}{7} x^2 y^{-1} \right) \cdot \left(\dfrac{14}{15} x^{-1} y^4 \right)$

40. $\left(\dfrac{5}{9} a^3 b^{-4} \right) \cdot \left(\dfrac{12}{25} a^{-2} b^2 \right)$

41. $4a^2(3a^2 - 5ab + b^2)$

42. $5bc(4b^2 - 3bc + c^2)$

43. $-3x^{-1}(-2x^3 + 3x^2 - x + 1)$

44. $2a^{-1}(4a^2 + 3a - 5)$

45. $(3a^2 + 2ab + b^2) \cdot (-ab)$

46. $(7y^2 - 3yz + z^2)(-4yz)$

47. $\dfrac{3}{5} a^2(5a - 15a^2 + 25a^3)$

48. $\dfrac{4}{9} z(12z + 21z^2 - 18z^3)$

Divide. Express your answers with only positive exponents.

49. $\dfrac{24x^5}{3x^3}$

50. $\dfrac{4y^7}{28y^5}$

51. $\dfrac{13x^4 y^2}{2x^4 y^7}$

52. $\dfrac{3p^5 q^3}{11p^9 q^3}$

53. $\dfrac{122a^{-3} b^3}{11a^2 b^{-2}}$

54. $\dfrac{17a^{-7} b^{-4}}{51a^{-2} b^{-7}}$

55. $\dfrac{(2x^2)^3}{6x}$

56. $\dfrac{(3y^4)^4}{12y^2}$

57. $\left(\dfrac{2x^2}{6x} \right)^3$

58. $\left(\dfrac{3y^4}{12y^2} \right)^4$

59. $\dfrac{(6x)^6}{(6x)^4}$

60. $\dfrac{(4y)^2}{(4y)^4}$

61. $\dfrac{(3a^{-2} b)^3}{6ab^2}$

62. $\dfrac{(4xy^{-3})^3}{16x^3 y}$

63. $\left(\dfrac{3a^2 b}{6ab^2} \right)^3$

64. $\left(\dfrac{4xy^3}{16x^3 y} \right)^3$

65. $\left(\dfrac{3a^2 b}{6ab^2} \right)^{-3}$

66. $\left(\dfrac{4xy^3}{16x^3 y} \right)^{-3}$

67. $\dfrac{(x^2 y^{-3} z)^4}{(2xyz^2)^2}$

68. $\dfrac{(3a^{-5} b^2 c^4)^3}{(a^2 b^3 c^2)^2}$

69. $\dfrac{7{,}309{,}800a^9}{0.000031a^3}$

70. $\dfrac{0.001321t^{-7}}{52{,}840{,}000t^{-10}}$

71. $\dfrac{2.35 \cdot 10^{-4} x^5}{4.7 \cdot 10^8 x^2}$

72. $\dfrac{10.54 \cdot 10^{12} m^7}{1.55 \cdot 10^{-5} m^2}$

73. $\dfrac{6x^3 + 12x^2 - 18x}{3x}$

74. $\dfrac{21a^4 - 14a^2 + 42}{7a^2}$

75. $\dfrac{4x^2 - 2x + 12}{8x}$

76. $\dfrac{25z^4 - 10z^3 + 45z^2 + 15z}{5z}$

77. $\dfrac{3.72x^4 - 6.96x^2 + 1.08}{1.2x^2}$

78. $\dfrac{7.578m - 10.525m^2 + 12.63m^3}{-4.21m^3}$

79. $\dfrac{9x^4 + 6x^3 y - 18x^2 y^2 - 24xy^3 + 72y^4}{-3xy}$

80. $\dfrac{12a^3 - 30a^2 b - 24ab^2 + 6b^3}{6a^2 b}$

81. Philbert's Pots has a production process with a fixed setup cost of $200.00 each time a production run is made. The production run can produce a maximum of 30 pots on a run. It cost $2.50 for the labor to produce a single pot. The cost of material is $2.00 per pot, reduced by the product of $0.05 times the number of pots for which material is purchased.

   a. Determine the cost function for producing a run of x pots, $C(x)$.

   b. If the pots can be sold for $13.50 each, determine the revenue function for selling x of them, $R(x)$.

c. Determine the profit function, $P(x)$.

d. Determine the average profit function (profit per pot), $A(x)$.

e. What is the average profit per pot if 20 are produced and sold? What if 30 pots are produced and sold?

82. America's Best Cellular, Incorporated, has a production process to manufacture ABC cellular phones with a setup cost of $500. A maximum of 150 phones can be produced on a production run. The cost of labor and materials for each phone is $20.

    a. Determine the cost function for producing a run of x cellular phones.

    b. The cellular phones sell for a price of $50. Determine the revenue function for selling x phones.

    c. Determine the profit function.

    d. Determine the average profit function (profit per phone).

    e. What is the average profit if 75 phones are sold? What if 100 phones are sold?

83. Write a polynomial for the perimeter of a rectangle whose width is 15 feet and whose length measures x feet more than the width. What is the perimeter if the additional length is 8 feet?

84. Write a polynomial for the perimeter of a triangle whose first side is 20 inches, whose second side is x inches longer than the first side, and whose third side is twice as long as the second side. What is the perimeter of the triangle if the additional length of the second side is 5 inches?

85. Write a polynomial for the difference in the surface area of a cube with edge x and the surface area of a sphere with a radius of $\frac{1}{2}$ of x. What is the difference in surface area if the cube measures 8 inches on a side?

86. A rectangular box has a length of 4 feet, a height of x feet, and a width of $2x$ feet. Write a polynomial for the difference in the surface area of the box and the surface area of a cube with a side measuring x feet. What is the difference in surface area if the height of the box is 1.5 feet?

87. Write a polynomial for the shaded area shown.

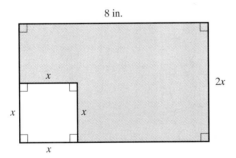

88. Write a polynomial for the shaded area shown.

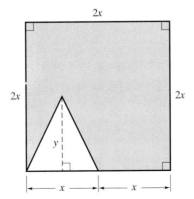

89. The neighborhood pool is shaped like a rectangle with a semicircle at each end. The length of the rectangle is 5 feet more than four times the radius of the semicircles. Write a polynomial to represent the area of the surface of the pool. Set up a table to determine the surface area of the pool as the radius of the semicircles varies from 8 feet to 12 feet in increments of 1 foot.

90. A patio is shaped like a rectangle with a triangle at one end. The length of the rectangle is 10 feet more than the width. The triangle's height and base are the same as the width of the rectangle. Write a polynomial to represent the area of the patio's surface. Set up a table to determine the area of the patio as the width of the rectangle varies from 8 feet to 12 feet in increments of 1 foot.

91. Amadou has a triangular deck behind his home. The base of the triangular deck measures four times the height. He plans to increase the base by 10 feet and to double the height.

   a. If the height of the current deck is x feet, what is the area of the deck?

   b. If Amadou changes the dimensions of the deck as planned, what will the new area be?

   c. What is the ratio of the planned area to the current area?

   d. Evaluate the three preceding functions if the height of Amadou's triangular deck now measures 10 feet.

92. Marissa has a square flower garden, which she wants to enlarge. She plans to double the length of one side and to increase the other side by 5 feet.

   a. If the original garden measures x feet on a side, what is its area?

   b. If Marissa changes the dimensions of the garden as planned, what will the new area be?

   c. What is the ratio of the area of the enlarged garden to the area of the current garden?

   d. Evaluate the three preceding functions if the flower garden now measures 8 feet on a side.

93. Pressure is measured in units of force per unit of area. For example, if an elephant weighs 7 tons, and each of her four feet is considered to be a circle with a radius of 8 inches, then the pressure on the floor would be 14,000 pounds divided by four times the area of one of the elephant's foot-pads, $4(\pi 8^2)$, or approximately 17.5 pounds per square inch. On the other hand, a women weighing 110 pounds and wearing high heels would exert a pressure of 110 divided by two times the area of her heel. (We make the simplifying assumption that her weight is distributed on her heels and not on the soles of her shoes.) Write a polynomial division expression for the pressure per square inch exerted by the woman's weight. Set up a table of values to evaluate this expression, for a heel radius that varies from 0.25 to 1 inch, in increments of 0.25 inches. For what radius of the heel is the woman's pressure on the floor approximately the same as the elephant's?

94. Assuming that a man's weight is fully distributed on his circular heels, the pressure exerted on the floor by a man weighing 175 pounds would be equal to his weight divided by the area of both of his heels. Write a polynomial division expression for the pressure per square inch exerted by his weight. Construct a table of values for a heel radius that varies from 1 to 1.5 inches, in increments of 0.05 inches. For what radius of the heel is the man's pressure on the floor approximately the same as the pressure of a bull elephant, as described in exercise 93?

95. A new home is offered for sale at a price of $80,000. The home is a one-story home whose length is twice its width. Write a polynomial division expression for the cost per square foot of the home. Evaluate the expression for widths beginning at 20 feet, incremented by 5 feet, up to 50 feet. What size home would correspond to a cost of approximately $33 per square foot?

96. A commercial building is listed to sell for $500,000. The building is a one-story building whose length is 1.5 times its width. Write a polynomial division expression for the cost per square foot of the building. Evaluate the expression for widths beginning at 100 feet, incremented by 50 feet, up to 250 feet. What size building corresponds to a cost of approximately $15 per square foot?

 Experiencing Algebra the Calculator Way

In the previous section, you were shown how the calculator can be used to check equivalence of algebraic expressions by graphing. Using the same technique, the calculator can be used to check the equivalence of one-variable polynomials after addition, subtraction, multiplication, or division. To do so, first store the original problem in Y1 and the resulting polynomial in Y2 in your calculator. Then graph the expressions separately, comparing the graphs. Finally, graph both expressions together, and use the TRACE command to verify that the two graphs are identical. The steps are outlined next.

Is $(3x^3 - x^2 + 4x - 5) + (3x^2 - 5x + 7) = 3x^3 + 2x^2 - x + 2$?

a. Set the screen to a decimal window.

b. Enter the original expression in Y1.

c. Graph the first expression.

d. Turn off the first graph and enter the resulting expression in Y2.

e. Graph the second expression.

f. The two graphs should be the same. Turn the Y1 graph on to look at both graphs simultaneously.

g. Trace the two graphs to determine equivalence, using the arrow keys to move along both graphs.

Use the same steps to check for equivalence of the following expressions.

1. Is $(3x^4 - x^3 + 2x^2 - 5) - (2x^4 + x^3 + x^2 - 4) = x^4 + x^2 - 9$?

2. Is $(3x^4 - x^3 + 2x^2 - 5) - (2x^4 + x^3 + x^2 - 4) = x^4 - 2x^3 + x^2 - 1$?

3. $2x^2(x^2 - 3x - 2) = 2x^4 - 6x^3 - 4x^2$?

4. Is $\left(\dfrac{1}{2}x\right)\left(2x + \dfrac{1}{3}\right) = x^2 - \dfrac{1}{6}x$?

For the next exercise, note that the screen setting for decimals does not show the graph very well. Try going back to the standard screen.

5. Is $-0.4x(7 - 5x + x^2) = 2.8x + 2x^2 - 0.4x^3$?

The same technique can also be used to check polynomial division when the polynomials involve only one variable. Use the technique to check the following polynomial divisions to see whether they are true or false.

6. Is $\dfrac{2x^3 - 6x^2 + 2x}{2x} = x^2 - 3x + 1$?

7. Is $\dfrac{-6x^2 + 9x}{-3x} = 2x + 3$?

8. Is $\dfrac{-8x^4 + 4x^3 - 8x^2 + 4x}{4x} = -2x^3 + x^2 - 2x + 4$?

9. Is $\dfrac{3x^4 - 3x^3 + 3x}{3x} = x^3 - x^2 + 1$?

 ## Experiencing Algebra the Group Way

Long Division of Polynomials

In order to divide a polynomial by another polynomial that is not a monomial, you can use the long division algorithm. First divide 25,461 by 123, using long division, to recall the steps. In your group, discuss the following example, and compare the steps to those you would follow if you were dividing one number by another using long division. Then work through the example, being sure that each member of the group understands the steps.

   Divide $4x^3 + 3x + 5$ by $2x - 3$. You will need to write any missing addends with 0 coefficients in order to keep the columns straight.

$$2x - 3 \overline{)4x^3 + 0x^2 + 3x + 5}$$ Write as long division. Write missing addend with 0 coefficient.

$$\begin{array}{r} 2x^2 \\ 2x - 3 \overline{)4x^3 + 0x^2 + 3x + 5} \end{array}$$ Divide the first term of the dividend by the first term of the divisor.

$$\begin{array}{r} 2x^2 \\ 2x - 3 \overline{)4x^3 + 0x^2 + 3x + 5} \\ 4x^3 - 6x^2 \end{array}$$ Multiply the partial quotient by the divisor.

$$\begin{array}{r} 2x^2 \\ 2x - 3 \overline{)4x^3 + 0x^2 + 3x + 5} \\ -(4x^3 - 6x^2) \\ \hline 6x^2 + 3x \end{array}$$ Subtract (change signs and add) and bring down the next term.

$$\begin{array}{r} 2x^2 + 3x \\ 2x - 3 \overline{)4x^3 + 0x^2 + 3x + 5} \\ -(4x^3 - 6x^2) \\ \hline 6x^2 + 3x \end{array}$$ Divide the first term of the new dividend by the first term of the divisor.

$$\begin{array}{r} 2x^2 + 3x \\ 2x - 3 \overline{\smash{\big)}\, 4x^3 + 0x^2 + 3x + 5} \\ -\underline{(4x^3 - 6x^2)} \\ 6x^2 + 3x \\ 6x^2 - 9x \end{array}$$

Multiply the partial quotient by the divisor.

$$\begin{array}{r} 2x^2 + 3x \\ 2x - 3 \overline{\smash{\big)}\, 4x^3 + 0x^2 + 3x + 5} \\ -\underline{(4x^3 - 6x^2)} \\ 6x^2 + 3x \\ -\underline{(6x^2 - 9x)} \\ 12x + 5 \end{array}$$

Subtract (change signs and add) and bring down the next term.

$$\begin{array}{r} 2x^2 + 3x + 6 \\ 2x - 3 \overline{\smash{\big)}\, 4x^3 + 0x^2 + 3x + 5} \\ -\underline{(4x^3 - 6x^2)} \\ 6x^2 + 3x \\ -\underline{(6x^2 - 9x)} \\ 12x + 5 \end{array}$$

Divide the first term of the new dividend by the first term of the divisor.

$$\begin{array}{r} 2x^2 + 3x + 6 \\ 2x - 3 \overline{\smash{\big)}\, 4x^3 + 0x^2 + 3x + 5} \\ -\underline{(4x^3 - 6x^2)} \\ 6x^2 + 3x \\ -\underline{(6x^2 - 9x)} \\ 12x + 5 \\ 12x - 18 \end{array}$$

Multiply the partial quotient by the divisor.

$$\begin{array}{r} 2x^2 + 3x + 6 + \dfrac{23}{2x - 3} \\ 2x - 3 \overline{\smash{\big)}\, 4x^3 + 0x^2 + 3x + 5} \\ -\underline{(4x^3 - 6x^2)} \\ 6x^2 + 3x \\ -\underline{(6x^2 - 9x)} \\ 12x + 5 \\ -\underline{(12x - 18)} \\ 23 \end{array}$$

Subtract (change signs and add). Write the remainder as a fraction in the quotient.

Now have each member of the group use long division to perform the following polynomial divisions.
Compare your work to be sure that each member of the group can use this method.

1. Divide $2x^2 + 11x - 21$ by $x + 7$.

2. $\dfrac{6x^2 - x + 9}{3x + 1}$

3. $\dfrac{3b^2 + 22b - 16}{b + 8}$

4. $\dfrac{x^3 - 1}{x - 1}$

5. Divide $x^2 + 10x + 25$ by $x + 3$.

6. $(x^4 - 81) \div (x + 3)$

Experiencing Algebra the Write Way

In this section, you were asked to subtract polynomials. The directions were written several different ways. You must be careful that you correctly determine which polynomial is being subtracted from which. For example, if you are asked to subtract $(5x^2 - 6)$ from $(11x^2 - 2x + 3)$, which of the following expressions is the correct one?

1. $5x^2 - 6 - 11x^2 - 2x + 3$

2. $11x^2 - 2x + 3 - 5x^2 - 6$

3. $(5x^2 - 6) - (11x^2 - 2x + 3)$

4. $(11x^2 - 2x + 3) - (5x^2 - 6)$

Explain why you think a particular expression is the correct one. Then describe the error(s) in the other three expressions.

10.3 More Polynomial Multiplication

Objectives

1 Multiply two binomials.

2 Multiply polynomials of two or more terms.

3 Multiply polynomials resulting in special products.

4 Model real-world situations using polynomials.

Application

The design of a swimming pool calls for the length to be twice its width. A 5-foot concrete walkway surrounds the pool. A customer would like to cover the walkway with ceramic tiles.

Swimming pool

a. Determine a function, $A(w)$, for the area covered by the walkway.

b. If each ceramic tile measures 12 inches by 6 inches, determine a function, $N(w)$, for the number of tiles needed to cover the walkway.

After completing this section, we will discuss this application further. See page 734.

In this section, we multiply polynomials when both factors have more than one term. First, we multiply two binomials.

---

1 Multiplying Binomials

To multiply binomials, we need to use the distributive law. For example,

$$\begin{aligned}
(x + 2)(x + 3) &= (x + 2)x + (x + 2)3 && \text{Distribute } (x + 2).\\
&= x^2 + 2x + 3x + 6 && \text{Distribute } x \text{ and } 3.\\
&= x^2 + 5x + 6 && \text{Collect like terms.}
\end{aligned}$$

or

$$\begin{aligned}
(x + 2)(x + 3) &= x(x + 3) + 2(x + 3) && \text{Distribute } (x + 3).\\
&= x^2 + 3x + 2x + 6 && \text{Distribute } x \text{ and } 2.\\
&= x^2 + 5x + 6 && \text{Collect like terms.}
\end{aligned}$$

or

$$x + 2 \quad \text{Vertical method}$$
$$\underline{x + 3}$$
$$3x + 6 \quad \text{Distribute 3.}$$
$$\underline{x^2 + 2x} \quad \text{Distribute } x.$$
$$x^2 + 5x + 6 \quad \text{Collect like terms.}$$

All three methods result in the same polynomial, $x^2 + 5x + 6$.

To multiply two binomial factors, use the distributive law to distribute the terms of one factor over the two terms of the second binomial factor.

> *Products with Two Binomial Factors*
>
> $$(a + b)(c + d) = a(c + d) + b(c + d)$$
> $$= ac + ad + bc + bd$$

For example,

$$(a + b)(c + d) = a(c + d) + b(c + d)$$

$$(x + 4)(x - 5) = x(x - 5) + 4(x - 5)$$
$$= x^2 - 5x + 4x - 20$$
$$= x^2 - x - 20$$

This process is sometimes called the **FOIL** method. This comes from the following labels:

| first term | last term | first term | last term | **First** terms | **Outside** terms | **Inside** terms | **Last** terms |

$$(a \ + \ b) \ (c \ + \ d) = ac \ + \ ad \ + \ bc \ + \ bd$$

outside term · inside term · inside term · outside term

For example,

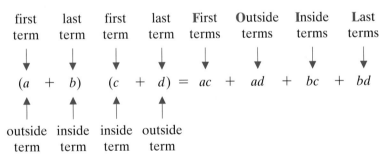

$$(x + 4)(x - 5) = x^2 - 5x + 4x - 20 = x^2 - x - 20$$

EXAMPLE 1 Multiply.

a. $(2x + 3)(4x - 1)$ **b.** $(x + 3)(x - 3)$ **c.** $(x + 5)^2$

Solution

$$\textbf{a.} \quad (2x + 3)(4x - 1) \overset{\text{F} \quad \text{O} \quad \text{I} \quad \text{L}}{=} 8x^2 - 2x + 12x - 3$$
$$= 8x^2 + 10x - 3 \qquad \text{Collect like terms.}$$

$$\textbf{b.} \quad (x + 3)(x - 3) \overset{\text{F} \quad \text{O} \quad \text{I} \quad \text{L}}{=} x^2 - 3x + 3x - 9$$
$$= x^2 + 0x - 9 \qquad \text{Collect like terms.}$$
$$= x^2 - 9$$

$$\textbf{c.} \quad (x + 5)^2 = (x + 5)(x + 5) \qquad \text{Expand.}$$
$$= x^2 + 5x + 5x + 25 \qquad \text{FOIL}$$
$$= x^2 + 10x + 25 \qquad \text{Collect like terms.} \quad \blacksquare$$

Experiencing Algebra the Checkup Way

In exercises 1–3, multiply.

1. $(a + 7)(7a + 1)$ **2.** $(2y - 1)(2y + 1)$ **3.** $(x - 5)^2$

4. When multiplying one binomial expression by another, you can use the FOIL method or the distributive law. Which do you prefer to use, and why?

---

2 Multiplying Polynomials

To multiply two polynomial factors, pick one factor and distribute its terms over all the terms of the second polynomial. We can do this several ways. Two examples are given next.

$$(x - 4)(x^2 + 2x - 1)$$
$$= x(x^2 + 2x - 1) - 4(x^2 + 2x - 1) \qquad \text{Distribute } (x^2 + 2x - 1).$$
$$= x^3 + 2x^2 - x - 4x^2 - 8x + 4 \qquad \text{Distribute } x \text{ and } -4.$$
$$= x^3 - 2x^2 - 9x + 4 \qquad \text{Collect like terms.}$$

or

$$\begin{array}{r} x^2 + 2x - 1 \\ \underline{x - 4} \\ -4x^2 - 8x + 4 \qquad \text{Distribute } -4. \\ \underline{x^3 + 2x^2 - x } \qquad \text{Distribute } x. \\ x^3 - 2x^2 - 9x + 4 \end{array}$$

Vertical method

> **Products with Polynomial Factors**
> To multiply two polynomial factors, use the distributive law to distribute the terms of one factor over the terms of the second polynomial factor.

EXAMPLE 2   Multiply.

     a. $(a^2 + 2a + 5)(a^2 - a + 4)$ **b.** $(x - 2)^3$

Solution

$$\textbf{a.} \quad (a^2 + 2a + 5)(a^2 - a + 4)$$
$$= a^2(a^2 - a + 4) + 2a(a^2 - a + 4) + 5(a^2 - a + 4) \qquad \text{Distribute.}$$
$$= a^4 - a^3 + 4a^2 + 2a^3 - 2a^2 + 8a + 5a^2 - 5a + 20 \qquad \text{Distribute.}$$
$$= a^4 + a^3 + 7a^2 + 3a + 20 \qquad \text{Simplify.}$$

b. $(x - 2)^3 = (x - 2)(x - 2)(x - 2)$ Expand.

$\qquad\qquad = \left[x(x - 2) - 2(x - 2)\right](x - 2)$ Distribute $(x - 2)$.

$\qquad\qquad = (x^2 - 2x - 2x + 4)(x - 2)$ Distribute x and 2.

$\qquad\qquad = (x^2 - 4x + 4)(x - 2)$ Collect like terms.

$\qquad\qquad = x(x^2 - 4x + 4) - 2(x^2 - 4x + 4)$ Distribute $(x^2 - 4x + 4)$.

$\qquad\qquad = x^3 - 4x^2 + 4x - 2x^2 + 8x - 8$ Distribute x and 2.

$\qquad\qquad = x^3 - 6x^2 + 12x - 8$ Collect like terms. ■

Experiencing Algebra the Checkup Way

In exercises 1–2, multiply.

1. $(x + 2)(3x^2 - 2x - 8)$ **2.** $(x + y)^3$

3. You have seen two methods for multiplying two polynomials. One is to use the distributive property repeatedly and the other is to perform vertical multiplication. Which would you choose to use and why?

---

3   Special Products   In previous exercises we determined certain products that we now identify as **special products**.

    The **product of a sum and difference of the same two terms** is considered a special product. To determine a rule for this product, complete the following set.

D I S C O V E R Y   5

Product of the Sum and Difference of the Same Two Terms
Multiply.

1. $(x + 5)(x - 5)$ **2.** $(3x + 1)(3x - 1)$ **3.** $(x + y)(x - y)$

Write a rule to determine by inspection the product of the sum and difference of the same two terms.

    The product of the sum and difference of the same two terms is the difference of the square of the first term and the square of the second term.

> *Product of the Sum and Difference of the Same Two Terms*
> $$(a + b)(a - b) = a^2 - b^2$$

We know this is true by determining the product algebraically:

$$(a + b)(a - b) = a^2 - ab + ab - b^2$$
$$= a^2 - b^2$$

For example, multiply $(x + 2)(x - 2)$.

$$(a + b)(a - b) = a^2 - b^2$$

$$(x + 2)(x - 2) = x^2 - 2^2 = x^2 - 4$$

The **square of a binomial** is also considered a special product. To determine a rule for this product, complete the following set.

DISCOVERY 6

Square of a Binomial

Rewrite in expanded form and multiply.

1. $(x + 5)^2$ **2.** $(3x - 1)^2$ **3.** $(x + y)^2$ **4.** $(x - y)^2$

Write a rule to determine by inspection the product for the square of a binomial.

The square of a binomial that is a sum of two terms is the square of the first term, plus two times the product of the first and last terms, plus the square of the last term. The square of a binomial that is a difference of two terms is the square of the first term, minus two times the product of the first and last terms, plus the square of the last term.

Square of a Binomial

$$(a + b)^2 = a^2 + 2ab + b^2$$
$$(a - b)^2 = a^2 - 2ab + b^2$$

We can also determine these products algebraically:

$$(a + b)^2 = (a + b)(a + b) \qquad (a - b)^2 = (a - b)(a - b)$$
$$= a^2 + ab + ab + b^2 \qquad\qquad = a^2 - ab - ab + b^2$$
$$= a^2 + 2ab + b^2 \qquad\qquad = a^2 - 2ab + b^2$$

For example, multiply $(x + 2)^2$ and $(x - 2)^2$.

$$(a + b)^2 = a^2 + 2 \quad a \quad b + b^2$$
$$\downarrow\ \downarrow \quad\ \downarrow \quad \downarrow\downarrow\downarrow \quad\ \downarrow$$
$$(x + 2)^2 = x^2 + 2 \cdot 2 \cdot x + 2^2 = x^2 + 4x + 4.$$

$$(a - b)^2 = a^2 - 2 \quad a \quad b + b^2$$
$$\downarrow\ \downarrow \quad\ \downarrow \quad \downarrow\downarrow\downarrow \quad\ \downarrow$$
$$(x - 2)^2 = x^2 - 2 \cdot 2 \cdot x + 2^2 = x^2 - 4x + 4.$$

 Helping Hand These special products are helpful to know, but can be found without memorizing the formulas by simply using the FOIL method of multiplying two binomials.

EXAMPLE 3 Multiply.

a. $(2x - 5)(2x + 5)$ **b.** $(2x + 5)^2$

Solution

a. This is the product of the sum and difference of the same two terms. The first term is $2x$ and the second term is 5.

$$(a \; + \; b)(a \; - \; b) = \; a^2 \; - \; b^2$$

$$(2x \; - \; 5)(2x \; + \; 5) = \; (2x)^2 \; - \; 5^2$$
$$= \; 4x^2 \; - \; 25$$

b. This is the square of a binomial. The binomial is a sum of $2x$ and 5.

$$(a \; + \; b)^2 = \; a^2 \; + \; 2 \; a \; b \; + \; b^2$$

$$(2x \; + \; 5)^2 = (2x)^2 \; + \; 2\,(2x)(5) \; + \; 5^2$$
$$= \; 4x^2 \; + \qquad 20x \; + \; 25 \qquad \blacksquare$$

 ## Experiencing Algebra the Checkup Way

In exercises 1–3, multiply.

1. $(3y - 7)(3y + 7)$ **2.** $(3y - 7)^2$ **3.** $(3y + 7)^2$

4. You can choose to learn the forms for special products, or you can choose to obtain the results by just applying the general rules for polynomial multiplication as described in previous sections of this chapter. Which do you prefer? Why?

---

4 Modeling the Real World   We have seen that many important quantities are expressed as products. Geometric areas are products of the sides of a rectangle, or the square of the side of a square, or the product of the base and the height of a parallelogram. Volumes are products of three dimensions, such as the width, length, and height of a rectangular solid, or the third power of the side of a cube. Calculations of these kinds of quantities often involve multiplying polynomials.

EXAMPLE 4   A rectangular garden plot has a length that is twice its width. Jay plans to increase the length by 5 feet and decrease the width by 2 feet. Write a polynomial representation of the area of the new garden plot in terms of the original width, w.

Solution

Let $w =$ original width (in feet)
      $2w =$ original length (in feet)

$w - 2 =$ new width (in feet)
$2w + 5 =$ new length (in feet)

The area is the product of the length and width.

$$(2w + 5)(w - 2) = 2w^2 - 4w + 5w - 10$$
$$= 2w^2 + w - 10$$

The new area is $(2w^2 + w - 10)$ square feet. ∎

EXAMPLE 5 Donya is making a rectangular toy box. She wants the length to be 6 inches more than the width and the height to be 3 inches more than the width. She plans to partition the inside of the toy box into three equal sections.
Find a polynomial representation for the volume of each section.

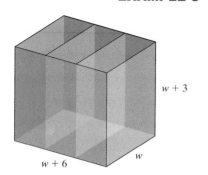

$w + 3$

$w + 6$ w

Solution

The volume of a rectangular solid is found by multiplying the length, width, and height.

Let w = width of the box in inches
$w + 6$ = length of the box in inches
$w + 3$ = height of the box in inches

A polynomial expression for the total volume is

$$w(w + 6)(w + 3).$$

To find the volume of one section, divide the total volume by 3.

$$\frac{w(w + 6)(w + 3)}{3}$$

Simplify this expression.

$$\frac{w(w^2 + 3w + 6w + 18)}{3} = \frac{w(w^2 + 9w + 18)}{3}$$
$$= \frac{w^3 + 9w^2 + 18w}{3}$$
$$= \frac{w^3}{3} + \frac{9w^2}{3} + \frac{18w}{3}$$
$$= \frac{1}{3}w^3 + 3w^2 + 6w$$

The volume of one section of the toy box is $\left(\frac{1}{3}w^3 + 3w^2 + 6w\right)$ cubic inches.
∎

Application

The design of a swimming pool calls for the length to be twice its width. A 5-foot concrete walkway surrounds the pool. A customer would like to cover the walkway with ceramic tiles.

a. Determine a function, $A(w)$, for the area covered by the walkway.
b. If each ceramic tile measures 12 inches by 6 inches, determine a function, $N(w)$, for the number of tiles needed to cover the walkway.

Discussion

a. Let $w =$ the width of the pool in feet

$2w =$ length of the pool in feet

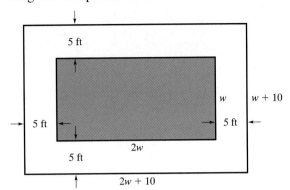

The walkway extends 5 feet on each side of the pool. Therefore, the width of the pool and the walkway is $(w + 10)$ feet. The length of the pool and walkway is $(2w + 10)$ feet.

The area of the pool and walkway is the length times the width.

$$(w + 10)(2w + 10) = (2w^2 + 30w + 100) \text{ square feet.}$$

The area of the pool is the width times the length, $w(2w)$, or $2w^2$ square feet.

A function for the area of the walkway, in square feet, is the area of the pool and walkway combined minus the area of the pool.

$$A(w) = (2w^2 + 30w + 100) - (2w^2)$$
$$A(w) = 30w + 100$$

b. Each tile measures 12 inches by 6 inches or 1 foot by 0.5 feet. The area of each tile is the product of 1 foot by 0.5 feet or 0.5 square feet.

A function for the number of tiles needed is the total area of the walkway divided by the area of each tile.

$$N(w) = \frac{30w + 100}{0.5}$$
$$N(w) = 60w + 200$$

∎

Experiencing Algebra the Checkup Way

1. Jay has another garden plot for flowers. It is a square garden. He wishes to make it rectangular by increasing one side by 4 feet to become the width, and by enlarging the other side to 3 feet more than 2 times its original measure to become the length. Write a polynomial expression to represent the area of the new flower garden in terms of its original side, s. What is the area of the new garden if it measured 5 feet on a side before the increase?

2. Donya makes a second toy box. For this box, the width is 5 inches more than twice the height and the length is 8 inches longer than the width. The box will be partitioned into two equal compartments. Find a polynomial representation for the volume of each compartment. What will be the volume of the box if the height of the box is 10 inches?

3. A rectangular garden has a length that is three times its width. A brick walkway around the garden measures 2 feet across. Determine a function for the area covered by the walkway. If each brick covers an area of 0.4 square feet, determine a function for the number of bricks needed to cover the walkway.

PROBLEM SET 10.3

Experiencing Algebra the Exercise Way

Multiply.

1. $(x + 3)(x + 8)$

2. $(a - 5)(a - 11)$

3. $(2x + 1)(3x - 4)$

4. $(5x + 3)(4x - 1)$

5. $(4 - x)(x + 2)$

6. $(6 + a)(a - 7)$

7. $(5 + x)(3 + 2x)$

8. $(4 + z)(1 + 7z)$

9. $(2x + 5)(3y - 2)$

10. $(5a - 2)(3b + 4)$

11. $(3x + 4y)(x - 2y)$

12. $(2a + 3b)(a - 4b)$

13. $(a - 2.4)(5a + 3.8)$

14. $(p - 1.7)(4p + 2.9)$

15. $(2x + 1.1)(3y + 3.2)$

16. $(5m - 4.9)(4n + 2.7)$

17. $\left(a + \dfrac{2}{3}\right)\left(a + \dfrac{1}{3}\right)$

18. $\left(x - \dfrac{1}{5}\right)\left(x + \dfrac{3}{5}\right)$

19. $\left(2x + \dfrac{1}{4}\right)\left(8x - \dfrac{1}{6}\right)$

20. $\left(\dfrac{2}{3}x - 5\right)\left(\dfrac{3}{5}x - 4\right)$

21. $(2x^2 - 3)(x^2 + 4)$

22. $(5x^3 + 1)(x^3 - 3)$

23. $(4x^2 + 3)(2x + 1)$

24. $(6x^3 - 5)(4x^2 - 3)$

25. $(2x + 3y^2)(3x^2 - 5y)$

26. $(4a^2 + 3b)(6a - 5b^2)$

27. $(3a^2 + 5b^3)(a^2 + b^3)$

28. $(7x^4 - 2y^3)(4x^4 - y^3)$

29. $(x + 1)(x^2 - x + 1)$

30. $(x - 1)(x^2 + x + 1)$

31. $(3x - 2)(2x^2 - 5x - 3)$

32. $(4x + 3)(x^2 - 5x - 2)$

33. $(x^2 + x + 1)(x^2 + 2x + 3)$

34. $(a^2 + a - 2)(a^2 - 2a + 1)$

35. $(a + b + c)^2$

36. $(a - b - c)^2$

37. $(z + 3)^3$

38. $(r + 2)^3$

39. $(3a - 2b)^3$

40. $(2x - 3y)^3$

41. $(x - 5)(x + 5)$

42. $(y + 12)(y - 12)$

43. $(3m + 7)(3m - 7)$

44. $(5p - 4)(5p + 4)$

45. $(2a + 3b)(2a - 3b)$

46. $(9p - 2q)(9p + 2q)$

47. $(4x - 1.5)(4x + 1.5)$

48. $(3z + 2.5)(3z - 2.5)$

49. $\left(\dfrac{2}{5}x - 1\right)\left(\dfrac{2}{5}x + 1\right)$

50. $\left(\dfrac{4}{7}y - 2\right)\left(\dfrac{4}{7}y + 2\right)$

51. $\left(\dfrac{1}{3}x + \dfrac{4}{5}\right)\left(\dfrac{1}{3}x - \dfrac{4}{5}\right)$

52. $\left(\dfrac{5}{7}y + \dfrac{3}{4}\right)\left(\dfrac{5}{7}y - \dfrac{3}{4}\right)$

53. $(x^2 + 7)(x^2 - 7)$

54. $(y^3 - 9)(y^3 + 9)$

55. $(2x^3 + 5y)(2x^3 - 5y)$

56. $(5a^5 - 2b^2)(5a^5 + 2b^2)$

57. $(m + 7)^2$

58. $(p + 6)^2$

59. $(x - y)^2$

60. $(u - v)^2$

61. $(2p + 9q)^2$

62. $(5m - 11n)^2$

63. $(6c - 5)^2$

64. $(8d + 3)^2$ **65.** $(3x^3 + 2)^2$ **66.** $(2z^2 - 5)^2$

67. $(2x^2 - 3y^3)^2$ **68.** $(5x^3 + 3y^2)^2$

69. A box is to be made out of a rectangular piece of cardboard that is 12 inches wide and 18 inches long. Squares, x inches on a side, are cut out of the corners, and the sides are bent upward.

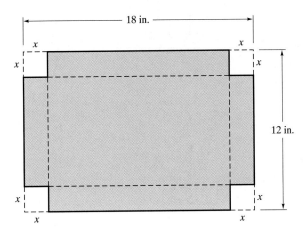

 a. Write expressions for the length, width, and height of the box.

 b. Write a simplified expression for the volume of the box.

 c. Write a simplified expression for the outside surface area of the box. (Note that the box does not have a top.)

 d. Find the volume and outside surface area of the box if squares measuring 2 inches on a side are cut from the corners.

70. A box is to be made out of a square piece of cardboard that is 10 inches on a side. Squares, y inches on a side, are cut out of the corners, and the sides are then bent upward.

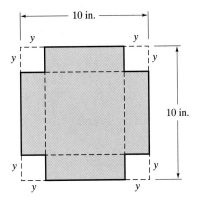

 a. Write expressions for the length, width, and height of the box.

 b. Write a simplified expression for the volume of the box.

 c. Write a simplified expression for the outside surface area of the box, which does not have a top.

 d. Find the volume and outside surface area of the box if squares measuring 1.5 inches on a side are cut from the corners.

71. Sammy wants to put a circular redwood deck around his circular pool. He wants the deck to be 5 feet wide. If the radius from the center of the pool to the outer edge of the deck is x feet, write a polynomial to represent the area of the deck by completing the following steps.

a. Find the area of the outer circle.

b. Find the area of the inner circle.

c. Find the difference of the two areas, which will be the area of the deck.

d. What is the exact area of the deck if the distance from the center of the pool to the outer edge of the deck is 22 feet?

72. A circular barbecue pit at the Butcher Shop Restaurant is surrounded by a concrete walkway. The distance from the center of the pit to the outer edge of the walkway is 6 feet.

a. Find the area of the outer circle.

b. Find the area of the inner circle.

c. Find the difference of the two areas, which will be the area of the walkway.

d. What is the exact area of the walkway if the distance from its inner edge to its outer edge is 3 feet?

73. Mike wants to enlarge his garage. It was built as a cube, with its height equal to its width equal to its length. He wants to increase the width by 5 feet and the length by 8 feet so that he can add a workshop.

a. What is the current volume of the garage if its original height measures x feet?

b. What will be the new volume of the garage?

c. What will be the ratio of the new volume to the old volume of the garage?

d. What is the ratio of the new volume to the old volume if the original garage had a height of 12 feet?

74. An office in the shape of a cube is to be enlarged. The width of the office is to be increased by 8 feet and the length is to measure twice the new width.

a. What is the current volume of the office if its original height measures x feet?

b. What will be the new volume of the office?

c. What will be the ratio of the new volume to the old volume of the office?

d. What is the ratio of the new volume to the old volume if the original office had a height of 9.5 feet?

Experiencing Algebra the Calculator Way

In previous sections, you were shown a technique for checking the equivalence of one-variable polynomial expressions by graphing. Use the technique to check the equivalence of the following expressions. Experiment with different zoom settings (decimal, standard, integer, and so on) to find the best setting to view each expression. If the simplified expression does not check, perform the multiplication to obtain the correct equivalent expression.

1. Is $(2x - 1)(2x + 1) = 2x^2 - 1$?

2. Is $(x + 1)(x - 1) = x^2 + x + 2$?

3. Is $(x - 2)(x - 1) = x^2 - 3x + 2$?

4. Is $(0.5x + 1)(4x - 0.8) = 2x^2 + 3.6x - 0.8$?

5. Is $\left(\frac{1}{2}x - 3\right)\left(2x + \frac{1}{3}\right) = x^2 - \frac{35}{6}x + 1$?

6. Is $(x^2 + 4)(x^2 - 1) = x^4 + 3x^2 - 4$?

7. Is $(x^2 + 1)(2x - 1) = 2x^3 - x^2 + 2x - 1$?

8. Is $(x^2 - 1)(0.3x - 1.4) = 0.3x^3 - 1.4x^2 - 0.3x - 1.4$?

Experiencing Algebra the Group Way

More about Special Products

In this section you have seen some special polynomials that are created by multiplication of binomials and/or polynomials. Some of these are listed here. Work together in your group to match each product with the correct polynomial. (Members of the group can carry out the indicated multiplications in order to find the match.)

1. $(A + B)(A - B)$ **A.** $A^2 + 2AB + B^2$

2. $(A + B)^2$ **B.** $A^2 - 2AB + B^2$

3. $(A - B)^2$ **C.** $A^2 - B^2$

4. $(A - 1)(A^2 + A + 1)$ **D.** $A^3 - B^3$

5. $(A + 1)(A^2 - A + 1)$ **E.** $A^3 + 1$

6. $(A - B)(A^2 + AB + B^2)$ **F.** $A^3 - 1$

7. $(A + B)(A^2 - AB + B^2)$ **G.** $A^3 + B^3$

Note that since $(A - B)(A + B) = A^2 - B^2$, $\dfrac{A^2 - B^2}{A + B} = A - B$, because division can be related to multiplication.

   Now, have each member of the group use the preceding relationships to perform the following division problems by inspection. (Again, remember that division is another way of stating a multiplication problem.) Compare your answers and agree on the correct result.

8. $(a^2 + 2ab + b^2) \div (a + b)$

9. $(x^3 - y^3) \div (x - y)$

10. $(x^3 + 1) \div (x^2 - x + 1)$

11. $(a^2 - b^2) \div (a + b)$

12. $(x^2 - 16x + 64) \div (x - 8)$

13. $(z^3 + 125) \div (z + 5)$

14. $(b^3 - 1) \div (b - 1)$

15. $(x^6 - y^6) \div (x^3 - y^3)$

16. $(4p^2 - 9q^2) \div (2p + 3q)$

17. $(8x^3 - 729) \div (2x - 9)$

Experiencing Algebra the Write Way

Pascal's Triangle

Blaise Pascal was a renowned mathematician who was born in 1623 and died in 1662. He showed phenomenal ability in mathematics at an early age. In 1653 he wrote extensively on the triangular arrangement of the coefficients of the powers of a binomial. The following exercise illustrates his findings.

Use the multiplication rule to express the following binomial powers as polynomials.

$(x + y)^0 =$

$(x + y)^1 =$

$(x + y)^2 =$

$(x + y)^3 =$

$(x + y)^4 =$

Next, complete the following chart, where each box entry is the sum of the two entries directly above the box.

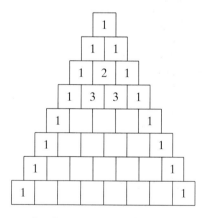

Compare the chart entries in a given row with the coefficients obtained in the preceding power expansions. Explain the relationship between the two. This chart is called Pascal's Triangle. Describe how to use the chart to easily rewrite a binomial such as $(x + y)$ raised to a power as a polynomial. Use the chart to write the polynomial expansion of $(x + y)^7$.

10.4 Common Factors and Factoring by Grouping

Objectives
1 Determine greatest common factors for sets of monomials.
2 Factor out greatest common monomial factors from polynomials.
3 Factor out greatest common polynomial factors from polynomials.
4 Factor polynomials by grouping.
5 Model real-world situations by factoring greatest common factors from polynomials.

Application

A horticulturalist working for Wilson's Nursery redesigned a square display area of width w feet, as shown in Figure 10.1. The designer approximated the numerical value for the area of the new rectangular design using a polynomial, $w^3 + 5w^2 + w + 5$. Factor the polynomial to determine the dimensions of the display in terms of the width of the original square, w. Describe the dimensions of the new design.

Figure 10.1

After completing this section, we will discuss this application further. See page 750.

The next few sections in this chapter deal with methods for rewriting polynomials as the products of simpler factors. These methods are important for simplifying complicated polynomials so we can use them more easily.

---

1 Determining the Greatest Common Factor

In Chapter 1 we stated that two numbers that are multiplied together are called factors of the product. For example,

since $1 \cdot 12 = 12$, then 1 and 12 are factors of 12.
since $2 \cdot 6 = 12$, then 2 and 6 are factors of 12.
since $3 \cdot 4 = 12$, then 3 and 4 are factors of 12.

Also, we may describe a factor of a given number as a number that divides into the given number evenly, or with a remainder of 0. For example, 2 is a factor of 12 because 2 divides into 12 with a remainder of 0.

To determine the integer factors of a number, divide the number by all the integers whose absolute value is less than or equal to the number itself. The integers that divide evenly are factors.

For example, determine all the positive integer factors of 24.

Divide 24 by the positive integers from 1 to 24.
The integers that divide with a remainder of 0 are as follows:

$$\begin{array}{cccccccc} 24 & 12 & 8 & 6 & 4 & 3 & 2 & 1 \\ 1\overline{)24} & 2\overline{)24} & 3\overline{)24} & 4\overline{)24} & 6\overline{)24} & 8\overline{)24} & 12\overline{)24} & 24\overline{)24} \end{array}$$

The positive integer factors of 24 are 1, 2, 3, 4, 6, 8, 12, and 24.

Since we are repeatedly dividing by consecutive integers, the calculator will do this quickly for us in a table.

To set up a table for integer factors of a number on your calculator:

- Set the table to automatically generate positive integers for the independent variable.
- Set the second column in the table to be the number divided by these positive integers, x.
- View the table to find the integer factors that are in the first column that correspond to an integer in the second column.

 Helping Hand Remember, there is no need to look beyond the numbers whose absolute value is the number itself.

For example, determine the integer factors of 24.

The integer factors of 24 are $-24, -12, -8 -6, -4, -3, -2, -1, 1, 2, 3,$ $4, 6, 8, 12,$ and 24, as shown in Figures 10.2a and 10.2b.

TECHNOLOGY

X	Y1	
1	24	
2	12	
3	8	
4	6	
5	4.8	
6	4	
7	3.4286	
X=1		

Figure 10.2a

X	Y1	
-7	-3.429	
-6	-4	
-5	-4.8	
-4	-6	
-3	-8	
-2	-12	
-1	-24	
X=-7		

Figure 10.2b

View the table.

[2nd] [TABLE]

For Figure 10.2a
Set the first column for integers.

[2nd] [TBLSET] [1] [ENTER] [1]
[ENTER] [ENTER] [▼] [ENTER]

Set the second column for the number divided by the integers in the first column.

Move down the table to determine additional positive integer factors of 24.

For Figure 10.2b
Move up the table to determine negative integer factors of 24.

The **greatest common factor (GCF)** for a set of numbers is the largest factor common to all the numbers.

To find the GCF for a set of numbers, determine the factors for each number in the set and then choose the largest factor common to all the sets of factors. For example, determine the GCF for 24, 36, and 72.

The factors of 24 are 1, 2, 3, 4, 6, 8, 12, 24.
The factors of 36 are 1, 2, 3, 4, 6, 9, 12, 18, 36.
The factors of 72 are 1, 2, 3, 4, 6, 8, 9, 12, 18, 36, 72.

largest common factor = 12

The GCF of 24, 36, and 72 is 12.

Now we need to determine a method to find the GCF for a set of monomials with only variable factors. Complete the following set of exercises.

D I S C O V E R Y   7

Greatest Common Factors for Monomials with Variable Factors

1. Write the following monomials in expanded form.

$x^3 = $ _____

$x^2 y = $ _____

$x^4 = $ _____

2. The variable common to the monomials x^3, $x^2 y$, and x^4 is __ .

3. There are __ of these variable factors common to the monomials x^3, $x^2 y$, and x^4.

4. The GCF for x^3, $x^2 y$, and x^4 is __ .

Write a rule to determine the GCF for a set of monomials with variable factors.

In viewing the expanded form of the monomials, we see that the common variable factor is repeated as a common factor for the number of times equal to the smallest exponent of that variable found in the monomials.

To find the GCF for a set of monomials with variable factors, determine the product of the common variable factors each having the smallest exponent common to that variable.

For example, determine the GCF for $a^3 b c^2$ and ac^4.

The variables a and c are common to both monomials. The smallest exponent of a common to both monomials is 1 and the smallest exponent of c common to both monomials is 2.

The GCF for $a^3 b c^2$ and ac^4 is the product $a^1 \cdot c^2$ or ac^2.

This process leads to an alternative method of finding the GCF for a set of numbers. Before we discuss this method, we need to define a **prime number** as a counting number greater than 1 that has exactly two different counting number factors, 1 and itself. The prime numbers less than 30 are

2, 3, 5, 7, 11, 13, 17, 19, 23, 29.

To factor a number *completely*, we write the number as a product of prime numbers. For example, factor 24 completely.

$$24 = 2 \cdot 2 \cdot 2 \cdot 3 = 2^3 \cdot 3$$

To find the GCF for a set of numbers, factor completely each number in the set and then determine the product of the common prime factors each having the smallest exponent to that prime number. For example, determine the GCF for 24, 36, and 72.

Write the prime factorization of each number.

$24 = 2 \cdot 2 \cdot 2 \cdot 3 = 2^3 \cdot 3$

$36 = 2 \cdot 2 \cdot 3 \cdot 3 = 2^2 \cdot 3^2$

$72 = 2 \cdot 2 \cdot 2 \cdot 3 \cdot 3 = 2^3 \cdot 3^2$

The prime factors common to all three numbers are 2 and 3. The smallest exponent of 2 is 2. The smallest exponent of 3 is 1.
  The GCF for 24, 36, and 72 is the product $2^2 \cdot 3^1$ or 12.

Determining the Greatest Common Factor
To find the GCF for a set of monomials, determine the product of

- the GCF for the coefficients;

- the GCF for each variable.

For example, determine the greatest common monomial factor for the monomials $24x^2yz^4$, $36x^3y^2z^3$, and $72x^2y^2z^2$.

The GCF for the coefficients of 24, 36, and 72 is 12.
  The GCF for the variable factors contains the smallest exponent common to each, or x^2, y, and z^2.
  $GCF = 12 \cdot x^2 \cdot y \cdot z^2$ or $12x^2yz^2$.

EXAMPLE 1   Determine the greatest common monomial factor for each set of monomials.

a. $12x^2y^4z^3$ and $30xy^3z^2$ **b.** $132a^2b^2c^2$ and $72a^2b^3$

Solution

a. $12x^2y^4z^3$ and $30xy^3z^2$
  The factors of 12 and 30 are small, and we should see that the GCF for the coefficients is 6.
  The GCF for the variable factors is xy^3z^2.
  The GCF for $12x^2y^4z^3$ and $30xy^3z^2$ is $6xy^3z^2$.

b. $132a^2b^2c^2$ and $72a^2b^3$
  The coefficients 132 and 72 are large, we will use the alternative method to find the GCF.

$132 = 2^2 \cdot 3 \cdot 11$ Factor each number completely.

$72 = 2^3 \cdot 3^2$

The GCF for the coefficients is $2^2 \cdot 3 = 12$.
  The GCF for the variable factors is a^2b^2.
  The GCF for $132a^2b^2c^2$ and $72a^2b^3$ is $12a^2b^2$. ∎

Experiencing Algebra the Checkup Way

Determine the greatest common monomial factor for each set of monomials.

1. $12a^2b^3c$; $18a^3bc^2$ **2.** $84x^3y^5z^2$; $210x^7y^3z^2$ **3.** $132pq$; $143p^3q^2r$; $77p^2r^3$

---

2 Factoring Out Greatest Common Monomial Factors

In Chapter 2 we reversed the distributive law in order to factor numeric expressions. The distributive law states that

$$a(b + c) = ab + ac \quad \text{or} \quad 2(3 + 4) = 2 \cdot 3 + 2 \cdot 4.$$

To reverse the law and factor,

$$ab + ac = a(b + c) \quad \text{or} \quad 2 \cdot 3 + 2 \cdot 4 = 2(3 + 4).$$

We are now ready to do the same for polynomials. (Later on, we will use this technique to simplify complicated rational expressions and equations.) To factor a polynomial completely, we first determine the greatest common factor (GCF) of its terms.

For example, factor $2x^2 + 4x + 6y$.

> The GCF of all the terms, $2x^2$, $4x$, and $6y$, is 2.
> Next, write each term as a product of the GCF and another factor.

$$2 \cdot x^2 + 2 \cdot 2x + 2 \cdot 3y$$

> Finally, reverse the distributive law and write a product of the GCF and a polynomial.

$$2(x^2 + 2x + 3y)$$

We can check all factoring by multiplying the factors and obtaining the original polynomial. This will verify that the product of the factors is equivalent to the original polynomial, but it will not verify that the polynomial is factored completely.

> *Factoring Out the GCF From a Polynomial*
> To factor out the GCF from a polynomial:
>
> - Determine the GCF for all the terms. If the GCF is 1, there is no need to continue.
> - Write each term as a product of the GCF and another factor.
> - Reverse the distributive law and write a product of the GCF and a polynomial.

Helping Hand If the first term of the polynomial is negative, write a product of the opposite of the GCF and a polynomial.

A polynomial factored completely will have no common factors in its terms. The polynomial $12x - 6y = 2(6x - 3y)$ is not factored completely because the terms in the polynomial factor $6x - 3y$ have a GCF, 3, and may be factored again. Therefore,

$$\begin{aligned}
12x - 6y &= 2(6x - 3y) \\
&= 2 \cdot 3(2x - y) \\
&= 6(2x - y)
\end{aligned}$$

Now $12x - 6y = 6(2x - y)$ is factored completely because the terms in the binomial $2x - y$ do not have a common factor.

EXAMPLE 2   Factor completely. Check the factors by multiplying.

    a. $-10x^4y^2 - 15xy^3 - 10x^2y^3$ **b.** $28a^3b^4 + 42a^4 - 14a^2b^5$

Solution

a. $-10x^4y^2 - 15xy^3 - 10x^2y^3$

> The GCF is $5xy^2$ but the first term is negative, so we write each term as a product of the opposite of the GCF, $-5xy^2$, and a factor.

$$= -5xy^2 \cdot 2x^3 + (-5xy^2) \cdot 3y + (-5xy^2) \cdot 2xy$$
$$= -5xy^2(2x^3 + 3y + 2xy)$$

> Write a product of the opposite of the GCF and a polynomial.

The check is left for you.

b. $28a^3b^4 + 42a^4 - 14a^2b^5$

> The GCF is $14a^2$.

$$= 14a^2 \cdot 2ab^4 + 14a^2 \cdot 3a^2 - 14a^2 \cdot b^5$$

> Write each term as a product of the GCF and a factor.

$$= 14a^2(2ab^4 + 3a^2 - b^5)$$

> Write a product of the GCF and a polynomial.

The check is left to you. ∎

✓ Experiencing Algebra the Checkup Way

Factor exercises 1–2 completely. Check the factors by multiplying.

1. $6a^3b^2 - 12a^2b^3 + 24a^2b^2$ **2.** $-8x^2y^3z - 24x^3y^2 + 36xyz$

3. How can you check to see that you have correctly factored a greatest common factor from a polynomial?

4. After you have factored a common factor from a polynomial, what should you do to be sure that you have factored the greatest common factor?

---

3   **Factoring Out Greatest Common Polynomial Factors**

A polynomial may have a smaller polynomial, other than a monomial, for the greatest common factor. For example,

> $2x(x + 1) + 3(x + 1)$ has two terms, $2x(x + 1)$ and $3(x + 1)$, and a GCF of $(x + 1)$.

To factor the polynomial $2x(x + 1) + 3(x + 1)$, we write a product of the GCF and another polynomial, or $(x + 1)(2x + 3)$.

     Remember, we should check to see that the product of the factors is equivalent to the simplification of the original polynomial. For example,

$$(x + 1)(2x + 3) = 2x^2 + 3x + 2x + 3 = 2x^2 + 5x + 3$$

is equivalent to the original polynomial

$$2x(x + 1) + 3(x + 1) = 2x^2 + 2x + 3x + 3 = 2x^2 + 5x + 3.$$

     If the polynomial is in one variable, a second method to check the factors would be to graph two functions, one defined by the original polynomial and one defined by the factored expression. The graphs should be equivalent, as shown in Figure 10.3.

TECHNOLOGY

Y1 = 2x(x + 1) + 3(x + 1)

Y2 = (x + 1)(2x + 3)

(−10, 10, −10, 10)

Figure 10.3

For Figure 10.3

Y=	2	X, T, θ, n	(	X, T, θ, n	+	1	)	+	3	(
X, T, θ, n	+	1	)
▼	(	X, T, θ, n	+	1	)	(	2	X, T, θ, n	+	3	)
▼	▲	◄	◄	ENTER	ENTER	ENTER	ENTER	GRAPH

The calculator will display a cursor as it graphs the second graph, which appears to trace the first graph. To confirm this, enter [TRACE].

Use the up and down arrow keys to determine the graphs are the same as you move along the graph with the left and right arrow keys.

EXAMPLE 3   Factor completely and check.

a. $3x(x^2 + 1) + 4(x^2 + 1)$ **b.** $5x^2(2x + 3y) - (2x + 3y)$

Solution

a. $3x(x^2 + 1) + 4(x^2 + 1) = (x^2 + 1)(3x + 4)$ The GCF is $(x^2 + 1)$. Write as a product of the GCF and a polynomial.

Y1 = 3x(x² + 1) + 4(x² + 1)

Y2 = (x² + 1)(3x + 4)

(−10, 10, −10, 10)

Multiplication check:
$$3x(x^2 + 1) + 4(x^2 + 1) = 3x^3 + 4x^2 + 3x + 4$$
$$(x^2 + 1)(3x + 4) = 3x^3 + 4x^2 + 3x + 4$$

Graphic check:
Graph Y1 = $3x(x^2 + 1) + 4(x^2 + 1)$ and Y2 = $(x^2 + 1)(3x + 4)$. Trace the graphs to verify that they are the same as shown to the left.

b. $5x^2(2x + 3y) - (2x + 3y) = (2x + 3y)(5x^2 - 1)$ The GCF is $(2x + 3y)$. Remember that $-(2x + 3y)$ is the same as $-1(2x + 3y)$.

The multiplication check is left for you. A graphic check is not possible because the polynomial has two variables. ∎

Experiencing Algebra the Checkup Way

Factor exercises 1–2 completely and check.

1. $7a(2a + b) + 4b(2a + b)$ **2.** $4x^2(3x - 2) - 3(3x - 2)$

3. What should you look for if you wish to factor a polynomial expression with fewer terms from a polynomial expression with more terms? That is, how would you recognize that there is a polynomial factor that can be extracted from a polynomial expression?

4 Factoring by Grouping

A polynomial may not appear to have a greatest common factor, such as the polynomial $2ax^2 + 4bx + axy + 2by$. However, if we rewrite this polynomial as a sum of two binomials, each binomial has a GCF.

$$2ax^2 + 4bx + axy + 2by$$
$$(2ax^2 + 4bx) + (axy + 2by)$$

The first binomial, $2ax^2 + 4bx$, has a GCF of $2x$. The second binomial, $axy + 2by$, has a GCF of y. Write each binomial as a product of the GCF and another binomial.

$$2x(ax + 2b) + y(ax + 2b)$$

Now the two terms $2x(ax + 2b)$ and $y(ax + 2b)$ have a GCF of $(ax + 2b)$. Factoring this GCF out of each term, we obtain

$$(ax + 2b)(2x + y).$$

This process is called **factoring by grouping**.
Remember to check the factoring by multiplying or graphing.

> *Factoring a Polynomial with Four Terms Using Grouping*
> To factor a polynomial with four terms using grouping:
>
> - Factor the GCF out of all terms.
> - Rewrite the polynomial as a sum of two binomials.
> - Write each binomial as a product of its GCF and another binomial.
> - Determine that the binomial in each group is the GCF of the resulting terms.
> - Write a product of the binomial (GCF) and another binomial.
> - If no common factor is found, a different grouping may be needed.

EXAMPLE 4 Factor completely and check.

a. $2x^2 - 10x + 7x - 35$ **b.** $3x^4 + 6x^2 - x^2 - 2$
c. $6x^2 - 3x + 12x - 6$

Solution

a. $2x^2 - 10x + 7x - 35$

$= (2x^2 - 10x) + (7x - 35)$ Group the terms.

$= 2x(x - 5) + 7(x - 5)$ Factor the GCF ($2x$ and 7) out of each group.

$= (x - 5)(2x + 7)$ Factor a common polynomial factor ($x - 5$) out of each term.

The check is left for you.

b. $3x^4 + 6x^2 - x^2 - 2$

$= (3x^4 + 6x^2) + (-x^2 - 2)$ Group the terms.

$= 3x^2(x^2 + 2) + (-1)(x^2 + 2)$ Factor out the GCF of each group ($3x^2$ and -1).

$= (x^2 + 2)(3x^2 - 1)$ Factor the polynomial factor ($x^2 + 2$) out of the remaining terms.

The check is left for you.

c. $6x^2 - 3x + 12x - 6$

$\quad = 3(2x^2 - x + 4x - 2)$ Factor out the GCF (3).

$\quad = 3[(2x^2 - x) + (4x - 2)]$ Group the terms.

$\quad = 3[x(2x - 1) + 2(2x - 1)]$ Factor out the GCF of each group.

$\quad = 3(2x - 1)(x + 2)$ Factor the polynomial factor $(2x - 1)$ out of the remaining terms.

The check is left for you. ■

Experiencing Algebra the Checkup Way

Factor completely and check.

1. $6x^2 - 10x + 9x - 15$

2. $2y^4 + 2y^2 - 5y^2 - 5$

3. $15a^3 - 20a^2 + 105a^2 - 140a$

4. $ax + ay + bx + by$

5 Modeling the Real World

It sometimes happens that the simplest way to model a complicated real-world situation gives rise to a complicated polynomial expression. But once you have the polynomial written down, you should always think about ways to factor the polynomial into simpler terms. This will make any operations you need to perform with the polynomial simpler and help you avoid errors.

EXAMPLE 5 Casey's father decided he would give his son a surprise birthday present. He wrote the following message:

> Every day for a week you will receive a gift of $5 more than you received the day before.

a. Write a polynomial for the total amount Casey will receive if he receives x dollars the first day. Simplify.

b. Factor out the GCF from your simplified expression in part (a).

c. Explain in your own words the meaning of the binomial factor.

Suppose Casey receives $10 the first day from his father.

d. Evaluate the polynomial in part (a) to determine the total amount Casey will receive in a week.

e. Evaluate the binomial factor found in part (b).

f. Show that the value obtained in part (e) has the meaning given in part (c).

Solution

a. Let x = amount received the first day
Casey will receive

$\quad x + (x + 5) + (x + 10) + (x + 15) + (x + 20) + (x + 25)$
$\quad + (x + 30)$ or $(7x + 105)$ dollars.

b. $7x + 105 = 7(x + 15)$

c. The binomial $(x + 15)$ is the average daily amount in dollars that Casey will receive for the 7 days.

d. $7x + 105 = 7(10) + 105 = 70 + 105 = 175$
If Casey receives $10 on the first day, he will receive $175 in a week from his father.

e. $x + 15 = 10 + 15 = 25$

f. Casey will receive an average of \$25 per day for a week. This will amount to

$$\frac{7 \text{ days}}{1 \text{ week}} \cdot \frac{\$25}{1 \text{ day}} = \frac{\$175}{1 \text{ week}}$$

or \$175 for the week, the same amount found in part (d). ∎

Application

A horticulturalist working for Wilson's Nursery redesigned a square display area of width w feet, as shown in Figure 10.4. The designer approximated the numerical value for the area of the new rectangular design using a polynomial, $w^3 + 5w^2 + w + 5$. Factor the polynomial to determine the dimensions of the display in terms of the width of the original square, w. Describe the dimensions of the new design.

Figure 10.4

Discussion

The polynomial to be factored has four terms, so we will factor it by grouping.

$$\begin{aligned} w^3 + 5w^2 + w + 5 &= \left(w^3 + 5w^2\right) + (w + 5) \qquad \text{Group the terms.} \\ &= w^2(w + 5) + 1(w + 5) \qquad \text{Factor the GCF out of each group.} \\ &= (w + 5)\left(w^2 + 1\right) \qquad \text{Factor a common polynomial out of the remaining terms.} \end{aligned}$$

One side is $(w + 5)$ feet, or 5 feet more than the original width. The other side is $\left(w^2 + 1\right)$ feet, or 1 foot more than the square of the original width. ∎

 Experiencing Algebra the Checkup Way

Katie gave up smoking as her New Year's resolution. Her dad told her that as an incentive, every month for 6 months, he would give her \$12 more than he gave her the month before if she continued not smoking.

1. Write a polynomial for the total amount of money Katie will receive if she receives x dollars after not smoking for one month.

2. Factor the polynomial and explain what each factor represents.

3. If her dad gives her \$50 the first month, how much will Katie receive if she doesn't smoke for the 6 months?

4. What is her average monthly amount received for not smoking? Does this check with your explanation in exercise 2?

PROBLEM SET 10.4

Experiencing Algebra the Exercise Way

Determine the greatest common monomial factor for each set of monomials.

1. $60a^2b^4c^3$; $50a^3bc^2$

2. $45x^2yz$; $90x^3yz^2$

3. $252x^3y^4$; $180x^2z$

4. $126u^3v^4$; $315u^5v^2$

5. $45pq^4$; $135r^4s$

6. $80c^5d^2$; $24a^2b^2$

7. $63xyz$; $98xyz$

8. $40a^2bc$; $250a^2bc$

9. $60a^2b^3c^3$; $90ab^2c$; $150a^2b^4c^2$

10. $120x^2y^4z^3$; $270x^2y^2z$; $750xy^2z$

Factor exercises 11–70 completely and check.

11. $4x + 12y$

12. $-7x + 21y$

13. $8x^3 - 4x^2 + 12x - 24$

14. $9d^5 - 12d^3 + 21d + 24$

15. $3a^4 - 5a^3 + 7a^2$

16. $-4p^5 - 9p^4 - 11p^3$

17. $-3x^5 - 9x^4 - 12x^3$

18. $5m^3 - 15m^2 + 30m$

19. $7x^4y^2 - 3x^2y + 9x^2y^4$

20. $-3u^3v + 4u^2v^2 - 8uv^3$

21. $8a^5b^3c + 4a^4b^2 + 16a^3c$

22. $7x^3y^5 - 21x^2y^4 + 63xy^3$

23. $66u^3v^4 - 88u^4v^3$

24. $-39c^2d^3 + 52c^3d^2$

25. $3x^3 + 5y^4$

26. $p^4 + 7q^2$

27. $5x(x + 3) - 4(x + 3)$

28. $3y(y + 7) - 5(y + 7)$

29. $x(2x + y) + 2y(2x + y)$

30. $3a(a + 3b) + b(a + 3b)$

31. $6x^2 + 10x + 21x + 35$

32. $15x^2 + 6x + 10x + 4$

33. $x^2 + 8x + x + 8$

34. $y^2 + 4y + y + 4$

35. $2a^2 + 3a - 2a - 3$

36. $2z^2 + 7z - 2z - 7$

37. $2x^2 + xy + 4xy + 2y^2$

38. $3p^2 + 9pq + pq + 3q^2$

39. $x^2 + xy - xy - y^2$

40. $m^2 + mn - mn - n^2$

41. $10xy - 55y + 24x - 132$

42. $28xy + 21y - 36x - 27$

43. $12ac + 3bc + 4ad + bd$

44. $10mp + 5np + 4mq + 2nq$

45. $2x^2y^2 + 3xy - 8xy - 12$

46. $7a^2b^2 - 2ab + 21ab - 6$

47. $-x^2 - 3x - xy - 3y$

48. $-a^2 - ab - 7a - 7b$

49. $x^4 + x^2y^2 + 2x^2y^2 + 2y^4$

50. $3p^4 - 3p^2q^2 + p^2q^2 - q^4$

51. $ac + bc + ad + bd$

52. $xy + y^2 + zx + zy$

53. $8x^2 + 4x + 24x + 12$

54. $21y^2 + 14y + 84y + 56$

55. $u^4 + u^3v - 2u^3v - 2u^2v^2$

56. $a^4 + a^3b + 2a^3b + 2a^2b^2$

57. $6a^4 + 6a^3b^2 + 6a^3b + 6a^2b^3$

58. $5c^5 + 5c^4d^2 + 5c^3d + 5c^2d^3$

59. $-4x^3 - 12x^2 - 2x^2 - 6x$

60. $-10y^3 + 50y^2 - 15y^2 + 75y$

61. $4x^2 + 6xz + 6xz + 9z^2$

62. $9u^2 + 12uv + 12uv + 16v^2$

63. $36a^2 - 30ab - 30ab + 25b^2$

64. $16x^2 + 12xy + 12xy + 9y^2$

65. $5m^3 + 5m^2n + 5m^2n + 5mn^2$

66. $7p^3 - 7p^2q - 7p^2q + 7pq^2$

67. $2x^3 + 3x + 8x^2 + 12$

68. $5c^4 + 7c - 15c^3 - 21$

69. $5a^2x + 2b^2x + 15a^2y + 6b^2y$

70. $2a^2c + 3b^2c + 14a^2d + 21b^2d$

71. Amy's dad promised her that for each soccer goal she made, he would give her $1 more than he gave her for her last soccer goal. She made nine goals during the season.

a. Write a polynomial for the total amount of money Amy will receive if she receives x dollars for her first goal.

  b. Factor out the GCF from the simplified expression in part (a).

  c. Explain what the factors in part (b) represent.

  d. If Amy's dad gave her $10 for her first goal, determine the total amount of money Amy received. Check your explanation in part (c), using this value for x.

72. Wynona started a program to quit smoking. She decided to limit herself to two fewer cigarettes than her limit from the day before. She was able to hold to the program.

  a. Write a polynomial for the total number of cigarettes she smoked during the first week if she smoked c cigarettes the first day.

  b. Factor out the GCF from the simplified expression in part (a).

  c. Explain what the factors in part (b) represent.

  d. If Wynona smoked 20 cigarettes the first day, determine the total number of cigarettes she smoked the first week. Does your explanation in part (c) check using this number? How many cigarettes did she smoke on the seventh day of the week?

73. In a sports program with n teams, it can be shown that the number of times each team must play every other team exactly two times in the program is given by $n^2 - n$.

  a. Factor the expression completely.

  b. Evaluate the original expression and the factored expression for a program that has 21 teams in it.

  c. Which expression was easier to evaluate and why?

74. It can be shown that in a sports program with n teams, the number of ways in which you can have three teams finish in the top three positions is given by $n^3 - 2n^2 - n + 2n$.

  a. Factor the expression completely.

  b. Evaluate the original expression and the factored expression for a program that has 11 teams in it.

  c. Which expression was easier to evaluate and why?

75. The area of a rectangle is numerically equal to the expression $x^2 + 7x - 3x - 21$. Factor the expression using grouping to determine algebraic expressions for the rectangle's width and length.

76. The area of a square is numerically equal to the expression $4x^2 + 6x + 6x + 9$. Factor the expression using grouping to determine an algebraic expression for the length of the square's sides.

Experiencing Algebra the Calculator Way

Factoring a Number into Prime Factors Using the Calculator

Graphing calculators can be programmed to perform certain operations. The following program[1] will factor a number into a product of prime factors. In order to place your calculator into a program edit mode, enter PRGM ▶ ▶ *to New, then* ENTER *. This will place the calculator into a mode so that you can enter a program. At each step, key in the instructions, and press Enter to move to the next step. If you make a mistake, use the arrow keys to move back up and correct it. Many of the instructions use keys with which you are already familiar. Any other programming instruction can be found by pressing the* PRGM *key and using the arrow keys to find the instruction, then pressing the* ENTER *key to select the instruction. Enter the following program.*

[1] By permission of Nan Burwell, Pellissippi State Technical Community College.

```
PROGRAM:PRIME
Input N
N→M
1→C
2→D
Lbl 1
M/D→B
If fpart(B)=0
Goto 2
C+2→D
D→C
If D≥√ (M)+1)
Goto 3
Goto 1
Lbl 2
ipart(B)→M
Disp D
Pause
If M = 1
Goto 3
Goto 1
Lbl 3
If M≠1
Disp M
If M=N
Disp "PRIME"
Disp "DONE"
```

Note: fPart(is found under the | MATH | key.

iPart(is found under the | MATH | key.

The equation sign and the inequality signs are found under the | 2nd | | Test | keys.

To run the program, enter | PRGM | | ▼ | *to go to the appropriate program, then press* | ENTER | *once to select the program, and again to execute the program. At the question mark prompt, key in the number to be factored, and press* | ENTER | *repeatedly until the calculator indicates the factoring is done. If you press* | ENTER | *again, the program will be restarted so that you can enter another number.*

Use the program to factor completely the following numbers:

1. 30   **2.** 108   **3.** 525

4. 1287   **5.** 1547   **6.** 4500

 Experiencing Algebra the Group Way

In some situations, you may want to factor a polynomial that does not have integer coefficients. In these situations, you may be able to factor out a common factor that is a fraction or a decimal, which will leave the remaining polynomial with integer coefficients. To illustrate, consider the following two examples.

Example 1: $\dfrac{1}{5}x^2 + \dfrac{2}{5}x + \dfrac{3}{5}x + \dfrac{6}{5} = \dfrac{1}{5}\left(x^2 + 2x + 3x + 6\right)$

The polynomial in the parentheses can now be factored by grouping.

Example 2: $0.3x^2 + 0.9x + 1.5x + 4.5 = 0.3\left(x^2 + 3x + 5x + 15\right)$

The polynomial in the parentheses can now be factored by grouping.

Each member of the group should try to factor a common factor from each of the following polynomials, and then try to factor completely the remaining polynomial. After completing the exercises, discuss your results with your group members. Come to agreement on the correct factoring for each expression.

1. $\dfrac{2}{5}x^2 + \dfrac{4}{5}x + \dfrac{2}{5}x + \dfrac{4}{5}$

2. $\dfrac{1}{3}a^2 - \dfrac{7}{3}a + \dfrac{7}{3}a - \dfrac{49}{3}$

3. $\dfrac{1}{4}x^2 + \dfrac{3}{4}x + \dfrac{3}{4}x + \dfrac{9}{4}$

4. $0.6b^2 - 2.1b + 0.2b - 0.7$

5. $0.9x^2 + 1.8x + 1.8x + 3.6$

6. $1.2y^2 + 1.8y - 1.8y - 2.7$

Experiencing Algebra the Write Way

Gennifer was asked to completely factor the polynomials listed. In each case, the answer she gave was incorrect. Explain what is wrong with each result.

1. $-8a - 4b = -4(2a - b)$

2. $5x^2 + 10x = 5\left(x^2 + 2x\right)$

3. $4x^2 + 3x + 4x + 3 = (4x + 3)(x + 0)$

4. $4y^3 - 6y^2 = 2^2 \cdot y^3 - 2 \cdot 3 \cdot y^2$

10.5 Factoring Trinomials of the Form $ax^2 + bx + c$

Objectives

1 Factor trinomials of the form $ax^2 + bx + c, a = 1$.

2 Factor trinomials of the form $ax^2 + bx + c, a \neq 1$, using the trial-and-error method.

3 Factor trinomials of the form $ax^2 + bx + c, a \neq 1$, using the ac method.

4 Model real-world situations by factoring trinomials.

Application

A telephone designer began with the plans of a square telephone with sides of x inches that covered an area of x^2 square inches. The newly designed rectangular phone covers an area of $\left(x^2 - 2x - 3\right)$ square inches. Determine the dimensions of the new phone in terms of x.

After completing this section, we will discuss this application further. See page 770.

In this section we continue our discussion of factoring. We will now factor a quadratic trinomial. A quadratic trinomial is a trinomial of the form $ax^2 + bx + c, a \neq 0$. The **leading coefficient** of the quadratic trinomial is a, the coefficient of the quadratic term, x^2.

1 Factoring Quadratic Trinomials, $a = 1$

To determine a process for factoring a quadratic trinomial, we need to determine a pattern. Complete the following set of exercises to discover the pattern.

DISCOVERY 8

Factoring Quadratic Trinomials

Multiply the following binomials to obtain a quadratic trinomial.

1. a. $(x + 3)(x + 2) =$ _____   **b.** $(3)(2) =$ _____

$3 + 2 =$ _____

2. a. $(x - 3)(x - 2) =$ _____   **b.** $(-3)(-2) =$ _____

$-3 + (-2) =$ _____

To factor a quadratic trinomial, we must reverse this process. Write a rule to determine the binomial factors needed to be multiplied to obtain the quadratic trinomial.

The first term in each binomial factor is x, or the square root of the quadratic term x^2. The second term in each of the binomial factors must be the factors of the constant term c. Their sum is the coefficient b.

We can see why this is true by using variables instead of numbers and multiplying.

$$\begin{array}{c} \quad\quad\;\; \mathbf{F} \quad\; \mathbf{O} \quad\;\; \mathbf{I} \quad\;\; \mathbf{L} \\ (x + m)(x + n) = x^2 + \;nx + mx\; + mn \quad \text{Use the FOIL method.} \end{array}$$

$$= x^2 + (n\; + \;m)x\; + mn \quad \begin{array}{l}\text{Factor a common factor out}\\ \text{of the middle two terms.}\end{array}$$

$$= x^2 + \quad\quad\; bx \quad\quad + \;c$$

This shows that $n + m = b$ and $mn = c$. In other words, look for two numbers whose product is c and whose sum is b.

Factoring a Quadratic Trinomial with a Leading Coefficient of 1
To factor a quadratic trinomial with a leading coefficient of 1,

$x^2 + bx + c = (x + m)(x + n)$ where $mn = c$ and $n + m = b$.

For example, factor $x^2 + x - 6$ completely.

Given $x^2 + x - 6$, $a = 1$, $b = 1$, and $c = -6$.

First determine the factors of c, -6. Next, add the pairs of factors to determine the sum of b, 1. It is easier to do this in a chart so that we do not omit any possibilities.

Factor	Factor	Sum of Factors
1	-6	-5
-1	6	5
2	-3	-1
-2	3	1 ←b

Choose the last pair of factors, -2 and 3, because their sum is 1 (b).

Therefore,

$$x^2 + x - 6 = (x - 2)(x + 3).$$

We should always check the factors by multiplication or graphing.
Multiplication check:

$$(x - 2)(x + 3) = x^2 + 3x - 2x - 6$$
$$= x^2 + x - 6 \qquad \text{Original polynomial}$$

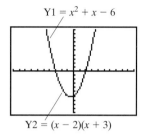

Y1 = $x^2 + x - 6$

Y2 = $(x - 2)(x + 3)$

$(-10, 10, -10, 10)$

Graphic check:
Let Y1 = $x^2 + x - 6$ and Y2 = $(x - 2)(x + 3)$. Trace the graphs
to verify that they are the same as shown to the left.

We could set up the previous chart on the calculator as shown in
Figure 10.5.

TECHNOLOGY

X	Y₁	Y₂
-2	3	1
-1	6	5
0	ERROR	ERROR
1	-6	-5
2	-3	-1
3	-2	1
4	-1.5	2.5

X = -2

Figure 10.5

For Figure 10.5
Set the first column for positive integer values.

| 2nd | TBLSET | 1 | ENTER | 1 | ENTER | ENTER | ▼ | ENTER |

Set the second column to be the number, c, divided by the independent
variable.

| Y= | (−) | 6 | ÷ | X, T, θ, n |

Set the third column to be the sum of the first two columns.

| ▼ | X, T, θ, n | + | VARS | ▶ | 1 | 1 |

View the table.

| 2nd | TABLE |

Use the arrows to move through the table to find a value in the Y2 column that is equal to b. The factors
are the integer values of x and Y1 corresponding to this value of b in Y2, −2 and 3.

To save us time in choosing possible factors, we need to see a pattern.
Complete the following set of exercises.

DISCOVERY 9

Determining Signs for the Factors of c
Factor a quadratic trinomial of the form $x^2 + bx + c$.

1. $x^2 + 5x + 6 = $ ____ ____
If c is positive and b is positive, then the factors of c are both _____ .

2. $x^2 - 5x + 6 = $ ____ ____
If c is positive and b is negative, then the factors of c are both _____ .

3. $x^2 + x - 6 = $ ____ ____
If c is negative and b is positive, then the factors of c have different
signs. The factor with the larger absolute value is _____ .

Continued

4. $x^2 - x - 6 = \underline{\quad}\,\underline{\quad}$

If c is negative and b is negative, then the factors of c have different signs. The factor with the larger absolute value is _____.

Write a rule to determine when the factors are positive or negative.

The signs of the factors are determined in the following way:

If c is positive, then the factors both have the same sign as b.
If c is negative, then the factors have different signs (the factor with the larger absolute value has the same sign as b).

EXAMPLE 1 Factor completely and check.

a. $z^2 + 11z + 24$ **b.** $x^2 + 4x - 7$ **c.** $2x^2 + 10x + 8$

Solution

a. $z^2 + 11z + 24$

$a = 1, b = 11$, and $c = 24$

Note: c is positive, so both factors have the sign of b, positive.
Write these factors of 24 (c).

Factor	Factor	Sum of Factors
1	24	25
2	12	14
3	8	11 $\leftarrow b$
4	6	10

$z^2 + 11z + 24 = (z + 3)(z + 8)$.

The check is left for you. *Note:* The variable z must be changed to x in order to graph the functions on your calculator.

To find the desired factors with your calculator, set up the following table. The factors are 3 and 8, as shown in Figure 10.6.

TECHNOLOGY

X	Y₁	Y₂
1	24	25
2	12	14
3	8	11
4	6	10
5	4.8	9.8
6	4	10
7	3.4286	10.429

X=3

Figure 10.6

For Figure 10.6

2nd | TBLSET | 1 | ENTER | 1 | ENTER | ENTER | ▼ | ENTER

Y= | 2 | 4 | ÷ | X, T, θ, n | ▼ | X, T, θ, n | + | VARS | ▶ | 1 | 1

2nd | TABLE

b. $x^2 + 4x - 7$

$a = 1, b = 4$, and $c = -7$

Note: c is negative, so the factors have different signs. The factor with the larger absolute value must be positive. Write these factors of -7 (c).

Factor	Factor	Sum of Factors
-1	7	6

The possible factors of -7 do not add to the desired sum of 4. Therefore, $x^2 + 4x - 7$ does not factor.

c. $2x^2 + 10x + 8$

First, factor out the common factor.

$$2(x^2 + 5x + 4)$$
$$a = 1, b = 5, \text{and } c = 4$$

Note: c is positive, so both factors must have the sign of b, positive. Write these factors of 4 (c).

Factor	Factor	Sum of Factors
1	4	5 $\leftarrow b$
2	2	4

$$2x^2 + 10x + 8 = 2(x^2 + 5x + 4)$$
$$= 2(x + 1)(x + 4)$$

The check is left for you. *Note:* If you multiply, multiply all three factors to check. ∎

The process of factoring used in this section can be applied to trinomials that are not quadratic. Any polynomial that can be written in the form $y^2 + by + c$, where y could be x^2, x^3, and so forth, can be factored in a similar manner.

> *Factoring a Quadratic-Like Trinomial with a Leading Coefficient of 1*
> To factor a quadratic-like trinomial with a leading coefficient of 1,
> $$y^2 + by + c = (y + m)(y + n)$$
> where $y = x^p$ and p is a positive integer greater than 1, $mn = c$, and $n + m = b$.

For example, factor $x^4 + 13x^2 + 36$.

This is not a quadratic trinomial, because the degree of the polynomial is 4. However, this is a quadratic-like trinomial with $y = x^2$ and $y^2 = (x^2)^2 = x^4$.

$$a = 1, b = 13, c = 36$$

Note: c is positive, so both factors must have the sign of b, positive.

Factor	Factor	Sum of Factors
1	36	37
2	18	20
3	12	15
4	9	13 ← b

Note that the first term in the binomials is y or x^2.

$$x^4 + 13x^2 + 36 = (x^2 + 4)(x^2 + 9)$$

Multiplication check:

$$(x^2 + 4)(x^2 + 9) = x^4 + 9x^2 + 4x^2 + 36$$
$$= x^4 + 13x^2 + 36$$

Experiencing Algebra the Checkup Way

Factor exercises 1–4 completely and check.

1. $b^2 - 12b + 35$ **2.** $c^2 - 5c - 24$ **3.** $6d^2 + 60d + 126$ **4.** $y^4 - 2y^2 - 3$

5. If a trinomial is quadratic-like, what must be true about the exponent of each of the three terms?

6. What do we mean by the quadratic term of a trinomial?

---

2 Factoring Quadratic Trinomials, $a \neq 1$

In this section we factor a quadratic trinomial, $ax^2 + bx + c$, where $a \neq 1$. First, let's review the multiplication problem that results in such a polynomial. For example,

$$\begin{array}{cccc} \text{F} & \text{O} & \text{I} & \text{L} \\ \downarrow & \downarrow & \downarrow & \downarrow \end{array}$$

$$(x + 3)(2x - 1) = 2x^2 - x + 6x - 3 = 2x^2 + 5x - 3$$

We want to reverse this multiplication by factoring the trinomial into two binomials. We call this the **trial-and-error method** because we make a guess and check to see if it is correct. For example, factor $2x^2 + 5x - 3$ completely.

The product of the first term in each binomial factor must equal $2x^2$. The product of the last term in each binomial factor must equal -3.

$$2x^2 + 5x - 3 = (\underline{\hphantom{xx}})(\underline{\hphantom{xx}})$$

First determine the possible factors that result in each.

$$2x^2 = x \cdot 2x \qquad \begin{aligned} -3 &= 1 \cdot -3 \\ &= -1 \cdot 3 \end{aligned}$$

Next fill in the binomial factors with all the possible combinations and multiply to find the middle term of the trinomial. Remember that the middle term is the sum of the product of the outer terms and the product of the inner terms.

$$2x^2 + 5x - 3 = (\underline{\quad}\;\underline{\quad})(\underline{\quad}\;\underline{\quad}) \qquad \text{Middle term}$$

$$(\underline{\;x\;} + \underline{\;1\;})(\underline{2x} - \underline{\;3\;}) \qquad -3x + 2x = -x$$
$$(\underline{\;x\;} - \underline{\;1\;})(\underline{2x} + \underline{\;3\;}) \qquad 3x - 2x = x$$
$$(\underline{2x} + \underline{\;1\;})(\underline{\;x\;} - \underline{\;3\;}) \qquad -6x + x = -5x$$
$$(\underline{2x} - \underline{\;1\;})(\underline{\;x\;} + \underline{\;3\;}) \qquad 6x - x = 5x$$

The factors $(2x - 1)(x + 3)$ result in the middle term $5x$. Multiply the two binomials to completely check your factors.

$$(2x - 1)(x + 3) = 2x^2 + 6x - x - 3 = 2x^2 + 5x - 3$$

A graphic check will result in equivalent graphs for the two functions $Y1 = 2x^2 + 5x - 3$ and $Y2 = (2x - 1)(x + 3)$.
Therefore, $2x^2 + 5x - 3 = (2x - 1)(x + 3)$.

Y1 = $2x^2 + 5x - 3$

Y2 = $(2x - 1)(x + 3)$

$(10, 10, -10, 10)$

Factoring a Quadratic Trinomial With a Leading Coefficient Not Equal to 1 Using the Trial-and-Error Method
To factor a quadratic trinomial using the trial-and-error method:

- Factor out the GCF from all terms.
- Determine the possible factors for the first term and the last term.
- Write a set of binomial factors for each combination of the factors.
- Multiply the factors to determine which set results in the middle term of the trinomial.

Check the factors by multiplying to obtain the original trinomial or by graphing the original polynomial and the factors as separate functions and determining that the graphs are equivalent.

For another example, factor $6x^2 + 19x + 8$ completely.

First, determine the factors for the first and last terms.

$$\begin{aligned} 6x^2 &= x \cdot 6x & 8 &= 1 \cdot 8 \\ &= 2x \cdot 3x & &= -1 \cdot -8 \\ &= -x \cdot -6x & &= 2 \cdot 4 \\ &= -2x \cdot -3x & &= -2 \cdot -4 \end{aligned}$$

Before we fill in the binomial factors, observe that we need to use only the positive factors because the trinomial has all positive terms. This eliminates half of the combinations.

$$\begin{aligned} 6x^2 &= x \cdot 6x & 8 &= 1 \cdot 8 \\ &= 2x \cdot 3x & &= 2 \cdot 4 \end{aligned}$$

Fill in the binomial factors with all the combinations and multiply to find the middle term of the original trinomial.

$$6x^2 + 19x + 8 = (\underline{\quad}\;\underline{\quad})(\underline{\quad}\;\underline{\quad}) \qquad \text{Middle term}$$

$$(\underline{\;x\;} + \underline{\;1\;})(\underline{6x} + \underline{\;8\;}) \qquad 8x + 6x = 14x$$
$$(\underline{\;x\;} + \underline{\;2\;})(\underline{6x} + \underline{\;4\;}) \qquad 4x + 12x = 16x$$

$(\underline{6x} + \underline{1})(\underline{\ x} + \underline{8})$ $48x + x = 49x$

$(\underline{6x} + \underline{2})(\underline{\ x} + \underline{4})$ $24x + 2x = 26x$

$(\underline{2x} + \underline{1})(\underline{3x} + \underline{8})$ $16x + 3x = 19x$

$(\underline{2x} + \underline{2})(\underline{3x} + \underline{4})$ $8x + 6x = 14x$

$(\underline{3x} + \underline{1})(\underline{2x} + \underline{8})$ $24x + 2x = 26x$

$(\underline{3x} + \underline{2})(\underline{2x} + \underline{4})$ $12x + 4x = 16x$

The factors $(2x + 1)(3x + 8)$ result in the correct middle term. Multiply the factors to check.

$$(2x + 1)(3x + 8) = 6x^2 + 16x + 3x + 8 = 6x^2 + 19x + 8$$

A graphic check with Y1 $= 6x^2 + 19x + 8$ and Y2 $= (2x + 1)(3x + 8)$ results in equivalent graphs.

Therefore, $6x^2 + 19x + 8 = (2x + 1)(3x + 8)$.

Y1 $= 6x^2 + 19x + 8$

Y2 $= (2x + 1)(3x + 8)$

$(-10, 10, -10, 10)$

Helping Hand We could have eliminated more of the combinations if we had been more observant. For example, six of the combinations had a common factor in one of the binomials. We know this is not possible because the original trinomial did not have a common factor. If we had observed this fact, we would have had only two possible combinations: $(6x + 1)(x + 8)$ and $(2x + 1)(3x + 8)$.

EXAMPLE 2   Factor completely. Check by multiplication or graphing.

a. $8x^2 - 26x + 15$ **b.** $6x^2 - 9x - 10$ **c.** $12x^2 - 14x - 6$

Solution

a. $8x^2 - 26x + 15$

First, determine the possible factors for the first and last terms.

$$8x^2 = x \cdot 8x \qquad 15 = 1 \cdot 15$$
$$= 2x \cdot 4x \qquad\quad = -1 \cdot -15$$
$$= 3 \cdot 5$$
$$= -3 \cdot -5$$

Next, fill in the binomial factors with all the possible combinations and multiply to find the correct middle term in the original trinomial.

Before we begin, observe that the middle term is negative. Therefore, the positive factors of 15 are not possible combinations, as they will result in only positive middle terms. This reduces the possibilities.

$$8x^2 = x \cdot 8x \qquad 15 = -1 \cdot -15$$
$$= 2x \cdot 4x \qquad\quad = -3 \cdot -5$$

$8x^2 - 26x + 15 = (\underline{\ \ } \underline{\ \ })(\underline{\ \ } \underline{\ \ })$ Middle term

$(\underline{\ x} - \underline{1})(\underline{8x} - \underline{15})$ $-15x - 8x = -23x$

$(\underline{\ x} - \underline{3})(\underline{8x} - \underline{5})$ $-5x - 24x = -29x$

$(\underline{8x} - \underline{1})(\underline{\ x} - \underline{15})$ $-120x - x = -121x$

$(\underline{8x} - \underline{3})(\underline{\ x} - \underline{5})$ $-40x - 3x = -43x$

$(\underline{2x} - \underline{1})(\underline{4x} - \underline{15})$ $-30x - 4x = -34x$

$$\underline{(2x - \underline{\ \ 3\ })(4x - \underline{\ \ 5\ })} \quad -10x - 12x = -22x$$
$$\underline{(4x - \underline{\ \ 1\ })(2x - \underline{\ 15})} \quad -60x - 2x = -62x$$
$$\underline{(4x - \underline{\ \ 3\ })(2x - \underline{\ \ 5\ })} \quad -20x - 6x = -26x$$

The factors $(4x - 3)(2x - 5)$ result in the middle term of $-26x$.

$$8x^2 - 26x + 15 = (4x - 3)(2x - 5)$$

The check is left for you.

b. $6x^2 - 9x - 10$

First, determine the possible factors for the first and last terms.

$$6x^2 = x \cdot 6x \qquad -10 = 1 \cdot -10$$
$$ = 2x \cdot 3x \qquad = -1 \cdot 10$$
$$ = 2 \cdot -5$$
$$ = -2 \cdot 5$$

Next, fill in the binomial factors with all the possible combinations and multiply to find the correct middle term in the original trinomial.

$$6x^2 - 9x - 10 = (\underline{\ \ \ }\ \underline{\ \ \ })(\underline{\ \ \ }\ \underline{\ \ \ }) \quad \text{Middle term}$$
$$\underline{(\ x + \underline{\ 1\ })(6x - \underline{10})}$$
$$\underline{(\ x - \underline{\ 1\ })(6x + \underline{10})}$$
$$\underline{(\ x + \underline{\ 2\ })(6x - \underline{\ 5\ })} \quad -5x + 12x = 7x$$
$$\underline{(\ x - \underline{\ 2\ })(6x + \underline{\ 5\ })} \quad 5x - 12x = -7x$$
$$\underline{(6x + \underline{\ 1\ })(\ x - \underline{10})} \quad -60x + x = -59x$$
$$\underline{(6x - \underline{\ 1\ })(\ x + \underline{10})} \quad 60x - x = 59x$$
$$\underline{(6x + \underline{\ 2\ })(\ x - \underline{\ 5\ })}$$
$$\underline{(6x - \underline{\ 2\ })(\ x + \underline{\ 5\ })}$$
$$\underline{(2x + \underline{\ 1\ })(3x - \underline{10})} \quad -20x + 3x = -17x$$
$$\underline{(2x - \underline{\ 1\ })(3x + \underline{10})} \quad 20x - 3x = 17x$$
$$\underline{(2x + \underline{\ 2\ })(3x - \underline{\ 5\ })}$$
$$\underline{(2x - \underline{\ 2\ })(3x + \underline{\ 5\ })}$$
$$\underline{(3x + \underline{\ 1\ })(2x - \underline{10})}$$
$$\underline{(3x - \underline{\ 1\ })(2x + \underline{10})}$$
$$\underline{(3x + \underline{\ 2\ })(2x - \underline{\ 5\ })} \quad -15x + 4x = -11x$$
$$\underline{(3x - \underline{\ 2\ })(2x + \underline{\ 5\ })} \quad 15x - 4x = 11x$$

Note: We did not find the middle term for the binomial factors with common factors.

No factors result in the middle term.

The trinomial $6x^2 - 9x - 10$ does not factor.

c. $12x^2 - 14x - 6$

First, factor out the greatest common factor, 2.

$$12x^2 - 14x - 6 = 2(6x^2 - 7x - 3)$$

Now determine the possible factors for the first and last terms.

$$6x^2 = x \cdot 6x \qquad -3 = 1 \cdot -3$$
$$ = 2x \cdot 3x \qquad = -1 \cdot 3$$

Next, fill in the binomial factors with all the possible combinations and multiply to find the correct middle term in the original trinomial.

$$6x^2 - 7x - 3 = (\underline{}\ \underline{})(\underline{}\ \underline{}) \qquad \text{Middle term}$$

$$(\underline{\ x}\ +\ \underline{1})(\underline{6x}\ -\ \underline{3})$$
$$(\underline{\ x}\ -\ \underline{1})(\underline{6x}\ +\ \underline{3})$$
$$(\underline{6x}\ +\ \underline{1})(\underline{\ x}\ -\ \underline{3}) \qquad -18x + x = -17x$$
$$(\underline{6x}\ -\ \underline{1})(\underline{\ x}\ +\ \underline{3}) \qquad 18x - x = 17x$$
$$(\underline{2x}\ +\ \underline{1})(\underline{3x}\ -\ \underline{3})$$
$$(\underline{2x}\ -\ \underline{1})(\underline{3x}\ +\ \underline{3})$$
$$(\underline{3x}\ +\ \underline{1})(\underline{2x}\ -\ \underline{3}) \qquad -9x + 2x = -7x$$
$$(\underline{3x}\ -\ \underline{1})(\underline{2x}\ +\ \underline{3}) \qquad 9x - 2x = 7x$$

Note: The binomial factors with common factors are not possible solutions. The factors $(3x + 1)(2x - 3)$ result in the correct middle term.

$$12x^2 - 14x - 6 = 2(3x + 1)(2x - 3)$$

The check is left for you. ∎

Quadratic-like trinomials are also found with the leading coefficient not equal to 1. Just as before, we factor them with the same procedure as quadratic trinomials. For example, factor $3x^4 + 2x^2 - 8$.

This is not a quadratic trinomial.
First, determine the possible factors for the first and last terms. Since the middle term is a factor of x^2, we will need to factor the first term $3x^4$ into factors of x^2.

$$3x^4 = x^2 \cdot 3x^2 \qquad -8 = 1 \cdot -8$$
$$= -1 \cdot 8$$
$$= 2 \cdot -4$$
$$= -2 \cdot 4$$

Next, fill in the binomial factors with all the possible combinations and multiply to find the correct middle term in the original trinomial.

$$3x^4 + 2x^2 - 8 = (\underline{}\ \underline{})(\underline{}\ \underline{}) \qquad \text{Middle term}$$

$$(\underline{x^2}\ +\ \underline{1})(\underline{3x^2}\ -\ \underline{8}) \qquad -8x^2 + 3x^2 = -5x^2$$
$$(\underline{x^2}\ -\ \underline{1})(\underline{3x^2}\ +\ \underline{8}) \qquad 8x^2 - 3x^2 = 5x^2$$
$$(\underline{x^2}\ +\ \underline{2})(\underline{3x^2}\ -\ \underline{4}) \qquad -4x^2 + 6x^2 = 2x^2$$

We do not need to continue, since we have found the needed middle term. The factors $(x^2 + 2)(3x^2 - 4)$ result in the correct middle term.

$$3x^4 + 2x^2 - 8 = (x^2 + 2)(3x^2 - 4)$$

The check is left for you.

Experiencing Algebra the Checkup Way

Factor exercises 1–4 completely and check.

1. $2x^2 - 9x - 5$ **2.** $15x^2 + 7x + 2$ **3.** $30x^2 + 65x + 30$ **4.** $6x^4 - 23x^2 + 20$

5. In this section, it was stated that if the original trinomial being factored does not have a common factor, then neither of the binomial factors can have a common factor. Explain why.

---

3 Factoring Quadratic Trinomials Using the *ac* Method

Sometimes another method may be easier to use to factor quadratic trinomials when the leading coefficient does not equal 1. This is an algorithm called the *ac* method. The **ac method** reverses the FOIL method by rewriting the middle term as a sum, using factors of the product of the coefficients a and c in the trinomial $ax^2 + bx + c$. For example,

$$\underset{\text{F}}{\downarrow} \quad \underset{\text{O}}{\downarrow} \quad \underset{\text{I}}{\downarrow} \quad \underset{\text{L}}{\downarrow}$$

$$(x + 3)(2x - 1) = 2x^2 - x + 6x - 3 = 2x^2 + 5x - 3.$$

We want to reverse this process entirely and obtain

$$2x^2 + 5x - 3 = 2x^2 - x + 6x - 3 = (x + 3)(2x - 1).$$

To do this, first determine the product of the coefficients a and c. Since $a = 2$ and $c = -3$, the product $ac = 2(-3) = -6$.

Next, determine the factors of ac (-6) whose sum is b (5).

This is the same procedure we used in factoring a quadratic trinomial with a leading coefficient of 1.

Factor	Factor	Sum of Factors
1	-6	-5
-1	6	5 $\leftarrow b$
2	-3	-1
-2	3	1

Remember, we can set up the table in the calculator as we did in the last section. The only difference is that we set the second column to be the product (ac) divided by x, as shown in Figure 10.7.

TECHNOLOGY

X	Y₁	Y₂
-1	6	5
0	ERROR	ERROR
1	-6	-5
2	-3	-1
3	-2	1
4	-1.5	2.5
5	-1.2	3.8

X= -1

Figure 10.7

For Figure 10.7

Use the arrow keys to move through the table. The integer values in the second column correspond to an integer factor in the first column. The third column is the sum of the first two columns.

We will use the factors -1 and 6, because their sum is the same as b, 5. Rewrite the middle term as a sum, using -1 and 6 as the new coefficients; that is,

$$2x^2 + 5x - 3 = 2x^2 - x + 6x - 3.$$

Factor the resulting polynomial using grouping.

$$\left(2x^2 - x\right) + (6x - 3) = x(2x - 1) + 3(2x - 1)$$ Factor a common factor from each group.

$$= (2x - 1)(x + 3)$$ Factor a common binomial from each term.

Check the results by multiplying.

$$(2x - 1)(x + 3) = 2x^2 + 6x - x - 3 = 2x^2 + 5x - 3$$

A graphic check with Y1 $= 2x^2 + 5x - 3$ and Y2 $= (2x - 1)(x + 3)$ results in equivalent graphs.

Therefore, $2x^2 + 5x - 3 = (2x - 1)(x + 3)$.

Y1 $= 2x^2 + 5x - 3$

Y2 $= (2x - 1)(x + 3)$

$(-10, 10, -10, 10)$

> *Factoring a Quadratic Trinomial with a Leading Coefficient Not Equal to 1 Using the ac Method*
> To factor a quadratic trinomial using the *ac* method:
>
> - Factor out the GCF from all terms.
>
> - Determine the product *ac*.
>
> - Determine the factors *m* and *n* of the product *ac* whose sum is *b*.
>
> - Rewrite the trinomial as a four-term polynomial, $ax^2 + mx + nx + c$.
>
> - Factor the resulting polynomial using grouping.
>
> Check the factors by multiplying to obtain the original trinomial or by graphing the original polynomial and the product of the factors as separate functions and determining that the graphs are equivalent.

For another example, factor $6x^2 + 19x + 8$ completely.

Since $a = 6$, $b = 19$, and $c = 8$, then $ac = 6 \cdot 8 = 48$.

Using a table, we determine the factors of the product that result in a sum of 19 (*b*). Remember, since *c* and *b* are both positive, we will not need to use the negative factors of 48.

Factor	Factor	Sum of Factors
1	48	49
2	24	26
3	16	19 ← *b*
4	12	16
6	8	14

The calculator will help us find the factors.

The factors 3 and 16 result in a sum of 19, as shown in Figure 10.8.

TECHNOLOGY

For Figure 10.8

2nd | TBLSET | 1 | ENTER | 1 | ENTER | ▼ | ENTER | ENTER

Y= | (| 6 | x | 8 |) | ÷ | X, T, θ, n | ▼ | X, T, θ, n | +

VARS | ▶ | 1 | 1 | 2nd | TABLE

Figure 10.8

Use the arrow keys to move through the table. The integer values in the second column correspond to an integer factor in the first column. The third column is the sum of the first two columns.

Rewrite the trinomial, using these factors as coefficients of the two new middle terms.

$$6x^2 + 19x + 8 = 6x^2 + 3x + 16x + 8$$
$$= (6x^2 + 3x) + (16x + 8) \quad \text{Group.}$$
$$= 3x(2x + 1) + 8(2x + 1) \quad \text{Factor out a common factor from each group.}$$
$$= (2x + 1)(3x + 8) \quad \text{Factor out a common binomial factor from each term.}$$

Check the factors by multiplying.

$$(2x + 1)(3x + 8) = 6x^2 + 16x + 3x + 8 = 6x^2 + 19x + 8$$

Y1 = $6x^2 + 19x + 8$

Y2 = $(2x + 1)(3x + 8)$

$(-10, 10, -10, 10)$

A graphic check with Y1 = $6x^2 + 19x + 8$ and Y2 = $(2x + 1)(3x + 8)$ results in equivalent graphs.

Therefore, $6x^2 + 19x + 8 = (2x + 1)(3x + 8)$.

EXAMPLE 3 Factor completely. Check by multiplication or graphing.

a. $8x^2 - 26x + 15$ **b.** $6x^2 - 9x - 10$ **c.** $12x^2 - 14x - 6$

Solution

a. $8x^2 - 26x + 15$

Since $a = 8$, $b = -26$, and $c = 15$, then $ac = 8 \cdot 15 = 120$.

Using a table, determine the factors of the product that result in a sum of -26 (b). We will need to use only the negative factors of ac, because c is positive and b is negative. *Note:* You may want to use the calculator table.

Factor	Factor	Sum of Factors
-1	-120	-121
-2	-60	-62
-3	-40	-43
-4	-30	-34
-5	-24	-29
-6	-20	$-26 \leftarrow b$
-8	-15	-23
-10	-12	-22

The factors -6 and -20 result in a sum of -26. Rewrite the trinomial using these factors as coefficients of the two new middle terms.

$$\begin{aligned}
8x^2 - 26x + 15 &= 8x^2 - 6x - 20x + 15 \\
&= \left(8x^2 - 6x\right) + \left(-20x + 15\right) && \text{Group.} \\
&= 2x(4x - 3) + (-5)(4x - 3) && \text{Factor out common factor.} \\
&= (4x - 3)(2x - 5) && \text{Factor out common binomial factor.}
\end{aligned}$$

The check is left for you.

$$8x^2 - 26x + 15 = (4x - 3)(2x - 5)$$

b. $6x^2 - 9x - 10$

Since $a = 6$, $b = -9$, and $c = -10$, then $ac = 6 \cdot -10 = -60$.

   Using a table, determine the factors of the product that result in a sum of -9 (b). *Note:* You may want to use the calculator table.

Factor	Factor	Sum of Factors
1	-60	-59
-1	60	59
2	-30	-28
-2	30	28
3	-20	-17
-3	20	17
4	-15	-11
-4	15	11
5	-12	-7
-5	12	7
6	-10	-4
-6	10	4

No set of factors result in a sum of -9. The trinomial does not factor.

   $6x^2 - 9x - 10$ does not factor.

c. $12x^2 - 14x - 6$

First, factor out the common factor of 2.

$$12x^2 - 14x - 6 = 2\left(6x^2 - 7x - 3\right)$$

Since $a = 6$, $b = -7$, and $c = -3$, then $ac = 6 \cdot -3 = -18$. Using a table, determine the factors of the product that result in a sum of -7 (b). *Note:* You may want to use the calculator table.

Factor	Factor	Sum of Factors	
1	-18	-17	
-1	18	17	
2	-9	-7	$\leftarrow b$
-2	9	7	
3	-6	-3	
-3	6	3	

The factors 2 and -9 result in a sum of -7. Rewrite the trinomial using these factors as coefficients of the two new middle terms.

$$12x^2 - 14x - 6 = 2(6x^2 - 7x - 3)$$
$$= 2(6x^2 + 2x - 9x - 3)$$
$$= 2[(6x^2 + 2x) + (-9x - 3)] \quad \text{Group.}$$
$$= 2[2x(3x + 1) - 3(3x + 1)] \quad \text{Factor out a common factor.}$$
$$= 2(3x + 1)(2x - 3) \quad \text{Factor out a common binomial factor.}$$

The check is left for you.

$$12x^2 - 14x - 6 = 2(3x + 1)(2x - 3) \quad \blacksquare$$

Quadratic-like trinomials also can be factored using this method. For example, factor $3x^4 + 2x^2 - 8$.

> This is not a quadratic trinomial. However, the same method may be used to factor this trinomial.
>   Since $a = 3, b = 2$, and $c = -8$, then $ac = 3 \cdot -8 = -24$. Using a table, determine the factors of the product that result in a sum of 2 (b). *Note:* You may want to use the calculator table.

Factor	Factor	Sum of Factors	
1	−24	−23	
−1	24	23	
2	−12	−10	
−2	12	10	
3	−8	−5	
−3	8	5	
4	−6	−2	
−4	6	2	← b

> The factors −4 and 6 result in a sum of 2. Rewrite the trinomial using these factors as coefficients of the two new middle terms.

$$3x^4 + 2x^2 - 8 = 3x^4 - 4x^2 + 6x^2 - 8$$
$$= (3x^4 - 4x^2) + (6x^2 - 8) \quad \text{Group.}$$
$$= x^2(3x^2 - 4) + 2(3x^2 - 4) \quad \text{Factor out a common factor.}$$
$$= (3x^2 - 4)(x^2 + 2) \quad \text{Factor out a common binomial factor.}$$

The check is left for you.

$$3x^4 + 2x^2 - 8 = (3x^2 - 4)(x^2 + 2)$$

Both the trial-and-error method and the ac method result in the same factors. As you work exercises, you will develop a sense as to which method is easier for you to use. At times one method is shorter than the other. At other times, either method will be about as difficult.

Experiencing Algebra the Checkup Way

Factor exercises 1–4 completely using the ac method of factoring a trinomial with a leading coefficient not equal to 1.

1. $2x^2 - 9x - 5$ **2.** $15x^2 + 7x + 2$ **3.** $30x^2 + 65x + 30$ **4.** $6x^4 - 23x^2 + 20$

5. If you had to factor a trinomial whose leading coefficient was not equal to 1, would you first try the trial-and-error method or the *ac* method? Explain your choice.

---

4 Modeling the Real World

Trinomials are used for modeling many real-world situations, such as the equation of motion for a projectile or the equation describing the impact that occurs in some kinds of collisions. In some cases, the trinomial can be factored using the methods described in this section, enabling us to solve the equations directly. In geometry problems, if the area of a figure is described by a trinomial, factoring it can help us determine the dimensions of the figure.

EXAMPLE 4

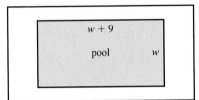

Mandy has designed a swimming pool area for a customer. The length of the pool is to be 9 feet more than the width. The pool is to have a concrete walk around it, with equal width on opposite sides. However, the walk is wider along one set of sides.

    Determine the two walk widths if her figures show that the total area covered by walk and pool is $(w^2 + 18w + 56)$ square feet, where w is the pool width.

Solution

To determine the outside dimensions of the walks, find the factors that are multiplied to obtain the total area, $w^2 + 18w + 56$.

$$w^2 + 18w + 56 = (w + 4)(w + 14)$$

The outside dimensions are $(w + 4)$ feet and $(w + 14)$ feet.

    The outside width is $(w + 4)$. To determine the width of the walk we subtract the pool width w, and divide by 2 (the walks along each side are equal).

$$\frac{(w + 4) - w}{2} = \frac{4}{2} = 2$$

The walk is 2 feet wide along the pool's length.

    The outside length is $(w + 14)$. To determine the width of the walk on this side we subtract the pool length, $w + 9$, and divide by 2.

$$\frac{(w + 14) - (w + 9)}{2} = \frac{5}{2} = 2\frac{1}{2}$$

The walk is $2\frac{1}{2}$ feet along the pool's width. ■

EXAMPLE 5

Carri has a triangular flower bed in the corner of her yard where the driveway enters the street at a 90-degree angle. The length of the flower bed along the driveway is twice the length of the flower bed along the street. She plans to increase the length of the sides of her flower bed along the driveway and street by the same number of feet. She has determined the area of the new flower bed will be $\left(x^2 + \frac{15}{2}x + \frac{25}{2}\right)$ square feet, given that x is the original number of feet on the street side of the flower bed.

a. Determine the length of the sides of the new flower bed in terms of x.
b. By how many feet does Carri plan to increase each side?

Solution

a. The area of a triangle is found by the formula $A = \frac{1}{2}bh$. Since the triangle is a right triangle, then the base and height are the lengths of the sides along the driveway and the street. To determine the length of these sides, we must factor the area given into the form $\frac{1}{2}bh$.

$$A \qquad\qquad \frac{1}{2} \qquad\qquad bh$$
$$\downarrow \qquad\qquad \downarrow \qquad\qquad \downarrow$$

$$x^2 + \frac{15}{2}x + \frac{25}{2} = \frac{1}{2}\left(2x^2 + 15x + 25\right) \qquad \text{Factor out the } \tfrac{1}{2}.$$

$$= \frac{1}{2}(x + 5)(2x + 5) \qquad \text{Factor the } bh \text{ into two binomials.}$$

The sides of the new triangular bed are $(x + 5)$ feet and $(2x + 5)$ feet.
b. Since the original dimensions of the flower bed were x feet and $2x$ feet, Carri planned to add 5 feet to each side. ∎

Application

A telephone designer began with the plans of a square telephone with sides of x inches that covered an area of x^2 square inches. The newly designed rectangular phone covers an area of $\left(x^2 - 2x - 3\right)$ square inches. Determine the dimensions of the new phone in terms of x.

Discussion

x is the length of the original side.
$x^2 - 2x - 3$ is the new area.

To determine the dimensions of the new telephone, factor the polynomial for the area into two factors.

$$x^2 - 2x - 3 = (x + 1)(x - 3)$$

The area of a rectangle is the product of its length and width. Therefore, the dimensions of the new phone are $(x + 1)$ inches by $(x - 3)$ inches. One side of the original phone was increased by 1 inch and the other side was decreased by 3 inches. ∎

Experiencing Algebra the Checkup Way

1. Mandy discovered that she had reversed the numbers on the constant term of the trinomial for area in Example 4. The trinomial should have been $w^2 + 18w + 65$. Rework the problem to find what the two widths of the walk should be.

2. Carri has another triangular garden on the other side of the driveway that has to be reduced. The length of the flower bed along the drive is three times the length along the street. She cut both sides of the triangle by the same amount. The reduced garden has an area equal to the polynomial $\frac{3}{2}x^2 - 8x + 8$, where x is the length of the small side of the original garden.

   a. Determine the sides of the reduced garden in terms of x.

   b. By how many feet did Carri reduce each side of the garden?

PROBLEM SET 10.5

Experiencing Algebra the Exercise Way

Factor completely and check.

1. $x^2 + 14x + 45$
2. $p^2 + 14p + 48$
3. $y^2 - 15y + 56$
4. $u^2 + 11u - 26$
5. $p^2 - 9p - 36$
6. $v^2 - 12v - 13$
7. $z^2 + 6z + 12$
8. $m^2 - 9m + 15$
9. $x^4 + 25x^2 + 144$
10. $b^4 + 29b^2 + 100$
11. $x^4 - 2x^2 - 3$
12. $d^4 + 18d^2 - 175$
13. $3a^2 + 48a + 165$
14. $7b^2 - 70b + 168$
15. $4c^2 + 44c - 104$
16. $7p^2 - 7p - 140$
17. $x^2 - 11xy + 24y^2$
18. $a^2 - 17ab + 72b^2$
19. $x^2 + 11xy - 12y^2$
20. $a^2 - 9ab - 90b^2$
21. $-3a^2 - 15ab - 18b^2$
22. $-5x^2 + 35xy - 60y^2$
23. $-2x^2 + 14xy + 36y^2$
24. $-6x^2 + 24xy + 126y^2$

Factor exercises 25–64 completely, using either the trial-and-error method or the ac method. Check your answers.

25. $3x^2 + 10x + 3$
26. $4x^2 + 12x + 7$
27. $2x^2 - 15x + 7$
28. $3x^2 - 34x + 11$
29. $3x^2 - x - 2$
30. $5x^2 - 2x - 3$
31. $5m^2 + 9m - 2$
32. $7p^2 + 34p - 5$
33. $2m^2 + 7m - 3$
34. $3t^2 - 12t + 4$
35. $4a^2 + 25a + 6$
36. $10c^2 + 41c + 4$
37. $9d^2 - 13d + 4$
38. $8b^2 - 17b + 9$
39. $6x^2 - 23x - 4$
40. $4x^2 - 31x - 8$
41. $8y^2 + 7y - 18$
42. $6z^2 + 19z - 20$
43. $6b^2 + 17b + 12$
44. $15a^2 + 28a + 12$
45. $20x^2 - 31x + 12$
46. $14z^2 + 13z - 12$
47. $18x^2 - 9x - 20$
48. $8x^2 - 22x - 63$
49. $18p^2 - 57p - 21$
50. $-63x^2 - 30x + 48$
51. $2x^4 + 11x^2 + 9$
52. $24x^4 - 22x^2 + 3$
53. $4m^4 + 13m^2 - 12$
54. $5z^4 + 39z^2 - 54$
55. $5x - 6x^2 + 56$
56. $21 - 5b - 4b^2$
57. $6x^2 + 5xy - 6y^2$
58. $14a^2 + 25ab + 6b^2$
59. $4u^2 - 39uv + 56v^2$
60. $3x^2 - 20xy + 32y^2$
61. $9x^4 + 13x^2y^2 + 4y^4$
62. $16x^4 + 41x^2y^2 + 25y^4$
63. $10x^2y^2 + xy - 21$
64. $21p^2q^2 - 2pq - 8$

65. The length of a rectangle is 8 inches more than its width. After both its length and width have been increased, the area of the larger rectangle is given by $\left(w^2 + 14w + 24\right)$ square inches, where w is the original width.

   a. Factor the polynomial to find the increased width and length.

   b. By how much was the width increased?

   c. By how much was the length increased?

66. A rectangular poster design has a width that is 5 inches less than its length. Its width is increased while its length is decreased. The area of the new poster is given by $(x^2 - 4x + 3)$ square inches, where x is the original length.

    a. Factor the polynomial to find the new width and length.

    b. By how much was the width increased?

    c. By how much was the length decreased?

67. A right triangle has its two legs increased by the same amount. After the increase, the area of the triangle is equal to the polynomial $(x^2 + \frac{21}{2}x + 20)$ square inches, where x is the length of the original triangle's small side.

    a. Determine the lengths of the legs of the enlarged triangle as a function of x.

    b. By how much were the legs increased?

    c. What is the expression for the length of the long leg of the original triangle?

68. A right triangle has its two legs decreased by the same amount. After the reduction, the area of the triangle is equal to the polynomial $(\frac{3}{2}x^2 - 12x + 24)$ square inches, where x is the length of the original triangle's small leg.

    a. Determine the lengths of the legs of the reduced triangle as a function of x.

    b. By how much were the legs decreased?

    c. What is the expression for the length of the long leg of the original triangle?

 Experiencing Algebra the Calculator Way

When using the *ac* method, if you store the values of a, b, and c from the trinomial $ax^2 + bx + c$ in your calculator, you can proceed from one trinomial to another without having to renter the expressions for Y1 and Y2. The following example illustrates the procedure.

    Factor $85x^2 - 91x - 72$ using the ac method.

    a. Store values for a, b, and c.

    b. Set Y1 $= \frac{ac}{x}$.

| Y= | AI PHA | A | × | ALPHA | C | ÷ | X, T, θ, n | ▼ |

    c. Set Y2 to test for the values of m and n that make $m + n = b$ a true statement.

| X, T, θ, n | + | VARS | ▶ | 1 | 1 | 2nd | TEST | 1 | ALPHA | B |

    d. Set your table as before, and view the table, scanning for a 1 in the Y2 column.

In this case, Y2 is 1 when the values of m and n are 45 and -136. Now you can use the grouping method to show that

$$85x^2 - 91x - 72 = 85x^2 - 136x + 45x - 72$$
$$= (85x^2 - 136x) + (45x - 72)$$
$$= 17x(5x - 8) + 9(5x - 8)$$
$$= (17x + 9)(5x - 8).$$

For subsequent problems, you need only store the new values for a, b, and c, and go directly to the table to find the new values of m and n.

Note that when you are scanning the table for the pair of numbers, there is some logic to follow in deciding whether to scan in the negative-integer direction or in the positive-integer direction. If the coefficient b is negative and c is positive, you will be searching for two negative integers, and will want to scan in that direction. If the coefficient c is negative, you may scan in either direction, since one of the integers will be positive and the other negative. If the coefficients b and c are both positive, you need only scan in the positive-integer direction, since the two integers will be positive.

Use this procedure to factor the following using the ac method. Be sure to factor completely.

1. $96x^2 - 16x - 2$ **2.** $24x^2 + 7x - 55$ **3.** $32x^2 + 102x + 81$

4. $72x^2 - 99x + 34$ **5.** $4p^4 + 109p^2 + 225$

Experiencing Algebra the Group Way

Each member of your group should use the methods of this section and the previous sections to factor the following trinomials completely. You will need to first factor out the greatest common factor; then you can factor the trinomial.

Discuss what you can do to make the following polynomials easier to factor. (Hint: Can you factor out a fraction as the greatest common factor?) Then factor completely.

1. $\dfrac{1}{3}x^2 + 4x + 9$ **2.** $\dfrac{1}{3}x^2 - 3x + 6$ **3.** $\dfrac{1}{4}x^2 - \dfrac{1}{2}x - \dfrac{15}{4}$

Discuss what you can do to make the following trinomials easier to factor. (Hint: Can you factor out a decimal factor as the greatest common factor?) Then factor completely.

4. $0.4p^2 + 3.6p + 5.6$ **5.** $0.2p^2 - 2.6p + 8$ **6.** $0.1u^2 + 0.6u - 2.7$

Discuss what you can do to make the following trinomials easier to factor. (Hint: How can you handle a negative sign in the leading coefficient?) Then factor completely.

7. $12x^6 + 24x^3 - 96$ **8.** $-24x^6 + 48x^3 + 192$ **9.** $0.5x^4 + 2.5x^2 + 2$

Experiencing Algebra the Write Way

1. Ned factored $-3x^2 - 15x + 312$ as $-3(x - 8)(x + 13)$. Lamar factored the same trinomial as $3(13 + x)(8 - x)$. Check to see whether the two answers multiply to the same trinomial. If they do, discuss how the two students may have obtained different answers, and try to identify the properties of real numbers that tell us that the two are equivalent expressions. State which answer you prefer and explain why.

2. Chuck used the *ac* method to factor the following trinomial. Study Chuck's answer and explain why he has not correctly factored the trinomial completely.

$6x^2 + 3x - 30 = (3x - 6)(2x + 5)$

10.6   General Strategies for Factoring

Objectives

1   Factor a difference of two squares.

2   Factor a perfect-square trinomial.

3   Factor a sum or difference of two cubes.

4   Factor any given polynomial completely.

5   Model real-world situations by factoring polynomials.

Application

The first telephone receivers had a cone-shaped mouthpiece. The mouthpiece volume was represented by the polynomial $\left(\frac{1}{3}\pi x^3 + \pi x^2\right)$ cubic inches, where x is the radius length in inches. Determine a polynomial for the height in terms of the radius.

After completing this section, we will discuss this application further. See page 783.

We are now ready to complete our discussion of factoring. However, before we finish this discussion, we have three additional types of polynomials to factor. Two of these polynomials are the results of the special products we previously multiplied.

1 Factoring a Difference of Two Squares

One special product consists of two factors, one the sum and the other the difference of the same two terms.

$$(a + b)(a - b) = a^2 - b^2$$

If we reverse this operation, we obtain two binomial factors.

> *Factoring the Difference of Two Squares*
> To factor the difference of two squares,
> $$a^2 - b^2 = (a + b)(a - b).$$

In order to do this factoring, we need to recognize a polynomial as the difference of two squares. The difference of two squares is a binomial consisting of the subtraction of two perfect-square terms, that is, $a^2 - b^2$. The factors for a difference of two squares are $(a + b)$ and $(a - b)$.

For example, factor $x^2 - 25$ completely.

$$a^2 - b^2 = (a + b)(a - b)$$

$$x^2 - 25 = (x)^2 - (5)^2 = (x + 5)(x - 5)$$

The factors may be checked by multiplication or by graphing, as in the last section.

EXAMPLE 1 Factor completely and check.

a. $4x^2 - 9y^2$ **b.** $3x^2 - 48$ **c.** $144 + x^2y^2$

Solution

a. $4x^2 - 9y^2 = (2x)^2 - (3y)^2$ Determine that $a = 2x$ and $b = 3y$.

$\qquad\qquad\quad = (2x + 3y)(2x - 3y)$ Write a product of the sum and difference of a and b.

The multiplication check is left for you.

b. $3x^2 - 48 = 3(x^2 - 16)$ Factor out the common factor.

$\qquad\qquad\quad = 3\left[(x)^2 - (4)^2\right]$ Determine that $a = x$ and $b = 4$.

$\qquad\qquad\quad = 3(x + 4)(x - 4)$ Write as a product of the sum and difference of a and b.

A multiplication or graphic check is left for you.

c. $144 + x^2 y^2$ will not factor. This is not a difference of squares but a *sum* of squares.

Remember that a variable term is a perfect square when its exponent is an even number. That is, x^4 is a perfect square of x^2 because $x^4 = \left(x^2\right)^2$ and x^6 is a perfect square of x^3 because $x^6 = \left(x^3\right)^2$.

Therefore, we can use this procedure to factor the difference of two squares if the variable terms have even exponents. For example, factor $m^4 - 81$.

$m^4 - 81 = \left(m^2\right)^2 - (9)^2$ Determine that $a = m^2$ and $b = 9$.

$\qquad\quad = \left(m^2 + 9\right)\left(m^2 - 9\right)$ Write as a product of the sum and difference of a and b.

$\qquad\quad = \left(m^2 + 9\right)\left[(m)^2 - (3)^2\right]$ Determine the perfect square terms of the second factor.

$\qquad\quad = \left(m^2 + 9\right)(m + 3)(m - 3)$ Write as a product of a sum and difference. ∎

Experiencing Algebra the Checkup Way

Factor exercises 1–5 completely and check.

1. $y^2 - 4$
2. $25x^2 - 16y^2$
3. $2z^2 - 18$
4. $a^2 + b^2$
5. $c^4 - 16$
6. What are the things you should look for in a polynomial in order to factor it as the difference of two squares?

---

2 Factoring a Perfect-Square Trinomial

Another special product is the square of a binomial.

$$(a + b)^2 = a^2 + 2ab + b^2$$
$$(a - b)^2 = a^2 - 2ab + b^2$$

We can reverse this operation by factoring the trinomial into a square of a binomial.

Factoring a Perfect-Square Trinomial
To factor a perfect-square trinomial,

$$a^2 + 2ab + b^2 = (a + b)^2$$

or

$$a^2 - 2ab + b^2 = (a - b)^2.$$

In order to do this factoring, we need to recognize when a polynomial is a perfect-square trinomial. In a perfect-square trinomial, the first and last terms are perfect squares, and the middle term is either positive or negative twice the product of the terms that are squared. That is, $a^2 + 2ab + b^2$ or $a^2 - 2ab + b^2$. The binomial factors for a perfect-square trinomial are $(a + b)^2$ or $(a - b)^2$. For example,

$$a^2 + 2\ a\ b + b^2 = (a + b)^2$$

$$x^2 + 10x + 25 = (x)^2 + 2(x)(5) + (5)^2 = (x + 5)^2$$

$$a^2 - 2\ a\ b + b^2 = (a - b)^2$$

$$x^2 - 10x + 25 = (x)^2 - 2(x)(5) + (5)^2 = (x - 5)^2$$

EXAMPLE 2 Factor completely and check.

a. $4x^2 + 12xy + 9y^2$ **b.** $3x^2 - 24xy + 48y^2$ **c.** $m^2 + 12m + 144$

Solution

a. $4x^2 + 12xy + 9y^2 = (2x)^2 + 2(2x)(3y) + (3y)^2$ Determine that $a = 2x$ and $b = 3y$.

$$= (2x + 3y)^2$$

The multiplication check is left for you.

b. $3x^2 - 24xy + 48y^2 = 3(x^2 - 8xy + 16y^2)$ Factor out a common factor.

$$= 3[(x)^2 - 2(x)(4y) + (4y)^2]$$ Determine that $a = x$ and $b = 4y$.

$$= 3(x - 4y)^2$$

A multiplication check is left for you.

c. $m^2 + 12m + 144$ does not factor. The first and last terms are perfect squares: m^2 and 12^2. However, the middle term is not $2(m)(12)$.

A perfect-square trinomial such as $x^4 - 18x^2 + 81$ can also be factored using this method. For example,

$$x^4 - 18x^2 + 81 = (x^2)^2 - 2(x^2)(9) + (9)^2$$ Determine that $a = x^2$ and $b = 9$.

$$= (x^2 - 9)^2$$
$$= (x^2 - 9)(x^2 - 9)$$ Expand the factors.
$$= (x + 3)(x - 3)(x + 3)(x - 3)$$ Factor each factor as a difference of two squares.

$$= (x + 3)^2(x - 3)^2$$

A multiplication or graphic check is left for you. ∎

Experiencing Algebra the Checkup Way

Factor exercises 1–5 completely and check.

1. $z^2 + 12z + 36$ **2.** $49a^2 + 42ab + 9b^2$ **3.** $5x^2 - 60x + 180$

4. $p^2 - 8p + 64$ **5.** $y^4 - 8y^2 + 16$

6. What should you look for in a polynomial in order to factor it as a perfect-square trinomial?

---

3 Factoring a Sum or Difference of Cubes A third type of polynomial that we need to be able to factor is the product of a binomial and a trinomial. Complete the following set of exercises to determine this product and discover a pattern you can use to factor it.

DISCOVERY 10	**Factoring a Sum or Difference of Two Cubes** Multiply. **1.** $(x + 5)(x^2 - 5x + 25)$ **2.** $(x - 5)(x^2 + 5x + 25)$ Write a rule to factor the sum or difference of two cubes.

The first product is a sum of two cubes. The second product is a difference of two cubes. In order to factor these polynomials, we turn these result around and write a binomial and trinomial factor.

> *Factoring the Sum or Difference of Two Cubes*
> To factor the sum or difference of two cubes,
> $$a^3 + b^3 = (a + b)(a^2 - ab + b^2)$$
> and
> $$a^3 - b^3 = (a - b)(a^2 + ab + b^2).$$

 Helping Hand The binomial factor has the same sign as the polynomial being factored. The middle term of the trinomial has the opposite sign of the polynomial being factored. The last term in the trinomial is always positive.

For example, factor $x^3 - 27$ completely.

$$a^3 - b^3 = (a - b)(a^2 + a\,b + b^2)$$

$$x^3 - 27 = (x)^3 - (3)^3 = (x - 3)[x^2 + x(3) + (3)^2]$$
$$= (x - 3)(x^2 + 3x + 9)$$

The factors may be checked by multiplication or by graphing.

EXAMPLE 3 Factor completely and check.

a. $m^3 + 64$ **b.** $27x^3 - 125y^3$

Solution

a. $m^3 + 64 = (m)^3 + (4)^3$ Determine $a = m$ and $b = 4$.

$= (m + 4)[m^2 - 4m + (4)^2]$ Write a product of a binomial factor and a trinomial factor.

$= (m + 4)(m^2 - 4m + 16)$ Simplify.

The check is left for you.

b. $27x^3 - 125y^3 = (3x)^3 - (5y)^3$ Determine $a = 3x$ and $b = 4$.

$= (3x - 5y)[(3x)^2 + (3x)(5y) + (5y)^2]$ Write a product of a binomial and a trinomial.

$= (3x - 5y)(9x^2 + 15xy + 25y^2)$ Simplify.

The check is left for you. ∎

Experiencing Algebra the Checkup Way

Factor exercises 1–3 completely and check.

1. $a^3 + 8$ **2.** $a^3 - 8$ **3.** $8x^3 + 27y^3$

4. When factoring a polynomial, how would you recognize it to be the sum or difference of two cubes?

---

4 Factoring Polynomials

In the previous sections, we discussed methods for factoring polynomials. We now discuss a general strategy to use when any given polynomial is to be factored. The following steps should be followed to completely factor a polynomial.

> *Steps to Factor a Polynomial Completely*
> **1.** Factor out the greatest common factor from all terms. Factor out -1 if the leading coefficient is negative.
>
>   Determine the type of polynomial remaining and factor as indicated for each. Repeat steps 2–4 until all polynomial factors (with the exception of the common monomial factor) do not factor.
>
> **2.** Binomial—Difference of two squares:
>
> $$a^2 - b^2 = (a + b)(a - b)$$
>
> Sum or difference of two cubes:
>
> $$a^3 + b^3 = (a + b)(a^2 - ab + b^2)$$
> $$a^3 - b^3 = (a - b)(a^2 + ab + b^2)$$
>
> Otherwise, it will not factor.
>
> **3.** Trinomial—Perfect square trinomial:
>
> $$a^2 + 2ab + b^2 = (a + b)^2$$
> $$a^2 - 2ab + b^2 = (a - b)^2$$
>
> Quadratic trinomial with leading coefficient 1:
>
> $$x^2 + bx + c = (x + m)(x + n),$$
> where $mn = c$ and $n + m = b$

Quadratic trinomial with leading coefficient greater than 1: trial-and-error method or *ac* method
Otherwise, it will not factor.

4. Four-term polynomial—Factor by grouping
Otherwise, it will not factor.

Check the factors by multiplying and obtaining the original polynomial or by graphing the original polynomial and the product of the factors as separate functions and determining that the graphs are equivalent.

EXAMPLE 4 Factor completely and check.

a. $3y^2 - 243$ **b.** $16y^4 - 200y + 625$
c. $6x^2 + 16x - 70$ **d.** $5x^3 + 12x^2 + 7x$
e. $2a^3b - 8a^2b^2 - 3a^2b^2 + 12ab^3$ **f.** $4x^2 + 14x + 49$
g. $15 + 8x + x^2$

Solution

a. $3y^2 - 243$
The GCF is 3. Therefore, factor out 3 from all terms.

$$3(y^2 - 81)$$

The remaining factor is a binomial; in fact, it is a difference of squares: $y^2 - 81 = (y)^2 - (9)^2 = (y + 9)(y - 9)$.

$$3(y + 9)(y - 9)$$

The remaining factors are binomials. However, neither is a difference of squares or difference of cubes. The binomials will not factor.
The check is left for you.

b. $16y^4 - 200y^2 + 625$
There are no common factors. The polynomial is a trinomial; in fact, it is a perfect-square trinomial: $(4y^2)^2 - 2(4y)(25) + (25)^2 = (4y^2 - 25)^2$.

$$(4y^2 - 25)^2$$

The remaining polynomial factors are binomials. Both are differences of squares, $4y^2 - 25 = (2y)^2 - (5)^2 = (2y + 5)(2y - 5)$, so we write the factors twice.

$$(2y + 5)(2y - 5)(2y + 5)(2y - 5)$$

or

$$(2y + 5)^2(2y - 5)^2$$

The remaining factors are binomials that will not factor.
The check is left for you.

c. $6x^2 + 16x - 70$
The GCF is 2. Therefore, factor 2 out of all terms.

$$2(3x^2 + 8x - 35)$$

The remaining factor is a trinomial with $a > 1$. Since $a = 3$ and $c = -35$ are not both prime, it will be easier to use the *ac* method: $ac = -105$.

Note: You may want to use the calculator table.

Factor	Factor	Sum of Factors
1	-105	-104
-1	105	104
3	-35	-32
-3	35	32
5	-21	-16
-5	21	16
7	-15	-8
-7	15	8 $\leftarrow b$

Rewrite the middle term of the trinomial, $8x$, as $-7x + 15x$ and factor by grouping.

$$2(3x^2 - 7x + 15x - 35)$$
$$= 2[(3x^2 - 7x) + (15x - 35)] \quad \text{Group terms.}$$
$$= 2[x(3x - 7) + 5(3x - 7)] \quad \text{Factor out a common factor from each group.}$$
$$= 2(3x - 7)(x + 5) \quad \text{Factor out a common binomial factor from each term.}$$

The remaining binomial factors will not factor.
  The check is left for you.

d. $5x^3 + 12x^2 + 7x$
The GCF is x. Factor x out of each term.

$$x(5x^2 + 12x + 7)$$

The remaining factor is a trinomial with $a > 1$. Since $a = 5$ and $c = 7$ are prime, we will use the trial-and-error method. Possible factors for the first and last terms are $5x^2 = x \cdot 5x$ and $7 = 1 \cdot 7$. Since $b = 12$ is a positive number, we will only use positive factors for 7. Filling in the blanks with possibilities and checking for the correct middle term will result in the following.

$x(\underline{\quad}\ \underline{\quad})(\underline{\quad}\ \underline{\quad})$ Middle term
$x(\underline{x} + \underline{1})(\underline{5x} + \underline{7})$ $7x + 5x = 12x$
$x(\underline{x} + \underline{7})(\underline{5x} + \underline{1})$ $x + 35x = 36x$

We choose $x(x + 1)(5x + 7)$ because it results in the correct middle term.

$$x(x + 1)(5x + 7)$$

The remaining binomial factors will not factor.
  The check is left for you.

e. $2a^3b - 8a^2b^2 - 3a^2b^2 + 12ab^3$
The GCF is ab. Factor ab out of each term.

$$ab(2a^2 - 8ab - 3ab + 12b^2)$$

The remaining polynomial has four terms. We will factor it by grouping.

$ab\left[(2a^2 - 8ab) + (-3ab + 12b^2)\right]$ Group terms.

$ab\left[2a(a - 4b) + (-3b)(a - 4b)\right]$ Factor out a common factor from each group.

$ab(a - 4b)(2a - 3b)$ Factor out a common binomial factor from each term.

The remaining binomial factors will not factor.
The check is left for you.

f. $4x^2 + 14x + 49$

There are no common factors. The polynomial is a trinomial. It looks similar to a perfect-square trinomial, but upon closer inspection it is not.

$$4x^2 + 14x + 49 \neq (2x)^2 + 2(2x)(7) + (7)^2$$

$$\uparrow$$
$$28x$$

It is a trinomial with $a > 1$. Since $a = 4$ and $c = 49$ are not prime, we will use the ac method: $ac = 196$. We will use a table to determine the factors, m and n, of the product 196 that will result in a sum of 14 (b). Since b is positive, we will only use the positive factors of 196. *Note:* You may want to use the calculator table.

Factor	Factor	Sum of Factors
1	196	197
2	98	100
4	49	53
7	28	35
14	14	28

Since no set of factors results in a sum of 14, the trinomial will not factor. $4x^2 + 14x + 49$ will not factor.

g. $15 + 8x + x^2$

There are no common factors. The polynomial is a trinomial that is not written in standard form. We will factor this trinomial by trial and error. Possible factors for the first and last terms are as follows:

$$15 = 1 \cdot 15 \qquad x^2 = x \cdot x$$
$$= 3 \cdot 5$$

Since $b = 8$ is a positive number, we will use only positive factors for 15. Filling in the blanks with possibilities and checking for the correct middle term results in the following.

$(\underline{\quad}\ \underline{\quad})(\underline{\quad}\ \underline{\quad})$ Middle term

$(\underline{1} + \underline{x})(\underline{15} + \underline{x})$ $x + 15x = 16x$

$(\underline{3} + \underline{x})(\underline{5} + \underline{x})$ $3x + 5x = 8x$

We choose $(3 + x)(5 + x)$ because this results in $8x$ for the middle term.

■

Experiencing Algebra the Checkup Way

Factor exercises 1–7 completely and check.

1. $10z^2 + 35z - 150$

2. $6a^3 + 26a^2 + 8a$

3. $4x^2 + 15x + 25$

4. $12x^3 - 60x^2y - 6x^2y + 30xy^2$

5. $-6a^2 + 24$

6. $81x^4 - 72x^2 + 16$

7. $12 - 17h - 5h^2$

8. What is the first step you should always look for when factoring a polynomial?

9. If you are factoring a binomial, for what forms should you be on the lookout?

10. When factoring a trinomial, for what forms should you be looking?

11. When factoring a polynomial with four terms, what method should you try to use?

---

5 Modeling the Real World

There are many mathematical relationships that cannot be described exactly by polynomials. However, many of these relationships can be approximated by polynomials, especially if we are interested in only a small domain of the variable. Because of this, factoring and simplifying polynomials is a very useful technique to learn.

EXAMPLE 5

Lynn wants to redesign the square deck on her house using all of the outside railing. However, she cannot use 9 square feet of the outdoor carpet because it has grease stains from the grill.

a. Determine the possible dimensions of Lynn's new deck in terms of the original side of length x feet.

b. If Lynn's original deck was 12 feet by 12 feet, determine the new deck's dimensions.

c. Using the dimensions found in part (b), draw two possible decks.

d. Determine the amount of railing for each deck in part (c).

e. If only the original railing is used, determine whether either drawing in part (c) is possible.

Solution

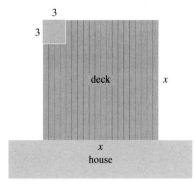

a. Since the length of the original deck (carpet) is x feet, the area of the original square deck is x^2.

The new deck (carpet) area is 9 square feet less than the original area, or $x^2 - 9$.

To determine the dimensions of the new deck, we must factor the area to determine the dimensions that were multiplied.

$$x^2 - 9 = (x)^2 - (3)^2 = (x + 3)(x - 3)$$

The resulting dimensions are $(x + 3)$ feet and $(x - 3)$ feet.

b. If $x = 12$, then the new deck's dimensions are 15 feet $(x + 3)$ by 9 feet $(x - 3)$.

c.

d. The first drawing will need $9 + 15 + 9$ or 33 feet of railing. The second drawing will need $15 + 9 + 15$ or 39 feet of railing.

e. The original deck had $12 + 12 + 12$ or 36 feet of railing. The first drawing in part (c) is the only possible deck using these conditions. ∎

Most real-world situations are not modeled by polynomials with integer coefficients. However, we may estimate the factors of these polynomials by rounding the coefficients to integers.

EXAMPLE 6 A tour agency offers special group package rates. One such offer is to give one free ticket if certain conditions are met. Another possibility is to reduce the cost of the ticket. A ticket agent uses a formula to determine that the revenue from a tour is represented by the polynomial $(149.95x - 0.99x^2)$, where x is the number of people participating. Round each coefficient to the nearest integer and factor. Determine from the factors whether a free ticket was offered or the cost of the tickets was reduced.

Solution

$x =$ number of people participating

$$149.95x - 0.99x^2 \approx 150x - x^2 \qquad \text{Round to integer coefficients.}$$
$$\approx x(150 - x) \qquad \text{Factor out the common factor.}$$

The revenue is the product of x participants times $(150 - x)$ dollars.

Therefore, the cost of the ticket is reduced and is approximately $150 minus $1 per participant. ∎

Application

The first telephone receivers had a cone-shaped mouthpiece. The mouthpiece volume was represented by the polynomial $\left(\frac{1}{3}\pi x^3 + \pi x^2\right)$ cubic inches, where x is the radius length in inches. Determine a polynomial for the height in terms of the radius.

Discussion

x is the radius length in inches.

$\frac{1}{3}\pi x^3 + \pi x^2$ is the volume of the mouthpiece.

The volume formula for a cone is $\frac{1}{3}\pi r^2 h$. In order to determine the height, factor out $\frac{1}{3}\pi x^2$ from the volume polynomial.

$$\frac{1}{3}\pi x^3 + \pi x^2 = \frac{1}{3}\pi x^2(x + 3)$$

Comparing the volume formula and the factored polynomial, we have

$$\frac{1}{3}\pi r^2 \quad h$$

$$\downarrow \qquad \downarrow$$

$$\frac{1}{3}\pi x^2(x + 3)$$

The radius is x inches and the height is $(x + 3)$ inches. ∎

Experiencing Algebra the Checkup Way

1. Lynn also has a square plot in her yard, measuring 16 feet on a side, which she wants to make into an outdoor sitting area. She plans to put a square patio in the plot for furniture, with the remainder of the plot landscaped as a garden.

   a. Determine a polynomial for the area of the plot available for landscaping if the patio measures p feet on a side.

   b. Factor the polynomial for the area. Use the factors to determine the dimensions of an equivalent rectangular garden area if the patio will be 7 feet on a side.

   c. Lynn sees an advertisement for garden plants that states the package contains enough plants for a 6-by-8-foot garden. Will the package be large enough for her garden?

2. A tray is made from a rectangular sheet of metal by cutting out squares from each corner and folding up the edges. If the volume of the tray is determined to be $(35x - 24x^2 + 4x^3)$ cubic inches, where x is the measure of the side of the squares removed from each corner, factor the expression for volume to obtain expressions for the height, width, and length of the tray. What are the dimensions of the tray if the squares cut from the corners measure 1 inch on a side?

PROBLEM SET 10.6

Experiencing Algebra the Exercise Way

Factor completely.

1. $x^2 - 100$
2. $y^2 - 64$
3. $121 - c^2$
4. $196 - b^2$
5. $49a^2 - 4$
6. $25z^2 - 9$
7. $25 - 4y^2$
8. $64 - 9x^2$
9. $16u^2 - 9v^2$
10. $36a^2 - 25b^2$
11. $7z^2 - 28$
12. $8x^2 - 8$
13. $25 + 4p^2$
14. $9y^2 + 4$
15. $x^4 - 625$
16. $a^4 - 1296$
17. $256 - z^4$
18. $625 - b^4$
19. $x^8 - 1$
20. $y^8 - 256$
21. $x^2 + 4x + 4$
22. $p^2 + 14p + 49$
23. $16z^2 + 40z + 25$
24. $36x^2 + 84x + 49$
25. $x^2 + 13x + 169$
26. $y^2 + 12y + 144$
27. $x^2 - 10x + 25$
28. $y^2 - 16y + 64$
29. $36z^2 - 60z + 25$
30. $64m^2 - 48m + 9$
31. $c^2 - 16d + 16d^2$
32. $z^2 - 20z + 25$
33. $a^4 - 32a^2 + 256$
34. $b^4 - 98b^2 + 2401$
35. $16x^4 - 72x^2 + 81$
36. $625y^4 - 200y^2 + 16$
37. $3x^2 + 24x + 48$
38. $16x^2 + 32x + 16$
39. $2a^2 - 12a + 18$
40. $5x^2 - 70x + 245$
41. $p^3 + 2p^2q + pq^2$
42. $y^2z^2 + 4yz^3 + 4z^4$
43. $2p^5 - 4p^3q^2 + 2pq^4$
44. $5u^5 - 40u^3v^2 + 80uv^4$
45. $m^5 + 2m^3n^2 + mn^4$
46. $p^7 + 2p^5q^2 + p^3q^4$
47. $x^3 - 27$
48. $z^3 - 343$
49. $a^3 + 64$
50. $m^3 + 1$
51. $27x^3 + 64y^3$
52. $125p^3 + 27q^3$

53. $8p^3 - 125q^3$

54. $27u^3 - 8v^3$

55. $p^4 + 64pq^3$

56. $125x^3y + y^4$

57. $81u^4 - 3uv^3$

58. $2a^3b - 54b^4$

In exercises 59–90, use the general strategy to factor completely. Check.

59. $3y^3 + 3y^2 + 3y$

60. $10x^3 + 35x^2 - 5x$

61. $10abc^2 + 15abc - 20ab$

62. $6xyz^2 + 10xyz - 6xy$

63. $-40a^2 - 24ab + 48ac$

64. $-28x^2 - 35xy + 21xz$

65. $108x^5 - 75x^3$

66. $32u^3 - 98u$

67. $-200x^3y + 32xy^3$

68. $-18a^3b + 128ab^3$

69. $x^3 - 16x^2 + 64x$

70. $z^3 - 10z^2 + 25z$

71. $12u^2v + 36uv^2 + 27v^3$

72. $50x^3 + 40x^2y + 8xy^2$

73. $3x^4 - 48x^2 + 7x^2 - 112$

74. $2x^4 - 18x^2 + 5x^2 - 45$

75. $4p^4 - 37p^2 + 9$

76. $9z^4 - 40z^2 + 16$

77. $2 + 8y - 42y^2$

78. $3 + 6y - 72y^2$

79. $4u^2v^2 + 36uv + 56$

80. $5a^2b^2 + 35ab + 60$

81. $32x^3 - 64x^2 - 28x^2 + 56x$

82. $15x^3 - 18x^2 - 60x^2 + 72x$

83. $12x^4 + 26x^3 - 30x^2$

84. $15z^4 + 10z^3 - 40z^2$

85. $x^6 - 5x^3y^3 + 3x^3y^3 - 15y^6$

86. $p^6 + 2p^3q^3 - 5p^3q^3 - 10q^6$

87. $x^4 - 5x^3 + 8x^2 - 40x$

88. $2y^4 + 6y^3 + 8y^2 + 24y$

89. $1 - k^8$

90. $256s^8 - 1$

91. A farmer leases you a plot of land for a garden. The plot is a square, but it contains a smaller square, 15 feet on a side, that cannot be used.

   a. Write a polynomial for the area of the land you will be able to garden, assuming the plot is x feet on a side.

   b. Factor the polynomial to find the dimensions of a rectangular plot with an equivalent area.

   c. If the square plot is 100 feet on a side, would you have more garden than another rectangular plot that measures 85 by 100 feet, which is available for the same rental fee?

92. A machinist must fabricate a square piece of metal that is y inches on a side, and which has a triangle cut out of it that has a base of x inches and a height of one-half the base.

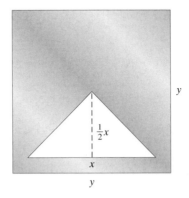

   a. Write a polynomial for the area of the metal square with the triangle removed.

   b. Factor the polynomial to find the dimensions of a rectangular piece of metal that would have an equivalent area.

   c. If the square is 12 inches on a side and the triangle has a base of 4 inches, what are the dimensions of a rectangle with an equivalent area?

Experiencing Algebra the Calculator Way

Following is a program[1] that will factor trinomials. Enter it into your calculator and try to factor some of the expressions presented earlier on the calculator. Once you create the program, when you execute it, it will ask you to enter the coefficients a, b, and c of the trinomial. The coefficients of the factors will be displayed, or else the calculator will tell you the trinomial is prime; that is, it does not factor.

Note: **The calculator should not be used as a crutch replacing your ability to factor with pencil and paper. Don't use this program in place of learning to factor. Instead use it as a tool to help you check your work and to assist you with those trinomials that would be tedious to factor by hand.**

Hints in programming FACTORER: ClrHome, Lbl, Disp, Input, If, Goto, and IS>(are found under $\boxed{\text{PRGM}}$ while you're entering the program; >, =, and ≤ are found in $\boxed{\text{2nd}}$ $\boxed{\text{MATH}}$ (that is, TEST); → is the $\boxed{\text{STO▶}}$ key; abs and Int(are in $\boxed{\text{MATH}}$ under NUM.

```
PROGRAM:FACTORER
Clrhome
Lbl 1
Disp "A(A>0)"
Input A
If A≤0
Goto 1
Disp "B"
Input B
Disp "C"
Input C
A*C→P
0→Y
−abs(P)→I
Lbl 2
If I = 0
I+1→I
If I+P/I=B
P/I→Y
IS>(I,abs(P))
Goto 2
If Y = 0
Goto 3
P/Y→X
1→I
Lbl 4
If (A/I=int((A/I))(X/I=int((X/I))
I→E
IS>(I,A)
Goto 4
A/E→G
Y/G→F
C/F→H
ClrHome
Disp "E,F,G,AND H OF"
Disp "(EX+F)(GX+H) ARE"
Disp E
```

[1] With the permission of Chuck Sterner, Pellissippi State Technical Community College.

Disp F
Disp G
Disp H
Goto 5
Lbl 3
Disp "PRIME"
Lbl 5

Experiencing Algebra the Group Way

Discuss how you would apply the techniques in this section to the following exercises, which contain coefficients that are fractions or decimals. Then have each member of the group factor completely, and compare your answers.

1. $z^2 - 1.44$

2. $\dfrac{9}{25}x^2 - \dfrac{16}{25}y^2$

3. $7.29 + 5.4p + p^2$

4. $x^2 - \dfrac{8}{5}x + \dfrac{16}{25}$

5. $y^3 - 13.824$

6. $\dfrac{8}{27}c^3 + 1$

7. For a real challenge, factor $a^6 - b^6$ two ways: first as the difference of two squares, $\left(a^3\right)^2 - \left(b^3\right)^2$, then as the difference of two cubes, $\left(a^2\right)^3 - \left(b^2\right)^3$. Factor completely and discuss your results.

Experiencing Algebra the Write Way

Perform the following two multiplications, which involve squares of binomials.

1. $\left(a^n + b^n\right)^2$

2. $\left(a^n - b^n\right)^2$

You should see that the results are two more recognizable forms that could be helpful when factoring. Write a description of how these two results, when turned around, could help you factor some trinomials.

Use your description to factor the following trinomials as illustrations of what you have described. Once you do the initial factoring, be sure to check to see whether the factors can be further factored.

3. $x^6 + 2x^3y^3 + y^6$

4. $p^8 - 2p^4q^4 + q^8$

CHAPTER 10	Summary

After completing this chapter, you should be able to define in your own words the following key terms, properties, and rules.

Terms
exponential expression
base
exponent
expanded form
special product
product of the sum and difference of
   the same two terms
square of a binomial

greatest common factor (GCF)
prime number
factoring by grouping
leading coefficient
trial-and-error method
ac method

Properties
Integer exponents

Rules
Rules for exponents
Addition and subtraction of
   polynomials
Multiplication of polynomials
Special products
Division of polynomials
Steps to factor a polynomial
   completely

CHAPTER 10	Review

Reflections

1. Explain the difference between expanded form and exponential form of an algebraic expression.

2. State the product rule for exponents and the power-to-a-power rule for exponents. How does one differ from the other?

3. What is the result of a product to a negative power? What is the result of a quotient to a negative power?

4. How does multiplying a polynomial by a monomial differ from dividing a polynomial by a monomial? In what sense are they alike?

5. Compare and contrast the operation of multiplying polynomials with that of factoring a polynomial.

10.1

Write in expanded form.

1. -5^2c^2 **2.** $(-5c)^2$ **3.** $4(x + y)^2z^0$ **4.** $\left(\dfrac{2}{3x}\right)^4$

Write with positive exponents.

5. $\dfrac{x(y - z)^{-1}}{z^{-3}}$ **6.** $3y^{-3} + 2y^{-2} + y^{-1} + 10y^0$

Multiply. Express your results with positive exponents.

7. $a^9 \cdot a^{-4}$ **8.** $(p + q)^{-3}(p + q)$

Divide. Express your results with positive exponents.

9. $\dfrac{t^{12}}{t^9}$ **10.** $\dfrac{m^{-2}}{m^{-4}}$ **11.** $\dfrac{(x + 3y)^{-5}}{(x + 3y)^{-4}}$ **12.** $\dfrac{72x^4y^5z}{24x^2y^4z^3}$

Simplify exercises 13–23. Express your results with positive exponents.

13. $\left(z^4\right)^3$ **14.** $\left(w^{-3}\right)^2$ **15.** $\left(p^{-2}\right)^{-4}$ **16.** $\left(a^3\right)^0$

17. $(-2a)^4$ **18.** $(-2a)^5$ **19.** $\left(\dfrac{-2x}{3z}\right)^3$ **20.** $\left(\dfrac{4a}{5b}\right)^{-2}$

21. $\left(a^2b^3c\right)^3$ **22.** $\left[(3x)^3\right]^2$ **23.** $\left[\left(\dfrac{m}{4n}\right)^2\right]^2$

24. A square is decreased in size by reducing each side to $\frac{1}{4}$ of its original length. Write expressions for the areas of the original square and of the reduced square. Compare the two areas.

25. A circular garden is increased in size by doubling its radius. Write expressions for the area of the original garden and for the area of the enlarged garden. Compare the two areas. What is the area of the enlarged garden if the original garden had a radius of 6 feet?

10.2

Add the polynomials.

26.
$$5x^4 + 3x^3 \qquad\quad + 6x - 3$$
$$4x^3 + 5x^2 \qquad\quad + 7$$
$$x^4 \qquad\quad - 3x^2 + x - 9$$
$$\underline{\qquad\quad x^3 + 2x^2 - 7x + 1}$$

27. Add $(4y^2 + 3y - 7)$, $(2y + 8)$, and $(5y^2 - 4y + 1)$.

28. $(3.57z^3 - 2.08z^2 + 8.77z - 1.99) + (4.73 - 2.98z + 5.64z^2)$

Subtract the polynomials as indicated.

29. $(4x^3 + 8x^2 - 6x + 2)$ less $(2x^3 + 12x^2 - x + 9)$

30. Subtract $(a^4 + 2a^3 + 3a^2 + 4a + 5)$ from $(5a^4 + a^3 + a^2 + a + 1)$.

31. $(65z^4 + 27z^2 + 36)$ decreased by $(16z^3 + 8z + 12)$

32. $\left(\dfrac{5}{8}b^4 + \dfrac{7}{8}b^3 - \dfrac{3}{4}b^2 + \dfrac{1}{2}b - \dfrac{1}{4}\right)$ minus $\left(\dfrac{1}{2}b^4 + \dfrac{3}{8}b^2 + \dfrac{1}{8}b\right)$

Multiply. Express your results with positive exponents.

33. $-3a^3b(5a^{-2}b^3)$
34. $6x^3(3x^2 + 2x - 7)$
35. $7a^{-2}(3a^6 + a^4 - 2a^2)$
36. $(-6.9x^3z^{-4})(3.4xz^3)$

In exercises 37–42, divide. Express your results with positive exponents.

37. $\dfrac{144x^6y^3z^4}{2x^5y^2z^6}$
38. $\dfrac{(2a^2)^3}{24a^5}$
39. $\left(\dfrac{27a^5b^3}{9a^2b^7}\right)^2$

40. $\dfrac{824{,}500{,}000\,y^{-5}}{0.0097y^7}$
41. $\dfrac{15b^4 - 10b^3 - 25b^2 + 5b}{-5b}$
42. $\dfrac{6ab^2 + 18a^2b}{3a^2b^2}$

43. A production process can produce up to 20 items on each run. The cost of producing the items consists of a fixed cost of $10.00 to set up the run and $3.50 per item for labor and materials. The items sell for $(10.00 - 0.25x)$ per item, where x is the number of items ordered.

    a. Write the cost function for producing x items, $C(x)$.

    b. Write a revenue function for selling x items, $R(x)$.

    c. Write the profit function, $P(x)$.

    d. Write the average profit function, $A(x)$.

    e. For what value of x will the profit function be maximized?

44. Write a polynomial for the perimeter of a rectangle whose length measures 20 meters and whose width measures x meters less than the length.

45. The length of a patio is 8 feet more than its width. A sandbox that measures 3 feet on a side is built on the patio. Write a polynomial for the area of the patio not covered by the sandbox. How many square feet of carpeting will be needed to cover the patio, excluding the sandbox, if the width of the patio is 9 feet?

10.3

In exercises 46–56, multiply.

46. $(y + 9)^2$
47. $(x^3 - 5)^2$
48. $(5x - 2)(x + 11)$
49. $(7 - z)(7 + z)$

50. $(y - 1.8)(y + 3.4)$
51. $(z^2 - 10)(z^2 + 10)$
52. $\left(\dfrac{4}{5}x - \dfrac{1}{2}\right)\left(\dfrac{4}{5}x + \dfrac{1}{2}\right)$
53. $(b - 4)^3$

54. $(2x + 1)(3x^2 + 5x - 4)$ **55.** $(a + b + c)^2$ **56.** $(a - 3)(a^2 + 3a + 9)$

57. The length of a box is 3 inches more than its height. Its width is 3 inches less than its height.

   a. Write expressions for the length, width, and height of the box.

   b. Write an expression for the volume of the box.

   c. Write an expression for the surface area of the box, including the top.

58. Andre plans to enlarge the deck on his house. The current deck is three times as long as its width. He plans to double the width and add 9 feet to the length.

   a. Write a polynomial for the current area of the deck.

   b. Write a polynomial for the area of the planned enlarged deck.

   c. What is the ratio of the planned area to the current area?

10.4

Factor exercises 59–63 completely and check.

59. $20a^6 - 28a^4 + 44a^2$ **60.** $22u^3v^2 + 22u^2v^3$ **61.** $3x^3 + 3x + x^2 + 1$

62. $7a^4 + 7a^2b^2 + 7a^2b^2 + 7b^4$ **63.** $15ac + 18ad + 20bc + 24bd$

64. It can be shown that the sum of the natural numbers from 1 to n equals $\frac{1}{2}n^2 + \frac{1}{2}n$.

   a. Factor the expression completely.

   b. Evaluate the original expression and the factored expression for the sum of the natural numbers from 1 to 12.

   c. Which expression was easier to evaluate and why?

65. The area of a rectangle is numerically equal to the polynomial

   $2x^2 - 6x + 5x - 15.$

   Factor the expression using the grouping method to determine algebraic expressions for the rectangle's width and length.

66. Because of a shortage of labor in a resort town, the owners of a fast-food restaurant offered to increase their employees' monthly salary by $10 for each additional month they remain employed. If an employee earns x dollars the first month, write a polynomial for her total pay for 7 months. Factor the GCF from the simplified expression. Interpret what the factors represent. If the employee's beginning salary is $960, determine her total pay for the 7 months. Check your interpretation for this beginning salary.

10.5

Factor completely and check.

67. $z^2 + 2z - 99$ **68.** $p^2 + 5pq - 66q^2$ **69.** $6a^2 + 96a + 234$ **70.** $x^4 + 8x^2 + 15$

71. $4q^3 - 28q^2 - 240q$ **72.** $x^2y^2 - 4xy - 117$ **73.** $-7x^2 + 98x - 168$

Factor exercises 74–77 completely, using either the trial-and-error method or the ac method.

74. $2x^2 - 11x + 5$ **75.** $6x^2 + 17x + 5$ **76.** $28a^2b^2 + 91ab + 21$ **77.** $-45x^3 - 102x^2 + 48x$

78. The base of a triangle measures twice its height. After the base and the height are increased, the enlarged triangle has an area numerically equal to the expression

   $2x^2 + 10x + \dfrac{21}{2},$

   where x is the height of the original triangle.

   a. Factor the expression to yield expressions for the base and height of the enlarged triangle.

   b. By how much was the base of the original triangle increased?

   c. How was the height of the original triangle increased?

79. A rectangle has a width that is 6 inches less than its length. After the width and length are increased, the larger rectangle has an area given by $\left(x^2 + 17x + 30\right)$ square inches, where x is the length of the original rectangle.

    a. Factor the polynomial to find the expressions for the increased length and width.

    b. By how much was the length increased?

    c. By how much was the width increased?

10.6

Factor exercises 80–99 completely.

80. $x^2 - 169$ **81.** $625 - a^2$ **82.** $12x^2 - 75$ **83.** $p^2 - q^2$

84. $p^2 + q^2$ **85.** $9x^2 - 25y^2$ **86.** $16x^4 - 81$ **87.** $p^2 + 12p + 36$

88. $q^2 - 16q + 64$ **89.** $c^3 + 27$ **90.** $8z^3 - 125$ **91.** $5h^3 + 40k^3$

92. $-12x^3 + 60x^2y - 75xy^2$ **93.** $7x^4 + 7x^3 + 7x^2$ **94.** $12x^3 - 243x$ **95.** $32x^3 + 32x^2 + 8x$

96. $24x^3 - 14x^2 - 90x$ **97.** $256x^4 - 288x^2 + 81$ **98.** $36x^4 - 25x^2 + 4$ **99.** $2x^4 + 14x^3 - 8x^2 - 56x$

100. The site for a memorial statue is a rectangular piece of land whose length is four times its width. The base of the statue is a square measuring 5 feet on a side.

    a. If x is the width of the site, write a polynomial for the area of land that will not be covered by the statue.

    b. Factor the polynomial to obtain the dimensions of a rectangular plot with an area equivalent to the uncovered area.

    c. If the site has a width of 80 feet, use the factors to find the dimensions of a rectangle with an area equivalent to the uncovered area.

CHAPTER 10   Mixed Review

Factor completely and check.

1. $z^2 + 9z - 90$ **2.** $a^2 - 18a + 72$ **3.** $x^2 + 14xy + 45y^2$

4. $5a^2 + 70a + 245$ **5.** $2a^2 + 8ab + 12b^2$ **6.** $x^4 + 10x^2 + 21$

7. $3q^3 - 33q^2 - 126q$ **8.** $-6x^2 + 42x + 360$ **9.** $10 + 7x + x^2$

10. $x^2 - 289$ **11.** $x^3 - 1$ **12.** $4x^2 - 64$

13. $u^2 + v^2$ **14.** $36x^2 - 49y^2$ **15.** $81x^4 - 1$

16. $p^2 + 22p + 121$ **17.** $q^2 - 30q + 225$ **18.** $27a^3 + 64b^3$

19. $27a^2b^2 - 72ab + 48$ **20.** $-50x^3 + 120x^2y - 72xy^2$ **21.** $8x^4 - 2x^3 + 6x^2 - 12x$

22. $35u^3v^2 + 25u^2v^3$ **23.** $2x^3 + 10x + x^2 + 5$ **24.** $m^2 - 2mn - 8mn + 16n^2$

25. $4a^4 + 8a^2b^2 + 8a^2b^2 + 16b^4$ **26.** $2x^2 - 13x + 11$ **27.** $24ac + 20ad + 18bc + 15bd$

28. $7x^2 - 19x - 6$ **29.** $10x^2 - 11x - 6$ **30.** $36a^2 + 66a + 24$

31. $-30x^2 - 28x + 32$ **32.** $12x^4 + 13x^2 + 3$ **33.** $54x^3 + 36x^2 + 6x$

34. $81x^4 - 72x^2 + 16$ **35.** $4x^4 - 61x^2 + 225$ **36.** $12x^3 + 18x^2 - 30x^2 - 45x$

37. $3x^4 + 15x^3 - 27x^2 - 135x$

Write with positive exponents.

38. $m^{-7}n^5$

39. $\dfrac{5^{-3}t^3}{4^{-3}s^4}$

40. $\dfrac{(d + 2e)^3}{(d - 2e)^{-2}}$

41. $2y^{-4} + 4y^{-3} + 6y^{-2} + 8y^{-1} + 10y^0$

Add the polynomials.

42. Add $(2y^2 + 4y - 3), (9y + 7),$ and $(8y^2 - 12y + 15)$.

43. $\left(\dfrac{3}{8}a^3 + \dfrac{3}{4}a^2 - \dfrac{5}{8}a + \dfrac{1}{4}\right) + \left(\dfrac{3}{4}a^3 + \dfrac{7}{16}a - \dfrac{5}{8}a^2 + \dfrac{11}{16}\right)$

44. Add $(4.9z^3 - 6.82z^2 + 12z - 11.07)$ and $(4.6 - 1.83z + 4.9z^2)$.

Subtract the polynomials as indicated.

45. $(2x^3 + 6x^2 - 9x + 13) - (4x^3 + 17x^2 - x + 6)$

46. Subtract $(5a^4 + 4a^3 + 3a^2 + 2a + 1)$ from $(6a^4 + 3a^2 + 4a + 5)$.

47. $(117z^4 + 43z^2 + 88)$ decreased by $(18z^3 + 50z + 32)$

Multiply. Express your results with positive exponents.

48. $11x^5 y^6 (13x^{-2} y^{-6})$

49. $-6x(2x^4 \quad 4x^3 + 6x^2 + 8x - 10)$

50. $9a^{-1}(4a^5 + 2a^3 - 3a)$

51. $(m - 11)(m + 11)$

52. $(z - 8)^2$

53. $(4a - 7)(a + 13)$

54. $(13 - x)(13 + x)$

55. $(b^3 + 4)^2$

56. $(t + 2)^3$

57. $(7x - 2)(x^2 + 4x - 3)$

58. $(p + q + r)^2$

59. $(b - 4)(b^2 + 4b + 16)$

Divide. Express your results with positive exponents.

60. $\dfrac{c^9}{c^6}$

61. $\dfrac{(a + 4b)^{-6}}{(a + 4b)^{-2}}$

62. $\dfrac{81x^5 y^7 z}{27x^2 y^6 z^2}$

63. $\dfrac{(3a^3)^3}{54a^7}$

64. $\left(\dfrac{21a^6 b^2}{7a^3 b^6}\right)^2$

65. $\dfrac{14b^4 - 21b^3 - 35b^2 + 28b}{-7b}$

66. $\dfrac{16cd^2 + 8c^2 d}{4c^2 d^2}$

Simplify exercises 67–79. Express your results with positive exponents.

67. $s^2 \cdot s^8$

68. $y^5 \cdot y^{-8}$

69. $(m + n)^5 (m + n)$

70. $(b^5)^7$

71. $(d^6)^{-3}$

72. $(x^0)^8$

73. $(-3d)^6$

74. $(-3d)^3$

75. $\left(\dfrac{m}{n}\right)^{-6}$

76. $(mn)^{-6}$

77. $(x^4 y^5 z)^4$

78. $[(4x)^2]^3$

79. $\left[\left(\dfrac{c}{2d}\right)^3\right]^2$

80. The area of a rectangle is numerically equal to the polynomial

$$8x^2 - 2x - 3.$$

Factor the expression using the grouping method to determine algebraic expressions for the rectangle's width and length.

81. The width of a rectangle is 2 inches less than its length. After the width and length are increased, the larger rectangle has an area given by $(6x^2 - 10x - 4)$ square inches, where x is the length of the original rectangle.

a. Factor the polynomial to find expressions for the increased length and width.

b. How was the length increased?

c. How was the width increased?

82. The base of a triangle is twice its height. After the base and the height are increased, the enlarged triangle has an area numerically equal to the expression

$$x^2 + 12x + 32,$$

where x is the height of the original triangle.

  a. Factor the expression to yield expressions for the base and height of the enlarged triangle.

  b. By how much was the base of the original triangle increased?

  c. By how much was the height of the original triangle increased?

83. The length of a rectangular box is 3 inches more than twice its height. The width of the box is equal to its height.

  a. Write expressions for the length, width, and height of the box.

  b. Write an expression for the volume of the box.

  c. Write an expression for the surface area of the box.

  d. What is the volume of the box if its height is 8 inches?

  e. What is the surface area of the box if its height is 8 inches?

84. A triangle has a base that is 5 cm more than twice its height.

  a. Write a polynomial to represent the area of the triangle if its height is x cm.

  b. What is the area of the triangle if its height is 12 cm?

85. A square patio measures x feet on a side. It will be enlarged to a width that is double the length of a current side, and a length that is 5 feet more than the new width.

  a. Write a polynomial for the current area of the patio.

  b. Write a polynomial for the enlarged area of the patio.

  c. What is the ratio of the enlarged area to the original area?

CHAPTER 10 | **Test**

Test Taking Tips

When studying for a test, you should try to improve your notes. Read your notes and textbook with pencil in hand. Identify and label according to categories. This chapter had many different methods for manipulating polynomials. If you organize your notes by the various methods, and work examples for each method, it will help you recall these methods during a test. Try to think of kinds of exercises to which you would apply each method. Compare the methods to see what the differences are. List key points that dictate the method to use. If something confuses you, place a big question mark next to it, and try to get help with the question before taking the test. Then go back and read the confusing material again to see if the help reduced your confusion.

Factor completely.

1. $81a^3 + 54a^2 + 9a$ **2.** $p^3 + 125$ **3.** $-8a^4b^2 - 36a^3b^3 - 16a^2b^4$

4. $a(a^2 + b^2) - 5b(a^2 + b^2)$ **5.** $15x^2 - 21xy + 10xy - 14y^2$ **6.** $64a^2 - 49b^2$

7. $25x^2 - 70x + 49$ **8.** $3x^3 - 27x^2 + 24x$ **9.** $x^2 - 4xy - 21y^2$

10. $14x^2 + 25x + 9$ **11.** $4x^4 + 27x^2 - 7$ **12.** $x^2 + 8x + 14$

Simplify and write with positive exponents.

13. $(2x - 1)(2x - 1)^8$ **14.** $3x^2y^0z^{-3}$ **15.** $(a + b)^3(a - b)^{-5}$

16. $(-2x^2y^{-1})^3$ **17.** $\dfrac{(3c - 7)^3}{(3c - 7)^5}$ **18.** $\left[\dfrac{(2p)^3}{3q}\right]^{-2}$

19. Add $\left(3y^2 + 16 - 7y + 5y^3\right)$ and $\left(7y + 6y^2 + 4y^4 - 11\right)$.

20. Subtract $\left(7x^5 + 23x^3 + 17x^2 - 39\right) - \left(2x^4 - 4x^2 - 2x - 9\right)$.

Multiply. Express your results with positive exponents.

21. $\left(-2p^3q^{-5}r^2\right)\left(5.7p^6q^7r\right)$ **22.** $-4t\left(2t^3 - 3t^2 - 8t + 6\right)$ **23.** $(9 - 5d)(9 + 5d)$

24. $(3x + 4)(5x - 7)$ **25.** $(4z - 3)\left(2z^2 - z + 5\right)$ **26.** $(x + 3)^2$

In exercises 27–29, divide. Express your results with positive exponents.

27. $\dfrac{24a^2b^{-3}c}{3ab^2c^{-2}}$

28. $\dfrac{\left(a^{-2}b^4\right)^3}{a^2b^5c}$

29. $\dfrac{15x^6 + 25x^5 - 5x^3}{5x^2}$

30. The width of a box is 4 inches more than its height. Its length is twice its height.

  a. Write a polynomial expression for its volume.

  b. Write a polynomial expression for its surface area, including its top.

  c. What is the volume and surface area if the box has a height of 5 inches?

31. David factored the following polynomial as shown:

$$12x^3 + 28x^2 - 27x - 63 = \left(12x^3 + 28x^2\right) + (-27x - 63)$$
$$= 4x^2(3x + 7) - 9(3x + 7)$$
$$= (3x + 7)\left(4x^2 - 9\right)$$

  a. Identify the method David used to factor the polynomial.

  b. Explain what is wrong with David's solution, and describe how you would correct the solution.

  c. What is the correct solution?

Solving Polynomial Equations and Inequalities in One Variable

N ow that we have learned how to work with polynomial expressions, including adding, subtracting, and factoring them, we can proceed to solve polynomial equations and inequalities. In this chapter we will examine numeric, graphic, and algebraic methods for solving polynomial equations, particularly quadratic equations and inequalities. Because the most precise of these methods is the algebraic approach, we will look at several ways of solving equations algebraically, including factoring, using the principle of square roots, completing the square, and using the quadratic formula.

Economists use many types of polynomial equations to model trends in sales and to forecast future sales. This information can be used to set interest rates for business loans or for deciding whether a company needs to borrow money in a short-term transaction. In this chapter we will look at some economic models that involve polynomial equations and show how they illustrate the methods of solution we describe.

11.1 Solving Equations Numerically and Graphically

Objectives

1 Identify polynomial equations in one variable.
2 Solve polynomial equations numerically.
3 Solve polynomial equations graphically.
4 Model real-world situations using polynomial equations and solve numerically or graphically.

Application

Using annual sales reports for Montgomery Ward Holdings for the years 1987 through 1995, a function to estimate annual sales in millions of dollars is $S(x) = 8x^3 - 91x^2 + 434x + 4789$, where x is the number of years after 1986. Determine when the annual sales will reach \$8,000 million.

After completing this section, we will discuss this application further. See page 809.

1 Identifying Polynomial Equations in One Variable

In this chapter, we will solve polynomial equations in one variable. A **polynomial equation in one variable**, or **polynomial equation**, is an equation that relates two polynomials. In an earlier chapter, we discussed polynomial equations in one variable with a degree of 1. These equations were of the form $ax + b = 0$, where $a \neq 0$. We called these linear equations in one variable or linear equations.

In this chapter, we discuss other polynomial equations. A polynomial equation with a degree of 2 is called a **quadratic equation in one variable** or **quadratic equation**. A quadratic equation is written in the form $ax^2 + bx + c = 0$, where $a \neq 0$. A polynomial equation with a degree of 3 is called a **cubic equation in one variable** or **cubic equation**. A cubic equation is written in the form $ax^3 + bx^2 + cx + d = 0$, where $a \neq 0$.

> *Standard Forms for Polynomial Equations*
> Given real numbers a, b, and c, where $a \neq 0$.
> A linear equation is written in the form
> $$ax + b = 0.$$
> A quadratic equation is written in the form
> $$ax^2 + bx + c = 0.$$
> A cubic equation is written in the form
> $$ax^3 + bx^2 + cx + d = 0.$$
> In general, a polynomial equation in one variable can be written in the form
> $$P(x) = 0,$$
> where $P(x)$ is a polynomial.

For example, the following equations are polynomial equations in one variable.

$$2x^3 + x^2 - 5x + 4 = 10 \quad \text{or} \quad 2x^3 + x^2 - 5x - 6 = 0 \qquad \text{Cubic}$$
$$x^2 - 7.4x = 2.36x^2 - 5.9 \quad \text{or} \quad 1.36x^2 + 7.4x - 5.9 = 0 \qquad \text{Quadratic}$$
$$\frac{1}{3}x^4 = \frac{2}{3}x^4 + \frac{7}{8}x^6 \quad \text{or} \quad \frac{7}{8}x^6 + \frac{1}{3}x^4 = 0 \qquad \text{Polynomial}$$

EXAMPLE 1 Determine whether each equation is a polynomial equation. Identify each polynomial equation as quadratic or cubic, when applicable.

a. $3x^2 + 5x^6 - 7x^{-3} = 4$ **b.** $6x^2 + 8 - 7x^3 = 12$

c. $\dfrac{3}{4}x = 2x^2$

Solution

a. $3x^2 + 5x^6 - 7x^{-3} = 4$ is not a polynomial equation because x has an exponent of -3, which is not a positive integer.

b. $6x^2 + 8 - 7x^3 = 12$, or, equivalently, $7x^3 - 6x^2 + 4 = 0$, is a cubic polynomial equation.

c. $\frac{3}{4}x = 2x^2$, or, equivalently, $2x^2 - \frac{3}{4}x = 0$, is a quadratic polynomial equation. ∎

Experiencing Algebra the Checkup Way

In exercises 1–6, determine whether each equation is a polynomial equation. Identify each polynomial equation as quadratic or cubic, when applicable.

1. $3x^2 - 5 = 4x + 2$

2. $x^{-2} + 4x - 7 = 0$

3. $2\sqrt{x} + 2x - 3 = 0$

4. $5x^3 - 2x^2 = 3x + 7$

5. $\dfrac{1}{4}x^2 + \dfrac{3}{4}x - \dfrac{5}{8} = 0$

6. $1.2x^3 - 3.7 = 5.6$

7. What is the difference between a polynomial expression and a polynomial equation?

8. What is meant by the degree of a polynomial equation?

---

2 Solving Polynomial Equations Numerically

In an earlier chapter, we determined whether a number was a solution of a linear equation by substituting the value of the possible solution for the variable and evaluating the two resulting expressions. If the resulting equation was true, the number substituted was called the **solution**. We do the same process for a polynomial equation. The set of all possible solutions is called the **solution set**. For example, given $x^2 - 3 = -x + 3$, determine whether 2 is a solution.

$$
\begin{array}{c|c}
x^2 - 3 = & -x + 3 \\
\hline
(2)^2 - 3 & -(2) + 3 \\
4 - 3 & 1 \\
1 &
\end{array}
$$

Therefore, 2 is a solution because the resulting equation, $1 = 1$, is true.

A linear equation that is not an identity has at most one solution. However, other polynomial equations may have more than one solution and still not be an identity.

In order to find other solutions of the equation $x^2 - 3 = -x + 3$, continue to substitute values for x and determine whether the resulting equations are true. A table of values is helpful in organizing this method.

Solving a Polynomial Equation Numerically
To solve a polynomial equation numerically:
Set up an extended table of values.

- The first column is labeled with the independent variable.
- The second column is labeled with the expression on the left side of the equation.
- The third column is labeled with the expression on the right side of the equation.

Complete the table.

- Substitute values for the independent variable.
- Evaluate the second and third columns.
- Continue until values for the two expressions (the numbers in the second and third columns) are equal.

The values for the independent variable (the number in the first column) that result in equivalent expressions are the solutions.

For example, a sample table to determine another solution of $x^2 - 3 = -x + 3$ could appear as follows:

x	$x^2 - 3$	$-x + 3$	
-4	$(-4)^2 - 3$ $16 - 3$ 13	$-(-4) + 3$ $4 + 3$ 7	$13 > 7$, so -4 is not a solution.
-3	$(-3)^2 - 3$ $9 - 3$ 6	$-(-3) + 3$ $3 + 3$ 6	$6 = 6$, so -3 is a solution.
-2	$(-2)^2 - 3$ $4 - 3$ 1	$-(-2) + 3$ $2 + 3$ 5	$1 < 5$, so -2 is not a solution.

According to the table, when -3 is substituted for the variable x, the two expressions are equivalent ($6 = 6$). Therefore, -3 is a second solution of the polynomial equation.

To solve a polynomial equation numerically for integer solutions on your calculator:

- Rename the independent variable as x.

Set up the table.

- Set up the first column for the independent variable by setting a minimum value and increments. Since we do not know the solution, we may want to start with 0. We will set the size of the increments at 1 to obtain integer values. Set the calculator to automatically perform the evaluations.
- Set up the second column of the table to be the expression on the left.
- Set up the third column of the table to be the expression on the right.

View the table.

- Move beyond the screen to view additional rows by using the up arrow for negative values and the down arrow for positive values of x that may be solutions.

The solutions are the x-values that determine equal Y1 and Y2 values. There may be more than one solution.

For example, solve $x^2 - 3 = -x + 3$ on your calculator.

Let Y1 $= x^2 - 3$ and Y2 $= -x + 3$.

The two solutions from the table are -3 and 2, as shown in Figure 11.1c.

TECHNOLOGY

Figure 11.1a   Figure 11.1b   Figure 11.1c

For Figure 11.1a

For Figure 11.1b

| 2nd | TBLSET | 0 | ENTER | (set minimum number to 0)

| 1 | ENTER | (independent variable values are increasing by 1)

| ENTER | ▼ | ENTER | (auto settings)

For Figure 11.1c

| 2nd | TABLE | results in the table. Use the up and down arrow keys to find the solutions, the x-values that determine Y1 $=$ Y2.

EXAMPLE 2   Solve numerically.

a. $x^2 + 6x + 5 = -2x - 7$ **b.** $a^3 + a^2 - 4a + 2 = 2a^2 + 2a + 2$

Calculator Numeric Solution

a. $x^2 + 6x + 5 = -2x - 7$

The solutions are -6 and -2 because when -6 and -2 are substituted for the variable in both expressions, the results are equivalent, as shown in Figure 11.2.

b. $a^3 + a^2 - 4a + 2 = 2a^2 + 2a + 2$

Rewrite as $x^3 + x^2 - 4x + 2 = 2x^2 + 2x + 2$.

Y1 $= x^3 + x^2 - 4x + 2$
Y2 $= 2x^2 + 2x + 2$.

TECHNOLOGY

X	Y1	Y2
-6	5	5
-5	0	3
-4	-3	1
-3	-4	-1
-2	-3	-3
-1	0	-5
0	5	-7

X = -6

$Y1 = x^2 + 6x + 5$
$Y2 = -2x - 7$

Figure 11.2

For Figure 11.2

| Y= | X, T, θ, n | x² | + | 6 | X, T, θ, n | + | 5 | ▼ | (–) | 2 |

| X, T, θ, n | – | 7 |

| 2nd | TBLSET | 0 | ENTER | 1 | ENTER | ENTER | ▼ | ENTER |

| 2nd | TABLE |

Use the arrow keys to find the solutions, −6 and −2.

The solutions are −2, 0, and 3 because when −2, 0, and 3 are substituted for the variable in both expressions, the results are equivalent. ■

Linear equations may have noninteger solutions, no solution, or an infinite number of solutions. This is also true for polynomial equations. To see examples of these cases in a numerical table, complete the following sets of exercises.

DISCOVERY 1

Polynomial Equations with Noninteger Solutions

$4x^2 - x - 3 = 3x$ does not have an integer solution. Complete the table of values given and compare the values obtained.

x	$4x^2 - x - 3$	$3x$	
−3	36	−9	36 > −9
−2			
−1			
0			
1			
2			
3			

Write a rule to determine that a solution of the equation lies between two integers given in the table.

The expression on the left is greater than the expression on the right for x-values of −3, −2, and −1. The expression on the left is less than the expression on the right for x-values of 0 and 1. Since each function is defined for all real numbers between −1 and 0, the expression on the left is equal to the expression on the right at some x-value between −1 and 0.

Also, the expression on the left is less than the expression on the right for x-values of 0 and 1, and the expression on the left is greater than the expression on the right for x-values of 2 and 3. Since each function is defined for all real numbers between 1 and 2, the expression on the left is equal to the expression on the right at some x-value between 1 and 2.

The solutions are noninteger; one solution is between −1 and 0, and the other solution is between 1 and 2.

DISCOVERY 2

Polynomial Equations with No Solution

Solve $x^2 + x + 10 = x^2 + x - 10$ numerically by completing the table of values given and comparing the values obtained.

x	$x^2 + x + 10$	$x^2 + x - 10$
0		
1		
2		
3		

Write a rule to explain the solution of the equation from viewing its table of values.

The expression on the right is always 20 less than the expression on the left. Therefore, it appears that the two expressions are never equal. The equation does not have a solution.

We can see why there is no solution if we rewrite the equation in standard form. The result of $x^2 + x + 10 = x^2 + x - 10$ is $20 = 0$, because the x^2 and x terms are eliminated from both sides of the equation. This result, $20 = 0$, is a contradiction.

DISCOVERY 3

Polynomial Equations with Many Solutions

Solve $2x^3 + 4x^2 + 5 = (x^3 + 3x^2 + 4) + (x^3 + x^2 + 1)$ numerically by completing the table of values given.

x	$2x^3 + 4x^2 + 5$	$(x^3 + 3x^2 + 4) + (x^3 + x^2 + 1)$
0		
1		
2		
3		

Write a rule to explain the solution of the equation from viewing its table of values.

The two expressions are equal for all values of the independent variable in the table. If we could view this table with all real-number values for x, the expressions would always be equal. Therefore, the solution of the equation is the set of all real numbers (the permissible replacements for the independent variable).

We can see why the solution set is all real numbers if we rewrite the equation in standard form. The result of $2x^3 + 4x^2 + 5 = (x^3 + 3x^2 + 4) + (x^3 + x^2 + 1)$ is $0 = 0$ because the x^2 and x terms are eliminated from both sides of the equation. This result, $0 = 0$, is an identity.

However, when solving numerically, certain polynomial equations may have a different result than we have found previously with linear equations. To see this, complete the following set of exercises.

D I S C O V E R Y   4

Polynomial Equations with No Real-Number Solutions

Solve $x^2 + x + 1 = 4x^2 + 4x + 4$ numerically by completing the table of values given and compare the values obtained.

x	$x^2 + x + 1$	$4x^2 + 4x + 4$
0		
1		
2		
3		

Write a rule to explain the solution of the equation from viewing its table of values.

The expression on the left is always less than the expression on the right. Therefore, the two expressions are never equal. It appears the equation does not have a solution. However, if we rewrite the equation in standard form, the result of $x^2 + x + 1 = 4x^2 + 4x + 4$ is $3x^2 + 3x + 3 = 0$. This does not result in a contradiction. The equation does not have a solution in the real-number system. We explain this result in more detail in Chapter 14.

EXAMPLE 3 Solve numerically, if possible.

a. $2(x^2 + 3x - 5) = 2x^2 + 2(3x - 5)$

b. $x^2 + 2x + 4 = 3x^2 + 6x + 12$

c. $x^3 + 5x^2 + 2x - 7 = x^3 + 5x^2 + 2$

d. $2x^2 + 7x - 4 = 2(x^2 + 3x + 1) + x$

a.

X	Y₁	Y₂
0	-10	-10
1	-2	-2
2	10	10
3	26	26
4	46	46
5	70	70
6	98	98

X=0

$-10 = -10$
$-2 = -2$
$10 = 10$
$26 = 26$
$46 = 46$
$70 = 70$
$98 = 98$

Y1 = $2(x^2 + 3x - 5)$
Y2 = $2x^2 + 2(3x - 5)$

b.

X	Y₁	Y₂
0	4	12
1	7	21
2	12	36
3	19	57
4	28	84
5	39	117
6	52	156

X=0

$4 < 12$
$7 < 21$
$12 < 36$
$19 < 57$
$28 < 84$
$39 < 117$
$52 < 156$

Y1 = $x^2 + 2x + 4$
Y2 = $3x^2 + 6x + 12$

c.

X	Y₁	Y₂
0	-7	2
1	1	8
2	25	30
3	71	74
4	145	146
5	253	252
6	401	398

X=0

$-7 < 2$
$1 < 8$
$25 < 30$
$71 < 74$
$145 < 146$
$253 > 252$
$401 > 398$

Y1 = $x^3 + 5x^2 + 2x - 7$
Y2 = $x^3 + 5x^2 + 2$

Calculator Numeric Solution

Enter the tables as in previous examples.

a. $2(x^2 + 3x - 5) = 2x^2 + 2(3x - 5)$
The expressions are equal for all x-values in the table. If we rewrite this equation in standard form, we obtain an identity, $0 = 0$. The permissible replacements for each expression are all real numbers. The solution set is all real numbers.

b. $x^2 + 2x + 4 = 3x^2 + 6x + 12$
The expression on the left is always less than the expression on the right. The expressions do not appear to be equal. If we rewrite this equation in standard form, we obtain an equation, $2x^2 + 4x + 8 = 0$. Therefore, there is no real-number solution.

c. $x^3 + 5x^2 + 2x - 7 = x^3 + 5x^2 + 2$
The expression on the left is less than the expression on the right for $x = 4$ and greater than the expression on the right for $x = 5$. A noninteger solution lies somewhere between 4 and 5.
Note: We will find the exact solution later in this section.

d.

X	Y₁	Y₂
0	-4	2
1	5	11
2	18	24
3	35	41
4	56	62
5	81	87
6	110	116

$$-4 < 2$$
$$5 < 11$$
$$18 < 24$$
$$35 < 41$$
$$56 < 62$$
$$81 < 87$$
$$110 < 116$$

X=0

$Y1 = 2x^2 + 7x - 4$
$Y2 = 2(x^2 + 3x + 1) + x$

d. $2x^2 + 7x - 4 = 2(x^2 + 3x + 1) + x$

The expression on the left is always 6 less than the expression on the right. It appears that the expressions will never be equal. If we rewrite this equation in standard form, we obtain an equation, $-6 = 0$. This is a contradiction. Therefore, there is no solution. ∎

Numerical Solutions of a Polynomial Equation
To solve a polynomial equation for integer solutions numerically, set up an extended table of values. In viewing the table, one of five possibilities will occur:

Integer solutions exist. The solutions are the integers in the first column that correspond to equal values in the second and third columns.

Noninteger solutions exist. When comparing corresponding values in the second and third columns, the order changes from "less than" to "greater than" or "greater than" to "less than". A noninteger solution is between the two integers in the first column that correspond to this change.

No solution exists. When comparing corresponding values in the second and third columns, a constant difference is found. The equation is a contradiction.

No real-number solution exists. When comparing corresponding values in the second and third columns, the value in one column is always less than the value in the other column. The equation is not a contradiction.

An infinite number of solutions exist. When comparing corresponding values in the second and third columns, the values are equal. The equation is an identity. The solution set consists of all numbers for which the equation is defined.

In conclusion, a polynomial equation may be solved numerically using a table of values. However, if the solution is noninteger, it will be difficult to find by this method. Also, it is difficult to know whether all possible solutions have been found.

 Experiencing Algebra the Checkup Way

Solve exercises 1–6 numerically.

1. $2x^2 + 6x = 4x + 12$

2. $b^3 + 3b^2 + 2b = 2b^2 + 6b + 4$

3. $6x^2 + 3x = 2x + 1$

4. $(3x - 4)(x + 1) = 3x^2 - x - 1$

5. $x^2 + 4x + 5 = 2x^2 + 8(x + 1) + 2$

6. $2(x^2 + 2x - 1) - x(x - 1) = 3x(x + 1) - 2(x^2 - x + 1)$

7. Explain the difference between integer solutions to a polynomial equation and noninteger solutions.

8. What are some of the limitations of the numerical method in solving a polynomial equation?

3 Solving Polynomial Equations Graphically

A second way to determine a real-number solution of an equation is to graph two functions. The functions to be graphed are written by using each expression in the equation as a rule for one of the functions. For the equation $x^2 + 2x = 8$, you would write the two functions $y_1 = x^2 + 2x$ and $y_2 = 8$. Complete the following set of exercises on your calculator.

Graphical Solutions
To solve the equation $x^2 + 2x = 8$, graph the functions $Y1 = x^2 + 2x$ and $Y2 = 8$ in a standard window. Sketch the graphs. Label the points of intersection of the graphs.

Write a rule to determine the solution of an equation from the graphs of the two functions.

Write a rule to determine the numeric value of each expression in the equation when the equation is evaluated with its solution.

The solutions, 2 and -4, of the equation $x^2 + 2x = 8$ are the x-coordinates of the points of intersection. The y-coordinates of the points of intersection are the values of each expression in the equation when x is replaced by the solution. Therefore, the values of the x-coordinates of the points of intersection of the two graphs are the solutions of the equation. The values of the y-coordinates of the points of intersection of the two graphs are the values obtained when both expressions are evaluated with the solution.

Solving a Polynomial Equation Graphically
To solve a polynomial equation graphically:

• Write two functions, using each expression in the equation as a rule.
• Graph both functions on the same coordinate plane by plotting points found in a table of values and connecting the points with a smooth curve to include all values in the domain of the functions.

The solutions of the equation are the x-coordinates of the points of intersection of the two graphs.

The y-coordinates of the points of intersection of the two graphs are the values obtained for both expressions when the equation is evaluated with the solutions.

For example, solve graphically $x^2 - 3 = -x + 3$.

Set up a table of values for each function.

x	$y = x^2 - 3$	y
-1	-2	-2
0	-3	-3
1	-2	-2
2	1	1

x	$y = -x + 3$	y
-1	4	4
0	3	3
1	2	2
2	1	1

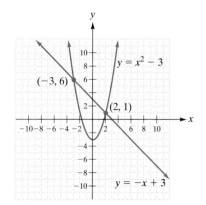

When plotted, the points result in the graph shown to the left.

The two solutions are the x-coordinates of the intersections, -3 and 2.

To solve a polynomial equation graphically on your calculator:

• Rename the independent variable as x and the dependent variable as y.
• Set the screen to the desired setting (integer, decimal, standard, or your choice).

- Enter the expression on the left side of the equation in Y1.
- Enter the expression on the right side of the equation in Y2.
- Graph.
- Find the point of intersection. Use the left and right arrow keys to locate the point of intersection. The up and down arrow keys move the cursor between graphs. Check the point of intersection by using these keys. You have found the intersection if the x-coordinate and y-coordinate do not change values when you change graphs.
- If an intersection cannot be found by tracing, or if you want to check the coordinates found by tracing, use the CALC function. The calculator will display the coordinates of the intersection.

The solutions of the equation are the x-coordinates of the points of intersection of the two graphs.

The y-coordinates of the points of intersection of the two graphs are the values obtained for both expressions when the equation is evaluated with the solutions. For example, graphically solve $x^2 - 3 = -x + 3$.

The two solutions are the x-coordinates of the intersections, -3 and 2, as shown in Figure 11.3.

TECHNOLOGY

$Y1 = x^2 - 3$

$(-3, 6)$ $(2, 1)$

$Y2 = -x + 3$

$(-47, 47, -31, 31)$

Figure 11.3

For Figure 11.3
Set the screen to the desired setting.

| ZOOM | 6 | ZOOM | 8 | ENTER |

Enter the expression on the left in Y1.

| Y= | X, T, θ, n | x² | − | 3 |

Enter the expression on the right in Y2.

| ▼ | (−) | X, T, θ, n | + | 3 |

Graph.

| GRAPH |

Trace.

| TRACE |

Use the arrow keys to determine the x-coordinates of the intersections.

EXAMPLE 4 Solve graphically.

a. $x^2 + 6x + 5 = -2x - 7$ **b.** $x^3 + x^2 - 4x + 2 = 2x^2 + 2x + 2$

Calculator Graphic Solution

$Y2 = 2x^2 + 2x + 2$

$(3, 26)$

$(-2, 6)$

$(0, 2)$

$Y1 = x^3 + x^2 - 4x + 2$

$(-10, 10, -30, 30)$

a. $x^2 + 6x + 5 = -2x - 7$
The two solutions are the x-coordinates of the intersections, -6 and -2, as shown in Figure 11.4.

b. $x^3 + x^2 - 4x + 2 = 2x^2 + 2x + 2$
The three solutions are the x-coordinates of the intersections: $-2, 0$, and 3, as shown to the left. ■

TECHNOLOGY

$Y1 = x^2 + 6x + 5$

$(-6, 5)$

$(-2, -3)$

$Y2 = -2x - 7$

$(-47, 47, -31, 31)$

Figure 11.4

For Figure 11.4

| Y= | X, T, θ, n | x² | + | 6 | X, T, θ, n | + | 5 | ▼ | (−) | 2 |

| X, T, θ, n | − | 7 | GRAPH | TRACE |

EXAMPLE 5 $4x^2 - 3x - 3 = x$ does not have integer solutions. Use the Intersect function on your calculator to find approximate solutions.

Calculator Graphic Solution

The two solutions are the x-coordinates of the intersections, -0.5 and 1.5, as shown in Figures 11.5a and 11.5b. ∎

Remember that polynomial equations may have an infinite number of solutions, no solutions, or no real-number solutions. Graphically solving polynomial equations may also result in these possibilities. Complete the following sets of exercises on your calculator.

DISCOVERY 6

Polynomial Equations with No Solution

Solve graphically the previous example of a polynomial equation with no solution, $x^2 + x + 10 = x^2 + x - 10$. Sketch the graph.

Write a rule to determine graphically when a polynomial equation has no solution.

The two graphs do not appear to intersect. Therefore, there is no ordered pair common to both functions. If we rewrite the equation in standard form, we obtain the contradiction $20 = 0$. There is no solution.

DISCOVERY 7

Polynomial Equations with Many Solutions

Solve graphically the previous example of a polynomial equation with a solution set of all real numbers, $2x^3 + 4x^2 + 5 = (x^3 + 3x^2 + 4) + (x^3 + x^2 + 1)$. Sketch the graph.

Write a rule to determine graphically when a polynomial equation has a solution of all real numbers.

TECHNOLOGY

Y2 = x   Y1 = 4x² − 3x − 3

Intersection
X=-.5   Y=-.5

(−10, 10, −10, 10)

Figure 11.5a

Y2 = x   Y1 = 4x² − 3x − 3

Intersection
X=1.5   Y=1.5

(−10, 10, −10, 10)

Figure 11.5b

For Figure 11.5a
Define the two expressions as rules for functions and enter into your calculator as in previous examples.

| ZOOM | 6 | ZOOM | 8 | ENTER | Y= |

| 4 | X, T, θ, n | x² | − | 3 | X, T, θ, n |

| − | 3 | ▼ | X, T, θ, n | GRAPH |

To change to a better picture, enter ZOOM

| 6 | TRACE |.

Use the arrow keys to find the intersection. This is not possible, so for each intersection enter 2nd   CALC

| 5 | and move as close to the intersection as possible.

| ENTER | ENTER | ENTER |.

For Figure 11.5b
Calculate the second intersection.

| 2nd | CALC | 5 |

Move as close to the intersection as possible.

| ENTER | ENTER | ENTER |

There is only one graph on the screen. (Actually, both graphs are the same.) Therefore, all ordered pairs on the graph are common to both functions, or all *x*-coordinates in the domain of the functions are solutions of the equation. If we rewrite the equation in standard form, the result is $0 = 0$, an identity. The solution set is all real numbers (the domain of the functions graphed).

DISCOVERY 8

Polynomial Equations with No Real-Number Solutions
Solve graphically the previous example of a polynomial equation with no real-number solution, $x^2 + x + 1 = 4x^2 + 4x + 4$. Sketch the graph.

Write a rule to explain graphically when a polynomial equation has no real-number solution.

The two graphs do not appear to intersect. Therefore, there is no ordered pair common to both graphed functions. If we rewrite the equation in standard form, we obtain the equation $3x^2 + 3x + 3 = 0$. This is not a contradiction. The equation does not have a solution in the real-number system. A further explanation for this case is given in Chapter 14.

EXAMPLE 6   Solve graphically.

a. $2(x^2 + 3x - 5) = 2x^2 + 2(3x - 5)$

b. $x^2 + 2x + 4 = 3x^2 + 6x + 12$

c. $2x^2 + 7x - 4 = 2(x^2 + 3x + 1) + x$

a.

$Y1 = 2(x^2 + 3x - 5)$

$Y2 = 2x^2 + 2(3x - 5)$

$(-47, 47, -31, 31)$

b.

$Y2 = 3x^2 + 6x + 12$

$Y1 = x^2 + 2x + 4$

$(-47, 47, -31, 31)$

c.

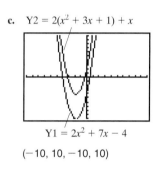

$Y2 = 2(x^2 + 3x + 1) + x$

$Y1 = 2x^2 + 7x - 4$

$(-10, 10, -10, 10)$

Calculator Graphic Solution

Define the two expressions as rules for functions and enter into your calculator, as in previous examples.

a. $2(x^2 + 3x - 5) = 2x^2 + 2(3x - 5)$
The graphs appear to be the same. Rewriting the equation results in $0 = 0$, an identity. The solution set is all real numbers (the domain of the graphed functions).

b. $x^2 + 2x + 4 = 3x^2 + 6x + 12$
The graphs do not appear to intersect. The standard form of the equation is $2x^2 + 4x + 8 = 0$. There is no real-number solution.

c. $2x^2 + 7x - 4 = 2(x^2 + 3x + 1) + x$
The graphs do not appear to intersect. Rewriting the equation results in a contradiction, $-6 = 0$. There is no solution. ∎

Graphical Solutions of Polynomial Equations
To solve a polynomial equation graphically, graph two functions defined by the expressions on the left and right sides of the equation. In viewing the graphs, one of four possibilities will occur:

One or more solutions exist. The graphs intersect. The solutions are the x-coordinates of the points of intersection.
No solution exists. The graphs do not appear to intersect. The original equation is a contradiction.
No real-number solution exists. The graphs do not appear to intersect. The original equation may be written in standard form.
An infinite number of solutions exist.
The graphs appear to coincide. The original equation is an identity. The solution set consists of all the numbers in the domain of the graphed functions.

In conclusion, we solve a polynomial equation graphically by graphing two functions. On a calculator, this method may be used to find noninteger solutions. Also, with this method we are better able to find all the solutions because we can see the number of points of intersection.

✓ **Experiencing Algebra the Checkup Way**

Solve exercises 1–6 graphically.

1. $x^2 + 7x = 3x + 21$

2. $x^3 + 2x^2 = x + 2$

3. $20x^2 + 4x = 15x + 3$

4. $(3x - 2)(x - 1) = 3x^2 - 5(x + 1)$

5. $x^2 - 2(3x - 5) = 3(x^2 - 6x) + 30$

6. $3(2x^3 + 2x^2) - (x + 2) + x^2 = 6x^3 + 7x^2 - x - 2$

7. In solving polynomial equations, sometimes we conclude that there are no solutions to the equation, and other times that there are no real-number solutions to the equation. What do you think is the difference between these two statements?

8. Once you graphically obtain the solutions of a polynomial equation, how can you check to be sure they are the solutions?

4 Modeling the Real World

An application of a quadratic equation is the vertical-position equation. The **vertical-position equation** is used to find the height of an object that was dropped or projected into the air. The height s of the object (in feet) is found using the equation $s = -16t^2 + v_0t + s_0$, where t is the time (in seconds), v_0 is the initial velocity, and s_0 is the initial height. Galileo discovered this formula in the late 1500's.

EXAMPLE 7

According to legend, Galileo simultaneously dropped two balls of different weights from the top of the Leaning Tower of Pisa in Italy, to see if they fell at the same rate or different rates. The Greek philosopher Aristotle had said that the heavier object would fall faster, and this was accepted as the truth for 2000 years. Galileo showed that if you neglect air resistance, they fall at the same rate. The Leaning Tower of Pisa is 179 feet tall; how long did it take for the balls to hit the ground?

Graphic Solution

Substitute values into the vertical-position equation. The balls hit the ground when they are 0 feet above ground level or when $s = 0$ feet, $v_0 = 0$ feet per second (the objects were dropped from rest), and $s_0 = 179$ feet.

$$s = -16t^2 + v_0t + s_0$$
$$0 = -16t^2 + 0t + 179$$
$$0 = -16t^2 + 179$$

The intersections of Y1 $= 0$ and Y2 $= -16x^2 + 179$ occur on the x-axis at $(3.34, 0)$ and $(-3.34, 0)$. The negative value of the x-intercept is not valid for this situation because we cannot have a negative value for time.

The objects were in the air about 3.34 seconds. ∎

Y2 $= -16x^2 + 179$

$(-3.34, 0)$ $(3.34, 0)$

Y1 $= 0$

$(-4.7, 4.7, -31, 310)$

Application

Using annual sales reports for Montgomery Ward Holdings for the years 1987 through 1995, a function to estimate annual sales in millions of dollars is $S(x) = 8x^3 - 91x^2 + 434x + 4789$, where x is the number of years after 1986. Determine when the annual sales will reach $8,000 million.

Discussion

Let $x =$ the number of years after 1986
$S(x) =$ annual sales in million dollars

$$S(x) = 8x^3 - 91x^2 + 434x + 4789$$
$$8000 = 8x^3 - 91x^2 + 434x + 4789 \quad \text{Substitute 8000 for } S(x).$$

According to the table, it appears that the annual sales reach $8000 million between 9 and 10 years after 1986. The annual sales in 1995 (1986 + 9) appear to be $7156 million. The annual sales in 1996 (1986 + 10) appear to be $8029 million. Therefore, in 1996 the annual sales for Montgomery Ward are projected to be approximately $8000 million.

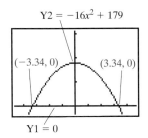

X	Y1	Y2
5	8000	5684
6	8000	5845
7	8000	6112
8	8000	6533
9	8000	7156
10	8000	8029
11	8000	9200

X=10

Y1 $= 8000$
Y2 $= 8x^3 - 91x^2 + 434x + 4789$

$Y2 = 8x^3 - 91x^2 + 434x + 4789$

$Y1 = 8000$

Intersection
X=9.9712794 Y=8000

(0, 12, 0, 10,000)

A graphical solution results in the same prediction, but visually shows the sales trend over the time period. ∎

Experiencing Algebra the Checkup Way

1. The Empire State Building is 1,250 feet tall. If King Kong dropped a banana from the top of the building, how long would it take for the banana to hit the ground?

2. Specifications for a shipping crate indicate that its ends be in the shape of a square, and the length of the crate must be 7 inches more than the width. Write and solve a polynomial equation to find the dimensions of the crate (to the nearest integer values) if the volume of the crate must be approximately 1300 square inches.

PROBLEM SET 11.1

Experiencing Algebra the Exercise Way

Determine whether each equation is a polynomial equation. Identify each polynomial equation as quadratic or cubic, where applicable.

1. $3x^3 - 2x^2 + x = 5$

2. $3y - 2y^{-1} + 4 = 0$

3. $3\sqrt{y} + y - 4 = 0$

4. $5.7x^3 - 1.9x^2 = 8.6x - 3.5$

5. $\frac{1}{4}x^4 + 3x^2 - \frac{3}{4} = 0$

6. $5(z - 1)^3 = 4(z - 1)^2$

7. $4(x - 2)(x + 7) = 16$

8. $3x + 5\sqrt{x} = 17$

9. $3x^{-2} - 5x = 4x^2$

10. $4a^3 + a^2 - 3a + 2 = 0$

11. $1.7x^2 + 3.2x = 5.7$

12. $\frac{2}{3}x^2 - \frac{5}{9}x = \frac{1}{6}$

Solve numerically.

13. $x^2 + 8 = 6x$

14. $x^2 - 6 = -x$

15. $x^3 = x$

16. $x^2 + 2x - 15 = 0$

17. $x^2 - 7 = x^2 + 3$

18. $x^2 - 3x + 2 - x(x - 3) + 7$

19. $x^2 + 5x + 1 = 1 + x(5 + x)$

20. $x(7 - x^2) + 6 = 6 + 7x - x^3$

21. $x^2 - 2x + 6 = 12 - 4x + 2x^2$

22. $x^2 + 2x + 4 = 1 - (x + 1)^2$

23. $\frac{1}{2}x^2 - x = 6 - 3x$

24. $\frac{1}{2}x^2 + 2x = \frac{3}{2}x + 6$

25. $2 - 0.2x^2 = 0.6x$

26. $6 + 2x - 0.4x^2 = 1.2x$

Solve graphically and check.

27. $x^2 - 3 = 6$

28. $x^2 - 8 = 8$

29. $x^2 - 3 = 2x$

30. $x^2 + 2x + 9 = 1 - 4x$

31. $x^3 = 4x$

32. $\frac{1}{2}x^3 = 4$

33. $x^2 - 3x - 10 = 0$

34. $x^3 + 3x^2 - x - 3 = 0$

35. $x^2 - 2x + 1 = x^2 - 2x - 3$

36. $3 - x^2 = 8 - x$

37. $x^2 + 1 = 3x^2 + 3$

38. $3 - x^2 = 6 - x^2$

39. $x(x + 3) = x^2 + 3x$

40. $(x + 1)^2 = x^2 + 2x + 1$

41. $4x^2 - x^3 = x^2 - 4x$

42. $x^3 - 6x + 2 = 2 - x^2$

43. $x^2 - 10x + 30 = \frac{1}{2}x^2 - 5x + 15$

44. $\frac{1}{2}x^2 + 5 = -\frac{1}{3}x^2 - 2$

45. $x^3 - 2x^2 + 1 = x^3 - 2x^2 + 9$ **46.** $-x^2 - 3 = -\dfrac{1}{3}x^2 - 1$

47. $x(x^2 - 3) - 5(x + 1) = x^3 - 8x - 5$

48. $(x - 2)(x^2 + 2x) = x^3 - 4x$ **49.** $4x^2 = 9$ **50.** $9x^2 = 16$

51. $10x^3 - 7x^2 - 4x = 3x - 4$ **52.** $4x^3 - 8x^2 = 7x - 5$ **53.** $x^2 - 0.9x - 10.36 = 0$

54. $x^2 - 5x + 3.36 = 0$ **55.** $x^3 + 3.7x^2 = 1.74x + 7.56$ **56.** $x^3 + 0.1x^2 + 5 = 6.02x + 6.2$

Use the position equation, $s = -16t^2 + v_0 t + s_0$, to solve.

57. A tightrope walker drops her hat from 40 feet above the ground. How many seconds will it take for the hat to hit the ground?

58. A gardener drops his pruning shears while trimming a tree. The gardener is 16 feet above the ground. How long will it take for the shears to hit the ground?

59. A tightrope walker throws a silver dagger vertically downward from 40 feet above the ground. If the initial velocity of the throw is 5 feet per second, how many seconds will it take for the dagger to hit the ground? (*Note:* $v_0 = -5$, since the object is thrown downward. If it had been thrown upward, the initial velocity would have been positive.)

60. A gardener tosses a pruned branch vertically downward to the ground from a height of 16 feet. If the initial velocity of the toss is 2 feet per second, how long will it take for the branch to hit the ground?

61. A tightrope walker throws a baton vertically upward at a velocity of 5 feet per second. If he is 40 feet above the ground, how many seconds will it take for the baton to hit the ground?

62. A gardener tosses a hammer vertically upward to shoo away a squirrel in a tree. It is released at a height of 6 feet above the ground with an initial velocity of 10 feet per second. He misses both the squirrel and the tree. How long will it take for the hammer to hit the ground?

Develop a polynomial equation for each situation and solve.

63. Blue Beagle Bus company advertises that groups may charter a bus by paying a fare of $30 per person, plus $1 per person for each unoccupied seat. The bus has 40 seats.

    a. Write a polynomial expression for the fare per person if there are x unsold seats on the bus.

    b. Write a polynomial expression for the number of people chartering the bus, given x unsold seats.

    c. Write a polynomial expression for the total revenue earned from the charter of the bus, given x unsold seats.

    d. Write a polynomial equation that sets the revenue at $1100 for a charter when there are x unsold seats.

    e. Solve the equation to obtain the nearest integer number of unsold seats that will yield a revenue of approximately $1100 for the charter. How many seats must be sold to meet this revenue goal?

64. The bus company described in exercise 63 offers another charter tour. The fare for this tour is $150 per person plus $5 per person for each unoccupied seat. This bus has 25 seats. Follow steps (a) through (e) to write a polynomial for the revenue if the company wants revenue to be $3500. How many seats must be sold to meet this revenue goal?

65. A statistical study attempted to relate the monthly sales (y) in a sales territory to the number of sales representatives (x) assigned to the territory. The polynomial equation derived from the study was $y = 11.55 + 20.67x - 1.35x^2$, where sales are recorded in thousands of dollars. How many sales reps should be assigned to a territory if the company wants monthly sales to reach $100,000?

66. Using the same statistical model described in exercise 65, how many sales reps should be assigned to a territory if the company wants monthly sales to reach $75,000?

67. Christie needs a crate that has a volume of approximately 2000 cubic inches. The width of the crate must be 1 inch more than the height. The length of the crate must be twice the height. Use a polynomial equation to find the dimensions to the nearest inch.

68. Marlena purchased 300 square feet of carpeting for her dining room. The room is rectangular, with a length that is 3 feet less than twice the width. What are the dimensions of the dining room to the nearest foot?

 Experiencing Algebra the Calculator Way

Using the ZBox Command to Improve a Graph's View

When solving a polynomial equation graphically, it is often necessary to experiment with different settings of the window to be able to see the graph clearly. As an example, solve the equation

$$x^3 + 5.2x^2 = 36.9 + 4.49x$$

using the following instructions.

1. Graph the expressions on the left and right sides of the equation using the decimal window. The graph appears to have the shape of a parabola, which is the shape for a quadratic function. But the expressions are cubic and linear, indicating this is not a good view.

2. Next, change to a standard window. More of the graph appears, but it still does not seem complete.

3. Change to an integer window. Much more of the graph appears, but it seems squeezed horizontally.

4. Change Xmin and Xmax by dividing each setting by 10.

This will spread out the graph. Then view the graph. This improves the graph, but it looks as if the window is still too small.

5. Change Ymin and Ymax by multiplying each setting by 2.

This will expand the graph in the y direction. Then view the graph. Now you see that the graph consists of a curve that is intersected by a straight line at two or more points.

6. Find the rightmost intersection. One solution of the equation is $x = 2.5$.

7. The left most intersection is still not clearly shown. Use $\boxed{\text{ZOOM}}$ $\boxed{1}$ to box the region where the two graphs meet. Draw a box by moving the cursor to the left upper corner of your box and pressing $\boxed{\text{ENTER}}$, then use the arrow keys right and down to draw a box. Press $\boxed{\text{ENTER}}$ again and the calculator will enlarge the box.

8. Now you can clearly see that the line intersects the curve at two points. This would be difficult to see otherwise. Find the two intersection points. The other two solutions are $x = -3.6$ and $x = -4.1$. After completing this exercise, restore the calculator window to the standard setting.

Use this approach to solve the following equations graphically. You can use other multipliers or divisors than those used in the preceding example.

1. $x^3 + 5x^2 + 4x + 20 = 5x^2 + 25x$; verify the solutions as $x = 1$, $x = 4$, and $x = -5$.
2. $x^3 + 3x^2 - 3x = x^2 - 2x + 2$; verify the solutions as $x = -2$, $x = -1$, and $x = 1$.
3. $x^3 - 2x^2 = 30x - x^2$; verify the solutions as $x = -5$, $x = 0$, $x = 6$.

Experiencing Algebra the Group Way

Another helpful technique for solving a polynomial equation graphically is to simplify the equation by placing it in standard form. To do this, move all terms to the left side of the equation, using the properties of equations. The equations will be of the form

$$ax^2 + bx + c = 0$$
$$ax^3 + bx^2 + cx + d = 0$$

and so on. Then store the left side of the equation in Y1 and set Y2 = 0 (since the right side of the equation is 0). When you graph, the solutions will be the x-coordinates of the points of intersection of the graphs of Y1 and Y2. However, since the graph of Y2 = 0 is the x-axis, the solutions will also be the x-coordinates of the x-intercepts of the graph of Y1. Each member of the group should try this method on the four equations in "Experiencing Algebra the Calculator Way" to find the solutions listed there. Discuss the pros and cons of both methods, and try to decide when you would choose to use one method or the other.

Experiencing Algebra the Write Way

When graphing the expressions on the left and right sides of a polynomial equation as two functions, you can identify both intercepts and intersection points. Define both terms, pointing out the differences between them and the similarities. Draw an example of a graph of the expressions on the left and right sides of a polynomial equation, labeling the intercepts and the intersection points. Can the intercepts and the intersection points occur at the same location? Explain.

11.2 Solving Equations Algebraically by Factoring

Objectives

1 Solve polynomial equations using the zero factor property.

2 Solve polynomial equations by factoring.

3 Model real-world situations using polynomial equations and solve by factoring.

Application

A report from the American Automobile Manufacturers Association summarizes motor vehicle factory sales. According to data in the report, retail sales for domestic cars (in millions of cars) may be approximated by the function $S(x) = 0.1x^2 - 0.7x + 7.6$, where x is the number of years after 1987. Using the given function, determine when the retail sales were 7 million domestic cars.

After completing this section, we will discuss this application further. See page 821.

In the preceding section we used numeric and graphic methods to solve polynomial equations. While such methods work, they are sometimes limited in their usefulness. Therefore, we need an algebraic method to solve these equations. One such method is to solve by factoring.

---

1 Solving Equations Using the Zero Factor Property

We begin by reviewing a property of real numbers that we discussed in Chapter 2. The zero property of multiplication stated that the product of a real number and 0 is 0. We can extend this property into another property called the zero factor property. The *zero factor property* states that if a product is 0, then one or both of the factors must be 0.

For example, $6 \cdot 0 = 0, 0 \cdot (-5) = 0$, or $0 \cdot 0 = 0$.

> *Zero Factor Property*
> If $ab = 0$, then either $a = 0$, $b = 0$, or both.

We can use this property to solve an equation of the form $P(x) = 0$ when $P(x)$ is in factored form, such as when $P(x) = (x + 5)(x - 2)$.

For example, solve $(x + 5)(x - 2) = 0$.

If $\underset{\uparrow}{(x + 5)}\underset{\uparrow}{(x - 2)} = 0$, then $\underset{\uparrow}{x + 5} = 0$, or $\underset{\uparrow}{x - 2} = 0$, or both.

$\quad\quad a \quad\quad b \quad\quad\quad\quad\quad a \quad\quad\quad\quad b$

We can now determine the solutions by solving the linear equations.

$$x + 5 = 0 \quad\quad \text{or} \quad\quad x - 2 = 0$$
$$x + 5 - 5 = 0 - 5 \quad\quad\quad x - 2 + 2 = 0 + 2$$
$$x = -5 \quad\quad\quad\quad\quad\quad x = 2$$

The solutions of the equation $(x + 5)(x - 2) = 0$ are -5 and 2.

We can check the solutions by substituting into the original equation.

Let $x = -5$.

$$\frac{(x + 5)(x - 2) \;= 0}{(-5 + 5)(-5 - 2) \;\big|\; 0}$$
$$(0)(-7)$$
$$0$$

Let $x = 2$.

$$\frac{(x + 5)(x - 2) = 0}{(2 + 5)(2 - 2) \;\big|\; 0}$$
$$(7)(0)$$
$$0$$

Both values result in true equations. Therefore, the solutions are -5 and 2.

EXAMPLE 1   Solve and check.

a. $(2x + 3)(5x - 4) = 0$ **b.** $x(x + 6)(3x - 2) = 0$

Algebraic Solution

a. $(2x + 3)(5x - 4) = 0$
Use the zero factor property.

$$2x + 3 = 0 \qquad \text{or} \qquad 5x - 4 = 0$$
$$2x + 3 - 3 = 0 - 3 \qquad\qquad 5x - 4 + 4 = 0 + 4$$
$$2x = -3 \qquad\qquad\qquad 5x = 4$$
$$x = -\frac{3}{2} \qquad\qquad\qquad x = \frac{4}{5}$$

The solutions of the equation are $-\frac{3}{2}$ and $\frac{4}{5}$.

Check on your calculator by substituting the values for the variable in the expression on the left side of the equation. The result should equal 0, the expression on the right side of the equation.

After substituting the solutions into the expression on the left, the results are 0. The solutions check.

b. $x(x + 6)(3x - 2) = 0$
We now have three factors equal to 0. The zero factor property can be expanded to more than two factors as well. Therefore, we set all three factors equal to 0.

$$x = 0 \qquad \text{or} \qquad x + 6 = 0 \qquad \text{or} \qquad 3x - 2 = 0$$
$$x = -6 \qquad\qquad\qquad x = \frac{2}{3}.$$

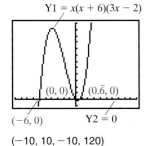

Y1 = $x(x + 6)(3x - 2)$

$(0, 0)$ $(0.\bar{6}, 0)$

$(-6, 0)$ Y2 = 0

$(-10, 10, -10, 120)$

The solutions of the equation are $0, -6$, and $\frac{2}{3}$.

A graphic check on the calculator results in three solutions: $0, -6$, and $\frac{2}{3}$.

∎

Experiencing Algebra the Checkup Way

Solve and check.

1. $(x + 7)(4x - 3) = 0$ **2.** $x(4x - 5)(x - 1) = 0$

2 Solving Equations by Factoring   As we know, most polynomial equations are not written in the factored form given in Example 1. We may have to use the algebra skills from previous chapters to manipulate the equation into this form.

Solving a Polynomial Equation Algebraically by Factoring
To solve a polynomial equation algebraically by factoring:

- Write the equation in the standard form $P(x) = 0$.
- Factor $P(x)$.
- Set each factor equal to 0 and solve for the variable.

Check the solutions by substitution or solving numerically or graphically.

For example, solve $x^2 + x - 6 = 0$.

$$x^2 + x - 6 = 0 \qquad \text{Standard form}$$
$$(x + 3)(x - 2) = 0 \qquad \text{Factor.}$$
$$x + 3 = 0 \quad \text{or} \quad x - 2 = 0 \qquad \text{Zero factor property}$$
$$x = -3 \qquad\qquad x = 2$$

Graphically check the solution by graphing the two functions determined by each side of the original equation. Let $Y1 = x^2 + x - 6$ and $Y2 = 0$

Y1 = $x^2 + x - 6$

$(-3, 0)$ $(2, 0)$

Y2 = 0

$(-10, 10, -10, 10)$

Helping Hand The second function, $Y2 = 0$, is the x-axis and cannot be seen as a line. Therefore, the function does not need to be graphed to determine the solution. We can graph Y1 and determine the x-intercepts.

The x-coordinates of the x-intercepts—that is, the intersections of the graph of Y1 and the x-axis—are -3 and 2. The solutions are -3 and 2.

If we cannot trace and find the intersection of the graph and the x-axis, the calculator will calculate it for us. Under the CALC function, choose Zero. Set an interval by choosing a left bound (a point on the graph to the left of the x-intercept) and a right bound (a point on the graph to the right of the x-intercept). Then select a guess between the two bounds. The calculator will display the x-intercept. The solutions (or **roots**) are the x-coordinates of each x-intercept.

EXAMPLE 2 Solve and check.

a. $x^2 - 9 = 0$ **b.** $4x^2 + 20x + 25 = 0$
c. $-10x^2 - 41x + 77 = 0$

Algebraic Solution

a.
$$x^2 - 9 = 0 \qquad \text{Standard form}$$
$$(x + 3)(x - 3) = 0 \qquad \text{Factor.}$$
$$x + 3 = 0 \quad \text{or} \quad x - 3 = 0 \qquad \text{Zero factor property}$$
$$x = -3 \qquad\qquad x = 3$$

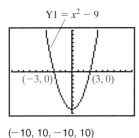

Y1 = $x^2 - 9$

$(-3, 0)$ $(3, 0)$

$(-10, 10, -10, 10)$

The equation solutions are -3 and 3.
The graphic check results in the graph of $Y1 = x^2 - 9$.
The x-coordinates of the x-intercepts are -3 and 3, the solutions.

b. $4x^2 + 20x + 25 = 0$ Standard form
$$(2x + 5)^2 = 0 \qquad \text{Factor.}$$

Set each factor equal to 0 and solve. Since the factor is squared, both factors are $2x + 5$. There is no need to solve two equations.

$$2x + 5 = 0$$

$$x = -\frac{5}{2}$$

Y1 = $4x^2 + 20x + 25$

$(-2.5, 0)$

$(-10, 10, -10, 10)$

The solution is $-\frac{5}{2}$. It is called a **double root**.

The graphic check results in the graph of Y1 = $4x^2 + 20x + 25$. There is only one x-intercept. The x-coordinate of the x-intercept, $-\frac{5}{2}$, is the solution. You need to use Zero under the CALC function to find the intercept.

Helping Hand A double root will always occur when the graphic check of an equation in standard form results in one x-intercept.

c. $\quad -10x^2 - 41x + 77 = 0 \quad$ Standard form

$-1(2x + 11)(5x - 7) = 0 \quad$ Factor.

Set each factor equal to 0 and solve. The common factor -1 cannot equal 0 because it is a constant.

$$2x + 11 = 0 \qquad \text{or} \qquad 5x - 7 = 0$$

$$x = -\frac{11}{2} \qquad\qquad x = \frac{7}{5}$$

```
-11/2→X: -10X²-41
X+77
               0
7/5→X: -10X²-41X+
77
               0
```

The solutions are $-\frac{11}{2}$ and $\frac{7}{5}$.

Check by substitution on your calculator.

Both solutions, $-\frac{11}{2}$ and $\frac{7}{5}$, when substituted for the variable, result in expressions equal to 0, the second expression value. ∎

EXAMPLE 3 Solve and check.

a. $6x^2 + 14x = 3x + 7$ **b.** $(x + 3)(x - 7) = -9$

c. $x^2 + 7x = -5$ **d.** $x^2 + 5x + 6 = -x^2 - 6$

e. $2x^3 + 4x^2 = 2(x^3 + 2x^2)$

Algebraic Solution

a. $6x^2 + 14x = 3x + 7$

Neither side of the equation is 0. Use the properties of equations to write the equation in standard form.

$$6x^2 + 14x - 3x - 7 = 3x + 7 - 3x - 7$$

$$6x^2 + 11x - 7 = 0$$

$$(3x + 7)(2x - 1) = 0 \qquad\qquad\qquad\qquad \text{Factor.}$$

$$3x + 7 = 0 \quad \text{or} \quad 2x - 1 = 0 \qquad \text{Zero factor property}$$

$$x = -\frac{7}{3} \qquad\qquad\qquad x = \frac{1}{2}$$

The equation solutions are $-\frac{7}{3}$ and $\frac{1}{2}$.

The calculator check by substitution results in equal values for the expressions on the left and the right when the solutions are substituted for the variable.

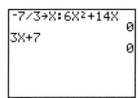

b. $(x + 3)(x - 7) = -9$

Neither side of the equation is 0. Multiply the expression on the left and then use the properties of equations to write the equation in standard form.

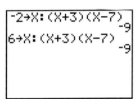

$$x^2 - 4x - 21 = -9$$

$$x^2 - 4x - 12 = 0 \qquad \text{Standard form}$$

$$(x + 2)(x - 6) = 0 \qquad \text{Factor.}$$

$$x + 2 = 0 \quad \text{or} \quad x - 6 = 0 \quad \text{Zero factor property}$$

$$x = -2 \qquad\qquad x = 6$$

The equation solutions are -2 and 6.

The calculator check by substitution results in a value of -9 for the expression on the left when the solutions are substituted for the variable. This is the value of the expression on the right.

c. $x^2 + 7x = -5$

Neither side of the equation is 0. Use the properties of equations to write the equation in standard form.

$$x^2 + 7x + 5 = 0$$

$Y1 = x^2 + 7x$
$Y2 = -5$
$(-0.807, -5)$
$(-6.193, -5)$
$(-47, 47, -31, 31)$

Factor the polynomial. (It is a trinomial with the leading coefficient equal to 1.) The polynomial does not factor.

We need to use another method. To solve graphically, graph the original equation expressions, $Y1 = x^2 + 7x$ and $Y2 = -5$. The x-coordinates of the intersections are approximately -6.193 and -0.807, the approximate solutions. Use Intersect under the CALC function.

d. $x^2 + 5x + 6 = -x^2 - 6$

Neither side of the equation is 0. Use the properties of equations to write the equation in standard form.

$$2x^2 + 5x + 12 = 0$$

Factor the polynomial. The polynomial does not factor. To determine the solution, we need to use a different method.

To solve graphically, graph the original equation expressions, $Y1 = x^2 + 5x + 6$ and $Y2 = -x^2 - 6$. The two graphs do not intersect.

$Y1 = x^2 + 5x + 6$
$Y2 = -x^2 - 6$
$(-47, 47, -31, 31)$

$Y1 = 2x^3 + 4x^2$

$Y2 = 2(x^3 + 2x^2)$

$(-10, 10, -10, 10)$

There is no real-number solution. (The equation can be written in standard form.)

e. $2x^3 + 4x^2 = 2(x^3 + 2x^2)$

Neither side of the equation is 0. Multiply the expression on the right and use the properties of equations to write the equation in standard form.

$$2x^3 + 4x^2 = 2x^3 + 4x^2$$
$$0 = 0$$

This is an identity. The solution set is all real numbers (the permissible values of the polynomial).

The graphic check results in two identical graphs. ∎

    ## Experiencing Algebra the Checkup Way

Solve exercises 1–7 and check.

1. $x^2 + 2x + 8 = (x + 1)^2 - 3$ 　　**2.** $a^2 - 81 = 0$ 　　**3.** $16x^2 + 24x + 9 = 0$

4. $4x^2 - 5x = 12x - 15$ 　　**5.** $(x + 4)(x - 2) = 16$ 　　**6.** $x^2 + 5x = 1$

7. $x^2 - 3x + 5 = x(x + 2) - 5(x - 1)$

8. When using the zero factor property to solve a polynomial equation, can you say that there is no solution if the standard form of the polynomial equation cannot be factored? Explain.

9. Assume that you are using the zero factor property to solve a polynomial equation. How can you tell that a polynomial equation has no solution? How can you tell that a polynomial equation has all real numbers as its solution? How can you tell that a polynomial equation has no real number as a solution?

---

3   Modeling the Real World

Geometry problems are common applications for polynomial equations. Use the formulas given to you in earlier chapters and solve them with the methods of this section. Be careful to evaluate the solutions to see whether they make sense within the constraints of the problem. Solutions of the equation sometimes may not make physical sense.

EXAMPLE 4

LaChung plans to make an open rectangular box from a flat piece of tin. He needs the length to be 5 feet more than the width. He plans to cut out square corners 3 feet on a side for the height of the box. He needs the box to hold 198 cubic feet of mulch.

a. Find the dimensions of the box.
b. Find the dimensions of the piece of tin needed.

Algebraic Solution

a. Let 　　$x =$ width of the box
　　　　$x + 5 =$ length of the box

The volume formula for a rectangular solid is $V = LWH$. Substitute values or expressions for the variables L, W, H, and V.

$$V = LWH$$
$$198 = (x + 5)(x)(3)$$
$$198 = 3x^2 + 15x \qquad \text{Simplify.}$$

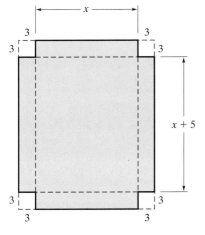

$$3x^2 + 15x - 198 = 0 \qquad \text{Standard form}$$
$$3(x^2 + 5x - 66) = 0 \qquad \text{Factor out the GCF.}$$
$$3(x - 6)(x + 11) = 0 \qquad \text{Factor the trinomial.}$$
$$x - 6 = 0 \quad \text{or} \quad x + 11 = 0 \qquad \text{Zero factor property}$$
$$x = 6 \qquad\qquad x = -11 \qquad \text{Solve.}$$

Since x is the width of the box, $x = -11$ is not an appropriate choice. Therefore, the width is 6 feet.

The length is $x + 5 = 6 + 5 = 11$ feet.

The box's dimensions are 11 feet by 6 feet by 3 feet.

b. The length of the tin must be 11 feet plus 6 feet (two 3-foot sections) or 17 feet.

The width of the tin must be 6 feet plus 6 feet (again, two 3-foot sections), or 12 feet. ∎

EXAMPLE 5 Phyllis plans to build a storage shed for her garden tools and lawn mower. She wants the length to be twice the width and the height to be 3 feet more than the width. Phyllis has enough materials to cover 340 square feet. She would like to use all the materials. Determine the possible dimensions of the shed.

Algebraic Solution

Let $W = $ width
    $2W = $ length
    $W + 3 = $ height

The surface area for a rectangular solid is given by the formula $SA = 2LW + 2WH + 2LH$.

$$340 = 2(2W)(W) + 2(W)(W + 3) + 2(2W)(W + 3) \qquad \text{Substitute expressions.}$$

$$340 = 4W^2 + 2W^2 + 6W + 4W^2 + 12W \qquad \text{Simplify.}$$

$$340 = 10W^2 + 18W$$

$$10W^2 + 18W - 340 = 0 \qquad \text{Standard form}$$

$$2(5W^2 + 9W - 170) = 0 \qquad \text{Factor out the GCF.}$$

$$2(5W^2 - 25W + 34W - 170) = 0 \qquad \text{Factor using the } ac \text{ method.}$$

$$2[5W(W - 5) + 34(W - 5)] = 0$$

$$2(W - 5)(5W + 34) = 0$$

$$W - 5 = 0 \quad \text{or} \quad 5W + 34 = 0 \qquad \text{Zero factor property}$$

$$W = 5 \qquad\qquad W = -\frac{34}{5}$$

The width is 5 feet. (A negative width is not possible, so we discard the solution $-\frac{34}{5}$ feet.) The length is twice the width, or 10 feet. The height is 3 feet more than the width, or 8 feet. ∎

Another application uses a formula introduced in Chapter 3 that relates the lengths of three sides of a right triangle. The **legs** of a right triangle are

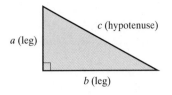

a (leg)

c (hypotenuse)

b (leg)

the two sides that form the right angle. The **hypotenuse** is the side opposite the right angle.

The **Pythagorean theorem** states that the sum of the squares of the lengths of the legs of a right triangle is equal to the square of the length of the hypotenuse.

In other words, $a^2 + b^2 = c^2$, where a and b are the lengths of the legs of a right triangle and c is the length of the hypotenuse.

EXAMPLE 6   George wants to lean a 10-foot ladder against a house at a height that is 2 feet more than the distance of the ladder from the house measured along the ground. Is this possible?

Algebraic Solution

(x+2) ft   10 ft

x ft

The distance from the house to the bottom of the ladder is x feet. The distance from the ground to the top of the ladder is $x + 2$ feet.

$$a^2 + b^2 = c^2$$
$$x^2 + (x + 2)^2 = 10^2 \qquad \text{Substitute expressions.}$$
$$x^2 + x^2 + 4x + 4 = 100 \qquad \text{Multiply.}$$
$$2x^2 + 4x - 96 = 0 \qquad \text{Write as } p(x) = 0.$$
$$2(x^2 + 2x - 48) = 0 \qquad \text{Factor.}$$
$$2(x - 6)(x + 8) = 0$$
$$x - 6 = 0 \quad \text{or} \quad x + 8 = 0 \qquad \text{Zero factor property}$$
$$x = 6 \qquad\qquad x = -8$$

The length of the distance along the ground from the house to the ladder is 6 feet. The distance from the ground to the top of the ladder is 8 feet. Yes, it is possible. ∎

Application

A report from the American Automobile Manufacturers Association summarizes motor vehicle factory sales. According to data in the report, retail sales for domestic cars (in millions of cars) may be approximated by the function $S(x) = 0.1x^2 - 0.7x + 7.6$, where x is the number of years after 1987. Using the given function, determine when the retail sales were 7 million domestic cars.

Discussion

Let $x =$ the number of years after 1987
$$S(x) = 0.1x^2 - 0.7x + 7.6$$

$$7 = 0.1x^2 - 0.7x + 7.6 \qquad \text{Substitute 7 for } S(x).$$
$$70 = x^2 - 7x + 76 \qquad \text{Multiply both sides of the equation by LCD of 10.}$$
$$0 = x^2 - 7x + 6 \qquad \text{Subtract 70 from both sides of the equation.}$$
$$0 = (x - 6)(x - 1) \qquad \text{Factor.}$$
$$x - 6 = 0 \quad \text{or} \quad x - 1 = 0 \qquad \text{Zero factor property.}$$
$$x = 6 \qquad\qquad x = 1$$

Retail sales were 7 million domestic cars at 1 year after 1987, or 1988, and again 6 years after 1987, or 1993. ∎

Experiencing Algebra the Checkup Way

1. For her art class, Trekisa needs to make a tray from a piece of poster board. From a rectangular piece of board, she must cut squares x inches on a side out of each corner, fold up the sides, and join them to make the tray. Her assignment is to make a tray that is 7 inches long, with a width that is 2 inches more than three times its height. The tray must have a volume of 35 cubic inches.

   a. Determine the dimensions of the tray.

   b. Determine the dimensions of the rectangular piece of posterboard.

2. Justin must make a box from balsa wood for an architecture class project. He is allowed to use 40 square inches of balsa wood for the project. The height of the box must be the same as its width. It must have a length that is 2 inches more than the width. What will be the dimensions of the box?

3. Steve is designing a sail for a sailboat he is building. The sail is a right triangle with a base of 9 feet. The hypotenuse of the sail will be 9 feet less than twice the height. What will be the height and hypotenuse of the sail?

4. The flow rate (Q) of water, in gallons per minute (gpm), is given by $Q = 29.7\, D^2 \sqrt{P}$, where D is the diameter of the nozzle, measured in inches, and P is the static pressure, in pounds per square inch (psi). Write an equation to find the diameter of the nozzle if the flow rate is 1188 gpm, and the static pressure is 100 psi. Find the nozzle diameter.

PROBLEM SET 11.2

Experiencing Algebra the Exercise Way

Solve exercises 1–50 and check.

1. $(x + 6)(x + 11) = 0$

2. $(p + 9)(p + 13) = 0$

3. $\left(\dfrac{3}{5}x - \dfrac{9}{20}\right)\left(x + \dfrac{2}{3}\right) = 0$

4. $\left(\dfrac{2}{3}x + \dfrac{4}{9}\right)\left(x - \dfrac{7}{9}\right) = 0$

5. $3x(x + 9)(2x - 5) = 0$

6. $9x(x - 4)(6x + 1) = 0$

7. $(7x - 49)(49x - 7) = 0$

8. $(5x - 45)(45x - 5) = 0$

9. $(4x + 3)(2x - 9)(x + 6) = 0$

10. $(2z + 7)(3z - 8)(z - 7) = 0$

11. $(0.2x + 6.8)(1.3x - 1.69) = 0$

12. $(1.4x + 4.2)(0.7x - 2.8) = 0$

13. $0 = x^2 + 10x + 24$

14. $z^2 + 13z + 40 = 0$

15. $x^2 + 33 = 14x$

16. $52 - 17x + x^2 = 0$

17. $4x^2 + 5x + 24x + 30 = 0$

18. $7x^2 + 8x + 14x + 16 = 0$

19. $5x^2 + 3x = 8$

20. $7x = 3x^2 - 20$

21. $15x^2 = 35x$

22. $63x = 18x^2$

23. $18x^2 - 3x = 5 - 30x$

24. $8x^2 + 12x = 14x + 21$

25. $16x^2 + 72x + 81 = 0$

26. $49x^2 - 28x + 4 = 0$

27. $4x^2 + 25x + 18 = 5x - 7$

28. $9x^2 + 29x + 8 = 5x - 8$

29. $b^2 + 7 = 71$

30. $c^2 - 5 = 139$

31. $9z^2 = 25$

32. $64p^2 = 81$

33. $x^2 + 10x + 20 = 0$

34. $x^2 + 11x + 20 = 0$

35. $(x + 1)^2 = 49$

36. $(x - 2)^2 = 36$

37. $(x - 3)(x - 2) = 42$

38. $(x - 5)(x + 4) = 22$

39. $(x - 7)(2x + 3) = 2(x^2 - 5x - 10) - (x + 1)$

40. $2(x^2 + 7x + 10) - x = (x + 4)(2x + 5)$

41. $(x + 3)^2 = x^2 + 6x + 11$

42. $(x - 6)(x + 9) = x^2 + 3x - 45$

43. $x^2 + (x + 3)^2 = 225$

44. $(x + 5)^2 + x^2 = 625$

45. $x^3 + 7x^2 - 9x - 63 = 0$

46. $z^3 + 5z^2 - 16z - 80 = 0$

47. $18x^3 + 45x^2 - 50x - 125 = 0$

48. $12p^3 + 36p^2 - 147p - 441 = 0$

49. $3x^3 - 3x^2 + 12x - 12 = 0$

50. $2x^3 - 16x^2 + 3x - 24 = 0$

51. Phil is designing a water trough for his ranch. It will be a rectangular box shape and must hold 72 cubic feet of water. He wants it to be 3 feet high, with a width that is 1 foot more than half its length.

   a. If the length is denoted by x, write an expression for the volume of the trough.

   b. Write an equation in terms of the volume and solve the equation for the dimensions of the trough.

52. A rectangular jewelry box is designed to have a height of 4 centimeters. Its length is 1 centimeter more than eight times its width.

   a. If the width is denoted by x, write an expression for the volume of the box.

   b. Write an equation for the volume of the box when it will hold 820 square centimeters and solve the equation for the dimensions of the box.

53. Michelle is designing drawers for a cabinet. She wants the drawer to have a width that is three times its height, and a length that is 2 inches more than four times the height. She will need wood for the four sides and the bottom.

   a. Write an expression for the surface area of the five sides for which she must obtain wood.

   b. If she figures that she needs 700 square inches of wood for the drawer, what are its dimensions?

54. A cardboard chute in the shape of a rectangular box is constructed with a width that is five times its height, and a length that is 2 units more than seven times its height. The chute is open on its two ends.

   a. Write an expression for the surface area of the chute.

   b. If the outer surface of the chute has a surface area of 828 square inches, what are the dimensions of the chute?

55. Steve designs a sail for his sailboat. It will be triangular, but not a right triangle. He wants the height to be 4 feet more than the base.

   a. Write an expression for the area of the sail.

   b. If the area of the sail is to be 30 square feet, what are the base and height of the sail?

56. The base of a triangular garden is 2 meters more than five times its height. The garden covers 260 square meters of ground.

   a. Write an expression for the area of the garden.

   b. What do the base and height of the garden measure?

57. A loading ramp is to be built from the ground to the loading dock. The cross-section of the ramp is a right triangle, with a base that is 6 feet more than the height and a hypotenuse that is 12 feet more than the height. Use the Pythagorean theorem to write a polynomial equation. Find the height, base, and hypotenuse of the ramp.

58. Marge and Gretchen are cutting out right triangles for a quilt they are making. The instructions call for the height of the triangles to be $\frac{3}{4}$ of the base, and the hypotenuse to be $\frac{1}{2}$ inch longer than the base. Write a polynomial equation. Find the lengths of the three sides of the triangles.

59. Claims adjusters are concerned with establishing who was at fault at an accident. To help them, they use skid marks to determine the speed of the vehicles. The formula used is

$$V^2 = 30FS,$$

where V is the velocity of the vehicle (in miles per hour), F is the coefficient of friction of the road in decimal form, and S is the skid length. Write an equation involving velocity if a car skidded 243 feet and the coefficient of friction of the road was 40%. What was the velocity of the vehicle?

60. Using the formula from exercise 59, write an equation for the velocity of a car that skidded 250 feet when the coefficient of friction of the road was 27%. What was the velocity of the car?

Experiencing Algebra the Calculator Way

When a polynomial equation does not factor easily, try solving it by graphing the left and right sides of the polynomial equation and finding the intersection points. The following are polynomials that can be factored but which might better be solved by graphing. First, see if you can factor, and if you cannot, try graphing to find the solution. Start with the standard window (Zoom 6) and then use the zoom-out and zoom-in features of the calculator to find the intersection points.

1. $x^2 - 133x + 4350 = 0$ 2. $12x^2 - 12x - 3672 = 0$ 3. $x^2 + 250x + 15625 = 0$ 4. $x^2 - 186x + 8649 = 0$

Experiment with very large ranges of window values for both Xmin and Xmax and Ymin and Ymax to graphically solve the next equation.

5. $13x^2 + 195x = 377x + 5655$

6. Some of the equations had a double root as a solution. What did you notice about the graph when this happened?

Experiencing Algebra the Group Way

Sometimes you can simplify a polynomial equation by substituting another variable for an expression in the equation. An example follows.

1. $(x + 3)^2 + 10(x + 3) + 25 = 0$
   Let $x + 3 = y$, yielding $y^2 + 10y + 25 = 0$, which factors into $(y + 5)^2 = 0$. Therefore, $y = -5$, and replacing y by $x + 3$, $x + 3 = -5$, which finally yields $x = -8$ as the solution of the original equation.

For the following exercises, each member of the group should try replacing the parenthetical expression with a single variable, factor and solve, and then replace the single variable with its parenthetical expression.

2. $(x - 4)^2 - 14(x - 4) + 49 = 0$ **3.** $2(a + 7)^2 + 11(a + 7) - 40 = 0$ **4.** $9(2b + 3)^2 - 64 = 0$

Share your solutions and agree on the correct results.

Experiencing Algebra the Write Way

In solving the equation

$$a^2 - 9a = 0,$$

Chantel factored the left side, used the zero factor property, and stated that the solutions of the equation were $a = 0$ and $a = 9$. On the other hand, Holly just divided both sides of the equation by a, and solved the resulting equation to get only one solution, $a = 9$. Which do you think is the correct way to solve the equation? Explain.

11.3 Solving Quadratic Equations Using Square Roots

Objectives

1 Simplify square-root expressions using the product rule for square roots.

2 Simplify square-root expressions using the quotient rule for square roots.

3 Solve quadratic equations in one variable algebraically using the principle of square roots.

4 Model real-world situations using quadratic equations and solve using the principle of square roots.

Application

According to annual reports of the Hearst Corporation from 1990 through 1995, the annual sales in millions of dollars may be approximated by the function $S(x) = 28x^2 + 2000$, where x is the number of years since 1991. Approximate when the chairman can predict sales to reach $2500 million.

After completing this section, we will discuss this application further. See page 833.

In the previous section, some quadratic equations had solutions that we could not determine by using the process of factoring. Therefore, we need to determine another algebraic method to find these solutions.

Before we begin, we need to review our definition of a square-root expression. A **square-root expression** is an expression in the form $\sqrt{a}$, where the symbol $\sqrt{}$ is called a **radical** and a is the **radicand**. For example, $\sqrt{36}$ is a numeric square root with a radicand of 36.

In Chapter 2, we evaluated square-root expressions with numerical radicands. That is, we determined a number whose square is the radicand. For example, evaluate $\sqrt{36}$.

Since both $(6)^2 = 36$ and $(-6)^2 = 36$, we need to distinguish between the two possible values, 6 and -6. We define $\sqrt{a}$ as the **principal square root** and $-\sqrt{a}$ as the **negative square root**. That is, $\sqrt{a}$ will always be a positive number and $-\sqrt{a}$ will always be a negative number. Therefore, $\sqrt{36} = 6$ because $(6)^2 = 36$, and $-\sqrt{36} = -6$ because $(-6)^2 = 36$.

Evaluating Square-Root Expressions
To evaluate a principal square root, $\sqrt{c^2} = |c|$.
To evaluate a negative square root, $-\sqrt{c^2} = -|c|$.

```
√(5)
         2.236067977
```

Figure 11.6

If the radicand cannot be written as the square of a number, we approximate the answer. We use the calculator to do this. For example, evaluate $\sqrt{5}$.

According to the results in Figure 11.6, $\sqrt{5} \approx 2.236$.

Also, remember that the radicand of a square root cannot be a negative number because there is no real number whose square is negative. For example, $\sqrt{-36}$ is not a real number.

---

1 Simplifying Square Roots Using the Product Rule

In earlier chapters, we also defined a square root as an exponential expression with an exponent of $\frac{1}{2}$. For example, $\sqrt{36} = 36^{1/2}$. Since square-root expressions are equivalent to rational exponential expressions, some properties of radicals correspond to properties of exponents. To see one of these properties, complete the following set of exercises.

DISCOVERY 9

Multiplication of Square Roots
Evaluate each expression on your calculator and compare the results obtained in the first column to the corresponding results in the second column.

1. a. $\sqrt{3} \cdot \sqrt{7} \approx$ ____   b. $\sqrt{21} \approx$ ____
2. a. $\sqrt{2} \cdot \sqrt{3} \approx$ ____   b. $\sqrt{6} \approx$ ____

Write a rule for multiplication of square roots.

The value of the expression in the first column is equivalent to the expression in the second column. The first value is the product of square roots. The second value is the square root of the product of the radicands in the first expression. Therefore, to multiply square roots, we multiply the radicands and then take the square root of the product.

Product Rule for Square Roots
For any real numbers $\sqrt{a}$ and $\sqrt{b}$,
$$\sqrt{a} \cdot \sqrt{b} = \sqrt{a \cdot b}.$$

We can show that this is true if we write the square-root expressions as rational exponential expressions and apply the product to a power rule for exponents. That is, for the exercises in the Discovery we would have the following:
$$\sqrt{3} \cdot \sqrt{7} = 3^{1/2} \cdot 7^{1/2} = (3 \cdot 7)^{1/2} = \sqrt{3 \cdot 7} = \sqrt{21}$$
$$\sqrt{2} \cdot \sqrt{3} = 2^{1/2} \cdot 3^{1/2} = (2 \cdot 3)^{1/2} = \sqrt{2 \cdot 3} = \sqrt{6}$$

In general,
$$\sqrt{a} \cdot \sqrt{b} = a^{1/2} \cdot b^{1/2} = (ab)^{1/2} = \sqrt{ab}.$$

To simplify square roots, we read the product rule from right to left: $\sqrt{ab} = \sqrt{a} \cdot \sqrt{b}$. For example, to simplify a square root, we rewrite the radicand as a product of a perfect square (preferably the largest possible perfect-square factor) and another factor. We then reverse the product rule by writing a product of square roots. Finally, we simplify the perfect square root. For example,

$$\sqrt{24} = \sqrt{4 \cdot 6} = \sqrt{4}\sqrt{6} = \sqrt{2^2}\sqrt{6} = 2\sqrt{6}.$$

EXAMPLE 1   Simplify $\sqrt{48}$ without a calculator. Check the results on your calculator.

Solution

$$\sqrt{48} = \sqrt{16 \cdot 3} = \sqrt{16}\sqrt{3} = 4\sqrt{3} \quad {\scriptstyle 16 = 4^2}$$

Helping Hand If we had not used the largest perfect-square factor, 16, we would need to simplify the expressions twice.

$$\sqrt{48} = \sqrt{4 \cdot 12} = \sqrt{4}\sqrt{12} = 2\sqrt{12} = 2\sqrt{4 \cdot 3} = 2\sqrt{4}\sqrt{3}$$
$$= 2 \cdot 2\sqrt{3} = 4\sqrt{3}$$

To check on your calculator, first evaluate the square-root expression found algebraically and then evaluate the given square-root expression. The results should be the same, as shown in Figure 11.7. ∎

Figure 11.7

Experiencing Algebra the Checkup Way

Simplify exercises 1–3 without using a calculator. Then check the results on your calculator.

1. $\sqrt{98}$ **2.** $\sqrt{3} \cdot \sqrt{12}$ **3.** $\sqrt{5} \cdot \sqrt{60}$

4. Explain the difference between finding the square root of a number and squaring a number.

5. What are the two operations that you can perform using the product rule for square roots?

---

2 Simplifying Square Roots Using the Quotient Rule

Square roots also have a property corresponding to the quotient rule for exponents. To see what it is, complete the following set of exercises.

DISCOVERY 10

Division of Square Roots

Evaluate each expression on your calculator and compare the results obtained in the first column to the corresponding results in the second column.

1. a. $\dfrac{\sqrt{9}}{\sqrt{3}} \approx$ ____   **b.** $\sqrt{3} \approx$ ____

2. a. $\dfrac{\sqrt{6}}{\sqrt{3}} \approx$ ____   **b.** $\sqrt{2} \approx$ ____

Write a rule for division of square roots.

The value of the expression in the first column is equivalent to the expression in the second column. The first value is the quotient of square roots. The second value is the square root of the quotient of the radicands in the first expression. Therefore, to divide square roots, we divide the radicands and then take the square root of the quotient.

> *Quotient Rule for Square Roots*
> For any real numbers $\sqrt{a}$ and $\sqrt{b}$ where $b \neq 0$,
>
> $$\frac{\sqrt{a}}{\sqrt{b}} = \sqrt{\frac{a}{b}}.$$

We can show that this is true if we write the square-root expressions as rational exponential expressions and apply the quotient rule for exponents. That is, for exercise 2 in the Discovery we would have the following:

$$\frac{\sqrt{6}}{\sqrt{3}} = \frac{6^{1/2}}{3^{1/2}} = \left(\frac{6}{3}\right)^{1/2} = \sqrt{\frac{6}{3}} = \sqrt{2}$$

For the general rule,

$$\frac{\sqrt{a}}{\sqrt{b}} = \frac{a^{1/2}}{b^{1/2}} = \left(\frac{a}{b}\right)^{1/2} = \sqrt{\frac{a}{b}}.$$

To simplify square roots, we read the quotient rule from right to left: $\sqrt{\frac{a}{b}} = \frac{\sqrt{a}}{\sqrt{b}}$. For example, to evaluate a square root having a fractional radicand, we reverse the quotient rule by writing a quotient of square roots. Then we simplify each square root using the product rule. For example,

$$\sqrt{\frac{5}{36}} = \frac{\sqrt{5}}{\sqrt{36}} = \frac{\sqrt{5}}{6}.$$

We must be careful when writing the final result. If the result is a fraction, it is conventional to write the denominator without radicals. The process of changing the fraction to an equivalent form without a radical denominator is called **rationalizing the denominator**. That is, we make the denominator a rational number.

For example, simplify

$$\sqrt{\frac{36}{5}} = \frac{\sqrt{36}}{\sqrt{5}} = \frac{6}{\sqrt{5}}.$$

To rationalize the denominator, we use the multiplication property of 1. That is, we multiply the numerator and denominator by the same value. We choose a value that results in the denominator having a perfect-square radicand, so that we can simplify it. Since the denominator is $\sqrt{5}$ and we want a perfect-square radicand, we can multiply the denominator by itself: $\sqrt{5}\,\sqrt{5} = \sqrt{25} = 5$. Therefore, rationalizing the denominator results in

$$\frac{6}{\sqrt{5}} = \frac{6}{\sqrt{5}} \cdot \frac{\sqrt{5}}{\sqrt{5}} = \frac{6\sqrt{5}}{5}.$$

EXAMPLE 2 Simplify without a calculator. Rationalize all denominators. Check your results on your calculator.

a. $\sqrt{\dfrac{3}{4}}$ **b.** $\sqrt{\dfrac{48}{50}}$

Solution

a. $\sqrt{\dfrac{3}{4}} = \dfrac{\sqrt{3}}{\sqrt{4}}\ \dfrac{\sqrt{3}}{2}$ 　　　　　　　　　　　　　　Quotient rule

b. $\sqrt{\dfrac{48}{50}} = \dfrac{\sqrt{48}}{\sqrt{50}} = \dfrac{\sqrt{16}\,\sqrt{3}}{\sqrt{25}\,\sqrt{2}} = \dfrac{4\sqrt{3}}{5\sqrt{2}}$ 　　Quotient rule

$\qquad\qquad = \dfrac{4\sqrt{3}}{5\sqrt{2}} \cdot \dfrac{\sqrt{2}}{\sqrt{2}} = \dfrac{4\sqrt{6}}{5\cdot 2}$ 　　Rationalize the denominator.

$\qquad\qquad = \dfrac{4\sqrt{6}}{10} = \dfrac{2\sqrt{6}}{5}$ 　　　　　Simplify.

A second method would be to reduce the fractional radicand before using the quotient rule.

$$\sqrt{\dfrac{48}{50}} = \sqrt{\dfrac{24}{25}} = \dfrac{\sqrt{24}}{\sqrt{25}} = \dfrac{\sqrt{4}\,\sqrt{6}}{\sqrt{25}} = \dfrac{2\sqrt{6}}{5}$$

To check on your calculator, first evaluate the square-root expression found algebraically and then evaluate the given square-root expression. The results should be the same.

a.
```
√(3)/2
          .8660254038
√(3/4)
          .8660254038
```

b.
```
(2√(6))/5
          .9797958971
√(48/50)
          .9797958971
```

■

Experiencing Algebra the Checkup Way

Simplify exercises 1–3 without a calculator. Rationalize all denominators. Check your results on your calculator.

1. $\sqrt{\dfrac{7}{64}}$ 　　　　**2.** $\sqrt{\dfrac{64}{7}}$ 　　　　**3.** $\sqrt{\dfrac{250}{45}}$

4. What does it mean to rationalize the denominator of a quotient?

5. What are the two operations you can perform using the quotient rule for square roots?

---

3 Solving Quadratic Equations Using the Square-Root Principle

We are now ready to determine a second algebraic method to solve a polynomial equation. In the previous section, we determined a solution of an equation such as $x^2 = 9$ by factoring. For example,

$$x^2 = 9$$
$$x^2 - 9 = 0$$
$$(x - 3)(x + 3) = 0$$
$$x - 3 = 0 \qquad \text{or} \qquad x + 3 = 0$$
$$x = 3 \qquad\qquad\qquad x = -3$$

The solutions are 3 and -3. We can write this as ± 3.

Another way to solve $x^2 = 9$ is to determine values for x that can be squared to equal 9. There are two such numbers: 3 and -3.

We are actually taking the square root of both sides of the equation in order to solve for the variable.

$$x^2 = 9$$
$$\sqrt{x^2} = \sqrt{9} \qquad \text{Take the square root of both sides.}$$
$$|x| = 3 \qquad \text{Evaluate.}$$
$$x = 3 \quad \text{or} \quad x = -3 \qquad \text{Solve the absolute value equation.}$$

This may also be written as $x = \pm 3$.

> *Principle of Square Roots*
> For any positive number b, if $a^2 = b$, then $a = \sqrt{b}$ or $a = -\sqrt{b}$.

We can also use this principle of square roots to determine solutions of equations such as $x^2 = 5$, when the squared variable does not equal a perfect square. (We could not solve this equation, $x^2 - 5 = 0$, by factoring over the rational numbers.)

> *Solving a Quadratic Equation Using the Principle of Square Roots*
> To solve a quadratic equation of the form $ax^2 + bx + c = 0$ when $b = 0$, that is, $ax^2 + c = 0$:
>
> • Solve for x^2.
>
> • Apply the principle of square roots.
>
> • Solve the resulting equations.

For example, solve $x^2 = 5$.

$$x = \sqrt{5} \quad \text{or} \quad x = -\sqrt{5}$$

The solutions are $\pm\sqrt{5}$, or approximately ± 2.236.

EXAMPLE 3   Solve and check.

a. $4x^2 - 9 = 0$ **b.** $x^2 = 0$ **c.** $x^2 = -5$
d. $(x + 2)^2 = 9$ **e.** $(x + 3)^2 - 3 = 2$ **f.** $x^2 - 4x + 4 = 5$

Algebraic Solution

a. $4x^2 - 9 = 0$

$$x^2 = \frac{9}{4} \qquad \text{Solve for } x^2.$$

$$x = \sqrt{\frac{9}{4}} \quad \text{or} \quad x = -\sqrt{\frac{9}{4}} \qquad \text{Principle of square roots}$$

$$x = \frac{3}{2} \qquad\qquad x = -\frac{3}{2}$$

Check by substitution.

$$4x^2 - 9 = 0$$

$$4\left(\frac{3}{2}\right)^2 - 9 \,\Big|\, 0$$

$$4\left(\frac{9}{4}\right) - 9$$

$$9 - 9$$

$$0$$

$$4x^2 - 9 = 0$$

$$4\left(-\frac{3}{2}\right)^2 - 9 \,\Big|\, 0$$

$$4\left(\frac{9}{4}\right) - 9$$

$$9 - 9$$

$$0$$

The solutions are $\pm\frac{3}{2}$.

b. $x^2 = 0$

$\quad x = 0$ Principle of square roots

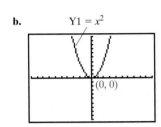

b. Y1 = x^2

(0, 0)

(−10, 10, −10, 10)

The solution is 0, because 0 is neither positive nor negative.
     Check by graphing.
     The solution is 0, the x-coordinate of the x-intercept.

c. $x^2 = -5$

The solution is not a real number, because there is no real number whose square is negative.
     Check by graphing. Let Y1 = x^2 and Y2 = −5.
     The graphs do not intersect. The equation in standard form is $x^2 + 5 = 0$. There is no real-number solution.

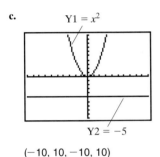

c. Y1 = x^2

Y2 = −5

(−10, 10, −10, 10)

d. This is a variable expression squared.

$$(x + 2)^2 = 9$$

$$x + 2 = \sqrt{9} \quad \text{or} \quad x + 2 = -\sqrt{9} \quad \text{Principle of square roots}$$

$$x + 2 = 3 \qquad\qquad x + 2 = -3$$

$$x = 1 \qquad\qquad\quad x = -5$$

The solutions are 1 and −5.
     The check is left to you.

e. $(x + 3)^2 - 3 = 2$

$$(x + 3)^2 = 5 \qquad\qquad \text{Solve for the squared expression, } (x + 3).$$

$$x + 3 = \sqrt{5} \quad \text{or} \quad x + 3 = -\sqrt{5} \qquad \text{Principle of square roots}$$

$$x = -3 + \sqrt{5} \qquad\qquad x = -3 - \sqrt{5}$$

$$x \approx -0.764 \qquad\qquad\quad x \approx -5.236$$

The solutions are $-3 \pm \sqrt{5}$, or approximately −0.764 and −5.236.
     The check is left for you.

f. The expression on the left is a perfect-square trinomial.

$$x^2 - 4x + 4 = 5$$

$$(x - 2)^2 = 5 \qquad\qquad \text{Factor into a binomial square.}$$

$$x - 2 = \sqrt{5} \quad \text{or} \quad x - 2 = -\sqrt{5} \qquad \text{Principle of square roots}$$

$$x = 2 + \sqrt{5} \qquad\qquad x = 2 - \sqrt{5}$$

$$x \approx 4.236 \qquad\qquad\quad x \approx -0.236$$

The solutions are $2 \pm \sqrt{5}$, or approximately 4.236 and -0.236. The check is left for you. ∎

 Experiencing Algebra the Checkup Way

Solve exercises 1–6 and check.

1. $x^2 = 16$

2. $9x^2 - 25 = 0$

3. $x^2 + 9 = 0$

4. $(x - 4)^2 = 16$

5. $(x - 1)^2 + 5 = 8$

6. $x^2 + 2x + 1 = 6$

7. How can you use the principle of square roots to solve a quadratic equation?

4   Modeling the Real World   The vertical-position equation, $s = -16t^2 + v_0 t + s_0$, can help us determine the height s of an object (in feet) dropped or projected into the air, where t is the time of motion (in seconds), v_0 is the object's initial velocity, and s_0 is its initial position. We can often solve this equation by factoring, but when the term v_0 equals 0, we can also solve this equation by applying the principle of square roots. Physically, this corresponds to an object whose initial speed is 0, meaning that it was dropped from rest.

EXAMPLE 4   Sadie enjoys bungee jumping. Her latest adventure was to free-fall from a 250-foot tower with a 100-foot bungee cord. Using the position equation, determine the length of time Sadie was free-falling on her first drop (before the bungee cord starts to stretch).

Algebraic Solution

The bungee cord starts to stretch after 100 feet. Therefore, Sadie is $250 - 100 = 150$ feet above the ground.

$$s = -16t^2 + v_0 t + s_0 \quad \text{Position equation}$$
$$150 = -16t^2 + 0t + 250 \quad s = 150, v_0 = 0 \text{ (free fall) } s_0 = 250$$
$$150 = -16t^2 + 250 \quad \text{Simplify.}$$
$$150 - 250 = -16t^2 \quad \text{There is no linear term } t. \text{ Solve for } t^2.$$
$$-100 = -16t^2$$
$$\frac{-100}{-16} = t^2$$
$$\frac{25}{4} = t^2$$
$$t = \pm\sqrt{\frac{25}{4}} \quad \text{Principle of square roots}$$
$$t = \frac{5}{2} \quad \text{The negative root is not possible because we are solving for a time.}$$
$$t = 2\frac{1}{2}$$

Sadie was free-falling about $2\frac{1}{2}$ seconds before the bungee cord began to stretch. ∎

EXAMPLE 5   A large boat is towing a smaller boat with a rope that spans 50 feet between hookups. If the rope is attached to the smaller boat at a point 10 feet below the level of attachment to the larger boat (see Figure 11.8), what is the distance between the boats?

Figure 11.8

Algebraic Solution

Let x = the distance between the boats

$$a^2 + b^2 = c^2 \qquad \text{Pythagorean theorem}$$

$$x^2 + 10^2 = 50^2 \qquad \text{Substitute 10 for } b \text{ and 50 for } c.$$

$$x^2 + 100 = 2500 \qquad \text{Simplify.}$$

$$x^2 = 2500 - 100 \qquad \text{Solve for } x^2.$$

$$x^2 = 2400 \qquad \text{Simplify.}$$

$$x = \pm\sqrt{2400} \qquad \text{Principle of square roots}$$

$$x = \sqrt{400 \cdot 6} \qquad \begin{array}{l}\text{Only the positive root is possible because we are}\\ \text{solving for a distance.}\end{array}$$

$$x = 20\sqrt{6} \qquad \text{Simplify.}$$

$$x \approx 48.99$$

The boats are $20\sqrt{6}$ feet apart, or approximately 49 feet. ∎

Application

According to annual reports of the Hearst Corporation from 1990 through 1995, the annual sales in millions of dollars may be approximated by the function $S(x) = 28x^2 + 2000$, where x is the number of years since 1991. Approximate when the chairman can predict sales to reach $2500 million.

Discussion

Let x = years since 1991
   $S(x)$ = annual sales in millions of dollars

$$S(x) = 28x^2 + 2000$$

$$2500 = 28x^2 + 2000 \qquad \text{Substitute 2500 for } S(x).$$

$$500 = 28x^2 \qquad \text{Solve for } x^2.$$

$$\frac{500}{28} = x^2$$

$$\frac{125}{7} = x^2$$

$$\pm\sqrt{\frac{125}{7}} = x \qquad \text{Principle of square roots}$$

$$x = \sqrt{\frac{125}{7}} \approx 4.2 \qquad \text{Use the positive root for predicting years after 1991.}$$

Approximately 4.2 years after 1991, the Hearst Corporation can expect to reach $2500 million in annual sales. This will be in $1991 + 5 = 1996$. (We added 5 years because the report is given annually and $2500 million will be reached after the fourth-year report has been made.) ∎

 Experiencing Algebra the Checkup Way

1. Modern skydivers typically free-fall from 12,000 feet above the ground until 2,500 feet, when they open their parachutes. They can maneuver in free-fall by controlling the position of their bodies. Use the position equation to determine the maximum length of time they would be free-falling.

2. A 3.5-foot metal rod is used to hook a disabled vehicle to a tow truck. The two hookups are separated by a horizontal distance of 2.8 feet. What is the vertical distance between the two hookups?

3. Use the mathematical model for annual sales in millions of dollars, $S(x) = 28x^2 + 2000$, where x is the number of years since 1991, to help the chairman of the Hearst Corporation predict in what year sales will reach $3500 million.

PROBLEM SET 11.3

 Experiencing Algebra the Exercise Way

Simplify without using a calculator. Rationalize all denominators. Check your results on your calculator.

1. $\sqrt{81}$ 2. $\sqrt{64}$ 3. $-\sqrt{100}$ 4. $-\sqrt{121}$

5. $\sqrt{3}\sqrt{27}$ 6. $-\sqrt{2}\sqrt{32}$ 7. $\sqrt{6}\sqrt{21}$ 8. $\sqrt{15}\sqrt{21}$

9. $\sqrt{147}$ 10. $-\sqrt{128}$ 11. $-\sqrt{125}$ 12. $\sqrt{27}$

13. $\sqrt{\dfrac{36}{49}}$ 14. $-\sqrt{\dfrac{25}{64}}$ 15. $\sqrt{\dfrac{11}{144}}$ 16. $\sqrt{\dfrac{7}{25}}$

17. $\sqrt{\dfrac{64}{13}}$ 18. $\sqrt{\dfrac{100}{11}}$ 19. $-\dfrac{\sqrt{28}}{\sqrt{9}}$ 20. $\dfrac{\sqrt{192}}{\sqrt{5}}$

21. $\dfrac{\sqrt{45}}{\sqrt{24}}$ 22. $\dfrac{\sqrt{150}}{\sqrt{56}}$ 23. $-\sqrt{\dfrac{18}{48}}$ 24. $-\sqrt{\dfrac{63}{75}}$

Solve and check.

25. $x^2 = 144$ 26. $x^2 = 121$ 27. $a^2 = 13$ 28. $b^2 = 15$

29. $q^2 = 98$ **30.** $p^2 = 200$ **31.** $2x^2 - 32 = 0$ **32.** $3x^2 - 27 = 0$

33. $4x^2 - 25 = 0$ **34.** $16y^2 - 49 = 0$ **35.** $9x^2 = 2$ **36.** $64x^2 - 1 = 0$

37. $x^2 + 4 = 6$ **38.** $5x^2 + 4 = 11$ **39.** $m^2 + 7 = 5$ **40.** $12 + v^2 = 5$

41. $(x - 5)^2 = 0$ **42.** $(2x - 7)^2 = 0$ **43.** $(z - 7)^2 = 4$ **44.** $(x + 6)^2 = 9$

45. $(4a - 3)^2 = 4$ **46.** $(3b - 5)^2 = 1$ **47.** $x^2 = 1.69$ **48.** $y^2 = 2.89$

49. $(x + 3)^2 - 1 = 3$ **50.** $(x - 6)^2 - 5 = 20$ **51.** $2(m - 4)^2 - 6 = 12$ **52.** $4(n + 9)^2 + 3 = 19$

53. $x^2 + 10x + 25 = 9$ **54.** $x^2 - 14x + 49 = 100$ **55.** $9x^2 - 6x + 1 = 144$ **56.** $25x^2 + 10x + 1 = 64$

57. $(x - 7)^2 - 5 = 1$ **58.** $(x - 12)^2 + 4 = 9$ **59.** $(2x + 1)^2 - 3 = 7$ **60.** $(4x - 5)^2 + 7 = 9$

61. $(x + 3)^2 - 6 = 6$ **62.** $(x - 15)^2 + 6 = 18$

Use the vertical-position equation to solve the following exercises.

63. A water balloon is dropped from a 400-foot tower. How long will it take for the balloon to reach the ground?

64. A brick falls from the top ledge of a building that is 576 feet tall. How long will it take for the brick to reach the ground?

65. How long will it take a skydiver to descend from 12,000 feet to 5,000 feet?

66. How long will it take a skydiver to descend from 11,000 feet to 3,500 feet?

Use the Pythagorean theorem to solve exercises 67–72.

67. A wheelchair ramp has a length of 61 inches. The horizontal distance of the ramp measures 60 inches. What is the vertical distance of the ramp?

68. Trent's kite is flying on 82 feet of string. His dad is standing directly below the kite and is 18 feet away from Trent. How high is the kite?

69. A traffic-control helicopter uses radar to determine that a car on a straight highway is 5000 feet away. The helicopter is 3000 feet above the highway. How far along the ground is the car from the helicopter?

70. A wire supporting a radio tower is attached to the top of the tower and to the ground. The wire is 130 meters long and it is attached to the ground 50 meters from the base of the tower. How tall is the tower?

71. The gable end of a roof is a right triangle with a span of 50 feet. The distance from the peak of the roof to either eave is the same. Find this distance.

x ft   x ft

50 ft

72. The diagonal of a square is 20 cm long. What is the perimeter of the square?

73. A company compiled data on its salespeople. The data were used to relate a salesperson's travel cost to the number of accounts handled. The mathematical model developed from the data estimated annual travel cost as $C(x) = 0.044x^2 + 4700$, where x is the number of accounts the salesperson manages. Use the model to estimate the number of accounts a salesperson should have if her annual travel costs are $9000.

74. Use the mathematical model in exercise 73 to estimate the number of accounts a salesperson should have if his annual travel costs are $6000.

Experiencing Algebra the Calculator Way

A popular algebra problem deals with sizes of pizza. In order to double the size (area) of a pizza, you must increase its diameter by a factor of $\sqrt{2}$; $d_2 = \sqrt{2}\, d_1$, where d_2 is the diameter of the pizza with doubled area and d_1 is the diameter of the original pizza. Thus, a pizza that is about twice as large as a 5-inch pizza will be 7 inches in diameter. With this in mind, complete the following table, rounding answers to the nearest inch.

Original Pizza Diameter	Twice-as-Large Pizza Diameter
5 inches	7 inches
6 inches	
7 inches	
8 inches	
9 inches	
10 inches	
11 inches	
12 inches	

Take the table with you the next time you go out for pizza, and use it for price comparisons!

Experiencing Algebra the Group Way

Sometimes you can factor a polynomial equation using radicals. As an example, the binomial $x^2 - 2$ can be thought of as the difference of x^2 and $(\sqrt{2})^2$, and can be factored into $(x - \sqrt{2})(x + \sqrt{2})$, using the rule for the difference of two squares. Discuss how to solve the following equations using this technique. Then have each member of the group solve the equations this way, and compare your results.

1. $(x - \sqrt{2})(x + \sqrt{2}) = 0$ **2.** $x^2 - 11 = 0$ **3.** $(x - 2\sqrt{3})(x + 2\sqrt{3}) = 0$

4. $x^2 - 18 = 0$ **5.** $2x(x^2 - 3) - 8(x^2 - 3) = 0$ **6.** $2x^3 - 9x^2 - 10x + 45 = 0$

Experiencing Algebra the Write Way

1. Rationalize the expression $\frac{7}{\sqrt{2}}$. Without using your calculator, do you know what a decimal approximation for $\sqrt{2}$ is? It is approximately equal to 1.414. If you had to evaluate the given expression without using your calculator, and using the decimal approximation given here, would you prefer to evaluate the given expression, or the expression after you rationalized it? Which would be easier to do with pencil and paper? Why? Without using your calculator, find a decimal approximation.

2. Suppose you wanted to add two expressions, $\frac{7}{\sqrt{2}}$ and $\frac{1}{\sqrt{3}}$. Rationalize each of these expressions. Which would be easier to add—the original expressions or the rationalized expressions? Give your reasons why. Can you write an exact expression for the sum?

11.4 Solving Quadratic Equations by Completing the Square

Objectives

1 Complete perfect-square trinomials.

2 Solve quadratic equations by completing the square.

3 Model real-world situations using quadratic equations and solve by completing the square.

Application

Publix Supermarkets, Inc., reports that annual sales have increased since 1986. A function to approximate annual sales in millions of dollars is $S(x) = 36x^2 + 288x + 4040$, where x is the number of years after 1986. In what year did annual sales reach $8000 million?

After completing this section, we will discuss this application further. See page 842.

1 Completing Perfect-Square Trinomials

As long as a variable expression is a perfect-square trinomial, which can be written as a binomial square, we can solve an equation using the principle of square roots. However, we may have an equation such as $x^2 + 6x = 2$ that has a variable expression, $x^2 + 6x$, that is not a perfect-square trinomial. We need to develop a method that will enable us to write an equivalent equation with a perfect-square trinomial.

First, we need to remember that a perfect-square trinomial is in the form $a^2 + 2ab + b^2$. Therefore, using this form to write a trinomial square in terms of x, substitute x for a.

$$a^2 + 2ab + b^2$$
$$x^2 + 2xb + b^2 \quad \text{Substitute } x \text{ for } a.$$
$$\text{or} \quad x^2 + 2bx + b^2 \quad \text{Rewrite the term } 2xb.$$

The coefficient of x is $2b$. Therefore, to determine a value for b we divide the coefficient of x by 2. Once we have the value for b, we square it and add it to the trinomial to make the trinomial a perfect square.

Using the expression $x^2 + 6x$ as an example, we can determine a value for b and then complete a perfect-square trinomial by adding to this expression a value for b^2.

$$6 = 2b \quad \text{The coefficient of } x, 6, \text{ is equal to } 2b.$$

$$\frac{6}{2} = \frac{2b}{2}$$

$$3 = b$$

Since $b = 3$, $b^2 = 3^2 = 9$. We need to add 9 to the expression $x^2 + 6x$ to obtain a perfect-square trinomial.

$$x^2 + 2bx + b^2 = x^2 + 2(3)(x) + 9$$
$$= x^2 + 6x + 9$$
$$= (x + 3)^2$$

EXAMPLE 1 Determine what value must be added to each of the following expressions to obtain a trinomial square.

    a. $x^2 - 3x$ **b.** $x^2 + \dfrac{2}{3}x$

Solution

    a. $x^2 - 3x$

The coefficient of x is -3. Dividing -3 by 2, we obtain a value for b, $\frac{-3}{2}$. Therefore, $b^2 = \left(\frac{-3}{2}\right)^2 = \frac{9}{4}$. We need to add $\frac{9}{4}$ to the expression to obtain a trinomial square: $x^2 - 3x + \frac{9}{4}$ or $\left(x - \frac{3}{2}\right)^2$.

    b. $x^2 + \dfrac{2}{3}x$

The coefficient of x is $\frac{2}{3}$. Dividing by 2 (or multiplying by $\frac{1}{2}$), we obtain a value for b, $\frac{2}{3} \cdot \frac{1}{2} = \frac{1}{3}$. Therefore, $b^2 = \left(\frac{1}{3}\right)^2 = \frac{1}{9}$. We need to add $\frac{1}{9}$ to the expression to obtain a trinomial square: $x^2 + \frac{2}{3}x + \frac{1}{9}$ or $\left(x + \frac{1}{3}\right)^2$. ∎

Experiencing Algebra the Checkup Way

In exercises 1–3, determine what value must be added to each expression to obtain a perfect square trinomial.

1. $x^2 + 8x$ **2.** $x^2 - 7x$ **3.** $x^2 - \dfrac{4}{5}x$

4. Explain what is meant by a perfect square trinomial.

2 Solving Quadratic Equations by Completing the Square

Now we are ready to solve the equation we introduced at the beginning of this section, $x^2 + 6x = 2$. To do this we will use a process called completing the square. **Completing the square** is a procedure used to determine a solution of an equation by rewriting the equation as a trinomial square equal to a rational number. For example, solve $x^2 + 6x = 2$ by completing the square.

$$x^2 + 6x = 2$$
$$x^2 + 6x + 9 = 2 + 9$$

Add 9 to both sides because that is the value for b^2 needed to complete the trinomial square on the left side of the equation.

$$(x + 3)^2 = 11$$

Rewrite the trinomial square as a binomial square.

$$x + 3 = \sqrt{11} \quad \text{or} \quad x + 3 = -\sqrt{11}$$

Principle of square roots

$$x = -3 + \sqrt{11} \qquad x = -3 - \sqrt{11}$$
$$x \approx 0.317 \qquad x \approx -6.317$$

The solutions are $-3 \pm \sqrt{11}$, or approximately 0.317 and -6.317.

Solving a Quadratic Equation by Completing the Square
To solve a quadratic equation by completing the square:

- Isolate the variable terms on one side of the equation.
- Divide both sides of the equation by the coefficient of x^2. (This is not needed if the coefficient is 1.)
- Determine the value needed to complete the square by dividing the coefficient of x by 2 and squaring the result.
- Add the value obtained to both sides of the equation.
- Rewrite the trinomial as a binomial square.
- Use the principle of square roots to determine the possible solutions and solve.

For example,

$$x^2 - 2x - 35 = 0$$
$$x^2 - 2x = 35$$

Isolate the variable terms.

$$x^2 - 2x + 1 = 35 + 1$$

Add the value needed to complete the square: $\left(\frac{-2}{2}\right)^2 = (-1)^2 = 1$.

$$(x - 1)^2 = 36$$

Binomial square

$$x - 1 = \sqrt{36} \quad \text{or} \quad x - 1 = -\sqrt{36}$$

Principle of square roots

$$x - 1 = 6 \qquad x - 1 = -6$$
$$x = 7 \qquad x = -5$$

The solutions are 7 and -5.

EXAMPLE 2   Solve and check.

a. $x^2 - 5x + 2 = 5$ **b.** $x^2 + 4x + 6 = 2$
c. $x^2 + x + 2 = 0$ **d.** $3x^2 + 7x - 8 = 0$

Algebraic Solution

a. $x^2 - 5x + 2 = 5$
$$x^2 - 5x = 3$$

Isolate the variable terms.

$$x^2 - 5x + \frac{25}{4} = 3 + \frac{25}{4}$$

Add the value needed to complete the square: $\left(-\frac{5}{2}\right)^2 = \frac{25}{4}$.

$$\left(x - \frac{5}{2}\right)^2 = \frac{37}{4}$$

Binomial square

$$x - \frac{5}{2} = \sqrt{\frac{37}{4}} \quad \text{or} \quad x - \frac{5}{2} = -\sqrt{\frac{37}{4}}$$

Principle of square roots

$$x - \frac{5}{2} = \frac{\sqrt{37}}{2} \qquad x - \frac{5}{2} = -\frac{\sqrt{37}}{2}$$

$$x = \frac{5}{2} + \frac{\sqrt{37}}{2} \qquad x = \frac{5}{2} - \frac{\sqrt{37}}{2}$$

$$x = \frac{5 + \sqrt{37}}{2} \qquad x = \frac{5 - \sqrt{37}}{2}$$

$$x \approx 5.541 \qquad x \approx -0.541$$

Y2 = 5   Y1 = $x^2 - 5x + 2$

$(-0.541, 5)$

$(5.541, 5)$

$(-10, 10, -10, 10)$

Check by substitution on your calculator. When the solutions are substituted for the variable, the expression equals 5, the expression on the right.

The solutions are $\frac{5 \pm \sqrt{37}}{2}$, or approximately 5.541 and −0.541.

Solve by graphing. Let Y1 = $x^2 - 5x + 2$ and Y2 = 5.

The solutions are approximately 5.541 and −0.541.

b. $x^2 + 4x + 6 = 2$

$$x^2 + 4x = -4$$ Isolate the variable terms.

$$x^2 + 4x + 4 = -4 + 4$$ Add the value needed to complete the square: $\left(\frac{4}{2}\right)^2 = 2^2 = 4$.

$$(x + 2)^2 = 0$$ Binomial square

$$x + 2 = 0$$ Principle of square roots

$$x = -2$$ Only one root equals 0.

The solution is −2 (a double root).

The check is left for you.

c. $x^2 + x + 2 = 0$

$$x^2 + x = -2$$ Isolate the variable terms.

$$x^2 + x + \frac{1}{4} = -2 + \frac{1}{4}$$ Add the value needed to complete the square: $\left(\frac{1}{2}\right)^2 = \frac{1}{4}$.

$$\left(x + \frac{1}{2}\right)^2 = -\frac{7}{4}$$

The solution is not a real number, because there is no real number whose square is negative.

d. $3x^2 + 7x - 8 = 0$

$$3x^2 + 7x = 8$$ Isolate the variable terms.

$$x^2 + \frac{7}{3}x = \frac{8}{3}$$ Divide by the coefficient of x^2.

$$x^2 + \frac{7}{3}x + \frac{49}{36} = \frac{8}{3} + \frac{49}{36}$$

Add the value needed to complete the square: $\left(\frac{7}{3} \cdot \frac{1}{2}\right)^2 = \left(\frac{7}{6}\right)^2 = \frac{49}{36}$.

$$\left(x + \frac{7}{6}\right)^2 = \frac{145}{36}$$

Binomial square

$$x + \frac{7}{6} = \sqrt{\frac{145}{36}} \quad \text{or} \quad x + \frac{7}{6} = -\sqrt{\frac{145}{36}}$$

Principle of square roots

$$x + \frac{7}{6} = \frac{\sqrt{145}}{6} \qquad x + \frac{7}{6} = -\frac{\sqrt{145}}{6}$$

$$x = -\frac{7}{6} + \frac{\sqrt{145}}{6} \qquad x = -\frac{7}{6} - \frac{\sqrt{145}}{6}$$

$$x = \frac{-7 + \sqrt{145}}{6} \qquad x = \frac{-7 - \sqrt{145}}{6}$$

$$x \approx 0.840 \qquad x \approx -3.174$$

```
(-7+√(145))/6→X:
3X²+7X-8
                  0
(-7-√(145))/6→X:
3X²+7X-8
              -2E-12
```

The solutions are $\frac{-7 \pm \sqrt{145}}{6}$, or approximately 0.840 and −3.174.

Note: The calculator checks of the solutions give values of 0 and −2E−12 (or −0.000000000002). The number −2E−12 is very close to 0, the expression on the right. ∎

Experiencing Algebra the Checkup Way

Solve exercises 1–5 by completing the square.

1. $x^2 + 8x = 2$ **2.** $5x^2 - 4x = 5$ **3.** $x^2 - x + 5 = 0$

4. $2x^2 + 3x = 9$ **5.** $x^2 - 16x = -64$

6. In order to use the method of completing the square to solve a quadratic equation, what must be true for the coefficient of the squared term? Is it always possible to write an equivalent equation that meets this condition? Explain.

---

3 Modeling the Real World

Completing the square is a very good general method for solving quadratic equations. It works with equations that can't be factored or with those that can be factored. Remember that when using the method of completing the square, you should always start by isolating the terms with the variable.

EXAMPLE 3

Go Away travel agency is preparing a special sale. The usual cost of a ticket is $150. The agency needs to collect $1000 to break even on the event. The agency wants to offer a special plan by reducing the ticket cost. If they advertise a reduction of $1 per person purchasing a ticket, determine the number of people that need to purchase this special offer so that the travel agency will break even.

Algebraic Solution

Let x = number of people purchasing tickets

       $150 - x$ = cost per ticket

The amount the agency will collect is the product of the number of people purchasing a ticket and the cost per ticket.

$$x(150 - x) = 1000$$

$$150x - x^2 = 1000$$

$$x^2 - 150x = -1000 \qquad \text{Divide both sides by } -1.$$

$$x^2 - 150x + (75)^2 = -1000 + (75)^2 \quad \text{Add } \left(\frac{150}{2}\right)^2 = (75)^2 \text{ to both sides.}$$

$$(x - 75)^2 = 4625$$

$$x = 75 \pm \sqrt{4625} = 75 \pm \sqrt{25 \cdot 185} = 75 \pm 5\sqrt{185}$$

$$x \approx 6.99 \quad \text{or} \quad x \approx 143.00$$

The agency will break even when 7 or 143 people purchase tickets. It is unlikely that the agency will sell tickets for $150 − $143 or $7 each. The logical answer is that they need to sell 7 tickets. (They most likely will limit the discount so that the cost does not fall below a certain number of dollars.) ∎

Application Publix Supermarkets, Inc., reports that annual sales have increased since 1986. A function to approximate annual sales in millions of dollars is $S(x) = 36x^2 + 288x + 4040$, where x is the number of years after 1986. In what year did annual sales reach $8000 million?

Discussion

Let $x = $ number of years after 1986
$S(x) = $ annual sales in million dollars

$$S(x) = 36x^2 + 288x + 4040$$

$$8000 = 36x^2 + 288x + 4040 \qquad \text{Substitute 8000 for } S(x).$$

$$3960 = 36x^2 + 288x \qquad \text{Subtract 4040 from both sides.}$$

$$110 = x^2 + 8x \qquad \text{Divide both sides by the leading coefficient, 36.}$$

$$110 + 16 = x^2 + 8x + 16 \qquad \text{Add } \left(\frac{8}{2}\right)^2 = 16 \text{ to both sides.}$$

$$126 = (x + 4)^2$$

$$\pm\sqrt{126} = x + 4$$

$$x = -4 \pm \sqrt{126}$$

$$x = -4 + \sqrt{126} \approx 7.2 \qquad \text{Use the positive root value.}$$

Annual sales for Publix Supermarkets reached $8000 million 7.2 years after 1986, or 1986 + 8 = 1994. (Remember to round up to the next year for any fractional part of the year.) ∎

✓ Experiencing Algebra the Checkup Way

1. A retailer advertises an item for $60 each. If more than one item is purchased, the price is reduced by $2 times the number of items purchased. The discount applies only if the total sale is $200 or more after the discount. The minimum price that the items can be sold for is $35 each. Find the number of items you should buy if you want the total purchase to be as close as possible to $200 without going under, so that the discount applies.

2. The demand for a product is changing because of a change in its unit price. A statistical study has determined that for a fairly wide price range, the demand $D(x)$ for the product can be approximated by $D(x) = 5x^2 - 156x + 1330$, where x represents the price per unit. Assume that the price can be set to any dollar amount up to $10 per item. For what price x, to the nearest dollar, will the demand for the product be 900 units?

PROBLEM SET 11.4

Experiencing Algebra the Exercise Way

Determine what value must be added to each expression to obtain a trinomial square.

1. $x^2 + 6x$

2. $x^2 - 8x$

3. $x^2 - 3x$

4. $x^2 + 3x$

5. $x^2 + \frac{3}{4}x$

6. $x^2 + \frac{3}{5}x$

7. $x^2 + x$

8. $x^2 - x$

9. $x^2 - 6x$

10. $x^2 + 8x$

11. $x^2 + 9x$

12. $x^2 - 5x$

13. $x^2 + \frac{8}{9}x$

14. $x^2 + \frac{6}{7}x$

15. $x^2 - 14x$

16. $x^2 + 10x$

Solve by completing the square.

17. $x^2 + 6x - 20 = 35$

18. $x^2 - 8x - 25 = 40$

19. $x^2 - 3x = 28$

20. $x^2 + 3x = 40$

21. $x^2 + \frac{4}{7}x + \frac{3}{49} = 0$

22. $x^2 + \frac{6}{5}x + \frac{8}{25} = 0$

23. $x^2 + x - 30 = 60$

24. $x^2 - x - 16 = 40$

25. $x^2 - 6x = 2$

26. $x^2 + 8x = 5$

27. $x^2 + 9x = 1$

28. $x^2 - 5x = 2$

29. $x^2 + \frac{8}{9}x = 2$

30. $x^2 + \frac{6}{7}x = 1$

31. $x^2 - x - 5 = 0$

32. $x^2 + x - 10 = 0$

33. $x^2 + x + 10 = 0$

34. $x^2 - x + 6 = 0$

35. $2x^2 + 6x - 1 = 0$

36. $4x^2 + 12x - 3 = 0$

37. $3x^2 + x - 7 = 0$

38. $5x^2 + 2x - 3 = 0$

39. $x^2 - 14x + 55 = 6$

40. $x^2 + 10x + 35 = 10$

41. $4x^2 - 20x + 30 = 5$

42. $9x^2 + 12x + 10 = 6$

43. $\frac{1}{2}x^2 + 5x - 2 = 0$

44. $\frac{1}{3}x^2 - 2x + 1 = 0$

45. $\frac{1}{3}x^2 + \frac{1}{9}x - \frac{1}{6} = 0$

46. $\frac{1}{2}x^2 - \frac{1}{6}x - \frac{3}{4} = 0$

47. $\frac{2}{3}x^2 - 2x - \frac{5}{6} = 0$

48. $\frac{3}{5}x^2 - 6x - \frac{9}{10} = 0$

Determine a quadratic equation for each situation, and solve the equation by completing the square.

49. Model cars sell for $20 each. To encourage sales, a discount is given so that the price is reduced by $1 times the number of cars purchased. How many cars can be purchased for a total cost of $75? The dealer does not intend to sell model cars for less than $12 each.

50. To discourage customers from hoarding Bean Buddies the local store sells them for $5 each, but adds a surcharge of 50 cents times the number of dolls purchased to the price of each doll. (A purchase of one doll costs $5.50, a purchase of two dolls costs $6.00 each, a purchase of three dolls costs $6.50 each, and so on.) Write a quadratic function for the cost of purchasing x dolls. How many Bean Buddies can be purchased for a total cost of $100?

51. The demand for a product is related to its price, x, by the polynomial function $D(x) = \frac{1}{3}x^2 - 64x + 3100$, where x is any price up to $50. At what value should the price be set in order to have a demand of 2000 units for the product? Round your answer to the nearest dollar.

52. Using the same demand function as in exercise 51, at what value should the price be set in order to have a demand of 1000 units for the product? Round your answer to the nearest dollar.

53. A large construction company studied the relationship between the size of a bid, x (in millions of dollars), and the cost to the company for preparing the bid, $C(x)$ (in thousands of dollars). A statistical analysis yielded the mathematical model $C(x) = 0.11x^2 + 3.08x + 11$. If the company spends $55,000 to prepare a bid, what should be the approximate size of the contract?

54. Using the same relationship as in exercise 53, what should be the approximate size of a contract if the cost of preparing the bid is $40,000?

55. The length of a rectangle is 4 inches more than its width. The area of the rectangle is 117 square inches. Find its dimensions.

56. The base of a triangle measures 8 cm more than its height. The area of the triangle is 90 square centimeters. Find the height and base of the triangle.

57. A foundation for a shed is to be rectangular, with a width that is 5 feet less than the length. The area of the foundation is to be approximately 85 square feet. Find the length and width of the foundation to the nearest tenth of a foot.

58. One leg of a right triangle is 8 feet longer than the other leg. The hypotenuse of the triangle is approximately 25 feet long. Find the lengths of the legs of the triangle to the nearest hundredth of a foot.

Use the vertical-position formula, $s = -16t^2 + v_0 t + s_0$, to write and solve a quadratic equation for the following exercises.

59. Starting 16 feet above the ground, a ball is thrown upward with an initial speed of 32 feet per second.

   a. Write a quadratic equation for the time it will take for the ball to reach the ground. (*Note:* Since the ball is thrown upward, the velocity will be positive; if it had been thrown downward, the velocity would be negative.)

   b. Complete the square to find an exact expression for the time it will take for the ball to reach the ground.

   c. Estimate the time to the nearest tenth of a second.

60. From a height of 8 feet, a projectile is fired upward with an initial speed of 88 feet per second.

   a. Write a quadratic equation for the time it will take for the projectile to reach the ground.

   b. Complete the square to find an exact expression for the time it will take for the projectile to reach the ground.

   c. Estimate the time to the nearest tenth of a second.

Experiencing Algebra the Calculator Way

Try to solve the following quadratic equations by completing the square. Then graph the equations by storing the left side in Y1 and the right side in Y2. In some cases you can find a real-number solution of the equation, and in other cases you cannot. Do you see a connection between those for which you cannot find a real-number solution and their graphs? Is there a connection between those for which you can find a real-number solution and their graphs? Now study your solutions obtained by completing the square. Do you see any connection for when you find a rational real-number solution and for when you find an irrational real-number solution?

1. $x^2 + 8x + 15 = 0$ **2.** $x^2 + 4x + 7 = 0$ **3.** $x^2 + x - 1 = 0$

4. $2x^2 + 11x + 12 = 0$ **5.** $2x^2 + 6x + 7 = 0$ **6.** $8x^2 + 8x - 5 = 0$

Experiencing Algebra the Group Way

The method of completing the square also works when the quadratic equation has decimal coefficients. Some of the application exercises in this section resulted in quadratic equations with decimal coefficients. Consider the following equation:

$$x^2 - 3.8x + 3.25 = 0$$

The steps for solving by completing the square are as follows.

Step 1. $x^2 - 3.8x = -3.25$

Step 2. $x^2 - 3.8x + 1.9^2 = -3.25 + 1.9^2$

Step 3. $(x - 1.9)^2 = 0.36$

Step 4. $x - 1.9 = \pm 0.6$

Step 5. $x = 1.9 \pm 0.6$

Step 6. $x = 1.9 + 0.6 = 2.5$ and $x = 1.9 - 0.6 = 1.3$

Each member of the group should use this method to solve the following quadratic equations, which have decimal coefficients. If the constant term is not a perfect square, leave your answers in radical form. Then compare your results and agree on the correct solution.

1. $x^2 - 5.6x + 6.15 = 0$ **2.** $x^2 + 1.4x = 17.15$ **3.** $x^2 + 3.8x + 3.12 = 0$

4. $x^2 + 0.4x = 1.3$ **5.** $x^2 - 0.16x = 2.4$

Experiencing Algebra the Write Way

You have seen that some quadratic equations can be solved by factoring and applying the zero factor property, while others can be solved by completing the square to make a square trinomial. If you are faced with solving a quadratic equation algebraically, discuss which method you would try to apply first, explaining your reasons why. Then discuss a situation in which the factoring method might not be best, where you would need to try completing the square. Finally, discuss when completing the square might not be best. You may wish to illustrate each situation with an example exercise from this section.

11.5 Solving Quadratic Equations Using the Quadratic Formula

Objectives

1 Solve quadratic equations using the quadratic formula.
2 Determine the number and type of solutions of quadratic equations using the discriminant.
3 Model real-world situations using quadratic equations and solve using the quadratic formula.

Application

A United Parcel Service (UPS) annual report on sales shows an increase in sales for the last 10 years of reporting. A function to approximate its sales in millions of dollars is $S(x) = 22x^2 + 1100x + 8800$, where x is the number of years after 1985. Approximate the year UPS will reach $22,500 million in annual sales.

After completing this section, we will discuss this application further. See page 853.

1 Solving Quadratic Equations Using the Quadratic Formula

When we have to repeat a process many times, it often saves time to develop a formula for the process. Therefore, instead of completing the square to solve a quadratic equation, we may want to determine a formula. To do this, we begin with the standard form of a quadratic equation in one variable, $ax^2 + bx + c = 0$, and repeat the process of completing the square, using letters instead of numbers, remembering that a, b, and c represent real numbers.

$$ax^2 + bx + c = 0$$
$$ax^2 + bx = -c \qquad \text{Isolate the variable terms.}$$
$$x^2 + \frac{b}{a}x = \frac{-c}{a} \qquad \text{Divide by the coefficient of } x^2.$$

Determine the value needed to complete the square. Multiply the coefficient of x by $\frac{1}{2}$ and square the result.

$$\frac{b}{a} \cdot \frac{1}{2} = \frac{b}{2a}$$
$$\left(\frac{b}{2a}\right)^2 = \frac{b^2}{4a^2}$$

Add $\dfrac{b^2}{4a^2}$ to both sides.

$$x^2 + \frac{b}{a}x + \frac{b^2}{4a^2} = \frac{-c}{a} + \frac{b^2}{4a^2}$$

Write the left side as a binomial square: $\left(x + \dfrac{b}{2a}\right)^2$. Simplify the right side:

$$\frac{-c}{a} + \frac{b^2}{4a^2} = \frac{-4ac}{4a^2} + \frac{b^2}{4a^2} = \frac{-4ac + b^2}{4a^2} \text{ or } \frac{b^2 - 4ac}{4a^2}.$$

$$\left(x + \frac{b}{2a}\right)^2 = \frac{b^2 - 4ac}{4a^2} \qquad \text{Binomial square.}$$

Use the principle of square roots to determine the solutions.

$$x + \frac{b}{2a} = \pm\sqrt{\frac{b^2 - 4ac}{4a^2}}$$

$$x + \frac{b}{2a} = \pm\frac{\sqrt{b^2 - 4ac}}{2a}$$

$$x = \frac{-b}{2a} \pm \frac{\sqrt{b^2 - 4ac}}{2a}$$

$$x = \frac{-b \pm \sqrt{b^2 - 4ac}}{2a}$$

The **quadratic formula** is usually written in the form $x = \dfrac{-b \pm \sqrt{b^2 - 4ac}}{2a}$.

Be careful when writing this that you write one fraction for the right side of the equation.

We can use this formula to solve any quadratic equation. To do this, first write the quadratic equation in standard form: $ax^2 + bx + c = 0$, with real numbers a, b, and c and $a \neq 0$. Then determine the values to substitute for a, b, and c.

> *Quadratic Formula*
> The quadratic formula used for solving a quadratic equation in standard form, $ax^2 + bx + c = 0$, with real numbers a, b, and c and $a \neq 0$, is
> $$x = \frac{-b \pm \sqrt{b^2 - 4ac}}{2a}.$$

For example, solve $2x^2 + 3x - 5 = 0$ using the quadratic formula.

$$x = \frac{-b \pm \sqrt{b^2 - 4ac}}{2a} \qquad a = 2, b = 3, \text{ and } c = -5$$

$$x = \frac{-3 \pm \sqrt{3^2 - 4(2)(-5)}}{2(2)} \qquad \text{Substitute values for } a, b, \text{ and } c.$$

$$x = \frac{-3 \pm \sqrt{9 + 40}}{4}$$

$$x = \frac{-3 \pm \sqrt{49}}{4}$$

$$x = \frac{-3 \pm 7}{4}$$

$$x = \frac{-3 + 7}{4} \qquad \text{or} \qquad x = \frac{-3 - 7}{4}$$

$$x = \frac{4}{4} \qquad\qquad\qquad x = -\frac{10}{4}$$

$$x = 1 \qquad\qquad\qquad x = -\frac{5}{2}$$

The solutions are 1 and $-\frac{5}{2}$.

Note: These solutions could have been determined by factoring.

EXAMPLE 1 Solve and check.

a. $2x^2 + 3x - 4 = 0$ **b.** $2x^2 + 4x = -2$

c. $2y^2 - 5y + 4 = 0$ **d.** $x^2 + 6x + 1 = 0$

Algebraic Solution

a. $2x^2 + 3x - 4 = 0$

$$x = \frac{-b \pm \sqrt{b^2 - 4ac}}{2a} \qquad a = 2, b = 3, \text{ and } c = -4$$

$$x = \frac{-3 \pm \sqrt{3^2 - 4(2)(-4)}}{2(2)}$$

$$x = \frac{-3 \pm \sqrt{9 + 32}}{4}$$

$$x = \frac{-3 \pm \sqrt{41}}{4}$$

$$x = \frac{-3 + \sqrt{41}}{4} \qquad \text{or} \qquad x = \frac{-3 - \sqrt{41}}{4}$$

$$x \approx 0.851 \qquad\qquad\qquad x \approx -2.351$$

```
(-3+√(41))/4→X:2
X²+3X-4
                0
(-3-√(41))/4→X:2
X²+3X-4
                0
```

```
.851→X:2X²+3X-4
        .001402
-2.351→X:2X²+3X-
4
        .001402
```

The solutions are $\frac{-3 \pm \sqrt{41}}{4}$, or approximately 0.851 and -2.351.
   Note: These solutions could not have been found by factoring. Check by substitution on your calculator.
   If we substitute the approximate solutions, we will not obtain an exact check.

b. $2x^2 + 4x = -2$

$2x^2 + 4x + 2 = 0$ Standard form

$$x = \frac{-b \pm \sqrt{b^2 - 4ac}}{2a} \qquad a = 2, b = 4, \text{ and } c = 2$$

$$x = \frac{-4 \pm \sqrt{4^2 - 4(2)(2)}}{2(2)}$$

$$x = \frac{-4 \pm \sqrt{16 - 16}}{4}$$

$$x = \frac{-4 \pm \sqrt{0}}{4}$$

$$x = \frac{-4}{4}$$

$$x = -1$$

The solution is -1.
   The check is left for you.

c. $2y^2 - 5y + 4 = 0$ This is a quadratic equation in terms of y.

$$y = \frac{-b \pm \sqrt{b^2 - 4ac}}{2a}$$

$$y = \frac{-(-5) \pm \sqrt{(-5)^2 - 4(2)(4)}}{2(2)} \qquad a = 2, b = -5, \text{ and } c = 4$$

$$y = \frac{5 \pm \sqrt{25 - 32}}{4}$$

$$y = \frac{5 \pm \sqrt{-7}}{4}$$

$\sqrt{-7}$ is not a real number. Therefore, the expressions $\frac{5 \pm \sqrt{-7}}{4}$ do not represent real numbers. There is no real-number solution.

d. $x^2 + 6x + 1 = 0$ Standard form

$$x = \frac{-b \pm \sqrt{b^2 - 4ac}}{2a} \qquad a = 1, b = 6, \text{ and } c = 1$$

$$x = \frac{-6 \pm \sqrt{6^2 - 4(1)(1)}}{2(1)}$$

$$x = \frac{-6 \pm \sqrt{36 - 4}}{2}$$

$$x = \frac{-6 \pm \sqrt{32}}{2}$$

$$x = \frac{-6 \pm 4\sqrt{2}}{2}$$

$$x = \frac{-6}{2} \pm \frac{4\sqrt{2}}{2} \qquad\qquad \text{Distributive law}$$

$$x = -3 \pm 2\sqrt{2}$$

The solutions are $-3 \pm 2\sqrt{2}$ or approximately -0.172 and -5.828. The check is left for you. ∎

 Experiencing Algebra the Checkup Way

Solve exercises 1–4 using the quadratic formula and check.

1. $2x^2 + x - 6 = 0$ **2.** $z^2 + z = 7$ **3.** $3(3p^2 - 4p) = -4$ **4.** $3k^2 + 2k + 5 = 3k$

5. The quadratic formula appears to be a single rule, yet sometimes there are two separate solutions, sometimes only one double root, and sometimes no real number. Explain how this is possible.

6. What does the symbol $\pm$ mean?

2 Determining Characteristics of Solutions Using the Discriminant

In previous examples, the solutions of a quadratic equation varied as to the number of solutions (two, one, or none) and the type of solution (rational, irrational, or no real number). At times, it is necessary only to determine the type and number of solutions. For example, if no real-number solution exists, there may not be any reason to attempt to solve the equation. Is there any way to determine the number and kind of solution without solving the equation? See if you can find an answer by completing the following set of exercises using the quadratic formula.

D I S C O V E R Y   1 1

Characteristics of the Quadratic-Formula Solution

In previous examples, we obtained the solutions for the given equations. Determine a value for the radicand, $b^2 - 4ac$, of the quadratic formula.

1. $2x^2 + 3x - 5 = 0$

$x = 1$ or $x = -\dfrac{5}{2}$

(two rational solutions)

$b^2 - 4ac = $ ____

2. $2x^2 + 3x - 4 = 0$

$x = \dfrac{-3 + \sqrt{41}}{4}$ or $x = \dfrac{-3 - \sqrt{41}}{4}$

(two irrational solutions)

$b^2 - 4ac = $ ____

3. $2x^2 + 4x + 2 = 0$

$x = -1$

(one rational solution)

$b^2 - 4ac = $ ____

4. $2y^2 - 5y + 4 = 0$

(no real-number solutions)

$b^2 - 4ac = $ ____

Write a rule to determine the number of and type of solutions of a quadratic equation by using $b^2 - 4ac$.

The radicand, $b^2 - 4ac$, determines the characteristics of the solutions of a quadratic equation. If the radicand is a perfect square ($\neq 0$), there will be two rational-number solutions. If the radicand is 0, there will be one rational-number solution. If the radicand is a positive number that is not a perfect square, then there will be two irrational-number solutions. If the radicand is a negative number, there will be no real-number solutions.

We can understand why this is true if we look at the entire quadratic formula, $x = \dfrac{-b \pm \sqrt{b^2 - 4ac}}{2a}$. The square root simplifies to a positive rational number if the radicand is a perfect square. In the formula, this results in a rational number being added to or subtracted from another rational number and then divided by a second rational number. The result is always two rational numbers.

The square root simplifies to 0 if the radicand is 0. In the formula, this results in 0 being added to or subtracted from another rational number and then divided by a second rational number. The result is always one rational number.

The square root remains if the radicand is a positive number that is not a perfect square. This results in an irrational number being added to or subtracted from a rational number and then divided by a second rational number. The result is always two irrational numbers.

The square root is not defined in the real-number system if the radicand is a negative number. Therefore, we cannot obtain a real-number solution.

We call the radicand, $b^2 - 4ac$, the **discriminant** of the quadratic equation $ax^2 + bx + c = 0$.

Determining the Characteristics of the Solution of a Quadratic Equation Using the Discriminant

Determine the value for the discriminant, $b^2 - 4ac$, for a quadratic equation in standard form, $ax^2 + bx + c = 0$, with rational numbers a, b, and c and $a \neq 0$. One of four possibilities will occur:

Discriminant	Number and Type of Real-Number Solutions
0	One rational-number solution
Perfect square, not equal to 0	Two rational-number solutions
Positive number, not a perfect square	Two irrational-number solutions
Negative number	No real-number solutions

For example, determine the characteristics of the solution of the quadratic equation $3x^2 - 7x + 12 = 0$.

$$b^2 - 4ac = (-7)^2 - 4(3)(12) \qquad a = 3, b = -7, \text{ and } c = 12$$
$$= 49 - 144$$
$$= -95$$

There are no real-number solutions of the equation because the discriminant value is negative.

EXAMPLE 2 Determine the characteristics of the solution of each quadratic equation. Do not solve the equation.

a. $15x^2 + 26x = 12$ **b.** $\dfrac{3}{4}x^2 - \dfrac{2}{3}x + \dfrac{1}{9} = 0$

c. $0.3x^2 - 0.6x + 0.3 = 0$

Solution

a.
$$15x^2 + 26x = 12$$
$$15x^2 + 26x - 12 = 0 \qquad \text{Standard form}$$
$$b^2 - 4ac = (26)^2 - 4(15)(-12) \qquad a = 15, b = 26, \text{ and } c = -12$$
$$= 1396$$

There are two irrational solutions, because 1396 is positive but not a perfect square.

b. $\dfrac{3}{4}x^2 - \dfrac{2}{3}x + \dfrac{1}{9} = 0$

$$b^2 - 4ac = \left(-\dfrac{2}{3}\right)^2 - 4\left(\dfrac{3}{4}\right)\left(\dfrac{1}{9}\right) \qquad a = \tfrac{3}{4}, b = -\tfrac{2}{3}, c = \tfrac{1}{9}$$
$$= \dfrac{1}{9}$$

There are two rational solutions, because $\tfrac{1}{9}$ is a perfect square.

Helping Hand If you prefer not to work with fractions, write an equivalent equation by multiplying by the LCD of 36. The new equivalent equation, $27x^2 - 24x + 4 = 0$ will have a discriminant value of 144, a perfect square as well.

c. $0.3x^2 - 0.6x + 0.3 = 0$

$$b^2 - 4ac = (-0.6)^2 - 4(0.3)(0.3) \quad a = 0.3, b = -0.6, c = 0.3$$
$$= 0$$

There is one rational solution, because the discriminant is 0. ∎

 ## Experiencing Algebra the Checkup Way

In exercises 1–4, determine the characteristics of the solution(s) of each quadratic equation. Do not solve the equation.

1. $0.1x^2 + x + 2.3 = 0$ **2.** $25x^2 - 60x + 36 = 0$ **3.** $3x^2 - 4x = 32$ **4.** $\dfrac{1}{2}x^2 + 3x + 17 = 0$

5. Under what conditions will a quadratic equation have rational numbers as solutions; irrational numbers as solutions; no real-number solutions?

---

3 Modeling the Real World

The compound-interest formula, $A = P(1 + r)^t$, is used to determine the compounded amount A given a principal P at an interest rate per time period r for t time periods. This formula can lead to various polynomial equations, including quadratic equations.

EXAMPLE 3

Due to the bank policy on education savings accounts, at age 18 Tommy must withdraw his education fund of $7,237. He plans to reinvest all of his fund at an annual interest rate such that this money will increase to a total of $8,000 in 2 years. Determine the annual interest rate at which he must reinvest his funds.

Algebraic Solution

Let r = interest rate.

$$A = P(1 + r)^t \qquad \text{Compound-interest formula}$$
$$8000 = 7237(1 + r)^2 \qquad A = 8000, P = 7237, t = 2$$
$$8000 = 7237(1 + 2r + r^2)$$
$$8000 = 7237 + 14{,}474r + 7237r^2$$
$$0 = 7237r^2 + 14{,}474r - 763 \qquad \text{Standard form}$$
$$r = \frac{-b \pm \sqrt{b^2 - 4ac}}{2a} \qquad \text{Quadratic formula}$$
$$r = \frac{-14{,}474 \pm \sqrt{14{,}474^2 - 4(7237)(-763)}}{2(7237)} \qquad \begin{matrix} a = 7237, b = 14{,}474, \\ \text{and } c = -763 \end{matrix}$$
$$r = \frac{-14{,}474 \pm \sqrt{231{,}584{,}000}}{14{,}474}$$
$$r \approx 0.0514 \approx 5.14\%$$

Tommy must reinvest his funds at approximately 5.14%. (Only the positive solution is used. The negative solution is nonapplicable.)

Note that the equation in this example could have also been easily solved using the principle of square roots. ∎

Application

A United Parcel Service (UPS) annual report on sales shows an increase in sales for the last 10 years of reporting. A function to approximate its sales in millions of dollars is $S(x) = 22x^2 + 1100x + 8800$, where x is the number of years after 1985. Approximate the year UPS will reach $22,500 million in annual sales.

Discussion

Let x = number of years after 1985
$S(x)$ = annual sales in millions of dollars

$$S(x) = 22x^2 + 1100x + 8800$$
$$22500 = 22x^2 + 1100x + 8800 \quad \text{Substitute 22500 for } S(x).$$
$$22x^2 + 1100x - 13700 = 0 \quad \text{Standard form}$$
$$x = \frac{-b \pm \sqrt{b^2 - 4ac}}{2a} \quad \text{Quadratic formula}$$
$$x = \frac{-1100 \pm \sqrt{1100^2 - 4(22)(-13700)}}{2(22)}$$
$$x \approx 10.3 \quad \text{or} \quad x \approx -60.3 \quad \text{Evaluate on your calculator.}$$

UPS reached approximately $22,500 million in annual sales 10.3 years after 1985, or $1985 + 11 = 1996$. ∎

Experiencing Algebra the Checkup Way

Set up a quadratic equation to represent each situation, and then use the quadratic formula to solve the equation.

1. Tommy considers investing his money in an aggressive mutual fund instead of in the bank. If he invests the $7,237 that he has on hand for 2 years, what equivalent annual interest rate must he realize in order to have the funds grow to $10,000?

2. Sometimes revenue functions are quadratic expressions. Assume that a manufacturer is supplying a dealer products at wholesale prices. Assume further that the minimum number of items per order is 25. One revenue function might be $R(x) = 3750 + 125x - x^2$, where $x + 25$ items are sold to the dealer at a price of $150 - x$ dollars each. For what values of x will the revenue be $4900? Which of the two solutions appears to be the most reasonable?

PROBLEM SET 11.5

Experiencing Algebra the Exercise Way

Use the quadratic formula to find the exact solution; then check.

1. $x^2 - 12x + 27 = 0$

2. $x^2 - 12x + 35 = 0$

3. $2x^2 + 3x - 15 = 2x + 6$

4. $3x^2 + 3x - 10 = x + 6$

5. $2z^2 + 11z + 5 = 0$

6. $3y^2 + 31y + 36 = 0$

7. $8(2p^2 - p + 1) = 7$

8. $5(5q^2 + 4q + 1) = 1$

9. $x^2 + 3x + 4 = 0$

10. $x^2 + x + 5 = 0$

11. $-5a^2 + 4a - 7 = 0$

12. $-3b^2 + b - 5 = 0$

13. $v^2 - 5v + 2 = 0$

14. $t^2 - 8t + 10 = 0$

15. $x(x - 4) + 1 = 0$

16. $x(x + 6) + 7 = 0$

17. $4x(x + 1) + 6 = 6 - x$

18. $3x(x - 3) - 2 = x - 2$

19. $3d^2 + 10 = 17$

20. $2r^2 + 4 = 19$

21. $16m = m^2 + 55$

22. $72 = -k^2 - 18k$

23. $(x - 4)(x + 4) = 2(x - 4)$

24. $6(x + 3) = (x - 3)(x + 3)$

25. $x^2 - 6.3x + 7.2 = 0$

26. $x^2 + 3.7x + 1.6 = 0$

27. $1.8 - 5.6x - x^2 = 0$

28. $6.2 + 1.8x - x^2 = 0$

29. $a^2 + 24.01 = 9.8a$

30. $b^2 + 14.2b = -50.41$

31. $1.7z^2 + 1.3z + 5.6 = 0$

32. $2.9t^2 - 5.2t + 8.1 = 0$

Evaluate the discriminant to determine the characteristics of the solution(s) of each quadratic equation. Do not solve the equation.

33. $x^2 - 11x + 24 = 0$

34. $x^2 + 8x + 21 = 0$

35. $a^2 + 12a + 36 = 0$

36. $b^2 - 3b - 8 = 0$

37. $z^2 = 4z - 5$

38. $y^2 + 81 = 18y$

39. $6x^2 - 11x - 7 = 0$

40. $5x^2 - 125 = 0$

41. $7p^2 - 15 = 0$

42. $10q^2 - 7q - 12 = 0$

43. $1 - 5x - 4x^2 = 0$

44. $6x - 5 = 3x^2$

45. $6.25z - 2.1 = 2.5z^2$

46. $2.1 - 1.3t - 4.3t^2 = 0$

47. $0.3x - 2.8 = 1.7x^2$

48. $x^2 = 8.6x - 18.49$

Use the compound-interest formula, $A = P(1 + r)^t$, to set up a quadratic equation for the following exercises, then solve the equation using the quadratic formula.

49. At what annual interest rate must $5000 be invested in order for it to compound to $6000 after 2 years?

50. In order for $1200 to grow to $1600 in 2 years, what must be the annual interest rate for the investment?

Solve the following quadratic revenue functions for the variable of interest.

51. The wholesale price of an item is reduced by $1 for each purchase over 50 items, from an initial selling price of $120 each. The revenue function $R(x) = 6000 + 70x - x^2$ represents the dollars received for selling $x + 50$ items, at a price of $120 - x$ dollars each, to a dealer. For what values of x will the revenue be $7125? Which answer appears more reasonable?

52. The wholesale price of an item is reduced by $1 for each purchase over 20 items, from an initial selling price of $200 per item. The revenue function $R(x) = 4000 + 180x - x^2$ represents the dollars received for selling $x + 20$ items, at a price of $200 - x$ dollars each, to a dealer. For what values of x will the revenue be $8500? Which answer appears more reasonable?

53. A statistical study of the consumer price index (CPI) for the years 1950 to 1993 yielded the polynomial function

$$y = 0.086x^2 - 9.34x + 277.78,$$

where y is the CPI (a percentage) and x is the number of years since 1950. Determine the year after 1950 in which the CPI was approximately 100%.

54. Using the function in exercise 53, determine the year after 1950 in which the CPI was approximately 125%.

 Experiencing Algebra the Calculator Way

The quadratic formula may be stored in a program for ease of use. The following program will use the quadratic formula to find the roots of a quadratic equation. To store the program in your calculator, enter the edit mode; press [PRGM] [▶] [▶] to NEW, then [ENTER] . This will place the calculator into a mode so that you can enter a program. At each step, enter in the instructions, and press [ENTER] to move to the next step. If you make a mistake, use the arrow keys to move back and forth and correct the error. Many of the instructions in the program are found by pressing the $\boxed{\text{PRGM}}$ key and using the arrow keys to find the instruction, then pressing the $\boxed{\text{ENTER}}$ key to select the instruction. Enter in the following program.

```
PROGRAM:QUADFORM
ClrHome
Disp "AX²+BX+C=0"
Disp "A=?"
Input A
Disp "B=?"
Input B
Disp "C=?"
Input C
ClrHome
B²-4AC→D
Disp "DISCRIMINANT="
Disp D
Disp "PRESS ENTER"
Pause
(-B/(2A))→R
If D>0
Goto 1
If D<0
Goto 2
Disp "DOUBLE ROOT="
Disp R
Goto 9
Lbl 1
((D)/(2A))→S
(R-S)→U
(R+S)→V
Disp "REAL ROOTS="
Disp U
Disp V
Goto 9
Lbl 2
((-D)/(2A))→S
Disp "IMAG.ROOTS:"
Disp "R+-S*I"
Disp "WHERE R="
Disp R
Disp "AND S="
Disp S
Lbl 9
```

To run the program, press $\boxed{\text{PRGM}}$ *and arrow down to the program with the name QUADFORM, then press* $\boxed{\text{ENTER}}$ $\boxed{\text{ENTER}}$ *to execute the program. The program will prompt you for the values of the coefficients when the equation is placed into standard form. After entering these values, the program will first show the value of the discriminant. When you press* $\boxed{\text{ENTER}}$ *, the program will display the solutions to the equation. If the equation has no real-number solutions, the program displays the solution in another number system, called imaginary numbers, which you may study later. To solve another equation, press* $\boxed{\text{ENTER}}$ *and the program will cycle back to the start. Press* $\boxed{\text{2nd}}$ $\boxed{\text{QUIT}}$ *to exit the program and return to the home screen.*

Use the program to complete the following table. Remember, the equation must be in standard form to determine the values of a, b, and c. When the solution is an irrational number, approximate the solution as a decimal to the nearest thousandth.

	Equation	Value of Discriminant	Types of Roots (Rational, Irrational, Not Real)	Number of Unlike Roots	Roots
1.	$x^2 + 6 = 5x$	1	rational	2	2, 3
2.	$9x^2 + 6x = -1$				
3.	$2x^2 + 1 = 7x$				
4.	$x^2 + 6x = -10$				
5.	$x^2 = 6 - x$				
6.	$5x^2 - 6x = 0$				
7.	$x^2 + 0.36 = 1.2x$				
8.	$1.7x^2 + x + 1.9 = 0$				
9.	$1.5x^2 + 1.2x = 3.6$				
10.	$\frac{1}{4}x^2 + x = \frac{1}{8}$				
11.	$x^2 - \frac{1}{6}x = \frac{1}{6}$				
12.	$\frac{1}{5}x^2 + \frac{2}{3}x = -\frac{7}{8}$				

Experiencing Algebra the Group Way

Although the arithmetic may become more tedious when solving a quadratic equation whose coefficients are fractions, the quadratic formula still applies. You can choose to solve the equation with the fractions, or you may choose to use the least common denominator to first clear the equation of fractions and then apply the quadratic formula.

Divide your group into two sections. Have one section solve the equations with the fractions, and have the other section clear the equations of fractions before solving. After solving the equations, discuss your results. Is it better to clear the fractions before solving the equations?

1. $\frac{5}{6}x^2 - \frac{4}{9}x - \frac{2}{3} = 0$ **2.** $\frac{1}{25}v^2 - \frac{2}{15}v + \frac{1}{9} = 0$ **3.** $\frac{3}{5}x^2 + \frac{5}{9} = \frac{2}{3}x$ **4.** $\frac{1}{4} - \frac{1}{2}x - \frac{1}{9}x^2 = 0$

Experiencing Algebra the Write Way

The term *discriminant* is an important term in this section. It is a derivative of the word *discriminate*. Look up this word in a dictionary and select the definition that most fits the use in this section. Then use the definition to explain why the discriminant is so important to the study of quadratic equations presented here.

11.6   More Real-World Models

Objectives   **1**   Model real-world situations using the Pythagorean theorem.
2   Model real-world situations by recognizing special triangles.
3   Solve formulas for a variable.

Application

East Side Motors is having a tent sale to reduce its year-end inventory. The maintenance workers read the tent installation directions. To install the 9-foot corner support pole, a tie-down rope is needed. The following figure illustrates the correct configuration.

Determine the length of the rope in the diagram.
   After completing this section, we will discuss this application further. See page 862.

We now have four algebraic methods as well as a numeric method and a graphic method to solve quadratic equations in one variable. First, let's review the strengths and weaknesses of these methods.

Method	Strengths	Weaknesses
Numeric	Easy to set up for integer values on a calculator	Time-consuming if completed by hand Will only determine solutions for the input values (usually integers)
Graphic	Easy to set up on a calculator Solution will always be found, if it exists	Appropriate range may be difficult to determine; graph may be hard to read Solution will be rounded for irrational and repeating fraction values
Algebraic	Exact solution will be found, if it exists	Time-consuming at times

After reviewing this list, we may want to rely more heavily on graphic and algebraic methods than on the numeric method. Now let us review the steps to solve a quadratic equation algebraically.

> *Algebraically Solving a Quadratic Equation in One Variable*
> To algebraically solve a quadratic equation in one variable, $ax^2 + bx + c = 0$, select one of the following methods.
>
> - If $b = 0$—that is, if the quadratic equation has no linear (x) term—solve for x^2 and use the principle of square roots to solve.
>
> - Factor $ax^2 + bx + c$ and use the zero factor property to solve, if possible.
>
> - If the quadratic expression will not factor, or is difficult to factor, use the quadratic formula or complete the square to solve.

1 Applying the Pythagorean Theorem

The Pythagorean theorem, $c^2 = a^2 + b^2$, can be used to determine the length of a side of a right triangle when a and b are the lengths of the legs and c is the length of the hypotenuse.

EXAMPLE 1

The Leaning Tower of Pisa is 179 feet tall, but was built on unstable ground. It began to tip while under construction and is now 15 feet out of perpendicular. Use the Pythagorean theorem to determine its present height.

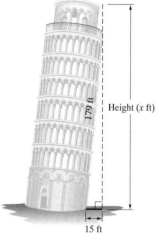

179 ft

Height (x ft)

15 ft

Algebraic Solution

$$a^2 + b^2 = c^2$$
$$(15)^2 + x^2 = (179)^2 \qquad \text{Substitute.}$$
$$x^2 = (179)^2 - (15)^2 \qquad \text{Solve for } x^2.$$
$$x^2 = 31{,}816 \qquad \text{Simplify.}$$
$$x = \pm\sqrt{31{,}816} \qquad \text{Principle of square roots}$$
$$x \approx 178.37 \qquad \text{A negative answer is not possible.}$$

The top of the Leaning Tower of Pisa is approximately 178.37 feet above ground. ∎

EXAMPLE 2

A baseball diamond is a 90-foot square. The batter bunts the ball down the third-base line. The third baseman charges the ball and catches it 40 feet from home plate. Find the distance he must throw the baseball to first base.

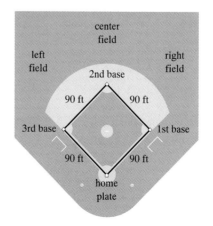

center field

left field

right field

2nd base

90 ft   90 ft

3rd base   1st base

90 ft   90 ft

home plate

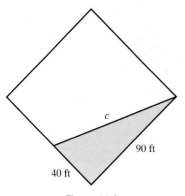

Figure 11.9

Algebraic Solution

Using Figure 11.9, we see that we have a right triangle with a 40-foot leg and a 90-foot leg. We must determine the length of the hypotenuse.

$$a^2 + b^2 = c^2$$
$$40^2 + 90^2 = c^2 \quad \text{Substitute.}$$
$$1600 + 8100 = c^2$$
$$9700 = c^2$$
$$\pm\sqrt{9700} = c \quad \text{Principle of square roots}$$
$$\pm 10\sqrt{97} = c$$

The third baseman must throw the baseball $10\sqrt{97}$ feet, or approximately 98.5 feet, to first base. ∎

EXAMPLE 3   One of the most memorable games in World Series history occurred on October 21, 1975. Carlton Fisk of the Boston Red Sox ended Game 6 at Fenway Park with a 12th inning home run over the wall called the Green Monster. The Green Monster is 315 feet from home plate.

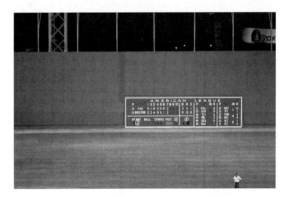

If Carlton hit the baseball at a height of 3 feet and the ball crossed the Green Monster at a point 318 feet away in a straight line from the bat, approximate the height of the ball above the ground as it crossed the wall.

Algebraic Solution

Let $x = $ the height of the ball as it crossed the Green Monster

Using Figure 11.10, we see that we have a right triangle.

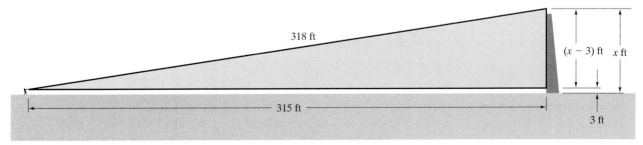

Figure 11.10

$$a^2 + b^2 = c^2$$

$$(x - 3)^2 + 315^2 = 318^2 \qquad \text{Substitute.}$$

$$(x - 3)^2 = 318^2 - 315^2 \qquad \text{Isolate the squared term.}$$

$$(x - 3)^2 = 1899 \qquad \text{Simplify.}$$

$$x - 3 = \pm\sqrt{1899} \qquad \text{Principle of square roots}$$

$$x = \pm\sqrt{1899} + 3$$

$$x \approx 46.6 \qquad \text{A negative solution does not represent a height.}$$

The ball crossed the Green Monster at a height of approximately 46.6 feet.

■

Experiencing Algebra the Checkup Way

1. The cross-section of an attic space atop a building is a right triangle from the peak to the base, where the horizontal distance is three times the height. If the distance from the peak to the eave is 15.8 feet, find the measure of the height and the base to the nearest tenth of a foot.

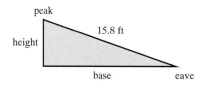

2. A quarterback completes a 22-yard pass to his receiver, who is at the sideline of the field. The quarterback is 15 yards from the sideline when he throws the pass. What is the forward distance of the pass?

3. Does the Pythagorean theorem apply to any triangle with sides measuring a, b, and c? Explain.

---

2 Special Triangles   Now we are ready to apply the Pythagorean theorem to some special triangles. First let's consider an isosceles right triangle. An **isosceles right triangle** has two **congruent** (equal) legs and two congruent (45°) angles opposite the congruent sides.

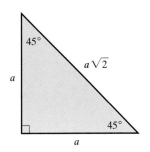

To determine the length of the hypotenuse in terms of the length of the congruent sides, we solve the Pythagorean theorem for c, substituting a for the length of each leg.

$$a^2 + b^2 = c^2$$

$$a^2 + a^2 = c^2 \quad \text{Substitute.}$$

$$2a^2 = c^2 \quad \text{Simplify.}$$

$$\pm\sqrt{2a^2} = c \quad \text{Principle of square roots}$$

$$\pm a\sqrt{2} = c \quad \text{Simplify.}$$

Therefore, the hypotenuse of an isosceles right triangle is $a\sqrt{2}$.

> *Isosceles Right Triangle (45°–45°–90°)*
> The length c of the hypotenuse of an isosceles right triangle is the length a of the congruent leg times $\sqrt{2}$.
>
> $$c = a\sqrt{2}$$

For example, determine the hypotenuse of an isosceles right triangle if the length of each congruent leg is 5 cm.

$$c = a\sqrt{2}$$

$$c = 5\sqrt{2} \quad \text{Substitute.}$$

The hypotenuse is $5\sqrt{2}$ cm, or approximately 7.071 cm.

EXAMPLE 4   Determine the length of each congruent leg of an isosceles right triangle if the hypotenuse is 5 cm.

Algebraic Solution

Substitute 5 for c in the formula and solve for a.

$$c = a\sqrt{2}$$

$$5 = a\sqrt{2} \quad \text{Substitute.}$$

$$\frac{5}{\sqrt{2}} = \frac{a\sqrt{2}}{\sqrt{2}} \quad \text{Divide both sides by } \sqrt{2}.$$

$$\frac{5}{\sqrt{2}} = a \quad \text{Simplify.}$$

$$\frac{5}{\sqrt{2}} \cdot \frac{\sqrt{2}}{\sqrt{2}} = a \quad \text{Rationalize the denominator.}$$

$$\frac{5\sqrt{2}}{2} = a \quad \text{Simplify.}$$

The congruent legs are $\frac{5\sqrt{2}}{2}$ cm, or approximately 3.536 cm. ∎

EXAMPLE 5   A single-engine airplane is flying at a low altitude. The pilot takes a reading on the power lines he is approaching. The angle between the horizontal and the power lines is 45°. The distance reading is 100 feet. If the pilot needs to clear the power lines at a height of 75 feet due to local regulations, will he need to adjust his present course?

Algebraic Solution

Let x = height above power lines

The hypotenuse is 100 feet.

$$c = a\sqrt{2} \qquad c = 100, a = x$$
$$100 = x\sqrt{2}$$
$$\frac{100}{\sqrt{2}} = x$$
$$\frac{100}{\sqrt{2}} \cdot \frac{\sqrt{2}}{\sqrt{2}} = x$$
$$\frac{100\sqrt{2}}{2} = x$$
$$50\sqrt{2} = x$$
$$x \approx 70.71 \text{ feet}$$

The pilot must adjust his altitude in order to clear the power lines at 75 feet.

∎

Application

East Side Motors is having a tent sale to reduce its year-end inventory. The maintenance workers read the tent installation directions. To install the 9-foot corner support pole, a tie-down rope is needed. The following figure illustrates the correct configuration.

Determine the length of the rope in the diagram.

Discussion

The triangle formed is a 45°–45°–90° triangle. The rope length is the hypotenuse, c.

Evaluate the formula $c = a\sqrt{2}$.

$$c = 9\sqrt{2} \qquad \text{Substitute 9 for } a.$$

$$c \approx 12.728$$

The rope in the diagram is $9\sqrt{2}$ feet, or approximately 12.728 feet.

Note: The rope will need additional length to connect to each end. ∎

Now let's consider an equilateral triangle. An **equilateral triangle** has three congruent (equal) sides and three congruent (60°) angles. If we draw an altitude for this triangle, it will bisect an angle and the side opposite the angle. Then we will have two congruent right triangles. The angles will measure 30°–60°–90° and the side opposite the 90° angle will be twice the length of the side opposite the 30° angle.

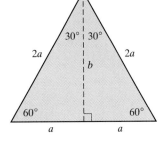

To determine the length of the second leg (the one opposite the 60° angle), we solve the Pythagorean theorem for b, substituting a for the length of the shorter leg and $2a$ for the length of the hypotenuse.

$$a^2 + b^2 = c^2$$
$$a^2 + b^2 = (2a)^2 \qquad \text{Substitute.}$$
$$a^2 + b^2 = 4a^2 \qquad \text{Simplify.}$$
$$b^2 = 4a^2 - a^2 \qquad \text{Subtract } a^2 \text{ from both sides.}$$
$$b^2 = 3a^2 \qquad \text{Simplify.}$$
$$b = \pm\sqrt{3a^2} \qquad \text{Principle of square roots}$$
$$b = \pm a\sqrt{3} \qquad \text{Simplify.}$$

Therefore, the side opposite the 60° angle of a 30°–60°–90° right triangle is $a\sqrt{3}$.

Right Triangle (30°–60°–90°)
The length c of the hypotenuse of a 30°–60°–90° triangle is twice the length a of the shorter side.

$$c = 2a$$

The length b of the longer leg of a 30°–60°–90° triangle is the length a of the shorter leg times $\sqrt{3}$.

$$b = a\sqrt{3}$$

For example, determine the length of the longer leg of a 30°–60°–90° triangle if the shorter leg is 5 inches.

Substitute 5 for a in the formula and solve for b.

$$b = a\sqrt{3}$$
$$b = 5\sqrt{3} \qquad \text{Substitute.}$$

The longer leg is $5\sqrt{3}$ inches, or approximately 8.660 inches.

EXAMPLE 6 Determine the length of the hypotenuse of a 30°–60°–90° triangle if the length of the side opposite the 60° angle is 5 inches.

Algebraic Solution

Use the formula for the longer side, $b = a\sqrt{3}$, substitute 5 for b, and solve for the shorter side, a.

$$b = a\sqrt{3}$$
$$5 = a\sqrt{3} \qquad \text{Substitute.}$$
$$\frac{5}{\sqrt{3}} = \frac{a\sqrt{3}}{\sqrt{3}} \qquad \text{Divide both sides by } \sqrt{3}.$$
$$\frac{5}{\sqrt{3}} = a \qquad \text{Simplify.}$$
$$\frac{5}{\sqrt{3}} \cdot \frac{\sqrt{3}}{\sqrt{3}} = a \qquad \text{Rationalize the denominator.}$$
$$\frac{5\sqrt{3}}{3} = a \qquad \text{Simplify.}$$

Now substitute for a in the formula for the hypotenuse, $c = 2a$.

$$c = 2a$$
$$c = 2\left(\frac{5\sqrt{3}}{3}\right) \qquad \text{Substitute.}$$
$$c = \frac{10\sqrt{3}}{3} \qquad \text{Simplify.}$$

Therefore, the hypotenuse is $\frac{10\sqrt{3}}{3}$ inches, or approximately 5.774 inches. ∎

EXAMPLE 7 It is recommended that an amateur diver stay within 30 feet of the water surface. An amateur diver carrying a homing device is alone in the water. A boat receiving his signal measures the distance to the diver at an angle from the water surface of 60° to be 40 feet. Is the diver out of this safety range?

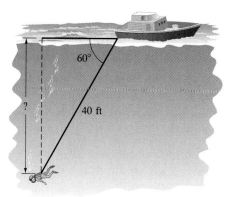

Algebraic Solution

The hypotenuse of the triangle (c) is 40 feet. We are looking for the side opposite the 60° angle (b).

$$c = 2a$$
$$40 = 2a \qquad \text{Substitute.}$$
$$20 = a$$

The shorter side is 20 feet.

$$b = a\sqrt{3}$$
$$b = 20\sqrt{3} \quad \text{Substitute.}$$
$$b \approx 34.64$$

The diver is approximately 34.64 feet below the water surface. He is below the safety level for amateur divers. ∎

Helping Hand Remember that the special-triangle formulas are derived from the Pythagorean theorem. Therefore, if you do not remember them, you can always use the Pythagorean theorem to solve the problem. It will just take more steps.

 Experiencing Algebra the Checkup Way

1. Determine the length of each congruent leg of an isosceles right triangle whose hypotenuse measures 6 mm.

2. To the nearest tenth of a foot, how far must a catcher throw the ball from home plate to the second base? Remember that a baseball diamond is a 90-foot square.

3. A ramp makes a 30° angle with the floor. If the vertical distance of the ramp is 3 feet, find the horizontal distance of the ramp and the ramp's length.

---

3 Solving Formulas   We can use the process for solving polynomial equations to solve formulas for variables. For example, solve the formula for the area of a circle, $A = \pi r^2$, for r.

$$A = \pi r^2 \qquad \text{Quadratic equation in terms of } r$$

$$\frac{A}{\pi} = r^2 \qquad \text{Divide both sides by } \pi.$$

$$r = \sqrt{\frac{A}{\pi}} \qquad \begin{array}{l}\text{Principle of square roots}\\ \text{Use the positive root for length of } r.\end{array}$$

EXAMPLE 8   Solve for the indicated variable.

a. Vertical-position formula, $s = -16t^2 + v_0t$ for t.

b. Cylinder surface area formula, $S = 2\pi r^2 + 2\pi rh$ for r.

Solution

a. Solve $s = -16t^2 + v_0t$ for t.

$$16t^2 - v_0t + s = 0 \qquad \begin{array}{l}\text{Quadratic equation in terms of } t\\ a = 16, b = -v_0, c = s\end{array}$$

$$t = \frac{-b \pm \sqrt{b^2 - 4ac}}{2a} \qquad \text{Quadratic formula}$$

$$t = \frac{-(-v_0) \pm \sqrt{(-v_0)^2 - 4(16)(s)}}{2(16)}$$

$$t = \frac{v_0 \pm \sqrt{v_0^2 - 64s}}{32}$$

b. Solve $S = 2\pi r^2 + 2\pi rh$ for r.

$$2\pi r^2 + 2\pi rh - S = 0 \quad \text{Quadratic equation in terms of } r$$
$$a = 2\pi, b = 2\pi h, c = -S$$

$$r = \frac{-b \pm \sqrt{b^2 - 4ac}}{2a} \quad \text{Quadratic formula}$$

$$r = \frac{-2\pi h \pm \sqrt{(2\pi h)^2 - 4(2\pi)(-S)}}{2(2\pi)}$$

$$r = \frac{-2\pi h \pm \sqrt{4\pi^2 h^2 + 8\pi S}}{4\pi}$$

$$r = \frac{-2\pi h \pm \sqrt{4(\pi^2 h^2 + 2\pi S)}}{4\pi}$$

$$r = \frac{-2\pi h \pm 2\sqrt{\pi^2 h^2 + 2\pi S}}{4\pi}$$

$$r = \frac{2(-\pi h \pm \sqrt{\pi^2 h^2 + 2\pi S})}{4\pi}$$

$$r = \frac{-\pi h \pm \sqrt{\pi^2 h^2 + 2\pi S}}{2\pi} \qquad \blacksquare$$

 ## Experiencing Algebra the Checkup Way

Solve each formula for the variable specified.

1. Area of a square, $A = s^2$, for the length of the side s.
2. Pythagorean theorem, $a^2 + b^2 = c^2$, for the length of side a.
3. Surface area of an open canister, $A = \pi r^2 + 2\pi rh$, for the radius r.

PROBLEM SET 11.6

 ## Experiencing Algebra the Exercise Way

Use the Pythagorean theorem to solve. Round your answers to the nearest tenth.

1. One leg of a right triangle measures 3 inches longer than the other leg. How long are the legs if the hypotenuse of the triangle is 15 inches long?

2. One leg of a right triangle is 1 foot less than twice the length of the other leg. If the hypotenuse of the triangle measures 17 feet, what are the lengths of the legs?

3. One leg of a right triangle measures 2 feet more than twice the length of the other leg. If the hypotenuse of the triangle measures 13 feet, how long are each of the legs?

4. The legs of a right triangle differ in length by 1 yard. If the hypotenuse of the triangle measures 29 yards, how long are the legs?

5. The hypotenuse of a right triangle measures 3 centimeters less than twice the length of one leg. The other leg measures 45 centimeters. Find the lengths of the unknown sides.

6. The hypotenuse of a right triangle is 4 inches less than 5 times the length of one leg. If the other leg measures 40 inches, find the lengths of the unknown sides.

7. A surveyor wants to measure the distance across a pond. The surveyor locates the points A, B, and C. She measures the distance from A to C, which is 99 yards, and the distance from A to B, which is 195 yards. Angle C is a right angle. Find the distance across the pond from C to B.

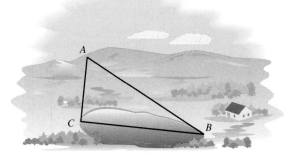

8. A surveyor wants to estimate the distance across a gorge. He measures the distance from G to H, which is 176 yards, and the distance from F to H, which is 274 yards. Angle G is a right angle. Find the distance across the gorge from F to G.

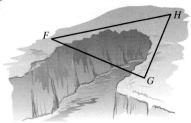

9. A contractor marks the foundation for a shed. The floor is a square with a diagonal measurement of 20 feet. In order to check that the sides are perpendicular, what should each side measure to the nearest tenth of a foot?

10. A contractor marks the foundation for a building. The floor is rectangular with a diagonal measurement of 25 feet. If the length is twice the width, what should each side measure to the nearest tenth of a foot?

11. A rectangular swimming pool measures 70 feet diagonally. The length is 5 feet less than three times the width. What are the dimensions of the pool?

12. A rectangular patio measures 36 feet diagonally. The length is 3 feet more than twice the width. What are the dimensions of the patio?

13. A slow-pitch softball diamond is a square, 65 feet on a side. What is the distance from first to third base?

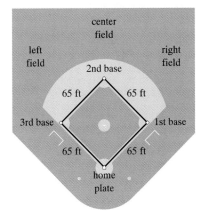

14. In a slow-pitch softball game, the pitcher fields the ball along the third-base line, 25 feet from home plate. She throws the ball to first base for the out. How far did she throw the ball?

15. In a slow-pitch softball game, the right fielder picks up a ground ball directly down the first-base line, and throws it to third base. The throw was estimated to be 97 feet. How far beyond first base did the fielder pick up the grounder?

16. In a slow-pitch softball game, the first baseman tags the runner out and throws to the third base-man for a double play. Her throw was estimated to be 82 feet. How far from first base did she tag the runner out?

17. A bridge that is 1 mile long expands during hot weather by 1 foot. If the bridge did not have expansion joints for this, how high would the center of the bridge rise?

$\frac{1}{2}$ mile $+ \frac{1}{2}$ foot $= 2640.5$ feet

?

1 mile $= 5280$ feet

18. A driveway is 50 feet long. During hot weather, it would expand 2 inches. If the driveway did not have expansion joints, how high would the center of the drive rise?

Use the properties of an isosceles right triangle to solve. Round your answers to the nearest hundredth.

19. Determine the length of the hypotenuse of an isosceles right triangle whose legs measure 3.75 meters.

20. What is the length of the hypotenuse of an isosceles right triangle whose legs measure 6.55 feet?

21. What will be the lengths of the legs of an isosceles right triangle whose hypotenuse measures 7.6 feet?

22. If the hypotenuse of an isosceles right triangle measures 14.9 centimeters, what are the lengths of its legs?

23. The top of a telephone pole is anchored with a guy wire that makes a 45-degree angle with the ground. If the pole is 20 feet high, how long is the guy wire?

24. A guy wire makes a 45-degree angle from the ground to the top of a pole. It is anchored 15 feet away from the base of the pole. How long is the guy wire?

25. A wire runs from the top of a building to the ground at a 45-degree angle. If the wire is 42.5 feet long, how high is the building?

26. A wire at a boot camp runs from the top of a tower to the ground at a 45-degree angle. If the wire is 145 feet long, how high is the tower?

27. An amateur diver is expected to stay within 30 feet of the water surface. His homing device sends a signal back to the boat at an angle of 45° from the water level and from a distance of 40 feet. Is the diver within the expected depth?

28. The amateur diver in exercise 27 moves further in the water and now sends a signal back to the boat at an angle of 45° from the water level but from a distance of 50 feet. Is the diver within the expected depth?

For the following exercises, assume the right triangles are 30°–60°–90° triangles, and use the properties of such triangles to solve. Round your answers to the nearest tenth.

29. Determine the lengths of the unknown sides of the triangle if the side opposite the 60° angle measures 18.6 inches.

30. If the side opposite the 60° angle measures 2.19 centimeters, find the lengths of the other sides of the triangle.

31. Given that the hypotenuse of the triangle measures 22 inches, what are the lengths of the legs?

32. What are the measures of the legs of the triangle if the hypotenuse measures 34 centimeters?

33. If the short leg of the triangle measures 21 centimeters, what are the lengths of the other sides?

34. What will be the lengths of the other sides when the length of the short leg of the triangle measures 8.2 inches?

35. An airplane is flying at an altitude of 4000 feet and is approaching the runway at a 30-degree angle. Find the horizontal distance to the setdown point on the runway and the slanted distance from the plane to the runway.

36. A kite is 120 feet above the ground. The string to the kite makes a 60-degree angle with the ground. Find the horizontal distance between the kite and its flyer and the length of the string between the kite and its flyer.

37. A guy wire reaches from the top of a pole to the ground at a 60-degree angle. The distance between the base of the pole and the point at which the wire is anchored to the ground measures 8 feet. Find the height of the pole and the length of the guy wire.

38. A telephone pole is 13 meters high. The pole is anchored with a guy wire that makes a 60-degree angle with the ground. How much wire is needed and how far from the base of the pole should it be anchored?

Solve each formula for the specified variable.

39. $E = mc^2$ for c

40. $A = 4\pi r^2$ for r

41. $V = \pi r^2 h$ for r

42. $F = \dfrac{mv^2}{R}$ for v

43. $E = \dfrac{1}{2}mv^2$ for v

44. $A = \dfrac{\pi r^2 S}{360}$ for r

45. $C = \dfrac{n(n-1)}{2}$ for n

46. $S = \dfrac{n(n+1)}{2}$ for n

47. $x^2 - y^2 = c^2$ for x

48. $x^2 + y^2 = r^2$ for x

49. $A = P(1+r)^2$ for r

50. $S = 16t^2 + gt$ for t

 ## Experiencing Algebra the Calculator Way

If the Pythagorean theorem is used repeatedly to solve problems, the instructions can be entered into a calculator to do so easily. In such applications, two of the three sides of the right triangle will be known. The equation $a^2 + b^2 = c^2$ can be solved for the unknown side. Store the values for the two variables that are known and enter the expression to be evaluated for the unknown side. An example follows.

> Find the distance a catcher must throw the baseball to first base if a batter bunts the ball 6.5 feet directly down the third-base line. For this example, the two legs of the triangle are 6.5 feet and 90 feet. The unknown side is the hypotenuse, $c = \sqrt{a^2 + b^2}$, where $a = 6.5$ and $b = 90$. The keystrokes for this calculation are [6] [.] [5] [STO▶] [ALPHA] [A] [ALPHA] [:] [9]
>
> [0] [STO▶] [ALPHA] [B] [ALPHA] [:] [2nd] [√] [ALPHA] [A] [x²] [+] [ALPHA]
>
> [B] [x²] [)] [ENTER] .
>
> The calculator returns an answer of 90.23441694; therefore, the catcher must throw the baseball 90.23 feet to first base. Then press [2nd] [ENTRY] to repeat the instruction and use the arrow keys to change the values stored.

Use this procedure to solve for the unknown side in the following exercises.

1. The hypotenuse of a right triangle measures 34.45 centimeters and one leg measures 23.87 centimeters. What is the length of the other leg?

2. The legs of a right triangle measure 184.8 and 5927.56 inches. What is the measure of the hypotenuse?

3. The hypotenuse of a right triangle is 5769 feet long, and one leg is 1800 feet long. How long is the other leg?

4. The legs of a right triangle are 9639 and 9720 decimeters long. What is the length of the hypotenuse?

5. The hypotenuse of a right triangle is $\frac{5}{64}$ feet long and one leg is $\frac{1}{16}$ feet long. What is the length of the other leg?

Experiencing Algebra the Group Way

The equation $x^2 + y^2 = z^2$, where x, y, and z are integers, is called a Diophantine equation. A Greek mathematician, Diophantus of Alexandria, proved that any set of three integers that satisfy this equation have the form

$$x = a^2 - b^2, \qquad y = 2ab, \qquad \text{and} \qquad z = a^2 + b^2,$$

where a and b are integers.

Select integers for a and b and generate triples for x, y and z that satisfy the Diophantine equation. Note that the Pythagorean theorem is an application of this equation. Each member of the group should generate five different sets of triples and sketch the right triangle that represents the relationship. For each triple generated, check to see that the Diophantine equation does in fact hold. Compare your results with other members of the group. How many different sets of triples did the group generate?

Experiencing Algebra the Write Way

Diophantus of Alexandria is listed in "Experiencing Algebra the Group Way" as a mathematician who worked with the relation we recognize as the Pythagorean theorem. The Pythagorean theorem, which was presented earlier in this section, is credited to the mathematician Pythagoras. The laws of falling bodies were discovered by Galileo Galilei, who reportedly dropped objects from the Leaning Tower of Pisa. Research the life of one of these mathematicians, and write a short summary of what you learn about them and their work.

11.7 Solving Quadratic Inequalities

Objectives

1 Identify quadratic inequalities in one variable.

2 Solve quadratic inequalities numerically.

3 Solve quadratic inequalities graphically.

4 Solve quadratic inequalities algebraically.

5 Model real-world situations using quadratic inequalities and solve.

Application

Kaiser Foundation Health Plan reports its net income (sales minus expenses) for the years from 1988 to 1995. The company CEO believes that the company has done well if its net income is at least $600 million. A function used to estimate the annual net income in millions of dollars is $I(x) = -28x^2 + 338x - 317$, where x is the number of years after 1987. Determine the years for which the CEO believes the company has done well.

After completing this section, we will discuss this application further. See page 885.

Earlier in this text, we solved linear inequalities in one variable. Remember that the solution set for a linear inequality contains an infinite number of solutions. Therefore, we describe the set as an inequality or in interval notation. For example,

Inequality	Interval	Inequality	Interval
$x < 1$	$(-\infty, 1)$	$x \leq 1$	$(-\infty, 1]$
$x > 1$	$(1, \infty)$	$x \geq 1$	$[1, \infty)$
$4 < x < 5$	$(4, 5)$	$4 \leq x < 5$	$[4, 5)$
$4 < x \leq 5$	$(4, 5]$	$4 \leq x \leq 5$	$[4, 5]$

1 Identifying Quadratic Inequalities in One Variable

In this section we will be solving quadratic inequalities in one variable. A **quadratic inequality in one variable** or **quadratic inequality** is written by replacing the equal symbol in a quadratic equation in one variable with an order symbol.

> *Standard Form for a Quadratic Inequality in One Variable*
> A quadratic inequality in standard form is written in one of the following forms:
>
> $$ax^2 + bx + c < 0$$
> $$ax^2 + bx + c > 0$$
> $$ax^2 + bx + c \leq 0$$
> $$ax^2 + bx + c \geq 0$$
>
> where a, b, and c are real numbers and $a \neq 0$.

Examples of quadratic inequalities are the following.

$$2x^2 + 3x - 5 < 0$$
$$-x^2 - 2x > 9$$
$$x^2 + 5x - 7 \leq 2x^2 + 4x + 15$$

EXAMPLE 1 Determine whether each inequality is a quadratic inequality.

a. $0.3x^3 + 5.1x^2 > x - 1.2$ **b.** $6x^{-2} + 5x^{-1} < 0$

Solution

a. $0.3x^3 + 5.1x^2 > x - 1.2$ is not a quadratic inequality, because it has a third-degree term (exponent of 3).

b. $6x^{-2} + 5x^{-1} < 0$ is not a quadratic inequality, because it has variables with negative exponents. ∎

Experiencing Algebra the Checkup Way

In exercises 1–4, determine whether each inequality is a quadratic inequality.

1. $2x + 3 \leq x^2 - 1$ **2.** $\dfrac{2}{3}x^2 - 3x \geq \dfrac{1}{4}$ **3.** $3x + 2x^{-2} > 4x^{-1} + 8$ **4.** $1.2\sqrt{x} - 3.3x^2 \leq 2.5x$

5. Explain the difference between a quadratic equation and a quadratic inequality.

2 Solving Quadratic Inequalities Numerically

We solved linear inequalities numerically for integer solutions by using a table of values. We will use the same method to solve a quadratic inequality in one variable for integer solutions.

> *Solving a Quadratic Inequality Numerically*
> To solve a quadratic inequality numerically for integer solutions:
> Set up an extended table of values.
>
> * The first column is labeled with the name of the independent variable.
> * The second column is labeled with the expression on the left side of the inequality.
> * The third column is labeled with the expression on the right side of the inequality.
>
> Complete the table.
>
> * Substitute values for the independent variable.
> * Evaluate the second and third column.
> * Continue until values for the two expressions (the numbers in the second and third column) result in a true inequality.
>
> The values for the independent variable (the numbers in the first column) that result in a true inequality are solutions for the inequality.

Helping Hand Not all solutions may be found by this method. We are limited to the numbers substituted for the independent variable.

To solve a quadratic inequality numerically for integer solutions on your calculator:

* Rename the independent variable as x.

Set up the table.

* Set up the first column for the independent variable by setting a minimum value and increments. Since we do not know the solution, we may want to start with 0. We will use 1 for the size of increments for integer values. Then set the calculator to automatically perform the evaluations.
* Set up the second column of the table to be the leftmost expression by entering the expression on the left side of the inequality in Y1.
* Set up the third column of the table to be the rightmost expression by entering the expression on the right side of the inequality in Y2.

View the table.

* Move beyond the screen to view additional rows by using the up and down arrows.

The solutions are the x-values that result in a true inequality.
   Note: As before, a complete solution set may not be found by this method.

For example, solve numerically $x^2 + 2x - 1 \geq 2$.

x	$x^2 + 2x - 1$	2	
-5	14	2	$14 \geq 2$
-4	7	2	$7 \geq 2$
-3	2	2	$2 \geq 2$
-2	-1	2	$-1 \not\geq 2$
-1	-2	2	$-2 \not\geq 2$
0	-1	2	$-1 \not\geq 2$
1	2	2	$2 \geq 2$
2	7	2	$7 \geq 2$
3	14	2	$14 \geq 2$

According to the table, when $-5, -4,$ and -3 are substituted into the inequality, the result is a true statement. Also, when $1, 2,$ and 3 are substituted into the inequality a true statement results. Therefore, there appear to be two sets of solutions: all integers less than or equal to -3, and all integers greater than or equal to 1.

A calculator table will find the integer solutions numerically. For example, solve $x^2 + 2x - 1 \geq 2$.

We obtain the same solution set: all integers less than or equal to -3 or greater than or equal to 1, as shown in Figure 11.11.

TECHNOLOGY

$Y1 = x^2 + 2x - 1$
$Y2 = 2$

Figure 11.11

For Figure 11.11
Set up the first column of the table.

| 2nd | TBLSET | 0 | ENTER | 1 | ENTER | ENTER | ▼ | ENTER |

Set up the second column in the table.

| Y= | X, T, θ, n | x² | + | 2 | X, T, θ, n | − | 1 |

Set up the third column in the table.

| ▼ | 2 |

View the table.

| 2nd | TABLE |

Use the up arrow key to view the table given.

The calculator table is very easy to generate and move through. However, only integer solutions are being found.

EXAMPLE 2   Solve for integer solutions numerically.

a. $x^2 + 3x - 4 \leq 2x + 2$ **b.** $3x^2 - x - 2 > 0$

c. $-x^2 + 6x > 3$

Calculator Numeric Solution

a. $x^2 + 3x - 4 \leq 2x + 2$

Let $Y1 = x^2 + 3x - 4$ and $Y2 = 2x + 2$.

X	Y1	Y2
-5	6	-8
-4	0	-6
-3	-4	-4
-2	-6	-2
-1	-6	0
0	-4	2
1	0	4
X=-5		

$6 \not\leq -8$
$0 \not\leq -6$
$-4 \leq -4$
$-6 \leq -2$
$-6 \leq 0$
$-4 \leq 2$
$0 \leq 4$

X	Y1	Y2
-1	-6	0
0	-4	2
1	0	4
2	6	6
3	14	8
4	24	10
5	36	12
X=5		

$0 \leq 4$
$2 \leq 6$
$14 \not\leq 8$
$24 \not\leq 10$
$36 \not\leq 12$

The solution set is all integers between -3 and 2, inclusive.

b. $3x^2 - x - 2 > 0$

Let $Y1 = 3x^2 - x - 2$ and $Y2 = 0$.

X	Y1	Y2
-3	28	0
-2	12	0
-1	2	0
0	-2	0
1	0	0
2	8	0
3	22	0
X=-3		

$28 > 0$
$12 > 0$
$2 > 0$
$-2 \not> 0$
$0 \not> 0$
$8 > 0$
$22 > 0$

The solution set is all integers less than 0 or greater than 1.

c. $-x^2 + 6x > 3$

Let $Y1 = -x^2 + 6x$ and $Y2 = 3$.

X	Y1	Y2
0	0	3
1	5	3
2	8	3
3	9	3
4	8	3
5	5	3
6	0	3
X=6		

$0 \not> 3$
$5 > 3$
$8 > 3$
$9 > 3$
$8 > 3$
$5 > 3$
$0 \not> 3$

The solution set is all integers between 1 and 5, inclusive. ∎

Helping Hand This method is not recommended, as it does not result in a complete solution set, only an integer solution set. However, this visualization may be used to check other methods.

 Experiencing Algebra the Checkup Way

Solve numerically for integer solutions.

1. $x^2 + 2x - 7 \geq 3x + 5$ **2.** $2x^2 + 5x - 3 < 0$ **3.** $-x^2 + 4 < x$

3 Solving Quadratic Inequalities Graphically

A second and more inclusive method for determining the solutions for an inequality is to graph two functions, y_1 and y_2. We will use the two expressions in the inequality as the rules of the functions. If we are solving a "less than" $(y_1 < y_2)$ inequality, we choose the x-values that correspond to the portion of the graph for which y_1 is below y_2. If we are solving a "greater than" $(y_1 > y_2)$ inequality, we choose the x-values that correspond to the portion of the graph for which y_1 is above y_2.

Solving a Quadratic Inequality Graphically
To solve a quadratic inequality graphically:

- Write two functions, y_1 and y_2, using the expressions on the left and right sides of the inequality as a rule.

- Graph both functions on the same coordinate plane.

- Determine the intersections, if they exist, of the y_1 and y_2 graphs.

- Locate the portion of the y_1 graph below the y_2 graph if the inequality is "less than." Locate the portion of the y_1 graph above the y_2 graph if the inequality is "greater than."

- Determine the x-coordinates for this portion of the graph.

  - If the portion is to the left of the intersection, then x is less than the x-coordinate of the intersection.

  - If the portion is to the right of the intersection, then x is greater than the x-coordinate of the intersection.

  - If the portion is between the left and right intersections, then x is greater than the x-coordinate of the left intersection and less than the x-coordinate of the right intersection.

The solution set of the inequality includes the x-coordinates of the points of intersection of the two graphs if the inequality contains equality.

To solve a quadratic inequality graphically on your calculator:

- Rename the independent variable as x.
- Set the screen to the desired setting.
- Enter the expression on the left side of the inequality in Y1.
- Enter the expression on the right side of the inequality in Y2.
- Graph.
- Find the points of intersection.
- Locate the portion of the Y1 graph below the Y2 graph if the inequality is "less than." Locate the portion of the Y1 graph above the Y2 graph if the inequality is "greater than."
- Determine the x-coordinates for this portion of the graph.
  - If the portion is to the left of the intersection, then x is less than the x-coordinate of the intersection.
  - If the portion is to the right of the intersection, then x is greater than the x-coordinate of the intersection.
  - If the portion is between the left and right intersections, then x is greater than the x-coordinate of the left intersection and less than the x-coordinate of the right intersection.

The solution set of the inequality includes the x-coordinates of the points of intersection of the two graphs if the inequality contains equality.

For example, solve graphically $x^2 + 2x - 1 \geq 2$.

Let $Y1 = x^2 + 2x - 1$ and $Y2 = 2$.

The solution contains the x-coordinates of the points of intersection, -3 and 1, because the inequality contains "equal to." The graph of Y1 is above the graph of Y2 to the left of the intersection point $(-3, 2)$ and to the right of the intersection point $(1, 2)$, as shown in Figures 11.12a, 11.12b, and 11.12c.

Therefore, the solution is $x \leq -3$ or $x \geq 1$. The solution set may be written in interval notation as $(-\infty, -3]$ or $[1, \infty)$. In mathematics we write this as $(-\infty, -3] \cup [1, \infty)$, where the symbol $\cup$ is called **union** and means "or."

TECHNOLOGY

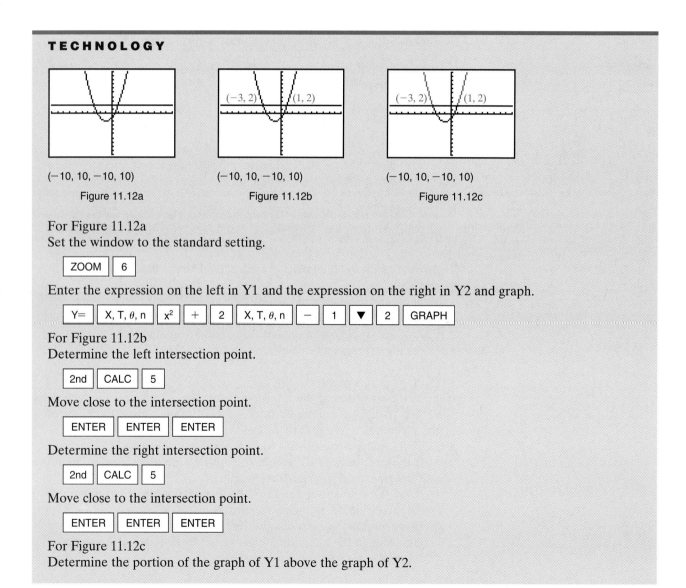

$(-10, 10, -10, 10)$

Figure 11.12a

$(-10, 10, -10, 10)$

Figure 11.12b

$(-10, 10, -10, 10)$

Figure 11.12c

For Figure 11.12a
Set the window to the standard setting.

| ZOOM | 6 |

Enter the expression on the left in Y1 and the expression on the right in Y2 and graph.

| Y= | X, T, θ, n | x² | + | 2 | X, T, θ, n | − | 1 | ▼ | 2 | GRAPH |

For Figure 11.12b
Determine the left intersection point.

| 2nd | CALC | 5 |

Move close to the intersection point.

| ENTER | ENTER | ENTER |

Determine the right intersection point.

| 2nd | CALC | 5 |

Move close to the intersection point.

| ENTER | ENTER | ENTER |

For Figure 11.12c
Determine the portion of the graph of Y1 above the graph of Y2.

EXAMPLE 3 Solve graphically.

    a. $x^2 + 3x - 4 \leq 2x + 2$ **b.** $3x^2 - x - 2 > 0$

    c. $-x^2 + 6x > 3$

Graphic Solution

a.

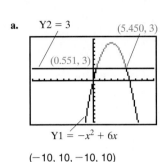

Y2 = 3   (5.450, 3)

(0.551, 3)

Y1 = $-x^2 + 6x$

(−10, 10, −10, 10)

a. $x^2 + 3x - 4 \leq 2x + 2$

Let Y1 = $x^2 + 3x - 4$ and Y2 = $2x + 2$.

    The solution contains both x-coordinates of the intersections because the inequality contains an "equal to." Since the inequality contains a "less than," we determine that Y1 is below Y2 between the points of intersection. Therefore, the solution set is $-3 \leq x \leq 2$ or $[-3, 2]$.

b. $3x^2 - x - 2 > 0$

Let Y1 = $3x^2 - x - 2$ and Y2 = 0. (This will graph a horizontal line on the x-axis.)

    The solution does not contain the x-coordinates of the points of intersection. Since the inequality is "greater than," we determine that Y1 is above Y2 to the left of the intersection point $\left(-\frac{2}{3}, 0\right)$ and to the right of the intersection point $(1, 0)$.

    Therefore, the solution set is $x < -\frac{2}{3}$ or $x > 1$. In interval notation, the solution is $\left(-\infty, -\frac{2}{3}\right) \cup (1, \infty)$.

b.

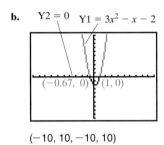

Y2 = 0   Y1 = $3x^2 - x - 2$

(−0.67, 0)   (1, 0)

(−10, 10, −10, 10)

c. $-x^2 + 6x > 3$

Let Y1 = $-x^2 + 6x$ and Y2 = 3.

    The solution does not contain the x-coordinates of the points of intersection. Since the inequality is "greater than," we determine that Y1 is above Y2 between the approximate points of intersection, (0.551, 3) and (5.450, 3).

    Therefore, the approximate solution set is $0.551 < x < 5.450$. In interval notation, the solution is approximately $(0.551, 5.450)$. ∎

c.

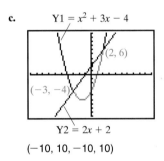

Y1 = $x^2 + 3x - 4$

(2, 6)

(−3, −4)

Y2 = $2x + 2$

(−10, 10, −10, 10)

There are special cases for linear inequalities where there is no solution or the solution is all real numbers. There are also special cases when working with quadratic inequalities. In fact, several types of solutions are possible. To see what they are, complete the following set of exercises on your calculator.

D I S C O V E R Y   1 2

Special Cases of Quadratic Inequalities

Graph the following functions. Label points of intersection if possible. Determine the solutions for the given inequalities.

1. $f(x) = -x^2 - 5$
    $g(x) = 0$
    a. $-x^2 - 5 > 0$ ____
    b. $-x^2 - 5 \geq 0$ ____
    c. $-x^2 - 5 < 0$ ____
    d. $-x^2 - 5 \leq 0$ ____

2. $h(x) = x^2 + 5x + 8$
    $j(x) = 0$
    a. $x^2 + 5x + 8 > 0$ ____
    b. $x^2 + 5x + 8 \geq 0$ ____
    c. $x^2 + 5x + 8 < 0$ ____
    d. $x^2 + 5x + 8 \leq 0$ ____

Continued

3. $y_1 = -x^2 - 10x - 25$
$y_2 = 0$
a. $-x^2 - 10x - 25 > 0$ ____
b. $-x^2 - 10x - 25 \geq 0$ ____
c. $-x^2 - 10x - 25 < 0$ ____
d. $-x^2 - 10x - 25 \leq 0$ ____

4. $y_1 = 2x^2 - 12x + 18$
$y_2 = 0$
a. $2x^2 - 12x + 18 > 0$ ____
b. $2x^2 - 12x + 18 \geq 0$ ____
c. $2x^2 - 12x + 18 < 0$ ____
d. $2x^2 - 12x + 18 \leq 0$ ____

The Discovery illustrates that some quadratic inequalities have no solution or a solution set consisting of all real numbers. Other solution sets contain only one value or all real numbers except one value.

EXAMPLE 4 Solve graphically.

a. $2x^2 \geq x^2$

b. $x^2 - 4x + 7 > -x^2 + 4x - 1$

c. $x^2 + 2 \leq 2$

Graphic Solution

a.

$(-10, 10, -10, 10)$

a. $2x^2 \geq x^2$
Let Y1 $= 2x^2$ and Y2 $= x^2$.
The solution contains the x-coordinate of the intersection point, $(0, 0)$, because the inequality contains equality. Since the inequality is "greater than," we determine that Y1 is above Y2 at all points to the left and to the right of the intersection. Therefore, the solution set is all real numbers.

b.

$(-10, 10, -10, 10)$

b. $x^2 - 4x + 7 > -x^2 + 4x - 1$
Let Y1 $= x^2 - 4x + 7$ and Y2 $= -x^2 + 4x - 1$.
The solution does not contain the x-coordinate of the intersection point, $(2, 3)$, because the inequality does not contain equality. Since the inequality is "greater than," we determine that Y1 is above Y2 at all points to the left of the intersection point and all points to the right of the intersection point.
Therefore, the solution set is all real numbers except 2, or $x \neq 2$. In interval notation, the solution is $(-\infty, 2) \cup (2, \infty)$.

c.

$(-10, 10, -10, 10)$

c. $x^2 + 2 \leq 2$
Let Y1 $= x^2 + 2$ and Y2 $= 2$.
The solution contains the x-coordinate of the intersection point, $(0, 2)$, because the inequality contains "equal to." Since the inequality is "less than," we determine that Y1 is not below Y2.
Therefore, the only solution is 0. ■

✓ Experiencing Algebra the Checkup Way

Solve exercises 1–6 graphically.

1. $x^2 + 2x - 7 \geq 3x + 5$

2. $2x^2 + 5x - 3 < 0$

3. $-x^2 + 4 < x$

4. $\dfrac{1}{2}x^2 + 2 \geq x^2 + 2$

5. $x^2 - 4x + 1 > -3$

6. $x^2 - 4x + 7 \leq -5 + 8x - 2x^2$

7. Describe what you might see if you graphically solved a quadratic inequality that had the following results:

   a. The solution set consists of all real numbers.

   b. The solution set consists of a single value.

   c. The solution set consists of an interval on the number line.

   d. There is no real-number solution.

---

4 Solving Quadratic Inequalities Algebraically

Several methods are available for solving a quadratic inequality algebraically. We will illustrate one method. Another method is described in the next "Experiencing Algebra the Group Way."

When we solved quadratic inequalities graphically, we first determined the points of intersection of the graphs. Algebraically, we need to determine these points by solving a quadratic equation. Remember, we have several methods available to do this. We call these points of equality **critical points**. These critical points are endpoints of possible interval solutions. After determining the possible intervals for the solution, we need only test one point in each interval. If one point in an interval is a solution, all points in the interval are solutions.

Solving a Quadratic Inequality Algebraically
To solve a quadratic inequality in one variable algebraically:

- Determine the critical points (points of equality) by solving a quadratic equation, replacing the inequality symbol with an equal symbol. Determine by the original inequality whether the points of equality are in the solution.

- Determine the possible intervals for the solution by using the critical points as endpoints.

- Test one value in each interval for a true statement. If the inequality is true for the value tested, then the inequality is true for all values on the interval.

Write the solution set as a union of all possible intervals.

For example, solve $x^2 + 2x - 1 \geq 2$.

Determine the critical points.

$$x^2 + 2x - 1 = 2 \qquad \text{Determine a quadratic equation.}$$
$$x^2 + 2x - 3 = 0 \qquad \text{Standard form}$$
$$(x + 3)(x - 1) = 0 \qquad \text{Solve by factoring.}$$
$$x + 3 = 0 \quad \text{or} \quad x - 1 = 0$$
$$x = -3 \qquad\qquad x = 1$$

The inequality contains equality, so the critical points are solutions. We include them in the intervals.

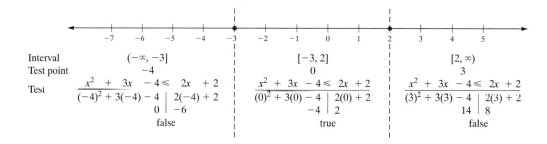

Interval	$(-\infty, -3]$	$[-3, 1]$	$[1, \infty)$
Test point	-4	0	3
Test	$x^2 + 2x - 1 \geq 2$ $\dfrac{(-4)^2 + 2(-4) - 1}{7} \bigg\| 2$	$x^2 + 2x - 1 \geq 2$ $\dfrac{(0)^2 + 2(0) - 1}{-1} \bigg\| 2$	$x^2 + 2x - 1 \geq 2$ $\dfrac{(3)^2 + 2(3) - 1}{14} \bigg\| 2$
	true	false	true

Therefore, the solution set is $(-\infty, -3] \cup [1, \infty)$.

EXAMPLE 5 Solve algebraically.

a. $x^2 + 3x - 4 \leq 2x + 2$ **b.** $3x^2 - x - 2 > 0$

c. $-x^2 + 6x > 3$

Algebraic Solution

a. $x^2 + 3x - 4 \leq 2x + 2$

Determine the critical points.

$$x^2 + 3x - 4 = 2x + 2$$
$$x^2 + x - 6 = 0$$
$$(x + 3)(x - 2) = 0$$
$$x = -3 \quad \text{or} \quad x = 2$$

The inequality contains equality, so the critical points are solutions. We include them in the intervals.

Interval	$(-\infty, -3]$	$[-3, 2]$	$[2, \infty)$
Test point	-4	0	3
Test	$x^2 + 3x - 4 \leq 2x + 2$ $\dfrac{(-4)^2 + 3(-4) - 4}{0} \bigg\| \dfrac{2(-4) + 2}{-6}$	$x^2 + 3x - 4 \leq 2x + 2$ $\dfrac{(0)^2 + 3(0) - 4}{-4} \bigg\| \dfrac{2(0) + 2}{2}$	$x^2 + 3x - 4 \leq 2x + 2$ $\dfrac{(3)^2 + 3(3) - 4}{14} \bigg\| \dfrac{2(3) + 2}{8}$
	false	true	false

Therefore, the solution is $[-3, 2]$.

b. $3x^2 - x - 2 > 0$

Determine the critical points.

$$3x^2 - x - 2 = 0$$
$$(3x + 2)(x - 1) = 0$$
$$x = -\frac{2}{3} \quad \text{or} \quad x = 1$$

The inequality does not contain equality. We do not include the critical points as solutions.

Interval	$\left(-\infty, -\frac{2}{3}\right)$	$\left(-\frac{2}{3}, 1\right)$	$(1, \infty)$
Test point	-1	0	2
Test	$\dfrac{3x^2 \; - \; x \; - \; 2 > 0}{3(-1)^2 - (-1) - 2 \;\big|\; 0}$	$\dfrac{3x^2 \; - \; x \; - \; 2 > 0}{3(0)^2 - (0) - 2 \;\big|\; 0}$	$\dfrac{3x^2 \; - \; x \; - \; 2 > 0}{3(2)^2 - (2) - 2 \;\big|\; 0}$
	$2 \;\big|$	$-2 \;\big|$	$8 \;\big|$
	true	false	true

Therefore, the solution is $\left(-\infty, -\frac{2}{3}\right) \cup (1, \infty)$.

c. $-x^2 + 6x > 3$

Determine the critical points.

$$-x^2 + 6x = 3$$
$$-x^2 + 6x - 3 = 0$$

This does not factor. We need to use the quadratic formula. Use $a = -1$, $b = 6$, and $c = -3$.

$$x = \frac{-b \pm \sqrt{b^2 - 4ac}}{2a}$$

$$x = \frac{-6 \pm \sqrt{6^2 - 4(-1)(-3)}}{2(-1)}$$

$$x = \frac{-6 \pm \sqrt{24}}{-2}$$

$$x = \frac{-6 \pm 2\sqrt{6}}{-2}$$

$$x = \frac{-6}{-2} \pm \frac{2\sqrt{6}}{-2}$$

$$x = 3 \pm \left(-\sqrt{6}\right)$$

$$x = 3 \pm \sqrt{6}$$

$$x \approx 0.551 \quad \text{or} \quad x \approx 5.450$$

The inequality does not contain equality. We do not include the critical points as solutions.

Interval	$(-\infty, 3 - \sqrt{6})$	$(3 - \sqrt{6}, 3 + \sqrt{6})$	$(3 + \sqrt{6}, \infty)$
Test point	0	1	6
Test	$\dfrac{-x^2 \; + \; 6x > 3}{-(0)^2 + 6(0) \;\big|\; 3}$	$\dfrac{-x^2 \; + \; 6x > 3}{-(1)^2 + 6(1) \;\big|\; 3}$	$\dfrac{-x^2 \; + \; 6x > 3}{-(6)^2 + 6(6) \;\big|\; 3}$
	$0 \;\big|$	$5 \;\big|$	$0 \;\big|$
	false	true	false

Therefore, the solution is $\left(3 - \sqrt{6}, 3 + \sqrt{6}\right)$. ∎

The special cases of quadratic inequalities may also be solved algebraically.

EXAMPLE 6   Solve algebraically.

a. $2x^2 \geq x^2$ **b.** $x^2 - 4x + 7 > -x^2 + 4x - 1$

c. $x^2 + 2 \leq 2$

Algebraic Solution

a. $2x^2 \geq x^2$

Determine the critical points.

$$2x^2 = x^2$$
$$x^2 = 0$$
$$x = 0$$

The inequality contains equality. We include the critical point as a solution.

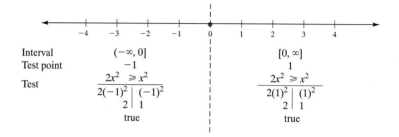

Therefore, the solution is $(-\infty, 0] \cup [0, \infty)$, which is equivalent to $(-\infty, \infty)$ or all real numbers.

b. $x^2 - 4x + 7 > -x^2 + 4x - 1$

Determine the critical points.

$$x^2 - 4x + 7 = -x^2 + 4x - 1$$
$$2x^2 - 8x + 8 = 0$$
$$2(x^2 - 4x + 4) = 0$$
$$2(x - 2)^2 = 0$$
$$x - 2 = 0$$
$$x = 2$$

The inequality does not contain equality. We do not include the critical point as a solution.

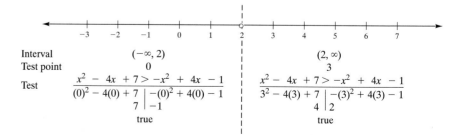

Therefore, the solution is $(-\infty, 2) \cup (2, \infty)$.

c. $x^2 + 2 \le 2$

Determine the critical points.

$$x^2 + 2 = 2$$
$$x^2 = 0$$
$$x = 0$$

The inequality contains equality. We include the critical point as a solution.

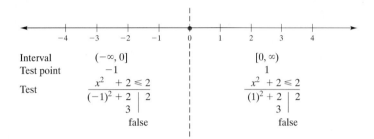

Interval	$(-\infty, 0]$	$[0, \infty)$
Test point	-1	1
Test	$\dfrac{x^2 \quad + 2 \le 2}{(-1)^2 + 2 \mid 2}$ $\qquad 3 \mid$	$\dfrac{x^2 \quad + 2 \le 2}{(1)^2 + 2 \mid 2}$ $\qquad 3 \mid$
	false	false

Therefore, the solution is neither possible interval. However, the critical point is a solution. The only solution is 0. ■

 ## Experiencing Algebra the Checkup Way

Solve exercises 1–6 algebraically.

1. $x^2 + 2x - 7 \ge 3x + 5$ **2.** $2x^2 + 5x - 3 < 0$ **3.** $-x^2 + 4 < x$

4. $\dfrac{1}{2}x^2 + 2 \ge x^2 + 2$ **5.** $x^2 - 4x + 1 > -3$ **6.** $x^2 - 4x + 7 \le -5 + 8x - 2x^2$

7. How do you determine the critical points of a quadratic inequality?

8. Why is it important to know the critical points of a quadratic inequality when solving the inequality algebraically?

---

5 Modeling the Real World
Inequalities often give us important information about the quantities related by a quadratic equation. If the equation describes the height of a thrown or falling object, an inequality might tell us when the object is higher or lower than a given height. If the equation describes a cost or sales function, an inequality might tell us the range of numbers of items we need to sell to make a profit. For these reasons, inequalities are very useful in business and science.

EXAMPLE 7
In a movie, a crash dummy is projected upward at a speed of 100 feet per second from the top of a 200-foot cliff. Determine the length of time the dummy is above the point of origin.

Algebraic Solution

Use the vertical-position function, $s(t) = -16t^2 + v_0 t + s_0$, for time t, v_0 as the initial velocity, and s_0 as the initial height, to write a function. Let $v_0 = 100$ and $s_0 = 200$. The position function then becomes

$$s(t) = -16t^2 + 100t + 200.$$

Use this position function to write an inequality. We want to know when the position is above—greater than—the point of origin, 200 feet. The dummy will be above the point of origin when $s(t) > 200$.

$$-16t^2 + 100t + 200 > 200$$

Determine the critical points.

$$-16t^2 + 100t + 200 = 200$$
$$-16t^2 + 100t = 0$$
$$-4t(4t - 25) = 0$$
$$-4t = 0 \quad \text{or} \quad 4t - 25 = 0$$
$$t = 0 \qquad\qquad t = \frac{25}{4}$$

The inequality does not contain equality, so the critical points are not solutions.

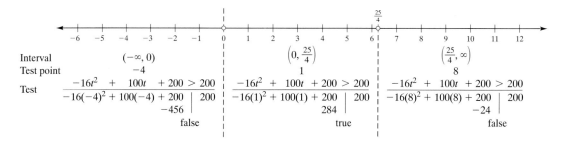

The solution is $0 < t < \frac{25}{4}$.

The dummy is above the point of origin between 0 and $\frac{25}{4}$ seconds, or between 0 and 6.25 seconds after projection. ∎

EXAMPLE 8 Elisa sells fruit drinks at the local fair. She has determined from past summers that the cost for x days of operation can be estimated by the cost function $C(x) = 2x^2 - 20x + 240$. Determine the number of days she can operate the stand at a cost of no more than $200.

Numeric Solution

We need to determine when the cost function is less than or equal to 200: $C(x) \le 200$.

$$2x^2 - 20x + 240 \le 200$$

Use the inequality $2x^2 - 20x + 240 \le 200$.

Since we only need to determine integer solutions, set up a table of values for x days. Let Y1 $= 2x^2 - 20x + 240$ and Y2 $= 200$.

According to Figure 11.13, Elisa should operate her stand for at least 3 days but not more than 7 days, to keep her cost at $200 or less.

Figure 11.13

Application

Kaiser Foundation Health Plan reports its net income (sales minus expenses) for the years from 1988 to 1995. The company CEO believes that the company has done well if its net income is at least $600 million. A function used to estimate the annual net income in millions of dollars is $I(x) = -28x^2 + 338x - 317$, where x is the number of years after 1987. Determine the years for which the CEO believes the company has done well.

$Y2 = 600$

$Y1 = -28x^2 + 338x - 317$

(4.12, 600)

(7.95, 600)

(0, 10, 0, 1000)

X	Y1	Y2
2	247	600
3	445	600
4	587	600
5	673	600
6	703	600
7	677	600
8	595	600

X=8

Discussion

Let x = number of years after 1987

$I(x)$ = annual net income in millions of dollars

$I(x) = -28x^2 + 338x - 317$

$-28x^2 + 338x - 317 \geq 600$ Net income is at least 600.

Let $Y1 = -28x^2 + 338x - 317$ and $Y2 = 600$.

The graph of the function representing the net income is above the graph of the constant function for x-values of 5, 6, and 7 years after 1987. This represents the years 1992, 1993, and 1994.

A numeric table of values confirms this. ∎

 ## Experiencing Algebra the Checkup Way

1. A baseball is thrown upward at a speed of 50 feet per second from the top of a tower that is 120 feet above the ground. Determine the length of time the baseball is no lower than the top of the tower.

2. The wholesale price of a computer is $600. The minimum order a dealer can place is 10 computers. For every additional computer above 10, the price per computer to the dealer is reduced by $20. If x represents the number of computers above 10 that are ordered, the price per computer will be $600 - 20x$, and the number ordered will be $10 + x$. The total revenue from the sale will be $R(x) = (600 - 20x)(10 + x)$. How many computers must be ordered for the revenue to be at least $7500?

3. Using data from the *Universal Almanac*, the growth in population of the Mexico City urban area can be approximated by the function $y = 0.006x^2 + 0.203x + 3.1$, where y is measured in millions of people and x is the number of years after 1950. Using this function, in what year would you expect the population of this area to first exceed 30 million people?

PROBLEM SET 11.7

Experiencing Algebra the Exercise Way

Determine whether each inequality is a quadratic inequality.

1. $2x^2 - 5 < 4x + 1$
2. $5a - 3 \geq 2a^{-2} + 7$
3. $1.3z - 2.8 > 4.3z^2$
4. $\frac{2}{3}x^3 + \frac{1}{7}x < \frac{5}{7}$

5. $4x^{-2} + 5x^{-1} \geq 2x + 1$
6. $x^2 > 0$
7. $\frac{1}{3}x^2 - \frac{5}{6}x > \frac{3}{4}$
8. $3x - 5 > x^2 + 8$

9. $2x^3 + 4 \leq x^2 + x$
10. $\frac{5}{9}x - \frac{2}{9}x^2 > \frac{2}{3}\sqrt{x} - \frac{5}{6}$
11. $3\sqrt{x} + 5x < x^2 - 5$
12. $5.4x^2 + 4.1x - 0.9 \geq 0$

Solve for integer solutions numerically.

13. $x^2 + 3x - 7 \geq x + 8$
14. $x^2 + 4x - 3 \leq 2x + 5$
15. $3x^2 + 9x + 7 < 11 - 2x$

16. $2x^2 + 4x - 8 < 2 + 3x$
17. $4x^2 - 13x - 7 > 18x + 1$
18. $3x^2 + 9x - 5 > 2x + 1$

Solve graphically.

19. $x^2 + 2x + 1 > 4$

20. $x^2 - 8x + 16 \geq 9$

21. $2x^2 + x - 3 < 7$

22. $x^2 - 2x - 8 \leq 2x - 3$

23. $24 + 5x - x^2 < -x + 8$

24. $14 + 5x - x^2 < -2x + 6$

25. $2x^2 - 5 \leq x^2 + 4$

26. $x^2 + 3x - 10 > 10 - 3x - x^2$

27. $\frac{1}{4}x^2 - 3 \geq x^2 + 2$

28. $5 - \frac{1}{5}x^2 \leq 1 - x^2$

29. $x^2 + 6x + 10 \geq -x^2 - 6x - 8$

30. $-x^2 - 4x \geq 4$

31. $x^2 - 4x + 8 \geq \frac{1}{4}x^2 - x + 5$

32. $x^2 - 8x + 15 \geq -x^2 + 8x - 17$

Solve exercises 33–54 algebraically.

33. $x^2 - 2x - 15 \geq 9$

34. $x^2 - 2x - 24 \leq 11$

35. $8 + 2x - x^2 > -7$

36. $10 + 3x - x^2 > -8$

37. $4x^2 - 12x + 9 \leq 4$

38. $4x^2 + 20x + 25 \geq 9$

39. $6 + 5x - x^2 < -8$

40. $20 + x - x^2 > -10$

41. $x^2 + 3 \geq -x + 15$

42. $\frac{1}{2}x^2 + 2 \leq 2x + 8$

43. $10 - 2x^2 < 4x + 4$

44. $7 - x^2 < -2x - 1$

45. $x^2 - x - 6 \leq 12 + 2x - 2x^2$

46. $2x^2 - 11x + 5 \geq -10 + 22x - 4x^2$

47. $x^2 - 3x + \frac{21}{4} \geq 2x^2 - 6x + \frac{15}{2}$

48. $-x^2 - 5x - \frac{17}{4} \leq -\frac{1}{5}x^2 - x + \frac{3}{4}$

49. $x^2 - x - \frac{7}{4} > -2x^2 + 2x - \frac{5}{2}$

50. $x^2 + 6x + 5 < -x^2 - 6x - 13$

51. $x^2 + 4x + 8 \geq 4$

52. $-x^2 + 8x - 14 \geq 2$

53. $2 + 4x - x^2 > 10 - 4x + x^2$

54. $-7 - 4x - \frac{1}{2}x^2 < x^2 + 8x + 17$

55. An egg is thrown upward from a stand that is 25 feet above the ground. The initial speed of the egg is 30 feet per second. For what length of time is the egg higher than the stand?

56. An arrow is projected upward with an initial velocity of 40 feet per second from a height of 220 feet above the ground. Determine the length of time the arrow is higher than the height at which it was released.

57. A rock is hurled upward with an initial velocity of 75 feet per second from a cliff that is 1200 feet high. For what time period is the height of the rock no more than 800 feet?

58. A golf ball is hit upward from a ledge that is 600 feet high. The initial speed of the ball is 60 feet per second. Determine the length of time when the height of the ball is no more than 200 feet.

59. Stereo sets wholesale for $78 each. The minimum order a dealer can place is 5 stereos. For every stereo over 5 ordered, the price per stereo is reduced $3. If $x + 5$ represents the number of stereos ordered, the price per stereo will be $78 - 3x$. Write the revenue function if $x + 5$ stereos are ordered. How many stereos must be ordered for the revenue to be at least $600?

60. Microwave ovens are sold at wholesale for $59.00 each, with a minimum order of 12 ovens. For every oven over 12, the price per oven is reduced $2.50. Let $x + 12$ represent the number of ovens ordered. Write a revenue function for a retailer who orders $x + 12$ ovens at $59 - 2.5x$ dollars each. How many ovens must be ordered for the revenue to be more than $700.00?

61. The cost to operate a booth at a flea market for x days is given by the cost function $C(x) = 3x^2 + x + 35$. How many days can the booth be operated at a cost of no more than $100?

62. The cost to run a stand at a farmers' market for x weeks is given by the cost function $C(x) = 5x^2 + 25x + 50$. For how many weeks can the stand be run with a cost of less than $250?

63. A statistical study related the hourly compensation costs for production workers in Japan as $y = 0.058x^2 - 0.79x + 6.125$, where y is the cost in U.S. dollars and x is the number of years after 1970. Use this function to estimate the years in which the hourly costs exceeded $10.

64. Use the function in exercise 63 to determine the years in which the hourly cost was below $6.75.

 ## Experiencing Algebra the Calculator Way

A. Using the TEST Function to Graphically Solve a Quadratic Inequality

You may use the TEST function of the calculator to determine whether a quadratic inequality is true or false. The calculator denotes a true statement as "1" and a false statement as "0." Using the TEST function, you can graph the number line solution. As an example, suppose you wish to solve the inequality $x^2 + 5x - 6 > 0$.

- Set the screen to integer coordinates for x and tenths coordinates for y:

| ZOOM | 6 | ZOOM | 8 | ENTER | WINDOW | ▼ | ▼ | ▼ | (−) | 3 | . | 1 |

| ENTER | 3 | . | 1 | ENTER | 1 | ENTER | 2nd | QUIT |

- Enter the inequality in Y1. The inequality symbols are found under the TEST menu:

| Y= | X, T, θ, n | x² | + | 5 | X, T, θ, n | − | 6 | 2nd | TEST | 3 | 0 |

- Graph:

| GRAPH |

The calculator will graph a y-coordinate of 1 for all true statements and a 0 for all false statements. This will appear as a line segment on the screen. You can imagine the graph as a number line representation of the solution intervals for the inequality. You will have to use your understanding of the endpoints to correctly interpret the graph. Use the procedure to check the solutions of the previous exercises.

B. Using the TEST Function to Numerically Solve a Quadratic Inequality

You have been shown how to use the TABLE function to numerically solve a quadratic inequality. Sometimes it is confusing to compare Y1 and Y2 to determine the correct order relation. There is a way to reduce this confusion. As an example, numerically solve $2 - 3x - x^2 > x - 5$ for integer solutions.

- Store the inequality Y2 > Y3 in Y1, the left side of the inequality in Y2, and the right side of the inequality in Y3. (This will make it easier to scan for values of x that make the inequality true.)

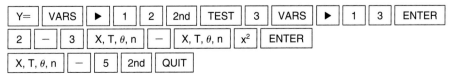

- Set the TBLSET to start at 0 and increment by 1 automatically.

- View the table, scanning up and down for various x-values. Wherever Y1 is equal to 1, the corresponding x-value is an integer solution for the inequality; wherever Y1 is equal to 0, the corresponding x-value is not a solution.

With this method, you no longer have to compare the Y2 and Y3 values to determine whether the x-value makes the inequality true or not. You see this immediately by reading the Y1 value.

Experiencing Algebra the Group Way

Solving a Quadratic Inequality Algebraically Using Sign Analysis

Another method to solve a quadratic inequality is to first write the quadratic inequality in standard form. If the corresponding quadratic equation can be factored, we can analyze the signs of the factors to determine whether a test point results in a true inequality. For example, solve $x^2 + 2x - 1 \geq 2$.

Write in standard form: $x^2 + 2x - 3 \geq 0$.
Determine the critical points by factoring.

$$x^2 + 2x - 3 = 0 \qquad \text{Standard form}$$
$$(x + 3)(x - 1) = 0 \qquad \text{Solve by factoring.}$$
$$x + 3 = 0 \quad \text{or} \quad x - 1 = 0$$
$$x = -3 \qquad\qquad x = 1$$

The inequality contains equality, so the critical points are solutions. We include them in the intervals.

Since we have written the inequality in standard form, we are testing to see whether the quadratic expression $x^2 + 2x - 3$ is greater than 0, or is a positive number. We can analyze the product without actually determining it because we know that the two factors must both have the same sign.

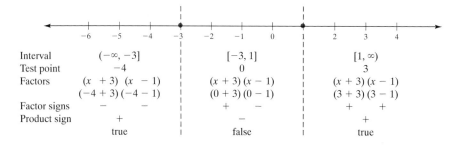

Interval	$(-\infty, -3]$	$[-3, 1]$	$[1, \infty)$
Test point	-4	0	3
Factors	$(x + 3)\ (x - 1)$	$(x + 3)\ (x - 1)$	$(x + 3)\ (x - 1)$
	$(-4 + 3)\ (-4 - 1)$	$(0 + 3)\ (0 - 1)$	$(3 + 3)\ (3 - 1)$
Factor signs	$-\qquad -$	$+\qquad -$	$+\qquad +$
Product sign	$+$	$-$	$+$
	true	false	true

Therefore, the solution set is $(-\infty, -3] \cup [1, \infty)$.

As another example, solve $x^2 + 3x - 4 \leq 2x + 2$ algebraically using sign analysis.

$$x^2 + 3x - 4 \leq 2x + 2$$
$$x^2 + x - 6 \leq 0 \qquad \text{Write in standard form.}$$
$$x^2 + x - 6 = 0 \qquad \text{Determine the critical points.}$$
$$(x + 3)(x - 2) = 0$$
$$x = -3 \quad \text{or} \quad x = 2$$

The inequality contains equality, so the critical points are solutions. We include them in the intervals.

Since we have written the inequality in standard form, we are testing to see whether the quadratic expression $x^2 + x - 6$ is less than 0, or is a negative number. We can analyze the product without actually determining it because we know that the two factors must have different signs.

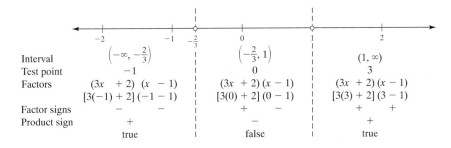

Interval	$(-\infty, -3]$	$[-3, 2]$	$[2, \infty)$
Test point	-4	0	3
Factors	$(x + 3)\ (x - 2)$	$(x + 3)\ (x - 2)$	$(x + 3)\ (x - 2)$
	$(-4 + 3)(-4 - 2)$	$(0 + 3)(0 - 2)$	$(3 + 3)(3 - 2)$
Factor signs	$-\qquad -$	$+\qquad -$	$+\qquad +$
Product sign	$+$	$-$	$+$
	false	true	false

Therefore, the solution is $[-3, 2]$.

As a final example, solve $3x^2 - x - 2 > 0$ using sign analysis.

$$3x^2 - x - 2 > 0$$

$$3x^2 - x - 2 = 0 \qquad \text{Determine the critical points.}$$

$$(3x + 2)(x - 1) = 0$$

$$x = -\frac{2}{3} \quad \text{or} \quad x = 1$$

The inequality does not contain equality. We do not include the endpoints as solutions.

Since we have written the inequality in standard form, we are testing to see whether the quadratic expression $3x^2 - x - 2$ is greater than 0, or is a positive number. We can analyze the product without actually determining it because we know that the two factors must have the same sign.

Interval	$\left(-\infty, -\frac{2}{3}\right)$	$\left(-\frac{2}{3}, 1\right)$	$(1, \infty)$
Test point	-1	0	3
Factors	$(3x + 2)\ (x - 1)$	$(3x + 2)(x - 1)$	$(3x + 2)(x - 1)$
	$[3(-1) + 2](-1 - 1)$	$[3(0) + 2](0 - 1)$	$[3(3) + 2](3 - 1)$
Factor signs	$-\qquad -$	$+\qquad -$	$+\qquad +$
Product sign	$+$	$-$	$+$
	true	false	true

Therefore, the solution is $\left(-\infty, -\frac{2}{3}\right) \cup (1, \infty)$.

Compare this method of solving with the method presented earlier in this section. Discuss in your group which of the two methods you prefer. Then have each member of the group use the algebraic method you prefer to solve the following exercises. Share your results.

1. $x^2 - 5x > 0$

2. $40 + 10x - 5x^2 \geq x^2 + 35x - 4$

3. $2m^2 + 15m - 40 < 6m + 16$

4. $z^2 + 12z - 25 \geq 3z + 11$

Experiencing Algebra the Write Way

When the graphical method is used to solve a quadratic inequality, the graph of the expression on the left, stored in Y1, may not intersect the graph of the expression on the right, stored in Y2. However, this does not necessarily mean that the inequality has no solutions. Sketch situations where this is so, and discuss conditions under which the inequality may have a solution.

CHAPTER 11	**Summary**

After completing this chapter, you should be able to define in your own words the following key terms, definitions, properties, and rules.

Terms

polynomial equation in one variable
polynomial equation
quadratic equation in one variable
quadratic equation
cubic equation in one variable
cubic equation
solution
solution set
vertical-position equation
root
double root
legs
hypotenuse
Pythagorean theorem
square-root expression
radical
radicand
principal square root
negative square root
rationalizing the denominator
completing the square
quadratic formula

discriminant
isosceles right triangle
congruent
equilateral triangle
quadratic inequality in one variable
quadratic inequality
union
critical points

Definitions

Standard forms for polynomial
  equations
Quadratic formula
Isosceles right triangle (45°–45°–90°)
Right triangle (30°–60°–90°)
Standard form for a quadratic
  inequality in one variable

Properties

Zero factor property
Product rule for square roots
Quotient rule for square roots
Principle of square roots

Rules

Solving a polynomial equation
  numerically
Solving a polynomial equation
  graphically
Solving a polynomial equation
  algebraically by factoring
Evaluating square-root
  expressions
Solving a quadratic equation using the
  principle of square roots
Solving a quadratic equation by
  completing the square
Determining the characteristics of the
  solution of a quadratic equation
  using the discriminant
Solving a quadratic inequality
  numerically
Solving a quadratic inequality
  graphically
Solving a quadratic inequality
  algebraically

CHAPTER 11	**Review**

Reflections

1. Define what is meant by a polynomial equation. What is the difference between a polynomial equation of degree two and one of degree three?

2. Explain how the zero factor property of real numbers can help you solve a polynomial equation algebraically.

3. Explain how the principle of square roots can help you solve a quadratic equation algebraically.

4. What is the quadratic formula and how is it used?

5. When can the Pythagorean theorem be used in modeling real-world situations?

6. What is the difference between a quadratic equation and a quadratic inequality? How do the solutions to each differ?

11.1

Solve numerically for integer solutions.

1. $2x^2 + 5x - 16 = 7x + 8$

2. $\frac{1}{3}x^2 + 5x + 6 = x - 3$

3. $0.7x^2 - 2.5x + 4.6 = 1.7x + 1.1$

Solve exercises 4–9 graphically.

4. $x^2 - 4x + 4 = 9$

5. $x^2 - 6 = \frac{1}{4}x^2 + 6$

6. $x^2 + 3x - 5 = 7 - 2x - x^2$

7. $-0.3x^2 + 4x + 5 = 2.2x - 11.5$ **8.** $x^2 + 8x + 8 = 0$ **9.** $\dfrac{1}{5}x^2 - 5x + 4 = 8 - \dfrac{1}{3}x^2$

10. An amateur scientist drops a lead weight from a platform 96 feet above the ground. How many seconds will it take for the weight to reach the ground?

11. The cost of producing x items is given by the mathematical model $C(x) = 8x^2 + 20x + 450$. How many items can be produced for $1850?

11.2

Solve exercises 12–19 algebraically by factoring.

12. $x^2 - 5 = x + 1$ **13** $6x^2 - x - 77 = 0$ **14.** $2x + 10 = x^2 - 5x + 2$

15. $x^2 - 7x - 60 = 0$ **16.** $3x^2 + 5x - 3 = 1 - 6x$ **17.** $6x^2 - 8x = 9x - 12$

18. $\dfrac{1}{4}x^2 + \dfrac{3}{2}x - \dfrac{19}{8} = \dfrac{3}{8}x + 2$ **19.** $9x^2 - 49 = 0$

20. Find the time it will take for a ball to reach the ground if it is thrown upward with an initial velocity of 48 feet per second from a height of 16 feet.

11.3

Simplify without using a calculator.

21. $\sqrt{25}$ **22.** $-\sqrt{49}$ **23.** $\sqrt{5}\sqrt{45}$ **24.** $\sqrt{15}\sqrt{21}$

25. $\sqrt{8}$ **26.** $\sqrt{\dfrac{64}{81}}$ **27.** $\sqrt{\dfrac{13}{25}}$ **28** $\sqrt{\dfrac{25}{3}}$

29. $\sqrt{\dfrac{2}{5}}$ **30.** $\sqrt{\dfrac{15}{21}}$ **31.** $\sqrt{\dfrac{6}{50}}$ **32.** $\dfrac{\sqrt{75}}{\sqrt{3}}$

Solve exercises 33–39 using the principle of square roots.

33. $4x^2 - 100 = 0$ **34.** $a^2 + 5 = 9$ **35.** $x^2 + 3 = 15$ **36.** $15 + b^2 = 7$

37. $(x - 4)^2 = 9$ **38.** $x^2 + 18x + 81 = 16$ **39.** $(z - 2)^2 + 5 = 7$

40. How long will it take a skydiver to free-fall from 10,000 feet to 6000 feet?

41. A boat ramp has a length of 35 feet. If the vertical distance of the ramp is 15 feet, what is the horizontal distance?

15 ft   35 ft   ?

42. A company has determined a mathematical model for annual sales in millions of dollars to be $s(x) = 28x^2 + 2000$, where x is the number of years after 1991. Determine the first year in which the company's annual sales will reach $3200 million.

11.4

Solve exercises 43–46 by completing the square.

43. $p^2 - 4p - 96 = 0$ **44.** $z^2 + 12z = -3$ **45.** $2x^2 - 5x - 12 = 0$ **46.** $x^2 + \dfrac{1}{2}x = 1$

47. The selling price of a collectible figurine is $20, but to discourage buyers from hoarding the figurines, a store adds a surcharge to the price. A customer may purchase the first three for $20 each, but the price for additional figurines is $20 plus $2 times the number in excess of three items. The cost of purchasing $x + 3$ figurines is $C(x) = 60 + x(20 + 2x)$. How many figurines can be purchased for $150? Solve by completing the square.

48. The length of a rectangle is 8 inches more than twice its width. The area of the rectangle is 90 square inches. Write a quadratic equation, and solve it by completing the square, to find the dimensions of the rectangle.

11.5
Use the quadratic formula to find exact solutions.

49. $x^2 - 2x - 63 = 0$ **50.** $x^2 = 3x + 3$ **51.** $25x^2 + 1 = 10x$ **52.** $z^2 + \dfrac{7}{20}z - \dfrac{3}{10} = 0$

53. $x^2 + 2.1x - 10.8 = 0$ **54.** $y^2 - 5y + 12 = 0$ **55.** $x^2 - 10x + 6 = 0$ **56.** $3a^2 - 4a - 12 = 0$

Evaluate the discriminant to determine the characteristics of the solution(s) of each quadratic equation. Do not solve the equation.

57. $x^2 + 2x + 10 = 0$ **58.** $x^2 + 20x + 55 = 2x - 26$

59. $x^2 = 10x + 75$ **60.** $x = x^2 - 11$

Use the compound-interest formula, $A = P(1 + r)^t$, to set up a quadratic equation for each situation and solve.

61. What must the annual interest rate be for $1000 to compound to $1166.40 after 2 years?

62. At what annual interest rate must $1000 be invested in order for it to compound to $1200 after 2 years?

63. The revenue function $R(x) = 600 + 26x - 2x^2$ represents the dollars received for selling $12 + x$ items at a price of $50 - 2x$ dollars per item. For what value of x will the revenue be approximately $450?

11.6
64. The two legs of a right triangle measure 11 inches and 60 inches. What is the length of the hypotenuse?

65. A surveyor wants to estimate the distance across a pond. She marks off a right triangle with the short leg spanning the pond. She measures the long leg to be 240 feet and the hypotenuse to be 250 feet. How wide is the pond?

66. A contractor has marked off the foundation for a rectangular patio. The width of the patio is to be 9 feet less than the length. The diagonal of the patio foundation is 45 feet. Find the dimensions of the patio. If the sides measure 27.5 feet and 35.4 feet, are the corners square?

67. What are the lengths of the legs of an isosceles right triangle whose hypotenuse measures 16.85 centimeters?

68. A rope attached to the top of a pole makes a 45 degree angle with the ground. If the pole is 7 feet high, how long is the rope?

69. Assume a right triangle is a 30°–60°–90° triangle. Determine the lengths of the sides of the triangle if the hypotenuse measures 20 inches.

Solve for the variable specified.

70. $A = \dfrac{1}{4}\pi d^2$ for d **71.** $a = bx^2 + c$ for x **72.** $s = -16t^2 + v_0 t + s_0$ for t

11.7
Solve numerically for integer solutions.

73. $x^2 + 6x - 9 \le 4x + 15$ **74.** $2x^2 + 3x - 8 > 6 + 4x - x^2$

Solve graphically.

75. $x^2 + 2x - 3 \ge 5$ **76.** $5 - x^2 \ge -4$ **77.** $x^2 - 2x - 1 < x + 3$

78. $x^2 + 3 < 1 - x^2$

79. $x^2 - 6x + 11 > -\frac{1}{2}x^2 + 3x - \frac{5}{2}$

80. $x^2 - 8x + 18 \leq \frac{1}{4}x^2 - 2x + 6$

81. $10 - 6x + x^2 < -4 + 6x - x^2$

Solve exercises 82–88 algebraically.

82. $x^2 - 4x + 4 < \frac{1}{4}x^2 - x + 3$

83. $x^2 + x - 6 \leq 12 - 2x - 2x^2$

84. $3 - z^2 > -2z$

85. $x^2 + 6x + 11 > -x^2 - 6x - 7$

86. $1 - 2x^2 \leq 1 - x^2$

87. $x^2 + 4x - 2 < -\frac{1}{2}x^2 - 2x - 8$

88. $p^2 - 6p - 1 < 0$

89. An item wholesales for $65. The minimum order is five items. For every item over five ordered, the wholesale price is reduced $2. If x represents the number of items over five ordered, the price will be $65 - 2x$, and the quantity ordered will be $x + 5$. Write the revenue function if $x + 5$ items are ordered. How many items must be ordered in order for the revenue to be at least $500?

90. The cost to rent a booth at a carnival for x days is given by the cost function $C(x) = 3x^2 + 25x + 50$. How many days can the booth be rented for a cost of no more than $200?

91. A dart is shot upward from a height 30 feet above the ground. The initial speed of the dart is 25 feet per second. For what length of time is the dart above the ground?

CHAPTER 11	**Mixed Review**

Simplify without using a calculator.

1. $-\sqrt{144}$

2. $\sqrt{125}$

3. $\sqrt{7}\sqrt{28}$

4. $\sqrt{\frac{121}{225}}$

5. $\sqrt{\frac{24}{135}}$

6. $\frac{\sqrt{63}}{\sqrt{28}}$

Solve graphically.

7. $x^2 - 4 = 2x - 1$

8. $3 - x^2 = -3 - \frac{1}{3}x^2$

9. $x^2 + 6x + 9 = 4$

10. $15x^2 + 13x - 72 = 0$

11. $2x + 10 = x^2 + 4x + 7$

12. $x^2 + 9x + 7 = 0$

13. $\frac{1}{6}x^2 - 2x + 7 = 9 - \frac{1}{4}x^2$

14. $x^2 - 6x - 40 = 0$

Solve numerically for integer solutions.

15. $2x^2 - x - 28 = x^2 + 3x + 17$

16. $3x^2 - 5x - 10 = 7x + 5$

Solve algebraically.

17. $12x^2 + 9x = 8x + 6$

18. $x^2 + 3x - 88 = 0$

19. $5x^2 + 14x - 6 = 8 - 19x$

20. $49x^2 - 16 = 0$

21. $5x^2 - 180 = 0$

22. $11 + b^2 = 2$

23. $(x - 9)^2 = 16$

24. $(p - 7)^2 + 6 = 9$

25. $z^2 + 12z = -33$

26. $m^2 + 7m + 12 = 9$

27. $b^2 + 2.4b - 4.32 = 0$

28. $q^2 - 7q - 78 = 0$

29. $x^2 + 20x + 84 = 0$

30. $2y^2 + 3y - 5 = 0$

31. $4x^2 + 16x - 2 = 0$

Use the quadratic formula to find the exact solution.

32. $4 + 8x + x^2 = 0$

33. $x^2 = 7x + 2$

34. $36q^2 + 25 = 60q$

35. $b^2 - 7b + 16 = 0$

36. $z^2 + 6z - 55 = 0$

37. $4m^2 + 7m = 36$

Solve for the variable specified.

38. $a = \dfrac{x(x + 1)}{2}$ for x

39. $x^2 + y^2 + z^2 = r^2$ for y

40. $A = 4\pi r^2$ for r

Solve for integer solutions numerically.

41. $x^2 + 2x - 7 \le 4x + 8$

42. $x^2 + 9x - 11 \le 4x + 3$

Solve algebraically.

43. $z^2 + 5z - 6 < 12 - 10z - 2z^2$

44. $m^2 - 15 > 2m$

45. $x^2 + 2x - 1 > -x^2 - 2x + 1$

46. $p^2 - 8p - 2 > 0$

47. $2x^2 - 5x - 11 \le 19 + 8x - x^2$

48. $3q^2 + 2q - 17 \ge 5q + 19$

Solve exercises 49–55 graphically.

49. $x^2 - 4x - 1 \ge x + 5$

50. $2 - x^2 > 5 + x^2$

51. $x^2 - 2x - 3 < 12$

52. $7 - x^2 > -9$

53. $x^2 + 4x - 2 > -5 - 4x - x^2$

54. $-x^2 - 10x - 27 < x^2 + 10x + 23$

55. $-x^2 + 6x - 7 > -\dfrac{1}{3}x^2 + 2x - 4$ **56.** $-x^2 + 6x - 6 \ge -\dfrac{1}{3}x^2 + 2x$

57. A student drops a notebook from 160 feet above ground level. How many seconds will it take for the notebook to reach the ground?

58. The cost of producing x items is given by the mathematical model $C(x) = 5x^2 + 75x + 875$. How many items can be produced for approximately $3500?

59. Find the time it will take for a rock to reach the ground if it is shot upward from a slingshot with an initial velocity of $v_0 = 64$ feet per second from a height of $s_0 = 32$ feet.

60. How long will it take a skydiver to free-fall from 11,000 feet to 4000 feet?

61. The hypotenuse of a right triangle measures 42.5 meters and one of its legs measures 34 meters. What is the measure of the other leg?

62. The area of a rectangle is 144 square cm. Its length measures 6 cm less than three times its width. Find the dimensions of the rectangle.

For exercises 63 and 64, use the compound-interest formula, $A = P(1 + r)^t$, to set up a quadratic equation for each situation and solve.

63. What must the annual interest rate be for $1200 to compound to $1323 after 2 years?

64. At what annual interest rate must $1200 be invested in order for it to compound to $1500 after 2 years?

65. The revenue function $R(x) = 850 + 35x - 5x^2$ represents the dollars received for selling $10 + x$ items at a price of $85 - 5x$ dollars per item. For what value of x will the revenue be approximately $650?

66. The two legs of a right triangle measure 20 inches and 48 inches. What is the length of the hypotenuse?

67. A surveyor wants to estimate the distance across a pond. She marks off a right triangle with the short leg spanning the pond. She measures the long leg to be 350 feet long and the hypotenuse to be 370 feet long. How wide is the pond?

68. One leg of a right triangle is 1 inch less than three times the length of the other leg. The hypotenuse of the triangle is 37 inches. Determine the lengths of the legs.

69. What are the lengths of the legs of an isosceles right triangle whose hypotenuse measures 14.21 centimeters?

70. A rope attached to the top of a pole makes a 45-degree angle with the ground. If the pole is 11 feet high, how long is the rope?

71. Assume that a right triangle is a 30°–60°–90° triangle. Determine the lengths of the sides of the triangle if the hypotenuse measures 32 inches.

72. The cost to rent a booth at a carnival for x days is given by the cost function $C(x) = 5x^2 + 20x + 100$. How many days can the booth be rented with a cost of no more than $500?

CHAPTER 11 | **Test**

Test-Taking Tips

Many students have failed a test at some point in their academic life. It is important that you respond to such a failure properly. Don't blame your teacher, your background, your past performance, your personal deficiencies, or other difficulties in your personal life. These are just excuses for the lack of success. Instead, make up your mind that you will do whatever it takes to master the skills being taught. Learn from your mistakes. If you can, meet with your instructor to review the test, with emphasis on the problems you missed. Try to see how you should have approached the problem. If your mistakes are careless mistakes, think of steps you can take to avoid these in the future. For example, if you make mistakes in transcribing the problem to your paper, make a vow always to check what you transcribe before you begin working the problem. If you make arithmetic mistakes, stop doing the arithmetic in your head. Instead do the work on paper, and use a calculator whenever you are permitted to do so. Remember that if you do your work neatly and in an orderly manner, it will help you understand the problem. The secret to being successful at mathematics is to be patient and to persevere.

Solve.

1. $x^2 - 4x - 9 = 2x + 7$

2. $2x^3 + 9x^2 - 23x - 66 = 0$

3. $4(x - 5)^2 + 7 = 71$

4. $x^2 - 6x + 13 = 0$

5. $2x^2 - 7x + 3 = 2x - 1$

6. $x^2 - 5x + 4 = 7 - 3x - x^2$

7. $x^2 - x - 6 \leq 6$

8. $(x + 3)(x - 2) < 3(x + 3)$

9. $2x^2 + 7x - 9 \geq 4x + 11$

In exercises 10–11, evaluate the discriminant, then find the exact roots, if possible.

10. $x^2 - 9x + 9 = 7x - 5$

11. $x^2 - 3x + 12 = 0$

12. Solve $s = at^2 + c$ for t.

13. Solve $x^2 - 2 = x + 4$

    a. numerically

    b. graphically

    c. algebraically

14. One leg of a right triangle is 4 inches longer than the other leg. The hypotenuse measures 20 inches. Find the lengths of the legs.

15. Keanu free-falls from 11,500 feet above the ground until he reaches 2600 feet, when he opens his parachute. Use the vertical-position equation, $s = -16t^2 + v_0t + s_0$, to determine the length of time Keanu was free-falling.

16. Use the compound-interest formula, $A = P(1 + r)^t$, to solve the following interest problem: What must the annual interest rate be for \$1400 to compound to \$1573 in 2 years?

17. E-Z Rental charges \$15 to rent a tiller plus a daily rental charge of \$25. The price for rental beyond the first day is reduced by \$2 times the number of additional days of rental. The total cost of is $C(x) = 40 + 25x - 2x^2$ if the tiller is rented for $x + 1$ days. If you can afford to spend no more than \$100 to rent the tiller, for how many additional days can you rent? (Assume rental is limited to no more than 7 days.)

18. Explain how to use the value of the discriminant of a quadratic equation to describe the characteristics of the solution(s) of the equation.

12

Rational Expressions, Functions, and Equations

I n this chapter, we define rational expressions and functions and perform operations on them. Since rational functions are simply ratios of two polynomials, the discussion follows naturally from the preceding chapters on polynomial expressions and functions. Once we've established the basic techniques for working with rational functions, we can show how to use them in equations and how to solve these equations.

Equations involving rational functions are extremely important in virtually all areas of applied mathematics. They are central to the basic description of electrical circuits, arising in all areas of electronic and computer design. Economic theory and business practice involve rational functions, as do medical practice, biology, and chemistry. We will discuss only the fundamental ideas of rational functions in this chapter, but you should be aware that they underlie the mathematical descriptions of most areas of modern technology.

12.1 Rational Expressions and Functions

Objectives

1 Identify rational expressions.

2 Determine the domain of rational functions.

3 Create a table of values for rational functions.

4 Graph rational functions using a set of ordered pairs.

5 Model real-world situations using rational functions.

Application

A solar-powered Mars rover vehicle can be controlled from Earth by sending it path commands. In developing the control system, the rational function $T(s) = \frac{2}{s^2+4s+5}$ arises. (The variable s represents a parameter whose meaning we will not discuss.) Set up a table of values for $T(s)$ when $s = -6, -5, -4, -3, -2, -1, 0, 1,$ and 2.

After completing this section, we will discuss this application further. See page 911.

---

1 Rational Expressions

In Chapter 1, we defined a **rational number** to be a number that can be written as a ratio $\frac{a}{b}$, where a and b are integers with $b \neq 0$. When a rational number is written in this form, we call the number a fraction. For example, $\frac{5}{8}$ is a rational number and a fraction. However, a rational number may be written in a form other than the ratio form. For example, 17 is a rational number, but is written as an integer. Also, 0.625 is a rational number, but is written in decimal form.

In this chapter, we discuss rational expressions. A **rational expression** can be written as a ratio $\frac{A}{B}$, where A and B are polynomials with $B \neq 0$. As we continue our discussion of rational expressions with variables in the denominator, we assume that the denominator does not equal 0. For example, $\frac{x+y}{2x}$ is a rational expression. When a rational expression is written in this form, we may also call the expression an **algebraic fraction**. Therefore, $\frac{x+y}{2x}$ is both a rational expression and an algebraic fraction. Just as rational numbers may be written in a form other than the ratio form, so can rational expressions. The polynomial $6x + 4$ may be written as the ratio $\frac{6x+4}{1}$, so it is considered a rational expression. However, it is not an algebraic fraction.

> *Rational Expression*
> A rational expression can be written in the form
>
> $$\frac{A}{B},$$
>
> where A and B are polynomials with $B \neq 0$.

Examples of rational expressions that are also algebraic fractions are $\frac{6}{xy}$ and $\frac{x^2+2x-15}{x+5}$.

Other kinds of expressions, such as $x^2 + \frac{5}{2z}$, are also rational expressions. To determine that this is true, we need to manipulate the expression. Since we do not yet have these skills, we will identify a rational expression as a sum of terms, each of which is a rational expression. The term x^2 can be written as a rational expression in the form $\frac{x^2}{1}$, and the term $\frac{5}{2z}$ is already in ratio form. Therefore, $x^2 + \frac{5}{2z}$ is a rational expression.

EXAMPLE 1   Identify each expression as rational or nonrational. If the expression is a rational expression, determine whether it is also an algebraic fraction.

a. $\dfrac{12 + \sqrt{x}}{x}$

b. $x^5 y + 9z$

c. $\dfrac{x^3 + x^2 - 3}{x - 5}$

d. a^{-3}

Solution

a. $\frac{12+\sqrt{x}}{x}$ is not a rational expression. The expression $12 + \sqrt{x}$ is not a polynomial, because it contains a square-root expression with a variable radicand, $\sqrt{x}$. Therefore, $\frac{12+\sqrt{x}}{x}$ is not a ratio of two polynomials.

b. $x^5 y + 9z$ is a rational expression, because it may be written as $\frac{x^5 y + 9z}{1}$ or $\frac{x^5 y}{1} + \frac{9z}{1}$. It is a polynomial, not an algebraic fraction.

c. $\frac{x^3 + x^2 - 3}{x - 5}$ is a rational expression and an algebraic fraction, because $\left(x^3 + x^2 - 3\right)$ and $(x - 5)$ are both polynomials.

d. a^{-3} is a rational expression and an algebraic fraction, because it can be written as $\frac{1}{a^3}$. ∎

Note: Example 1b is a polynomial and also a rational expression. According to the definition of rational expressions, all polynomial expressions are rational expressions. However, since we have already studied polynomial expressions, we will limit our main discussion in this chapter to nonpolynomial rational expressions (algebraic fractions).

Experiencing Algebra the Checkup Way

Identify each expression as rational or nonrational. For each one that is rational, determine whether it is also an algebraic fraction.

1. $\dfrac{x^2 + 2x + 1}{x + 1}$

2. $\dfrac{3\sqrt[5]{x} + 2x}{x + 3}$

3. $x^2 + \dfrac{9}{x - 3}$

4. $4x^3 - 2x^2 + x - 5$

5. $4x^{-2}$

6. $\dfrac{2xy}{z}$

7. All algebraic fractions are rational expressions, but not all rational expressions are algebraic fractions. Explain why.

---

2 Determining the Domain of Rational Functions

A special type of relation, a rational relation, equates a rational expression in one independent variable to a dependent variable. For example, $y = \frac{9}{x}$ and $y = \frac{x^2 - 4}{x + 2}$ are rational relations. Some rational relations are also functions and, therefore, may be written using function notation, such as $f(x) = \frac{9}{x}$ and $g(x) = \frac{x^2 - 4}{x + 2}$.

> **Rational Function**
> A rational function can be written in the form
>
> $$f(x) = \frac{A(x)}{B(x)},$$
>
> where $A(x)$ and $B(x)$ are polynomial functions with $B(x) \neq 0$.

Examples of **rational functions** are as follows:

$$f(x) = \frac{6}{x}$$

$$g(x) = \frac{x + 2}{x + 1}$$

$$h(x) = \frac{x^2 + 2x - 15}{x + 5}$$

$$j(x) = \frac{5}{x} + \frac{4}{x^2}$$

The domain of a polynomial function is all real numbers. However, this may not be true for a rational function. Sometimes, substituting certain values for the independent variable in a rational expression results in undefined values for the fractional term. Such numbers must be excluded from the domain. We do this by identifying them as restrictions on the domain or **restricted values**. We need to be able to determine these restricted values. Complete the following set of exercises to determine a method for finding the restrictions on the domain of a rational function.

DISCOVERY 1

Restricted Values

1. Complete the following tables of values for the given rational functions.

    a. $f(x) = \dfrac{6}{x}$ **b.** $g(x) = \dfrac{x+2}{x-1}$ **c.** $h(x) = \dfrac{x^2 - x - 2}{x-2}$

x	$f(x)$		x	$g(x)$		x	$h(x)$
-3			-3			-3	
-2			-2			-2	
-1			-1			-1	
0			0			0	
1			1			1	
2			2			2	
3			3			3	

2. Determine the restricted values of each function.
    a.   **b.**   **c.**
    Graph on a calculator screen $(-9.4, 9.4, 1, -6.2, 6.2, 1, 1)$ the given rational functions. Trace each function's graph.
3. What happens when you reach the point on a graph for the restricted x-values found above?

Write a rule to determine the restricted values of a rational function by viewing its table of values.
    Write a rule to determine the restricted values of a rational function by viewing its graph.
    Write a rule to determine the restricted values of a rational function algebraically.

The restrictions on the domain of a rational function are the numbers that result in undefined values for the rational expression. On the function's graph, the restricted values (x-values) of the function do not have corresponding function values. This occurs because the function cannot be evaluated when the denominator of the rational expression is 0. Therefore, to determine the restricted values algebraically, set the expression in the denominator of the rational expression equal to 0 and solve for x.

We have discovered three methods—numeric, graphic, and algebraic—of determining the restricted values from the domain of a rational function. The numeric and graphic methods have limitations as to their effectiveness, so they should be used as a check of the algebraic method.

To determine algebraically the restricted values of a rational function:

- Set the expression in the denominator equal to 0.
- Solve for the independent variable.

This method will find all the restricted values.

To determine numerically, on your calculator, the restricted integer values of a rational function, set up a table of values.

- Rename the independent variable as x and the dependent variable as y.
- Enter the rational expression as Y1.
- Set up the table values. Enter the minimum integer value and an increment of 1 (for integer values). Set the calculator to automatically perform the evaluations.
- View the table and move through the table with the up and down arrows.

Restricted integer values are the x-values that result in errors in the table. This method will only determine integer values.

To determine graphically, on your calculator, the restricted values of a rational function:

- Enter the equation in Y1.
- Graph the equation.
- Trace the equation by using the left or right arrow keys.

The x-values that have no corresponding y-values are restricted values for the rational function. This will determine x-values according to the calculator window setting.

For example, determine the restricted values and then state the domain of the rational function $f(x) = \frac{x^2-4}{x-2}$.

Algebraically	*Numerically*	*Graphically*

$$x - 2 = 0$$
$$x = 2$$

X	Y1
0	2
1	3
2	ERROR
3	5
4	6
5	7
6	8

X=0

$$Y1 = \frac{x^2 - 4}{x - 2}$$

The function is not defined at $x = 2$.

$$Y1 = \frac{x^2 - 4}{x - 2}$$

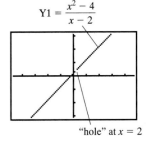

"hole" at $x = 2$

$(-47, 47, -31, 31)$

The graph has a "hole" at $x = 2$.

The restricted value is 2.

The domain is all real numbers not equal to 2.

$x \neq 2$ Inequality notation

$(-\infty, 2) \cup (2, \infty)$ Interval notation

Helping Hand The union symbol ($\cup$) joins the two intervals and is read "or," meaning that the elements in the domain are in the first interval or in the second interval.

EXAMPLE 2   Determine algebraically the restricted values and then state the domain of the given rational functions. Check your answer numerically or graphically.

a. $h(x) = \dfrac{x+4}{x^2 - x - 20}$ **b.** $j(x) = \dfrac{6}{x^2 + 12}$ **c.** $m(x) = \dfrac{3x+1}{5x-8}$

Solution

a. $h(x) = \dfrac{x+4}{x^2 - x - 20}$

To determine the restricted values, set the denominator equal to 0 and solve for x by factoring.

$$x^2 - x - 20 = 0$$

$$(x+4)(x-5) = 0$$

$$x + 4 = 0 \quad \text{or} \quad x - 5 = 0$$

$$x = -4 \qquad\qquad x = 5$$

The restricted values are -4 and 5.

Domain: All real numbers not equal to -4 or 5
$$x \neq -4 \quad \text{or} \quad x \neq 5$$
$$(-\infty, -4) \cup (-4, 5) \cup (5, \infty)$$

Since the restricted values are integers, check the answer numerically. Let $Y1 = \frac{x+4}{x^2-x-20}$ and view the table.

X	Y1	
-4	ERROR	
-3	-.125	
-2	-.1429	
-1	-.1667	
0	-.2	
1	-.25	
2	-.3333	
X= -4		

X	Y1	
-1	-.1667	
0	-.2	
1	-.25	
2	-.3333	
3	-.5	
4	-1	
5	ERROR	
X=5		

The function values for $x = -4$ and $x = 5$ are undefined.
The restricted values are -4 and 5. The answer checks.

b. $j(x) = \dfrac{6}{x^2 + 12}$

To determine the restricted values, set the denominator equal to 0 and solve for x.

$$x^2 + 12 = 0$$

The expression on the left does not factor. Also, note that if we subtract 12 from both sides, we obtain $x^2 = -12$. There is no real number whose square is a negative number. Therefore, there are no restricted values in the real-number system.

Domain: All real numbers
$$(-\infty, \infty)$$

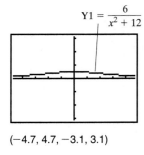

$Y1 = \dfrac{6}{x^2 + 12}$

$(-4.7, 4.7, -3.1, 3.1)$

Let's check this graphically.

The graphed function does not appear to have any "holes" in it. Therefore, the answer checks.

c. $m(x) = \dfrac{3x + 1}{5x - 8}$

To determine the restricted values, set the denominator equal to 0 and solve for x.

$$5x - 8 = 0$$
$$5x = 8$$
$$x = \dfrac{8}{5}$$

The restricted value is $\frac{8}{5}$.

Domain: All real numbers not equal to $\frac{8}{5}$
$$x \neq \tfrac{8}{5}$$
$$\left(-\infty, \tfrac{8}{5}\right) \cup \left(\tfrac{8}{5}, \infty\right)$$

$Y1 = \dfrac{3x + 1}{5x - 8}$

Y1=(3X+1)/(5X-8)

X=1.6   Y=

$(-9.4, 9.4, -6.2, 6.2)$

Since the restricted value is not an integer, we cannot use a table of integer values. Check graphically.

The function is not defined for $x = 1.6$ or $\frac{8}{5}$. The answer checks. ∎

Experiencing Algebra the Checkup Way

In exercises 1–4, determine algebraically the restricted values and then state the domain of the given rational functions. Check your answer numerically or graphically.

1. $s(x) = \dfrac{x^2 + x - 12}{x + 4}$ **2.** $g(x) = \dfrac{x + 8}{x^2 + x - 12}$ **3.** $C(x) = \dfrac{8x}{x^2 + 1}$ **4.** $a(b) = \dfrac{4}{2b - 3}$

5. What does it mean to say that a rational function has restricted values?

3   Creating a Table of Values

Now that we can determine the domain of a rational function, we want to evaluate the function for values in its domain. To do this, we set up an extended table of values.

Helping Hand In section 9.2, we set up tables of values for polynomial functions. We follow the same steps for setting up a table of values for a rational function.

For example, evaluate the function $y = \frac{5}{x} + \frac{4}{x^2}$ for three values in its domain.

Set up a table of values. Choose any permissible value for x, the independent variable, and obtain a value for y, the dependent variable, by solving the equation. We will use -1, 1, and 2 for x-values. *Note:* We cannot use the restricted value of 0.

x	$y = \dfrac{5}{x} + \dfrac{4}{x^2}$	y
-1	$y = \dfrac{5}{-1} + \dfrac{4}{(-1)^2}$ $y = -5 + 4$ $y = -1$	-1
1	$y = \dfrac{5}{1} + \dfrac{4}{1^2}$ $y = 5 + 4$ $y = 9$	9
2	$y = \dfrac{5}{2} + \dfrac{4}{2^2}$ $y = \dfrac{5}{2} + 1$ $y = \dfrac{7}{2}$	$\dfrac{7}{2}$

Therefore, $(-1, -1)$, $(1, 9)$, and $\left(2, \frac{7}{2}\right)$ are three ordered-pair solutions of the rational function $y = \frac{5}{x} + \frac{4}{x^2}$.

On your calculator, set up a table of value functions to evaluate the function $y = \frac{5}{x} + \frac{4}{x^2}$.

X	Y1
-1	-1
0	ERROR
1	9
2	3.5
3	2.1111
4	1.5
5	1.16

X = -1

$$Y1 = \frac{5}{x} + \frac{4}{x^2}$$

Helping Hand This table was generated using the Auto mode for TBLSET. However, the Ask mode could also be used. See "Experiencing Algebra the Calculator Way" in this section.

EXAMPLE 3 Evaluate the function $p(x) = \frac{x^2 - 4}{x - 2}$ for $x = -1, 0$, and 1.

Solution

x	$p(x) = \dfrac{x^2 - 4}{x - 2}$	$p(x)$
-1	$p(-1) = \dfrac{(-1)^2 - 4}{-1 - 2}$ $p(-1) = \dfrac{-3}{-3}$ $p(-1) = 1$	1
0	$p(0) = \dfrac{0^2 - 4}{0 - 2}$ $p(0) = \dfrac{-4}{-2}$ $p(0) = 2$	2
1	$p(1) = \dfrac{1^2 - 4}{1 - 2}$ $p(1) = \dfrac{-3}{-1}$ $p(1) = 3$	3

X	Y1	
-1	1	
0	2	
1	3	
2	ERROR	
3	5	
4	6	
5	7	

X= -1

$Y1 = \dfrac{x^2 - 4}{x - 2}$

Therefore, $(-1, 1), (0, 2)$, and $(1, 3)$ are three solutions of the rational function. To use your calculator rewrite $p(x)$ as y and evaluate the function for integer values of x beginning with -1. ∎

Experiencing Algebra the Checkup Way

Evaluate the function for the three given values.

1. $y = \dfrac{30}{x^3} + \dfrac{6}{x}$ for $x = -1, 1, 2$

2. $g(x) = \dfrac{x}{x + 4}$ for $x = -2, 0, 2$

4 Graphing Rational Functions

Rational functions have an infinite number of possible solutions. In order to illustrate these solutions, we use a graph. When we graphed linear functions, we needed two points to determine the linear pattern and one additional point for a check point. To graph quadratic functions, we determined the vertex and several points to the left and right of it in order to see the pattern. To graph a rational function, determine the restricted values. These values will not have corresponding function values. Then graph several points to the left and right of each restricted value to see a pattern. This may be a very lengthy process by hand.

To graph a rational function:

- Determine the restrictions on the domain.
- Determine a table of values by choosing x-values less than and greater than the restricted values. Pay close attention to the x-values close to the restricted values.
- Graph the function by plotting the sample set of ordered pairs from the table of values and connecting the points with a smooth curve determined by the pattern seen. Be careful not to cross the vertical line where x is equal to a restricted value, because the restricted values do not have corresponding function values.

Note: The calculator TABLE function in Ask mode will set up this table.

To graph a rational function on your calculator:

- Enter the equation in Y1.
- Choose an appropriate viewing screen (integers, decimals, standard, or set your own values) and graph.
- Determine individual solutions. Trace and move the cursor using the left and right arrow keys.

Helping Hand The calculator window setting is very important to the "picture" you receive. You should carefully consider your choices.

For example, graph the rational function $y = \frac{5}{x} + \frac{4}{x^2}$.

The restricted value is 0. Therefore, complete a table of values by choosing x-values less than 0, such as $-0.01, -0.1, -0.5, -1, -2, -3, -4, -5,$ and -6, and x-values greater than 0, such as $0.01, 0.1, 0.5, 1, 2, 3, 4, 5,$ and 6.

x	y		x	y
-6	-0.722		0.01	40500
-5	-0.84		0.1	450
-4	-1		0.5	26
-3	-1.222		1	9
-2	-1.5		2	3.5
-1	-1		3	2.111
-0.5	6		4	1.5
-0.1	350		5	1.16
-0.01	39500		6	0.944

Graph the ordered pairs found in the table of values and connect the points with a smooth curve. Do *not* connect across the vertical line when x is equal to the restricted value 0, or $x = 0$.

$$y = \frac{5}{x} + \frac{4}{x^2}$$

(2, 3.5)
(3, 2.111)
(6, 0.944)
(4, 1.5)
(−5, −0.84) (−1, −1)
(−6, −0.722)
(5, 1.16)
(−4, −1)
(−3, −1.222)
(−2, −1.5)

On your calculator, graph the rational function $y = \dfrac{5}{x} + \dfrac{4}{x^2}$.

$$Y1 = \frac{5}{x} + \frac{4}{x^2}$$

$(-47, 47, -31, 31)$

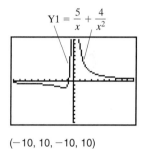

$$Y1 = \frac{5}{x} + \frac{4}{x^2}$$

$(-10, 10, -10, 10)$

EXAMPLE 4   Graph the rational functions.

a. $p(x) = \dfrac{x^2 - 4}{x - 2}$ **b.** $y = \dfrac{x^2 - x - 15}{x + 3}$

Solution

a. $p(x) = \dfrac{x^2 - 4}{x - 2}$

The restricted value is 2. Set up a table of values using x-values less than and greater than the restricted value 2.

x	$p(x)$		x	$p(x)$
−1	1		2.01	4.01
0	2		2.1	4.1
1	3		2.5	4.5
1.5	3.5		3	5
1.9	3.9		4	6
1.99	3.99		5	7

Graph the ordered pairs found in the table of values and connect the points with a smooth curve. Again, do not cross the vertical line $x = 2$.

Therefore, there is a "hole" in the graph at $x = 2$. It should be enclosed with an open dot to show that it is not included in the linear graph.

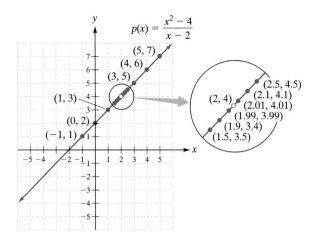

b. $y = \dfrac{x^2 - x - 15}{x + 3}$

The restricted value is -3. Set up a table of values using x-values less than and greater than the restricted value -3.

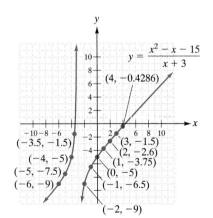

x	y
-6	-9
-5	-7.5
-4	-5
-3.5	-1.5
-3.1	22.9
-3.01	292.99

x	y
-2.99	-307
-2.9	-36.9
-2.5	-12.5
-2	-9
-1	-6.5
0	-5
1	-3.75
2	-2.6
3	-1.5
4	-0.4286

Graph the ordered pairs found in the table of values and connect the points with a smooth curve. Do not connect across the vertical line $x = -3$.

Calculator Solution

Helping Hand It is always a good idea to look at your table of values as well as your calculator graph. Your calculator graphs may be misleading without proper settings.

a. Enter the equation in Y1, graph, and choose the best viewing screen. The integer screen is not a good picture.

Note: The standard screen does not show the "hole" because it is an integer value for *x*.

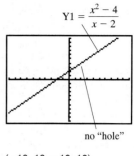

$(-47, 47, -31, 31)$ $(-10, 10, -10, 10)$

b. Enter the equation in Y1, graph, and choose the best viewing screen. The integer screen is not a good picture. The decimal screen shows very little of the graph. The standard screen adds an extra line in the graph. Also, notice that the graph appears to be defined at $x = -3$, a restricted value.

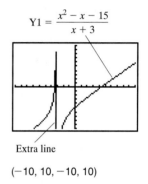

$(-47, 47, -31, 31)$ $(-4.7, 4.7, -3.1, 3.1)$ $(-10, 10, -10, 10)$

The extra line is due to the fact that the calculator is in connected mode. It connected the two parts of the graph across the vertical line, $x = -3$. To graph only points, change the calculator to dot mode, as shown in Figure 12.1. ■

TECHNOLOGY

$(-10, 10, -10, 10)$

Figure 12.1

For Figure 12.1

Set the calculator to dot mode.

| MODE |

Arrow down and to the right to Dot.

Highlight Dot and press | ENTER |.

Now press | GRAPH |.

Experiencing Algebra the Checkup Way

Graph the rational functions in exercises 1–4.

1. $y = \dfrac{8}{x^2} + \dfrac{24}{x^3}$ **2.** $h(x) = \dfrac{x^2 + 8x + 15}{x + 3}$ **3.** $g(x) = \dfrac{x^2 - 5x + 8}{x - 2}$ **4.** $c(x) = \dfrac{2}{x} + \dfrac{7}{2x}$

5. Do you think a graph presents a more complete description of the solutions to a rational function than a table of values does? Explain.

---

5 Modeling the Real World   Rational expressions occur in many models of real-world problems. One common example comes from the distance-traveled formula, $d = rt$, where d is the distance traveled by a moving object; r is its average rate, or speed (which we assume to be constant); and t is the time of travel. If we solve this equation for the time t, we get the rational expression $t = \dfrac{d}{r}$.

EXAMPLE 5   Margaret breaks her leg during her vacation and requires surgery. She wants to have the surgery at home. The hospital she is in is 3 miles from the airport. The flight home is 625 miles. The air attendant states that the average plane speed is three times the average speed of ground transportation in an ambulance.

Hospital   Airport   Home
|← 3 mi →|←——————————— 625 mi ———————————→|

a. Let $x =$ the speed of the ambulance
Write a function, $T(x)$, for the total time traveled to arrive at Margaret's home airport.
b. Graph the function.
c. If the ambulance speed from the hospital to the airport was 65 mph, estimate to the nearest hundredth of an hour the total time traveled to Margaret's home airport.
d. If Margaret travels 4 hours to reach her home airport, estimate to the nearest mile per hour the average speed of the ambulance from the hospital to the airport.

Solution

a. Since $t = \dfrac{d}{r}$, we determine the following from the problem:

Time traveled by the ambulance is $\dfrac{3}{x}$.

Time traveled by the plane is $\dfrac{625}{3x}$.

The total time traveled is the sum of the two times, or $T(x) = \dfrac{3}{x} + \dfrac{625}{3x}$.

b.

$$Y1 = \frac{3}{x} + \frac{625}{3x}$$

$(-10, 84, -10, 114)$

c. Evaluate $T(65)$. According to the graph, when x is 65, $T(x)$ is approximately 3.25.

$$Y1 = \frac{3}{x} + \frac{625}{3x}$$

X=65   Y=3.2512821

$(-10, 84, -10, 114)$

The total time traveled is approximately 3.25 hours when the ambulance speed is 65 mph.

d. Trace the calculator graph. When $T(x) \approx 4$, then x is approximately 53.

$$Y1 = \frac{3}{x} + \frac{625}{3x}$$

X=53   Y=3.9874214

$(-10, 84, -10, 114)$

The average ambulance speed is approximately 53 mph when the total time traveled is 4 hours. ∎

Application

A solar-powered Mars rover vehicle can be controlled from Earth by sending it path commands. In developing the control system, the rational function $T(s) = \frac{2}{s^2 + 4s + 5}$ arises. (The variable s represents a parameter whose meaning we will not discuss.) Set up a table of values for $T(s)$ when $s = -6$, $-5, -4, -3, -2, -1, 0, 1$, and 2.

Discussion

Let $Y1 = \frac{2}{x^2 + 4x + 5}$.

X	Y1
‐6	.11765
‐5	.2
‐4	.4
‐3	1
‐2	2
‐1	1
0	.4
X=‐6	

X	Y1
‐4	.4
‐3	1
‐2	2
‐1	1
0	.4
1	.2
2	.11765
X=2	

■

Experiencing Algebra the Checkup Way

A trucking company makes a delivery 270 miles away. The truck travels 60 miles on rural roads and 210 miles on interstate highways. The average speed of the truck on the interstate is 10 miles per hour less than twice its average speed on the rural roads.

a. Letting x be the average speed on the rural roads, write a function $T(x)$ for the total time of the delivery trip.

b. Graph the function on your calculator.

c. If the average speed on the rural road was 35 mph, use the graph to estimate to the nearest tenth of an hour the total time of the delivery trip.

d. If the total time of the trip was 6 hours, use the graph to find the average speed on the rural roads and calculate the average speed on the interstate.

PROBLEM SET 12.1

Experiencing Algebra the Exercise Way

Determine whether each expression is rational or nonrational. For each one that is rational, determine whether it is also an algebraic fraction.

1. $\dfrac{x^2 + 10x + 25}{x + 5}$

2. $\dfrac{x + 4\sqrt{x} + 7}{x - 2}$

3. $z - 4 - \dfrac{25}{z - 4}$

4. $0.8a^2 - 0.2a + 1.2$

5. $\dfrac{x + 3}{\sqrt{x} - 2}$

6. $6x - 3x^{-1}$

7. $6x^2 + 17x - 3$

8. $\dfrac{\sqrt{x} + 3}{5x}$

9. $\dfrac{11}{3xy}$

10. $\dfrac{\sqrt{x^2 + 4}}{x - 6}$

11. $3x^{-2} + 4x^{-1} + 3 - x$

12. $\dfrac{1}{2}x^2 - \dfrac{3}{4}x + \dfrac{7}{8}$

13. $\dfrac{0.5x + 7}{1.2x - 4}$

14. $a + 7 - \dfrac{6}{a + 1}$

15. $\dfrac{2 - 3\sqrt{x}}{2x}$

16. $\dfrac{4}{7 - xy}$

Determine algebraically the restricted values and then state the domain of each rational function. Check your answer numerically or graphically.

17. $y = \dfrac{3 - x}{x}$

18. $y = \dfrac{1 - x}{x^2 + 8x + 15}$

19. $h(x) = \dfrac{x - 5}{x^2 - 11x + 30}$

20. $g(x) = \dfrac{4x^2 + 1}{2x^2 + 6x}$

21. $C(x) = \dfrac{x + 7}{x^2 - 4}$

22. $y = \dfrac{5x^2 - 2}{x^3 - 4x^2 - x + 4}$

23. $y = \dfrac{2x^2 + 7}{x^2 - 5x}$

24. $b(x) = \dfrac{x + 7}{5x}$

25. $f(x) = \dfrac{x + 2}{x^3 - 2x^2 + 4x - 8}$

26. $y = \dfrac{55}{x^2 + 4x + 4}$

27. $f(x) = \dfrac{7}{2x^2 + 17x + 35}$

28. $y = \dfrac{12}{25x^2 + 30x + 9}$

29. $y = \dfrac{x^2 - 3x}{8x^2 + 6x - 9}$

30. $F(x) = \dfrac{x^3 - 8}{4x^3 + 20x^2 - 64x - 320}$

31. $y = \dfrac{4x}{4x^2 + 36x + 81}$

32. $g(x) = \dfrac{7x - 3}{14x^2 + 25x + 9}$

33. $h(x) = \dfrac{6 - x}{x^2 - 22x + 121}$

34. $y = \dfrac{5x + 2}{x^2 + 3x + 4}$

35. $y = \dfrac{3x^2}{9x^2 - 25}$

36. $y = \dfrac{9x^3}{6x^2 + 13x - 15}$

37. $C(x) = \dfrac{5x^3 + 1}{2x^3 + 4x^2 - 18x - 36}$

38. $y = \dfrac{2x^2 + 1}{16x^2 - 49}$

39. $y = \dfrac{3x + 8}{2x^2 + 5x + 7}$

40. $f(x) = \dfrac{9 - 2x}{9x^2 - 24x + 16}$

41. $y = \dfrac{x + 4}{2x + 3}$

42. $g(x) = \dfrac{8x^2 + 19}{10x^2 + 3x - 18}$

Evaluate each function for $x = -3, -1, 0, 1, 3$, if possible.

43. $y = \dfrac{6}{x} + \dfrac{9}{x^2}$

44. $y = \dfrac{25x^2 - 4}{5x + 2}$

45. $h(x) = \dfrac{x^2 - 49}{x - 7}$

46. $g(x) = \dfrac{4x}{x^3 + 1}$

47. $y = \dfrac{2x}{x^2 + 3}$

48. $f(x) = \dfrac{9}{x} - \dfrac{36}{x^2}$

49. $y = \dfrac{50}{x^2} + \dfrac{15}{x}$

50. $g(x) = \dfrac{2x^2 + 5}{3x + 1}$

51. $f(x) = \dfrac{x^2 + 1}{x - 3}$

52. $z(x) = \dfrac{6x^2 - x - 35}{2x - 5}$

53. $R(x) = \dfrac{2x^2 + 7x + 6}{x + 2}$

54. $y = \dfrac{x + 3}{x^2} - \dfrac{5}{x}$

In exercises 55–62, graph each rational function.

55. $y = \dfrac{8}{x}$

56. $y = \dfrac{1 - x}{x + 1}$

57. $y = \dfrac{x - 5}{x + 3}$

58. $g(x) = \dfrac{x^2 + 3}{x^2 + x - 2}$

59. $f(x) = \dfrac{2x + 3}{x^2 - 2x - 3}$

60. $c(x) = \dfrac{x^2 + x - 2}{x + 2}$

61. $g(x) = \dfrac{2x^2 - 5x + 2}{x - 2}$

62. $y = -\dfrac{4}{x}$

63. Joey has entered an amateur triathlon competition. One leg of the race is a 26-mile stretch where he will run. Another leg of the race is a 110-mile stretch where he will bicycle. Joey figures that he can bike 20 miles per hour faster than he can run.

|← 1 mi →| |← 110 mi →| |← 26 mi →|

  a. Letting x be his average running speed, write a function for the total time it will take him to complete these two legs of the race.

  b. Graph the function.

  c. If Joey's average running speed is 9 miles per hour, use the graph to estimate, to the nearest tenth of an hour, the total time to complete these two legs of the race.

  d. If the total time to complete these two legs of the race is 8 hours, use the graph to estimate Joey's average running speed and then determine his biking speed.

64. In Joey's amateur triathlon competition, another leg of the competition is a swim race. For this competition, he must swim 1 mile upriver and then return. The speed of the river current is 2 miles per hour.

  a. Letting x be Joey's swimming speed in still water, write a function for the total time it will take him to swim up the river and back.

  b. Graph the function in the window $(0, 9.4, 1, 0, 6.2, 1, 1)$.

c. If Joey's swimming speed in still water is 2.5 mph, how long will it take him to complete this leg of the competition? Round your answer to the nearest tenth of an hour.

d. If Joey wants to complete this leg of the competition in 1.5 hours, how fast should he be able to swim in still water?

65. A robot and camera are designed to harvest fruit from a tree. The camera and robot are connected in a feedback loop by a minicomputer, according to the feedback function $F(s) = \frac{10}{(s+3)^2}$. (The variable s represents a parameter whose meaning we will not discuss.) Set up a table of values for $F(s)$ when $s = -4, -3, -2, -1, 0, 1, 2, 3,$ and 4, if possible.

Gripper

Camera

66. The sensor on a four-wheel-drive vehicle uses a closed-loop control system to maintain a constant speed of the wheel. The feedback function is $F(s) = \frac{10(s+3)}{s(s+1)}$. (The variable s represents a parameter whose meaning we will not discuss.) Set up a table of values for the function, using $s = -3, -2, -1, 0, 1, 2,$ and 3, if possible.

 Experiencing Algebra the Calculator Way

A convenient way to obtain solutions of a rational function is to use the TABLE function while in the Ask mode. In this section of the text, this method was suggested as an alternative method for incrementing values of x. To use this feature, first store the rational function in Y1. Then set the TBLSET to "Ask" for the independent variable. Once the TBLSET has been set, use the TABLE command to obtain a pair of values for any value of the independent variable that you wish. Use this approach to find the solutions specified for the following rational equations.

1. $y = \frac{6}{x-3} + \frac{6}{x+3}$; find (4,), (8,) and (10,).

2. $y = \frac{x^2 - 9}{x-3}$; find (−6,), (−1,), (0,), (2,), (3,), and (5,).

3. $y = \frac{x^2 + 9}{x-3}$; find (−6,), (−1,), (0,), (2,), (3,), and (5,).

4. $y = \frac{12x^2}{3x}$; find (−5,), (−2,), (0,), (1,), (3,), and (6,).

5. $y = \frac{3x}{12x^2}$; find (−5,), (−2,), (0,), (1,), (3,), and (6,).

6. $y = \dfrac{x^2 + x - 20}{x^2 + 6x + 5}$; find $(-2.5, \quad), (-1.3, \quad), (0, \quad), (1.8, \quad), (2.7, \quad), (5.9, \quad)$.

7. $y = \dfrac{x - 4}{x + 1}$; find $(-2.5, \quad), (-1.3, \quad), (0, \quad), (1.8, \quad), (2.7, \quad), (5.9, \quad)$.

Experiencing Algebra the Group Way

One common application that involves rational expressions is to consider the average cost of producing items. In earlier chapters, we saw that often we can express the cost of producing x items as a linear function. For example, if there is a setup cost of $500 to prepare for production, and a variable cost of $12 per item produced, the cost of producing x items is given by the function $c(x) = 12x + 500$. The average cost of producing x items is given by the function $c_{ave}(x) = \frac{12x + 500}{x}$. Graph this function using a window of $(0, 940, 100, 0, 62, 10, 1)$.

1. Discuss what this graph indicates about the average cost of producing x items.

    a. Does the average cost increase or decrease as the number of items produced increases? What does this mean?

    b. As x gets arbitrarily large, what value does the average cost approach? You can trace along the curve to explore this.

    c. Do you think there is a limit to how low the average cost will drop as x gets larger?

2. Have the group set up a table of values to see what happens as x increases. Use the TABLE setting to fill in the column for $c_{ave}(x)$. (The $p_{ave}(x)$ column will be completed later.)

x	$c_{ave}(x)$	$p_{ave}(x)$
100		
200		
300		
400		
500		
1000		
1500		
2000		
2500		
3000		

3. Do you think the average cost of producing x items will ever become less than $12? Discuss what you think is happening. This is an example of a limit. It is a concept that you will encounter in many mathematics applications.

4. Suppose all the items produced sold for $50 each. Write a revenue function $r(x)$.

5. Use the cost and revenue functions to define a profit function $p(x) = r(x) - c(x)$, assuming the producer can sell all the items produced.

6. Finally, write an average profit function $p_{ave}(x) = \frac{p(x)}{x}$.

Graph the function and complete the table of values as you did previously to see what you can determine about the behavior of this function as the number of items produced and sold increases.

7. These functions represent a mathematical model of a real-world situation. Discuss what this exercise has shown you with regard to using mathematics to model a real-world process.

Experiencing Algebra the Write Way

In the study of statistics, the *average* of a set of observations (that is, numbers) is calculated as the total of the observations divided by the number of observations in the set. Symbolically,

$$ave = \frac{total}{n},$$

where n is the number of observations in the set. Consider the restrictions on the divisor in this rational expression. Obviously, n cannot equal 0. What does this mean in terms of collecting observations and calculating averages? Does it make sense that this should be a restricted value? What would be the minimum number of observations to calculate an average?

Also in the study of statistics, the *variability* in a set of observations is calculated as the total of squared deviations from the average, divided by the number of observations less 1. Don't be concerned if you don't understand all the terminology in this definition. We are really interested only in what is happening with the divisor. Symbolically,

$$var = \frac{total\ of\ squares}{n - 1}.$$

What values are restricted on the divisor in this rational expression? Can you measure variability in numbers if you have 0 observations? What if you have only one observation? Again, do the restrictions make sense in the context of the application? Write a short summary of your understanding of the questions raised in this application.

12.2 Multiplication and Division of Rational Expressions

Objectives

1 Simplify rational expressions.

2 Multiply rational expressions.

3 Divide rational expressions.

4 Model real-world situations using expressions involving multiplication and division of rational expressions.

Application The inverse-square law is used to describe the gravitational force between two objects. That is, gravitational force is proportional to the expression $\frac{1}{d^2}$, where d is the distance between the centers of mass of two objects.

a. Write a proportional expression for the amount of gravitational force between the earth and a meteor if their centers of mass are x miles apart.

b. Write a proportional expression for the amount of gravitational force between the earth and a meteor if the distance x miles between their centers of mass is doubled; if it is tripled.

c. What is the effect on the gravitational force if the distance between two objects is doubled? If it is tripled?

After completing this section, we will discuss this application further. See page 925.

---

1 Simplifying Rational Expressions

We are now ready to simplify rational expressions that are algebraic fractions. We simplify these expressions using the same procedures as with numeric fractions.

To write equivalent rational expressions, we need to review a property of real numbers discussed in Chapter 2. The multiplication identity property states that the product of a real number and 1 is the real number itself. We use this property to write equivalent rational numbers, which are numbers that have the same value.

To write an equivalent numeric fraction in simplest form, we factor out the greatest common factor (GCF) of the numerator and denominator, rewrite the GCF as 1, and eliminate the factor of 1 using the identity property. For example, simplify $\frac{6}{14}$.

$$\frac{6}{14} = \frac{2 \cdot 3}{2 \cdot 7} \quad \text{Factor out the GCF, 2.}$$

$$= \frac{2}{2} \cdot \frac{3}{7}$$

$$= 1 \cdot \frac{3}{7} \quad \text{Rewrite the GCF as 1.}$$

$$= \frac{3}{7}$$

The multiplication identity property is also true for rational expressions. It allows us to write equivalent rational expressions using the same procedure as with numeric fractions. **Equivalent rational expressions** have the same value for any permissible replacement of the independent variable. Complete the following set of exercises to see the meaning of this definition.

D I S C O V E R Y   2

Simplified Expressions and Restricted Values

To simplify $\frac{6x^2}{14x}$, complete the following steps.

$$\frac{6x^2}{14x} = \frac{2x \cdot 3x}{2x \cdot 7} \qquad \text{Factor out the GCF, } 2x.$$

$$= \frac{2x}{2x} \cdot \frac{3x}{7}$$

$$= 1 \cdot \frac{3x}{7} \qquad \text{Rewrite the GCF as 1.}$$

$$= \frac{3x}{7}$$

Check the equivalence of the expressions $\frac{6x^2}{14x}$ and $\frac{3x}{7}$ by graphing. Let $Y1 = \frac{6x^2}{14x}$ and $Y2 = \frac{3x}{7}$.

1. Both graphs appear to be coinciding. However, look at a table of values for $x = -3, -2, -1, 0, 1, 2,$ and 3. What do you see?

2. Determine the restricted values for each expression.

3. Explain why the two expressions are equivalent for all values except when $x = 0$.

Note that the original expression to be simplified had a restricted value of $x \neq 0$, but the simplified expression did not have a restricted value. The permissible values for x in the original expression are all real numbers except 0. The permissible values for x in the simplified expression are all real numbers. Therefore, the two expressions are said to be equivalent expressions for their permissible values.

Another property of multiplication that is often useful in simplifying rational expressions is the multiplication property of -1. The multiplication property of -1 states that the product of a real number and -1 is the opposite of the number itself. This is useful in simplifying rational expressions when the numerator and denominator are opposites.

Helping Hand Two polynomials are opposites if every term of one polynomial corresponds to an opposite term in the second polynomial.

For example, simplify $\frac{x-1}{1-x}$.

The numerator and denominator are opposites because x and $-x$ are corresponding terms, as well as 1 and -1. Therefore, if we rewrite the denominator as a product of -1 and its opposite, we can factor out a 1 from the expression.

$$\frac{x - 1}{1 - x} = \frac{x - 1}{-1(-1 + x)}$$ Rewrite the denominator as a product of −1 and its opposite.

$$= \frac{x - 1}{-1(x - 1)}$$ Rearrange the binomial factor in the denominator.

$$= \frac{x - 1}{x - 1} \cdot \frac{1}{-1}$$

$$= 1 \cdot -1$$ Rewrite the GCF as 1.

$$= -1$$

If the numerator or denominator polynomials contain more than one term, it is necessary to factor them in order to find the GCF. For example, simplify $\frac{5x+15}{10x-25}$.

$$\frac{5x + 15}{10x - 25} = \frac{5(x + 3)}{5(2x - 5)}$$ Factor the numerator and denominator.

$$= \frac{5}{5} \cdot \frac{x + 3}{2x - 5}$$ Write a product, one factor containing the GCF of the numerator and denominator and the other containing the remaining factors.

$$= 1 \cdot \frac{x + 3}{2x - 5}$$ Rewrite the GCF as 1.

$$= \frac{x + 3}{2x - 5}$$

> *Simplifying Rational Expressions*
> To simplify rational expressions:
>
> - Factor the numerator and denominator.
> - Write a product of two rational expressions, one factor containing the GCF of the numerator and denominator and the other containing the remaining factors.
> - Rewrite the factor containing the GCF as 1.
> - Multiply.
>
> $$\frac{A}{B} = \frac{k \cdot C}{k \cdot D} = \frac{k}{k} \cdot \frac{C}{D} = \frac{C}{D},$$
>
> where A, B, C, and D are polynomials, $B \neq 0$, $D \neq 0$, and k is the GCF of A and B.

EXAMPLE 1   Simplify.

a. $\dfrac{x^2 - 5x - 14}{x^2 - 8x + 7}$ **b.** $\dfrac{16 - x^4}{x^3 - 2x^2 + 4x - 8}$

Solution

a. $\dfrac{x^2 - 5x - 14}{x^2 - 8x + 7} = \dfrac{(x + 2)(x - 7)}{(x - 1)(x - 7)}$ Factor the numerator and denominator.

$$= \frac{x - 7}{x - 7} \cdot \frac{x + 2}{x - 1}$$ Write a product, one factor containing the GCF of the numerator and denominator and the other containing the remaining factors.

$$= 1 \cdot \frac{x+2}{x-1} \qquad \text{Rewrite the GCF as 1.}$$

$$= \frac{x+2}{x-1} \qquad \text{Multiply.}$$

b. $\dfrac{16-x^4}{x^3-2x^2+4x-8} = \dfrac{(2-x)(2+x)(4+x^2)}{(x-2)(x^2+4)}$ Factor the numerator and denominator.

$$= \frac{-1(x-2)(2+x)(4+x^2)}{(x-2)(x^2+4)} \qquad \text{Rewrite the factor } 2-x=-1(x-2).$$

$$= \frac{(x-2)(4+x^2)}{(x-2)(x^2+4)} \cdot \frac{-1(2+x)}{1}$$

Write a product, one factor containing the GCF of the numerator and denominator and the other containing the remaining factors. Note: $4+x^2 = x^2+4$.

$$= 1 \cdot \frac{-1(2+x)}{1} \qquad \text{Rewrite the GCF as 1.}$$

$$= -1(2+x) \text{ or } -2-x \qquad \text{Multiply.} \blacksquare$$

Note: You may be aware of a process called **cancellation**. It may be used to reduce the number of steps in simplifying rational expressions. However, cancellation must be used properly and with great care. The process involves dividing out common *factors* from the numerator and denominator. For example,

Example 1a could have been worked as follows:

$$\frac{x^2-5x-14}{x^2-8x+7} = \frac{(x+2)(x-7)}{(x-1)(x-7)} \qquad \text{Factor the numerator and denominator.}$$

$$= \frac{(x+2)\cancel{(x-7)}}{(x-1)\cancel{(x-7)}} \qquad \text{Cancel or divide out a common factor of } (x-7). \textit{Note: } \frac{x-7}{x-7}=1.$$

$$= \frac{x+2}{x-1}$$

 Helping Hand The remaining *x-terms* cannot be canceled. We can cancel or divide out *factors* only. We cannot cancel terms.

Caution
To simplify a rational expression by cancellation, the numerator and denominator must be factored. Only factors can be canceled or divided out.

Experiencing Algebra the Checkup Way

Simplify exercises 1–4.

1. $\dfrac{12x^2 y^2 z}{28x^3 yz}$

2. $\dfrac{3a - 6}{9a + 12}$

3. $\dfrac{x^2 - 6x + 8}{x^2 - 10x + 24}$

4. $\dfrac{25 - x^2}{x^3 - 5x^2 + 7x - 35}$

5. What is the difference between a factor and a term of a polynomial?

6. When simplifying a rational expression, you can cancel only factors, not terms. Why?

---

2 Multiplying Rational Expressions

To multiply numeric fractions, we multiply the numerators together, multiply the denominators together, and simplify, if necessary, the resulting fraction. For example,

$$\frac{3}{4} \cdot \frac{5}{7} = \frac{3 \cdot 5}{4 \cdot 7} = \frac{15}{28}.$$

We use the same procedure for multiplication of rational expressions.

> *Multiplying Rational Expressions*
> To multiply rational expressions:
>
> - Multiply the numerators.
> - Multiply the denominators.
> - Factor the numerator and denominator.
> - Simplify the resulting rational expression.
>
> $$\frac{A}{B} \cdot \frac{C}{D} = \frac{AC}{BD},$$
>
> where A, B, C, and D are polynomials with $B \neq 0$ and $D \neq 0$.

For example,

$$\frac{6x}{5} \cdot \frac{3y}{4x} = \frac{6x \cdot 3y}{5 \cdot 4x} = \frac{18xy}{20x} = \frac{2x}{2x} \cdot \frac{9y}{10} = 1 \cdot \frac{9y}{10} = \frac{9y}{10}.$$

EXAMPLE 2 Multiply and simplify.

a. $\dfrac{x + 4}{x - 5} \cdot \dfrac{x}{x + 1}$

b. $\dfrac{2x - 3}{x^2 - 9} \cdot \dfrac{x - 3}{6x^2 - 7x - 3}$

Solution

a. $\dfrac{x + 4}{x - 5} \cdot \dfrac{x}{x + 1} = \dfrac{(x + 4)x}{(x - 5)(x + 1)}$ Multiply numerators and denominators.

or $\dfrac{x^2 + 4x}{x^2 - 4x - 5}$ It is not necessary to complete the multiplication.

b. $\dfrac{2x - 3}{x^2 - 9} \cdot \dfrac{x - 3}{6x^2 - 7x - 3}$

$= \dfrac{(2x - 3)(x - 3)}{(x^2 - 9)(6x^2 - 7x - 3)}$ Multiply numerators and denominators.

$$= \frac{(2x - 3)(x - 3)}{(x - 3)(x + 3)(2x - 3)(3x + 1)} \qquad \text{Factor.}$$

$$= \frac{(2x - 3)(x - 3)}{(2x - 3)(x - 3)} \cdot \frac{1}{(x + 3)(3x + 1)} \qquad \text{Factor out the GCF.}$$

$$= \frac{1}{(x + 3)(3x + 1)} \qquad \text{Multiply.} \quad \blacksquare$$

Just as we may cancel in simplification of algebraic fractions, we may use this canceling process with care in multiplication of algebraic fractions. To do this, we simplify by cancellation before we multiply.

To multiply rational expressions using cancellation:

- Factor the numerators and denominators.
- Cancel, or divide out, common factors in pairs—one from the numerator and one from the denominator.
- Multiply the remaining factors.

The product will not need to be simplified after all common factors are canceled. For example, the product in Example 2b may be found by this method.

$$\frac{2x - 3}{x^2 - 9} \cdot \frac{x - 3}{6x^2 - 7x - 3}$$

$$= \frac{2x - 3}{(x + 3)(x - 3)} \cdot \frac{x - 3}{(2x - 3)(3x + 1)} \qquad \text{Factor.}$$

$$= \frac{\cancel{2x - 3}}{(x + 3)\cancel{(x - 3)}} \cdot \frac{\cancel{x - 3}}{\cancel{(2x - 3)}(3x + 1)} \qquad \text{Cancel out factors.}$$

$$= \frac{1}{(x + 3)(3x + 1)} \qquad \text{Multiply.}$$

 Experiencing Algebra the Checkup Way

Multiply and simplify.

1. $\dfrac{8x}{15y} \cdot \dfrac{3y^3}{4x^3}$

2. $\dfrac{x - 1}{x + 1} \cdot \dfrac{x + 4}{x^2}$

3. $\dfrac{10x + 4}{x^2 - 16} \cdot \dfrac{x + 4}{5x^2 - 18x - 8}$

3 Dividing Rational Expressions

To divide numeric fractions, we multiply by the reciprocal of the divisor and simplify the resulting fraction, if necessary. For example,

$$\frac{3}{4} \div \frac{5}{7} = \frac{3}{4} \cdot \frac{7}{5} = \frac{3 \cdot 7}{4 \cdot 5} = \frac{21}{20}.$$

We use the same procedure for division of rational expressions.

Dividing Rational Expressions
To divide rational expressions:

- Multiply by the reciprocal of the divisor.
- Factor the numerator and denominator.

- Simplify the resulting rational expression.

$$\frac{A}{B} \div \frac{C}{D} = \frac{A}{B} \cdot \frac{D}{C} = \frac{AD}{BC},$$

where A, B, C, and D are polynomials with $B \neq 0$, $D \neq 0$, and $C \neq 0$.

For example,

$$\frac{15a^3b}{2cd} \div \frac{20ac^2}{3d} = \frac{15a^3b}{2cd} \cdot \frac{3d}{20ac^2} = \frac{45a^3bd}{40ac^3d} = \frac{5ad}{5ad} \cdot \frac{9a^2b}{8c^3} = \frac{9a^2b}{8c^3}.$$

EXAMPLE 3   Divide and simplify.

a. $\dfrac{2x+1}{2x^2-8} \div \dfrac{2x+1}{x^4-16}$

b. $\dfrac{x^2+8x+12}{x^2+12} \div (x+6)$

Solution

a. $\dfrac{2x+1}{2x^2-8} \div \dfrac{2x+1}{x^4-16}$

$= \dfrac{2x+1}{2x^2-8} \cdot \dfrac{x^4-16}{2x+1}$ Rewrite as multiplication by reciprocal of divisor.

$= \dfrac{(2x+1)(x^4-16)}{(2x^2-8)(2x+1)}$ Multiply numerators and denominators.

$= \dfrac{(2x+1)(x^2+4)(x+2)(x-2)}{2(x+2)(x-2)(2x+1)}$ Factor to simplify.

$= \dfrac{(2x+1)(x+2)(x-2)}{(2x+1)(x+2)(x-2)} \cdot \dfrac{x^2+4}{2}$ Factor out the GCF.

$= \dfrac{x^2+4}{2}$ Multiply.

b. $\dfrac{x^2+8x+12}{x^2+12} \div (x+6)$

$= \dfrac{x^2+8x+12}{x^2+12} \cdot \dfrac{1}{x+6}$ Rewrite as multiplication by the reciprocal of the divisor.

$= \dfrac{x^2+8x+12}{(x^2+12)(x+6)}$ Multiply numerators and denominators.

$= \dfrac{(x+6)(x+2)}{(x^2+12)(x+6)}$ Factor to simplify.

$= \dfrac{x+6}{x+6} \cdot \dfrac{x+2}{x^2+12}$ Factor out the GCF.

$= \dfrac{x+2}{x^2+12}$ Multiply. ∎

We may also use the canceling process, with care, in division of rational expressions.

To divide rational expressions using cancellation:

- Multiply by the reciprocal of the divisor.
- Factor the numerators and denominators.
- Cancel, or divide out, common factors in pairs—one from the numerator and one from the denominator.
- Multiply the remaining factors.

The product will not need to be simplified after all common factors are canceled. For Example 3a,

$$\frac{2x + 1}{2x^2 - 8} \div \frac{2x + 1}{x^4 - 16}$$

$$= \frac{2x + 1}{2x^2 - 8} \cdot \frac{x^4 - 16}{2x + 1}$$ Rewrite as multiplication.

$$= \frac{2x + 1}{2(x + 2)(x - 2)} \cdot \frac{(x^2 + 4)(x + 2)(x - 2)}{2x + 1}$$ Factor.

$$= \frac{\cancel{2x + 1}}{2\cancel{(x + 2)}\cancel{(x - 2)}} \cdot \frac{(x^2 + 4)\cancel{(x + 2)}\cancel{(x - 2)}}{\cancel{2x + 1}}$$ Cancel out common factors.

$$= \frac{x^2 + 4}{2}$$ Multiply.

 Helping Hand Remember, we cancel common factors. This means we must be canceling in a multiplication problem. Therefore, *always* change the division problem to multiplication *before* canceling factors.

 ## Experiencing Algebra the Checkup Way

Divide and simplify exercises 1–3.

1. $\dfrac{25x^3 y^2}{z^2} \div \dfrac{20xy^3}{z^3}$ **2.** $\dfrac{5a + 7}{3x^2 - 3} \div \dfrac{10a + 14}{9x^4 - 9}$ **3.** $\dfrac{5x^2 + 19x - 4}{x^2 - 4} \div (5x - 1)$

4. Why must you first change a division problem to a multiplication problem before performing any cancellation of factors?

---

4 Modeling the Real World   We've seen that rational expressions are very common in models of real-world situations. The ability to simplify these expressions makes it much easier to work with them in multiplication and division, saving time and possible errors.

EXAMPLE 4   Julia read a puzzle to her math class.

> Pick a number.
> Multiply the number by 4.
> Add 64.
> Divide by the sum of the number and 16.

Julie told the class that the answer is 4.
    Analyze the puzzle algebraically.
    How did Julia know the answer?

Solution

Let $x =$ the number

$$\frac{4x + 64}{x + 16} = \frac{4\cancel{(x + 16)}}{\cancel{x + 16}} = 4$$

The result of the puzzle is always 4. ∎

EXAMPLE 5   Balto the rescue dog traveled a distance of 125 miles.

a. Write an expression for the time traveled if Balto traveled at a speed of x mph.
b. Write an expression for the new distance Balto traveled if he kept the time constant but increased the speed 10 mph.

Solution

a. $t = \dfrac{d}{r}$ Distance-traveled formula solved for t

   $t = \dfrac{125}{x}$ Substitute 125 for d and x for r.

An expression for the time Balto traveled is $\frac{125}{x}$ hours.

b. The new rate is $x + 10$. The time is still $\frac{125}{x}$.

   $d = rt$ Distance-traveled formula

   $d = (x + 10)\left(\dfrac{125}{x}\right)$

   $d = \dfrac{125(x + 10)}{x}$

An expression for the distance Balto traveled is $\frac{125(x+10)}{x}$ miles. ∎

Application

The inverse-square law is used to describe the gravitational force between two objects. That is, gravitational force is proportional to the expression $\frac{1}{d^2}$, where d is the distance between the centers of mass of two objects.

a. Write a proportional expression for the amount of gravitational force between the earth and a meteor if their centers of mass are x miles apart.
b. Write a proportional expression for the amount of gravitational force between the earth and a meteor if the distance x miles between their centers of mass is doubled; if it is tripled.
c. What is the effect on the gravitational force if the distance between two objects is doubled? If it is tripled?

Discussion

a. Let $x =$ distance in miles between the centers of mass. Given $\frac{1}{d^2}$, we substitute x for d. $\frac{1}{x^2}$ is proportional to the gravitational force if the distance is x miles.

b. Let $x =$ distance in miles between the centers of mass

$2x =$ distance doubled

Given $\frac{1}{d^2}$, we substitute $2x$ for d. $\frac{1}{(2x)^2} = \frac{1}{4x^2}$ is proportional to the gravitational force if the distance is doubled.

Let $x =$ distance in miles between the centers of mass

$3x =$ distance tripled

Given $\frac{1}{d^2}$, we substitute $3x$ for d. $\frac{1}{(3x)^2} = \frac{1}{9x^2}$ is proportional to the gravitational force if distance is tripled.

c. If the distance between two objects is doubled, then the expression changes from $\frac{1}{x^2}$ to $\frac{1}{4x^2}$. Since $\frac{1}{4x^2} = \frac{1}{4} \cdot \frac{1}{x^2}$, the gravitational force is proportional to one-fourth of the original force.

If the distance between two objects is tripled, then the expression changes from $\frac{1}{x^2}$ to $\frac{1}{9x^2}$. Since $\frac{1}{9x^2} = \frac{1}{9} \cdot \frac{1}{x^2}$, the gravitational force is proportional to one-ninth of the original force. ∎

Experiencing Algebra the Checkup Way

1. Glenda plays a game with her students. She tells them to start with their ages, multiply them by 2, and add 6. Then she tells them to divide the result by 2 and add 7. She asks each student what number he or she has and then she can tell them their age. Write an algebraic expression for the result of Glenda's game, and explain how she can tell the students' ages from this.

2. Reza traveled 150 miles.

a. Write an expression for his average rate of speed if it took x hours for the trip.

b. If he were to double his rate of speed and increase his time by 1 hour, write an expression for the new distance he would travel.

PROBLEM SET 12.2

Experiencing Algebra the Exercise Way

Simplify.

1. $\dfrac{36x^3 y^2 z}{54x^2 y^5}$

2. $\dfrac{21x^3 y^4}{35x^5 yz^2}$

3. $\dfrac{-56a^3 b^2}{84a^2 b^2 c}$

4. $\dfrac{99ab^5 c}{-72a^3 b^2}$

5. $\dfrac{9x - 27}{18x - 6}$

6. $\dfrac{8x + 16}{24x + 12}$

7. $\dfrac{8 - z}{z - 8}$

8. $\dfrac{x - y}{y - x}$

9. $\dfrac{5x^2 y^3 + 10xy^4}{15xy^2 - 20x^2 y^2}$

10. $\dfrac{15x^2 y - 9x^3 y}{6x^2 y^2 + 3xy^3}$

11. $\dfrac{-6x + 9y - 3z}{3x - 21y + 3z}$

12. $\dfrac{-7x + 28y - 14z}{14x - 7y + 7z}$

13. $\dfrac{x^2 - 8x + 12}{x^2 - 10x + 24}$

14. $\dfrac{x^2 - 6x + 9}{x^2 - 10x + 21}$

15. $\dfrac{x^2 - x - 6}{x^2 + 9x + 14}$

16. $\dfrac{x^2 + 12x + 32}{x^2 - x - 20}$

17. $\dfrac{3x^2 + 7x + 2}{3x^2 - 11x - 4}$

18. $\dfrac{2x^2 + 11x + 5}{2x^2 - 17x - 9}$

19. $\dfrac{6x^2 - x - 2}{4x^2 - 4x - 3}$

20. $\dfrac{10x^2 + 7x - 12}{8x^2 + 2x - 15}$

21. $\dfrac{8x^2 + 12x + 4}{24x^2 - 40x - 16}$

22. $\dfrac{12x^2 + 6x - 6}{27x^2 + 45x - 18}$

23. $\dfrac{2x^2 + xy - y^2}{3x^2 + 4xy + y^2}$

24. $\dfrac{5x^2 - 6xy + y^2}{4x^2 - 3xy - y^2}$

25. $\dfrac{64 - x^2}{x^3 + 2x^2 - 64x - 128}$

26. $\dfrac{25 - x^2}{x^3 + 3x^2 - 25x - 75}$

27. $\dfrac{2x^2 - 7x - 15}{x^3 - 5x^2 + 11x - 55}$

28. $\dfrac{3x^2 - 17x - 28}{x^3 - 7x^2 + 9x - 63}$

Multiply and simplify.

29. $\dfrac{12a^2b^2}{35cd^2} \cdot \dfrac{49c^2d^2}{27ab^3}$

30. $\dfrac{15a^3b^2}{16c^3d^5} \cdot \dfrac{24c^3d^3}{25ab^4}$

31. $\dfrac{-2x^3}{5y^2} \cdot \dfrac{15xy^2}{8x^2}$

32. $\dfrac{12x}{15y^3} \cdot \dfrac{-5xy^5}{26x^4}$

33. $(2.6x^2) \cdot \dfrac{3.1x}{y^2}$

34. $\dfrac{7x^2y}{6z} \cdot 9$

35. $\dfrac{1}{3} \cdot \dfrac{2a^2}{3b}$

36. $\dfrac{7a^3}{3b^2} \cdot \dfrac{2}{5}$

37. $\dfrac{x + 5}{x} \cdot \dfrac{x^3}{x + 4}$

38. $\dfrac{x^3}{x - 11} \cdot \dfrac{x + 15}{x^2}$

39. $\dfrac{3x + 2}{x + 4} \cdot \dfrac{x - 4}{3x + 2}$

40. $\dfrac{x + 7}{4x + 3} \cdot \dfrac{4x + 3}{x - 7}$

41. $\dfrac{x + 7}{2x + 1} \cdot \dfrac{5x + 2}{x}$

42. $\dfrac{3x + 5}{x} \cdot \dfrac{x + 4}{2x + 9}$

43. $\dfrac{x^2 - x - 6}{2x^2 + 3x + 1} \cdot \dfrac{2x^2 - x - 1}{x^2 + 5x + 6}$

44. $\dfrac{x^2 + 8x + 15}{3x^2 - 5x - 2} \cdot \dfrac{3x^2 + 7x + 2}{x^2 - 2x - 15}$

45. $\dfrac{x^2 - xy - 2y^2}{x^2 - 9y^2} \cdot \dfrac{x^2 - 3xy}{x^2 - y^2}$

46. $\dfrac{xy - 5y^2}{x^2 - 4y^2} \cdot \dfrac{x^2 - xy - 2y^2}{x^2 - 25y^2}$

Divide and simplify exercises 47–70.

47. $\dfrac{54a^3b^2}{c} \div \dfrac{36ab^2}{c}$

48. $\dfrac{49a^4b^2}{c^2} \div \dfrac{56a^3b^3}{c^2}$

49. $\dfrac{-21x^2y^3}{z} \div \dfrac{7xy^2}{z^2}$

50. $\dfrac{33x^3y}{z^3} \div \dfrac{-11x^5y^3}{z^2}$

51. $(32ab^2) \div \dfrac{8ab^3}{c}$

52. $(21a^2b^4) \div \dfrac{7ab^2}{c^2}$

53. $\dfrac{21x^2y^2}{z^3} \div (-3xy^3)$

54. $\dfrac{-34x^3y}{z^2} \div (17x^2y^4)$

55. $\dfrac{a + 4}{9a^2 - 1} \div \dfrac{5a + 20}{3a + 1}$

56. $\dfrac{7a + 21}{36a^2 - 1} \div \dfrac{a + 3}{6a - 1}$

57. $\dfrac{x^2 - 16}{5y - 2} \div \dfrac{x + 4}{25y^2 - 4}$

58. $\dfrac{x^2 - 49}{4y + 3} \div \dfrac{x + 7}{16y^2 - 9}$

59. $\dfrac{2x^2 - 5x - 3}{x^2 - 5x - 14} \div \dfrac{3x^2 + 10x + 3}{x^2 - 4x - 21}$

60. $\dfrac{x^2 - 2x - 8}{2x^2 + x - 3} \div \dfrac{3x^2 + 8x + 4}{2x^2 - 5x - 12}$

61. $\dfrac{8x^2 + 2x - 3}{4x^2 - 1} \div (4x + 3)$

62. $\dfrac{15x^2 + 16x + 4}{9x^2 - 4} \div (5x + 2)$

63. $(x + 9) \div \dfrac{2x^2 + 19x + 9}{3x + 4}$

64. $(x + 11) \div \dfrac{2x^2 + 17x - 55}{5x - 2}$

65. $\dfrac{1}{3x - 5} \div \dfrac{1}{x + 7}$

66. $\dfrac{5}{4x + 3} \div \dfrac{7}{2x + 1}$

67. $\dfrac{x^2 + 3xy}{7xy + 2y^2} \div \dfrac{x^2 + 4xy + 3y^2}{7x^2 - 5xy - 2y^2}$

68. $\dfrac{x^2 + 7xy + 10y^2}{3x^2 - 4xy - 4y^2} \div \dfrac{x^2 + 5xy}{3xy + 2y^2}$

69. $\dfrac{4x + 8y}{3x - 12y} \div \dfrac{4x + 4y}{6x + 6y}$

70. $\dfrac{5x + 35y}{6x + 18y} \div \dfrac{5x - 10y}{8x + 24y}$

71. Katarina drove a distance of 170 miles. If her average rate of travel (speed) was x miles per hour, write a rational expression for her time of travel. If she had traveled for the same amount of time, but had decreased her average speed by 10 mph, write an expression for the distance she would have traveled. How far would she have traveled at the reduced speed if her original speed was 50 miles per hour?

72. Brian traveled 155 miles. Write an expression for his time of travel if his average speed was x mph. If he travels the same length of time, but increases his speed by 8 mph, write an expression for the distance he would travel. How far would he travel at the increased speed if his original speed was 45 miles per hour?

73. A box has a volume given by the formula $V = LWH$. If the volume of the box is $15x^3 + 7x^2 - 2x$ cubic inches, its height is x inches, and its width is $3x + 2$ inches, use the volume formula to determine an expression for the length in terms of the height x inches. If the height of the box measures 4 inches, what are its other dimensions?

74. A cylindrical can has a volume given by the formula $V = \pi r^2 h$. If a can has a volume of $6\pi x^3 - 5\pi x^2$ cubic inches, and its radius is x inches, use the volume formula to determine an expression for the height of the can in terms of the radius x inches. If the radius of the can measures 1.5 inches, what is its height?

75. The fixed cost of producing an item is $300 and the variable cost is $5 per item produced. The revenue received for selling the item is $25 per item.

   a. Write a cost function and a revenue function for producing and selling x items.

   b. Write an expression for the ratio of revenue to cost for x items, and simplify.

   c. If a production run produces 40 items, what is the value of the revenue-to-cost ratio?

76. The fixed cost of producing an item is $175 and the variable cost is $25 per item produced. The revenue received for selling the item is $75 per item.

   a. Write a cost function and a revenue function for producing and selling x items.

   b. Write an expression for the ratio of cost to revenue for x items, and simplify.

   c. If a production run produces 50 items, what is the value of the cost-to-revenue ratio?

 Experiencing Algebra the Calculator Way

Earlier in the text, we showed how you could use the graphing features of your calculator to check your work on simplification of algebraic expressions. The technique can also be used when you are performing operations on rational expressions in a single variable. Consider the following example.

Simplify $\frac{x^3+3x^2-4x-12}{x^3+2x^2-9x-18}$. Using the methods in this section, you should be able to show that the expression simplifies to $\frac{x-2}{x-3}$ for any permissible replacements for x. To check this on your calculator, store the original expression in Y1 and the simplified expression in Y2. Graph each expression separately to see whether they yield the same graph. Then graph them simultaneously to see that the graphs do in fact coincide. If they do, you have completed the check to see that you have correctly simplified the expression. As you trace the graphs, you should notice that the only place in which they differ is in the restricted values. The first graph has three restricted values while the second graph, the simplification, has only one restricted value.

When you simplify a rational expression, the simplified expression may be a linear function of the form
$ax + b$. *Complete the following table to determine how the expressions simplify, and check your*
simplification for equivalence by tracing the graphs as described.

	Expression	Restricted Values	Algebraically Simplified Expression	Is the Simplified Function Linear?
1.	$\dfrac{x^2 - 9}{x - 3}$			
2.	$\dfrac{x^2 + 9}{x - 3}$			
3.	$\dfrac{12x^2}{3x}$			
4.	$\dfrac{3x}{12x^2}$			
5.	$\dfrac{5x^2 - 10x}{5x}$			
6.	$\dfrac{2x^2 - 3x}{2x^2 - 5x}$			
7.	$\dfrac{4 - x}{x - 4}$			
8.	$\dfrac{x^2 + x - 20}{x^2 + 6x + 5}$			
9.	$\dfrac{x^3 - 6x^2 - 16x}{2x}$			
10.	$\dfrac{2x^2 - 3x - 20}{x - 4}$			

Experiencing Algebra the Group Way

In performing operations with rational expressions, you may have the operations of multiplication
and division occurring in the same expression. When this happens, you must remember the rules on
order of operations, and perform the operations just as you would for rational numbers. Each
member of the group should perform the operations and simplify the following expressions. Discuss
among yourselves what operations should be done in what order. Compare your answers and agree
on the correct final result for each exercise.

1. $\dfrac{12x^2 y^3}{25z^2} \cdot \dfrac{15z^3}{6xy^5} \div \dfrac{12xy^2}{35z}$

2. $\dfrac{7a^2 b^2}{9c} \div \dfrac{14ac^2}{3b^3} \cdot \dfrac{b^3 c^2}{2a^2}$

3. $\dfrac{x^2 + 2x - 3}{x + 5} \cdot \dfrac{x + 4}{x^2 - 1} \div \dfrac{x^2 + x - 12}{x^2 + 4x - 5}$

4. $\dfrac{2x^3 + x^2}{3x - 2} \div \dfrac{2x^2 + 11x + 5}{x^2 + 5x} \cdot \dfrac{3x^2 + 19x - 14}{x^2 + 6x + 5}$

Experiencing Algebra the Write Way

In "Experiencing Algebra the Calculator Way," the rational expression $\frac{x^3+3x^2-4x-12}{x^3+2x^2-9x-18}$ was said to simplify to $\frac{x-2}{x-3}$. Prove to yourself that this is so. It was further stated that the original expression had more restricted values than the simplified expression. Determine what the restricted values are for both expressions. Finally, discuss the implications of this difference in restricted values for the two expressions. If you simplify a rational expression, which should you use as the restricted values in the domain of the function: those from the simplified expression or those from the original expression? Explain your reasons for your answer.

12.3 Addition and Subtraction of Rational Expressions

Objectives

1 Add and subtract rational expressions with like denominators.

2 Determine the least common denominator for a set of rational expressions.

3 Write equivalent rational expressions using the least common denominator as the new denominator.

4 Add and subtract rational expressions with unlike denominators.

5 Model real-world situations using expressions involving addition and subtraction of rational expressions.

Application

George Ferris constructed the Ferris wheel for the 1893 Columbian Exposition in Chicago. To keep a steady-state speed for the ride, he set up a control system. A function for the wheel and motor dynamics can be expressed by the sum of the expressions $\frac{1}{s^2+6s+8}$ and $\frac{1}{s+4}$, where s represents an electronic parameter. Determine the sum of the expressions.

After completing this section, we will discuss this application further. See page 940.

1 Adding Rational Expressions with Like Denominators

Now that we can multiply rational expressions, we are ready to add and subtract them. To add or subtract numeric fractions with like denominators, we add or subtract the numerators to obtain the numerator of the answer. The denominator of the answer is the like denominator. We simplify the result, if necessary. For example,

$$\frac{2}{5} + \frac{1}{5} = \frac{2+1}{5} = \frac{3}{5} \quad \text{and} \quad \frac{2}{5} - \frac{1}{5} = \frac{2-1}{5} = \frac{1}{5}.$$

We use the same procedure for adding and subtracting rational expressions.

> *Adding and Subtracting Rational Expressions with Like Denominators*
> To add rational expressions:
>
> - Add the numerators.
> - Use the like denominator for the denominator of the sum.
>
> $$\frac{A}{B} + \frac{C}{B} = \frac{A+C}{B},$$
>
> where A, B, and C are polynomials with $B \neq 0$.
> To subtract rational expressions:
>
> - Subtract the numerators.
> - Use the like denominator for the denominator of the difference.
>
> $$\frac{A}{B} - \frac{C}{B} = \frac{A-C}{B},$$
>
> where A, B, and C are polynomials with $B \neq 0$.
> Remember to simplify the answer, if possible.

For example,

$$\frac{2x}{5y} + \frac{x^2}{5y} = \frac{2x + x^2}{5y} \quad \text{or} \quad \frac{x(2+x)}{5y} \qquad \text{Add.}$$

$$\frac{7ab}{2a} - \frac{-3a^2}{2a} = \frac{7ab - (-3a^2)}{2a} = \frac{7ab + 3a^2}{2a} \qquad \text{Subtract.}$$

$$= \frac{a(7b + 3a)}{2a} = \frac{a}{a} \cdot \frac{7b + 3a}{2} = \frac{7b + 3a}{2} \qquad \text{Simplify.}$$

EXAMPLE 1   Add or subtract and simplify.

a. $\dfrac{2x}{x+3} + \dfrac{6}{x+3}$ **b.** $\dfrac{3x}{3x^2 - 13x + 14} - \dfrac{7}{3x^2 - 13x + 14}$

c. $\dfrac{x+4}{x^2 + 3x - 4} - \dfrac{x-1}{x^2 + 3x - 4}$

Solution

a. $\dfrac{2x}{x+3} + \dfrac{6}{x+3} = \dfrac{2x + 6}{x+3}$ Add numerators.

$$= \frac{2\cancel{(x+3)}}{\cancel{x+3}} \qquad \text{Factor.}$$

$$= 2 \qquad \text{Simplify.}$$

b. $\dfrac{3x}{3x^2 - 13x + 14} - \dfrac{7}{3x^2 - 13x + 14}$

$$= \frac{3x - 7}{3x^2 - 13x + 14} \qquad \text{Subtract numerators.}$$

$$= \frac{3x - 7}{(3x - 7)(x - 2)} \qquad \text{Factor.}$$

$$= \frac{1}{x - 2} \qquad \text{Simplify.}$$

c. $\dfrac{x + 4}{x^2 + 3x - 4} - \dfrac{x - 1}{x^2 + 3x - 4}$

$$= \frac{(x + 4) - (x - 1)}{x^2 + 3x - 4} \qquad \text{Subtract numerators.}$$

$$= \frac{5}{x^2 + 3x - 4}$$

 Helping Hand Be careful when subtracting numerators with more than one term. It is helpful to use parentheses to group the numerators, as in Example 1c.

 ## Experiencing Algebra the Checkup Way

Add or subtract and simplify exercises 1–4.

1. $\dfrac{5xy}{3z} - \dfrac{7x}{3z}$

2. $\dfrac{3x}{x + 7} + \dfrac{21}{x + 7}$

3. $\dfrac{x + 5}{2x^2 + 5x - 12} + \dfrac{x - 8}{2x^2 + 5x - 12}$

4. $\dfrac{2x + 7}{x^2 + 3x - 18} - \dfrac{x + 7}{x^2 + 3x - 18}$

5. What must be true before you can add or subtract rational expressions?

6. After adding or subtracting rational expressions, what should you do to the result (in addition to checking your work)?

---

2 Determining the Least Common Denominator

In order to add or subtract numeric fractions, we must verify that the fractions must have like denominators. If they do not, we must change them to equivalent fractions with a common denominator. The **least common denominator (LCD)** is the smallest number for which each denominator is a factor. That is, the LCD is the smallest number divisible by each of the denominators.

To determine the least common denominator for a set of fractions, first factor each of the denominators into its prime factors. Next, write a product consisting of each different denominator factor, using the largest exponent that occurred for each factor.

For example, determine the LCD for $\frac{7}{12}$ and $\frac{1}{30}$.

Factor the denominators:

$12 = 2^2 \cdot 3$

$30 = 2 \cdot 3 \cdot 5$

The different denominator factors are 2, 3, and 5. The greatest exponent of 2 is 2, of 3 is 1, and of 5 is 1.

Multiply:

$\text{LCD} = 2^2 \cdot 3 \cdot 5 = 60$

We use the same procedure for finding the LCD of rational expressions.

Determining the Least Common Denominator

To determine the least common denominator for a set of rational expressions:

• Factor each denominator into its prime factors.

• Write a product consisting of each different factor, using the greatest exponent that occurs for each.

For example, determine the least common denominator for $\frac{7x}{8xy^3}$ and $\frac{3z}{20x^2y}$.

Factor the denominators:

$$8xy^3 = 2^3 \cdot x \cdot y^3$$
$$20x^2y = 2^2 \cdot 5 \cdot x^2 \cdot y$$

The different denominator factors are 2, 5, x, and y. The greatest exponent of 2 is 3, of 5 is 1, of x is 2, and of y is 3.

Multiply:

$$\text{LCD} = 2^3 \cdot 5 \cdot x^2 \cdot y^3 = 40x^2y^3$$

EXAMPLE 2   Determine the least common denominator for the following sets of rational expressions.

a. $\dfrac{3x}{x+3}$ and $\dfrac{2x}{x+2}$ **b.** $\dfrac{x+5}{4x^2-9}$ and $\dfrac{3x-1}{2x^2-x-3}$

c. $\dfrac{2}{x-2}$ and $\dfrac{-2}{-x+2}$

Solution

a. $\dfrac{3x}{x+3}$ and $\dfrac{2x}{x+2}$

The denominators do not factor. Therefore, we use both denominators as factors for the LCD.

$$\text{LCD} = (x+3)(x+2)$$

There is no need to multiply these factors.

b. $\dfrac{x+5}{4x^2-9}$ and $\dfrac{3x-1}{2x^2-x-3}$

Factor the denominators:

$$4x^2 - 9 = (2x+3)(2x-3)$$
$$2x^2 - x - 3 = (2x-3)(x+1)$$
$$\text{LCD} = (2x+3)(2x-3)(x+1)$$

c. $\dfrac{2}{x-2}$ and $\dfrac{-2}{-x+2}$

Notice that the denominators are opposites. Therefore, either denominator may be considered the LCD. ■

Experiencing Algebra the Checkup Way

In exercises 1–4, determine the least common denominator for each set of rational expressions.

1. $\dfrac{5x}{12x^2 y}$ and $\dfrac{4z}{15xy^3}$

2. $\dfrac{5}{x+4}$ and $\dfrac{7x}{x-5}$

3. $\dfrac{x-1}{25x^2-1}$ and $\dfrac{2x+5}{15x^2-2x-1}$

4. $\dfrac{7}{x-5}$ and $\dfrac{8}{5-x}$

5. When you find the least common denominator for a set of rational expressions, what is the meaning of the word *least*?

6. To find the least common denominator for a set of rational expressions, you should first factor the expressions into prime factors. What is the meaning of the word *prime*?

---

3 Writing Equivalent Rational Expressions with the LCD

Now that we can determine the LCD for a set of rational expressions, we are ready to change the expressions to equivalent expressions, with the LCD as the new denominators. We use the multiplication identity property to do this.

Recall the procedure for writing equivalent numeric fractions. First, we must determine the factor needed to multiply the original denominator in order to obtain the new denominator. Next, multiply the original numeric fraction by a factor of 1 (using the needed factor as the numerator and denominator).

For example, write an equivalent numeric fraction with a denominator of 20 for $\frac{3}{4}$.

$$\frac{3}{4} = \frac{?}{20}$$
Since $20 = 4 \cdot 5$, we need a factor of 5.

$$\frac{3}{4} = \frac{3}{4} \cdot \frac{5}{5} = \frac{15}{20}$$
Multiply by a factor of 1, $\frac{5}{5}$.

We use the same procedure for writing equivalent rational expressions.

> *Determining Equivalent Rational Expressions*
> To determine an equivalent rational expression:
>
> - Factor the denominator of the original rational expression and the new desired denominator (LCD).
> - Determine the factors needed to multiply the original denominator to obtain the desired denominator.
> - Multiply the original rational expression by a factor of 1, using the factors found in the preceding step as the numerator and denominator.

For example, write an equivalent rational number with a denominator of $40x^2 y^3$ for $\frac{7x}{8xy^3}$.

$$\frac{7x}{8xy^3} = \frac{?}{40x^2 y^3}$$

Factor the denominators:

$$40x^2 y^3 = 2^3 \cdot 5 \cdot x^2 \cdot y^3$$
$$8xy^3 = 2^3 \cdot x \cdot y^3$$

Helping Hand It is easier to see the "needed" factors if we arrange the factors in the same order, leaving a space for the missing factors, such as 5.

The given denominator, $8xy^3$, must be multiplied by $5x$ to obtain the desired denominator, $40x^2y^3$.

$$\frac{7x}{8xy^3} \cdot \frac{5x}{5x} = \frac{35x^2}{40x^2y^3}$$

EXAMPLE 3 Write an equivalent rational expression with the given LCD.

a. $\dfrac{3x}{x+3}$; LCD $= x^2 + 5x + 6$

b. $\dfrac{x+5}{4x^2-9}$; LCD $= 4x^4 + 4x^3 - 9x^2 - 9x$

c. $\dfrac{2}{x-2}$; LCD $= 2 - x$

Solution

a. $\dfrac{3x}{x+3}$; LCD $= x^2 + 5x + 6$

Factor the denominators:

$$x^2 + 5x + 6 = (x+3)(x+2)$$
$$x + 3 \qquad = x + 3 \qquad\qquad x + 3 \text{ does not factor.}$$

The given denominator must be multiplied by $(x+2)$ to obtain the desired denominator.

$$\frac{3x}{x+3} \cdot \frac{x+2}{x+2} = \frac{3x^2 + 6x}{x^2 + 5x + 6}$$

b. $\dfrac{x+5}{4x^2-9}$; LCD $= 4x^4 + 4x^3 - 9x^2 - 9x$

Factor the denominators:

$$4x^4 + 4x^3 - 9x^2 - 9x = x(2x+3)(2x-3)(x+1)$$
$$4x^2 - 9 \qquad\qquad = (2x+3)(2x-3)$$

The given denominator must be multiplied by $x(x+1)$ to obtain the desired denominator.

$$\frac{x+5}{4x^2-9} \cdot \frac{x(x+1)}{x(x+1)} = \frac{x^3 + 6x^2 + 5x}{4x^4 + 4x^3 - 9x^2 - 9x}$$

c. $\dfrac{2}{x-2}$; LCD $= 2 - x$

The denominators do not factor. However, they are opposites. Therefore, the given denominator must be multiplied by -1 to obtain the desired denominator.

$$\frac{2}{x-2} \cdot \frac{-1}{-1} = \frac{-2}{-x+2} \text{ or } \frac{-2}{2-x} \qquad\blacksquare$$

Experiencing Algebra the Checkup Way

Write an equivalent rational expression with the given least common denominator.

1. $\dfrac{-4x}{3xy^2}$; LCD $= 12x^2y^2$

2. $\dfrac{2x}{x+5}$; LCD $= x^2 + 9x + 20$

3. $\dfrac{2x+1}{x^2-16}$; LCD $= x^3 + 7x^2 - 16x - 112$

4. $\dfrac{7}{x-5}$; LCD $= 5x - x^2$

---

4 Adding and Subtracting Rational Expressions with Unlike Denominators

To add or subtract numeric fractions with unlike denominators, we change the fractions to equivalent fractions with like denominators and add or subtract. For example, to add $\frac{7}{12} + \frac{1}{30}$, we use the LCD, 60, that we found earlier.

$$\frac{7}{12} + \frac{1}{30} = \frac{7}{12} \cdot \frac{5}{5} + \frac{1}{30} \cdot \frac{2}{2} \qquad \text{Change to like denominators.}$$

$$= \frac{35}{60} + \frac{2}{60}$$

$$= \frac{37}{60} \qquad\qquad\qquad \text{Add numerators.}$$

We use the same procedure for addition and subtraction of rational expressions.

> *Adding and Subtracting Rational Expressions with Unlike Denominators*
>
> To add rational expressions:
>
> • Change the rational expressions to equivalent expressions with like denominators.
>
> • Add the numerators.
>
> • Use the like denominator for the denominator of the sum:
>
> $$\frac{A}{B} + \frac{C}{B} = \frac{A+C}{B},$$
>
> where A, B, and C are polynomials with $B \neq 0$.
>
> To subtract rational expressions:
>
> • Change the rational expressions to equivalent expressions with like denominators.
>
> • Subtract the numerators.
>
> • Use the like denominator for the denominator of the difference:
>
> $$\frac{A}{B} - \frac{C}{B} = \frac{A-C}{B},$$
>
> where A, B, and C are polynomials with $B \neq 0$.
>
> Remember to simplify the answer, if possible.

For example,

$$\frac{7x}{8xy^3} + \frac{3x^2}{20x^2y} = \frac{7x}{8xy^3} \cdot \frac{5x}{5x} + \frac{3x^2}{20x^2y} \cdot \frac{2y^2}{2y^2}$$ We found the LCD, $40x^2y^3$, earlier.

$$= \frac{35x^2}{40x^2y^3} + \frac{6x^2y^2}{40x^2y^3}$$ Change to like denominators.

$$= \frac{35x^2 + 6x^2y^2}{40x^2y^3}$$ Add numerators.

$$= \frac{35 + 6y^2}{40y^3} \cdot \frac{x^2}{x^2}$$ Simplify.

$$= \frac{35 + 6y^2}{40y^3}$$

EXAMPLE 4   Add or subtract and simplify.

a. $\dfrac{3x}{x + 3} + \dfrac{2x}{x + 2}$ **b.** $\dfrac{5}{x + 4} + \dfrac{x - 4}{x^2 + 8x + 16}$

c. $\dfrac{2}{x - 2} + \dfrac{2}{2 - x}$ **d.** $\dfrac{x + 5}{4x^2 - 9} - \dfrac{x - 1}{2x^2 - x - 3}$

e. $\dfrac{x}{x + 3} - \dfrac{2x}{x - 3} + \dfrac{x^2 + 10x + 3}{x^2 - 9}$

Solution

a. $\dfrac{3x}{x + 3} + \dfrac{2x}{x + 2}$

Neither denominator factors. LCD $= (x + 3)(x + 2)$. Multiply the first rational expression by $\frac{x+2}{x+2}$ and the second rational expression by $\frac{x+3}{x+3}$.

$$= \frac{3x(x + 2)}{(x + 3)(x + 2)} + \frac{2x(x + 3)}{(x + 2)(x + 3)}$$

$$= \frac{3x^2 + 6x}{(x + 3)(x + 2)} + \frac{2x^2 + 6x}{(x + 2)(x + 3)}$$ Multiply each numerator. Do not multiply the denominator until after addition.

$$= \frac{5x^2 + 12x}{(x + 3)(x + 2)}$$ Add numerators.

$$= \frac{x(5x + 12)}{(x + 3)(x + 2)}$$ Factor to determine if the expression will simplify.

b. $\dfrac{5}{x + 4} + \dfrac{x - 4}{x^2 + 8x + 16} = \dfrac{5}{x + 4} + \dfrac{x - 4}{(x + 4)^2}$ Factor the denominators.

The first denominator does not factor. Use the denominator, $x + 4$, as a factor.

The second denominator does factor.

$$x^2 + 8x + 16 = (x + 4)^2$$

The largest power of the common factor, $x + 4$, is 2. Therefore, LCD $= (x + 4)^2$. Multiply the first expression by $\frac{x+4}{x+4}$.

$$= \frac{5(x + 4)}{(x + 4)(x + 4)} + \frac{x - 4}{(x + 4)^2} \qquad (x + 4)^2 = (x + 4)(x + 4)$$

$$= \frac{5x + 20}{(x + 4)^2} + \frac{x - 4}{(x + 4)^2} \qquad \text{Multiply.}$$

$$= \frac{6x + 16}{(x + 4)^2} \qquad \text{Add numerators.}$$

$$= \frac{2(3x + 8)}{(x + 4)^2} \qquad \text{Factor to simplify.}$$

c. $\dfrac{2}{x - 2} + \dfrac{2}{2 - x}$

The denominators do not factor. However, they are opposites: $x - 2$ and $2 - x$. Therefore, either denominator may be used as the LCD. We will use $x - 2$. Multiply the second expression by $\frac{-1}{-1}$.

$$= \frac{2}{x - 2} + \frac{2(-1)}{(2 - x)(-1)}$$

$$= \frac{2}{x - 2} + \frac{-2}{x - 2} \qquad \text{Multiply.}$$

$$= \frac{2 - 2}{x - 2} \qquad \text{Subtract numerators.}$$

$$= \frac{0}{x - 2} = 0 \qquad \text{Simplify.}$$

d. $\dfrac{x + 5}{4x^2 - 9} - \dfrac{x - 1}{2x^2 - x - 3} = \dfrac{(x + 5)}{(2x + 3)(2x - 3)} - \dfrac{(x - 1)}{(2x - 3)(x + 1)}$

Factor the denominators:

$$4x^2 - 9 = (2x + 3)(2x - 3)$$
$$2x^2 - x - 3 = (2x - 3)(x + 1)$$

LCD $= (2x + 3)(2x - 3)(x + 1)$. Multiply the first expression by $\frac{x+1}{x+1}$ and the second expression by $\frac{2x+3}{2x+3}$.

$$= \frac{(x + 5)(x + 1)}{(2x + 3)(2x - 3)(x + 1)} - \frac{(x - 1)(2x + 3)}{(2x - 3)(x + 1)(2x + 3)}$$

$$= \frac{x^2 + 6x + 5}{(2x + 3)(2x - 3)(x + 1)} - \frac{2x^2 + x - 3}{(2x - 3)(x + 1)(2x + 3)} \qquad \text{Multiply.}$$

$$= \frac{(x^2 + 6x + 5) - (2x^2 + x - 3)}{(2x + 3)(2x - 3)(x + 1)} \qquad \text{Subtract numerators.}$$

$$= \frac{x^2 + 6x + 5 - 2x^2 - x + 3}{(2x + 3)(2x - 3)(x + 1)}$$

$$= \frac{-x^2 + 5x + 8}{(2x + 3)(2x - 3)(x + 1)} \qquad \text{Simplify.}$$

e. $\dfrac{x}{x + 3} - \dfrac{2x}{x - 3} + \dfrac{x^2 + 10x + 3}{x^2 - 9} = \dfrac{x}{x + 3} - \dfrac{2x}{x - 3} + \dfrac{x^2 + 10x + 3}{(x + 3)(x - 3)}$

Factor the denominators. LCD $= (x + 3)(x - 3)$. Multiply the first expression by $\frac{x-3}{x-3}$ and the second expression by $\frac{x+3}{x+3}$.

$$= \frac{x(x-3)}{(x+3)(x-3)} - \frac{2x(x+3)}{(x-3)(x+3)} + \frac{x^2+10x+3}{(x+3)(x-3)}$$

$$= \frac{x^2-3x}{(x+3)(x-3)} - \frac{2x^2+6x}{(x-3)(x+3)} + \frac{x^2+10x+3}{(x+3)(x-3)} \qquad \text{Multiply.}$$

$$= \frac{(x^2-3x)-(2x^2+6x)+(x^2+10x+3)}{(x+3)(x-3)} \qquad \text{Subtract numerators.}$$

$$= \frac{x^2-3x-2x^2-6x+x^2+10x+3}{(x+3)(x-3)}$$

$$= \frac{x+3}{(x+3)(x-3)} \qquad \text{Simplify.}$$

$$= \frac{1}{x-3} \qquad \text{Simplify.} \blacksquare$$

 ## Experiencing Algebra the Checkup Way

Add or subtract and simplify.

1. $\dfrac{5}{6x^2y} + \dfrac{9}{2xy^2}$

2. $\dfrac{2x}{x-3} + \dfrac{5x}{x-8}$

3. $\dfrac{5}{x-4} - \dfrac{3}{4-x}$

4. $\dfrac{x}{x^2+10x+21} + \dfrac{3}{x^2+8x+15}$

5. $\dfrac{x}{x-4} - \dfrac{3}{x+4} + \dfrac{6x}{x^2-16}$

---

5   Modeling the Real World

Geometric formulas are often written as rational expressions. For example, the area of a rectangle is $A = LW$, where L is the rectangle's length and W is its width. We can solve for L to obtain $L = \frac{A}{W}$, which is a rational expression. This formula is very useful for modeling practical situations where you want to determine the dimensions of some rectangular object with a given area.

EXAMPLE 5

Two rectangular bins are arranged side by side, as shown in the following figures. The area of the smaller bin is 25 square feet and the area of the larger bin is 36 square feet. Determine the total length of the two bins in terms of the width W.

a.

b.

c.

Solution

a. The length of the smaller bin is $\frac{25}{W}$ feet. The length of the larger bin is $\frac{36}{W}$ feet. The total length is $\frac{25}{W} + \frac{36}{W} = \frac{61}{W}$ feet.

b. The length of the smaller bin is $\frac{25}{2W}$ feet. The length of the larger bin is $\frac{36}{W}$ feet. The total length is $\frac{25}{2W} + \frac{36}{W} = \frac{25}{2W} + \frac{72}{2W} = \frac{97}{2W}$ feet.

c. The length of the smaller bin is $\frac{25}{W}$ feet. The length of the larger bin is $\frac{36}{W+10}$ feet. The total length is $\frac{25}{W} + \frac{36}{W+10} = \frac{25W+250}{W(W+10)} + \frac{36W}{W(W+10)} = \frac{61W+250}{W(W+10)}$ feet. ∎

Application George Ferris constructed the Ferris wheel for the 1893 Columbian Exposition in Chicago. To keep a steady-state speed for the ride, he set up a control system. A function for the wheel and motor dynamics can be expressed by the sum of the expressions $\frac{4}{s^2+6s+8}$ and $\frac{1}{s+4}$, where s represents an electronic parameter. Determine the sum of the expressions.

Discussion

$$\frac{4}{s^2+6s+8} + \frac{1}{s+4}$$

$$= \frac{4}{(s+2)(s+4)} + \frac{1}{s+4}$$
Factor the denominators.
LCD $= (s+2)(s+4)$

$$= \frac{4}{(s+2)(s+4)} + \frac{1(s+2)}{(s+4)(s+2)}$$
Multiply the expression on the right by $\frac{s+2}{s+2}$.

$$= \frac{4}{(s+2)(s+4)} + \frac{s+2}{(s+4)(s+2)}$$
Multiply.

$$= \frac{4+(s+2)}{(s+2)(s+4)}$$
Add numerators.

$$= \frac{s+6}{(s+2)(s+4)}$$
∎

 Experiencing Algebra the Checkup Way

1. The width of a rectangle is given by $\frac{x-1}{5x}$ yards and its length is given by $\frac{x+1}{3x}$ yards. Find an expression for its perimeter.

2. A second rectangle has a width given by $\frac{x+1}{2x}$ yards and a length given by $\frac{3x+2}{x}$ yards. Find an expression for its perimeter.

3. Find the difference between the two perimeters.

PROBLEM SET 12.3

Experiencing Algebra the Exercise Way

Add and simplify.

1. $\dfrac{5}{x} + \dfrac{8}{x}$

2. $\dfrac{3}{x} + \dfrac{9}{x}$

3. $\dfrac{5}{x} + \dfrac{8}{-x}$

4. $\dfrac{3}{-x} + \dfrac{9}{x}$

5. $\dfrac{2x}{5xy} + \dfrac{3x}{5xy}$

6. $\dfrac{b}{4ab} + \dfrac{3b}{4ab}$

7. $\dfrac{x-1}{x+6} + \dfrac{x+1}{x+6}$

8. $\dfrac{x-5}{x+12} + \dfrac{2x+5}{x+12}$

9. $\dfrac{2b}{b^2-25} + \dfrac{10}{b^2-25}$

10. $\dfrac{21}{z^2-49} + \dfrac{3z}{z^2-49}$

11. $\dfrac{x-5}{x+3} + \dfrac{x+5}{x+3} + \dfrac{x+9}{x+3}$

12. $\dfrac{x-2}{2x+1} + \dfrac{3x+1}{2x+1} + \dfrac{4x+5}{2x+1}$

13. $\dfrac{3x-2}{x-5} + \dfrac{x+8}{5-x}$

14. $\dfrac{x+4}{7-x} + \dfrac{4x-17}{x-7}$

15. $\dfrac{a^2}{a-3} + \dfrac{9}{3-a}$

16. $\dfrac{25}{5-c} + \dfrac{c^2}{c-5}$

17. $\dfrac{5x}{x^2-9} + \dfrac{15}{9-x^2}$

18. $\dfrac{3x-4}{x^2-1} + \dfrac{3-4x}{1-x^2}$

19. $\dfrac{3}{2x} + \dfrac{7}{6x^2}$

20. $\dfrac{9}{5x^2} + \dfrac{3}{10x^3}$

21. $\dfrac{3x+1}{x-6} + \dfrac{x-4}{2x-12}$

22. $\dfrac{2x-3}{x+9} + \dfrac{x+2}{2x+18}$

23. $\dfrac{2x}{2x-3} + \dfrac{6x+9}{4x^2-9}$

24. $\dfrac{2x-1}{5x+2} + \dfrac{4-10x}{25x^2-4}$

25. $\dfrac{7}{3x-5} + \dfrac{4}{3x+5}$

26. $\dfrac{5}{2x-3} + \dfrac{7}{2x+3}$

27. $\dfrac{7}{x-5} + \dfrac{x+1}{x^2-10x+25}$

28. $\dfrac{2}{x-8} + \dfrac{3x+4}{x^2-16x+64}$

29. $\dfrac{b+8}{b} + \dfrac{b}{b+8}$

30. $\dfrac{a-3}{2a} + \dfrac{2a}{a-3}$

31. $\dfrac{x-2}{4x+12} + \dfrac{2x+1}{x^2-9}$

32. $\dfrac{x-1}{x^2-4} + \dfrac{2x-1}{3x+6}$

33. $\dfrac{x+7}{x^2+2x-15} + \dfrac{8-x}{x^2+9x+20}$

34. $\dfrac{3}{x^2+8x+7} + \dfrac{4-x}{x^2+5x-14}$

35. $\dfrac{3a-b}{a^2b} + \dfrac{a+2b}{ab^2}$

36. $\dfrac{p-q}{pq^2} + \dfrac{p+q}{p^2q}$

37. $\dfrac{3x}{x-2y} + \dfrac{4y}{2y-x}$

38. $\dfrac{x}{5x-y} + \dfrac{3y}{y-5x}$

39. $\dfrac{5x+2y}{x^2-9y^2} + \dfrac{6}{x+3y}$

40. $\dfrac{2x+y}{4x^2-9y^2} + \dfrac{7}{2x-3y}$

41. $\dfrac{8}{x^2+6xz+9z^2} + \dfrac{2}{x^2-9z^2}$

42. $\dfrac{5}{x^2-4y^2} + \dfrac{3}{x^2+4xy+4y^2}$

Subtract and simplify.

43. $\dfrac{4}{d} - \dfrac{9}{d}$

44. $\dfrac{3}{b} - \dfrac{11}{b}$

45. $\dfrac{9xy}{7x^2y} - \dfrac{2xy}{7x^2y}$

46. $\dfrac{2xy}{5xy^2} - \dfrac{7xy}{5xy^2}$

47. $\dfrac{2x-3}{x+9} - \dfrac{x-3}{x+9}$

48. $\dfrac{5x-4}{x+8} - \dfrac{2x-1}{x+8}$

49. $\dfrac{4x-13}{x-5} - \dfrac{2x-3}{x-5}$

50. $\dfrac{3x+5}{x-6} - \dfrac{x+17}{x-6}$

51. $\dfrac{x+3}{x+11} - \dfrac{2x-8}{x+11}$

52. $\dfrac{x+2}{x+13} - \dfrac{3x-7}{x+13}$

53. $\dfrac{z^2}{z+4} - \dfrac{16}{z+4}$

54. $\dfrac{c^2}{c+7} - \dfrac{49}{c+7}$

55. $\dfrac{3c}{c^2-9} - \dfrac{9}{c^2-9}$

56. $\dfrac{5b}{b^2-4} - \dfrac{10}{b^2-4}$

57. $\dfrac{5x+1}{2x+3} - \dfrac{x+2}{2x+3} - \dfrac{2x-5}{2x+3}$

58. $\dfrac{2x+5}{3x-4} - \dfrac{x+4}{3x-4} - \dfrac{3x-2}{3x-4}$

59. $\dfrac{7x+5}{x-2} - \dfrac{x-1}{2-x}$

60. $\dfrac{2x-3}{x-7} - \dfrac{x+4}{7-x}$

61. $\dfrac{3x}{x^2-4} - \dfrac{6}{4-x^2}$

62. $\dfrac{5a}{a^2-36} - \dfrac{30}{36-a^2}$

63. $\dfrac{6x-3}{3x+15} - \dfrac{x-1}{x+5}$

64. $\dfrac{3x+7}{2x+3} - \dfrac{x+4}{6x+9}$

65. $\dfrac{7}{2x-5} - \dfrac{9}{2x+5}$

66. $\dfrac{9}{3x-1} - \dfrac{4}{3x+1}$

67. $\dfrac{6}{x^2+12x+36} - \dfrac{2x+1}{x+6}$

68. $\dfrac{3}{x^2-14x+49} - \dfrac{x-4}{x-7}$

69. $\dfrac{x}{8-x} - \dfrac{8-x}{x}$

70. $\dfrac{x-10}{x} - \dfrac{x}{x-10}$

71. $\dfrac{x+2}{3x+12} - \dfrac{x-4}{x^2-16}$

72. $\dfrac{7}{x^2-9} - \dfrac{9}{x^2+3x}$

73. $\dfrac{11}{b^2-9} - \dfrac{7}{2b^2-b-15}$

74. $\dfrac{14}{a^2-25} - \dfrac{9}{2a^2-9a-5}$

75. $\dfrac{7}{5ab^2} - \dfrac{15}{10a^2b} - \dfrac{3}{2b}$

76. $\dfrac{5}{16x^2y} - \dfrac{2}{24xy} - \dfrac{7}{6xy^2}$

77. $\dfrac{4p-q}{p+3q} - \dfrac{p+2q}{p+3q}$

78. $\dfrac{2x-z}{x+5z} - \dfrac{x-4z}{x+5z}$

79. $\dfrac{7}{x^2+6xy+9y^2} - \dfrac{2}{x^2-9y^2}$

80. $\dfrac{8}{x^2+10xy+25y^2} - \dfrac{3}{x^2-25y^2}$

Add or subtract and simplify exercises 81–92.

81. $\dfrac{x}{x+5} - \dfrac{4}{x-5} + \dfrac{10x}{x^2-25}$

82. $\dfrac{6z}{z^2-81} - \dfrac{3}{z-9} + \dfrac{2z}{z+9}$

83. $1 + \dfrac{x-9}{x+10}$

84. $3 + \dfrac{x}{3x+1}$

85. $5 - \dfrac{4}{2x+7}$

86. $1 - \dfrac{x}{x+4}$

87. $\dfrac{2x-3}{x+7} - 1$

88. $\dfrac{5x+8}{9x-2} - 4$

89. $\dfrac{3}{x+3} + x + 5$

90. $x + 3 + \dfrac{2}{x+1}$

91. $2x + 1 - \dfrac{3}{x-4}$

92. $\dfrac{5x}{4x-1} - 5x$

93. In Figure 12.2 (a), the smaller rectangle has an area of 20 square feet, and the larger rectangle has an area of 45 square feet. Given the lengths shown, find an expression for the sum of the two widths of the rectangles in terms of L. Repeat the exercise for Figure 12.2 (b).

(a)

(b)

Figure 12.2

94. In Figure 12.3 (a), the smaller rectangular box has a volume of 60 cubic inches, while the larger rectangular box has a volume of 200 cubic inches. Given the lengths shown, find an expression for the difference in the two widths in terms of L. Repeat the exercise for Figure 12.3 (b).

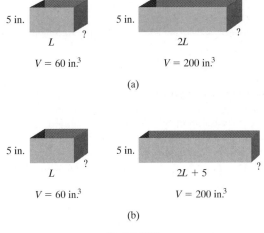

Figure 12.3

95. The width of a rectangle is given by $\frac{24}{x-1}$ feet and its length is given by $\frac{72}{x+1}$ feet. Find an expression for its perimeter.

96. The base of a trapezoid measures $\frac{60}{x+3}$ inches, its top measures $\frac{42}{x+3}$ inches, and its sides measure $\frac{9}{x}$ inches and $\frac{21+x}{2x}$ inches. Find an expression for its perimeter.

97. A company receives \$55 for each widget it sells. To produce the widgets, the company has a setup cost of \$100 and a cost per widget of \$25.

   a. Write a rational expression for the ratio of revenue to cost for producing and selling x widgets.

   The company also produces gadgets, which sell for \$40 each. These have a setup cost of \$800 and a production cost of \$20 per gadget.

   b. Write a rational expression for the ratio of revenue to cost for producing and selling x gadgets.

   c. Write a rational expression for the difference of the two ratios, widgets less gadgets.

   d. What is the difference in the two ratios if 100 of each are produced and sold? Express the result in fractional form.

98. A company gives discounts for multiple purchases. Its revenue for selling x items is $r(x) = 25x - x^2$ and its cost of production for the items is $c(x) = 5x + 10$.

   a. Write a rational expression for the ratio of revenue to cost for producing and selling items.

   The company sells another product with discounts, so that its revenue function for selling x items is $r(x) = 20x - x^2$. Its cost function for producing x items is $c(x) = 4x$.

   b. Write a rational expression for the ratio of revenue to cost for producing and selling x of these items.

   c. Write a rational expression for the difference of the two ratios.

   d. What is the difference in the two ratios if 20 of each product are produced and sold? Express the result in fractional form.

99. An automatic control system that measures blood sugar and controls a pump to inject insulin in a diabetic person is represented by the sum of the two rational expressions $\frac{2}{s}$ and $\frac{-1}{s+1}$, where s is a parameter. Determine the sum of the expressions.

100. An automatic control system for antilock brakes on a four-wheel-drive vehicle is represented by the sum of the two rational expressions $\frac{-20}{s+1}$ and $\frac{30}{s}$, where s is a parameter. Determine the sum of the expressions.

Experiencing Algebra the Calculator Way

You can use your calculator to check your operations on rational expressions.

First, perform the operation algebraically. For example, given the original expression $\frac{2}{x-3} + \frac{5x}{x+3}$, algebraically determine the simplified expression $\frac{5x^2 - 13x + 6}{x^2 - 9}$.

Next, check for equivalence of the original and simplified expressions by graphing. Set the screen to an appropriate window setting. Enter the original expression in Y1. Graph the original expression. Turn off the original graph and enter the simplified expression in Y2. Graph the simplified expression. The two graphs should be the same except for possible "holes" (restricted values). Then graph both expressions and trace the graphs to determine equivalence.

An alternate check would be to view the table of values. After storing the original and simplified expressions in Y1 and Y2, view the table. If the expressions are equivalent, the two columns of the table should have identical values, except for restricted values.

Use these procedures to check your solutions to the following exercises.

1. $\dfrac{x+3}{x} + \dfrac{x-2}{x-1}$

2. $\dfrac{x+3}{x} - \dfrac{x-2}{x-1}$

3. $\dfrac{x+2}{x-2} + \dfrac{x-2}{x^2-4}$

4. $\dfrac{x+2}{x-2} - \dfrac{x-2}{x^2-4}$

5. $\dfrac{x+3}{x^2+x-6} + \dfrac{x-3}{x^2-5x+6}$

6. $\dfrac{x+3}{x^2+x-6} - \dfrac{x-3}{x^2-5x+6}$

Experiencing Algebra the Group Way

A. Order of Operations and Rational Expressions

The order-of-operations procedures also apply to rational expressions. When simplifying an expression, you would first work within parentheses; then you would operate on exponents; next you would do all multiplications and divisions, moving left to right; and last you would do all additions and subtractions, moving left to right. Of course, you would reduce the rational expressions at each step whenever possible.

Each member of the group should try this on the following expressions. Afterward, discuss the order in which you performed the operations, share your results, and agree on the correct result for each exercise.

1. $\dfrac{4x^2}{x^2-4} \div \dfrac{2x}{x-2} - \dfrac{x-3}{x} \cdot \dfrac{5x}{x^2-9}$

2. $\dfrac{4x^2}{x^2-4} + \dfrac{2x}{x-2} \cdot \dfrac{x-3}{x} \cdot \dfrac{5x}{x^2-9}$

3. $\left(\dfrac{2}{x+2}\right)^2 \cdot \dfrac{x^2-4}{4} + x \div \dfrac{x}{x-2}$

4. $\left(\dfrac{2}{x+2}\right)^2 - \dfrac{x^2-4}{4} \cdot x \cdot \dfrac{x}{x-2}$

5. $\dfrac{3}{a^2b} \cdot \left(\dfrac{2a}{b}\right)^2 - \dfrac{5b^2}{a} \div \dfrac{4b^3}{a^2}$

6. $\dfrac{3}{a^2b} \cdot \left(\dfrac{2a}{b}\right)^2 \cdot \dfrac{5b^2}{a} \div \dfrac{4b^3}{a^2}$

B. Complex Rational Expressions

Fractions that contain rational expressions within the numerator and/or the denominator are **complex rational expressions**. When you encounter such an expression, remember that you can rewrite the fraction as a division problem, then use the methods of this and the previous section to simplify. Each member of the group should perform the following operations and simplify the expressions. Then share with one another the order in which you performed the operations and come to agreement on the correct final result.

7. $\dfrac{\dfrac{3xy}{2z^2}}{\dfrac{9x^3y}{8z}}$

8. $\dfrac{2x + \dfrac{1}{x}}{5x}$

9. $\dfrac{\dfrac{a+b}{a-b}}{\dfrac{a^2+2ab+b^2}{a^2-b^2}}$

10. $\dfrac{\dfrac{2x}{5} - \dfrac{5}{x}}{\dfrac{2x}{5} + \dfrac{1}{15x}}$

11. $\dfrac{\dfrac{2}{x} + \dfrac{x}{2}}{\dfrac{y}{3} - \dfrac{3}{y}}$

12. $\dfrac{\dfrac{1}{a^2} + \dfrac{2}{ab}}{\dfrac{3}{ab^2} + \dfrac{1}{b}}$

Experiencing Algebra the Write Way

Many mathematical models use rational expressions to explain behavior of physical objects. Listed here are several simple mathematical models that use rational expressions.

1. If two resistors R_1 and R_2 (measured in ohms) are connected in parallel, then the combined resistance R_T (in ohms) is given by $\frac{1}{R_T} = \frac{1}{R_1} + \frac{1}{R_2}$.

2. The combined capacitance C of two capacitors C_1 and C_2 connected in series is given by $\frac{1}{C} = \frac{1}{C_1} + \frac{1}{C_2}$.

3. If two blood vessels share common endpoints (connected in parallel) and if r_1 and r_2 are the resistances of the two vessels to the flow of blood (measured in dynes), then the combined resistance of the vessels is given by $\frac{1}{r} = \frac{1}{r_1} + \frac{1}{r_2}$.

4. The force F required to stretch a spring is given by $F = kx$, where x is the distance the spring stretches and k is the spring constant of the spring. If two springs with spring constants of k_1 and k_2 are connected in sequence, the spring constant k of the combination is given by $\frac{1}{k} = \frac{1}{k_1} + \frac{1}{k_2}$.

5. The focal length f of a lens is related to the distances from the lens q and p of the object and of the image by the formula $\frac{1}{f} = \frac{1}{p} + \frac{1}{q}$.

6. If two lenses with focal lengths of f_1 and f_2 are placed in contact with one another, the focal length of the combination is given by $\frac{1}{f} = \frac{1}{f_1} + \frac{1}{f_2}$.

Search in the library for a reference that discusses one of these applications. Or, if you prefer, find a reference on another mathematical model that involves rational expressions. Describe the model you find. If the reference contains an example that uses the model, summarize the example in a brief written report. Be sure to include the title, author, publisher, and call number of the reference you found.

12.4 Solving Rational Equations in One Variable Numerically and Graphically

Objectives
1 Identify rational equations in one variable.
2 Solve rational equations in one variable numerically.
3 Solve rational equations in one variable graphically.
4 Model real-world situations using rational equations in one variable.

Application

In the process of developing a control system for automatically controlling insulin injections, a function $C(s)$ representing the percent of blood sugar concentrate in the human body was developed, $C(s) = \frac{s+2}{s(s+1)}$, where s represents a parameter. If the normal blood sugar concentration is 0.1%, determine a real-number value for s.

After completing this section, we will discuss this application further. See page 958.

---

1 Rational Equations in One Variable

A **rational equation in one variable**, or **rational equation**, is an equation that can be written in the form of a rational expression, containing one variable, that is equal to 0. We are now ready to solve such equations.

> *Standard Form for a Rational Equation in One Variable*
> A rational equation in one variable is written in the form
>
> $$R(x) = 0,$$
>
> where $R(x)$ is a rational expression.

For example, the following are rational equations in one variable.

$$\frac{2}{x} = \frac{x}{8}, \qquad \text{Standard form, } \frac{2}{x} - \frac{x}{8} = 0.$$

$$\frac{x+2}{x+1} = \frac{x+1}{x}, \qquad \text{Standard form, } \frac{x+2}{x+1} - \frac{x+1}{x} = 0.$$

$$\frac{5}{x} + \frac{x-5}{3x} - \frac{x^2-9}{x+3} = 0 \qquad \text{Already written in standard form.}$$

EXAMPLE 1 Determine whether each equation is rational.

a. $3x^2 + 5x^6 - 7x^3 = 0$ **b.** $6x^{-2} + 8 - 7x^{-3} = 12$

c. $x^{3/4} = 2x^2$

Solution

a. $3x^2 + 5x^6 - 7x^3 = 0$ is a polynomial equation, but it is also a rational equation, because each term can be written as a rational expression with a denominator of 1.

$$\frac{3x^2}{1} + \frac{5x^6}{1} - \frac{7x^3}{1} = 0$$

b. $6x^{-2} + 8 - 7x^{-3} = 12$ is a rational equation, because an expression that contains a variable with a negative exponent can be written as a rational expression.

$$6x^{-2} = \frac{6}{x^2} \quad \text{and} \quad 7x^{-3} = \frac{7}{x^3}$$

Therefore, $\frac{6}{x^2} + 8 - \frac{7}{x^3} - 12 = 0$.

c. $x^{3/4} = 2x^2$ is not a rational equation, because an expression containing a variable base with a fractional exponent cannot be written as a rational expression. ∎

Experiencing Algebra the Checkup Way

In exercises 1–6, determine whether each equation is rational.

1. $\dfrac{1}{\sqrt{x}} = \dfrac{x}{2}$

2. $4z^2 - 3z - 1 = 0$

3. $a + 2 = a^{1/2}$

4. $\dfrac{5}{x} + 3 = \dfrac{x}{7}$

5. $\dfrac{3}{2x} + \dfrac{1}{x-2} = 5$

6. $3m^{-2} + 4m^{-1} = -6$

7. Explain the difference between a rational equation and a rational expression.

---

2 Solving Rational Equations Numerically

In previous chapters, we determined whether a number was a solution of an equation in one variable by substituting the number for the variable and evaluating the two resulting expressions. If the resulting equation was true, the number substituted was called a solution. The set of all possible solutions is called the solution set. We do the same process for a rational equation in one variable. For example, given $-\frac{1}{x} + \frac{3}{x} = -x + 3$, determine whether 2 is a solution.

$$-\frac{1}{x} + \frac{3}{x} = -x + 3$$

$-\dfrac{1}{2} + \dfrac{3}{2}$	$-(2) + 3$
1	1

Therefore, 2 is a solution because the resulting equation, $1 = 1$, is true.

To find other solutions of this equation, $-\frac{1}{x} + \frac{3}{x} = -x + 3$, we continue to substitute possible values for x and determine whether the resulting equations are true. Remember that any numbers resulting in an undefined value for the rational terms are restricted values. Restricted values are *never* solutions of rational equations. A table of values is helpful in organizing this method.

Solving a Rational Equation Numerically
To solve a rational equation numerically:
Determine the restricted values for the independent variable.

Set up an extended table of values:

- The first column is labeled with the name of the independent variable.
- The second column is labeled with the expression on the left side of the equation.
- The third column is labeled with the expression on the right side of the equation.

Complete the table:

- Substitute values for the independent variable.
- Evaluate the second and third columns.

Continued

> • Continue until values for the two expressions (the numbers in the second and third columns) are equal.
>
> The values for the independent variable (the number in the first column) used to find these equivalent expressions are the solutions.

For example, a sample table to determine another solution of the equation $-\frac{1}{x} + \frac{3}{x} = -x + 3$ could appear as follows:

Note: 0 is a restricted value for the equation.

x	$-\dfrac{1}{x} + \dfrac{3}{x}$	$-x + 3$	
-1	$-\dfrac{1}{-1} + \dfrac{3}{-1}$ -2	$-(-1) + 3$ 4	$-2 \neq 4$
1	$-\dfrac{1}{1} + \dfrac{3}{1}$ 2	$-(1) + 3$ 2	$2 = 2$

According to the table, when 1 is substituted for the variable, the two expressions are equivalent ($2 = 2$). Therefore, 1 is another solution of the rational equation.

To solve a rational equation numerically on your calculator:

• Rename the independent variable as x.

Set up the table.

• Set up the first column for the independent variable by setting a minimum value and increments. Since we do not know the solution, we may want to start with 0. Use increments of 1 to obtain integer values. Set the calculator to perform the evaluations automatically.
• Set up the second column of the table to be the expression on the left. Enter the expression on the left side of the equation in Y1.
• Set up the third column of the table to be the expression on the right. Enter the expression on the right side of the equation in Y2.

View the table.

• Move beyond the screen to view additional rows by using the up and down arrows.

The integer solutions are the x-values that determine equal values for Y1 and Y2. There may be more than one solution.

For example, solve $-\frac{1}{x} + \frac{3}{x} = -x + 3$ on your calculator.

The solutions are the *x*-values that correspond to Y1 = Y2. The two integer solutions from the table are 1 and 2.

EXAMPLE 2   Solve numerically.

a. $2x^{-1} = \dfrac{x}{8}$

b. $\dfrac{a}{a - 2} = \dfrac{a + 1}{a - 3}$

c. $\dfrac{x + 4}{x^2 + 3x - 4} + \dfrac{x + 1}{x - 1} = \dfrac{x + 2}{2x - 4}$

Calculator Numeric Solution

a. $2x^{-1} = \dfrac{x}{8}$

Since $2x^{-1} = 2\left(\frac{1}{x}\right) = \frac{2}{x}$, 0 is a restricted value.

Let $Y1 = 2x^{-1}$ and $Y2 = \dfrac{x}{8}$.

X	Y1	Y2
-4	-.5	-.5
-3	-.6667	-.375
-2	-1	-.25
-1	-2	-.125
0	ERROR	0
1	2	.125
2	1	.25
X= -4		

X	Y1	Y2
-2	-1	-.25
-1	-2	-.125
0	ERROR	0
1	2	.125
2	1	.25
3	.6667	.375
4	.5	.5
X=4		

The solutions are −4 and 4, because when −4 and 4 are substituted for the variable in both expressions, the resulting values are equal.

b. $\dfrac{a}{a - 2} = \dfrac{a + 1}{a - 3}$

Restricted values are 2 and 3. Rewrite the equation in terms of *x*.

$$\frac{x}{x - 2} = \frac{x + 1}{x - 3}$$

The solution is 1, because when 1 is substituted for the variable in both expressions, the resulting values are equal.

X	Y1	Y2
0	0	-.3333
1	-1	-1
2	ERROR	-3
3	3	ERROR
4	2	5
5	1.6667	3
6	1.5	2.3333
X=0		

$Y1 = \dfrac{x}{x - 2}$

$Y2 = \dfrac{x + 1}{x - 3}$

X	Y₁	Y₂
-2	0	0
-1	-.5	-.1667
0	-2	-.5
1	ERROR	-1.5
2	4	ERROR
3	2.5	2.5
4	2	1.5

X=-2

$$Y1 = \frac{x + 4}{x^2 + 3x - 4} + \frac{x + 1}{x - 1} \quad Y2 = \frac{x + 2}{2x - 4}$$

c. $$\frac{x + 4}{x^2 + 3x - 4} + \frac{x + 1}{x - 1} = \frac{x + 2}{2x - 4}$$

Restricted values are −4, 1, and 2.

The solutions are −2 and 3, because when −2 and 3 are substituted for the variable in both expressions, the resulting values are equal. ∎

EXAMPLE 3 $x^{-2} - 3 = -x + 3$ does not have an integer solution. Set up a table of values on your calculator and determine that there is no integer solution.

X	Y₁	Y₂
2	-2.75	1
3	-2.889	0
4	-2.938	-1
5	-2.96	-2
6	-2.972	-3
7	-2.98	-4
8	-2.984	-5

X=8

$$Y1 = x^{-2} - 3$$
$$Y2 = -x + 3$$

Calculator Numeric Solution

−2.75 < 1
−2.889 < 0
−2.938 < −1
−2.96 < −2
−2.972 > −3
−2.98 > −4
−2.984 > −5

We cannot find an integer value for x that corresponds to Y1 = Y2. However, for x-values less than or equal to 5, Y1 < Y2, and for x-values greater than or equal to 6, Y1 > Y2. Since x-values are not restricted between 5 and 6, a solution occurs between 5 and 6, when Y1 = Y2. ∎

We see that a table of values cannot help us determine a noninteger solution, but can help us approximate it. We need a different method to find the exact solution.

Some polynomial equations have no solution or an infinite number of solutions. This is also true for rational equations. Complete the following sets of exercises to determine when these possibilities occur.

D I S C O V E R Y   3

Rational Equations with No Solution

Solve $\frac{x+4}{x-1} = \frac{x-4}{x-1}$ numerically by completing the table of values.

x	$\dfrac{x + 4}{x - 1}$	$\dfrac{x - 4}{x - 1}$
−3		
−2		
−1		
0		
1		
2		
3		

Write a rule to explain the solution of the equation from viewing its table of values.

It appears that the expression on the right, Y1, is never equal to the expression on the left, Y2. The x-values less than the restricted value of 1 correspond to Y1 < Y2. The x-values greater than the restricted value of 1 correspond to Y1 > Y2. Since the restricted value is between these ranges, an alternative method is needed to confirm that there is no solution of the equation.

DISCOVERY 4

Rational Equations with Many Solutions

Solve $\frac{3}{x} = \frac{6}{2x}$ numerically by completing the table of values.

x	$\dfrac{3}{x}$	$\dfrac{6}{2x}$
-3		
-2		
-1		
0		
1		
2		
3		

Write a rule to explain the solution of the equation from viewing its table of values.

The two expressions are equal for every value of the independent variable in the table. The domain for the independent variable is all real numbers not equal to 0. Therefore, it appears that the solution set of the equation is all real numbers not equal to 0. We call this type of rational equation an identity. An identity is an equation for which all permissible replacements of the variable result in a true equation.

EXAMPLE 4 Solve numerically.

a. $\dfrac{3x - 15}{6 + 3x} = \dfrac{x - 10}{x + 2}$

b. $\dfrac{7x}{5} - \dfrac{x + 7}{x + 5} = \dfrac{7x^2 + 30x - 35}{5x + 25}$

Calculator Numeric Solution

a. $\dfrac{3x - 15}{6 + 3x} = \dfrac{x - 10}{x + 2}$

The restricted value is -2.

The expressions Y1 and Y2 do not appear to be equal. However, for all x-values less than the restricted value of -2, Y1 < Y2, and for all x-values greater than -2, Y1 > Y2. We need another method to confirm that there is no solution.

b. $\dfrac{7x}{5} - \dfrac{x + 7}{x + 5} = \dfrac{7x^2 + 30x - 35}{5x + 25}$

The restricted value is -5.

The expressions are always equal in the table, so it appears that the solution set is all real numbers not equal to -5, the restricted value. The equation is an identity. ∎

X	Y1	Y2	
-5	3.3333	5	3.3333 < 5
-4	4.5	7	4.5 < 7
-3	8	13	8 < 13
-2	ERROR	ERROR	
-1	-6	-11	-6 > -11
0	-2.5	-5	-2.5 > -5
1	-1.333	-3	-1.333 > -3

X=-5

$Y1 = \dfrac{3x - 15}{6 + 3x}$

$Y2 = \dfrac{x - 10}{x + 2}$

X	Y1	Y2
0	-1.4	-1.4
1	.06667	.06667
2	1.5143	1.5143
3	2.95	2.95
4	4.3778	4.3778
5	5.8	5.8
6	7.2182	7.2182

X=0

$Y1 = \dfrac{7x}{5} - \dfrac{x + 7}{x + 5}$

$Y2 = \dfrac{7x^2 + 30x - 35}{5x + 25}$

Numerical Solutions of a Rational Equation
To solve a rational equation for integer solutions numerically, set up an extended table of values. In viewing the table, one of four possibilities will occur:

Continued

Integer solutions exist. The solutions are the integers in the first column that correspond to equal values in the second and third columns.

Noninteger solutions exist. When comparing corresponding values in the second column to the third column, the order changes from "less than" to "greater than" or "greater than" to "less than," and the restricted value does not occur at this change. A noninteger solution occurs between the two consecutive integers in the first column that correspond to this change.

It appears no solution exists. When comparing corresponding values in the second and third columns, there does not appear to be a change in order for two consecutive integers, or a change occurs but the restricted value occurs at this change.

An infinite number of solutions exist. When comparing corresponding values in the second and third columns, the values are equal. The equation is an identity. The solution set is all numbers for which the equation is defined.

In conclusion, a rational equation may be solved numerically using a table of values. However, if the solution is noninteger or does not exist, it will be difficult to find by this method. Also, it is difficult to know whether all possible solutions have been found.

Experiencing Algebra the Checkup Way

In exercises 1–6, solve numerically for integer solutions if possible.

1. $3x^{-1} = \dfrac{x}{12}$

2. $2b + 3 = b + \dfrac{8}{b + 1}$

3. $\dfrac{t}{t + 3} = \dfrac{t - 2}{t - 1}$

4. $1 + \dfrac{10}{u} = \dfrac{3}{u} - 1$

5. $\dfrac{x + 3}{x + 1} = \dfrac{x + 4}{x + 1}$

6. $\dfrac{2}{p + 1} = \dfrac{4}{2p + 2}$

7. What is the difference between solving a rational equation and evaluating a rational expression? Is one operation related to the other?

---

3 Solving Rational Equations Graphically

We may solve a rational equation graphically, using the same procedure as with linear and polynomial equations. That is, graph two functions defined by the expressions on the left and right sides of the equation. The *x*-coordinates of the points of intersection of the graphs are the solutions.

Solving a Rational Equation Graphically
To solve a rational equation graphically:

• Write two functions, using each expression in the equation as a rule.

• Graph both functions on the same coordinate plane by plotting points found in a table of values and connecting the points with a smooth curve to include all values in the domain of the functions.

Remember not to connect points across the vertical lines represented by $x = a$, where a is a restricted value.

The solutions of the equation are the x-coordinates of the points of intersection of the two graphs.

The y-coordinates of the points of intersection of the two graphs are the values obtained for both expressions when the equation is evaluated with the solutions.

For example, solve graphically $-\frac{1}{x} + \frac{3}{x} = -x + 3$.

For the equation $-\frac{1}{x} + \frac{3}{x} = -x + 3$, we write the two functions as $y_1 = -\frac{1}{x} + \frac{3}{x}$ and $y_2 = -x + 3$. Set up a table of values for each function. The restricted value for the function y_1 is $x = 0$.

x	$y = -\dfrac{1}{x} + \dfrac{3}{x}$	y
-4	$y = -\dfrac{1}{-4} + \dfrac{3}{-4}$	$-\dfrac{1}{2}$
-3	$y = -\dfrac{1}{-3} + \dfrac{3}{-3}$	$-\dfrac{2}{3}$
-2	$y = -\dfrac{1}{-2} + \dfrac{3}{-2}$	-1
-1	$y = -\dfrac{1}{-1} + \dfrac{3}{-1}$	-2
-0.5	$y = -\dfrac{1}{-0.5} + \dfrac{3}{-0.5}$	-4
-0.1	$y = -\dfrac{1}{-0.1} + \dfrac{3}{-0.1}$	-20
0.1	$y = -\dfrac{1}{0.1} + \dfrac{3}{0.1}$	20
0.5	$y = -\dfrac{1}{0.5} + \dfrac{3}{0.5}$	4
1	$y = -\dfrac{1}{1} + \dfrac{3}{1}$	2
2	$y = -\dfrac{1}{2} + \dfrac{3}{2}$	1
3	$y = -\dfrac{1}{3} + \dfrac{3}{3}$	$\dfrac{2}{3}$
4	$y = -\dfrac{1}{4} + \dfrac{3}{4}$	$\dfrac{1}{2}$

x	$y = -x + 3$	y
-1	$y = -(-1) + 3$	4
0	$y = -(0) + 3$	3
1	$y = -(1) + 3$	2
2	$y = -(2) + 3$	1
3	$y = -(3) + 3$	0

Plotting these points results in the following graph: (Remember not to cross the $x = 0$ line with the graph of the first equation.)

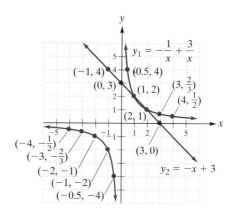

The two solutions are the *x*-coordinates of the intersections, 1 and 2.

To solve a rational equation graphically on your calculator:

- Rename the independent variable as *x*.
- Set the screen to the desired setting (integer, decimal, standard, or your choice).
- Enter the expression on the left side of the equation in Y1.
- Enter the expression on the right side of the equation in Y2.
- Graph.
- Find the points of intersection.

The solutions of the equation are the *x*-coordinates of the points of intersection of the two graphs.

The *y*-coordinates of the points of intersection of the two graphs are the values obtained for both expressions when the equation is evaluated with the solutions.

For example, solve graphically $-\frac{1}{x} + \frac{3}{x} = -x + 3$ on a decimal screen.

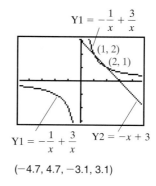

$$(-4.7, 4.7, -3.1, 3.1)$$

The two solutions are the *x*-coordinates of the intersections: 1 and 2.

EXAMPLE 5   Solve graphically.

a. $2x^{-1} = \dfrac{x}{8}$

b. $\dfrac{a}{a-2} = \dfrac{a+1}{a-3}$

c. $\dfrac{x+4}{x^2+3x-4} + \dfrac{x+1}{x-1} = \dfrac{x+2}{2x-4}$

Calculator Graphic Solution

a. $2x^{-1} = \dfrac{x}{8}$

$(-4.7, 4.7, -3.1, 3.1)$

The two solutions are the *x*-coordinates of the intersections: -4 and 4.

b. $\dfrac{a}{a-2} = \dfrac{a+1}{a-3}$

Rewrite in terms of *x* and graph.

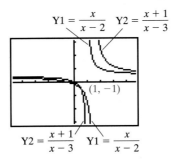

$(-9.4, 9.4, -6.2, 6.2)$

The solution is the *x*-coordinate of the intersection: 1.

c. $\dfrac{x+4}{x^2+3x-4} + \dfrac{x+1}{x-1} = \dfrac{x+2}{2x-4}$

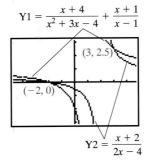

$(-4.7, 4.7, -3.1, 3.1)$

The two solutions are the *x*-coordinates of the intersections: -2 and 3. ∎

EXAMPLE 6 $x^{-2} - 3 = -x + 3$ does not have an integer solution. Use the Intersect function on your calculator to find the approximate solutions.

$Y2 = -x + 3$ $Y1 = x^{-2} - 3$

$(-0.395, 3.395)$ $(0.423, 2.577)$

$(5.972, -2.972)$

$(10, 10, -10, 10)$

Calculator Graphic Solution

The three approximate solutions are the *x*-coordinates of the intersections: $-0.395, 0.423,$ and $5.972.$ ∎

Remember that some rational equations may be contradictions or identities. Graphically solving rational equations may also result in these possibilities. Complete the following sets of exercises on your calculator.

DISCOVERY 5

Rational Equations with No Solution
Solve graphically the previous example of a rational equation with no solution, $\frac{x+4}{x-1} = \frac{x-4}{x-1}$. Sketch the graph.
    Write a rule to determine that a rational equation has no solution from its graph.

The two functions do not appear to intersect. There is no ordered pair common to both functions; therefore, it appears that there is no solution of the equation.

DISCOVERY 6

Rational Equations with Many Solutions
Solve graphically the previous example of a rational equation with many solutions, $\frac{3}{x} = \frac{6}{2x}$. Sketch the graph.
    Write a rule to determine that a rational equation has many solutions from its graph.

It appears that there is only one graph on the screen. Actually, both graphs are the same. Therefore, all ordered pairs on the graph are common to both functions, or all *x*-coordinates are solutions of the equation. The solution set is all real numbers not equal to 0 (the domain of the graphed functions).

EXAMPLE 7 Solve graphically.

a. $\dfrac{3x - 15}{6 + 3x} = \dfrac{x - 10}{x + 2}$

b. $\dfrac{7x}{5} - \dfrac{x + 7}{x + 5} = \dfrac{7x^2 + 30x - 35}{5x + 25}$

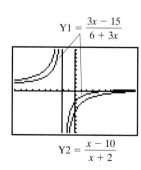

$Y1 = \dfrac{3x - 15}{6 + 3x}$

$Y2 = \dfrac{x - 10}{x + 2}$

$(-10, 10, -10, 10)$
Connected mode

Calculator Graphic Solution

Define the two expressions as rules for functions and enter into your calculator, as in previous examples.

a. $\dfrac{3x - 15}{6 + 3x} = \dfrac{x - 10}{x + 2}$

The graphs do not appear to intersect. There does not appear to be a solution. Another method is needed to confirm this.

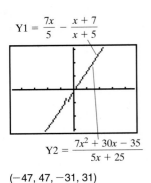

$Y1 = \dfrac{7x}{5} - \dfrac{x+7}{x+5}$

$Y2 = \dfrac{7x^2 + 30x - 35}{5x + 25}$

$(-47, 47, -31, 31)$

b. $\dfrac{7x}{5} - \dfrac{x+7}{x+5} = \dfrac{7x^2 + 30x - 35}{5x + 25}$

The graphs are the same. The solution set is all real numbers not equal to -5 (the domain of the graphed functions). ∎

Graphical Solutions of a Rational Equation
To solve a rational equation graphically, graph two functions defined by the expressions on the left and right sides of the equation. In viewing the graphs, one of three possibilities will occur:

One or more solutions exist.
The graphs intersect. The solutions are the x-coordinates of the points of intersection.
No solution exists.
The graphs do not appear to intersect.
An infinite number of solutions exist.
The graphs appear to coincide. The solution set is all numbers in the domains of the graphed functions.

In conclusion, we solve a rational equation by graphing two functions. With a calculator, this method may be used to find noninteger solutions. Also, using this method we are better able to find all the solutions because we can see the number of points of intersection. We can also determine that the graphs do not appear to intersect and that certain equations probably do not have solutions.

 Experiencing Algebra the Checkup Way

Solve exercises 1–6 graphically.

1. $3x^{-1} = \dfrac{x}{12}$

2. $2y + 3 = y + \dfrac{8}{y+1}$

3. $\dfrac{x}{x+3} = \dfrac{x-2}{x-1}$

4. $1 + \dfrac{10}{W} = \dfrac{3}{W} - 1$

5. $\dfrac{k+3}{k+1} = \dfrac{k+4}{k+1}$

6. $\dfrac{2}{x+1} = \dfrac{4}{2x+2}$

7. Compare the solutions for these six exercises with the answers for the same six exercises in the previous checkup exercises. For which exercises were you able to find a solution graphically but not numerically? Why?

---

4 Modeling the Real World

We previously used the simple-interest formula, $I = PRT$, where I is the amount of simple interest, P is the amount of principal, R is the rate of interest, and T is the amount of time. When this formula is solved for the principal, it gives rise to the rational equation $P = \frac{I}{RT}$. This relationship is another example of writing rational expressions to model real-world situations.

EXAMPLE 8 At the end of a 2-year investment of $2000, Chantell had earned simple interest of $125 on one investment and $130 on a second investment. She remembered that the second investment earned 0.25% higher interest than the first investment. What were the two simple-interest rates?

Graphic Solution

Let $\quad x =$ interest rate for the first investment (in decimal form)
$x + 0.0025 =$ interest rate of the second investment

The time T is 2 years.

The first investment interest was $125.

The second investment interest was $130.

Since $P = \frac{I}{RT}$,

$$P_1 = \frac{125}{x(2)} \qquad \text{First investment principal}$$

$$P_2 = \frac{130}{(x + 0.0025)2} \qquad \text{Second investment principal}$$

$$Y1 = \frac{125}{2x} + \frac{130}{2(x + 0.0025)}$$

(0.0625, 2000)

$Y2 = 2000$

(0, 1.175, 0, 3100)

The total principal was $2000. Therefore, $P_1 + P_2 = 2000$.

$$\frac{125}{x(2)} + \frac{130}{(x + 0.0025)2} = 2000$$

Graph both expressions in the equation on your calculator using a window of (0, 1.175, 0.1, 0, 3100, 100, 1).

The x-coordinate of the point of intersection of the graphs is the solution: 0.0625.

Chantell earned an interest rate of 0.0625 or 6.25% on the first investment and an interest rate of $0.0625 + 0.0025 = 0.65$ or 6.5% on the second investment. ∎

Application

In the process of developing a control system for automatically controlling insulin injections, a function $C(s)$ representing the percent of blood sugar concentrate in the human body was developed, $C(s) = \frac{s+2}{s(s+1)}$ where s represents a parameter. If the normal blood sugar concentration is 0.1%, determine a real-number value for s.

Discussion

Let $C(s) = 0.1$.

$$0.1 = \frac{s + 2}{s(s + 1)}$$

$$Y2 = \frac{x + 2}{x(x + 1)}$$

(10.84, 0.1)

$Y1 = 0.1$

(0, 20, 0, 1)

Let Y1 = 0.1 and Y2 = $\frac{x + 2}{x(x + 1)}$.

The solution is approximately 10.84. ∎

✓ Experiencing Algebra the Checkup Way

1. At the end of a 3-year investment period, Akim earned $225 in simple interest. He also earned $225 on a second investment for a 2-year period. The second investment offered a reduced interest rate, since it was a shorter investment period. The simple-interest rate was 0.5% less than that for the longer period. If he invested a total of $4000 in the two investments, what were the two simple-interest rates?

2. Joey is planning strategy for his amateur Iron Man competition. He trains on a 35-mile-long bike trail and is able to complete the trail in 1.5 hours. The competition will use a bike trail that is 56 miles long. If he wants to be able to bike at the same rate, determine how many additional hours, x, it will take to complete the competition trail.

PROBLEM SET 12.4

Experiencing Algebra the Exercise Way

Determine whether each equation is rational.

1. $x^{-3} + 2x^{-2} - x^{-1} = 5$ **2.** $c^{-1/3} + 5 = 2c$ **3.** $\dfrac{1}{x+7} + \dfrac{1}{x} = 5$ **4.** $\dfrac{1}{5+x} = \dfrac{\sqrt{2x-1}}{x^2}$

5. $v^{1/2} + 3v = 10$ **6.** $\dfrac{4.7}{x} - \dfrac{1.2}{x^2} = 2.6$ **7.** $\dfrac{\sqrt{2x+7}}{x} = \dfrac{1}{3-x}$ **8.** $\dfrac{4}{\sqrt{5x}} = \dfrac{1}{\sqrt{2}} - \dfrac{3}{\sqrt{2x}}$

9. $\dfrac{2.7}{z^2} - \dfrac{5.3}{z} + 0.9 = 0$ **10.** $\dfrac{\sqrt{5}}{2h^2} = 4 - \dfrac{\sqrt{3}}{h}$ **11.** $\dfrac{1}{3x^2} + \dfrac{5}{6x} = \dfrac{8}{9}$ **12.** $3x^{-2} = 5 + x^{-1}$

13. $\dfrac{5}{\sqrt{3m}} + \dfrac{7}{\sqrt{m}} = \dfrac{1}{\sqrt{5}}$ **14.** $\dfrac{3}{5n^2} + \dfrac{2}{n} = \dfrac{7}{11}$ **15.** $\dfrac{\sqrt{3}}{x^2} + \dfrac{\sqrt{2}}{x} = 7$ **16.** $\dfrac{1}{4x+1} + \dfrac{4}{3x} = 7$

Solve numerically for integer solutions if possible.

17. $\dfrac{q}{7} = 7q^{-1}$ **18.** $\dfrac{x}{3} = 27x^{-1}$ **19.** $\dfrac{3(x-3)}{2x+1} = \dfrac{x-3}{x+1}$

20. $2d - 11 = \dfrac{d^2 - 5d - 6}{d+1}$ **21.** $\dfrac{5}{6} = \dfrac{7}{x} - \dfrac{1}{3}$ **22.** $\dfrac{8x+1}{8x} - \dfrac{1}{2} = \dfrac{5}{8}$

23. $\dfrac{5}{2s} = \dfrac{4}{s} - \dfrac{1}{2}$ **24.** $\dfrac{5}{x} - \dfrac{1}{3} = \dfrac{11}{3x}$ **25.** $\dfrac{4}{x+8} - \dfrac{3}{x+2} = \dfrac{-5}{56}$

26. $\dfrac{5}{x+2} - \dfrac{3}{2x} = \dfrac{1}{2}$ **27.** $\dfrac{2G+5}{G-1} = 9$ **28.** $\dfrac{3e+11}{e+4} = 2$

29. $\dfrac{b-4}{b+2} = \dfrac{1}{4}$ **30.** $\dfrac{c+7}{c-1} = 3$ **31.** $\dfrac{z-3}{z-4} = \dfrac{7}{z-4}$

32. $\dfrac{p+3}{p-4} = \dfrac{-30}{p+2}$ **33.** $\dfrac{1}{x+6} + \dfrac{1}{x-6} = \dfrac{6}{x^2-36}$ **34.** $\dfrac{5}{2x-3} + \dfrac{5}{2x+3} = \dfrac{-40}{4x^2-9}$

35. $\dfrac{-5}{a-2} = \dfrac{1+a}{2-a}$ **36.** $\dfrac{3+b}{7-b} = \dfrac{1}{3(b+5)}$ **37.** $\dfrac{1}{x-1} + \dfrac{4}{x^2-1} = 1$

38. $\dfrac{2}{x+2} - \dfrac{4}{x^2-4} = 2$ **39.** $\dfrac{a-3}{a-1} + \dfrac{3}{a+1} = \dfrac{(a+3)(a-2)}{a^2-1}$ **40.** $\dfrac{5}{b-3} - \dfrac{2}{b^2-9} = \dfrac{5b+13}{b^2-9}$

41. $\dfrac{3}{x-5} + \dfrac{3}{x^2-25} = \dfrac{3x+1}{x^2-25}$ **42.** $\dfrac{3}{x+4} + \dfrac{2}{x+2} = \dfrac{5x+9}{x^2+6x+8}$

Solve exercises 43–70 graphically.

43. $\dfrac{1}{3} = \dfrac{x+1}{x+2} - \dfrac{1}{2}$ **44.** $\dfrac{4x+3}{3x-1} - \dfrac{3}{4} = \dfrac{4}{5}$ **45.** $\dfrac{5}{c} + c = \dfrac{21}{2}$ **46.** $\dfrac{8}{d} - 2d = \dfrac{10}{3}$

47. $\dfrac{9}{x} - \dfrac{2}{x} = 21$ **48.** $\dfrac{17}{x} = 6 + \dfrac{5}{x}$ **49.** $\dfrac{3}{k} = \dfrac{17}{4} - \dfrac{2}{5k}$ **50.** $\dfrac{1}{2x} - \dfrac{9}{x} = -17$

51. $\dfrac{x}{3} = \dfrac{x}{7} + \dfrac{2}{3}$ **52.** $\dfrac{h}{7} = \dfrac{3h}{5} - \dfrac{16}{21}$ **53.** $\dfrac{x+5}{x-3} = \dfrac{1+x}{2-x}$ **54.** $\dfrac{x+9}{x-2} = \dfrac{3+x}{7-x}$

55. $\dfrac{3-z}{7-z} = \dfrac{15}{z-5}$ **56.** $\dfrac{18}{5-z} = \dfrac{8-z}{2-z}$ **57.** $\dfrac{1}{x+3} + \dfrac{1}{x} = 2$ **58.** $\dfrac{1}{x+2} - \dfrac{1}{x} = 3$

59. $w^{-3} + 2w^{-2} - w^{-1} = 1$ **60.** $3v^{-2} = 5 + v^{-1}$ **61.** $2.7x = 5.3 - \dfrac{0.9}{x}$ **62.** $\dfrac{4.7}{x} - \dfrac{1.2}{x^2} = 2.6$

63. $\dfrac{1}{3u^2} + \dfrac{5}{6u} = \dfrac{8}{9}$

64. $\dfrac{3}{5x^2} + \dfrac{2}{x} = \dfrac{7}{11}$

65. $\dfrac{\sqrt{3}}{x^2} + \dfrac{\sqrt{2}}{x} = 7$

66. $\dfrac{\sqrt{5}}{2w^2} = 4 - \dfrac{\sqrt{3}}{w}$

67. $\dfrac{3x + 7}{x - 1} = \dfrac{3x - 3}{x - 1}$

68. $\dfrac{1}{t + 5} - \dfrac{1}{t + 3} = \dfrac{-6}{t^2 + 8t + 15}$

69. $\dfrac{b + 4}{b - 2} = \dfrac{b^2 + 3b - 4}{b^2 - 3b + 2}$

70. $\dfrac{x - 5}{2x + 3} = \dfrac{x^2 - 7x + 10}{2x^2 - x - 6}$

71. Tony's employer deducts a percentage of Tony's gross pay to pay part of his medical benefits insurance. Currently, he is paying $85.56 per month. Tony's gross pay will be reduced by $1200.00 per month while he takes some time off to help his wife with the birth of a new baby. The company will reduce his benefit payment proportionally. His new monthly insurance will be $53.22. Write a rational equation for x, his monthly gross pay before the reduction, and solve it (to the nearest $5.00).

72. Bethann is able to save $3000 per year from her gross salary. She has been offered another position paying $8000 more per year, and figures she will be able to save $4000 per year. If this is the same proportional savings amount, write a rational equation for her current annual gross pay, x, and solve it to find her current pay and her new pay.

73. Maurice drove his car at a constant rate for 132 miles in one time period and 225 miles in a second time period. The second time period was 1.6 hours longer than the first. Write a rational equation for the length of time of the first period, x, and solve it to find the two times to the nearest tenth of an hour.

74. A marathon runner completed one practice run of 17 miles in a given time, and another run of 21 miles in a time that was 0.3 of an hour longer. If the runner's speed was a constant for the two runs, write a rational equation using x as the time of the first run. Solve this equation to find the two times of the practice runs.

75. In order to diversify her savings, Marianne placed part of her money into one account that paid her $286 simple interest for 2 years, and the remainder in another account that paid her $117 simple interest for 2 years. The first account was able to offer her 2% more simple interest than the second account could. If she invested a total of $3500, what were the annual interest rates she received?

76. Roger invested some of his savings in an account that paid him 6% simple interest annually, amounting to $420. He invested other savings in an account that paid him 5% simple interest annually, amounting to $367.50. The money in the second account was invested for 18 months longer than that for the first account. What were the two time periods for the investments, if the total invested in both accounts was $5600?

77. Two blood vessels in a human body are connected in parallel. The combined resistance R of the blood vessels to the flow of blood is related to the resistances r_1 and r_2 of the individual vessels by the mathematical model $\dfrac{1}{R} = \dfrac{1}{r_1} + \dfrac{1}{r_2}$. If the combined resistance is 11.5 dynes and the resistance of the first vessel is 20.5 dynes, what is the resistance of the second vessel to the nearest tenth of a dyne?

flow of blood

78. When two springs are connected in sequence, the spring constant of the combination K is related to the spring constants k_1 and k_2 of the individual springs by the mathematical model $\dfrac{1}{K} = \dfrac{1}{k_1} + \dfrac{1}{k_2}$. If the constant for the combination is 1.5 pounds per inch and the constant for the first spring is 6 pounds per inch, what is the constant for the second spring?

k_1

k_2

Experiencing Algebra the Calculator Way

A. Using the TEST Key When Solving Numerically

When solving numerically, the expression on the left side of the rational equation is stored in Y1 and the expression on the right side in Y2. Solutions to the equation are those values of the variable that make the two expressions equal. Sometimes it is difficult to find the equal values. An alternative method is to store the expressions on the left and right sides in Y2 and Y3, and store the test relation, Y2 $=$ Y3, in Y1. Then scan Y1 in the table of values for a value of 1, which indicates that the test relation is true, and the corresponding value of the variable will be the solution of the rational equation. As an example, use this procedure to solve the rational equation $\frac{x+7}{x+4} = \frac{5}{x-1} + \frac{3}{x^2+3x-4}$.

Step 1. Store the test relation Y2 $=$ Y3 in Y1.

| Y= | VARS | ▶ | 1 | 2 | 2nd | TEST | 1 | VARS | ▶ | 1 | 3 | ENTER |

Step 2. Store the expression on the left in Y2 and the expression on the right in Y3.

```
Plot1 Plot2 Plot3
\Y1=Y2=Y3
\Y2=(X+7)/(X+4)
\Y3=5/(X-1)+3/(X
2+3X-4)
\Y4=
\Y5=
\Y6=
```

Step 3. Use the TABLE function to generate the table, starting at $x = 0$ and incrementing in units of 1.

Step 4. Scan the table until you find a value of Y1 that is equal to 1. This indicates that for the corresponding x-value, the expressions on left and right are equal (thus, Y2 $=$ Y3). Verify by moving the cursor over to display Y2 and Y3. You have found a solution of the rational equation.

X	Y1	Y2
0	0	1.75
1	ERROR	1.6
2	0	1.5
3	0	1.4286
4	0	1.375
5	1	1.3333
6	0	1.3

X=5

X	Y2	Y3
0	1.75	-5.75
1	1.6	ERROR
2	1.5	5.5
3	1.4286	2.7143
4	1.375	1.7917
5	1.3333	1.3333
6	1.3	1.06

Y3=1.33333333333

Try this approach on some of the exercises in this section for which you were instructed to solve numerically.

B. Changing the Window When Solving Graphically

When graphing rational equations, it is sometimes helpful to use a window other than those given under the zoom options. You can change the window to any setting you choose. But if you want to retain the properties of the decimal window or the integer window, it is best to change the windows by adjusting the settings by a constant. Consider the following examples.

1. Solve graphically the rational equation $6x + 6 = \frac{-(11x+1)}{x+1}$.

a. Begin by storing the left side of the equation in Y1 and the right side in Y2. Then view the graph with a standard window.

b. Since this graph is not easy to read, try the decimal window. This is also difficult to read, so try the integer window. This begins to show the graph more completely. However, the graph seems close to the y-axis. A better view might be to change Xmin and Xmax by dividing the values by 10.

(Note that if you don't care to enter the division, you could mentally divide and enter the new settings for the x-axis.)

c. This yields a clear view of the graph, with the intersection points easily visible. Now the intersection points can be easily determined using the CALC function: $x = -3.5$ and $x = -\frac{1}{3}$.

2. Solve graphically the rational equation $\frac{1}{4x+1} + \frac{4}{3x} = 3$.

a. Store the expressions on the left and right sides of the equation in Y1 and Y2. Again, first try the standard window to view the graph.

b. This is not a clear view of the graph, so try the decimal window. The graph extends to the upper edge of the window, so we should double the Ymin and Ymax.

(Again, note that you could multiply mentally and enter the new settings for the y-axis.)

c. The view is better, but an important part of the graph is close to the y-axis. It would help to enlarge this portion of the graph by dividing the Xmin and the Xmax by 5.

d. The two intersection points are clearly visible and can be found to be $x = -\frac{2}{9}$ and $x = \frac{1}{2}$.

3. Application problems may dictate special conditions on the range and domain of a rational equation. For example, suppose a biker covers a distance of 64 miles in one race, and a distance of 78 miles in another race. The second race took her 0.6 of an hour longer to complete. If her rate of speed was the same for both races, find her two times. As before, the relation $r = \frac{d}{t}$ yields the rational equation $\frac{64}{t} = \frac{78}{t+0.6}$, where t is the time of the first race.

a. Store the expressions on the left and right sides of the equation in Y1 and Y2, after changing the variable from t to x. Start with the standard window. The graph is not easily seen. Change to the integer window. The graph is seen in the first and third quadrants.

b. Since we are concerned only with nonnegative times and rates of speed, we want to deal with only the first quadrant. We can change the window by adding values to Xmin, Xmax, Ymin, and Ymax. If you look at the window, you see we must add 47 to make Xmin 0 and add 31 to make Ymin 0. We will not change the scale.

c. While the graph is better, it can be improved by dividing Xmin and Xmax by 10. Note that since Xmin was already at 0, it was not necessary to divide by 10.

d. Now you can find the intersection point that yields a solution of $t = 2.7$ hours for the first race and $t + 0.6 = 3.3$ hours for the second race.

From these examples, you should see that you can change the domain, the range, or both, of any of the window options by multiplying, dividing, adding, or subtracting a constant. If you use the same constant for each operation on the domain or range, you preserve the properties of the windows (for example, keeping integer values or decimal values or avoiding distortion in the graph).

Experiencing Algebra the Group Way

When graphing a rational equation, the restricted values play an important role in the graph. To illustrate this, consider the rational equation in one variable given by $\frac{2}{x-1} = \frac{-2}{x+3}$.

Graph the equation by hand, using a table of values to graph first the left side of the equation, and another table of values to graph the right side of the equation, both on the same coordinate system.

Complete the following table of values, then graph the points.

x	-7	-5	-3	-1	0	$\dfrac{1}{2}$	$\dfrac{3}{4}$
$y = \dfrac{2}{x-1}$							

x	$\dfrac{5}{4}$	$\dfrac{3}{2}$	2	3	5	7	9
$y = \dfrac{2}{x-1}$							

Notice that the graph never crosses the line where $x = 1$. This is a restricted value of our equation. You could imagine a vertical line drawn at $x = 1$, and the graph approaches this line as your values for x get closer to 1. Such a line is called an asymptote. A vertical asymptote is generally drawn as a dotted line. In this exercise draw a dotted vertical line at $x = 1$.

Next, let's draw the graph of the right side of our equation. The restricted value is $x = -3$, so there will be an asymptote at this value. Indicate it by drawing a dotted line. Complete the table of values and graph the points.

x	-11	-9	-7	-5	-4	$-\dfrac{7}{2}$	$-\dfrac{13}{4}$
$y = \dfrac{-2}{x+3}$							

x	$-\dfrac{11}{4}$	$-\dfrac{5}{2}$	-2	-1	1	3	5
$y = \dfrac{-2}{x+3}$							

Have each member of the group find the solution of the original rational equation by locating the intersection point of the two functions. This exercise should introduce you to the value of drawing vertical asymptotes at restricted values in order to more easily draw the graphs. Then try this approach on the following exercises. Discuss your results and agree on the correct solutions to the equations.

1. $\dfrac{-1}{x+2} = \dfrac{1}{x-2}$ **2.** $\dfrac{1}{2x-1} = \dfrac{2}{x+1}$

Experiencing Algebra the Write Way

In solving a rational equation graphically, you sometimes encounter an identity. In this case, the graph of the left side of the rational equation is the same as the graph of the right side of the equation. You might quickly assume that all real numbers are solutions of the equation. However, this is not exactly true. There may be numbers that do not satisfy the equation. Write a short paragraph describing what you must look for when you encounter a rational equation that is an identity and what qualifications you must make on your statement of the solutions in this situation.

12.5 Solving Rational Equations in One Variable Algebraically

Objectives
1 Solve rational equations algebraically.
2 Model real-world situations using rational equations.

Application

A formula for the total resistance R in a parallel circuit is $R^{-1} = r_1^{-1} + r_2^{-1}$, where R = total resistance, r_1 = resistance of the first resistor, and r_2 = resistance of the second resistor.

a. Solve the formula for R.
b. A typical light bulb has a resistance of about 100 ohms. An iron has a resistance of 15 ohms. If a light bulb and an iron are connected in a parallel circuit, determine the total resistance.

After completing this section, we will discuss this application further. See page 970.

1 Solving Rational Equations Algebraically

We are now ready to solve rational equations in one variable algebraically. We have already solved linear equations with fractional coefficients. To simplify these equations, we applied the multiplication property of equations. The multiplication property of equations states that if both sides of an equation are multiplied by the same nonzero expression, the result is an equivalent equation. We used this property to clear the fractions by multiplying by the least common denominator of all the fractions. For example, solve $\frac{1}{2}x + \frac{3}{4}x = \frac{2}{3}x + 7$.

$$\frac{1}{2}x + \frac{3}{4}x = \frac{2}{3}x + 7 \qquad \text{The LCD is 12.}$$

$$12\left(\frac{1}{2}x + \frac{3}{4}x\right) = 12\left(\frac{2}{3}x + 7\right) \qquad \text{Multiply by 12.}$$

$$12\left(\frac{1}{2}x\right) + 12\left(\frac{3}{4}x\right) = 12\left(\frac{2}{3}x\right) + 12(7) \qquad \text{Distribute 12.}$$

$$6x + 9x = 8x + 84$$

$$15x = 8x + 84$$

$$7x = 84 \qquad \text{Subtract 8}x.$$

$$x = 12 \qquad \text{Divide by 7.}$$

We use the same procedure for rational equations. However, we need to be aware of the restricted values for the equation.

> *Solving a Rational Equation Algebraically*
> To solve a rational equation in one variable algebraically:
>
> - Determine the restricted values for the equation.
> - Multiply both sides of the equation by the least common denominator of all terms.
> - Solve the resulting equation.
> - Discard any solutions that are restricted values.
>
> Check the solution by substitution or by solving numerically or graphically.

For example, solve $\frac{2}{x} + \frac{4}{2x} = \frac{3}{x} + 1$.

$$\frac{2}{x} + \frac{4}{2x} = \frac{3}{x} + 1 \qquad \text{The restricted value is 0. The LCD is 2}x.$$

$$2x\left(\frac{2}{x} + \frac{4}{2x}\right) = 2x\left(\frac{3}{x} + 1\right) \qquad \text{Multiply by 2}x.$$

$$2x\left(\frac{2}{x}\right) + 2x\left(\frac{4}{2x}\right) = 2x\left(\frac{3}{x}\right) + 2x(1) \qquad \text{Distribute 2}x.$$

$$4 + 4 = 6 + 2x$$

$$8 = 6 + 2x$$

$$2 = 2x \qquad \text{Subtract 6.}$$

$$1 = x \qquad \text{Divide by 2.}$$

Check the solution by substitution.

$$\frac{2}{x} + \frac{4}{2x} = \frac{3}{x} + 1$$

$\dfrac{2}{1} + \dfrac{4}{2(1)}$	$\dfrac{3}{1} + 1$
$2 + 2$	$3 + 1$
4	4

The solution is 1, because when 1 is substituted for the variable in both expressions, the resulting expressions are equal.

EXAMPLE 1 Solve.

a. $\dfrac{a}{a-2} = \dfrac{a+1}{a-3}$ **b.** $x^{-2} - 2 = 2$

c. $1 - \dfrac{4}{x+2} = \dfrac{2x}{x+2}$ **d.** $\dfrac{2}{x+3} - \dfrac{x+1}{x^2+5x+6} = \dfrac{4}{x^2-4}$

Algebraic Solution

a.
$$\frac{a}{a-2} = \frac{a+1}{a-3}$$
Restricted values are 2 and 3. The LCD is $(a-2)(a-3)$.

$$\cancel{(a-2)}(a-3)\left(\frac{a}{\cancel{a-2}}\right) = (a-2)\cancel{(a-3)}\left(\frac{a+1}{\cancel{a-3}}\right)$$
Multiply by the LCD.

$$(a-3)a = (a-2)(a+1)$$
Simplify.

$$a^2 - 3a = a^2 - a - 2$$
Simplify.

$$-2a = -2$$
Subtract a^2 and add a.

$$a = 1$$
Divide by -2.

Since the solution is an integer, check by solving numerically. Let $Y1 = \frac{x}{x-2}$ and $Y2 = \frac{x+1}{x-3}$.

The solution is 1.

X	Y₁	Y₂
0	0	-.3333
1	-1	-1
2	ERROR	-3
3	3	ERROR
4	2	5
5	1.6667	5
6	1.5	2.3333
X=0		

b.
$$x^{-2} - 2 = 2$$

$$\frac{1}{x^2} - 2 = 2$$
Rewrite without the negative exponent. The restricted value is 0. The LCD is x^2.

$$x^2\left(\frac{1}{x^2} - 2\right) = 2x^2$$
Multiply by x^2.

$$x^2\left(\frac{1}{x^2}\right) - 2x^2 = 2x^2$$
Distribute.

$$1 - 4x^2 = 0$$
Subtract $2x^2$.

$$(1 + 2x)(1 - 2x) = 0$$
Factor.

$$1 + 2x = 0 \quad \text{or} \quad 1 - 2x = 0$$
Use the zero factor property.

$$x = -\frac{1}{2} \qquad x = \frac{1}{2}$$
Solve.

Y2 = 2

(0.5, 2)

(−0.5, 2)

Y1 = x⁻² − 2

(−4.7, 4.7, −3.1, 3.1)

Check by graphing on a calculator decimal screen.
The solutions are $-\frac{1}{2}$ and $\frac{1}{2}$.

c.
$$1 - \frac{4}{x+2} = \frac{2x}{x+2}$$
The restricted value is −2. The LCD is $(x+2)$.

$$(x+2)\left(1 - \frac{4}{x+2}\right) = (x+2)\left(\frac{2x}{x+2}\right)$$
Multiply by the LCD.

$$(x + 2)(1) - (x + 2)\left(\frac{4}{x + 2}\right) = (x + 2)\left(\frac{2x}{x + 2}\right) \quad \text{Distribute the LCD.}$$

$$x + 2 - 4 = 2x$$

$$x - 2 = 2x$$

$$-2 = x \qquad \text{Subtract } x.$$

We determined that -2 is a restricted value. Therefore, it cannot be a solution. We call -2 an **extraneous solution**. This is the reason it is very important to determine the restricted values for the equation first. This equation has no solution.

d.
$$\frac{2}{x + 3} - \frac{x + 1}{x^2 + 5x + 6} = \frac{4}{x^2 - 4} \qquad \begin{array}{l}\text{Restricted} \\ \text{values are} \\ -3, -2, \text{ and } 2.\end{array}$$

$$\frac{2}{x + 3} - \frac{x + 1}{(x + 3)(x + 2)} = \frac{4}{(x + 2)(x - 2)} \qquad \begin{array}{l}\text{Factor each} \\ \text{denominator to} \\ \text{find the LCD.}\end{array}$$

$$(x + 2)(x - 2)(x + 3)\left(\frac{2}{x + 3} - \frac{x + 1}{(x + 3)(x + 2)}\right) =$$

$$(x + 2)(x - 2)(x + 3)\left(\frac{4}{(x + 2)(x - 2)}\right) \qquad \begin{array}{l}\text{Multiply by the} \\ \text{LCD, } (x + 2) \\ (x - 2)(x + 3).\end{array}$$

$$(x + 2)(x - 2)\cancel{(x + 3)}\left(\frac{2}{\cancel{x + 3}}\right) - \cancel{(x + 2)}(x - 2)\cancel{(x + 3)}\left(\frac{x + 1}{\cancel{(x + 3)}\cancel{(x + 2)}}\right) =$$

$$\cancel{(x + 2)}\cancel{(x - 2)}(x + 3)\left(\frac{4}{\cancel{(x + 2)}\cancel{(x - 2)}}\right) \qquad \begin{array}{l}\text{Distribute the} \\ \text{LCD.}\end{array}$$

$$(x + 2)(x - 2)2 - (x - 2)(x + 1) = (x + 3)4$$

$$(2x^2 - 8) - (x^2 - x - 2) = 4x + 12$$

$$x^2 + x - 6 = 4x + 12$$

$$x^2 - 3x - 18 = 0 \qquad \begin{array}{l}\text{Subtract} \\ 4x \text{ and } 12.\end{array}$$

$$(x - 6)(x + 3) = 0 \qquad \text{Factor.}$$

$$x - 6 = 0 \quad \text{or} \quad x + 3 = 0 \qquad \begin{array}{l}\text{Use the} \\ \text{zero factor} \\ \text{property.}\end{array}$$

$$x = 6 \qquad\qquad x = -3 \qquad \text{Solve.}$$

X	Y1	Y2
0	.5	-1
1	.33333	-1.333
2	.25	ERROR
3	.2	.8
4	.16667	.33333
5	.14286	.19048
6	.125	.125

X=0

$$Y1 = \frac{2}{x + 3} - \frac{x + 1}{x^2 + 5x + 6}$$

$$Y2 = \frac{4}{x^2 - 4}$$

Note: $x = -3$ is an extraneous solution. We only need to check the solution 6. A numeric check is used because the solution is an integer.

The solution is 6. ∎

An alternative method may be used to solve Example 1a. The rational equation to be solved, $\frac{a}{a-2} = \frac{a+1}{a-3}$, consists of two expressions, each of which is an algebraic fraction: $\frac{a}{a-2}$ and $\frac{a+1}{a-3}$. This special type of rational equation is called a proportion. To solve a proportion, we can equate the cross-products; that is, multiply the numerator of one fraction and the denominator of the

$$\frac{a}{a-2} = \frac{a+1}{a-3}$$

other fraction, and solve the remaining equation. For example, solve Example 1a as a proportion.

$$a(a-3) = (a+1)(a-2) \quad \text{Equate the cross-products.}$$

$$a^2 - 3a = a^2 - a - 2 \quad \textit{Note: this is the same as the equation in the previous solution.}$$

$$-3a = -a - 2 \quad \text{Subtract } a^2 \text{ from both sides.}$$

$$-2a = -2 \quad \text{Add } a \text{ to both sides.}$$

$$a = 1 \quad \text{Divide both sides by } -2.$$

Some rational equations are contradictions and have no solution. Other rational equations are identities and have an infinite number of solutions. We determine these situations algebraically the same way as we did for linear and quadratic equations.

EXAMPLE 2 Solve.

a. $\dfrac{3x-15}{6+3x} = \dfrac{x-10}{x+2}$ $\qquad$ **b.** $\dfrac{3}{x} = \dfrac{6}{2x}$

Algebraic Solution

a.
$$\frac{3x-15}{6+3x} = \frac{x-10}{x+2} \qquad \text{The restricted value is } -2.$$

$$\frac{3x-15}{3(2+x)} = \frac{x-10}{x+2} \qquad \text{Factor the denominators.}$$

$$3(x+2)\left(\frac{3x-15}{3(2+x)}\right) = 3(x+2)\left(\frac{x-10}{x+2}\right) \qquad \text{Multiply by the LCD, } 3(x+2).$$

$$3x - 15 = 3x - 30$$

$$-15 = -30 \qquad \text{Subtract } 3x.$$

Since $-15 \neq -30$ the equation is a contradiction. There is no solution.

b.
$$\frac{3}{x} = \frac{6}{2x} \qquad \text{The restricted value is } 0.$$

$$2x\left(\frac{3}{x}\right) = 2x\left(\frac{6}{2x}\right) \qquad \text{Multiply by the LCD, } 2x.$$

$$6 = 6$$

Since $6 = 6$, the equation is an identity. The solution set is all real numbers not equal to 0. (0 is the restricted value for the equation.) ∎

You should be very careful to use the LCD to eliminate denominators in equations only. For example, solve $\frac{2}{x} + \frac{3}{x} = 1$.

$$x\left(\frac{2}{x} + \frac{3}{x}\right) = x(1)$$

$$2 + 3 = x$$

$$5 = x$$

A word of caution must be given before we continue. *Expressions multiplied by the LCD will not result in equivalent expressions.* For example, given the expression $\frac{2}{x} + \frac{3}{x}$, we find the sum to be the expression $\frac{5}{x}$. However, multiplying the expression $\frac{2}{x} + \frac{3}{x}$ by x results in $x(\frac{2}{x} + \frac{3}{x}) = x(\frac{2}{x}) + x(\frac{3}{x}) = 2 + 3 = 5$. These are not equivalent results. Therefore, we cannot simplify a rational expression by multiplying by the LCD.

Helping Hand You can *solve* a rational *equation* by multiplying by the LCD. However, you cannot *simplify* a rational *expression* by multiplying through by the LCD.

Algebraic Solutions of Rational Equations
To solve a rational equation algebraically, determine the restricted values, multiply both sides of the equation by the LCD of all fractional terms, and solve the resulting equation. One of three possibilities will occur:

One or more solutions exist.
No solution exists. The solution process results in a contradiction.
An infinite number of solutions exist. The solution set is all real numbers not equal to the restricted values. The solution process results in an identity.

 Experiencing Algebra the Checkup Way

Solve exercises 1–5 and check.

1. $\dfrac{7}{2x} + \dfrac{3}{x} = 2 - \dfrac{3}{2x}$

2. $\dfrac{x - 10}{x - 1} = \dfrac{10 - 2x}{2 - 2x}$

3. $\dfrac{2x}{x - 3} = \dfrac{6}{x - 3} + 1$

4. $\dfrac{6}{3x + 3} = \dfrac{2}{x + 1}$

5. $\dfrac{x + 2}{x - 3} - \dfrac{15}{x^2 - x - 6} = \dfrac{2}{x - 3}$

6. How can you tell whether a rational equation has extraneous solutions?

7. When solving a rational equation algebraically, how can you tell whether the equation has no solutions?

8. When solving a rational equation algebraically, how can you tell whether the equation has all real numbers as solutions, excluding restricted values?

---

2 Modeling the Real World

In earlier sections we discussed some of the many important real-life situations that could be represented as rational expressions, including geometric relationships, the distance traveled at a constant rate, and simple interest. The useful thing about representing these situations as rational expressions is that we can fit them into rational equations. Then we can solve the equations to determine quantities of interest from given data.

EXAMPLE 3

Olando would like to increase the size of his triangular sail for his sailboat by increasing the length of its base. He wants to increase the present area of 30 ft^2 by an additional 10 ft^2. Determine the number of feet he must add to the present 6-foot base in order to add an additional 10 ft^2 to the area.

Algebraic Solution

The heights of both triangular sails remain unchanged, so they are equal. The formula for the area of a triangle is $A = \frac{1}{2}bh$. Solve the formula for h.

$$A = \frac{1}{2}bh$$

$$2 \cdot A = 2 \cdot \frac{1}{2}bh \qquad \text{Multiply both sides by the LCD, 2.}$$

$$2A = bh$$

$$\frac{2A}{b} = \frac{bh}{b} \qquad \text{Divide both sides by } b.$$

$$\frac{2A}{b} = h$$

The height of the original triangle is $h = \frac{2A}{b} = \frac{2 \cdot 30}{6} = \frac{60}{6} = 10$.
Let $x =$ number of feet added to the base
The height of the new triangular sail is

$$h = \frac{2A}{b} = \frac{2 \cdot (30 + 10)}{6 + x} = \frac{80}{6 + x}.$$

Since the two heights are equal, we can write the equation

$$10 = \frac{80}{6 + x}.$$

$$(6 + x)10 = (\cancel{6 + x})\frac{80}{\cancel{6 + x}} \qquad \text{Multiply both sides by the LCD, } (6 + x).$$

$$60 + 10x = 80 \qquad \text{Simplify.}$$

$$60 + 10x - 60 = 80 - 60 \qquad \text{Subtract 60 from both sides.}$$

$$10x = 20$$

$$\frac{10x}{10} = \frac{20}{10} \qquad \text{Divide both sides by 10.}$$

$$x = 2$$

Two feet must be added to the original base in order to add 10 ft^2 to the area of the sail. ∎

Application

A formula for the total resistance R in a parallel circuit is $R^{-1} = r_1^{-1} + r_2^{-1}$, where $R =$ total resistance, $r_1 =$ resistance of the first resistor, and $r_2 =$ resistance of the second resistor.

a. Solve the formula for R.
b. A typical light bulb has a resistance of about 100 ohms. An iron has a resistance of 15 ohms. If a light bulb and an iron are connected in a parallel circuit, determine the total resistance.

Discussion

a. $R^{-1} = r_1^{-1} + r_2^{-1}$

$$\frac{1}{R} = \frac{1}{r_1} + \frac{1}{r_2} \qquad \text{Write as a rational equation.}$$

$$\frac{1}{R}(Rr_1r_2) = \left(\frac{1}{r_1} + \frac{1}{r_2}\right)(Rr_1r_2) \qquad \text{Multiply by the LCD, } Rr_1r_2.$$

$$\frac{1}{\cancel{R}}(\cancel{R}r_1r_2) = \left(\frac{1}{\cancel{r_1}}\right)(R\cancel{r_1}r_2) + \left(\frac{1}{\cancel{r_2}}\right)(Rr_1\cancel{r_2}) \quad \text{Distributive property}$$

$$r_1r_2 = Rr_2 + Rr_1$$

$$r_1r_2 = R(r_2 + r_1) \qquad\qquad \text{Factor.}$$

$$R = \frac{r_1r_2}{r_1 + r_2} \qquad\qquad \text{Divide both sides by } (r_1 + r_2).$$

b. $R = \dfrac{r_1r_2}{r_1 + r_2}$

$$R = \frac{(100)(15)}{100 + 15} \qquad \text{Substitute 100 for } r_1 \text{ and 15 for } r_2.$$

$$R = \frac{1500}{115}$$

$$R = \frac{300}{23}$$

The total resistance is $\frac{300}{23}$ ohms. ∎

Experiencing Algebra the Checkup Way

Two resistors are wired in parallel and the total resistance of the circuit is 12 ohms. Find the resistance of the two resistors when the resistance of the second resistor is 10 ohms more than the resistance of the first resistor.

PROBLEM SET 12.5

Experiencing Algebra the Exercise Way

Solve exercises 1–74 algebraically and check numerically, graphically, or by substitution.

1. $\dfrac{1}{a} = \dfrac{5}{9} + \dfrac{2}{3}$

2. $\dfrac{5}{7} - \dfrac{3}{b} = \dfrac{1}{3}$

3. $\dfrac{2}{z} = \dfrac{4}{7} - \dfrac{2}{3}$

4. $\dfrac{4}{y} = \dfrac{1}{3} + \dfrac{3}{5}$

5. $\dfrac{11}{x} - \dfrac{3}{4} = \dfrac{5}{8}$

6. $\dfrac{3}{x} = \dfrac{5}{8} - \dfrac{3}{4}$

7. $1 - \dfrac{8}{x} = \dfrac{10}{x}$

8. $1 - \dfrac{12}{x} = \dfrac{2}{x}$

9. $1 + \dfrac{7}{x} = \dfrac{19}{x}$

10. $1 + \dfrac{9}{x} = \dfrac{11}{x}$

11. $\dfrac{1}{3} = \dfrac{5}{x} + \dfrac{7}{3x}$

12. $\dfrac{1}{4} = \dfrac{3}{x} + \dfrac{3}{4x}$

13. $\dfrac{1}{2} = \dfrac{5}{2x} - \dfrac{6}{x}$

14. $\dfrac{1}{3} = \dfrac{3}{2x} - \dfrac{1}{x}$

15. $\dfrac{9}{x - 3} = 1$

16. $\dfrac{11}{x + 6} = 1$

17. $2 = \dfrac{6}{x - 2}$

18. $3 = \dfrac{4}{x - 5}$

19. $\dfrac{x - 4}{2x + 3} = \dfrac{5}{21}$

20. $\dfrac{x - 1}{3x + 2} = \dfrac{6}{13}$

21. $\dfrac{1}{x - 6} = \dfrac{17}{2x + 3}$

22. $\dfrac{17}{2x - 5} = \dfrac{47}{4x + 3}$

23. $\dfrac{8}{2x - 3} + \dfrac{4}{x} = 0$

24. $\dfrac{17}{5x + 2} - \dfrac{2}{x} = 0$

25. $\dfrac{8}{x-2} = \dfrac{6}{x}$

26. $\dfrac{1}{x+1} = \dfrac{4}{3x}$

27. $\dfrac{2x+3}{x+4} = \dfrac{5}{x+4}$

28. $\dfrac{3x+1}{x+7} = \dfrac{4}{x-2}$

29. $\dfrac{16}{x} = x$

30. $\dfrac{81}{x} = x$

31. $\dfrac{z}{7} - \dfrac{7}{z} = 0$

32. $\dfrac{2}{y} = \dfrac{y}{32}$

33. $\dfrac{10}{k} + 3 = k$

34. $m = \dfrac{28}{m} - 3$

35. $b = 8 - \dfrac{16}{b}$

36. $b + \dfrac{1}{16b} = -\dfrac{1}{2}$

37. $a + \dfrac{10}{a} = \dfrac{1}{a} - 6$

38. $c + 2 = 14 - \dfrac{36}{c}$

39. $\dfrac{x}{3} + \dfrac{5}{x} = \dfrac{1}{x} - \dfrac{8}{3}$

40. $\dfrac{x}{5} + \dfrac{3}{x} = -\dfrac{13}{5} - \dfrac{5}{x}$

41. $\dfrac{x}{4} + \dfrac{4}{x} = 3 - \dfrac{4}{x}$

42. $\dfrac{x}{4} + \dfrac{1}{2x} = \dfrac{7}{4} - \dfrac{1}{x}$

43. $\dfrac{y}{5} - \dfrac{21}{5y} = 1 + \dfrac{3}{y}$

44. $\dfrac{z}{5} - \dfrac{2}{z} = \dfrac{2}{5} + \dfrac{1}{z}$

45. $\dfrac{x+7}{x+9} = \dfrac{x}{x+1}$

46. $\dfrac{x+8}{x+4} = \dfrac{x+1}{x-1}$

47. $\dfrac{x-6}{x+5} = \dfrac{x-4}{3x+2}$

48. $\dfrac{x+3}{4x-1} = \dfrac{x+7}{1-4x}$

49. $x^{-1} - 5 = 7$

50. $6 = 2 + 8x^{-1}$

51. $x^{-1} + \dfrac{2}{3} = \dfrac{3}{5}$

52. $x^{-1} + \dfrac{3}{7} = \dfrac{5}{8}$

53. $x^{-2} - 6 = 3$

54. $x^{-2} + 3 = 19$

55. $1 - 4x^{-1} = 60x^{-2}$

56. $14x^{-2} = 1 + 5x^{-1}$

57. $\dfrac{9}{x-7} + 3 = \dfrac{2x-5}{x-7}$

58. $3 + \dfrac{5}{x+3} = \dfrac{2x+1}{x+3}$

59. $\dfrac{x+2}{3} = \dfrac{x^2-x+7}{3x-6}$

60. $\dfrac{5x-2}{3} = \dfrac{5x^2+14x+2}{3x+9}$

61. $\dfrac{x-3}{x+4} = \dfrac{14}{x^2+6x+8}$

62. $\dfrac{z+4}{z+1} = \dfrac{30}{z^2-2z-3}$

63. $\dfrac{25}{p^2+p-12} = \dfrac{p+4}{p-3}$

64. $\dfrac{q+3}{q-4} = \dfrac{42}{q^2-2q-8}$

65. $\dfrac{m-2}{m+1} = \dfrac{7m+22}{m^2+6m+5}$

66. $\dfrac{x+6}{x-4} = \dfrac{5x-3}{x^2-7x+12}$

67. $\dfrac{1-4x}{1-x} + 2 = \dfrac{6x-3}{x-1}$

68. $\dfrac{2x-1}{x-1} - 1 = \dfrac{5x-7}{x-1} - 4$

69. $2 + \dfrac{z+2}{2z+1} = \dfrac{3z+6}{2z+1} + 1$

70. $\dfrac{x+5}{x-6} + \dfrac{1}{2} = \dfrac{3x+4}{2x-12}$

71. $\dfrac{2}{x-4} + \dfrac{5x}{x^2-16} = \dfrac{1}{x+4}$

72. $\dfrac{5}{x-1} - \dfrac{3}{x+1} = \dfrac{2x}{x^2-1}$

73. $\dfrac{1}{x+5} + \dfrac{21}{x^2-25} = 2$

74. $\dfrac{1}{x-9} + \dfrac{1}{8} = \dfrac{3}{x^2-81}$

75. A circuit has two resistors wired in parallel. The resistance of one resistor is 5 ohms less than twice the resistance of the other resistor. The total resistance of the circuit is 6 ohms. Find the resistance of each resistor.

76. Two resistors in a circuit are wired in parallel. The resistance of the second resistor is 5 ohms more than three times the resistance of the first resistor. The total resistance of the circuit is 4 ohms. Find the resistance of each resistor.

77. The student nature club has spent $120 of its $300 in funds preparing for an Earth Day celebration. The club's budget allocated 45% of all funds to be spent on the celebration. If the club does not want to touch its remaining funds, but instead has a fund-raiser to raise additional funds, how much money should be raised and spent on the celebration to bring the percentage up to 45% of all funds?

78. Felix has raised $75 for his club's fund-raiser. So far, all the members have raised a total of $200, including Felix's contributions. Felix wants to make a last-ditch effort to raise enough additional money so that his contribution will be 50% of the total raised. If no other members raise additional funds, how much more must Felix raise to bring his percentage up to 50% of the total?

79. Timmy's triangular play area is to be enlarged by increasing the height of the triangle. The goal is to increase the current 60 square feet area by an additional 45 square feet. How many feet must be added to the current 8-foot height to accomplish this?

80. Jim wants to extend his current rectangular deck by increasing its width. The current deck has an area of 403 square feet. How many feet can be added to the current width of 15.5 feet in order to add an additional 117 square feet to the area?

 ## Experiencing Algebra the Calculator Way

In addition to the numeric, graphic, and algebraic methods for solving rational equations, the calculator contains a "solve" feature that can be used to find solutions. To use this feature, first store the left side of the equation in Y1 and the right side of the equation in Y2. Then key in the expression

solve (Y1-Y2, x, n),

where n is an initial guess close to where you might expect the solution to be, and "solve" is a function selected from the calculator's catalog of functions. The keystrokes to solve the equation $\frac{7}{2x} + \frac{3}{x} = 2 - \frac{3}{2x}$ are listed.

1. Store the two sides of the equation in Y1 and Y2.

2. Enter 2nd CATALOG and arrow down to the "solve(" line. Press ENTER .

3. Complete the parentheses by entering Y1-Y2, x, n, and) as follows:

VARS ▶ 1 1 − VARS ▶ 1 2 , X, T, θ, n , 3) ENTER

where 3 is our initial guess at the solution. The calculator returns a 4, which is the actual solution.

Once you have entered these keystrokes, you can reuse them for a new equation without having to repeat the keystrokes.

4. Change what you have stored in Y1 and Y2, using the new left-hand and right-hand expressions of the new equation. Press 2nd QUIT .

5. Press 2nd ENTRY , which will repeat the "solve" instruction, and change the initial guess appropriately. Press ENTER and the calculator will yield a solution for the new equation.

Try this approach on some of the preceding exercises. The shortcomings of this method are that you must know how many solutions to seek and you must know approximately where the solutions are. If your initial guess is far from the actual solution, the calculator will time out and give you an error message, since it uses an iterative approach to find the solution. These shortcomings underscore the need to know other methods to solve a rational equation.

Experiencing Algebra the Group Way

Sometimes it is possible to rewrite a rational equation to make it easier to solve. As an example, suppose you were trying to solve the equation $2\left(\frac{a}{a+1}\right)^2 + 5\left(\frac{a}{a+1}\right) - 3 = 0$.

Rather than deal with the equation as it is, let's substitute an x wherever you see $\frac{a}{a+1}$; that is, let $x = \frac{a}{a+1}$. The equation becomes $2x^2 + 5x - 3 = 0$. This equation can easily be solved by factoring. The solutions are $x = \frac{1}{2}$ and $x = -3$.

Now we can use the relation $x = \frac{a}{a+1}$ to solve for a. The relation yields two equations: $\frac{1}{2} = \frac{a}{a+1}$ and $-3 = \frac{a}{a+1}$.

You can use the methods of this section to solve these two equations algebraically to yield the solutions: $a = 1$ and $a = -\frac{3}{4}$.

Discuss how you would use this substitution technique to solve the following rational equations. Then have each member of the group solve the equations, and compare your results to decide on the correct final answers.

1. $\left(\dfrac{a-1}{a+1}\right)^2 - 25 = 0$ **2.** $10\left(\dfrac{z+3}{z}\right)^2 = 11\left(\dfrac{z+3}{z}\right) + 6$

3. $9\left(\dfrac{b-5}{b-7}\right)^2 - 20\left(\dfrac{b-5}{b-7}\right) + 15 = 10\left(\dfrac{b-5}{b-7}\right) - 1$

Experiencing Algebra the Write Way

Work the following two problems.

1. Solve the equation algebraically.

$$\frac{7}{2x} + \frac{3}{x} = 2 - \frac{3}{2x}$$

2. Simplify the expression algebraically.

$$\frac{7}{2x} + \frac{3}{x} + 2 - \frac{3}{2x}$$

Discuss the difference between the two exercises, and explain why the algebraic methods you would employ in exercise 1 cannot be used in exercise 2.

12.6 More Real-World Models

Objectives   1 Solve real-world models involving rates.

2 Solve real-world models involving proportions.

3 Solve real-world models involving geometric proportions.

Application

A formula for the combined heat conductivity, K_c, when insulation is added to a wall or ceiling is $\frac{1}{K_c} = \frac{1}{K_1} + \frac{1}{K_2}$, where K_1 is the heat conductivity of the wall or ceiling and K_2 is the heat conductivity of the insulation being added.

a. Add the expressions given in the right side of the formula.
b. If the heat conductivity for a ceiling is 0.63 and the desired combined heat conductivity is 0.42, determine the heat conductivity for the insulation being added.

After completing this section, we will discuss this application further. See page 981.

We now know three methods to solve a rational equation: numeric, graphic, and algebraic. We have also solved several types of real-world models with each of these methods. However, many other types of models can be solved with these methods.

In this section, we discuss some common types of real-world models involving rational equations. Remember, there is no set way to work all problems. Also, once a rational equation is written for the problem, it may be solved with any of the methods we have learned.

Let's review the method we have been using to answer a question about a real-world model.

Solving Real-World Models
To solve an application problem:

- Read and understand the problem.
- Define a variable for the unknown quantity and define other quantities in terms of the variable, if possible.
- Write an equation with the given information.
- Solve the equation either numerically, graphically, or algebraically.
- Check the solution.
- Write an answer for the question in a complete sentence.

---

1   Solving Rate Problems

A **ratio** is the quotient of two quantities. A **rate** is a ratio used to compare different kinds of measurements, one of which is time, such as miles per hour. Rate of work is one type of problem that leads to solving a rational equation. This type of problem is usually referred to as a work problem.

Before we begin, we need to be able to determine a rate of work. We know that if a painter needs 4 hours to paint a room, then in one hour $\frac{1}{4}$ of the job is completed. In two hours, $\frac{2}{4} = \frac{1}{2}$ of the job is completed. If we use this information, we determine the rate of work by solving any one of the following equations.

$$\text{time} \cdot \text{rate} = \text{job completed}$$

$$1 \cdot x = \frac{1}{4} \qquad\qquad \tfrac{1}{4} \text{ of job completed}$$

$$2 \cdot x = \frac{1}{2} \qquad\qquad \tfrac{1}{2} \text{ of job completed}$$

$$3 \cdot x = \frac{3}{4} \qquad\qquad \tfrac{3}{4} \text{ of job completed}$$

$$4 \cdot x = 1 \qquad\qquad \text{entire job completed}$$

All of the equations solved for x result in $x = \frac{1}{4}$. Therefore, the rate of work is $\frac{1}{4}$ job per hour.

> *Rate of Work*
> If a task can be completed in x hours, then the rate of work is $\frac{1}{x}$ of the task per hour.

Next, we need to understand that if more than one person or machine is working on a task, the total rate of work is the sum of the individual rates. For example, two painters are painting a room. The first painter paints at a rate of $\frac{1}{4}$ room per hour and his helper paints at a rate of $\frac{1}{6}$ room per hour. Determine the total rate of work.

The sum of the two rates is

$$\frac{1}{4} + \frac{1}{6} = \frac{3}{12} + \frac{2}{12} = \frac{5}{12}.$$

Therefore, the total rate of work is $\frac{5}{12}$ room per hour.

EXAMPLE 1 Michelangelo working alone can paint a room in 4 hours. His helper, Leonardo, would need 6 hours to do the job alone. Determine the number of hours required for the two painters to paint the room together.

Algebraic Solution

Let x = number of hours needed to paint the room together

$\frac{1}{4}$ is the rate of work for Michelangelo.

$\frac{1}{6}$ is the rate of work for Leonardo.

$\frac{1}{x}$ is the rate of work for both painters working together.

The sum of the individual rates equals the total rate.

$$\frac{1}{4} + \frac{1}{6} = \frac{1}{x}$$ The restricted value is 0.

$$12x\left(\frac{1}{4} + \frac{1}{6}\right) = 12x\left(\frac{1}{x}\right)$$ Multiply by the LCD.

$$12x\left(\frac{1}{4}\right) + 12x\left(\frac{1}{6}\right) = 12x\left(\frac{1}{x}\right)$$ Distribute the LCD.

$$3x + 2x = 12$$

$$5x = 12$$

$$x = \frac{12}{5} \quad \text{or} \quad 2\frac{2}{5}$$

Y1 $= \frac{1}{4} + \frac{1}{6}$

(2.4, 0.41$\overline{6}$)

Y2 $= \frac{1}{x}$

$(-4.7, 4.7, -3.1, 3.1)$

It would take $2\frac{2}{5}$ hours for the painters to paint the room if they work together. Check your solution graphically on your calculator. The solution is 2.4. ∎

EXAMPLE 2   Normally, it takes 3 minutes to fill a sink. However, today the drain does not close properly and allows water to drain as it is being filled. Therefore, the sink is filled at the end of 5 minutes. If the water is turned off, determine the number of minutes that water will remain in the sink.

Solution

Let $x =$ number of minutes it takes to drain the sink

$\frac{1}{3}$ is the rate of work for filling the sink.

$\frac{1}{x}$ is the rate of work for draining the sink.

$\frac{1}{5}$ is the rate of work for filling and draining at the same time.

The difference of the individual rates equals the combined rate.

$$\frac{1}{3} - \frac{1}{x} = \frac{1}{5}$$ The restricted value is 0.

$$15x\left(\frac{1}{3} - \frac{1}{x}\right) = 15x\left(\frac{1}{5}\right)$$ Multiply by the LCD.

$$15x\left(\frac{1}{3}\right) - 15x\left(\frac{1}{x}\right) = 15x\left(\frac{1}{5}\right)$$ Distribute the LCD.

$$5x - 15 = 3x$$

$$2x = 15$$

$$x = \frac{15}{2} \quad \text{or} \quad 7\frac{1}{2}$$

Y2 $= \frac{1}{5}$

(7.5, 0.2)

Y1 $= \frac{1}{3} - \frac{1}{x}$

$(-9.4, 9.4, -3.1, 3.1)$

It takes $7\frac{1}{2}$ minutes to drain the sink. Therefore, water will remain in the sink for $7\frac{1}{2}$ minutes.

Check your solution graphically on your calculator. The solution is 7.5. ∎

 Experiencing Algebra the Checkup Way

1. Merle can mow the lawn around his farmhouse in 2 hours. His wife, Glenna, can do the same job in 1.6 hours. Assuming they have two lawn mowers and can work together without getting in each other's way, how long will it take them to mow the lawn together?

2. Water is being pumped out of a storage tank at a rate that would empty the tank in 2 hours. At the same time, water is being pumped into the tank at an unknown rate. If an empty tank can be filled in 5 hours while water is being simultaneously pumped out, how long would it take to fill an empty tank if no water is pumped out?

---

2 Solving Proportion Problems

Two ratios that are equal in value may be written as a rational equation called a **proportion**. In order for the two ratios to be equal, the numerator and the denominator of each ratio must be written in the same order. For example, $\frac{\text{cost}}{\text{weight}} = \frac{\text{cost}}{\text{weight}}$, but $\frac{\text{cost}}{\text{weight}} \neq \frac{\text{weight}}{\text{cost}}$.

EXAMPLE 3

The Wright family invited eight family members for Thanksgiving dinner. The 16.3-pound baked spiral-cut ham cost $80.69. Two additional family members will eat Christmas dinner. The Christmas ham weighs 20.1 pounds. If the cost per pound did not change between Thanksgiving and Christmas, determine the cost of the Christmas ham.

Algebraic Solution

Let x = cost of the Christmas ham

The cost per pound for the Thanksgiving ham $\left(\frac{\text{cost}}{\text{weight}}\right)$ is $\frac{80.69}{16.3}$.

The cost per pound for the Christmas ham $\left(\frac{\text{cost}}{\text{weight}}\right)$ is $\frac{x}{20.1}$.

The ratios of cost per pound are the same for the Thanksgiving and Christmas hams.

$$\frac{80.69}{16.3} = \frac{x}{20.1}$$

$$1621.869 = 16.3x \quad \text{Equate the cross-products.}$$

$$99.50 \approx x$$

The Christmas ham cost about $99.50.

Check your solution graphically on your calculator. The solution is 99.5. ∎

$Y1 = \frac{80.69}{16.3}$

(99.50, 4.95)

$Y2 = \frac{x}{20.1}$

(0, 188, 0, 31)

EXAMPLE 4

Justin is practicing batting a baseball with his mother. He has hit 10 out of 20 pitches. His goal is to hit 60% of the pitches. How many consecutive pitches must he hit to raise his average to 60%?

Algebraic Solution

Let x = number of consecutive pitches he must hit

The current ratio of hits to pitches $\left(\frac{\text{hits}}{\text{pitches}}\right)$ is $\frac{10}{20}$.

The ratio after x consecutive hits $\left(\frac{\text{hits}}{\text{pitches}}\right)$ is $\frac{10+x}{20+x}$.

The desired ratio of hits to pitches is 60%, or $\frac{60}{100}$.

$Y1 = \dfrac{10 + x}{20 + x}$

$Y2 = \dfrac{60}{100}$

The proportion is as follows:

$$\frac{10 + x}{20 + x} = \frac{60}{100}$$

$$1000 + 100x = 1200 + 60x \qquad \text{Equate the cross-products.}$$

$$40x = 200$$

$$x = 5$$

Justin must hit five consecutive pitches to raise his average to 60%.
Check your solution numerically on your calculator. The solution is 5. ∎

Experiencing Algebra the Checkup Way

1. Jose was paid $55.13 for 4.5 hours of work. How much would he have earned if he had worked an 8-hour shift?

2. Michelle has scored 6 out of 10 baskets from the free-throw line. How many more consecutive baskets must she make in order to bring her average up to 75%?

---

3 Solving Geometric Proportions

Geometric figures can be proportional. One example of proportional figures is similar triangles. **Similar triangles** are triangles with congruent corresponding angles and proportional corresponding sides. The symbol for similar is ∼. For example,

$$\triangle ABC \sim \triangle DEF \text{ is read "triangle } ABC \text{ is similar to triangle } DEF."$$

In Figure 12.4, sides AB and DE, BC and EF, and AC and DF are corresponding sides. **Corresponding sides** are in the same position in the figure. **Corresponding angles** are A and D, B and E, and C and F.

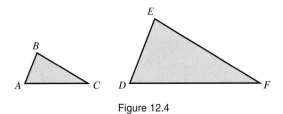

Figure 12.4

The ratio of the measure of any side of one triangle and the measure of the corresponding side on the second triangle are always constant. For example,

$$\frac{AB}{DE} = \frac{BC}{EF} = \frac{AC}{DF}.$$

 Helping Hand Compare sides from the same triangle in the same order in the ratio $\left(\frac{\triangle ABC}{\triangle DEF}\right)$.

Therefore, if two sides of one triangle and one corresponding side of a second triangle are known, the second corresponding side may be found using a proportion.

EXAMPLE 5 Given the following similar triangles, $\triangle ABC \sim \triangle DEF$, determine the length of the unknown labeled side.

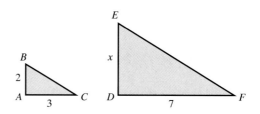

Algebraic Solution

Since $\triangle ABC \sim \triangle DEF$, we have three pairs of corresponding sides that are proportional. However, only two pairs of corresponding sides have their dimensions labeled.

$$\frac{AB}{DE} = \frac{AC}{DF} \quad \text{Compare corresponding sides } \left(\frac{\triangle ABC}{\triangle DEF}\right).$$

$$\frac{2}{x} = \frac{3}{7} \quad \text{Substitute values.}$$

$$3x = 14$$

$$x = \frac{14}{3}$$

The length of the unknown side is $\frac{14}{3}$.

A calculator graph results in the solution of approximately 4.667. ∎

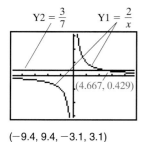

$Y2 = \frac{3}{7}$ $Y1 = \frac{2}{x}$

(4.667, 0.429)

$(-9.4, 9.4, -3.1, 3.1)$

EXAMPLE 6 To determine the height of a tree, Sam stood next to it and had Kyle measure the length of his shadow and the tree's shadow. Use Figure 12.5 to determine the height of the tree.

Algebraic Solution

We first must determine that the triangles formed are similar; that is, that the angle measurements of corresponding angles are equal.

We know that the tree and Sam both form right angles with the ground. From geometry, we know that the angles formed by the sun striking the tree and Sam are equal. From geometry, we also know that the sum of the angles of a triangle is 180 degrees and the sums of the two known angles are equal. Therefore, the third angles must be equal.

The corresponding sides are therefore proportional, because the corresponding angles are congruent. Let x equal the height of the tree.

$$\frac{7.5}{3} = \frac{x}{5.5} \quad \text{Compare corresponding sides}$$

$$3x = 41.25$$

$$x = 13.75$$

The height of the tree is 13.75 feet.

A calculator graph results in the solution of 13.75. ∎

Figure 12.5

$Y1 = \frac{5.5}{3}$

(13.75, 1.833)

$Y2 = \frac{x}{7.5}$

$(-47, 47, -31, 31)$

Application

A formula for the combined heat conductivity, K_c, when insulation is added to a wall or ceiling is $\frac{1}{K_c} = \frac{1}{K_1} + \frac{1}{K_2}$, where K_1 is the heat conductivity of the wall or ceiling and K_2 is the heat conductivity of the insulation being added.

a. Add the expressions given in the right side of the formula.

b. If the heat conductivity for a ceiling is 0.63 and the desired combined heat conductivity is 0.042, determine the heat conductivity for the insulation being added.

Discussion

a. $\dfrac{1}{K_1} + \dfrac{1}{K_2} = \dfrac{K_2}{K_1 K_2} + \dfrac{K_1}{K_1 K_2}$ 　　Change the fractions to like denominators.

$$= \dfrac{K_2 + K_1}{K_1 K_2}$$

b. $\dfrac{1}{K_c} = \dfrac{K_2 + K_1}{K_1 K_2}$

$\dfrac{1}{0.042} = \dfrac{K_2 + 0.63}{0.63 K_2}$ 　　Let $K_c = 0.042$ and $K_1 = 0.63$.

$0.63 K_2 = 0.042 (K_2 + 0.63)$ 　　Equate cross-products.

$0.63 K_2 = 0.042 K_2 + 0.02646$ 　　Distribute.

$0.588 K_2 = 0.02646$ 　　Subtract $0.042 K_2$ from both sides.

$K_2 = 0.045$ 　　Divide both sides by 0.588.

The insulation being added to the ceiling needs to have a heat conductivity of 0.045 in order for the combined heat conductivity to be 0.042. ∎

✓ Experiencing Algebra the Checkup Way

1. $\triangle ABC \sim \triangle DEF$. Use proportions to find the lengths of the unknown sides.

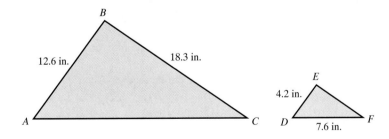

2. A tower stands 20 feet high and casts a shadow of 18 feet. An antenna mounted on top of the tower casts a shadow with the tower of 27 feet. Find the height of the antenna.

PROBLEM SET 12.6

Experiencing Algebra the Exercise Way

1. Miriam can type a report in 3 hours. Saul can type the same report in 4.2 hours. Assuming they can work together to get the report done, how long will it take them?

2. Paul can wax his car in 45 minutes. His big brother John can do the job in 30 minutes. If they work together, how long will it take them to wax Paul's car?

3. It takes Jacques twice as long to clean the house as it does his wife, Simone. When they work together, they can clean the house in $3\frac{1}{3}$ hours. How long does it take each of them to do the job alone?

4. When Mary Lynne cleans the pool, it takes her an hour longer than it does when Joe cleans the pool. If they can clean the pool in $1\frac{1}{2}$ hours when they work together, how long does it take each of them working alone?

5. Work records show that Felix averages 9 hours to do a certain plumbing job, while Oscar averages 6 hours to do the same job. How long would you expect them to take to do the job together?

6. JoAnne can grade a set of test papers in 15 minutes. Bob can grade the same number of test papers in 25 minutes. How long will it take them to grade the set of papers working together?

7. A tank is filled by two separate pipelines. When the red pipeline is used alone to fill the tank, it takes 4 hours. When the blue pipeline is used alone to fill the tank, it takes 7 hours. How long would it take if both pipelines are used together to fill the tank?

8. A tank can be drained by two separate drains. When the large drain is used alone, it takes 5 hours to drain the tank. When the smaller drain is used alone, it takes 7.5 hours to drain the tank. If both drains are used together, how long will it take to drain the tank?

9. A gas supply line is used to fill storage tanks. Gas line A can fill the tank in $\frac{2}{3}$ of the time it takes gas line B to fill the tank. Together, the lines can fill the tank in $4\frac{4}{5}$ hours. How long does it take each line alone to fill the tank?

10. Two water supply lines can be used to fill the neighborhood pool. Used alone, the second line takes an hour and a half longer than the first line to fill the pool. Together, they can fill the pool in $4\frac{1}{2}$ hours. How long does it take each line used alone to fill the pool?

11. Arsenio bought 15.75 shares of a mutual fund for $1000. How many shares can he buy for $1800 at the same price per share?

12. Julio bought $1100 worth of stock at $55\frac{7}{8}$ per share. How much money did he recover if later he sold the stock for $49\frac{3}{8}$ per share?

13. Ricki has earned 45 points out of 60 extra-credit points in her math class. If she completes all of the additional assignments for full credit, how many additional extra-credit points must there be if she wants her average for extra credit to be 80%?

14. A 2.5-liter mixture of diluted vinegar was made by combining 0.8 liter of vinegar with distilled water. How much more pure vinegar must be added to the mixture to bring the percent of vinegar in the mixture up to 40%?

In Figure 12.6, △PQR ~ △XYZ. Use these triangles for exercises 15, 17, and 19, and find the measures of the unknown sides of the similar triangles, given the information provided. In Figure 12.7, △JKL ~ △MNO. Use these triangles for exercises 16, 18, and 20, and find the measures of the unknown sides of the similar triangles, for the information given.

Figure 12.6

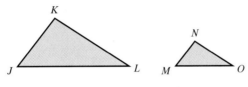

Figure 12.7

15. $\overline{PQ}$ measures 24 inches, $\overline{QR}$ measures 12 inches, $\overline{XZ}$ measures 3 inches, and $\overline{YZ}$ measures 2 inches.

16. $\overline{JK}$ measures 7 mm, $\overline{JL}$ measures 35 mm, $\overline{NO}$ measures 8 mm, and $\overline{MO}$ measures 10 mm.

17. $\overline{QR}$ measures 4.4 cm, $\overline{PR}$ measures 5.875 cm, $\overline{XY}$ measures 4.03 cm, and $\overline{XZ}$ measures 2.35 cm.

18. $\overline{KL}$ measures 32.4 yards, $\overline{JL}$ measures 43.92 yards, $\overline{MN}$ measures 6.9 yards, and $\overline{NO}$ measures 13.5 yards.

19. $\overline{PQ}$ measures $10\frac{5}{16}$ feet, $\overline{PR}$ measures $5\frac{5}{8}$ feet, $\overline{XY}$ measures $4\frac{1}{8}$ feet, and $\overline{YZ}$ measures $1\frac{3}{4}$ feet.

20. $\overline{JK}$ measures $9\frac{7}{18}$ feet, $\overline{KL}$ measures $20\frac{1}{24}$ feet, $\overline{MN}$ measures $4\frac{1}{3}$ feet, and $\overline{MO}$ measures $13\frac{1}{2}$ feet.

21. Bridgette was walking along a beach edged by a cliff. She wondered how high the cliff was, so she paced the distance from its base to the tip of its shadow. The shadow measured 35 paces, so she estimated the shadow to be 35 feet long. Then she estimated her shadow to be 4 feet long. If Bridgette is 5.5 feet tall, what is the estimated height of the cliff, based on this information?

22. In late afternoon, a 6-foot lamppost casts a 14-foot shadow. How high is a flagpole if it casts a 35-foot shadow?

 ## Experiencing Algebra the Calculator Way

You have learned several calculator-based methods for solving rational equations, including the following:

1. *Graphical solution.* Store the left side of the rational equation in Y1 and the right side of the equation in Y2. Graph the two functions and find the intersection point, which represents the solution.

2. *Numerical solution.* Again, store the left and right sides of the equations using the [Y=] key, and then use the [TABLE] key to generate pairs of values and scan through until you find a pair that is equal.

3. *Numerical solution.* After storing the left and right sides of the equations using the $\boxed{\text{Y=}}$ key, use the "solve" function to find the solution. This technique was described in "Experiencing Algebra the Calculator Way."

Try these three techniques on the following application exercises. Also solve algebraically. List some of the advantages and disadvantages of the three calculator methods and the algebraic method, illustrated by your example exercises. Try to remain flexible in your use of the methods.

1. A rectangle has an area of 25 square feet. Letting x represent the length of the rectangle, write a function for the perimeter of the rectangle in terms of x. What are the dimensions of the rectangle if its perimeter is 25 feet?

2. It takes Becky twice as long to paint a fence as it takes Tom. Together they can paint the fence in 4 hours. How long would it take each of them working alone?

3. In a 24-hour period, Huck rafted 144 miles down the river. At the same rate of speed, how many more hours will it take Huck to complete his trip of 200 miles down river?

4. Aunt Polly bakes and sells cookies to support herself. She figures that each baking cycle costs her $9.00 to prepare for baking, and $0.55 for each dozen cookies she bakes. Write a function to estimate the average cost for each dozen cookies Aunt Polly bakes. How many dozen cookies should she bake to spend an average of $0.75 per dozen?

Experiencing Algebra the Group Way

Many applications involve the use of formulas, which often are rational equations with several variables, and often you must solve the formula for the variable of interest.

Divide your group into two teams. Have one team work the odd-numbered exercises and the other team work the even-numbered exercises. Solve each formula for the variable specified. Compare your answers with those of your teammates to agree on the final result. Then share your work with the other members of your group.

1. $t = \dfrac{d}{r}$ for r

2. $h = \dfrac{2A}{b + B}$ for A

3. $\dfrac{1}{R} = \dfrac{1}{r_1} + \dfrac{1}{r_2}$ for r_2

4. $\dfrac{x}{y} = \dfrac{y}{z}$ for z

5. $\dfrac{x}{a} + \dfrac{y}{b} = 1$ for a

6. $\dfrac{1}{x} + \dfrac{1}{kx} = 1$ for k.

7. $\dfrac{1}{x} + \dfrac{1}{x + c} = 1$ for c

8. $P = \dfrac{A}{(1 + i)^t}$ for A

9. $S = \dfrac{n(a + L)}{2}$ for L

10. $E^2 = \dfrac{z^2 s^2}{n}$ for n

Experiencing Algebra the Write Way

In this section you learned that in some instances, you can use cross-products to solve a rational equation. Consider each of the following equations. For which equations can you use cross-products? Explain your reasons.

1. $\dfrac{2}{x} = \dfrac{6}{x + 1}$

2. $\dfrac{2}{x} = \dfrac{6}{x} + 1$

3. $x^2 - \dfrac{1}{x} = \dfrac{x + 1}{3}$

4. $\dfrac{x^2 - 1}{x} = \dfrac{x + 1}{3}$

CHAPTER 12	Summary

After completing this chapter, you should be able to define in your own words the following key terms, definitions, and rules.

Terms
rational number
rational expression
algebraic fraction
rational function
restricted values
equivalent rational expressions
cancellation
least common denominator
complex rational expressions
rational equation in one variable
extraneous solution

ratio
rate
proportion
similar triangles
corresponding sides
corresponding angles

Definitions
Rate of work

Rules
Simplifying rational expressions

Multiplying rational expressions
Dividing rational expressions
Adding and subtracting rational
   expressions
Determining the least common
   denominator
Determining equivalent rational
   expressions
Solving a rational equation numerically
Solving a rational equation graphically
Solving a rational equation
   algebraically

CHAPTER 12	Review

Reflections

1. What is the difference between a polynomial expression and a rational expression?

2. What does it mean to cancel when multiplying rational expressions? Can you cancel when dividing rational expressions? Explain.

3. What must be true before you can add or subtract two rational expressions?

4. What is the difference between a rational equation and a rational expression?

5. How do restricted values affect the solutions to a rational equation?

6. When solving a rational equation algebraically, how can you tell there are no solutions? How can you tell there are many solutions? How can you tell there are extraneous solutions?

12.1

Determine whether each expression is a rational expression.

1. $3 + \dfrac{x - 5}{x^2 + 6x + 9}$

2. $x^2 - \dfrac{\sqrt{x} + 3x}{x + 1}$

3. $5x^2 - 3x + 2 - 4x^{-1}$

4. $2x + 5$

Algebraically determine the restricted values and then state the domain of each rational equation.

5. $y = \dfrac{-3}{x^2}$

6. $f(x) = \dfrac{2x + 7}{x^2 + 5x - 24}$

7. $y = \dfrac{5}{4x^2 + 9}$

8. $y = \dfrac{5}{4x^2 - 9}$

Evaluate each function for $x = -2, -1, 0, 1,$ and 2, if possible.

9. $y = \dfrac{180}{x^2} + \dfrac{30}{x}$

10. $g(x) = \dfrac{x + 3}{x^2 - x - 2}$

Graph each rational function.

11. $p(x) = 1 - \dfrac{4}{x} - \dfrac{21}{x^2}$

12. $y = \dfrac{x^2 - 3x - 10}{x^2 - x - 12}$

13. Bob and Gretchen took turns driving on a rural highway. Bob's average speed was 10 miles per hour greater than Gretchen's average speed. Bob drove 125 miles of the trip and Gretchen drove 80 miles of the trip.

   a. Letting x be Gretchen's average speed, write a function $t(x)$ for the total time of the trip.

b. Graph the function.

c. If Gretchen's average speed was 30 miles per hour, estimate the total time of the trip to the nearest tenth of an hour.

d. If the time of the trip was 4.5 hours, what was Gretchen's average speed and Bob's average speed?

12.2

Simplify.

14. $\dfrac{-56x^3yz}{126x^2y^3z}$

15. $\dfrac{5p - 15}{15p + 25}$

16. $\dfrac{15x - 3x^2}{6x^3 - 30x^2}$

17. $\dfrac{2x^2 + x - 15}{4x^2 + 13x + 3}$

18. $\dfrac{b^2 - 49}{b^3 + 7b^2 + 2b + 14}$

Multiply and simplify.

19. $\dfrac{9x^3}{35y} \cdot \dfrac{-5y^2}{6x^5}$

20. $\dfrac{a + 5}{a - 4} \cdot (a + 1)$

21. $\dfrac{4m - 4}{m^2 - 25} \cdot \dfrac{m - 5}{2m^2 + 5m - 7}$

22. $\dfrac{a - 5}{a + 4} \cdot \dfrac{a + 4}{5 - a}$

23. $\dfrac{7x^2y}{5y - 3x} \cdot \dfrac{3x - 5y}{42xy^3}$

24. $\dfrac{2m + 6}{9m + 45} \cdot \dfrac{-3m - 15}{10m + 30}$

Divide exercises 25–33 and simplify.

25. $\dfrac{14z^5}{25x^2y^3} \div \dfrac{-7z^3}{15xy^4}$

26. $\dfrac{27a^2b}{8cd} \div \dfrac{9c^2d}{16ab^2}$

27. $\dfrac{x^2 + 4x + 3}{5x^2 + 5} \div \dfrac{x^2 - 3x + 2}{x^4 - 1}$

28. $\dfrac{3x^2y}{z^3} \div (2xyz)$

29. $(21a^2bc) \div \dfrac{3ab}{2c}$

30. $\dfrac{x^2 - 4}{x^2 + 4} \div (x - 2)$

31. $(2x^2 - x - 3) \div \dfrac{2x^2 - 7x + 6}{2x^2 - x - 6}$

32. $\dfrac{a + 3}{a + 6} \div \dfrac{a + 2}{a + 4}$

33. $\dfrac{x - 11}{x - 3} \div \dfrac{11 - x}{3 - x}$

34. Mario traveled 220 miles. If the trip took t hours, write an expression for his average rate of speed. If he cuts his average speed in half and adds 2 hours to his time, write an expression for the new distance he would travel.

35. A box has a volume given by $4x^3 + 12x^2$ cubic inches. The base of the box is a square with each side measuring $2x$ inches. Find the height of the box.

36. The fixed cost (setup cost) to produce an item is $500 and the variable cost per item produced is $40. The revenue received for selling each item produced is $80 per item.

a. Write a cost function and a revenue function for producing and selling x items.

b. Write an expression for the ratio of cost to revenue for x items and simplify.

12.3

Add or subtract exercises 37–50 and simplify.

37. $\dfrac{3y}{5x} + \dfrac{7y^2}{5x}$

38. $\dfrac{5b^3}{7a} - \dfrac{2b}{7a}$

39. $\dfrac{x - 8}{2x - 5} + \dfrac{3x - 2}{2x - 5}$

40. $\dfrac{10x^2 + 3x + 5}{4x^2 - 9} - \dfrac{2 - 7x}{4x^2 - 9}$

41. $\dfrac{4}{5x^3y} + \dfrac{7}{15x^2y^2}$

42. $\dfrac{5x}{x - 8} + \dfrac{2x}{x + 4}$

43. $\dfrac{8}{2x - 1} - \dfrac{4}{x + 5}$

44. $\dfrac{7}{x - y} + \dfrac{4}{y - x}$

45. $\dfrac{4x}{9x^2 - 16} + \dfrac{2}{15x - 20}$

46. $\dfrac{5}{2x^2 - 5x - 3} + \dfrac{7}{3x^2 - 11x + 6}$

47. $\dfrac{7}{2x - 18} - \dfrac{3x + 4}{x^2 - 81}$

48. $\dfrac{8}{2x^2 + x - 6} - \dfrac{2}{3x^2 + 4x - 4}$

49. $\dfrac{7}{x + 5} + \dfrac{6}{x - 5} + \dfrac{8}{5 - x}$

50. $\dfrac{7x}{x + 2} - \dfrac{11}{3x} - \dfrac{5}{6}$

51. The lengths of the sides of a triangle are given by the rational expressions $\frac{x-1}{x+1}$, $\frac{x-3}{x}$, and $\frac{x+1}{2x}$. Add the lengths to find an expression for the perimeter of the triangle.

52. The perimeter of a rectangle is given by the rational expression $\frac{14x^2+14x+6}{x(x+1)}$. If the width of the rectangle is given by the expression $\frac{3x}{x+1}$, use subtraction to find an expression for the length of the rectangle.

12.4
Determine whether each equation is rational.

53. $\dfrac{2x+3}{6} = \dfrac{5}{\sqrt{x}-1}$

54. $\dfrac{x^2+6x-7}{x^2-6x+5} = \dfrac{2x+1}{x^2}$

55. $2x^2+5x-15=0$

56. $3x-7=4x^{1/3}$

57. $5x^{-2}+3x^{-1}+4=18$

58. $\dfrac{2}{x}-\dfrac{5}{x-3}=17$

Solve for integer solutions numerically, if possible.

59. $x+3=\dfrac{3x-26}{2-x}$

60. $\dfrac{3}{x+3}=\dfrac{6}{2x+6}$

61. $\dfrac{x}{8}=\dfrac{2}{x}$

62. $\dfrac{x}{x+5}=\dfrac{x+8}{x+5}$

Solve exercises 63–67 graphically.

63. $\dfrac{x}{4}=\dfrac{16}{x}$

64. $\dfrac{7-x}{2-x}=\dfrac{x+9}{x-2}$

65. $x+2=\dfrac{6x+19}{x+2}$

66. $1+\dfrac{5}{x}=\dfrac{3x+10}{3x}+\dfrac{5}{3x}$

67. $4x=\dfrac{12-x}{x+3}$

68. A delivery van travels at a constant rate of speed. One leg of the trip was a 70-mile drive. A second leg of the trip was 91 miles and took 0.6 of an hour longer. Letting x be the time for the first trip, write a rational equation and solve it to find the two times for the trip.

69. Two resistors are in a parallel circuit. One resistor has a resistance that is 5 ohms more than twice the resistance of the other resistor. The total resistance of the circuit is 30 ohms. Find the resistances of the two resistors to the nearest ohm.

12.5
Solve exercises 70–84 algebraically.

70. $\dfrac{4}{3x}=1-\dfrac{17}{3x}$

71. $\dfrac{5}{2x+4}=\dfrac{2x+1}{2}$

72. $\dfrac{3x+7}{2x-4}=\dfrac{11}{3}$

73. $\dfrac{z}{50}-\dfrac{2}{z}=0$

74. $b=1+\dfrac{30}{b}$

75. $a+\dfrac{13}{a}=-\dfrac{3}{a}-8$

76. $x^{-2}-18=7$

77. $1=12p^{-2}+p^{-1}$

78. $\dfrac{x-2}{x-6}+3=\dfrac{3x-14}{x-6}$

79. $\dfrac{3}{m+4}+\dfrac{7}{m^2-16}=2$

80. $\dfrac{x+5}{x-2}=\dfrac{x+8}{2(x+3)-(x+8)}$

81. $\dfrac{a}{a+5}=\dfrac{a-4}{a-3}$

82. $\dfrac{2x}{x+3}=1-\dfrac{7}{x+3}$

83. $\dfrac{2}{(3x+5)-(2x+1)}=\dfrac{8}{3(x+5)+(x+1)}$

84. $\dfrac{7}{x+3}+\dfrac{2x-1}{x^2+x-6}=\dfrac{5x-2}{x^2-4}$

85. Two resistors are wired in parallel in a circuit. The resistance of the second resistor is 10 ohms less than the resistance of the first resistor, and the total resistance of the circuit is 12 ohms. Find the two resistances.

86. Maya and her roommate place equal amounts of money into their joint account to pay bills. Maya placed $85 into the account, and when she counts the money, she finds the total is $210. Her roommate has evidently added money to the account. How much more money must she add to the account to make her share 50%?

12.6

87. Norman can install drywall in an average-sized room in 6 hours. His assistant can do the room in 8 hours. How long will it take them to do the room working together?

88. Lucy and Viv are packaging candy on an assembly line. It takes Lucy 10 minutes longer to pack a crate of candy than it takes Viv to do the same. If they work together to pack the crate, they can do so in 30 minutes. How long does it take Lucy and Viv each to do the job alone?

89. One production line can fill a barrel full of chocolate drops in 10 minutes. Another production line can fill the barrel in 15 minutes. How long will it take both lines to fill a barrel working together?

90. One production line takes twice as long to produce widgets as does a high-speed production line. When orders backlog, both production lines must be run. If it takes both lines working together $3\frac{1}{2}$ hours to produce an order, how long would it take each line working alone?

91. Solomon earned $18.50 for distributing 30 catalogs. If the proportion holds, how much would he earn to distribute 100 catalogs?

92. A diluted alcohol solution is made by mixing 1.5 cups of pure grain alcohol with 12 cups of water. How many more cups of pure alcohol should be added to the solution to make it a 25% alcohol solution?

93. $\triangle GHI \sim \triangle JKL$. Use the triangles to find the measures of the missing sides of the similar triangles, given the following information.

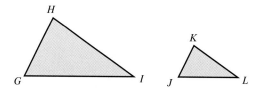

a. $\overline{GH}$ measures 4 inches, $\overline{HI}$ measures 8 inches, $\overline{JK}$ measures 7 inches, and $\overline{JL}$ measures 21 inches.

b. $\overline{GH}$ measures $3\frac{1}{2}$ feet, $\overline{GI}$ measures 13 feet, $\overline{JK}$ measures $2\frac{5}{8}$ feet, and $\overline{KL}$ measures $5\frac{13}{16}$ feet.

c. $\overline{HI}$ measures 9.22 *cm*, $\overline{GI}$ measures 14.08 *cm*, $\overline{KL}$ measures 2.305 *cm*, and $\overline{JK}$ measures 1.88 *cm*.

94. A surveyor sighted along similar triangles to determine the height of a bluff. He was standing 120 feet away from the bluff and 15 feet away from his surveying partner, who was holding the surveyor rod. The top of the 6-foot rod was in line with the top of the bluff from his point of view. How high was the bluff?

95. In the "Case of the Musgrave Ritual," Sherlock Holmes needs to know where the shadow of an elm tree falls at a certain time of day "when the sun is over the oak tree." However, the tree was struck by lightning and is gone. Fortunately, the owner of the estate knows that the elm was 64 feet tall because he had used trigonometry to determine this before the tree fell. Holmes quickly fashioned a 6-foot rod and measured its shadow to be 9 feet. He then determined what the length of the shadow of the oak tree would have been. It was elementary, my dear student. What was the length of the tree's shadow?

CHAPTER 12 | Mixed Review

Evaluate each function for $x = -2, -1, 0, 1,$ and 2, if possible.

1. $y = \dfrac{45}{x^2} + \dfrac{15}{x}$

2. $g(x) = \dfrac{x + 5}{x^2 + 5x + 4}$

Graph each rational function.

3. $p(x) = 2 - \dfrac{3}{x} - \dfrac{2}{x^2}$

4. $y = \dfrac{x^2 - 5x - 6}{x^2 + 4x - 5}$

Solve numerically for integer solutions, if possible.

5. $x + 5 = \dfrac{x - 11}{2 - x}$

6. $\dfrac{x + 4}{2x + 1} = \dfrac{x - 4}{(x + 1) + x}$

7. $5 = \dfrac{3(x + 5)}{x + 3} + \dfrac{4x}{2x + 6}$

8. $\dfrac{x}{16} = \dfrac{4}{x}$

Solve graphically.

9. $\dfrac{1}{2} - \dfrac{3}{2x} = \dfrac{1}{2} + \dfrac{1}{2x} - \dfrac{2}{x}$

10. $5x = \dfrac{9x + 4}{x + 2}$

11. $\dfrac{x}{3} = \dfrac{27}{x}$

12. $\dfrac{4 - x}{3 - x} = \dfrac{x + 11}{x - 3}$

13. $\dfrac{x + 8}{2} = \dfrac{2x + 11}{x + 1}$

Determine algebraically the restricted values and then state the domain of each rational equation.

14. $y = \dfrac{5}{9x^2 + 25}$

15. $y = \dfrac{5}{9x^2 - 25}$

16. $g(x) = \dfrac{x + 5}{3x}$

17. $h(x) = \dfrac{5x - 7}{3x^2 + 2x - 8}$

Simplify.

18. $\dfrac{3x^2 + 19x + 20}{2x^2 + 13x + 15}$

19. $\dfrac{k^2 - 25}{k^3 - 5k^2 + 6k - 30}$

20. $\dfrac{-72x^4 y^2 z}{96xy^6 z}$

21. $\dfrac{7q - 21}{14q + 28}$

22. $\dfrac{12x^2 - 6x^3}{9x^3 - 36x}$

Add or subtract and simplify.

23. $\dfrac{7}{3x + 2} - \dfrac{2}{x - 3}$

24. $\dfrac{14}{a - b} + \dfrac{9}{b - a}$

25. $\dfrac{7b}{3a} + \dfrac{5b^2}{3a}$

26. $\dfrac{3p^2}{4m} - \dfrac{2p}{4m}$

27. $\dfrac{5}{4x^2 y^3} + \dfrac{3}{6x^2 y}$

28. $\dfrac{x}{x + 3} + \dfrac{4x}{x - 5}$

29. $\dfrac{2x}{4x^2 - 25} + \dfrac{1}{6x - 15}$

30. $\dfrac{7}{2x^2 + 5x - 3} + \dfrac{5}{3x^2 + 11x + 6}$

31. $\dfrac{3z - 5}{2z - 7} + \dfrac{z - 9}{2z - 7}$

32. $\dfrac{10x^2 - 8x}{25x^2 - 16} - \dfrac{5x - 4}{25x^2 - 16}$

33. $\dfrac{3}{x + 6} + \dfrac{2}{x - 6} + \dfrac{4}{6 - x}$

34. $\dfrac{x}{x + 1} - \dfrac{3}{2x} - \dfrac{3}{4}$

35. $\dfrac{5}{2x + 10} - \dfrac{2x + 1}{x^2 - 25}$

36. $\dfrac{3}{4x^2 - 17x + 15} - \dfrac{2}{5x^2 - 19x + 12}$

Multiply and simplify.

37. $\dfrac{m^2 - 36}{2m^2 + 9m + 10} \cdot \dfrac{3m + 6}{m - 6}$

38. $\dfrac{z - 3}{z - 7} \cdot \dfrac{7 - z}{z - 3}$

39. $\dfrac{8a^4}{21b} \cdot \dfrac{-35b^3}{12a^7}$

40. $(2c + 3) \cdot \dfrac{c + 7}{c + 3}$

41. $\dfrac{3b - 4a}{24ab^3} \cdot \dfrac{8a^2 b}{4a - 3b}$

42. $\dfrac{5p + 20}{12p + 96} \cdot \dfrac{-9p - 72}{15p + 60}$

Divide and simplify.

43. $\dfrac{22g^8}{15h^3 k^2} \div \dfrac{-11g^4}{10hk^3}$

44. $\dfrac{18p^2 q^2}{25m^2 n} \div \dfrac{3mn^3}{5pq^5}$

45. $(15m^3 np^2) \div \dfrac{2mn}{5p}$

46. $\dfrac{4x^2 - 9}{4x^2 + 9} \div (2x + 3)$

47. $\dfrac{x^2 - x - 6}{2x^2 + 8} \div \dfrac{x^2 - 5x + 6}{x^4 - 16}$

48. $\dfrac{5a^2 b^3}{c^5} \div (3a^2 bc^2)$

49. $\dfrac{z - 3}{z - 6} \div \dfrac{z + 4}{z + 8}$

50. $\dfrac{k - 7}{k - 12} \div \dfrac{7 - k}{12 - k}$

51. $(2x^2 + 9x - 5) \div \dfrac{2x^2 + 3x - 2}{2x^2 + 5x + 2}$

Solve.

52. $\dfrac{4}{7} - \dfrac{1}{y} = \dfrac{9}{28}$

53. $\dfrac{7}{3x} = 2 - \dfrac{17}{3x}$

54. $\dfrac{9}{2x + 3} = -3$

55. $\dfrac{23}{18} = \dfrac{4}{9} + \dfrac{5}{m}$

56. $\dfrac{4}{x - 1} = \dfrac{5x - 16}{7}$

57. $\dfrac{7x - 2}{3x + 5} = 16$

58. $2 - \dfrac{4}{x + 3} = \dfrac{x + 2}{x + 3}$

59. $\dfrac{5}{m + 3} + \dfrac{8}{m^2 - 9} = \dfrac{3}{5}$

60. $\dfrac{16}{2x + 6} = \dfrac{5}{x}$

61. $35 = p^{-2} + 2p^{-1}$

62. $\dfrac{x - 6}{x - 4} = \dfrac{x + 7}{2(x + 3) - (x + 10)}$

63. $\dfrac{a}{a - 7} = \dfrac{a + 1}{a - 2}$

64. $1 - \dfrac{6}{x} = \dfrac{6}{x} - \dfrac{1}{2} + \dfrac{21}{2x}$

65. $\dfrac{4x + 7}{3} - \dfrac{x + 6}{5} = \dfrac{4x - 1}{5}$

66. $1 + 7x^{-1} = 3$

67. $\dfrac{2x}{x - 4} = 1 + \dfrac{9}{x - 4}$

68. $\dfrac{10}{x + 5} - \dfrac{24}{x^2 + x - 20} = \dfrac{1}{x^2 - 16}$

69. $\dfrac{2}{(x + 3) + (x - 9)} = \dfrac{3}{2(x + 4) + (x - 17)}$

70. Dave can hang wallpaper in a room and finish in 10 hours. Joan can do the same room and finish in 7 hours. How long will it take them to paper the room working together?

71. A diluted glue mixture is made by mixing 2 pints of glue with 7 pints of distilled water. How many more pints of glue are needed to bring the mixture up to a 30% glue solution?

72. Tina earned $42 in tips from waiting on 9 tables. If this rate holds, how much in tips would she earn waiting on 15 tables?

73. Antonio drove 120 miles in t hours. Write an expression for his average rate of speed. If he reduces his average speed to $\frac{2}{3}$ of his original speed and adds 1 hour to his time, write an expression for the new distance he could travel.

74. A tree casts a shadow of 18 feet. At the same time of day, a mailbox that is 4 feet high casts a shadow of 3 feet. How high is the tree?

75. A box has a width of x inches and a length that is five times the width. If the volume of the box is $10x^3 + 5x^2$ cubic inches, write an expression for the height of the box.

76. One production line takes $1\frac{1}{2}$ hours longer to fill an order than a second production line takes. When both lines are used, the order can be filled in $3\frac{1}{3}$ hours. How long does it take each line working alone to fill the order?

77. The lengths of the sides of a triangle are given by the expressions $\frac{6}{x-3}$, 3, and $\frac{x-1}{x}$. Find an expression for the perimeter of the triangle.

78. Latoya has two roommates. Each pays $\frac{1}{3}$ of the bills. Latoya has added \$70 to the amount her roommates collected, and the total was \$250. How much more does Latoya have to add to the money to make her contribution $\frac{1}{3}$ of the total?

79. Elaine claimed a mileage charge of \$65.50 on her expense report. Her company reimburses employees at the rate of 24 cents per mile. Determine the approximate number of miles that Elaine drove on her business trip.

80. Two resistors are connected in parallel. The total resistance of the circuit is 25 ohms. If one resistor has a resistance that is 12 ohms more than the resistance of the other resistor, what are the two resistances to the nearest ohm?

CHAPTER 12 | Test

Test-Taking Tips

Many students have been conditioned to think they should use only their textbook when they need a reference to help them with their math difficulties. This is not true. Even though your instructor may emphasize the adopted text, remember that you can always seek other explanations of the same material in other textbooks. When you have difficulty understanding a concept, go to the library and check other math textbooks to see how they present the material. You may find that you more readily understand the examples in another text. Or you may find that another author has a manner of explanation that fits better with your style of learning. When students decide to check another text, it is often an eye-opener for them, and they find to their delight that they have a much better grasp of the material they are studying. Also, other texts will provide you with many more exercises that you can use to rehearse and prepare for the test.

Determine the restricted values and then state the domain of each rational equation.

1. $y = \dfrac{x-7}{2x^2 + 6x}$

2. $g(x) = \dfrac{x^2 - 4x - 21}{x^2 - 5x - 36}$

3. Graph the rational function $f(x) = \dfrac{x+4}{x-2}$.

Simplify.

4. $\dfrac{24x + 56}{9x^2 - 49}$

5. $\dfrac{2z^3 - 18z}{z^3 + 3z^2 + 9z + 27}$

Perform the operations and simplify.

6. $\dfrac{5}{x^2 + 4x} + \dfrac{2}{x^2 + x - 12}$

7. $\dfrac{5x^2 - 40x}{20x^2 + 30x} \div \dfrac{x^2 - 64}{2x^2 + 19x + 24}$

8. $\dfrac{2x + 1}{x^2 + 5x} - \dfrac{x - 4}{x^2 + 10x + 25}$

9. $\dfrac{24x^2 y}{x^2 - xy - 2y^2} \cdot \dfrac{3x^2 - 12xy + 12y^2}{16x^3 y}$

10. Solve $x - 5 = \dfrac{5 - x}{x}$

    a. numerically   **b.** graphically   **c.** algebraically

Solve exercises 11–17.

11. $\dfrac{16}{x-3} = \dfrac{x-3}{x}$

12. $\dfrac{b}{5} + \dfrac{1}{2} = \dfrac{1}{5} - \dfrac{11}{10b}$

13. $\dfrac{3}{m} - \dfrac{m}{75} = 0$

14. $6 + 14x^{-1} + 4x^{-2} = 0$

15. $\dfrac{x^2 + 6x + 9}{4x + 20} = \dfrac{x+6}{x+5}$

16. $\dfrac{2}{x+2} = \dfrac{3}{x+3}$

17. $2 + \dfrac{10.68}{x} + \dfrac{10.72}{x^2} = \dfrac{1}{x} + \dfrac{5.34}{x^2} + \dfrac{5.36}{x^3}$

18. Chris wants to estimate the height of a tree that casts a shadow measuring 32.5 feet. She knows that a 7-foot pole in the yard casts a shadow of 10.5 feet. What is the height of the tree?

19. Jack can rake the leaves in his yard in 6 hours. When Jill helps him, they can rake the leaves in 2 hours and 24 minutes (that is, $2\frac{2}{5}$ hours). How long would it take Jill to rake the leaves alone?

20. Explain why a rational equation can be solved algebraically by multiplying both sides of the equation by the least common denominator (LCD), but a rational expression cannot be simplified by multiplying by the LCD.

13

Radical Expressions, Expressions Containing Rational Exponents, Radical Functions, and Radical Equations

We have discussed radicals and numbers with rational exponents in several previous chapters. In this chapter, we examine algebraic expressions that involve radicals and rational exponents. We use the properties of radicals and rational exponents to see how to perform mathematical operations on these expressions. Then we study radical equations in one variable and use standard numerical, graphical, and algebraic methods to solve these equations.

Radical equations occur in many common real-life situations. For example, the geometric formulas for determining the dimensions of a square or circular object with a given area involve square roots. The geometric formulas for determining the dimensions of a cubic or spherical object from a given volume involve cube roots. Aside from geometry, many kinds of data from statistical analysis can be described by radical expressions. Also, many relations in physics involve radical expressions; for example, the diameter of a meteor crater is proportional to the cube root of the meteor's energy near ground level. We will use these kinds of expressions to illustrate concepts throughout this chapter.

13.1 Evaluating Radical Expressions and Expressions Containing Rational Exponents

Objectives

1 Evaluate radical expressions with a real-number radicand.

2 Evaluate expressions of the form $a^{1/n}$, where a is a real number and n is a positive integer greater than 1.

3 Evaluate expressions of the form $a^{m/n}$, where a is a real number, m is an integer not equal to 0, and n is a positive integer greater than 1.

4 Model real-world situations with expressions involving radicals or rational exponents.

Application

According to annual reports from the Amway Corporation, the number of employees of the company can be estimated by the expression $6257\sqrt[3]{x}$, where x is the number of years after 1988. Approximate the number of employees for the year 1992.

After completing this section, we will discuss this application further. See page 1003.

1 Evaluating Radical Expressions

In Chapter 2, we defined a radical expression. A **radical expression** is an expression that can be written in the form $\sqrt[n]{a}$, where n (an integer greater than 1) is the **index** (the plural form is *indices*) and a is the radicand. The symbol $\sqrt{}$ is called the radical sign. If the index is 2, it is conventional not to write it. For example, the following are radical expressions with numerical radicands.

$\sqrt{64}$ This is read: The square root of 64.

$\sqrt[3]{64}$ This is read: The cube root of 64.

$\sqrt[6]{64}$ This is read: The sixth root of 64.

$\sqrt[7]{64}$ This is read: The seventh root of 64.

We revisited square-root expressions in Chapter 11 and evaluated square roots with numerical radicands. Now we will revisit the other radical expressions. The process of evaluating radicals with even and odd indices is different. We call radicals with even indices **even roots**. Radicals with odd indices are called **odd roots**.

Square roots are examples of even roots. In general, to evaluate even roots, we follow the same rules as square roots.

- The radicand of an even root cannot be a negative number because all real numbers when raised to an even power are positive. (For additional discussion, see Chapter 14.)
- The principal root, $\sqrt[n]{a}$, is always a positive value.
- The negative root, $-\sqrt[n]{a}$, is always a negative value.

For example,

$\sqrt[4]{-2}$ does not represent a real number.
The principal root $\sqrt[4]{81} = 3$, because $3^4 = 81$.
The negative root $-\sqrt[4]{81} = -3$, because $-\sqrt[4]{81}$ is the opposite of the principal root $\sqrt[4]{81}$.

To evaluate odd roots, we do not have to worry about cases such as principal roots, negative roots, or nonreal numbers. For example,

$$\sqrt[3]{64} = 4, \text{ because } 4^3 = 64.$$
$$\sqrt[3]{-64} = -4, \text{ because } (-4)^3 = -64.$$

> *Evaluating Radical Expressions with Numerical Radicands*
> To evaluate a radical expression $\sqrt[n]{a}$:
>
> - If n is an integer > 1 and $a = 0$, then the result is 0.
> - If n is an even integer >1 and $a < 0$, then the result is not a real number.
> - If n is an even integer >1 and $a > 0$, then $\sqrt[n]{a} = |b|$ if $b^n = a$.
> - If n is an odd integer >1, $\sqrt[n]{a} = b$ if $b^n = a$.

If the radicand cannot be written as a power of the index, we approximate the answer. We can use a calculator to do this. For example, evaluate $\sqrt[7]{64}$.

Since we cannot determine a number that can be raised to the seventh power to equal 64, we must use a calculator to approximate the answer.

Therefore, $\sqrt[7]{64} \approx 1.811$ because $(1.811)^7 \approx 64$.

EXAMPLE 1 Evaluate to the nearest thousandth, if possible.

a. $\sqrt[3]{-125}$ b. $\sqrt{12}$
c. $-\sqrt[4]{16}$ d. $\sqrt[4]{-16}$

Solution

a. $\sqrt[3]{-125} = -5$, because $(-5)^3 = -125$.
b. $\sqrt{12} \approx 3.464$, because $(3.464)^2 \approx 12$.
c. $-\sqrt[4]{16} = -2$
    Since $2^4 = 16$, then $-\sqrt[4]{16} = -(2) = -2$. This is the negative root.
d. $\sqrt[4]{-16}$ is not a real number, because the radicand is negative and the root is even.

See Figures 13.1a and 13.1b for calculator solutions. ∎

TECHNOLOGY

Figure 13.1a

ERR:NONREAL ANS
1:Quit
2:Goto

The value is not a real number.

Figure 13.1b

For Figure 13.1a

For Figure 13.1b

d. [4] [MATH] [5] [(−)] [1] [6] [ENTER]

The error message "NONREAL ANS" means that we are attempting to take an even root of a negative number.

Experiencing Algebra the Checkup Way

Evaluate exercises 1–6 to the nearest thousandth, if possible.

1. $\sqrt[4]{81}$ 2. $-\sqrt[4]{81}$ 3. $\sqrt[4]{-81}$

4. $\sqrt[3]{-64}$ 5. $\sqrt[3]{64}$ 6. $\sqrt{117}$

7. Explain the difference between finding the square root of a number and squaring a number.

8. When a negative number is multiplied as a factor an even number of times, what will be the sign of the result? Use this fact to explain why the radicand of an even root must be a positive number if the solution is to be a real number.

9. When a negative number is multiplied as a factor an odd number of times, what will be the sign of the result? Use this fact to explain why the radicand of an odd root may be a positive number or a negative number.

---

2 Expressions with Rational Exponents Having Numerators of 1

In Chapter 2, we discussed expressions with a rational exponent having a numerator of 1. Such an expression can be written in the form $a^{1/n}$, where n is an integer not equal to 0 and a is the base. For example,

$64^{1/2}$, $64^{1/3}$, and $64^{1/6}$ are expressions with numerical bases and positive rational exponents having numerators of 1.
$64^{-1/2}$, $64^{-1/3}$, and $64^{-1/6}$ are expressions with numerical bases and negative rational exponents having numerators of 1.

We defined an expression with a rational exponent having a numerator of 1 to be a radical expression.

> *Expressions with Rational Exponents Having a Numerator of 1*
>
> $$a^{1/n} = \sqrt[n]{a}$$
>
> $$a^{-1/n} = \frac{1}{a^{1/n}} = \frac{1}{\sqrt[n]{a}}, a \neq 0$$
>
> where a is a real number and n is a positive integer > 1.

To evaluate an expression with a rational exponent having a numerator of 1, write an equivalent radical expression.

- If the rational exponent is positive, then $a^{1/n} = \sqrt[n]{a}$, where n is a positive integer.

- If the rational exponent is negative, then $a^{-1/n} = \frac{1}{a^{1/n}} = \frac{1}{\sqrt[n]{a}}$, where n is a positive integer and $a \neq 0$.
- Evaluate the resulting expression.

For example, given that $8^2 = 64$, $4^3 = 64$, and $2^6 = 64$,

$$64^{1/2} = \sqrt{64} = 8 \qquad 64^{-1/2} = \frac{1}{64^{1/2}} = \frac{1}{\sqrt{64}} = \frac{1}{8}$$

$$64^{1/3} = \sqrt[3]{64} = 4 \qquad 64^{-1/3} = \frac{1}{64^{1/3}} = \frac{1}{\sqrt[3]{64}} = \frac{1}{4}$$

$$64^{1/6} = \sqrt[6]{64} = 2 \qquad 64^{-1/6} = \frac{1}{64^{1/6}} = \frac{1}{\sqrt[6]{64}} = \frac{1}{2}$$

EXAMPLE 2 Given that $5^4 = 625$ and $4^5 = 1024$, write the following expressions as radical expressions and evaluate, if possible.

a. $625^{1/4}$ **b.** $-625^{1/4}$ **c.** $(-625)^{1/4}$

d. $1024^{1/5}$ **e.** $-1024^{1/5}$ **f.** $(-1024)^{1/5}$

Solution

a. $625^{1/4} = \sqrt[4]{625} = 5$ $5^4 = 625$

b. $-625^{1/4} = -\sqrt[4]{625} = -5$ The negative sign is not with the base, and therefore indicates a negative root.

c. $(-625)^{1/4} = \sqrt[4]{-625}$, which is not a real number.   The radicand is negative and the index is even.

d. $1024^{1/5} = \sqrt[5]{1024} = 4$ $4^5 = 1024$

e. $-1024^{1/5} = -\sqrt[5]{1024} = -4$ The negative sign is not with the base, and therefore indicates a negative root.

f. $(-1024)^{1/5} = \sqrt[5]{-1024} = -4$ $(-4)^5 = -1024$

To check Example 2a, 2b, and 2c on your calculator, enter each exponential expression, as shown in Figures 13.2a and 13.2b.

TECHNOLOGY

```
625^(1/4)
              5
-625^(1/4)
             -5
```

Figure 13.2a

```
ERR:NONREAL ANS
1:Quit
2:Goto
```

The value is not a real number.

Figure 13.2b

For Figure 13.2a

a. `6` `2` `5` `^` `(` `1` `÷` `4` `)` `ENTER`

b. `(−)` `6` `2` `5` `^` `(` `1` `÷` `4` `)` `ENTER`

For Figure 13.2b

c. `(` `(−)` `6` `2` `5` `)` `^` `(` `1` `÷` `4` `)` `ENTER`

Calculator solutions for Examples 2d, 2e, and 2f are shown in the figure to the left. ∎

EXAMPLE 3 Given that $5^4 = 625$ and $4^5 = 1024$, write the following expressions as radical expressions and evaluate, if possible. Express your answers as fractions.

a. $625^{-1/4}$ **b.** $-625^{-1/4}$ **c.** $(-625)^{-1/4}$

d. $1024^{-1/5}$ **e.** $-1024^{-1/5}$ **f.** $(-1024)^{-1/5}$

Solution

a. $625^{-1/4} = \dfrac{1}{625^{1/4}} = \dfrac{1}{\sqrt[4]{625}} = \dfrac{1}{5}$

b. $-625^{-1/4} = -\dfrac{1}{625^{1/4}} = -\dfrac{1}{\sqrt[4]{625}} = -\dfrac{1}{5}$

c. $(-625)^{-1/4} = \dfrac{1}{(-625)^{1/4}} = \dfrac{1}{\sqrt[4]{-625}}$, which is not a real number.

d. $1024^{-1/5} = \dfrac{1}{1024^{1/5}} = \dfrac{1}{\sqrt[5]{1024}} = \dfrac{1}{4}$

e. $-1024^{-1/5} = -\dfrac{1}{1024^{1/5}} = -\dfrac{1}{\sqrt[5]{1024}} = -\dfrac{1}{4}$

f. $(-1024)^{-1/5} = \dfrac{1}{(-1024)^{1/5}} = \dfrac{1}{\sqrt[5]{-1024}} = \dfrac{1}{-4} = -\dfrac{1}{4}$

To check on your calculator, enter each exponential expression and convert the answer to fractional notation, as shown for Examples 3a and 3b in Figure 13.3.

TECHNOLOGY

```
625^(-1/4)▸Frac
                1/5
-625^(-1/4)▸Frac
               -1/5
```

For Figure 13.3

a. [6] [2] [5] [^] [( ] [(−)] [1] [÷] [4] [ )] [MATH] [1]
[ENTER]

b. [(−)] [6] [2] [5] [^] [( ] [(−)] [1] [÷] [4] [ )] [MATH] [1]
[ENTER]

Figure 13.3

In Example 3c, $(-625)^{-1/4}$ is not a real number. A calculator check results in the error message, "NONREAL ANS."

Calculator checks for Examples 3d, 3e, and 3f are shown in the following figures.

If the radicand cannot be written as a power of the index, approximate the answer. Use your calculator to do this. For example,

$$64^{1/7} = \sqrt[7]{64} \approx 1.811$$

$$64^{-1/7} = \frac{1}{64^{1/7}} = \frac{1}{\sqrt[7]{64}} \approx 0.552$$

Helping Hand Since we must use the calculator, we do not need to change to an equivalent radical expression.

EXAMPLE 4   Evaluate. Round to the nearest thousandth.

a. $625^{1/5}$ **b.** $-1024^{-1/4}$

Calculator Solution

a. $625^{1/5} \approx 3.624$ **b.** $-1024^{-1/4} \approx -0.177$ ∎

✓ Experiencing Algebra the Checkup Way

Write as a radical expression and evaluate, if possible.

1. $16^{1/4}$ **2.** $-16^{1/4}$ **3.** $(-16)^{1/4}$

Write as a radical expression and evaluate, if possible. Express your answer as a fraction.

4. $125^{-1/3}$ **5.** $-125^{-1/3}$ **6.** $(-125)^{-1/3}$

Evaluate exercises 7–8 to the nearest thousandth.

7. $500^{1/4}$ **8.** $650^{-1/3}$

9. Describe the relationship between a radical expression and an expression with a rational exponent whose numerator is equal to 1.

---

3 Expressions with a Rational Exponent Having a Numerator Not Equal to 1

Some expressions have a rational exponent with a numerator not equal to 1, such as $4^{3/2}$. We need to be able to evaluate such an expression. Complete the following set of exercises with your calculator to discover a rule for writing an equivalent radical expression from an expression containing a rational exponent.

D I S C O V E R Y   1

Radicals and Rational Exponents

Evaluate each expression and compare the results obtained in each row.

1. a. $4^{3/2} = $ _____   **b.** $\left(\sqrt{4}\right)^3 = $ _____   **c.** $\sqrt{4^3} = $ _____

2. a. $64^{2/3} = $ _____   **b.** $\left(\sqrt[3]{64}\right)^2 = $ _____   **c.** $\sqrt[3]{64^2} = $ _____

3. a. $8^{4/3} = $ _____   **b.** $\left(\sqrt[3]{8}\right)^4 = $ _____   **c.** $\sqrt[3]{8^4} = $ _____

4. a. $(-8)^{4/3} = $ _____   **b.** $\left(\sqrt[3]{-8}\right)^4 = $ _____   **c.** $\sqrt[3]{(-8)^4} = $ _____

Write a rule for converting an expression with a rational exponent to a radical expression.

In each row, the two radical expressions have the same value as the expression with a rational exponent. (*Note:* On some calculators this is not true. If this is the case with your calculator, see the "Helping Hand" on page 1001.) As we already know, the base of the expression with a rational exponent is the radicand of the radical expression, and the denominator of the rational exponent is the index of the radical expression. The numerator of the rational exponent is the power to which the radical expression is raised, or the power to which the radicand is raised.

We can confirm this by rewriting the radical expression as an expression with a rational exponent and simplifying using the power-to-a-power rule for exponents. For example, in the first "Discovery" exercise,

$$\left(\sqrt{4}\right)^3 = \left(4^{1/2}\right)^3 = 4^{3/2} \quad \text{or} \quad \sqrt{4^3} = \left(4^3\right)^{1/2} = 4^{3/2}$$

Therefore, $4^{3/2} = \left(\sqrt{4}\right)^3 = \sqrt{4^3}$.

In general,

$$\left(\sqrt[n]{a}\right)^m = \left(a^{1/n}\right)^m = a^{m/n} \quad \text{or} \quad \sqrt[n]{a^m} = \left(a^m\right)^{1/n} = a^{m/n}$$

Therefore, $a^{m/n} = \left(\sqrt[n]{a}\right)^m = \sqrt[n]{a^m}$.

> **Rational Exponents**
>
> $$a^{m/n} = \sqrt[n]{a^m} \quad \text{or} \quad \left(\sqrt[n]{a}\right)^m,$$
>
> where a is a real number, $a^{1/n}$ is defined, m and n have no common factors other than 1, m is an integer $\neq 0$, and n is a positive integer >1.

To write an equivalent radical expression for an expression with a positive rational exponent:

- Write the base as the radicand.
- Write the denominator of the rational exponent as the index of the radical.
- Write the numerator of the rational exponent as either the power of the radicand or the power of the radical expression.

For example, write $25^{3/2}$ as a radical expression and evaluate.

$$25^{3/2} = \sqrt{25^3} = \sqrt{15{,}625} = 125 \quad \text{or} \quad 25^{3/2} = \left(\sqrt{25}\right)^3 = (5)^3 = 125$$

 Helping Hand The order of taking the power does not matter.

As another example, write $16^{-3/4}$ as a radical expression and evaluate.

First, write the expression with a positive exponent.

$$16^{-3/4} = \frac{1}{16^{3/4}} = \frac{1}{\left(\sqrt[4]{16}\right)^3} = \frac{1}{(2)^3} = \frac{1}{8}$$

EXAMPLE 5 Write as an equivalent radical expression and evaluate.

    a. $4^{3/2}$ **b.** $(-32)^{3/5}$

    c. $12^{2/5}$ **d.** $-32^{-4/5}$

Solution

Each of these expressions is written in the following solutions as an equivalent radical expression. We chose to write the numerator of the fraction as a power of the radical expression. However, if the numerator is written as the power of the radicand, the result is the same.

a. $4^{3/2} = \left(\sqrt{4}\right)^3 = 2^3 = 8$

b. $(-32)^{3/5} = \left(\sqrt[5]{-32}\right)^3 = (-2)^3 = -8$

c. $12^{2/5} = \left(\sqrt[5]{12}\right)^2 \approx 2.702$

Calculate on your calculator, because 12 cannot be written as a power of the index 5.

d. $-32^{-4/5} = -\dfrac{1}{32^{4/5}} = -\dfrac{1}{\left(\sqrt[5]{32}\right)^4} = -\dfrac{1}{2^4} = -\dfrac{1}{16}$

Write as a positive exponent first.

To check on your calculator, enter the exponential expression, as shown in the following figures.

Helping Hand Some calculators are not programmed to evaluate exponential expressions with negative bases and rational exponents having an odd-number denominator and an integer numerator not equal to 1. Therefore, for Example 5b, enter the exponential expression as a power to a power, $\left[(-32)^{1/5}\right]^3$ or $\left[(-32)^3\right]^{1/5}$, or rewrite the expression as an equivalent radical expression, $\left(\sqrt[5]{-32}\right)^3$ or $\sqrt[5]{(-32)^3}$.

Experiencing Algebra the Checkup Way

Rewrite exercises 1–4 as radical expressions and evaluate.

1. $16^{3/2}$

2. $(-125)^{5/3}$

3. $15^{3/2}$

4. $-125^{-5/3}$

5. When given an expression with a rational exponent, explain how the numerator and the denominator of the exponent are used to transform the expression into a radical expression.

4   Modeling the Real World   In geometry, the formula for the area A of a square of side s is $A = s^2$. If we are given the area of a square, we calculate the length of its side as $s = \pm\sqrt{A}$, but since we know s must be a positive number, $s = \sqrt{A}$. Similarly, we can use the formula for the area of a circle to find the radius r of a circle of area A, $r = \sqrt{\frac{A}{\pi}}$. If we write down the formula for the volume of a cube, we can also use that to find the edge length of a cube given its volume.

We can also write these formulas as expressions containing rational exponents. These are very useful equations for determining the dimensions you need to create square or circular objects of a given area, or cubic or spherical objects of a given volume. Remember, that in all cases, you need to perform the operations on the units of measurement as well as on the given numbers.

EXAMPLE 6   The base of the Great Pyramid at Giza, Egypt, is a square with area 570,000 square feet. What is the length of one of its sides?

Solution

In the introduction to this section, we derived the formula $s = \sqrt{A}$, where A is the area of a square and s is the length of a side of the square.

$$s = \sqrt{A}$$

$$s = \sqrt{570,000} \quad \text{Substitute 570,000 for } A.$$

$$s \approx 754.983$$

One side of the Great Pyramid is approximately 755 feet. ■

EXAMPLE 7   **a.** The volume V of a sphere with radius of length r is $V = \frac{4}{3}\pi r^3$. Write a formula for r in terms of V.
b. The geodesic dome of the Spaceship Earth at the Epcot Center has a volume of 2.2×10^6 cubic feet. Assuming it is a sphere, what is its diameter?

Solution

a. $V = \dfrac{4}{3}\pi r^3$

$3V = 4\pi r^3$ Multiply both sides by 3.

$\dfrac{3V}{4\pi} = r^3$ Divide both sides by 4π.

$\sqrt[3]{\dfrac{3V}{4\pi}} = r$ Take the cube root of both sides.

or $r = \sqrt[3]{\dfrac{3V}{4\pi}}$

b. We will use the formula derived in Example 7a to determine the radius of the dome.

$$r = \sqrt[3]{\dfrac{3V}{4\pi}}$$

$$r = \sqrt[3]{\dfrac{3(2.2 \times 10^6)}{4\pi}}$$

$$r \approx 80.68$$

The diameter is twice the radius, or $d = 2r$.

$$d = 2r$$

$$d \approx 2(80.68)$$

$$d \approx 161.36$$

The diameter of the geodesic dome is approximately 161.36 feet. ∎

Application

According to annual reports from the Amway Corporation, the number of employees of the company can be estimated by the expression $6257\sqrt[3]{x}$, where x is the number of years after 1988. Approximate the number of employees for the year 1992.

Discussion

Given the expression $6257\sqrt[3]{x}$, where x is the number of years after 1988, we substitute 4, the number of years 1992 is after 1988, for x and evaluate.

$$6257\sqrt[3]{x} = 6257\sqrt[3]{4} \approx 9932.368$$

The Amway Corporation had approximately 9932 employees in 1992. ∎

Experiencing Algebra the Checkup Way

1. The base of the Washington Monument has an area of 0.2 square miles or approximately 5,600,000 square feet. If the base is a square, what is the length of one side?

2. The area covered by the dome of Saint Peter's Basilica in Rome is approximately 19,360 square feet. Write a formula for the radius of a circle in terms of its area A. Use the formula to estimate the radius of the dome. What is the dome's diameter?

3. The number of employees of the Amway Corporation is estimated by the expression $6257 \sqrt[3]{x}$, where x is the number of years after 1988. Assuming that this mathematical model still applies for the year 2000, approximate the number of employees in the year 2000.

PROBLEM SET 13.1

 Experiencing Algebra the Exercise Way

Evaluate to the nearest thousandth, if possible.

1. $\sqrt{81}$

2. $\sqrt{49}$

3. $\sqrt{1.44}$

4. $\sqrt{1.69}$

5. $\sqrt{\dfrac{4}{9}}$

6. $\sqrt{\dfrac{25}{36}}$

7. $\sqrt[3]{\dfrac{-1}{27}}$

8. $\sqrt[3]{\dfrac{-8}{27}}$

9. $-\sqrt[4]{625}$	**10.** $-\sqrt[4]{2401}$	**11.** $\sqrt[4]{-625}$	**12.** $\sqrt[4]{-2401}$
13. $\sqrt[3]{216}$	**14.** $\sqrt[3]{1331}$	**15.** $\sqrt[3]{-216}$	**16.** $\sqrt[3]{-1331}$
17. $-\sqrt[3]{216}$	**18.** $-\sqrt[3]{1331}$	**19.** $\sqrt{110}$	**20.** $\sqrt{200}$
21. $-\sqrt{110}$	**22.** $-\sqrt{200}$	**23.** $\sqrt{-110}$	**24.** $\sqrt{-200}$
25. $\sqrt[3]{110}$	**26.** $\sqrt[3]{200}$	**27.** $-\sqrt[3]{110}$	**28.** $-\sqrt[3]{200}$
29. $\sqrt[5]{20}$	**30.** $\sqrt[6]{25}$	**31.** $\sqrt[3]{12.5}$	**32.** $\sqrt[4]{72.8}$

Write as a radical expression and evaluate, if possible.

33. $36^{1/2}$	**34.** $100^{1/2}$	**35.** $216^{1/3}$	**36.** $729^{1/3}$
37. $-81^{1/4}$	**38.** $-625^{1/4}$	**39.** $(-81)^{1/4}$	**40.** $(-625)^{1/4}$
41. $-8^{1/3}$	**42.** $-27^{1/3}$	**43.** $(-8)^{1/3}$	**44.** $(-27)^{1/3}$

Write as a radical expression and evaluate, if possible. Express your answer as a fraction.

45. $36^{-1/2}$	**46.** $100^{-1/2}$	**47.** $216^{-1/3}$	**48.** $729^{-1/3}$
49. $81^{-1/4}$	**50.** $625^{-1/4}$	**51.** $-81^{-1/4}$	**52.** $(-625)^{-1/4}$
53. $8^{-1/3}$	**54.** $27^{-1/3}$	**55.** $(-8)^{-1/3}$	**56.** $(-27)^{-1/3}$

Write as a radical expression and evaluate to the nearest thousandth.

57. $522^{1/2}$	**58.** $478^{1/3}$	**59.** $522^{1/4}$	**60.** $478^{1/5}$
61. $522^{-1/3}$	**62.** $478^{-1/2}$	**63.** $522^{-1/5}$	**64.** $478^{-1/4}$

Write as a radical expression and evaluate, if possible. Express your results as integers or fractions.

65. $27^{4/3}$	**66.** $25^{3/2}$	**67.** $(-27)^{4/3}$	**68.** $(-25)^{3/2}$
69. $27^{-4/3}$	**70.** $25^{-3/2}$	**71.** $-27^{-4/3}$	**72.** $-25^{-3/2}$
73. $4^{5/2}$	**74.** $9^{3/2}$	**75.** $8^{7/3}$	**76.** $125^{5/3}$
77. $4^{-7/2}$	**78.** $16^{-5/2}$	**79.** $-16^{3/2}$	**80.** $-64^{3/2}$
81. $(-9)^{3/2}$	**82.** $(-4)^{3/2}$	**83.** $-81^{-3/2}$	**84.** $-36^{-3/2}$

Write exercises 85–94 as radical expressions and approximate to the nearest thousandth, if possible.

85. $28^{5/4}$	**86.** $36^{5/4}$	**87.** $(-21)^{4/3}$	**88.** $(-15)^{2/3}$
89. $5^{-2/3}$	**90.** $7^{-2/3}$	**91.** $-42^{-2/3}$	**92.** $-36^{-2/3}$
93. $(-88)^{3/8}$	**94.** $(-66)^{5/6}$		

95. A painting is in the shape of a square. Find the length of a side in each situation.

    a. The painting is a mural whose area is 289 square feet.

    b. The painting is a canvas whose area is 90.25 square inches.

    c. The painting is a locket whose area is 115 square millimeters.

96. A canvas cover has a square shape. Find the length of a side in each situation.

    a. The canvas covers an area of 529 square yards.

    b. The canvas covers an area of 110.25 square centimeters.

    c. The canvas covers an area of 45 square feet.

97. A puddle of standing water has the shape of a circle. Find the exact length of the radius of the puddle in each situation. Then approximate the length to the nearest thousandth.

    a. The puddle has an area of 196π square inches.

    b. The puddle has an area of 49 square yards.

    c. The puddle has an area of 108 square meters.

98. Find the exact length of the radius of a circular metal ring that encloses the area listed. Then approximate the length to the nearest thousandth.

    a. The metal ring encloses an area of 225π square decimeters.

    b. The metal ring encloses an area of 361 square feet.

    c. The metal ring encloses an area of 200 square centimeters.

99. A wooden box is shaped like a cube. Find the length of a side of the box for each situation. Round your answers to the nearest hundredth.

    a. The volume of the box is 1728 cubic inches.

    b. The volume of the box is 120 cubic meters.

100. A bundle of paper has the shape of a cube. Find the length of a side of the bundle for each situation. Round your answers to the nearest hundredth.

    a. The volume of the bundle is 9261 cubic centimeters.

    b. The volume of the bundle is 500 cubic feet.

101. A balloon has a spherical shape. Find the radius and diameter for each situation.

    a. The volume of the balloon is 288π cubic decimeters.

    b. The volume of the balloon is 250 cubic yards.

102. A mesh wire cage has the shape of a sphere. Find the radius and diameter of the cage for each situation.

    a. The cage encloses a volume of 972π cubic inches.

    b. The cage encloses a volume of 1000 cubic meters.

103. The area covered by the dome of St. Paul's Cathedral in London is approximately 8200 square feet. What is the radius of the dome? What is its diameter?

104. The area of the square floor of the central building of the Taj Mahal is approximately 377,000 square feet. What is the length of one of its sides?

Experiencing Algebra the Calculator Way

In the Application for this section, you were given a mathematical model to estimate the number of employees in the Amway Corporation, based on data in their annual reports. The estimate is given by the expression $6257\sqrt[3]{x}$, where x is the number of years after 1988. Sometimes this information is best summarized in a table (for example, if you were preparing a report on your findings). You can use the TABLE feature of your calculator to generate a table of values to show what this company's employment is estimated to be for years after 1988. To do so, let x represent the number of years after 1988, set Y1 equal to $1988 + x$, and set Y2 equal to $6257\sqrt[3]{x}$. Then generate the table. Complete the following table using this approach.

x	Year	Number of Employees
1	1989	
2	1990	
3	1991	
4	1992	9932
5	1993	
6	1994	
7	1995	
8	1996	
9	1997	
10	1998	
11	1999	
12	2000	

When we use a mathematical model this way to estimate some future value, we assume that conditions that led to past data will continue in the future. When you think of this model, what assumptions do you think you would have to make in order to use the estimates?

Experiencing Algebra the Group Way

When considering the relationship between radicals and expressions with rational exponents, it was stated that

$$a^{m/n} = \sqrt[n]{a^m} \quad \text{or} \quad \left(\sqrt[n]{a}\right)^m \qquad \text{for any real number } a.$$

In previous exercises, a was usually an integer or a decimal. However, it can also be a fraction. For example,

$$\left(\frac{4}{9}\right)^{5/2} = \left(\sqrt{\frac{4}{9}}\right)^5 = \left(\frac{2}{3}\right)^5 = \frac{32}{243}.$$

Discuss how you would evaluate the following expressions. Then have each member of the group perform the evaluation, using the example as a guide. Compare your results and decide on the correct answers.

1. $\left(\dfrac{9}{16}\right)^{3/2}$ 2. $\left(\dfrac{8}{27}\right)^{4/3}$ 3. $\left(\dfrac{32}{243}\right)^{3/5}$ 4. $\left(\dfrac{36}{49}\right)^{3/2}$ 5. $\left(\dfrac{1}{81}\right)^{5/4}$ 6. $\left(\dfrac{49}{25}\right)^{3/2}$

Remember that a fraction raised to a negative exponent is equivalent to the reciprocal of the fraction raised to the opposite of the negative exponent (that is, a positive exponent). Discuss how you would use this fact to evaluate the following expressions. Have each member of the group evaluate the expressions, and compare your results to decide on the correct answers.

7. $\left(\dfrac{4}{9}\right)^{-3/2}$ **8.** $\left(\dfrac{8}{125}\right)^{-2/3}$ **9.** $\left(\dfrac{1}{32}\right)^{-4/5}$ **10.** $\left(\dfrac{25}{49}\right)^{-3/2}$ **11.** $\left(\dfrac{4}{25}\right)^{-1/2}$ **12.** $\left(\dfrac{27}{8}\right)^{-4/3}$

Experiencing Algebra the Write Way

In the definition of rational exponents,

$$a^{m/n} = \sqrt[n]{a^m} = \left(\sqrt[n]{a}\right)^m,$$

it was stated that n is a positive integer greater than 1.

1. Consider what would happen if $n = 1$. Describe what this would do to the expression $a^{m/n}$, and why this value is excluded from the definition.

2. Next, consider what would happen if $n = 0$. What would this do to the expression $a^{m/n}$, and why is this value excluded from the definition?

3. Explain why we don't need to consider negative integer values for n.

4. Finally, when considering an expression of the form $a^{m/n}$, you should express the exponent $\frac{m}{n}$ in lowest terms. Why?

13.2   Radical Functions and Their Graphs

Objectives

1 Identify radical relations and functions.

2 Determine the domain of radical functions.

3 Create tables of values for radical functions.

4 Graph radical functions using a set of ordered pairs.

5 Model real-world situations using radical functions.

Application The absolute luminosity (brightness) of a main-sequence star (a star similar to our Sun) is proportional to the 3.5 power of its mass. The function $L = M^{3.5}$, where M is the mass of a star, can be used to compare the absolute luminosity L of main-sequence stars.

a. Set up a table of values for stars whose mass is 1, 10, and 100 times the mass of the Sun ($M_\odot$). That is, let $M = 1M_\odot$, $10M_\odot$, and $100M_\odot$.

b. According to the table in part (a), if the mass of a star is 10 times the mass of another star, approximately (to the nearest thousand) how much brighter will it be?

After completing this section, we will discuss this application further. See page 1020.

In the preceding section, we evaluated radical expressions with numerical radicands. However, radical expressions may also have radicands that contain variables, such as $\sqrt{x}$ or $\sqrt[3]{2x + 5}$. The related expressions written with rational exponents are $x^{1/2}$ and $(2x + 5)^{1/3}$.

1 Radical Relations and Functions

In this section we discuss a special type of relation, a **radical relation**. A radical relation equates a radical expression in one independent variable to a dependent variable—for example, $y = \sqrt{x}$ or $y = \sqrt[3]{2x + 5}$. Since a radical expression can be written as an expression with a rational exponent, these relations may also be written as $y = x^{1/2}$ and $y = (2x + 5)^{1/3}$. Some radical relations are also **radical functions** and can be written in function notation, such as $f(x) = \sqrt{x}$ and $f(x) = x^{1/2}$.

> *Radical Function*
> A radical function can be written in the form
>
> $$f(x) = A(x),$$
>
> where $A(x)$ is a radical expression with the variable x in the radicand.

For example, the following are radical functions.

$$f(x) = \sqrt{x + 2} + 5 \qquad s(x) = 5x^{3/5} - 1$$
$$g(x) = 4\sqrt[3]{x + 2} \qquad h(x) = (x + 2)^{3/4}$$

EXAMPLE 1 State whether each function is a radical function.

a. $f(x) = \sqrt{5}x$ **b.** $p(x) = \left(\sqrt{x + 3}\right)^5$ **c.** $m(x) = 6^{1/2}x^2 + 4$

Solution

a. $f(x) = \sqrt{5}x$ is not a radical function, because the radicand does not contain a variable. This is a linear equation.

b. $p(x) = \left(\sqrt{x + 3}\right)^5$ is a radical function, because the radicand contains the independent variable x.

c. $m(x) = 6^{1/2}x^2 + 4$ is not a radical function. When the function is written in the form $m(x) = \sqrt{6}x^2 + 4$, the radicand does not contain a variable. This is a quadratic equation. ∎

Experiencing Algebra the Checkup Way

State whether each function in exercises 1–6 is a radical function.

1. $f(x) = 2\sqrt{x} + 5$ **2.** $y = \sqrt{2x} + 5$ **3.** $g(t) = 4t^{1/3} - 7$

4. $f(b) = 4^{2/3}b - 9$ **5.** $y = (\sqrt[3]{x} + 1)^2$ **6.** $p(x) = (2x + 5)^{4/5}$

7. How does a radical function differ from a polynomial function?

---

2 Determining the Domain of a Radical Function

In Chapter 12, we saw that rational functions had values excluded from their domain. We called such restrictions on the domain **restricted values**. Radical functions may have values restricted from their domains as well. Sometimes, substituting values for the independent variable in a radical expression results in values that are not real numbers. (In this chapter we are concerned with only the real-number system. Another number system is discussed in Chapter 14.) Complete the following set of exercises to determine a method for finding these restricted values.

DISCOVERY 2

Restricted Values

1. Complete the following tables of values for the given radical functions.

a. $f(x) = \sqrt{x}$

x	$f(x)$
-3	
-2	
-1	
0	
1	

b. $g(x) = \sqrt[4]{x + 1}$

x	$g(x)$
-3	
-2	
-1	
0	
1	

c. $h(x) = \sqrt[3]{x}$

x	$h(x)$
-3	
-2	
-1	
0	
1	

d. $j(x) = \sqrt[5]{x + 1}$

x	$j(x)$
-3	
-2	
-1	
0	
1	

2. Determine the restriction on the domain for each function, if possible.

   a.   **b.**

   c.   **d.**

3. The functions in exercises 1a and 1b are defined by even roots. The functions in exercises 1c and 1d are defined by odd roots. Which functions have restricted values?

    Graph the given radical functions with restricted values on a decimal calculator screen. Trace each function's graph.

4. What happens when you reach the point on the graph for the restricted x-values found above?

Continued

Write a rule to determine the restrictions on the domain of a radical function by viewing its table of values.

Write a rule to determine the restrictions on the domain of a radical function by viewing its graph.

Write a rule to determine the restrictions on the domain of a radical function algebraically.

First, the radical functions defined by even roots have restricted values. In viewing a table of values, the numbers restricted from the domain of a radical function are the numbers that result in nonreal numbers when evaluating the radical expression. When we view the function's graph, the restricted values of the function do not have corresponding function values. Since these restricted values occur when the function is evaluated for a nonreal value, and this is when the radicand of an even root is negative, or less than 0, we can determine the restricted values of even roots algebraically by setting the radicand less than 0 and solving for the independent variable.

The corresponding functions defined by expressions with exponents have restrictions on the domain when the rational exponent has an even denominator. This is equivalent to a radical expression with an even index. Therefore, to determine the restricted values algebraically, write an inequality with the base or radicand less than 0 and solve for the independent variable.

We have discovered three methods—numeric, graphic, and algebraic—for determining the restrictions on the domain of a radical function. The numeric and graphic methods have limitations as to their effectiveness. They should be used primarily as a check of the algebraic method.

To determine algebraically the restricted values of a radical function with an even index:

• Set the expression in the radicand less than 0.
• Solve for the independent variable.

This method will find all the restricted values.

To determine numerically on your calculator the restricted integer values of a radical function, set up a table of values.

• Rename the independent variable as x and the dependent variable as y.
• Enter the radical expression in Y1.
• Set up the table of values. Enter the minimum integer value and an increment of 1 (for integer values). Set the calculator to automatically perform the evaluations.
• View the table and move through the table with the up and down arrows.

Restricted integer values are the x-values that result in nonreal values (ERROR in the table). This will only determine integer values.

To determine graphically on your calculator the restricted values of a radical function:

• Enter the equation in Y1.
• Graph the equation.
• Trace the equation using the left and right arrow keys.

The x-values that have no corresponding y-values are restricted values for the radical function. The x-values found by this method will vary according to the window setting of your calculator.

For example, determine the restricted values and then state the domain of the radical function $y = \sqrt[4]{3x}$.

Algebraically	*Numerically*	*Graphically*
$3x < 0$	Y1 = $\sqrt[4]{3x}$	Y1 = $\sqrt[4]{3x}$
$x < 0$		

Numerically:

X	Y1
-3	ERROR
-2	ERROR
-1	ERROR
0	0
1	1.3161
2	1.5651
3	1.7321

X= -3

The function is not defined for *x*-values less than 0.

Graphically: Y1 = $\sqrt[4]{3x}$

(−4.7, 4.7, −3.1, 3.1)

The graph of the function does not exist for *x*-values less than 0.

The restricted values are all real numbers less than 0.
    The domain is all real numbers greater than or equal to 0.

$x \geq 0$ Inequality notation

$[0, \infty)$ Interval notation

Helping Hand If we want to find the domain directly, without going through the separate step of finding the restricted values, we set the radicand ≥ 0 and solve for the independent variable.

EXAMPLE 2   Determine the restricted values algebraically, if they exist, and then state the domain of the given radical functions. Check your answers numerically or graphically.

a. $y = \sqrt[3]{x + 5} + \sqrt[3]{x - 8}$ **b.** $f(x) = \sqrt{x + 5} + \sqrt{x - 8}$

c. $y = (x - 7)^{2/5}$ **d.** $g(x) = (3x + 4)^{3/4}$

Solution

a. $y = \sqrt[3]{x + 5} + \sqrt[3]{x - 8}$
    There are no restricted values, because the index of the radical, 3, is odd.

    Domain: All real numbers
            $(-\infty, \infty)$

Since there are no restricted values, check graphically.
    The graph appears to be continuous and has no "holes" for restricted values.

Y1 = $\sqrt[3]{x + 5} + \sqrt[3]{x - 8}$

(−47, 47, −31, 31)

b. $f(x) = \sqrt{x + 5} + \sqrt{x - 8}$

There are restricted values because the index of the radical expressions, 2, is even. To determine the restricted values, set both of the radicands less than 0 and solve for x.

$$x + 5 < 0 \qquad \text{or} \qquad x - 8 < 0$$
$$x < -5 \qquad\qquad\qquad x < 8$$

According to these inequalities, the restricted values are all real numbers less than -5 or all real numbers less than 8. The restricted values are all real numbers less than 8 since this restriction covers both inequalities.

Domain: All real numbers greater than or equal to 8
$$x \geq 8$$
$$[8, \infty)$$

Check numerically. Let Y1 $= \sqrt{x + 5} + \sqrt{x - 8}$.

X	Y1	
0	ERROR	
1	ERROR	
2	ERROR	
3	ERROR	
4	ERROR	
5	ERROR	
6	ERROR	
X=0		

X	Y1	
6	ERROR	
7	ERROR	
8	3.6056	
9	4.7417	
10	5.2872	
11	5.7321	
12	6.1231	
X=12		

The table shows that restricted integer values are less than 8.

c. $y = (x - 7)^{2/5}$

There are no restricted values because the denominator of the rational exponent, 5, is odd.

Domain: All real numbers
$$(-\infty, \infty)$$

Since there are no restricted values, check graphically.
 The graph appears to be continuous and has no "holes" for restricted values.

Y1 $= (x - 7)^{2/5}$

$(-47, 47, -31, 31)$

d. $g(x) = (3x + 4)^{3/4}$

There are restricted values because the denominator of the rational exponent is even. To determine the restricted values, set the base of the expression less than 0 and solve for x.

$$3x + 4 < 0$$
$$x < -\frac{4}{3}$$

The restricted values are all real numbers less than $-\frac{4}{3}$.

Domain: All real numbers greater than or equal to $-\frac{4}{3}$
$$x \geq -\frac{4}{3}$$
$$\left[-\frac{4}{3}, \infty\right)$$

X	Y₁	
-1.6	ERROR	
-1.5	ERROR	
-1.4	ERROR	
-1.3	.17783	
-1.2	.50297	
-1.1	.76529	
-1	1	

X= -1

Since the restricted values are less than a fraction, check numerically by selecting x-values close to $-\frac{4}{3}$. This will not be an exact check.

In viewing the table, x-values less than -1.333 or $-\frac{4}{3}$ are restricted. It appears that the restricted values are $x < -1.333$. ∎

✔ Experiencing Algebra the Checkup Way

In exercises 1–4, determine the restricted values and then state the domain of the given functions.

1. $y = (x + 2)^{2/3}$ **2.** $y = (x + 2)^{1/2}$ **3.** $g(x) = \sqrt{x + 1} + \sqrt{x - 3}$ **4.** $f(x) = (2x - 8)^{3/4}$

5. What values must be restricted from the domain of a radical function?

6. When will a radical function have restrictions on its domain?

7. When you graph a radical function on your calculator, how can you tell whether there are restrictions on its domain?

---

3 Creating a Table of Values

Now that we can determine the domain of a radical function, we want to evaluate the function for values in its domain. In order to do this, we set up an extended table of values. For example, evaluate $y = 2\sqrt{3x + 10}$ for three values in its domain.

Set up a table of values. Choose any permissible value for x, the independent variable, and obtain a value for y, the dependent variable, by evaluating the right side. The domain of the function is the set of all real numbers greater than or equal to $-\frac{10}{3}$. Therefore, we choose to use the integers $-3, -2,$ and -1 for x-values.

x	$y = 2\sqrt{3x + 10}$	y
-3	$y = 2\sqrt{3(-3) + 10}$ $y = 2\sqrt{1}$ $y = 2$	2
-2	$y = 2\sqrt{3(-2) + 10}$ $y = 2\sqrt{4}$ $y = 4$	4
-1	$y = 2\sqrt{3(-1) + 10}$ $y = 2\sqrt{7}$ $y \approx 5.2915$	5.2915

X	Y₁	
-3	2	
-2	4	
-1	5.2915	
0	6.3246	
1	7.2111	
2	8	
3	8.7178	

X= -3

Y1 = 2√3x + 10

Figure 13.4

Therefore, $(-3, 2)$, $(-2, 4)$, and $(-1, 5.2915)$ are three ordered-pair solutions for the radical function.

On your calculator, evaluate $y = 2\sqrt{3x + 10}$. The Auto mode for TBLSET is shown in Figure 13.4.

EXAMPLE 3 Evaluate each function for the three given x-values.

a. $y = -3x^{3/4}$ for $x = 0, 1, 2$

b. $m(x) = \sqrt[3]{2x - 9}$ for $x = -1, 0, 1$

c. $y = 5(x + 1)^{2/3}$ for $x = -1, 0, 1$

Solution

a.

x	$y = -3x^{3/4}$	y
0	$y = -3(0)^{3/4}$ $y = -3(0)$ $y = 0$	0
1	$y = -3(1)^{3/4}$ $y = -3(1)$ $y = -3$	-3
2	$y = -3(2)^{3/4}$ $y = -3(\sqrt[4]{2})^3$ $y \approx -5.045$	-5.045

Therefore, $(0, 0)$, $(1, -3)$, and $(2, -5.045)$ are three solutions.

b.

x	$m(x) = \sqrt[3]{2x - 9}$	$m(x)$
-1	$m(-1) = \sqrt[3]{2(-1) - 9}$ $m(-1) = \sqrt[3]{-11}$ $m(-1) \approx -2.224$	-2.224
0	$m(0) = \sqrt[3]{2(0) - 9}$ $m(0) = \sqrt[3]{-9}$ $m(0) \approx -2.08$	-2.08
1	$m(1) = \sqrt[3]{2(1) - 9}$ $m(1) = \sqrt[3]{-7}$ $m(1) \approx -1.913$	-1.913

Therefore, $(-1, -2.224)$, $(0, -2.08)$, and $(1, -1.913)$ are three solutions.

c.

x	$y = 5(x + 1)^{2/3}$	y
-1	$y = 5(x + 1)^{2/3}$ $y = 5(-1 + 1)^{2/3}$ $y = 0$	0
0	$y = 5(x + 1)^{2/3}$ $y = 5(0 + 1)^{2/3}$ $y = 5$	5
1	$y = 5(x + 1)^{2/3}$ $y = 5(1 + 1)^{2/3}$ $y \approx 7.937$	7.937

Therefore, $(-1, 0)$, $(0, 5)$, and $(1, 7.937)$ are three solutions.

Calculator Solution

The Auto mode for TBLSET is used to generate the following tables. The ASK mode could have been used.

a.

X	Y1
0	0
1	-3
2	-5.045
3	-6.839
4	-8.485
5	-10.03
6	-11.5

X=6

$Y1 = -3x^{3/4}$

b.

X	Y1
-1	-2.224
0	-2.08
1	-1.913
2	-1.71
3	-1.442
4	-1
5	1

X=-1

$Y1 = \sqrt[3]{2x - 9}$

c.

X	Y1
-1	0
0	5
1	7.937
2	10.4
3	12.599
4	14.62
5	16.51

X=-1

$Y1 = 5(x + 1)^{2/3}$

■

✓ Experiencing Algebra the Checkup Way

In exercises 1–4, evaluate each function for the given values.

1. $y = -3\sqrt{2x + 7}$ for $x = -3, -1, 1, 3$

2. $g(x) = \dfrac{2}{3}x^{3/4}$ for $x = -1, 0, 1, 4, 16$

3. $b = \sqrt[4]{8a + 1}$ for $a = 0, 5, 10$

4. $y = 3(x - 1)^{4/5}$ for $x = -31, 0, 1, 33$

5. When setting up a table of values for a radical function, how can you choose values to use for the independent variable?

---

4 Graphing Radical Functions

Radical functions have an infinite number of possible solutions. We use a graph to illustrate these solutions. As with any function, to graph a radical function we determine the domain and then use these values to plot ordered-pair solutions. We need to determine enough ordered pairs so that we can see the pattern. This may be a very lengthy process by hand.

To graph a radical function:

- Determine the restricted values of the domain.
- Determine a table of values by choosing enough *x*-values in the domain to see a pattern. Pay close attention to the *x*-values close to the restricted values.
- Graph the function by plotting the sample set of ordered pairs from the table of values and connecting the points with a smooth curve determined by the pattern seen. Be careful not to cross the vertical line where *x* is equal to a restricted value, because the restricted values do not have corresponding function values.

Note: The calculator TABLE function in Ask mode will set up this table.

To graph a radical function on your calculator:

- Enter the equation in Y1.
- Choose an appropriate viewing screen (integer, decimal, standard, or set your own values) and graph.

• Determine individual solutions. Trace and move the cursor using the left and right arrow keys.

Helping Hand The calculator window setting is very important to the picture you receive. You should carefully consider your choices.

For example, graph the radical function $y = 2\sqrt{3x + 10}$.

Complete a table of values by choosing x-values in the domain, which is the set of all real numbers greater than or equal to $-\frac{10}{3}$.

x	y
$-\dfrac{10}{3}$	0
-3.2	1.2649
-3.1	1.6733
-3	2
-2	4
-1	5.2915
0	6.3246
1	7.2111
2	8
3	8.7178

Graph the ordered pairs found in the table of values, connecting the points with a smooth curve.

$Y1 = 2\sqrt{3x + 10}$

$(-47, 47, -31, 31)$

Figure 13.5

Use your calculator to graph the radical function $y = 2\sqrt{3x + 10}$, as shown in Figure 13.5. ■

EXAMPLE 4 Graph each radical function.

a. $y = -3x^{3/4}$ **b.** $m(x) = \sqrt[3]{2x - 9}$ **c.** $y = 5(x + 1)^{2/3}$

Solution

a. $y = -3x^{3/4}$

Set up a table of values using x-values in the domain, which is the set of all real numbers greater than or equal to 0.

x	y
0	0
0.1	-0.5335
0.5	-1.784
1	-3
2	-5.045
3	-6.839
4	-8.485
5	-10.03
6	-11.5
7	-12.91

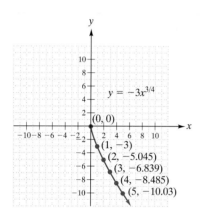

Graph the ordered pairs found in the table of values and connect the points with a smooth curve.

b. $m(x) = \sqrt[3]{2x - 9}$

Set up a table of values using x-values in the domain, which is the set of all real numbers.

x	y
-2	-2.351
-1	-2.224
0	-2.08
1	-1.913
2	-1.71
3	-1.442
4	-1
5	1
6	1.4422
7	1.71
8	1.9129

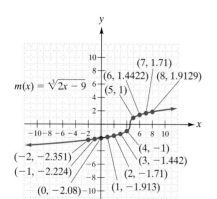

Graph the ordered pairs found in the table of values and connect the points with a smooth curve.

c. $y = 5(x + 1)^{2/3}$

Set up a table of values using x-values in the domain, the set of all real numbers.

x	y
-3	7.937
-2	5
-1	0
0	5
1	7.937
2	10.4

Graph the ordered pairs found in the table of values and connect the points with a smooth curve.

Calculator Solution

a.

$(-47, 47, -31, 31)$

b.

$(-47, 47, -31, 31)$

c.

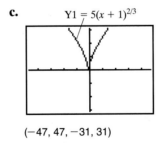

$(-47, 47, -31, 31)$ ∎

  Experiencing Algebra the Checkup Way

In exercises 1–4, graph each radical function.

1. $y = 2\sqrt{x} + 2$ 　　　**2.** $f(x) = \sqrt{2x - 3}$ 　　　**3.** $y = -2x^{3/4}$ 　　　**4.** $y = 3x^{2/3}$

5. Describe the procedure you would follow to graph a radical function with pencil and paper. What would you do differently if the function has restrictions on its domain?

5 Modeling the Real World

We have seen that many geometric formulas can give rise to radical functions, such as determining the dimensions of a square or a cube given its area or volume, respectively. Often a graph of the radical function makes it easier for us to determine other values of the dimensions, given different initial data.

EXAMPLE 5   The formula for the length of the side of a square is $s = A^{1/2}$, where A is the area of the square.

   a. Set up a table of values for the A-values 0, 4, 9, and 16.
   b. Graph on your calculator, using the integer window, and check the solutions found in part (a).
   c. Use the graph to determine the length of a side of a square if the area is 12 square feet.

Solution

b.

Y1 $= x^{1/2}$

(4, 2)
(9, 3)
(0, 0)
(16, 4)

$(-47, 47, -31, 31)$

a.

A	s
0	0
4	2
9	3
16	4

c.

Y1 $= x^{1/2}$

X=12   Y=3.4641016

$(-47, 47, -31, 31)$

b. Let $x = A$ and $y = s$. Then $y = x^{1/2}$. Let Y1 $= x^{1/2}$ and graph.
   Trace the graph to determine the ordered pairs found in part (a).
c. To determine the length of a side given the area, trace the graph to determine the y-coordinate (length of side) that corresponds to the x-coordinate (area) when $x = 12$.
   The approximate length of a side of a square when the area is 12 square feet is 3.464 feet.   ■

Application   The absolute luminosity (brightness) of a main-sequence star (a star similar to our Sun) is proportional to the 3.5 power of its mass. The function $L = M^{3.5}$, where M is the mass of a star, can be used to compare the absolute luminosity L of main-sequence stars.

   a. Set up a table of values for stars whose mass is 1, 10, and 100 times the mass of the Sun ($M_\odot$). That is, let $M = 1M_\odot, 10M_\odot$, and $100M_\odot$.
   b. According to the table in part (a), if the mass of a star is 10 times the mass of another star, approximately (to the nearest thousand) how much brighter will it be?

Discussion

X	Y1
1	1
10	3162.3
100	1E7

X=

a. Let Y1 $= x^{3.5}$ and use the Ask mode of TblSet to generate the table of values.
b. In comparing the absolute luminosity for two stars of mass $M = 1M_\odot$ and $M = 10M_\odot$, the second star has 10 times more mass than the first. The second star's brightness has increased from 1 to 3162, or to approximately 3000 times as bright as the first star.
   When we compare $M = 10M_\odot$ and $M = 100M_\odot$ (the mass increased 10 times), the luminosity increases from 3162 to 10,000,000. The brightness increases $\frac{10,000,000}{3162} \approx 3162$, or approximately 3000 times.   ■

Experiencing Algebra the Checkup Way

1. The radius of a circle is a function of its area A,

$$r = \left(\frac{A}{\pi}\right)^{1/2}.$$

   a. Set up a table of values with A equal to integer values from 1 to 10.

   b. Graph and check your solutions from part (a).

   c. Determine the radius of a circle whose area is 8.5 square feet.

2. Graph the function $L = M^{3.5}$, used to compare the absolute luminosity L of a main-sequence star whose mass is $M_\odot$. Use a calculator window of (0, 94, 0, 620,000). Trace the graph to find the absolute luminosity of stars with masses of 1, 4, 16, and 64 times the mass of the Sun. Use these numbers to determine how the absolute brightness of a main-sequence star changes as the mass increases by a factor of 4.

PROBLEM SET 13.2

Experiencing Algebra the Exercise Way

Identify each function as radical or nonradical.

1. $y = \sqrt{5x + 7}$
2. $f(x) = 5\sqrt{4x - 7} + 8$
3. $f(x) = 2\sqrt{3x + 1} - 5$
4. $f(b) = (2b + 5)^{2/3}$
5. $y = 5\sqrt[3]{x} - 7$
6. $g(x) = 2\sqrt{x} + 17$
7. $y = (3x - 5)^{4/5}$
8. $h(x) = 9 + 2^{1/3}x$
9. $g(x) = 7^{1/2}x + 5$
10. $y = 13 - \sqrt{7x}$

Determine the restricted values and then state the domain of each function.

11. $y = \sqrt{x - 3}$
12. $y = 5 + 4\sqrt{x}$
13. $y = \sqrt[3]{x - 3}$
14. $f(x) = (5 - 4x)^{3/4}$
15. $f(x) = (7 - 2x)^{2/3}$
16. $g(x) = (5 - 4x)^{2/3}$
17. $h(x) = (7 - 2x)^{3/4}$
18. $y = \sqrt{3x - 1} - \sqrt{x + 2}$
19. $y = 2\sqrt{x} + 3$
20. $y = 2 + \sqrt[3]{3x + 5}$
21. $y = \sqrt{2x + 1} - \sqrt{x - 3}$
22. $f(x) = 2 + \sqrt{3x + 5}$
23. $y = \left(\sqrt[3]{5x + 9}\right)^4$
24. $y = \left(\sqrt[5]{3 - 4x}\right)^2$
25. $y = \left(\sqrt[4]{3x + 2}\right)^5$
26. $y = \left(\sqrt{7x - 5}\right)^3$

Evaluate each function using four values from the domain.

27. $x = \sqrt{x + 7}$
28. $y = 3\sqrt{4 - x}$
29. $f(x) = \sqrt[3]{5x + 21}$
30. $g(x) = 2 - 5\sqrt{x + 1}$
31. $y = 1 + 6\sqrt{x - 9}$
32. $y = \sqrt[3]{x} + 3$
33. $h(x) = 2\sqrt{2 - 3x}$
34. $f(x) = \sqrt{2x + 1}$
35. $g(x) = \sqrt{2x - 1} + 2$
36. $y = 9 - 4\sqrt{x}$
37. $y = 5(x + 2)^{2/3}$
38. $y = -2(x - 2)^{2/3}$
39. $y = -2(x - 1)^{3/2}$
40. $y = 4(x + 1)^{3/2}$

Graph the functions in exercises 41–58.

41. $y = \sqrt{x}$
42. $y = 3\sqrt{x}$
43. $y = \sqrt[3]{x} - 10$
44. $y = 2\sqrt[3]{x} + 5$
45. $y = 5\sqrt{x} + 10$
46. $y = 6 - 3\sqrt{x}$
47. $f(x) = \sqrt{x - 5}$
48. $h(x) = \sqrt{2x + 5}$
49. $g(x) = \sqrt[3]{8x}$
50. $p(x) = -\sqrt[3]{4x}$
51. $y = 5 - x^{3/2}$
52. $y = x^{3/2} + 2$
53. $y = x^{3/4} + 2$
54. $y = 2 - x^{3/4}$
55. $y = 3 - x^{2/3}$
56. $y = x^{2/3} - 3$
57. $y = x^{4/5} + 1$
58. $y = x^{2/5} + 1$

59. Find the lengths of the sides of a series of squares with an area starting at 10 square feet, increasing by 10 square feet, up to a maximum area of 100 square feet.

60. Find the radii of a series of circles with areas beginning at 10 square feet, increasing by 10 square feet, up to a maximum area of 100 square feet.

61. In statistical analyses, data are often summarized in tables called frequency tables. When designing such a table, rules of thumb are used to decide on the number of rows in the table. One such rule is that r, the number of rows in the table, should be equal to the square root of n, the number of pieces of data collected. Graph this relation for values of n ranging from 0 to 400. How many rows should you have in a frequency table for 250 pieces of data?

62. In statistics, if a set of data consists of the integers from 1 to n, the variability of the numbers is given by

$$s = \sqrt{\frac{n(n + 1)}{12}}$$

Graph this relation for values of n ranging from 1 to 250. What is the variability of the integers from 1 to 150?

63. Claims adjusters and highway patrol officers use the lengths of skid marks to determine the speed of a vehicle involved in an accident. The velocity, V, in miles per hour is estimated as $V = \sqrt{12S}$, where S is the length of the skid mark in feet, and the coefficient of friction of the road is assumed to be 40%. Graph this function for values of the domain between 0 and 300 feet. If a car leaves a skid mark that is 250 feet long, what would you estimate the speed of the car to be?

64. If the coefficient of friction on a road is 35%, the velocity, V, in miles per hour of a car that leaves a skid mark of S feet is given by the mathematical model $V = \sqrt{10.5S}$. Graph this function for values of the domain between 0 and 300 feet. If a car leaves a skid mark that is 200 feet long, what would you estimate the speed of the car to be?

 Experiencing Algebra the Calculator Way

When you graph a radical function expressed in the form of an expression with a rational exponent, you must be sure that the calculator displays the complete graph. Some calculators show only a portion of the graph. The TI-83 calculator will display the complete graph, but earlier versions may not. However, you may be able to obtain the complete graph with minor adjustments when entering the function. To explore this further, graph each of the following equations using an integer or decimal window.

1. $y = x^{4/5}$ **2.** $y = \left(x^{1/5}\right)^4$ **3.** $y = \left(x^4\right)^{1/5}$

4. $y = \left(\sqrt[5]{x}\right)^4$ **5.** $y = \sqrt[5]{x^4}$

With some calculators, the first graph appears only in the first quadrant of your screen, while the other graphs appear in both the first and second quadrants of the screen. If you were to construct a table of values for exercise 1 and graph it on the coordinate plane, you would see that the graph should appear in both the first and second quadrants of the screen. If the calculator does not display this complete graph, it is an erroneous graph. The graphs of exercises 2, 3, 4, and 5 should appear correctly on the calculator.

This illustrates that when you enter a function with a fractional exponent into the calculator, if your calculator has this peculiarity, you must separate the numerator and the denominator of the fractional exponent into two exponents. It does not matter which one you place inside the grouping symbol and which outside.

Also, you know that the radical expressions in exercises 4 and 5 are equivalent to the expression with a rational exponent in exercise 1. This offers you two additional ways to store expressions in your calculator to obtain the correct graph. This problem does not occur if the denominator of the fractional exponent is an even number.

Experiencing Algebra the Group Way

In the study of physics, kinetic energy is defined as the capability for performing work as a result of the motion of a body. One means to calculate kinetic energy, E_k, is the formula $E_k = \frac{1}{2}\left(\frac{W}{g}\right)v^2$, where W is the weight of the object, g is the acceleration due to gravity, and v is the velocity of the object. If the kinetic energy is specified, the formula can be solved for the velocity needed to obtain the desired level of energy, $v = \sqrt{\frac{2gE_k}{W}}$. Kinetic energy can be measured in terms of the number of foot-pounds of work done. One foot-pound of work is equivalent to the energy required to move an object weighing 1 pound a distance of 1 foot.

Suppose we have a 3200-pound automobile, the acceleration due to gravity is 32 ft/sec², and the kinetic energy is given in the following table. How would you calculate the speed of the automobile required to achieve the level of kinetic energy given? Discuss how you could use the TABLE feature of your calculator to complete the table. Then have each member of your group complete the table. Compare your results and agree on the correct values.

E_k, ft-lbs	310,000	320,000	330,000	340,000	350,000
v, ft/sec					

E_k, ft-lbs	360,000	370,000	380,000	390,000	400,000
v, ft/sec					

A speed of 60 miles per hour is equivalent to a speed of 88 feet per second. Which level of kinetic energy in the table would require a speed close to 60 miles per hour?

Many applications in the physical sciences involve mathematical models containing radical expressions. It is important that you understand how to work with these expressions for later uses.

Experiencing Algebra the Write Way

For certain values of x, $\sqrt{x^2} = x$, and for certain other values of x, $\sqrt{x^2} = -x$. Identify the values of x that make each statement true. Then explain how you determined your answer.

13.3 Properties of Rational Exponents

Objectives
1. Evaluate exponential expressions with rational exponents using properties of exponents.
2. Simplify exponential expressions with rational exponents using properties of exponents.
3. Model real-world situations using exponential expressions containing rational exponents.

Application

The Stefan-Boltzmann law states that the temperature of a star is equal to the expression $\left(\frac{F}{\sigma}\right)^{1/4}$ where F is the energy flux (amount of energy that leaves the surface) of the star and the Greek letter σ (pronounced *sigma*) is a constant. Write an expression for the total temperature of two stars if one star's energy flux is twice the other.

After completing this section, we will discuss this application further. See page 1028.

---

1 Evaluating Rational Exponents

The properties of exponents that we used earlier with integer exponents also apply to rational exponents. Let's review these.

> *Properties of Rational Exponents*
>
> $$a^{-n} = \frac{1}{a^n}$$ Definition of a negative exponent
>
> $$\frac{1}{a^{-n}} = a^n$$ Definition of a negative exponent
>
> $$a^m \cdot a^n = a^{m+n}$$ Product rule
>
> $$\frac{a^m}{a^n} = a^{m-n}$$ Quotient rule
>
> $$\left(a^m\right)^n = a^{mn}$$ Power-to-a-power rule
>
> $$(ab)^m = a^m b^m$$ Product-to-a-power rule
>
> $$\left(\frac{a}{b}\right)^m = \frac{a^m}{b^m}$$ Quotient-to-a-power rule
>
> $$\left(\frac{a}{b}\right)^{-m} = \left(\frac{b}{a}\right)^m$$ Quotient-to-a-negative-power rule
>
> In these expressions, a and b are nonzero real expressions for which both sides of the equation represent real numbers and m and n are rational expressions.

For example, evaluate the expression $\left(7^4\right)^{1/2}$ using the properties of exponents.

$$\left(7^4\right)^{1/2} = 7^{4 \cdot 1/2} = 7^2 = 49 \quad \text{Power-to-a-power rule}$$

EXAMPLE 1 Use the properties of exponents to evaluate. Check using your calculator.

a. $25^{3/4} \cdot 25^{-1/4}$ **b.** $\dfrac{16^{3/8}}{16^{1/8}}$ **c.** $2^{1/2} \cdot 8^{1/2}$

d. $\left(\dfrac{3^5}{2^{10}}\right)^{-2/5}$

Solution

a. $25^{3/4} \cdot 25^{-1/4} = 25^{3/4 + (-1/4)} = 25^{1/2} = 5$ Product rule

b. $\dfrac{16^{3/8}}{16^{1/8}} = 16^{3/8 - 1/8} = 16^{1/4} = 2$ Quotient rule

c. $2^{1/2} \cdot 8^{1/2} = (2 \cdot 8)^{1/2} = 16^{1/2} = 4$ Product-to-a-power rule

d. $\left(\dfrac{3^5}{2^{10}} \right)^{-2/5} = \dfrac{3^{5(-2/5)}}{2^{10(-2/5)}} = \dfrac{3^{-2}}{2^{-4}}$ Quotient-to-a-power rule

$\qquad\qquad\quad = \dfrac{2^4}{3^2} = \dfrac{16}{9}$ Definition of a negative exponent

A second way to evaluate this expression is to use the quotient-to-a-negative-power rule first, and then use the quotient-to-a-power rule.

$$\left(\frac{3^5}{2^{10}} \right)^{-2/5} = \left(\frac{2^{10}}{3^5} \right)^{2/5} = \frac{2^{10(2/5)}}{3^{5(2/5)}} = \frac{2^4}{3^2} = \frac{16}{9}$$

To check on your calculator, carefully enter the expressions into the calculator. Remember to enclose the rational exponents in parentheses.

```
25^(3/4)*25^(-1/
4)
                5
16^(3/8)/16^(1/8
)
                2
```

```
2^(1/2)*8^(1/2)
                4
(3^5/2^10)^(-2/5
)▶Frac
             16/9
```

Experiencing Algebra the Checkup Way

Use the properties of exponents to evaluate exercises 1–4. Check using your calculator.

1. $36^{5/6} \cdot 36^{-1/3}$ **2.** $\dfrac{8^{7/12}}{8^{1/4}}$ **3.** $3^{1/3} \cdot 9^{1/3}$ **4.** $\left(\dfrac{5^2}{3^4} \right)^{-3/2}$

5. Explain the difference between an integer exponent and a rational exponent. Give examples of each.

---

2   Simplifying Expressions with Rational Exponents

To simplify an exponential expression with a rational exponent and a variable base, we use the same rules we used for evaluating an exponential expression with a numerical base.

However, suppose we are evaluating an expression whose exponent has an even-numbered denominator, such as $x^{1/2}$. We must be sure that the variable represents only nonnegative numbers, because an even root is not defined for a negative number.

Similarly, suppose we are evaluating an expression whose exponent is negative, such as $x^{-1/3}$. We must be sure that the variable represents only nonzero numbers, because we rewrite negative exponents as the reciprocal of the base and a positive power, $\left(\frac{1}{x} \right)^{1/3}$. If the variable x is zero, the reciprocal $\frac{1}{x}$ is undefined.

In this text, we will assume the variable base does not represent values for which the expression is undefined.

EXAMPLE 2 Simplify using the properties of exponents. Write each result with positive exponents.

a. $x^{1/2}x^{-1/4}$ **b.** $\dfrac{y^{5/8}}{y^{1/4}}$ **c.** $(xy)^{3/4}$ **d.** $\left(\dfrac{x}{y}\right)^{-2/3}$

Solution

a. $x^{1/2}x^{-1/4} = x^{1/2+(-1/4)} = x^{1/4}$ Product rule

b. $\dfrac{y^{5/8}}{y^{1/4}} = y^{5/8-1/4} = y^{3/8}$ Quotient rule

c. $(xy)^{3/4} = x^{3/4}y^{3/4}$ Product-to-a-power rule

d. $\left(\dfrac{x}{y}\right)^{-2/3} = \dfrac{x^{-2/3}}{y^{-2/3}}$ Quotient-to-a-power rule

        $= \dfrac{y^{2/3}}{x^{2/3}}$ Definition of a negative exponent

A second way to evaluate this expression is to use the quotient-to-a-negative-power rule first, and then use the quotient-to-a-power rule.

$$\left(\frac{x}{y}\right)^{-2/3} = \left(\frac{y}{x}\right)^{2/3} = \frac{y^{2/3}}{x^{2/3}} \quad \blacksquare$$

Using combinations of the properties of exponents allows us to simplify more complicated expressions. For example, simplify the expression $(25x^4y^3)^{1/2}$ using the properties of exponents.

$$(25x^4y^3)^{1/2} = 25^{1/2}(x^4)^{1/2}(y^3)^{1/2} \quad \text{Product-to-a-power rule}$$
$$= 25^{1/2}x^{4\cdot1/2}y^{3\cdot1/2} \quad \text{Power-to-a-power rule}$$
$$= 5x^2y^{3/2}$$

When we combine the properties of exponents, we may simplify the expression in different orders of steps and still obtain the correct results. Therefore, do not be concerned if you apply the properties of exponents in a different order from what you see in the examples, as long as you obtain the same results.

EXAMPLE 3 Simplify. Write the result using positive exponents.

a. $(2x^{3/4}y)(3x^{2/3}y^{5/8})$ **b.** $\left(\dfrac{5x^{1/10}}{x^{-2/5}}\right)^5$ **c.** $n^{1/3}(n^{2/3} + n^{3/4})$

Solution

a. $(2x^{3/4}y)(3x^{2/3}y^{5/8}) = (2\cdot3)x^{3/4+2/3}y^{1+5/8}$ Product rule

                       $= 6x^{17/12}y^{13/8}$

b. $\left(\dfrac{5x^{1/10}}{x^{-2/5}}\right)^5 = \dfrac{(5x^{1/10})^5}{(x^{-2/5})^5}$ Quotient-to-a-power rule

         $= \dfrac{5^5x^{(1/10)5}}{x^{(-2/5)5}}$ Product-to-a-power rule, power-to-a-power rule

         $= \dfrac{5^5x^{1/2}}{x^{-2}}$

$$= 5^5 x^{1/2-(-2)} \qquad \text{Quotient rule}$$

$$= 5^5 x^{5/2} \quad \text{or} \quad 3125 x^{5/2}$$

c. $n^{1/3}(n^{2/3} + n^{3/4}) = n^{1/3+2/3} + n^{1/3+3/4} \qquad \text{Product rule}$

$$= n + n^{13/12} \qquad\qquad\qquad\qquad \blacksquare$$

Experiencing Algebra the Checkup Way

Simplify exercises 1–7. Write the results using positive exponents.

1. $(x^9)^{1/3}$

2. $x^{1/3} \cdot x^{-1/6}$

3. $\dfrac{z^{2/3}}{z^{1/6}}$

4. $\left(\dfrac{p}{q}\right)^{-3/5}$

5. $(4a^2 b^3)^{1/2}$

6. $\left(\dfrac{8x^{2/3}}{4x^{-2/3}}\right)^3$

7. $a^{1/2}(a^{1/4} - a^{2/3})$

8. In the expression $x^{3/4}$, what restrictions are placed on values of x because of the even denominator in the exponent?

9. In the expression $x^{-2/3}$, what restrictions are placed on the values of x because of the negative exponent?

10. Explain why it is important to be aware of restrictions on the base of an expression with rational exponents whenever conditions such as those illustrated in exercises 8 and 9 are present.

---

3 Modeling the Real World

In our daily lives we often need to increase or decrease the size of objects in the shape of geometric figures. For instance, we might want to increase the size of a room or decrease the size of a fenced area for a pet. We may know the desired area and must determine the dimensions. We usually need to evaluate exponential expressions in order to determine these lengths.

EXAMPLE 4 The formula $s = A^{1/2}$ is used to determine the length of the side of a square given the area A.

a. If the area of a square doubles, how is the length of a side affected? (The ratio of the areas is 2 to 1. What is the ratio of the new side to the original side?)

b. If the area of a square triples, how is the length of a side affected? (The ratio of the areas is 3 to 1. What is the ratio of the new side to the original side?)

c. If the area of a square is multiplied by a factor of 4, determine the ratio of the length of a new side to the length of the original side.

Solution

a. Let $A = $ the original area of a square
$s_1 = $ the length of the original side
Then $2A = $ the area of the new square (the area doubled)
$s_2 = $ the length of the new side

Using the formula $s = A^{1/2}$, we have

$s_1 = A^{1/2}$ for the original side.

$s_2 = (2A)^{1/2} = 2^{1/2} A^{1/2}$ for the new side.

The ratio of the new side to the original side is

$$\frac{s_2}{s_1} = \frac{2^{1/2} A^{1/2}}{A^{1/2}} = \frac{2^{1/2}}{1},$$

or approximately $\frac{1.414}{1}$, when the ratio of the new area to the original area is $\frac{2}{1}$.

b. Let $A =$ the original area of a square
$s_1 =$ the length of the original side
Then $3A =$ the area of the new square (the area tripled)
$s_3 =$ the length of the new side

Using the formula $s = A^{1/2}$, we have

$$s_1 = A^{1/2} \quad \text{for the original side.}$$

$$s_3 = (3A)^{1/2} = 3^{1/2}A^{1/2} \quad \text{for the new side.}$$

The ratio of the new side to the original side is

$$\frac{s_3}{s_1} = \frac{3^{1/2}A^{1/2}}{A^{1/2}} = \frac{3^{1/2}}{1},$$

or approximately $\frac{1.732}{1}$, when the ratio of the new area to the original area is $\frac{3}{1}$.

c. In part (a), when the ratio of the areas is $\frac{2}{1}$, the ratio of the lengths of the sides is $\frac{2^{1/2}}{1}$, or $\frac{1.414}{1}$. In part (b), when the ratio of the areas is $\frac{3}{1}$, the ratio of the lengths of the sides is $\frac{3^{1/2}}{1}$, or $\frac{1.732}{1}$.

Therefore, if the area is increased x times, the ratio of the areas is $\frac{x}{1}$. The ratio of the length of the new side to the length of the original side is $\frac{x^{1/2}}{1}$. The ratio of the length of the new side to the length of the original side when the ratio of the areas is $\frac{4}{1}$ is $\frac{4^{1/2}}{1}$ or $\frac{2}{1}$. ∎

Application The Stefan-Boltzmann law states that the temperature of a star is equal to the expression $\left(\frac{F}{\sigma}\right)^{1/4}$, where F is the energy flux (amount of energy that leaves the surface) of the star and the Greek letter σ (pronounced *sigma*) is a constant. Write an expression for the total temperature of two stars if one star's energy flux is twice the other.

Discussion

Let $x =$ the amount of energy flux of the first star
$2x =$ the amount of energy flux of the second star

$$\left(\frac{x}{\sigma}\right)^{1/4} = \text{the temperature of the first star}$$

$$\left(\frac{2x}{\sigma}\right)^{1/4} = \text{the temperature of the second star}$$

The total temperature is the sum of the individual temperatures.

$$\left(\frac{x}{\sigma}\right)^{1/4} + \left(\frac{2x}{\sigma}\right)^{1/4} = \frac{x^{1/4}}{\sigma^{1/4}} + \frac{2^{1/4}x^{1/4}}{\sigma^{1/4}} \qquad \text{Quotient-to-a-power rule}$$

$$= \frac{x^{1/4} + 2^{1/4}x^{1/4}}{\sigma^{1/4}} \qquad \text{Add rational expressions.}$$

$$= \frac{x^{1/4}(1 + 2^{1/4})}{\sigma^{1/4}} \qquad \text{Factor the numerator.}$$

$$= \left(1 + 2^{1/4}\right) \frac{x^{1/4}}{\sigma^{1/4}} \qquad \text{Rewrite product as factors.}$$

$$= \left(1 + 2^{1/4}\right)\left(\frac{x}{\sigma}\right)^{1/4} \qquad \text{Quotient-to-a-power rule}$$

$$\approx 2.189\left(\frac{x}{\sigma}\right)^{1/4} \qquad \text{Evaluate.}$$

The total temperature of the two stars is approximately $2.189\left(\frac{x}{\sigma}\right)^{1/4}$, or about 2.189 times the temperature of the first star. ∎

Experiencing Algebra the Checkup Way

1. The formula $r = \left(\frac{A}{\pi}\right)^{1/2}$ is used to determine the length of the radius of a circle whose area is A.

   a. If the area of a circle is doubled, how is the radius of the circle affected? (The ratio of the area is 2 to 1; what is the ratio of the new radius to the original radius?)

   b. If the area of the circle is tripled, how is the radius of the circle affected? (The ratio of the area is 3 to 1; what is the ratio of the new radius to the original radius?)

   c. If the area of the circle is multiplied by 4, determine the ratio of the lengths of the radii.

2. A tank of water has an opening near its base. The flow of water from the opening has a velocity (in feet per second) given by the expression $v = (64.4h)^{0.5}$, where h is the height of the water above the opening.

   a. Write an expression for the velocity of the water flow when the height of water in the tank is doubled.

   b. Determine an expression for the difference between the velocities—that is, the velocity of the water flow when its height is doubled less the velocity of the water flow from the original height.

PROBLEM SET 13.3

Experiencing Algebra the Exercise Way

Evaluate using the properties of exponents. Check using a calculator.

1. $9^{-1/2}$ **2.** $81^{-1/4}$ **3.** $\dfrac{1}{8^{-1/3}}$ **4.** $\dfrac{1}{16^{-1/4}}$

5. $27^{1/3} \cdot 27^{4/3}$ **6.** $64^{1/4} \cdot 64^{5/4}$ **7.** $\dfrac{32^{4/5}}{32^{1/5}}$ **8.** $\dfrac{64^{5/6}}{64^{1/3}}$

9. $\left(125^{1/2}\right)^{2/3}$ **10.** $\left(256^{1/3}\right)^{3/4}$ **11.** $3^{1/2} \cdot 12^{1/2}$ **12.** $5^{1/3} \cdot 25^{1/3}$

13. $\left(\dfrac{8}{27}\right)^{1/3}$ **14.** $\left(\dfrac{27}{125}\right)^{2/3}$ **15.** $\left(\dfrac{9}{16}\right)^{-1/2}$ **16.** $\left(\dfrac{81}{16}\right)^{-3/4}$

17. $\left[\left(2^{1/2}\right)\left(8^{1/2}\right)\right]^{-3/2}$ **18.** $\left[\left(2^{1/2}\right)\left(32^{1/2}\right)\right]^{-4/3}$

Simplify. Write the results using positive exponents.

19. $x^{-2/3}$ **20.** $x^{-5/6}$ **21.** $\dfrac{12}{y^{-3/4}}$

22. $\dfrac{2}{y^{-4/7}}$ **23.** $z^{2/3} \cdot z^{3/4}$ **24.** $z^{3/4} \cdot z^{7/8}$

25. $\dfrac{p^{5/6}}{p^{2/3}}$ **26.** $\dfrac{x^{5/9}}{x^{2/3}}$ **27.** $\left(b^{3/4}\right)^{8/9}$

28. $\left(z^{2/5}\right)^{15/16}$

29. $\left(x^2 y\right)^{3/4}$

30. $\left(pq^3\right)^{5/6}$

31. $\left(\dfrac{x^2}{y^3}\right)^{5/6}$

32. $\left(\dfrac{a^4}{b^3}\right)^{7/12}$

33. $\left(\dfrac{a}{b}\right)^{-1/3}$

34. $\left(\dfrac{m}{n}\right)^{-3/4}$

35. $c^{3/5} \cdot c^{-4/5}$

36. $k^{5/7} \cdot k^{-3/7}$

37. $\left(8a^5 b^6\right)^{2/3}$

38. $\left(16c^{8/9} d^2\right)^{3/4}$

39. $\left(5a^{3/4} b^{2/5}\right)\left(2a^{1/3} b^{2/5}\right)$

40. $\left(3x^{1/5} y^{1/3}\right)\left(-2x^{3/5} y^{1/4}\right)$

41. $\left(\dfrac{m^{3/7}}{2m^{-2/7}}\right)^2$

42. $\left(\dfrac{4z^{5/9}}{z^{-2/9}}\right)^3$

43. $\left(3a^{1/3} b^2 c^{1/6}\right)^{-2}\left(2a^{4/3} b^{1/4} c^{5/6}\right)^3$

44. $\left(2x^{4/9} y^{3/4} z\right)^{-3}\left(2x^{2/3} y^{1/4} z^3\right)^2$

45. $x^{1/4}\left(x^{2/3} - x^{4/5}\right)$

46. $z^{2/3}\left(z^{1/4} - z^{1/3}\right)$

47. $2x^{2/5}\left(x^{1/5} + 3y^{2/5}\right)$

48. $5a^{2/7}\left(3a^{1/7} - b^{4/7}\right)$

49. $a^{1/4} b^{1/3}\left(3 - a^{1/2} b^{5/6}\right)$

50. $x^{1/4} y^{3/4}\left(x^{1/2} y^{3/8} - 4\right)$

51. $\left(x^{1/2} - y^{1/2}\right)\left(x^{1/3} + y^{1/3}\right)$

52. $\left(c^{2/3} - d^{2/3}\right)\left(c^{1/2} + d^{1/2}\right)$

53. $\left(x^{1/4} + y^{1/4}\right)\left(x^{1/4} - y^{1/4}\right)$

54. $\left(p^{3/4} - q^{3/4}\right)\left(p^{3/4} + q^{3/4}\right)$

55. $\left(x^2 + y^2\right)\left(x^{1/2} - y^{1/2}\right)$

56. $\left(a^{2/3} + b^{2/3}\right)(a - b)$

57. $\left(x^{1/3} + 2\right)\left(x^{1/3} - 2\right)$

58. $\left(4 - z^{1/4}\right)\left(4 + z^{1/4}\right)$

59. $\left(x^{1/4} + 2\right)^2$

60. $\left(x^{1/3} + 3\right)^2$

61. $\left(x - y^{1/2}\right)^2$

62. $\left(x^{1/2} - y\right)^2$

63. $\left(a^{1/2} + b^{1/2}\right)^2$

64. $\left(c^{1/2} - d^{1/2}\right)^2$

65. The length s of the side of a cube is related to the volume V of the cube by the formula $s = V^{1/3}$. How should you increase the length of a side in order to increase the volume of the cube to eight times its original volume?

66. The length s of the side of a cube is related to the surface area A of the cube by the formula $s = \left(\dfrac{A}{6}\right)^{1/2}$. How should you increase the length of a side in order to increase the surface area of the cube to nine times its original area?

67. The time t (in second) it would take an object to fall to the ground from a distance d (in feet) above the ground is given by the formula $t = \left(\dfrac{d}{16.1}\right)^{1/2}$. If you triple the height from which you drop the object, how does this increase the time it will take the object to fall to the ground? (Hint: Determine the difference of the time at given distances of d and $3d$.)

68. Using the formula from exercise 67, what will be the increase in the time it will take the object to fall to the ground if you quadruple the height from which you drop the object?

Experiencing Algebra the Calculator Way

The calculator can help you check to see whether you have correctly simplified expressions with rational exponents, when the expressions involve only a single variable. Store the original expression in Y1 and the simplified expression in Y2. Graph Y1 and then graph Y2, separately, and compare the graphs. Next, graph both expressions simultaneously to see that the graphs coincide. If they do, your simplified expression is equivalent to the original expression.

Simplify the following expressions, using only positive exponents, and check by graphing.

1. $\left(x^3\right)^{2/3}$

2. $\left(x^3\right)^{-2/3}$

3. $\dfrac{x^4}{x^{9/4}}$

4. $\dfrac{x^2}{x^{7/2}}$

5. $x^{3/4}\left(x^{3/2} - x^{2/3}\right)$

6. $\left(x^{1/3} + 1\right)\left(x^{1/3} - 1\right)$

Experiencing Algebra the Group Way

Have you ever wondered how wind chill factors are calculated? A mathematical model to calculate wind chill temperature is given by

$$T_w = \dfrac{\left(10.45 + 6.686x^{1/2} - 0.447x\right)(T - 91.4)}{22.034} + 91.4,$$

where T is the actual temperature in Fahrenheit degrees and x is the wind velocity in miles per hour. This is an example of a mathematical model that is used widely to communicate weather conditions to the general public. You may recall hearing a local weather forecaster speak of wind chill factors when reporting the weather.

Discuss how you could use the calculator to evaluate this model for given values of temperature T and wind velocity x. Then work together to store this model in the calculator under Y1, using x for the wind velocity and T for the temperature. Next, store a value for T using the $\boxed{\text{STO}\blacktriangleright}$ key.

Finally, use the TABLE function to read wind chill temperatures for the values of x listed in the following table. Complete the table.

Fahrenheit Temperature, T	Wind Velocity, x	Wind Chill Temperature, T_w
30° F	10 mph	16°F
30°F	20 mph	
30°F	30 mph	
30°F	40 mph	
35°F	10 mph	22°F
35°F	20 mph	
35°F	30 mph	
35°F	40 mph	
40°F	10 mph	28°F
40°F	20 mph	
40°F	30 mph	
40°F	40 mph	

Experiencing Algebra the Write Way

In the exercises in this section, you were asked to simplify the expression $\left(a^{1/2} + b^{1/2}\right)^2$. If you simplified this expression correctly, you saw that the result was *not* $(a + b)$. This is an important point to remember. Explain why the result is not $(a + b)$. Would you expect $\left(c^{1/2} - d^{1/2}\right)^2$ to be equal to $(c - d)$? Explain.

13.4 Properties of Radicals

Objectives
1 Simplify radical expressions using the product rule for radicals.
2 Simplify radical expressions using the quotient rule for radicals.
3 Model real-world situations using expressions containing radical expressions.

Application

Dancers and basketball players have great jumping abilities and seem to "hang in the air." The relationship between hang time t and the vertical height of the jump is given by the equation $t = 2\sqrt{\frac{2d}{g}}$, where d is the vertical height and g is the amount of acceleration due to gravity.

a. If the time is measured in seconds and d is the vertical height in feet, then g is the acceleration due to gravity in feet per second squared, or 32 feet per second squared. Write a formula for the hang time using these units of measurement.

b. According to the *Guinness Book of Records*, Darrell Griffith, a basketball player, made a standing vertical jump in 1976 of 4 feet. Determine his hang time using the formula found in part (a).

After completing this section, we will discuss this application further. See page 1042.

Since radical expressions are equivalent to exponential expressions with rational exponents, there are properties of radicals that correspond to properties of exponents. We have already defined two of these properties for square roots: the product rule and the quotient rule. We now extend these definitions for all radical expressions.

1 **Simplifying Radical Expressions Using the Product Rule**

The product rule for square roots states that for any real numbers $\sqrt{a}$ and $\sqrt{b}$, $\sqrt{a} \cdot \sqrt{b} = \sqrt{a \cdot b}$. For example,

$$\sqrt{3} \cdot \sqrt{2} = \sqrt{3 \cdot 2} = \sqrt{6}.$$

Complete the following set of exercises to determine wheter this rule is true for all radical expressions.

DISCOVERY 3

Multiplication of Radicals with Like Indices

Approximate each expression and compare the results obtained in the first column to the corresponding results in the second column.

1. a. $\sqrt[3]{-3} \cdot \sqrt[3]{8} \approx$ _____   b. $\sqrt[3]{-24} \approx$ _____
2. a. $\sqrt[4]{6} \cdot \sqrt[4]{8} \approx$ _____   b. $\sqrt[4]{48} \approx$ _____

Write a rule for multiplication of radicals with like indices.

The value of the expression in the first column is equivalent to the value of the expression in the second column. The first value is the product of roots with the same indices. The second value is the root of the product of the radicands in the first expression. Therefore, to multiply radicals with like indices, we multiply the radicands and then take the root of the product.

Product Rule for Radicals
For any real numbers $\sqrt[n]{a}$ and $\sqrt[n]{b}$ and index n (an integer greater than 1),
$$\sqrt[n]{a} \cdot \sqrt[n]{b} = \sqrt[n]{a \cdot b}.$$

We can show that this is true if we rewrite the radical expressions as exponential expressions with rational exponents and apply the product-to-a-power rule for exponents. That is, for the preceding "discovery" exercises, we would have the following:

$$\sqrt[3]{-3} \cdot \sqrt[3]{8} = (-3)^{1/3} \cdot 8^{1/3} = (-3 \cdot 8)^{1/3} = (-24)^{1/3} = \sqrt[3]{-24}$$
$$\sqrt[4]{6} \cdot \sqrt[4]{8} = 6^{1/4} \cdot 8^{1/4} = (6 \cdot 8)^{1/4} = 48^{1/4} = \sqrt[4]{48}$$

For the general rule, $\sqrt[n]{a} \cdot \sqrt[n]{b} = a^{1/n} b^{1/n} = (ab)^{1/n} = \sqrt[n]{ab}.$
To simplify radicals, we read the product rule from right to left:
$\sqrt[n]{ab} = \sqrt[n]{a} \cdot \sqrt[n]{b}.$

Simplifying Radical Expressions—Condition 1
If a radical expression has a radicand with a perfect nth factor and an index of n, it can be simplified.

For example, to simplify a cube root, we rewrite the radicand as a product of a perfect-cube (preferably the largest possible perfect cube factor) and another factor. We then reverse the product rule by writing a product of cube roots. Finally, we simplify the perfect-cube root. For example,

$$\sqrt[3]{24} = \sqrt[3]{8 \cdot 3} = \sqrt[3]{8} \; \sqrt[3]{3} = \sqrt[3]{2^3} \; \sqrt[3]{3} = 2\sqrt[3]{3}$$

We simplify other roots with the same process.

EXAMPLE 1   Simplify without a calculator. Check the results on your calculator.

a. $\sqrt{48}$ **b.** $\sqrt[3]{54}$
c. $\sqrt[4]{80}$ **d.** $\sqrt[5]{-96}$

Solution

a. $\sqrt{48} = \sqrt{16 \cdot 3} = \sqrt{16} \; \sqrt{3} = \sqrt{4^2} \; \sqrt{3} = 4\sqrt{3}$

 Helping Hand If we had not used the largest perfect square factor, 16, but used a factor of 4, we would need to simplify the expression twice.

$$\sqrt{48} = \sqrt{4 \cdot 12} = \sqrt{4} \; \sqrt{12} = 2\sqrt{12} = 2\sqrt{4 \cdot 3} = 2\sqrt{4} \; \sqrt{3}$$
$$= 2 \cdot 2\sqrt{3} = 4\sqrt{3}$$

b. $\sqrt[3]{54} = \sqrt[3]{27 \cdot 2} = \sqrt[3]{27} \; \sqrt[3]{2} = \sqrt[3]{3^3} \; \sqrt[3]{2} = 3\sqrt[3]{2}$
c. $\sqrt[4]{80} = \sqrt[4]{16 \cdot 5} = \sqrt[4]{16} \; \sqrt[4]{5} = \sqrt[4]{2^4} \; \sqrt[4]{5} = 2\sqrt[4]{5}$
d. $\sqrt[5]{-96} = \sqrt[5]{-32 \cdot 3} = \sqrt[5]{-32} \; \sqrt[5]{3} = \sqrt[5]{(-2)^5} \; \sqrt[5]{3} = -2\sqrt[5]{3}$

To check these results on your calculator, first evaluate the result found algebraically and then evaluate the given radical expression. The two values should be the same.

a. First, enter the algebraic result, $4\sqrt{3}$.
Second, enter the given radical expression, $\sqrt{48}$.

```
4√(3)
          6.92820323
√(48)
          6.92820323
```

b.
```
3³√(2)
          3.77976315
³√(54)
          3.77976315
```

c.
```
2*4 ˣ√5
          2.990697562
4 ˣ√80
          2.990697562
```

d.
```
-2*5 ˣ√3
          -2.491461879
5 ˣ√ -96
          -2.491461879
```
∎

Before we expand this simplification to variable radicands, we must remember that evaluating even roots always results in a positive number. Therefore, $\sqrt{x^2} = |x|$ and $\sqrt[4]{x^4} = |x|$. If we assume that no radicand is formed by raising negative quantities to even powers, there will be no need to write these results with absolute values.

In this text, we will assume that no radicand is formed by raising negative quantities to even roots. Therefore, the results will not be written using absolute values.

We simplify radical expressions with variable radicands using the same procedure. In addition to rewriting the numerical coefficient as a product with a perfect root factor, we also rewrite the variables as products with a perfect root factor. (A perfect root factor is a factor whose exponent is a multiple of the index of the radical.)

Perfect squares of variables must have an exponent that is a multiple of 2. For example, x^2, x^4, and x^6 are perfect squares because $x^2 = (x)^2$, $x^4 = (x^2)^2$ and $x^6 = (x^3)^2$. Likewise, perfect-cube roots of variables must have an exponent that is a multiple of 3, such as x^3, x^6 or $(x^2)^3$, and x^9 or $(x^3)^3$. A perfect nth root must have an exponent that is a multiple of n.

To determine the exponent of the largest perfect root factor for a variable, determine the largest multiple of the index that is less than or equal to the variable exponent. For example, the largest perfect-square factor for x^5 is x^4, because 4 is the largest multiple of 2 less than the exponent 5. Therefore, $x^5 = x^4 \cdot x$. The largest perfect-cube factor for x^5 is x^3, because 3 is the largest multiple of 3 less than the exponent 5. Therefore, $x^5 = x^3 \cdot x^2$.

To simplify a radical expression with a variable radicand, such as $\sqrt{x^5}$ or $\sqrt[3]{x^5}$, first rewrite the radicand as a product of a perfect root and another factor; then, write the radical expression as a product of radical expressions; finally, simplify the perfect root factor. For example,

$$\sqrt{x^5} = \sqrt{x^4 \cdot x} = \sqrt{x^4}\sqrt{x} = \sqrt{(x^2)^2}\sqrt{x} = x^2\sqrt{x}$$
$$\sqrt[3]{x^5} = \sqrt[3]{x^3}\sqrt[3]{x^2} = x\sqrt[3]{x^2}$$

We can extend this procedure to simplify variable radicands with numerical coefficients. For example,

$$\sqrt{16x^2 y^4} = \sqrt{16 \cdot x^2 \cdot y^4} \qquad \text{Find the perfect-square factors of the radicand.}$$

$$= \sqrt{16}\sqrt{x^2}\sqrt{y^4}$$

$$= \sqrt{4^2}\sqrt{x^2}\sqrt{(y^2)^2}$$

$$= 4xy^2$$

$$\sqrt{8a^3b^5} = \sqrt{4 \cdot 2 \cdot a^2 \cdot a \cdot b^4 \cdot b}$$ Find the perfect-square factors of the radicand.

$$= \sqrt{4}\sqrt{2}\sqrt{a^2}\sqrt{a}\sqrt{b^4}\sqrt{b}$$

$$= \sqrt{2^2}\sqrt{2}\sqrt{a^2}\sqrt{a}\sqrt{(b^2)^2}\sqrt{b}$$

$$= 2\sqrt{2}a\sqrt{ab^2}\sqrt{b}$$

$$= 2ab^2\sqrt{2ab}$$ Regroup and multiply.

EXAMPLE 2   Simplify.

a. $\sqrt{50xy^{15}z^4}$ **b.** $\sqrt[3]{64a^3b^6c^{14}}$ **c.** $\sqrt{3x^2 + 12x + 12}$

Solution

a. $\sqrt{50xy^{15}z^4} = \sqrt{25 \cdot 2 \cdot x \cdot y^{14} \cdot y \cdot z^4}$ Find the perfect-square factors of the radicand.

$$= \sqrt{25}\sqrt{2}\sqrt{x}\sqrt{y^{14}}\sqrt{y}\sqrt{z^4}$$

$$= \sqrt{5^2}\sqrt{2}\sqrt{x}\sqrt{(y^7)^2}\sqrt{y}\sqrt{(z^2)^2}$$

$$= 5\sqrt{2}\sqrt{x}y^7\sqrt{y}z^2$$

$$= 5y^7z^2\sqrt{2xy}$$ Regroup and multiply.

b. $\sqrt[3]{64a^3b^6c^{14}} = \sqrt[3]{64 \cdot a^3 \cdot b^6 \cdot c^{12} \cdot c^2}$ Find the perfect-cube factors of the radicand.

$$= \sqrt[3]{64}\sqrt[3]{a^3}\sqrt[3]{b^6}\sqrt[3]{c^{12}}\sqrt[3]{c^2}$$

$$= \sqrt[3]{4^3}\sqrt[3]{a^3}\sqrt[3]{(b^2)^3}\sqrt[3]{(c^4)^3}\sqrt[3]{c^2}$$

$$= 4ab^2c^4\sqrt[3]{c^2}$$

c. $\sqrt{3x^2 + 12x + 12} = \sqrt{3(x^2 + 4x + 4)}$ This radicand has terms, not factors. To simplify, factor the radicand.

$$= \sqrt{3(x + 2)^2}$$

$$= \sqrt{(x + 2)^2}\sqrt{3}$$

$$= (x + 2)\sqrt{3}$$

Note: Our assumption that no radicand is formed by raising negative quantities to even roots allows us to write the result, $|x + 2|\sqrt{3}$, without absolute values. ■

Now that we understand the principle of simplifying radical expressions, we introduce a second method of simplifying radical expressions with variable radicands. Let's discover this method in the following exercise.

DISCOVERY 4

Simplifying Radical Expressions

Observe the following steps to simplify a radical expression. The process consists of writing the radical expression as an expression with a fractional exponent and using the properties of exponents.

Simplify $\sqrt[3]{x^{14}}$.

$$\sqrt[3]{x^{14}} = x^{14/3}$$ Write an equivalent exponential expression with rational exponents.

$$= x^{4\,2/3}$$ Write the exponent as mixed number.

$$= x^{4+2/3}$$ Write the exponent as a sum.

$$= x^4 \cdot x^{2/3}$$ Product rule for exponents

$$= x^4 \sqrt[3]{x^2}$$ Write an equivalent radical expression.

Therefore, $\sqrt[3]{x^{14}} = x^4 \sqrt[3]{x^2}$.

Write a rule to simplify a radical expression using the results of this process.

Note that we write the exponent as a mixed number. The final simplification is the product of the variable raised to the whole-number part of the mixed number, and the root of the variable raised to the numerator of the fractional part of the mixed number.

For example, simplify $\sqrt{x^5}$.

$$\sqrt{x^5} = x^{5/2} = x^{2\,1/2}$$ Write the expression with a mixed-number exponent.

$$= x^2 x^{1/2}$$ Product rule

$$= x^2 \sqrt{x}$$ Write the expression with radicals.

Now, let's complete the examples from Example 2 by this method.

EXAMPLE 3   Simplify.

a. $\sqrt{50xy^{15}z^4}$ **b.** $\sqrt[3]{64a^3b^6c^{14}}$

Solution

a. $\sqrt{50xy^{15}z^4} = (50xy^{15}z^4)^{1/2}$ Write the expression with rational exponents.

$$= 50^{1/2}x^{1/2}y^{15/2}z^2$$ Power-to-a-power rule

$$= 50^{1/2}x^{1/2}y^{7\,1/2}z^2$$ Write the improper fraction as a mixed number.

$$= 50^{1/2}x^{1/2}y^7 y^{1/2}z^2$$ Product rule

$$= 5\sqrt{2}\sqrt{x}y^7\sqrt{y}z^2$$ Write the expression with radicals.

$$= 5y^7z^2\sqrt{2xy}$$ Regroup and simplify.

b. $\sqrt[3]{64a^3b^6c^{14}} = (64a^3b^6c^{14})^{1/3}$ Write the expression with rational exponents.

$$= 64^{1/3}a^1b^2c^{14/3}$$ Power-to-a-power rule

$$= 64^{1/3}ab^2c^{4\,2/3}$$ Write the improper fraction as a mixed number.

$$= 64^{1/3}ab^2c^4c^{2/3}$$ Product rule

$$= 4ab^2c^4\sqrt[3]{c^2}$$ Write the expression with radicals. ∎

We also use the product rule for radicals to multiply radical expressions with the same index. For example,

$$\sqrt{2}\sqrt{5} = \sqrt{10}$$
$$\sqrt{8x}\sqrt{3x} = \sqrt{24x^2} = \sqrt{4}\sqrt{6}\sqrt{x^2} = 2x\sqrt{6}$$

 Helping Hand To use this rule, the index of each radical must be the same.

EXAMPLE 4 Multiply and simplify.

a. $\left(2x\sqrt{3y}\right)\left(4\sqrt{6xy}\right)$ **b.** $\sqrt{2x - 6}\cdot\sqrt{x - 3}$

c. $2\sqrt[3]{4a^2b^5}\cdot 3ab\sqrt[3]{12ab^2}$

Solution

a. $\left(2x\sqrt{3y}\right)\left(4\sqrt{6xy}\right) = 2x\cdot 4\sqrt{3y\cdot 6xy}$ Multiply nonradical factors and radical factors.

$$= 8x\sqrt{18xy^2}$$
$$= 8x\sqrt{9\cdot 2\cdot x\cdot y^2}$$ Factor.
$$= 8x\cdot 3y\sqrt{2x}$$ Simplify.
$$= 24xy\sqrt{2x}$$

b. $\sqrt{2x - 6}\cdot\sqrt{x - 3} = \sqrt{(2x - 6)(x - 3)}$

$$= \sqrt{2(x - 3)(x - 3)}$$ Factor.
$$= \sqrt{2(x - 3)^2}$$
$$= (x - 3)\sqrt{2}$$ Simplify.

c. $2\sqrt[3]{4a^2b^5}\cdot 3ab\sqrt[3]{12ab^2}$

$$= 2\cdot 3ab\sqrt[3]{4a^2b^5\cdot 12ab^2}$$ Multiply nonradical factors and radical factors.
$$= 6ab\sqrt[3]{48a^3b^7}$$
$$= 6ab\sqrt[3]{8\cdot 6\cdot a^3\cdot b^6\cdot b}$$ Factor.
$$= 6ab\cdot 2ab^2\sqrt[3]{6b}$$ Simplify.
$$= 12a^2b^3\sqrt[3]{6b}$$ ■

Experiencing Algebra the Checkup Way

Simplify without a calculator. Check the results on your calculator.

1. $\sqrt{192}$ **2.** $\sqrt[3]{-40}$ **3.** $\sqrt[4]{162}$

Simplify exercises 4–7.

4. $\sqrt{98x^4y^3z^9}$ **5.** $\left(3a\sqrt{5b}\right)\left(2\sqrt{5ab}\right)$

6. $\sqrt{5x + 10}\cdot\sqrt{2x + 4}$ **7.** $4x\sqrt[3]{12xy^7}\cdot 3y\sqrt[3]{36x^2y^4}$

8. Why must we assume that radicands of even-indexed radicals are nonnegative?

9. What does the term "perfect nth root factor of a radicand" mean?

2 Simplifying Radical Expressions Using the Quotient Rule

The quotient rule for square roots states that for any real numbers $\sqrt{a}$ and $\sqrt{b}$, $\frac{\sqrt{a}}{\sqrt{b}} = \sqrt{\frac{a}{b}}$. For example, $\frac{\sqrt{6}}{\sqrt{2}} = \sqrt{\frac{6}{2}} = \sqrt{3}$. To determine whether we can extend this rule to all radical expressions, complete the following set of exercises.

D I S C O V E R Y   5

Division of Radicals with Like Indices

Approximate each expression and compare the results obtained in the first column to the corresponding results in the second column.

1. a. $\dfrac{\sqrt[3]{8}}{\sqrt[3]{2}} \approx$ _____   **b.** $\sqrt[3]{4} \approx$ _____

2. a. $\dfrac{\sqrt[4]{16}}{\sqrt[4]{2}} \approx$ _____   **b.** $\sqrt[4]{8} \approx$ _____

Write a rule for division of radicals with like indices.

The value of the expression in the first column is equivalent to the expression in the second column. The first value is the quotient of roots with the same indices. The second value is the root of the quotient of the radicands in the first expression. Therefore, to divide radicals with like indices, we divide the radicands and then take the root of the quotient.

> *Quotient Rule for Radicals*
> For any real numbers $\sqrt[n]{a}$ and $\sqrt[n]{b}$ and index n (an integer greater than 1),
> $$\frac{\sqrt[n]{a}}{\sqrt[n]{b}} = \sqrt[n]{\frac{a}{b}}.$$

We can show this is true if we rewrite the radical expressions as exponential expressions with rational exponents and apply the quotient rule for exponents. That is, for the preceding "Discovery" exercises we would have the following:

$$\frac{\sqrt[3]{8}}{\sqrt[3]{2}} = \frac{8^{1/3}}{2^{1/3}} = \left(\frac{8}{2}\right)^{1/3} = \sqrt[3]{\frac{8}{2}} = \sqrt[3]{4}$$

$$\frac{\sqrt[4]{16}}{\sqrt[4]{2}} = \frac{16^{1/4}}{2^{1/4}} = \left(\frac{16}{2}\right)^{1/4} = \sqrt[4]{\frac{16}{2}} = \sqrt[4]{8}$$

For the general rule, $\dfrac{\sqrt[n]{a}}{\sqrt[n]{b}} = \dfrac{a^{1/n}}{b^{1/n}} = \left(\dfrac{a}{b}\right)^{1/n} = \sqrt[n]{\dfrac{a}{b}}.$

To simplify radicals, we read the product rule from right to left:

$$\sqrt[n]{\frac{a}{b}} = \frac{\sqrt[n]{a}}{\sqrt[n]{b}}.$$

> *Simplifying Radical Expressions—Condition 2*
> If a radical expression has a fractional radicand, it can be simplified.

For example, to evaluate a cube root with a fractional radicand, we reverse the quotient rule by writing a quotient of cube roots. Then we simplify each cube root. For example,

$$\sqrt[3]{\frac{5}{8}} = \frac{\sqrt[3]{5}}{\sqrt[3]{8}} = \frac{\sqrt[3]{5}}{2}$$

We must be careful when writing the final result. If the result is a fraction, it is conventional to write the denominator without radicals. The process of changing the fraction to an equivalent form without a radical denominator is called **rationalizing the denominator**. That is, we make the denominator a rational number. Rationalizing the denominator makes it easier to add or subtract radical expressions because the denominators are rational numbers and not radicals.

> *Simplifying Radical Expressions—Condition 3*
> If a radical expression has a denominator containing a radical, it can be rationalized.

For example,

$$\sqrt[3]{\frac{8}{5}} = \frac{\sqrt[3]{8}}{\sqrt[3]{5}} = \frac{2}{\sqrt[3]{5}} \text{ is not fully simplified.}$$

To rationalize the denominator, we use the multiplication property of 1— that is, we multiply the numerator and denominator by the same value. We choose a value that will result in the denominator being a perfect root, so that we can simplify it. Since the denominator is $\sqrt[3]{5}$ and we want a perfect-cube root, we can multiply this expression by its square, $\left(\sqrt[3]{5}\right)^2$ or $\sqrt[3]{5^2}$. Therefore, rationalizing the denominator results in

$$\frac{2}{\sqrt[3]{5}} = \frac{2}{\sqrt[3]{5}} \cdot \frac{\sqrt[3]{5^2}}{\sqrt[3]{5^2}} = \frac{2\sqrt[3]{5^2}}{\sqrt[3]{5^3}} = \frac{2\sqrt[3]{25}}{5}.$$

We evaluate and simplify other roots with the same process.

EXAMPLE 5 Simplify without a calculator. Rationalize all denominators. Check the result on your calculator.

a. $\sqrt{\dfrac{3}{4}}$ **b.** $\sqrt{\dfrac{63}{50}}$ **c.** $\sqrt[5]{\dfrac{64}{5}}$

Solution

a. $\sqrt{\dfrac{3}{4}} = \dfrac{\sqrt{3}}{\sqrt{4}} = \dfrac{\sqrt{3}}{2}$ Quotient rule

b. $\sqrt{\dfrac{63}{50}} = \dfrac{\sqrt{63}}{\sqrt{50}} = \dfrac{\sqrt{9}\sqrt{7}}{\sqrt{25}\sqrt{2}} = \dfrac{3\sqrt{7}}{5\sqrt{2}}$ Quotient rule

$\qquad = \dfrac{3\sqrt{7}}{5\sqrt{2}} \cdot \dfrac{\sqrt{2}}{\sqrt{2}} = \dfrac{3\sqrt{14}}{5\sqrt{4}} = \dfrac{3\sqrt{14}}{5\cdot2} = \dfrac{3\sqrt{14}}{10}$ Rationalize the denominator.

c. $\sqrt[5]{\dfrac{64}{5}} = \dfrac{\sqrt[5]{64}}{\sqrt[5]{5}} = \dfrac{\sqrt[5]{32}\sqrt[5]{2}}{\sqrt[5]{5}} = \dfrac{2\sqrt[5]{2}}{\sqrt[5]{5}}$ Quotient rule

$\qquad = \dfrac{2\sqrt[5]{2}}{\sqrt[5]{5}} \cdot \dfrac{\sqrt[5]{5^4}}{\sqrt[5]{5^4}} = \dfrac{2\sqrt[5]{2 \cdot 5^4}}{\sqrt[5]{5^5}} = \dfrac{2\sqrt[5]{1250}}{5}$ Rationalize the denominator.

To check these results on your calculator, first evaluate the result found algebraically and then evaluate the given radical expression. The two values should be the same.

a.
```
√(3)/2
        .8660254038
√(3/4)
        .8660254038
```

b.
```
(3√(14))/10
        1.122497216
√(63/50)
        1.122497216
```

c.
```
(2*5*√(1250))/5
        1.665106415
5*√(64/5)
        1.665106415
```

EXAMPLE 6   Simplify. Rationalize all denominators.

$$\textbf{a. } \sqrt{\frac{16ab}{3c}} \qquad\qquad \textbf{b. } \sqrt{\frac{72x^3 y^2}{15xy}} \qquad\qquad \textbf{c. } \sqrt[3]{\frac{35m^2}{12np^2}}$$

Solution

a.
$$\sqrt{\frac{16ab}{3c}} = \frac{\sqrt{16ab}}{\sqrt{3c}} = \frac{4\sqrt{ab}}{\sqrt{3c}} \qquad \text{Quotient rule}$$

$$= \frac{4\sqrt{ab}}{\sqrt{3c}} \cdot \frac{\sqrt{3c}}{\sqrt{3c}} = \frac{4\sqrt{3abc}}{\sqrt{(3c)^2}} = \frac{4\sqrt{3abc}}{3c} \qquad \begin{array}{l}\text{Rationalize the} \\ \text{denominator.}\end{array}$$

b. First simplify the radicand before applying the quotient rule.

$$\sqrt{\frac{72x^3 y^2}{15xy}} = \sqrt{\frac{24x^2 y}{5}} = \frac{\sqrt{24x^2 y}}{\sqrt{5}} \qquad \text{Quotient rule}$$

$$= \frac{\sqrt{24x^2 y}}{\sqrt{5}} \cdot \frac{\sqrt{5}}{\sqrt{5}} = \frac{\sqrt{120x^2 y}}{\sqrt{5^2}} = \frac{2x\sqrt{30y}}{5} \qquad \begin{array}{l}\text{Rationalize the} \\ \text{denominator.}\end{array}$$

c.
$$\sqrt[3]{\frac{35m^2}{12np^2}} = \frac{\sqrt[3]{35m^2}}{\sqrt[3]{12np^2}} \qquad \text{Quotient rule}$$

To determine the factor needed to rationalize the denominator, we first determine the smallest perfect cube that is divisible by the numerical factor of the radicand, 12. The smallest perfect cube divisible by 12 is 216 = 6^3. 216 divided by 12 is 18. Therefore, 18 is the needed numerical factor. Each variable factor must also be a perfect cube. We determine the variable factors needed to be n^2 and p. The cube root of $18n^2 p$ is the factor needed to rationalize the denominator.

$$= \frac{\sqrt[3]{35m^2}}{\sqrt[3]{12np^2}} \cdot \frac{\sqrt[3]{18n^2 p}}{\sqrt[3]{18n^2 p}} = \frac{\sqrt[3]{630m^2 n^2 p}}{\sqrt[3]{216n^3 p^3}} = \frac{\sqrt[3]{630m^2 n^2 p}}{6np} \qquad \blacksquare$$

We also use the quotient rule for radicals to divide radical expressions with the same index. For example,

$$\frac{\sqrt{72}}{\sqrt{2}} = \sqrt{\frac{72}{2}} = \sqrt{36} = 6$$

$$\frac{\sqrt{245x^3}}{\sqrt{5x}} = \sqrt{\frac{245x^3}{5x}} = \sqrt{49x^2} = 7x$$

EXAMPLE 7 Divide and simplify. Rationalize all denominators.

a. $\dfrac{\sqrt{3y}}{\sqrt{6xy}}$ 　　　　 b. $\dfrac{2a\sqrt{5a}}{4\sqrt{6ab^2}}$ 　　　　 c. $\dfrac{\sqrt[3]{4a^2b^5}}{\sqrt[3]{12ab^2}}$

Solution

a. $\dfrac{\sqrt{3y}}{\sqrt{6xy}} = \sqrt{\dfrac{3y}{6xy}} = \sqrt{\dfrac{1}{2x}}$ 　　　　　　　　 Quotient rule

$\qquad = \sqrt{\dfrac{1}{2x}} \cdot \sqrt{\dfrac{2x}{2x}} = \sqrt{\dfrac{2x}{(2x)^2}} = \dfrac{\sqrt{2x}}{2x}$ 　　 Rationalize the denominator.

b. $\dfrac{2a\sqrt{5a}}{4\sqrt{6ab^2}} = \dfrac{a\sqrt{5a}}{2b\sqrt{6a}}$ 　　　　　　　　　 Simplify.

$\qquad = \dfrac{a}{2b}\sqrt{\dfrac{5a}{6a}} = \dfrac{a}{2b}\sqrt{\dfrac{5}{6}}$ 　　　　　 Quotient rule

$\qquad = \dfrac{a}{2b}\sqrt{\dfrac{5}{6}} \cdot \sqrt{\dfrac{6}{6}} = \dfrac{a}{2b}\sqrt{\dfrac{30}{36}} = \dfrac{a}{2b} \cdot \dfrac{\sqrt{30}}{6} = \dfrac{a\sqrt{30}}{12b}$ 　Rationalize the denominator.

c. $\dfrac{\sqrt[3]{4a^2b^5}}{\sqrt[3]{12ab^2}} = \sqrt[3]{\dfrac{4a^2b^5}{12ab^2}} = \sqrt[3]{\dfrac{ab^3}{3}} = b\sqrt[3]{\dfrac{a}{3}}$ 　　Quotient rule

$\qquad = b\sqrt[3]{\dfrac{a}{3}} \cdot \sqrt[3]{\dfrac{3^2}{3^2}} = b\sqrt[3]{\dfrac{9a}{3^3}} = \dfrac{b\sqrt[3]{9a}}{3}$ 　Rationalize the denominator. ∎

Experiencing Algebra the Checkup Way

Simplify without a calculator. Rationalize all denominators. Check your results on your calculator.

1. $\sqrt{\dfrac{13}{16}}$ 　　　　 **2.** $\sqrt{\dfrac{27}{20}}$ 　　　　 **3.** $\sqrt[3]{\dfrac{27}{2}}$

Simplify exercises 4–9. Rationalize all denominators.

4. $\sqrt{\dfrac{25xy}{2z}}$ 　　　 **5.** $\sqrt{\dfrac{18a^2b^3}{14ab^2}}$ 　　　 **6.** $\sqrt[3]{\dfrac{6x}{10y^2z}}$

7. $\dfrac{\sqrt{5x}}{\sqrt{10xy}}$ 　　　 **8.** $\dfrac{4b\sqrt{3ab}}{12\sqrt{15a^2b}}$ 　　　 **9.** $\dfrac{\sqrt[3]{2c^3d}}{\sqrt[3]{8cd^4}}$

10. What does it mean to rationalize the denominator of a radical expression?

---

3 Modeling the Real World　Another example of a radical expression we may encounter is found in a formula for the length of time (in seconds) that it takes for a pendulum to swing from one side of its vertical rest position to the other and back (called its period). This time, T, is determined by the length (in feet) of its suspension, L, according to the formula $T = 2\pi\sqrt{\dfrac{L}{32}}$. The motion of a pendulum in a grandfather clock can be modeled by this formula. However, with some simplifying assumptions, many other kinds of motion can also be modeled with this formula, such as the swaying of a skyscraper in a strong wind or the swinging of a person's leg while walking.

EXAMPLE 8 Yueling practices daily for the 10 km walk. She swings each arm in a forward-and-back motion as she walks. If the length of her arm is 2 feet, determine the time it takes her arm to complete the forward-and-back motion and return to its original starting position, assuming that her arms swing in a pendulum motion and not by her own efforts.

Solution

We will model this motion as a pendulum and use the formula $T = 2\pi \sqrt{\frac{L}{32}}$.

$$T = 2\pi \sqrt{\frac{L}{32}}$$

$$T = 2\pi \sqrt{\frac{2}{32}} \qquad \text{Substitute 2 for } L.$$

$$T = 2\pi \sqrt{\frac{1}{16}} \qquad \text{Simplify the radicand.}$$

$$T = 2\pi \cdot \frac{1}{4} \qquad \text{Simplify the radical factor.}$$

$$T = \frac{\pi}{2} \qquad \text{Multiply and simplify.}$$

The forward-and-back motion of Yueling's arm takes $\frac{\pi}{2}$ seconds, or approximately 1.57 seconds.

Note that Yueling's arm is not a true pendulum because it may swing faster or slower due to her own effort. ∎

Application

Dancers and basketball players have great jumping abilities and seem to "hang in the air." The relationship between hang time t and the vertical height of the jump is given by the equation $t = 2\sqrt{\frac{2d}{g}}$, where d is the vertical height and g is the amount of acceleration due to gravity.

a. If the time is measured in seconds and d is the vertical height in feet, then g is the acceleration due to gravity in feet per second squared, or 32 feet per second squared. Write a formula for the hang time using these units of measurement.

b. According to the *Guinness Book of Records*, Darrell Griffith, a basketball player, made a standing vertical jump in 1976 of 4 feet. Determine his hang time using the formula found in part (a).

Discussion

a. Use the given equation for hang time and substitute 32 for g, then simplify.

$$t = 2\sqrt{\frac{2d}{g}}$$

$$t = 2\sqrt{\frac{2d}{32}}$$

$$t = 2\sqrt{\dfrac{d}{16}} \quad \text{Simplify.}$$

$$t = 2\dfrac{\sqrt{d}}{\sqrt{16}} \quad \text{Quotient rule}$$

$$t = 2\dfrac{\sqrt{d}}{4} \quad \text{Simplify.}$$

$$t = \dfrac{\sqrt{d}}{2}$$

An equation for the hang time t (in seconds) is $t = \frac{\sqrt{d}}{2}$, where d is the vertical height in feet.

b. Use the equation for hang time found in part (a), $t = \frac{\sqrt{d}}{2}$, and substitute 4 for d.

$$t = \dfrac{\sqrt{d}}{2}$$

$$t = \dfrac{\sqrt{4}}{2}$$

$$t = \dfrac{2}{2}$$

$$t = 1$$

Darrell Griffith's hang time for a vertical jump of 4 feet was 1 second. ■

Experiencing Algebra the Checkup Way

1. The pendulum in a grandfather clock is 16 inches long ($1\frac{1}{3}$ feet long). What is the period of the pendulum?

2. The amount of current I (in amperes) passing through a circuit is related to the amount of power P (in watts) it uses and the resistance R (in ohms) in the circuit according to the formula $I = \sqrt{\frac{P}{R}}$. How many amps of current pass through a circuit if it uses 1000 watts of power and the resistance of the circuit is 3 ohms?

PROBLEM SET 13.4

Experiencing Algebra the Exercise Way

Simplify without a calculator. Check your results on your calculator.

1. $\sqrt{28}$ **2.** $\sqrt{75}$ **3.** $\sqrt[3]{-686}$ **4.** $\sqrt[3]{-192}$

5. $\sqrt[4]{112}$ **6.** $\sqrt[4]{7203}$ **7.** $\sqrt[5]{-6250}$ **8.** $\sqrt[5]{-1944}$

Simplify.

9. $\sqrt{20x^4 y^3 z^2}$ **10.** $\sqrt{12x^3 y^9 z^8}$ **11.** $\sqrt[3]{72m^5 n^9}$ **12.** $\sqrt[3]{108p^7 q^8}$

13. $\sqrt[4]{162x^4 y^5}$ **14.** $\sqrt[4]{80a^6 b^8}$ **15.** $\sqrt[5]{486a^6 b^{10} c^2}$ **16.** $\sqrt[5]{729x^2 y^8 z^{15}}$

17. $\sqrt{5x^2 + 30x + 45}$ **18.** $\sqrt{3x^3 + 6x^2 + 3x}$

Multiply and simplify.

19. $\sqrt{7x} \cdot \sqrt{14y}$ **20.** $\sqrt{6x} \cdot \sqrt{12y}$ **21.** $2\sqrt{7xy} \cdot x\sqrt{14y}$

22. $-3\sqrt{7pq} \cdot 2\sqrt{3p^4q}$

23. $\sqrt{7x + 14y} \cdot \sqrt{3x + 6y}$

24. $\sqrt{p^2 + 2pq} \cdot \sqrt{3p + 6q}$

25. $\sqrt{x + 2} \cdot \sqrt{x^2 + 3x + 2}$

26. $\sqrt{x - 7} \cdot \sqrt{x^2 - 6x - 7}$

27. $\sqrt{x^2 + x - 2} \cdot \sqrt{x^2 + 3x - 4}$

28. $\sqrt{x^2 + 6x + 8} \cdot \sqrt{x^2 - 16}$

29. $\sqrt[3]{-4x^4y^2} \cdot \sqrt[3]{6xy}$

30. $\sqrt[3]{-25x^4y} \cdot \sqrt[3]{10x^2y^7}$

Simplify without a calculator. Rationalize all denominators. Check your results on your calculator.

31. $-\sqrt{\dfrac{36}{49}}$

32. $-\sqrt{\dfrac{25}{81}}$

33. $\sqrt{\dfrac{1210}{1440}}$

34. $\sqrt{\dfrac{1690}{1960}}$

35. $-\sqrt{\dfrac{8}{27}}$

36. $-\sqrt{\dfrac{27}{125}}$

37. $\sqrt[3]{\dfrac{4}{125}}$

38. $\sqrt[3]{\dfrac{5}{512}}$

39. $\sqrt[3]{-\dfrac{9}{25}}$

40. $\sqrt[3]{-\dfrac{10}{49}}$

41. $\sqrt[5]{\dfrac{1}{16}}$

42. $\sqrt[5]{\dfrac{1}{81}}$

Simplify. Rationalize all denominators.

43. $\sqrt{\dfrac{4x^2}{9y^2}}$

44. $\sqrt{\dfrac{25x}{49y^2}}$

45. $\sqrt{\dfrac{3x}{25y^2}}$

46. $\sqrt{\dfrac{5p}{49q^2}}$

47. $\sqrt{\dfrac{4xy}{5z}}$

48. $\sqrt{\dfrac{36ab}{7c}}$

49. $\sqrt{\dfrac{2x^2}{6}}$

50. $\sqrt{\dfrac{7z^4}{35}}$

51. $\sqrt[3]{\dfrac{27x^3}{y^6}}$

52. $\sqrt[3]{\dfrac{-64x^6y^3}{z^9}}$

53. $\sqrt[3]{\dfrac{3}{25x^2}}$

54. $\sqrt[3]{\dfrac{7}{36a^2}}$

55. $\sqrt[3]{\dfrac{3x^2y}{5xy^2z}}$

56. $\sqrt[3]{\dfrac{4a^2b^2c}{7ab^2c^2}}$

Divide and simplify. Rationalize all denominators.

57. $\dfrac{\sqrt{5}}{\sqrt{x}}$

58. $\dfrac{\sqrt{10}}{\sqrt{y}}$

59. $\dfrac{\sqrt{4x}}{\sqrt{8xy}}$

60. $\dfrac{\sqrt{5a}}{\sqrt{15ab}}$

61. $\dfrac{\sqrt{z^3}}{\sqrt{8}}$

62. $\dfrac{\sqrt{p^3}}{\sqrt{27}}$

63. $\dfrac{\sqrt{ab^4}}{\sqrt{a^2b}}$

64. $\dfrac{\sqrt{c^2d}}{\sqrt{c^3d^4}}$

65. $\dfrac{3x\sqrt{5x^2y}}{6\sqrt{15x^3y}}$

66. $\dfrac{5p\sqrt{3pq^2}}{15\sqrt{6pq^3}}$

67. $\dfrac{\sqrt[3]{3}}{\sqrt[3]{x^2}}$

68. $\dfrac{\sqrt[3]{7}}{\sqrt[3]{a^2}}$

69. $\dfrac{\sqrt[3]{3x}}{\sqrt[3]{12xy}}$

70. $\dfrac{\sqrt[3]{6b}}{\sqrt[3]{24ab}}$

71. $\dfrac{\sqrt[3]{-8xy^2z^2}}{\sqrt[3]{3x^2y^2z}}$

72. $\dfrac{\sqrt[3]{-27a^2bc^4}}{\sqrt[3]{5a^2b^2c^3}}$

73. Find the period of a pendulum whose length is 7 feet.

74. Find the period of a pendulum whose length is 12 feet.

75. Use the pendulum formula to model the motion of a man's leg as he walks. If his leg measures 3 feet from his heel to his hip, determine the time it takes his leg to complete the forward-and-back motion to return to its starting position.

76. A boy's leg measures 1.6 feet from his heel to his hip. Use the pendulum formula to determine the time it takes his leg to complete the forward-and-back motion to return to its starting position as he walks.

For the following exercises, use the formula given in the preceding "Experiencing Algebra the Checkup Way": $I = \sqrt{\dfrac{P}{R}}$, where $I =$ amount of current in amperes, $P =$ amount of power in watts, and $R =$ amount of resistance in ohms.

77. How many amperes of current flow through a circuit with a resistance of 300 ohms that uses 10,800 watts of power?

78. How many amperes of current flow through a circuit with a resistance of 250 ohms that uses 20,250 watts of power?

79. Find the current flowing through a resistance of 10 ohms with 425 watts of power.

80. Find the current flowing through a resistance of 15 ohms with 880 watts of power.

Experiencing Algebra the Calculator Way

You can use the TABLE feature of your calculator to check your work after simplifying a radical expression, if the expression contains a single variable. First, change the variable to x. Then store the original expression in Y1 and your simplified expression in Y2. Generate a table of values, and compare the values for Y1 and Y2. If they are the same, it would indicate that your simplification is correct. Use this approach to check after simplifying the following expressions.

1. $\sqrt[3]{2x^2} \cdot \sqrt[3]{108x}$

2. $3\sqrt{12a^2} \cdot \sqrt{6a^4}$

3. $\sqrt{x^2 + 10x + 25}$

4. $\sqrt{b^3 + 6b^2 + 9b}$

5. $\sqrt{2x^2 - 4x + 2}$

6. $\sqrt{\dfrac{36x^2}{27x^3}}$

Experiencing Algebra the Group Way

In this section, you saw an interesting application that involves a radical expression from the study of physics. It concerns the movement of the simple pendulum. If T is the period of the pendulum, then $T = 2\pi\sqrt{\frac{L}{g}}$, where L is the length of the pendulum and g is the acceleration of gravity. Given that the acceleration of gravity is 32 feet per second squared, the formula becomes $T = 2\pi\sqrt{\frac{L}{32}}$. Store this formula in Y1, using the variable x for the length, and complete the following table, which relates the period of a pendulum (seconds) to its length (feet).

L	0.25	0.50	0.75	1.00	1.25	1.50	1.75	2.00
T								

Graph the ordered pairs on a coordinate plane.

An interesting experiment would be to attempt to verify these results. Discuss among your group how you would design an experiment to check out your table. Since it would be difficult to measure a fraction of a second, you will need to think about how you might do this. Share your design with the class.

Experiencing Algebra the Write Way

The following examples illustrate the use of rational exponents to simplify radical expressions involving different indices. In each of the examples, an incorrect step has been made, which yields a result that is not equivalent to the original expression. You may use the TABLE feature described in "Experiencing Algebra the Calculator Way" to see that they are not equivalent to the original expression. Try to determine where the error has been made and describe the incorrect step.

1. $\sqrt[3]{x^2}\,\sqrt[5]{x^3} = x^{2/3} \cdot x^{3/5} = x^{(2+3)/(3+5)} = x^{5/8} = \sqrt[8]{x^5}$

2. $\sqrt[3]{x^2}\,\sqrt[5]{x^3} = x^{3/2} \cdot x^{5/3} = x^{9/6 + 10/6} = x^{19/6} = \sqrt[6]{x^{19}}$
$= \sqrt[6]{x^{18} \cdot x} = x^3\sqrt[6]{x}$

3. $\dfrac{\sqrt[5]{x^3}}{\sqrt[3]{x^2}} = \dfrac{x^{3/5}}{x^{2/3}} = x^{3/5 - 2/3} = x^{(3-2)/(5-3)} = x^{1/2} = \sqrt{x}$

13.5 Operations on Radicals

Objectives

1 Add and subtract radical expressions.
2 Multiply radical expressions.
3 Divide radical expressions and rationalize a denominator having two terms.
4 Model real-world situations using expressions involving addition or subtraction of radicals.

Application

The Hephaesteion was a temple built by the Greeks in the fifth century B.C. The ratio of its width to its height is approximated by the expression $\frac{2}{\sqrt{5}-1}$. This number is called the golden ratio. Early Greeks believed that rectangles with this ratio were aesthetically pleasing to the eye. Rationalize the denominator of the expression.

After completing this section, we will discuss this application further. See page 1053.

1 Adding and Subtracting Radical Expressions

We are now ready to add and subtract radical expressions. We need to develop a property of radicals for addition and subtraction. Let's discuss addition and subtraction of like radicals. **Like radicals** have the same index and radicands. The expression $2\sqrt{3} + 5\sqrt{3}$ contains two terms with like radicals, $2\sqrt{3}$ and $5\sqrt{3}$. The coefficients of the radicals in the expression are 2 and 5, respectively. To determine a rule for the sum or difference of like radicals, complete the following set of exercises.

DISCOVERY 6

Addition and Subtraction of Radical Expressions with Like Radicals

Approximate each expression and compare the results obtained in the first column to the corresponding results in the second column.

1. a. $\sqrt{2} + \sqrt{2} \approx$ ____   **b.** $2\sqrt{2} \approx$ ____
2. a. $2\sqrt{2} + \sqrt{2} \approx$ ____   **b.** $3\sqrt{2} \approx$ ____
3. a. $3\sqrt{2} - 2\sqrt{2} \approx$ ____   **b.** $\sqrt{2} \approx$ ____
4. a. $\sqrt[3]{2} + \sqrt[3]{2} \approx$ ____   **b.** $2\sqrt[3]{2} \approx$ ____
5. a. $2\sqrt[3]{2} + \sqrt[3]{2} \approx$ ____   **b.** $3\sqrt[3]{2} \approx$ ____
6. a. $3\sqrt[3]{2} - 2\sqrt[3]{2} \approx$ ____   **b.** $\sqrt[3]{2} \approx$ ____

Write a rule for addition and subtraction of like radicals.

Each expression in the first column is the sum or difference of like radicals. The expression in the second column has the same like radical as the first column, but is multiplied by the sum or difference of the coefficients in the first column. The corresponding values in each column are the same. Therefore, to add (or subtract) like radicals, we add (or subtract) the coefficients of each like radical.

We can show this is true by using the distributive law, as we did when we combined like terms. For example,

$$2x + x = 2x + 1x = (2 + 1)x = 3x \qquad \text{Like terms}$$
$$2\sqrt{2} + \sqrt{2} = 2\sqrt{2} + 1\sqrt{2} = (2 + 1)\sqrt{2} = 3\sqrt{2} \qquad \text{Like radicals}$$

 Helping Hand Just as we cannot add or subtract unlike terms, such as $2x + y$, we cannot add or subtract unlike radicals, such as $2\sqrt{2} + \sqrt{3}$.

> *Addition and Subtraction of Like Radicals*
> To add or subtract like radicals:
> $$a\sqrt{x} + b\sqrt{x} = (a + b)\sqrt{x}$$
> $$a\sqrt{x} - b\sqrt{x} = (a - b)\sqrt{x}$$

For example,

$$5\sqrt{3x} + 2\sqrt{3x} = 7\sqrt{3x}$$
$$8\sqrt[3]{5} - 2\sqrt[3]{5} = 6\sqrt[3]{5}$$

EXAMPLE 1   Add or subtract as indicated.

a. $2\sqrt{xy} + 3\sqrt[3]{xy} - 4\sqrt[3]{xy} - \sqrt{xy}$
b. $3x\sqrt{y} - 5x\sqrt{y} + 4x\sqrt{y}$
c. $5a\sqrt[3]{abc} + 4\sqrt[3]{abc}$

Solution

a. $2\sqrt{xy} + 3\sqrt[3]{xy} - 4\sqrt[3]{xy} - \sqrt{xy}$
$\quad = 2\sqrt{xy} - \sqrt{xy} + 3\sqrt[3]{xy} - 4\sqrt[3]{xy}$ Rearrange terms.
$\quad = (2 - 1)\sqrt{xy} + (3 - 4)\sqrt[3]{xy}$ Subtract coefficients.
$\quad = \sqrt{xy} - \sqrt[3]{xy}$

b. $3x\sqrt{y} - 5x\sqrt{y} + 4x\sqrt{y}$
$\quad = (3x - 5x + 4x)\sqrt{y}$ Add and subtract coefficients.
$\quad = 2x\sqrt{y}$

c. $5a\sqrt[3]{abc} + 4\sqrt[3]{abc} = (5a + 4)\sqrt[3]{abc}$ Add coefficients. ■

Sometimes we need to simplify the radical expressions to have like radical terms.

EXAMPLE 2   Add or subtract as indicated.

a. $5\sqrt{32} - \sqrt{72}$ **b.** $3ab\sqrt{ab} + 2b\sqrt{a^3 b} - a\sqrt{4ab^3}$

c. $\sqrt{2} + \sqrt{\dfrac{1}{2}}$

Solution

a. $5\sqrt{32} - \sqrt{72} = 5 \cdot 4\sqrt{2} - 6\sqrt{2}$ Simplify radical expressions.

$$= 20\sqrt{2} - 6\sqrt{2}$$

$$= 14\sqrt{2}$$ Subtract coefficients.

b. $3ab\sqrt{ab} + 2b\sqrt{a^3b} - a\sqrt{4ab^3}$

$$= 3ab\sqrt{ab} + 2ab\sqrt{ab} - 2ab\sqrt{ab}$$ Simplify radical expressions.

$$= (3ab + 2ab - 2ab)\sqrt{ab}$$ Add and subtract coefficients.

$$= 3ab\sqrt{ab}$$

c. $\sqrt{2} + \sqrt{\dfrac{1}{2}} = \sqrt{2} + \dfrac{\sqrt{1}}{\sqrt{2}}$ Quotient rule

$$= \sqrt{2} + \frac{\sqrt{1}}{\sqrt{2}} \cdot \frac{\sqrt{2}}{\sqrt{2}}$$ Rationalize the denominator.

$$= \sqrt{2} + \frac{\sqrt{2}}{2}$$

$$= \sqrt{2} + \frac{1}{2}\sqrt{2}$$

$$= \left(1 + \frac{1}{2}\right)\sqrt{2}$$ Add coefficients.

$$= \frac{3}{2}\sqrt{2}$$ ∎

Experiencing Algebra the Checkup Way

In exercises 1–6, add or subtract as indicated.

1. $3\sqrt{ab} + 5\sqrt[4]{ab} - 4\sqrt{ab} + 2\sqrt[4]{ab}$ **2.** $3p\sqrt{q} - 7p\sqrt{q} + 8p\sqrt{q}$ **3.** $5m\sqrt[3]{mn} + 2\sqrt[3]{mn}$

4. $2\sqrt{48} + \sqrt{75}$ **5.** $6xy\sqrt{xy} + 5y\sqrt{x^3y} - 4x\sqrt{9xy^3}$ **6.** $\sqrt{3} - \sqrt{\dfrac{1}{3}}$

7. Define what is meant by the term *like radicals*. Give examples of like radicals and unlike radicals.

8. Explain what a coefficient of a radical term is.

9. What must you do to the radical terms of an addition or subtraction problem before collecting like terms? Why?

---

2 Multiplying Radicals   We have already multiplied radical expressions with one term. We use the properties of radicals to simplify these. We are now ready to expand our multiplication of radicals to radical expressions that may have more than one term.

To multiply, we use the distributive law, as we did to multiply polynomial expressions with more than one term. For example,

$$2(x + 3) = 2x + 6$$ Polynomial expression

$$\sqrt{2}\left(\sqrt{x} + \sqrt{3}\right) = \sqrt{2x} + \sqrt{6}$$ Radical expression

$$(x + 3)(x - 4) = x^2 - 4x + 3x - 12$$ Polynomial expression

$$= x^2 - x - 12$$

$$\left(\sqrt{x} + 3\right)\left(\sqrt{x} - 4\right) = \sqrt{x^2} - 4\sqrt{x} + 3\sqrt{x} - 12$$ Radical expression

$$= x - \sqrt{x} - 12$$

EXAMPLE 3   Multiply and simplify.

a. $3\sqrt[3]{x}\left(4\sqrt[3]{x^2}-2\right)$

b. $\left(\sqrt{2}-\sqrt{xy}\right)\left(\sqrt{5}+\sqrt{xy}\right)$

c. $\left(\sqrt{2}+\sqrt{3}\right)^2$

d. $\left(\sqrt{x}-2\right)^2$

Solution

a. $3\sqrt[3]{x}\left(4\sqrt[3]{x^2}-2\right)=12\sqrt[3]{x^3}-6\sqrt[3]{x}$ Distributive law

$\qquad\qquad\qquad = 12x - 6\sqrt[3]{x}$

b. $\left(\sqrt{2}-\sqrt{xy}\right)\left(\sqrt{5}+\sqrt{xy}\right)$

$\qquad = \sqrt{10}+\sqrt{2xy}-\sqrt{5xy}-\sqrt{(xy)^2}$ FOIL method

$\qquad = \sqrt{10}+\sqrt{2xy}-\sqrt{5xy}-xy$

c. $\left(\sqrt{2}+\sqrt{3}\right)^2$

$\qquad = \left(\sqrt{2}+\sqrt{3}\right)\left(\sqrt{2}+\sqrt{3}\right)$ Expand factors.

$\qquad = \sqrt{4}+\sqrt{6}+\sqrt{6}+\sqrt{9}$ FOIL method

$\qquad = 2 + 2\sqrt{6}+3$

$\qquad = 5 + 2\sqrt{6}$

However, we should have noticed that this is a special product, $(a+b)^2 = a^2 + 2ab + b^2$.

$$\left(\sqrt{2}+\sqrt{3}\right)^2 = \left(\sqrt{2}\right)^2 + 2\sqrt{2}\sqrt{3}+\left(\sqrt{3}\right)^2 = 2 + 2\sqrt{6}+3$$
$$= 5 + 2\sqrt{6}$$

d. $\left(\sqrt{x}-2\right)^2 = \left(\sqrt{x}\right)^2 - 2\cdot\sqrt{x}\cdot 2 + 2^2 = x - 4\sqrt{x}+4$ ∎

The product of the sum and difference of two terms is the difference of their squares.

$$(a+b)(a-b) = a^2 - b^2$$

The expressions $a + b$ and $a - b$ are called **conjugates** of each other. When we multiply conjugates that contain square roots, we obtain an interesting result. Complete the following set of exercise to discover this result.

D I S C O V E R Y   7

Conjugates

Multiply and simplify.

1. $\left(\sqrt{2}+\sqrt{3}\right)\left(\sqrt{2}-\sqrt{3}\right)$ **2.** $\left(2+\sqrt{x}\right)\left(2-\sqrt{x}\right)$

What did you notice about the products?

In these exercises, we noticed that the factors contained square roots but the product did not contain a square root.

We can see why this is true if we multiply $\left(\sqrt{x}+\sqrt{y}\right)\left(\sqrt{x}-\sqrt{y}\right)$, using the special product

$$(a+b)(a-b) = a^2 - b^2.$$
$$\left(\sqrt{x}+\sqrt{y}\right)\left(\sqrt{x}-\sqrt{y}\right) = \left(\sqrt{x}\right)^2 - \left(\sqrt{y}\right)^2$$
$$= x - y$$

This is true only for radicals involving square roots. We will use conjugates in the next section to rationalize denominators.

Experiencing Algebra the Checkup Way

Multiply exercises 1–6 and simplify. Where possible, check for equivalence of your results using your calculator.

1. $7\sqrt[3]{x}\left(5\sqrt[3]{x^2} + 4\sqrt[3]{x}\right)$

2. $\left(\sqrt{3} - \sqrt{ab}\right)\left(\sqrt{7} + \sqrt{ab}\right)$

3. $\left(\sqrt{10} + \sqrt{5}\right)\left(\sqrt{10} - \sqrt{5}\right)$

4. $\left(11 + \sqrt{z}\right)\left(11 - \sqrt{z}\right)$

5. $\left(\sqrt{10} + \sqrt{5}\right)^2$

6. $\left(\sqrt{z} - 5\right)^2$

7. Describe what we mean by a conjugate of a radical expression. Give an example.

8. What special result is obtained when multiplying conjugate expressions?

---

3 Dividing Radicals We have already divided radical expressions with one term. We used the properties of radicals to simplify these. We are now ready to expand our division of radicals to radical expressions that may have more than one term.

To divide a radical expression by a single-term radical expression, we use the distributive law, as we did to divide polynomial expressions. For example,

$$\frac{x + 6}{2} = \frac{x}{2} + \frac{6}{2} \qquad \text{Polynomial expression}$$

$$= \frac{1}{2}x + 3$$

$$\frac{\sqrt{x} + \sqrt{6}}{\sqrt{2}} = \frac{\sqrt{x}}{\sqrt{2}} + \frac{\sqrt{6}}{\sqrt{2}} \qquad \text{Radical expression}$$

$$= \frac{\sqrt{x}}{\sqrt{2}} \cdot \frac{\sqrt{2}}{\sqrt{2}} + \sqrt{3} \qquad \text{Simplify and rationalize the denominator.}$$

$$= \frac{\sqrt{2x}}{2} + \sqrt{3} \quad \text{or} \quad \frac{1}{2}\sqrt{2x} + \sqrt{3}$$

To divide a radical expression with square roots by a radical expression containing two terms with square roots, we use the multiplication property of 1 and conjugates. Remember that the product of conjugates with at least one square-root term results in an expression without square roots. Therefore, this division process will rationalize the denominator. For example,

$$\frac{\sqrt{5}}{\sqrt{3} + \sqrt{2}} = \frac{\sqrt{5}}{\sqrt{3} + \sqrt{2}} \cdot \frac{\sqrt{3} - \sqrt{2}}{\sqrt{3} - \sqrt{2}} \qquad \begin{array}{l}\text{Multiplication by 1}\\ \text{Use the conjugate of the}\\ \text{denominator as numerator and}\\ \text{denominator of the factor of 1.}\end{array}$$

$$= \frac{\sqrt{5}\left(\sqrt{3} - \sqrt{2}\right)}{\left(\sqrt{3} + \sqrt{2}\right)\left(\sqrt{3} - \sqrt{2}\right)} \qquad \text{Multiply.}$$

$$= \frac{\sqrt{15} - \sqrt{10}}{\left(\sqrt{3}\right)^2 - \left(\sqrt{2}\right)^2} \qquad \text{Distribute and simplify.}$$

$$= \frac{\sqrt{15} - \sqrt{10}}{3 - 2}$$

$$= \frac{\sqrt{15} - \sqrt{10}}{1}$$

$$= \sqrt{15} - \sqrt{10}$$

EXAMPLE 4   Divide and simplify.

a. $\dfrac{2\sqrt{x} + \sqrt{5}}{\sqrt{x} - 2\sqrt{2}}$ b. $\dfrac{\sqrt{3} + \sqrt{7}}{\sqrt{3} - \sqrt{7}}$

Solution

a. $\dfrac{2\sqrt{x} + \sqrt{5}}{\sqrt{x} - 2\sqrt{2}}$

$= \dfrac{2\sqrt{x} + \sqrt{5}}{\sqrt{x} - 2\sqrt{2}} \cdot \dfrac{\sqrt{x} + 2\sqrt{2}}{\sqrt{x} + 2\sqrt{2}}$

Multiplication by 1
Use the conjugate of the denominator as numerator and denominator of the factor of 1.

$= \dfrac{(2\sqrt{x} + \sqrt{5})(\sqrt{x} + 2\sqrt{2})}{(\sqrt{x} - 2\sqrt{2})(\sqrt{x} + 2\sqrt{2})}$

Multiply.

$= \dfrac{2\sqrt{x^2} + 4\sqrt{2x} + \sqrt{5x} + 2\sqrt{10}}{(\sqrt{x})^2 - (2\sqrt{2})^2}$

Use the FOIL method and simplify.

$= \dfrac{2x + 4\sqrt{2x} + \sqrt{5x} + 2\sqrt{10}}{x - 8}$

b. $\dfrac{\sqrt{3} + \sqrt{7}}{\sqrt{3} - \sqrt{7}} = \dfrac{\sqrt{3} + \sqrt{7}}{\sqrt{3} - \sqrt{7}} \cdot \dfrac{\sqrt{3} + \sqrt{7}}{\sqrt{3} + \sqrt{7}}$

Multiplication by 1
Use the conjugate of the denominator as numerator and denominator of the factor of 1.

$= \dfrac{(\sqrt{3} + \sqrt{7})(\sqrt{3} + \sqrt{7})}{(\sqrt{3} - \sqrt{7})(\sqrt{3} + \sqrt{7})}$

Multiply.

$= \dfrac{(\sqrt{3})^2 + 2\sqrt{21} + (\sqrt{7})^2}{(\sqrt{3})^2 - (\sqrt{7})^2}$

FOIL method

$= \dfrac{3 + 2\sqrt{21} + 7}{3 - 7}$

$= \dfrac{10 + 2\sqrt{21}}{-4}$

$= \dfrac{2(5 + \sqrt{21})}{2(-2)}$

Factor the numerator and denominator to simplify the fraction.

$= \dfrac{5 + \sqrt{21}}{-2}$

$= \dfrac{5 + \sqrt{21}}{-2} \cdot \dfrac{-1}{-1}$

Multiplication by 1
Use −1 as the numerator and denominator in order to eliminate a negative denominator.

$= \dfrac{-5 - \sqrt{21}}{2}$ ∎

Experiencing Algebra the Checkup Way

Divide exercises 1–4 and simplify. Check for equivalence of your result using your calculator.

1. $\dfrac{\sqrt{6x} + \sqrt{15}}{\sqrt{3}}$

2. $\dfrac{\sqrt{13}}{\sqrt{5} + \sqrt{2}}$

3. $\dfrac{\sqrt{6} + \sqrt{2}}{\sqrt{6} - \sqrt{2}}$

4. $\dfrac{8\sqrt{x} - \sqrt{3}}{\sqrt{x} + 2\sqrt{3}}$

5. Suppose one radical expression involving square roots is being divided by another radical expression with two terms involving square roots. What is accomplished by multiplying both the numerator and the denominator by the conjugate of the denominator? Why would this be desirable?

---

4 Modeling the Real World

When we use geometric formulas involving radicals, we encounter values that are not perfect-square radicands, but are irrational numbers instead. Evaluating complicated radical expressions can be tricky, even with a calculator; it is usually a good idea to simplify these radical expressions using the rules for radicals we've discussed in this section.

EXAMPLE 5

Fernando plans to increase the size of a square fenced area in his yard. The present area is 48 square feet. He plans to increase the fenced area to 108 square feet and keep the shape as a square. Determine the amount of additional fencing that Fernando needs to purchase. (Round your answer to the nearest foot.)

Solution

Determine the length of the sides of the present area and the new area.

Present area: $\quad s = \sqrt{A}$ $\qquad$ New area: $\quad s = \sqrt{A}$

$$s = \sqrt{48} \qquad\qquad\qquad s = \sqrt{108}$$
$$s = \sqrt{16 \cdot 3} \qquad\qquad\quad s = \sqrt{36 \cdot 3}$$
$$s = 4\sqrt{3} \qquad\qquad\qquad s = 6\sqrt{3}$$

Determine the amount of fencing for both areas. Use the perimeter formula.

Present area: $\quad P = 4s$ $\qquad$ New area: $\quad P = 4s$

$$P = 4 \cdot 4\sqrt{3} \qquad\qquad\quad P = 4 \cdot 6\sqrt{3}$$
$$P = 16\sqrt{3} \qquad\qquad\qquad P = 24\sqrt{3}$$

The difference in the new perimeter and the present perimeter is the amount of fencing needed.

$$24\sqrt{3} - 16\sqrt{3} = 8\sqrt{3} \approx 13.86$$

Fernando needs $8\sqrt{3}$ feet of additional fencing or approximately 14 feet of fencing. ■

Application

The Hephaesteion was a temple built by the Greeks in the fifth century B.C. The ratio of its width to its height is approximated by the expression $\frac{2}{\sqrt{5}-1}$. This number is called the golden ratio. Early Greeks believed that rectangles with this ratio were aesthetically pleasing to the eye. Rationalize the denominator of the expression.

Discussion

$$\frac{2}{\sqrt{5}-1} = \frac{2}{\sqrt{5}-1} \cdot \frac{\sqrt{5}+1}{\sqrt{5}+1} \qquad \text{Use the conjugate of the denominator as the numerator and denominator of the factor of 1.}$$

$$= \frac{2(\sqrt{5}+1)}{(\sqrt{5}-1)(\sqrt{5}+1)} \qquad \text{Multiply.}$$

$$= \frac{2(\sqrt{5}+1)}{4}$$

$$= \frac{\sqrt{5}+1}{2}$$

The golden ratio is $\frac{\sqrt{5}+1}{2}$.

Note: In "Experiencing Algebra the Calculator Way" in section 5.5, you were given this form of the golden ratio. ■

 Experiencing Algebra the Checkup Way

Sandra purchased enough baseboard to surround her sunporch floor, which was a square measuring 350 square feet. Julie purchased baseboard for her sunporch, which was also a square measuring 224 square feet. What is the difference in the amounts of baseboard the women purchased? Ignore cuts in the baseboard for doors.

Sandra

Julie

PROBLEM SET 13.5

 Experiencing Algebra the Exercise Way

Add or subtract as indicated.

1. $2\sqrt{28} - \sqrt{63}$

2. $5\sqrt{24} - \sqrt{54}$

3. $\sqrt{10} - \sqrt{\dfrac{1}{10}}$

4. $\sqrt{13} + \sqrt{\dfrac{1}{13}}$

5. $\sqrt[3]{24} - 4\sqrt[3]{3}$

6. $2\sqrt[3]{250} + \sqrt[3]{54}$

7. $5\sqrt{75} - 2\sqrt{27} + \sqrt{48}$

8. $4\sqrt{80} - 2\sqrt{45} + \sqrt{20}$

9. $5\sqrt{x} + 9\sqrt{x}$

10. $8\sqrt{bc} - 10\sqrt{bc}$

11. $\sqrt{25x} + \sqrt{36x}$

12. $\sqrt{64p} + \sqrt{144p}$

13. $\sqrt{8x^3} - \sqrt{50x^3}$

14. $\sqrt{48y^5} - \sqrt{75y^5}$

15. $\sqrt{9a} + \sqrt{16a^3}$

16. $\sqrt{121b^3} - \sqrt{16b}$

17. $7a\sqrt{b} + 9a\sqrt{b} - 2a\sqrt{b}$

18. $2x\sqrt{y} - 5x\sqrt{y} + 4x\sqrt{y}$

19. $5\sqrt{pq} - 4\sqrt[3]{pq} + 2\sqrt{pq} + 11\sqrt[3]{pq}$

20. $4\sqrt[3]{ab} - 3\sqrt{ab} - 5\sqrt{ab} + 2\sqrt[3]{ab}$

21. $7y\sqrt{x^3y} + 3x\sqrt{xy^3} - 4xy\sqrt{xy}$

22. $5d\sqrt{c^3d} - 8c\sqrt{cd^3} + 2cd\sqrt{cd}$

23. $2x\sqrt[3]{x^2y^4z} - 3y\sqrt[3]{x^5yz}$

24. $6x\sqrt[4]{xy^5z^2} + y\sqrt[4]{x^5yz^2}$

Multiply and simplify.

25. $\sqrt{7}(\sqrt{5} - \sqrt{7})$

26. $\sqrt{5}(\sqrt{6} + \sqrt{5})$

27. $\sqrt{3}(\sqrt{x} - \sqrt{5})$

28. $2\sqrt{5}(\sqrt{7} + \sqrt{a})$

29. $3\sqrt{a}(2\sqrt{a} - 5)$

30. $8\sqrt{c}(3\sqrt{c} + 4)$

31. $2\sqrt[3]{x}(4\sqrt[3]{x^2} - 6\sqrt[3]{x})$

32. $7\sqrt[3]{a}(5\sqrt[3]{a} - 2\sqrt[3]{a^2})$

33. $(\sqrt{3} - 5\sqrt{6})(2\sqrt{3} + \sqrt{8})$

34. $(3\sqrt{6} + 2)(\sqrt{5} - 4\sqrt{3})$

35. $(\sqrt{3} - \sqrt{x})(\sqrt{2} + \sqrt{x})$

36. $(\sqrt{2} - \sqrt{z})(\sqrt{5} + \sqrt{z})$

37. $(5 - \sqrt{6})(5 + \sqrt{6})$

38. $(\sqrt{11} + \sqrt{12})(\sqrt{11} - \sqrt{12})$

39. $(12 + \sqrt{p})(12 - \sqrt{p})$

40. $(13 - \sqrt{q})(13 + \sqrt{q})$

41. $(\sqrt{2x} + \sqrt{3y})(\sqrt{2x} - \sqrt{3y})$

42. $(\sqrt{6x} + \sqrt{3y})(\sqrt{6x} - \sqrt{3y})$

43. $(\sqrt{a} + 4)^2$

44. $(\sqrt{bc} + 5)^2$

45. $(3\sqrt{b} - 2)^2$

46. $(9\sqrt{c} - 3)^2$

47. $(\sqrt{x} - \sqrt{y})^2$

48. $(\sqrt{2x} - \sqrt{3y})^2$

Divide and simplify.

49. $\dfrac{\sqrt{21x} - \sqrt{14}}{\sqrt{7}}$

50. $\dfrac{\sqrt{10x} + \sqrt{30}}{\sqrt{5}}$

51. $\dfrac{\sqrt{a} - 12}{\sqrt{a}}$

52. $\dfrac{9 + \sqrt{b}}{\sqrt{b}}$

53. $\dfrac{\sqrt{x} + \sqrt{y} + \sqrt{z}}{\sqrt{x}}$

54. $\dfrac{\sqrt{ab} - \sqrt{ac} + \sqrt{bc}}{\sqrt{b}}$

55. $\dfrac{18}{\sqrt{6} + \sqrt{3}}$

56. $\dfrac{24}{\sqrt{10} + \sqrt{2}}$

57. $\dfrac{\sqrt{3} + \sqrt{2}}{\sqrt{3} - \sqrt{2}}$

58. $\dfrac{\sqrt{3} - \sqrt{2}}{\sqrt{3} + \sqrt{2}}$

59. $\dfrac{3x}{\sqrt{x} - 2}$

60. $\dfrac{4w}{3 - \sqrt{w}}$

61. $\dfrac{3b - 4}{\sqrt{3b} - 2}$

62. $\dfrac{ab - 1}{\sqrt{ab} + 1}$

63. $\dfrac{\sqrt{x} + 3}{\sqrt{x} - 3}$

64. $\dfrac{6 - \sqrt{p}}{6 + \sqrt{p}}$

65. $\dfrac{3\sqrt{x} - 4}{4 - 3\sqrt{x}}$

66. $\dfrac{3 - 5\sqrt{x}}{5\sqrt{x} - 3}$

67. One painting on a square canvas measures 490 square inches. A second painting on a square canvas measures 810 square inches. How many more inches of frame will the second painting require over that required for the first painting?

68. The footprint of one computer is a square measuring 150 square inches. The footprint of a second computer is also a square, but it measures 216 square inches. By how many inches does the perimeter of the footprint for the second computer exceed that of the first? (*Note:* The footprint of a computer is the base upon which it rests.)

69. A box in the shape of a cube has a volume of 1750 cubic inches. It contains a smaller box shaped like a cube, with a volume of 896 cubic inches. Determine the difference in the perimeters of the bases of the two boxes.

70. A pair of stacking tables in the shapes of cubes consists of one whose volume is 2000 cubic inches and another whose volume is 6750 cubic inches. Determine the difference in the perimeters of the bases of the two tables.

Experiencing Algebra the Calculator Way

Operations with radicals represent another situation in which the calculator can be helpful to check your results, if the radical expressions contain only a single variable. By storing the original expression in Y1 and your simplified result in Y2, and comparing the graphs for equivalence, you can see whether your result is correct. You may also use the TABLE function to explore equivalence of the two expressions. Simplify the following expressions and use this method of checking your results for equivalence.

1. $\left(3\sqrt[3]{x} + 5\sqrt{x}\right) + \left(\sqrt[3]{x} - 3\sqrt{x}\right) + \left(4\sqrt{x} + 7\right)$

2. $\left(2\sqrt{x} + 7\right) - \left(\sqrt{x} + 9\right)$

3. $2\sqrt[3]{x}\left(3\sqrt[3]{2x} + 5\right)$

4. $\left(2\sqrt{x} + 3\sqrt{2x}\right)\left(\sqrt{x} + \sqrt{2x}\right)$

5. $\dfrac{x - 16}{\sqrt{x} + 4}$

6. $\dfrac{21}{\sqrt{x} - 7}$

7. $\left(3\sqrt{x} + 5\right)\left(\sqrt{x} - 7\right) + 3\sqrt{x} - 6$

Experiencing Algebra the Group Way

The coefficients in radical addition and subtraction are not limited to integer values. They may be decimal or fraction values also. When combining the coefficients, use the rules for adding and subtracting decimals and fractions. Discuss the steps you would follow to perform the addition and subtraction for each of the following exercises. Then have each member of the group determine the result. Compare your results and agree on the final answers.

1. $3.7\sqrt{x} + 5.8\sqrt{x}$

2. $2.8\sqrt{10x} + 1.6\sqrt{90x}$

3. $6.1\sqrt{7x^2} - 2.3\sqrt{28x^2}$

4. $5.2\sqrt{75a} - 2.7\sqrt{27a} + \sqrt{48a}$

5. $\dfrac{3}{4}\sqrt{p} - \dfrac{5}{6}\sqrt{p}$

6. $\dfrac{1}{3}\sqrt{3x} + \dfrac{7}{9}\sqrt{27x}$

7. $\dfrac{3}{4}\sqrt{5a^2} - \dfrac{5}{8}\sqrt{20a^2}$

8. $\dfrac{2}{3}\sqrt{32b} + \dfrac{5}{6}\sqrt{18b} - \dfrac{3}{4}\sqrt{8b}$

Experiencing Algebra the Write Way

Consider the following two exercises.

1. $\sqrt[3]{2x^2}\left(\sqrt[3]{4x^2} + 5\right) = \sqrt[3]{8x^4} + 5\sqrt[3]{2x^2} = 2\sqrt[3]{x^4} + 5\sqrt[3]{2x^2}$

2. $\dfrac{\sqrt[3]{15x^5} + \sqrt[3]{24x^4} + \sqrt[3]{9x^3} - 3\sqrt[3]{6x^2} + 2\sqrt[3]{18x}}{\sqrt[3]{3x}} = \sqrt[3]{5x^4} + \sqrt[3]{8x^3} + \sqrt[3]{3x^2} - 3\sqrt[3]{2x} + 2\sqrt[3]{6}$

Are the exercises completed? If not, describe what remains to be done, and why. Then present the final result, if different from that given. Write a short description of the steps that must be conducted to obtain the final result for each of the exercises. Finish the description by stating what you should look for when you think you have completed simplifying a radical expression.

13.6   **Solving Radical Equations in One Variable Numerically and Graphically**

Objectives
1. Identify radical equations in one variable.
2. Solve radical equations in one variable numerically.
3. Solve radical equations in one variable graphically.
4. Model real-world situations using radical equations in one variable.

Application

Using the data given by TVB 1992–93 & McCann-Erickson[1], an expression to estimate the local television advertising volume in millions of dollars is

[1] Sources: TVB 1992–93 & McCann-Erickson, *The 1995 Information Please Business Almanac and Sourcebook.*

$3619 \sqrt[3]{x}$, where x is the number of years after 1981. An expression to estimate the spot television advertising volume in millions of dollars is $4257\sqrt[4]{x}$ where x is the number of years after 1981. Determine graphically the year the local television advertising volume equals the spot television advertising volume.

After completing this section, we will discuss this application further. See page 1067.

---

1 Radical Equations in One Variable

We are now ready to solve radical equations in one variable. A **radical equation in one variable**, or *radical equation*, can be written in the form of an expression, containing radicals with variables in the radicands, that is equal to 0. Since an exponential expression with a rational exponent is equivalent to a radical expression, a radical equation may also be written in the form of an exponential expression, which has a variable base with a rational exponent, that is equal to 0.

> *Standard Form for a Radical Equation in One Variable*
> A radical equation in one variable is written in the form
>
> $$D(x) = 0,$$
>
> where $D(x)$ is (1) an expression containing radicals with a variable in the radicand or (2) an exponential expression with a variable base and a rational exponent.

The following examples are radical equations in one variable:

$$\sqrt{2x + 5} = 5, \text{ because } \sqrt{2x + 5} - 5 = 0.$$

$$\sqrt[3]{x + 3} = 5\sqrt[3]{x - 2}, \text{ because } \sqrt[3]{x + 3} - 5\sqrt[3]{x - 2} = 0.$$

$$(2x + 7)^{2/5} = x - 3, \text{ because } (2x + 7)^{2/5} - x + 3 = 0 \text{ or}$$
$$\sqrt[5]{(2x + 7)^2} - x + 3 = 0.$$

EXAMPLE 1   State whether each of the following equations is a radical equation.

a. $\sqrt[5]{x + 3} = 2x$ **b.** $\sqrt{3}x + x = 0$ **c.** $x^{3/4} = 2x^2$

Solution

a. $\sqrt[5]{x + 3} = 2x$ is a radical equation, because $\sqrt[5]{x + 3} - 2x = 0.$

b. $\sqrt{3}x + x = 0$ is not a radical equation, because the radicand does not contain a variable.

c. $x^{3/4} = 2x^2$ is a radical equation, because $x^{3/4} - 2x^2 = 0$ is equivalent to $\sqrt[4]{x^3} - 2x^2 = 0.$ ■

Experiencing Algebra the Checkup Way

State whether each of the following equations is a radical equation.

1. $\sqrt{5} + x = 7$ **2.** $\sqrt[3]{2x} = x + 3$ **3.** $5x - 3 = x^{2/3}$

4. What is the difference between a radical equation and a radical expression?

---

2 Solving Radical Equations Numerically

In previous chapters, we determined whether a number was a solution of a polynomial equation or a rational equation in one variable by substituting the value for the possible solution into the variable and evaluating the two resulting expressions. If the resulting equation was true, the number substituted was called a solution. We do the same for a radical equation in one variable. For example, given $\sqrt{x + 3} = x + 1$, determine whether -2 is a solution.

$$\frac{\sqrt{x + 3} = x + 1}{\begin{array}{c|c} \sqrt{-2 + 3} & -2 + 1 \\ \sqrt{1} & -1 \\ 1 & \end{array}}$$

Therefore, -2 is not a solution, because the resulting values for the expressions, 1 and -1, are not equal.

In order to find a solution of the equation $\sqrt{x + 3} = x + 1$, we continue to substitute possible values for x and determine whether the resulting equations are true. Remember that certain numbers are restricted values for the radical terms and result in values not defined in the real-number system. Restricted values are *never* solutions of radical equations. A table of values is helpful in organizing this method.

> *Solving a Radical Equation Numerically*
> To solve a radical equation numerically:
> Determine the restricted values for the independent variable in each radical expression.
>> Set up an extended table of values:
>
> • The first column is labeled with the name of the independent variable.
> • The second column is labeled with the expression on the left side of the equation.
> • The third column is labeled with the expression on the right side of the equation.
>
> Complete the table:
>
> • Substitute values for the independent variable.
> • Evaluate the second and third columns.
> • Continue until values for the two expressions (the numbers in the second and third columns) are equal.
>
> *Continued*

The values for the independent variable (the number in the first column) used to find these equivalent expressions are the solutions.

For example, a sample table to determine the integer solutions of $\sqrt{x + 3} = x + 1$ could appear as follows.

The restricted values for the radical expression are all real numbers less than -3.

x	$\sqrt{x + 3}$	$x + 1$
-1	1.4142	0
0	1.7321	1
1	2	2
2	2.2361	3

According to the table, when 1 is substituted for the variable, x, the two expressions are equal $(2 = 2)$. Therefore, 1 is a solution of the radical equation.

To solve a radical equation numerically on your calculator:

- Rename the independent variable as x.

Set up the table.

- Set up the first column for the independent variable by setting a minimum value and the size of increments. Since we do not know the solution, we may want to start with 0. Use increments of 1 to obtain integer values. Set the calculator to automatically perform the evaluations.
- Set up the second column of the table to be the expression on the left. Enter the expression on the left side of the equation in Y1.
- Set up the third column of the table to be the expression on the right. Enter the expression on the right side of the equation in Y2.

View the table.

- Move beyond the screen to view additional rows by using the up and down arrows.

The integer solutions are the x-values that determine equal values for Y1 and Y2. For example, solve $\sqrt{x + 3} = x + 1$ on your calculator.

The solution occurs when Y1 $=$ Y2. The solution from the table is 1, as shown in Figures 13.6a, 13.6b, and 13.6c.

TABLE SETUP
TblStart=0
⊿Tbl=1
Indpnt: **Auto** Ask
Depend: **Auto** Ask

Figure 13.6a

Plot1	Plot2	Plot3
\Y₁=√(X+3)		
\Y₂=X+1		
\Y₃=		
\Y₄=		
\Y₅=		
\Y₆=		
\Y₇=		

Figure 13.6b

X	Y₁	Y₂
0	1.7321	1
1	2	2
2	2.2361	3
3	2.4495	4
4	2.6458	5
5	2.8284	6
6	3	7
X=0		

Figure 13.6c

EXAMPLE 2 Solve numerically.

a. $\sqrt{4(2x-1)} = x - 3$ **b.** $\sqrt[3]{x^2 + 8x + 7} = x + 1$

c. $x - 7 = (x + 1)^{3/4}$

Calculator Numeric Solution

a. $\sqrt{4(2x-1)} = x - 3$

The restricted values for the radical expression are all real numbers less than $\frac{1}{2}$.

The solution is 13, because when 13 is substituted for the variable in both expressions, the resulting values are equal.

b. $\sqrt[3]{x^2 + 8x + 7} = x + 1$

There are no restricted values for the radical expression.

The solutions are -3, -1, and 2, because when -3, -1, and 2 are substituted for the variable in both expressions, the resulting values are equal.

c. $x - 7 = (x + 1)^{3/4}$

The restricted values for the radical expression are all real numbers less than -1.

The solution is 15, because when 15 is substituted for the variable in both expressions, the resulting values are equal. ∎

a.

X	Y₁	Y₂
8	7.746	5
9	8.2462	6
10	8.7178	7
11	9.1652	8
12	9.5917	9
13	10	10
14	10.392	11
X=13		

Y1 = $\sqrt{4(2x-1)}$
Y2 = $x - 3$

b.

X	Y₁	Y₂
-3	-2	-2
-2	-1.71	-1
-1	0	0
0	1.9129	1
1	2.5198	2
2	3	3
3	3.42	4
X=-3		

Y1 = $\sqrt[3]{x^2 + 8x + 7}$
Y2 = $x + 1$

c.

X	Y₁	Y₂
9	2	5.6234
10	3	6.0401
11	4	6.4474
12	5	6.8463
13	6	7.2376
14	7	7.622
15	8	8
X=15		

Y1 = $x - 7$
Y2 = $(x + 1)^{3/4}$

EXAMPLE 3 $\sqrt[5]{x + 3} = 2x$ does not have an integer solution. Set up a table of values on your calculator and determine that there is no integer solution.

Calculator Numeric Solution

We cannot find a value for x that corresponds to Y1 = Y2. However, for x-values less than or equal to 0, Y1 > Y2, and for x-values greater than or equal to 1, Y1 < Y2. Since the x-values are not restricted between 0 and 1, this means that a solution occurs between 0 and 1 when Y1 = Y2. ∎

X	Y₁	Y₂
-3	0	-6
-2	1	-4
-1	1.1487	-2
0	1.2457	0
1	1.3195	2
2	1.3797	4
3	1.431	6
X=0		

0 > -6
1 > -4
1.1487 > -2
1.2457 > 0
1.3195 < 2
1.3797 < 4
1.431 < 6

Y1 = $\sqrt[5]{x + 3}$
Y2 = $2x$

Some polynomial and rational equations had no solution or an infinite number of solutions. This is also true for radical equations. Complete the following sets of exercises to find rules to explain these situations.

D I S C O V E R Y   8

Radical Equations with No Solution

Solve $\sqrt{x + 2} - 5 = \sqrt{x + 2} + 8$ numerically by completing the table of values given.

x	$\sqrt{x + 2} - 5$	$\sqrt{x + 2} + 8$
-3		
-2		
-1		
0		
1		
2		
3		

Write a rule to explain the solution of the equation from viewing its table of values.

It appears that the expression on the left is never equal to the expression on the right. In fact, the expression on the left is always 13 less than the expression on the right. Therefore, the equation does not appear to have a solution. We will need to confirm this by using an alternative method of solving.

D I S C O V E R Y   9

Radical Equations with Many Solutions

Solve $\sqrt{x} = \sqrt[6]{x^3}$ numerically by completing the table of values given.

x	$\sqrt{x}$	$\sqrt[6]{x^3}$
0		
1		
2		
3		

Write a rule to explain the solution of the equation from viewing its table of values.

The two expressions are equal for every value of the independent variable in the table. The domain for the independent variable is all real numbers greater than or equal to 0. Therefore, it appears that the solution set of the equation is all real numbers greater than or equal to 0.

EXAMPLE 4   Solve numerically.

a. $(x + 2)^{2/3} = -3$ **b.** $(x + 1)^{2/3} = (x^2 + 2x + 1)^{1/3}$

c. $\sqrt{x + 3} = \sqrt[4]{(x + 3)^2}$ **d.** $\sqrt{x + 3} - 2 = \sqrt[4]{(x + 3)^2}$

Calculator Numeric Solution

Enter the tables as in previous examples.

a. $(x + 2)^{2/3} = -3$

a.

X	Y1	Y2
-5	2.0801	-3
-4	1.5874	-3
-3	1	-3
-2	0	-3
-1	1	-3
0	1.5874	-3
1	2.0801	-3

X= -5

Y1 = $(x + 2)^{2/3}$
Y2 = -3

The expressions do not appear to be equal. The expression on the left is always less than the expression on the right. The equation does not appear to have a solution. We will confirm this algebraically in the next section of this chapter.

b. $(x + 1)^{2/3} = (x^2 + 2x + 1)^{1/3}$

X	Y1	Y2
0	1	1
1	1.5874	1.5874
2	2.0801	2.0801
3	2.5198	2.5198
4	2.924	2.924
5	3.3019	3.3019
6	3.6593	3.6593
X=0		

$$1 = 1$$
$$1.5874 = 1.5874$$
$$2.0801 = 2.0801$$
$$2.5198 = 2.5198$$
$$2.924 = 2.924$$
$$3.3019 = 3.3019$$
$$3.6593 = 3.6593$$

Y1 $= (x + 1)^{2/3}$ Y2 $= (x^2 + 2x + 1)^{1/3}$

The expressions are always equal for values in the table, so it appears that the solution set is all real numbers, the domain of the independent variable.

c. $\sqrt{x + 3} = \sqrt[4]{(x + 3)^2}$

X	Y1	Y2
-5	ERROR	1.4142
-4	ERROR	1
-3	0	0
-2	1	1
-1	1.4142	1.4142
0	1.7321	1.7321
1	2	2
X= -5		

$$0 = 0$$
$$1 = 1$$
$$1.4142 = 1.4142$$
$$1.7321 = 1.7321$$
$$2 = 2$$

Y1 $= \sqrt{x + 3}$ Y2 $= \sqrt[4]{(x + 3)^2}$

The expressions are always equal for values in the table, so it appears that the solution set is all real numbers greater than or equal to -3, the domain of the independent variable.

d. $\sqrt{x + 3} - 2 = \sqrt[4]{(x + 3)^2}$

X	Y1	Y2
0	-.2679	1.7321
1	0	2
2	.23607	2.2361
3	.44949	2.4495
4	.64575	2.6458
5	.82843	2.8284
6	1	3
X=0		

$$-.2679 < 1.7321$$
$$0 < 2$$
$$.23607 < 2.2361$$
$$.44949 < 2.4495$$
$$.64575 < 2.6458$$
$$.82843 < 2.8284$$
$$1 < 3$$

Y1 $= \sqrt{x + 3} - 2$ Y2 $= \sqrt[4]{(x + 3)^2}$

The expression on the left is always 2 less than the expression on the right. The equation does not appear to have a solution. We will confirm this algebraically in the next section of this chapter. ■

Numerical Solutions of a Radical Equation
To solve a radical equation numerically for integer solutions, set up an extended table of values. In viewing the table, one of five possibilities will occur:

Integer solutions exists. The solutions are the integers in the first column that correspond to equal values in the second and third columns.
Noninteger solutions exist. When comparing corresponding values in the second and third columns, the order changes from "less than" to "greater than" or "greater than" to "less than," and the restricted

> value does not occur at this change. A noninteger solution occurs between the two consecutive integers in the first column that correspond to this change.
>
> **No solution exists.** When comparing corresponding values in the second and third columns, one column is always less than the other column.
>
> **An infinite number of solutions exist.** When comparing corresponding values in the second and third columns, the values are equal. The solution set is all numbers for which the equation is defined.

There are limitations on solving numerically. One limitation is that the solutions found are only integer solutions. Another limitation is the difficulty in determining whether an equation has no solution or a noninteger solution.

 ## Experiencing Algebra the Checkup Way

Solve exercises 1–5 numerically.

1. $x = \sqrt[3]{3 + x - 3x^2}$ **2.** $(x + 2)^{2/3} = x - 16$ **3.** $\sqrt[3]{2x + 3} = 2x - 3$ **4.** $\sqrt[4]{x^6} = \sqrt{x^3} + 5$

5. $\sqrt[4]{4x^2 + 4x + 1} = (2x + 1)^{1/2}$

6. When solving a radical equation numerically, there may be infinitely many solutions. How can you tell whether this is so?

7. When solving a radical equation numerically, there may appear to be no solutions. How can you tell whether this is so?

8. When solving a radical equation numerically, there may be a non-integer solution. How can you tell whether this is so?

---

3 Solving Radical Equations Graphically

A second method of solving an equation is to graph two functions. The functions to be graphed are written by using each expression in the equation as a rule for one of the functions. The x-coordinates of the points of intersection are the solutions.

> *Solving a Radical Equation Graphically*
> To solve a radical equation graphically:
>
> • Write two functions, using each expression in the equation as a rule.
>
> • Graph both functions on the same coordinate plane by plotting points found in a table of values and connecting the points with a smooth curve to include all values in the domain of the functions. Remember not to connect points across vertical lines represented by $x = a$, where a is a restricted value.
>
> The solutions of the equation are the x-coordinates of the points of intersection of the two graphs.
>
> The y-coordinates of the points of intersection of the two graphs are the values obtained for both expressions when the equation is evaluated with the solutions.

For example, solve graphically $\sqrt{x + 3} = x + 1$.

Set up a table of values for each function.

$y = \sqrt{x + 3}$ $\qquad\qquad$ $y = x + 1$

x	y
−3	0
−2	1
−1	1.4142
0	1.7321
1	2
2	2.2361

x	y
−1	0
0	1
1	2
2	3
3	4

Plotting these points results in the following graph:

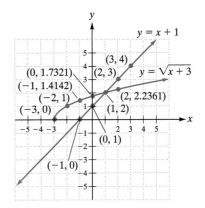

The solution is the x-coordinate of the intersection, 1.

To solve a radical equation graphically on your calculator:

- Rename the independent variable as x.
- Set the screen to the desired setting (integer, decimal, standard, or your choice).
- Enter the expression on the left side of the equation in Y1.
- Enter the expression on the right side of the equation in Y2.
- Graph.
- Find the point of intersection.

The solutions of the equation are the x-coordinates of the points of intersection of the two graphs.

The y-coordinates of the points of intersection of the two graphs are the values obtained for both expressions when the equation is evaluated with the solutions. For example, solve graphically $\sqrt{x + 3} = x + 1$.

The solution is the x-coordinate of the intersection, 1, as shown in Figure 13.7.

Y2 = x + 1   Y1 = $\sqrt{x + 3}$

(−10, 10, −10, 10)

Figure 13.7

EXAMPLE 5 Solve graphically.

a. $\sqrt{4(2x - 1)} = x - 3$ $\qquad\qquad$ b. $\sqrt[3]{x^2 + 8x + 7} = x + 1$

c. $x - 7 = (x + 1)^{3/4}$

Calculator Graphic Solution

a. $\sqrt{4(2x - 1)} = x - 3$

$(-47, 47, -31, 31)$

The solution is the x-coordinate of the intersection, 13.

b. $\sqrt[3]{x^2 + 8x + 7} = x + 1$

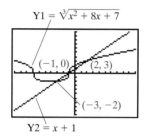

$(-10, 10, -10, 10)$

The solutions are the x-coordinates of the intersections, $-3, -1$, and 2.

c. $x - 7 = (x + 1)^{3/4}$

$(-47, 47, -31, 31)$

The solution is the x-coordinate of the intersection, 15. ∎

EXAMPLE 6 $\sqrt[5]{x + 3} = 2x$ does not have an integer solution. Use the Intersect function on your calculator to find an approximate solution.

Calculator Graphic Solution

$(-4.7, 4.7, -3.1, 3.1)$

The approximate solution is the x-coordinate of the intersection, 0.648. ∎

Remember that radical equations may have no solution or infinitely many solutions. Solving radical equations graphically also results in these possibilities. Complete the following sets of exercises on your calculator to determine when these possibilities occur.

DISCOVERY 10

Radical Equations with No Solution

Solve graphically the previous example of a radical equation with no solution, $\sqrt{x+2} - 5 = \sqrt{x+2} + 8$. Sketch the graph.

Write a rule to determine from its graph a radical equation with no solution.

The two functions do not appear to intersect. Therefore, there is no ordered pair common to both functions. The equation does not appear to have a solution. Once again, we will confirm this algebraically in the next section.

DISCOVERY 11

Radical Equations with Many Solutions

Solve graphically the previous example of a radical equation with many solutions, $\sqrt{x} = \sqrt[6]{x^3}$. Sketch the graph.

Write a rule to determine from its graph a solution of a radical equation with many solutions.

It appears that there is only one graph on the screen. Actually, both graphs are the same. You can verify this by tracing and using the arrow keys to move from one graph to another. Therefore, all ordered pairs on the graph are in common to both functions, and all x-coordinates are solutions of the equation. The solution set is all real numbers greater than or equal to 0 (the domain of the graphed functions).

EXAMPLE 7 Solve graphically.

a. $(x+2)^{2/3} = -3$ **b.** $(x+1)^{2/3} = \left(x^2 + 2x + 1\right)^{1/3}$

c. $\sqrt{x+3} = \sqrt[4]{(x+3)^2}$ **d.** $\sqrt{x+3} - 2 = \sqrt[4]{(x+3)^2}$

Calculator Graphic Solution

Define the two expressions as rules for functions and enter into your calculator, as in previous examples.

a. $(x+2)^{2/3} = -3$

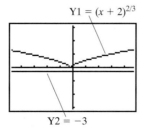

$(-47, 47, -31, 31)$

The graphs do not appear to intersect. The equation does not appear to have a solution. We will confirm this algebraically in the next section of this chapter.

b. $(x + 1)^{2/3} = (x^2 + 2x + 1)^{1/3}$

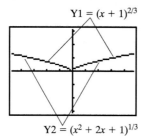

$Y1 = (x + 1)^{2/3}$

$Y2 = (x^2 + 2x + 1)^{1/3}$

$(-47, 47, -31, 31)$

The graphs appear to be the same. The solution set is all real numbers (the domain of the graphed functions).

c. $\sqrt{x + 3} = \sqrt[4]{(x + 3)^2}$

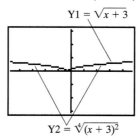

$Y1 = \sqrt{x + 3}$

$Y2 = \sqrt[4]{(x + 3)^2}$

$(-47, 47, -31, 31)$

The graphs are the same when $x \geq -3$. The equation is an identity. The solution set is all real numbers greater than or equal to -3 (the domain of the graphed functions).

d. $\sqrt{x + 3} - 2 = \sqrt[4]{(x + 3)^2}$

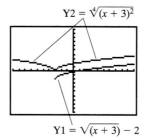

$Y2 = \sqrt[4]{(x + 3)^2}$

$Y1 = \sqrt{(x + 3)} - 2$

$(-10, 10, -10, 10)$

The graphs do not appear to intersect. The equation does not appear to have a solution. We will confirm this algebraically in the next section of this chapter. ∎

Graphical Solutions of a Radical Equation
To solve a radical equation graphically, graph two functions, defined by the expressions on the left and right sides of the equation. In viewing the graphs, one of four possibilities will occur:

One or more solutions exist. The graphs intersect. The solutions are the x-coordinates of the points of intersection.

> **No solution exists.** The graphs do not appear to intersect.
> **An infinite number of solutions exist.** The graphs appear to coincide. The solution set is all numbers in the domains of both of the graphed functions.

To summarize, we solve a radical equation graphically by graphing two functions. With a calculator, we may use this method to find noninteger solutions. Also, using this method, we are better able to find all the solutions because we can see the number of points of intersection. We can also determine that the graphs do not intersect and that certain equations do not appear to have solutions.

 Experiencing Algebra the Checkup Way

Solve exercises 1–5 graphically.

1. $x = \sqrt[3]{3 + x - 3x^2}$ **2.** $(x + 2)^{2/3} = x - 16$ **3.** $\sqrt[3]{2x + 3} = 2x - 3$ **4.** $\sqrt[4]{x^6} = \sqrt{x^3} + 5$
5. $\sqrt[4]{4x^2 + 4x + 1} = (2x + 1)^{1/2}$

6. When graphing the expressions on the left and right sides of a radical equation, the graphs may appear to coincide. If so, what does this indicate about solutions to the equation?

7. When graphing the expressions on the left and right sides of a radical equation, the graphs may not appear to intersect. If so, what does this indicate about solutions to the equation?

---

4 Modeling the Real World

We have seen that analyzing geometric situations often involves the use of radicals. If the radicand is not a particular number, but is a variable instead, we may wind up having to solve radical equations to determine the geometric dimensions. Solving these radical equations by graphing is often useful, particularly when we want to compare several solutions.

EXAMPLE 8

Dione's art instructor asked her to design a triangular flag with sides measuring $\sqrt{x}$ feet, $\sqrt{x + 7}$ feet, and $\sqrt{x + 16}$ feet. The flag is to be bound such that its perimeter is 12 feet. Determine the dimensions of the flag.

Graphic Solution

The perimeter is the distance around the triangular flag. Therefore, an equation for the perimeter is $\sqrt{x} + \sqrt{x + 7} + \sqrt{x + 16} = 12$. Graphing the two expressions in the equation, we obtain the graph to the left.

The x-coordinate of the intersection is 9. The solution is 9. The dimensions are $\sqrt{x} = \sqrt{9} = 3$ feet, $\sqrt{x + 7} = \sqrt{9 + 7} = \sqrt{16} = 4$ feet, and $\sqrt{x + 16} = \sqrt{9 + 16} = \sqrt{25} = 5$ feet. ∎

$Y1 = \sqrt{x} + \sqrt{x + 7} + \sqrt{x + 16}$

Intersection
X=9   Y=12

$Y2 = 12$

$(-47, 47, -31, 31)$

Application

Using the data given by TVB 1992–93 & McCann-Erickson[1], an expression to estimate the local television advertising volume in millions of dollars is

---

[1] Sources: TVB 1992–93 & McCann-Erickson, *The 1995 Information Please Business Almanac and Sourcebook.*

$3619 \sqrt[3]{x}$, where x is the number of years after 1981. An expression to estimate the spot television advertising volume in millions of dollars is $4257 \sqrt[4]{x}$, where x is the number of years after 1981. Determine graphically the year the local television advertising volume equals the spot television advertising volume.

Y2 = $4257\sqrt[4]{x}$

Y1 = $3619\sqrt[3]{x}$

Intersection
X=7.0174739 Y=6928.6536

(0, 20, 0, 10,000)

Discussion

To determine the year when the local television advertising volume equals the spot television advertising volume, we equate the two given expressions, $3619 \sqrt[3]{x} = 4257 \sqrt[4]{x}$. Graph each expression as a function of y.

The x-coordinate of the intersection of the graphs is approximately 7. Therefore, 7 years after 1981, in 1988, the volumes will be equal. ∎

 ## Experiencing Algebra the Checkup Way

Archie's math teacher instructed him to design a triangular garden plot with the lengths of two sides given by the expressions $\sqrt{x}$ feet and $\sqrt{3x + 36}$ feet, and with the third side measuring 9 feet. She told him that the perimeter of the plot is given by the expression $\sqrt{20x + 9}$ feet. Archie must find the lengths of the two unknown sides of the triangular plot, and the length of the perimeter of the garden plot. Solve Archie's problem.

PROBLEM SET 13.6

Experiencing Algebra the Exercise Way

State whether each equation is a radical equation.

1. $\sqrt{2x + 3} = x + 1$
2. $4x + 1 = 5x - \sqrt[3]{18}$
3. $3x - \sqrt{7} = 2x + 1$
4. $3x - 5^{2/3} = 0$
5. $x^{2/3} + \sqrt{3} = 0$
6. $3x^2 + x - 2 = 0$
7. $x + 5^{3/4} = 0$
8. $x - 5 = \sqrt{3x + 7}$
9. $x^2 - 3x + 2 = 0$
10. $x^{2/3} = 4 - 2\sqrt[3]{x^2}$
11. $x^{1/3} + 5\sqrt[3]{x} = 12$
12. $2x^{3/4} - \sqrt{8} = 0$

Solve numerically.

13. $\sqrt{5x + 4} = x - 4$
14. $\sqrt[4]{4x^2 + 28x + 49} = (2x + 7)^{1/2}$
15. $(2x + 1)^{2/3} = \sqrt[3]{4x^2 + 4x + 1}$
16. $x - 3 = \sqrt{3x - 5}$
17. $(5 - 2x)^{1/2} = \sqrt[4]{4x^2 - 20x + 25}$
18. $\sqrt[3]{9x^2 - 6x + 1} = (\sqrt[3]{3x - 1})^2$

Solve graphically.

19. $\sqrt{x} = 3$
20. $\sqrt{x} = 4$
21. $\sqrt{x - 2} = 3$
22. $\sqrt{x + 7} = 4$
23 $\sqrt{3x + 1} = \sqrt{26 - 2x}$
24. $\sqrt{2x + 1} = \sqrt{13 - x}$
25. $\sqrt{3x + 7} = x - 1$
26. $\sqrt{6x + 1} = 9 - x$
27. $x^3 = \sqrt[3]{x}$
28. $8x^3 = \sqrt[3]{2x}$
29. $(x + 2)^2 = \sqrt{x + 2}$
30. $(x - 2)^3 = \sqrt[3]{x - 2}$
31. $\sqrt{2x + 1} = 2x + 1$
32. $\sqrt{x - 4} = x - 4$
33. $(3x + 5)^{1/2} = \sqrt{3x - 5}$
34. $(x + 1)^{1/2} = \sqrt{x - 1}$
35. $\sqrt[3]{x^2 + 6x + 9} = (x + 3)^{2/3}$
36. $(3 - x)^{2/3} = \sqrt[3]{x^2 - 6x + 9}$
37. $\sqrt{x - 3} = \sqrt[4]{x^2 - 6x + 9}$
38. $\sqrt{x} = \sqrt[4]{x^2}$
39. $\sqrt[3]{(x + 1)^2} = \sqrt[3]{x^2 - 2x + 1}$
40. $\sqrt[3]{(x + 4)^2} = x$
41. $(x + 2)^{3/2} = x + 20$
42. $3 - x = (x - 2)^{3/2}$
43. $\sqrt[3]{x^2 - 6x + 9} = x + 9$
44. $2x + 5 = \sqrt[3]{x^2 - 4x + 4}$
45. $x + 5 = \sqrt[3]{4x + 5}$
46. $\sqrt[3]{2x + 3} = 3 - x$
47. $\sqrt{x} = 4.23$
48. $\sqrt{2x + 3} = 5.07$

49. $3x + 1 = \sqrt[3]{2x - 5}$

50. $\sqrt[3]{3 - x} = 3x$

51. $\sqrt[3]{2x + 3} = \sqrt{4 - x}$

52. $\sqrt{3 - x} = \sqrt[3]{x - 2}$

53. $(5x + 7)^{2/3} = (x - 6)^{3/4}$

54. $(x - 4)^{3/4} = (4x - 3)^{2/3}$

55. $3x + 2 = \sqrt{9x^2 + 12x + 4}$

56. $\sqrt{4x^2 - 20x + 25} = 5 - 2x$

57. Li's math teacher assigned her the problem of designing a silver jewelry box. The box must have a rectangular base with a width of $\sqrt{x + 4}$ inches and a length of $\sqrt{3x}$ inches. The perimeter of the base must be 20 inches. Help Li determine the dimensions of the base of the box.

58. José's math teacher instructed him to design a jewelry box made of pewter. The box must have a rectangular base with a width of $\sqrt{x + 9}$ inches and a length of $\sqrt{3x}$ inches. The base must have a perimeter of 30 inches. Help José find the dimensions of the base of the box.

For the following exercises, use the relation $t = \sqrt{\frac{2d}{32.2}}$, where t is the time (in seconds) it would take for an object to reach the ground when it is dropped from a height of d (in feet). (Note: To solve the equation graphically, the window for the domain will have to be increased to display values in the thousands.)

59. An apple was dropped from near the top of the Washington Monument. It took 5.845 seconds for the apple to fall to the ground. We don't recommend that you try this experiment, but what does this time tell you about the height from which the apple was dropped?

60. A shock-resistant watch was dropped from the top of the Empire State Building and took 8.81 seconds to fall to the ground. From what height was the watch dropped?

Experiencing Algebra the Calculator Way

The graphing calculator easily solves complicated radical equations, such as those that involve more than one radical or those that involve radicals with indices greater than 2. Some of these are presented in the followiing exercises. Graph and solve using your calculator.

1. $\sqrt{x - 2} + 1 = \sqrt{x - 1}$

2. $\sqrt{x - 1} = \sqrt{x} - 1$

3. $\sqrt[3]{x - 6} = x$

4. $\sqrt[4]{x + 4} = 1$

5. $\sqrt{x - 3} + 1 = \sqrt{x - 1}$

6. $\sqrt[3]{x^2 - 5} - 3 = -1$

7. $\sqrt{x - 1} + x = \sqrt{x} + 1$

8. $\sqrt[4]{x^2 - x + 2} = 2$

9. $\sqrt{2(2x + 1)} - 1 = \sqrt{2(x + 1)}$

10. $1 + 3\sqrt{2x - 3} = 3\sqrt{15} + 1$

11. $\sqrt{4 - 18x} = 2x^2 - 5x - 18$

12. $\sqrt{\dfrac{5x + 9}{3x - 8}} = \dfrac{x - 1}{x - 4}$

13. $\sqrt[3]{3x + 4} = \sqrt{36 - x}$

14. $\sqrt[4]{3x + 4} = \sqrt[3]{12 - x}$

15. $\sqrt[4]{1 - 5x} = x^2 + x - 4$

Experiencing Algebra the Group Way

Although it may be easy to solve a radical equation graphically, sometimes a table of values is more useful to understand the mathematical model of a real-world situation. For example, you may be more interested in how radical expressions behave over their domain of values, rather than which value of the domain equates two expressions. The following example illustrates this. Use your calculator to generate the table requested, and then have your group discuss the questions that follow.

Local television advertising volume in millions of dollars is given by the expression $3619 \sqrt[3]{x}$, where x is the number of years after 1981. Spot television advertising volume in millions of dollars is given by the expression $4257\sqrt[4]{x}$, with x defined the same way. Complete the following table of values for these two measures.

Year	Local Advertising Volume, $3619\sqrt[3]{x}$	Spot Advertising Volume, $4257\sqrt[4]{x}$	Difference, Spot Less Local
1982			
1983			
1984			
1985			
1986			
1987			
1988			
1989			
1990			
1991			

Answer the following questions comparing these two advertising forms over the years listed in the table.

1. In what years did spot television advertising volume exceed local television advertising volume?
2. In what years did local television advertising volume exceed spot television advertising volume?
3. In what year was the difference between the two volumes at its greatest?
4. Which form of advertising first reached a volume exceeding $6000 million? In which year did this occur?

Experiencing Algebra the Write Way

Write a paragraph to summarize what you would see if you were graphically solving a radical equation where each of the following situations existed:

1. The equation had no real-number solutions.
2. The equation had one solution.
3. The equation had more than one solution, but no more than a finite number of solutions.
4. The equation had an infinite number of solutions.
5. The equation had all real numbers as solutions.

13.7 Solving Radical Equations in One Variable Algebraically

Objectives
1. Solve square-root equations in one variable algebraically.
2. Solve radical equations in one variable algebraically.
3. Solve equations containing variable expressions with rational exponents algebraically.
4. Model real-world situations using radical equations in one variable.

Application

An explosion of energy E (in ft-lbs) creates a crater whose diameter d (in feet) is found using the formula $d = kE^{1/3}$, where k is a constant.

a. The explosion of 1 ton of TNT has an energy of 3.1×10^9 ft-lbs and creates a crater with a diameter of 30 feet. Determine a value for the constant k.

b. The Barringer meteor crater near Winslow, Arizona, is 4000 feet in diameter. Determine the energy of its explosion. (Use the value for k found in part (a).)

After completing this section, we will discuss this application further. See page 1080.

1 Solving Square-Root Equations

To solve an equation containing a radical expression or an exponential expression, we must determine a process that reverses the effect of raising a number to a power. Complete the following exercises to discover a pattern involving powers.

DISCOVERY 12

Principle of Powers

Complete the following statements with true or false.

1. If $\quad 8 = 8 \quad$ is true, then $\quad (8)^2 = (8)^2 \quad$ is ____.

2. If $5 + 3 = 8 \quad$ is true, then $(5 + 3)^2 = (8)^2 \quad$ is ____.

3. If $5 + 3 = 4 \cdot 2$ is true, then $(5 + 3)^2 = (4 \cdot 2)^2$ is ____.

4. If $\quad 8 = 8 \quad$ is true, then $\quad (8)^3 = (8)^3 \quad$ is ____.

5. If $5 + 3 = 8 \quad$ is true, then $(5 + 3)^3 = (8)^3 \quad$ is ____.

6. If $5 + 3 = 4 \cdot 2$ is true, then $(5 + 3)^3 = (4 \cdot 2)^3 \quad$ is ____.

7. If $\quad 8 = 8 \quad$ is true, then $\quad (8)^{2/3} = (8)^{2/3} \quad$ is ____.

8. If $5 + 3 = 8 \quad$ is true, then $(5 + 3)^{2/3} = (8)^{2/3} \quad$ is ____.

9. If $5 + 3 = 4 \cdot 2$ is true, then $(5 + 3)^{2/3} = (4 \cdot 2)^{2/3}$ is ____.

Write a rule for determining a true equation using powers.

If we begin with an equation that is true and we raise both expressions contained in the equation to the same power, the result is a true equation.

Principle of Powers
If $a = b$, then $a^n = b^n$.

We use this principle to solve algebraically equations in one variable that contain radicals and rational exponents. For example, solve $\sqrt{2x} = 6$.

$\sqrt{2x} = 6$ Restricted values are all real numbers less than 0.

$(\sqrt{2x})^2 = 6^2$ Square both sides.

$2x = 36$

$x = 18$

Check the solution by substitution.

$$\frac{\sqrt{2x} = 6}{\begin{array}{c|c} \sqrt{2(18)} & 6 \\ \sqrt{36} & \\ 6 & \end{array}}$$

The solution is 18.

A radical equation containing a square-root expression equal to a negative number does not have a real-number solution. For example, solve $\sqrt{2x} = -6$.

$\sqrt{2x}$ is a principal root and represents a nonnegative number. Therefore, the expression $\sqrt{2x}$ cannot equal the negative number -6. We say that the equation has no real-number solution.

We must always check our solutions when using the principle of powers in solving. At times, extraneous solutions may be obtained. Remember, extraneous solutions are results obtained in solving that are not solutions of the original equation. For example,

$\sqrt{x + 6} = x$ Restricted values are all real numbers less than -6.

$(\sqrt{x + 6})^2 = x^2$ Square both sides.

$x + 6 = x^2$

$x^2 - x - 6 = 0$ Standard form for a polynomial equation

$(x - 3)(x + 2) = 0$

$x = 3$ or $x = -2$

Check the solutions by substitution.

$$\frac{\sqrt{x + 6} = x}{\begin{array}{c|c} \sqrt{3 + 6} & 3 \\ 3 & \end{array}} \qquad\qquad \frac{\sqrt{x + 6} = x}{\begin{array}{c|c} \sqrt{-2 + 6} & -2 \\ 2 & \end{array}}$$

The solution is 3.   Since $2 \neq -2$, -2 is not a solution.

Applying the principle of powers resulted in a true equation, but one that is not equivalent to the original equation. This can be shown as follows:

$x = 1$ (This equation has one solution, 1.)

$x^2 = 1^2$ or $x^2 = 1$ (This equation has two solutions, 1 and -1.)

Not all solutions of the squared equation are solutions of the original equation. However, all solutions of the original equation *are* solutions of the squared equation. This means that we have an extraneous solution of -1 after squaring the original equation.

Helping Hand We must check the final solutions to determine if they are solutions of the original equation.

EXAMPLE 1 Solve algebraically and check numerically, graphically, or by substitution.

a. $\sqrt{3x + 10} - x = 4$ **b.** $2\sqrt{5x} + 1 = 11$

c. $\sqrt{5a + 4} = \sqrt{4a - 3}$ **d.** $\sqrt{x} + 2 = \sqrt{x + 5}$

Algebraic Solution

a. $\sqrt{3x + 10} - x = 4$

Restricted values for the radical expression are all real numbers less than $\frac{-10}{3}$.

$$\sqrt{3x + 10} = x + 4$$ Add x to both sides.

$$\left(\sqrt{3x + 10}\right)^2 = (x + 4)^2$$ Square both sides.

$$3x + 10 = x^2 + 8x + 16$$

$$x^2 + 5x + 6 = 0$$ Set the quadratic expression equal to 0.

$$(x + 3)(x + 2) = 0$$ Factor.

$$x = -3 \quad \text{or} \quad x = -2$$ Set each factor equal to 0 and solve.

X	Y1	Y2
-4	ERROR	4
-3	4	4
-2	4	4
-1	3.6458	4
0	3.1623	4
1	2.6056	4
2	2	4

X= -4

Y1 = $\sqrt{3x + 10} - x$
Y2 = 4

Since both solutions are integers, check numerically on your calculator. The solutions are -3 and -2.

b. $2\sqrt{5x} + 1 = 11$ Restricted values for the radical expression are all real numbers less than 0.

$$2\sqrt{5x} = 10$$ Subtract 1 from both sides.

$$\frac{2\sqrt{5x}}{2} = \frac{10}{2}$$ Divide both sides by 2.

$$\sqrt{5x} = 5$$

$$\left(\sqrt{5x}\right)^2 = 5^2$$ Square both sides.

$$5x = 25$$

$$x = 5$$ Divide both sides by 5.

Check by substitution

$$\begin{array}{c|c} 2\sqrt{5x} + 1 = 11 & \\ \hline 2\sqrt{5(5)} + 1 & 11 \\ 2\sqrt{25} + 1 & \\ 2 \cdot 5 + 1 & \\ 11 & \end{array}$$

The solution is 5.

c. $\sqrt{5a + 4} = \sqrt{4a - 3}$ Restricted values for the radical expressions are all real numbers less than $\frac{3}{4}$.

$$\left(\sqrt{5a + 4}\right)^2 = \left(\sqrt{4a - 3}\right)^2$$ Square both sides.

$$5a + 4 = 4a - 3$$

$$a = -7$$

The possible solution is a restricted value. There is no real-number solution.

d. $\sqrt{x} + 2 = \sqrt{x + 5}$ Restricted values for the radical expressions are all real numbers less than 0.

$$\left(\sqrt{x} + 2\right)^2 = \left(\sqrt{x + 5}\right)^2$$ Square both sides.

$$x + 4\sqrt{x} + 4 = x + 5$$

$$4\sqrt{x} = 1$$ Isolate the radical term.

$$\left(4\sqrt{x}\right)^2 = (1)^2$$ Square both sides.

$$16x = 1$$

$$x = \frac{1}{16}$$

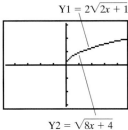

Check by substitution on your calculator.
The solution is $\frac{1}{16}$. ∎

When solving numerically and graphically, some radical equations appear to have no solution or to have infinitely many solutions, as in the next example.

EXAMPLE 2   Solve algebraically and check graphically.

a. $\sqrt{2x} + 3 = \sqrt{2x} - 5$ **b.** $2\sqrt{2a + 1} = \sqrt{8a + 4}$

Algebraic Solution

a. $\sqrt{2x} + 3 = \sqrt{2x} - 5$ Restricted values for the radical expressions are all real numbers less than 0.

$$3 = -5$$ Isolate the radical expression by subtracting $\sqrt{2x}$.

This is a contradiction. There is no solution.
Check graphically on your calculator.
The graphs do not appear to intersect. There is no solution.

Y1 = √2x + 3

Y2 = √2x − 5

(−47, 47, −31, 31)

b. $2\sqrt{2a + 1} = \sqrt{8a + 4}$ Restricted values for the radical expressions are all real numbers less than $\frac{-1}{2}$.

$$\left(2\sqrt{2a + 1}\right)^2 = \left(\sqrt{8a + 4}\right)^2$$ Square both sides.

$$4(2a + 1) = 8a + 4$$

$$8a + 4 = 8a + 4$$

$$4 = 4$$ Subtract 8a from both sides.

This is an identity. The solution set is all real numbers greater than or equal to $-\frac{1}{2}$.
Check graphically on your calculator.
The graphs are coinciding. There are infinitely many solutions. The solution set is all real numbers greater than or equal to $-\frac{1}{2}$. ∎

Y1 = 2√2x + 1

Y2 = √8x + 4

(−47, 47, −31, 31)

 Experiencing Algebra the Checkup Way

Solve exercises 1–8 algebraically and check.

1. $\sqrt{5x} = 2$

2. $\sqrt{x + 12} = x$

3. $x - \sqrt{5x - 16} = 2$

4. $3\sqrt{2x} + 2 = 8$

5. $\sqrt{2z + 1} = \sqrt{z - 4}$

6. $\sqrt{x + 9} = \sqrt{x} + 1$

7. $\sqrt{x + 1} + 2 = \sqrt{x + 1} - 3$

8. $\sqrt{x^2 + 6x + 9} = x + 3$

9. The principle of powers states that if an equation is true, and if you raise the expressions on the left and right sides of the equation to the same power, you obtain another equation that is true. Does this mean that the new equation has the same solutions as the original equation? Explain your answer.

---

2 Solving Other Radical Equations

To solve other radical equations we use the same procedure as with square-root equations, except we raise each expression to the power of the index. For example, solve $\sqrt[3]{3x} = 6$.

$$\sqrt[3]{3x} = 6 \qquad \text{There are no restricted values because the index of the radical is odd.}$$

$$\left(\sqrt[3]{3x}\right)^3 = (6)^3 \qquad \text{Cube both sides.}$$

$$3x = 216$$

$$x = 72$$

Check by substitution.

$$\frac{\sqrt[3]{3x} = 6}{\begin{array}{c|c} \sqrt[3]{3(72)} & 6 \\ \sqrt[3]{216} & \\ 6 & \end{array}}$$

The solution is 72.

> **Solving a Radical Equation Algebraically Using the Principle of Powers**
> To solve an equation algebraically using the principle of powers:
>
> - Determine the restricted values for the independent variable for each radical expression.
>
> - Isolate a radical term on one side of the equation.
>
> - Raise both expressions in the equation to the power of the index of the isolated radical term; that is, to the second power for square roots, to the third power for cube roots, and so on.
>
> - Solve the resulting equation. (If the resulting equation contains a radical, this process must be repeated.)
>
> Always check the solutions numerically, graphically, or by substitution.

EXAMPLE 3 Solve algebraically and check numerically, graphically, or by substitution.

    a. $\sqrt[4]{x - 5} = 2$ **b.** $\sqrt[3]{x^2 + 12x} + 5 = 9$

Algebraic Solution

    a. $\sqrt[4]{x - 5} = 2$ Restricted values for the radical expression are all real numbers less than 5.

$$\left(\sqrt[4]{x - 5}\right)^4 = (2)^4 \qquad \text{Raise to the fourth power on both sides.}$$

$$x - 5 = 16$$

$$x = 21$$

Check by substitution.

$$\sqrt[4]{x-5} = 2$$

$$\begin{array}{c|c} \sqrt[4]{21-5} & 2 \\ \sqrt[4]{16} & \\ 2 & \end{array}$$

The solution is 21.

b. $\sqrt[3]{x^2 + 12x} + 5 = 9$ There are no restricted values.

$\sqrt[3]{x^2 + 12x} = 4$ Subtract 5 from both sides.

$\left(\sqrt[3]{x^2 + 12x}\right)^3 = (4)^3$ Cube both sides.

$x^2 + 12x = 64$ Simplify.

$x^2 + 12x - 64 = 0$ Standard form of a quadratic equation.

$(x + 16)(x - 4) = 0$ Factor.

$x = -16$ or $x = 4$ Solve.

Y1 = $\sqrt[3]{x^2 + 12x}$ + 5

$(-16, 9)$ $(4, 9)$

Y2 = 9

$(-47, 47, -31, 31)$

To check graphicaly on your calculator, graph Y1 = $\sqrt[3]{x^2 + 12x} + 5$ and Y2 = 9. The x-coordinates of the intersections are -16 and 4. The solutions are -16 and 4. ∎

Experiencing Algebra the Checkup Way

Solve exercises 1–3 algebraically and check.

1. $\sqrt[3]{4x} = 2$ **2.** $\sqrt[4]{x-3} = 2$ **3.** $\sqrt[3]{x^2 + 6x} + 2 = 5$

4. When using the principle of powers to solve a radical equation, how do you decide what power to apply to the expressions on the left and right sides of the original radical equation?

---

3 Solving an Equation with Rational Exponents

To solve an equation involving an expression with a rational exponent, we use the principle of powers. To obtain an integer exponent, we raise both expressions in the equation to the denominator of the fractional exponent. That is, if we have $x^{2/3}$ with a rational exponent, we raise it to a power of 3, $\left(x^{2/3}\right)^3$. By the power-to-a-power property of exponents, we can simplify this expression to $\left(x^{2/3}\right)^3 = x^2$.

> *Solving an Equation with a Rational Exponent Algebraically Using the Principle of Powers*
> To solve an equation algebraically using the principle of powers:
>
> • Determine the restricted values for the independent variable.
>
> • Isolate a term with an exponential expression on one side of the equation.
>
> • Raise both expressions in the equation to the power of the denominator of the exponent.
>
> • Solve the resulting equation. (If the resulting equation contains a rational exponential expression, this process must be repeated.)
>
> Always check the solutions numerically, graphically, or by substitution.

For example, solve $x^{2/3} = 4$.

$$x^{2/3} = 4 \qquad \text{There are no restricted values.}$$
$$\left(x^{2/3}\right)^3 = 4^3 \qquad \text{Raise both sides to a power of 3.}$$
$$x^2 = 64$$
$$x = \pm 8 \qquad \text{Principle of square roots}$$

Check by substitution.

$$\begin{array}{c|c} x^{2/3} = 4 \\ \hline (8)^{2/3} & 4 \\ 4 & \end{array} \qquad\qquad \begin{array}{c|c} x^{2/3} = 4 \\ \hline (-8)^{2/3} & 4 \\ 4 & \end{array}$$

The solution is 8.   The solution is -8.

In the example, we used the principle of square roots to solve the equation $x^2 = 64$ and obtain $x = \pm 8$. Before we continue, we need to expand the principle of square roots to a rule for all roots. There are two different cases we need to consider: first, if the exponent is even, and second, if the exponent is odd.

Principle of Roots

If n is a positive even integer, b is a positive number, and $a^n = b$, then $a = \sqrt[n]{b}$ or $a = -\sqrt[n]{b}$.

If n is a positive even integer, b is a negative number, and $a^n = b$, then a is not a real number.

If n is a positive even integer, b is 0, and $a^n = b$, then $a = 0$.

If n is a positive odd integer, b is a real number, and $a^n = b$, then $a = \sqrt[n]{b}$.

The principle of roots will allow us to solve equations such as the following:

a. $x^4 = 16$ **b.** $x^4 = 0$ **c.** $x^4 = -16$
    $x = \pm\sqrt[4]{16}$ $x = 0$ x is not a real
    $x = \pm 2$ number.

d. $x^3 = 8$ **e.** $x^3 = -8$
    $x = \sqrt[3]{8}$ $x = \sqrt[3]{-8}$
    $x = 2$ $x = -2$

EXAMPLE 4   Solve algebraically and check numerically, graphically, or by substitution.

a. $(x + 2)^{3/4} = 8$ **b.** $(x + 2)^{4/3} = 3$ **c.** $(x - 2)^{-3/2} = \dfrac{1}{8}$

Algebraic Solution

a. $(x + 2)^{3/4} = 8$ Restricted values are all real numbers less than -2.
    $\left[(x + 2)^{3/4}\right]^4 = (8)^4$ Raise both sides to a power of 4.
      $(x + 2)^3 = 4096$
         $x + 2 = \sqrt[3]{4096}$ Principle of roots
         $x + 2 = 16$
             $x = 14$

a.

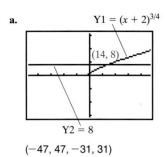

$Y1 = (x + 2)^{3/4}$

$(14, 8)$

$Y2 = 8$

$(-47, 47, -31, 31)$

b.

c.

To check graphically on your calculator, graph $Y1 = (x + 2)^{3/4}$ and $Y2 = 8$. The x-coordinate of the intersection is 14.

The solution is 14.

b.
$$(x + 2)^{4/3} = 3$$ There are no restricted values.
$$[(x + 2)^{4/3}]^3 = 3^3$$ Raise both sides to a power of 3.
$$(x + 2)^4 = 27$$
$$x + 2 = \pm \sqrt[4]{27}$$ Principle of roots
$$x = -2 \pm \sqrt[4]{27}$$ Subtract 2 from both sides.

Check by substitution on your calculator.
The solutions are $-2 \pm \sqrt[4]{27}$.

c.
$$(x - 2)^{-3/2} = \frac{1}{8}$$ Restricted values are all real numbers less than 2.

$$[(x - 2)^{-3/2}]^2 = \left(\frac{1}{8}\right)^2$$ Raise both sides to a power of 2.

$$\frac{1}{(x - 2)^3} = \frac{1}{64}$$ Write as a positive exponent.

$$(x - 2)^3 = 64$$ Cross-multiply to solve the proportion.
$$x - 2 = \sqrt[3]{64}$$ Principle of roots
$$x - 2 = 4$$
$$x = 6$$

Check numerically on your calculator. $Y1 = (x - 2)^{-3/2}$ and $Y2 = \frac{1}{8}$.
The solution is 6. ∎

In section 13.6, we determined that the equation $(x + 2)^{2/3} = -3$ did not appear to have a solution. Now let's confirm that this is true algebraically.

EXAMPLE 5 Solve $(x + 2)^{2/3} = -3$.

Algebraic Solution

$$(x + 2)^{2/3} = -3$$ Restricted values are all real numbers less than -2.
$$[(x + 2)^{2/3}]^3 = (-3)^3$$ Raise both sides to a power of 3.
$$(x + 2)^2 = -27$$

There is no real-number solution for the equation, because according to the principle of roots, the square of $(x + 2)$ cannot be a negative number. ∎

In the previous section, we could not determine that the equation did not have a real-number solution because our graph represents only real-number coordinates.

✓ **Experiencing Algebra the Checkup Way**

Solve exercises 1–4 algebraically and check.

1. $x^{3/5} = 8$ **2.** $(x + 5)^{3/2} = 27$ **3.** $(x - 1)^{-3/4} = 8$ **4.** $(3 - x)^{2/3} + 3 = 2$

5. To solve an equation with rational exponents, you may need to use the principle of powers and then the principle of roots. Explain the difference between these two principles.

4 Modeling the Real World

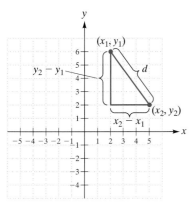

Figure 13.8

In earlier chapters, we studied the Pythagorean theorem, $a^2 + b^2 = c^2$, where a and b are the lengths of the legs of a right triangle and c is the length of the hypotenuse. We will expand the uses of the Pythagorean theorem in this chapter.

An application of the Pythagorean theorem is used to determine the distance between two points in a rectangular coordinate system.

Before we begin, we must determine a method to evaluate the distance between two points that lie on the same vertical or horizontal line. To determine the distance between two points that lie on a vertical line, we take the absolute value of the difference between the two y-coordinates of the points. For example, the vertical distance between $(4, 2)$ and $(4, -3)$ is

$$|2 - (-3)| = |2 + 3| = |5| = 5$$

The distance between the two points is 5.

To determine the distance between two points that lie on a horizontal line, we take the absolute value of the difference between the two x-coordinates of the points. For example, the horizontal distance between $(1, 3)$ and $(4, 3)$ is

$$|1 - 4| = |-3| = 3$$

The distance between the two points is 3.

To determine the distance between two points that do not lie on a horizontal or vertical line, we apply the Pythagorean theorem. See Figure 13.8.

$$\text{Let } a = |x_2 - x_1| \text{ and } b = |y_2 - y_1|$$
$$a^2 + b^2 = c^2$$
$$(x_2 - x_1)^2 + (y_2 - y_1)^2 = d^2 \quad \text{Substitute.}$$

Note: We do not need the absolute value symbols because we are squaring the number. It does not matter whether the number is positive or negative; the squaring will always result in a positive number.

$$\pm \sqrt{(x_2 - x_1)^2 + (y_2 - y_1)^2} = d \quad \text{Principle of powers}$$

or

$$\sqrt{(x_2 - x_1)^2 + (y_2 - y_1)^2} = d$$

We do not write the negative square root because we cannot have a negative length when measuring distance.

Distance Formula
The distance d between any two points on a coordinate plane (x_1, y_1) and (x_2, y_2) is

$$d = \sqrt{(x_2 - x_1)^2 + (y_2 - y_1)^2}.$$

For example, determine the distance between the points $(2, 3)$ and $(5, 1)$.

Let $x_1 = 2$, $y_1 = 3$, $x_2 = 5$, and $y_2 = 1$.
$$d = \sqrt{(x_2 - x_1)^2 + (y_2 - y_1)^2}$$
$$d = \sqrt{(5 - 2)^2 + (1 - 3)^2} \quad \text{Substitute.}$$

$$d = \sqrt{3^2 + (-2)^2}$$
$$d = \sqrt{9 + 4}$$
$$d = \sqrt{13}$$

The distance between the two points is $\sqrt{13}$, or approximately 3.606.

EXAMPLE 6   Determine the possible y-coordinates of a point 5 units from $(-1, 4)$ with an x-coordinate of 2.

Algebraic Solution

Let $x_1 = 2$ and y_1 be the missing y-coordinate.
Let $x_2 = -1$ and $y_2 = 4$.

$$d = \sqrt{(x_2 - x_1)^2 + (y_2 - y_1)^2}$$

$$5 = \sqrt{(-1 - 2)^2 + (4 - y_1)^2} \qquad \text{Substitute.}$$

$$5 = \sqrt{(-3)^2 + (4 - y_1)^2}$$

$$5 = \sqrt{9 + 16 - 8y_1 + y_1^2}$$

$$5 = \sqrt{25 - 8y_1 + y_1^2}$$

$$5^2 = \left(\sqrt{25 - 8y_1 + y_1^2}\right)^2 \qquad \text{Square both sides.}$$

$$25 = 25 - 8y_1 + y_1^2$$

$$0 = -8y_1 + y_1^2 \qquad \text{Standard form for a quadratic equation}$$

$$0 = y_1(-8 + y_1) \qquad \text{Factor.}$$

$$y_1 = 0 \quad \text{or} \quad y_1 = 8 \qquad \text{Solve.}$$

The two possible points are $(2, 0)$ or $(2, 8)$. ∎

Application   An explosion of energy E (in ft-lbs) creates a crater whose diameter d (in feet) is found using the formula $d = kE^{1/3}$, where k is a constant.

a. The explosion of 1 ton of TNT has an energy of 3.1×10^9 ft-lbs and creates a crater with a diameter of 30 feet. Determine a value for the constant k.

b. The Barringer meteor crater near Winslow, Arizona, is 4000 feet in diameter. Determine the energy of its explosion. (Use the value for k found in part (a).)

Discussion

a. Use the given formula.

$$d = kE^{1/3}$$

$$30 = k(3.1 \times 10^9)^{1/3} \qquad \text{Substitute 30 for } d \text{ and } 3.1 \times 10^9 \text{ for } E.$$

$$k = \frac{30}{(3.1 \times 10^9)^{1/3}} \qquad \text{Solve for k.}$$

$$k \approx 0.02$$

b.
$$d = kE^{1/3}$$

$$4000 = 0.02E^{1/3} \qquad \text{Substitute 4000 for } d \text{ and 0.02 for } k.$$

$$4000^3 = (0.02E^{1/3})^3 \qquad \text{Cube both sides.}$$

$$64{,}000{,}000{,}000 = 0.000008E$$
$$8{,}000{,}000{,}000{,}000{,}000 = E$$
$$\text{or } E = 8 \times 10^{15}$$

The energy of the meteor explosion that caused the crater near Winslow was approximately 8×10^{15} ft-lbs. ■

Experiencing Algebra the Checkup Way

1. Determine the distance between the two points $(5, -2)$ and $(5, 7)$.
2. Determine the distance between the two points $(-4, -5)$ and $(3, -5)$.
3. Determine the distance between the two points $(-2, 1)$ and $(3, 4)$.
4. Find the possible y-coordinates of a point that is 10 units away from the point $(6, 5)$ and has an x-coordinate of -2.

PROBLEM SET 13.7

Experiencing Algebra the Exercise Way

Solve algebraically and check.

1. $\sqrt{x} - 3 = 5$
2. $\sqrt{x} - 5 = 2$
3. $\sqrt{x} + 1.7 = 4.5$
4. $\sqrt{x} - 2.4 = 3.8$
5. $\sqrt{x} + 8 = 5$
6. $\sqrt{x} + 11 = 10$
7. $\sqrt{3x} - 4 = 2$
8. $\sqrt{7x} - 2 = 12$
9. $9 - 3\sqrt{2z} = 0$
10. $15 - 5\sqrt{6z} = 0$
11. $3\sqrt{6x} + 1 = 10$
12. $4\sqrt{3x} + 3 = 15$
13. $\sqrt{x + 5} = 3$
14. $\sqrt{3 + x} = 5$
15. $\sqrt{2x + 5} + 4 = 9$
16. $\sqrt{3x + 1} + 2 = 5$
17. $\sqrt{3x + 4} - 2 = 6$
18. $\sqrt{5x + 4} - 3 = 5$
19. $\sqrt{5 - 4x} = x$
20. $\sqrt{x + 30} = x$
21. $\sqrt{6x - 5} = \sqrt{4x + 5}$
22. $\sqrt{3x + 7} = \sqrt{5x - 2}$
23. $3\sqrt{x + 2} = \sqrt{x + 10}$
24. $4\sqrt{x + 3} = \sqrt{x + 18}$
25. $x = 3 + 2\sqrt{x - 4}$
26. $x = 3 + 2\sqrt{2x - 10}$
27. $x = \sqrt{21 - x} - x^2 + 3$
28. $\sqrt{(4x + 5)(x + 1)} = 5 + x$
29. $\sqrt{x^2 - 14x + 49} = 7 - x$
30. $\sqrt{4x^2 - 12x + 9} = 3 - 2x$
31. $x = \sqrt{2x + 7}$
32. $\sqrt{8 - 3x} + x = 0$
33. $5 + \sqrt{25 - 2x} = x$
34. $7 + \sqrt{49 - 2x} = x$
35. $\sqrt{x} - 3 = \sqrt{x - 27}$
36. $\sqrt{x} - 8 = \sqrt{x - 64}$
37. $\sqrt{x - 7} = 7 - \sqrt{x}$
38. $\sqrt{x + 15} = 3 + \sqrt{x}$
39. $\sqrt{2x + 5} - 7 = \sqrt{5 + 2x} + 3$
40. $\sqrt{4x + 3} - 5 = \sqrt{3 + 4x} + 9$
41. $\sqrt{2x + 3} = 1 - \sqrt{x + 5}$
42. $\sqrt{3x - 2} = 1 + \sqrt{x + 3}$
43. $\sqrt[3]{3x} = -6$
44. $\sqrt[3]{6x} = -3$
45. $\sqrt[4]{2x} = 10$
46. $\sqrt[4]{2x - 10} = 4$
47. $\sqrt[5]{2x} = -2$
48. $\sqrt[5]{9x} = -3$
49. $\sqrt[3]{x} + 3 = 1$
50. $\sqrt[3]{x} - 7 = -5$
51. $\sqrt[4]{x} + 1 = 5$
52. $\sqrt[4]{x} + 3 = 6$
53. $\sqrt[3]{2x + 1} = 3$
54. $\sqrt[3]{3x + 2} = -4$
55. $\sqrt[4]{x - 5} = 2$
56. $\sqrt[4]{x - 7} = 3$
57. $\sqrt[5]{2x - 5} = 3$
58. $\sqrt[3]{3x - 1} = 2$
59. $\sqrt[3]{x^2 + 7x + 7} = 9$
60. $\sqrt[4]{x^2 + 24x + 2} = 5$
61. $\sqrt[3]{3x - 5} = \sqrt[4]{2x + 4}$
62. $\sqrt[4]{5x - 7} = \sqrt[4]{x + 5}$
63. $\sqrt[4]{5x - 2} = 2\sqrt[4]{3}$
64. $\sqrt[3]{3x + 6} = 3\sqrt[3]{2}$
65. $x = \sqrt[4]{18x^2 - 81}$
66. $x = \sqrt[4]{8x^2 - 16}$
67. $\sqrt[3]{2x} + \sqrt[4]{3x} = 0$
68. $\sqrt[3]{5x} + \sqrt[3]{x} = 0$
69. $\sqrt[3]{3x - 5} + \sqrt[4]{x - 3} = 0$
70. $\sqrt[4]{x + 3} + \sqrt[4]{2x + 1} = 0$
71. $\sqrt[3]{3x - 5} + \sqrt[3]{x - 3} = 0$
72. $\sqrt[3]{5x - 2} + \sqrt[3]{3x - 2} = 0$

73. $\sqrt[4]{7x-1} - \sqrt[4]{x+11} = 0$

74. $\sqrt[4]{8x-1} - \sqrt[4]{x+6} = 0$

75. $x^{4/3} = 16$

76. $x^{2/3} = 25$

77. $(x+6)^{2/5} = 4$

78. $(x+8)^{2/3} = 16$

79. $(x-4)^{3/4} = 27$

80. $(x-9)^{3/2} = 64$

81. $x^{-2/3} = 4$

82. $x^{-3/4} = 27$

83. $(x-5)^{-3/4} = 27$

84. $(4x+5)^{3/4} = 125$

85. $(5x-3)^{-2/3} = \dfrac{1}{25}$

86. $(6x-1)^{-3/4} = \dfrac{1}{64}$

87. $x^{2/3} + 5 = 3$

88. $x^{4/5} + 6 = 4$

89. $x^{3/4} - 7 = 1$

90. $x^{3/5} - 6 = 21$

In exercises 91–96, find the distance on the coordinate plane between the points for the coordinate pairs listed.

91. $(8, -3)$ and $(8, 2)$

92. $(-2, 3)$ and $(-2, 11)$

93. $(-3, 6)$ and $(5, 6)$

94. $(-9, -1)$ and $(-2, -1)$

95. $(-3, -4)$ and $(2, 5)$

96. $(-5, 7)$ and $(3, -4)$

97. Find the possible y-coordinates of a point that has an x-coordinate of 8 and is 13 units away from $(3, 4)$.

98. Find the possible y-coordinates of a point that has an x-coordinate of -13 and is 17 units away from $(2, -3)$.

99. Find the possible x-coordinates of a point that has a y-coordinate of -1 and is 10 units away from the point $(-2, 5)$.

100. Find the possible x-coordinates of a point that has a y-coordinate of 1 and is 5 units away from $(1, -3)$.

101. Find the possible y-coordinates of a point that has an x-coordinate of 6 and is 5 units away from $(-2, 1)$.

102. Find the possible x-coordinates of a point that has a y-coordinate of 1 and is 2 units away from $(1, 9)$.

103. One of the largest known craters believed to have been produced by a meteorite was discovered in northwestern Quebec, Canada. The circular pit is approximately 2.5 miles in diameter, or 13,200 feet. Use the formula presented in this section to determine the energy of the explosion when the meteor struck.

104. Use the formula in this section to determine the energy of the explosion of a meteor that creates a crater having a diameter of 5,000 feet.

105. Civil engineers relate the crushing load L (in tons) for a square wooden pillar that has a thickness T (in inches) and a height H (in feet) by using the mathematical model $T = \left(\frac{LH^2}{25}\right)^{1/4}$. If a square wooden pillar has a thickness of 4 inches and a height of 8 feet, what is its crushing load?

106. Use the formula in exercise 105 to find the crushing load of a wooden pillar that is 6 inches thick and 10 feet tall.

Experiencing Algebra the Calculator Way

The calculator can easily find solutions of radical equations or exponential equations where the algebraic solutions are very difficult and sometimes impossible to find. Use your calculator to solve the following equations by storing the left side of the equation in Y1 and the right side of the equation in Y2. Then graph to find the intersection points of the two functions.

1. $(\sqrt[4]{2x+1})(\sqrt[3]{x-13}) = 9$

2. $\sqrt[5]{3x+2} - \sqrt[4]{8x+1} = -1$

3. $\dfrac{\sqrt{3x+4}}{\sqrt[4]{x-4}} = \sqrt[3]{4x-16}$

4. $\sqrt[3]{2x+1} = \sqrt[4]{3x^2}$

5. $x^{3/2} + 2x^{1/2} - 7 = 0$

6. $3x^{2/3} - 5x^{1/3} - 9 = 0$

Experiencing Algebra the Group Way

You have learned methods for solving many different types of equations:

1. linear equations, by isolating the variable;

2. polynomial equations, by factoring and using the zero factor rule;

3. rational equations, by multiplying through by the least common denominator; and

4. radical and exponential equations, by applying the power principle and the root principle.

In some cases, you may have a combination of these equation types, which you can solve by creatively applying the techniques you have learned. Discuss how you would approach the following exercises. Then try to solve the equations using these methods. Compare your results to agree on the final solutions.

1. $\sqrt{m + \dfrac{1}{m}} = \dfrac{5\sqrt{2}}{7}$ 　　 **2.** $\dfrac{\sqrt{5k+1}}{\sqrt{5k-1}} = \dfrac{\sqrt{51}}{7}$ 　　 **3.** $\dfrac{\sqrt{3}}{\sqrt{2z-3}} = \sqrt{\dfrac{3}{z}}$

4. $\sqrt{2 + \sqrt{p}} = 4$ 　　 **5.** $\dfrac{\sqrt{a-7}}{2} = \dfrac{4}{\sqrt{a+5}}$ 　　 **6.** $\sqrt{\dfrac{1}{t} + \dfrac{1}{t+2}} = \dfrac{\sqrt{15}}{6}$

Experiencing Algebra the Write Way

In this chapter, you have seen how you can solve radical equations numerically, graphically, and algebraically. Consider the following equations. For each equation, how would you choose the method to use? Explain your answer carefully. It is not enough to say, "I picked the easiest method." Explain how you knew that one method was easier to use than another. Then use the method to solve the equation. If the method does not easily provide an answer, strategize about a second choice.

1. $\sqrt[4]{x} = \dfrac{2}{3}$ 　　　　 **2.** $\sqrt{3x+4} + 2 = \sqrt{2x^2 + 4}$ 　　　 **3.** $x = \sqrt{3x+4}$

CHAPTER 13 | Summary

After completing this chapter, you should be able to define in your own words the following key terms, properties, and rules.

Terms
radical expression
index
even roots
odd roots
radical relation
radical function
restricted values
rationalizing the denominator
like radicals
conjugates
radical equation in one variable

standard form for a radical
　　equation
distance formula

Properties
Properties of rational exponents
Product rule for radicals
Quotient rule for radicals
Principle of powers
Principle of roots

Rules
Evaluating radical expressions with
　　numerical radicands
Simplifying radical expressions
Addition and subtraction of like
　　radicals
Solving a radical equation numerically
Solving a radical equation graphically
Solving a radical equation
　　algebraically
Solving an equation with a rational
　　exponent algebraically

CHAPTER 13 | Review

Reflections
1. What is the relationship between a radical expression with a variable in its radicand and a variable expression with a rational exponent?

2. How can you determine restricted values for a radical function?

3. What does it mean to rationalize a radical expression?

4. When operating with radical expressions involving square roots, sometimes it is important to be able to determine the conjugate of an expression. What is the conjugate of a radical expression? When is it necessary to work with the conjugate of a radical expression?

5. When solving a radical equation numerically, how can you tell that there are an infinite number of solutions?

6. When solving a radical equation graphically, how can you tell that there are no real-number solutions?

7. When solving a radical equation algebraically, how can you tell whether a solution is an extraneous solution?

In these exercises, we will assume that the variable base of an exponential expression or a variable radicand does not represent values for which the expression is not defined.

13.1

Evaluate to the nearest thousandth, if possible.

1. $\sqrt{225}$ **2.** $\sqrt{2.89}$ **3.** $\sqrt{\dfrac{49}{64}}$

4. $\sqrt[3]{-\dfrac{27}{125}}$ **5.** $-\sqrt[4]{1296}$ **6.** $\sqrt[4]{-1296}$

7. $\sqrt{150}$ **8.** $\sqrt[3]{-35}$ **9.** $\sqrt[5]{125}$

In exercises 10–17, write each expression as a radical expression and evaluate, if possible.

10. $(-64)^{1/3}$ **11.** $-16^{1/4}$ **12.** $(-16)^{1/4}$ **13.** $-64^{-1/3}$

14. $-64^{4/3}$ **15.** $(-64)^{3/2}$ **16.** $16^{-3/4}$ **17.** $(-16)^{-3/4}$

18. Find the length of a side of a square picture frame that encloses an area of 121 square inches.

19. Find the length of the side of a cube-shaped box whose volume is $\frac{125}{216}$ cubic yards.

20. Find the radius and diameter of a rubber ball whose volume is 65.45 cubic centimeters.

13.2

Determine the restricted values and then state the domain of each radical function.

21. $y = \sqrt{2x - 7}$ **22.** $y = \sqrt[3]{2x - 7}$ **23.** $y = (4x + 9)^{3/4}$

In exercises 24–25, use a table of values to graph each radical function.

24. $f(x) = 2\sqrt{x}$ **25.** $y = x^{3/2} + 1$

26. In statistics, the variability of the integers 1 to n is calculated as $s = \sqrt{\dfrac{n(n+1)}{12}}$. Calculate the variability of the integers from 1 to 23.

27. When the coefficient of friction on a road is 30%, the velocity, V, in miles per hour of a car that leaves a skid mark of S feet is given by the mathematical model $V = \sqrt{9S}$. Graph this function for values of S between 0 and 200 feet. What would you estimate the speed of a car to be if it leaves a skid mark that is 150 feet long?

13.3

Evaluate, using the properties of exponents.

28. $\dfrac{1}{4^{-1/2}}$ **29.** $8^{2/3} \cdot 8^{5/3}$ **30.** $\dfrac{9^{7/3}}{9^{2/3}}$

31. $\left(\dfrac{4}{9}\right)^{-3/2}$ **32.** $\left[(3^{1/2})(27^{1/2})\right]^{-3/2}$ **33.** $(64^{2/3})^{3/4}$

Simplify exercises 34–39. Write your results using positive exponents.

34. $\dfrac{x^{2/3}}{x^{5/6}}$ **35.** $y^{2/5} \cdot y^{-3/10}$ **36.** $\left(z^{3/5}\right)^{5/9}$

37. $\left(\dfrac{a^3}{b^6}\right)^{-5/12}$ **38.** $\left(8x^6 y^9\right)^{4/3}$ **39.** $\left(2a^{3/4} b^{1/3}\right)\left(3a^{1/3} b^{2/3}\right)$

40. How should the length of the side of a square be changed to increase the area of the square to 5 times its original size?

13.4
Simplify without a calculator. Check the results on your calculator.

41. $\sqrt{6300}$　　　　**42.** $\sqrt[3]{-320}$　　　　**43.** $\sqrt[4]{162}$

Simplify.

44. $\sqrt{45x^4 y^7 z^2}$　　　**45.** $\sqrt[3]{-64x^2 y^7}$　　　**46.** $\sqrt{12x^2 - 36x + 27}$

Multiply and simplify.

47. $\sqrt{2x} \cdot \sqrt{8x^3}$　　**48.** $\sqrt[3]{-2a^2 b} \cdot \sqrt[3]{20a^2 b^5}$　　**49.** $\sqrt{x^2 - 2xy} \cdot \sqrt{3x - 6y}$

Simplify without a calculator, rationalizing all denominators.

50. $\sqrt{\dfrac{25}{64}}$　　　**51.** $\sqrt{\dfrac{13}{289}}$　　　**52.** $\sqrt{\dfrac{27}{343}}$

53. $\sqrt[3]{\dfrac{6}{25}}$　　　**54.** $\dfrac{\sqrt{50}}{\sqrt{60}}$

Simplify and rationalize.

55. $\sqrt{\dfrac{25a^2}{64b^4}}$　　**56.** $\sqrt{\dfrac{16m}{5}}$　　**57.** $\sqrt[3]{\dfrac{3z^3}{4x^2 y}}$　　**58.** $\dfrac{4a\sqrt{5ab^2}}{12\sqrt{10ab^3}}$

59. Find the period of a pendulum whose length is 3 feet.

13.5
Add or subtract as indicated.

60. $3\sqrt{5} - 2\sqrt{5} + 7\sqrt{5} - \sqrt{5}$　　**61.** $7\sqrt{11} + 2\sqrt{44}$　　**62.** $\sqrt{15} + \sqrt{\dfrac{1}{15}}$

63. $5\sqrt[3]{16} - \sqrt[3]{54}$　　**64.** $\sqrt{49x} - \sqrt{25x}$　　**65.** $4b\sqrt{a^3 b} - 7a\sqrt{ab^3} + 8ab\sqrt{ab}$

Multiply and simplify.

66. $\sqrt{7}\left(\sqrt{14} - \sqrt{7}\right)$　　**67.** $\sqrt{2a}\left(6 + \sqrt{2a}\right)$　　**68.** $\left(2 - \sqrt{5}\right)\left(4 + \sqrt{5}\right)$

69. $\left(\sqrt{5x} + \sqrt{7y}\right)\left(\sqrt{5x} - \sqrt{7y}\right)$　　**70.** $\left(\sqrt{x} + 8\right)^2$　　**71.** $3\sqrt[3]{x}\left(2\sqrt[3]{x^2} + \sqrt[3]{x}\right)$

Divide exercises 72–77 and simplify.

72. $\dfrac{\sqrt{15x} - \sqrt{30}}{\sqrt{5}}$　　**73.** $\dfrac{\sqrt{z} - 5}{\sqrt{z}}$　　**74.** $\dfrac{24}{\sqrt{5} + 2}$

75. $\dfrac{\sqrt{x} + 2}{\sqrt{x} - 2}$　　**76.** $\dfrac{2\sqrt{x} - 5}{5 - 2\sqrt{x}}$　　**77.** $\dfrac{2x - 9}{\sqrt{2x} - 3}$

78. One square mirror measures 720 square inches. A larger square mirror measures 1620 square inches. How much more framing material will the second mirror require over that required for the first mirror?

13.6
Solve numerically.

79. $\sqrt{3x - 5} = x - 3$　　**80.** $\sqrt{6x} - 1 = (6x)^{1/2}$　　**81.** $\sqrt{x^2 + 10x + 25} = x + 5$

Solve exercises 82–85 graphically.

82. $\sqrt{2x - 7} = 2x - 7$　　**83.** $\sqrt{x^2 + 2x + 1} = x + 1$

84. $(x + 4)^{3/2} = \sqrt[3]{2x + 3}$　　**85.** $(x + 5)^{3/5} = (4x - 1)^{2/3}$

86. For her algebra class, Miss Grundy assigned Reggie the task of designing a box whose base has a width defined by the expression $\sqrt{7x + 4}$ and a length defined by the expression $x - 2$. She further required the base of the box to have a perimeter equal to 60 inches. Help Reggie find the dimensions of the base.

87. The time t, in seconds it would take for an object to fall a distance d in feet is given by the expression $t = \sqrt{\frac{2d}{32.2}}$. From what height did a peach drop if it took 6 seconds to fall to the ground?

13.7
Solve algebraically and check.

88. $2\sqrt{3x} + 3 = 15$
89. $\sqrt{4x - 3} = x - 2$
90. $2\sqrt{x + 5} = \sqrt{5x + 9}$
91. $\sqrt{x + 6} + 3 = \sqrt{5x - 1}$
92. $\sqrt{x + 8} = \sqrt{x - 2}$
93. $\sqrt[3]{2x} = -4$
94. $\sqrt[4]{x + 3} = 3$
95. $(x + 7)^{2/5} = 4$
96. $x^{-3/2} = 8$
97. $2x^{2/3} - 5 = 1$

In exercises 98–101, find the distance on the coordinate plane between the points for the coordinate pairs listed.

98. $(4, -3)$ and $(4, 7)$
99. $(-2, -4)$ and $(7, -4)$
100. $(6, 2)$ and $(9, 6)$
101. $(-3, -1)$ and $(4, 8)$

102. Find the possible y-coordinates of a point that is 5 units away from the point $(3, -2)$ and has an x-coordinate of 6.

103. If the coefficient of friction on a road is 35%, the velocity, V, in miles per hour of a car that leaves a skid mark of S feet is given by the mathematical model $V = \sqrt{10.5S}$. What would be the length of the skid mark of a car traveling 40 miles per hour if the car had to suddenly stop?

CHAPTER 13 | Mixed Review

Evaluate to the nearest thousandth, if possible.

1. $\sqrt{196}$
2. $\sqrt{4.41}$
3. $\sqrt[3]{-\frac{27}{64}}$
4. $\sqrt[4]{256}$
5. $\sqrt[4]{-256}$
6. $\sqrt[3]{-29}$

Write as a radical expression and evaluate, if possible.

7. $121^{1/2}$
8. $(-125)^{1/3}$
9. $-81^{1/4}$
10. $(-81)^{1/4}$
11. $729^{5/6}$
12. $(-729)^{5/6}$
13. $(-8)^{-2/3}$
14. $(-81)^{-3/4}$

Use the properties of exponents to evaluate.

15. $\frac{1}{9^{-1/2}}$
16. $27^{2/3} \cdot 27^{5/3}$
17. $\frac{6^{7/3}}{6^{2/3}}$
18. $(36^{2/3})^{3/4}$
19. $\left(\frac{9}{16}\right)^{-3/2}$
20. $\left[(3^{1/2})(12^{1/2})\right]^{-3/2}$

Simplify without a calculator, rationalizing all denominators.

21. $-\sqrt{\frac{72}{98}}$
22. $\sqrt{\frac{15}{144}}$
23. $\sqrt{\frac{50}{338}}$
24. $\sqrt[3]{-\frac{64}{125}}$
25. $\sqrt{150}$
26. $\sqrt[3]{-448}$
27. $\sqrt[4]{48}$
28. $\sqrt[5]{-486}$

Perform the indicated operations and simplify.

29. $\sqrt{15} \cdot \sqrt{35}$
30. $\sqrt{\frac{3}{7}} - \sqrt{\frac{7}{3}}$
31. $6\sqrt{13} + 3\sqrt{52}$

32. $4\sqrt{7} - 3\sqrt{7} + 11\sqrt{7} - \sqrt{7}$

33. $\sqrt{3}\left(\sqrt{6} - \sqrt{3}\right)$

34. $\left(7 - \sqrt{3}\right)\left(9 + \sqrt{3}\right)$

35. $\left(\sqrt{10} - \sqrt{5}\right)\left(\sqrt{10} + \sqrt{5}\right)$

36. $6\sqrt[3]{375} + 2\sqrt[3]{24}$

Simplify. Write your results using positive exponents.

37. $\dfrac{x^{2/3}}{x^{3/4}}$

38. $z^{3/5} \cdot z^{-3/2}$

39. $\left(\dfrac{p^4}{q^8}\right)^{-5/16}$

40. $\left(27x^9 y^{12}\right)^{4/3}$

41. $\sqrt{72x^6 y^3 z^4}$

42. $\sqrt[3]{-64x^2 y^7}$

43. $2\sqrt{3xy} \cdot y\sqrt{6x}$

44. $\sqrt[3]{-3a^5 b^5} \cdot \sqrt[3]{18ab^2}$

45. $\sqrt{10x + 35y} \cdot \sqrt{2x + 7y}$

46. $\sqrt{\dfrac{36x^2}{49y^4}}$

47. $\sqrt{\dfrac{25z}{3}}$

48. $\sqrt[3]{\dfrac{-27a}{b^3}}$

49. $\dfrac{\sqrt{6a}}{\sqrt{12ab}}$

50. $\dfrac{\sqrt{x^3 y^2}}{\sqrt{x^4 y^5}}$

51. $\sqrt{121x} - \sqrt{81x}$

52. $16d\sqrt{c^3 d} - 11c\sqrt{cd^3} + 9cd\sqrt{cd}$

53. $\left(\sqrt{a} + 9\right)^2$

54. $\sqrt{6a}\left(3 + \sqrt{6a}\right)$

55. $\left(\sqrt{3x} + \sqrt{2y}\right)\left(\sqrt{3x} - \sqrt{2y}\right)$

56. $2\sqrt[3]{x^2}\left(3\sqrt[3]{x} + 5\sqrt[3]{x^2}\right)$

57. $\dfrac{\sqrt{18x} - \sqrt{42}}{\sqrt{6}}$

58. $\dfrac{\sqrt{m} - 9}{\sqrt{m}}$

59. $\dfrac{18}{\sqrt{7} + 2}$

60. $\dfrac{3 + \sqrt{x}}{3 - \sqrt{x}}$

61. $\dfrac{7 - 3\sqrt{a}}{3\sqrt{a} - 7}$

62. $\dfrac{25 - 7x}{5 - \sqrt{7x}}$

Graph each radical function. State the restricted values on the domain.

63. $f(x) = 5 - \sqrt{x}$

64. $y = x^{3/2} - 3$

Solve exercises 65–80.

65. $\sqrt{x^2 + 8x + 16} = x + 4$

66. $\sqrt{x - 2} = x - 2$

67. $\sqrt{x^2 + 6x + 9} = x + 3$

68. $(x - 1)^{3/2} = \sqrt[3]{2x + 5}$

69. $(x + 4)^{3/5} = (5x - 1)^{2/3}$

70. $\sqrt{x} + 2 = 11$

71. $3\sqrt{5x + 7} = 52$

72. $\sqrt{3x + 1} = x - 3$

73. $2\sqrt{x + 9} = \sqrt{9x + 1}$

74. $\sqrt{2x + 1} + 2 = \sqrt{6x + 1}$

75. $\sqrt{10 - x} = \sqrt{3 - x}$

76. $\sqrt[3]{3x} = -6$

77. $\sqrt[4]{x + 2} = 3$

78. $(x + 5)^{2/5} = 9$

79. $x^{-3/2} = 27$

80. $3x^{2/3} - 7 = 2$

81. Find the length of a side of a square napkin whose area is 529 square inches.

82. In statistics, the variability of the integers 1 to n is calculated as $s = \sqrt{\dfrac{n(n+1)}{12}}$. Calculate the variability of the integers from 1 to 27.

83. The time t in seconds it would take for a pear to fall a distance d in feet is given by the expression $t = \sqrt{\dfrac{2d}{32.2}}$. From what height did the pear fall if it took 4 seconds to reach the ground?

84. Using the formula for the period T of a pendulum of length L, $T = 2\pi\sqrt{\dfrac{L}{32}}$, find the period of a pendulum whose length is 3.5 feet.

Find the distance on the coordinate plane between the points for the coordinate pairs listed in exercises 85–88.

85. $(6, -3)$ and $(6, 7)$

86. $(-4, 8)$ and $(2, 8)$

87. $(5, -1)$ and $(9, 2)$

88. $(5, 7)$ and $(-2, 10)$

89. Find the possible x-coordinates of a point that has a y-coordinate of -2 and is 4 units away from $(2, 8)$.

90. Find the possible y-coordinates of a point that has an x-cordinate of 7 and is 5 units away from $(3, 2)$.

CHAPTER 13 | **Test**

Test-Taking Tips

When preparing for a test, it is usually helpful to go back to previous chapters that you have studied and do a cursory review of that material. In mathematics, each chapter builds upon previous chapters. By reviewing previous chapters, you are reinforcing what you learned before and what you have been tested on before. One way to review would be to study the practice tests from previous chapters. If you find you are stuck on any exercises, then go back and study some examples similar to the exercise. You will be reinforcing the skills that you are assumed to have mastered, and these may help you when you take the test on new material.

Evaluate, if possible. Round decimal answers to the nearest thousandth.

1. $\sqrt{196}$ **2.** $\sqrt{2.25}$ **3.** $\sqrt[4]{21}$ **4.** $\sqrt{-25}$ **5.** $\sqrt[3]{\dfrac{-8}{125}}$

Use the properties of exponents to evaluate.

6. $16^{5/2} \cdot 16^{-1/4}$ **7.** $\left(81^{4/3}\right)^{3/8}$ **8.** $64^{2/3}$ **9.** $\left(\dfrac{8}{27}\right)^{-2/3}$

In Exercises 10–17, simplify. Express your results as a single radical expression wherever possible. Rationalize all denominators. (Assume that the variable base of an exponential expression or a variable radicand does not represent values for which the expression is not defined.)

10. $\dfrac{x^{4/5}}{x^{3/10}}$ **11.** $\left(\sqrt{2x} - \sqrt{5y}\right)\left(\sqrt{2x} + \sqrt{5y}\right)$ **12.** $\sqrt{6x^3 y} \cdot \sqrt{15xy^2}$

13. $\sqrt{\dfrac{3z^3}{2xy^2}}$ **14.** $\dfrac{\sqrt{50xy^3}}{\sqrt{98x^3 y^2}}$ **15.** $\sqrt{81x} + 2\sqrt{25x} - 3\sqrt{16x}$

16. $5\sqrt[3]{x}\left(2\sqrt[3]{x^2} + 3\sqrt[3]{x}\right)$ **17.** $\dfrac{\sqrt{x} + 4}{\sqrt{x} + 1}$

18. Solve $(x + 4)^{1/3} + 3 = 2$.

    a. numerically   **b.** graphically   **c.** algebraically

Solve exercises 19–22.

19. $3\sqrt{x} - 5 = 13$ **20.** $\sqrt{3x + 1} = x - 1$

21. $\sqrt{x^2 + 10x + 25} = x + 5$ **22.** $\sqrt{5x + 1} - 2 = \sqrt{x + 1}$

23. Graph the radical function $f(x) = \sqrt{x + 7} - 3$ and state the restricted values on the domain.

In exercises 24–25, find the distance on the coordinate plane between the points for the coordinate pairs listed.

24. $(3, -2)$ and $(3, 5)$ **25.** $(2, -3)$ and $(5, 4)$

26. A square tablecloth measures 2000 square inches. A larger square tablecloth measures 3125 square inches. How much more border will the larger tablecloth require over that required by the smaller tablecloth?

27. Explain how you would determine the restricted values in the domain of a radical function where the index of the radical is an even number. Use an example to illustrate your explanation. Then explain how you would describe the domain of a radical function.

CHAPTERS 1–13 | Cumulative Review

Simplify and write with positive exponents.

1. $2^0 x^{-1} y^2$

2. $\left(3x^{1/2} y^{3/4}\right)^2$

3. $\left(\dfrac{(2s)^2}{3t}\right)^{-3}$

Simplify.

4. $\left(2x^3 + 6x^2 y - 2xy^2 + y^3\right) + \left(3x^3 + 4xy^2 - y^3\right)$

5. $\left(1.2a^2 - 3.6ab + b^2\right) - \left(4a^2 + 2.71ab - 3.4b^2\right)$

6. $\left(6.8m^2 n\right)\left(-2mn^2 p\right)$

7. $(3a - b)(2a + 4b)$

8. $(2x + 3)(2x - 3)$

9. $(2x + 3)^2$

10. $\dfrac{-15x^2 y^3 z}{3xyz}$

11. $\dfrac{2m^2 n + 4mn - 8n^2}{2m^2 n}$

12. $\dfrac{x^2 + 2x - 3}{x^2 - 9}$

13. $\dfrac{x}{x + 2} + \dfrac{3}{x - 2}$

14. $\dfrac{1}{x + 2} - \dfrac{3}{x - 3} - \dfrac{x + 3}{x^2 + x - 12}$

15. $\dfrac{2a - 5}{a + 2} \cdot \dfrac{2a^2 + 3a - 2}{4a^2 - 25}$

16. $\dfrac{2x}{2x^2 + 9x + 4} \div \dfrac{4x^2 y}{x^2 + 9x + 20}$

17. $\sqrt{8y} + \sqrt{2y} - 2\sqrt{18y}$

18. $\sqrt[3]{25a^4 b} \cdot \sqrt[3]{5ab}$

19. $\left(\sqrt{3} - \sqrt{5}\right)\left(\sqrt{3} + \sqrt{5}\right)$

20. $\dfrac{\sqrt{21abc^3}}{\sqrt{7a^3 b}}$

21. $\dfrac{\sqrt{x} + 2}{\sqrt{x} - 1}$

22. $x^{1/2}\left(x^{2/3} - x^{3/4}\right)$

Factor exercises 23–25 completely, if possible.

23. $16a^2 - 25b^2$

24. $x^2 - 2x - 8$

25. $3x^2 - 9x - 30$

26. Given $f(x) = -x^2 + 3x - 1$, find $f(-2)$.

Graph and label as indicated. Determine the domain and range of each function.

27. $f(x) = -3.2x + 1$; three points on the graph

28. $y = x^2 + 4x + 6$; vertex, y-intercept, enough points to determine the curve, and the axis of symmetry

29. $g(x) = -2x^2 + x + 1$; vertex, x-intercept, y-intercept, enough points to determine the curve, and the axis of symmetry

30. $y = \dfrac{x^2 - 4}{x + 2}$; enough points to determine the curve

31. $h(x) = \dfrac{2}{x}$; enough points to determine the curve

32. $y = 2\sqrt{x}$; enough points to determine the curve

33. $a(x) = x^{2/3} + 2$; enough points to determine the curve

Solve.

34. $2(x + 3) - 4(x - 1) = x - 2$

35. $2.4x - 1.2(2x - 3) = 3.6$

36. $x^2 + 2x - 15 = 0$

37. $2t^2 + 3t = 4$

38. $\dfrac{x + 1}{x - 1} = \dfrac{x + 3}{x + 2}$

39. $\dfrac{2}{x^2} + \dfrac{3}{2x^2} = \dfrac{1}{8}$

40. $\sqrt{2x - 3} + 5 = 9$

Solve. Write the solution set in interval notation.

41. $2x^2 - 9x - 18 < 0$

Solve.

42. $3x - 4y = 3$
$x + y = 8$

In exercises 43–44, write a linear equation for a line that satisfies the given conditions.

43. Passes through the points $(3, -5)$ and $(-4, 2)$

44. Perpendicular to $2x + 3y = 5$ and passes through $(-2, 1)$

45. Write a quadratic equation for a curve that passes through the points $(0, -4)$, $(-4, 0)$, and $(1, 0)$.

46. The diagonal of a rectangle measures 20 feet. The length of the rectangle is 4 feet more than the width. Find the dimensions of the rectangle.

47. Determine the possible y-coordinates of a point 5 units from $(-3, 4)$ with an x-coordinate of 0.

48. Kevin can rake the leaves in his yard in 5 hours. His sister Elizabeth can rake the leaves in her yard in 4 hours. It is 12:00 noon. Can Kevin and Elizabeth, working together, be through raking leaves before their mother arrives home at 2:30?

49. A small business spends $1,000 on production equipment. Each item produced costs $0.55 to produce and is sold for $1.25. How many items must be sold before the business breaks even?

50. A skydiver free-falls from a height of 10,000 feet above the ground. He opens his parachute at a height of 2,500 feet. Use the vertical-position equation to determine the length of time he is free-falling.

14

Complex Numbers

We stated in previous chapters that square roots of negative numbers are not defined in the real-number system. This meant that we could not find a real-number solution for several kinds of equations. However, mathematicians found a way around this limitation by extending the real-number system, using a new kind of number called imaginary numbers. The combination of real numbers and imaginary numbers is called the complex-number system.

Do not be confused by the name *imaginary*. Imaginary numbers are useful in many practical applications, especially in describing electricity and electronic devices. We will not try to explain these applications in this text, though we will state some applied equations that involve imaginary numbers. Instead we will focus on adding, subtracting, multiplying, and dividing complex numbers. Finally, we will show how the use of complex numbers can help us solve equations with no real-number solution.

14.1 The Complex-Number System

14.2 Equations with Imaginary-Number Solutions

14.1   The Complex Number System

Objectives

1 Write imaginary numbers.
2 Perform operations on imaginary numbers.
3 Write complex numbers.
4 Perform operations on complex numbers.
5 Model real-world situations using complex numbers.

Application

In a particular electronic circuit, the voltage, V, is $6.375 - 3.150i$ volts and the impedance, Z, is $2.145 + 1.112i$ ohms. Find the magnitude of the current, I, across this part of the circuit, using the equation $V = IZ$.

After completing this section, we will discuss this application further. See page 1104.

The key to working with square roots of negative numbers is to isolate the factor of -1 in the radicand. Then we can proceed to work with the rest of the number, carrying this factor along as if it were a variable. We illustrate this idea by first introducing and operating with imaginary numbers. Then we combine imaginary numbers with real numbers to form complex numbers and work with them.

1 Writing Imaginary Numbers

In this new system, we define a number to be the principal square root of -1. This number is the **imaginary unit i**.

> *Definition of i*
> The imaginary unit $i = \sqrt{-1}$.
> Therefore, $i^2 = -1$.

Using this definition and the product rule for square roots, we can define the square root of any negative real number in terms of i. For example, write $\sqrt{-5}$ in terms of i.

$$\sqrt{-5} = \sqrt{-1 \cdot 5} \qquad \text{Isolate a factor of } -1 \text{ in the radicand.}$$
$$= \sqrt{-1} \cdot \sqrt{5} \qquad \text{Product rule for square roots}$$
$$= i\sqrt{5} \quad \text{or} \quad \sqrt{5}i \qquad \text{Substitute } i \text{ for } \sqrt{-1}.$$

This process leads us to the definition for the square root of a negative real number in terms of i.

> *Square Root of a Negative Number*
> $\sqrt{-b} = \sqrt{b}\,i$, where b is any positive real number.

Helping Hand Be careful when writing the expression $\sqrt{b}\,i$ with the square root first. It can be hard to see that i is not under the square-root symbol. Therefore, when writing the expression on paper, you may want to write it with the i first, as $i\sqrt{b}$.

The calculator can be set to write the square root of a negative number in terms of i. For example, write $\sqrt{-5}$ in terms of i, as shown in Figure 14.1.

TECHNOLOGY

√(-5)
     2.236067977i
√(5)i
     2.236067977i

Figure 14.1

For Figure 14.1
Change the calculator to $a + bi$ mode.

| MODE | ▼ | ▼ | ▼ | ▼ | ▼ | ▼ | ▶ | ENTER |

Return to the home screen.

| 2nd | QUIT |

Enter the square-root expression to be written in terms of i.

| 2nd | √ | (−) | 5 |) | ENTER |

This is an approximate decimal value for $\sqrt{5}\,i$. Enter this value to check.

| 2nd | √ | 5 |) | 2nd | i | ENTER |

For ease in reading approximate values, set the calculator to the number of decimal places you want to round to. For example, round to two decimal places the values found in Figure 14.1, as shown in Figure 14.2.

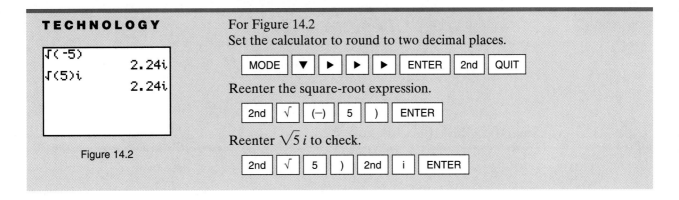

TECHNOLOGY

√(-5)
     2.24i
√(5)i
     2.24i

Figure 14.2

For Figure 14.2
Set the calculator to round to two decimal places.

| MODE | ▼ | ▶ | ▶ | ▶ | ENTER | 2nd | QUIT |

Reenter the square-root expression.

| 2nd | √ | (−) | 5 |) | ENTER |

Reenter $\sqrt{5}\,i$ to check.

| 2nd | √ | 5 |) | 2nd | i | ENTER |

EXAMPLE 1   Write in terms of i.

     a. $\sqrt{-36}$ **b.** $\sqrt{-\dfrac{9}{16}}$ **c.** $\sqrt{-8}$

Solution

a. $\sqrt{-36} = \sqrt{36}\,i$ Write the square root of a negative number in terms of *i*.

$\qquad\qquad = 6i$ $\sqrt{36} = 6$

b. $\sqrt{-\dfrac{9}{16}} = \sqrt{\dfrac{9}{16}}\,i$ Write the square root of a negative number in terms of *i*.

$\qquad\qquad = \dfrac{3}{4}i$ $\sqrt{\frac{9}{16}} = \frac{3}{4}$

c. $\sqrt{-8} = \sqrt{8}\,i$ Write the square root of a negative number in terms of *i*.

$\qquad\qquad = 2\sqrt{2}i \quad \text{or} \quad 2i\sqrt{2}$ $\sqrt{8} = 2\sqrt{2}$

Check on your calculator. Round approximate values to two decimal places, as shown in Figures 14.3a and 14.3b. ∎

TECHNOLOGY

Figure 14.3a

Figure 14.3b

For Figure 14.3a

Set the calculator to round to two decimal places and to *a* + *bi* mode.

MODE ▼ ▶ ▶ ▶ ENTER ▼

▼ ▼ ▼ ▼ ▶ ENTER

Return to the home screen.

2nd QUIT

Enter the square-root expression to be written in terms of *i*.

a. 2nd √ (−) 3 6) ENTER

b. 2nd √ (−) 9 ÷ 1 6) MATH 1 ENTER

For Figure 14.3b

c. 2nd √ (−) 8) ENTER

This is an approximate value for $2\sqrt{2}\,i$. Enter this value to check.

2 2nd √ 2) 2nd i ENTER

 Experiencing Algebra the Checkup Way

Write the expressions in exercises 1–3 in terms of i.

1. $\sqrt{-49}$ **2.** $\sqrt{-\dfrac{4}{81}}$ **3.** $\sqrt{-27}$

4. Explain the difference between the following two radicals.

    a. $-\sqrt{16}$ **b.** $\sqrt{-16}$

5. What is an imaginary number?

2 Operations on Imaginary Numbers

Figure 14.4

When we perform operations with imaginary numbers, we must first write all square roots of negative numbers in terms of i. Even though the symbol i is *not* a variable, we can then treat it as a variable when performing operations.

Before we begin, we need to evaluate i raised to powers greater than 2. For example, evaluate i^1 and i^2 on your calculator, as shown in Figure 14.4.

Complete the following set of exercises with your calculator to discover the results of raising i to powers greater than 2.

DISCOVERY 1

Powers of i

1. Evaluate the following expressions.

$i^1 = \underline{\quad i \quad}$ $i^2 = \underline{\quad -1 \quad}$

   a. $i^3 = \underline{\quad\quad}$ **b.** $i^4 = \underline{\quad\quad}$

   c. $i^5 = \underline{\quad\quad}$ **d.** $i^6 = \underline{\quad\quad}$

2. Look for a pattern and predict the following.

$i^7 = \underline{\quad\quad}$

Check your predictions on your calculator. Were you correct? The calculator value is written in scientific notation. If you evaluate the calculator value, it should be approximately $-i$.

3. Predict a value for i^8 and check your results again.

$i^8 = \underline{\quad\quad}$

Look for a pattern and then write a rule for evaluating i to any power.

The values for the powers of i repeat the pattern $i, -1, -i, 1, i, \ldots$.
To determine the value of i raised to a power, divide the power by 4.

- If the remainder is 1, the value of the expression is i.
- If the remainder is 2, the value of the expression is -1.
- If the remainder is 3, the value of the expression is $-i$.
- If the remainder is 0, the value of the expression is 1.

We can see that this is true algebraically.

$$i^1 = i$$
$$i^2 = -1$$
$$i^3 = (i^2)(i) = (-1)(i) = -i$$
$$i^4 = (i^3)(i) = (-i)(i) = -i^2 = -(-1) = 1$$
$$i^5 = (i^4)(i) = (1)(i) = i$$
$$\vdots$$

We can add, subtract, multiply, and divide imaginary numbers:

Addition $ai + bi = (a + b)i$ Add the coefficients of i.

Subtraction $ai - bi = (a - b)i$ Subtract the coefficients of i.

Multiplication $\quad (ai)(bi) = (ab)i^2 \qquad$ Multiply the coefficients of i.
Remember that $i \cdot i = i^2$.

$$= (ab)(-1) \quad \text{Substitute } -1 \text{ for } i^2.$$

$$= -ab \qquad \text{Simplify.}$$

Division $\qquad \dfrac{ai}{bi} = \dfrac{a}{b} \qquad\qquad$ Simplify.

 Helping Hand We do not need to memorize these patterns. Simply perform the operations, treating i as a variable.

For example,

$$\sqrt{-2}\,\sqrt{-18} = \sqrt{2}i \cdot \sqrt{18}i \qquad \text{Write each square root of a negative number in terms of } i.$$

$$= \sqrt{36}\,i^2 \qquad\qquad \text{Product rule for radicals}$$

$$= 6 \cdot -1 \qquad\qquad \text{Substitute } -1 \text{ for } i^2.$$

$$= -6$$

 Helping Hand Remember to write the square roots of a negative number in terms of i before you perform operations with imaginary numbers. For example, $\sqrt{-2} \cdot \sqrt{-18} \neq \sqrt{36}$.

EXAMPLE 2 Perform the indicated operation.

a. $\sqrt{-27} + \sqrt{-12}$ **b.** $2\sqrt{-63} - 3\sqrt{-28}$ **c.** $\dfrac{\sqrt{-25}}{\sqrt{-16}}$

d. $\sqrt{-2}\,\sqrt{-3}\,\sqrt{-5}$ **e.** $\left(\sqrt{-3} + \sqrt{-4}\right)\left(\sqrt{-2} - \sqrt{-6}\right)$

Solution

a. $\sqrt{-27} + \sqrt{-12} = \sqrt{27}i + \sqrt{12}i \qquad$ Write the square root of a negative number in terms of i.

$$= 3\sqrt{3}i + 2\sqrt{3}i \qquad \text{Simplify the radicals.}$$

$$= 5\sqrt{3}i$$

b. $2\sqrt{-63} - 3\sqrt{-28} = 2\sqrt{63}i - 3\sqrt{28}i \qquad$ Write the square root of a negative number in terms of i.

$$= 2 \cdot 3\sqrt{7}i - 3 \cdot 2\sqrt{7}i \qquad \text{Simplify the radicals.}$$

$$= 6\sqrt{7}i - 6\sqrt{7}i \qquad\qquad \text{Multiply.}$$

$$= 0$$

c. $\dfrac{\sqrt{-25}}{\sqrt{-16}} = \dfrac{\sqrt{25}i}{\sqrt{16}i} \qquad$ Write the square root of a negative number in terms of i.

$$= \dfrac{5i}{4i} \qquad \text{Simplify the radicals.}$$

$$= \dfrac{5}{4} \qquad \text{Simplify.}$$

d. $\sqrt{-2}\,\sqrt{-3}\,\sqrt{-5} = \sqrt{2}i \cdot \sqrt{3}i \cdot \sqrt{5}i$ Write the square root of a negative number in terms of i.

$$= \sqrt{30}i^3$$ Product rule for square roots

$$= (\sqrt{30})(-i)$$ Substitute $-i$ for i^3.

$$= -\sqrt{30}i$$

e. $(\sqrt{-3} + \sqrt{-4})(\sqrt{-2} - \sqrt{-6})$

$$= (\sqrt{3}i + \sqrt{4}i)(\sqrt{2}i - \sqrt{6}i)$$ Write the square root of a negative number in terms of i.

$$= \sqrt{6}i^2 - \sqrt{18}i^2 + \sqrt{8}i^2 - \sqrt{24}i^2$$ FOIL method

$$= \sqrt{6}i^2 - 3\sqrt{2}i^2 + 2\sqrt{2}i^2 - 2\sqrt{6}i^2$$ Simplify the radicals.

$$= \sqrt{6}(-1) - 3\sqrt{2}(-1) + 2\sqrt{2}(-1) - 2\sqrt{6}(-1)$$ Substitute -1 for i^2.

$$= -\sqrt{6} + 3\sqrt{2} - 2\sqrt{2} + 2\sqrt{6}$$ Multiply.

$$= \sqrt{6} + \sqrt{2}$$

We can check these operations on the calculator. Set your calculator to round to two decimal places and to $a + bi$ mode, then enter the expression. Answers with radicals are approximated and can be checked by entering the exact answer and comparing the two results.

a. $\sqrt{-27} + \sqrt{-12} \approx 8.66i$ Approximate value for $5\sqrt{3}i$

```
√(-27)+√(-12)
              8.66i
5√(3)i
              8.66i
```

b. $2\sqrt{-63} - 3\sqrt{-28} = 0$ **c.** $\dfrac{\sqrt{-25}}{\sqrt{-16}} = \dfrac{5}{4}$

```
2√(-63)-3√(-28)
              0.00
√(-25)/√(-16)►Fr
ac
               5/4
```

d. $\sqrt{-2}\,\sqrt{-3}\,\sqrt{-5} \approx -5.48i$ Approximate value for $-\sqrt{30}i$

e. $\left(\sqrt{-3} + \sqrt{-4}\right)\left(\sqrt{-2} - \sqrt{-6}\right) \approx 3.86$ Approximate value for $\sqrt{6} + \sqrt{2}$

```
((√(-3)+√(-4))(√(
-2)-√(-6))
              3.86
√(6)+√(2)
              3.86
```

■

 ## Experiencing Algebra the Checkup Way

In exercises 1–5, perform the indicated operation.

1. $\sqrt{-4} + \sqrt{-64}$ **2.** $5\sqrt{-20} - 3\sqrt{-125}$ **3.** $\dfrac{\sqrt{-100}}{\sqrt{-121}}$

4. $\sqrt{-6}\,\sqrt{-10}\,\sqrt{-15}$ **5.** $\left(\sqrt{-5} - \sqrt{-6}\right)\left(\sqrt{-2} - \sqrt{-15}\right)$

6. Is the imaginary number i a variable? Explain.

7. How is the imaginary number i treated the same as a variable?

---

3 Complex Numbers

As we performed operations on imaginary numbers in the last section, we obtained values expressed in different forms. For example, some of the results were real numbers and others were expressions that contained the imaginary number i. Together they make up the **complex-number system**.

> *Standard Form for a Complex Number*
> A complex number is written in the standard form
>
> $$a + bi,$$
>
> where a and b are real numbers.
>
> If $b = 0$, then $a + 0i = a$ is a real number.
> If $b \neq 0$, then $a + bi$ is an imaginary number.
> If $a = 0$ and $b \neq 0$, then $0 + bi = bi$ is a pure imaginary number.
>
> We call a the real part and b the imaginary part.

In summary, the set of complex numbers consists of two mutually exclusive subsets: real numbers and imaginary numbers. Remember that two sets are mutually exclusive when any number that belongs to one set does not belong to the other set. To visualize the set of complex numbers, we add the set of imaginary numbers to the set of real numbers that we viewed in Figure 2.7.

Complex numbers

Real numbers

Rational numbers

Integers

Whole numbers

Natural numbers
or
Counting numbers

Irrational numbers

Imaginary numbers

EXAMPLE 3 Determine the real part and the imaginary part for each of the following complex numbers. Identify any real number or pure imaginary number.

a. $5\sqrt{3}i$ **b.** 0 **c.** $\dfrac{5}{4}$

d. $-30i$ **e.** $-\sqrt{6} + \sqrt{10}i$ **f.** $-3\sqrt{6} + \sqrt{2}$

Solution

a. $5\sqrt{3}i$ is a pure imaginary number. The real part is 0 and the imaginary part is $5\sqrt{3}$.

b. 0 is a real number. The real part is 0 and the imaginary part is 0.

c. $\dfrac{5}{4}$ is a real number. The real part is $\dfrac{5}{4}$ and the imaginary part is 0.

d. $-30i$ is a pure imaginary number. The real part is 0 and the imaginary part is -30.

e. $-\sqrt{6} + \sqrt{10}i$ is a complex number. The real part is $-\sqrt{6}$ and the imaginary part is $\sqrt{10}$.

f. $-3\sqrt{6} + \sqrt{2}$ is a real number. The real part is $-3\sqrt{6} + \sqrt{2}$ and the imaginary part is 0. ■

Experiencing Algebra the Checkup Way

In exercises 1–6, state the real part and the imaginary part for each complex number. Identify any real number or pure imaginary number.

1. $\sqrt{3} - 2\sqrt{5}$ **2.** $12i$ **3.** 1244

4. $\dfrac{\sqrt{7}}{8}$ **5.** $9 - \sqrt{6}i$ **6.** $-2\sqrt{17}i$

7. Every real number is also a complex number, but not all complex numbers are real numbers. Explain.

4 Operations on Complex Numbers

Two complex numbers $a + bi$ and $c + di$ are equal if and only if $a = c$ and $b = d$. For example,

$$\sqrt{4} + \sqrt{-3} \text{ and } 2 + \sqrt{3}i \text{ are equal because } \sqrt{4} = 2 \text{ and}$$
$$\sqrt{-3} = \sqrt{3}i.$$

We can add and subtract complex numbers by adding the real parts and the imaginary parts separately.

$$(a + bi) + (c + di) = (a + c) + (b + d)i$$
$$(a + bi) - (c + di) = (a - c) + (b - d)i$$

Again, we treat i as a variable and perform the operations in the same manner as adding and subtracting binomials.

EXAMPLE 4   Add or subtract. Write your answer in standard form for a complex number.

a. $(2 + 3i) + (-4 + 5i)$ **b.** $7 - (2 + i)$ **c.** $-2i - (3 - 2i)$

Solution

```
(2+3i)+(-4+5i)
               -2+8i
7-(2+i)
               5-i
-2i-(3-2i)
               -3
```

a. $(2 + 3i) + (-4 + 5i) = [2 + (-4)] + (3 + 5)i = -2 + 8i$

b. $7 - (2 + i) = 7 - 2 - i = 5 - i$

c. $-2i - (3 - 2i) = -2i - 3 + 2i = -3$

Calculator checks for Examples 4a, 4b, and 4c are shown in the figure. ∎

We multiply complex numbers by using the distributive property. Remember, this leads to the FOIL method for binomials.

Helping Hand Remember to simplify powers of i. Write the products in standard form for complex numbers.

EXAMPLE 5   Multiply. Write your answer in standard form for a complex number.

a. $2(3 - 4i)$ **b.** $3i(6 + i)$ **c.** $(-5 + 2i)(7 - 6i)$

Solution

a. $2(3 - 4i) = 6 - 8i$ Distributive property

b. $3i(6 + i) = 18i + 3i^2$ Distributive property

$\quad\quad\quad\quad = 18i + 3(-1)$

$\quad\quad\quad\quad = 18i - 3$

$\quad\quad\quad\quad = -3 + 18i$

```
2(3-4i)
               6-8i
3i(6+i)
               -3+18i
(-5+2i)(7-6i)
               -23+44i
```

c. $(-5 + 2i)(7 - 6i) = -35 + 30i + 14i - 12i^2$ FOIL method

$\quad\quad\quad\quad\quad\quad = -35 + 30i + 14i - 12(-1)$

$\quad\quad\quad\quad\quad\quad = -35 + 30i + 14i + 12$

$\quad\quad\quad\quad\quad\quad = -23 + 44i$

Calculator checks for Examples 5a, 5b, and 5c are shown in the figure. ∎

When we multiplied the sum and difference of the same two terms using binomials, we obtained a special product. Similarly, the product of $a + bi$ and $a - bi$ results in a special product. To determine this product, complete the following set of exercises.

DISCOVERY 2

Product of $a + bi$ and $a - bi$
Multiply.

1. $(2 + 3i)(2 - 3i)$ **2.** $(-4 + i)(-4 - i)$

Write a rule to determine by inspection the product of $a + bi$ and $a - bi$.

The product is a real number, the sum of the squares of a and b. Complex numbers of the form $a + bi$ and $a - bi$ are called **complex conjugates**.

> *Product of Complex Conjugates*
> $$(a + bi)(a - bi) = a^2 + b^2$$

We can verify this result by multiplying $a + bi$ and $a - bi$ algebraically.

$$(a + bi)(a - bi) = a^2 - abi + abi - b^2 i^2$$
$$= a^2 - abi + abi - b^2(-1)$$
$$= a^2 - abi + abi + b^2$$
$$= a^2 + b^2$$

Helping Hand Be careful not to confuse this product with the special product for real numbers $(a + b)(a - b) = a^2 - b^2$.

The following pairs of complex numbers are examples of complex conjugates.

$2 + 3i$	and	$2 - 3i$
$-4 - i$	and	$-4 + i$
5 (or $5 + 0i$)	and	5 (or $5 - 0i$)
$2i$ (or $0 + 2i$)	and	$-2i$ (or $0 - 2i$)

To divide a complex number by a nonzero real number, we use the distributive property, as we did with binomials.

$$\frac{a + bi}{c} = \frac{a}{c} + \frac{bi}{c} = \frac{a}{c} + \frac{b}{c}i$$

However, to divide two complex numbers $\frac{a + bi}{c + di}$, multiply the numerator and denominator by the conjugate of the denominator, $c - di$.

$$\frac{a + bi}{c + di} = \frac{(a + bi)(c - di)}{(c + di)(c - di)}$$

EXAMPLE 6   Divide. Write your answer in standard form for a complex number.

a. $\dfrac{3 + 9i}{3}$ **b.** $\dfrac{2 - 3i}{4 + i}$ **c.** $\dfrac{-2 + 4i}{5i}$

Solution

a. $\dfrac{3 + 9i}{3} = \dfrac{3}{3} + \dfrac{9i}{3}$ Distributive property

$= 1 + 3i$

b. $\dfrac{2 - 3i}{4 + i} = \dfrac{(2 - 3i)(4 - i)}{(4 + i)(4 - i)}$

Multiply the numerator and denominator by the conjugate of the denominator.

$= \dfrac{8 - 2i - 12i + 3i^2}{16 + 1}$

$(a + b)(a - b) = a^2 + b^2$, when $a = 4$ and $b = 1$

$= \dfrac{8 - 2i - 12i + 3(-1)}{16 + 1}$

$= \dfrac{8 - 2i - 12i - 3}{17}$

$= \dfrac{5 - 14i}{17}$

$= \dfrac{5}{17} - \dfrac{14}{17}i$

Standard form

c. $\dfrac{-2 + 4i}{5i} = \dfrac{(-2 + 4i)(-5i)}{(5i)(-5i)}$

Conjugate of the denominator $5i$ or $0 + 5i$ is $0 - 5i$ or $-5i$.

$= \dfrac{10i - 20i^2}{25}$

$(5i)(-5i) = -25i^2 = -25(-1) = 25$

$= \dfrac{10i - 20(-1)}{25}$

$= \dfrac{10i + 20}{25}$

$= \dfrac{10}{25}i + \dfrac{20}{25}$

$= \dfrac{2}{5}i + \dfrac{4}{5}$

$= \dfrac{4}{5} + \dfrac{2}{5}i$

Standard form

Note: We could have multiplied by i or $-i$ instead of $-5i$. For example, if we multiplied by i we would have the following:

$\dfrac{-2 + 4i}{5i} = \dfrac{(-2 + 4i)(i)}{(5i)(i)}$

$= \dfrac{-2i + 4i^2}{5i^2}$

$= \dfrac{-2i + 4(-1)}{5(-1)}$

$= \dfrac{-2i - 4}{-5}$

$= \dfrac{-2i}{-5} + \dfrac{-4}{-5}$

$= \dfrac{2}{5}i + \dfrac{4}{5} \quad \text{or} \quad \dfrac{4}{5} + \dfrac{2}{5}i$

Check on your calculator, as shown in the following figures.

a.

Set your calculator to round to two decimal places. Check by entering the exact answer and comparing results.

b.
```
(2-3i)/(4+i)
           .29-.82i
(5/17)-(14/17)i
           .29-.82i
```

c.
```
(-2+4i)/(5i)
           .80+.40i
(4/5)+(2/5)i
           .80+.40i
```

■

 Experiencing Algebra the Checkup Way

Add or subtract.

1. $(15 - 12i) + (11 + 7i)$ **2.** $11 - (5 - 3i)$ **3.** $21i - (8 + i)$

Multiply.

4. $i(12 + 3i)$ **5.** $(8 - 4i)(9 + 2i)$ **6.** $(7 + 3i)(7 - 3i)$

Divide exercises 7–9.

7. $\dfrac{24 - 18i}{6}$ **8.** $\dfrac{7 - 8i}{2i}$ **9.** $\dfrac{5}{8 - i}$

10. Explain the difference between the conjugate of a radical expression and the conjugate of a complex number. How are these two kinds of conjugates used?

5 Modeling the Real World

In previous chapters, we examined an important formula, called Ohm's law, $V = IR$, that applies to direct-current (DC) circuits, such as electricity you get from connecting a battery. However, there is another kind of electric circuit, called an alternating-current (AC) circuit, that is used to provide the electric power in houses, offices, and industry. The electrical quantities in an AC circuit, such as voltage and current, can be described by complex numbers.

In an AC circuit, Ohm's law takes on a slightly different form, $V = IZ$. The quantity V is still called the voltage and the quantity I is still called current, though both these quantities may be complex numbers. The quantity Z is called the impedance, and includes other electrical properties that we won't discuss, as well as the resistance R, which is the same as in DC circuits. When engineers work with the AC form of Ohm's law, they often have to determine the magnitude of the voltage, which is denoted as $|V|$. If the voltage is given in the complex form $a + bi$, the magnitude of the voltage is the principal square root of the sum of the squares of the real part and the imaginary part, or $|V| = \sqrt{a^2 + b^2}$. We will solve a couple of problems using these equations to give you practice in working with complex numbers.

EXAMPLE 7

In a particular circuit, the current, I, is $2 - 3i$ amperes and the impedance, Z, is $6 + 2i$ ohms. Find the magnitude of the total voltage $|V|$ across this part of the circuit.

Solution

The formula for total voltage is $V = IZ$.

$$V = IZ$$
$$V = (2 - 3i)(6 + 2i)$$
$$V = 12 + 4i - 18i - 6i^2$$
$$V = 12 + 4i - 18i - 6(-1)$$
$$V = 12 + 4i - 18i + 6$$
$$V = 18 - 14i$$

The total voltage is $18 - 14i$ volts.

The magnitude of the total voltage is $|V| = \sqrt{a^2 + b^2}$, where $a = 18$ and $b = -14$.

$$|V| = \sqrt{(18)^2 + (-14)^2} \approx 22.8 \quad \text{Use a calculator to approximate to two decimal places.}$$

The magnitude of the total voltage is approximately 22.8 volts. ∎

Application

In a particular electronic circuit, the voltage, V, is $6.375 - 3.150i$ volts and the impedance, Z, is $2.145 + 1.112i$ ohms. Find the magnitude of the current, I, across this part of the circuit, using the equation $V = IZ$.

Discussion

We will use a calculator to solve this exercise, to simplify the calculations.

$$V = IZ$$
$$6.375 - 3.150i = I(2.145 + 1.112i) \quad \text{Substitute the given values for } V \text{ and } Z.$$
$$I = \frac{6.375 - 3.150i}{2.145 + 1.112i} \quad \text{Solve for } I.$$
$$I \approx 1.742 - 2.372i$$

Note: Set your calculator to round to three decimal places (the number of decimal places given in the problem).

The magnitude of the current $|I| = \sqrt{a^2 + b^2}$, where $a = 1.742$ and $b = -2.372$.

$$|I| = \sqrt{(1.742)^2 + (-2.372)^2} \approx 2.943$$

The magnitude of the current is approximately 2.943 amperes. ∎

Experiencing Algebra the Checkup Way

1. Find the magnitude of the total voltage across a circuit when the current is $4 - 2i$ amperes and the impedance is $5 + 3i$ ohms.

2. Find the magnitude of the current across a circuit when the voltage is $5.4 - 3.1i$ volts and the impedance is $2.2 - 1.2i$ ohms.

PROBLEM SET 14.1

Experiencing Algebra the Exercise Way

Write in terms of i.

1. $\sqrt{-100}$ **2.** $\sqrt{-144}$ **3.** $\sqrt{-\dfrac{16}{49}}$ **4.** $\sqrt{-\dfrac{36}{121}}$

5. $\sqrt{-32}$ **6.** $\sqrt{-75}$ **7.** $2\sqrt{-50}$ **8.** $-3\sqrt{-98}$

Perform the indicated operations.

9. $\sqrt{-9} + \sqrt{-16}$ **10.** $\sqrt{-25} + \sqrt{-81}$ **11.** $\sqrt{-25} - \sqrt{-100}$

12. $\sqrt{-36} - \sqrt{-49}$ **13.** $7\sqrt{-36} + 9\sqrt{-4}$ **14.** $5\sqrt{-16} + 2\sqrt{-9}$

15. $2\sqrt{-121} - 3\sqrt{-9}$ **16.** $3\sqrt{-144} - 2\sqrt{-25}$ **17.** $\dfrac{\sqrt{-144}}{\sqrt{-225}}$

18. $\dfrac{\sqrt{-64}}{\sqrt{-100}}$ **19.** $\sqrt{-5}\,\sqrt{-8}\,\sqrt{-10}$ **20.** $\sqrt{-3}\,\sqrt{-5}\,\sqrt{-15}$

21. $(\sqrt{-6} + \sqrt{-4})(\sqrt{-3} - \sqrt{-8})$ **22.** $(\sqrt{-3} + \sqrt{-10})(\sqrt{-5} - \sqrt{-6})$ **23.** $(\sqrt{-5} - \sqrt{-7})(\sqrt{-5} + \sqrt{-7})$

24. $(\sqrt{-3} + \sqrt{-11})(\sqrt{-3} - \sqrt{-11})$

Determine the real part and the imaginary part for each complex number. Identify any real number or pure imaginary number.

25. $\dfrac{5}{7}$ **26.** $5\sqrt{3}i$ **27.** $2i$ **28.** $2\sqrt{3} - \sqrt{5}$

29. $\sqrt{3} - 5i$ **30.** $\dfrac{\sqrt{3}}{2}$ **31.** -6 **32.** $7 + \sqrt{3}i$

33. $2\sqrt{5}i$ **34.** $-14i$ **35.** $-4\sqrt{7} + \sqrt{11}$ **36.** -17

Add or subtract. Write your answer in standard form for a complex number.

37. $(3 + 5i) + (-8 - i)$ **38.** $(9 - 17i) + (-11 + 8i)$ **39.** $(6 + 2i) - (3 + 3i)$

40. $(14 + 3i) - (5 - 6i)$ **41.** $8i - (5 - 6i)$ **42.** $19i - (4 + 3i)$

43. $(4 - 5i) - (3 - 5i)$ **44.** $(6 + 8i) - (6 + 2i)$ **45.** $(7 + i) - 6$

46. $(13 + 2i) - 15$ **47.** $10 + (3 + 5i)$ **48.** $22 - (4 + 7i)$

49. $\left(\dfrac{1}{2} + 5i\right) + \left(3 - \dfrac{2}{3}i\right)$ **50.** $\left(\dfrac{3}{8} + 6i\right) + \left(\dfrac{1}{8} - 7i\right)$ **51.** $(4.5 + 6.7i) - (2.88 - 4.68i)$

52. $(12.7 - 3.63i) + (4.6 + 12.7i)$ **53.** $(2\sqrt{3} - \sqrt{2}i) + (5\sqrt{3} + 2\sqrt{2}i)$ **54.** $(5\sqrt{5} + \sqrt{3}i) - (7\sqrt{5} + 8\sqrt{3}i)$

Multiply. Write your answer in standard form for a complex number.

55. $-7(4 + 9i)$ **56.** $5(-7 - 11i)$ **57.** $5i(8 - 2i)$

58. $-7i(3 + 12i)$ **59.** $(4 - 3i)(6 + 5i)$ **60.** $(9 + 6i)(5 - 4i)$

61. $(5 + 7i)(5 - 7i)$ **62.** $(11 - 3i)(11 + 3i)$ **63.** $(-6 - i)(-6 + i)$

64. $(-5 + 2i)(-5 - 2i)$ **65.** $5.6(2.1 - 8.7i)$ **66.** $4.7i(3.2 + 6i)$

67. $(0.4 - 3.1i)(5.7 + 0.8i)$ **68.** $(2.5 + 3.4i)(1.2 - 0.6i)$ **69.** $\left(\dfrac{3}{5} + \dfrac{1}{2}i\right)\left(\dfrac{2}{5} - \dfrac{2}{3}i\right)$

70. $\left(\dfrac{3}{4} - \dfrac{2}{3}i\right)\left(\dfrac{3}{5} + \dfrac{1}{3}i\right)$ **71.** $\sqrt{2}i(\sqrt{2} + \sqrt{3}i)$ **72.** $-3\sqrt{3}i(\sqrt{6} - \sqrt{15}i)$

73. $(\sqrt{3} - \sqrt{5}i)(\sqrt{3} + \sqrt{5}i)$ **74.** $(\sqrt{7} + 2\sqrt{6}i)(\sqrt{7} - 2\sqrt{6}i)$

Divide exercises 75–88. Write your answer in standard form for a complex number.

75. $\dfrac{7 + 21i}{7}$

76. $\dfrac{16 + 48i}{8}$

77. $\dfrac{-4 + 7i}{3 - i}$

78. $\dfrac{47 + 13i}{5 + 2i}$

79. $\dfrac{6 - 5i}{2i}$

80. $\dfrac{12 + 9i}{-6i}$

81. $\dfrac{16.2 - 13.5i}{2.7i}$

82. $\dfrac{9.03 + 6.45i}{4.3i}$

83. $\dfrac{21.2 - 10.4i}{4.5 + i}$

84. $\dfrac{-19.7 + 21.5i}{1 + 7.4i}$

85. $\dfrac{\sqrt{6} + \sqrt{14}i}{\sqrt{2}i}$

86. $\dfrac{\sqrt{15} - \sqrt{21}i}{\sqrt{3}i}$

87. $\dfrac{2 + 5\sqrt{6}i}{2\sqrt{3} + \sqrt{2}i}$

88. $\dfrac{23 + 4\sqrt{10}i}{\sqrt{5} + 2\sqrt{2}i}$

89. Find the magnitude of the total voltage, V, across a circuit if the current, I, is $3 + 5i$ amperes and the impedance, Z, is $5 + 4i$ ohms. Use the formula $V = IZ$.

90. What is the total voltage, V, across a circuit when the current, I, is $5 - i$ amperes and the impedance, Z, is $8 + 2i$ ohms?

91. Use the formula $I = \frac{V}{Z}$ to find the magnitude of the current, I, across a circuit when the voltage V, is $18 + i$ volts and the impedance, Z, is $2 + 3i$ ohms.

92. Find the magnitude of the current, I, across a circuit when the voltage, V, is $40 + 44i$ volts and the impedance, Z, is $6 + 4i$ ohms.

 ## Experiencing Algebra the Calculator Way

Now that you have learned to set your calculator to complex-number mode, you can investigate how the calculator handles roots of negative numbers when the index of the radical is something other than 2. Use the complex-number setting for the following exercises.

Simplify.

1. $\sqrt{-25}$

2. $\sqrt[3]{-27}$

3. $\sqrt[4]{-64}$

4. $\sqrt[5]{-32}$

5. $\sqrt[4]{-324}$

6. $\sqrt[4]{-40{,}000}$

When you have your calculator in complex-number mode, you can use the fraction key to change decimal values to fractions. For example, convert $0.25 - 0.8i$ to fractional notation by entering the expression, followed by

| MATH | 1 | ENTER | ,

which results in the expression, $\frac{1}{4} - \frac{4}{5}i$.

Convert the following complex numbers to fractional notation.

7. $1.5 - 3.5i$

8. $0.4 + 3.2i$

9. $-1.8i$

The calculator also can determine the magnitude of a complex number, as required in Example 7 in this section. Remember that the magnitude of $a + bi$ is calculated as $\sqrt{a^2 + b^2}$. For example, to find the magnitude of $3 + 4i$, enter the following.

| MATH | ▶ | ▶ | 5 | 3 | + | 4 | 2nd | i |) | ENTER |

The calculator returns a value of 5 for the magnitude of $3 + 4i$. Use this feature to find the magnitude of the following complex numbers.

10. $6 + 8i$

11. $6 - 8i$

12. $2 - 5i$

13. 22

14. $-7i$

15. $\sqrt{3}i$

Experiencing Algebra the Group Way

Discuss how you would solve each of the following exercises. Then implement the approach your group agrees upon. Once you obtain a solution, discuss how you would check your solution. Carry out the check to verify that you have found the correct answer.

For each of the following exercises, determine the real part, a, and the imaginary part, b, of the complex number. Set your calculator to complex-number mode and use the calculator to check your operations on the complex numbers.

1. $(a + bi) - (1 - 8i) = 3 + 5i$

2. $(a + bi) + (3 - 2i) = 8 + 5i$

3. $(a + bi)(2 + 5i) = 38 + 8i$

4. $(a + bi) \div (3 + 7i) = 5 + 2i$

5. $(6.2 + 4.1i) + (a + bi) = 10 + 5.6i$

6. $\left(\dfrac{1}{2} + 2i\right) - (a + bi) = -\dfrac{1}{4} + 7i$

7. $\left(3 + \dfrac{1}{2}i\right)(a + bi) = 2 - \dfrac{35}{6}i$

8. $(7 + 43.4i) \div (a + bi) = (5 + 2i)$

Experiencing Algebra the Write Way

In this section we saw that the product of complex conjugates gives the result $(a + bi)(a - bi) = a^2 + b^2$. This result can be used to solve the equation $x^2 + 4 = 0$ in the complex-number system. Explain each step used to solve the equation and state the algebraic principle involved. Then explain why this equation has a solution in the set of complex numbers, but not in the set of real numbers.

14.2 Equations with Imaginary-Number Solutions

Objectives

1 Solve quadratic equations with imaginary-number solutions using the principle of square roots.

2 Solve quadratic equations with imaginary-number solutions using the quadratic formula.

3 Model real-world situations using quadratic equations with imaginary-number solutions.

Application

In designing an electronic feedback system, the function $G(s) = \frac{3(s+2)}{s(s+1)}$ was derived. Let $G(s) = -1$ and solve the resulting equation for s.

After completing this section, we will discuss this application further. See page 1111.

In previous chapters of this text, we solved equations for real-number solutions. In this section, we determine imaginary-number solutions of equations.

1 Solving Quadratic Equations Using the Square-Root Principle

Some quadratic equations can be solved using the principle of square roots. That is,

for any positive number b, if $a^2 = b$, then $a = \pm \sqrt{b}$.

This principle limited us to a positive number b in order to obtain real-number solutions. For example, solve $x^2 = 1$.

$$x^2 = 1$$
$$x = \pm 1$$

However, to solve the equation $x^2 = -1$, we need a new principle.

> *Principle of Square Roots for Imaginary-Number Solutions*
> For any negative number b, if $a^2 = b$, then $a = \pm \sqrt{b}i$.

Now we can solve the equation $x^2 = -1$.

$$x^2 = -1$$
$$x = \pm \sqrt{1}i$$
$$x = \pm i$$

We can check the solutions by substitution.

Let $x = i$.

$$\frac{x^2 = -1}{\begin{array}{c|c} (i)^2 & -1 \\ -1 & \end{array}}$$

Let $x = -i$.

$$\frac{x^2 = -1}{\begin{array}{c|c} (-i)^2 & -1 \\ i^2 & \\ -1 & \end{array}}$$

Both solutions check.

EXAMPLE 1 Solve.

a. $x^2 + 6 = 0$ **b.** $2x^2 + 16 = 0$
c. $(x + 3)^2 + 16 = 0$ **d.** $3(2x - 3)^2 = -15$

Solution

a. $x^2 + 6 = 0$

$$x^2 = -6 \qquad \text{Subtract 6 from both sides.}$$
$$x = \pm \sqrt{6}i \qquad \text{Principle of square roots for imaginary-number solutions}$$

Check by substitution.

Let $x = \sqrt{6}i$.

$$\frac{x^2 + 6 = 0}{\begin{array}{c|c} (\sqrt{6}i)^2 + 6 & 0 \\ (\sqrt{6})^2(i)^2 + 6 & \\ (6)(-1) + 6 & \\ -6 + 6 & \\ 0 & \end{array}}$$

Let $x = -\sqrt{6}i$.

$$\frac{x^2 + 6 = 0}{\begin{array}{c|c} (-\sqrt{6}i)^2 + 6 & 0 \\ (-\sqrt{6})^2(i)^2 + 6 & \\ (6)(-1) + 6 & \\ -6 + 6 & \\ 0 & \end{array}}$$

Both solutions check.

b. $2x^2 + 16 = 0$

$$2x^2 = -16 \qquad \text{Subtract 16 from both sides.}$$

$$\frac{2x^2}{2} = -\frac{16}{2} \qquad \text{Divide both sides by 2.}$$

$$x^2 = -8 \qquad \text{Simplify.}$$

$$x = \pm\sqrt{8}i \qquad \text{Principle of square roots for imaginary-number solutions}$$

$$x = \pm 2\sqrt{2}i \qquad \text{Simplify.}$$

```
2√(2)i→X:2X²+16
                 0
-2√(2)i→X:2X²+16
                 0
```

Check by substitution on your calculator.

c. $(x + 3)^2 + 16 = 0$

$$(x + 3)^2 = -16 \qquad \text{Subtract 16 from both sides.}$$

$$x + 3 = \pm\sqrt{16}i \qquad \text{Principle of square roots for imaginary-number solutions}$$

$$x + 3 = \pm 4i \qquad \text{Simplify.}$$

$$x = -3 \pm 4i \qquad \text{Subtract 3 from both sides.}$$

The check is left for you.

d. $3(2x - 3)^2 = -15$

$$(2x - 3)^2 = -5 \qquad \text{Divide both sides by 3.}$$

$$2x - 3 = \pm\sqrt{5}i \qquad \text{Principle of square roots for imaginary-number solutions}$$

$$2x = 3 \pm \sqrt{5}i \qquad \text{Add 3 to both sides.}$$

$$x = \frac{3 \pm \sqrt{5}i}{2} \qquad \text{Divide both sides by 2.}$$

$$x = \frac{3}{2} \pm \frac{\sqrt{5}}{2}i \qquad \text{Standard form}$$

The check is left for you. ∎

Experiencing Algebra the Checkup Way

Solve exercises 1–4.

1. $x^2 + 8 = 0$ **2.** $5x^2 + 20 = 0$ **3.** $(x - 4)^2 + 27 = 0$ **4.** $-6(3z + 1)^2 = 12$

5. In solving quadratic equations that have imaginary-number solutions, what steps are the same as when you solve equations with real-number solutions? What steps are different and why?

2 Solving Quadratic Equations Using the Quadratic Formula

A second method of solving quadratic equations in the standard form, $ax^2 + bx + c = 0$, is to use the quadratic formula.

$$x = \frac{-b \pm \sqrt{b^2 - 4ac}}{2a}$$

When we solved quadratic equations using the quadratic formula, we found that some equations had no real-number solutions. These situations occurred when the discriminant was a negative number. Now we can see that these solutions are imaginary numbers.

EXAMPLE 2 Solve.

a. $3x^2 + 8x + 15 = 0$

b. $\dfrac{y-2}{y-5} = \dfrac{4}{y+4}$

Solution

a. $3x^2 + 8x + 15 = 0$

$$x = \frac{-b \pm \sqrt{b^2 - 4ac}}{2a}$$ Quadratic formula

$$x = \frac{-8 \pm \sqrt{8^2 - 4(3)(15)}}{2(3)}$$ $a = 3, b = 8,$ and $c = 15$

$$x = \frac{-8 \pm \sqrt{64 - 180}}{6}$$

$$x = \frac{-8 \pm \sqrt{-116}}{6}$$

$$x = \frac{-8 \pm \sqrt{116}i}{6}$$ Write the square root of a negative number in terms of i.

$$x = \frac{-8 \pm \sqrt{4 \cdot 29}i}{6}$$ Simplify the radical.

$$x = \frac{-8 \pm 2\sqrt{29}i}{6}$$

$$x = -\frac{8}{6} \pm \frac{2\sqrt{29}i}{6}$$

$$x = -\frac{4}{3} \pm \frac{\sqrt{29}}{3}i$$

```
(-4/3)+(√(29)i/3
)→X:3X²+8X+15
                0
(-4/3)-(√(29)i/3
)→X:3X²+8X+15
                0
```

Check the two imaginary-number solutions by substitution on your calculator.

b.
$$\frac{y-2}{y-5} = \frac{4}{y+4}$$

$$y^2 + 4y - 2y - 8 = 4y - 20$$ Cross-multiply.

$$y^2 - 2y + 12 = 0$$ Standard form of a quadratic equation (in terms of y)

$$y = \frac{-b \pm \sqrt{b^2 - 4ac}}{2a}$$ Quadratic formula

$$y = \frac{-(-2) \pm \sqrt{(-2)^2 - 4(1)(12)}}{2(1)}$$ $a = 1, b = -2,$ and $c = 12$

$$y = \frac{2 \pm \sqrt{4 - 48}}{2}$$

$$y = \frac{2 \pm \sqrt{-44}}{2}$$

$$y = \frac{2 \pm \sqrt{44}i}{2}$$ Write the square root of a negative number in terms of i.

$$y = \frac{2 \pm \sqrt{4 \cdot 11}i}{2}$$ Simplify the radical.

$$y = \frac{2 \pm 2\sqrt{11}i}{2}$$

$$y = \frac{2}{2} \pm \frac{2\sqrt{11}i}{2}$$

$$y = 1 \pm \sqrt{11}i$$

```
1+√(11)i→Y:(Y-2)
/(Y-5)
            .56-.37i
4/(Y+4)
            .56-.37i
```

Check the two imaginary-number solutions by substitution on your calculator. The check of $1 + \sqrt{11}i$ is shown to the left. ∎

Experiencing Algebra the Checkup Way

Solve exercises 1–2.

1. $5x^2 + 3x + 9 = 0$ **2.** $\dfrac{x + 4}{x - 6} = \dfrac{2}{x + 8}$

3. In the quadratic formula, what is the discriminant?

4. If the solutions to a quadratic equation are imaginary numbers, what is true about the discriminant?

3 Modeling the Real World

In the preceding section, we saw that imaginary numbers occur in the study of electricity. However, imaginary-number solutions of equations also occur in other scientific fields of study. We must remember that imaginary numbers do have meanings in these areas, although we will not try to explain them in this text.

EXAMPLE 3

In studying the motion of biological cells and viruses, we must solve the equation $3.0 = 2.5p - 12.6p^2$. Determine the solution set of the equation.

Solution

$$3.0 = 2.5p - 12.6p^2$$

$$12.6p^2 - 2.5p + 3.0 = 0$$ Standard form of a quadratic equation

$$p = \frac{-b \pm \sqrt{b^2 - 4ac}}{2a}$$ Quadratic formula

$$p = \frac{-(-2.5) \pm \sqrt{(-2.5)^2 - 4(12.6)(3.0)}}{2(12.6)}$$ $a = 12.6$, $b = -2.5$, and $c = 3.0$

$$p = \frac{2.5 \pm \sqrt{-144.95}}{25.2}$$

$$p = \frac{2.5 \pm \sqrt{144.95}i}{25.2}$$ Write the square root of a negative number in terms of i. ∎

Application

In designing an electronic feedback system, the function $G(s) = \frac{3(s+2)}{s(s+1)}$ was derived. Let $G(s) = -1$ and solve the resulting equation for s.

Discussion

$$G(s) = \frac{3(s + 2)}{s(s + 1)}$$

$$-1 = \frac{3(s + 2)}{s(s + 1)} \qquad \text{Substitute } -1 \text{ for } G(s).$$

$$-s(s + 1) = 3(s + 2) \qquad \text{Cross-multiply.}$$

$$-s^2 - s = 3s + 6 \qquad \text{Simplify.}$$

$$0 = s^2 + 4s + 6$$

$$s^2 + 4s + 6 = 0 \qquad \text{Standard form of a quadratic equation}$$

$$s = \frac{-b \pm \sqrt{b^2 - 4ac}}{2a} \qquad \text{Quadratic formula}$$

$$s = \frac{-4 \pm \sqrt{4^2 - 4(1)(6)}}{2(1)} \qquad a = 1, b = 4, \text{ and } c = 6$$

$$s = \frac{-4 \pm \sqrt{-8}}{2}$$

$$s = \frac{-4 \pm \sqrt{8}i}{2} \qquad \text{Write the square root of a negative number in terms of } i.$$

$$s = \frac{-4 \pm 2\sqrt{2}i}{2} \qquad \text{Simplify the radical.}$$

$$s = -\frac{4}{2} \pm \frac{2\sqrt{2}i}{2}$$

$$s = -2 \pm \sqrt{2}i \ \blacksquare$$

Experiencing Algebra the Checkup Way

In the electronic feedback system, the function $G(s) = \frac{3(s+2)}{s(s+1)}$ is derived. Solve the resulting equation if $G(s) = -2$.

PROBLEM SET 14.2

Experiencing Algebra the Exercise Way

Solve exercises 1–48.

1. $x^2 + 9 = 0$
2. $x^2 + 25 = 0$
3. $a^2 + 7 = 0$
4. $b^2 + 11 = 0$
5. $z^2 + 5 = 1$
6. $m^2 + 18 = 2$
7. $3p^2 + 75 = 0$
8. $4q^2 + 64 = 0$
9. $4d^2 + 12 = 0$
10. $5c^2 + 10 = 0$
11. $(t + 1)^2 + 9 = 0$
12. $(s - 3)^2 + 36 = 0$
13. $4(x - 5)^2 + 22 = 2$
14. $2(x + 3)^2 + 21 = 5$
15. $4(2x + 5)^2 = -16$
16. $3(2y - 1)^2 = -75$
17. $y^2 + 1.44 = 0$
18. $z^2 + 5.76 = 0$
19. $(x - 1.2)^2 = -0.36$
20. $(x + 2.7)^2 = -1.21$
21. $2(z + 2.5)^2 + 10.58 = 0$
22. $3(y - 1.4)^2 + 7.68 = 0$
23. $x^2 + \frac{9}{16} = 0$
24. $x^2 + \frac{25}{49} = 0$
25. $\left(b - \frac{1}{2}\right)^2 + \frac{1}{4} = 0$
26. $\left(c + \frac{2}{3}\right)^2 + \frac{9}{16} = 0$
27. $x^2 + 2x + 4 = 0$
28. $x^2 - 6x + 14 = 0$

29. $b^2 - 10b + 27 = 0$ **30.** $x^2 + 14x + 51 = 0$ **31.** $4y^2 + 4y + 5 = 0$ **32.** $9x^2 + 24x + 17 = 0$

33. $9p^2 - 12p + 8 = 0$ **34.** $16z^2 - 8z + 7 = 0$ **35.** $x^2 - 2.4x + 3.44 = 0$ **36.** $m^2 + 4.2m + 7.41 = 0$

37. $2y^2 - 2y + 1.22 = 0$ **38.** $3z^2 + 3.6z + 1.35 = 0$ **39.** $x^2 - \dfrac{2}{3}x + \dfrac{13}{36} = 0$ **40.** $x^2 + \dfrac{1}{2}x + \dfrac{25}{144} = 0$

41. $4z^2 + \dfrac{4}{3}z + \dfrac{2}{9} = 0$ **42.** $9x^2 + 3x + \dfrac{13}{16} = 0$ **43.** $\dfrac{x}{x-2} = \dfrac{5}{x+3}$ **44.** $\dfrac{a}{a-9} = \dfrac{4}{a+7}$

45. $\dfrac{y+7}{y-3} = \dfrac{6}{y+4}$ **46.** $\dfrac{b+5}{b-6} = \dfrac{8}{b+1}$ **47.** $\dfrac{z-5}{z(z+3)} = \dfrac{4}{5}$ **48.** $\dfrac{c-9}{c(c+3)} = \dfrac{2}{3}$

49. In designing an electronic feedback system, the function $G(s) = \frac{3(s+2)}{s(s+1)}$ is used. Suppose we let $G(s) = -3$. Solve the resulting equation for s.

50. Using the function from exercise 49, solve the resulting equation if $G(s) = -\frac{3}{2}$.

51. In analyzing the laminar flow of fluids, energy loss is calculated using the constant, where $K = 1.00 - 2.67r + r^2$, where r is the ratio of cross-sectional areas. Let $K = -1.75$ and solve the resulting equation for r.

52. Using the relation in exercise 51, let $K = -2.50$ and solve the resulting equation for r.

Experiencing Algebra the Calculator Way

In this section, we saw that it is easy to check imaginary solutions to quadratic equations using your calculator. You can minimize keystrokes by using the 2nd   ENTRY feature of the calculator to repeat an instruction, which you can then edit. As an example, if you solve the equation $x^2 + 6x + 13 = 0$, the solutions are $x = -3 \pm 2i$. To check these solutions, enter the following.

The calculator returns a 0, indicating that the imaginary number is a solution. Next, press 2nd

 ENTRY to repeat the instruction, change the addition sign of the solution to a subtraction sign, and

press ENTER again. The calculator returns a 0 again, indicating that the second imaginary number

is also a solution.
Use this method to check your solutions to the following equations.

1. $x^2 - 10x + 34 = 0$ **2.** $x^2 + 14x + 65 = 0$ **3.** $4x^2 + 20x + 26 = 0$ **4.** $16x^2 - 8x + 10 = 0$

Experiencing Algebra the Group Way

In your group, discuss how you would solve the equation $x^3 + 1 = 0$ if the solutions were in the real-number system. How many solutions are there in the real-number system? Then factor the left side of the equation, and discuss how you would solve the equation in the imaginary-number system. You should see that there are three distinct solutions in the imaginary-number system. What are they? Discuss how you would check the solutions. Now use what you have discovered to solve the following equations in the imaginary-number system.

1. $x^3 + 8 = 0$ **2.** $2z^3 + 250 = 0$ **3.** $a^3 + 0.125 = 0$ **4.** $y^3 + \dfrac{1}{8} = 0$

Experiencing Algebra the Write Way

Fractal geometry is an area of mathematics that uses complex numbers to draw extraordinary pictures called fractals. While you may not have the math skills to fully understand the principles that underlie the process, you may still enjoy the amazing pictures obtained. In the library, find a reference on fractals. You may want to search for some of the most popular drawings, such as the Mandelbrot set or the Sierpinski triangle.

Write a short description of what you have found. Include the title and author of the text you reference, and the library call number of the text. Some texts provide programs that can be entered into a graphing calculator to reproduce the designs. You may want to try to do so.

CHAPTER 14 | Summary

After completing this chapter, you should be able to define in your own words the following key terms, definitions, and rules.

Terms
imaginary unit *i*
complex-number system
complex conjugates

Definitions
Square root of a negative number
Standard form for a complex
  number

Rules
Product of complex conjugates
Principle of square roots for
  imaginary-number solutions

CHAPTER 14 | Review

Reflections
1. What is the difference between the real-number system and the complex-number system?
2. Explain the process to add or subtract two complex numbers.
3. Can you use the FOIL method to multiply two complex numbers? If so, explain how.
4. How can you form the conjugate of a complex number?
5. How is the conjugate of a complex number used to perform division of complex numbers?
6. What is the principle of square roots for imaginary numbers? How is it used to solve quadratic equations?
7. When using the quadratic formula to solve a quadratic equation, how does the discriminant tell you that the solutions will be imaginary numbers?

14.1
Write in terms of i.

1. $\sqrt{-64}$

2. $\sqrt{-\dfrac{25}{49}}$

3. $\sqrt{-6.25}$

4. $\sqrt{-50}$

5. $\sqrt{-\dfrac{81}{2}}$

6. $-5\sqrt{-32}$

Perform the indicated operations.

7. $\sqrt{-25} + \sqrt{-49}$

8. $\sqrt{-144} - \sqrt{-64}$

9. $2\sqrt{-36} + 6\sqrt{-81}$

10. $11\sqrt{-4} - 3\sqrt{-36}$

11. $\dfrac{\sqrt{-169}}{\sqrt{-225}}$

12. $\sqrt{-2}\,\sqrt{-6}\,\sqrt{-75}$

13. $\sqrt{-2}\,(\sqrt{-6} + \sqrt{75})$

14. $(\sqrt{-2} + \sqrt{-18})(\sqrt{-4} - \sqrt{-9})$

15. $(\sqrt{-7} + \sqrt{-11})(\sqrt{-7} - \sqrt{-11})$

Determine the real part and the imaginary part for each complex number. Then identify any real number or pure imaginary number.

16. $-\sqrt{3}i$

17. $\dfrac{\sqrt{11}}{3}$

18. $\sqrt{13} - 2i$

19. $4\sqrt{2} + 1$

20. $3 - 17i$

21. -43

In exercises 22–38, perform the indicated operations. Write your answer in standard form.

22. $(17 + 4i) + (12 - 6i)$

23. $-15i(3 - 6i)$

24. $(12 - 3i) - (1 + i)$

25. $(2 + 5i)(-3 + 4i)$

26. $(3 + 11i)(3 - 11i)$

27. $6 - (2 + 12i)$

28. $\dfrac{12 + 15i}{3}$

29. $\dfrac{14 - 21i}{-7i}$

30. $\dfrac{41 + i}{5 - 2i}$

31. $\left(\dfrac{3}{5} - 5i\right) + \left(\dfrac{2}{5} + 2i\right)$

32. $(13.7 + 0.29i) - (14.92 + 1.5i)$

33. $(5\sqrt{7} + 8\sqrt{13}i) + (3\sqrt{7} - 2\sqrt{13}i)$

34. $\sqrt{6}i(\sqrt{3} - \sqrt{6}i)$

35. $\left(\dfrac{2}{3} - \dfrac{3}{5}i\right)\left(\dfrac{1}{2} + \dfrac{1}{3}i\right)$

36. $5.8i(1.9 - 2i)$

37. $\dfrac{\sqrt{10} + 5\sqrt{3}i}{\sqrt{5}}$

38. $\dfrac{18 - 11\sqrt{6}i}{3\sqrt{2} + \sqrt{3}i}$

39. What is the magnitude of the total voltage, V, across a circuit if the current, I, is $5 + 4i$ amperes and the impedance, Z, is $9 - 2i$ ohms? Use the formula $V = IZ$. Round your answer to the nearest tenth of a volt.

40. Use the formula $Z = \dfrac{V}{I}$ to find the magnitude of the impedance, Z, when the voltage, V, is $33 + 19i$ volts and the current, I, is $5 + 2i$ amperes. Express your answer as a simplified radical.

14.2
Solve exercises 41–63.

41. $x^2 + 100 = 0$

42. $y^2 + 15 = 0$

43. $z^2 + 10 = 1$

44. $5t^2 + 125 = 0$

45. $3a^2 + 33 = 0$

46. $(r - 5)^2 + 36 = 0$

47. $7(x + 2)^2 + 23 = 2$

48. $3(4x + 1)^2 = -27$

49. $u^2 + 4.84 = 0$

50. $(v - 3.4)^2 + 3.24 = 0$

51. $c^2 + \dfrac{36}{121} = 0$

52. $\left(m + \dfrac{2}{5}\right)^2 + \dfrac{16}{25} = 0$

53. $x^2 - 10x + 29 = 0$

54. $4y^2 + 4y + 10 = 0$

55. $z^2 + 16z + 17 = 0$

56. $9x^2 - 12x + 40 = 0$

57. $x^2 - 2.4x + 2.65 = 0$

58. $4x^2 + 4x + 5.84 = 0$

59. $x^2 - \dfrac{3}{2}x + \dfrac{5}{8} = 0$

60. $4x^2 - 12x + \dfrac{85}{9} = 0$

61. $\dfrac{x}{x - 5} = \dfrac{10}{x + 1}$

62. $\dfrac{y + 4}{y - 8} = \dfrac{9}{y + 6}$

63. $\dfrac{b - 8}{b(b + 7)} = \dfrac{2}{3}$

64. An electronic feedback system has the process $G(s) = \dfrac{3(s+10)}{s(s+5)}$. Let $G(s) = -1$ and solve the equation for s.

CHAPTER 14	**Mixed Review**

Determine the real part and the imaginary part for each complex number. Then identify any real number or pure imaginary number.

1. $-\dfrac{\sqrt{23}}{5}$

2. $\sqrt{29} + 5i$

3. $16 + 22i$

4. $-3\sqrt{5} - 7$ **5.** $\sqrt{31}i$ **6.** $-\pi$

Write in terms of i.

7. $\sqrt{-169}$ **8.** $\sqrt{-\dfrac{64}{81}}$ **9.** $\sqrt{-\dfrac{25}{6}}$

10. $10\sqrt{-80}$ **11.** $\sqrt{-6.25}$ **12.** $-\sqrt{-108}$

Perform the indicated operations. Write your answer in standard form.

13. $(22.3 - 1.33i) + (8.55 - 2.9i)$ **14.** $\sqrt{-64} + \sqrt{-4}$ **15.** $\sqrt{-196} - \sqrt{-100}$

16. $\left(\dfrac{3}{4} + \dfrac{1}{2}i\right)\left(\dfrac{4}{9} - 2i\right)$ **17.** $-1.5i(2.9 - 4i)$ **18.** $7\sqrt{-25} + 3\sqrt{-64}$

19. $\sqrt{-2}\sqrt{-6}\sqrt{-48}$ **20.** $(\sqrt{-3} - \sqrt{-10})(\sqrt{-5} + \sqrt{-6})$

21. $(\sqrt{-13} + \sqrt{-17})(\sqrt{-13} - \sqrt{-17})$

22. $(21 - i) - (7 + i)$ **23.** $(9 - 3i)(-9 + 3i)$ **24.** $(-2 + 12i)(-2 - 12i)$

25. $3i - (5 + 7i)$ **26.** $\dfrac{24 - 16i}{-8}$ **27.** $\dfrac{18 - 27i}{9i}$

28. $\dfrac{32 - 9i}{2 - 3i}$ **29.** $\left(\dfrac{5}{6} - 7i\right) + \left(\dfrac{5}{6} + i\right)$ **30.** $\sqrt{10}i(\sqrt{5} - \sqrt{2}i)$

31. $\dfrac{\sqrt{30} + 6\sqrt{2}i}{\sqrt{6}}$ **32.** $\dfrac{12i + \sqrt{10}}{2\sqrt{5} + \sqrt{2}i}$ **33.** $\dfrac{\sqrt{-289}}{\sqrt{-841}}$

Solve exercises 34–45.

34. $\dfrac{d - 11}{d(d + 9)} = \dfrac{5}{8}$ **35.** $x^2 + 10.24 = 0$ **36.** $(m + 7)^2 + 25 = 0$

37. $4(y - 3)^2 + 29 = 5$ **38.** $x^2 - 16x + 67 = 0$ **39.** $9y^2 + 30y + 32 = 0$

40. $a^2 + 100 = 19$ **41.** $6b^2 + 78 = 0$ **42.** $4x^2 + 12x + 10.96 = 0$

43. $x^2 + \dfrac{5}{4}x + \dfrac{7}{16} = 0$ **44.** $\dfrac{y + 9}{y + 1} = \dfrac{5}{y - 7}$ **45.** $\left(y + \dfrac{3}{7}\right)^2 + \dfrac{25}{49} = 0$

46. Use the formula $Z = \frac{V}{I}$ to find the magnitude of the current, I, when the voltage, V, is $30 + 52i$ volts and the impedance, Z, is $9 + 5i$ ohms. Round your answer to the nearest tenth of an ampere.

47. An electronic feedback system has the process $G(s) = \frac{3(s+10)}{s(s+5)}$. Let $G(s) = -2$ and solve the resulting equation for s.

CHAPTER 14 | **Test**

Test-Taking Tips

Doing well on tests requires perseverance in the classroom. Attend all classes and take full class notes. Research shows that successful students never cut class and usually record at least 64% of what is discussed in class. Failing students record half as much and often miss class. Missing one class puts you behind in the course by at least two lessons. Can you see why? It is important to stay current. Do not allow yourself to fall behind in homework or study, or the entire course will become an effort and a struggle to catch up. Participate in the class by asking questions. Instructors welcome student questions. If necessary, see the instructor outside of class if you do not understand a lesson and can't get your questions answered in class. Do not delay in getting help with difficult concepts.

Perform the indicated operations. Write your answer in standard form.

1. $\sqrt{-64} + \sqrt{-9}$ **2.** $3\sqrt{-100} - 2\sqrt{-49}$ **3.** $\sqrt{-2}\sqrt{-7}\sqrt{-56}$

4. $\sqrt{-2}\left(\sqrt{-7} - \sqrt{56}\right)$

5. $\dfrac{\sqrt{-225}}{\sqrt{-289}}$

6. $\left(\sqrt{-6} - \sqrt{-13}\right)\left(\sqrt{-6} + \sqrt{-13}\right)$

7. $(8 + 2i)(-5 + i)$

8. $\dfrac{29 + 29i}{5 - 2i}$

9. $(22.47 - 13.6i) - (12.2 - 7.32i)$

10. $\sqrt{15i}\left(\sqrt{3} + \sqrt{5i}\right)$

11. $\dfrac{44 + 16i}{2i}$

12. $\left(\dfrac{1}{2} + \dfrac{3}{7}i\right)\left(\dfrac{14}{15} - \dfrac{7}{9}i\right)$

Solve exercises 13–19.

13. $x^2 + 196 = 0$

14. $(t + 2)^2 + 15 = 0$

15. $d^2 + \dfrac{4}{49} = 0$

16. $2z^2 + 5 = 2.12$

17. $x^2 - 6x + 17 = 0$

18. $9x^2 - 6x + 7 = 0$

19. $\dfrac{y - 2}{y(y + 1)} = \dfrac{4}{7}$

20. What is the magnitude of the total voltage, V, across a circuit if the current, I, is $8 + 3i$ amperes and the impedance, Z, is $11 - 3i$ ohms? Use the formula $V = IZ$ and round your answer to the nearest tenth of a volt.

21. Explain the difference between the real-number system and the complex-number system.

15

Exponential and Logarithmic Functions and Equations

I n this chapter we introduce two new types of functions: the exponential function and the logarithmic function. We show how to use the properties of exponents to perform operations with these functions and how to solve equations involving them. Exponential and logarithmic functions have a special relationship: each is the inverse function of the other. We begin this chapter by discussing what inverse functions are, when they exist, and how we can find them.

Exponential and logarithmic functions are used to model many important real-world situations in business and science. Exponential models of growth and decay describe situations as varied as compound interest, population growth, and radioactive decay. Logarithms are used to describe the magnitudes of earthquakes, sound levels, and the acidity of a chemical solution. We discuss some of these applications throughout this chapter.

15.1 Inverse Functions

15.2 Exponential Functions

15.3 Logarithmic Functions

15.4 Properties of Logarithms

15.5 Solving Exponential and Logarithmic Equations

15.1   Inverse Functions

Objectives   1 Determine the inverse of a relation.

2 Determine whether a function is a one-to-one function.

3 Graph inverse functions.

4 Determine the inverse of a function.

5 Model real-world situations using inverse functions.

Application

Currency exchange rates vary daily. According to a recent report, a function to determine the number of British pounds given x United States dollars was $f(x) = 0.59172x$. Determine the inverse function $f^{-1}(x)$ and explain its meaning.

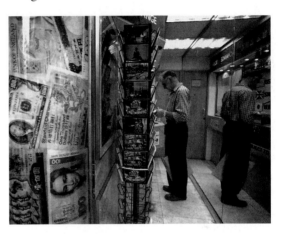

After completing this section, we will discuss this application further. See page 1130.

1 Determining the Inverse of a Relation

In Chapter 4 we defined a relation as a set of ordered pairs. For example, the set of ordered pairs a biologist obtains when Celsius temperatures are converted to Fahrenheit temperatures,

$$T = \{(20, 68), (21, 69.8), (22, 71.6), (23, 73.4)\},$$

is a relation.

If we reverse the order in each ordered pair, another useful relation results. For example, the set of ordered pairs a biologist obtains when Fahrenheit temperatures are converted to Celsius temperatures,

$$\{(68, 20), (69.8, 21), (71.6, 22), (73.4, 23)\},$$

is also a relation.

This second relation is called the **inverse** of the relation T and is denoted T^{-1}.

$$T = \{(20, 68), (21, 69.8), (22, 71.6), (23, 73.4)\}$$
$$T^{-1} = \{(68, 20), (69.8, 21), (71.6, 22), (73.4, 23)\}$$

Helping Hand Do *not* confuse the inverse notation T^{-1} with exponential notation. The -1 is *not* an exponent.

> *Inverse of a Relation Written as Ordered Pairs*
> To determine the inverse of a relation written as a set of ordered pairs, interchange the coordinates for the independent and dependent variables in the original relation.

EXAMPLE 1 Determine the inverses of the following relations.

 a. $f = \{(3, 6), (5, 10), (4, 8), (0, 0)\}$

 b. $A = \{(1, 2), (-2, 3), (4, -5), (0, 2)\}$

Solution

 a. $f = \{(3, 6), (5, 10), (4, 8), (0, 0)\}$

  $f^{-1} = \{(6, 3), (10, 5), (8, 4), (0, 0)\}$

 b. $A = \{(1, 2), (-2, 3), (4, -5), (0, 2)\}$

  $A^{-1} = \{(2, 1), (3, -2), (-5, 4), (2, 0)\}$ ∎

Recall that a relation can also be written as an equation in two variables. To determine the inverse of a relation expressed in this form, we follow the same procedure as with ordered pairs: interchange the independent and dependent variables. We can get the standard form of the inverse relation by solving the new equation for the new dependent variable.

> *Inverse of a Relation Written as an Equation*
> To determine the inverse of a relation written as an equation, interchange the independent and dependent variables in the original equation and solve for the new dependent variable.

For example, given $x =$ Celsius temperature, $y =$ Fahrenheit temperature, and the relation $y = \frac{9}{5}x + 32$, determine the inverse relation.

 Interchange the variables. Let $x =$ Fahrenheit temperature and $y =$ Celsius temperature.

$$x = \frac{9}{5}y + 32$$

 Solve for y.

$$x - 32 = \frac{9}{5}y$$

$$\frac{5}{9}(x - 32) = y \quad \text{or} \quad y = \frac{5}{9}(x - 32)$$

EXAMPLE 2   Determine the inverse relations.

a. $y = 3x + 5$ **b.** $y = x^2 - 2$

Solution

a. $y = 3x + 5$

$$x = 3y + 5 \qquad\qquad \text{Interchange the variables.}$$

$$x - 5 = 3y \qquad\qquad \text{Solve for } y.$$

$$\frac{x - 5}{3} = y \quad \text{or} \quad y = \frac{1}{3}x - \frac{5}{3}$$

b. $y = x^2 - 2$

$$x = y^2 - 2 \qquad\qquad \text{Interchange the variables.}$$

$$x + 2 = y^2 \qquad\qquad \text{Solve for } y.$$

$$\pm\sqrt{x + 2} = y \quad \text{or} \quad y = \pm\sqrt{x + 2} \quad \blacksquare$$

 Experiencing Algebra the Checkup Way

In exercises 1–4, determine the inverse for each relation.

1. $g = \{(1, 0.5), (2, 1), (3, 1.5), (4, 2), (5, 2.5), (6, 3)\}$ **2.** $K = \left\{\left(\frac{1}{2}, 3\right), \left(\frac{2}{3}, 4\right), \left(\frac{3}{4}, 5\right), \left(\frac{4}{5}, 4\right), \left(\frac{5}{6}, 3\right)\right\}$

3. $y = -4x + 1$ **4.** $y = 3x^2 + 6$

5. The inverse of the function $f(x)$ is denoted by $f^{-1}(x)$. What does the notation $\left[f(x)\right]^{-1}$ indicate? Describe the differences in the two notations.

**2 Determining
One-to-One Functions**

In Chapter 4 we also defined a function. A function is a relation in which every element in the domain corresponds to only one element in the range. In Example 1, we determined the inverse relation of the two functions f and A.

$$f = \{(3, 6), (5, 10), (4, 8), (0, 0)\}$$

$$A = \{(1, 2), (-2, 3), (4, -5), (0, 2)\}$$

The inverse of the function f is a function.

$$f^{-1} = \{(6, 3), (10, 5), (8, 4), (0, 0)\}$$

However, the inverse of the function A is not a function because an element in the domain of the inverse relation, 2, is paired with two different elements in the range, 1 and 0.

$$A^{-1} = \{(2, 1), (3, -2), (-5, 4), (2, 0)\}$$

Complete the following set of exercises to see when the inverse of a function is also a function.

D I S C O V E R Y   1

Inverses of Functions Written as Ordered Pairs

Use the following functions to complete the following exercises.

a. $F = \{(0, 2), (1, 5), (2, 8), (3, 11)\}$

b. $G = \{(0, 2), (1, 3), (-1, 3), (-2, 6)\}$

1. List the domain and range for each function and draw a line to connect each element in the domain with its corresponding element in the range.
   a. $F = \{(0, 2), (1, 5), (2, 8), (3, 11)\}$
      Domain: Range:
   b. $G = \{(0, 2), (1, 3), (-1, 3), (-2, 6)\}$
      Domain: Range:

2. Determine the inverse of each function.
   a. $F = \{(0, 2), (1, 5), (2, 8), (3, 11)\}$
   b. $G = \{(0, 2), (1, 3), (-1, 3), (-2, 6)\}$

3. List the domain and range for each inverse and draw a line to connect each element in the domain with its corresponding element in the range.
   a. $F = \{(0, 2), (1, 5), (2, 8), (3, 11)\}$
      Domain: Range:
   b. $G = \{(0, 2), (1, 3), (-1, 3), (-2, 6)\}$
      Domain: Range:

4. Is the inverse a function?
   a. $F = \{(0, 2), (1, 5), (2, 8), (3, 11)\}$
   b. $G = \{(0, 2), (1, 3), (-1, 3), (-2, 6)\}$

Write a rule to determine from viewing a set of ordered pairs when the inverse of a function is also a function.

The inverse of the first function, F, is also a function. The inverse of the second function, G, is not a function. The range of the function becomes the domain of its inverse. In order for each element in the domain of the inverse to be paired with only one element in the range, each element in the range of the function must be paired with only one element in the domain. The function is then called a **one-to-one function**. The inverse of a one-to-one function is a function.

One-to-One Function
A function is a one-to-one function if no two different ordered pairs have the same second coordinate.

Helping Hand A one-to-one function is a set of ordered pairs in which no two different ordered pairs have the same first coordinate or the same second coordinate.

EXAMPLE 3   Determine whether the inverses of the following functions are functions.

a. $h = \{(2.75, 3.25), (0.5, 3.25), (-2.25, 2.75)\}$

b. $R = \{(0, 1.5), (1, 2.5), (3, 4.5)\}$

Solution

a. $h = \{(2.75, 3.25), (0.5, 3.25), (-2.25, 2.75)\}$
   The function h is not one-to-one because the second coordinate 3.25 is repeated in two ordered pairs. The inverse of h is not a function.

b. $R = \{(0, 1.5), (1, 2.5), (3, 4.5)\}$
   The function R is one-to-one because no two ordered pairs have the same first coordinate or the same second coordinate. The inverse of R is a function. ■

In Example 2, we determined the inverse of two functions written in equation form:

a. $y = 3x + 5$ **b.** $y = x^2 - 2$

The inverse of the first function, $y = \frac{1}{3}x - \frac{5}{3}$, is a function. However, the inverse of the second function, $y = \pm\sqrt{x + 2}$, is not a function. If we graph each of the inverses, we can check to see that one is a function and that one is not a function by using the vertical-line test.

a.

b.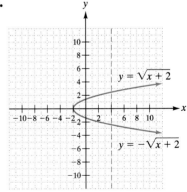

Note: All sample vertical lines drawn for part (a) intersect the graph once. A sample vertical line is drawn for part (b) that intersects the graph more than once.

However, we can also determine whether the inverse of a function is a function from the graph of the function itself. Complete the following set of exercises to see when a function is one-to-one, or has an inverse that is a function.

DISCOVERY 2

Graphs of One-to-One Functions

The following are graphs of one-to-one functions. Draw a horizontal line through more than one point on the graph, if possible.

1.

2.

3.

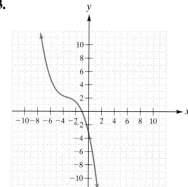

Write a rule for determining a one-to-one function from the graph of a function by drawing a horizontal line through points on the graph.

Check your rule on the following graph of a function, which is not one-to-one.

4.

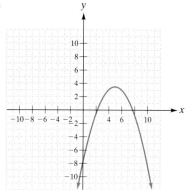

All possible horizontal lines cross the graphs of the one-to-one functions only once. It is possible to draw a horizontal line that crosses the function that is not one-to-one more than once.

Horizontal-Line Test
If a horizontal line can be drawn such that it intersects the graph of a function more than once, the graph does not represent a one-to-one function. If it is not possible to draw such a horizontal line, then the graph represents a one-to-one function.

We know that this rule is true because if we graph two distinct ordered pairs with the same *y*-coordinate, they will lie on the same horizontal line. However, a one-to-one function does not have two ordered pairs with the same *y*-coordinate.

Helping Hand According to the vertical-line test for functions, it is not possible to draw a vertical line that intersects the graph of a function more than once. According to the horizontal-line test for one-to-one functions, it is not possible to draw a horizontal line that intersects the graph of a one-to-one function more than once. Therefore, it is not possible to draw a vertical or horizontal line that intersects the graph of a one-to-one function more than once.

EXAMPLE 4 Determine whether the following graphs represent one-to-one functions.

a.

b.

c.
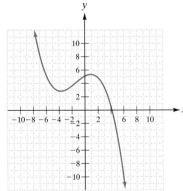

Solution

a. The graph does not represent a function because a vertical line intersects the graph more than once.
b. The graph represents a one-to-one function because all possible vertical and horizontal lines cross the graph only once.

    c. The graph is a function because it passes the vertical-line test, but a horizontal line can be drawn that intersects the graph more than once. Therefore, it is not a one-to-one function. ∎

 Experiencing Algebra the Checkup Way

Determine whether the inverse of each function is a function.

1. $B = \{(0, -3), (2, 1), (4, 5), (6, 9), (8, 13)\}$

2. $G = \{(-2, 5), (-1, 2), (0, 1), (1, 2), (2, 5)\}$

Determine whether the graphs in exercises 3–5 represent one-to-one functions.

3.

4.

5.

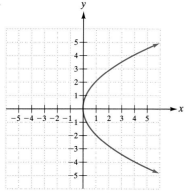

6. For what purpose is the vertical-line test used?

7. For what purpose is the horizontal-line test used?

8. Every one-to-one function is a relation, but not every relation is a one-to-one function. Explain why this is so.

---

3 Graphing Inverse Functions

We interchange the coordinates of the ordered pairs of a one-to-one function to obtain its inverse function. Therefore, the domain and range of a one-to-one function and its inverse function also interchange. If we graph a one-to-one function and its inverse function on the same coordinate plane, as well as graph the line $y = x$, we obtain an interesting picture. For example,

Graph the function $f = \{(2,3), (0,4), (-2,1)\}$.

Graph the inverse function $f^{-1} = \{(3,2), (4,0), (1,-2)\}$.

Graph the equation $y = x$.

When we graph the function f and its inverse function f^{-1} on the same coordinate plane, we see that the points graphed are the same distance, on either side, from the line for the equation $y = x$. This line is called the **line of symmetry**. This visualization can help us determine whether we have graphed a function and its inverse function correctly.

Note: This symmetry is easier to see if you fold your graph paper along the line of symmetry. The graph of the function and the graph of its inverse should match.

EXAMPLE 5 Graph on your calculator the following function and its inverse, as well as the line of symmetry $y = x$.

$$f(x) = x + 4$$
$$f^{-1}(x) = x - 4$$

Solution

Note that the graphs for $y = x + 4$ and $y = x - 4$ appear to be symmetric about the line $y = x$. ∎

 Helping Hand You need to be careful because looks are sometimes deceiving. However, you can trace the two lines to determine that the coordinates of the ordered pairs also interchange. For example, the ordered pair $(6, 10)$ lies on the graph of $y = x + 4$ and the ordered pair $(10, 6)$ lies on the graph of the inverse $y = x - 4$.

✓ Experiencing Algebra the Checkup Way

1. On your calculator, graph the following function, its inverse, and the line of symmetry $y = x$.

$$f(x) = 2x - 4 \quad \text{and} \quad f^{-1}(x) = \frac{1}{2}x + 2$$

2. What does the line of symmetry $y = x$ mean to you?

4 Determining an Inverse Function If a one-to-one function $f(x)$ is defined by an equation, we can determine the inverse function $f^{-1}(x)$ in the same way we obtained an inverse for a relation. To determine the inverse of a function $f(x)$:

- Replace $f(x)$ with y.
- Interchange x and y.
- Solve the resulting equation for y.
- Replace y with $f^{-1}(x)$.

EXAMPLE 6 Determine the inverse function $f^{-1}(x)$. Graph the function, its inverse, and the line of symmetry $y = x$ on your calculator to check.

a. $f(x) = \sqrt[3]{2x}$

b. $f(x) = \dfrac{2}{3x} + 4$

Solution

a. $f(x) = \sqrt[3]{2x}$

$y = \sqrt[3]{2x}$ Replace $f(x)$ with y.

$x = \sqrt[3]{2y}$ Interchange x and y.

$x^3 = 2y$ Solve for y.

$y = \dfrac{1}{2}x^3$

$f^{-1}(x) = \dfrac{1}{2}x^3$ Replace y with $f^{-1}(x)$.

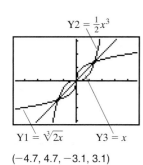

Y2 $= \frac{1}{2}x^3$

Y1 $= \sqrt[3]{2x}$ Y3 $= x$

$(-4.7, 4.7, -3.1, 3.1)$

Check by graphing on your calculator.

b. $f(x) = \dfrac{2}{3x} + 4$

$y = \dfrac{2}{3x} + 4$ Replace $f(x)$ with y.

$x = \dfrac{2}{3y} + 4$ Interchange x and y.

$x - 4 = \dfrac{2}{3y}$ Subtract 4 from both sides.

$3y(x - 4) = 3y\left(\dfrac{2}{3y}\right)$ Multiply both sides by $3y$.

$3xy - 12y = 2$ Simplify.

$y(3x - 12) = 2$ Factor out a common factor of y.

$\dfrac{y(3x - 12)}{3x - 12} = \dfrac{2}{3x - 12}$ Divide both sides by $(3x - 12)$.

$y = \dfrac{2}{3x - 12}$ Simplify.

The calculator check is very difficult to visualize because of the asymptotes in the graphs. Check to see whether the coordinates are reversed in the ordered pairs of the two functions, as shown in Figures 15.1a, 15.1b, and 15.1c. ■

 Experiencing Algebra the Checkup Way

In exercises 1–2, determine the inverse of each function. Then graph the function and its inverse and the line of symmetry.

1. $f(x) = -2x + 6$ **2.** $g(x) = x^3$

3. When is the inverse of a function not a function?

4. How can you test to find whether a given function has an inverse that is a function?

5 Modeling the Real World   We have seen many times in this course that important relations in business, science, and social studies are functions. We can write inverse functions for many of them, just as we've learned in this section. It is often helpful to interpret the meaning of these inverse functions in terms of the original situation.

TECHNOLOGY

$Y1 = \dfrac{2}{3x} + 4$ $Y3 = x$

$Y2 = \dfrac{2}{3x - 12}$

$(-9.4, 9.4, -6.2, 6.2)$

Figure 15.1a

$Y1 = \dfrac{2}{3x} + 4$ $Y3 = x$

$Y2 = \dfrac{2}{3x - 12}$

$(-9.4, 9.4, -6.2, 6.2)$

Figure 15.1b

$Y1 = \dfrac{2}{3x} + 4$ $Y3 = x$

$Y2 = \dfrac{2}{3x - 12}$

$(-9.4, 9.4, -6.2, 6.2)$

Figure 15.1c

For Figure 15.1a
Change the window setting to $(-9.4, 9.4, -6.2, 6.2)$.
Enter Y1, Y2, and Y3.

For Figure 15.1b
Trace the inverse function (Y2) to an integer-valued x-coordinate such as 5.

  [TRACE] [▼]

Move the cursor to the point $(5, 0.66666667)$.

For Figure 15.1c
Since the coordinates in the ordered pair $(5, 0.66666667)$ were interchanged from the function (Y1), calculate the x-value of 0.66666667 $\left(\text{or } \frac{2}{3}\right)$ for the function to obtain the ordered pair $(0.6666667, 5)$.

  [2nd] [CALC] [1] [2] [÷] [3] [ENTER]

This change in your point of view can sometimes provide new insights into your mathematical model.

EXAMPLE 7   Marvin is paid a salary of \$300 per week plus a commission of 6% of his total sales.

  a. Write a function $S(x)$ to represent Marvin's weekly income.
  b. Determine the inverse function $S^{-1}(x)$.
  c. Interpret the meaning of the inverse function $S^{-1}(x)$.

Solution

  a. Marvin's income is \$300 plus 6% of his weekly sales.
    Let $x =$ the amount of Marvin's weekly sales
      $S(x) = 300 + 0.06x$

  b. $S(x) = 300 + 0.06x$

        $y = 300 + 0.06x$ Let $y = S(x)$.

        $x = 300 + 0.06y$ Interchange x and y.

      $x - 300 = 0.06y$ Solve for y.

$$\frac{x - 300}{0.06} = y \qquad \text{Divide both sides by 0.06.}$$

$$\frac{50}{3}x - 5000 = y$$

$$S^{-1}(x) = \frac{50}{3}x - 5000 \qquad \text{Replace } y \text{ with } S^{-1}(x).$$

c. The inverse function $S^{-1}(x)$ represents the amount of Marvin's weekly sales in terms of his total pay for the week. ∎

Application Currency exchange rates vary daily. According to a recent report, a function to determine the number of British pounds given x United States dollars was $f(x) = 0.59172x$. Determine the inverse function $f^{-1}(x)$ and explain its meaning.

Discussion

$$f(x) = 0.59172x$$

$$y = 0.59172x \qquad \text{Substitute } y \text{ for } f(x).$$

$$x = 0.59172y \qquad \text{Interchange } x \text{ and } y.$$

$$\frac{x}{0.59172} = \frac{0.59172y}{0.59172} \qquad \text{Solve for } y.$$

$$\frac{1}{0.59172}x = \frac{0.59172y}{0.59172}$$

$$1.69x \approx y$$

$$y \approx 1.69x$$

$$f^{-1}(x) \approx 1.69x \qquad \text{Substitute } f^{-1}(x) \text{ for } y.$$

The inverse function is used to determine the number of United States dollars given x British pounds. ∎

 Experiencing Algebra the Checkup Way

Dimitri invests $1200 in a fund that pays 5% simple interest per year.
a. Write a function $I(x)$ to represent the interest earned after x years.
b. Determine the inverse function $I^{-1}(x)$.
c. Interpret the meaning of the inverse function.

PROBLEM SET 15.1

 Experiencing Algebra the Exercise Way

Determine the inverse for each relation.

1. $h = \{(-3, 5), (-2, 4), (-1, 3), (0, 2), (1, 1), (2, 0)\}$

2. $d = \{(5, 25), (4, 16), (3, 9), (2, 4), (1, 1), (0, 0)\}$

3. $A = \{(3, 6), (2, 7), (1, 8), (0, 8), (-1, 7), (-2, 6)\}$

4. $J = \{(-4, 1), (3, 2), (-2, 1), (1, 2), (0, 1), (-1, 2)\}$

5. $M = \left\{ \left(\frac{1}{5}, 1.3\right), \left(\frac{3}{5}, 2.3\right), (1, 3.3), \left(\frac{7}{5}, 4.3\right), \left(\frac{9}{5}, 5.3\right), \left(\frac{11}{5}, 6.3\right) \right\}$

6. $P = \{(14, 0.2), (24, 0.4), (34, 0.6), (44, 0.8), (54, 1.0)\}$

7. $y = 2x - 8$ **8.** $y = 3x + 6$ **9.** $y = -3x + 2$ **10.** $y = 5 - 2x$

11. $y = \dfrac{3}{4}x + 9$ **12.** $y = -\dfrac{2}{3}x + \dfrac{4}{3}$ **13.** $y = 0.125x - 2.5$ **14.** $y = 1.8 - 0.4x$

15. $y = x^2 - 2$ **16.** $y = x^3 + 1$

Determine whether the inverse of each function is a function.

17. $k = \{(5, 2), (10, 4), (15, 8), (20, 16), (25, 32)\}$ **18.** $j = \{(-8, 3), (-9, 4), (-10, 5), (-11, 4), (-12, 3)\}$

19. $Q = \{(-2, 0), (-4, 2), (-6, 4), (-8, 2), (-10, 0)\}$ **20.** $P = \{(1, 16), (2, 15), (3, 14), (4, 13), (5, 12)\}$

Determine whether each graph represents a one-to-one function.

21.

22.

23.

24.

25.

26.
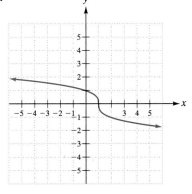

Determine the inverse of each function. Then use your calculator to graph the function, its inverse, and the line of symmetry $y = x$.

27. $g(x) = 3x - 6$

28. $f(x) = -4x + 2$

29. $y = \dfrac{2}{3}x - 4$

30. $y = -\dfrac{2}{5}x + 4$

31. $h(x) = x^2 - 1$

32. $r(x) = 2 - x^2$

33. $y = \dfrac{1}{3}x^3 - 4$

34. $y = \dfrac{1}{4}x^3 + 2$

Write a function to represent each situation. Then determine the inverse of the function. Interpret what the inverse of the function represents.

35. Julia is paid $1500 per month plus a commission of 2% of the value of all stock transactions she handles. What is Julia's monthly income?

36. Harvey earns $125 per week plus an average of 15% of his sales in tips waiting tables. What are his weekly earnings?

37. Antonio drives at an average speed of 55 miles per hour. What distance does he travel in a given amount of time?

38. Grace operates a machine that cuts 30 pairs of jeans per hour. How many pairs of jeans can she cut in a given amount of time?

39. Priscilla borrowed $2000 from her parents. They agreed that until she repays the loan, they will charge her 0.5% simple interest per month. What is the total amount Priscilla will repay?

40. Kimberly purchased a bond for $1500. The bond pays 0.4% simple interest per month. How much will Kimberly earn for the bond?

 Experiencing Algebra the Calculator Way

The calculator can draw the inverse of a function without your having to derive the inverse algebraically. As an example, graph the function $y = \frac{1}{2}x^3 + 3$. Do so by storing the function in Y1 and graph using the standard window setting. Now draw the inverse by entering the following:

| 2nd | DRAW | ▼ | ▼ | ▼ | ▼ | ▼ | ▼ | ▼ | ENTER | VARS | ▶ | 1 | 1 | ENTER |

The calculator will draw the inverse of the function on the same graph as the function. Once you have algebraically determined the inverse, you can check it by first graphing the function (stored in Y1), then graphing your algebraically derived inverse (stored in Y2), and finally instructing the calculator to draw the inverse of the original function. If the graph of your inverse and the calculator's inverse coincide, this verifies that you have correctly determined the inverse. (Note: You will not be able to trace to verify that the two graphs of inverse functions coincide, but you can visually check.) For the following exercises, first find the inverse algebraically, graph the function and its inverse, and then check using this feature of your calculator.

1. $y = 0.3x^2 - 4$

2. $f(x) = 0.1x^3 + 2x$

3. $g(x) = 5\sqrt{x} - 1.5$

4. $y = \dfrac{1}{x} + 2$

 Experiencing Algebra the Group Way

To help you understand inverse functions, you should draw the graphs of some functions without using your calculator. Each member of the group should set up a coordinate system on a sheet of graph paper. Label the x-axis and the y-axis and mark the scale on each. Use an integer scale. Then graph the line of symmetry on the graph using a black marker. Now have each member of the group select one of the following functions. Graph the function using a blue marker. (You may need to use a table of values to draw the graph.) Then algebraically find the inverse of the function. Graph the inverse using a green marker. Share your graph with the other members of the group. Make sure that all members of the group have correctly drawn their graphs.

1. $y = \dfrac{1}{2}x + 5$ **2.** $y = x^2 - 5$ **3.** $y = x^3 + 2x^2 - x - 2$

4. $y = x^5 - 5x^3 + 4x$ **5.** $y = 5 - x$ **6.** $y = \dfrac{2}{x}$

Experiencing Algebra the Write Way

In this section, you were cautioned not to confuse the notation $f^{-1}(x)$ with the notation $[f(x)]^{-1}$. Discuss what each notation means, using an example for each. Then use a dictionary to find definitions for the words *inverse* and *reciprocal*, and relate these definitions to what you have studied.

15.2 Exponential Functions

Objectives

1 Identify exponential functions.
2 Evaluate exponential functions.
3 Graph exponential functions.
4 Graph the natural exponential function.
5 Model real-world situations using exponential functions.

Application

The population of the United States (in thousands) may be approximated by the exponential function $f(x) = (227{,}429.74)1.01^x$, where x is the number of years after 1980.

a. Graph this function.
b. According to the graph, what is the estimated population of the United States in the year 2002?

After completing this section, we will discuss this application further. See page 1142.

1 Identifying Exponential Functions

In previous chapters we studied polynomial functions, rational functions, and radical functions. Each of these functions has a term with a variable base and a rational-number exponent.

$$f(x) = x^2 \qquad g(x) = x^{-2} \qquad h(x) = x^{1/2}$$

Polynomial function   Rational function   Radical function

In this section we examine a function that has a term with a rational-number base and a variable exponent, the reverse of what we previously studied.

$$f(x) = 2^x \qquad g(x) = 2^{-x} \qquad h(x) = \left(\dfrac{1}{2}\right)^x$$

We call each of these functions an **exponential function**.

> *Exponential Function*
> An exponential function f can be written in the form
>
> $$f(x) = a^x,$$
>
> where $a > 0$ and $a \neq 1$, and x is any real number.

Note the restrictions on the base a. The base must be positive and not equal to 1. A base of 1 results in the constant function $f(x) = 1^x$ or $f(x) = 1$.

EXAMPLE 1 For each function, state whether it is an exponential function or not.

a. $y = 5^x$ **b.** $f(x) = x^{-5/3}$ **c.** $g(x) = 0^x$

Solution

a. $y = 5^x$ is an exponential function, because it has a rational-number base and a variable exponent.

b. $f(x) = x^{-5/3}$ is not an exponential function, because the base is a variable. In fact, this is a radical function.

c. $g(x) = 0^x$ is not an exponential function, because it has a base of 0. ∎

Experiencing Algebra the Checkup Way

For each function, state whether it is an exponential function or not.

1. $h(x) = x^{2/3}$ **2.** $k(x) = \left(\dfrac{2}{3}\right)^x$ **3.** $y = 1^x$

2 Evaluating Exponential Functions

To evaluate an exponential function, we substitute the value for the independent variable and evaluate the resulting numeric expression. The resulting numeric expression will be an exponential expression containing a real-number exponent. We already know how to evaluate an exponential expression with a rational exponent. For example,

$$a^3 = a \cdot a \cdot a \qquad a^{-2} = \frac{1}{a^2} \qquad a^{3/4} = \left(\sqrt[4]{a}\right)^3$$

Therefore

$$2^3 = 2 \cdot 2 \cdot 2 = 8 \qquad 5^{-2} = \frac{1}{5^2} = \frac{1}{25} \qquad 16^{3/4} = \left(\sqrt[4]{16}\right)^3 = 2^3 = 8$$

We also may need to evaluate an exponential expression with an irrational exponent, such as $a^{\sqrt{3}}$. For example, evaluate $2^{\sqrt{3}}$.

Since $\sqrt{3} \approx 1.732$, we can approximate $2^{\sqrt{3}}$ by evaluating $2^{1.7}$, or $2^{1.73}$, or $2^{1.732}$, and so on, depending on the accuracy we require.

However, since we are using a calculator to perform these operations, we can also enter the expression with an irrational exponent and obtain an approximation with the accuracy of our calculator display.

```
2^1.7
        3.249009585
2^1.73
        3.317278183
2^1.732
        3.321880096
```

```
2^√(3)
        3.321997085
```

EXAMPLE 2 Evaluate the function $g(x) = 8^x$ at the given values.

a. $g(2)$ **b.** $g(-2)$ **c.** $g\left(\dfrac{2}{3}\right)$ **d.** $g(\sqrt{2})$

Solution

a. $g(2) = 8^2 = 64$

b. $g(-2) = 8^{-2} = \dfrac{1}{8^2} = \dfrac{1}{64}$

c. $g\left(\dfrac{2}{3}\right) = 8^{2/3} = \left(\sqrt[3]{8}\right)^2 = 2^2 = 4$

d. $g(\sqrt{2}) = 8^{\sqrt{2}} \approx 18.93050099$

A calculator is needed for this last evaluation.

Solution

```
Y₁(2)
              64
Y₁(-2)▶Frac
            1/64
```

```
Y₁(2/3)
               4
Y₁(√(2))
       18.93050099
```

Y1 = 8ˣ   Y1 = 8ˣ   ∎

Experiencing Algebra the Checkup Way

In exercises 1–4, evaluate the function $h(x) = 4^x$ at the given values.

1. $h(3)$

2. $h(-3)$

3. $h\left(\dfrac{3}{2}\right)$

4. $h(\sqrt{3})$

5. Are there any real-number values of x for which the function $h(x) = 4^x$ cannot be evaluated?
(*Hint:* Consider each of the subsets of numbers that make up the real-number system.)

3 Graphing Exponential Functions

We graph a function by first determining the domain of the function and then evaluating the function for values in its domain. We do not need to determine the domain of an exponential function because it is given to us in the definition; that is, x is a real number. Therefore, the domain is the set of all real numbers.

To graph an exponential function in the form $f(x) = a^x$, set up a table of values using real-number values for x, plot the points, and connect them with a smooth curve. For example, graph $f(x) = 8^x$.

x	$f(x)$
-3	$\dfrac{1}{512}$
-2	$\dfrac{1}{64}$
-1	$\dfrac{1}{8}$
0	1
1	8
2	64
3	512

Y1 = 8^x

(−4.7, 4.7, −3.1, 3.1)

On your calculator, you obtain the same graph.

Exponential functions can also be written in the form $f(x) = a^{-x}$, where $a > 0$ and $a \neq 1$. These functions are equivalent to other functions written in the form $f(x) = a^x$, where $a > 0$ and $a \neq 1$. Complete the following set of exercises on your calculator to determine this relationship.

DISCOVERY 3

Equivalent Exponential Functions

1. Graph each exponential function on a decimal window.

   a. $f(x) = 2^x$ **b.** $f(x) = 2^{-x}$

   c. $f(x) = \left(\dfrac{1}{2}\right)^x$ **d.** $f(x) = \left(\dfrac{1}{2}\right)^{-x}$

2. Match the graphs of the functions.

   Write a rule to determine equivalent functions.

The functions $f(x) = 2^{-x}$ and $f(x) = \left(\frac{1}{2}\right)^x$ are equivalent. The functions $f(x) = 2^x$ and $f(x) = \left(\frac{1}{2}\right)^{-x}$ are also equivalent.

Algebraically, using the properties of exponents, we can show that the exponential expression $a^{-x} = \left(\frac{1}{a}\right)^x$ and $a^x = \left(\frac{1}{a}\right)^{-x}$, where $a > 0$, $a \neq 1$, and x is a rational number.

$a^{-x} = \left(a^{-1}\right)^x$	Power-to-a-power rule
$a^{-x} = \left(\dfrac{1}{a}\right)^x$	Definition of a negative exponent
$a^x = \left(a^{-1}\right)^{-x}$	Power-to-a-power rule
$a^x = \left(\dfrac{1}{a}\right)^{-x}$	Definition of a negative exponent

Now let's graph the function $f(x) = \left(\frac{1}{8}\right)^x = 8^{-x}$. Determine the function's domain and range, the graph's y-intercept, and whether the function is increasing or decreasing.

x	$f(x)$
−3	512
−2	64
−1	8
0	1
1	$\dfrac{1}{8}$
2	$\dfrac{1}{64}$
3	$\dfrac{1}{512}$

$Y1 = 8^{-x}$

$(-4.7, 4.7, -3.1, 3.1)$

On your calculator, you obtain the same graph.

Exponential functions and their graphs have several common characteristics. Some of these characteristics are common to all exponential functions and others are common to certain sets of functions. Two of these characteristics are determined by the value of the base a. Complete the following set of exercises to discover the common characteristics of exponential functions and their graphs.

DISCOVERY 4

Effect of the Base a on an Exponential Graph

1. Sketch the graphs of the following exponential functions of the form $f(x) = a^x$, where $a > 0$, on the same coordinate plane. Use the decimal window.

   a. $f(x) = 2^x$ **b.** $f(x) = 5^x$ **c.** $f(x) = 10^x$

   d. $f(x) = \left(\dfrac{1}{2}\right)^x$ **e.** $f(x) = \left(\dfrac{1}{5}\right)^x$ **f.** $f(x) = \left(\dfrac{1}{10}\right)^x$

Use the graphs to answer the following questions.
2. The domain of all the functions is _____.
3. The range of all the functions is _____.
4. Are all the functions one-to-one?
5. Determine the y-intercept of each function.
6. Determine the x-intercept of each function.
7. In exercise 1a–1c, $a > 1$. The function is <u>increasing/decreasing</u>. The larger the value of a, the <u>steeper/shallower</u> the graph.
8. In exercises 1d–1f, $0 < a < 1$. The function is <u>increasing/decreasing</u>. The smaller the value of a (as a approaches 0), the <u>steeper/shallower</u> the graph.

The exponential function $y = a^x$, where $a > 1$, is always increasing. The larger the value of a, the steeper the function's graph. The exponential function $y = a^x$, where $0 < a < 1$, is always decreasing. The smaller the value of a, the steeper the function's graph. All exponential functions have a domain of all real numbers and a range of all positive real numbers, and their graphs have a y-intercept of $(0, 1)$. Exponential functions have no x-intercept.

Let's summarize the information we observe about the exponential function $f(x) = a^x$ and its corresponding graph.

Characteristics of an Exponential Function and Its Graph
Given the exponential function $f(x) = a^x$ and its graph, we know the following characteristics.

    Domain   All real numbers
    Range   All positive real numbers

    The function is one-to-one.

    y-intercept $(0, 1)$
    x-intercept   There is no x-intercept. The graph of the function approaches but does not reach the x-axis.

If $a > 1$ then the function is always increasing.
If $0 < a < 1$, then the function is always decreasing.

EXAMPLE 3 Graph each function.

a. $g(x) = 8^{2x}$ **b.** $h(x) = 8^{-2x}$

Calculator Solution

a.

$(-4.7, 4.7, -3.1, 3.1)$

b.

$(-4.7, 4.7, -3.1, 3.1)$ ∎

Experiencing Algebra the Checkup Way

In exercises 1–2, graph each exponential function.

1. $y = 2^{3x}$ **2.** $y = 2^{-3x}$

3. Why are negative numbers excluded from the range of the exponential function $y = a^x$, $a > 0$?

---

4 The Natural Exponential Function In all of the examples of exponential functions we have discussed, we have chosen to use a rational-number base. However, an irrational-number base could have been chosen. In fact, many applications of exponential functions involve a special irrational number as the base. This number occurs often in nature and in human activity, including the description of continuously compounded interest, the decay rates of radioactive elements, and even the growth rates of bacterial populations. Complete the following set of exercises to explore this special irrational number.

DISCOVERY 5

The irrational number e

1. Complete the following table of values for the function

$$y = \left(1 + \frac{1}{x}\right)^x.$$

x	y
1	
10	
100	
1000	
10,000	
100,000	
1,000,000	

Continued

2. As the *x*-value increases, the value of the function approaches the value _____. This value is an approximate value for the irrational number *e*.

The irrational number we discovered is denoted by the symbol *e* and is called the **natural base**. Rounded to five decimal places, the value of *e* is 2.71828. The calculator gives us a more accurate value to nine decimal places, as shown in Figure 15.2.

TECHNOLOGY

For Figure 5.2

| 2nd | e^x | 1 |) | ENTER |

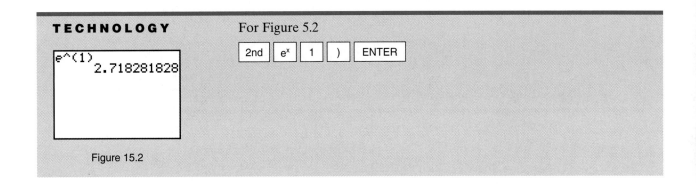

```
e^(1)
       2.718281828
```

Figure 15.2

The irrational number *e* is used to describe the **natural exponential function** $f(x) = e^x$. Remember, the base *e* is a positive number greater than 1. Therefore, the domain of the function is the set of all real numbers. The range is the set of all positive real numbers. The graph of the function has a *y*-intercept at (0, 1) and is always increasing. Calculate a table of values on your calculator and use the coordinates to graph the function. Check your graph on your calculator.

Let Y1 = e^x.

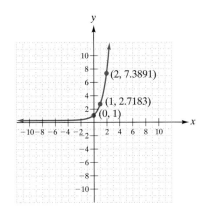

X	Y1
-3	.04979
-2	.13534
-1	.36788
0	1
1	2.7183
2	7.3891
3	20.086

X=-3

(2, 7.3891)
(1, 2.7183)
(0, 1)

Y1 = e^x

(−4.7, 4.7, −3.1, 3.1)

EXAMPLE 4 Graph the function $f(x) = 2e^x$.

Calculator Solution

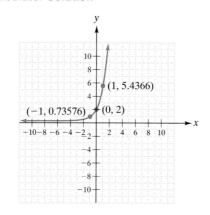

Y1 = 2e^x

(1, 5.4366)

(−1, 0.73576)   (0, 2)

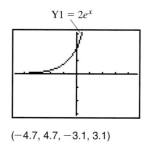

Y1 = 2e^x

(−4.7, 4.7, −3.1, 3.1)

Experiencing Algebra the Checkup Way

In exercises 1–2, graph each function and label the y-intercept.

1. $y = 0.5e^x$ **2.** $y = e^{-x}$

3. The number e is an irrational number. What does this mean?

---

5 Modeling the Real World

In the first discussion of this section, we explained that an exponential function $y = a^x$ is different from a polynomial function $y = x^a$. Now let's examine the graphs of these two functions to see exactly how different they are.

DISCOVERY 6

Comparing Exponential and Polynomial Functions

1. Determine a table of values for the following functions using integer values in the domain from −5 to 15.
   a. The exponential function $y = 2^x$
   b. The polynomial function $y = x^2$
2. Compare the tables of values. When $x = 2$ and $x = 4$, both function values are equal. For x-values greater than 4, which function is increasing at a faster rate?

The exponential function $y = 2^x$ increases at a faster rate than the polynomial function $y = x^2$. Therefore, we use an exponential function to describe situations that change quickly over a large range of domain values.

Exponential functions are used to model many types of relationships that occur in the real world. These relationships range from calculation of the balance in a savings account, or the amount owed on a loan, to predictions of population models.

In Chapter 3, we first discussed the calculation of interest. Remember the formula for simple interest, $I = Prt$, where P is the amount of principal, r is the rate of interest per time period, and t is the number of time periods. Compound interest is based on taking the interest accumulated in one time period and adding it to the principal before determining the interest of the next time period.

Let $t = 1$ year. At the end of 1 year, the amount is the principal plus the interest.

$$P + Prt = P + Pr(1)$$
$$= P + Pr$$
$$= P(1 + r).$$

If this amount is left at the same interest rate for one more year, the total amount is the last amount plus the interest.

$$P(1 + r) + [P(1 + r)]rt = P(1 + r) + [P(1 + r)]r(1)$$
$$= P(1 + r) + Pr(1 + r)$$
$$= P(1 + r)(1 + r)$$
$$= P(1 + r)^2$$

If we continue this pattern, at the end of 3 years the amount is $P(1 + r)^3$. Therefore, we can arrive at the formula given for the compounded amount A,

$$A = P(1 + r)^t,$$

where $P =$ principal, $r =$ interest per time period, and $t =$ the number of time periods.

EXAMPLE 5 Alex plans to invest $10,000 at an annual compounded rate of 8%. Determine the amount of his investment at the end of 2 years.

Solution

Use the compounded formula with $P = 10,000$, $r = 0.08$, and $t = 2$.

$$A = P(1 + r)^t$$
$$A = 10,000(1 + 0.08)^2$$
$$A = 10,000(1.08)^2$$
$$A = 11,664$$

Alex will have $11,664 in his account at the end of 2 years. ∎

Continuously compounded interest is the case of compound interest with very short periods, so that the addition of interest occurs on a continuous basis. A formula for the continuously compounded amount A is

$$A = Pe^{rt},$$

where $P =$ principal, $t =$ number of years, and $r =$ annual interest rate compounded continuously.

EXAMPLE 6 Alex plans to invest $10,000 at a rate of 8% compounded continuously. Determine the amount of his investment at the end of 2 years.

Solution

Use the continuously compounded formula with $P = 10,000$, $r = 0.08$, and $t = 2$.

$$A = Pe^{rt}$$

$$A = 10,000e^{(0.08)(2)}$$

$$A = 10,000e^{0.16}$$

$$A \approx 11735.11$$

```
10000→P:.08→R:2→
T:Pe^(RT)
        11735.10871
```

Alex will have approximately \$11,735.11 in his account at the end of 2 years. ■

Application

The population of the United States (in thousands) may be approximated by the exponential function $f(x) = (227,429.74)1.01^x$, where x is the number of years after 1980.

a. Graph this function.
b. According to the graph, what is the estimated population of the United States in the year 2002?

Discussion

a.   Y1 = (227429.74)1.01^x

(0, 47, 0, 620,000)

Y1 = (227429.74)1.01^x

```
X=22          Y=283085.4
```

(0, 47, 0, 620,000)

b. Let $x = 2002 - 1980 = 22$ and use the value function.

According to the model, the population of the United States will be approximately 283,085.4 thousand people, or 283,085,400, in the year 2002. ■

 Experiencing Algebra the Checkup Way

1. Cindy invests \$5,000 at an annual compounded interest rate of 6%. How much will she have after 4 years?

2. If Cindy had invested the \$5,000 at a continuously compounded rate of 6%, how much would she have after 4 years?

3. Using data reported in the *Statistical Abstract of the United States*, the total business expenditures in the United States for new plants and equipment can be estimated by the exponential function

$$y = (295.6)1.055^x,$$

where x is the number of years after 1980 and y is billions of dollars. Graph this function. Use the function to estimate the expenditures for the year 2000.

PROBLEM SET 15.2

Experiencing Algebra the Exercise Way

For each function, state whether it is an exponential function or not.

1. $y = 7^x$

2. $d(x) = x^{1.5}$

3. $f(x) = 0.3^x$

4. $y = 22.3^x$

5. $g(x) = x^{0.3}$

6. $y = x^4$

7. $y = 1.57^x$

8. $y = 12^x$

9. $y = x^{-3}$

10. $T(x) = \left(\dfrac{5}{8}\right)^x$

11. $R(x) = \left(\dfrac{2}{3}\right)^x$

12. $b(x) = 1.5^x$

Evaluate the function $g(x) = 16^x$ at the given values.

13. $g(3)$

14. $g(4)$

15. $g(-2)$

16. $g(-1)$

17. $g\left(\dfrac{1}{2}\right)$

18. $g\left(\dfrac{3}{4}\right)$

19. $g(\sqrt{2})$

20. $g(0)$

Evaluate the function $h(x) = 0.64^x$ at the given values.

21. $h(0.3)$

22. $h(1.5)$

23. $h\left(-\dfrac{1}{3}\right)$

24. $h\left(\dfrac{5}{6}\right)$

25. $h(-\sqrt{2})$

26. $h(\sqrt{5})$

Graph each exponential function.

27. $f(x) = 4^x$

28. $C(x) = 3^x$

29. $g(x) = 4^{-x}$

30. $D(x) = 3^{-2x}$

31. $h(x) = 4^{2x}$

32. $F(x) = 3^{2x-1}$

33. $j(x) = 4^{(1/2)x}$

34. $K(x) = 3^{x/4}$

35. $k(x) = 4^{x-1}$

36. $L(x) = 3^x + 1$

37. $m(x) = 4^x - 1$

38. $M(x) = 3^{x+1} - 1$

39. $y = e^{(1/2)x}$

40. $y = e^{0.2x}$

41. $y = \dfrac{1}{2}e^x$

42. $y = 0.2e^x$

43. $y = e^{(-1/2)x}$

44. $y = e^{-0.2x}$

45. $y = e^x + \dfrac{1}{2}$

46. $y = e^{0.2x} + 0.2$

47. $y = \dfrac{1}{2}e^{(1/2)x}$

48. $y = 0.2e^{0.2x}$

In exercises 49–52, write a function for the total value of the investment. Graph the function and answer the question.

49. Jerome received his annual bonus of $6,000, which he invested at an annually compounded interest rate of 5.5%. How much was the investment after 7 years?

50. Marissa received a $3,000 commission for landing a book contract with a major school. She invested the money at an annually compounded interest rate of 6.2%. What was the investment worth after 4 years?

51. Jolene inherited $8,000, which she invested at a continuously compounded interest rate of 4.8%. How much did she earn after 5 years?

52. Marty's regional sales netted her a commission of $4500. If she invests the money at a continuously compounded interest rate of 7.5%, how much will the investment be worth after 10 years?

53. Data reported in the *Statistical Abstract of the United States* suggest that total passenger miles for the U.S. scheduled airline industry can be estimated by the mathematical model

$$y = (281.49)1.047^x,$$

where x is the number of years after 1980 and y is the number of passenger miles in billions. Graph this function. What does the model predict as the number of passenger miles for the year 2005?

54. The national health expenditures can be estimated by the mathematical model

$$y = (78.16)1.115^x,$$

where x is the number of years after 1970 and y is the total expenditures in billions of dollars. Graph this function. What does the model predict the expenditures will be for the year 2000?

Experiencing Algebra the Calculator Way

The calculator allows you to easily explore more complicated mathematical models that involve exponential expressions. Graph the following functions and study the effects of the operations indicated.

1. a. $f(x) = e^x$ **b.** $g(x) = e^{-x}$

2. a. $h(x) = e^x + e^{-x}$ **b.** $j(x) = e^x - e^{-x}$

3. a. $k(x) = (e^x)(e^{-x})$ **b.** $m(x) = e^x \div e^{-x}$

4. a. $F(x) = e^{(1/2)x}$ **b.** $G(x) = e^{(-1/2)x}$

5. a. $H(x) = e^{(1/2)x} + e^{(-1/2)x}$ **b.** $J(x) = e^{(1/2)x} - e^{(-1/2)x}$

6. a. $K(x) = (e^{(1/2)x})(e^{(-1/2)x})$ **b.** $M(x) = (e^{(1/2)x}) \div (e^{(-1/2)x})$

Could you have predicted any of these results? Which rules of exponents apply to these exercises? See if you can use the rules of exponents to write a simplified form of some of these functions. Then check your results by graphing.

Experiencing Algebra the Group Way

In "Experiencing Algebra the Exercise Way," a mathematical model was presented to predict passenger miles for U.S. scheduled airlines. The model was given as $y = (281.49)1.047^x$, where x is the number of years after 1980 and y is the number of passenger miles in billions. The actual data used to develop this model are presented in the following table. Use your calculator to determine the predicted number of passenger miles for each of the years shown.

Year	Actual Passenger Miles (in billions)	Predicted Passenger Miles
1985	336.4	
1986	366.5	
1987	404.5	
1988	423.3	
1989	432.7	
1990	457.9	
1991	448.0	
1992	478.1	

In your group, discuss how well you think the predicted values compare with the actual values. Discuss how to measure the goodness of fit of the actual data with the predicted values. Would you feel comfortable using the model to predict passenger miles for other years? Explain.

Experiencing Algebra the Write Way

The definition of an exponential function $f(x) = a^x$ specifies that a must be positive and must not equal 1. Consider an exponential equation with a negative base, such as $y = (-2)^x$. Set up a table of values using integer values of x. What do you notice about the values of y? Does this equation behave like an exponential function? Can you understand why the base of an exponential expression cannot be negative? Explain.

Next, consider an exponential function with a base of 1—for example, $y = 1^x$. What does the table of values look like for this equation? Can you see why it is excluded from the discussion of exponential functions? Explain.

Finally, consider the functions $f(x) = -2^x$, $g(x) = (-2)^x$, and $h(x) = 2^x$. Are any of these functions the same? Which of the functions is an exponential function? Graph each function separately using a decimal window. Trace the graphs. What do the graphs show? Does this example further confirm the rule that the base of an exponential function must be positive? Explain.

15.3 Logarithmic Functions

Objectives
1 Identify logarithmic functions.
2 Evaluate logarithms.
3 Graph logarithmic functions.
4 Model real-world situations using logarithmic functions.

Application

The magnitude R, measured on the Richter scale, of an earthquake of intensity I is defined by the function $R = \log \frac{I}{I_0}$, where I_0 is the intensity of a very small vibration in the Earth used as a standard. The San Francisco earthquake of 1906 had a magnitude of 8.3 on the Richter scale. Eighty-three years later, in 1989, San Francisco had another earthquake measuring 7.1.

a. Determine the intensity of each earthquake.

b. The difference on the Richter scale of the 1906 and 1989 earthquakes is 1.2. Determine the ratio of the intensity of the 1906 earthquake to the 1989 earthquake.

After completing this section, we will discuss this application further. See page 1156.

---

1 Identifying Logarithmic Functions

In section 15.1, we introduced the concept of the inverse of a function. The horizontal-line test states that if it is not possible to draw a horizontal line that intersects the graph of a function more than once, then the graph represents a one-to-one function. A one-to-one function has an inverse function.

According to the horizontal-line test, all exponential functions are one-to-one and, therefore, have inverse functions.

Let's determine the inverse function of the exponential function.

$f(x) = a^x$	Exponential function
$y = a^x$	Replace $f(x)$ with y.
$x = a^y$	Interchange x and y.
$y = $ the power to which we raise a to obtain x	Solve for y.

In order to write this mathematically, we define the **logarithm of x with base a** to be the power to which we raise a to get x.

> *Logarithm of x with base a*
> The logarithm of x with base a is written in the form $\log_a x$ and is defined as
>
> $$y = \log_a x \quad \text{if and only if} \quad x = a^y,$$
>
> where a and x are positive real numbers and $a \neq 1$.

Now we can write the inverse function of the exponential function, $f(x) = a^x$, as

$$y = \log_a x$$
$$\text{or} \quad f^{-1}(x) = \log_a x.$$

One example of an exponential function and its inverse function is

$$g(x) = 2^x \quad \text{and} \quad g^{-1}(x) = \log_2 x.$$

We have now identified a new function called the **logarithmic function**, which is the inverse of the exponential function.

> *Logarithmic Function with Base a*
> The logarithmic function with base a can be written in the form
>
> $$f(x) = \log_a x,$$
>
> where a and x are positive real numbers and $a \neq 0$.

EXAMPLE 1 Determine the logarithmic function that is the inverse of the given exponential function.

   a. $f(x) = 5^x$ \qquad\qquad **b.** $g(x) = 10^x$

   Solution

   a. Given $f(x) = 5^x$, $f^{-1}(x) = \log_5 x$.

   b. Given $g(x) = 10^x$, $g^{-1}(x) = \log_{10} x$. ∎

 Experiencing Algebra the Checkup Way

In exercises 1–2, determine the logarithmic function that is the inverse of the given exponential function.

1. $f(x) = 3^x$ \qquad\qquad **2.** $h(x) = 13^x$

3. What is wrong with the statement, "The inverse function for the exponential function $F(x) = 7^x$ is the logarithmic function $F^{-1}(x) = \log_x 7$"? How can you guard against making this mistake?

---

2 Evaluating Logarithms According to the definition of the logarithm of x with base a, the two equations $y = \log_a x$ and $x = a^y$ are equivalent. For example,

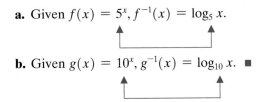

$$y = \log_a x \qquad x = a^y$$
$$3 = \log_2 8 \qquad 8 = 2^3$$

Therefore, by definition, *a logarithm is an exponent.*

To evaluate a logarithm $\log_a x$, ask the question, "To what power must a be raised to obtain x?" For example, evaluate $\log_3 9$.

The power to which 3 must be raised to obtain 9 is 2. Therefore, since $3^2 = 9$, then $\log_3 9 = 2$.

EXAMPLE 2 Evaluate.

   a. $\log_2 32$ \qquad\qquad **b.** $\log_4 2$ \qquad\qquad **c.** $\log_3 \dfrac{1}{3}$

Solution

a. $\log_2 32$

The power to which 2 must be raised to obtain 32 is 5. Therefore, since $2^5 = 32$, then $\log_2 32 = 5$.

b. $\log_4 2$

The power to which 4 must be raised to obtain 2 is $\frac{1}{2}$. Therefore, since $4^{1/2} = 2$, then $\log_4 2 = \frac{1}{2}$.

c. $\log_3 \dfrac{1}{3}$

The power to which 3 must be raised to obtain $\frac{1}{3}$ is -1. Therefore, since $3^{-1} = \frac{1}{3}$, then $\log_3 \frac{1}{3} = -1$. ■

When evaluating logarithms, we sometimes encounter certain special cases. These special cases are properties of all logarithms. Complete the following set of exercises to identify these properties.

DISCOVERY 7

Properties of Logarithms

Determine the following logarithms in the form $\log_a x$.

1. a. $\log_3 1$ **b.** $\log_5 1$

2. a. $\log_3 3$ **b.** $\log_5 5$

3. a. $\log_3(3^2)$ **b.** $\log_5(5^2)$

4. a. $\log_3(-1)$ **b.** $\log_5(-1)$

5. a. $\log_3 0$ **b.** $\log_5 0$

6. In exercise 1, $x = 1$. The logarithms are _____ .

7. In exercise 2, $x = a$, the base. The logarithms are _____ .

8. In exercise 3, $x = a^2$, the base squared. The logarithms are _____ .

9. In exercise 4, $x = -1$. The logarithms are _____ .

10. In exercise 5, $x = 0$. The logarithms are _____ .

The properties discovered in these exercises come directly from the definition of a logarithm.

Properties of Logarithms

For any positive real numbers a and x, where $a \neq 1$, logarithms have the following properties.

$\log_a 1 = 0$	because $a^0 = 1$.
$\log_a a = 1$	because $a^1 = a$.
$\log_a a^x = x$	because $a^x = a^x$.
$\log_a(-1)$ is undefined	because a is a positive number and there is no power to which a can be raised to obtain a negative number.
$\log_a 0$ is undefined	because a is a positive number and there is no power to which a can be raised to obtain 0.

The base of a logarithm can be any positive real number except 1. However, one base that appears more often than other rational numbers is the base 10. A base 10 logarithm is called the **common logarithm**.

Common Logarithm
The common logarithm of a number x is $\log_{10} x$ or $\log x$.

 Helping Hand When we write $\log x$, the base is understood to be 10.

The calculator has a special key for evaluating the common logarithm. For example, evaluate $\log_{10} 100$ and check your results on your calculator.

$\log_{10} 100 = 2$, because $10^2 = 100$, as shown in Figure 15.3.

Figure 15.3

EXAMPLE 3 Evaluate and check on your calculator.

a. $\log 1$ **b.** $\log 0.01$ **c.** $\log 20$ **d.** $\log 0$

Solution

a. $\log 1 = 0$ Because $10^0 = 1$.

b. $\log 0.01 = -2$ Because $10^{-2} = \frac{1}{10^2} = \frac{1}{100} = 0.01$.

c. $\log 20 \approx 1.301$ You must evaluate this on your calculator, because 10 cannot easily be raised to a power to obtain 20.

d. $\log 0$ is undefined.

 Helping Hand The calculator will return an error message when the logarithm is undefined.

The logarithm with base e is called the **natural logarithm**. It is written using the special symbol $\ln x$, and is read "el en of x."

Natural Logarithm
The natural logarithm of a number x is $\log_e x$ or $\ln x$.

All the properties of logarithms listed in this section are also true for natural logarithms.

Properties of Natural Logarithms
For any positive real number x, natural logarithms have the following properties.

$\ln 1 = 0$	because $e^0 = 1$.
$\ln e = 1$	because $e^1 = e$.
$\ln e^x = x$	because $e^x = e^x$.
$\ln(-1)$ is undefined	because e is a positive number and there is no power to which e can be raised to obtain a negative number.
$\ln 0$ is undefined	because e is a positive number and there is no power to which e can be raised to obtain 0.

The calculator has a special key for evaluating the natural logarithm. For example, evaluate $\ln e^2$ and check your results on your calculator.

$\ln e^2 = 2$, because a property of logarithms states that $\ln e^x = x$ and in this case $x = 2$, as shown in Figure 15.4.

TECHNOLOGY

For Figure 15.4

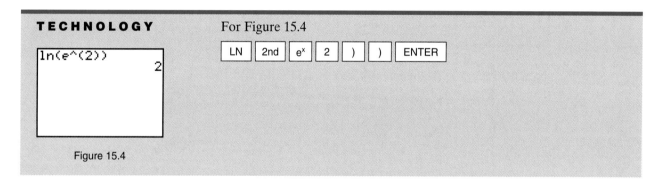

| LN | 2nd | e^x | 2 |) |) | ENTER |

Figure 15.4

EXAMPLE 4 Evaluate $\ln \frac{1}{e^2}$ and check on your calculator.

Solution

$$\ln \frac{1}{e^2} = \ln e^{-2} = -2$$ ∎

To evaluate logarithms with bases other than 10 and e on the calculator, we need to introduce the **change-of-base formula**. It can be shown that $\log_a x$ can be written as a quotient of logarithms with a base other than a.

Change-of-Base Formula
For any positive real numbers a, b, and x, where $a \neq 1$ and $b \neq 1$, then

$$\log_a x = \frac{\log_b x}{\log_b a} \quad \text{or} \quad \log_a x = \frac{\ln x}{\ln a}.$$

To evaluate logarithms with bases other than 10 and *e*:

- Use the change-of-base formula with common logarithms.

$$\log_a x = \frac{\log_{10} x}{\log_{10} a}$$

or

- Use the change-of-base formula with natural logarithms.

$$\log_a x = \frac{\ln x}{\ln a}$$

Helping Hand Note that the original logarithm has base *a* and the quotient has log *a* or ln *a* in the denominator (base). This will help you to remember the location of *a* in the quotient.

For example, write $\log_3 4$ using the change-of-base formula and common logarithms and evaluate on your calculator.

$$\log_3 4 = \frac{\log 4}{\log 3}$$

Therefore, $\log_3 4 \approx 1.262$ or $3^{1.262} \approx 4$.

EXAMPLE 5   Evaluate $\log_5 12$

    a. using the change-of-base formula and natural logarithms.
    b. using the change-of-base formula and common logarithms.

Calculator Solution

a. $\log_5 12 = \dfrac{\ln 12}{\ln 5} \approx 1.544$ **b.** $\log_5 12 = \dfrac{\log 12}{\log 5} \approx 1.544$

Note: We obtain the same value in 5a and 5b. ∎

✓ Experiencing Algebra the Checkup Way

Evaluate.

1. $\log_2 16$ **2.** $\log_4 \dfrac{1}{64}$

Evaluate exercises 3–7 and check on your calculator.

3. $\log 1000$ **4.** $\log 0.001$ **5.** $\log -1$ **6.** $\ln e^4$ **7.** $\ln \dfrac{1}{e^4}$

8. Evaluate $\log_8 24$ using
    a. natural logarithms.   **b.** common logarithms.

9. Explain the difference between the common logarithm of a number and the natural logarithm of a number. Are these the only two forms of logarithms we can use?

---

3   Graphing Logarithmic Functions   We are now ready to graph a logarithmic function. We illustrate two methods of setting up a table of values for the logarithmic function.

The first method involves setting up a table of values for the inverse of the logarithmic function (the exponential function), which is usually easier to evaluate than the logarithmic function. Reversing the coordinates will then determine the table of values for the logarithmic function.

To set up a table of values for a logarithmic function:

- Identify the inverse function (the exponential function).
- Set up a table of values for the exponential function.
- Reverse the coordinates in the ordered pairs to determine the ordered pairs of the logarithmic function.

For example, graph the logarithmic function $f(x) = \log_8 x$.

The inverse function is the exponential function $f^{-1}(x) = 8^x$. The domain of this inverse function is all real numbers. (We set up a table of values for this function in Section 15.2.)

$$f^{-1}(x) = 8^x \qquad\qquad f(x) = \log_8 x$$

x	$f^{-1}(x)$
-3	$\dfrac{1}{512}$
-2	$\dfrac{1}{64}$
-1	$\dfrac{1}{8}$
0	1
1	8
2	64
3	512

Reverse coordinates $\longrightarrow$

x	$f(x)$
$\dfrac{1}{512}$	-3
$\dfrac{1}{64}$	-2
$\dfrac{1}{8}$	-1
1	0
8	1
64	2
512	3

Note: In Figure 15.5, we graphed both the exponential function and the logarithmic function. We also graphed $y = x$, the line of symmetry, to illustrate that the graphs represent inverse functions.

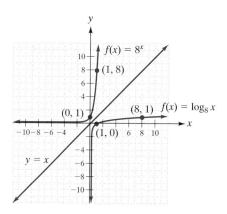

Figure 15.5

The second method to complete a table of values for the logarithmic function involves substituting values for the independent variable and evaluating the function. First, determine the domain of the logarithmic function. Since it is the inverse of an exponential function, we reverse the domain and range of the two functions.

Exponential Function				*Logarithmic Function*
Domain	←	all real numbers	→	Range
Range	←	all positive real numbers	→	Domain

Therefore, the domain of a logarithmic function is the set of all positive real numbers.

To complete the table of values, we may need to use a calculator. Also, remember to use the change-of-base formula, when needed.

To set up a table of values for a logarithmic function:

- Substitute positive real-number values from the domain of the function for the independent variable.
- Determine values for the dependent variable by evaluating the resulting expression.

For example, graph the logarithmic function $f(x) = \log_8 x$.

Use your calculator to determine a table of values for the function, using the change-of-base formula. Let $f(x) = \log_8 x = \frac{\ln x}{\ln 8}$.

x	$f(x)$
0.001	−3.322
0.01	−2.215
0.1	−1.107
0.5	−0.333
1	0
2	0.333
3	0.528
4	0.667
5	0.774
6	0.862

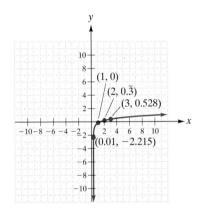

To graph a logarithmic function on your calculator, enter the function in Y1 using the change-of-base formula.

For example, graph the logarithmic function $f(x) = \log_8 x$.

Let $f(x) = \log_8 x = \frac{\ln x}{\ln 8}$.

We also have logarithmic functions identified by a common logarithm and a natural logarithm.

$Y1 = \log_8 x = \frac{\ln x}{\ln 8}$

$(-4.7, 4.7, -3.1, 3.1)$

> *Common Logarithmic Function*
> The common logarithmic function is written in the form
>
> $$f(x) = \log_{10} x \quad \text{or} \quad f(x) = \log x,$$
>
> where x is a positive real number.

> *Natural Logarithmic Function*
> The natural logarithmic function is defined as $f(x) = \log_e x$ and is written in the form
>
> $$f(x) = \ln x,$$
>
> where x is a positive real number.

EXAMPLE 6   Graph.

a. $y = \log x$ **b.** $g(x) = \ln x$

Solution

a. For $y = \log x$, we illustrate the first graphical method.

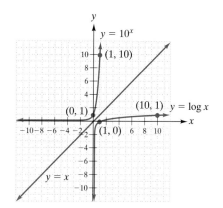

$$f^{-1}(x) = 10^x \qquad\qquad f(x) = \log x$$

x	$f^{-1}(x)$
-3	0.001
-2	0.01
-1	0.1
0	1
1	10
2	100
3	1000

Reverse coordinates $\longrightarrow$

x	$f(x)$
0.001	-3
0.01	-2
0.1	-1
1	0
10	1
100	2
1000	3

b. For $g(x) = \ln x$, we illustrate the second graphical method.

x	$g(x)$
0.001	-6.908
0.01	-4.605
0.1	-2.303
0.5	-0.693
1	0
2	0.693
3	1.099
4	1.386
5	1.609
6	1.792

Calculator Solution

a.

Y1 = log *x*

(−4.7, 4.7, −3.1, 3.1)

b.

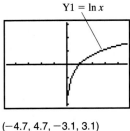

Y1 = ln *x*

(−4.7, 4.7, −3.1, 3.1)   ∎

We can summarize the characteristics of a logarithmic function and its graph by remembering that a logarithmic function is an inverse of an exponential function. Therefore, the domain and range are interchanged.

Characteristics of a Logarithmic Function and Its Graph
Given the logarithmic function $f(x) = \log_a x$ and its graph, we know the following characteristics.

Domain	All positive real numbers
Range	All real numbers

The function is one-to-one.

y-intercept	There is no *y*-intercept. The graph of the function approaches but does not reach the *y*-axis.
x-intercept	$(1, 0)$

If $a > 1$, then the function is always increasing.
If $0 < a < 1$, then the function is always decreasing.

Experiencing Algebra the Checkup Way

In exercises 1–3, graph each logarithmic function using a table of values.

1. $f(x) = \log_3 x$ **2.** $g(x) = \log(3x)$ **3.** $h(x) = \ln(3x)$

4. Explain the relationship between the domain and range of an exponential function and the domain and range of its inverse function—that is, the corresponding logarithmic function.

---

4 Modeling the Real World

Logarithmic functions are used to model many different real-world situations, especially when the independent variable can take a wide range of values. The reason for this is that the values of the logarithmic function change slowly over a large range of domain values. Examples of logarithmic functions are found in many of the sciences. For instance, the magnitude of an earthquake is measured on a Richter scale, which uses a logarithmic function to describe motion from millionths of an inch to tens of feet. The loudness of a sound, from the merest whisper to the roar of thunder, is measured in decibels, which are defined by a logarithmic function.

Another important application of common logarithms is found in chemistry. The pH value of a substance is its measure of acidity or alkalinity. Pure water has a pH value of 7.0. A pH value greater than 7.0 represents an alkaline substance, and a pH value less than 7.0 represents an acidic substance.

The pH of a substance is defined by the function

$$pH = -\log[H^+],$$

where $[H^+]$ is the hydrogen ion concentration in moles per liter.

EXAMPLE 7   Orange juice has a hydrogen ion concentration of 6.3×10^{-4} moles per liter. Determine its pH.

Calculator Solution

Substitute in the formula 6.3×10^{-4} for $[H^+]$.

$$pH = -\log[H^+]$$
$$pH = -\log(6.3 \times 10^{-4})$$
$$pH \approx 3.2 \qquad \blacksquare$$

```
-log(6.3*10^(-4)
)
      3.200659451
```

EXAMPLE 8   Crackers have a pH value of 8.4. Determine their hydrogen ion concentration.

Solution

Substitute in the formula 8.4 for pH.

$$pH = -\log[H^+]$$
$$8.4 = -\log[H^+]$$
$$-8.4 = \log[H^+] \qquad \text{Divide both sides by } -1.$$
$$10^{-8.4} = [H^+] \qquad \text{Write as an exponential equation.}$$
$$4.0 \times 10^{-9} \approx [H^+]$$

Note: This calculator value is rounded to one decimal place.   ∎

```
10^(-8.4)
  3.981071706E-9
```

Application

The magnitude R, measured on the Richter scale, of an earthquake of intensity I is defined by the function $R = \log \frac{I}{I_0}$, where I_0 is the intensity of a very small vibration in the Earth used as a standard. The San Francisco earthquake of 1906 had a magnitude of 8.3 on the Richter scale. Eighty-three years later, in 1989, San Francisco had another earthquake measuring 7.1.

a. Determine the intensity of each earthquake.
b. The difference on the Richter scale of the 1906 and 1989 earthquakes is 1.2. Determine the ratio of the intensity of the 1906 earthquake to the 1989 earthquake.

Discussion

a. Use the formula $R = \log \dfrac{I}{I_0}$ with $R = 8.3$ and $R = 7.1$.

$$R = \log \dfrac{I}{I_0} \qquad\qquad R = \log \dfrac{I}{I_0}$$

$$8.3 = \log \dfrac{I}{I_0} \qquad\quad 7.1 = \log \dfrac{I}{I_0} \qquad \text{Substitute values.}$$

$$10^{8.3} = \dfrac{I}{I_0} \qquad\qquad 10^{7.1} = \dfrac{I}{I_0} \qquad \text{Write exponential equations.}$$

$$I = 10^{8.3} I_0 \qquad\qquad I = 10^{7.1} I_0$$

The intensity of the 1906 earthquake was $10^{8.3} I_0$, and the intensity of the 1989 earthquake was $10^{7.1} I_0$.

b. The ratio of the intensity of the 1906 earthquake to the intensity of the 1989 earthquake is $\dfrac{10^{8.3} I_0}{10^{7.1} I_0} = \dfrac{10^{8.3}}{10^{7.1}} \approx 15.8$.

The intensity of the 1906 earthquake was approximately 15.8 times as great as that of the 1989 earthquake.

Note: These magnitudes have been revised. See the following "Experiencing Algebra the Checkup Way" for additional information. ∎

Experiencing Algebra the Checkup Way

1. Pure water has a pH value of 7.0. What is its hydrogen ion concentration?

2. Until 1979, an earthquake of magnitude 8.5 on the Richter scale was thought to be the most powerful possible. Since then, improvements in seismic measuring techniques have enabled scientists to refine the scale. Now 9.5 is considered to be the practical limit to measuring an earthquake's magnitude. As a result, the magnitude of the Alaskan earthquake of 1964 has been revised upward to 9.2 on the Richter scale. How does its intensity compare with that of the 1989 San Francisco earthquake, which had a magnitude of 7.1 on the Richter scale?

3. The refinement of the Richter scale also downgraded the magnitude of the 1906 San Francisco earthquake from 8.3 to 7.9. How has the intensity of this earthquake been affected by this downgrade?

PROBLEM SET 15.3

Experiencing Algebra the Exercise Way

Determine the inverse logarithmic function for each exponential function Note: k and b are constants.

1. $f(x) = 11^x$ **2.** $h(x) = 15^x$ **3.** $g(x) = 6^x$ **4.** $p(x) = 29^x$

5. $H(x) = k^x$ **6.** $J(x) = b^x$

Evaluate.

7. $\log_2 64$ **8.** $\log_2 128$ **9.** $\log_3 243$ **10.** $\log_3 729$

11. $\log_4 256$ **12.** $\log_5 125$ **13.** $\log_2 \dfrac{1}{8}$ **14.** $\log_4 \dfrac{1}{16}$

15. $\log_4 0.25$ **16.** $\log_2 0.125$ **17.** $\log_3 \dfrac{1}{81}$ **18.** $\log_5 \dfrac{1}{125}$

Evaluate and check on your calculator.

19. $\log 10$

20. $\log 10,000$

21. $\log 0.0001$

22. $\log 0.000001$

23. $\ln e^3$

24. $\ln e^7$

25. $\ln e^{-5}$

26. $\ln e^{-8}$

27. $\ln \dfrac{1}{e^5}$

28. $\ln \dfrac{1}{e^7}$

Evaluate using your calculator.

29. $\log 15$

30. $\log 23$

31. $\log \dfrac{1}{12}$

32. $\log \dfrac{1}{19}$

33. $\log 1.35$

34. $\log 12.5$

35. $\ln 14$

36. $\ln 27$

37. $\ln 2.85$

38. $\ln 11.6$

39. $\ln \dfrac{1}{5}$

40. $\ln \dfrac{1}{15}$

Evaluate each logarithm, using common logarithms to change the base.

41. $\log_4 12$

42. $\log_5 28$

43. $\log_2 10$

44. $\log_4 100$

45. $\log_5 2.88$

46. $\log_3 14.7$

47. $\log_5 \dfrac{2}{3}$

48. $\log_3 \dfrac{3}{5}$

Evaluate each logarithm, using natural logarithms to change the base.

49. $\log_8 15$

50. $\log_6 35$

51. $\log_3 5.9$

52. $\log_7 3.75$

53. $\log_5 \dfrac{1}{7}$

54. $\log_{12} \dfrac{1}{3}$

In exercises 55–60, create a table of values and graph.

55. $f(x) = \log_5 x$

56. $F(x) = \log_7 x$

57. $g(x) = \log(x + 2)$

58. $G(x) = \log(x - 2)$

59. $h(x) = \ln(x + 2)$

60. $H(x) = \ln(x - 2)$

61. Rainwater typically has a pH of 6.2. Determine its hydrogen ion concentration.

62. Acid rain in many parts of the world has a pH value as low as 3. What is the hydrogen ion concentration of this level of acid rain?

63. Determine the pH value of seawater if its hydrogen ion concentration is 3.2×10^{-9} moles per liter.

64. What is the pH value of milk whose hydrogen ion concentration is 4×10^{-7} moles per liter?

65. An estimated 50,000 earthquakes of magnitude 3.5 occur worldwide each year. How do these compare in intensity with the 1906 San Francisco earthquake, which had a magnitude of 8.3 on the Richter scale?

66. Annually there are approximately 800 earthquakes worldwide with a magnitude of 5.5 on the Richter scale. How do these compare in intensity with the 1989 San Francisco earthquake, which had a magnitude of 7.1 on the Richter scale?

Experiencing Algebra the Calculator Way

Use your calculator to graph the following logarithmic functions.

1. $f(x) = \log x$

2. $g(x) = \log(x + 1)$

3. $h(x) = \log x + \log(x + 1)$

4. $k(x) = \log[x(x + 1)]$

5. $j(x) = \log x - \log(x + 1)$

6. $m(x) = \log\left(\dfrac{x}{x + 1}\right)$

Compare the graphs of exercises 3 and 4. Then compare the graphs of exercises 5 and 6. Do the graphs appear to be the same? How can you check this using your calculator? If the graphs are the same, does this suggest a relationship for the log of a product or the log of a quotient? How would you state this relationship? Are there any restrictions on the domains of the functions?

Experiencing Algebra the Group Way

Graph the logarithmic functions in exercises 1–2. Then discuss the questions presented to help you better understand the graphs of logarithmic functions.

1. $f(x) = \log(x - 2)$

2. $g(x) = \log(2 - x)$

3. Describe the domain of each function.

4. How are the two graphs related?

Experiencing Algebra the Write Way

1. Explain the difference between $\log_3 5$ and $\log_5 3$. Evaluate using your calculator to help you see the difference.

2. Explain the difference between the functions $y = \log x + 2$ and $y = \log(x + 2)$. Graph the functions on your calculator to help you see the difference.

3. How does the domain of the function $y = \log x + 2$ differ from the domain of the function $y = \log(x + 2)$?

15.4 Properties of Logarithms

Objectives 1 Rewrite logarithmic expressions using the properties of logarithms.

2 Model real-world situations using logarithms.

Application If you change the speakers in your stereo system, going from large speakers to smaller ones, there will be a response peak.

To determine the peak response, you must evaluate the expression.

$$20\left[\log 2.6 + \log Q_s + 0.35\left(\log V_a - \log V_b\right)\right],$$

where V_a = volume of the larger speaker, V_b = volume of the smaller speaker, and Q_s is the Q of the system. Condense this logarithmic expression.

After completing this section, we will discuss this application further. See page 1163.

---

1 Using Properties of Logarithms

In section 15.3, we discussed properties of logarithms that were derived from the definition of logarithms. In order to rewrite logarithmic expressions, we need to expand this list of properties. Since we know that logarithms are exponents, by definition, we should expect to have properties of logarithms that correspond to the properties of exponents that we discussed in Chapter 10. That is,

$$a^m a^n = a^{m+n} \qquad \text{Product rule}$$

$$\frac{a^m}{a^n} = a^{m-n} \qquad \text{Quotient rule}$$

$$\left(a^m\right)^n = a^{mn} \qquad \text{Power-to-a-power rule}$$

Complete the following set of exercises on your calculator to discover these properties.

DISCOVERY 8

Product, Quotient, and Power Rules of Logarithms
Approximate each expression and compare the results obtained in the left column to the corresponding results in the right column.

1. Product rule
  a. $\log(3 \cdot 4) \approx$ _____
  c. $\ln(2 \cdot 5) \approx$ _____

  b. $\log 3 + \log 4 \approx$ _____
  d. $\ln 2 + \ln 5 \approx$ _____

2. Quotient rule
  a. $\log \dfrac{3}{4} \approx$ _____

  c. $\ln \dfrac{2}{5} \approx$ _____

  b. $\log 3 - \log 4 \approx$ _____

  d. $\ln 2 - \ln 5 \approx$ _____

Continued

3. Power rule
  a. $\log 3^4 \approx$ ____   **b.** $4 \log 3 \approx$ ____
  c. $\ln 2^5 \approx$ ____   **d.** $5 \ln 2 \approx$ ____

Write the following rules of logarithms.

4. Product rule
5. Quotient rule
6. Power rule

For the product rule, the logarithm of a product is equal to the sum of the logarithms of the factors. For the quotient rule, the logarithm of a quotient is equal to the difference of the logarithm of the numerator minus the logarithm of the denominator. For the power rule, the logarithm of a base raised to a power is equal to the product of the power and the logarithm of the base.

> *Product, Quotient, and Power Rules of Logarithms*
> Assume that m and n are any real number, variable, or expression, where $m > 0$ and $n > 0$. Also, assume that $a > 0$, $a \neq 1$, and c is a real number.
>
> | | **Logarithm with Base a** | **Natural Logarithm** |
> |----------------|------------------------------|------------------------|
> | Product rule | $\log_a mn = \log_a m + \log_a n$ | $\ln mn = \ln m + \ln n$ |
> | Quotient rule | $\log_a \dfrac{m}{n} = \log_a m - \log_a n$ | $\ln \dfrac{m}{n} = \ln m - \ln n$ |
> | Power rule | $\log_a m^c = c \log_a m$ | $\ln m^c = c \ln m$ |

 Helping Hand There is no property of logarithms that can be used to simplify the log of a sum or difference, $\log_a(m + n)$ or $\log_a(m - n)$.

We can use the properties of logarithms stated in this section and section 15.3 to rewrite logarithms. We will be working with variable expressions as well as numeric ones.

We will assume that the variables do not represent values for which the expression is not defined.

First, we **expand** a logarithm by using the properties stated previously and writing a sum, a difference, or a product. For example, expand the logarithmic expression $\log 3x$.

$$\log 3x = \log 3 + \log x \quad \text{Product rule}$$

EXAMPLE 1 Expand each logarithmic expression.

  a. $\log_2 \dfrac{x}{3}$ **b.** $\log_5 x^3$

Solution

  a. $\log_2 \dfrac{x}{3} = \log_2 x - \log_2 3 \quad \text{Quotient rule}$

  b. $\log_5 x^3 = 3 \log_5 x \qquad\qquad \text{Power rule} \blacksquare$

We **condense** a logarithm by using the properties stated previously, reading right to left. In other words, we write a product, quotient, or power. For example, condense the logarithmic expression $\ln 2 - \ln x$.

$$\ln 2 - \ln x = \ln \frac{2}{x} \qquad \text{Quotient rule}$$

EXAMPLE 2 Condense each logarithmic expression.

    a. $\ln 2 + \ln x + \ln y$ **b.** $2 \ln y$

Solution

    a. $\ln 2 + \ln x + \ln y = \ln 2xy$ Product rule

    b. $2 \ln y = \ln y^2$ Power rule ∎

We can combine the rules of exponents to rewrite more complicated expressions. Remember, the logarithms must have the same base in order to apply the rules of logarithms.

EXAMPLE 3 Expand the logarithmic expression $\log_3 \sqrt{3x}$.

Solution

$$\log_3 \sqrt{3x} = \log_3 (3x)^{1/2} \qquad \text{Definition of square root}$$

$$= \frac{1}{2} \log_3 3x \qquad \text{Power rule}$$

$$= \frac{1}{2} \left(\log_3 3 + \log_3 x \right) \qquad \text{Product rule}$$

$$= \frac{1}{2} \log_3 3 + \frac{1}{2} \log_3 x \qquad \text{Distribute } \tfrac{1}{2}.$$

$$= \frac{1}{2} (1) + \frac{1}{2} \log_3 x \qquad \log_3 3 = 1$$

$$= \frac{1}{2} + \frac{1}{2} \log_3 x \qquad\qquad\qquad ∎$$

EXAMPLE 4 Condense the logarithmic expression $2 \ln(2x + 3) + \ln(x + 3) - \ln x$.

Solution

$$2 \ln(2x + 3) + \ln(x + 3) - \ln x$$

$$= \ln(2x + 3)^2 + \ln(x + 3) - \ln x \qquad \text{Power rule}$$

$$= \ln(2x + 3)^2(x + 3) - \ln x \qquad \text{Product rule}$$

$$= \ln \frac{(2x + 3)^2(x + 3)}{x} \qquad \text{Quotient rule} ∎$$

Experiencing Algebra the Checkup Way

Expand each logarithmic expression.

1. $\log_5 11x$　　　　　　　　**2.** $\ln \dfrac{x}{y}$

In exercises 3–4, condense each logarithmic expression.

3. $\log x + \log y - \log z$　　**4.** $-3 \ln x$
5. Expand the logarithmic expression $\log_5 5x^2$.
6. What does it mean to expand a logarithmic expression?
7. What does it mean to condense a logarithmic expression?

---

2 Modeling the Real World　　Condensing logarithmic expressions is an important skill needed to solve logarithmic equations. However, condensing logarithms may simplify the evaluation of expressions by enabling us to calculate a single logarithm instead of calculating more than one logarithm in an expression. The accuracy of our results in evaluating one expression (rounding once) may be greater than when we evaluate an expression in which we round more than one value.

EXAMPLE 5　　The power gain, in decibels, of an electronic device is determined by the logarithmic expression $10(\log P_0 - \log P_i)$, where P_0 is the output power, in watts, and P_i is the input power, in watts.

a. Condense the expression using the rules of logarithms.
b. Determine the power gain of an amplifier with an output of 25.0 W and an input of 0.625 W.

Solution

a. $10(\log P_0 - \log P_i) = 10\left[\log\left(\dfrac{P_0}{P_i}\right)\right]$　　Quotient rule

$$= \log\left(\dfrac{P_0}{P_i}\right)^{10}$$　　Power rule

b. $\log\left(\dfrac{P_0}{P_i}\right)^{10} = \log\left(\dfrac{25.0}{0.625}\right)^{10} \approx 16.021 \text{ dB } \blacksquare$

Application

If you change the speakers in your stereo system, going from large speakers to smaller ones, there will be a response peak.
　　To determine the peak response, you must evaluate the expression

$$20\left[\log 2.6 + \log Q_s + 0.35(\log V_a - \log V_b)\right],$$

where V_a = volume of the larger speaker, V_b = volume of the smaller speaker, and Q_s is the Q of the system. Condense this logarithmic expression.

Discussion

$$20\left[\log 2.6 + \log Q_s + 0.35(\log V_a - \log V_b)\right]$$
$$= 20\left[\log 2.6 + \log Q_s + 0.35 \log \left(\dfrac{V_a}{V_b}\right)\right]$$　　Quotient rule

$$= 20\left[\log 2.6 + \log Q_s + \log\left(\frac{V_a}{V_b}\right)^{0.35}\right]$$ Power rule

$$= 20\log\left[(2.6)(Q_s)\left(\frac{V_a}{V_b}\right)^{0.35}\right]$$ Product rule

$$= \log\left[2.6Q_s\left(\frac{V_a}{V_b}\right)^{0.35}\right]^{20}$$ Power rule ∎

 Experiencing Algebra the Checkup Way

In exercises 1 and 2, use the rules of logarithms to expand the right side of each application from geometry.

1. $\ln A = \ln(\pi r^2)$ **2.** $\log A = \log\left(\frac{1}{2}bh\right)$

3. Light passing through a transparent solution follows the model

$y = c(\ln I_0 - \ln I),$

where c is a constant related to the solution, I_0 is the intensity of the light striking the solution, and I is the intensity at a depth of y units in the solution.

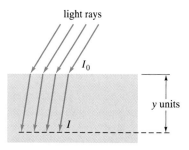

light rays

I_0

y units

I

a. Use the rules of logarithms to condense the right side of the model.

b. If $c = 8.5$ for a solution, find the depth y when the intensity at the surface is three times the intensity at the depth of y units.

PROBLEM SET 15.4

 Experiencing Algebra the Exercise Way

Expand each logarithmic expression.

1. $\log 12a$ **2.** $\ln 25c$ **3.** $\ln x^3$ **4.** $\log z^3$

5. $\log_5 \frac{x}{5}$ **6.** $\log_7 \frac{7}{y}$ **7.** $\log \frac{2x^2}{y}$ **8.** $\log \frac{x^2}{5y^3}$

9. $\log_3 x^3 y^2$ **10.** $\log_2 a^2 b^4$ **11.** $\ln \sqrt[3]{xy^2}$ **12.** $\log \sqrt[4]{x^3 y}$

13. $\log \frac{\sqrt{2x}}{\sqrt[3]{y}}$ **14.** $\ln \frac{\sqrt[3]{3x^2}}{\sqrt{2y}}$ **15.** $\log_3 3a$ **16.** $\log_5 5z$

17. $\log_5 10xy$ **18.** $\log_3 \frac{xy}{6}$ **19.** $\log_a(ab^2)$ **20.** $\log_6(3ab^2)$

Condense each logarithmic expression.

21. $\log x + \log(x + 5)$ **22.** $\log(x - 1) + \log(x + 1)$ **23.** $2\ln x + 3\ln y$

24. $3 \ln b - 2 \ln c$

25. $2 \log_3(x + 3) - \log_3(x - 1)$

26. $5 \log_5(a - 5) + 2 \log_5 a$

27. $\dfrac{1}{2} \ln x - \dfrac{1}{5} \ln(x + 1)$

28. $\dfrac{1}{4} \log z - \dfrac{1}{3} \log(z + 5)$

29. $\log xy - \log xz$

30. $2 \log pq - \log p$

Use the mathematical model for power gain, $G = \log\left(\frac{P_0}{P_i}\right)^{10}$, where P_0 is the output power in watts and P_i is the input power in watts, for the following exercises.

31. Determine the power gain G, in decibels, for an amplifier with an output P_0 of 20 watts and an input P_i of 1.5 watts.

32. What is the power gain G, in decibels, of an amplifier with an output P_0 of 30 watts and an input P_i of 2 watts?

Use the mathematical model for light passing through a transparent liquid, $y = c \ln \frac{I_0}{I}$, where I_0 is the intensity of light striking a solution, I is the intensity at a depth of y units in the solution, and c is a related constant, for the following exercises.

33. If $c = 12$ for a liquid, find the depth y when the surface intensity I_0 is 3.5 times the intensity at the depth of y units.

34. If $c = 10$ for a liquid, at what depth y will the surface intensity be 6 times the intensity at the depth?

If money is continuously compounded, the amount in the account will grow to k times the original investment in $t = \frac{\ln k}{r}$ years when the annual rate of interest is r. Use this model for the following exercises.

35. How long will it take the amount invested to triple if the annual interest rate is 5%?

36. At an annual interest rate of 4.5%, how long will it take an investment to double in value?

37. How long will it take an investment to increase to four times the original investment if the annual interest rate is 9%?

38. If the annual interest rate is 10%, how long will it take an investment to increase in value by a factor of 3.5 times its original value?

 Experiencing Algebra the Calculator Way

You were told that the log of a sum or a difference does not usually simplify. To investigate this, graph the functions in exercises 1–4 on your calculator using a decimal window.

1. $\log 3x$

2. $\log x + \log 2x$

3. $\log(x^2 - x)$

4. $\log x^2 - \log x$

5. Compare the graphs of exercises 1 and 2. Are they equivalent?

6. Compare the graphs of exercises 3 and 4. Are they equivalent?

7. What is wrong with the statement, $\log (A + B) = \log A + \log B$?

8. What is wrong with the statement, $\log (A - B) = \log A - \log B$?

 Experiencing Algebra the Group Way

When an amount of money P is invested into an account that pays interest compounded annually at a rate of interest r, the amount A in the account after t years is given by the mathematical model $A = P(1 + r)^t$. If you wish to determine the amount of time it will take to double your investment, you would set A equal to $2P$ and solve for t: $2P = P(1 + r)^t$. You can take the logarithm of both sides of this equation, and then use the rules of logarithms to expand and solve for t. Work together to show that the solution to this equation is

$$t = \frac{\log 2}{\log(1 + r)}.$$

Next, use this model to complete the following table.

r	3%	3.5%	4%	4.5%	5%	5.5%	6%	6.5%
t								

Use the table to discuss the following questions.

1. How long will it take to double an investment when interest is compounded annually at 4.5%?
2. How long will it take to double an investment when interest is compounded annually at 6%?

Discuss how to find the mathematical model that would tell you the length of time it would take to triple an investment. Could you have developed the model using natural logarithms instead of common logarithms? Try it and see.

Experiencing Algebra the Write Way

One of the most useful applications of exponential and logarithmic expressions is the determination of the half-life of chemical elements. Find a library reference that discusses half-life and write a short summary of what you find. Be sure to cite the call number of the reference.

15.5 Solving Exponential and Logarithmic Equations

Objectives

1 Identify exponential and logarithmic equations in one variable.
2 Solve exponential and logarithmic equations in one variable numerically.
3 Solve exponential and logarithmic equations in one variable graphically.
4 Solve exponential and logarithmic equations in one variable algebraically.
5 Model real-world situations using exponential and logarithmic equations in one variable.

Application

According to Newton's law of cooling, the temperature T of a body t minutes after it is placed in surroundings having a constant temperature T_0 is determined by the function $T(t) = T_0 + Ce^{-kt}$, where C is the difference between the initial temperature and the surrounding temperature and k is the cooling constant.

a. Boiling water (100°C) is placed in a freezer at 0°C. After 25 minutes, the water temperature is 50°C. Determine the constant of cooling.
b. Determine the temperature of the water after 2 hours.

After completing this section, we will discuss this application further. See page 1179.

1 Exponential and Logarithmic Equations in One Variable

If we take the logarithm of an expression, we call the expression the **argument** of the logarithm. For example, the expression $(2x + 1)$ is the argument of $\log(2x + 1)$. A **logarithmic equation in one variable**, or **logarithmic equation**, is an equation with a logarithmic expression having a variable in the argument of the logarithm. For example, the following are logarithmic equations.

$$\log_3 x = 5 \qquad \ln(x + 1) = \ln 5$$

An **exponential equation in one variable**, or **exponential equation**, is an equation with an exponential expression with a variable exponent. For example, the following are exponential equations.

$$4^x = 26 \qquad e^x = e^{2x-3}$$

EXAMPLE 1   Identify each equation as exponential, logarithmic, or neither.

a. $\ln 3 = x + 4$ \qquad b. $10e^x = 100$ \qquad c. $x^5 + 6 = \log 10$

Solution

a. $\ln 3 = x + 4$ is neither a logarithmic nor an exponential equation. The logarithmic argument does not contain a variable; therefore, $\ln 3$ represents a number. This is a linear equation.

b. $10e^x = 100$ is an exponential equation, because the exponent of the exponential expression contains a variable.

c. $x^5 + 6 = \log 10$ is neither a logarithmic nor an exponential equation. The exponential expression does not have a variable exponent, and the logarithmic expression is a number. This is a polynomial equation. ■

Experiencing Algebra the Checkup Way

In exercises 1–4, identify each equation as exponential, logarithmic, or neither.

1. $8 - x = e^2$ \qquad **2.** $2 + \log x = 5$ \qquad **3.** $2^x = 4^{x+3}$ \qquad **4.** $\log 5 = x - 1$

5. What is the difference between an exponential equation in one variable and a logarithmic equation in one variable?

---

2   Solving Equations Numerically

In previous chapters, we determined whether a number was a solution of an equation in one variable by substituting the number for the variable and evaluating the two resulting expressions. If the resulting equation was true, the number substituted was called a solution. The set of all possible solutions is called the solution set. We do the same process for exponential and logarithmic equations.

To solve an equation numerically, we expand this process and use a table of values. We continue to substitute permissible values for the independent variable and determine whether the resulting equations are true. Remember that any numbers resulting in an undefined value for the terms are restricted values. Restricted values are *never* solutions of equations.

> *Solving an Exponential or Logarithmic Equation Numerically*
> To solve an exponential or logarithmic equation numerically:
>
> - Determine the restricted values for the independent variable.
> - Set up an extended table of values.
> - Complete the table.
>   - Substitute permissible values for the independent variable.
>   - Evaluate the second and third columns.
>   - Continue until values for the two expressions (the numbers in the second and third columns) are equal.
>
> *Continued*

The values for the independent variable (the number in the first column) used to find these equivalent expressions are the solutions.

For example, solve the equation $\ln(x + 1) + \ln(x - 2) = \ln 10$.

Note: Natural logarithms are defined for positive values only. Therefore, to determine the domain, solve the inequalities $x + 1 > 0$ and $x - 2 > 0$, or $x > -1$ and $x > 2$. In order to satisfy both inequalities at the same time, we choose the domain to be the set of all real numbers greater than 2. Set up a table of values using this domain.

x	$\ln(x + 1) + \ln(x - 2)$	$\ln 10$	
3	1.3863	2.3026	$1.3863 \neq 2.3026$
4	2.3026	2.3026	$2.3026 = 2.3026$

According to the table, when 4 is substituted for the variable, the two expressions are equivalent ($2.3026 = 2.3026$). Therefore, 4 is a solution of the equation.

To solve an exponential or logarithmic equation numerically on your calculator:

- Rename the independent variable as x.
- Set up the table.
- View the table.

The integer solutions are the x-values that determine equal values for Y1 and Y2. There may be more than one solution.
For example, solve the equation $\ln(x + 1) + \ln(x - 2) = \ln 10$.

Let Y1 $= \ln(x + 1) + \ln(x - 2)$ and Y2 $= \ln 10$.
The solution is the x-value that corresponds to Y1 $=$ Y2. The integer solution from the table is 4.

The solutions of the exponential or logarithmic equations may not be integer solutions. In addition, the equation may not have a real-number solution or may have an infinite number of real-number solutions. These possible solution sets are determined by the same process as in previous chapters.

X	Y1	Y2
0	ERROR	2.3026
1	ERROR	2.3026
2	ERROR	2.3026
3	1.3863	2.3026
4	2.3026	2.3026
5	2.8904	2.3026
6	3.3322	2.3026

X=4

EXAMPLE 2 Solve numerically.

a. $4^x = 2^{x+1}$
b. $\log x^4 - \log x = 3 \log x$
c. $5e^x + 3 = 6$
d. $\log_5 x = x + 5$

Calculator Numeric Solution

a. $4^x = 2^{x+1}$
Let Y1 $= 4^x$ and Y2 $= 2^{x+1}$.
The solution is 1, because when 1 is substituted for the variable in both expressions, the resulting values are equal.

b. $\log x^4 - \log x = 3 \log x$
Let Y1 $= \log x^4 - \log x$ and Y2 $= 3 \log x$.

a.
X	Y1	Y2
0	1	2
1	4	4
2	16	8
3	64	16
4	256	32
5	1024	64
6	4096	128

X=0

b.
X	Y1	Y2
0	ERROR	ERROR
1	0	0
2	.90309	.90309
3	1.4314	1.4314
4	1.8062	1.8062
5	2.0969	2.0969
6	2.3345	2.3345

X=0

c.

X	Y₁	Y₂
-2	3.6767	6
-1	4.8394	6
0	8	6
1	16.591	6
2	39.945	6
3	103.43	6
4	275.99	6

X = -1

$3.6767 < 6$
$4.8394 < 6$
$8 > 6$
$16.591 > 6$
$39.945 > 6$
$103.43 > 6$
$275.99 > 6$

d.

X	Y₁	Y₂
1	0	6
2	.43068	7
3	.68261	8
4	.86135	9
5	1	10
6	1.1133	11
7	1.2091	12

X = 1

$0 < 6$
$.43068 < 7$
$.68261 < 8$
$.86135 < 9$
$1 < 10$
$1.1133 < 11$
$1.2091 < 12$

The expressions are always equal in the table, so it appears that the solution set is all real numbers greater than 0, the domain of the functions listed in the table.

c. $5e^x + 3 = 6$

Let $Y1 = 5e^x + 3$ and $Y2 = 6$.

We cannot find an integer value for x that corresponds to $Y1 = Y2$. However, for x-values less than or equal to -1, $Y1 < Y2$, and for x-values greater than or equal to 0, $Y1 > Y2$. Since x-values are not restricted between -1 and 0, a noninteger solution occurs between -1 and 0, when $Y1 = Y2$.

d. $\log_5 x = x + 5$

Let $Y1 = \log_5 x$ and $Y2 = x + 5$. Remember to enter $Y1$ as $\frac{\log x}{\log 5}$.

The expressions $Y1$ and $Y2$ do not appear to be equal. For all values in the table, $Y1 < Y2$. There does not appear to be a solution. ∎

Numerical Solutions of an Exponential or Logarithmic Equation

To solve an equation for integer solutions numerically, set up an extended table of values. In viewing the table, one of four possibilities will occur:

Integer solutions exist. The solutions are the integers in the first column that correspond to equal values in the second and third columns.

Noninteger solutions exist. When comparing corresponding values in the second and third columns, the order changes from "less than" to "greater than" or "greater than" to "less than," and the restricted value does not occur at this change. A noninteger solution occurs between the two consecutive integers in the first column that correspond to this change.

It appears that no solution exists. When comparing corresponding values in the second and third columns, there does not appear to be a change in order for two consecutive integers, or a change occurs but the restricted value occurs at this change.

An infinite number of solutions exist. When comparing corresponding values in the second and third columns, the values are equal. The equation is an identity. The solution set is all numbers for which the equation is defined.

In conclusion, an exponential or logarithmic equation may be solved numerically using a table of values. However, if the solution is not an integer or does not exist, it will be difficult to find using this method.

Experiencing Algebra the Checkup Way

Solve exercises 1–5 numerically.

1. $3^{a-2} = 9^a$

2. $\log 4x^2 = \log x + \log 4x$ **3.** $2\ln(x - 1) = \ln 16$

4. $2^{x(x+2)} = 2^{(x+1)^2}$

5. $\log_3 x = 2 - x$

6. What does it mean to solve an exponential equation or a logarithmic equation by the numerical method?

7. What are the limitations of the numerical method for solving an exponential or logarithmic equation in one variable?

3 Solving Equations Graphically

We may solve an exponential or logarithmic equation graphically, using the same procedure we used previously with other equations. That is, graph two functions, defined by the left side and the right side of the equation. The x-coordinates of the points of intersection of the graphs are the solutions.

> *Solving an Exponential or Logarithmic Equation Graphically*
> To solve an exponential or logarithmic equation graphically:
>
> • Write two functions, using each side of the equation as a rule.
> • Graph both functions on the same coordinate plane by plotting points found in a table of values and connecting the points with a smooth curve, to include all values in the domain of the functions.
>
> The solutions of the equation are the x-coordinates of the points of intersection of the two graphs.
> The y-coordinates of the points of intersection of the two graphs are the values obtained for both expressions when the equation is evaluated with the solutions.

For example, solve the equation $\ln(x + 1) + \ln(x - 2) = \ln 10$ graphically.

For the equation $\ln(x + 1) + \ln(x - 2) = \ln 10$, we write the two functions $y_1 = \ln(x + 1) + \ln(x - 2)$ and $y_2 = \ln 10$.

Set up a table of values for each function.

The domain of the function y_1 is $x > 2$. (We determined this in the last objective.)

x	$\ln(x + 1) + \ln(x - 2)$	y
3	$\ln(3 + 1) + \ln(3 - 2)$	1.3863
4	$\ln(4 + 1) + \ln(4 - 2)$	2.3026
5	$\ln(5 + 1) + \ln(5 - 2)$	2.8904
6	$\ln(6 + 1) + \ln(6 - 2)$	3.3322

x	$y = \ln 10$	y
3	$y = \ln 10$	2.3026
4	$y = \ln 10$	2.3026
5	$y = \ln 10$	2.3026
6	$y = \ln 10$	2.3026

Graph.

The solution is the x-coordinate of the intersection, 4.

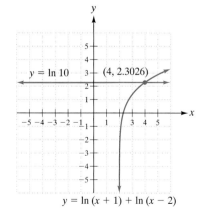

$y = \ln (x + 1) + \ln (x - 2)$

To solve an exponential or logarithmic equation graphically on your calculator:

• Rename the independent variable as x and the dependent variable as y.
• Enter the left side of the equation in Y1.
• Enter the right side of the equation in Y2.
• Graph.
• Find the points of intersection.

The solutions of the equation are the x-coordinates of the points of intersection of the two graphs.

The y-coordinates of the points of intersection of the two graphs are the values obtained for both expressions when the equation is evaluated with the solutions.

For example, solve $\ln(x + 1) + \ln(x - 2) = \ln 10$ graphically on your calculator.

Y1 = ln (x + 1) + ln (x − 2)
Y2 = ln 10

(−10, 10, −10, 10)

Let $Y1 = \ln(x + 1) + \ln(x - 2)$ and $Y2 = \ln 10$.
The solution is the x-coordinate of the intersection, 4.

Solving exponential or logarithmic equations graphically may also result in graphs that do not intersect (corresponding to a contradiction) or that coincide (corresponding to an identity).

EXAMPLE 3 Solve graphically.

a. $4^x = 2^{x+1}$ **b.** $\log x^4 - \log x = 3 \log x$
c. $5e^x + 3 = 6$ **d.** $\log_5 x = x + 5$

Calculator Graphic Solution

a. $4^x = 2^{x+1}$

Y1 = 4^x Y2 = 2^{x+1}

(−10, 10, −10, 10)

The solution is the x-coordinate of the intersection, 1.

b. $\log x^4 - \log x = 3 \log x$

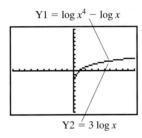

Y1 = $\log x^4 - \log x$

Y2 = $3 \log x$

(−10, 10, −10, 10)

The graphs are the same. The solution set is all real numbers greater than 0, the domain of the functions graphed.

c. $5e^x + 3 = 6$

Y1 = $5e^x + 3$ Y2 = 6

(−10, 10, −10, 10)

The solution is the x-coordinate of the intersection, or approximately −0.51.

d. $\log_5 x = x + 5$

Y2 = $x + 5$ Y1 = $\log_5 x$

$(-10, 10, -10, 10)$

The graphs do not appear to intersect. There does not appear to be a solution. ∎

Graphical Solutions of an Exponential or Logarithmic Equation
To solve an equation graphically, graph two functions, defined by the left and right sides of the equation. In viewing the graphs, one of three possibilities will occur:

One or more solutions exist. The graphs intersect. The solutions are the x-coordinates of the points of intersection.
No solution exists. The graphs do not appear to intersect.
An infinite number of solutions exists. The graphs appear to coincide. The solution set is all numbers in the domains of the graphed functions.

In conclusion, we solve an exponential or logarithmic equation by graphing two functions. When we use a calculator, this method may be used to find noninteger solutions. Also, with this method we are better able to find all the solutions because we can see the number of points of intersection. We can also determine that the graphs do not intersect and that certain equations do not have solutions.

Experiencing Algebra the Checkup Way

Solve exercises 1–5 graphically.

1. $3^{a-2} = 9^a$ **2.** $\log 4x^2 = \log x + \log 4x$ **3.** $2 \ln(x - 1) = \ln 16$

4. $2^{x(x+2)} = 2^{(x+1)^2}$ **5.** $\log_3 x = 2 - x$

6. What does it mean to solve an exponential or logarithmic equation by graphing?

7. What is the advantage of the graphing method over the numerical method for solving an exponential or logarithmic equation?

---

4 Solving Equations Algebraically

We are now ready to solve exponential and logarithmic equations algebraically. To solve these equations, we need to discuss certain properties of exponential and logarithmic equations. Complete the following set of exercises to discover two of these properties.

D I S C O V E R Y   9

Properties of Exponential and Logarithmic Equations

Complete the following statements with "true" or "false."

1. a. If $2 = 2$ is true, then $5^2 = 5^2$ is _____.
b. If $2 = 2$ is true, then $12^2 = 12^2$ is _____.
c. If $2 = 2$ is true, then $e^2 = e^2$ is _____.

Write a rule for determining a true equation using exponentials.

2. a. If $2 = 2$ is true, then $\log_5 2 = \log_5 2$ is _____.
b. If $2 = 2$ is true, then $\log_{12} 2 = \log_{12} 2$ is _____.
c. If $2 = 2$ is true, then $\ln 2 = \ln 2$ is _____.

Write a rule for determining a true equation using logarithms.

If we begin with an equation that is true and write an exponential expression for each side of the equation, using the same base and the original expressions as exponents, the result is a true equation. If we begin with an equation that is true and take the same logarithm of both expressions contained in the equation, the result is a true equation.

> *Properties of Exponential and Logarithmic Equations*
> For a positive real number a, where $a \neq 1$, and real numbers x and y, the following properties are true.
>
> **1. a.** If $a^x = a^y$, then $x = y$.
> **b.** If $x = y$ then $a^x = a^y$.
>
> For positive real numbers x, y, and a, where $a \neq 1$, the following properties are true.
>
> **2. a.** If $\log_a x = \log_a y$, then $x = y$.
> **b.** If $x = y$, then $\log_a x = \log_a y$.

First, we will discuss solving exponential equations. Our first example is an exponential equation that is written with both sides having exponential expressions with the same base. We use property 1a to solve this exponential equation by equating the exponents. For example, solve $4^x = 4^3$.

$$4^x = 4^3$$

$x = 3$ Equate the exponents of both sides.

Our second example is an exponential equation that cannot be written with both sides having exponential expressions with the same base. To solve this type of equation, we choose a logarithm, usually log or ln, and equate the logarithms of both sides using property 2b. We may need to use the inverse property of logarithms, $\log_a a^x = x$ or $\ln e^x = x$, as well as $a^{\log_a x} = x$ or $e^{\ln x} = x$, to simplify the equations. For example, solve $4^x = 5$.

$$4^x = 5$$

$\ln 4^x = \ln 5$ Equate the natural logarithms of both sides.

$x \ln 4 = \ln 5$ Power rule

$$x = \frac{\ln 5}{\ln 4}$$ Divide both sides by ln 4.

$x \approx 1.16$

> *Solving an Exponential Equation Algebraically*
> To solve an exponential equation algebraically:
>
> - Write both sides of the equation as exponential expressions with the same base, equate the exponents, and solve for the variable.
>
> or
>
> - Isolate the exponential expression, take the logarithms of both sides, and solve for the variable.

EXAMPLE 4 Solve algebraically.

a. $2^x = 32$ **b.** $e^x = 72$ **c.** $5e^{2x} = 8$

Algebraic Solution

a. $2^x = 32$

$2^x = 2^5$ Rewrite 32 with the same base as the expression on the left, or 2: $32 = 2^5$.

$x = 5$ Equate the exponents of both sides.

Check by substitution.

$$\frac{2^x \;=\; 32}{2^5 \;\big|\; 32}$$
$$32$$

The solution checks.

b. $e^x = 72$

$\ln e^x = \ln 72$ Equate the natural logarithms of both sides.

$x = \ln 72$ Inverse property of natural logarithms

$x \approx 4.277$

$Y2 = 72$ $Y1 = e^x$

Intersection
X=4.2766661 Y=72

$(-10, 10, -10, 100)$

Check by solving graphically.
The solution checks.

c. $5e^{2x} = 8$

$e^{2x} = \dfrac{8}{5}$ Divide both sides by 5.

$\ln e^{2x} = \ln \dfrac{8}{5}$ Equate the natural logarithms of both sides.

$2x = \ln \dfrac{8}{5}$ Inverse property of natural logarithms

$x = \dfrac{\ln \dfrac{8}{5}}{2}$ Divide both sides by 2.

$x \approx 0.235$

$Y1 = 5e^{2x}$ $Y2 = 8$

Intersection
X=.23500181 Y=8

$(-10, 10, -10, 10)$

Check by solving graphically.
The solution checks. ∎

We use property 2a to solve logarithmic equations by equating the arguments of logarithms with the same base. For example, solve $\ln(x + 3) = \ln 2$.

$$\ln(x + 3) = \ln 2$$

$x + 3 = 2$ Equate the arguments of the logarithms of both sides.

$x = -1$ Subtract 3 from both sides.

To solve a logarithmic equation that cannot be written with the same base, we choose an exponent and equate the exponential expressions of both sides, using property 1b. We may need to use the inverse property of exponentials, $a^{\log_a x} = x$ or $e^{\ln x} = x$, to simplify the equations. For example, solve $\log_7(2x) = 6$.

$$\log_7 2x = 6$$

$7^{\log_7(2x)} = 7^6$ Equate the exponential expressions of both sides.

$2x = 7^6$ Inverse property of exponentials

$x = \dfrac{7^6}{2}$ Divide both sides by 2.

$x = 58824.5$

We also could have solved this equation by writing an equivalent exponential equation for the given logarithmic equation. For example, $\log_7(2x) = 6$ yields

$$7^6 = 2x \qquad \frac{7^6}{2} = x \qquad x = 58824.5$$

Solving a Logarithmic Equation Algebraically
To solve a logarithmic equation algebraically:

- Write both sides of the equation with logarithmic expressions with the same base, equate the arguments, and solve for the variable.

or

- Isolate the logarithmic expression, exponentiate both sides, and solve for the variable.

EXAMPLE 5   Solve algebraically.

a. $\log x + \log(x - 2) = \log 8$ **b.** $3 \ln 2x = 9$

Algebraic Solution

$$\log x + \log(x - 2) = \log 8$$

$\log[x(x - 2)] = \log 8$ Product rule.

$x(x - 2) = 8$ Equate the arguments of the logarithms of both sides.

$$x^2 - 2x - 8 = 0$$

$$(x - 4)(x + 2) = 0$$

$x - 4 = 0$ or $x + 2 = 0$

$x = 4$ $x = -2$

a.

Y1 = log x + log (x − 2)
Y2 = log 8

Intersection
X=4   Y=.90308999

(10, 10, 10, 10)

Check by solving graphically.

According to the graph, there is only one solution, 4. Note that -2 is a restricted value and cannot be a solution.

Y2 = 9   Y1 = 3 ln 2x

Intersection
X=10.042768 Y=9

$(-10, 20, -10, 20)$

b. $3 \ln 2x = 9$

$\ln 2x = 3$ — Divide both sides by 3.

$e^{\ln 2x} = e^3$ — Write both sides as an exponential expression using base e and the original expression as an exponent.

$2x = e^3$ — Inverse property of exponentials

$x = \dfrac{e^3}{2}$ — Divide both sides by 2.

$x \approx 10.043$

Check by solving graphically.
The solution checks. ∎

It is possible that an exponential equation or a logarithmic equation does not have a solution. Also, the solution set can consist of more than one solution. These results can be determined by observing that an equation is a contradiction or an identity. For example, solve $\log x^4 - \log x = \log x^3$.

$$\log x^4 - \log x = \log x^3$$

$$\log\left(\frac{x^4}{x}\right) = \log x^3 \qquad \text{Quotient rule}$$

$$\log x^3 = \log x^3 \qquad \text{Simplify.}$$

$$x^3 = x^3 \qquad \text{Equate the arguments of the logarithms of both sides.}$$

$$x^3 - x^3 = x^3 - x^3 \qquad \text{Subtract } x^3 \text{ from both sides.}$$

$$0 = 0$$

This is an identity. The equation appears to have an infinite number of solutions. The solution set is all positive real numbers, the permissible values for the variables in the equation.

Algebraic Solutions of an Exponential or Logarithmic Equation
To solve an exponential or logarithmic equation algebraically, determine the restricted values and solve. One of three possibilities will occur:

One or more solutions exist.
No solution exists. The solution process results in a contradiction.
An infinite number of solutions exist. The solution set is all real numbers not equal to the restricted values. The solution process results in an identity.

Experiencing Algebra the Checkup Way

Solve exercises 1–7 algebraically.

1. $3^x = 81$

2. $e^x = 3$

3. $2e^x = 7$

4. $\ln 2 + 2 \ln x = \ln(6 - x)$

5. $5 + \log 3x = 7$

6. $\log 4x^2 = \log x + \log 4x$

7. $2^{x(x+2)} = 2^{(x+1)^2}$

8. What does it mean to solve an exponential or logarithmic equation in one variable by the algebraic method?

9. What advantage is there in using the algebraic method over the numerical or graphical methods to solve an exponential or logarithmic equation?

5 Modeling the Real World

In section 15.2, we determined the balance in an account earning continuously compounded interest. This is one example of a quantity that increases over time according to the **exponential growth** model. A similar **exponential decay** model represents a quantity that steadily decreases over time. Examples of these models are found in biology, chemistry, and business, as well as other physical and social sciences.

The exponential growth model is represented by the function $A(t) = A_0 e^{kt}$, where $A(t)$ is the amount present at time t, A_0 is the initial amount present, and k represents the growth constant ($k > 0$). The exponential decay model is represented by the same function except the growth factor is negative ($k < 0$).

EXAMPLE 6

According to the U.S. Census Bureau, the population of the United States in 1996 was 265.455 million people with a projected population increase to 392.031 million people in 2050.

a. Determine the growth constant.
b. Write an exponential growth function to model the U.S. population.
c. Use the function in part (b) to estimate the U.S. population 30 years after 1996, or in 2026.

Algebraic Solution

a. $A(t) = A_0 e^{kt}$ Exponential growth function; t = number of years after 1996,

$392.031 = 265.455\, e^{k(54)}$ $A(t) = 392.031$, $A_0 = 265.455$, $t = 2050 - 1996 = 54$

$\dfrac{392.031}{265.455} = e^{54k}$ Divide both sides by 265.455.

$\ln \dfrac{392.031}{265.455} = \ln e^{54k}$ Equate the natural logarithms of both sides.

$\ln \dfrac{392.031}{265.455} = 54k$ Inverse property of natural logarithms

$k = \dfrac{1}{54} \ln \dfrac{392.031}{265.455}$ Divide both sides by 54.

$k \approx 0.007$

The growth constant is about 0.007.

b. $A(t) = A_0 e^{kt}$ Exponential growth function; t = number of years after 1996

$A(t) \approx 265.455 e^{0.007t}$ $A(t)$ = population in millions, $A_0 = 265.455$ million, $k \approx 0.007$, t = number of years after 1996

c. $A(t) \approx 265.455 e^{0.007t}$

$A(30) \approx 265.455 e^{0.007(30)}$ Substitute 30 for t.

$A(30) \approx 327.4860094$

The population of the United States will be approximately 327.486 million in 2026. ∎

EXAMPLE 7

The gross national product has risen exponentially over the past years. The gross national product can be approximated by the exponential growth model $A(t) = A_0 e^{0.035t}$, where t is the number of years after 1990 and A_0 is the gross national product for 1990. Determine when the 1990 gross national product will double.

Algebraic Solution

$$A_0 = \text{the gross national product in 1990}$$

$$2A_0 = \text{double the 1990 gross national product}$$

Therefore, let $A(t) = 2A_0$ and solve for t.

$$A(t) = A_0 e^{0.035t}$$

$$2A_0 = A_0 e^{0.035t}$$

$2 = e^{0.035t}$ Divide both sides by A_0.

$\ln 2 = \ln e^{0.035t}$ Equate the natural logarithms of both sides.

$\ln 2 = 0.035t$ Inverse property of natural logarithms

$t = \dfrac{\ln 2}{0.035}$ Divide both sides by 0.035.

$t \approx 19.8$

The 1990 gross national product will double in about 20 years. ∎

If a quantity grows exponentially, the amount of time it takes to increase to twice its original amount is called the **doubling time**. Note that the amount originally present does not affect this time.

If a quantity decays exponentially, the amount of time it takes to become half of its original amount is called the **half-life**. As with doubling time, the amount originally present does not affect this time.

EXAMPLE 8 Carbon-14 (C-14) is a radioactive form of carbon found in all living organisms. After an organism dies, the C-14 present begins to decay. The rate of decay appears to be steady. The half-life of C-14 is about 5730 years. The exponential decay function can be used to approximate the amount of C-14 present t years after an organism dies.

a. Determine the decay factor.
b. If a fossil is found with $\frac{1}{3}$ the C-14 of its living form, determine the time since the organism died.

Algebraic Solution

a. A_0 = the original amount of C-14 present

$$\frac{1}{2} A_0 = \text{half the original amount of C-14 present}$$

Therefore, let $A(t) = \frac{1}{2} A_0$ and $t = 5730$, then solve for k.

$$A(t) = A_0 e^{kt}$$

$$\frac{1}{2} A_0 = A_0 e^{k \cdot 5730}$$

$$\frac{1}{2} = e^{5730k} \qquad\qquad \text{Divide both sides by } A_0.$$

$$\ln \frac{1}{2} = \ln e^{5730k} \qquad\qquad \text{Equate the natural logarithms of both sides.}$$

$$\ln \frac{1}{2} = 5730k \qquad\qquad \text{Inverse property of natural logarithms}$$

$$k = \left(\ln \frac{1}{2} \right)\left(\frac{1}{5730} \right) \qquad\qquad \text{Divide both sides by 5730.}$$

$$k \approx -0.000121$$

The decay constant is about -0.000121.

b. $\dfrac{1}{3} A_0$ = one-third of the amount of the original C-14

$$A(t) = A_0 e^{kt}$$

$$\frac{1}{3} A_0 \approx A_0 e^{-0.000121t}$$

$$\frac{1}{3} \approx e^{-0.000121t} \qquad\qquad \text{Divide both sides by } A_0.$$

$$\ln \frac{1}{3} \approx \ln e^{-0.000121t} \qquad\qquad \text{Equate the natural logarithms of both sides.}$$

$$\ln \frac{1}{3} \approx -0.000121t \qquad\qquad \text{Inverse property of natural logarithms}$$

$$t \approx \left(\ln \frac{1}{3} \right)\left(\frac{1}{-0.000121} \right) \qquad\qquad \text{Divide both sides by } -0.000121.$$

$$t \approx 9079.44$$

The organism has been dead about 9079 years. ∎

Application

According to Newton's law of cooling, the temperature T of a body t minutes after it is placed in surroundings having a constant temperature T_0 is determined by the function $T(t) = T_0 + Ce^{-kt}$, where C is the difference between the initial temperature and the surrounding temperature and k is the cooling constant.

a. Boiling water (100°C) is placed in a freezer at 0°C. After 25 minutes the water temperature is 50°C. Determine the constant of cooling.

b. Determine the temperature of the water after 2 hours.

Discussion

a. $T(t) = T_0 + Ce^{-kt}$

$50 = 0 + 100e^{-k \cdot 25}$ Substitute 50 for $T(t)$, 0 for T_0, 100 for C, and 25 for t.

$50 = 100e^{-25k}$

$\dfrac{1}{2} = e^{-25k}$ Divide both sides by 100.

$\ln \dfrac{1}{2} = \ln e^{-25k}$ Equate the natural logarithms of both sides.

$\ln \dfrac{1}{2} = -25k$ Inverse property of natural logarithms

$k = -\dfrac{1}{25} \ln \dfrac{1}{2}$ Divide both sides by −25.

$k \approx 0.0277$

The constant of cooling is about 0.0277.

b. $T(120) \approx 0 + 100e^{-0.0277(120)}$ Substitute 120 minutes for t, 0 for T_0, 100 for C, and −0.0277 for k.

$T(120) \approx 3.6$

The temperature is about 3.6°C after 2 hours. ∎

Experiencing Algebra the Checkup Way

1. The U.S. Census Bureau estimated the total female population of the United States to be 127.798 million on July 1, 1990. This population had grown to 136.570 million on July 1, 1997. Use the exponential growth model to develop a mathematical model to estimate the total female population t years after 1990. What does the model predict the total female population will be in 2020, 30 years from 1990?

2. The gross national product growth model is

$A(t) = A_0 e^{0.035t}$,

where t is the number of years after 1990 and A_0 is the gross national product for 1990. When will the gross national product triple in value?

3. Radium-226 has a half-life of 1620 years. Determine the decay factor of radium-226. How long will it take for a store of radium-226 to diminish to 90 percent of its original amount?

4. Use Newton's law of cooling to determine the time it would take boiling water to cool to 20°C when placed in a freezer at 0°C.

PROBLEM SET 15.5

Experiencing Algebra the Exercise Way

Identify each equation as exponential, logarithmic, or neither.

1. $-3 + \log x^2 = 1$ **2.** $2e^x - 5 = 3$ **3.** $e^3 + x = 2x - 1$ **4.** $\log x^3 + 3 = 5$

5. $e^{2x} - 1 = 5$ **6.** $\log 8 + x = \log 10$ **7.** $x = \log 4 + \log 7$ **8.** $x + e^2 = 1$

Solve exercises 9–70.

9. $5^{2x} = 625$

10. $3^{x+2} = 81$

11. $e^t = 2$

12. $e^{3t} + 5 = 7$

13. $5^x = 1$

14. $3^m = 0.5$

15. $3e^{-x} = 2$

16. $e^{-2x} + 1 = 5$

17. $(2^{3x})(2^5) = 2^8$

18. $(5^x)(5^{x+3}) = 5^4$

19. $2^x = 2^{3x-6}$

20. $e^{3x-1} = e^{2x+3}$

21. $5^{2x(x-2)} = 5^{3(x-1)}$

22. $7^{a^2+4} = 7^{5a}$

23. $e^{x(x-2)} = e^{x+10}$

24. $3^{2x(x+6)} = 3^{5(x+3)}$

25. $3^{x+x(x-3)} = 3^{(x-1)^2}$

26. $5^{(x+3)^2} = 5^{x(x+6)}$

27. $8^{5(x-3)} = 8^{4(x-2)}8^{(x-7)}$

28. $e^{a+7} = e^{3a+4}e^{3-2a}$

29. $3^{3x} = 9^{x+1}$

30. $5^{x+7} = 25^{x-2}$

31. $5^{2b+5} = 5^4$

32. $7^{3c-1} = 7^{c+9}$

33. $3^{2x^2} \cdot 3^{5x} = 27$

34. $5^{3x^2} \cdot 5^{5x} = 25$

35. $e^{0.5x} = 4$

36. $10^{1.5x} = 8$

37. $(3.5)^x = 12$

38. $(4.3)^z - 5 = 1$

39. $\log_5 c = 5$

40. $3 \log_2 b = 12$

41. $\log x = 0$

42. $\log x = 1$

43. $\ln z = 0$

44. $\ln y = 2$

45. $\log_3 k = 2$

46. $2 \log_5 x = 8$

47. $\log_5 x = -3$

48. $\log_3 k + 5 = 1$

49. $\log_3(a + 2) = 2$

50. $\log_2(3a - 7) = 3$

51. $2 \ln x = 1$

52. $-5 \ln x = 10$

53. $\log x + 4 = 2$

54. $3 \log x - 5 = 1$

55. $5 \ln z + 4 = 4$

56. $\ln x + 2 = 3$

57. $\ln x + \ln(x + 1) = \ln 12$

58. $\ln x + \ln(2x - 5) = \ln 25$

59. $2 \ln(p - 5) = \ln 9$

60. $\ln 16 = 2 \ln(x - 7)$

61. $\log 2x + \log 3x = \log 6 + 2 \log x$

62. $3 \log x - \log x = 2 \log x$

63. $\ln x + \ln(x + 2) = 2 \ln(x + 2)$

64. $2 \ln(x + 2) = \ln(x + 2) + \ln 2$

65. $\log(x + 4) - \log x = \log 2$

66. $\log(x + 3) - \log x = \log 5$

67. $\log x - \log(x + 6) = -1$

68. $\log_2 x - \log_2(x + 6) = -2$

69. $\log_3(x + 16) - \log_3 x = 2$

70. $\ln(x^2 - 3x + 2) - \ln(x - 1) = \ln 5$

71. The U.S. Census Bureau reported the total male population of the United States to be 121.600 million on July 1, 1990. It reported that the population had grown to 131.005 million on July 1, 1997. Use the exponential growth function to model the growth in the male population since 1990. What does the model predict the male population will be in the year 2025?

72. In 1984, the number of households with computers was 6.980 million. This number grew exponentially to 22.605 million in 1993. Use the growth function to model the growth in households with computers since 1984. If this growth continues, what does the model predict this number will be in the year 2010?

73. Per capita income in the United States has grown exponentially over the last decade. Per capita income can be estimated by the growth model $A(t) = A_0 e^{0.0307t}$, where t is the number of years after 1990 and A_0 is per capita income for 1990. If the trend continues, in what year will per capita income double its 1990 value?

74. Using the growth model in exercise 73, in what year will per capita income increase to 1.5 times its value in 1990?

75. Uranium-238 has a half-life of 4.5 billion years. Determine the decay factor of uranium-238. How long will it take for a sample of uranium-238 to diminish to 98% of its original amount?

76. Using the information in exercise 75, determine how long it will take for a sample of uranium-238 to diminish to 90% of its original amount.

Experiencing Algebra the Calculator Way

Graphically solve the equation $e^{x(x+2)} = e^{(x+1)^2}$ using your calculator. If you enter the expressions as shown below, you may notice that the calculator indicates that the graphs cross at $x \approx -1.414214$.

However, if you attempt to solve the same equation algebraically, there is no solution. The reason may be inappropriate placement of parentheses when entering the expressions into the calculator. Let's explore the ways you can enter the right-hand expression into your calculator. When you press the e^x key, the calculator starts a set of parentheses for you. If you follow this with the expression $x + 1$, close the parentheses, and square it, the calculator assumes that this is equivalent to the expression $\left(e^{(x+1)}\right)^2$. To instruct the calculator that the expression $(x + 1)$ is to be squared, you must enclose the squared expression in another pair of parentheses: $e^{((x+1)^2)}$. To verify this, enter all three expressions into your calculator and graph each separately, then compare the graphs. The keystrokes needed to enter all three follow.

| Y= | 2nd | e^x | X, T, θ, n | + | 1 |) | x^2 | ENTER |

| (| 2nd | e^x | X, T, θ, n | + | 1 |) |) | x^2 | ENTER |

| 2nd | e^x | (| X, T, θ, n | + | 1 |) | x^2 |) | GRAPH |

You should notice that the graphs of Y1 and Y2 are identical. This indicates that when you square an exponent of e, the calculator assumes that the entire exponential expression is to be squared. The graph of Y3 is different from the other two. This indicates that if you want the exponent of e to be squared, you must use an additional set of parentheses to enclose the entire squared exponent. Be careful that you do this. Remember that it is safer to use an additional set of parentheses to be sure the calculator behaves as you wish. Just be sure that the parentheses do not change the meaning of your expression.

 Experiencing Algebra the Group Way

Many situations may fit into the exponential growth model. Some of these include the spread of the AIDS virus, world population growth, growth of bacteria, sales of compact discs, sales of computers, growth of the value of stocks or portfolios, values of collectibles such as art or sports cards, and so forth. Have each member of the group collect data on a variable that may be experiencing exponential growth. You can search the statistical abstracts and reference books in your library. Then work together to develop a mathematical model to represent the growth. Check the model against the data you collected. Finally, use the model to predict a future value of the variable. Share your results.

Experiencing Algebra the Write Way

In this section, you saw examples of exponential growth models and exponential decay models. Describe the two models and when it would be appropriate to use either. Then describe a situation that would be an appropriate application of each model.

CHAPTER 15	Summary

After completing this chapter, you should be able to define in your own words the following key terms, definitions, properties, and rules.

Terms
inverse
one-to-one function
line of symmetry
exponential function
natural base
natural exponential function
logarithm of x with base a
logarithmic function
common logarithm
natural logarithm
change-of-base formula
expand
condense
argument
logarithmic equation in one
    variable
exponential equation in one
    variable

exponential growth
exponential decay
doubling time
half-life

Definitions
exponential function
logarithm of x with base a
logarithmic function with base a
common logarithm
natural logarithm
common logarithmic function
natural logarithmic function

Properties
Characteristics of an exponential
    function and its graph
Properties of logarithms
Properties of natural logarithms

Characteristics of a logarithmic
    function and its graph
Properties of exponential and
    logarithmic equations

Rules
Horizontal-line test
Change-of-base formula
Product rule of logarithms
Quotient rule of logarithms
Power rule of logarithms
Solving an exponential or logarithmic
    equation numerically
Solving an exponential or logarithmic
    equation graphically
Solving an exponential equation
    algebraically
Solving a logarithmic equation
    algebraically

CHAPTER 15	Review

Reflections
1. What do we mean by the inverse of a relation?
2. How can you construct the inverse of a relation?
3. What is a one-to-one function?
4. What is an exponential function?
5. What is a logarithmic function?
6. What are the two most frequently used values for the base of a logarithmic function?
7. State the following rules of logarithms:
    a. The product rule   **b.** The quotient rule   **c.** The power rule

15.1
Determine the inverse of each relation.

  1. $h = \{(2, 4.5), (4, 3.5), (6, 2.5), (8, 1.5), (10, 0.5)\}$
  2. $y = 3x - 9$ **3.** $y = x^2 + 1$ **4.** $y = x^3 - 1$

Determine whether the inverse of each function is a function.

5. $P = \{(9, 1), (8, 2), (7, 3), (6, 1), (5, 2), (4, 3)\}$

6. $Q = \{(1, 9), (2, 8), (3, 7), (4, 6), (5, 5), (6, 4), (7, 3)\}$

Determine whether each graph represents a one-to-one function.

7.

8.

9.

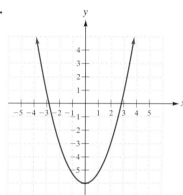

Determine the inverse of each function. Sketch the graph of the function, its inverse, and the line of symmetry.

10. $f(x) = \dfrac{3}{4}x - 3$

11. $y = x^3 + 8$

Write a function to represent each situation. Determine the inverse of the function and interpret what the inverse function represents.

12. Motomo is paid $570 per week plus 3% commission on the value of all sales she handles. What is Motomo's weekly income?

13. Valecia can complete an average of 15 algebra problems in one hour. What is the average number of problems she can complete in a given number of hours?

15.2

Determine whether each function is an exponential function.

14. $f(x) = 2^x$

15. $y = x^2$

Evaluate the function $g(x) = 1.21^x$ at the given values.

16. $g(2)$

17. $g(-1)$

18. $g(0)$

19. $g\left(\dfrac{1}{2}\right)$

20. $g(0.3)$

21. $g(\sqrt{2})$

In exercises 22–24, graph each function.

22. $f(x) = 5^x - 1$

23. $g(x) = 9^{(1/2)x}$

24. $y = 2e^{0.5x}$

25. Paul invested his holiday bonus of $1000 into an account that paid 4% interest compounded annually. Write a function for the total value of his investment. Graph the function. How much was the investment worth after 4 years?

26. The mathematical model $y = (78.16)1.115^t$ predicts national health expenditures in the United States, where t is the number of years after 1970 and y is total expenditures in billions of dollars. What does the model predict that expenditures will be for the year 2005?

15.3

Determine the logarithmic function that is the inverse of each exponential function.

27. $h(x) = 8^x$

28. $A(x) = Ae^{kx}$

Evaluate.

29. $\log 100$

30. $\log_2 16$

31. $\log_3 \dfrac{1}{27}$

32. $\log 1.5$

33. $\ln e^4$

34. $\ln 10$

35. $\ln e^{-2}$

36. $\log \dfrac{3}{5}$

37. $\log_5 15$

Create a table of values for each function and graph.

38. $y = \log_3 x$

39. $f(x) = \ln(x - 2)$

The pH value of a substance is defined by the function

$$pH = -\log[H^+],$$

where $[H^+]$ is the hydrogen ion concentration in moles per liter. Use this relation to answer the following questions.

40. The hydrogen ion concentration of lemon juice is 6.2×10^{-3} moles per liter. What is its pH value?

41. The pH value of blood is typically 7.4. What is its hydrogen ion concentration?

15.4

Write each logarithmic expression in expanded form.

42. $\log 2x^4$

43. $\log_7 \dfrac{7x}{y}$

44. $\ln 25x^2 y^3 z$

45. $\ln \dfrac{\sqrt[3]{2x^2 y}}{\sqrt{yz}}$

In exercises 46–49, write each logarithmic expression in condensed form.

46. $\log(x - 3) + \log(x + 3)$

47. $5 \ln x - 3 \ln y$

48. $\dfrac{1}{3} \log x - \dfrac{1}{2} \log y$

49. $\log ab - \log bc + \log cd$

50. Money invested at a continuously compounded interest rate r will grow to k times the original investment in t years, where $t = \frac{\ln k}{r}$. How long will it take an investment to triple in value if the annual interest rate is 6%?

15.5

Identify each equation as exponential, logarithmic, or neither.

51. $e^x + 5 = 7$

52. $\ln 7 - x = \ln 3$

53. $\log x^2 + 2 = \log x$

54. $x = e^3 - 1$

55. $2^x + 7 = 2^{3x}$

56. $y = \log_2 5 - e^2$

Solve exercises 57–75.

57. $3^{x+1} = 243$

58. $e^{-5t} - 2 = 3$

59. $12^a = 1$

60. $(3^{2x})(3^5) = 3^8$

61. $e^{2x(x-3)} = e^{2(x-2)(x-1)}$

62. $4^{x^2+2x} = 64$

63. $5^{2x-3} = 5^{x+9} \cdot 5^{x-12}$

64. $10^{2.3x} = 4$

65. $\log_7 a = 49$ **66.** $5\log_3 x = 45$ **67.** $\ln z = 1$ **68.** $\log b = 0$

69. $\log k = -3$ **70.** $5 + \log_2 x = 3$ **71.** $3\ln x = 1$ **72.** $\ln(2x^2 + 7x) = \ln 15$

73. $2\log(x - 2) = \log 9$ **74.** $\log x + \log(x + 4) = 2\log(x + 2)$ **75.** $7\ln x - \ln x^3 = 4\ln x$

76. Census data reported that the total expenditures for health care were \$697.5 billion in 1990 and had grown exponentially to \$949.4 billion in 1994. Use the growth function $A(t) = A_0 e^{kt}$ to model the growth in health care expenditures since 1990. If this growth continues, what will be the estimated health care expenditures in the years 2000, 2005, and 2010?

77. The decay function for carbon-14 (C-14) is approximated as $A(t) = A_0 e^{kt}$, where $k \approx -0.000121$. If skeletal remains are found with $\frac{2}{3}$ of the C-14 of the living form, determine the time since the body's demise.

CHAPTER 15	**Mixed Review**

Evaluate.

1. $\log 0.001$ **2.** $\log_7 343$ **3.** $\log_2 \dfrac{1}{64}$

4. $\log 5.1$ **5.** $\ln e^{-3}$ **6.** $\ln 100$

7. $\ln e$ **8.** $\ln \dfrac{4}{7}$ **9.** $\log_3 36$

Write each logarithmic expression in expanded form.

10. $\log 3x^2 y$ **11.** $\log_3 \dfrac{9a}{b}$ **12.** $\ln 100p^3 q^2 r$ **13.** $\log \dfrac{\sqrt[5]{6x^3}}{\sqrt{xy}}$

Write each logarithmic expression in condensed form.

14. $\log(x^2 - 9) - \log(x + 3)$ **15.** $2\log c - 5\log d$

16. $\dfrac{1}{2}\ln x - 3\ln y$ **17.** $\log 2xy - \log xz + \log 3yz$

Determine the inverse of each relation.

18. $y = 5 - x$ **19.** $y = 1 - x^2$ **20.** $y = 4 - x^3$

21. $y = 2 - \dfrac{4}{5}x$ **22.** $m(x) = 5^x$ **23.** $G(x) = ab^x$, a and b are constants.

Evaluate the function $g(t) = 1 + \left(\dfrac{4}{9}\right)^t$ at the given values.

24. $g(3)$ **25.** $g(-1)$ **26.** $g(0)$

27. $g\left(\dfrac{1}{2}\right)$ **28.** $g(1.5)$ **29.** $g(-\sqrt{3})$

Graph each function.

30. $m(x) = 3^x - 2$ **31.** $k(x) = 8^{(1/3)x}$ **32.** $y = -2e^{0.4x}$ **33.** $y = \log_2 x - 2$

34. $g(x) = \log(x + 1)$

Solve.

35. $\log_6 b = 216$

36. $2 \log_3 z = 6$

37. $\log z = 1$

38. $\ln b = 0$

39. $\log 2m = -4$

40. $-1 + \log_3 x = 4$

41. $2 \log x = 1$

42. $\log(2x^2 + 3x) = \log 9$

43. $2 \ln(x + 3) = \ln 4$

44. $\log 4x + \log(x + 1) = 2 \log(2x + 1)$ **45.** $2 \log a + \log a^4 = 6 \log a$

46. $5^{x-3} = 125$

47. $e^{-t} + 4 = 5$

48. $7^a = e$

49. $(6^7)(6^{3x}) = 6^2$

50. $e^{x(x+6)} = e^{(x+5)(x+1)}$

51. $2^{x^2} \cdot 2^{-3x} = 16$

52. $7^{2x-6} = (7^{3x-11})(7^{5-x})$

53. $10^{1.8x} = 9$

In exercises 54 and 55, write a function to represent each situation. Determine the inverse of the function and interpret what the inverse function represents.

54. Diana earns $1200 per month plus 2.5% commission on all of her sales at a furniture gallery. What is Diana's monthly income?

55. Carlyle averages 95 kilometers per hour on his auto trip through Germany. How far can he travel in a given number of hours?

56. Kristin invested her inheritance of $8500 into an account that paid 6.5% interest compounded annually. Write a function for the total value of her investment. Graph the function. How much was the investment worth after 10 years?

57. The mathematical model $y = 2.490e^{0.0673t}$ predicts the number of basic and cable TV systems in the United States, where t is the number of years after 1970 and y is the number of systems, in thousands. What does the model predict the number of systems will be for the year 2010, assuming the same rate of growth? Does it seem reasonable to assume that the number of these systems will continue to grow this way?

The pH value of a substance is defined by the function

$$pH = -\log[H^+],$$

*where $[H^+]$ is the hydrogen ion concentration in moles per liter.
    Use this relation to answer exercises 58–59.*

58. The hydrogen ion concentration of apple juice is 1.6×10^{-4} moles per liter. What is its pH value?

59. The pH value of gastric juice is typically 1.6. What is its hydrogen ion concentration?

60. Money invested at a continuously compounded interest rate r will grow to k times the original investment in t years, where $t = \frac{\ln k}{r}$. How long will it take an investment to double in value if the annual interest rate is 5.6%?

61. Revenues for public elementary and secondary schools totaled $96.9 billion in 1980 and grew exponentially to $207.8 billion in 1990. Use the growth function $A(t) = A_0 e^{kt}$ to model the growth in revenues since 1980. If this growth continues, what will be the estimated revenues in the years 2000, 2005, and 2010?

62. The decay function for carbon-14 (C-14) is approximated as $A(t) = A_0 e^{kt}$ where $k \approx -0.000121$. If the remains of a living organism are found with 40% of the C-14 of its living form, determine the time since the organism died.

CHAPTER 15 | **Test**

Test-Taking Tips

If math is your most challenging subject, make sure to study it before all other subjects. Do not leave it until the last. You must study math when you are most alert and fresh. You will do better and you will recall more of what you have studied. It has been shown that if you take a few minutes' break every half-hour while you are studying, it will refresh you and help you retain more of the information. Begin each study session with a review of previous material studied. This will keep your math skills polished. Read your text before attempting to do the assigned exercises. Always check your answers with those provided in the text. If you cannot reconcile your answer with that in the text, be sure to mark the exercise so that you can ask about it in class. Try to look ahead at some of the material that will be presented in the next class, so that it will not be difficult to understand when your instructor presents it.

1. Graph the function $f(x) = x^3$, its inverse, and the line of symmetry.

2. Graph $f(x) = 2^x + 1$.

3. Graph $g(x) = \ln(x + 2)$.

4. Find the inverse of the function $F(x) = 2x - 8$.

Evaluate $g(x) = 16^{(1/2)x}$ at the given values.

5. $g(-1)$ **6.** $g(0)$ **7.** $g(4)$

8. $g(0.3)$ **9.** $g(\sqrt{3})$

Write the expanded form of each expression.

10. $\log 3x^2 y^3 z$ **11.** $\log_3 \dfrac{9a^2}{b}$

Write the condensed form of each expression.

12. $2 \log x + \log(x - 4)$ **13.** $\dfrac{1}{2} \ln x - 2 \ln y$

14. Solve $9^x = 3^{x+1}$

 a. numerically. **b.** graphically. **c.** algebraically.

Solve exercises 15–18.

15. $(2^{3x})(2^{-2}) = 8$ **16.** $2 \ln a = 3.1$ **17.** $2 \log x + \log x^4 = 6 \log x$ **18.** $9^x = 5$

19. Pedro earns $400 per week plus a commission of 3% of all sales he makes at the appliance store.

 a. Write a function for his total weekly income.

 b. Determine the inverse of the function.

 c. Interpret what the inverse of the function represents.

20. Kate discovered a bank deposit book that her deceased grandfather had owned. The bank book indicated that he had made a single deposit of $2000 into an account that paid 5% interest compounded annually. Write a function for the amount of money that is in the account after x years. What was the investment worth after 20 years?

21. Money invested at a continuously compounded interest rate r will grow to k times the original investment in t years, where $t = \frac{\ln k}{r}$. How long will it take an investment to double in value if the annual interest rate is 7.5%?

22. What do we mean by the common logarithm of a number?

CHAPTERS 1–15 | Cumulative Review

Simplify and write with positive exponents.

1. $5^{-2}x^0y^2$

2. $(-2x^{-3}y^2)^2$

3. $\left(\dfrac{4x^{3/4}}{x^{-1/4}}\right)^2$

Simplify.

4. $(3.2a^2 - 2.6ab + 1.7b^2) - (4a^2 + 2.6ab - b^2)$

5. $(4.5x^2y)(-2y^2z)$

6. $(3x + 2y)(3x - 2y)$

7. $(2x + 6)(2x - 3)$

8. $(x - 4)^2$

9. $\dfrac{25x^2y^4z^2}{-5xyz}$

10. $\dfrac{2r^2s + 4rs - 8s^2}{2rs}$

11. $\dfrac{x^2 - x - 6}{x^2 - 9}$

12. $\dfrac{x}{x + 2} + \dfrac{3}{x - 2} + \dfrac{x - 1}{x^2 - 4}$

13. $\dfrac{1}{x + 4} - \dfrac{x}{x - 2}$

14. $\dfrac{2m - 3}{m + 1} \cdot \dfrac{2m^2 + 5m + 3}{4m^2 - 9}$

15. $\dfrac{16x}{y^3 + y^2 - 12y} \div \dfrac{4x^2y}{y^2 - y - 20}$

16. $\sqrt{18x} - \sqrt{50x} + 4\sqrt{8x}$

17. $\sqrt[3]{16a^2b^2} \cdot \sqrt[3]{8ab^2}$

18. $(\sqrt{2} - \sqrt{3})(\sqrt{2} + \sqrt{3})$

19. $\dfrac{\sqrt{32xy^2z}}{\sqrt{8x^3y}}$

20. $\dfrac{\sqrt{x} + 4}{\sqrt{x} - 3}$

21. $x^{2/3}(x^{3/4} - x^{1/3})$

Factor completely, if possible.

22. $25m^2 - 36n^2$

23. $2x^2 - 4x - 16$

24. $x^2 + 6x - 6$

Graph and label as indicated. Determine the domain and range of each function.

25. $f(x) = \dfrac{2}{3}x + 1$; three points on the graph

26. $y = x^2 + 5x + 4$; vertex, y-intercept, x-intercept, enough points to determine the curve, and the axis of symmetry

27. $y = \dfrac{x^2 + 4}{x + 2}$; enough points to determine the curve

28. $h(x) = \sqrt{x - 5}$; enough points to determine the curve

29. $g(x) = x^{2/3} + 3$; enough points to determine the curve

30. $y = 3^x$; enough points to determine the curve

31. $f(x) = \ln(x - 3)$; enough points to determine the curve

Solve.

32. $2(x - 5) - (x + 4) = 2x - 8$

33. $2(x + 3.1) = (x - 4.2) + (x - 6)$

34. $x^2 - 2x - 12 = 12$

35. $x^2 - 5x + 9 = 0$

36. $\dfrac{x + 1}{x + 2} = \dfrac{x - 1}{x + 3}$

37. $4\sqrt{x + 1} - 14 = -2$

38. $e^{2x-4} = e^{x(x-2)}$

39. $2\log_3 x = \log_3 5$

Solve. Write the solution set in interval notation.

40. $2x - 3 < 3(x - 4)$

41. $x^2 + 2x \geq 2$

Solve.

42. $3x - 2y = 4$
$x + y = 8$

In exercises 43–44, write a linear equation for a line that satisfies the given conditions.

43. Passes through the points $(3, -1)$ and $(-2, 2)$

44. Is perpendicular to $x + 4y = 2.3$ and passes through $(-2, 1)$

45. Write a quadratic equation for a curve that passes through the points $(0, -6)$, $(-4, 0)$, and $(1, 0)$.

46. Given $f(x) = \dfrac{2}{3}x + 6$, find $f^{-1}(x)$.

47. Happy Recipe Company bought a rebuilt copier for \$525 to reproduce its latest recipe book. If it costs \$5 per book for materials to print the books and each book sells for \$15, determine the break-even point where the revenue exceeds the cost.

48. Nathan has 15 feet of landscaping timbers to place diagonally across his rectangular flower garden. If he wants to use all of the timbers and have the length of the garden be 3 feet more than the width, determine the dimensions of the garden.

49. A tank is drained by two separate drains. When the drain on the left is used alone, it takes 4 hours to drain the tank. When the drain on the right is used alone, it takes 6.5 hours to drain the tank. How long will it take to drain the tank if both drains are used? (Round your answer to the nearest tenth of an hour.)

50. If money is continuously compounded, the amount in the account will grow to k times the original investment in $t = \frac{\ln k}{r}$ years when the annual rate of interest is r. How long will it take the amount invested to triple if the annual interest rate is 4.5%?

Answers to Selected Exercises

Chapter 1

PROBLEM SET 1.1

Experiencing Algebra the Exercise Way

1. (a) integer, rational   **(b)** natural, whole, integer, rational   **(c)** natural, whole, integer, rational
(d) rational   **2. (a)** natural, whole, integer, rational   **(b)** rational   **(c)** natural, whole, integer, rational
(d) rational   **3. (a)** whole, integer, rational   **(b)** rational   **(c)** rational   **(d)** rational
4. (a) natural, whole, integer, rational   **(b)** integer, rational   **(c)** rational   **(d)** rational

5. $3; 1.75; -2; -1.25$ **6.** $1\frac{1}{8}; -\frac{3}{4}; -2; 1\frac{7}{8}; 1\frac{3}{4}$ **7.** -345.67 **8.** -17 **9.** $5; -5; -2$ **10.** $2; -13$

11. 5 and 6   **12.** -2 and -1 **13.**

14.

15. $<$ **16.** $<$ **17.** $>$ **18.** $<$ **19.** $>$ **20.** $>$
21. $<$ **22.** $<$ **23.** $<$ **24.** $>$ **25.** $>$ **26.** $<$
27. $=$ **28.** $=$ **29.** $>$ **30.** $<$ **31.** $<$ **32.** $>$

33. T   **34.** F   **35.** F   **36.** F   **37.** F   **38.** T   **39.** F   **40.** F   **41.** F   **42.** F   **43.** F
44. F   **45.** F   **46.** T   **47.** T   **48.** F   **49.** F   **50.** T   **51.** $0.295 < 0.7$ **52.** $0.06 > -2.56$

53. $-1 > -5$ **54.** $24 < 25$ **55.** $0.4 = \frac{2}{5}$ **56.** $-\frac{43}{50} = -0.86$ **57.** 15.34 **58.** 25 **59.** 15.34

60. 25 **61.** $3\frac{1}{3}$ **62.** 25 **63.** $3\frac{1}{3}$ **64.** 25 **65.** -23 **66.** -25 **67.** -23 **68.** -25 **69.** -15

70. $-\frac{1}{2}$ **71.** 25 **72.** 35 **73.** $-\frac{3}{2}$ **74.** $-\frac{5}{4}$ **75.** loss of $712 million $= -712$

76. loss of $8.28\% = -8.28$

Experiencing Algebra the Calculator Way

1. F   **2.** F   **3.** F   **4.** F   **5.** F   **6.** F   **7.** F   **8.** T   **9.** T   **10.** F   **11.** F   **12.** T   **13.** F
14. T

PROBLEM SET 1.2

Experiencing Algebra the Exercise Way

1. 2   **2.** 12   **3.** -13 **4.** -15 **5.** -31 **6.** -58 **7.** 0   **8.** 0   **9.** 39   **10.** -33 **11.** -547
12. 682   **13.** 6.66   **14.** 3.16   **15.** -1.3 **16.** -2.8 **17.** 1.37   **18.** 2.09   **19.** -3.37 **20.** -11.4

21. -1.25 **22.** -23.5 **23.** 0   **24.** 0   **25.** $-\frac{11}{10}$ **26.** $-\frac{19}{28}$ **27.** $-\frac{11}{18}$ **28.** $-\frac{7}{24}$ **29.** $\frac{4}{9}$

30. $\frac{1}{2}$ **31.** $\frac{2}{3}$ **32.** $-\frac{3}{4}$ **33.** 0   **34.** 0   **35.** $\frac{11}{12}$ **36.** $2\frac{13}{15}$ **37.** $-3\frac{3}{4}$ **38.** $-2\frac{1}{2}$ **39.** -64

40. -98 **41.** -9 **42.** 35   **43.** -7.01 **44.** -7.01 **45.** $-\frac{5}{12}$ **46.** $-\frac{17}{20}$ **47.** 1241   **48.** -355

49. $1500 + 150 + 150 + 150 + (-75) + (-500) + (-200) + 12 = 1187$; The net balance of Lindsay's account is \$1187. **50.** $500 + 75 + 50 + 100 + (-125) + 35 = 635$; The balance of the account is \$635.
51. $-148{,}561 + 5{,}253{,}628 = 5{,}105{,}067$; The census for 1990 of Cook County, Illinois was 5,105,067.
52. $-226{,}156 + 2{,}337{,}843 = 2{,}111{,}687$; The census for 1990 of Wayne County, Michigan was 2,111,687.

53. $8 + \left(-4\frac{3}{4}\right) + 22\frac{1}{2} = 25\frac{3}{4}$; Heath had a net gain of $25\frac{3}{4}$ yards.

54. $5\frac{1}{4} + \left(-6\frac{1}{2}\right) + 32 + 2\frac{1}{4} = 33$; Heath had a net gain of 33 yards.

55. $-255 + 375 + (-575) + 1525 = 1070$; Karin is \$1070 above her quota because 1070 is a positive number.
56. $385 + 285 + (-555) + (-405) + 265 + 575 = 550$; Karin is \$550 above her quota.
57. $-2.5 + 1.25 + (-1.8) + (-2.5) = -5.55$; Beth lost 5.55 pounds in four weeks.
58. $-3.5 + (-2.6) + 2.25 + 0 = -3.85$; Brent lost 3.85 pounds in four weeks.
59. $378 + 322 + 218 = 918$; Liu drove 918 miles. **60.** $33.6 + 25.9 + 28.3 = 87.8$; The tour was 87.8 miles.
61. $25 + 8 + (-12) + 17 = 38$; Julio had 38 chips at the end of the third hand.

62. $72.38 + (-5.95) + (-12.75) + 35 + (-7.81) = 80.87$; Julianne has \$80.87 in the petty cash fund at the end of the day. **63.** $\frac{1}{2} + \frac{1}{4} + 1 + 1 + \frac{1}{2} = 3\frac{1}{4}$; The recipe requires $3\frac{1}{4}$ cups of dry ingredients.

64. $1\frac{1}{4} + \frac{3}{4} + \frac{1}{2} + 2\frac{1}{4} = 4\frac{3}{4}$; The pattern uses $4\frac{3}{4}$ yards of material.

Experiencing Algebra the Calculator Way

A **1.** $7\frac{6}{7}$ **2.** $-2\frac{69}{113}$ **3.** $2\frac{253}{487}$ **4.** $-5\frac{13}{19}$ **B** **1.** $-7\frac{31}{3036}$ **2.** $-3\frac{889}{3036}$ **3.** $3\frac{889}{3036}$

4. $7\frac{31}{3036}$ **5.** $37\frac{213}{323}$ **6.** $-5\frac{281}{323}$ **7.** $5\frac{281}{323}$ **8.** $-37\frac{213}{323}$ **9.** 329.985 **10.** -545.9315

11. -329.9185 **12.** 545.9315 **13.** $1{,}986{,}482$ **14.** $199{,}532$ **15.** $-199{,}532$ **16.** $-1{,}986{,}482$

PROBLEM SET 1.3

Experiencing Algebra the Exercise Way

1. -16 **2.** -46 **3.** 13 **4.** -15 **5.** -7 **6.** 14 **7.** 30 **8.** -16 **9.** 65 **10.** 57
11. -547 **12.** 682 **13.** 3.7 **14.** -8.2 **15.** -6.83 **16.** 5.71 **17.** 1.17 **18.** 4.4 **19.** -1.25
20. 23.5 **21.** 2.46 **22.** 5.4 **23.** -1.26 **24.** -3.04 **25.** $-\frac{1}{10}$ **26.** $\frac{5}{28}$ **27.** $-\frac{17}{18}$ **28.** $-\frac{11}{24}$
29. $\frac{13}{9}$ **30.** $\frac{7}{6}$ **31.** $\frac{2}{3}$ **32.** $\frac{3}{4}$ **33.** $\frac{2}{3}$ **34.** $-\frac{6}{7}$ **35.** $-\frac{18}{7}$ **36.** $-\frac{7}{5}$ **37.** $\frac{3}{2}$ **38.** $\frac{9}{8}$
39. $-\frac{16}{5}$ **40.** $-\frac{10}{3}$ **41.** $-\frac{4}{3}$ **42.** $-\frac{7}{4}$ **43.** 38 **44.** -6 **45.** 43 **46.** 29 **47.** 9.21
48. 16.32 **49.** 14.3 **50.** 35.2 **51.** $-\frac{7}{12}$ **52.** $\frac{25}{12}$ **53.** 1008 **54.** 7479 **55.** -4 **56.** 234
57. $-\frac{1}{5}$ **58.** $-\frac{1}{15}$ **59.** 15.35 **60.** -2.81 **61.** $98 - (-90) = 188$; The range is 188°F.
62. $44 - (-56) = 100$; The range is 100°F. **63.** $130 - (-180) = 310$; The change of the mean surface temperature is 310°C. **64.** $350 - (-170) = 520$; The change of the mean surface temperature is 520°C.
65. $20{,}320 - (-282) = 20{,}602$; The difference is 20,602 feet.
66. $163 - (-2) = 165$; The difference is 165 meters.
67. $420.35 + 185.00 + 75.00 + (-50.00) + (-120.00) + (-12.55) + (-110.76) + (-5.50) = 381.54$; Rolanda's current balance is \$381.54. **68.** $485.26 + 325.00 + (-50.00) + (-40.00) + (-10.00) + (-175.00) + (-14.59) + (-35.76) + (-3.75) = 481.16$; Daryl's current balance is \$481.16.

69. $20 + \left(-2\frac{1}{2}\right) + \left(-1\frac{2}{3}\right) + (-1) + \left(-2\frac{1}{4}\right) = 12\frac{7}{12}$; Betty has $12\frac{7}{12}$ cups of flour left.

70. $15\frac{3}{4} + \left(-1\frac{1}{2}\right) + (-3) + \left(-2\frac{3}{4}\right) + \left(-\frac{2}{3}\right) = 7\frac{5}{6}$; $7\frac{5}{6}$ yards remain on the bolt of fabric.

71. $25 + (-5.75) + 15 + (-12.50) + (-4.50) + 2.35 = 19.60$; There is $19.60 left in the petty cash fund.

72. $25 + (-12.5) + (-8.25) + 15 + (-5.5) = 13.75$; 13.75 gallons of liquid fertilizer remains in the tank.

73. $19.95 + 19.95 + 19.95 + (-25) + (-59.27) + (-19.95) = -44.37$; Rosie lost $44.37 that morning.

74. $39.95 + 27.95 + 19.99 + (-175) + (-29.95) + (-14.95) = -132.01$; Richard lost $132.01 that hour.

Experiencing Algebra the Calculator Way

1. $3\frac{889}{3036}$ **2.** $7\frac{31}{3036}$ **3.** $-7\frac{31}{3036}$ **4.** $-3\frac{889}{3036}$ **5.** $-5\frac{281}{323}$ **6.** $37\frac{213}{323}$ **7.** $-37\frac{213}{323}$ **8.** $5\frac{281}{323}$

9. 545.9315 **10.** -329.9185 **11.** -545.9315 **12.** 329.9185 **13.** $-199{,}532$ **14.** $-1{,}986{,}482$

15. $1{,}986{,}482$ **16.** $199{,}532$

PROBLEM SET 1.4

Experiencing Algebra the Exercise Way

1. -135 **2.** -224 **3.** 128 **4.** 605 **5.** -125 **6.** -9 **7.** 153 **8.** 128 **9.** 0 **10.** 0

11. -0.968 **12.** -1 **13.** 0.34 **14.** 68.4 **15.** 7.29 **16.** 5 **17.** -12.5 **18.** -1.083 **19.** $\frac{5}{24}$

20. $\frac{22}{51}$ **21.** $-\frac{5}{4}$ **22.** $-\frac{16}{21}$ **23.** $\frac{1}{7}$ **24.** 1 **25.** $-\frac{3}{28}$ **26.** $-\frac{25}{51}$ **27.** 0 **28.** 0 **29.** 0 **30.** 0

31. positive   **32.** positive   **33.** negative   **34.** positive   **35.** positive   **36.** negative   **37.** negative

38. negative   **39.** 4800 **40.** $60{,}000$ **41.** $-\frac{4}{75}$ **42.** $\frac{4}{75}$ **43.** 1.144 **44.** 0.638 **45.** -14 **46.** 0

47. 0 **48.** $-\frac{93}{2}$ **49.** 0 **50.** 0 **51.** $12 \cdot 225 = 2700$; Steve pays $2700 in rent each year.

52. $65 \cdot 13 = 845$; Tricia's loan was $845.   **53.** $(0.22)(-645) = -141.90$; Sara has $-141.90 deducted every two weeks.; $(6)(-141.9) = -851.40$; This amounts to $-851.40 every 12 weeks.   **54.** $-5 \times 9 \times 6 = -270$; Ron will bet $270 in a week.   **55.** $(4)\left(-4\frac{1}{2}\right) = -18$; Heath lost 18 yards on these four sacks.

56. $(-1.75)(5) = -8.75$; Joanne is charged $8.75.   **57.** $(4.5)(4)(7) = 126$; The track athlete will run 126 miles in four weeks.   **58.** $\left(1\frac{1}{4}\right)(2)(7) = 17\frac{1}{2}$; The athlete trains $17\frac{1}{2}$ hours in two weeks.   **59.** $(20)(25) = 500$; There are 500 soldiers in each group.   **60.** $(8)(22) = 176$; There are 176 guests at the reception.

61. $(10)(3)(4) = 120$; There are 120 people riding in the cars.   **62.** $(12)(4)(3) = 144$; There are 144 soldiers riding in the tanks.   **63.** $(0.05)(40)\left(1\frac{1}{2}\right)(3) = 9$; Sammy earns $9 for his work.   **64.** $(0.25)(20)(6) = 30$; Melanie earns $30 for her troop.   **65.** $(4)(3)(20) = 240$; Nellie will be able to store 240 CD's.

66. $(5)(5)(24) = 600$; Omar can expect to store 600 books.   **67.** $(50)\left(8\frac{1}{2}\right)(4) = 1700$; George drove approximately 1700 miles.   **68.** $\left(9\frac{1}{2}\right)\left(1\frac{3}{4}\right)(5) = 83\frac{1}{8}$; Michele will hike $83\frac{1}{8}$ miles.

69. $(24)(0.59)(14) = 198.24$; The total retail value for the vegetables is $198.24.

70. $(12)(18)(12)(-0.35) = -907.2$; The cost the distributor incurs for this order is $907.20.

71. $(100)\left(2\frac{3}{4}\right)(12) = 3300$; Drucilla will pay her parents $3300.   **72.** $(175)(10)(12) = 21{,}000$; The annuity will pay Keith $21,000.   **73.** $(8)(6)(4)(24) = 4608$; 4608 ounces will be needed to fill the order.

74. $(12)(12)(4)(18) = 10{,}368$; 10,368 ounces will fill the order.

1. $9\dfrac{291}{506}$ **2.** $-9\dfrac{291}{506}$ **3.** $-9\dfrac{291}{506}$ **4.** $9\dfrac{291}{506}$ **5.** $345\dfrac{305}{323}$ **6.** $-345\dfrac{305}{323}$ **7.** $-345\dfrac{305}{323}$ **8.** $345\dfrac{305}{323}$

9. $-47{,}298.74651$ **10.** $47{,}298.74651$ **11.** $-47{,}298.74651$ **12.** $47{,}298.74651$ **13.** $976{,}049$

14. $-976{,}049$ **15.** $-976{,}049$ **16.** $976{,}049$

PROBLEM SET 1.5

Experiencing Algebra the Exercise Way

1. -15 **2.** -14 **3.** 8 **4.** 5 **5.** 17 **6.** 8 **7.** 0 **8.** 0 **9.** -1 **10.** -1 **11.** -200

12. -90 **13.** 8.5 **14.** 17.1 **15.** 81 **16.** 0.05 **17.** 1 **18.** -1 **19.** -5 **20.** -1

21. undefined **22.** undefined **23.** -0.8 **24.** -16 **25.** -0.3 **26.** -0.005 **27.** $\dfrac{96}{125}$ **28.** $\dfrac{33}{34}$

29. $-\dfrac{20}{9}$ **30.** $-\dfrac{33}{5}$ **31.** $-\dfrac{19}{21}$ **32.** $-\dfrac{21}{25}$ **33.** $\dfrac{7}{9}$ **34.** $\dfrac{18}{25}$ **35.** $\dfrac{25}{16}$ **36.** $\dfrac{36}{25}$ **37.** $-\dfrac{64}{21}$

38. $-\dfrac{27}{17}$ **39.** 0 **40.** 0 **41.** undefined **42.** undefined **43.** 1 **44.** $-\dfrac{4}{9}$ **45.** $\dfrac{2}{9}$ **46.** $-\dfrac{7}{16}$

47. -42 **48.** -14 **49.** 0 **50.** undefined **51.** -800 **52.** -540 **53.** 0.486 **54.** 9.3 **55.** $\dfrac{4}{3}$

56. 1 **57.** $\dfrac{20 + \left(-3\frac{1}{2}\right) + 8\frac{3}{4} + 12}{4} = 9\dfrac{5}{16}$; Heath averaged $9\dfrac{5}{16}$ yards per play.

58. $\dfrac{16 + 3 + (-7) + \left(-6\frac{1}{2}\right)}{4} = 1\dfrac{3}{8}$; Andy averaged $1\dfrac{3}{8}$ yards per play.

59. $\dfrac{3.5 + 2.0 + 0.5 + (-1.5) + (-2.5) + 3.5 + 4.0 + (-4.0) + 3.5 + 2.5 + 3.5}{11} = 1.3\overline{6}$; Professor Chip's
average rating was approximately 1.36 points. **60.** $75 \div 20 = 3.75$; Miss Bundy's average rating was
3.75 points.; $-18.75 \div 15 = -1.25$; Mr. Rooney's average rating was -1.25 points.

61. $364 \div 26 = 14$; There will be 14 soldiers in each row. **62.** $54 \div 3 = 18$; There will be 18 rows of cars.

63. $479 \div 60 = 7.98\overline{3}$; It will take Michael approximately 8 hours to drive to New Orleans.

64. $868 \div 14 = 62$; Thelma and Louise's average speed must be 62 mph. **65.** $3200 \div 12 = 266.\overline{6}$;
The distributor will have 266 full packs. **66.** $1450 \div 8 = 181.25$; The market has 181 full cartons.

67. $659 \div 19.4 \approx 33.97$; Al will use approximately 34 gallons of gas. **68.** $659 \div 38 \approx 17.34$; Al's gas mileage
on the trip was approximately 17.34 mpg. **69.** $47{,}500 \div 40 = 1187.5$; 1187 bottles can be filled.

70. $2800 \times 16 \div 98 \approx 457.14$; 457 boxes can be filled.

71. $16{,}000{,}000 \text{ seconds} \times \dfrac{1 \text{ minute}}{60 \text{ seconds}} \times \dfrac{1 \text{ hour}}{60 \text{ minutes}} \times \dfrac{1 \text{ day}}{24 \text{ hours}} \approx 185.2$; It will take a little over 185 days.

72. $20{,}000{,}000 \div 60 \div 60 \div 24 \div 7 \approx 33.1$; It will take a little over 33 weeks. **73.** $850 \div 35 \approx 24.3$; It will
take Anita 25 weeks to pay her mother. **74.** $1200 \div 45 = 26.\overline{6}$; It will take Sonya 27 weeks to save for college.

75. $\dfrac{335 \div (3 \times 20)}{6 \text{ cabinets}} \approx 5.6$; Billie will need 6 CD cabinets to store her collection. **76.** $650 \div (3 \times 125) = 1.7$;
Bruce will need 2 CD cabinets to store his collection. **77.** $1{,}035{,}900{,}000 \div 4 = 258{,}975{,}000$; The estimated
expenditure for a quarter was \$258,975,000. **78.** $(1350 \div 50) \times 1000 \approx 37.04$; It would take Phillipe Petit
approximately 37 minutes to complete a 1000 foot walk.

Experiencing Algebra the Calculator Way

1. $\dfrac{513}{1564}$ **2.** $-\dfrac{513}{1564}$ **3.** $-\dfrac{513}{1564}$ **4.** $\dfrac{513}{1564}$ **5.** $\dfrac{2567}{3515}$ **6.** $-\dfrac{2567}{3515}$ **7.** $-\dfrac{2567}{3515}$ **8.** $\dfrac{2567}{3515}$

9. -4.055 **10.** 4.055 **11.** -4.055 **12.** 4.055 **13.** 0.817 **14.** -0.817 **15.** -0.817 **16.** 0.817

Reflections

1–7. Answers will vary.

Exercises

1. -15: integer, rational; 1000: natural, whole, integer, rational; 0: whole, integer, rational; -2000: integer rational; 13: natural, whole, integer, rational; $-\dfrac{15}{17}$: rational; 12.97: rational; $3\dfrac{5}{8}$: rational; $\dfrac{12}{4} = 3$: natural, whole, integer, rational   **2.** $3; 0; -2; 1$

3.

$$-3 \quad -2\tfrac{1}{2} \quad -1.1 \quad 0 \quad \tfrac{3}{4} \quad 1\tfrac{1}{2} \quad 2.5 \quad 4$$

4. $>$ **5.** $>$ **6.** $<$ **7.** $<$ **8.** $<$ **9.** $=$ **10.** $>$ **11.** $<$ **12.** $<$ **13.** $<$ **14.** $>$ **15.** $>$ **16.** $>$

17. $<$ **18.** $<$ **19.** $<$ **20.** True   **21.** False   **22.** True   **23.** $-49 < -23$ **24.** $\dfrac{13}{17} > \dfrac{252}{529}$

25. $-\dfrac{1729}{50} = -34.58$ **26.** $-\dfrac{17}{33}$ **27.** 67 **28.** -16.85 **29.** $5\dfrac{1}{2}$ **30.** 32.698 **31.** -257 **32.** -14

33. -38 **34.** 16 **35.** -4529 **36.** 38.86 **37.** $-\dfrac{2}{3}$ **38.** $\dfrac{50}{3}$ **39.** $1\dfrac{3178}{3225}$ **40.** $-335{,}597$ **41.** 14.017

42. $\dfrac{58}{63}$ **43.** -44.668 **44.** $166{,}867$ **45.** 56.328 **46.** $-\dfrac{166}{345}$ **47.** -123 **48.** -145 **49.** $-\dfrac{67}{24}$

50. $650 + (-250) + 1200 + (-700) = 900$; Willie is \$900 above quota at the end of the four weeks.

51. $65 + (-100) = -35$; The resultant will be pointing 35 km west.   **52.** 26

53. $-\dfrac{53}{56}$ **54.** -2.4 **55.** -3.97 **56.** 0 **57.** $-\dfrac{5}{3}$ **58.** $-\dfrac{197}{336}$ **59.** $-2{,}977{,}581$ **60.** -2564

61. $\dfrac{47}{165}$ **62.** 124.92 **63.** 945 **64.** 8 **65.** 0 **66.** 28.9 **67.** 3 **68.** $\dfrac{43}{12}$ **69.** -47 **70.** 7.75

71. $1\dfrac{43}{45}$ **72.** $735.66 + (-276.12) + (-187.05) + (-68.57) + 75.00 + 185.00 + 50 + (-4.65) + (-12.00)$ $= 497.27$; Cleta has \$497.27 left in her account at the end of the month.   **73.** $14{,}494 - (-282) = 14{,}776$; The difference in elevation between these two points is 14,776 feet.   **74.** $28\dfrac{1}{4} - 22\dfrac{1}{2} = 5\dfrac{3}{4}$; John's gain per share was $\$5\dfrac{3}{4}$.   **75.** 78 **76.** -105 **77.** $\dfrac{37}{7}$ **78.** -1 **79.** -0.922 **80.** 0 **81.** -25 **82.** -680

83. $-2{,}444{,}209$ **84.** $\dfrac{11}{570}$ **85.** 8.4048 **86.** $3{,}477{,}285$ **87.** approximately 60.988 **88.** $705{,}012$

89. $-\dfrac{2}{13}$ **90.** approximately -7.011 **91.** $-638{,}775$ **92.** 0 **93.** $-64{,}000$ **94.** 7.04 **95.** $-\dfrac{5}{6}$

96. 0 **97.** $(14)(36)(16) = 8064$; 8064 ounces of cleanser will be required to process the order.

98. $(22.5)(45) = 1012.5$; The bill for labor will be \$1012.50   **99.** -55 **100.** 26 **101.** 235 **102.** $-\dfrac{5}{6}$

103. -4.59 **104.** 0 **105.** undefined   **106.** 13.7 **107.** -21.033 **108.** $-\dfrac{1}{8}$ **109.** -537 **110.** 219

111. $1\dfrac{5}{22}$ **112.** $\dfrac{65}{119}$ **113.** 6.94 **114.** -294 **115.** -100 **116.** -9.24 **117.** $-\dfrac{13}{17}$

118. $\dfrac{10 + (-5) + 8 + 1 + (-12)}{5} = 0.4$; David's score is 0.4 points above the class average.

119. $\dfrac{625 + 690 + 620 + 590 + 630 + 660}{6} = 635.83$; A fair monthly rent would be \$635.83.

120. $345 \div 18.7 \approx 18.45$; Clarence's average mileage is approximately 18.45 mpg.

CHAPTER 1 MIXED REVIEW

1. $-\dfrac{9}{25}$ **2.** 102   **3.** -3.7 **4.** $-4\dfrac{6}{7}$ **5.** -0.085 **6.** 7   **7.** -1457 **8.** 0.17   **9.** $1\dfrac{5}{26}$ **10.** $-1\dfrac{3}{8}$

11. 2371   **12.** 12,147   **13.** 0.055   **14.** $\dfrac{159}{455}$ **15.** -19.356 **16.** -2.1 **17.** -182 **18.** $-\dfrac{19}{39}$

19. -2.48 **20.** $-\dfrac{3}{11}$ **21.** 1.03   **22.** $\dfrac{3}{25}$ **23.** $\dfrac{11}{34}$ **24.** 999,000   **25.** -474 **26.** $\dfrac{11}{81}$

27. 15.977   **28.** 4545   **29.** $\dfrac{2}{11}$ **30.** -2 **31.** -0.0054 **32.** 0   **33.** -2925 **34.** 88   **35.** 8437

36. $\dfrac{1}{16}$ **37.** 31.6316   **38.** 4,800,000   **39.** 1467.73   **40.** 0   **41.** 235   **42.** $-\dfrac{1}{3}$ **43.** -3.7

44. indeterminate   **45.** undefined   **46.** -56.8 **47.** 8.2   **48.** $\dfrac{34}{55}$ **49.** -67 **50.** 2.5   **51.** 204

52. $\dfrac{15}{28}$ **53.** $\dfrac{1}{45}$ **54.** $>$ **55.** $<$ **56.** $>$ **57.** $<$ **58.** $>$ **59.** $=$ **60.** $<$ **61.** $>$ **62.** $<$

63. $<$ **64.** $>$ **65.** $>$ **66.** 8.103   **67.** $-\dfrac{19}{35}$ **68.** 53.4   **69.** -83 **70.** $\dfrac{109}{30}$ **71.** -30

72. -33.38 **73.** $7\dfrac{17}{42}$ **74.** $-35,640$ **75.** 96   **76.** $-\dfrac{2}{5}$ **77.** 0   **78.** -385 **79.** -16.5 **80.** -6

81.

82. $75 < 76$ **83.** $\dfrac{1}{7} > -\dfrac{2}{5}$ **84.** $\dfrac{13}{25} = 0.52$

85. The business made a profit of \$92,000.; The business lost \$15,000.

86. The average weekly change is 0 for the four weeks.   **87.** Approximately 117 credits can run per minute.

88. It takes $7\dfrac{1}{2}$ gallons of water to fill ten 10-gallon hats.

89. Captain Picard had 582 more people in his command.   **90.** 5376 footballs will be needed.

CHAPTER 1 TEST

1. 15   **2.** 0, 15   **3.** 0, 15, -17 **4.** 0, $-\dfrac{1}{3}$, 15, $-4\dfrac{1}{5}$, 0.546, -17 **5.** $<$ **6.** $>$ **7.** $=$ **8.** $\dfrac{1}{4} < \dfrac{5}{16}$

9. $-2.3 > -3.2$ **10.** $0.06 = \dfrac{3}{50}$ **11.** 13.37   **12.** 20   **13.** -20 **14.** -36 **15.** $\dfrac{3}{95}$ **16.** -3.602

17. $\dfrac{2}{5}$ **18.** -4409 **19.** -45.78 **20.** $-17,128,272$ **21.** -1011.55 **22.** 91   **23.** $-\dfrac{4}{3}$

24. undefined   **25.** 0   **26.** 2   **27.** -14.45 **28.** 0   **29.** $-\dfrac{1}{42}$ **30.** 5.1   **31.** $-6\dfrac{21}{37}$ **32.** -3

33.

34. $500 + (-123.75) + (-56.80) + (-95.87) + 250 = 473.58$; Sally's current account balance is \$473.58.

35. $0.24 \times 675 = 162$; Regina will have \$162 per week deducted.

36. If the signs are the same, the product is positive. If the signs are different, the product is negative.

37. If the sum of the negative signs is even, the product is positive. If the sum of the negative signs is odd, the product is negative.

Chapter 2

PROBLEM SET 2.1

Experiencing Algebra the Exercise Way

1. 15^6 **2.** $(-31)^4$ **3.** $\left(-\dfrac{1}{5}\right)^4$ **4.** $\left(\dfrac{4}{7}\right)^5$ **5.** $(3.7)^3$ **6.** $(-2.2)^4$ **7.** 0^7 **8.** 1^7 **9.** positive

10. positive   **11.** negative   **12.** negative   **13.** negative   **14.** negative   **15.** negative   **16.** negative

17. $3 \cdot 3 \cdot 3 \cdot 3 = 81$ **18.** $2 \cdot 2 \cdot 2 \cdot 2 \cdot 2 \cdot 2 = 64$ **19.** $(-3)(-3)(-3)(-3) = 81$

20. $(-2)(-2)(-2)(-2)(-2)(-2) = 64$ **21.** $-(3 \cdot 3 \cdot 3 \cdot 3) = -81$ **22.** $-(2 \cdot 2 \cdot 2 \cdot 2 \cdot 2 \cdot 2) = -64$

23. $-[(-3)(-3)(-3)(-3)] = -81$ **24.** $-[(-2)(-2)(-2)(-2)(-2)(-2)] = -64$ **25.** $(-4)(-4)(-4) = -64$

26. $(-3)(-3)(-3)(-3)(-3) = -243$ **27.** $-[(-4)(-4)(-4)] = 64$ **28.** $-[(-3)(-3)(-3)(-3)(-3)] = 243$

29. 6.25 **30.** 0.16 **31.** -0.125 **32.** -0.027 **33.** $-\dfrac{9}{49}$ **34.** $-\dfrac{16}{81}$ **35.** $\dfrac{64}{27}$ **36.** $\dfrac{27}{8}$ **37.** 0

38. 0 **39.** 1 **40.** 1 **41.** -1 **42.** -1 **43.** 1 **44.** 1 **45.** $38{,}950{,}081$ **46.** $923{,}521$

47. -1.469 **48.** -3.375 **49.** $\dfrac{64}{729}$ **50.** $\dfrac{81}{256}$ **51.** $\dfrac{3125}{7776}$ **52.** $\dfrac{512}{729}$ **53.** $-69{,}343{,}957$

54. $-4{,}984{,}209{,}207$ **55.** 126.325 **56.** 0.0025 **57.** -102.495 **58.** $-34{,}509.358$ **59.** $-1{,}640{,}401.445$

60. $35{,}672{,}895.98$ **61.** 1256 **62.** $-\dfrac{4}{17}$ **63.** -13.06 **64.** $3\dfrac{16}{37}$ **65.** 1 **66.** 1 **67.** -1 **68.** -1

69. $\dfrac{1}{49}$ **70.** $\dfrac{1}{64}$ **71.** $\dfrac{81}{16}$ **72.** 16 **73.** 25 **74.** 6.25 **75.** $-\dfrac{1}{121}$ **76.** $-\dfrac{1}{144}$ **77.** $-\dfrac{1}{12}$

78. $-\dfrac{1}{11}$ **79.** $\dfrac{1}{97}$ **80.** $\dfrac{1}{52}$ **81.** $-\dfrac{1296}{625}$ **82.** $-\dfrac{2401}{81}$ **83.** 0.056 **84.** -66.639 **85.** $-\dfrac{81}{400}$

86. $-\dfrac{4096}{6561}$ **87.** $-\dfrac{343}{8}$ **88.** 0.004 **89.** $\dfrac{125}{216}$ **90.** -0.004 **91.** -0.006 **92.** $\dfrac{12}{61}$

93. $(3.5)^3 = 42.875$; The volume of the pit is 42.875 ft^3.   **94.** $(15)^3 = 3375$; The volume of the block of ice is 3375 in^3.   **95.** $(6.5)^2 = 42.25$; Aladdin's magic carpet will cover 42.25 ft^2.   **96.** $(4.25)^2 = 18.0625$; The canvas will cover 18.0625 yd^2 of ground.   **97.** $(755)^2 = 570{,}025$; The Great Pyramid covers $570{,}025$ ft^2 of ground.   **98.** Blue $= 36$ ft^2; White $= 64$ ft^2; Red $= 125$ ft^2

Experiencing Algebra the Calculator Way

1. $24{,}137{,}569$ **2.** $-24{,}137{,}569$ **3.** $24{,}137{,}569$ **4.** $1{,}419{,}857$ **5.** $-1{,}419{,}857$ **6.** $-1{,}419{,}857$

7. $-191{,}102{,}976$ **8.** $-\dfrac{16}{6561}$ **9.** $\dfrac{16}{6561}$ **10.** $27{,}606.520$ **11.** $-27{,}606.520$ **12.** 0.098

13. -0.098 **14.** $-\dfrac{279{,}841}{1296}$ **15.** $\dfrac{83{,}521}{256}$ **16.** $-\dfrac{83{,}521}{256}$ **17.** -0.020 **18.** 0.020 **19.** $-18{,}691.288$

20. $18{,}691.288$ **21.** 62.389 **22.** $\dfrac{19{,}487{,}171}{2187}$ **23.** $-\dfrac{4{,}574{,}296}{9261}$ **24.** $29{,}394{,}751.66$

PROBLEM SET 2.2

Experiencing Algebra the Exercise Way

1. 2.345×10^{10} **2.** 1.83×10^{19} **3.** -2.03415×10^{14} **4.** -1.5395×10^{19} **5.** 1.76×10^{-8} **6.** 1.3×10^{-14}
7. -6.591×10^{-6} **8.** -7.2193×10^{-10} **9.** 3.6943×10^{0} **10.** 9.98031×10^{0} **11.** -4.7502×10^{0}
12. -1.40001×10^{0} **13.** $6.3 \times 10^{17} = 630{,}000{,}000{,}000{,}000{,}000$ **14.** $3.076 \times 10^8 = 307{,}600{,}000$
15. $-7.1103 \times 10^5 = -711{,}030$ **16.** $-1.005 \times 10^{11} = -100{,}500{,}000{,}000$ **17.** $-3.7 \times 10^{-5} = -0.000037$
18. $-8.405 \times 10^{-7} = -0.0000008405$ **19.** $1.966 \times 10^{-2} = 0.01966$ **20.** $5.555 \times 10^{-6} = 0.000005555$
21. $4.356 \times 10^{0} = 4.356$ **22.** $6.055 \times 10^{0} = 6.055$ **23.** $-9.95 \times 10^{0} = -9.95$ **24.** $-8.103 \times 10^{0} = -8.103$

25. 27,000,000   **26.** 5,470,000,000   **27.** −4,005,000   **28.** −899,050,000   **29.** 0.0000004056
30. 0.0000666   **31.** −0.00030303   **32.** −0.00000000511   **33.** 1.26   **34.** 3.69   **35.** −4.5   **36.** −8.81
37. $1,024,769,000,000   **38.** $271,638,000,000   **39.** $7.53131 × 10^{11} or $753,131,000,000
40. $2.650724 × 10^{-1}$ or 0.2650724   **41.** $1.4438 × 10^7$ crimes; $2.55458 × 10^8$ population; $5.6518 × 10^{-2}$ ratio;
In 1992, there were about 0.056518 crimes per person in the U.S.   **42.** $2.38 × 10^4$ murders; $9.3166 × 10^{-5}$ ratio;
In 1992, there were $9.3166 × 10^{-5}$ murders per person in the U.S.   **43.** $1.878285 × 10^6$ American Indian;
$2.487 × 10^8$ total population; 0.755% of population were American Indian.   **44.** $2.177 × 10^6$ deaths; 0.875%
of the U.S. population died.   **45.** $9.4259425 × 10^{10}$ or 94,259,425,000 cups of fruit were consumed in a year.
46. $2.54887815 × 10^{10}$ pounds; 25,488,781,500 pounds of fresh fruit will be consumed.
47. 2,650,000,000 Christmas cards will be sold in 1996.   **48.** 925,000,000 Valentine's Day cards were sold.
49. Each pyramid at Giza would weigh over $1.2 × 10^{10}$ pounds.   **50.** $2 × 10^6$; The Egyptians had to move
$2 × 10^6$ blocks.   **51.** The Great Wall of China is $1.9536 × 10^7$ feet long.   **52.** $1.0979641 × 10^7$;
The Grand Coulee Dam contains $1.0979641 × 10^7$ cubic yards of concrete.

Experiencing Algebra the Calculator Way

1. (a) 6.022 E23   **(b)** 602,200,000,000,000,000,000,000   **(c)** scientific notation; takes up less room
(d) 1.2044 E26   **(e)** $1.2044 × 10^{26}$
2. (a) $5.642151 × 10^9$ **(b)** 5.642151 E9   **(c)** $1.6926453 × 10^{10}$ **(d)** 16,926,453,000

PROBLEM SET 2.3

Experiencing Algebra the Exercise Way

1. 6   **2.** 9   **3.** 16   **4.** 18   **5.** −5   **6.** −7   **7.** 0.8   **8.** 0.9   **9.** $\frac{7}{9}$ **10.** $\frac{8}{11}$ **11.** $-\frac{4}{3}$

12. $-\frac{6}{7}$ **13.** 1   **14.** −1   **15.** 0   **16.** 0   **17.** not a real number   **18.** not a real number

19. between 3 and 4 or approximately 3.162   **20.** between 4 and 5 or approximately 4.690
21. between −2 and −1 or approximately −1.732   **22.** between −4 and −3 or approximately −3.742
23. −34.641   **24.** −46.583   **25.** 3.240   **26.** 7.078   **27.** −0.316   **28.** 0.804   **29.** 2.370   **30.** 2.898
31. −1.581   **32.** −0.632   **33.** 4   **34.** 2   **35.** 12   **36.** 21   **37.** 10.726   **38.** 16.288   **39.** −5
40. −4   **41.** −6   **42.** −5   **43.** 1.604   **44.** −3.185   **45.** not a real number   **46.** not a real number

47. −1.662   **48.** −2.247   **49.** 1.833   **50.** 2.252   **51.** $\frac{1}{2}$ **52.** $\frac{2}{5}$ **53.** $-\frac{2}{5}$ **54.** $-\frac{9}{11}$ **55.** −1.395

56. −1.340   **57.** −1.5   **58.** $2\frac{2}{3}$

59.

60.

61. Each side is 13.5 feet.   **62.** Each side is 18.7 feet.   **63.** Jennie will need about 9.434 feet of logs.
64. Jennie will need 17 feet of logs.   **65.** The current will be approximately 0.173 ampere.
66. The current will be approximately 0.289 ampere.   **67.** The speed was approximately 31.6 mph.
68. The speed was approximately 49 mph.   **69.** The speed was approximately 56 mph.
70. Yes, the car was going faster than 65 mph.   **71.** The flow rate is approximately 42.264 gallons per minute.
72. The flow rate is approximately 84 gallons per minute.

Experiencing Algebra the Calculator Way

1. 593   **2.** −237   **3.** $\frac{41}{51}$ **4.** 26.378   **5.** $-\frac{8}{9}$ **6.** 65   **7.** not a real number   **8.** −155

9. 6.8   **10.** 1.772   **11.** 44.710   **12.** 0.816

PROBLEM SET 2.4

Experiencing Algebra the Exercise Way

1. $27^{1/3} = 3$ **2.** $125^{1/3} = 5$ **3.** $(-27)^{1/3} = -3$ **4.** $(-125)^{1/3} = -5$ **5.** $-(27)^{1/3} = -3$

6. $-(125)^{1/3} = -5$ **7.** $-(-27)^{1/3} = 3$ **8.** $-(-125)^{1/3} = 5$ **9.** $-(256)^{1/4} = -4$ **10.** $-(729)^{1/6} = -3$

11. $(-256)^{1/4}$ is not a real number   **12.** $(-729)^{1/6}$ is not a real number   **13.** $(250)^{1/5} \approx 3.017$

14. $(200)^{1/5} \approx 2.885$ **15.** $(-39.304)^{1/3} = -3.4$ **16.** $-(39.304)^{1/3} = -3.4$ **17.** $(-5.6)^{1/4}$ is not a real number

18. $-(-5.6)^{1/4}$ is not a real number   **19.** $75.85^{1/5} \approx 2.377$ **20.** $-(-75.85)^{1/5} \approx 2.377$ **21.** $\left(\dfrac{64}{343}\right)^{1/3} = \dfrac{4}{7}$

22. $\left(\dfrac{125}{512}\right)^{1/3} = \dfrac{5}{8}$ **23.** $\left(\dfrac{12}{13}\right)^{1/4} \approx 0.980$ **24.** $\left(\dfrac{5}{6}\right)^{1/4} \approx 0.955$ **25.** $\left(\dfrac{1}{243}\right)^{1/5} = \dfrac{1}{3}$ **26.** $\left(\dfrac{1}{32}\right)^{1/5} = \dfrac{1}{2}$

27. $(289)^{1/2} = 17$ **28.** $(961)^{1/2} = 31$ **29.** $(-1024)^{1/5} = -4$ **30.** $(-7776)^{1/5} = -6$

31. $(187.4161)^{1/4} = 3.7$ **32.** $(133.6336)^{1/4} = 3.4$ **33.** $\left(\dfrac{16}{2401}\right)^{1/4} = \dfrac{2}{7}$ **34.** $\left(\dfrac{625}{4096}\right)^{1/4} = \dfrac{5}{8}$

35. $(6859)^{1/3} = 19$ **36.** $(12,167)^{1/3} = 23$ **37.** $-(4096)^{1/4} = -8$ **38.** $-(14,641)^{1/4} = -11$

39. $-(4.85)^{1/4} \approx -1.484$ **40.** $-(14.51)^{1/4} \approx -1.952$ **41.** $\left(\dfrac{841}{1225}\right)^{1/2} = \dfrac{29}{35}$ **42.** $\left(\dfrac{1089}{1369}\right)^{1/2} = \dfrac{33}{37}$

43. $(614,656)^{1/4} = 28$ **44.** $(20,736)^{1/4} = 12$ **45.** $(-5832)^{1/3} = -18$ **46.** $(-13,824)^{1/3} = -24$

47. $(-5.55)^{1/5} \approx -1.409$ **48.** $(-12.03)^{1/5} \approx -1.645$ **49.** $\left(-2\dfrac{1}{7}\right)^{1/5} \approx -1.165$ **50.** $\left(-3\dfrac{5}{9}\right)^{1/5} \approx -1.289$

51. $(3125)^{1/5} = 5$ **52.** $(32,768)^{1/5} = 8$ **53.** $-(841)^{1/2} = -29$ **54.** $-(3025)^{1/2} = -55$

55. $(-17.576)^{1/3} = -2.6$ **56.** $(-6.859)^{1/3} = -1.9$ **57.** $-\left(3\dfrac{3}{5}\right)^{1/4} \approx -1.377$ **58.** $-\left(4\dfrac{8}{15}\right)^{1/4} \approx -1.459$

59. Each side is 5 yards.   **60.** Each side is 4.5 meters.   **61.** Each side is approximately 1.442 feet.
62. Each side is approximately 2.466 feet.   **63.** Each side is approximately 3.464 feet.
64. The pond is approximately 7.071 feet by 7.071 feet by 2 feet.   **65.** Each side is approximately 614.003 feet.
66. The diagonal is approximately 868.332 feet.   **67.** The radius is approximately 78.583 feet.
68. The radius is approximately 339.921 feet.

Experiencing Algebra the Calculator Way

1. $(57,392)^{1/5} \approx 8.949$ **2.** $-(37,652)^{1/4} \approx -13.930$ **3.** $(\pi)^{1/3} \approx 1.465$ **4.** $\left(13\dfrac{15}{19}\right)^{1/2} \approx 3.713$

5. $\left(-23\dfrac{15}{17}\right)^{1/7} \approx -1.574$ **6.** $\left(\dfrac{2197}{3375}\right)^{1/3} = \dfrac{13}{15}$ **7.** $(299821.9536)^{1/4} = 23.4$ **8.** $(0.1)^{1/2} \approx 0.316$

9. $\left(\dfrac{1}{5}\right)^{1/5} \approx 0.725$

PROBLEM SET 2.5

Experiencing Algebra the Exercise Way

1. b   **2.** f   **3.** c   **4.** a   **5.** f   **6.** d   **7.** b   **8.** c   **9.** a   **10.** e   **11.** e   **12.** b
13. d   **14.** b   **15.** g   **16.** i   **17.** h   **18.** g   **19.** j   **20.** h   **21.** i   **22.** j

23. $-12, 3, 6.2, -3.5, -\dfrac{5}{9}, \dfrac{3}{5}; \dfrac{1}{12}, -\dfrac{1}{3}, -\dfrac{1}{6.2}, \dfrac{1}{3.5}, \dfrac{9}{5}, -\dfrac{5}{3}$ **24.** $-24, 5, 1.5, -4.2, -\dfrac{6}{7}, \dfrac{8}{11}; \dfrac{1}{24}, -\dfrac{1}{5}, -\dfrac{1}{1.5}, \dfrac{1}{4.2}, \dfrac{7}{6}, -\dfrac{11}{8}$

25. $1.9 + (-4.33)$ **26.** $\dfrac{4}{11} + \dfrac{15}{99}$ **27.** $-65(58)$ **28.** $\left(5\dfrac{2}{3}\right)\left(4\dfrac{1}{3}\right)$ **29.** $[5.6(-3.7)](1.1)$

30. $40 \cdot (35 \cdot 17)$ **31.** $\dfrac{5}{13} + \left(\dfrac{8}{13} + \dfrac{1}{13} \right)$ **32.** $[-35 + (-54)] + (-99)$ **33.** $\left(\dfrac{3}{8} \right)\left(\dfrac{5}{7} \right) - \left(\dfrac{3}{8} \right)\left(\dfrac{1}{9} \right)$

34. $-23(31) + (-23)(25)$ **35.** $2.7(-1.5) + 2.7(3.2)$ **36.** $\left(1\dfrac{1}{4} \right)\left(5\dfrac{1}{2} \right) - \left(1\dfrac{1}{4} \right)\left(3\dfrac{1}{8} \right)$ **37.** $\dfrac{217}{7} - \dfrac{175}{7}$

38. $\dfrac{-78}{6} + \dfrac{108}{6}$ **39.** $-15 - 19.3$ **40.** $-5.7 - 0.06$ **41.** $\dfrac{6}{7} + \dfrac{5}{9}$ **42.** $51 + 19$ **43.** $-1\dfrac{1}{7} + 2\dfrac{1}{5}$

44. $-89 + 17$ **45.** $-19.37 - 15.043$ **46.** $-2\dfrac{1}{4} - 3\dfrac{5}{8}$ **47.** $15(17 + 21)$ **48.** $81(22 + 4)$

49. $-3(14 + 21)$ **50.** $-13(21 + 16)$ **51.** $-6(12 - 13)$ **52.** $-5(45 - 7)$ **53.** $-3(15 + 17)$
54. $-2(38 + 15)$ **55.** -79 **56.** -129 **57.** 1 **58.** 30 **59.** -10 **60.** -15 **61.** 3 **62.** 2
63. -1.7 **64.** 12.7 **65.** -38 **66.** -38 **67.** 19.2 **68.** 6.6 **69.** -139 **70.** -106 **71.** 121

72. -11 **73.** -22.15 **74.** -3 **75.** 78 **76.** 66 **77.** $\dfrac{64}{135}$ **78.** $\dfrac{27}{80}$ **79.** $\dfrac{73}{72}$ **80.** $\dfrac{1}{3}$ **81.** -53

82. -221 **83.** 24 **84.** 115 **85.** 2 **86.** 4 **87.** 10 **88.** 8 **89.** 0 **90.** 0 **91.** undefined

92. undefined   **93.** $\dfrac{87 + 80 + 92 + 76 + 100}{5} = 87$; Holly's average grade on the tests was 87.

94. $\dfrac{85 + 70 + 91 + 95 + 80}{5} = 84.2$; Monica's average is 84.2.   **95.** $\dfrac{675 + 375 + 545 + 390}{4} = 496.25$;

Estrelita's average weekly sales was $496.25.   **96.** $\dfrac{2650 + 4700 + 3500}{3} \approx 3617$; Karen's average monthly

sales was approximately $3617.   **97.** $\dfrac{168 - 136}{12} = 2\dfrac{2}{3}$ pounds; Marilyn lost an average $2\dfrac{2}{3}$ pounds per week.

98. $\dfrac{210 - 195}{8} = 1\dfrac{7}{8}$; Brian's average weekly gain was 1.875 pounds.

99. "Can't Buy Me Love" sold 7 million records; "Do They Know It's Christmas" sold 7 million records; "We Are the World" sold 7 million records; "I Will Always Love You" sold 13.5 million records; "White Christmas" sold 30 million records; Total records sold was 64.5 million.
100. "Rock Around the Clock" sold 17 million records; "It's Now or Never" sold 10 million records; "Hound Dog" sold 9 million records; "Diana" sold 9 million records; The difference was 8 million singles.

Experiencing Algebra the Calculator Way

1. $-1,403,590$ **2.** 5.124 **3.** -619.905 **4.** 3.556 **5.** $\dfrac{1187}{742}$ **6.** undefined   **7.** 735 **8.** 5

9. undefined   **10.** 0

CHAPTER 2 REVIEW

Reflections

1–12. Answers will vary.

Exercises

1. 12^{10} **2.** $\left(\dfrac{5}{11} \right)^5$ **3.** (a) positive   (b) negative   (c) negative   (d) negative   (e) negative

(f) positive   **4.** 256 **5.** 1.44 **6.** $2\dfrac{10}{27}$ **7.** 0 **8.** 1 **9.** -243 **10.** 81 **11.** -0.008 **12.** $\dfrac{16}{9}$

13. 1 **14.** -1 **15.** $-39,135,393$ **16.** $-\dfrac{16,807}{243}$ **17.** 0.011 **18.** $9,834,496$ **19.** $\dfrac{729}{4096}$ **20.** $-\dfrac{2401}{81}$

21. 1 **22.** 1 **23.** -1 **24.** 15 **25.** -15 **26.** -15 **27.** 1 **28.** indeterminate   **29.** 1

30. 0 **31.** 1 **32.** 3.079 **33.** 1 **34.** $229,384$ **35.** $\dfrac{1}{144}$ **36.** $-\dfrac{1}{144}$

37. 5.562×10^{-15} **38.** $-\dfrac{1}{729}$ **39.** $-\dfrac{1}{729}$ **40.** $-\dfrac{8}{19}$ **41.** $\dfrac{16}{49}$ **42.** 1 **43.** -1 **44.** 0.171

45. $\dfrac{512}{343}$ **46.** Yes; There will be enough plants to fill the garden. **47.** 15.625 ft^3 of mulch will fill the bin.

48. 1.89×10^{-7} **49.** 1.89×10^{17} **50.** -5.6×10^{-4} **51.** -2.7085×10^{10} **52.** $5.89 \times 10^{11} = 589{,}000{,}000{,}000$

53. $4.02 \times 10^{-7} = 0.000000402$ **54.** $-1.3 \times 10^7 = -13{,}000{,}000$ **55.** $-7.093 \times 10^{-5} = -0.00007093$

56. $\$5.904822 \times 10^{12}$ **57.** $\$237{,}000{,}000$; The U.S. GNP exceeds the Solomon Islands GNP by $\$5.904585 \times 10^{12}$.

58. 0.000008 m **59.** Michael Jackson's album sold over 4.0×10^7 copies. **60.** 9 **61.** 0.8 **62.** $\dfrac{3}{5}$

63. -7 **64.** not a real number **65.** 1.13 **66.** -21.7 **67.** $-\dfrac{24}{37}$ **68.** 1.595 **69.** 3.873

70. not a real number **71.** 3 **72.** 0.5 **73.** $\dfrac{2}{3}$ **74.** -30 **75.** -1 **76.** -1.9 **77.** -1.585

78.

79. The diamond is 27 meters on a side.
80. The box is 4.5 inches on a side. **81.** $16^{1/4} = 2$
82. $(-16)^{1/4}$ is not a real number **83.** $-(9)^{1/2} = -3$

84. $\left(-3\dfrac{53}{1024}\right)^{1/5} = -\dfrac{5}{4}$ **85.** $(-123)^{1/7} \approx -1.989$ **86.** $20^{1/5} \approx 1.821$

87. The diagonal is approximately 30.406 inches long. **88.** c **89.** k **90.** f **91.** a **92.** j **93.** b

94. d **95.** h **96.** e **97.** g **98.** i **99.** $-8, 12, -\dfrac{3}{17}, \dfrac{5}{3}, \dfrac{1}{8}, -\dfrac{1}{12}, \dfrac{17}{3}, -\dfrac{3}{5}$ **100.** $12.4 + (-33.05)$

101. $\left(2\dfrac{4}{19}\right)\left(1\dfrac{9}{10}\right)$ **102.** $[132 + (-207)] + 391$ **103.** $\dfrac{3}{7} \cdot \left(\dfrac{14}{15} \cdot \dfrac{5}{9}\right)$ **104.** $-2.6(-1.9) - 2.6(3.2)$

105. $\dfrac{5}{6}\left(-\dfrac{3}{5}\right) + \dfrac{5}{6}\left(-\dfrac{4}{15}\right)$ **106.** $\dfrac{1687}{7} - \dfrac{1372}{7}$ **107.** $-2.7 - 3.09$ **108.** $296 + 132$ **109.** $-14.2 - 10.9$

110. $-32 + 51$ **111.** $21(18 + 47)$ **112.** $5(19 - 17)$ **113.** 83 **114.** 10.3 **115.** -334 **116.** 117

117. 29 **118.** -118 **119.** 16 **120.** 0 **121.** undefined **122.** 132 ft^2 will not be covered by the rug.

123. Mary will need approximately 41.205 feet of lace. **124.** The daily temperature was 74°F.

125. Richard lost 2.1 pounds per week on average.

CHAPTER 2 MIXED REVIEW

1. $(-9)^7 = -4{,}782{,}969$ **2.** $(-5.5)^4 = 915.0625$ **3.** $4.75 \times 10^{-6} = 4.75 \text{ E}{-6}$ **4.** $3.554 \times 10^{17} = 3.554 \text{ E17}$

5. $-9.2 \times 10^{-5} = -9.2 \text{ E}{-5}$ **6.** $-1.00505 \times 10^8 = -1.00505 \text{ E8}$ **7.** $1.12 \times 10^9 = 1{,}120{,}000{,}000$

8. $7.94 \times 10^{-12} = 0.00000000000794$ **9.** $-6.876 \times 10^4 = -68{,}760$ **10.** $-2.35 \times 10^{-7} = -0.000000235$

11. $2197^{1/3} = 13$ **12.** $32^{1/5} = 2$ **13.** $(-81)^{1/4}$ is not a real number **14.** $(-125)^{1/5} = -2.627$

15. $\left(-\dfrac{64}{125}\right)^{1/3} = -\dfrac{4}{5}$ **16.** $-(121)^{1/2} = -11$ **17.** $10^{1/4} \approx 1.778$ **18.** $-(4521.2176)^{1/4} = -8.2$

19. $42(15 - 23)$ **20.** $-31(12 + 42)$ **21.** 248 **22.** -0.16 **23.** -20 **24.** 267 **25.** 10 **26.** 662

27. 86 **28.** 0 **29.** undefined **30.** 169 **31.** 5252.335 **32.** $\dfrac{121}{25}$ **33.** 0 **34.** 1 **35.** -125

36. 625 **37.** -415.654 **38.** $-\dfrac{343}{125}$ **39.** 1 **40.** -1 **41.** 81 **42.** $-\dfrac{1}{243}$ **43.** 19.4481 **44.** 1

45. 1 **46.** -1 **47.** 22 **48.** -22 **49.** -22 **50.** -1 **51.** indeterminate **52.** -1 **53.** 0

54. 1 **55.** 65.02 **56.** 1 **57.** 2,333,145 **58.** 1 **59.** $-\dfrac{11}{65}$ **60.** 1 **61.** $\dfrac{1}{400}$ **62.** $\dfrac{1}{400}$

63. $-\dfrac{1}{400}$ **64.** $\dfrac{1}{216}$ **65.** $-\dfrac{1}{216}$ **66.** $-\dfrac{1}{216}$ **67.** $\dfrac{25}{64}$ **68.** 1 **69.** -1 **70.** 50

71. not a real number **72.** -20 **73.** 2.13 **74.** $\dfrac{4}{17}$ **75.** $-\dfrac{21}{38}$ **76.** $2\dfrac{1}{3}$ **77.** 1.2 **78.** -0.112

79. -47.282 **80.** -4 **81.** $\dfrac{3}{2}$ **82.** -6.5 **83.** $1\dfrac{1}{3}$ **84.** -1.904 **85.** 0.693 **86.** 1.265

87. -1.395 **88.** $\dfrac{3}{4}$ **89.** -1.6 **90.** -1.25 **91.**

92. $-24, 15, -\dfrac{4}{9}, \dfrac{5}{8}, \dfrac{1}{24}, -\dfrac{1}{15}, \dfrac{9}{4}, -\dfrac{8}{5}$;

93. The porch's area is $196\ \text{ft}^2$. **94.** The volume of the fruit cellar is $216\ \text{ft}^3$. **95.** 1.176946×10^9
96. $987,000,000$ **97.** The dimensions of the tarpaulin are approximately 17.321 feet on each side.
98. The dimensions of the tree house are 7 feet on each side. **99.** Katie's average cost per frame was $41.50.
100. Cecilia's salary increased on average $1687.50 yearly.

CHAPTER 2 TEST

1. 5.239×10^{15} **2.** -2.03×10^{-6} **3.** $5,070,000$ **4.** -0.0000000104

5.

6. -49 **7.** $\dfrac{4}{3}$ **8.** b **9.** c **10.** a **11.** 2.25 **12.** 81

13. $\dfrac{256}{81}$ **14.** 1 **15.** 0 **16.** -64 **17.** -4.008 **18.** 1

19. 1 **20.** indeterminate **21.** $\dfrac{64}{9}$ **22.** 1 **23.** -14 **24.** $\dfrac{6}{11}$ **25.** -1.897 **26.** $\dfrac{8}{3}$ **27.** $1\dfrac{2}{3}$

28. -72.2 **29.** 11 **30.** 20 **31.** 0 **32.** 22.25; The garden will have $22.25\ \text{ft}^2$ in excess.
33. 2.241×10^{11}; The GNP of Switzerland exceeds that of Romania by 2.241×10^{11} or $224,100,000,000.
34. Take the positive power of the reciprocal.
35. Raise the radical expression to the power that is the reciprocal of the index.

Chapter 3

PROBLEM SET 3.1

Experiencing Algebra the Exercise Way

For problems 1–20, let each $x, y, z =$ some number **1.** $25 - x$ **2.** $x - 25$ **3.** $\dfrac{3}{4}x$ **4.** $0.25x$

5. $x \div 15$ **6.** $55 \div x$ **7.** $2.5x - 19.59 \div x$ **8.** $x^2 + 3x$ **9.** $12x - 25$ **10.** $8x - 3$

11. $x + y + 2xy$ **12.** $3x + 80$ **13.** $(x + y + z) \div 3$ **14.** $\dfrac{1}{3}(x - 5)$ **15.** $2x - 5$ **16.** $5x + 4$

17. $\dfrac{1}{3}x + 6$ **18.** $3x - \dfrac{10}{x}$ **19.** $2x \div (x + 5)$ **20.** $xy - 8$ **21.** $6a + 2c$ **22.** $3300x$

23. $9.5x + 12.25y$ **24.** $200x + 50y - 750$ For problems 25–40, answers will vary. One possibility given.
25. The sum of a number and 27. **26.** Eight subtracted from a number. **27.** The quotient of 35 divided by some number. **28.** The sum of three different numbers. **29.** Three-fifths of a number.

30. The quotient of two numbers plus 3. **31.** 12.50 subtracted from some number. **32.** The sum of $\dfrac{2}{3}$ of

some number added to $\dfrac{1}{3}$ of another number. **33.** The difference of 14 and the product of a number times 5.

34. The product of 2 and π and some number. **35.** The product of 3.14 and some number.

36. A number divided by 12 subtracted from -25. **37.** One-half of the sum of two different numbers. **38.** The sum of one number squared plus another number squared. **39.** The sum of three different grades divided by 3. **40.** The difference of end reading minus begin reading divided by gallons. **41.** -10
42. -34 **43.** 7 **44.** 13 **45.** -3.1 **46.** 1.82 **47.** 54.21 **48.** 20.7 **49.** -51 **50.** -81 **51.** $\dfrac{41}{2}$

52. $\dfrac{103}{3}$ **53.** 392 **54.** 67.2 **55.** $\dfrac{64}{15}$ **56.** 66 **57.** 14.28 **58.** $\dfrac{5}{3}$ **59.** 44 **60.** 57 **61.** 20.25

62. 14.76 **63.** 1 **64.** 5 **65.** 13 **66.** 7 **67.** 1.7 **68.** 4.8 **69.** 10.7 **70.** 13.8 **71.** -2
72. indeterminate **73.** 4 **74.** 2 **75.** $4x + 0.75y$; The revenue from the tickets was $750.
76. The daily charge for 5 days and 600 miles is $435.00. **77.** πd; The circumference of the pool is approximately 37.7 feet. **78.** $2\pi r$; The circumference is approximately 18.8 feet.

Experiencing Algebra the Calculator Way

1. (a) $\dfrac{27}{28}$ **(b)** $\dfrac{290}{3}$ **(c)** $\dfrac{31}{365}$ **2. (a)** 1134.115 **(b)** 1773.547 **(c)** 0.008 **(d)** 2.405

(e) 39.716 **(f)** 31,415.927 **3. (a)** 200 **(b)** 5 **(c)** 4 **(d)** 1.414 **(e)** 1 **(f)** 4

4. (a) 7 **(b)** -11 **(c)** -16 **(d)** 8 **(e)** -7 **(f)** indeterminate **5. (a)** 2 **(b)** $\dfrac{1}{2}$ **(c)** $\dfrac{5}{14}$

(d) $\dfrac{65}{134}$ **(e)** undefined **(f)** 0

PROBLEM SET 3.2

Experiencing Algebra the Exercise Way

1. (a) 2 **(b)** $12, -11$ **(c)** none **2. (a)** 3 **(b)** $3, 4, 13$ **(c)** none **3. (a)** 4 **(b)** $-15, 12, -1, 9$
(c) $-15y$ and $-y$ **4. (a)** 6 **(b)** $3, 5, -2, 1, 3, -6$ **(c)** $3x$ and x; $5z$ and $3z$; -2 and -6 **5. (a)** 4
(b) $2, -6, 1, 12$ **(c)** $-6x$ and x **6. (a)** 5 **(b)** $3, 1, -1, 1, 4$ **(c)** y^3 and $4y^3$ **7. (a)** 3
(b) $3.4, -11.2, -0.3$ **(c)** $3.4a$ and $-0.3a$ **8. (a)** 4 **(b)** $\dfrac{2}{5}, \dfrac{1}{10}, -\dfrac{3}{10}, \dfrac{1}{5}$ **(c)** $\dfrac{2}{5}m$ and $-\dfrac{3}{10}m$; $\dfrac{1}{10}n$ and $\dfrac{1}{5}n$
9. (a) 3 **(b)** $2, 3, 6$ **(c)** $3(n-5)$ and $6(n-5)$ **10. (a)** 4 **(b)** $3, -2, -7, -1$ **(c)** $3(p+q)$ and
$-2(p+q)$ **11. (a)** 4 **(b)** $1, 3, -1, 7$ **(c)** none **12. (a)** 4 **(b)** $1, -1, 6, -3$ **(c)** none
13. $71x$ **14.** $46v$ **15.** $18a$ **16.** $87q$ **17.** $x + 14$ **18.** $52a + 109$ **19.** $x^3 + x + 6$
20. $7h^3 - 2h^2 - 9$ **21.** $-12 - 10yz + 5xz$ **22.** $24mn - 23 + 37np + 37mp$ **23.** $1.87a + 6.78b$

24. $17.348z - 44.004x$ **25.** $-\dfrac{1}{2}x + \dfrac{1}{2}$ **26.** $\dfrac{13}{8}z + \dfrac{7}{32}$ **27.** $7x^3 - 2x^2y - 4xy^2 + 9y^3$

28. $10d^5 - 10d^3e^2 + 14d^2e^3 - 16e^5$ **29.** $\dfrac{65}{42}x + \dfrac{19}{42}y$ **30.** $-\dfrac{118}{99}a + \dfrac{134}{99}b$

31. $13.74a^2 - 10.08b^2 + 2.35ab + 8.45$ **32.** $29.3m^3 - 9.2n^2 - 8.2mn$
33. $35a^3 - 41b^3 + 5ab + 4a^2 - 7b^2 + 5$ **34.** $7m^3 + 29n^2 - 14mn + 16m^2 - 11n^3$ **35.** $a - 3$
36. $x + 1$ **37.** $15w - 5$ **38.** $14k - 17$ **39.** $3.6x + 4.8$ **40.** $6.7y - 4.2$ **41.** $66x - 79$
42. $25 - 10t$ **43.** $-29d + 7c$ **44.** $-57r + 22t$ **45.** $2.3z + 1.3$ **46.** $0.7x - 4.4$ **47.** $-72 - 43y$
48. $718z - 91$ **49.** $-x + 6y + 3z$ **50.** $40a + 33b + 14c$ **51.** $13z - 7$ **52.** $-216p + 114$
53. $2.3y + 0.8z$ **54.** $-1.92t - 12.8r$ **55.** 0 **56.** $2x - 2y$ **57.** 0 **58.** 0 **59.** $2a$ **60.** $-10m$
61. Willy needs 1232 feet of fencing. **62.** Joshua needs 216 inches of stripping.
63. Rusty needs 294 square inches of balsa wood. **64.** Tammy needs 1176 square inches of foil.
65. Profit $= 13.5 + 0.9x$; Carl will realize a $238.50 profit on the job.
66. Net $\$ = 23 + 30x$; Pete will realize a profit of $128 on the job.
67. Gain $= 2.75 + 1.5x$; The net profit is $8.75 for a 4-ounce letter.
68. Return $= 7 + 1.5x$; Tillie will have a net return of $175 on a 112-page manuscript.
69. Cost $= 10.4895x$; Change $= 50 - 10.4895x$; Laurie will pay $31.47 for the 3 CD's and get $18.53 in change.
70. Return $= 10.5x - 18.5$; Mary Lynne will earn $212.50 from the shirts.

71. \$ made $= 9x + 4.5y$; \$855 was made on the dinner.
72. \$ made $= 30.5x + 20.5y$; The company will make \$886 from the tour.

Experiencing Algebra the Calculator Way

1. $-5.342x - 11.8105$ **2.** $1492x - 3996$ **3.** $-\dfrac{21}{260}x - \dfrac{33}{52}y$ **4.** $-1\dfrac{32}{75}x + 2\dfrac{13}{50}$ **5.** $0.91x + 1.0035$
6. $-1018.3646x - 119.3616$ **7.** $x + 3$

PROBLEM SET 3.3

Experiencing Algebra the Exercise Way

1. $62xy$ **2.** $496rs$ **3.** $-960ab$ **4.** $-605xy$ **5.** $220mn$ **6.** $-3nm$ **7.** $3.01st$ **8.** $-0.272xy$
9. $-\dfrac{10}{27}cd$ **10.** $-\dfrac{2}{9}mn$ **11.** $48a + 84$ **12.** $130x + 325$ **13.** $-30x - 45$ **14.** $-60z - 12$
15. $20z + 56$ **16.** $2a + 410$ **17.** $7.7x - 16.06$ **18.** $3.96a - 2.88$ **19.** $33.6z + 40$ **20.** $24.5a + 105$
21. $-\dfrac{6}{7}m + \dfrac{1}{2}$ **22.** $-\dfrac{3}{22}z + \dfrac{15}{4}$ **23.** $\dfrac{5}{3}b - \dfrac{3}{4}$ **24.** $\dfrac{-5}{2}y + \dfrac{20}{3}$ **25.** $\dfrac{5}{12}d + \dfrac{3}{8}$ **26.** $4x + \dfrac{1}{14}$
27. $15x^2 + 12xy$ **28.** $6x^2 + 12xy$ **29.** $36cd + 84d^2$ **30.** $20x^2 + 28xy$ **31.** $1.98m^2 - 3.24mn$
32. $5.81zy - 3.43z^2$ **33.** $-\dfrac{9}{17}a^2 - \dfrac{3}{5}ab$ **34.** $\dfrac{1}{6}m^2 - \dfrac{7}{10}mn$ **35.** $\dfrac{3}{8}m^2 - \dfrac{3}{2}mn$ **36.** $\dfrac{5}{16}ab - \dfrac{5}{2}b^2$
37. $12p$ **38.** $14x$ **39.** $-3x$ **40.** $-4z$ **41.** $2z$ **42.** $2b$ **43.** $-2c$ **44.** $-3m$ **45.** $-\dfrac{1}{4}x$
46. $-\dfrac{5}{36}y$ **47.** $\dfrac{1}{6}a$ **48.** $\dfrac{3}{4}b$ **49.** $5x$ **50.** $5a$ **51.** $-0.2s$ **52.** $-2.4x$ **53.** $-11.1q$ **54.** $23.5a$
55. $-\dfrac{1}{9}m$ **56.** $-\dfrac{1}{7}c$ **57.** $3x + 5$ **58.** $-6m - 3n$ **59.** $-3b + \dfrac{1}{2}c$ **60.** $0.3m - n$
61. $12a + 3b - 15c$ **62.** $-15x - 4y + 25z$ **63.** $-73a + 78b - 60c$ **64.** $-51x + 252y - 249z$
65. $40.3x - 6.7y$ **66.** $65.8p - 18.2q$ **67.** $\dfrac{5}{12}p - \dfrac{55}{84}q$ **68.** $-\dfrac{11}{24}a - \dfrac{1}{18}b$ **69.** $11 + 4x + 4y$
70. $-51x + 31y - 19$ **71.** $-24a - 30b - 17c + 18$ **72.** $-117x - 77y - 31z + 33$
73. $6x + 60y - 132z$ **74.** $4a + 26b - 64c$ **75.** $7a + 8c$ **76.** $6x - 13y$ **77.** $0.7m - 8.4n$
78. $-7.48a + 13.9b$ **79.** Surface area $= 10w^2$; The surface area is 40 square feet
80. Surface area $= 10w^2$; The surface area is 1440 square inches   **81.** Expense $= 275x + 0.2y + 100$; \$1325
is the total trip expense.   **82.** Expense $= 223x + 0.25y + 150$; The total trip expense is \$1006.50.
83. Expense $= 200x + 0.22y + 550$; \$1032.50 is the total expense.   **84.** Expense $= 450 + 285x + 0.36y$;
The total expense is \$1671.   **85.** Cost $= 124x + 44$; The total cost is \$912.
86. Price $= 109.8x$; The total price is \$2635.20.

Experiencing Algebra the Calculator Way

1. $165,459x + 618,940y$ **2.** $49.6a + 90.82b$ **3.** $4400.226x + 4191.8788y - 170,736.5727$ **4.** $\dfrac{123}{8}x - \dfrac{123}{10}y$

5. $5.12ac$ **6.** -50.9 **7.** $16.5y$ **8.** $-\dfrac{4}{9}y$ **9.** $-\dfrac{2}{3}$ **10.** $-\dfrac{3}{2}y$ **11.** $7c$ **12.** $\dfrac{1}{3}x - \dfrac{3}{7}y$

PROBLEM SET 3.4

Experiencing Algebra the Exercise Way

1. equation   **2.** expression   **3.** expression   **4.** equation   **5.** equation   **6.** expression   **7.** equation
8. expression   **9.** expression   **10.** equation   **11.** true   **12.** true   **13.** false   **14.** false
15. false   **16.** true   **17.** true   **18.** false   **19.** false   **20.** false   **21.** false   **22.** true

23. false **24.** true **25.** false **26.** false **27.** yes **28.** no **29.** no **30.** no **31.** no
32. yes **33.** yes **34.** yes **35.** yes **36.** no **37.** no **38.** yes **39.** yes **40.** no

41. $7 + 6(5) = 3(7) + 4^2$ **42.** $\dfrac{21}{-3} = 8 - 15$ **43.** $x + 6 = 15$ **44.** $2x - 5 = x + 2$ **45.** $2x = 12$

46. $\dfrac{x}{12} = 2200$ **47.** $x^2 - 21 = 100$ **48.** $2x - 100 = x + 50$ **49.** $2(x + 5^2) = x + 100$

50. $\dfrac{1}{2}x + 60 = 200$ **51.** $2(x + 2) = 4 + 2x$ **52.** $3(x - 6) = 3x - 18$ **53.** $17 + \dfrac{x}{2} = 4 + 3x$

54. $x^2 + x = 2x$ **55.** $p = d + \pi r$ **56.** $r = \dfrac{d}{t}$ **57.** $I = A - P$ **58.** $A = P + I$

Experiencing Algebra the Calculator Way

1. true **2.** true **3.** false **4.** false **5.** true **6.** true **7.** false **8.** true **9.** true
10. false **11.** false **12.** true **13.** true **14.** yes **15.** no **16.** yes **17.** yes

---

PROBLEM SET 3.5

Experiencing Algebra the Exercise Way

1. 468 in^2; 104 in. **2.** 600 mm^2; 160 mm **3.** 24 cm^2; 20 cm **4.** 40 ft^2; 26 ft **5.** $\dfrac{25}{4}$ ft^2; 10 ft

6. 31.36 m^2; 22.4 m **7.** 3060 m^2; 242 m **8.** 3705 in^2; 368 in. **9.** 100 ft^2; 52 ft **10.** 660 cm^2; 120 cm
11. 86.6 in^2; 33.0 in. **12.** 23.8 ft^2; 17.3 ft **13.** 15 ft^3; 46 ft^2 **14.** 72 ft^3; 108 ft^2 **15.** 421.875 in^3; 337.5 in^2
16. 551.368 cm^3; 403.44 cm^2 **17.** 35.3 in^3; 61.3 in^2 **18.** 117.8 in^3; 133.5 in^2 **19.** 4189 cm^3; 1257 cm^2
20. 524 in^3; 314 in^2 **21.** 0.049 ft^3; 0.817 ft^2 **22.** 33.51 cm^3; 64.38 cm^2 **23.** 320 cm^3 **24.** 4 ft^3 **25.** 25°

26. 19° **27.** 115° **28.** 56° **29.** 79° **30.** 45° **31.** 58 in. **32.** 34 m **33.** $6\dfrac{1}{2}$ cm **34.** $\dfrac{25}{36}$ yard

35. 7.69 mm **36.** 12.85 m **37.** John will need to cover 189 ft^2. **38.** The triangle contains 54 ft^2 of space.; The perimeter is 36 feet. **39.** The area of coverage is 2704 in^2.; Gretchen will need 208 inches of fringe material. **40.** The area of the tablecloth is 50.3 ft^2.; Karen Ann will need 25.1 feet of lace edging.
41. Linda had 102 ft^2 of sod removed.; She needed 41 feet of border. **42.** The deck contains 225 ft^2 of space.; Marcos will need 56 feet of latticework. **43.** The square footage of the area is 78.5 ft^2.; The border will be 31.4 feet. **44.** The area of the floor of the wine cellar is 112 ft^2. **45.** The lot is 55,000 ft^2.
46. Rick will have 360 ft^2 of driveway.; He will need 84 feet of timber. **47.** The box will hold 16 ft^3 of toys.; Jim painted 40 ft^2 of surface area, using 2 pints of paint. **48.** The cheese ball contains 33.5 in^3 of cheese.; 50.3 in^2 of pecans cover the ball. **49.** The barrel contains 12.6 ft^3 of space.; 31.4 ft^2 of surface area will need to be painted. **50.** The cube contains 15.625 ft^3 of ice.; The surface area is 37.5 ft^2. **51.** The tank will hold 4188.8 in^3 of gas.; The surface area is 1256.6 in^2. **52.** The volume of the crate is 16 ft^3.; The outer surface contains 40 ft^2 of wood. **53.** The case contains 5832 in^3, with a surface area of 1944 in^2.
54. It will take 1005.3 in^3 of pellets.; The surface area is 603.2 in^2.

55. The volume of the paperweight is $28\dfrac{7}{12}$ in^3. **56.** The volume of the bag is 84.8 in^3.

57. The third angle is 85°. **58.** The third angle is 60°. **59.** The pitch of the roof is 40°.
60. The angle formed with the driveway is 20°. **61.** The other angle is 135°. **62.** The other angle is 120°.
63. The diagonal must measure 10 feet. **64.** The diagonal measure must be 13 feet.

Experiencing Algebra the Calculator Way

Students should develop other programs for various formulas.

Experiencing Algebra the Exercise Way

1. JoAnne paid $162.50 in interest.   **2.** Jack paid $385 in interest.   **3.** Simple interest is better.
4. Simple interest is better.   **5.** The option in exercise 1 is the best choice.   **6.** The option in exercise 6 is the best choice.   **7.** $2.92 of interest is earned.   **8.** The interest will be $2 and the total will be $102.
9. $48 in interest is paid.   **10.** The simple interest is $144.   **11.** Steve earned $376.20 in interest.
12. Sharona earned $1558.27 in interest.   **13.** Chauncie had $1610.21 in interest.   **14.** Chelsea earned $472.46 in interest.   **15.** The interest earned will be $374.59.   **16.** The interest earned will be $463.51.
17. The interest is $189.31.   **18.** The interest is $452.38.   **19.** The interest is $929.89.
20. The interest is $3410.14.   **21.** The temperature is 77°F.   **22.** The temperature is 87.8°F.
23. The temperature is $33\frac{1}{3}$°C.   **24.** The temperature is 18.9°C.   **25.** The temperature is 212°F.
26. The temperature is 1945.4°F.   **27.** The temperature is 203°F.   **28.** The temperature is 5370.8°F.
29. The temperature is −38.87°C.   **30.** The temperature is 356.58°C.   **31.** The temperature is 28.9°C.
32. The temperature is 22.8°C.   **33.** The distance covered was 522.5 miles.   **34.** The trip was 511.5 miles.
35. He drove 223.806 miles.   **36.** He drove 460.848 miles.   **37.** The pie is 56 feet high.
38. The banana is 850 ft from the ground.   **39.** The baseball is 131 ft high.   **40.** The fire cracker is 4 ft high.
41. It will take 1.924 seconds.   **42.** It will take 2.221 seconds.   **43.** The period is 1.666 seconds.
44. The period is 2.127 seconds.   **45.** The period is 0.962 seconds.   **46.** The period is 1.859 seconds.
47. The leg takes 1.756 seconds.; Eydie's speed is 2.28 feet per second.   **48.** The stride takes 5.554 seconds.; Gargantua is running 10.8 feet per second.

Experiencing Algebra the Calculator Way

Number of Years (n)	Amount earned (A)	Interest $= A - 80{,}000$
5	$122,367	$42,367
10	$187,172	$107,172
15	$286,296	$206,296
20	$437,916	$357,916
25	$669,832	$589,832
30	$1,024,568	$944,568

CHAPTER 3 REVIEW

Reflections

1–9. Answers will vary.

Exercises

1. $55x + 4$ **2.** $55(x + 4)$ **3.** $\frac{3}{4}(x + 35)$ **4.** $\frac{3}{4}x + 35$ **5.** $2x - 20$ **6.** $20 - 2x$ **7.** $2500 + 275n$

8. $\frac{650}{h}$ **9.** $200 + 5.5k$ For problems 10–18, answers will vary. One possibility is given.

10. The sum of 5 and a number.   **11.** The difference of 8 and 6 times some number.
12. The product of 9 and a number, divided by 6.   **13.** Two-thirds of the difference of a number and 75.
14. The square of one number added to another number.   **15.** The product of three different numbers.

16. 15   **17.** −48   **18.**   **19.** 2   **20.** $\frac{4}{15}$ **21.** undefined   **22.** 79.48   **23.** 325   **24.** 225   **25.** −225

26. 225   **27.** $1200 + 75m$; Sandi will have $2100 after 12 months.; Yes, she will have enough money.

28. $3; 3x^2, -16x, 35$ **29.** $4; 5x, 12, -3y, -16$ **30.** $3; 2(x + 1), -4(y + 2), -4$ **31.** $3; a^2, 2ab, b^2$
32. $3, -2, 4, 9; 3x$ and $4x, -2y$ and $9y$ **33.** $2, -1, 3, -5; 2a^2$ and $3a^2$ **34.** $2.4, 5.1, 6.2; 2.4x$ and $6.2x$

35. $4, -2, 2; 4(a + b)$ and $-2(a + b)$ **36.** $-11c$ **37.** $0.2z$ **38.** $24x - 42$ **39.** $\dfrac{1}{12}x + \dfrac{7}{8}y$

40. $9x^2 + 28xy + 5y^2 - 2$ **41.** $-19p + 21$ **42.** $3a + 7$ **43.** $7a + 8b$
44. $2.75(x + y) - (1.25x + 1.5y) = 1.5x + 1.25y$; The net profit is $930.
45. $20 - 5.3x$; Katie received $4.10 in change.   **46.** $8.75x - 52.65$; Margaret's net profit is $227.35.

47. $70ab$ **48.** $8.2m$ **49.** $-7.6a + 9.4ab$ **50.** $-\dfrac{5}{14}x + \dfrac{1}{9}y$ **51.** $6x^2 - 34xy$ **52.** $41m$

53. $-\dfrac{3}{16}z$ **54.** $18.3ab$ **55.** $-77.22a$ **56.** $3a - 4b + 2c$ **57.** $129x + 3y$ **58.** $-12x - 21y - 31$

59. $10a - 26b - 3c + 15$ **60.** Tom: x; Charles: $2x - 5$; Jim: $x + 7$; All three: $4x + 2$; 182 is the pushups total.
61. $335x + 0.2y$; The total cost is $1409.   **62.** expression   **63.** equation   **64.** equation   **65.** expression
66. false   **67.** true   **68.** true   **69.** false   **70.** no   **71.** yes   **72.** yes   **73.** yes   **74.** no

75. $3 + 2(27 - 15) = 3^3$ **76.** $5 + 4x = 65 + \dfrac{x}{4}$ **77.** 208 m^2; 68 m   **78.** 880 in^2; 128 in.

79. 225 cm^2; 60 cm   **80.** 65 m^2; 34 m   **81.** 9450 yard^2; 425 yard   **82.** 467.59 ft^2; 76.65 ft
83. 6615 in^3; 2478 in^2 **84.** 3112.136 mm^3; 1278.96 mm^2 **85.** 54,965.3 in^3; 8143.01 in^2

86. 145,124.7 cm^3; 13,355.04 cm^2 **87.** 117.3 cm^3; 151.6 cm^2 **88.** $66\dfrac{2}{3}$ in^3 **89.** The other angle is 122°.

90. The other angle is 32°.   **91.** The third angle is 25°.   **92.** The hypotenuse is 29 in.
93. The hypotenuse is 29.89 cm.   **94.** Dan should order 5100 ft^2 of sod and 252 ft of fencing.
95. The garden will have about 197.9 ft^2.   **96.** The two 10-in. pizzas are the better deal.
97. The truck will hold 80 ft^3.   **98.** The surface area is approximately 113.1 ft^2.   **99.** The other angle is 50°.
100. The diagonal must be 22.5 feet.   **101.** The total amount of the loan is $956.25
102. The interest is $9472.01.   **103.** The amount of interest is $9347.92.   **104.** The temperature is 122°F.

105. The temperature is $26\dfrac{2}{3}$°C.   **106.** LuAnn traveled 356.5 miles.   **107.** The wedding bouquet is 36 feet

above the ground.   **108.** The height is 128 feet after 2 seconds.; The height is 144 feet after 3 seconds.;
The height is 128 feet after 4 seconds.; The height is 80 feet after 5 seconds.   **109.** The period is 2.72 seconds.
110. The first option is the better choice.

CHAPTER 3 MIXED REVIEW

1. $4; 12x, y, -z, 23$ **2.** $3; 3(a - 2), 5(b - 4), 75$ **3.** $5; 12, -7x, 14x, -18, x$ **4.** $1, -2, -5, 4, -1, 6;$
x and $4x, -2y$ and $-y, -5$ and 6 **5.** $1, 2, -3, 6, 1; b^2$ and $-3b^2, 2b$ and $6b$ **6.** -54 **7.** 54 **8.** -54
9. 54 **10.** 324 **11.** -324 **12.** 324 **13.** -324 **14.** 10.77033 **15.** 4 **16.** not a real number
17. 0 **18.** 35 **19.** undefined   **20.** true   **21.** true   **22.** false   **23.** true   **24.** yes   **25.** no
26. yes   **27.** yes   **28.** no   **29.** no   **30.** $17h$ **31.** $8m + 10$ **32.** $27x - 8 + 15y$
33. $15x^4 + x^3 - 7x^2 - 46x - 1$ **34.** $10.9a + 3.4b$ **35.** $-27y + 15$ **36.** $4g + 4$ **37.** $-x - 2y - 15z$

38. $-42xy$ **39.** $\dfrac{3}{10}a + \dfrac{9}{20}b$ **40.** $25.36z$ **41.** $8x - 12y + 17z$ **42.** $-\dfrac{7}{25}v$ **43.** $3x - 4y + 6z$

44. $35.9x - 49.3y$ **45.** $-144a + 132b - 252$ **46.** $-30x + 45$ **47.** $2(x + 50) - \dfrac{1}{2}x$ **48.** $11 + \dfrac{1}{4}x$

49. $x^2 + 2x = x + 306$ **50.** $225 + 45x$; Lakeetha will make $5625 in earnings.   **51.** $500 + 145n - 15n$;
Carmen has $2450 deposited after 15 weeks.; She has a $1825 balance after the withdrawal.

52. (a) Beatrice: x; Marie: $2x - 5$; Ann: $\dfrac{1}{2}x$; Magdalene: x

(b) Beatrice: $100 + 25x$; Marie: $100 + 25(2x - 5)$; Ann: $100 + 25\left(\dfrac{1}{2}x\right)$; Magdalene: $100 + 25x$

(c) $100 + 25x + 100 + 25(2x - 5) + 100 + 25\left(\dfrac{1}{2}x\right) + 100 + 25x$

(d) $275 + 112.5x$ **(e)** \$2525 total money is earned.   **53.** Fred must buy 16,000 ft^2 of sod.

54. Chums's pool will hold 1413.7 ft^3 of water.   **55.** The temperature is $35\dfrac{5}{9}$°C.   **56.** You will have \$31,600.67 over 10 years.   **57.** Randy bicycled 16.25 miles.   **58.** The hypotenuse is 193 mm.   **59.** The can's volume is about 12.44 in^3.; The can's surface area is about 31.91 in^2.   **60.** The ball is 70 feet after 1 second.; The ball is 102 feet after 2 seconds.; The ball is 102 ft after 3 seconds.; The ball is 70 ft after 4 seconds.; The ball is 6 feet after 5 seconds.   **61.** Answer will vary. Possible answer: The sum of $\dfrac{2}{3}$ times a number and 25.

62. Answer will vary. Possible answer: Seven times the difference of a number and 45, added to 15.
63. equation   **64.** expression   **65.** expression   **66.** equation   **67.** The complementary angle is 5°.
68. The supplementary angle is 137°.   **69.** The third angle is 91°.

CHAPTER 3 TEST

1. $\dfrac{x}{12}$ **2.** $\dfrac{12}{x}$ **3.** $1.08x$; \$16.20   **4.** Answer will vary. Possible answer: b subtracted from the square of a
5. 1   **6.** -8 **7.** 36   **8.** -36 **9.** 36   **10.** 8 terms   **11.** $y^3, -5y^2, 15y, 7y^2, 4y, 6y^3$ **12.** $-3, -12$
13. $1, -5, 15, -3, 7, -12, 4, 6$ **14.** y^3 and $6y^3$, $-5y^2$ and $7y^2$, $15y$ and $4y$, -3 and -12 **15.** $\dfrac{5}{6}x + \dfrac{29}{18}y - \dfrac{5}{9}$
16. $6p - q$ **17.** $-5x + 9$ **18.** $6a^2 + 12ab - 16ac$ **19.** no   **20.** yes   **21.** The tool box's volume is 12 ft^3.; The outside surface area is 34 ft^2.   **22.** Tracy's account will have \$18,050.03 in 40 years.
23. The supplementary angle is 102°.   **24.** The hypotenuse is 52 inches.   **25.** The temperature is 77°F.
26. Answer will vary. Possible answer: The area is the space contained within the boundaries, whereas the perimeter is the distance around the boundaries.

Chapter 4

PROBLEM SET 4.1

Experiencing Algebra the Exercise Way

1.

x	y
-2	-6
-1	-1
0	4
1	9
2	14
3	19

2.

x	y
-3	18
-2	10
-1	2
0	-6
1	-14

3.

x	y
-15	-11
-10	-8
-5	-5
0	-2
5	1
10	4
15	7

4.

x	y
-18	-11
-9	-4
0	3
9	10
18	17
27	24
36	31

5.

x	y
−2	−3
−1	−0.7
0	1.6
1	3.9
2	6.2

6.

x	y
−3	5.2
−1	−4.4
0	−9.2
1	−14
3	−23.6

7.

x	y
−1	2
−4	1
−7	0
−10	−1
−13	−2

8.

x	y
−10	−2
−4	−1
2	0
8	1
14	2

For problems 9–16, answers will vary. One possibility is given.

9.

x	y
−2	−20
−1	−14
0	−8
1	−2
2	4

10.

x	y
−2	37
−1	26
0	15
1	4
2	−7

11.

x	y
−14	−6
−7	−4
0	−2
7	0
14	2

12.

x	y
−16	11
−8	8
0	5
8	2
16	−1

13.

x	y
−2	11.3
−1	6.7
0	2.1
1	−2.5
2	−7.1

14.

x	y
−2	−22
−1	−11.4
0	−0.8
1	9.8
2	20.4

15.

x	y
−6	−5
−2	−2
0	$-\frac{1}{2}$
2	1
6	4

16.

x	y
−11	−6
−3	−3
5	0
13	3
21	6

17.

x	y
−2	−37
0	−13
2	11

18.

x	y
−1	21
1	3

19.

y	z
−3	4
0	5
3	6

20.

q	p
−8	−11
0	−4
8	3

21.

b	a
−1	−8.5
0	5.7
1	19.9

22.

n	m
−2	−7.5
−1	−5.6
0	−3.7

23.

x	y
−3	10
−2	3
−1	0
0	1
1	6
2	15
3	28

24.

x	y
−2	−44
−1	−24
0	−10
1	−2
2	0
3	−4
4	−14

25.

x	y
−1	−5
0	−12
1	−7

26.

x	y
6	−100
7	−145
8	−198
9	−259

27.

x	y
−1	−2
1	undefined

28.

x	y
1	$-\frac{3}{2}$
3	undefined

29.

H	V
1	8
3	24
5	40
7	56
9	72

30.

s	V
1	1
2	8
3	27
4	64
5	125
6	216

31.

t	I
1	225
2	450
3	675
4	900
5	1125
6	1350
7	1575
8	1800
9	2025
10	2250
11	2475
12	2700

32.

t	I
1	210
3	630
5	1050
7	1470
9	1890
11	2310
13	2730
15	3150

33.

R	I
1	9
2	4.5
3	3
4	2.25
5	1.8
6	1.5
7	$\frac{9}{7}$
8	1.125
9	1

34.

R	V
2	10
3	15
4	20
5	25
6	30
7	35
8	40
9	45

35. $(-2, 1.6), (-1, 2.8), (0, 4), (1, 5.2), (2, 6.4)$
36. $(-4, 7.2), (-2, 6.6), (0, 6), (2, 5.4), (4, 4.8)$
37. $\left(\frac{1}{6}, \frac{5}{6}\right), \left(\frac{1}{5}, \frac{4}{5}\right), \left(\frac{1}{4}, \frac{3}{4}\right), \left(\frac{1}{3}, \frac{2}{3}\right), \left(\frac{1}{2}, \frac{1}{2}\right)$
38. $(1, 1), (2, 3), (3, 6), (4, 10), (5, 15)$ **39.** $(2, 8), (4, 16), (6, 24), (8, 32), (10, 40)$
40. $(4, 6), (6, 4), (8, 2), (9.5, 0.5)$ **41.** domain: $\{3, 5, 7, 9\}$;
range: $\{15.8, 17.8, 19.8, 21.8\}$ **42.** domain: $\{11, 15, 19, 23\}$; range: $\{8, 12, 16, 20\}$
43. domain: $\{4\}$; range: $\{-3, -1, 1, 3, ...\}$

44. domain: $\{3, 2, 1, 0, -1, ...\}$; range: $\{-1\}$ **45.** domain: $\{2\}$; range: $\{..., -2, -1, 0, 1, 2, ...\}$
46. domain: $\{..., -2, -1, 0, 1, 2, ...\}$; range: $\{0\}$ **47.** domain: $\{2, 4, 6\}$; range: $\{3, 11, 19\}$
48. domain: $\{10, 20, 30\}$; range: $\{35, 65, 95\}$ **49.** domain: all real numbers; range: all real numbers
50. domain: all real numbers; range: all real numbers **51.** domain: all real numbers; range: all real numbers ≥ 1
52. domain: all real numbers; range: all real numbers ≥ -2
53. domain: all real numbers ≥ 2; range: all real numbers ≥ 0 **54.** domain: all real numbers ≥ -2;
range: all real numbers ≥ 0 **55.** domain: all real numbers $x \neq 2$; range: all real numbers $y \neq 0$
56. domain: all real numbers $x \neq 4$; range: all real numbers $y \neq 0$ **57.** domain: all real numbers $s > 0$;
range: all real numbers $V > 0$ **58.** domain: all real numbers $t \geq 0$; range: all real numbers $d \geq 0$
59. $s = -16t^2 + 50$; His position will be s feet high t seconds after the jump. **60.** $s = -16t^2 + 10t$;
Its position is s feet high t seconds after launch. **61.** $(1, 65), (2, 130), (3, 195), (4, 260)$; This distance traveled
(in miles) after 1, 2, 3, and 4 hours is 65, 130, 195, and 260 respectively. **62.** $(2.5, 78), (2.75, 70.91), (3, 65)$,
$(3.25, 60), (3.5, 55.71)$; If David completes the trip in 2.5, 2.75, 3, 3.25, or 3.5 hours, he was traveling at 78, 70.91,
65, 60, and 55.71 miles per hour respectively.

Experiencing Algebra the Calculator Way

1. $Y1 = 2.75x - 15.8$

X	Y1
-250	-703.3
-200	-565.8
-150	-428.3
-100	-290.8
-50	-153.3
0	-15.8
50	121.7

Y1■2.75X-15.8

X	Y1
100	259.2
150	396.7
200	534.2
250	671.7

Y1■2.75X-15.8

2. $Y1 = 3x^3 + 5x^2 + 7x + 9$

X	Y1
-5	-276
-3.873	-117.4
-3.142	-56.66
-3	-48
-2	-9
-1.442	.30467
0	9

Y1■3X^3+5X²+7X+9

X	Y1
2	67
3.1416	173.36
3.1623	176

Y1■3X^3+5X²+7X+9

3. $Y1 = (2x + 1)^4$

X	Y1
25	6.77E6
30	1.38E7
35	2.54E7
40	4.3E7
45	6.86E7
50	1.04E8

Y1=(2X+1)^4

4. $Y1 = (8)2\pi x + 2\pi x^2$

X	Y1
2	125.66
2.5	164.93
3	207.35
3.5	252.9
4	301.59
4.5	353.43
5	408.41

Y1=8*2πX+2πX²

5. $Y1 = 12000(1.075)^x$

X	Y1
1	12900
2	13868
3	14908
4	16026
5	17228
6	18520
7	19909

Y1=12000(1.075)...

X	Y1
8	21402
9	23007
10	24732
11	26587
12	28581

Y1=12000(1.075)...

6. $Y1 = 12000e^{(0.075x)}$

X	Y1
1	12935
2	13942
3	15028
4	16198
5	17460
6	18820
7	20286

Y1=12000e^(0.07...

X	Y1
8	21865
9	23568
10	25404
11	27383
12	29515

Y1=12000e^(0.07...

PROBLEM SET 4.2

Experiencing Algebra the Exercise Way

1.

2.

3.

4.

5.

6.

7.

8.

9.

10.

11.

12.

13.

14.

15.

16.

17.

18.

19.

20.

21. $A(8, 2), B(-9, 7), C(0, 0), D(-2, -3), E(0, 4), F(5, -6), G(-5, 0)$
22. $A(-7, -6), B(2, 4), C(-5, 2), D(0, -9), E(5, -5), F(9, -7), G(6, 0)$ **23.** quadrant II   **24.** quadrant III
25. quadrant I   **26.** quadrant IV   **27.** quadrant III   **28.** quadrant II   **29.** y-axis   **30.** x-axis
31. quadrant IV   **32.** quadrant I   **33.** x-axis   **34.** y-axis   **35.** x-axis   **36.** origin   **37.** quadrant I
38. quadrant II   **39.** y-axis   **40.** x-axis   **41.** quadrant IV   **42.** quadrant III   **43.** quadrant III
44. x-axis   **45.** y-axis   **46.** quadrant IV

47.

48.

49.

50.

51.

52.

53.

54.

55.

56.

57.

58.

59.

60.

61.

62.

63.

64.

65.

66.

67.

68.

69. domain: all real numbers; range: all real numbers ≤ -1 **70.** domain: all real numbers ≥ 3; range: all real numbers

71. domain: all real numbers; range: all real numbers ≥ 3

72. domain: $\{3\}$; range: all real numbers

73. domain: 1960 through 1992; range: approximately 45% to 62%; The domain represents the time period between the years 1960 and 1992 during which the data was collected. The range represents the percent of the adult population who identify themselves as Democrats for each year.   **74.** domain: 1980 through 1992; range: approximately 280 to 450; The domain represents the time period between the years 1980 and 1992 during which the data was collected. The range represents the number of aggravated assaults (per 100,000 inhabitants) in the U.S. for each year.   **75.** domain: all real numbers $0 \leq x \leq 2.5$; range: all real numbers $0 \leq y \leq 100$; The domain represents the time that has passed from 0 seconds to 2.5 seconds. The range represents the height from 100 feet to 0 feet.

76. domain: 0 to approximately 5; range: 0 to approximately 2.5; The domain represents the length in feet of a pendulum. The range represents the period in seconds of the pendulum's arc swing.

Experiencing Algebra the Calculator Way

A   **1.** Integer setting   **2.** Decimal setting   **3.** Standard setting

B   **1.** $Y1 = 0.6x - 1.2$ **2.** $Y1 = -0.5x + 2.2$ **3.** $Y1 = |x| - 2$

$(-2, -2.4), (-1, -1.8),$
$(0, -1.2), (1, -0.6), (2, 0)$

$(-2, 3.2), (-1, 2.7),$
$(0, 2.2), (1, 1.7), (2, 1.2)$

$(-2, 0), (-1, -1),$
$(0, -2), (1, -1), (2, 0)$

4. $Y1 = |x - 2|$

$(-2, 4), (-1, 3),$
$(0, 2), (1, 1), (2, 0)$

5. $Y1 = x - 2$

$(-2, -4), (-1, -3),$
$(0, -2), (1, -1), (2, 0)$

6. exercise 3:
    exercise 4: MATH ▶ 1 X,T,θ,n − 2) ;
    exercise 5: X,T,θ,n − 2

Experiencing Algebra the Exercise Way

1. not a function **2.** function **3.** function **4.** function **5.** not a function **6.** not a function
7. function **8.** function **9.** function **10.** function **11.** function **12.** function **13.** not a function
14. not a function **15.** function **16.** function **17.** function **18.** function **19.** not a function
20. not a function **21.** function **22.** function **23.** function **24.** function **25.** function
26. not a function **27.** not a function **28.** function **29.** function **30.** not a function **31.** 112
32. 1012 **33.** -128 **34.** -328 **35.** 60 **36.** -36 **37.** 7 **38.** 14 **39.** $20a + 12$
40. $-20a + 12$ **41.** $20a + 52$ **42.** $-20a + 52$ **43.** $20a - 68$ **44.** $-20a + 92$
45. $20a + 20b + 12$ **46.** $20b + 20a + 12$ **47.** 75 **48.** 3 **49.** 53 **50.** 11 **51.** 11.82 **52.** 4.62
53. $\dfrac{173}{25}$ **54.** $\dfrac{93}{25}$ **55.** $\dfrac{203}{25}$ **56.** $147\dfrac{1}{2}$ **57.** $2b^2 - 4b + 5$ **58.** $2b^2 + 4b + 5$ **59.** 6 **60.** 9
61. 24 **62.** 12 **63.** 4.5 **64.** 8.7 **65.** 22.5 **66.** 9.03 **67.** 7 **68.** 11 **69.** 23 **70.** 5
71. 10 **72.** 7 **73.** 3 **74.** 2 **75.** $\sqrt{-10}$, which is not a real number
76. $\sqrt{-85}$, which is not a real number **77.** 4.5 **78.** 4.6 **79.** $\dfrac{7}{2}$ **80.** $\dfrac{21}{5}$

81. $f(x) = 1500 + 35x$; The production run costs \$15,500.
82. $f(x) = 25{,}000 + 550x$; The cost of production is \$1,675,000.
83. $f(x) = 125x - 470$; The net revenue is \$49,530.
84. $f(x) = 1200x - 185$; The net revenue will be \$59,815.
85. $f(x) = 175x - 3x^2$; If 22 customers make reservations for the tour, the company will make \$2398.
86. $f(x) = (375 + 25x)(40 - x)$; The total monthly rental receipts will be \$16,650. **87.** $f(x) = 5 + 4x$;
The cost of 12 used CD's will be \$53. **88.** $f(x) = 35 + 1.5x$; The cost of 18 comics will be \$47.
89. $f(x) = 39 + 25x$; The charge for renting a truck for 3 days will be \$114.
90. $f(x) = 475 + 165x$; Susie's week's pay will be \$1135. **91.** $f(x) = 2.5 + x$; The charge is \$9.50.
92. $f(x) = 140 + 18.5x$; There will be a \$1527.50 charge for a party of 75 guests.

Experiencing Algebra the Calculator Way

exercises 1–6

X	Y1
65	278916
⁻83	⁻5.6E5
3.1416	45.017
1.4142	7.2426
5634	1.8E11
⁻3.142	⁻23.28

Y1◻X^3+X²+X+1

exercises 7–12

X	Y1
⁻8	4
0	4
⁻4	0
.8	4.8
⁻6.3	2.3
.75	4.75

Y1◻√(X²+8X+16)

exercises 13–18

X	Y1
10	1
⁻5	⁻.5
20	.33333
5.5	10
5	ERROR
.2	⁻1.042

Y1◻5/(X−5)

Experiencing Algebra the Exercise Way

1. (a) $(-2, 0), (6, 0)$ **(b)** $(0, 3)$ **(c)** $x < 2$ **(d)** $x > 2$ **(e)** 4 **(f)** none
2. (a) $(-1, 0), (3, 0)$ **(b)** $(0, -2)$ **(c)** $x > 1$ **(d)** $x < 1$ **(e)** none **(f)** -3
3. (a) $(-5, 0), (-1, 0), (4, 0)$ **(b)** $(0, -1)$ **(c)** $x < -3, x > 2$ **(d)** $-3 < x < 2$ **(e)** 2 **(f)** -3
4. (a) $(-3, 0), (1, 0), (5, 0)$ **(b)** $(0, -1)$ **(c)** $-1 < x < 3$ **(d)** $x < -1, x > 3$ **(e)** 3 **(f)** -2

5. $y = 3x - 6$

x-intercept: $(2, 0)$
y-intercept: $(0, -6)$

6. $y = 4x + 8$

x-intercept: $(-2, 0)$
y-intercept: $(0, 8)$

7. $y = \frac{1}{2}x + 1$

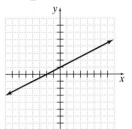

x-intercept: $(-2, 0)$
y-intercept: $(0, 1)$

8. $y = \frac{2}{3}x + 4$

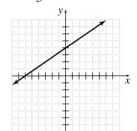

x-intercept: $(-6, 0)$
y-intercept: $(0, 4)$

9. $y = 1.2x - 6$

x-intercept: $(5, 0)$
y-intercept: $(0, -6)$

10. $y = 0.2x + 1$

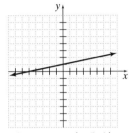

x-intercept: $(-5, 0)$
y-intercept: $(0, 1)$

11. $f(x) = -12x + 24$

x-intercept: $(2, 0)$
y-intercept: $(0, 24)$

12. $F(x) = 15x - 45$

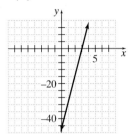

x-intercept: $(3, 0)$
y-intercept: $(0, -45)$

13. $f(x) = 9x + 15$

x-intercept: $\left(-\frac{5}{3}, 0\right)$

y-intercept: $(0, 15)$

14. $G(x) = -8x + 36$

x-intercept: $\left(\frac{9}{2}, 0\right)$

y-intercept: $(0, 36)$

15. $y = x^2 - 9$

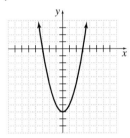

x-intercepts: $(3, 0)$,
$(-3, 0)$
y-intercept: $(0, -9)$

16. $y = x^2 - 16$

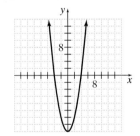

x-intercepts: $(4, 0)$,
$(-4, 0)$
y-intercept: $(0, -16)$

17. $y = x^2 + 6x + 9$

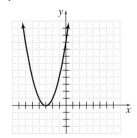

x-intercept: $(-3, 0)$

y-intercept: $(0, 9)$

18. $y = x^2 - 4x + 4$

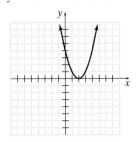

x-intercept: $(2, 0)$

y-intercept: $(0, 4)$

19. $y = 4x^2 + 4x + 1$

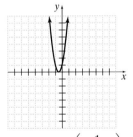

x-intercept: $\left(-\frac{1}{2}, 0\right)$

y-intercept: $(0, 1)$

20. $y = 4x^2 - 12x + 9$

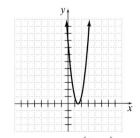

x-intercept: $\left(\frac{3}{2}, 0\right)$

y-intercept: $(0, 9)$

21. $g(x) = x^2 + 10x - 3$

x-intercepts: $(-10.29, 0)$, $(0.29, 0)$
y-intercept: $(0, -3)$

22. $f(x) = 0.4x^2 - 0.4x - 6.5$

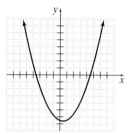

x-intercepts: $(-3.56, 0)$, $(4.56, 0)$
y-intercept: $(0, -6.5)$

23. $H(x) = x^2 - 5x - 24$

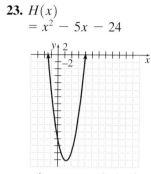

x-intercepts: $(-3, 0)$, $(8, 0)$
y-intercept: $(0, -24)$

24. $g(x) = 2x^2 + 13x - 70$

x-intercepts: $(-10, 0)$, $(3.5, 0)$
y-intercept: $(0, -70)$

25. $y = x^3 + x^2 - 2x$

x-intercepts: $(-2, 0)$, $(0, 0)$, $(1, 0)$
y-intercept: $(0, 0)$

26. $y = x^3 + 4x^2 + 3x$

x-intercepts: $(-3, 0)$, $(-1, 0)$, $(0, 0)$
y-intercept: $(0, 0)$

27. $f(x) = x^3 + 2x^2 - x - 2$

x-intercepts: $(-2, 0)$, $(-1, 0)$, $(1, 0)$
y-intercept: $(0, -2)$

28. $f(x) = x^3 + x^2 - 4x - 4$

x-intercepts: $(-2, 0)$, $(-1, 0)$, $(2, 0)$
y-intercept: $(0, -4)$

29. $h(x) = |x| - 6$

x-intercepts: $(-6, 0)$, $(6, 0)$

y-intercept: $(0, -6)$

30. $f(x) = |2x| - 6$

x-intercepts: $(-3, 0)$, $(3, 0)$

y-intercept: $(0, -6)$

31. $y = |2x - 3| - 1$

x-intercepts: $(1, 0), (2, 0)$

y-intercept: $(0, 2)$

32. $y = 5 - |3x + 1|$

x-intercepts: $(-2, 0)$, $\left(1\frac{1}{3}, 0\right)$

y-intercept: $(0, 4)$

33. $y = |x^2 - 2| - 1$

x-intercept: $(-1.73, 0)$,
$(-1, 0), (1, 0), (1.73, 0)$
y-intercept: $(0, 1)$

34. $y = |x^2 - 3| - 1$

x-intercept: $(-2, 0)$,
$(-1.41, 0), (1.41, 0)$,
$(2, 0)$
y-intercept: $(0, 2)$

35. $y = 2x + 8$

increasing for all
x-values

36. $y = 4 - x$

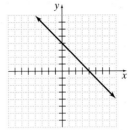

decreasing for all
x-values

37. $f(x) = 3 - 2x$

decreasing for all
x-values

38. $g(x) = x - 2$

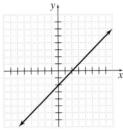

increasing for all
x-values

39. $y = 1 - x^2$

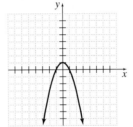

increasing for $x < 0$
decreasing for $x > 0$
relative maximum is 1

40. $y = x^2 + 1$

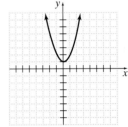

increasing for $x > 0$
decreasing for $x < 0$
relative minimum is 1

41. $g(x) = x^2 + 4x + 3$

increasing for $x > -2$
decreasing for $x < -2$
relative minimum is -1

42. $h(x) = 4x - 5 - x^2$

increasing for $x < 2$
decreasing for $x > 2$
relative maximum is -1

43. $y = |x + 3|$

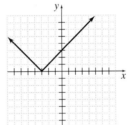

increasing for $x > -3$
decreasing for $x < -3$
relative maximum is 0

44. $y = |x| + 3$

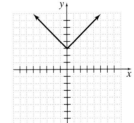

increasing for $x > 0$
decreasing for $x < 0$
relative minimum is 3

45. $f(x) = x^2 + 2x^2 - x - 2$

increasing for $x < -1.55$ and $x > 0.22$
decreasing for $-1.55 < x < 0.22$
relative maximum ≈ 0.63
relative minimum ≈ -2.11

46. $p(x) = -x^3 - x^2 + 4x - 4$

decreasing for $x < -1.54$ and $x > 0.87$
increasing for $-1.54 < x < 0.87$
relative minimum ≈ -8.88
relative maximum ≈ -1.94

47. $(4, 7)$ **48.** $(8, 1)$ **49.** $(-2, 3)$ **50.** $(-1, -2)$ **51.** $(-0.75, 5.75)$ **52.** $(-2.\overline{6}, 10.\overline{6})$
53. $(3.8, 12)$ **54.** $(3, 5)$ **55.** $(-1, 3), (1, 3)$ **56.** $(-5, 9), (5, 9)$ **57.** $(1, 3), (3, 11)$
58. $(-4, -2), (-1, 4)$ **59.** $(-2, -1), (4, 2)$ **60.** $(-3, -3), (6, 6)$ **61.** $(-7, 2), (7, 2)$
62. $(4, 4), (-12, 4)$
63. $Y1 = 5x - 50$ **64.** $Y1 = 50{,}000 - 5000x$

increasing for $x > 0$ decreasing for $0 < x < 10$
65. $Y1 = 400x - 10x^2$ for $0 < x \le 25$ **66.** $Y1 = 100x - x^2$ for $0 < x \le 65$

increasing for $0 < x < 50$ increasing for $0 < x < 20$
decreasing for $50 < x < 65$ decreasing for $20 < x < 25$
relative maximum at $x = 50$ relative maximum at $x = 20$

67. (a) $f(x) = 4x + 50$ **(b)** $g(x) = 10x$
   (c) $Y1 = 4x + 50$ **(d)** At $x = 8.3$ containers, the cost for producing and the cost
         $Y2 = 10x$ for selling is the same at \$83.33. This means that
                                               9 containers must be sold to cover the costs of production.

intersection at $(8.\overline{3}, 83.\overline{3})$

68. (a) $f(x) = 12x + 100$ **(b)** $g(x) = 24x$
   (c) $Y1 = 12x + 100$ **(d)** At $x = 8.\overline{3}$ carvings, the cost and revenue is equal at \$200.
         $Y2 = 24x$ This means that 9 carvings must be sold to cover the costs
                                               of production.

intersection at $(8.\overline{3}, 200)$

69. (a) $f(x) = 200 + 50x;\ g(x) = 75x$ **(c)** At 8 credit hours, the pay is the same, at \$600.
   (b) $Y1 = 4x + 50x$
         $Y2 = 75x$

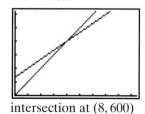

intersection at $(8, 600)$

70. (a) $f(x) = 25 + 10x$; $g(x) = 15x$ **(c)** At 5 lawns, the pay is the same, at $75.
   (b) $Y1 = 25 + 10x$
       $Y2 = 15x$

intersection at $(5, 75)$

Experiencing Algebra the Calculator Way

For problems 1–3, graphs will vary. **1.** $(-4.\overline{6}, 1.\overline{4})$ and $(6, 5)$ **2.** $(-5, -1)$ and $(5, -1)$
3. $(-6, 18)$ and $(6, 18)$

CHAPTER 4 REVIEW

Reflections

1–8. Answers will vary.

Exercises

Answers will vary.

1.

a	b
−3	13
−2	11
−1	9
0	7
1	5
2	3
3	1

2.

x	y
9	10
6	8
3	6
0	4
−3	2
−6	0
−9	−2

3.

x	y
−3	−2.4
−2	−2
−1	−1.6
0	−1.2
1	−0.8
2	−0.4
3	0

4.

b	a
−2	21
−1	10
1	6
2	13

5.

x	y
−18	−30,190
−7	−1898
0	−22
6	962
21	45,002
22.5	55,457.375

6.

x	y
−2	21
−1	12
0	5
1	0
2	3
3	4

7.

x	y
−2.7	7.994
−1.9	−4.054
−0.6	−13.804
0	−14.2
0.8	−10.696
1.5	−3.85
2.4	10.136

8. Answers will vary.
Possible answer:

x	y
−1	−33
0	−21
1	−9
2	3
3	15

9. Answers will vary.
Possible answer:

x	y
−2	7.7
−1	6.1
0	4.5
1	2.9
2	1.3

10. Answers will vary.
Possible answer:

x	y
−4	−12
−2	−9
0	−6
2	−3
4	0

11. Answers will vary.
Possible answer:

x	y
−4	17
−2	13
0	9
2	5
4	1

12.

x	y
−3	91
−1	15
1	−21
3	−17

13.

x	y
−15	−1
−10	2
−5	5
0	8
5	11
10	14
15	17

14.

x	y
−3	−64.2
−2	−47.1
−1	−30
0	−12.9
1	4.2
2	21.3
3	38.4

15.

x	y
−6	155
−2	39
0	17
3	29
8	169
11	325

16.

r	A
4	50.265
6	113.097
8	201.062
10	314.159

17.

r	V
3	339.3
6	678.6
9	1017.9
12	1357.2

18.

a	b
10	80
20	70
30	60
40	50
45	45

19.

t	A
2	2247.2
3	2382.03
4	2524.95

20.

F	C
−23	−30.6
−14	−25.6
0	−17.8
41	5
50	10
59	15
100	37.8

21.

t	d
2	130
3	195
4	260
5	325
6	390
7	455

22. $(-10, 37), (-5, 22), (0, 7), (5, -8), (10, -23)$
23. $(-8, 0), (-7, 1), (-4, 2), (1, 3), (8, 4)$
24. $(-6, -5), (-3, -3), (0, -1), (3, 1), (6, 3)$
25. $(2, 1), (4, 2), (6, 3), (8, 4), (10, 5)$ **26.** domain: $\{1, 3, 5, 7, 9\}$; range: $\{2, 6, 10, 14, 18\}$
27. domain: $\{..., -6, -4, -2, 0, 2, 4, 6, ...\}$; range: $\{..., 6, 4, 2, 0, -2, -4, -6, ...\}$
28. domain: $\{-5, -4, -3, -2, -1\}$; range: $\{-1, 3, 7, 11, 15\}$
29. domain: all real numbers; range: all real numbers ≥ 2.5
30. domain: all real numbers ≥ -5; range: all real numbers ≥ 0
31. domain: all real numbers $x \neq 1$; range: all real numbers $y \neq 0$
32. domain: all real numbers; range: all real numbers
33. domain: all real numbers ≥ 0; range: all real numbers ≥ 0

34.

35.

36.

37.

38.

39.

40. $A(5, 3)$ **41.** $B(-2, -5)$ **42.** $C(2, -2)$
43. $D(-3, 5)$ **44.** $E(5, 0)$ **45.** $F(0, -4)$
46. $G(0, 0)$ **47.** quadrant I   **48.** quadrant III
49. quadrant IV   **50.** quadrant II   **51.** x-axis
52. y-axis   **53.** origin

54.   **55.**   **56.**   **57.**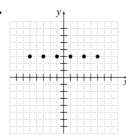

58. domain: all real numbers; range: all real numbers ≤ 2 **59.** domain: all real numbers; range: $\{-3\}$
60. domain: all real numbers; range: all real numbers   **61.** domain: all real numbers ≤ 2;
range: all real numbers ≥ 0 **62.** domain: all real numbers; range: all real numbers ≥ 0
63. domain: all real numbers; range: all real numbers ≤ 0 **64.** domain: years 1970 to 1993;
range: all real numbers $65 \leq y \leq 85$; For a year (independent variable) the energy consumption (dependent
variable) is graphed.   **65.** domain: integers 1 to 7; range: $\{40, 50, 55, 60\}$; The domain represents the number
of children from one family enrolled in the childcare center. The range represents the charge in dollars for a
week's care for the children from a family.   **66.** domain: all real numbers > 0; range: all real numbers > 0;
The length of a side (independent variable) and its corresponding area (dependent variable) is graphed.
67. not a function   **68.** function   **69.** function   **70.** not a function   **71.** function   **72.** not a function
73. No   **74.** Yes   **75.** -39 **76.** 97   **77.** 3   **78.** 27.8   **79.** $-4a + 1$ **80.** $4b + 13$ **81.** 44

82. 14   **83.** -2.25 **84.** $5a^2 + a - 4$ **85.** $5a^2 - a - 4$ **86.** $-\dfrac{63}{16}$ **87.** 3   **88.** 5   **89.** 11

90. $f(x) = 4500 + 17x$; The cost of producing 1200 widgets is \$24,900.   **91.** $f(x) = 50 + 25x$; The cost of a
4-day rental is \$150.   **92.** $f(x) = 1500 + 125x$; The charge for a training session for 20 employees is \$4,000.
93. $f(x) = 1.5x - 15$; He will make a profit of \$187.50.   **94. (a)** $(-5, 0), (1, 0), (6, 0)$ **(b)** $(0, 1)$
(c) $x < -3, x > 3$ **(d)** $-3 < x < 3$ **(e)** 3   **(f)** -3

95. $y = 3x + 9$ **96.** $y = 6 - x$ **97.** $y = \dfrac{3}{4}x - 9$ **98.** $y = x^2 - 0.36$

x-intercept: $(-3, 0)$
y-intercept: $(0, 9)$

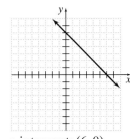
x-intercept: $(6, 0)$
y-intercept: $(0, 6)$

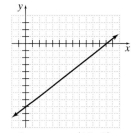
x-intercept: $(12, 0)$
y-intercept: $(0, -9)$

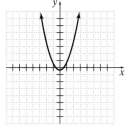
x-intercept: $(-0.6, 0)$,
$(0.6, 0)$
y-intercept: $(0, -0.36)$

99. $y = |x| - 4$

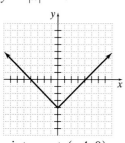

x-intercept: $(-4, 0)$, $(4, 0)$
y-intercept: $(0, -4)$

100. $y = 4x - 3$

increasing for all values of x

101. $h(x) = 6 - 2x$

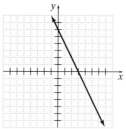

decreasing for all values of x

102. $y = 3 - x^2$

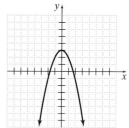

increasing for $x < 0$
decreasing for $x > 0$
relative maximum is 3

103. $y = |x| + 2$

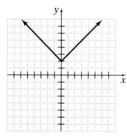

increasing for $x > 0$
decreasing for $x < 0$
relative minimum is 2

104. $y = |x^2 - 1|$

increasing for
$-1 < x < 0, x > 1$
decreasing for $x < -1$,
$0 < x < 1$
relative maximum is 1
relative minima are $0, 0$

105. $(3, 4)$ **106.** $(-2, -2), (3, 3)$
107. $(-7, 2), (-3, 2)$

108. $f(x) = 10.45x$

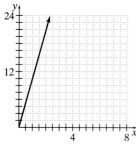

increasing for $x > 0$

109. $f(x) = 216 - 4.5x$

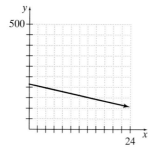

decreasing for $x > 0$

110. $Y1 = 325 + 325x - 15x^2$

increasing for $0 < x < 7$

111. (a) $f(x) = 400 + 65x$
　　　$g(x) = 100x$
(b) $Y1 = 400 + 65x$
　　　$Y2 = 100x$

intersect at approximately $(11.4, 1143)$
(c) At about 11.4 credit hours the stipend
is the same at about \$1143 for both options.

112. (a) $f(x) = 500 + 12x$
　　　$g(x) = 25x$
(b) $Y1 = 500 + 12x$
　　　$Y2 = 25x$

intersect at approximately $(38.5, 961.5)$
(c) At about 38.5 items, the cost to produce and
the revenue is equal at about \$961.5 each. This
means 39 items must be sold to break even.

CHAPTER 4 MIXED REVIEW

1. 0　　**2.** 18　　**3.** 7.2　　**4.** 11.7　　**5.** $b + 9$　　**6.** $-h + 8$　　**7.** 0　　**8.** 0　　**9.** -6.25

10. $v^2 - 3v - 4$　　**11.** $v^2 + 3v - 4$　　**12.** $-\dfrac{14}{9}$　　**13.** 4　　**14.** 8　　**15.** 16　　**16.** Yes　　**17.** No

18. Yes　　**19.** No　　**20.** Yes

21. $y = 5x - 10$

x-intercept at $(2, 0)$
y-intercept at $(0, -10)$
increasing for all x-values

22. $y = 8 - 2x$

x-intercept at $(0, 8)$
y-intercept at $(4, 0)$
decreasing for all x-values

23. $y = 4.8x - 1.2$

x-intercept at $(0.25, 0)$
y-intercept at $(0, -1.2)$
increasing for all x-values

24. $y = \dfrac{2}{5}x + 4$

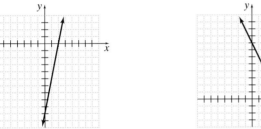

x-intercept at $(-10, 0)$
y-intercept at $(0, 4)$
increasing for all x-values

25. $y = x^2 - 1.21$

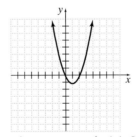

x-intercepts at $(-1.1, 0)$ and $(1.1, 0)$
y-intercept at $(0, -1.21)$
increasing for $x > 0$
decreasing for $x < 0$
relative minimum is -1.21

26. $y = 2 - |x|$

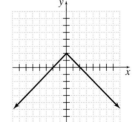

x-intercepts at $(-2, 0)$, $(2, 0)$
y-intercept at $(0, 2)$
increasing for $x < 0$
decreasing for $x > 0$
relative maximum is 2

27. $(-3, -4)$　　**28.** $(0, 0), (3, 9)$　　**29.** $(-1, 2), (3, 6)$　　**30.** domain: $\{2, 4, 6, 8, 10\}$; range: $\{1, 2, 3, 4, 5\}$
31. domain: $\{..., -6, -4, -2, 0, 2, 4, 6, ...\}$; range: $\{3\}$　　**32.** domain: $\{-5, -4, -3, -2, -1\}$; range: $\{25, 16, 9, 4, 1\}$

33. domain: all real numbers; range: all real numbers ≥ -1.5 **34.** domain: all real numbers ≥ 8; range: all real numbers ≥ 0 **35.** domain: all real numbers $x \neq 0$; range: all real numbers 0
36. domain: all real numbers; range: all real numbers   **37.** domain: all real numbers $\leq +3$; range: all real numbers ≥ 0 **38.** domain: all real numbers; range: all real numbers ≥ 0
39. domain: all real numbers; range: all real numbers ≤ 3 **40.** $(-6, 60), (-3, 36), (0, 12), (3, -12), (6, -36)$
41. $(3, 1), (2, 2), (1, \sqrt{7}), (0, \sqrt{10}), (-1, \sqrt{13}), (-2, 4)$ **42.** $(-7, 1), (0, 5), (7, 9), (14, 13), (21, 17)$

43.

x	y
−2	33
0	−5
2	5

44.

x	y
−8	−11
−4	−8
0	−5
4	−2
8	1

45.

x	y
−2	25.2
−1	20.5
0	15.8
1	11.1
2	6.4

46.

x	y
−2	35
$-\frac{3}{4}$	0
0	−15
$\frac{3}{4}$	−25.5
5	0

47.

x	y
−15	−3164
−5	−104
0	1
5	156
15	3616
25	16,276

48.

x	y
−6	95
−3	20
0	1
3	32
6	119
9	260

49.

x	y
−3.7	63.014
−2.2	26.504
−0.7	10.694
0	10.4
0.8	15.584
2.3	41.174
3.8	87.464

50. Answers will vary. Possible answer:

x	y
−1	22
0	17
1	12

51. Answers will vary. Possible answer:

x	y
−1	−6.1
0	−1.6
1	2.9

52. Answers will vary. Possible answer:

x	y
−4	2
0	3
4	4

53. Answers will vary. Possible answer:

x	y
−3	19
0	10
3	1

54. $\left(\frac{1}{4}, 1.5708\right), \left(\frac{1}{2}, 3.1416\right), (1, 6.2832), \left(\frac{3}{2}, 9.4248\right), (2, 12.566)$

55.

s	A
3	9
5	25

56.

H	V
1	2
1.25	2.5
1.5	3
1.75	3.5
2	4

57.

a	b
30	150
60	120
90	90
120	60
150	30

58.

t	I
2	240
3	360
4	480

59.

C	F
−10	14
−5	23
0	32
5	41
10	50
15	59
20	68
25	77

60. $f(x) = 2500 + 12x$; The production run will cost $22,300.
61. $f(x) = 15 + 2x$; It will cost $35 to rent the grinder for 10 hours.
62. $f(x) = 275 + 9.5x$; A luncheon for 135 employees will cost $1557.50.
63. $f(x) = -185 + 4x$; The net profit for the game will be $1055.

64. $Y1 = 250 - 3.5x$

decreasing for $0 < x < 71.43$

65. $Y1 = 1000 + 50x$

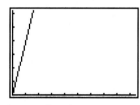

increasing for $x > 0$

66. $Y1 = x(100 - x)$

increasing for $0 < x < 50$
decreasing for $50 < x < 100$

67. (a) $f(x) = 25,000 + 5000x$
$g(x) = 6000x$
(b) $Y1 = 25,000 + 5000x$
$Y2 = 6000x$

intersect at $(25, 150,000)$
(c) At 25 years, the money received is the same at $150,000.

68. (a) $f(x) = 22x + 600$
$g(x) = 75x$
(b) $Y1 = 22x + 600$
$Y2 = 75x$

intersect at approximately $(11.32, 849.06)$
(c) At about 11.32 appliances the total acquisition cost and total revenue are equal at about $849.06. This means 12 appliances must be sold to break even.

CHAPTER 4 PRACTICE TEST

1.

x	y
−9	0
0	−9
3	60

2. $y = |2x|$

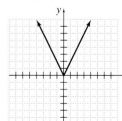

3. all real numbers   **4.** all real numbers ≥ 0
5. Yes; All possible vertical lines cross the graph a maximum of one time.   **6.** $x > 0$ **7.** $x < 0$
8. none   **9.** 0   **10.** $(0, 0)$ **11.** $(0, 0)$
12. $A(1, 2), B(-2, -4), C(-5, 3), D(2, -5), E(0, -2)$
13. quadrant IV   **14.** 8   **15.** 3   **16.** $a + 5$
17. $-\frac{1}{2}b + 6$ **18.** $f(x) = 450 + 21.5x$
19. The cost is $5825.   **20.** $(2, -4)$

21. Answers will vary. Possible answer: Each point in the plane corresponds to an ordered pair. The first number denotes the distance and direction along the x-axis. The second number denotes the distance and direction along the y-axis.

CUMULATIVE REVIEW CHAPTERS 1–4

1. 12　　**2.** 0, 12　　**3.** $-\dfrac{2}{3}$; 0; 12; $1\dfrac{4}{5}$; -0.33　　**4.** $\sqrt{7}$　　**5.** $>$　　**6.** $>$　　**7.** $<$

8.

9. -15　**10.** -2.56　**11.** 3　**12.** $-\dfrac{31}{24}$

13. $-1\dfrac{37}{40}$　**14.** $\dfrac{63}{640}$　**15.** -62.208　**16.** 0

17. 96　**18.** 31　**19.** -6.2　**20.** 0　**21.** -8　**22.** $\dfrac{4}{5}$　**23.** -1.095　**24.** not a real number

25. 1.051　**26.** 1　**27.** 1　**28.** indeterminate　**29.** -4096　**30.** 4096　**31.** $\dfrac{16}{9}$　**32.** 3.05×10^{-6}

33. -4.2356×10^6　**34.** 0.0356　**35.** 678,000,000　**36.** $(3125)^{1/4} \approx 7.4767$　**37.** $2\sqrt{2}$

38. **(a)** 6　**(b)** $a^3, -2a^2, a, -2a^3, 7a$　**(c)** -5　**39.** $4y + z$

40. $\dfrac{3}{4}y - \dfrac{43}{48}$　**41.** No　**42.**

43. all real numbers; all real numbers ≥ 3
44. Yes; since all possible vertical lines cross the graph a maximum of one time.　**45.** $x > 0$
46. The minimum is 3 at $x = 0$.　**47. (a)** -2
(b) $\dfrac{1}{3}a + \dfrac{1}{3}h - 5$　**48.** The volume is 13.78125 ft³.
49. Kelsie's interest is $119.41.

50. $C(x) = 35 + 2.80x$; The cost of producing 150 ornaments in one production run is $455.

Chapter 5

PROBLEM SET 5.1

Experiencing Algebra the Exercise Way

1. linear　**2.** linear　**3.** nonlinear　**4.** linear　**5.** linear　**6.** nonlinear　**7.** nonlinear
8. nonlinear　**9.** linear　**10.** linear　**11.** 14　**12.** 5　**13.** -6　**14.** -8　**15.** 7　**16.** 0
17. all real numbers　**18.** noninteger between 0 and 1　**19.** no solution　**20.** no solution
21. no solution　**22.** all real numbers　**23.** noninteger between 0 and 1　**24.** all real numbers
25. -3　**26.** all real numbers　**27.** no solution　**28.** 2　**29.** all real numbers　**30.** -1　**31.** 15
32. all real numbers　**33.** no solution　**34.** -8　**35.** 3　**36.** approximately 0.727　**37.** all real numbers
38. no solution　**39.** The number of miles is 80.　**40.** The number of pages is 20.　**41.** The factory should
produce 20 pairs of shoes.　**42.** The number of hours is 8.　**43.** She can spend $29.
44. She should lose 1 pound.　**45.** The dimensions are 5 feet by 8 feet.
46. The lengths are 2.8 inches and 11.2 inches　**47.** Any number of rolls will have the same charge for both.
48. There is no number of hours for which the fee will be equal.

Experiencing Algebra the Calculator Way

A　**1.** 22　**2.** -12　**3.** 250　**4.** -500　**B**　Students should experiment with same exercises.

Experiencing Algebra the Exercise Way

1. 18   **2.** −104   **3.** 116   **4.** 76   **5.** −7.98   **6.** −4.606   **7.** $\frac{14}{9}$ **8.** 0   **9.** −3   **10.** 50

11. −16.85   **12.** 22.6   **13.** $-\frac{14}{5}$ **14.** $\frac{32}{7}$ **15.** 36   **16.** 123   **17.** $-\frac{17}{16}$ **18.** $\frac{17}{30}$ **19.** −90

20. 0   **21.** 81   **22.** −62   **23.** −0.02   **24.** −3.7   **25.** $\frac{2}{5}$ **26.** −16   **27.** 4.88   **28.** −69.2

29. −57   **30.** $16\frac{1}{5}$ **31.** 3   **32.** 17   **33.** about −2.398   **34.** −10   **35.** $\frac{1}{3}$ **36.** $-\frac{5}{7}$ **37.** 14

38. −41   **39.** 6.3   **40.** −1   **41.** 0   **42.** −1   **43.** 6 servings remain in the box.
44. He can have 700 calories.   **45.** His gross pay was $2351.58.   **46.** It was marked down $41.46.

47. She should borrow $1\frac{3}{4}$ cups.   **48.** He can work $4\frac{5}{12}$ hours.   **49.** There was $4.37 sales tax.

50. It was reduced by 32,221 people.   **51.** She must buy 45 feet; no, she will not have enough.
52. The loan value is $93,000.   **53.** There were 480 paid admissions.   **54.** The price was about $250.06.
55. They must sell 580 packets.   **56.** It will take 18 months.   **57.** The estate was worth $75,400.
58. The price was about $5.99.   **59.** The height is 17.5 feet.   **60.** The height must be 5 feet.
61. The height must be about 6 feet.   **62.** The radius is about 16 inches   **63.** You must place $6400 into savings.   **64.** The average speed was about 65.8 mph.   **65.** The quarterly profits were $63,650.
66. The jackpot was $45,990,000.   **67.** Her sales were $1350.   **68.** Her sales were $120,000.

Experiencing Algebra the Calculator Way

1. about 461.2 feet   **2.** $1733.22   **3.** about 55.3 inches   **4.** about $6400   **5.** $2\frac{1}{8}$ per share

6. 6 pieces   **7.** about 12 gallons   **8.** about 123 square feet   **9.** 62.5 grams
10. 60 grams; does not agree; difference may be round-off error   **11.** about 16.7 feet per second

Experiencing Algebra the Exercise Way

1. −2   **2.** −44   **3.** 0   **4.** 4.5   **5.** 3.3   **6.** 5   **7.** 0   **8.** 10.2   **9.** about 7.21   **10.** 1

11. $\frac{1}{2}$ **12.** $\frac{2}{3}$ **13.** 2   **14.** −1   **15.** 30   **16.** −2   **17.** 1   **18.** 0   **19.** 8   **20.** −3

21. all real numbers   **22.** all real numbers   **23.** no solution   **24.** no solution   **25.** all real numbers
26. no solution   **27.** −6.6   **28.** all real numbers   **29.** no solution   **30.** 6   **31.** no solution

32. 8   **33.** 6   **34.** all real numbers   **35.** no solution   **36.** 10   **37.** $\frac{10}{9}$ **38.** $\frac{28}{3}$ **39.** $-\frac{1}{18}$

40. $\frac{9}{5}$ **41.** −120   **42.** −66   **43.** $-\frac{8}{13}$ **44.** $-\frac{3}{8}$ **45.** 107.5   **46.** 3.6   **47.** 0   **48.** 8.8

49. −0.05   **50.** 70   **51.** You could drive about 1250 miles.   **52.** You could drive 1727.5 miles.
53. The monthly payments would be $85.50.   **54.** The monthly charge would be $140.

55. There were 12 liters of 30% solution.   **56.** There were $2\frac{1}{2}$ gallons of 40% solution.

57. Her brothers average weekly earnings are $352.55.   **58.** His profit last year was $8988.
59. There is no value of sales for which the two are equal.   **60.** The cost are the same for any number of days.
61. The plans are the same for any amount of total sales.
62. There is no number of miles for which the two plans cost the same.

1. The sales were $652.80.   **2.** She should administer 3.5 tablets.   **3.** He needs 3 sheets.

PROBLEM SET 5.4

Experiencing Algebra the Exercise Way

1. $s = \dfrac{P}{4}$ **2.** $b = \dfrac{A}{h}$ **3.** $d = \dfrac{C}{\pi}$ **4.** $r = \dfrac{C}{2\pi}$ **5.** $L = \dfrac{V}{WH}$ **6.** $W = \dfrac{V}{LH}$ **7.** $L = \dfrac{S - 2WH}{2W + 2H}$

8. $H = \dfrac{S - 2LW}{SL + 2W}$ **9.** $h = \dfrac{V}{\pi r^2}$ **10.** $h = \dfrac{S - 2\pi r^2}{2\pi r}$ **11.** $C = \dfrac{5}{9}(F - 32)$ **12.** $F = \dfrac{9}{5}C + 32$

13. $P = \dfrac{I}{rt}$ **14.** $r = \dfrac{I}{Pt}$ **15.** $P = \dfrac{A}{(1 + i)^t}$ **16.** $P = \dfrac{A}{e^{rt}}$ **17.** $g = \dfrac{v}{t}$ **18.** $t = \dfrac{v}{g}$ **19.** $R = \dfrac{V}{I}$

20. $m = \dfrac{E}{c^2}$ **21.** $m = x - zs$ **22.** $s = \dfrac{x - m}{z}$ **23.** $y = -\dfrac{4}{3}x$ **24.** $y = -\dfrac{1}{3}x$ **25.** $y = \dfrac{1}{2}x$

26. $y = \dfrac{1}{3}x$ **27.** $y = -x$ **28.** $y = x$ **29.** $y = -\dfrac{5}{4}x + 5$ **30.** $y = -x - 3$ **31.** $y = -x - 7$

32. $y = 13x - 13$ **33.** $y = \dfrac{1}{2}x + 2$ **34.** $y = -\dfrac{8}{7}x - 8$ **35.** $y = x - 1$ **36.** $y = 3x - 2$

37. $y = 4x - 19$ **38.** $y = -4x + 13$ **39.** $y = -2x + 8$ **40.** $y = 3x + 35$ **41.** $y = -x - 6$

42. $y = -5x - 62$ **43.** $y = \dfrac{2}{3}x + 10$ **44.** $y = -\dfrac{3}{4}x$ **45.** $y = -\dfrac{2}{3}x - \dfrac{1}{3}$ **46.** $y = \dfrac{4}{9}x + \dfrac{1}{6}$

47. $x = \dfrac{1}{5}y - 3$ **48.** $x = -y - 1$ **49.** $x = -\dfrac{1}{2}y + 4$ **50.** $x = \dfrac{1}{9}y + 3$ **51.** $x = -\dfrac{7}{6}y + \dfrac{28}{3}$

52. $x = \dfrac{11}{4}y + \dfrac{55}{4}$ **53.** $x = \dfrac{9}{5}y + \dfrac{6}{5}$ **54.** $x = -4y + \dfrac{11}{3}$ **55.** $x = \dfrac{1}{m}y - \dfrac{b}{m}$ **56.** $x = \dfrac{1}{m}y - \dfrac{a}{m} + b$

57. $P = 200 + 85m; m = \dfrac{1}{85}P - \dfrac{40}{17}$; It will take 24 months to payoff $2240.; It will take 12 months to payoff

$1200.   **58.** $c = 75 + 35h; h = \dfrac{1}{35}c - \dfrac{15}{17}$; Richard worked 12 hours for $495.; Richard worked 16.5 hours

for $652.50.   **59.** $T = 22c + 12.50; c = \dfrac{1}{22}T - \dfrac{25}{44}$; She can spend about $1.02 on each student for a $35 party.;

She can spend about $1.70 on each student for a $50 party.   **60.** $T = 175 + 14c; c = \dfrac{1}{14}T - \dfrac{25}{2}$; They can

spend about $35.71 for each member if they raise $675. They can spend about $58.92 on each member if they

raise $1000.   **61.** $B = 75 + 3T; T = \dfrac{1}{3}B - 25$; Ted's weekly earnings are about $216.67 when his boss

averages $725 per week; Ted's weekly earnings are $400 when his boss averages $1275 per week.

62. $M = 1.5F - 0.75; F = \dfrac{2}{3}M + \dfrac{1}{2}$; Females would average $8.80 per hour if males earned $12.45 per hour.;

Females would average $14.50 per hour if males earned $21 per hour.   **63.** $C = 75 + 65d; d = \dfrac{1}{65}C - \dfrac{15}{13}$;

The equipment could be rented for 2 days for under $250.; The equipment could be rented for 5 days for under

$400.   **64.** $D = 60h + 50; h = \dfrac{1}{60}D - \dfrac{5}{6}$; There are 9.67 hours remaining if the total distance is 630 miles.;

There are 8.5 hours remaining if the total distance is 560 miles.

65. $V = 15h; h = \dfrac{V}{15};$ The height should be 4 feet for a volume of 60 cubic feet.; The height should be $6\frac{2}{3}$ feet for a volume of 100 cubic feet.   **66.** $S = 30 + 16h; h = \dfrac{1}{16}S - \dfrac{15}{8};$ The height would be 3.5 feet if the total surface area is 86 square feet.; The height would be 5.625 feet if the total surface area was 120 square feet.

Experiencing Algebra the Calculator Way

1. $P = \dfrac{A}{e^{rt}};$ The amount to invest is about \$7985.16; \$7985.16; \$7297.89; \$6376.28; \$5827.48; \$17,617.20; \$15,315.66; \$12,414.63; \$10,792.76

PROBLEM SET 5.5

Experiencing Algebra the Exercise Way

1. The doses are 6 grains, 8 grains, and 10 grains.   **2.** The doses are 16 cc, 15 cc, 14 cc, 13 cc and 12 cc.
3. The number awarded at each stage is 3 prizes, 5 prizes, 7 prizes, and 9 prizes.   **4.** The number awarded each day are 2 prizes, 4 prizes, 6 prizes, 8 prizes, and 10 prizes.   **5.** The lowest grade was 81 points and the highest grade was 88 points.   **6.** The ratings are $-4, -2, 0, 2,$ and 4.   **7.** The angles measure $50°, 60°,$ and $70°.$

8. The angles measure $70°, 70°,$ and $40°.$ **9.** Each side measures $9\frac{3}{4}$ inches.   **10.** The sides measure 2.5 cm, 5 cm, and 4 cm.   **11.** The sides measure 6 feet, 6 feet, and 4 feet.   **12.** The sides measure $15\frac{1}{5}$ meters, $15\frac{1}{5}$ meters, and $7\frac{3}{5}$ meters.   **13.** The dimensions are 85 yards by 115 yards.   **14.** Each side measures $\frac{1}{4}$ inch.

15. The dimensions are 95 cm by 52.25 cm.   **16.** The dimensions are 8 inches by 18 inches.
17. The dimensions should be 8 feet by 40 feet.; It will cover 320 square feet of yard.   **18.** Each side would be 24 feet.; Yes, 576 ft^2 of area is greater than 320 ft^2 of area.   **19.** The dimensions are about 13.7 feet by 68.6 feet; the area of this run is larger than the run in exercise 17.   **20.** Each side measures 32 feet.; The area is 1024 square feet.   **21.** The angles measure $37°, 111°,$ and $32°.$ **22.** The angles measure $30°, 60°,$ and $90°.$
23. The amount borrowed was \$4000.; The interest was \$500.   **24.** The amount borrowed was \$1200.; The interest was \$108.   **25.** You must invest about \$4587.16.   **26.** About \$11,160.71 should be invested.
27. He should invest about \$454,545.   **28.** About \$7421.15 should be invested.   **29.** \$9500 was invested at 8%.; \$5500 was invested at 6.5%.   **30.** About \$7494.74 was invested at 9.2%.; About \$7505.26 was invested at 3.5%.

31. $A = 1.07P; P = \dfrac{A}{1.07};$ About \$1261.68 should be invested to have \$1350.; About \$2336.45 should be invested to have \$2500.   **32.** $P = 1.11L; L = \dfrac{P}{1.11};$ You will receive \$1200 as a loan if the payback is \$1332.; You will receive about \$720.72 as a loan if the payback is \$800.   **33.** The original price was \$85.
34. The original price was about \$129.99.; The amount of the reduction was about \$19.50.   **35.** The original cost was about \$12.47.   **36.** The dealer paid \$200.   **37.** The markup percentage was 80%.
38. The markup percentage was 40%.   **39.** The regular price is \$260.   **40.** The regular price is \$73.75.
41. The SRP should be about \$19,230.77.   **42.** The SRP should be about \$10,582.35.   **43.** The original price is about \$59.96 if the sale price is \$53.96.; The original price is about \$109.94 if the sale price is \$98.95.
44. The subtotal is about \$25 when the total cost is \$27.19.; The subtotal is \$132 when the total cost is \$143.55.
45. His hourly wage before the increase was about \$13.45.   **46.** Her salary before the increase was about \$30,660.38.   **47.** The bill before the gratuity was added was about \$124.56.   **48.** The bill before the gratuity was added was about \$228.65.

Experiencing Algebra the Calculator Way

1.

width

length

2. Let x = length in inches

3.

$\frac{\sqrt{5}-1}{2}x$

x

4. $323.61 = 2x + 2Gx$

5. The length is about 100 inches.   **6.** The width is about 61.804 inches.
7. The perimeter is 323.61 inches after rounding.

PROBLEM SET 5.6

Experiencing Algebra the Exercise Way

1. -9 and -3 **2.** -2 and 16   **3.** -13 and 13   **4.** no solution   **5.** 1 and 5   **6.** -3 and 7
7. -5 and -1 **8.** 0 and 1   **9.** -3 **10.** -1 **11.** -9 and 9   **12.** -9 and 9   **13.** -4 and 2
14. 2 and 4   **15.** -3 and 1   **16.** 1 and 5   **17.** -2 and 0   **18.** -3 and -1 **19.** -47 and 5
20. -10 and 48   **21.** -41 and 3   **22.** -19 and 17   **23.** -3.92 and 8.26   **24.** 21.931 and 23.729
25. -1.133 and 0.333   **26.** -7.4375 and 5.6875   **27.** no solution   **28.** -6 **29.** 32   **30.** no solution
31. -8.677 and -1.333 **32.** -0.5 and 5.5   **33.** -138 and 138   **34.** -2400 and 2400   **35.** no solution
36. -0.009 and 0.009   **37.** -41.67 and 41.67   **38.** no solution   **39.** $-14\frac{5}{9}$ and $14\frac{5}{9}$ **40.** $-\frac{11}{12}$ and $\frac{11}{12}$
41. -864 and -292 **42.** -774 and 168   **43.** -1221 and 2663   **44.** 527 and 775   **45.** 5 and 53
46. $-\frac{7}{2}$ and $\frac{43}{2}$ **47.** no solution   **48.** no solution   **49.** -42 and 70   **50.** $-\frac{73}{2}$ and $\frac{67}{2}$ **51.** -6 and 2
52. $-\frac{33}{2}$ and $\frac{1}{2}$ **53.** -16 and -8 **54.** $\frac{3}{2}$ and $\frac{13}{2}$ **55.** The maximum depth of Lake Superior is either
513 feet or 1333 feet.; The maximum depth is 1333 feet.   **56.** The maximum depth of the Caspian Sea is either
3363 feet or 7267 feet. The Caspian Sea is 3363 feet deep.   **57.** The minimum and maximum heights the
clothes will fit are 5 feet 3 inches and 6 feet 3 inches.   **58.** The limits are 5 feet 9 inches and 6 feet 5 inches.
59. The minimum and maximum percentages are 39% and 45%.   **60.** The minimum and maximum
percentages are 43.5% and 52.5%.   **61.** The range is from 130 pounds to 134 pounds.

62. The range is from 0.95 pounds to 1.05 pounds.   **63.** The lengths range from $5\frac{1}{4}$ inches to $5\frac{3}{4}$ inches.

64. The lengths range from 25.375 inches 25.625 inches.   **65.** The possible values for the extreme score are
49 and 93.   **66.** The range of scores is from 38 points to 94 points.   **67.** The pairs of ages are 35 and 47
or 47 and 59.   **68.** The monthly sales for the other brand are either 9,600,000 bottles or 14,600,000 bottles.

Experiencing Algebra the Calculator Way

1. 0.5   **2.** no solution   **3.** 4 and -13 **4.** 1.5   **5.** -7.5 and 7.5

CHAPTER 5 REVIEW

Reflections

1–8. Answers will vary.

Exercises

1. nonlinear   **2.** linear   **3.** linear   **4.** nonlinear   **5.** linear   **6.** nonlinear   **7.** -6 **8.** 6
9. 3   **10.** noninteger between -3 and -2 **11.** all real numbers   **12.** no solution   **13.** 2   **14.** -2
15. all real numbers   **16.** no solution   **17.** 2.4   **18.** The two offers are equivalent at 10 hours.
19. The fourth week donation should be $2165.   **20.** The sides measure 7.75 feet, 7.75 feet, and 10.75 feet.

21. 26   **22.** $\frac{32}{39}$ **23.** -2 **24.** 2.933   **25.** -68 **26.** -38.5 **27.** 105   **28.** $\frac{16}{25}$ **29.** 12

30. -2.98 **31.** 3.5 **32.** There were 58 passes given.   **33.** There were 280 graduates.
34. They must sell 5334 books.   **35.** The total proceeds were $42,630.   **36.** -14 **37.** 2 **38.** -3.4
39. 1.4 **40.** $\dfrac{2}{3}$ **41.** $-\dfrac{11}{6}$ **42.** all real numbers   **43.** no solution   **44.** You can drive 909 miles.
45. The annual depreciation is about $17,857.   **46.** The offers are the same at 15 hours.   **47.** $h = \dfrac{2A}{b + B}$
48. $W = \dfrac{S - 2LH}{2L + 2H}$ **49.** $x = -\dfrac{7}{6}y + 7$ **50.** $y = \dfrac{6}{5}x - \dfrac{22}{15}$ **51.** $A = 6000 + 8000n; n = \dfrac{A - 6000}{8000};$
It will last 9 years if the amount is $78,000.; It will last 15 years if the amount is $126,000.
52. The lengths should be 10 inches, 12 inches, and 14 inches.   **53.** The lengths should be 11 inches, 12 inches,
and 13 inches.   **54.** The dimensions are 30 feet by 90 feet.   **55.** It should be invested for 6 years.
56. You should invest $10,000.   **57.** The suit's retail price should have been $262.50.   **58.** The artist was
paid $25.   **59.** 23 and -23 **60.** no solution   **61.** 0   **62.** 7   **63.** 8 and 16   **64.** no solution
65. $-\dfrac{1}{2}$ and $\dfrac{15}{2}$ **66.** 1 and 13   **67.** no solution   **68.** -2 and 4   **69.** The permissible limits on the part
are 62.75 mm and 62.83 mm.   **70.** The limits on the percentage of voters are 45% and 53%.

CHAPTER 5 MIXED REVIEW

1. all real numbers   **2.** no solution   **3.** -4 **4.** 3   **5.** 3.1   **6.** 2   **7.** noninteger between -4 and -3
8. -3 **9.** all real numbers   **10.** -2 **11.** no solution   **12.** linear   **13.** nonlinear   **14.** nonlinear
15. linear   **16.** linear   **17.** nonlinear   **18.** -348 **19.** $\dfrac{3}{10}$ **20.** 32   **21.** -72.3 **22.** -14
23. -14.59 **24.** 7   **25.** -444 **26.** $-\dfrac{2}{3}$ **27.** 7.49   **28.** 8.7   **29.** 6.4   **30.** $-\dfrac{1}{8}$ **31.** $\dfrac{11}{7}$
32. 6   **33.** 1.5   **34.** all real numbers   **35.** no solution   **36.** -3 **37.** 0 and 8   **38.** no solution
39. $-\dfrac{14}{5}$ and 2   **40.** 4 and 10   **41.** -5 and 3   **42.** -31 and 31   **43.** no solution   **44.** 0
45. $x = 2y + 0.3$ **46.** $y = -\dfrac{1}{6}x + \dfrac{1}{4}$ **47.** $h = \dfrac{S - 2\pi r^2}{2\pi r}$ **48.** $P = \dfrac{I}{rt}$ **49.** The two possible
heights are 683 feet and 1023 feet. The bank is 1023 feet.   **50.** The limits are 67 and 77 points.
51. The subtotal was about $65.58.; The total bill was about $70.99.   **52.** He expects to receive $14,125.
53. She worked 1250 hours.   **54.** An employee needs 120 houses.   **55.** The annual depreciation is $11,750.
56. She needs an additional $414.   **57.** The pieces should be 5 inches, 6 inches, 7 inches, and 8 inches.
58. The pieces should be 3 inches, 5 inches, 7 inches, and 9 inches.   **59.** The original price was about $305.82.
60. The simple interest rate should be 6.5%.   **61.** You should invest $12,500.   **62.** The dimensions are
16.8 feet by 25.2 feet.   **63.** The price before tax was about $299.; Sales tax was about $26.16.
64. $A = 40 + 22.5h; h = \dfrac{A - 40}{22.5};$ A job that cost $208.75 lasts 7.5 hours.; A job that cost $85 lasts 2 hours.
65. The angle made with the width of the rug is 55°.

CHAPTER 5 TEST

1. linear   **2.** nonlinear   **3.** nonlinear   **4.** linear   **5.** no solution   **6.** -3 **7.** -2.079
8. all real numbers   **9.** $1\dfrac{3}{4}$ **10.** -10 and 4   **11.** no solution   **12.** The pieces should be cut into
sections measuring 14 inches, 15 inches, and 16 inches.   **13.** His monthly payments will be $135.
14. The price before it went on sale was about $239.93.   **15.** $W = \dfrac{P - 2L}{2};$ The width is 7.6 inches.
16. The measures of the angles are 40°, 50°, and 90°.   **17.** The limits on the true percent are 49% and 55%.

18. 1500 liters of 60% apple juice must be added.   **19.** The two payment plans will be equal for $7500 of sales.

20. The two plans will cost the same if the job lasts $16\frac{2}{3}$ hours.   **21.** Answers will vary.

Chapter 6

| PROBLEM SET 6.1 |

Experiencing Algebra the Exercise Way

1. linear; $5x + 7y = 35$; $a = 5, b = 7; c = 35$ **2.** linear; $\sqrt{3}x + 2y = 6; a = \sqrt{3}, b = 2, c = 6$

3. nonlinear   **4.** linear; $8x + 3y = -24; a = 8, b = 3, c = -24$ **5.** nonlinear   **6.** nonlinear

7. linear; $-\frac{5}{6}x + y = -2; a = -\frac{5}{6}, b = 1, c = -2$ **8.** linear; $-5x + y = 10; a = -5, b = 1, c = 10$

9. linear; $y = 4; a = 0, b = 1, c = 4$ **10.** linear; $5x + 6y = 15; a = 5, b = 6, c = 15$ **11.** linear;
$2x = 5; a = 2, b = 0, c = 5$ **12.** linear; $5y = 14; a = 0, b = 5, c = 14$ **13.** linear; $4.2x + 0.3y = 1.4$;
$a = 4.2, b = 0.3, c = 1.4$ **14.** linear; $-1.5x + 4.5y = 10.5; a = -1.5, b = 4.5, c = 10.5$

15. not a solution   **16.** solution   **17.** solution   **18.** not a solution   **19.** solution   **20.** not a solution
21. not a solution   **22.** solution   **23.** solution   **24.** not a solution   **25.** solution   **26.** not a solution
27. not a solution   **28.** solution   **29.** not a solution   **30.** solution   **31.** not a solution   **32.** solution
33. Answers will vary. Possible answer: $(-6, -3), (0, -2)$, and $(6, -1)$ **34.** Answers will vary.
Possible answer: $(-7, 4), (0, 3)$, and $(7, 2)$ **35.** Answers will vary. Possible answer: $(-8, 6), (0, 1)$, and $(8, -4)$
36. Answers will vary. Possible answer: $(-8, -11), (0, -4)$, and $(8, 3)$ **37.** Answers will vary.
Possible answer: $(-1, -1), (2, 3)$, and $(5, 7)$ **38.** Answers will vary. Possible answer: $(-1, -1), (4, 1)$, and $(9, 3)$
39. Answers will vary. Possible answer: $(0, 8), (1, 8)$, and $(2, 8)$ **40.** Answers will vary.
Possible answer: $(0, 4), (1, 4)$, and $(2, 4)$ **41.** Answers will vary. Possible answer: $(-1, -6.8), (0, -4.2)$, and
$(1, -1.6)$ **42.** Answers will vary. Possible answer: $(-1, -10.2), (0, -3.4)$, and $(1, 3.4)$

43. Answers will vary.   **44.** Answers will vary.   **45.** Answers will vary.   **46.** Answers will vary.
Possible answer: Possible answer: Possible answer: Possible answer:

            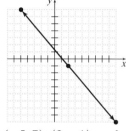

$(0, 3), (1, 1)$, and $(0, -6), (1, -1)$, and $(-3, -7), (0, -2)$, and $(-5, 7), (2, -1)$, and
$(2, -1)$ are three $(2, 4)$ are three $(3, 3)$ are three $(9, -9)$ are three
possible solutions.   possible solutions.   possible solutions.   possible solutions.

47. Answers will vary. Possible answer:

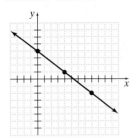

$(0, 4)$, $(4, 1)$, and $(8, -2)$ are three possible solutions.

48. Answers will vary. Possible answer:

$(-6, -8)$, $(0, -3)$, and $(6, 2)$ are three possible solutions.

49. Answers will vary. Possible answer:

$(-3, -10)$, $(2, 4)$, and $(7, 18)$ are three possible solutions.

50. Answers will vary. Possible answer:

$(-7, 18)$, $(3, -1)$, and $(13, -20)$ are three possible solutions.

51. Answers will vary. Possible answer:

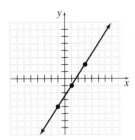

$(-1, -4)$, $(1, -1)$, and $(3, 2)$ are three possible solutions.

52. Answers will vary. Possible answer:

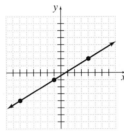

$(-6, -4)$, $(-1, -1)$, and $(4, 2)$ are three possible solutions.

53. Answers will vary. Possible answer:

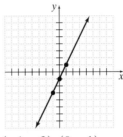

$(-1, -3)$, $(0, -1)$, and $(1, 1)$ are three possible solutions.

54. Answers will vary. Possible answer:

$(-1, -5)$, $(0, -7)$, and $(1, -9)$ are three possible solutions.

55. Answers will vary. Possible answer:

$(-1, -4)$, $(0, -4)$, and $(1, -4)$ are three possible solutions.

56. Answers will vary. Possible answer:

$(-1, 6)$, $(0, 6)$, and $(1, 6)$ are three possible solutions.

57. **(a)** $(1, 0)$, $(2, 5)$, $(4, 15)$

(b)

(c) A crew of 5 people would pack 20 boxes per minute.

(d) Answers will vary. Possible answer: There is probably a maximum number of boxes that can be packed by a large number of people maybe given the size of the packing plant.

58. (a) $(0, 100)$, $(6, 85)$, $(10, 75)$

(b)

(c) The score for missing 12 questions would be 70.

(d) domain: 0 to 40

59. (a) She would earn $81.

(b) No, she should be paid $65.

(c) She would be paid $25.

(d) Answers will vary. Possible answer: Domain: 0 to 50; Range: 25 to 425

60. (a) The student would receive a score of 165 points.

(b) Yes

(c) The student would receive a score of 165 points.

(d) domain: 0 to 40

61. (a) $(2, 6)$, $(3.5, 10.5)$, $(10.5, 31.5)$

(b)

(c) The border would be 12 inches.

(d) Yes, all equilateral triangles have three sides of equal measure.

62. (a) $(15, 50)$, $(25, 70)$, $(10, 40)$

(b)

(c) The perimeter would be 60 cm.

(d) Yes, it is a linear equation.

63. (a) The cost would be $325.

(b) The cost would be $362.50.

(c) yes   **(d)**

x	$D(x)$
0	250
5	268.75
10	287.50
15	306.25
20	325
25	343.75
30	362.50
35	381.25
40	400
45	418.75
50	437.50

64. (a) She will earn $600.

(b) She will earn $425.

(c) yes   **(d)**

x	$P(x)$
0	300
2	350
4	400
6	450
8	500
10	550
12	600
14	650
16	700
18	750
20	800

65. Answers will vary. Possible answer: $(5, 225)$, $(10, 350)$, $(15, 475)$; The cost of producing 5 items, 10 items, and 15 items is $225, $350, and $475, respectively.

66. Answers will vary. Possible answer: $(5, 750)$, $(10, 500)$, $(15, 250)$; The outstanding balance of a loan with payments of 5 months, 10 months, and 15 months is $750, $500, and $250, respectively.

Experiencing Algebra the Calculator Way

1. not a solution   **2.** not a solution   **3.** solution

4.

x	y
1.5	3.7245
1.6	4.0966
1.7	4.4687
1.8	4.8408
1.9	5.2129
2.0	5.585

5.

x	y
0	-5
7	-1.75
14	1.5
21	4.75
28	8
35	11.25

6. $(0, -1.41), (2, 2.05), (4, 5.51), (6, 8.98), (8, 12.44)$

7. $(1, 0.20), (2, 0.39), (3, 0.59), (4, 0.79), (5, 0.98)$

8. $Y1 = 9.64x$

X	Y₁
5	48.2
10	96.4
15	144.6
20	192.8
25	241
30	289.2
35	337.4

X=35

X	Y₁
40	385.6
45	433.8
50	482
55	530.2
60	578.4
65	626.6
70	674.8

X=70

X	Y₁
75	723
80	771.2
85	819.4
90	867.6
95	915.8
100	964

X=100

PROBLEM SET 6.2

Experiencing Algebra the Exercise Way

1. x-intercept: $(-2, 0)$
y-intercept: $(0, 4)$

2. x-intercept: $(-5, 0)$
y-intercept: $(0, 1)$

3. x-intercept: $(4, 0)$
y-intercept: $(0, 2)$

4. x-intercept: $(-5, 0)$
y-intercept: $(0, -5)$

5. x-intercept: $(0, 0)$
y-intercept: $(0, 0)$

6. x-intercept: $(0, 0)$
y-intercept: $(0, 0)$

7. x-intercept: $(3, 0)$
y-intercept: none

8. x-intercept: $(-4, 0)$
y-intercept: none

9. x-intercept: none
y-intercept: $(0, 1)$

10. x-intercept: none
y-intercept: $(0, -4)$

11.

x-intercept: $(4.8, 0)$
y-intercept: $(0, -24)$

12.
x-intercept: $(5.25, 0)$
y-intercept: $(0, 21)$

13.
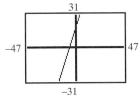
x-intercept: $(-6, 0)$
y-intercept: $(0, 18)$

14.

x-intercept: $(-5.5, 0)$
y-intercept: $(0, -33)$

15.

x-intercept: $(6, 0)$
y-intercept: $(0, 7.5)$

16.
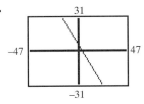
x-intercept: $(4, 0)$
y-intercept: $(0, 6.4)$

17.

x-intercept: $(5.6, 0)$
y-intercept: $(0, -4)$

18.
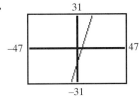
x-intercept: $(5, 0)$
y-intercept: $(0, -15)$

19.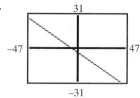

x-intercept: $(-5, 0)$
y-intercept: $(0, -3.\overline{3})$

20.

x-intercept: $(-16, 0)$
y-intercept: $(0, -2)$

21. x-intercept: $(4, 0)$
y-intercept: ; $\left(0, \dfrac{12}{5}\right)$

22. $(9, 0)$
y-intercept: $(0, 7)$

23. x-intercept: $\left(\dfrac{7}{2}, 0\right)$

y-intercept: $(0, -2)$

24. x-intercept: $(31, 0)$

y-intercept: $(0, -31)$

25. x-intercept: $\left(-\dfrac{27}{2}, 0\right)$

y-intercept: $(0, -3)$

26. x-intercept: $(-3, 0)$

y-intercept: $\left(0, -\dfrac{9}{2}\right)$

27. x-intercept: $(6, 0)$
y-intercept: $(0, 4)$

28. x-intercept: $(-9, 0)$
y-intercept: $(0, -15)$

29. x-intercept: $(0, 0)$
y-intercept: $(0, 0)$

30. x-intercept: $(0, 0)$
y-intercept: $(0, 0)$

31. x-intercept: $(10, 0)$
y-intercept: none

32. x-intercept: $(5, 0)$;
y-intercept: none

33. x-intercept: none
y-intercept: $(0, 11)$

34. x-intercept: none
y-intercept: $(0, -5)$

35. $(0, -24)$ **36.** $(0, 2)$ **37.** $(0, -15)$ **38.** $(0, -16)$ **39.** $(0, 0)$ **40.** $(0, 0)$ **41.** $(0, -2)$
42. $(0, 3)$ **43.** $(0, 0)$ **44.** $(0, 0)$ **45.** $(0, 9)$ **46.** $(0, -8)$ **47.** $(0, 0)$ **48.** $(0, 0)$

49.

50.

51.

52.

53.

54.

55.

56.

57.

58.

59.

60.

61.

62.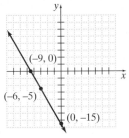

63. $y = -40x + 200$; The x-intercept is $(5, 0)$ which represents after 5 hours, there will be 0 miles left. The y-intercept is $(0, 200)$ which represents after 0 hours, there are 200 miles to travel.

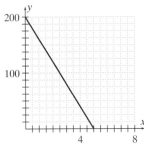

The destination is 100 miles away after 2.5 hours.

64. $y = -20x + 370$; The x-intercept is $(18.5, 0)$ which represents after 18.5 weeks, Joel owes \$0. The y-intercept is $(0, 370)$ which represents after 0 weeks, Joe owes \$370

After 11 weeks, Joe owes \$150.

65. $y = -4x + 150$; The x-intercept is $(37.5, 0)$ which represents after 37.5 minutes, the tank is empty. The y-intercept is $(0, 150)$ which represents after 0 minutes, the tank is full.

After 20 minutes, there are 70 gallons remaining.

66. $y = -3x + 50$; The x-intercept is $\left(16\frac{2}{3}, 0\right)$ which represents at $16\frac{2}{3}$ hours, the tank is empty. The y-intercept is $(0, 50)$ which represents at 0 hours, the tank has 50 gallons in it.

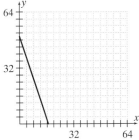

After 8 hours, the tank has 26 gallons in it.

67. The x-intercept is $(0, 0)$. The y-intercept is $(0, 0)$. The cost of producing 0 units is \$0.; The cost of producing 50 units is \$250.; The cost of producing 75 units is \$375.

68. The x-intercept is $(0, 0)$.; The y-intercept is $(0, 0)$.; The net profit from caring for 0 lawns is \$0.; The net profit for caring for 25 lawns is \$100.; The net profit for caring for 40 lawns is \$160.

Experiencing Algebra the Calculator Way

1.

x-intercept: $(29.\overline{3}, 0)$
y-intercept: $(0, -15)$

2.

x-intercept: $(13.168, 0)$
y-intercept: $(0, 33.71)$

3.

x-intercept: $(-17.\overline{7}, 0)$
y-intercept: $(0, 32)$

4.

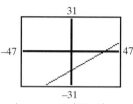

x-intercept: $(32, 0)$
y-intercept: $(0, -17.\overline{7})$

5. At 0°C, the Fahrenheit temperature is 32°F.; At 0°F, the Celsius temperature is $-17.\overline{7}$°C.

PROBLEM SET 6.3

Experiencing Algebra the Exercise Way

1. negative; $-\dfrac{3}{2}$ **2.** undefined   **3.** zero   **4.** positive; $\dfrac{7}{2}$ **5.** positive; $\dfrac{1}{6}$ **6.** zero   **7.** undefined

8. negative; $-\dfrac{5}{2}$ **9.** $\dfrac{2}{3}$ **10.** $-\dfrac{9}{5}$ **11.** 0   **12.** undefined   **13.** undefined   **14.** $\dfrac{15}{7}$ **15.** -2

16. 0   **17.** $-\dfrac{4}{5}$ **18.** $\dfrac{5}{3}$ **19.** -6 **20.** 0.4   **21.** $\dfrac{19}{12}$ **22.** $-\dfrac{63}{44}$ **23.** The slope is 21 and the

y-intercept is $(0, 15)$.   **24.** The slope is -19 and the y-intercept is $(0, 28)$.   **25.** The slope is $\dfrac{11}{15}$ and the

y-intercept is $\left(0, -\dfrac{21}{25}\right)$.   **26.** The slope is $-\dfrac{5}{9}$ and the y-intercept is $\left(0, \dfrac{17}{18}\right)$.   **27.** The slope is 5.95 and

the y-intercept is $(0, -2.01)$.   **28.** The slope is -3.6 and the y-intercept is $(0, 14.8)$.

29. The slope is -1255 and the y-intercept is $(0, 85,600)$.   **30.** The slope is 45 and the y-intercept is $(0, 1250)$.

31. The slope is 4 and the y-intercept is $(0, -16)$.   **32.** The slope is -8 and the y-intercept is $(0, 13)$.

33. The slope is 0 and the y-intercept is $(0, -2)$.   **34.** The slope is 0 and the y-intercept is $(0, -22)$.

35. The slope is 3 and the y-intercept is $(0, -4)$.   **36.** The slope is $-\dfrac{7}{3}$ and the y-intercept is $(0, 2)$.

37. The slope is $\dfrac{5}{2}$ and the y-intercept is $\left(0, -\dfrac{7}{2}\right)$.   **38.** The slope is $\dfrac{4}{3}$ and the y-intercept is $\left(0, \dfrac{5}{3}\right)$.

39. The slope is 0 and the y-intercept is $\left(0, -4\dfrac{7}{8}\right)$.   **40.** The slope is undefined and no y-intercept.

41.

42.

43.

44.

45.

46.

47.

48.

49.

50.

51.

52.

53.

54.

55.

56.

57.

58.

59.

60.

61.

62.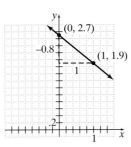

63. The grade of the advertised terrain is 35%.
64. The grade of the terrain is 25%.
65. The pitch of the roof is 27.5%.
66. The pitch of the roof is approximately 42%.

67. Their average speed was
7 miles per hour.; $y = 7x$

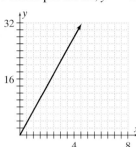

They would travel 17.5 miles.

68. His average speed was
96 km per hour.; $y = 96x$

He would travel 384 km.

69. (a) $-\dfrac{579}{9}$ **(b)** $y = -\dfrac{579}{9}x + 1624$ **(d)** $Y1 = -\dfrac{579}{9} + 1624$

(c)

Answers will vary.

70. (a) $-\dfrac{691}{9}$ **(b)** $y = -\dfrac{691}{9}x + 1745$ **(d)** $Y1 = -\dfrac{691}{9}x + 1745$

(c)

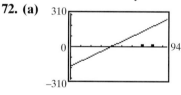

Answers will vary.

71. (a)

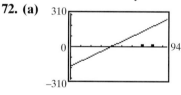

(b) 24.8; The actual value is (15, 25) which
is very close.

(c)

x	actual y	predicted y	difference
27	30	32.72	-2.72
22	26	29.42	-3.42
15	25	24.8	0.2
35	42	38	4
30	38	34.7	3.3
52	40	49.22	-9.22
35	32	38	-6
55	54	51.2	2.8
40	50	41.3	8.7
40	43	41.3	1.7

72. (a)

(b) 129.07; It is off by 9.07 pounds.

(c)

x	actual y	predicted y	difference
65	105	119.65	-14.65
65	125	119.65	5.35
62	110	105.52	4.48
67	120	129.07	-9.07
69	140	138.49	1.51
65	135	119.65	15.35
61	95	100.81	-5.81
67	130	129.07	0.93

Answers will vary.

73. (a)

(b) At $x = 10$, $y = 72$
$x = 20$, $y = 64$
$x = 40$; $y = 48$
$x = 64$, $y = 28.8$

(c) Demand decreases as price increases.

(d) At a price of $100 or more, demand is 0.

74. (a)

(b) At $x = 10$, $y = 6.25$
$x = 20$, $y = 12.5$
$x = 40$, $y = 25$
$x = 64$, $y = 40$

(c) As price increases, supply increases.

(d) No; Answers will vary.

Experiencing Algebra the Calculator Way

1. (a) $m = 4, b = 0$
(b) $m = 2, b = 0$
(c) $m = \frac{1}{2}, b = 0$

2. (a) $m = -4, b = 0$
(b) $m = -2, b = 0$
(c) $m = -\frac{1}{2}, b = 0$

3. (a) $m = 4, b = 9$
(b) $m = 4, b = 0$
(c) $m = 4, b = -9$

4. (a) $m = -4, b = 9$
(b) $m = -4, b = 0$
(c) $m = -4, b = 9$

The y-intercept, $(0, 0)$, is the same. The slopes are different, but all are positive. The graphs rise at different rates, but all cross at $(0, 0)$.

The y-intercept is the same at $(0, 0)$. The slopes use different, but all are negative. The graphs decline at different rates but all cross at $(0, 0)$.

The slopes are the same. The y-intercepts are different. They are all parallel, but cross the y-axis at different points.

The slopes are the same. The y-intercepts are different. They are parallel, but cross the y-axis at different points.

PROBLEM SET 6.4

Experiencing Algebra the Exercise Way

1. intersecting and perpendicular   **2.** intersecting and perpendicular   **3.** parallel   **4.** parallel
5. only intersecting   **6.** only intersecting   **7.** coinciding   **8.** coinciding   **9.** only intersecting
10. only intersecting   **11.** parallel   **12.** coinciding   **13.** intersecting and perpendicular
14. intersecting and perpendicular   **15.** parallel   **16.** only intersecting   **17.** parallel   **18.** parallel
19. coinciding   **20.** coinciding   **21.** coinciding   **22.** only intersecting   **23.** only intersecting
24. parallel   **25.** only intersecting   **26.** parallel   **27. (a)** $y = 0.25x + 3.5$ **(b)** $y = 0.25x$

(c) no break-even point   **(d)** $y = \frac{1}{3}x$ **(e)** At 42 candy bars, Brook will break-even.

(f) At 10 candy bars, Brook will break-even. **(g)** At about 5.45 candy bars, Brook will break-even. At 6 candy bars, Brook will start making a profit. **(h)** Answers will vary. **28. (a)** $y = 285 + 200x$ **(b)** $y = 200x$ **(c)** no break-even point **(d)** $y = 300x$ **(e)** At 2.85 radios, Joe will break-even. At 3 radios, Joe will make a profit. **(f)** At 3.5 radios, Joe will break-even. **(g)** Answers will vary.

29. $y_1 = 35 + 0.25x, m = 0.25, b = 35$;
$y_2 = 60; m = 0, b = 60$;
Their graphs will intersect because the slopes are not equal.;

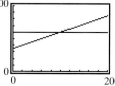

The intersection is $(100, 60)$. At 100 miles, the prices are equal at $60 per day.

30. $y_1 = 65, m = 0, b = 65$;
$y_2 = 15 + 10x, m = 10, b = 15$
Their graphs will intersect because the slopes are not equal.;

The intersection is $(5, 65)$. At 5 hours, the costs will be equal at $65.

31. $y_1 = 50 + 2x, m = 2, b = 50$; $y_2 = 75, m = 0, b = 75$; $x = 8, m =$ undefined, $b =$ none; Yes, y_1 intersects with $x = 8$ and y_2 intersects with $x = 8$ because each has a different slope. $x = 8$ is perpendicular to y_2 because one is vertical and the other is horizontal. The intersection of y_1 and $x = 8$ is $(8, 66)$. At 8 years, she will receive $66. The intersection of y_2 and $x = 8$ is $(8, 75)$. At 8 years, she will receive $75. The intersection of y_1 and y_2 is $(12.5, 75)$. At $12\frac{1}{2}$ years she will receive the same either way, $75.

32. $y_1 = 0.26x, m = 0.26, b = 0$; $y_2 = 8 + 0.02x, m = 0.02, b = 8$; $x = 30, m =$ undefined, $b =$ none; Yes, $x = 30$ will intersect each y_1 and y_2 because they have different slopes. No, $x = 30$ is not perpendicular to either y_1 or y_2. y_1 and y_2 intersect at $\left(33\frac{1}{3}, 8\frac{2}{3}\right)$. At $33\frac{1}{3}$ words, the cost is the same either way, $8.67. y_1 and $x = 30$ intersect at $(30, 7.8)$. At 30 words, the cost is $7.80. y_2 and $x = 30$ intersect at $(30, 8.6)$. At 30 words, the cost is $8.60.

33. $y_1 = 10x; m = 10, b = 0$; $y_2 = 15(x - 4), m = 15, b = -60$; $y_3 = 150; m - 0, b = 150$; y_1 and y_2 intersect at $(12, 120)$. At 12 seconds, Speedie will catch Archie at a distance of 120 feet or before the end zone 150 feet away.

34. $y_1 = 18x; y_2 = 21.5(x - 0.75)$; At a distance of about 82.9 miles, Tom will overtake Victor.

Experiencing Algebra the Calculator Way

1. $-10; 10; 1; -10; 10; 1$ **2.** $-47; 47; 10; -31; 31; 10$ **3.** $0; 94; 10; 0; 62; 10$ **4.** $-470; 470; 100; -310; 310; 100$

PROBLEM SET 6.5

Experiencing Algebra the Exercise Way

1. $y = \frac{3}{2}x - 1$ **2.** $y = \frac{1}{2}x + 1$ **3.** $x = -5$ **4.** $x = 4\frac{1}{2}$ **5.** $y = -3x$ **6.** $y = 3\frac{1}{3}$

7. $y = -\frac{3}{2}$ **8.** $y = -\frac{1}{5}x - 3$ **9.** $y = -\frac{2}{5}x + 4$ **10.** $y = -\frac{1}{7}x - 9$ **11.** $y = \frac{5}{9}x$

12. $y = \frac{1}{7}x - 1$ **13.** $y = 4x - \frac{3}{4}$ **14.** $y = 11x + \frac{1}{2}$ **15.** $y = -4.1x + 0.5$ **16.** $y = -6.2x - 2.2$

17. $y = -33$ **18.** $y = -4x$ **19.** $y = \frac{2}{3}x - 5$ **20.** $y = -2x + 8$ **21.** $y = -3x + 4$

22. $y = \frac{4}{3}x + 5$ **23.** $y = -1.7x + 3.6$ **24.** $y = 1.4x - 3.3$ **25.** $y = -\frac{3}{2}x - \frac{1}{2}$ **26.** $y = 6$

27. $x = -1$ **28.** $y = -5x + 11$ **29.** $y = 2x + 3$ **30.** $y = \frac{2}{7}x + \frac{20}{7}$ **31.** $y = 2$ **32.** $x = 2$

33. $y = \dfrac{5}{14}x + \dfrac{51}{14}$ **34.** $y = \dfrac{14}{27}x - \dfrac{8}{27}$ **35.** $y = -\dfrac{3}{2}x$ **36.** $y = -\dfrac{9}{2}x + \dfrac{67}{4}$ **37.** $y = -\dfrac{42}{13}x + \dfrac{21}{13}$

38. $y = \dfrac{35}{11}x + \dfrac{129}{11}$ **39.** $y = x + 0.4$ **40.** $y = -19x + 25$ **41.** $y = \dfrac{3}{8}x + 4$ **42.** $y = -\dfrac{5}{3}x$

43. $y = 3x - \dfrac{13}{6}$ **44.** $y = -0.8x + 4.2$ **45.** $y = -\dfrac{1}{3}x + 7$ **46.** $y = \dfrac{1}{6}x + 2.4$

47. $y = -\dfrac{1}{5}x - 27$ **48.** $y = -\dfrac{7}{5}x$

49. (a) $m = -0.676$
  (b) $y = -0.676x + 42.4$

  (c) The percent is predicted to be 26.852%.
  It is fairly close.
  (d) The percent is predicted to be 15.36%.
  (e) In year 2027, the predicted percentage
  becomes close to zero. Answers will vary.

50. (a) $m = -0.94$
  (b) $y = -0.94x + 51.9$

  (c) The percentage is predicted to be 33.1%.
  It is fairly close.
  (d) The percent is predicted to be 14.3%.
  (e) In year 2020, the predicted percentage
  becomes close to zero. Answers will vary.

51. $y = x + 273$; A Kelvin temperature of 373 corresponds to 100°C. **52.** $y = x + 460$; The Rankine temperature that corresponds to 75°F is 535. **53.** $y = 2.6x + 12.8$ **54.** $y = -3.8x + 21.6$
55. $y = -0.005x + 52.5$ **56.** $y = -0.008x + 55$; Answers will vary. **57.** $y = 1000x - 1000$;

The prediction is 9000 sales. **58.** $y = -\dfrac{81}{140}x + \dfrac{1515}{28}$; The prediction is about 13.6 years.

59. $y = 120x + 5470$; The predicted enrollment in 1996 is 6190 students.; Yes, this is a good estimate.;
The predicted enrollment in 2000 would be 6670 students. **60.** $y = -250,000x + 5,125,000$; The predicted business is $5,125,000 in 1990.; This is a good estimate.; The predicted business would be $2,625,000 in 2000.

Experiencing Algebra the Calculator Way

1. $y = 55x + 265$ **2.** $y = 32x - 863$ **3.** $y = 2.670054945x + 6.4$ **4.** $y = 5x - 0.75$
5. $y = 3.5x + 38.5$ **6.** $y = -0.\overline{6}x + 8.\overline{6}$

CHAPTER 6 REVIEW

Reflections

1–9. Answers will vary.

Exercises

1. linear; $0.6x - y = -2.3$ **2.** nonlinear **3.** linear; $3x - 6y = -12$ **4.** linear; $4x - 2y = 2$
5. nonlinear **6.** linear; $6y = 19$ **7.** solution **8.** not a solution **9.** not a solution **10.** solution
11. Answers will vary. Possible answer: $(-1, 10)$, $(0, 8)$, and $(1, 6)$
12. Answers will vary. Possible answer: $(-13, -15)$, $(0, -7)$, and $(13, 1)$
13. Answers will vary. Possible answer: $(0, -9)$, $(1, -9)$, and $(2, -9)$

14. Answers will vary. Possible answer:

$(0, -12)$, $(1, -3)$, and $(2, 6)$ are three possible solutions.

15. Answers will vary. Possible answer:

$(-3, 6)$, $(0, 2)$, and $(3, -2)$ are three possible solutions.

16. Answers will vary. Possible answer:

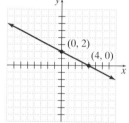

$(-1, -2)$, $(0, -2)$, and $(1, -2)$ are three possible solutions.

17. Answers will vary. Possible answer:

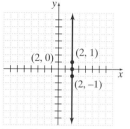

$(2, -1)$, $(2, 0)$, and $(2, 1)$ are three possible solutions.

18. (a)

(b) She will receive $235 for a job that is 30 pages long.

19. (a) He would earn $110.   **(b)** No, he should be paid $155.

(c) He would be paid $20.   **20.** x-intercept: $(-3, 0)$; y-intercept: $(0, -2)$

21. x-intercept: $(-10, 0)$; y-intercept: $(0, 4)$ **22.** $(0, 4)$ **23.** $(0, 0)$

24.

25.

26.

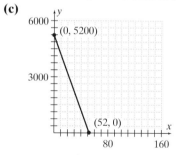

27. (a) $y = 5200 - 100x$

(b) The x-intercept is $(52, 0)$. At 52 weeks, the balance is $0.; The y-intercept is $(0, 5200)$. At 0 weeks, the balance is $5200.

(c)

(d) There is $2000 in the account.

28. (a) $y = 50 - 0.5x$

(b) The x-intercept is $(100, 0)$. After 100 plays, Bryon has $0 left.; The y-intercept is $(0, 50)$. After 0 plays, Bryon has $50.

(c)

(d) He has $20 left.

29. 0   **30.** $\dfrac{9}{2}$ **31.** $-\dfrac{8}{5}$ **32.** undefined   **33.** $\dfrac{1}{2}$ **34.** $-\dfrac{5}{3}$ **35.** 0   **36.** undefined

37. The slope is 23 and the y-intercept is $(0, -51)$.   **38.** The slope is -3.05 and the y-intercept is $(0, 2.97)$.

39. The slope is $-\dfrac{6}{5}$ and the y-intercept is $\left(0, \dfrac{12}{5}\right)$.   **40.** The slope is 0 and the y-intercept is $\left(0, -\dfrac{9}{2}\right)$.

41.

42.

43.

44.

45.

46.

47.

48.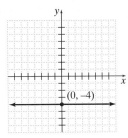

49. (a) 9.5 **(b)** $y = 9.5x + 62$

(c)   **(d)** The predicted grade would be about 76 points.

At $x = 3$, $y = 90$. The prediction is not very close to 98.
At $x = 2$, $y = 81$. The prediction is fairly close to 80.

50. only intersecting   **51.** coinciding   **52.** parallel   **53.** parallel   **54.** intersecting and perpendicular
55. only intersecting   **56.** intersecting and perpendicular   **57.** intersecting and perpendicular

58. (a) $y = 35x + 85$ **(b)** $y = 35x$ **(c)** ; There is no break-even point.
(d) $y = 60x$

(e) ; The break-even point is at $(3.4, 204)$. He will start making a profit when he sells the fourth calculator.   **(f)** J.R. should sell the calculators for $60 each.

59. $y = -\dfrac{1}{4}x + 1$ **60.** $y = -2x + 3$ **61.** $y = \dfrac{3}{5}x - 2$ **62.** $y = -3.5$ **63.** $x = 2.6$

64. $y = -5x + 7$ **65.** $y = \dfrac{3}{11}x + \dfrac{28}{11}$ **66.** $y = \dfrac{1}{3}x + \dfrac{14}{3}$ **67.** $y = 4x - 3$ **68.** $y = -\dfrac{1}{2}x + 5$

69. (a) $y = \dfrac{5}{2}x + 10$

(b) The prediction is 22.5 thousands of records sold. This is not very close to the actual sales.

1. Answers will vary. Possible answer:

2. Answers will vary. Possible answer:

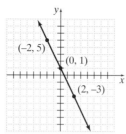

3. Answers will vary. Possible answer:

4.

5.

6.

7.

8.

9.

10.

11.

12.

13.

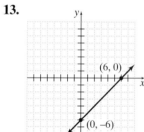

14. only intersecting   **15.** only intersecting   **16.** parallel

17. intersecting and perpendicular   **18.** coinciding

19. intersecting and perpendicular   **20.** parallel

21. Answers will vary. Possible answer: $(-1, 8)$, $(0, 8)$, and $(1, 8)$

22. Answers will vary. Possible answer: $(-9, 0)$, $(0, 8)$, and $(9, 16)$

23. Answers will vary. Possible answer: $(-11, -17)$, $(0, -8)$, and $(11, 1)$

24. linear; $x - y = 0$ **25.** nonlinear   **26.** linear; $1.3x - y = 0.5$

27. linear; $15x - y = 0$ **28.** linear; $5x - 8y = -21$ **29.** nonlinear

30. solution   **31.** solution   **32.** solution   **33.** not a solution   **34.** solution   **35.** not a solution

36. The slope is undefined.; There is no y-intercept.   **37.** The slope is $-\dfrac{3}{2}$.; The y-intercept is $(0, -5)$.

38. The slope is 3.; The y-intercept is $(0, -2)$.   **39.** The slope is 0.; The y-intercept is $(0, 0)$.

40. The slope is 13.; The y-intercept is $(0, -15)$.   **41.** The slope is -5.03.; The y-intercept is $(0, 7.92)$.

42. 0   **43.** undefined   **44.** -3 **45.** $\dfrac{13}{6}$ **46.** $y = 4x - 18$ **47.** $y = -\dfrac{1}{4}x - \dfrac{5}{4}$

48. $y = -\dfrac{2}{3}x + 5$ **49.** $x = 4.1$ **50.** $y = -3x - 8$ **51.** $y = 8$ **52.** $y = 4x + 4.8$

53. $y = 3x - 2$ **54.** $y = 2x + 2$

55. (a) $y = \dfrac{21}{22}x + \dfrac{102}{11}$ (b) The predicted score of about 86 is not very close to the actual score of 78.

56. (a)

(b) See the graph in part a.; Frank would receive $26 for 8 innings. Frank would receive $30 for 10 innings.

57. (a) $y = -5x + 180$ **(b)** The x-intercept is $(36, 0)$. After 36 hours, the tank is empty.; The y-intercept is $(0, 180)$. After 0 hours, the tank has 180 gallons.

(c)

(d) After 16 hours, 100 gallons remain in the tank.

58. (a) $y = 25x + 15$ **(b)** The trainer would earn $65.   **(c)** He would earn $52.50.

59. (a) $c(x) = 0.75x + 225$ **(b)** $r(x) = 2x$

(c)

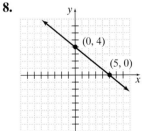

The break-even point is $(180, 360)$.
Revenue equals cost at 180 bows.

(d) No, 150 is less than 180.; Yes, 200 is greater than 180.; She must sell at least 180 bows.

60. The grade of the hill is 48%.

CHAPTER 6 TEST

1. solution   **2.** not a solution   **3.** linear   **4.** linear   **5.** nonlinear   **6.** nonlinear

7. Answers will vary.   **8.**   **9.**   **10.** 0   **11.** $-\dfrac{2}{7}$ **12.** 1

Possible answer:

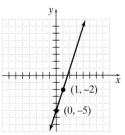

13. undefined   **14.** only intersecting   **15.** parallel   **16.** coinciding   **17.** intersecting and perpendicular

18. The slope is $\dfrac{3}{4}$.; The y-intercept is $(0, 3)$.   **19.** The slope is -1.; The y-intercept is $(0, 3)$.

20. $y = -\dfrac{5}{3}x + \dfrac{13}{3}$ **21.** $y = 9x + 7$ **22.** $y = 6x + 8$ **23.** $y = \dfrac{1}{3}x + \dfrac{7}{3}$

24. $y = 1450 - 150x$ **25.** Answers will vary.

At $x = 4$, $y = 850$;
After 4 months, his
remaining loan is $850.

Chapter 7

PROBLEM SET 7.1

Experiencing Algebra the Exercise Way

1. solution   **2.** solution   **3.** solution   **4.** not a solution   **5.** not a solution   **6.** not a solution
7. not a solution   **8.** solution   **9.** not a solution   **10.** not a solution   **11.** $(0, -2)$
12. all ordered pairs (x, y) that satisfy $x + 3y = 3$ **13.** $(5, -1)$ **14.** $(3, 0)$ **15.** no solution
16. $(-4, 4)$ **17.** all ordered pairs (x, y) that satisfy $x - y = -1$ **18.** no solution   **19.** $(-2, 2)$

20. $(0, 1)$ **21.** $(1, 2)$ **22.** all ordered pairs (x, y) that satisfy $y = -\dfrac{2}{3}x - 2$ **23.** no solution

24. $(1, -3)$ **25.** all ordered pairs (x, y) that satisfy $y = \dfrac{1}{2}x + 2$ **26.** no solution   **27.** $(2, 3)$

28. no solution   **29.** $(1, 4)$ **30.** $(2, 3)$ **31.** no solution   **32.** $(-3, -1)$ **33.** $(2, 1)$ **34.** $(2, -1)$

35. all ordered pairs (x, y) that satisfy $y = x - 7$ **36.** $(0, 3)$ **37.** no solution   **38.** no solution
39. (a) Turtle Rental: $y = 39.95 + 0.25(x - 150)$; Snail Rental: $y = 79.95 + 0.15(x - 200)$
(b) $(475, 121.2)$ **(c)** If Ahmet drives less than 475 miles, Turtle Rental is a better deal. If Ahmet drives more
than 475 miles, Snail Rental is a better deal.   **(d)** Turtle Rental   **(e)** Snail Rental
40. (a) Turtle Rental: $y = 49.95 + 0.3x$; Snail Rental: $y = 19.95 + 0.4x$ **(b)** $(300, 139.95)$
(c) If Ahmet drives less than 300 miles, Snail Rental is a better deal. If Ahmet drives more than 300 miles,
Turtle Rental is a better deal.   **(d)** Snail Rental   **(e)** Turtle Rental
41. (a) Bulk rate: $y = 75 + 0.226x$; First class: $y = 0.32x$ **(b)** approximately $(798, 255)$
(c) When there are more than 798 pieces of mail it is more cost effective to use bulk-rate.;
The graph representing bulk-rate is lower than that representing first-class for values of x greater than 798.
(d) When there are less than 798 pieces of mail it is more cost effective to use first-class.; The graph
representing first-class is lower than that representing bulk-rate for values of x less than 798.
42. (a) With coupon book: $y = 50 + 13.5x$; Without coupon book: $y = 17.5x$ **(b)** $(12.5, 218.75)$
(c) It will be beneficial to purchase the coupon book if you will purchase 13 or more dinners.
(d) It will be more cost effective not to purchase the coupon book if you will purchase 12 or fewer dinners.;
The two options are equal at the intersection of 12.5 dinners, with a cost of $218.75.

43. $x + y = 500$; $y = 3x$; The car payment is \$125 and the rent payment is \$375.   **44.** $330x + 450y = 7800$; $x + y = 20$; There should be 10 1-bedroom apartments and 10 2-bedroom apartments.   **45.** $x + y = 40$; $7x + 8.2y = 298$; She should work 15 hours at the job that pays \$8.20 per hour, and 25 hours at the job paying \$7.00 per hour.   **46.** $18x + 22y = 316$; $y = 3 + x$; His wages are \$6.25 per hour and \$9.25 per hour.

47. $L = 2W - 25$; $2L + 2W = 550$; The width is 100 feet and the length is 175 feet.   **48.** $W = \dfrac{1}{2}L + 5$; $2W + 2L = 310$; The width is 55 feet and the length is 100 feet.   **49.** $y = 2x + 1$; $x + y = 22$; Shania had 7 records and Reba had 15 records.   **50.** $y = x + 5$; $x + y = 21$; There were 8 cups and 13 saucers.

Experiencing Algebra the Calculator Way

1. $\approx(-1.05, -1.33)$ **2.** $\approx(-5.94, -10.68)$ **3.** $\approx(-8.42, -115.3)$ **4.** $\approx(3.21, 0.86)$ **5.** no solution   **6.** all ordered pairs (x, y) that satisfy $y = \dfrac{-x + 7}{3}$ **7.** $\approx(-6.88, 395.63)$ **8.** $\approx(15.71, 575)$ **9.** $(30, 9000)$

PROBLEM SET 7.2

Experiencing Algebra the Exercise Way

1. $(12, -7)$ **2.** $(4, 1)$ **3.** $(5, 0)$ **4.** $\left(\dfrac{5}{2}, \dfrac{3}{2}\right)$ **5.** $(-5, -5)$ **6.** $(1, -1)$ **7.** no solution

8. all ordered pairs (x, y) that satisfy $y = 2x + 3$ **9.** $(16, 13)$ **10.** $(2, -2)$ **11.** $\left(-\dfrac{13}{5}, -\dfrac{8}{5}\right)$

12. $(4, 9)$ **13.** $(-8, -1)$ **14.** no solution   **15.** $\left(\dfrac{3}{2}, \dfrac{5}{2}\right)$ **16.** $(-3, -7)$ **17.** all ordered pairs (x, y) that satisfy $y = -3x + 2$ **18.** $(4, -7)$ **19.** $(-4, 5)$ **20.** $(0, -2)$ **21.** $(4, 11)$ **22.** $(5, -1)$ **23.** $(2, -15)$ **24.** no solution   **25.** all ordered pairs (x, y) that satisfy $x - y = -1$ **26.** all ordered pairs (x, y) that satisfy $x + 3y = 3$ **27.** $(1, 2)$ **28.** $(1, -3)$ **29.** $(-2, 2)$ **30.** $(8, 7)$ **31.** all ordered pairs (x, y) that satisfy $y = \dfrac{1}{2}x + 2$ **32.** all ordered pairs (x, y) that satisfy $x = -\dfrac{3}{2}y - 3$

33. no solution   **34.** no solution   **35.** $(2, 3)$ **36.** $(2, 3)$ **37.** $(2, 1)$ **38.** $(2, -1)$

39. all ordered pairs (x, y) that satisfy $y = x - 7$ **40.** $\left(\dfrac{3}{2}, \dfrac{9}{4}\right)$ **41.** no solution   **42.** no solution

43. $(14, -5)$ **44.** $(9, 2)$ **45.** $2W + 2L = 146$; $L = 2W - 11$; The width is 28 feet and the length is 45 feet.   **46.** $2W + 2L = 2100$; $L = 3W + 50$; The width is 250 feet and the length is 800 feet.   **47.** $x + y = 90$; $y = 4x - 10$; The angles measure 20° and 70°.   **48.** $x + y = 180$; $y - x = 40$; The angles measure 70° and 110°.   **49.** $x + x + y = 180$; $y = x + x + 20$; The angles measure 40°, 40°, and 100°.   **50.** $x + x + y = 180$; $y = x + 15$; The angles measure 55°, 55°, and 70°.   **51.** $R = 2r + 5$; $2\pi R = 283$; The radius of each measures 20 inches and 45 inches.   **52.** $2\pi R = 163$; $R = 3r - 10$; The radius of each measures 12 cm and 26 cm.   **53.** $x + y = 100{,}000$; $0.07x + 0.06y = 6450$; She borrowed \$45,000 at 7% simple interest and \$55,000 at 6% simple interest.   **54.** $1500x + 1200y = 117.90$; $y = x + 0.003$; The interest rate was 4.2$\overline{3}$% for the \$1500 investment and 4.5$\overline{3}$% for the \$1200 investment.   **55.** $x + y = 15$; $y = 25 - x$; There is no solution.   **56.** $x + y = 12$; $y = 12 - x$; The solutions are all ordered pairs (x, y) that satisfy $x + y = 12$, where $x =$ acres of alfalfa and $y =$ acres of wheat.   **57.** $x + y = 1.4155 \times 10^{12}$; $y = x + 1.687 \times 10^{11}$; The amounts are \$6.234 $\times 10^{11}$ from individual income taxes and \$7.921 $\times 10^{11}$ from other sources.   **58.** $\dfrac{x + y}{2} = 2.75 \times 10^{-10}$; $y - x = 4.5 \times 10^{-10}$; The diameters are 5×10^{-11} m for helium and 5×10^{-10} m for cesium.

Experiencing Algebra the Calculator Way

1. $(153.75, 225.85)$ 2. $\left(\dfrac{28}{55}, \dfrac{37}{66}\right)$ 3. $(0.0983, -1.0768)$ is not a solution.   4. $(-2897.65, 1725.85)$

5. $\left(\dfrac{13}{35}, -\dfrac{17}{55}\right)$ is not a solution.   6. $\left(-\dfrac{78}{85}, \dfrac{28}{51}\right)$ is not a solution is not a solution.

PROBLEM SET 7.3

Experiencing Algebra the Exercise Way

1. $(-2, 2)$ 2. $(3, -7)$ 3. $(5, 2)$ 4. $(-3, -1)$ 5. $(-3, -9)$ 6. $(8, 2)$ 7. $(8, -2)$ 8. $(-3, 5)$

9. $(4, 3)$ 10. $(-1, -2)$ 11. $(7, -9)$ 12. $(-8, 7)$ 13. $(-3, 12)$ 14. $(13, -2)$ 15. $\left(\dfrac{13}{10}, \dfrac{29}{10}\right)$

16. $\left(\dfrac{4}{5}, -\dfrac{7}{5}\right)$ 17. $\left(-\dfrac{19}{5}, \dfrac{12}{5}\right)$ 18. $\left(\dfrac{9}{2}, -\dfrac{3}{2}\right)$ 19. $\left(\dfrac{21}{5}, \dfrac{7}{2}\right)$ 20. $\left(-\dfrac{9}{5}, -\dfrac{17}{5}\right)$ 21. $\left(\dfrac{13}{10}, \dfrac{33}{10}\right)$

22. $\left(-\dfrac{41}{10}, \dfrac{7}{10}\right)$ 23. $\left(\dfrac{2}{3}, \dfrac{3}{4}\right)$ 24. $\left(\dfrac{3}{5}, \dfrac{5}{6}\right)$ 25. $\left(\dfrac{3}{8}, -\dfrac{3}{4}\right)$ 26. $\left(\dfrac{7}{9}, -\dfrac{5}{8}\right)$ 27. all ordered pairs

(x, y) that satisfy $y = \dfrac{3}{2}x - 9$ 28. all ordered pairs (x, y) that satisfy $y = \dfrac{6}{5}x + 2$ 29. no solution

30. no solution   31. $(30, -2)$ 32. $(20, 8)$ 33. $(10, 10)$ 34. $(40, -10)$ 35. $(-400, -700)$

36. $(-250, 550)$ 37. $\left(\dfrac{44}{5}, \dfrac{33}{5}\right)$ 38. $\left(\dfrac{43}{10}, -\dfrac{23}{10}\right)$ 39. $(52, 48)$ 40. $(63, 57)$ 41. $(7, 4)$

42. $(5, 9)$ 43. $(40, 70)$ 44. $(80, 20)$ 45. $(80, 120)$ 46. $(76, 138)$

47. $x + y = 683; 1.5x + 5y = 2645;$ There were 220 students who attended the game.   48. $x + y = 56;$ $30x + 45y = 2190;$ There were 22 senior citizens and 34 others.   49. $x - y = 50; 8.5x + 5y = 3462.5;$ They sold 275 cookbooks and 225 calendars.   50. $x + y = 5.5; 6x + 4y = 29.5;$ They sold her 3.75 pounds of ham and 1.75 pounds of cheese.   51. $x + y = 16{,}500; 0.05x + 0.0725y = 1000;$ She should invest $8722.22 at 5% and $7777.78 at 7.25%.   52. $x + y = 11{,}000; 0.05x + 0.0725y = 600;$ She should invest $8777.78 at 5% and $2222.22 at 7.5%.   53. $x + y = 385; 2x + 2y = 770;$ The solution is any number of adults, x, and any number of children, y, where $x + y = 385$.   54. $x + y = 8.95; 2x + 2y = 13.95;$ There is no solution.   55. $2x + 2y = 620; 2x + 2(y + 90) = 800;$ The solutions are any number of yards, x, and any number of yards, y, where $x + y = 310$.   56. $R - r = 10; 2\pi R = 2\pi r + 20\pi;$ The solutions are any radius, r, and any radius, R, when $R - r = 10$.   57. $x + x + y = 180; y = 90 - 2x;$ There is no solution.

58. $x + y = 180; y - x = 30;$ The angles are 75° and 105°.   59. $y = x + 4.864 \times 10^7; \dfrac{x + y}{2} = 1.1728 \times 10^8;$ The distances from the sun are 9.296×10^7 miles for Earth and 1.416×10^8 miles for Mars.

60. $y = 3.6302 \times 10^9 + x; \dfrac{x + y}{2} = 1.851 \times 10^9;$ The distances from the sun are 3.59×10^7 miles for Mercury and 3.661×10^9 miles for Pluto.

Experiencing Algebra the Calculator Way

1. $(352, 126)$ 2. $(73, 88)$ 3. $(-1.08, -3.462)$ 4. $(0.088, 4750)$ 5. $\left(\dfrac{17}{36}, -\dfrac{41}{76}\right)$ 6. $\left(\dfrac{3}{5}, -\dfrac{2}{5}\right)$

PROBLEM SET 7.4

Experiencing Algebra the Exercise Way

1. $x + y = 30; 0.9x + 1.5y = 1.25(30);$ She should mix 12.5 pounds of peanuts with 17.5 pounds of candy.
2. $0.1x + 0.25(100) = 0.15y; x + 100 = y;$ There should be 200 ten cent pogs and 300 total pogs in the mix.

3. $x + y = 65; 5x + 10y = 365;$ There are 57 \$5 bills and 8 \$10 bills.   **4.** $x + y = 35; 20x + 50y = 1300;$ There are 15 \$20 bills and 20 \$50 bills.   **5.** $x + y = 130; 0.65x + 0y = 0.35(130);$ The mixture should have 70 gallons of concentrate and 60 gallons of water.   **6.** $x + 0.35y = 0.5(5); x + y = 5;$ 1.2 gallons should be drained and replaced with antifreeze.   **7.** $450 = 3(x + y); 450 = 5(x - y);$ The speed of the plane with no wind is 120 mph and the speed of the wind is 30 mph.   **8.** $y = 4x; y = 3(x + 40);$ His speed the first time was 120 mph and the distance was 480 miles.   **9.** $4.5x + 7.5y = 3937.5; x + y = 625;$ There were 250 children and 375 adults.   **10.** $5.5x + 10y = 5355; x = 2y;$ There were 510 children and 255 adults.

11. $x + y = 5; 0.7x + 0.4y = 0.5(5);$ He should mix $1\frac{2}{3}$ pints of 70% weed killer and $3\frac{1}{3}$ pints of 40% weed killer.   **12.** $x + y = 200; 0.043x + 0y = 0.02(200);$ He should mix 93 gallons of 4.3% butterfat milk with 107 gallons of skim milk.   **13.** $9.5x + 7y = 8.5(20); x + y = 20;$ He should use 12 pounds of French vanilla coffee and 8 pounds of hazelnut coffee.   **14.** $x + y = 10; 3.5x + 7.5y = 5(10);$ The blend contained 6.25 pounds of orange spice tea and 3.75 pounds of lemon honey tea.
15. $x + y = 10,000; 0.085x + 0.07y = 752.5;$ She invested \$3500 at 8.5% and \$6500 at 7%.
16. $x + y = 10,000; 0.07x + 0.0825y = 725;$ He borrowed \$2000 at 7% and \$8000 at 8.25%.

17. $x = 2y; 11 = 3x + 60y;$ He walked for $\frac{1}{3}$ hour and rode for $\frac{1}{6}$ hour.   **18.** $x = y; 12x + 3y = 30;$

The time spent canoeing was 2 hours, and time spent hiking was 2 hours, and the distance traveled by canoe was 24 miles.   **19.** $x + y = 30; 5x + 12y = 250;$ She can buy 16 azaleas and 14 rhododendeous.
20. $x + y = 50; x + 2.5y = 95;$ She should order 20 hot dogs and 30 burgers.
21. $15x + 20y = 320; 18x + 24y = 384;$ The solutions are any wage, x, and any wage, y, where $15x + 20y = 320.$ **22.** $2x + 4y = 132; 3x + 6y = 180;$ There is no solution.

Experiencing Algebra the Calculator Way

1. (a) $R(x) = 25x$
(b) $C(x) = 10x + 1500$
(c) 6000

0, 0, 200

2. (a) $R(x) = 45x$
(b) $C(x) = 25x + 2500$
(c) 7000

0, 0, 150

3. The graphs intersect at approximately (75.7, 2458.3). The break-even point is at producing and selling 76 purses

Intersection
X=75.662651 _Y=2458.2795

(d) The graphs intersect at (100, 2500). The break-even point is at producing and selling 100 lamps.
(e) The solution checks.

(d) The graphs intersect at (125, 5625). The break-even point is at producing and selling 125 tables.
(e) The solution checks.

CHAPTER 7 REVIEW

Reflections

1–8. Answers will vary.

Exercises

1. solution   **2.** solution   **3.** not a solution   **4.** not a solution   **5.** not a solution   **6.** solution
7. not a solution   **8.** solution   **9.** $(7, 3)$ **10.** $(-4, 2)$ **11.** $(-2, -1)$ **12.** $(3, -4)$ **13.** no solution

14. all ordered pairs $(x. y)$ that satisfy $y = \frac{3}{2}x - 6$ **15.** $(1, -3)$ **16.** no solution   **17.** all ordered pairs (x, y) that satisfy $2x - 11 = 3$ or $x = 7$ **18.** all ordered pairs (x, y) that satisfy $y - 1 = 4$ or $y = 5$
19. $(-3, 4)$ **20.** $(5, -5)$ **21.** $(-3, -5)$ **22.** $(5, 1)$
23. $x + y = 500 - 120; y = x + 40;$ There were 50 more Democrats than Independents.

24. $2W + 2L = 116.6; 2(W + 4.7) + 2(L - 2.9) = 120.2;$ The solution is all ordered pairs (W, L) that satisfy $2W + 2L = 116.6.$ **25.** $\left(-\dfrac{3}{4}, \dfrac{5}{8}\right)$ **26.** $\left(\dfrac{1}{5}, \dfrac{16}{5}\right)$ **27.** no solution **28.** $(-53, -62)$ **29.** $(27, -41)$

30. all ordered pairs (x, y) that satisfy $y = 3x + 7$ **31.** $\left(\dfrac{15}{19}, \dfrac{10}{19}\right)$ **32.** $(575, 823)$ **33.** $(30, 6)$

34. $(-10, 2)$ **35.** $\left(\dfrac{17}{8}, -\dfrac{29}{8}\right)$ **36.** $\left(120, \dfrac{3}{4}\right)$ **37.** $x + y = 90; y = 2x + 12;$ The difference in the angles is 38°. **38.** $L = 3W - 2.5; 2W + 2L = 31.8;$ The area is 51.98 cm². **39.** $x + y = 10,000,000; 0.045x + 0.06y = 487,500;$ She invested \$7,500,000 at 4.5% simple interest and \$2,500,000 at 6% simple interest. **40.** $(7, -15)$ **41.** $(6, 6)$ **42.** $(-4, 15)$

43. $(-3, -4)$ **44.** no solution **45.** $\left(\dfrac{133}{31}, -\dfrac{2}{31}\right)$ **46.** $(4, 8)$ **47.** all ordered pairs (x, y) that satisfy $y = \dfrac{5}{7}x + 1$ **48.** $\left(\dfrac{5}{9}, -\dfrac{7}{9}\right)$ **49.** $\left(\dfrac{7}{8}, \dfrac{21}{8}\right)$ **50.** $(10, 5)$ **51.** $(350, -650)$ **52.** $x + y = 100;$ $0.25x + 0.3y = 0.27(100);$ The amounts are 60 pounds of 25% copper and 40 pounds of 30% copper. **53.** $x + y = 40; 250x + 400y = 12,700;$ She will have more of the small offices. She will have 22 small offices and 18 large offices. **54.** $y = x + 5.328 \times 10^{24}; \dfrac{x + y}{2} = 3.306 \times 10^{24};$ The mass of Mars is 6.42×10^{23} kg and the mass of Earth is 5.97×10^{24} kg. **55.** $25x + 35y = 5500; x + y = 200;$ The plant should order 150 components from Supplier A and 50 components from Supplier B. **56.** $x + y = 150;$ $0.1x + 0.05y = 0.08(150);$ He should use 90 pounds of 10% nitrogen with 60 pounds of 5% nitrogen. **57.** $0.49x + 0.99y = 0.69(200); x + y = 200;$ They should mix 120 pounds of broccoli with 80 pounds of cauliflower. **58.** $x + y = 10; 65x + 45y = 600;$ He drove 487.5 miles on the interstate. **59.** $y = 217.26(x + 1.603); y = 217.50(x + 1.598);$ The speed of the current was 2.929 mps and the distance of the race was 984.46 meters. **60.** $C(x) = 400 + 5x; R(x) = 8.5x;$ The break-even point is at about 114 items.; When the company produces and sells less than 114 items, cost exceeds revenue. When the company produces and sells at least 115 items, revenue exceeds cost. **61.** $A(x) = 150 + 0.25x; B(x) = 175 + 0.2x;$ He must drive more than 500 miles.

CHAPTER 7 MIXED REVIEW

1. $(-14, -6)$ **2.** all ordered pairs (x, y) that satisfy $y = \dfrac{4}{5}x - 6$ **3.** $(8, -10)$ **4.** $(1200, 900)$

5. $(-6, 21)$ **6.** $(-2, -1)$ **7.** no solution **8.** $\left(\dfrac{87}{26}, -\dfrac{5}{26}\right)$ **9.** $(6, -20)$ **10.** $(3, 7)$

11. $\left(-\dfrac{3}{7}, \dfrac{6}{7}\right)$ **12.** $\left(\dfrac{27}{8}, -\dfrac{21}{8}\right)$ **13.** $(3, -2)$ **14.** no solution **15.** $(-4, 2)$ **16.** $(3, -3)$

17. no solution **18.** all ordered pairs (x, y) satisfying $y = -4x - 3$ **19.** all ordered pairs (x, y) that satisfy $x + 7 = 3$ or $x = -4$ **20.** all ordered pairs (x, y) that satisfy $y + 9 = 7$ or $y = -2$ **21.** $(6, 5)$ **22.** $(-3, -2)$ **23.** $(5, -2)$ **24.** $(-2, 2)$ **25.** $(1, 1)$ **26.** $(-6, -1)$ **27.** $(44, -23)$ **28.** $(-12, 5)$

29. $(-38, 43)$ **30.** all ordered pairs (x, y) that satisfy $y = 4x - 7$ **31.** $\left(\dfrac{1}{6}, -\dfrac{5}{6}\right)$ **32.** $\left(-\dfrac{3}{5}, -\dfrac{12}{5}\right)$

33. $\left(\dfrac{20}{9}, \dfrac{1}{9}\right)$ **34.** $(723, -491)$ **35.** $\left(\dfrac{19}{8}, -\dfrac{21}{8}\right)$ **36.** $\left(180, \dfrac{5}{9}\right)$ **37.** no solution **38.** $(120, 180)$

39. not a solution **40.** solution **41.** solution **42.** solution **43.** not a solution **44.** solution **45.** not a solution **46.** not a solution **47.** $x + y = 200; 0.15x + 0.35y = 0.27(200);$ 80 pounds of 15% brass; 120 pounds of 35% brass; 40 pounds more of the 35% alloy will be used. **48.** $8x + 12y = 7300;$ $y = x + 150;$ She will receive \$2200 for all of the 1-bedroom apartments and \$5100 for all of the 2-bedroom apartments. **49.** $x + y = 180; y = x + 10;$ The smaller angle measures 85°. **50.** $y = x + 5; 4x + 4y = 100;$ The areas of the squares will be 100 in² and 225 in².

51. $x + y = 700; 0.7x + 0.4y = 400$; There were 100 more women surveyed.
52. $x + y = 180; y = 3x + 12$; The angles measure 42° and 138°.
53. $x + y = 30; 0.15x + 0.25y = 0.21(30)$; She should use 12 cc of 15% and 18 cc of 25%.
54. $3.5 = \frac{1}{2}x + \frac{1}{3}y; 4 = \frac{2}{3}x + \frac{1}{3}y$; He walked at 3 mph and jogged at 6 mph.   **55.** $x + y = 50$;
$8.5x + 12.5y = 9.5(50)$; The shop should mix 37.5 pounds of gourmet coffee with 12.5 pounds of dutch chocolate.   **56.** $10.75x + 6.5y = 181; x + y = 20$; She should work 12 hours at \$10.75 per hour; 8 hours at \$6.50 per hour.   **57.** $y = x(400 + 40); y = (x + 1)(400 - 40)$; The distance traveled was 1980 miles.
58. $U(x) = 39.95 + 0.15x; B(x) = 19.95 + 0.22x$; You must drive at least 286 miles in order for U Rent It to be less costly.   **59.** $C(x) = 7.5 + 2.5x; R(x) = 6.5x$; The shop keeper must produce and sell at least 19 items in order not to lose money.

CHAPTER 7 TEST

1. solution   **2.** all ordered pairs (x, y) that satisfy $y = 4$ **3.** no solution   **4.** $(2, 1)$ **5.** $(-2, 4)$
6. no solution   **7.** $\left(\frac{1}{4}, -\frac{3}{8}\right)$ **8.** no solution   **9.** $(8, 0)$ **10.** $\left(\frac{34}{19}, \frac{13}{19}\right)$ **11.** The break-even point
is at $91\frac{2}{3}$ items.; After producing and selling 92 items, the factory's revenue will be greater than its cost.

12. $y = 3x; y = 2(x + 4)$; Kenny's rate was 8 mph and the distance to Dolly was 24 miles.
13. $6x + 8y = 58; 10x + 5y = 55$; The computer takes 3 nanoseconds per addition and 5 nanoseconds per multiplication.   **14.** $x + y = 30; 1.25x + 2y = 1.5(30)$; He should mix 20 pounds of raisins with 10 pounds of peanuts.   **15.** $x + y = 90; y = 2x$; The angles measure 30° and 60°.
16. $x + y = 100; 0.5x + 0.1y = 0.3(100)$; She should mix 50 cc of 50% solution and 50 cc of 10% solution.
17. One solution exists; no solution exists; an infinite number of solutions exist. Answers will vary.

Chapter 8

PROBLEM SET 8.1

Experiencing Algebra the Exercise Way

1. linear   **2.** linear   **3.** nonlinear   **4.** nonlinear   **5.** linear   **6.** linear   **7.** linear   **8.** linear
9. linear   **10.** nonlinear   **11.** nonlinear   **12.** nonlinear   **13.** nonlinear   **14.** linear   **15.** linear
16. linear
17.

$[6, \infty]$
19.
$(-\infty, 12)$
21.

$\left(-\frac{13}{5}, \infty\right)$

18.

$(-\infty, 9]$
20.
$(-7, \infty)$
22.

$\left(-\infty, 3\frac{5}{6}\right)$

23.

$\left(-\infty, 4\frac{2}{3}\right)$

24.

$\left[\frac{16}{3}, \infty\right)$

25.

12.59

$(-\infty, 12.59)$

26.

5.1

$[5.1, \infty)$

27.

−6.7

$(-6.7, \infty)$

28.

45.65

$(-\infty, 45.65)$

29.

$(5, 13)$

30.

$(-2, -1)$

31.

$(2, 8)$

32.

$[3, 6)$

33.

$(-4, 0]$

34.

$[0, 5)$

35.

$[-1, 6)$

36.

$(2, 7]$

37.

$[2, 7]$

38.

$[15, 30]$

39.

$\left(\frac{2}{5}, 3\frac{1}{3}\right]$

40.

$\left[-1\frac{3}{4}, \frac{2}{3}\right]$

41.

−2.5   3.5

$[-2.5, 3.5)$

42.

−6.5   −1.5

$(-6.5, -1.5)$

43.

$\left[\frac{4}{5}, 4.5\right]$

44.

$\left(-2.5, \frac{2}{5}\right)$

45. (a) $; (-\infty, 4.5)$ **(b)** $x \le 3; (-\infty, 3]$

(c) $x < -2;$ **(d)** $; [5.7, \infty)$

(e) $z > -7; (-7, \infty)$ **(f)** $z > 2;$

(g) $; (2, 8)$ **(h)** $-3 \le y < 2; [-3, 2)$

(i) $0 \le y \le 9;$ **46. (a)** $a < -9;$

(b) $a \le 5; (-\infty, 5]$ **(c)** $; \left(-\infty, \dfrac{1}{2}\right)$

(d) $b \ge 0;$ **(e)** $b > -4; (-4, \infty)$

(f) $; (2.7, \infty)$ **(g)** $4 < c < 11;$

(h) $0 \le c < 5; [0, 5)$ **(i)** $; [-5, -1]$

47. $39.95 + 0.2x \le 150$ **48.** $300 + 22x < 1000$ **49.** $800 < 450 + 0.05x$ **50.** $15x - 125 \ge 250$
51. $150 \le 25 + 12.5x \le 200$ **52.** $200 \le 4.5x - 350 \le 500$

Experiencing Algebra the Calculator Way

1.   **2.**   **3.**   **4.**

5.   **6.**   **7.**

PROBLEM SET 8.2

Experiencing Algebra the Exercise Way

1. integers less than 24   **2.** integers greater than -2 **3.** no solution   **4.** all integers
5. integers equal to and greater than 0   **6.** integers less than -6 **7.** all integers   **8.** no solution
9. $x \ge -2$ **10.** $x \le 2$ **11.** $x > -4$ **12.** $x > 2$ **13.** $x \le 3$ **14.** $x \ge 2$ **15.** all real numbers
16. all real numbers   **17.** no solution   **18.** no solution   **19.** $(-3, \infty)$ **20.** $(-\infty, 13)$

21. $(-\infty, -4)$ **22.** $(-\infty, -38)$ **23.** $(-\infty, 0]$ **24.** $\left(-\infty, \dfrac{28}{5}\right]$ **25.** $(2, \infty)$ **26.** $(7, \infty)$

27. $(3.3, \infty)$ **28.** $(5, \infty)$ **29.** $(0, \infty)$ **30.** $(10.2, \infty)$ **31.** $[6, \infty)$ **32.** $(-\infty, 6.\overline{53658}]$

33. $\left[-\dfrac{749}{92}, \infty\right)$ **34.** $(-\infty, 1]$ **35.** $\left(\dfrac{1}{2}, \infty\right)$ **36.** $\left(-\infty, -\dfrac{1}{4}\right)$ **37.** $(8, \infty)$ **38.** $(-\infty, -3)$

39. $(8.8, \infty)$ **40.** $(0, \infty)$ **41.** $\left(-\infty, -\dfrac{1}{162}\right]$ **42.** $\left[-\dfrac{3}{8}, \infty\right)$ **43.** $(-120, \infty)$ **44.** $(-66, \infty)$

45. no solution   **46.** no solution   **47.** all real numbers   **48.** all real numbers   **49.** $(107.5, \infty)$

50. $(3.6, \infty)$ **51.** $\dfrac{73 + 97 + 82 + 89 + 95 + x}{6} \ge 87;$ His score must be 86 or greater.

52. $\dfrac{38 + 62 + 56 + 42 + x}{5} > 50$; She must earn more than $52.

53. $9.75x + 5200 \le 7500$; He can work 235 hours or less.   **54.** $22 + 3.5x \le 55$; He can use the grinder 9 hours or less.   **55.** $165x \le 2000$; The number of people can be 12 or less.   **56.** $12.5x + 87.5 \le 120$; She can buy 1 or 2 sweaters.   **57.** $x + x + 150 + 2x + 50 \le 1200$; She can have no more than 250 calories for breakfast, 400 calories for lunch, and 550 calories for dinner.   **58.** $x + 2x - 10 \ge 110$; Tommy must work 40 or more hours.; Shawn must work 70 or more hours.   **59.** $8.5x + 6.5(120 - x) \le 950$; She can order 85 or fewer meat plates.   **60.** $25 + 0.22x > 15 + 0.35x$; You can drive 76 or fewer miles.

61. $2x + \dfrac{3}{4}x + 30 - 4 \le 185$; The width must be 57 or fewer feet.   **62.** $2x + 2(2x + 15) \le 240$; The width must b 35 or fewer feet.   **63.** $300 + 0.05(x - 1000) > 500 + 0.05(x - 2000)$; There are no values of sales that plan A will pay more than plan B.   **64.** $37x + 125 < (25 + 12)x + 175$; Any number of sweaters will cost less.   **65.** The years are 1990 to the present.   **66.** The years are 1987 to the present.

Experiencing Algebra the Calculator Way

Answers will vary.

PROBLEM SET 8.3

Experiencing Algebra the Exercise Way

1. linear; $x + 1.7y > 4.6$; $a = 1, b = 1.7, c = -4.6$ **2.** nonlinear   **3.** nonlinear
4. linear; $-5x + 10y \ge 15$; $a = -5, b = 10, c = 15$ **5.** nonlinear   **6.** nonlinear
7. linear; $6x - 2y > 1$; $a = 6, b = -2, c = 1$ **8.** nonlinear   **9.** linear; $4x - y \le -16$; $a = 4, b = -1, c = -16$ **10.** linear; $-4.2x + 3.5y < -2.8$; $a = -4.2, b = 3.5, c = -2.8$
11. linear; $6x + 15y \le 7$; $a = 6, b = 15, c = 7$ **12.** linear; $x + 2y < 12$; $a = 1, b = 2, c = 12$

13. $y < -2x + 3$ **14.** $y > 5x - 6$ **15.** $y \le \dfrac{5}{3}x - 2$ **16.** $y \ge -\dfrac{8}{7}x + 2$

   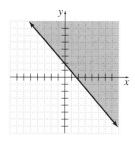

17. $y < -\dfrac{3}{4}x + 4$ **18.** $y < \dfrac{5}{6}x - 3$ **19.** $y \ge 2.8x - 1.6$ **20.** $y \ge -1.9x + 4.7$

21. $y > \dfrac{3}{2}x - \dfrac{5}{2}$

22. $y > \dfrac{3}{5}x - \dfrac{2}{5}$

23. $y \geq 2x - 1$

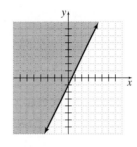

24. $y \leq -2x - 7$

25. $y > -4$

26. $y > 6$

27. $x \leq 1$

28. $x \leq 5$

29. $y \geq -\dfrac{3}{5}x + \dfrac{12}{5}$

30. $y \geq -\dfrac{7}{9}x + 7$

31. $y > -x - 7$

32. $y < x - 3$

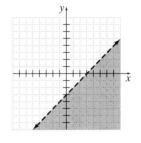

33. $y < -\dfrac{1}{3}x - 3$

34. $y < -\dfrac{4}{3}x - 4$

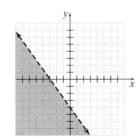

35. $y \leq -\dfrac{3}{8}x + 3$

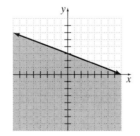

36. $y \geq \dfrac{2}{3}x - 6$

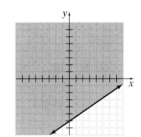

37. $y \geq \dfrac{6}{7}x + \dfrac{5}{7}$

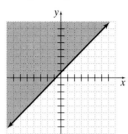

38. $y \leq \dfrac{9}{10}x - \dfrac{13}{20}$

39. $y < 0.5625x$

40. $y > -3x$

41. $y < 5.4$

42. $y > 0.25$

43. $y < x - 9$

44. $y > x + 9$

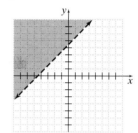

45. $y < -x - 9$

46. $y > -x + 9$

47. $y \leq x$

48. $y \geq -x$

49. $25x + 12y \leq 225$

ordered pairs in the shaded region; Yes; No

50. $12x + 18y \leq 240$

ordered pairs in the shaded region; Yes; No

51. $2x + 2y \leq 220$

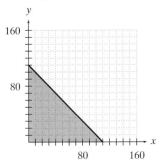

ordered pairs in the
shaded region; No; Yes

52. $2(10x + 10y) \leq 2400$

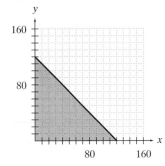

ordered pairs in the
shaded region; No; Yes

53. $15x + 12y \geq 400$

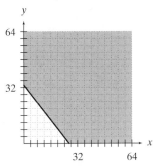

ordered pairs in the
shaded region; No; Yes

54. $15x + 10y \geq 75$

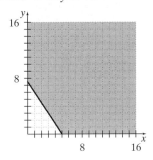

ordered pairs in the
shaded region; Yes; Yes

55. $4.5x + 2y \geq 250$

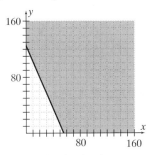

ordered pairs in the
shaded region; No; Yes

56. $160x + 65y \leq 2000$

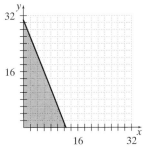

ordered pairs in the
shaded region; Yes; No

Experiencing Algebra the Calculator Way

1. $x < 10$

2. $x < 5$

3. $x > \dfrac{14}{5}$

4. $x \geq 2.7$

5. $x \leq \pi$

6. $x \leq 3 - \sqrt{2}$

PROBLEM SET 8.4

Experiencing Algebra the Exercise Way

1.

2.

3.

4.

5.

6.

7.

8.

9.

10.

11.

12.

13.

14.

15.

16.

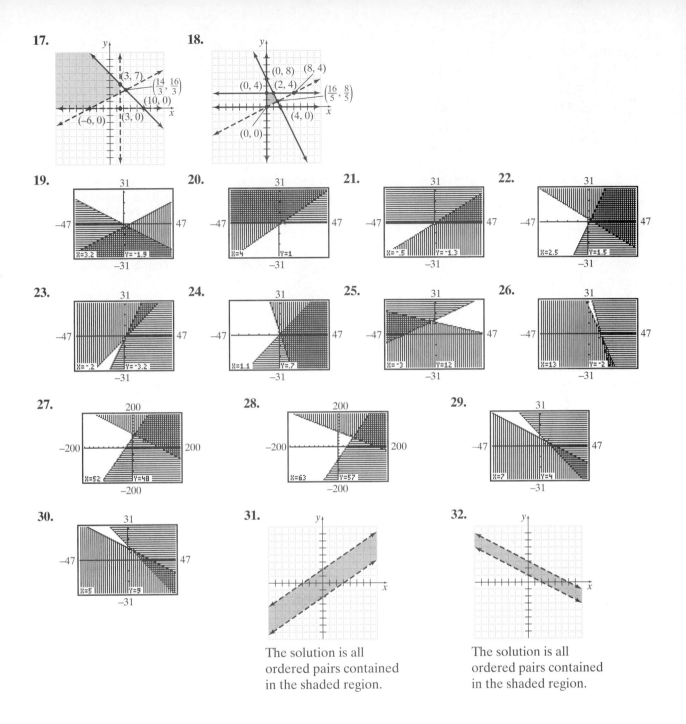

17.

18.

19.

20.

21.

22.

23.

24.

25.

26.

27.

28.

29.

30.

31.

The solution is all ordered pairs contained in the shaded region.

32.

The solution is all ordered pairs contained in the shaded region.

33.

There are no ordered pairs that satisfy this system of linear inequalities.

34.

There are no ordered pairs that satisfy this system of linear inequalities.

35.

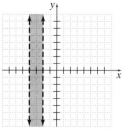

The solution is all ordered pairs contained in the shaded region.

36.

The solution is all ordered pairs contained in the shaded region.

37.

The solution is all ordered pairs below and including the boundary line

$2x + y = -1$.

38.

The solution is all ordered pairs below the boundary line

$y = x - 9$.

39.

The solution is all ordered pairs on the line $3y = x + 6$ or

$y = \frac{1}{3}x + 2$.

40.

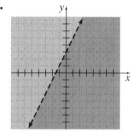

There are no ordered pairs that satisfy this system of linear

inequalities.

41.

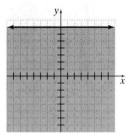

The solution is all ordered pairs below the line $y = 7$.

42.

The solution is all ordered pairs above and including the boundary line $y = 3x + 4$.

43. $2x + 2y \leq 100$
  $y \geq x + 10$
  $x \geq 0$
  $y \geq 0$

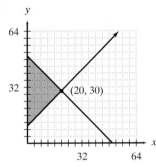

Possible answer:
10 feet by 30 feet

44. $2x + 2y \leq 100$
  $y \geq 2x$
  $x \geq 0$
  $y \geq 0$

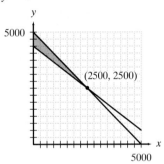

Possible answer:
5 feet by 25 feet

45. $x + y \leq 3000$
  $0.06x + 0.08y \geq 200$
  $x \geq 0$
  $y \geq 0$

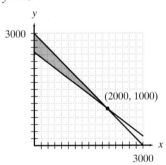

Possible answer:
$1000 at 6%;
$2000 at 8%

46. $x + y \leq 5000$
  $0.06x + 0.08y \leq 350$
  $x \geq 0$
  $y \geq 0$

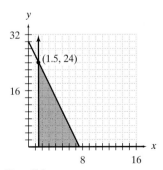

Possible answer:
$1000 at 6%;
$4000 at 8%

47. $x + y \leq 20$
  $6.5x + 8.25y \geq 150$
  $x \geq 0$
  $y \geq 0$

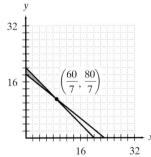

Possible answer:
He could work 6 hours on
the first job and 14 hours
on the second job.; No; Yes

48. $20x + 5y \leq 150$
  $x \geq 1.5$
  $y \geq 0$

Possible answer:
3 hours and 10 guests;
Yes; No

49. $1.75x + 2.25y \leq 200$
$x \geq 50$
$y \geq 25$

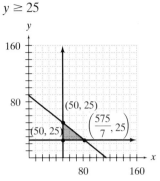

Possible answer:
75 servings of lasagna
and 30 servings of veal;
Yes; No

50. $0.05x > 0.01x + y$
$x \geq 25,000$
$y \geq 1399$

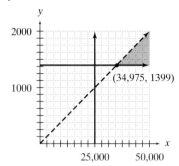

Possible answer:
45,000 copies and
$1600 machine cost;
No; Yes

Experiencing Algebra the Calculator Way

1.
2.
3.
4.

5.
6.

CHAPTER 8 REVIEW

Reflections

1–7. Answers will vary.

Exercises

1. nonlinear   **2.** linear   **3.** linear   **4.** nonlinear   **5.** linear   **6.** nonlinear   **7.** linear   **8.** linear

9.
$(-\infty, 3)$

10.
$(-2, \infty)$

11.
$(-\infty, -5]$

12.
$[-3.5, \infty)$

13.
$(-2, 4)$

14.
$(-1, 0]$

15.

$[3, 5.5]$

16.

$\left(2\frac{1}{2}, 8\right)$

17.

$\left[-2.3, -1\frac{1}{3}\right]$

18. $(30 + 25)x \geq 300$ **19.** $x + 2x + \frac{1}{4}(2x) < 200{,}000$

20. $60 + 0.18x < 0.32x$ **21.** integers less than -6 **22.** integers greater than 6

23. integers less than or equal to 3   **24.** integers greater than or equal to -2

25. $x > 2$
$(2, \infty)$

26. $x \leq 2.4$
$(-\infty, 2.4]$

27. no solution

28. all real numbers
$(-\infty, \infty)$

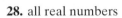

29. $(259, \infty)$ **30.** $\left(-\infty, \frac{32}{39}\right)$ **31.** $(-14, \infty)$ **32.** no solution   **33.** $(-\infty, -3.4]$ **34.** $[1.4, \infty)$

35. $(0, \infty)$ **36.** no solution   **37.** $49.95 + 0.18x \leq 150$; The number of miles driven should be less than or equal to 555 miles.   **38.** $\dfrac{2100 + 1300 + 1650 + 1250 + 1725 + x}{6} > 1500$; His sales should be greater than $975.   **39.** $2x + 2(x + 4) \leq 40$; The width can be no more than 8 feet.   **40.** linear; $x + 2y < 12$; $a = 1$, $b = 2$, $c = 12$ **41.** linear; $6x - 9y > -5$; $a = 6$, $b = -9$, $c = -5$ **42.** nonlinear

43. linear; $3x - 14y > -29$; $a = 3$, $b = -14$; $c = -29$ **44.** nonlinear   **45.** nonlinear

46. $y < -2x + 8$ **47.** $y > \frac{3}{5}x - 6$ **48.** $y \leq \frac{1}{4}x + 3$ **49.** $y \geq 3$

50. $y < -2$

51. $x > 2$

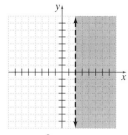

52. $y < \frac{2}{3}x - 2$

53. $y \geq -4x + 11$

54. $y \geq 0.5x - 2$

55. $y > -\frac{2}{3}x - 10$

56. $y > -x - 2$

57. $y > -9x + 6$

58. $4x + 6y \leq 85$

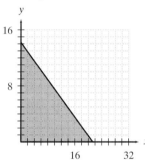

Possible answer: 15 rhododendrons and 2 azaleas or 10 rhododendrons and 5 azaleas

59. $5x - 3y \geq 80$

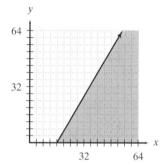

Possible answer: 40 correct and 3 incorrect or 30 correct and 0 incorrect

60.

61.

62.

63.

64.

no solution

65.

no solution

66.

67.

68.

69.

70.

71.

72.

73.

74.

75.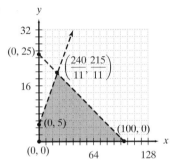

76. $4x + 6y \le 85$
$y + 4 \le x$
$x \ge 0$
$y \ge 0$

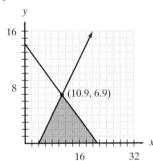

Possible answer:
15 rhododendrons and
2 azaleas

77. $0.05x + 0.06y \ge 225$
$x + y \le 4000$
$x \ge 0$
$y \ge 0$

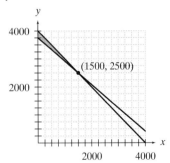

Possible answer:
$200 at 5% and $3800
at 6%

CHAPTER 8 MIXED REVIEW

1.

$(-\infty, -2)$

2.

$(7, \infty)$

3.

$(-1, 3)$

4.

$[2.6, \infty)$

5.

$\left(-\infty, 3\frac{2}{3}\right]$

6.

$\left(-2.4, 4\frac{1}{3}\right]$

7. integers less than -4 **8.** integers greater than 8   **9.** integers less than or equal to -3

10. integers less than or equal to 14

11. $x > 2$

$(2, \infty)$

12. $x \leq -4.2$

$(-\infty, -4.2]$

13. all real numbers

$(-\infty, \infty)$

14. no solution

15. $(-186, \infty)$

16. $\left(\frac{23}{34}, \infty\right)$ **17.** $(7, \infty)$ **18.** no solution   **19.** $[-2.8, \infty)$ **20.** $(-\infty, -3.7]$ **21.** $(-\infty, -1)$

22. $(-\infty, \infty)$

23.

24.

25.

26.

27.

28.

29.

30.

31.

32.

33.

34.

35.

36.

37.

38.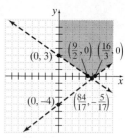

39. $y > \dfrac{9}{5}x - 9$

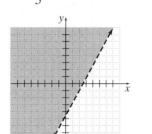

40. $y > \dfrac{4}{3}x - 5$

41. $y \le \dfrac{2}{3}x + 3$

42. $y \ge -5$

43. $y > \dfrac{5}{3}$

44. $x < -16$

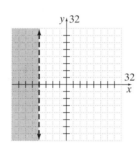

45. $y < \dfrac{1}{7}x - 3$

46. $y \ge -0.5x + 3$

47. $y \ge \dfrac{8}{3}x - 8$

48. $y > -\dfrac{3}{4}x - 3$

49. $y > x - 7$

50. $y > -5x + 7$

51. $y \geq 2x$
$x + y \leq 540$
$x \geq 0$
$y \geq 0$

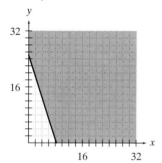

Possible answer:
100 acres of oats and
400 acres of wheat

52. $3x + 5y \geq 6000$
$y \geq x + 75$
$x \geq 0$
$y \geq 0$

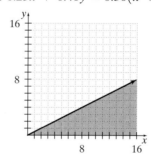

Possible answer:
$1000 for an efficiency;
$1500 for a regular
apartment

53. $255 + 2.5x < 12.5x$; To make a profit at least 26 packs must be sold.;
Possible answer: There were 27 packs sold.

54. $\dfrac{45 + 36 + 52 + 48 + 31 + x}{6} < 42$; Her sixth phone bill must be less than $40.;
Possible answer: Her phone bill should be $35.

55. $18x > 600$; The length must be greater than $33\frac{1}{3}$ inches.; Possible answer: The length is 40 inches.

56. $3x + y \geq 25$

Possible answer:
10 wins and 5 ties

57. $0.25x + 0.40y \leq 0.30(x + y)$

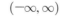

Possible answer:
10 liters of 25% solution and
2 liters of 40% solution

CHAPTER 8 TEST

1. linear   **2.** nonlinear   **3.** linear   **4.** linear   **5.** no solution

6.

$(-\infty, -4)$

7.

$(-\infty, \infty)$

8.

$-\frac{8}{3}$

$\left(-\infty, -\frac{8}{3}\right]$

9. $y < -2x + 5$

10. $x < 4$

11.

(4, 0)

12.

$\left(\frac{9}{7}, \frac{1}{7}\right)$

13.

14.

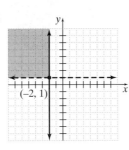

(−2, 1)

15. $\dfrac{83 + 72 + x}{3} \geq 80$; The score must be at least 85.;

Possible answer: The score is 90 points.

16. $5x + 2y \geq 20$

Possible answer:
5 good deeds and
5 activity sheets

17. $0.04x + 0.08y \geq 400$
$x + y \leq 6000$
$x \geq 0$
$y \geq 0$

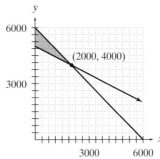

(2000, 4000)

Possible answer:
$500 at 4% and $5500 at 8%

18. Answers will vary.

CUMULATIVE REVIEW CHAPTERS 1–8

1. 9   **2.** −9   **3.** $-\dfrac{3}{4}$ **4.** $\dfrac{64}{9}$ **5.** $-\dfrac{3}{2}$ **6.** $\dfrac{9}{40}$ **7.** −6   **8.** 35   **9.** undefined   **10.** $-2x + 2$

11. $-2x + 6$ **12.**

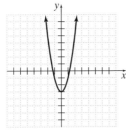

13. The domain of the relation is all real numbers. The range of the relation is all real numbers ≥ -3.

14. The relation is a function since all possible vertical lines cross the graph a maximum of one time.

15. The relative minimum value is −3 at $x = 0$. There is no relative maximum.

16. The relation is increasing for all $x > 0$, and decreasing for all $x < 0$.

17. The x-intercepts are $(-1.225, 0)$ and $(1.225, 0)$. The y-intercept is $(0, -3)$.   **18.** $\dfrac{8}{7}$ **19.** -2

20. All real numbers   **21.** 2 and -8 **22.** $x = 0$

23. $x > -3; (-3, \infty)$

24. $x \leq -\dfrac{2}{5}; \left(-\infty, -\dfrac{2}{5}\right]$ **25.** no solution

26.   **27.**   **28.**   **29.**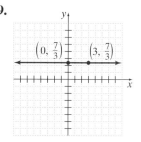

30.   **31.** Intersecting and perpendicular lines.   **34.**
32. $(-9, -23)$
33. All ordered pairs which satisfy $y = -2x + 4$.

One solution is $(1, 0)$.

35. -5 **36.** undefined   **37.** 2   **38.** 0   **39.** $y = -\dfrac{1}{3}x - \dfrac{7}{3}$ **40.** $y = -\dfrac{2}{3}x + \dfrac{22}{3}$ **41.** 5.34×10^6

42. 0.00012   **43.** -0.00004783 **44.** $L = \dfrac{P}{2} - W$ **45.** 2   **46.** Lance should invest \$25,227.28.

47. The smaller angle measures $21\dfrac{2}{3}°$ and the larger angle measures $68\dfrac{1}{3}°$.   **48.** Mike should mix $3\dfrac{1}{3}$ pounds of Hazelnut Coffee and $6\dfrac{2}{3}$ pounds of Cinnamon Coffee.   **49.** April must score at least 80 on the last test to get a B in her Algebra class.   **50.** $c(x) = 35 + 1.50x$; The cost of renting a chainsaw for 12 hours is \$53.

Chapter 9

PROBLEM SET 9.1

Experiencing Algebra the Exercise Way

1. Yes   **2.** No   **3.** Yes   **4.** No   **5.** No   **6.** Yes   **7.** Yes   **8.** No   **9.** Yes   **10.** Yes   **11.** No
12. Yes   **13.** Yes   **14.** No   **15.** No   **16.** Yes   **17.** No   **18.** Yes   **19.** Yes   **20.** Yes
21. trinomial   **22.** polynomial   **23.** monomial   **24.** binomial   **25.** binomial   **26.** trinomial
27. polynomial   **28.** monomial   **29.** trinomial   **30.** monomial   **31.** binomial   **32.** binomial
33. monomial   **34.** binomial   **35.** trinomial   **36.** binomial   **37.** degrees of terms: 0,1; degree of polynomial: 1   **38.** degree of term: 0; degree of polynomial: 0   **39.** degree of term: 0; degree of polynomial: 0
40. degrees of terms: 4, 6; degree of polynomial: 6   **41.** degree of term: 0, degree of polynomial: 0
42. degrees of terms: 2, 2; degree of polynomial: 2   **43.** degrees of terms: 5, 4, 0; degree of polynomial: 5

44. degrees of terms: 1, 0; degree of polynomial: 1   **45.** degrees of terms: 2, 2; degree of polynomial: 2
46. degrees of terms: 9, 6, 5; degree of polynomial: 9   **47.** degrees of terms: 15, 12, 7; degree of polynomial: 15
48. degree of term: 2; degree of polynomial: 2   **49.** $a^3 + 3a^2 - 2a + 5$ **50.** $4a^9 - 2a^6 + 3a^3 - 17$
51. $-\dfrac{8}{15}x^4 + \dfrac{4}{5}x^3 + \dfrac{2}{15}x$ **52.** $-p^5 - p^4 + p^3 + p^2 - p - 1$ **53.** $3.06x^4 + 0.1x^3 + 4.6x^2 - 1.72$
54. $23x^9 + 15x^7 + 9x^5 + 5x^3 + 7x + 33$ **55.** $11 - 2b + 7b^2 - 6b^3$ **56.** $x^2 - 4x^3 + x^4 + 6x^5 - 8x^6$
57. $\dfrac{1}{14}x - \dfrac{5}{14}x^3 + \dfrac{1}{7}x^5$ **58.** $-1 - q + q^2 + q^3 - q^4 - q^5$ **59.** $-2.77 + 3.2x^3 + 9.76x^5 + 0.5x^7$
60. $4 - 2x + 4x^2 - 2x^3 - 4x^4 + x^5$ **61. (a)** 33   **(b)** 21   **(c)** 1   **62. (a)** 35   **(b)** -1 **(c)** 1
63. (a) 37   **(b)** 37   **(c)** 0   **64. (a)** 15   **(b)** -15 **(c)** 27   **65. (a)** -2.4 **(b)** 9.0375
(c) -20.4625 **66. (a)** 4   **(b)** 21.204   **(c)** -11.3 **67. (a)** 0   **(b)** $-\dfrac{77}{24}$ **(c)** 0   **68. (a)** -2

(b) 0   **(c)** $34\dfrac{2}{3}$ **69.** The perimeter measures $4x + 1$ units.; The perimeter measures 33 inches.

70. The surface area measures $4\pi x^2$ square units.; The surface area measures 64π in². **71.** The surface area measures $2x^2 + 12x$ square units.; The surface area measures 22.5 m². **72.** The surface area measures $30h + 100$ square units.; The surface area measures 205 in². **73.** The total area is $x^2 + 12x + 21$ m².

74. The total area is $x^2 + \dfrac{1}{2}xy + y^2$ square units. **75.** The area not covered by the patio is $lw - 300$ ft².;

The area not covered by the patio is 8700 ft². **76.** The area not covered by the pool is $lw - \pi r^2$ square units.; The area not covered by the pool is approximately 811.4 m². **77.** The square of the length of the hypotenuse is $x^2 + y^2$ square feet.; The square of the length of the hypotenuse is 65 ft², so the hypotenuse is equal to $\sqrt{65}$ feet. **78.** The square of the length of the leg is $x^2 - y^2$.; The square of the length of the leg is 64 ft², so the length of the leg is 8 feet. **79.** The replacement cost is $12x^2$ dollars.; The replacement cost is $1728.
80. The replacement cost is $12\pi r^2$ dollars.; The replacement cost is about $5428.67.
81. (a) Revenue $= 200 + 12x^2$ **(b)** Cost $= 75 + 2.75x^2$ **(c)** The revenue is $2900.; The cost is $693.75.; The net return is $2206.25. **82. (a)** Revenue $= 350 + 15lw$ **(b)** Cost $= 100 + 5.25lw$ **(c)** The revenue is $4440.; The cost is $1517.50.

Experiencing Algebra the Calculator Way

1. $\{-192, -32, -8, 24\}$ **2.** $\{-432, -108, -24\}$
3. $\{0.229, 0.06725, -32.625, -0.016\}$ or $\left\{\dfrac{229}{1000}, \dfrac{269}{4000}, -\dfrac{261}{8}, -\dfrac{2}{125}\right\}$

PROBLEM SET 9.2

Experiencing Algebra the Exercise Way

1.

x	y
-2	4
-1	0
0	-6
1	-8
2	0

2.

x	y
-2	0
-1	8
0	6
1	0
2	-4

3.

x	y
-2	-3
-1	-2
0	1
1	6
2	13

4.

x	y
-2	13
-1	6
0	1
1	-2
2	-3

5. all real numbers   **6.** all real numbers   **7.** all real numbers less than or equal to 5
8. all real numbers less than or equal to 9   **9.** all real numbers greater than or equal to -5
10. all real numbers greater than or equal to -7 **11.** all real numbers   **12.** all real numbers
13. all real numbers less than 21   **14.** all real numbers greater than or equal to -3.1
15. $f(-2) = 38$ **16.** $f(-1) = 16$ **17.** $f(2) = -14$ **18.** $f(3) = -52$ **19.** $g(-1.7) = -30.2501$
20. $g(-1.9) = -37.2843$ **21.** $g(2564.5) \approx 4.5528 \times 10^{10}$ **22.** $g(3079.8) \approx 7.8859 \times 10^{10}$

23. $g(1.5) = 4.2875$ **24.** $g(1.8) = 10.4864$ **25.** $g(1.1995) \approx -0.0001799$ **26.** $g(0) = -6.7$

27. $h\left(-\dfrac{3}{2}\right) = -\dfrac{73}{16}$ **28.** $h\left(-\dfrac{1}{2}\right) = -\dfrac{17}{16}$ **29.** $h\left(\dfrac{5}{2}\right) = \dfrac{55}{16}$ **30.** $h\left(\dfrac{7}{2}\right) = \dfrac{207}{16}$

31. (a) When 5, 10, 15, 20, 25, and 30 watches are ordered, the revenue is \$625, \$1000, \$1125, \$1000, \$625, and \$0, respectively.   **(b)** The range is all real numbers less than or equal to 1125.   **(c)** This range shows us that the maximum revenue would be \$1125.   **32. (a)** When the space is rented for 10, 20, 30, 40, 50, and 60 months, the cost is \$2500, \$4000, \$4500, \$4000, \$2500, and \$0, respectively.   **(b)** The range is all real numbers less than or equal to 4500.   **(c)** This range shows us that the maximum cost would be \$4500, and there is a value of x for which the cost is \$0.

33.

Age (x)	63	65	70	75	80	85
Days $(S(x))$	4.131	5.135	7.26	8.835	9.86	10.335

(a) The function predicted a stay of 10 days for an 85-year-old woman, which is not a very good prediction of the actual data of an 8-day stay for an 85-year-old woman.   **(b)** The function predicted a stay of 7 days for a 70-year-old woman, which is a fairly good prediction of the actual data of a 6-day stay, but not as good for a 9-day stay.   **(c)** Answers will vary.

34.

Age (x)	35	40	45	50	55	60	65	70
Premium $(P(x))$	224.05	675.20	802.35	928	1374.65	2464.80	4520.95	7865.60

(a) The prediction is not very good.   **(b)** The prediction is relatively close.   **(c)** Answers will vary.
35. The domain is all real numbers between 0 and 8.; The rocket is in the air for 8 seconds before it explodes. It explodes before it reaches the maximum value or the function.; The range is all real numbers less than or equal to 1136.; The maximum height will be 1136 feet.   **36.** The domain is all real numbers between 0 and 10.; The rocket is in the air for 10 seconds before it explodes.; The range is all real numbers less than or equal to 1426.25.; The maximum height will be at 1426.25 feet.

Experiencing Algebra the Calculator Way

1. The domain is all real numbers greater than or equal to zero.
2. The range is all real numbers between 0 and approximately 456,518.
3. Her estimated sales are \$403,592.64, which is very close to the actual sales of \$402,000.
4.

x	Actual Sales	Predicted Sales, $S(x)$	Difference (\$)
0.8	\$102,000	\$105,747.36	−3747.36
1.1	\$195,000	\$182,222.04	12,777.96
1.4	\$265,000	\$249,305.04	15,694.96
1.5	\$237,000	\$269,579	−32,597
2.2	\$345,000	\$382,278.16	−37,278.16
3.0	\$533,000	\$448,466	84,534
3.6	\$473,000	\$454,279.04	18,720.96
4.4	\$402,000	\$403,592.64	−1592.64
4.5	\$298,000	\$392,561	−94,561
5.5	\$263,000	\$224,851	38,149

; Answers will vary.

PROBLEM SET 9.3

Experiencing Algebra the Exercise Way

1. nonquadratic   **2.** quadratic   **3.** nonquadratic   **4.** quadratic   **5.** quadratic   **6.** quadratic
7. quadratic   **8.** nonquadratic   **9.** quadratic   **10.** quadratic   **11.** quadratic   **12.** nonquadratic
13. nonquadratic   **14.** quadratic   **15.** quadratic   **16.** nonquadratic

17–26.

	a	b	c	graph wide/narrow	graph concave upward/downward	graph vertex	axis of symmetry
17.	-5	10	1	narrow	downward	$(1, 6)$	$x = 1$
18.	6	-6	-5	narrow	upward	$(0.5, -6.5)$	$x = 0.5$
19.	0.6	6	-2	wide	upward	$(-5, -17)$	$x = -5$
20.	-1	6	-2	neither	downward	$(3, 7)$	$x = 3$
21.	2	3	5	narrow	upward	$(-0.75, 3.875)$	$x = -0.75$
22.	-3	6	-5	narrow	downward	$(1, -2)$	$x = 1$
23.	$-\frac{1}{4}$	1	-3	wide	downward	$(2, -2)$	$x = 2$
24.	$\frac{1}{3}$	2	-1	wide	upward	$(-3, -4)$	$x = -3$
25.	1	8	1	neither	upward	$(-4, -15)$	$x = -4$
26.	-0.4	2.4	-1.1	wide	downward	$(3, 2.5)$	$x = 3$

27.

$f(x) = 2x^2 + 5x - 7$

28.

$y = 2x^2 + 6x - 5$

29.

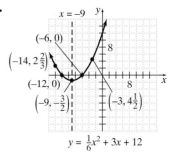

$y = \frac{1}{6}x^2 + 3x + 12$

30.

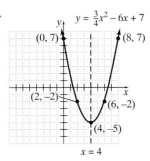

$y = \frac{3}{4}x^2 - 6x + 7$

31.

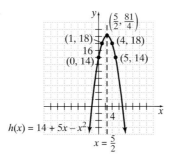

$h(x) = 14 + 5x - x^2$

32.

$f(x) = 11 - 4x + x^2$

33.

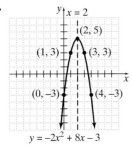

$y = -2x^2 + 8x - 3$

34.

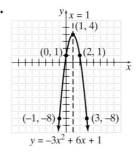

$y = -3x^2 + 6x + 1$

35.

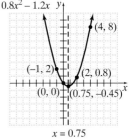

$g(x) = 0.8x^2 - 1.2x$

36.

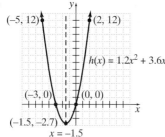

$(-5, 12)$ $(2, 12)$

$h(x) = 1.2x^2 + 3.6x$

$(-3, 0)$ $(0, 0)$

$(-1.5, -2.7)$

$x = -1.5$

37.

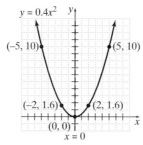

$y = 0.4x^2$

$(-5, 10)$ $(5, 10)$

$(-2, 1.6)$ $(2, 1.6)$

$(0, 0)$

$x = 0$

38.

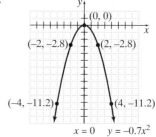

$(0, 0)$

$(-2, -2.8)$ $(2, -2.8)$

$(-4, -11.2)$ $(4, -11.2)$

$x = 0$ $y = -0.7x^2$

39.

$(-2, 9)$ $(2, 9)$

$y = 3x^2 - 3$

$(-1, 0)$ $(1, 0)$

$(0, -3)$

$x = 0$

40.

$(0, 3)$

$(-1, -3)$ $(1, -3)$

$y = -6x^2 + 3$

$(-2, -21)$ $(2, -21)$

$x = 0$

41.

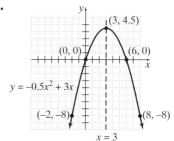

$(3, 4.5)$

$(0, 0)$ $(6, 0)$

$y = -0.5x^2 + 3x$

$(-2, -8)$ $(8, -8)$

$x = 3$

42.

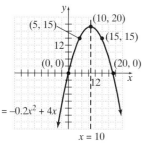

$(10, 20)$

$(5, 15)$ $(15, 15)$

12

$(0, 0)$ $(20, 0)$

12

$y = -0.2x^2 + 4x$

$x = 10$

43. $Y1 = -16x^2 + 12x + 24$

30

0 Maximum X=.37500192 Y=26.25 5
0

The vertex is approximately $(0.375, 26.25)$.; The maximum height is 26.25 feet.; The apple will hit the ground after approximately 1.7 seconds.

44. $Y1 = -16x^2 + 80x$

110

0 Maximum X=2.5531985 Y=99.954719 10
0

The vertex is $(2.5, 100)$.; The football will reach a maximum height of 100 feet after 2.5 seconds.; The football will hit the ground after 5 seconds.

45. $Y1 = 140x - x^2$

5000

0 Maximum X=70.212766 Y=4899.9547 150
0

The vertex is $(70, 4900)$.; The room has a maximum area of 4900 ft² when the width is 70 feet.

46. $Y1 = 120x - 2x^2$

2000

0 Maximum X=29.999996 Y=1800 100
0

The vertex is $(30, 1800)$; The pen has a maximum area of 1800 ft² when the length of two sides are each 30 feet.

47. $Y1 = 5x^2 - 80x + 400$

500

0 Minimum X=8.0000018 Y=80 25
0

The vertex is $(8, 80)$.; At a height of 8 inches the square of the hypotenuse will be minimized at 80 in².

48. $Y1 = x^2 + 10x$

35

-20 20

Minimum X=-4.999999 Y=-25
-35

The vertex is $(-5, -25)$.; No, the vertex does not have any physical meaning.

49. $Y1 = 46x - x^2$

The vertex is $(23, 529)$.; At $x = \$23$ the revenue will beat a maximum of $529.

50. $Y1 = 200 + 25x - 0.5x^2$

The vertex is $(25, 512.5)$.; At 25 bicycles, cost will be at a maximum of $512.50. The cost for producing more than 25 bicycles goes down as the number of bicycles increases.

Experiencing Algebra the Calculator Way

1.

2.

3.

4.

5.

6.

Answers may vary.

PROBLEM SET 9.4

Experiencing Algebra the Exercise Way

1. $y = x^2 + 2x - 8$

$y = x^2 + 2x - 8$

2. $y = -x^2 + 2x + 3$

$y = -x^2 + 2x + 3$

3. $y = 2x^2 + 7x - 4$

$y = 2x^2 + 7x - 4$

4. $y = 3x^2 + x - 2$

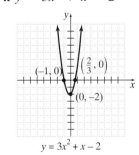

$y = 3x^2 + x - 2$

5. $y = -\dfrac{1}{3}x^2 + 3$

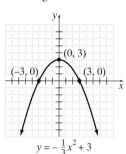

$y = -\dfrac{1}{3}x^2 + 3$

6. $y = -\dfrac{1}{16}x^2 + 1$

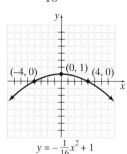

$y = -\dfrac{1}{16}x^2 + 1$

7. $y = \dfrac{1}{2}x^2 + x - 4$

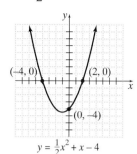

$y = \dfrac{1}{2}x^2 + x - 4$

8. $y = \dfrac{1}{3}x^2 - \dfrac{1}{3}x - 2$

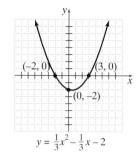

$y = \dfrac{1}{3}x^2 - \dfrac{1}{3}x - 2$

9. $y = -\dfrac{1}{6}x^2 + \dfrac{2}{3}$

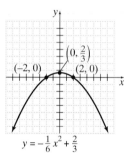

$y = -\dfrac{1}{6}x^2 + \dfrac{2}{3}$

10. $y = -\dfrac{1}{8}x^2 - \dfrac{1}{8}x + \dfrac{1}{4}$

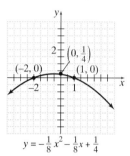

$y = -\dfrac{1}{8}x^2 - \dfrac{1}{8}x + \dfrac{1}{4}$

11. $y = -\dfrac{8}{9}x^2 + \dfrac{40}{9}x - 2$

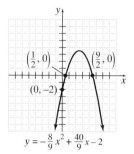

$y = -\dfrac{8}{9}x^2 + \dfrac{40}{9}x - 2$

12. $y = -\dfrac{9}{2}x^2 - \dfrac{3}{2}x + 1$

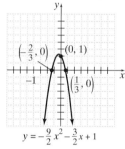

$y = -\dfrac{9}{2}x^2 - \dfrac{3}{2}x + 1$

13. $y = x^2 - 2x - 15$

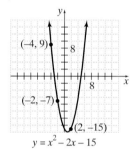

$y = x^2 - 2x - 15$

14. $y = x^2 + 3x - 18$

$y = x^2 + 3x - 18$

15. $y = 2x^2 - 3x - 9$

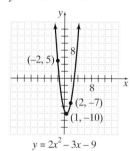

$y = 2x^2 - 3x - 9$

16. $y = 3x^2 - 11x - 4$

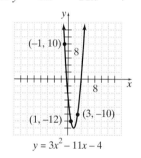

$y = 3x^2 - 11x - 4$

17. $= \dfrac{1}{3}x^2 - 2x + 5$

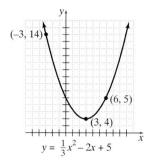

$y = \dfrac{1}{3}x^2 - 2x + 5$

18. $y = \dfrac{3}{4}x^2 + x - 4$

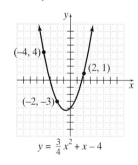

$y = \dfrac{3}{4}x^2 + x - 4$

19. $y = -x^2 + 4x + 3$

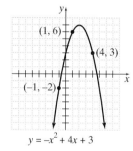

$y = -x^2 + 4x + 3$

20. $y = -x^2 - 2x + 5$

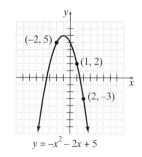

$y = -x^2 - 2x + 5$

21. $y = -2x^2 - 4x - 5$ **22.** $y = -\frac{1}{2}x^2 + 3x - 7$ **23.** $y = \frac{1}{2}x^2 + 4x + 10$ **24.** $y = \frac{1}{3}x^2 - 4x + 16$

$y = -2x^2 - 4x - 5$

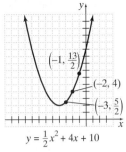

$y = -\frac{1}{2}x^2 + 3x - 7$

$y = \frac{1}{2}x^2 + 4x + 10$

$y = \frac{1}{3}x^2 - 4x + 16$

25. $s(t) = -16t^2 + 12t + 150$
The ball will hit the ground in approximately 3.46 seconds.

26. $s(t) = -16t^2 + 18t + 220$
The pie will hit the ground in approximately 4.31 seconds.

27. $s(t) = -16t^2 + 400$
The dummy will hit the ground in 5 seconds.

28. $s(t) = -16t^2 + 600$
The toy will hit the ground in approximately 6.12 seconds.

29. $s(t) = -2.7t^2 + 2000$
The package will touch the surface at approximately 27.22 seconds.

30. $s(t) = -2.7t^2 + 25t + 3000$
The probe will reach the surface in approximately 38.28 seconds.

31. $f(x) = 0.07795x^2 - 0.92376x + 23.06$; In the year 2000, the production is predicted to be 35.766 trillion cubic feet. Answers will vary. **32.** $f(x) = 0.01288x^2 + 1.6696x + 53.11$; In the year 1997, the production is predicted to be 85.22 trillion cubic feet. Answers will vary. **33.** $f(x) = 5.03x^2 + 211.1x + 738$; In 1995, the prediction is 11,598 franchises. This is fairly close to 10,953. Answers will vary.
34. $f(x) = 0.001\bar{6}x^2 + 0.09\bar{6}x + 2.7$; The prediction for 1990 is about 9.23 million. This is fairly close to 9.9 million. Answers will vary.

35. (a) $f(x) = -x^2 + 20x$ **(b)** $Y1 = -x^2 + 20x$

(c) The vertex is at (10, 100). The maximum area that can be covered is 100 square yards when the width is 10 yards.

36. (a) $f(x) = x^2 + 4x$ **(b)** $Y1 = x^2 + 4x$

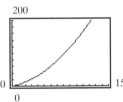

(c) domain: all real numbers > 0; The height of the sailcloth can be any real number greater than 0.

Experiencing Algebra the Calculator Way

1. $y = 0.54x^2 + 0.7x - 1.2$ **2.** $y = 50x^2 + 609x + 108$ **3.** $y = 60x^2 + 61x - 65$

CHAPTER 9 REVIEW

Reflections

1–8. Answers will vary.

Exercises

1. Yes; monomial **2.** Yes; binomial **3.** No **4.** Yes; polynomial **5.** No **6.** Yes; trinomial
7. The degrees of the terms are 1, 3, 0.; The degree of the polynomial is 3. **8.** The degrees of the terms are

3, 2, 0.; The degree of the polynomial is 3.   **9.** The degrees of the terms are 1, 0.; The degree of the polynomial is 1.   **10.** The degree of the term is 1.; The degree of the polynomial is 1.   **11.** The degree of the terms are 2, 1, 0.; The degree of the polynomial is 2.   **12.** $11y^4 + 9y^3 + 5y^2 - 6y + 12$ **13.** $-p + 5$

14. $\frac{1}{4}z^4 + \frac{1}{3}z^3 + \frac{1}{2}z^2 + z + 1$ **15.** $-2.3b^5 - 9.1b^3 + 0.6b + 1.8$ **16.** 0   **17.** -90 **18.** -98

19. 0   **20.** 0   **21.** -1 **22.** -1 **23.** 0   **24.** -1 **25.** 3   **26.** 1   **27.** The perimeter is $2w + 2w^2$ units.; The perimeter is 112 yards.   **28.** The perimeter is $x^2 + 4x + 1$ units.; The perimeter is 33 inches.

29. The total area is $a^2 + 20a$ in^2.   **30.** The shaded area is $-\frac{1}{2}x^2 + 10x$ in^2.

31. The area of the lawn not covered by the garden is $z^2 - \frac{1}{2}xy$ square feet.; The area is 6370 ft^2.

32. (a) The charge for a room is $500 + 40lw$ dollars.   (b) The cost to build a room is $275 + 12lw$ dollars.
(c) The revenue is $15,500.; The cost is $4775.; The net return is $10,725.

33.

x	y
-3	-18
-2	0
-1	4
0	0
1	-6
2	-8
3	0

34. The range is all real numbers.
35. The range is all real numbers greater than or equal to -12.5.
36. The range is all real numbers.
37. The range is all real numbers greater than or equal to -9.
38. $f(-2) = -36$ **39.** $f(0) = -4$ **40.** $f(2) = 20$
41. $f\left(-\frac{1}{2}\right) = -\frac{45}{8}$ **42.** $f(1.7) = 11.249$

43. (a) The revenue for 5, 10, 15, 20, and 25 shirts is $47.50, $70, $67.50, $40, and $-$12.50, respectively. Answers will vary.   (b) The cost for 5, 10, 15, and 20 shirts is $20, $40, $60, and $80, respectively.
(c) The profit from 5, 10, 15, and 20 shirts is $27.50, $30, $7.50, and $-$40, respectively.
(d) Answers will vary.

44.

Gallons (x)	900	1000	1100	1200	1300	1400
Cost (y)	16,970	17,000	17,010	17,000	16,970	16,920

; Answers will vary.

45. quadratic   **46.** nonquadratic   **47.** nonquadratic   **48.** quadratic

49–52.

	a	b	c	graph wide/narrow	graph concave upward/ downward	graph vertex	axis of symmetry
49.	$-\frac{1}{4}$	$\frac{1}{2}$	1	wide	downward	$(1, \frac{5}{4})$	$x = 1$
50.	-2	4	0	narrow	downward	$(1, 2)$	$x = 1$
51.	$\frac{1}{3}$	1	0	wide	upward	$(-\frac{3}{2}, -\frac{3}{4})$	$x = -\frac{3}{2}$
52.	3	-3	1	narrow	upward	$(\frac{1}{2}, \frac{1}{4})$	$x = \frac{1}{2}$

53.

54.

55.

56.

$(-4, -16)$; No, the vertex has no physical meaning.

57.

The vertex is (30, 450).; The revenue is at a maximum of $450 when 30 photos are ordered.

58. The vertex is $(1.875, 176.25)$.; The egg reaches a maximum height of 176.25 feet at 1.875 seconds.; The egg will reach the ground in approximately 5.19 seconds. **59.** $y = x^2 - 5x - 24$
60. $y = -2x^2 + 9x + 5$ **61.** $y = x^2 - 7x + 6$
62. $s(t) = -16t^2 + 32t + 160$; The hammer will reach the ground at approximately 4.3 seconds.

63. $f(x) = 0.00325x^2 + 0.015x + 3.525$; In 1980, 1970, and 1960, the predictions are 25.525 million, 20.5 million, and 16.125 million, respectively.; Answers will vary.; In the year 2000, the prediction is 37.525 million.

CHAPTER 9 MIXED REVIEW

1. 0 **2.** −30 **3.** −60 **4.** 0 **5.** 0 **6.** −2 **7.** 5 **8.** 5 **9.** −5
10. (a) binomial; Degree of each term is 0, 2.; Degree of polynomial is 2.; $3x^2 + 5$
(b) polynomial; Degree of each term is 2, 3, 0, 1.; Degree of polynomial is 3.; $-5a^3 + 15a^2 + a + 4$
(c) polynomial; Degree of each term is 4, 1, 0, 5, 2.; Degree of polynomial is 5.; $x^5 + 5x^4 - 3x^2 + x - 2$
11. (a) trinomial; Degree of each term is 2, 1, 0.; Degree of polynomial is 2.
(b) polynomial; Degree of each term is 3, 2, 3, 0, 4.; Degree of polynomial is 4.
(c) monomial; Degree of term is 3.; Degree of polynomial is 3.
12. 0 **13.** 12 **14.** 0 **15.** 0 **16.** −31.824
17.

x	y
−3	0
−2	16
−1	12
0	0
1	−8
2	0
3	36

18. The range is all real numbers.
19. The range is all real numbers greater than or equal to −6.75.
20. The range is all real numbers.
21. The range is all real numbers greater than or equal to −87.04.

22. $x = -\dfrac{7}{4}$

23. $x = 2$

24. $x = 0$

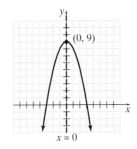

25–28.

	a	b	c	graph wide/narrow	graph concave upward/downward	graph vertex	axis of symmetry
25.	$\frac{1}{3}$	$\frac{2}{3}$	1	wide	upward	$(-1, \frac{2}{3})$	$x = -1$
26.	-3	6	0	narrow	downward	$(1, 3)$	$x = 1$
27.	$-\frac{1}{4}$	1	3	wide	downward	$(2, 4)$	$x = 2$
28.	2	4	-6	narrow	upward	$(-1, -8)$	$x = -1$

29. $y = x^2 + 8x + 24$ **30.** $y = x^2 - 5x - 36$ **31.** $y = 3x^2 - 5x - 12$ **32.** The polynomial for the perimeter is $2w^3 + 2w + 10$ units.; The perimeter is 70 feet.   **33.** The perimeter is $x^2 + 3x - 10$ units.; The perimeter is 120 cm.   **34.** The polynomial for the total area is $x^2 + 11x$ square units.

35. The polynomial for the shaded area is $\dfrac{24 + \pi}{8}x^2$ square units.

36. The polynomial is $xy - \pi z^2$ square feet.; The area measures approximately 3798.9 ft^2.
37. (a) The cost is $1.5lw$ dollars.   **(b)** The net return is $800 - 1.5lw$ dollars.   **(c)** The net return will be \$575.
38. (a)

x	$P(x)$
0	0
1	12
2	28
3	48
4	72
5	100
6	132
7	168

(b) Answers will vary.

39. (a) The predicted GPA is 3.19875.
(b)

GMAT score, z	500	550	600	650	700	750
GPA in MBA, y	3.575	3.55975	3.504	3.40775	3.271	3.09375

(c) As the entrance exam score goes up, the student's predicted performance goes down.

40. $Y1 = -0.8x^2 + 1500$
$Y2 = 0$

The object will reach the ground in approximately 43.3 seconds.

41. $f(x) = 0.0006x^2 - 0.016x + 1.68$; In 1930 and 1990, the predicted divorce rate per 1000 population is 1.74 and 5.1, respectively.; Answers will vary.; In the year 2000 the prediction is 6.08 per 1000 population.

CHAPTER 9 TEST

1. monomial   **2.** polynomial   **3.** binomial   **4.** 5   **5.** 5   **6.** $x^5 + 3x^4 + 9x^2 + 14x + 15$
7. $-\dfrac{4}{9} + a - \dfrac{5}{6}a^2 - \dfrac{2}{3}a^3$ **8.** -72 **9.** -2 **10.** -224
11. The total cost will be $16.5lw + 75$ dollars; The total cost will be \$680.   **12.** 0   **13.** -6

14. 4   **15.**

16. The vertex is $(2, -8)$.

17. The range is all real numbers greater than or equal to -8.

18. Yes; The graph of the relation passes the vertical line test.

19–20.

	a	b	c	graph wide/narrow	graph concave upward/downward	graph vertex	axis of symmetry
19.	$\frac{1}{2}$	2	3	wide	upward	$(-2, 1)$	$x = -2$
20.	3	-3	$\frac{1}{4}$	narrow	upward	$(\frac{1}{2}, -\frac{1}{2})$	$x = \frac{1}{2}$

21. $y = x^2 - 6x + 8$ **22.** $y = 2x^2 - x + 3$ **23.** Answers will vary.

Chapter 10

PROBLEM SET 10.1

Experiencing Algebra the Exercise Way

1. $4 \cdot 4 \cdot 4 \cdot a \cdot a$ **2.** $-3 \cdot b \cdot b \cdot b$ **3.** $(-3x)(-3x)(-3x)(-3x)$ **4.** $(-4c)(-4c)(-4c)$

5. $a \cdot a \cdot a \cdot c \cdot c \cdot c \cdot c \cdot c$ **6.** $x \cdot x \cdot y$ **7.** $\left(\frac{3x}{4}\right)\left(\frac{3x}{4}\right)\left(\frac{3x}{4}\right)$ **8.** $\left(\frac{2}{3}\right)\left(\frac{2}{3}\right) \cdot x \cdot x \cdot x$

9. $5(x + y)(x + y)$ **10.** $-4(p - q)(p - q)$ **11.** $\frac{1}{p^3}$ **12.** $\frac{1}{q^2}$ **13.** q^5 **14.** $2p^3$ **15.** $\frac{q^5}{p^3}$

16. $\frac{2p^3}{q^2}$ **17.** $\frac{q^5}{p^3}$ **18.** $\frac{p^3}{q^2}$ **19.** $\frac{64n^3}{81m^2}$ **20.** $\frac{32y^4}{25x^3}$ **21.** $\frac{81n^3}{64m^2}$ **22.** $\frac{25y^4}{32x^3}$ **23.** $\frac{-4(m + n)^2}{5(m - n)}$

24. $\frac{5(a - b)^3}{7(a + b)^2}$ **25.** $\frac{5(m - n)}{4(m + n)^2}$ **26.** $\frac{-35(a + b)^2}{(a - b)^3}$ **27.** $\frac{1}{a^3} + \frac{2}{a^2} - \frac{3}{a} + 4$ **28.** $\frac{1}{x^3} + \frac{1}{x^2} - \frac{1}{x}$

29. x^{13} **30.** a^{23} **31.** y^8 **32.** b^{16} **33.** $\frac{1}{z^5}$ **34.** $\frac{1}{c^8}$ **35.** $\frac{1}{p^9}$ **36.** $\frac{1}{d^{11}}$ **37.** 1   **38.** 1

39. $(x + 3)^3$ **40.** $(x + 9)^{13}$ **41.** p^5 **42.** a^4 **43.** y **44.** x^4 **45.** $\frac{1}{b^2}$ **46.** $\frac{1}{t^3}$ **47.** $(2x - 3)^5$

48. $(4x + 7)^7$ **49.** $(p + q)^3$ **50.** $(xy + 2)^6$ **51.** $\frac{1}{(4 - x)^5}$ **52.** $\frac{1}{(15 - 3t)^8}$ **53.** $\frac{1}{(z - 5)^3}$

54. $\frac{1}{(r + s)^3}$ **55.** a^{30} **56.** m^{28} **57.** c^8 **58.** p^6 **59.** $(x + y)^6$ **60.** $(a + 2b)^{12}$ **61.** $\frac{1}{(a - b)^4}$

62. $\frac{1}{(c - 3d)^5}$ **63.** 1   **64.** 1   **65.** $625m^4$ **66.** $81k^4$ **67.** $\frac{b^4}{d^4}$ **68.** $\frac{m^5}{n^5}$ **69.** $p^{21}q^{21}$ **70.** $x^9y^9z^9$

71. $\frac{81b^4}{c^4}$ **72.** $\frac{125y^3}{z^3}$ **73.** $64c^6$ **74.** $16c^4$ **75.** $\frac{y^3}{64x^3}$ **76.** $\frac{b^5}{243a^5}$ **77.** $\frac{q^4}{81p^4}$ **78.** $\frac{d^2}{25c^2}$

79. $p^{15}q^{21}$ **80.** k^8m^{12} **81.** $1024a^{10}$ **82.** $81t^4$ **83.** $\frac{x^6}{64y^6}$ **84.** $\frac{729z^6}{w^6}$

85. The original area is x^2 square units; The enlarged area is $25x^2$ square units; The enlarged area is 25 times bigger.; If the original side is 6 feet, the original area and enlarged area are 36 ft^2 and 900 ft^2, respectively.

86. The original area is x^2 square units; The enlarged area is $6.76x^2$ square units; The enlarged area is 6.76 times bigger; If the original side is 12 feet, then the original area and enlarged area are 144 ft^2 and 973.44 ft^2, respectively.

87. The volume of the original bin is x^3 cubic units; The volume of the enlarged bin is $64x^3$ cubic units; The volume of the enlarged bin is 64 times greater.; If the original side measures 1.5 feet, then the volumes of the original bin and enlarged bin are 3.375 ft^3 and 216 ft^3, respectively.

88. The volume of the original block is x^3 cubic units; The volume of the smaller block is $0.512x^3$ cubic units; The volume of the smaller block is 0.512 times the volume of the larger block. If the original side is 22 inches, then the volume of the original block and smaller block are 10,648 in^3 and 5451.776 in^3, respectively.

Experiencing Algebra the Calculator Way

1. They are not equivalent.   **2.** They are equivalent.   **3.** They are equivalent.   **4.** They are not equivalent.
5. They are not equivalent.   **6.** They are equivalent.

PROBLEM SET 10.2

Experiencing Algebra the Exercise Way

1. $4x^4 + 9x^3 + 5x^2 - 42x + 28$ **2.** $5b^3 - 4$ **3.** $9x^4 + 3x^3 - 10x^2 - 3x + 9$ **4.** $z^3 + z^2 + 5z + 6$
5. $-3x^2y + 6y^3 + 15x^3$ **6.** $4a^3 + 6a^2b - ab^2 + 7b^3$ **7.** $a^3 + 8a^2 - 7a - 1$ **8.** $3x^2 + 12$
9. $\frac{2}{3}y^4 + \frac{5}{3}y^3 + \frac{19}{9}y^2 + \frac{1}{2}y - \frac{22}{9}$ **10.** $\frac{13}{12}x^3 - \frac{2}{3}x^2 - \frac{1}{4}x + \frac{19}{12}$ **11.** $18.77x^3 - 1.23x^2 + 3.81x + 9.735$
12. $0.7y^3 + 6.2y^2 - 4.4y + 0.3$ **13.** $5117a^3 + 50998a^2 - 1816a + 2095$ **14.** $50b^2 + 200$
15. $3a + 4b + 5c + 6d$ **16.** $5x + y + 11z$ **17.** $2z^3 + 27z^2 - 51z + 114$ **18.** $-3a^2 - 5a + 15$
19. $a^4 - a^3 + a^2 - a$ **20.** $b^7 + b^5 + b^3 + b$ **21.** $7x^2 - 3x - 39$ **22.** $-5y^3 + 8y - 11$
23. $-5a^3 - 6a^2 - 12a + 14$ **24.** $x^3 - 2x^2 + 3x + 9$ **25.** $42x^3 - 30x^2y + 3xy^2 + 11y^3$
26. $51p^3 + 26p^2q - 16pq^2 + 41q^3 + 10$ **27.** $4a - 2b + 7c - 6d$ **28.** $12x + 5y + 8z$
29. $\frac{3}{14}x^2 - \frac{19}{42}x - \frac{26}{21}$ **30.** $\frac{7}{24}x^3 + \frac{11}{24}x^2 - \frac{1}{4}x - \frac{1}{3}$ **31.** $9x^3 + 0.8x^2y - 14xy^2 + 68y^3$
32. $2.48x^2 - 12.51xy - 8.75y^2$ **33.** $4683z^2 - 4403z + 7187$ **34.** $-86b^3 + 178b^2 - 1344b + 1591$
35. $\frac{-42}{q^3}$ **36.** $39xy^3$ **37.** $\frac{6.02x^5}{y^2}$ **38.** $15.39y^3$ **39.** $\frac{2}{5}xy^3$ **40.** $\frac{4a}{15b^2}$ **41.** $12a^4 - 20a^3b + 4a^2b^2$
42. $20b^3c - 15b^2c^2 + 5bc^3$ **43.** $6x^2 - 9x + 3 - \frac{3}{x}$ **44.** $8a + 6 - \frac{10}{a}$ **45.** $-3a^3b - 2a^2b^2 - ab^3$
46. $-28y^3z + 12y^2z^2 - 4yz^3$ **47.** $3a^3 - 9a^4 + 15a^5$ **48.** $\frac{16}{3}z^2 + \frac{28}{3}z^3 - 8z^4$ **49.** $8x^2$ **50.** $\frac{y^2}{7}$
51. $\frac{13}{2y^5}$ **52.** $\frac{3}{11p^4}$ **53.** $\frac{122b^5}{11a^5}$ **54.** $\frac{b^3}{3a^5}$ **55.** $\frac{4x^5}{3}$ **56.** $\frac{27y^{14}}{4}$ **57.** $\frac{x^3}{27}$ **58.** $\frac{y^8}{256}$ **59.** $36x^2$
60. $\frac{1}{16y^2}$ **61.** $\frac{9b}{2a^7}$ **62.** $\frac{4}{y^{10}}$ **63.** $\frac{a^3}{8b^3}$ **64.** $\frac{y^6}{64x^6}$ **65.** $\frac{8b^3}{a^3}$ **66.** $\frac{64x^6}{y^6}$ **67.** $\frac{x^6}{4y^{14}}$ **68.** $\frac{27c^8}{a^{19}}$
69. $(2.358 \times 10^{11})a^6$ **70.** $(2.5 \times 10^{-11})t^3$ **71.** $(5 \times 10^{-13})x^3$ **72.** $(6.8 \times 10^{17})m^5$ **73.** $2x^2 + 4x - 6$
74. $3a^2 - 2 + \frac{6}{a^2}$ **75.** $\frac{1}{2}x - \frac{1}{4} + \frac{3}{2x}$ **76.** $5z^3 - 2z^2 + 9z + 3$ **77.** $3.1x^2 - 5.8 + \frac{0.9}{x^2}$
78. $-\frac{1.8}{m^2} + \frac{2.5}{m} - 3$ **79.** $-\frac{3x^3}{y} - 2x^2 + 6xy + 8y^2 - \frac{24y^3}{x}$ **80.** $\frac{2a}{b} - 5 - \frac{4b}{a} + \frac{b^2}{a^2}$
81. (a) $C(x) = 200 + 4.45x$ **(b)** $R(x) = 13.5x$ **(c)** $P(x) = 9.05x - 200$ **(d)** $A(x) = 9.05 - \frac{200}{x}$
(e) The average profit per pot if 20 and 30 are produced is $-\$0.95$ and $\$2.38$, respectively.
82. (a) $C(x) = 500 + 20x$ **(b)** $R(x) = 50x$

(c) $P(x) = 30x - 500$ **(d)** $A(x) = 30 - \dfrac{500}{x}$ **(e)** The average profit if 75 phones and 100 phones are sold is about \$33.33 and \$25, respectively.   **83.** $60 + 2x$ feet; The perimeter is 76 feet.
84. $80 + 3x$ inches; The perimeter is 95 inches.   **85.** $6x^2 - \pi x^2$ square units; The difference is approximately 182.9 in^2.   **86.** $24x - 2x^2$ square feet; The difference is 31.5 ft^2.   **87.** $16x - x^2$ square inches

88. $4x^2 - \dfrac{xy}{2}$ square units   **89.** $(\pi + 8)r^2 + 10r$ square feet   **90.** $\dfrac{3}{2}x^2 + 10x$ square feet

r (feet)	Area (feet)^2
8	793.06
9	992.47
10	1214.16
11	1458.13
12	1724.39

x (feet)	Area (feet)^2
8	176
9	211.5
10	250
11	291.5
12	336

91. (a) $2x^2$ square feet   **(b)** $4x^2 + 10x$ square feet   **(c)** $2 + \dfrac{5}{x}$ **(d)** The current area is 200 ft^2; The planned area is 500 ft^2; The ratio is $\dfrac{5}{2}$.   **92. (a)** x^2 square feet   **(b)** $2x^2 + 10x$ square feet

(c) $2 + \dfrac{10}{x}$ **(d)** The original area was 64 ft^2; The new area is 208 ft^2; The ratio is $\dfrac{13}{4}$.

93. $\dfrac{55}{\pi r^2}$ pounds per square inch

r (inch)	Pounds per square inch
0.25	280.1
0.50	70.0
0.75	31.1
1.00	17.5

For a radius of 1 inch, the woman's pressure on the floor approximates the elephant's.

94. $\dfrac{175}{2\pi r^2}$ pounds per square inch

r (inches)	Pounds per square inch
1.0	27.9
1.05	25.3
1.10	23.0
1.15	21.1
1.20	19.3
1.25	17.8
1.30	16.5
1.35	15.3
1.40	14.2
1.45	13.2
1.50	12.4

For a radius of 1.25 inches, the pressure is approximately the same as the elephant's.

95. $\dfrac{40{,}000}{w^2}$ cost per square foot

w (feet)	Cost per square foot
20	100
25	64
30	44.44
35	32.65
40	25
45	19.75
50	16

A home with a size of 35 ft by 70 ft would cost approximately $33 per square foot.

96. $\dfrac{500{,}000}{1.5w^2}$ cost per square foot

w (feet)	Cost per square foot
100	33.33
150	14.81
200	8.33
250	5.33

A building with a size of 150 ft by 225 ft would cost approximately $15 per square foot.

Experiencing Algebra the Calculator Way

1. No   **2.** Yes   **3.** Yes   **4.** No   **5.** No   **6.** Yes   **7.** No   **8.** No   **9.** Yes

---

PROBLEM SET 10.3

Experiencing Algebra the Exercise Way

1. $x^2 + 11x + 24$ **2.** $a^2 - 16a + 55$ **3.** $6x^2 - 5x - 4$ **4.** $20x^2 + 7x - 3$ **5.** $-x^2 + 2x + 8$
6. $a^2 - a - 42$ **7.** $2x^2 + 13x + 15$ **8.** $7z^2 + 29z + 4$ **9.** $6xy - 4x + 15y - 10$
10. $15ab + 20a - 6b - 8$ **11.** $3x^2 - 2xy - 8y^2$ **12.** $2a^2 - 5ab - 12b^2$ **13.** $5a^2 - 8.2a - 9.12$
14. $4p^2 - 3.9p - 4.93$ **15.** $6xy + 6.4x + 3.3y + 3.52$ **16.** $20mn + 13.5m - 19.6n - 13.23$

17. $a^2 + a + \dfrac{2}{9}$ **18.** $x^2 + \dfrac{2}{5}x - \dfrac{3}{25}$ **19.** $16x^2 + \dfrac{5}{3}x - \dfrac{1}{24}$ **20.** $\dfrac{2}{5}x^2 - \dfrac{17}{3}x + 20$ **21.** $2x^4 + 5x^2 - 12$
22. $5x^6 - 14x^3 - 3$ **23.** $8x^3 + 4x^2 + 6x + 3$ **24.** $24x^5 - 18x^3 - 20x^2 + 15$
25. $6x^3 - 10xy + 9x^2y^2 - 15y^3$ **26.** $24a^3 - 20a^2b^2 + 18ab - 15b^3$ **27.** $3a^4 + 8a^2b^3 + 5b^6$
28. $28x^8 - 15x^4y^3 + 2y^6$ **29.** $x^3 + 1$ **30.** $x^3 - 1$ **31.** $6x^3 - 19x^2 + x + 6$
32. $4x^3 - 17x^2 - 23x - 6$ **33.** $x^4 + 3x^3 + 6x^2 + 5x + 3$ **34.** $a^4 - a^3 - 3a^2 + 5a - 2$
35. $a^2 + b^2 + c^2 + 2ab + 2bc + 2ac$ **36.** $a^2 + b^2 + c^2 - 2ab - 2ac + 2bc$ **37.** $z^3 + 9z^2 + 27z + 27$
38. $r^3 + 6r^2 + 12r + 8$ **39.** $27a^3 - 54a^2b + 36ab^2 - 8b^3$ **40.** $8x^3 - 36x^2y + 54xy^2 - 27y^3$
41. $x^2 - 25$ **42.** $y^2 - 144$ **43.** $9m^2 - 49$ **44.** $25p^2 - 16$ **45.** $4a^2 - 9b^2$ **46.** $81p^2 - 4q^2$
47. $16x^2 - 2.25$ **48.** $9z^2 - 6.25$ **49.** $\dfrac{4}{25}x^2 - 1$ **50.** $\dfrac{16}{49}y^2 - 4$ **51.** $\dfrac{1}{9}x^2 - \dfrac{16}{25}$ **52.** $\dfrac{25}{49}y^2 - \dfrac{9}{16}$
53. $x^4 - 49$ **54.** $y^6 - 81$ **55.** $4x^6 - 25y^2$ **56.** $25a^{10} - 4b^4$ **57.** $m^2 + 14m + 49$
58. $p^2 + 12p + 36$ **59.** $x^2 - 2xy + y^2$ **60.** $u^2 - 2uv + v^2$ **61.** $4p^2 + 36pq + 81q^2$
62. $25m^2 - 110mn + 121n^2$ **63.** $36c^2 - 60c + 25$ **64.** $64d^2 + 48d + 9$ **65.** $9x^6 + 12x^3 + 4$
66. $4z^4 - 20z^2 + 25$ **67.** $4x^4 - 12x^2y^3 + 9y^6$ **68.** $25x^6 + 30x^3y^2 + 9y^4$

69. (a) length: $(18 - 2x)$ in.; width: $(12 - 2x)$ in.; height: (x) in.
(b) The volume is $(4x^3 - 60x^2 + 216x)$ in³.   **(c)** The surface area is $(-4x^2 + 216)$ in².
(d) The volume is 224 in³ and the surface area is 200 in².

70. (a) length: $(10 - 2y)$ in.; width: $(10 - 2y)$ in.; height: y in.   **(b)** The volume is $(4y^3 - 40y^2 + 100y)$ in³.
(c) The surface area is $(-4y^2 + 100)$ in².   **(d)** The volume is 73.5 in³ and the surface area is 91 in².
71. (a) (πx^2) ft²   **(b)** $[\pi(x - 5)^2]$ ft²   **(c)** The area of the deck is $(10\pi x - 25\pi)$ ft².
(d) The area is (195π) ft².

72. (a) (36π) ft^2 **(b)** $\left[\pi(6-x)^2\right]$ ft^2 **(c)** The area of the deck is $(12\pi x - \pi x^2)$ ft^2.
(d) The area is (27π) ft^2.

73. (a) The old volume is x^3 ft^3. **(b)** The new volume is $(x^3 + 13x^2 + 40x)$ ft^3.

(c) The ration is $\dfrac{x^2 + 13x + 40}{x^2}$. **(d)** The ratio is $\dfrac{85}{36}$.

74. (a) The old volume is x^3 ft^3. **(b)** The new volume is $(2x^3 + 32x^2 + 128x)$ ft^3.

(c) The ratio is $\dfrac{2x^2 + 32x + 128}{x^2}$. **(d)** The ratio is $\dfrac{2450}{361}$.

Experiencing Algebra the Calculator Way

1. not equivalent; $4x^2 - 1$ **2.** not equivalent; $x^2 - 1$ **3.** equivalent **4.** equivalent

5. not equivalent; $x^2 - \dfrac{35}{6}x - 1$ **6.** equivalent **7.** equivalent

8. not equivalent; $0.3x^3 - 1.4x^2 - 0.3x + 1.4$

PROBLEM SET 10.4

Experiencing Algebra the Exercise Way

1. $10a^2bc^2$ **2.** $45x^2yz$ **3.** $36x^2$ **4.** $63u^3v^2$ **5.** 45 **6.** 8 **7.** $7xyz$ **8.** $-10a^2bc$ **9.** $30ab^2c$
10. $30xy^2z$ **11.** $4(x+3y)$ **12.** $-7(x-3y)$ **13.** $4(2x^3 - x^2 + 3x - 6)$
14. $3(3d^5 - 4d^3 + 7d + 8)$ **15.** $a^2(3a^2 - 5a + 7)$ **16.** $-p^3(4p^2 + 9p + 11)$
17. $-3x^3(x^2 + 3x + 4)$ **18.** $5m(m^2 - 3m + 6)$ **19.** $x^2y^2(7x^2 - 3 + 9y^2)$
20. $-uv(3u^2 - 4uv + 8v^2)$ **21.** $4a^3(2a^2b^3c + ab^2 + 4c)$ **22.** $7xy^3(x^2y^2 - 3xy + 9)$
23. $22u^3v^3(3v + 4u)$ **24.** $-13c^2d^2(3d - 4c)$ **25.** does not factor **26.** does not factor
27. $(x+3)(5x-4)$ **28.** $(y+7)(3y-5)$ **29.** $(2x+y)(x+2y)$ **30.** $(a+3b)(3a+b)$
31. $(3x+5)(2x+7)$ **32.** $(5x+2)(3x+2)$ **33.** $(x+8)(x+1)$ **34.** $(y+4)(y+1)$
35. $(2a+3)(a-1)$ **36.** $(2z+7)(z-1)$ **37.** $(2x+y)(x+2y)$ **38.** $(p+3q)(3p+q)$
39. $(x+y)(x-y)$ **40.** $(m+n)(m-n)$ **41.** $(2x-11)(5y+12)$ **42.** $(4x+3)(7y-9)$
43. $(4a+b)(3c+d)$ **44.** $(2m+n)(5p+2q)$ **45.** $(2xy+3)(xy-4)$ **46.** $(7ab-2)(ab+3)$
47. $-1(x+3)(x+y)$ **48.** $-1(a+b)(a+7)$ **49.** $(x^2+y^2)(x^2+2y^2)$
50. $(p+q)(p-q)(3p^2+q^2)$ **51.** $(a+b)(c+d)$ **52.** $(x+y)(y+z)$ **53.** $4(2x+1)(x+3)$
54. $7(3y+2)(y+4)$ **55.** $u^2(u+v^2)(u-2)$ **56.** $a^2(a+b)(a+2b)$ **57.** $6a^2(a+b^2)(a+b)$
58. $5c^2(c+d^2)(c^2+d)$ **59.** $-2x(x+3)(2x+1)$ **60.** $-5y(y-5)(2y+3)$ **61.** $(2x+3z)^2$
62. $(3u+4v)^2$ **63.** $(6a-5b)^2$ **64.** $(4x+3y)^2$ **65.** $5m(m+n)^2$ **66.** $7p(p-q)^2$
67. $(2x^2+3)(x+4)$ **68.** $(5c^3+7)(c-3)$ **69.** $(5a^2+2b^2)(x+3y)$ **70.** $(2a^2+3b^2)(c+7d)$
71. (a) She will receive $(9x+36)$ dollars. **(b)** $9(x+4)$. **(c)** The bonomial $(x+4)$ is the average amount in dollars that she will receive for each of her 9 goals.. **(d)** She will receive $126.
72. (a) She smoked $(7c-42)$ cigarettes the first week. **(b)** $7(c-6)$ **(c)** The binomial $(c-6)$ represents the average number of cigarettes she smoked for each of 7 days. **(d)** She smoked 98 cigarettes; Yes; She smoked 8 cigarettes on the seventh. **73. (a)** $n(n-1)$ **(b)** Each equals 420 times.
(c) The factored expression was easier to evaluate; Answers will vary. **74. (a)** $n(n-2)(n-1)$
(b) Each equals 7980 times. **(c)** The factored expression was easier to evaluate; Answers will vary.
75. The rectangle's length is $(x+7)$ units and width is $(x-3)$ units.
76. The length of the square's side is $(2x+3)$ units.

Experiencing Algebra the Calculator Way

1. $30 = 2 \cdot 3 \cdot 5$ **2.** $108 = 2^2 \cdot 3^2$ **3.** $525 = 3 \cdot 5^2 \cdot 7$ **4.** $1287 = 3^2 \cdot 11 \cdot 13$ **5.** $1547 = 7 \cdot 13 \cdot 17$
6. $4500 = 2^2 \cdot 3^2 \cdot 5^3$

Experiencing Algebra the Exercise Way

1. $(x + 5)(x + 9)$ **2.** $(p + 6)(p + 8)$ **3.** $(y - 7)(y - 8)$ **4.** $(u - 2)(u + 13)$ **5.** $(p + 3)(p - 12)$
6. $(v + 1)(v - 13)$ **7.** does not factor **8.** does not factor **9.** $(x^2 + 9)(x^2 + 16)$
10. $(b^2 + 4)(b^2 + 25)$ **11.** $(x^2 + 1)(x^2 - 3)$ **12.** $(d^2 - 7)(d^2 + 25)$ **13.** $3(a + 5)(a + 11)$
14. $7(b - 4)(b - 6)$ **15.** $4(c - 2)(c + 13)$ **16.** $7(p + 4)(p - 5)$ **17.** $(x - 3y)(x - 8y)$
18. $(a - 8b)(a - 9b)$ **19.** $(x - y)(x + 12y)$ **20.** $(a + 6b)(a - 15b)$ **21.** $-3(a + 2b)(a + 3b)$
22. $-5(x - 3y)(x - 4y)$ **23.** $-2(x + 2y)(x - 9y)$ **24.** $-6(x + 3y)(x - 7y)$ **25.** $(3x + 1)(x + 3)$
26. does not factor **27.** $(x - 7)(2x - 1)$ **28.** $(x - 11)(3x - 1)$ **29.** $(x - 1)(3x + 2)$
30. $(x - 1)(5x + 3)$ **31.** $(m + 2)(5m - 1)$ **32.** $(p + 5)(7p - 1)$ **33.** does not factor
34. does not factor **35.** $(a + 6)(4a + 1)$ **36.** $(c + 4)(10c + 1)$ **37.** $(d - 1)(9d - 4)$
38. $(b - 1)(8b - 9)$ **39.** $(x - 4)(6x + 1)$ **40.** $(x - 8)(4x + 1)$ **41.** $(y + 2)(8y - 9)$
42. $(z + 4)(6z - 5)$ **43.** $(2b + 3)(3b + 4)$ **44.** $(5a + 6)(3a + 2)$ **45.** $(5x - 4)(4x - 3)$
46. $(2z + 3)(7z - 4)$ **47.** $(3x - 4)(6x + 5)$ **48.** $(2x - 9)(4x + 7)$ **49.** $3(2p - 7)(3p + 1)$
50. $-3(7x + 8)(3x - 2)$ **51.** $(2x^2 + 9)(x^2 + 1)$ **52.** $(4x^2 - 3)(6x^2 - 1)$ **53.** $(m^2 + 4)(4m^2 - 3)$
54. $(z^2 + 9)(5z^2 - 6)$ **55.** $-1(2x - 7)(3x + 8)$ **56.** $-1(b + 3)(4b - 7)$ **57.** $(2x + 3y)(3x - 2y)$
58. $(2a + 3b)(7a + 2b)$ **59.** $(u - 8v)(4u - 7v)$ **60.** $(x - 4y)(3x - 8y)$ **61.** $(x^2 + y^2)(9x^2 + 4y^2)$
62. $(x^2 + y^2)(16x^2 + 25y^2)$ **63.** $(2xy + 3)(5xy - 7)$ **64.** $(3pq - 2)(7pq + 4)$
65. (a) The increased width is $(w + 2)$ in. and the increased length is $(w + 12)$ in.
(b) The width was increased by 2 in. **(c)** The length was increased by 4 in.
66. (a) The new width is $(x - 3)$ in. and the new length is $(x - 1)$ in. **(b)** The width was increased by 2 in.
(c) The length was decreased by 1 in.
67. (a) The lengths of the legs are $(x + 8)$ in. and $(2x + 5)$ in. **(b)** They were each increased by 8 in.
(c) The expression is $(2x - 3)$ in.
68. (a) The lengths of the legs are $(x - 4)$ in. and $(3x - 12)$ in. **(b)** They were each decreased by 4 in.
(c) The expression is $(3x - 8)$ in.

Experiencing Algebra the Calculator Way

1. $2(4x - 1)(12x + 1)$ **2.** $(3x + 5)(8x - 11)$ **3.** $(2x + 3)(16x + 27)$ **4.** $(3x - 2)(24x - 17)$
5. $(p^2 + 25)(4p^2 + 9)$

Experiencing Algebra the Exercise Way

1. $(x + 10)(x - 10)$ **2.** $(y + 8)(y - 8)$ **3.** $(11 + c)(11 - c)$ **4.** $(14 + b)(14 - b)$
5. $(7a + 2)(7a - 2)$ **6.** $(5z + 3)(5z - 3)$ **7.** $(5 + 2y)(5 - 2y)$ **8.** $(8 + 3x)(8 - 3x)$
9. $(4u + 3v)(4u - 3v)$ **10.** $(6a + 5b)(6a - 5b)$ **11.** $7(z + 2)(z - 2)$ **12.** $8(x + 1)(x - 1)$
13. does not factor **14.** does not factor **15.** $(x^2 + 25)(x + 5)(x - 5)$ **16.** $(a^2 + 36)(a + 6)(a - 6)$
17. $(16 + z^2)(4 + z)(4 - z)$ **18.** $(25 + b^2)(5 + b)(5 - b)$ **19.** $(x^4 + 1)(x^2 + 1)(x + 1)(x - 1)$
20. $(y^4 + 16)(y^2 + 4)(y + 2)(y - 2)$ **21.** $(x + 2)^2$ **22.** $(p + 7)^2$ **23.** $(4z + 5)^2$ **24.** $(6x + 7)^2$
25. does not factor **26.** does not factor **27.** $(x - 5)^2$ **28.** $(y - 8)^2$ **29.** $(6z - 5)^2$
30. $(8m - 3)^2$ **31.** does not factor **32.** does not factor **33.** $(a + 4)^2(a - 4)^2$ **34.** $(b + 7)^2(b - 7)^2$
35. $(2x + 3)^2(2x - 3)^2$ **36.** $(5y + 2)^2(5y - 2)^2$ **37.** $3(x + 4)^2$ **38.** $16(x + 1)^2$ **39.** $2(a - 3)^2$
40. $5(x - 7)^2$ **41.** $p(p + q)^2$ **42.** $z^2(y + 2z)^2$ **43.** $2p(p + q)^2(p - q)^2$ **44.** $5u(u + 2v)^2(u - 2v)^2$
45. $m(m^2 + n^2)^2$ **46.** $p^3(p^2 + q^2)^2$ **47.** $(x - 3)(x^2 + 3x + 9)$ **48.** $(z - 7)(z^2 + 7z + 49)$
49. $(a + 4)(a^2 - 4a + 16)$ **50.** $(m + 1)(m^2 - m + 1)$ **51.** $(3x + 4y)(9x^2 - 12xy + 16y^2)$
52. $(5p + 3q)(25p^2 + 15pq + 9q^2)$ **53.** $(2p - 5q)(4p^2 + 10pq + 25q^2)$
54. $(3u - 2v)(9u^2 + 6uv + 4v^2)$ **55.** $p(p + 4q)(p^2 - 4pq + 16q^2)$ **56.** $y(5x + y)(25x^2 - 5xy + y^2)$
57. $3u(3u - v)(9u^2 + 3uv + v^2)$ **58.** $2b(a - 3b)(a^2 + 3ab + 9b^2)$ **59.** $3y(y^2 + y + 1)$
60. $5x(2x^2 + 7x - 1)$ **61.** $5ab(2c^2 + 3c - 4)$ **62.** $2xy(3z^2 + 5z - 3)$ **63.** $-8a(5a + 3b - 6c)$

64. $-7x(4x + 5y - 3z)$ **65.** $3x^3(6x + 5)(6x - 5)$ **66.** $2u(4u + 7)(4u - 7)$

67. $-8xy(5x + 2y)(5x - 2y)$ **68.** $-2ab(3a + 8b)(3a - 8b)$ **69.** $x(x - 8)^2$ **70.** $z(z - 5)^2$

71. $3v(2u + 3v)^2$ **72.** $2x(5x + 2y)^2$ **73.** $(x + 4)(x - 4)(3x^2 + 7)$ **74.** $(x + 3)(x - 3)(2x^2 + 5)$

75. $(p + 3)(p - 3)(2p + 1)(2p - 1)$ **76.** $(z + 2)(z - 2)(3z + 2)(3z - 2)$ **77.** $-2(3y - 1)(7y + 1)$

78. $-3(4y - 1)(6y + 1)$ **79.** $4(uv + 2)(uv + 7)$ **80.** $5(ab + 3)(ab + 4)$ **81.** $4x(x - 2)(8x - 7)$

82. $3x(5x - 6)(x - 4)$ **83.** $2x(x + 3)(6x - 5)$ **84.** $5z^2(z + 2)(3z - 4)$ **85.** $(x^3 - 5y^3)(x^3 + 3y^3)$

86. $(p^3 + 2q^3)(p^3 - 5q^3)$ **87.** $x(x - 5)(x^2 + 8)$ **88.** $2y(y + 3)(y^2 + 4)$

89. $(1 + k^4)(1 + k^2)(1 + k)(1 - k)$ **90.** $(16s^4 + 1)(4s^2 + 1)(2s + 1)(2s - 1)$

91. (a) The garden area is $(x^2 - 225)$ ft^2. **(b)** The rectangular plot has dimensions of $(x + 15)$ ft by $(x - 15)$ ft. **(c)** Yes, the plot that is 100 ft on each side has a larger garden area than the 85 by 100 foot plot.

92. (a) The area is $\left(y^2 - \frac{1}{4}x^2 \right)$ in^2. **(b)** An equivalent area is a rectangle measuring $\left(y + \frac{1}{2}x \right)$ in. by $\left(y - \frac{1}{2}x \right)$ in. **(c)** The dimensions are 14 in. by 10 in.

Experiencing Algebra the Calculator Way

Answers will vary.

CHAPTER 10 REVIEW

Reflections

1–5. Answers will vary.

Exercises

1. $-5c^2 \cdot c \cdot c$ **2.** $(-5c)(-5c)$ **3.** $4(x + y)(x + y)$ **4.** $\left(\frac{2}{3x}\right)\left(\frac{2}{3x}\right)\left(\frac{2}{3x}\right)\left(\frac{2}{3x}\right)$ **5.** $\frac{xz^3}{y - z}$

6. $\frac{3}{y^3} + \frac{2}{y^2} + \frac{1}{y} + 10$ **7.** a^5 **8.** $\frac{1}{(p + q)^2}$ **9.** t^3 **10.** m^2 **11.** $\frac{1}{x + 3y}$ **12.** $\frac{3x^2 y}{z^2}$ **13.** z^{12}

14. $\frac{1}{w^6}$ **15.** p^8 **16.** 1 **17.** $16a^4$ **18.** $-32a^5$ **19.** $-\frac{8x^3}{27z^3}$ **20.** $\frac{25b^2}{16a^2}$ **21.** $a^6 b^9 c^3$ **22.** $729x^6$

23. $\frac{m^4}{256n^4}$ **24.** Area of original square: x^2 square units; Area of reduced square: $\frac{x^2}{16}$ square units; The smaller area is $\frac{1}{16}$ of the original area. **25.** Area of original garden: πr^2 square units; Area of enlarged garden: $4\pi r^2$ square units; The enlarged garden has an area that is 4 times that of the original garden.; The garden has an area of 144π ft^2. **26.** $6x^4 + 8x^3 + 4x^2 - 4$ **27.** $9y^2 + y + 2$ **28.** $3.57z^3 + 3.56z^2 + 5.79z + 2.74$

29. $2x^3 - 4x^2 - 5x - 7$ **30.** $4a^4 - a^3 - 2a^2 - 3a - 4$ **31.** $65z^4 - 16z^3 + 27z^2 - 8z + 24$

32. $\frac{1}{8}b^4 + \frac{7}{8}b^3 - \frac{9}{8}b^2 + \frac{3}{8}b - \frac{1}{4}$ **33.** $-15ab^4$ **34.** $18x^5 + 12x^4 - 42x^3$ **35.** $21a^4 + 7a^2 - 14$

36. $-\frac{23.46x^4}{z}$ **37.** $\frac{72xy}{z^2}$ **38.** $\frac{a}{3}$ **39.** $\frac{9a^6}{b^8}$ **40.** $\frac{85{,}000{,}000{,}000}{y^{12}}$ **41.** $-3b^3 + 2b^2 + 5b - 1$

42. $\frac{2}{a} + \frac{6}{b}$ **43. (a)** $C(x) = 10 + 3.5x$ **(b)** $R(x) = (10 - 0.25x)x$ **(c)** $P(x) = -0.25x^2 + 6.5x - 10$

(d) $A(x) = 0.25x + 6.5 - \frac{10}{x}$ **(e)** $x = 13$ **44.** The perimeter is $(80 - 2x)$ meters.

45. Area $= x^2 + 8x - 9$; The patio needs 144 ft^2 of carpeting. **46.** $y^2 + 18y + 81$ **47.** $x^6 - 10x^3 + 25$

48. $5x^2 + 53x - 22$ **49.** $49 - z^2$ **50.** $y^2 + 1.6y - 6.12$ **51.** $z^4 - 100$ **52.** $\frac{16}{25}x^2 - \frac{1}{4}$

53. $b^3 - 12b^2 + 48b - 64$ **54.** $6x^3 + 13x^2 - 3x - 4$ **55.** $a^2 + b^2 + c^2 + 2ab + 2bc + 2ac$

56. $a^3 - 27$ **57. (a)** length: $(x + 3)$ in.; width: $(x - 3)$ in.; height: x in.   **(b)** The volume is $(x^3 - 9x)$ in^3.
(c) The surface area is $(6x^2 - 18)$ in^2.   **58. (a)** The current area is $3x^2$ ft^2.   **(b)** The new area is
$(6x^2 + 18x)$ ft^2.   **(c)** The ratio is $\dfrac{2x + 6}{x}$.   **59.** $4a^2(5a^4 - 7a^2 + 11)$ **60.** $22u^2v^2(u + v)$

61. $(x^2 + 1)(3x + 1)$ **62.** $7(a^2 + b^2)^2$ **63.** $(5c + 6d)(3a + 4b)$ **64. (a)** $\dfrac{1}{2}n(n + 1)$

(b) The sum is 78.   **(c)** The factored expression is easier to evaluate.; Answers will vary.
65. The width is $(x - 3)$ units and the length is $(2x + 5)$ units.
66. $x + (x + 10) + (x + 20) + (x + 30) + (x + 40) + (x + 50) + (x + 60)$; $7(x + 30)$; The employee
earns an average of $(x + 30)$ dollars for each of 7 months.; The salary is $6930.   **67.** $(z - 9)(z + 11)$
68. $(p - 6q)(p + 11q)$ **69.** $6(a + 3)(a + 13)$ **70.** $(x^2 + 3)(x^2 + 5)$ **71.** $4q(q + 5)(q - 12)$
72. $(xy + 9)(xy - 13)$ **73.** $-7(x - 2)(x - 12)$ **74.** $(x - 5)(2x - 1)$ **75.** $(2x + 5)(3x + 1)$
76. $7(ab + 3)(4ab + 1)$ **77.** $-3x(3x + 8)(5x - 2)$ **78. (a)** The base is $(2x + 7)$ units and the height
is $(2x + 3)$ units.   **(b)** The base was increased by 7 units.   **(c)** The height was increased by $(x + 3)$ units.
79. (a) The new length is $(x + 15)$ units and the new width is $(x + 2)$ units.   **(b)** It was increased by 15 units.
(c) It was increased by 8 units.   **80.** $(x + 13)(x - 13)$ **81.** $(25 + a)(25 - a)$ **82.** $3(2x + 5)(2x - 5)$
83. $(p + q)(p - q)$ **84.** does not factor   **85.** $(3x + 5y)(3x - 5y)$ **86.** $(4x^2 + 9)(2x + 3)(2x - 3)$
87. $(p + 6)^2$ **88.** $(q - 8)^2$ **89.** $(c + 3)(c^2 - 3c + 9)$ **90.** $(2z - 5)(4z^2 + 10z + 25)$
91. $5(h + 2k)(h^2 + 2hk + 4k^2)$ **92.** $-3x(2x - 5y)^2$ **93.** $7x^2(x^2 + x + 1)$ **94.** $3x(2x + 9)(2x - 9)$
95. $8x(2x + 1)^2$ **96.** $2x(4x - 9)(3x + 5)$ **97.** $(4x + 3)^2(4x - 3)^2$
98. $(3x + 2)(3x - 2)(2x + 1)(2x - 1)$ **99.** $2x(x + 7)(x - 2)(x + 2)$
100. (a) The land area not covered is $(4x^2 - 25)$ ft^2.
(b) The dimensions would be $(2x + 5)$ ft by $(2x - 5)$ ft.   **(c)** The dimensions would be 165 ft by 155 ft.

CHAPTER 10 MIXED REVIEW

1. $(z + 15)(z - 6)$ **2.** $(a - 6)(a - 12)$ **3.** $(x + 9y)(x + 5y)$ **4.** $5(a + 7)^2$ **5.** $2(a^2 + 4ab + 6b^2)$
6. $(x^2 + 3)(x^2 + 7)$ **7.** $3q(q - 3)(q + 14)$ **8.** $-6(x + 5)(x - 12)$ **9.** $(x + 2)(x + 5)$
10. $(x + 17)(x - 17)$ **11.** $(x - 1)(x^2 + x + 1)$ **12.** $4(x + 4)(x - 4)$ **13.** does not factor
14. $(6x + 7y)(6x - 7y)$ **15.** $(9x^2 + 1)(3x + 1)(3x - 1)$ **16.** $(p + 11)^2$ **17.** $(q - 15)^2$
18. $(3a + 4b)(9a^2 + 12ab + 16b^2)$ **19.** $3(3ab - 4)^2$ **20.** $-2x(5x - 6y)^2$ **21.** $2x(4x^3 - x^2 + 3x - 6)$
22. $5u^2v^2(7u + 5v)$ **23.** $(x^2 + 5)(2x + 1)$ **24.** $(m - 2n)(m - 8n)$ **25.** $4(a^2 + 2b^2)^2$
26. $(x - 1)(2x - 11)$ **27.** $(6c + 5d)(4a + 3b)$ **28.** $(x - 3)(7x + 2)$ **29.** $(2x - 3)(5x + 2)$
30. $6(2a + 1)(3a + 4)$ **31.** $-2(3x + 2)(5x - 8)$ **32.** $(3x^2 + 1)(4x^2 + 3)$ **33.** $6x(3x + 1)^2$
34. $(3x + 2)^2(3x - 2)^2$ **35.** $(2x + 5)(2x - 5)(x + 3)(x - 3)$ **36.** $3x(2x + 3)(2x - 5)$

37. $3x(x + 5)(x + 3)(x - 3)$ **38.** $\dfrac{n^5}{m^7}$ **39.** $\dfrac{64t^3}{125s^4}$ **40.** $(d + 2e)^2(d - 2e)^2$

41. $\dfrac{2}{y^4} + \dfrac{4}{y^3} + \dfrac{6}{y^2} + \dfrac{8}{y} + 10$ **42.** $10y^2 + y + 19$ **43.** $\dfrac{9}{8}a^3 + \dfrac{1}{8}a^2 - \dfrac{3}{16}a + \dfrac{15}{16}$
44. $4.9z^3 - 1.92z^2 + 10.17z - 6.47$ **45.** $-2x^3 - 11x^2 - 8x + 7$ **46.** $a^4 - 4a^3 + 2a + 4$
47. $117z^4 - 18z^3 + 43z^2 - 50z + 56$ **48.** $143x^3$ **49.** $-12x^5 + 24x^4 - 36x^3 - 48x^2 + 60x$
50. $36a^4 + 18a^2 - 27$ **51.** $m^2 - 121$ **52.** $z^2 - 16z + 64$ **53.** $4a^2 + 45a - 91$
54. $169 - x^2$ **55.** $b^6 + 8b^3 + 16$ **56.** $t^3 + 6t^2 + 12t + 8$ **57.** $7x^3 + 26x^2 - 29x + 6$

58. $p^2 + q^2 + r^2 + 2pq + 2qr + 2pr$ **59.** $b^3 - 64$ **60.** c^3 **61.** $\dfrac{1}{(a + 4b)^4}$ **62.** $\dfrac{3x^3y}{z}$

63. $\dfrac{a^2}{2}$ **64.** $\dfrac{9a^6}{b^8}$ **65.** $-2b^3 + 3b^2 + 5b - 4$ **66.** $\dfrac{4}{c} + \dfrac{2}{d}$ **67.** s^{10} **68.** $\dfrac{1}{y^3}$ **69.** $(m + n)^6$

70. b^{35} **71.** $\dfrac{1}{d^{18}}$ **72.** 1   **73.** $729d^6$ **74.** $-27d^3$ **75.** $\dfrac{n^6}{m^6}$ **76.** $\dfrac{1}{m^6n^6}$ **77.** $x^{16}y^{20}z^4$

78. $4096x^6$ **79.** $\dfrac{c^6}{64d^6}$ **80.** The width is $(2x + 1)$ units and the length is $(4x - 3)$ units.

81. **(a)** The new length is $(3x + 1)$ in. and the new width is $(2x - 4)$ in.
(b) The length was increased by $(2x + 1)$ in.   **(c)** The width was increased by $(x - 2)$ in.
82. **(a)** The base is $(2x + 16)$ units and the height is $(x + 4)$ units.
(b) The base was increased by 16 units.   **(c)** The height was increased by 4 units.
83. **(a)** length: $(2x + 3)$ in.; width: x in.; height: x in.   **(b)** The volume is $(2x^3 + 3x^2)$ in^3.
(c) The surface area is $(10x^2 + 12x)$ in^2.   **(d)** The volume is 1216 in^3.   **(e)** The surface area is 736 in^2.

84. **(a)** The area is $\left(x^2 + \dfrac{5}{2}x \right)$ cm^2.   **(b)** The area is 174 cm^2.   **85.** **(a)** The current area is x^2 ft^2.

(b) The new area will be $(4x^2 + 10x)$ ft^2.   **(c)** The ratio is $\dfrac{4x + 10}{x}$.

CHAPTER 10 TEST

1. $9a(3a + 1)^2$ **2.** $(p + 5)(p^2 - 5p + 25)$ **3.** $-4a^2b^2(a + 4b)(2a + b)$ **4.** $(a^2 + b^2)(a - 5b)$
5. $(5x - 7y)(3x + 2y)$ **6.** $(8a + 7b)(8a - 7b)$ **7.** $(5x - 7)^2$ **8.** $3x(x - 1)(x - 8)$
9. $(x + 3y)(x - 7y)$ **10.** $(2x + 1)(7x + 9)$ **11.** $(x^2 + 7)(2x + 1)(2x - 1)$ **12.** does not factor
13. $(2x - 1)^9$ **14.** $\dfrac{3x^2}{z^3}$ **15.** $\dfrac{(a + b)^3}{(a - b)^5}$ **16.** $\dfrac{-8x^6}{y^3}$ **17.** $\dfrac{1}{(3c - 7)^2}$ **18.** $\dfrac{9q^2}{64p^6}$
19. $4y^4 + 5y^3 + 9y^2 + 5$ **20.** $7x^5 - 2x^4 + 23x^3 + 21x^2 + 2x - 30$ **21.** $-11.4p^9q^2r^3$
22. $-8t^4 + 12t^3 + 32t^2 - 24t$ **23.** $81 - 25d^2$ **24.** $15x^2 - x - 28$ **25.** $8z^3 - 10z^2 + 23z - 15$

26. $x^2 + 6x + 9$ **27.** $\dfrac{8ac^3}{b^5}$ **28.** $\dfrac{b^7}{a^8c}$ **29.** $3x^4 + 5x^3 - x$ **30.** **(a)** The volume is $(2x^3 + 8x^2)$ in^3.
(b) The surface area is $(10x^2 + 24x)$ in^2.   **(c)** The volume is 450 in^3; The surface area is 370 in^2.
31. **(a)** factor by grouping   **(b)** He did not factor completely.   **(c)** $(3x + 7)(2x + 3)(2x - 3)$

Chapter 11

PROBLEM SET 11.1

Experiencing Algebra the Exercise Way

1. polynomial; cubic   **2.** not a polynomial   **3.** not a polynomial   **4.** polynomial; cubic   **5.** polynomial
6. polynomial; cubic   **7.** polynomial; quadratic   **8.** not a polynomial   **9.** not a polynomial
10. polynomial; cubic   **11.** polynomial; quadratic   **12.** polynomial; quadratic   **13.** 2 and 4
14. -3 and 2   **15.** $-1, 1,$ and 0   **16.** -5 and 3   **17.** no solution   **18.** no solution
19. all real numbers   **20.** all real numbers   **21.** no real-number solution
22. no real-number solution   **23.** -6 and 2   **24.** -4 and 3   **25.** -5 and 2   **26.** -3 and 5
27. -3 and 3   **28.** -4 and 4   **29.** -1 and 3   **30.** -4 and -2 **31.** $-2, 0,$ and 2   **32.** 2   **33.** -2 and 5
34. $-3, -1,$ and 1   **35.** no solution   **36.** no real-number solution   **37.** no real-number solution
38. no solution   **39.** all real numbers   **40.** all real numbers   **41.** $-1, 0,$ and 4   **42.** $-3, 0,$ and 2
43. no real-number solution   **44.** no real-number solution   **45.** no solution

46. no real-number solution   **47.** all real numbers   **48.** all real numbers   **49.** $-\dfrac{3}{2}$ and $\dfrac{3}{2}$ **50.** $-\dfrac{4}{3}$ and $\dfrac{4}{3}$

51. $-0.8, 0.5,$ and 1   **52.** $-1, 0.5,$ and 2.5   **53.** -2.8 and 3.7   **54.** 0.8 and 4.2   **55.** $-3.6, -1.5,$ and 1.4
56. $-2.4, -0.2,$ and 2.5   **57.** It will hit the ground in approximately 1.58 seconds.
58. They will hit the ground in 1 second.   **59.** The dagger will hit the ground in approximately 1.43 seconds.
60. The branch will hit the ground in approximately 0.94 seconds.   **61.** It will hit the ground in 1.75 seconds.
62. The hammer will hit the ground in 1 second.
63. **(a)** $30 + x$ **(b)** $40 - x$ **(c)** $1200 + 10x - x^2$ **(d)** $1100 = 1200 + 10x - x^2$
(e) There should be 16 unsold seats and 24 sold seats.   **64.** **(a)** $150 + 5x$ **(b)** $25 - x$
(c) $3750 - 25x - 5x^2$ **(d)** $3500 = 3750 - 25x - 5x^2$ **(e)** There should be 5 unsold seats and 20 sold seats.

65. There is no real-number solution.   **66.** There should be between 5 and 11 sales reps.
67. The dimensions are about 20 in. by 11 in. by 10 in.   **68.** The dimensions are 23 ft by 13 ft.

Experiencing Algebra the Calculator Way

Students should verify solutions with the calculator.

PROBLEM SET 11.2

Experiencing Algebra the Exercise Way

1. -11 and -6 **2.** -13 and -9 **3.** $-\dfrac{2}{3}$ and $\dfrac{3}{4}$ **4.** $-\dfrac{2}{3}$ and $\dfrac{7}{9}$ **5.** $-9, 0,$ and $\dfrac{5}{2}$ **6.** $-\dfrac{1}{6}, 0,$ and 4

7. $\dfrac{1}{7}$ and 7 **8.** $\dfrac{1}{9}$ and 9 **9.** $-6, -\dfrac{3}{4},$ and $\dfrac{9}{2}$ **10.** $-\dfrac{7}{2}, \dfrac{8}{3},$ and 7 **11.** -34 and 1.3 **12.** -3 and 4

13. -6 and -4 **14.** -8 and -5 **15.** 3 and 11 **16.** 4 and 13 **17.** -6 and $-\dfrac{5}{4}$ **18.** -2 and $-\dfrac{8}{7}$

19. $-\dfrac{8}{5}$ and 1 **20.** $-\dfrac{5}{3}$ and 4 **21.** 0 and $\dfrac{7}{3}$ **22.** 0 and $\dfrac{7}{2}$ **23.** $-\dfrac{5}{3}$ and $\dfrac{1}{6}$ **24.** $-\dfrac{3}{2}$ and $\dfrac{7}{4}$ **25.** $-\dfrac{9}{4}$

26. $\dfrac{2}{7}$ **27.** $-\dfrac{5}{2}$ **28.** $-\dfrac{4}{3}$ **29.** -8 and 8 **30.** -12 and 12 **31.** $-\dfrac{5}{3}$ and $\dfrac{5}{3}$ **32.** $-\dfrac{9}{8}$ and $\dfrac{9}{8}$

33. approximately -7.24 and -2.76 **34.** approximately -8.70 and -2.30 **35.** -8 and 6 **36.** -4 and 8
37. -4 and 9 **38.** -6 and 7 **39.** all real numbers   **40.** all real numbers   **41.** no solution
42. no solution   **43.** -12 and 9 **44.** -20 and 15 **45.** $-7, -3,$ and 3 **46.** $-5, -4,$ and 4

47. $-\dfrac{5}{2}, -\dfrac{5}{3},$ and $\dfrac{5}{3}$ **48.** $-3.5, -3,$ and 3.5 **49.** 1 **50.** 8

51. (a) The volume is $\left(\dfrac{3}{2}x^2 + 3x\right)$ ft^3.   **(b)** The dimensions are 6 ft by 3 ft by 4 ft.

52. (a) The volume is $(32x^2 + 4x)$ cm^3.   **(b)** The dimensions are 5 cm by 4 cm by 41 cm.
53. (a) The surface area is $(26x^2 + 10x)$ in^2.   **(b)** The dimensions are 15 in. by 5 in. by 22 in.
54. (a) The surface area is $(84x^2 + 24x)$ units^2.   **(b)** The dimensions are 3 in. by 15 in. by 23 in.

55. (a) The area is $\left(\dfrac{1}{2}x^2 + 2x\right)$ ft^2.   **(b)** The dimensions are 6 ft base, 10 ft height.

56. (a) The area is $\left(\dfrac{5}{2}x^2 + x\right)$ m^2.   **(b)** The dimensions are: 10 m height, 52 m base.

57. $(x + 12)^2 = x^2 + (x + 6)^2$; The measurements are: 18 ft height, 24 ft base, and 30 ft hypotenuse.

58. $\left(x + \dfrac{1}{2}\right)^2 = x^2 + \left(\dfrac{3}{4}x\right)^2$; The measurements are: 2 in. base, $1\dfrac{1}{2}$ in. height, and $2\dfrac{1}{2}$ in. hypotenuse.
59. $V^2 = 30(0.40)(243)$; The vehicle was traveling at 54 mph.
60. $V^2 = 30(0.27)(250)$, The vehicle was traveling at 45 mph.

Experiencing Algebra the Calculator Way

1. 58 and 75   **2.** -17 and 18   **3.** -125 **4.** 93   **5.** -15 and 29   **6.** Answers will vary.

PROBLEM SET 11.3

Experiencing Algebra the Exercise Way

1. 9   **2.** 8   **3.** -10 **4.** -11 **5.** 9   **6.** -8 **7.** $3\sqrt{14}$ **8.** $3\sqrt{35}$ **9.** $7\sqrt{3}$ **10.** $-8\sqrt{2}$
11. $-5\sqrt{5}$ **12.** $3\sqrt{3}$ **13.** $\dfrac{6}{7}$ **14.** $-\dfrac{5}{8}$ **15.** $\dfrac{\sqrt{11}}{12}$ **16.** $\dfrac{\sqrt{7}}{5}$ **17.** $\dfrac{8\sqrt{13}}{13}$ **18.** $\dfrac{10\sqrt{11}}{11}$

19. $-\dfrac{2\sqrt{7}}{3}$ **20.** $\dfrac{8\sqrt{15}}{5}$ **21.** $\dfrac{\sqrt{30}}{4}$ **22.** $\dfrac{5\sqrt{21}}{14}$ **23.** $-\dfrac{\sqrt{6}}{4}$ **24.** $-\dfrac{\sqrt{21}}{5}$ **25.** ± 12 **26.** ± 11

27. $\pm\sqrt{13}$ **28.** $\pm\sqrt{15}$ **29.** $\pm 7\sqrt{2}$ **30.** $\pm 10\sqrt{2}$ **31.** ± 4 **32.** ± 3 **33.** $\pm\dfrac{5}{2}$ **34.** $\pm\dfrac{7}{4}$

35. $\pm\dfrac{\sqrt{2}}{3}$ **36.** $\pm\dfrac{1}{8}$ **37.** $\pm\sqrt{2}$ **38.** $\pm\dfrac{\sqrt{35}}{5}$ **39.** no real-number solution

40. no real-number solution   **41.** 5   **42.** $\dfrac{7}{2}$ **43.** 5 and 9   **44.** -9 and -3 **45.** $\dfrac{1}{4}$ and $\dfrac{5}{4}$

46. $\dfrac{4}{3}$ and 2   **47.** ± 1.3 **48.** ± 1.7 **49.** -5 and -1 **50.** 1 and 11   **51.** 1 and 7   **52.** -11 and -7

53. -8 and -2 **54.** -3 and 17   **55.** $-\dfrac{11}{3}$ and $\dfrac{13}{3}$ **56.** $-\dfrac{9}{5}$ and $\dfrac{7}{5}$ **57.** $7 \pm \sqrt{6}$ **58.** $12 \pm \sqrt{5}$

59. $\dfrac{-1 \pm \sqrt{10}}{2}$ **60.** $\dfrac{5 \pm \sqrt{2}}{4}$ **61.** $-3 \pm 2\sqrt{3}$ **62.** $15 \pm 2\sqrt{3}$

63. It will take 5 seconds for the balloon to hit the ground.   **64.** It will reach the ground in 6 seconds.

65. It will take $\dfrac{5\sqrt{70}}{2}$ or approximately 20.9 seconds.   **66.** It will take $\dfrac{25\sqrt{3}}{2}$ or approximately 21.65 seconds.

67. It is 11 inches high.   **68.** The kite is 80 feet high.   **69.** The distance is 4000 feet.
70. The tower is 120 meters tall.   **71.** The distance is $25\sqrt{2}$ or approximately 35.36 feet.
72. The perimeter is $40\sqrt{2}$ or approximately 56.57 cm.   **73.** She manages about 313 accounts.
74. He manages about 172 accounts.

Experiencing Algebra the Calculator Way

7 in., 8 in., 10 in., 11 in., 13 in., 14 in., 16 in., 17 in.

PROBLEM SET 11.4

Experiencing Algebra the Exercise Way

1. 9   **2.** 16   **3.** $\dfrac{9}{4}$ **4.** $\dfrac{9}{4}$ **5.** $\dfrac{9}{64}$ **6.** $\dfrac{9}{100}$ **7.** $\dfrac{1}{4}$ **8.** $\dfrac{1}{4}$ **9.** 9   **10.** 16   **11.** $\dfrac{81}{4}$ **12.** $\dfrac{25}{4}$

13. $\dfrac{16}{81}$ **14.** $\dfrac{9}{49}$ **15.** 49   **16.** 25   **17.** -11 and 5   **18.** -5 and 13   **19.** -4 and 7   **20.** -8 and 5

21. $-\dfrac{3}{7}$ and $-\dfrac{1}{7}$ **22.** $-\dfrac{4}{5}$ and $-\dfrac{2}{5}$ **23.** -10 and 9   **24.** -7 and 8   **25.** $3 \pm \sqrt{11}$ **26.** $-4 \pm \sqrt{21}$

27. $\dfrac{-9 \pm \sqrt{85}}{2}$ **28.** $\dfrac{5 \pm \sqrt{33}}{2}$ **29.** $\dfrac{-4 \pm \sqrt{178}}{9}$ **30.** $\dfrac{-3 \pm \sqrt{58}}{7}$ **31.** $\dfrac{1 \pm \sqrt{21}}{2}$ **32.** $\dfrac{-1 \pm \sqrt{41}}{2}$

33. no real-number solution   **34.** no real-number solution   **35.** $\dfrac{-3 \pm \sqrt{11}}{2}$ **36.** $\dfrac{-3 \pm 2\sqrt{3}}{2}$

37. $\dfrac{-1 \pm \sqrt{85}}{6}$ **38.** -1 and $\dfrac{3}{5}$ **39.** 7   **40.** -5 **41.** $\dfrac{5}{2}$ **42.** $-\dfrac{2}{3}$ **43.** $-5 \pm \sqrt{29}$ **44.** $3 \pm \sqrt{6}$

45. $\dfrac{-1 \pm \sqrt{19}}{6}$ **46.** $\dfrac{1 \pm \sqrt{55}}{6}$ **47.** $\dfrac{3 \pm \sqrt{14}}{2}$ **48.** $\dfrac{10 \pm \sqrt{106}}{2}$ **49.** The number of cars is 15.

50. $f(x) = 0.5x^2 + 5x$; A total of 10 dolls can be purchased.   **51.** The price should be set at \$19.
52. The price should be set at \$42.   **53.** The contract should be about \$10,400,000.
54. The contract should be for about \$7,400,000.   **55.** The width is 9 in. and the length is 13 in.
56. The height is 10 cm and the base is 18 cm.   **57.** The length is 12.1 ft and the width is 7.1 ft.
58. The lengths of the legs are 13.22 ft and 21.22 ft.   **59.** (a) $0 = -16t^2 + 32t + 16$
(b) It will take $1 + \sqrt{2}$ seconds.   **(c)** It will take approximately 2.4 seconds.

60. (a) $0 = -16t^2 + 88t + 8$ **(b)** It will take $2.75 + \sqrt{8.0625}$ seconds.
(c) It will take approximately 5.6 seconds.

Experiencing Algebra the Calculator Way

1. -5 and -3 **2.** no real-number solution   **3.** approximately -1.618 and 0.618 **4.** -4 and -1.5
5. no real-number solution   **6.** approximately -1.435 and 0.435

PROBLEM SET 11.5

Experiencing Algebra the Exercise Way

1. 3 and 9   **2.** 5 and 7   **3.** $-\dfrac{7}{2}$ and 3   **4.** $-\dfrac{8}{3}$ and 2   **5.** -5 and $-\dfrac{1}{2}$ **6.** -9 and $-\dfrac{4}{3}$ **7.** $\dfrac{1}{4}$

8. $-\dfrac{2}{5}$ **9.** no real-number solution   **10.** no real-number solution   **11.** no real-number solution

12. no real-number solution   **13.** $\dfrac{5 \pm \sqrt{17}}{2}$ **14.** $4 \pm \sqrt{6}$ **15.** $2 \pm \sqrt{3}$ **16.** $-3 \pm \sqrt{2}$

17. $-\dfrac{5}{4}$ and 0   **18.** 0 and $\dfrac{10}{3}$ **19.** $\pm\dfrac{\sqrt{21}}{3}$ **20.** $\pm\dfrac{\sqrt{30}}{2}$ **21.** 5 and 11   **22.** -12 and -6

23. -2 and 4   **24.** -3 and 9   **25.** 1.5 and 4.8   **26.** -3.2 and -0.5 **27.** $-2.8 \pm \sqrt{9.64}$
28. $0.9 \pm \sqrt{7.01}$ **29.** 4.9   **30.** -7.1 **31.** no real-number solution   **32.** no real-number solution
33. two rational solutions   **34.** no real-number solution   **35.** one rational solution
36. two irrational solutions   **37.** no real-number solution   **38.** one rational solution
39. two rational solutions   **40.** two rational solutions   **41.** two irrational solutions
42. two rational solutions   **43.** two irrational solutions   **44.** no real-number solution
45. two rational solutions   **46.** two irrational solutions   **47.** no real-number solution
48. one rational solution   **49.** The interest rate must be about 9.5%.
50. The interest rate must be about 15.5%.   **51.** The values are 25 and 45.; Answers will vary.
52. The values are 30 and 150.; Answers will vary.   **53.** The year was 1975.   **54.** The year was 1970.

Experiencing Algebra the Calculator Way

Equation	Value of Discriminant	Types of Roots	Number of Unlike Roots	Roots
1. $x^2 + 6 = 5x$	1	rational	2	2, 3
2. $9x^2 + 6x = -1$	0	rational	1	$-\frac{1}{3}$
3. $2x^2 + 1 = 7x$	41	irrational	2	0.149, 3.351
4. $x^2 + 6x = -10$	-4	not real	2	not real
5. $x^2 = 6 - x$	25	rational	2	$-3, 2$
6. $5x^2 - 6x = 0$	36	rational	2	0, 1.2
7. $x^2 + 0.36 = 1.2x$	0	rational	1	0.6
8. $1.7x^2 + x + 1.9 = 0$	-11.92	not real	2	not real
9. $1.5x^2 + 1.2x = 3.6$	23.04	rational	2	$-2, 1.2$
10. $\frac{1}{4}x^2 + x = \frac{1}{8}$	1.125	irrational	2	$-4.121, 0.121$
11. $x^2 - \frac{1}{6}x = \frac{1}{6}$	$0.69\overline{4}$	rational	2	$-0.\overline{3}, 0.5$
12. $\frac{1}{5}x^2 + \frac{2}{3}x = -\frac{7}{8}$	$-0.2\overline{5}$	not real	2	not real

Experiencing Algebra the Exercise Way

1. The legs are 9 inches and 12 inches. **2.** The legs are 8 feet and 15 feet. **3.** The legs are 5 feet and 12 feet.
4. The legs are 21 yards and 20 yards. **5.** The leg is 28 cm and the hypotenuse is 53 cm.
6. The leg is 9 inches and the hypotenuse is 41 inches. **7.** The distance is 168 yards.
8. The distance is 210 yards. **9.** They should each measure approximately 14.1 feet.
10. The width is approximately 11.2 feet and the length is approximately 22.4 feet.
11. The width is about 23.6 feet and the length is about 65.8 feet. **12.** The width is about 14.9 feet and the
length is about 32.8 feet. **13.** The distance is about 91.9 feet. **14.** She threw the ball 69.6 feet.
15. It was 7 feet beyond first base. **16.** The first baseman was 15.0 feet from first base.
17. It would rise approximately 51.4 inches. **18.** It would rise about 24.5 inches.
19. The hypotenuse measures approximately 5.30 m. **20.** The hypotenuse measures approximately 9.26 feet.
21. The lengths are approximately 5.37 feet. **22.** The lengths are approximately 10.54 cm.
23. The wire is approximately 28.28 feet. **24.** The wire is approximately 21.21 feet.
25. The building is approximately 30.05 feet tall. **26.** The tower is approximately 102.53 feet high.
27. Yes, 28.28 feet is less than 30 feet. **28.** No, 35.36 feet is greater than 30 feet.
29. The lengths are approximately 10.7 in. and 21.5 in. **30.** The lengths are approximately 1.3 cm and 2.5 cm.
31. The lengths are 11 in. and approximately 19.1 in. **32.** The lengths are 17 cm and approximately 29.4 cm.
33. The lengths are 42 cm and approximately 36.4 cm. **34.** The lengths are 16.4 in. and approximately 14.2 in.
35. The horizontal distance is about 6928.2 ft and the slanted distance is 8000 ft.
36. The horizontal distance is approximately 69.3 ft and the length of string is approximately 138.6 ft.
37. The height of the pole is approximately 13.9 ft and the length of the wire is 16 ft. **38.** The amount of
wire is approximately 15.0 m and it should be anchored approximately 7.5 m from the base of the pole.

39. $c = \pm \dfrac{\sqrt{Em}}{m}$ **40.** $r = \pm \dfrac{\sqrt{A\pi}}{2\pi}$ **41.** $r = \pm \dfrac{\sqrt{V\pi h}}{\pi h}$ **42.** $v = \pm \dfrac{\sqrt{FRm}}{m}$ **43.** $v = \pm \dfrac{\sqrt{2Em}}{m}$

44. $r = \pm \dfrac{6\sqrt{10A\pi S}}{\pi S}$ **45.** $n = \dfrac{1 \pm \sqrt{1 + 8C}}{2}$ **46.** $n = \dfrac{-1 \pm \sqrt{1 + 8S}}{2}$ **47.** $x = \pm \sqrt{y^2 + c^2}$

48. $x = \pm \sqrt{r^2 - y^2}$ **49.** $r = -1 \pm \dfrac{\sqrt{AP}}{P}$ **50.** $t = \dfrac{-g \pm \sqrt{g^2 + 64S}}{32}$

Experiencing Algebra the Calculator Way

1. approximately 24.84 cm **2.** 5930.44 in. **3.** 5481 ft **4.** 13,689 dm **5.** $\dfrac{3}{64}$ ft

Experiencing Algebra the Exercise Way

1. quadratic inequality **2.** not a quadratic inequality **3.** quadratic inequality
4. not a quadratic inequality **5.** not a quadratic inequality **6.** quadratic inequality
7. quadratic inequality **8.** quadratic inequality **9.** not a quadratic inequality
10. not a quadratic inequality **11.** not a quadratic inequality **12.** quadratic inequality
13. all integers less than or equal to −5 and greater than or equal to 3 **14.** all integers greater than or equal
to −4 and less than or equal to 2 **15.** all integers greater than −4 and less than 1
16. all integers greater than −3 and less than 2 **17.** all integers less than 0 or greater than 8
18. all integers less than −3 or greater than 0 **19.** $(-\infty, -3) \cup (1, \infty)$ **20.** $(-\infty, 1] \cup [7, \infty)$
21. $(-2.5, 2)$ **22.** $[-1, 5]$ **23.** $(-\infty, -2) \cup (8, \infty)$ **24.** $(-\infty, -1) \cup (8, \infty)$ **25.** $[-3, 3]$
26. $(-\infty, -5) \cup (2, \infty)$ **27.** no solution **28.** no solution **29.** $(-\infty, \infty)$ **30.** −2 **31.** $(-\infty, \infty)$
32. $(-\infty, \infty)$ **33.** $(-\infty, -4] \cup [6, \infty)$ **34.** $[-5, 7]$ **35.** $(-3, 5)$ **36.** $(-3, 6)$ **37.** $\left[\dfrac{1}{2}, \dfrac{5}{2}\right]$
38. $(-\infty, -4] \cup [1, \infty)$ **39.** $(-\infty, -2) \cup (7, \infty)$ **40.** $(-5, 6)$ **41.** $(-\infty, -4] \cup [3, \infty)$ **42.** $[-2, 6]$

43. $(-\infty, -3) \cup (-1, \infty)$ **44.** $(-\infty, -2) \cup (4, \infty)$ **45.** $[-2, 3]$ **46.** $\left(-\infty, \dfrac{1}{2}\right] \cup [5, \infty)$ **47.** $\dfrac{3}{2}$

48. $(-\infty, \infty)$ **49.** $\left(-\infty, \dfrac{1}{2}\right) \cup \left(\dfrac{1}{2}, \infty\right)$ **50.** no solution **51.** $(-\infty, \infty)$ **52.** 4 **53.** no solution

54. $(-\infty, -4) \cup (-4, \infty)$ **55.** The egg is higher than the stand between 0 and $\dfrac{15}{8}$ seconds.

56. The arrow is above the point of origin between 0 and $\dfrac{5}{2}$ seconds.

57. The rock is no more than 800 feet from about 7.866 seconds to 11.316 seconds.
58. The ball is no more than 200 feet from about 7.215 seconds to 8.279 seconds.
59. $R(x) = -3x^2 + 63x + 390$; The number ordered must be greater than 9 and less than 22 stereos.
60. $R(x) = -2.5x^2 + 29x + 708$; The number ordered must be at least 12 but less than 24 ovens.
61. The booth can be operated from 1 day to 4 days. **62.** The stand can be operated from 1 week to 4 weeks.
63. The years are from 1988 and on. **64.** The years were from 1970 to 1985.

Experiencing Algebra the Calculator Way

Answers will vary.

CHAPTER 11 REVIEW

Reflections

1–6. Answers will vary.

Exercises

1. -3 and 4 **2.** -9 and -3 **3.** 1 and 5 **4.** -1 and 5 **5.** -4 and 4 **6.** -4 and 1.5
7. -5 and 11 **8.** approximately -6.83 and -1.17 **9.** approximately -0.74 and 10.12
10. It will reach the ground in approximately 2.45 seconds. **11.** 12 items can be produced. **12.** -2 and 3
13. $-\dfrac{7}{2}$ and $\dfrac{11}{3}$ **14.** -1 and 8 **15.** -5 and 12 **16.** -4 and $\dfrac{1}{3}$ **17.** $\dfrac{4}{3}$ and $\dfrac{3}{2}$ **18.** $\dfrac{5}{2}$ and -7

19. $\pm\dfrac{7}{3}$ **20.** The ball will hit the ground in approximately 3.3 seconds. **21.** 5 **22.** -7 **23.** 15

24. $3\sqrt{35}$ **25.** $2\sqrt{2}$ **26.** $\dfrac{8}{9}$ **27.** $\dfrac{\sqrt{13}}{5}$ **28.** $\dfrac{5\sqrt{3}}{3}$ **29.** $\dfrac{\sqrt{10}}{5}$ **30.** $\dfrac{\sqrt{35}}{7}$ **31.** $\dfrac{\sqrt{3}}{5}$
32. 5 **33.** ± 5 **34.** ± 2 **35.** $\pm 2\sqrt{3}$ **36.** no real-number solution **37.** 1 and 7
38. -13 and -5 **39.** $2 \pm \sqrt{2}$ **40.** It will take $5\sqrt{10}$ seconds or approximately 15.8 seconds.
41. The horizontal distance is $10\sqrt{10}$ ft or approximately 31.6 ft. **42.** The year will be 1998.
43. -8 and 12 **44.** $-6 \pm \sqrt{33}$ **45.** $-\dfrac{3}{2}$ and 4 **46.** $\dfrac{-1 \pm \sqrt{17}}{4}$ **47.** 3 figurines can be purchased.

48. $x^2 + 4x - 45 = 0$; The dimensions are 5 in. by 18 in. **49.** -7 and 9 **50.** $\dfrac{3 \pm \sqrt{21}}{2}$ **51.** $\dfrac{1}{5}$

52. $-\dfrac{3}{4}$ and $\dfrac{2}{5}$ **53.** -4.5 and 2.4 **54.** no real-number solution **55.** $5 \pm \sqrt{19}$ **56.** $\dfrac{2 \pm 2\sqrt{10}}{3}$

57. no real-number solution **58.** one rational solution **59.** two rational solutions
60. two irrational solutions **61.** The interest rate would be 8%. **62.** The interest is about 9.5%.
63. For a value of 17.33, the revenue will be approximately $450. **64.** The hypotenuse is 61 in.
65. The pond is 70 feet wide. **66.** The dimensions are 36 ft by 27 ft.; No, the corners are not square.
67. The length of the legs is $8.425\sqrt{2}$ cm, or approximately 11.91 cm.
68. The rope is $7\sqrt{2}$ ft or approximately 9.9 feet. **69.** The lengths of the sides are 10 in. and $10\sqrt{3}$ in.

70. $d = \dfrac{2\sqrt{\pi A}}{\pi}$ **71.** $x = \pm\dfrac{\sqrt{b(a - c)}}{b}$ **72.** $t = \dfrac{-v_0 \pm \sqrt{(v_0)^2 + 64(s_0 - s)}}{-32}$

73. all integers greater than or equal to -6 and less than or equal to 4
74 all integers less than -2 or greater than 2
75. $(-\infty, -4] \cup [2, \infty)$ **76.** $[-3, 3]$ **77.** $(-1, 4)$ **78.** no solution **79.** $(-\infty, 3) \cup (3, \infty)$ **80.** 4
81. $(1.59, 4.41)$ **82.** $\left(2 - \frac{2}{3}\sqrt{6}, 2 + \frac{2}{3}\sqrt{6}\right)$ **83.** $[-3, 2]$ **84.** $(-1, 3)$ **85.** $(-\infty, -3) \cup (-3, \infty)$
86. $(-\infty, \infty)$ **87.** no solution **88.** $(3 - \sqrt{10}, 3 + \sqrt{10})$ **89.** $R(x) = -2x^2 + 55x + 325$; The order must be greater than 8 items but less than 29 items. **90.** The booth can be rented up to 4 days.
91. The dart is above the ground from 0 seconds to approximately 2.358 seconds.

CHAPTER 11 MIXED REVIEW

1. -12 **2.** $5\sqrt{5}$ **3.** 14 **4.** $\frac{11}{15}$ **5.** $\frac{2\sqrt{10}}{15}$ **6.** $\frac{3}{2}$ **7.** -1 and 3 **8.** -3 and 3 **9.** -5 and -1

10. $-2\frac{2}{3}$ and $1\frac{4}{5}$ **11.** -3 and 1 **12.** approximately -8.14 and -0.86 **13.** approximately -0.85 and 5.65

14. -4 and 10 **15.** -5 and 9 **16.** -1 and 5 **17.** $-\frac{3}{4}$ and $\frac{2}{3}$ **18.** -11 and 8 **19.** -7 and $\frac{2}{5}$

20. $\pm\frac{4}{7}$ **21.** ± 6 **22.** no real-number solution **23.** 5 and 13 **24.** $7 \pm \sqrt{3}$ **25.** $-6 \pm \sqrt{3}$

26. $\frac{-7 \pm \sqrt{37}}{2}$ **27.** -3.6 and 1.2 **28.** -6 and 13 **29.** -14 and -6 **30.** $-\frac{5}{2}$ and 1 **31.** $\frac{-4 \pm 3\sqrt{2}}{2}$

32. $-4 \pm 2\sqrt{3}$ **33.** $\frac{7 \pm \sqrt{57}}{2}$ **34.** $\frac{5}{6}$ **35.** no real-number solution **36.** -11 and 5 **37.** -4 and $\frac{9}{4}$

38. $x = \frac{-1 \pm \sqrt{1 + 8a}}{2}$ **39.** $y = \sqrt{r^2 - x^2 - z^2}$ **40.** $r = \pm\frac{\sqrt{A\pi}}{2\pi}$ **41.** all integers greater than or equal to -3 and less than or equal to 5 **42.** all integers greater than or equal to -7 and less than or equal to 2
43. $(-6, 1)$ **44.** $(-\infty, -3) \cup (5, \infty)$ **45.** $(-\infty, -1 - \sqrt{2}) \cup (-1 + \sqrt{2}, \infty)$
46. $(-\infty, 4 - 3\sqrt{2}) \cup (4 + 3\sqrt{2}, \infty)$ **47.** $\left[-\frac{5}{3}, 6\right]$ **48.** $(-\infty, -3] \cup [4, \infty)$ **49.** $(-\infty, -1] \cup [6, \infty)$
50. no solution **51.** $(-3, 5)$ **52.** $(-4, 4)$ **53.** $(-\infty, -3.58) \cup (-0.42, \infty)$ **54.** $(-\infty, -5) \cup (-5, \infty)$
55. $(0.88, 5.12)$ **56.** 3 **57.** The notebook will reach the ground in $\sqrt{10}$ seconds or approximately 3.16 seconds. **58.** The number is about 16 items. **59.** It will reach the ground in $2 + \sqrt{6}$ seconds or approximately 4.45 seconds. **60.** It will take $\sqrt{437.5}$ seconds or approximately 20.92 seconds.
61. The other leg is 25.5 meters. **62.** The dimensions are 8 cm by 18 cm. **63.** The interest rate is 5%.
64. The interest rate is approximately 11.8%. **65.** A value of about 11 will yield a revenue of about $650.
66. The hypotenuse is 52 inches. **67.** The pond is 120 ft wide. **68.** The legs measure 12 in. and 35 in.
69. They each measure $7.105\sqrt{2}$ cm or approximately 10 cm.
70. The rope is $11\sqrt{2}$ feet long or approximately 15.6 feet. **71.** The sides measure 16 in. and $16\sqrt{3}$ in.
72. The booth can be rented up to 7 days.

CHAPTER 11 TEST

1. -2 and 8 **2.** $-5.5, -2,$ and 3 **3.** 1 and 9 **4.** no real-number solution **5.** 0.5 and 4

6. -0.82 and 1.82 **7.** $[-3, 4]$ **8.** all integers greater than -3 and less than 5 **9.** $(-\infty, -4) \cup \left[\frac{5}{2}, \infty\right)$

10. two irrational solutions; $8 \pm 5\sqrt{2}$ **11.** no real-number solutions **12.** $t = \pm\frac{\sqrt{a(s - c)}}{a}$

13. **(a)** -2 and 3 **(b)** -2 and 3 **(c)** -2 and 3 **14.** The legs are 12 in. and 16 in.
15. Keanu was free-falling for about 24 seconds. **16.** The interest rate must be approximately 6%.
17. You can rent for up to 3 additional days. **18.** Answers will vary.

Chapter 12

PROBLEM SET 12.1

Experiencing Algebra the Exercise Way

1. rational expression and an algebraic fraction   **2.** not a rational expression   **3.** rational expression

4. rational expression   **5.** not a rational expression   **6.** rational expression   **7.** rational expression

8. not a rational expression   **9.** rational expression and an algebraic fraction   **10.** not a rational expression

11. rational expression   **12.** rational expression   **13.** rational expression and an algebraic fraction

14. rational expression   **15.** not a rational expression   **16.** rational expression and an algebraic fraction

17. $0; x \neq 0$ **18.** -5 and $-3; x \neq -5, x \neq -3$ **19.** 5 and $6; x \neq 5, x \neq 6$ **20.** -3 and $0; x \neq -3, x \neq 0$

21. -2 and $2; x \neq -2, x \neq 2$ **22.** $-1, 1,$ and $4; x \neq -1, x \neq 1, x \neq 4$ **23.** 0 and $5x \neq 0; x \neq 5$ **24.** $0; x \neq 0$

25. $2; x \neq 2$ **26.** $-2; x \neq -2$ **27.** -5 and $-\dfrac{7}{2}; x \neq -5; x \neq -\dfrac{7}{2}$ **28.** $-\dfrac{3}{5}; x \neq -\dfrac{3}{5}$

29. $-\dfrac{3}{2}$ and $\dfrac{3}{4}; x \neq -\dfrac{3}{2}, x \neq \dfrac{3}{4}$ **30.** $-5, -4,$ and $4; x \neq -5, x \neq -4, x \neq 4$ **31.** $-\dfrac{9}{2}; x \neq -\dfrac{9}{2}$

32. $-\dfrac{9}{7}$ and $-\dfrac{1}{2}; x \neq -\dfrac{9}{7}, x \neq -\dfrac{1}{2}$ **33.** $11; x \neq 11$ **34.** no restricted values; all real numbers

35. $-\dfrac{5}{3}$ and $\dfrac{5}{3}; x \neq -\dfrac{5}{3}, x \neq \dfrac{5}{3}$ **36.** -3 and $\dfrac{5}{6}; x \neq -3, x \neq \dfrac{5}{6}$ **37.** $-3, -2,$ and $3; x \neq -3, x \neq -2, x \neq 3$

38. $-\dfrac{7}{4}$ and $\dfrac{7}{4}; x \neq -\dfrac{7}{4}, x \neq \dfrac{7}{4}$ **39.** no restricted values; all real numbers   **40.** $\dfrac{4}{3}; x \neq \dfrac{4}{3}$

41. $-\dfrac{3}{2}; x \neq -\dfrac{3}{2}$ **42.** $-\dfrac{3}{2}$ and $\dfrac{6}{5}; x \neq -\dfrac{3}{2}, x \neq \dfrac{6}{5}$ **43.** $(-3, -1), (-1, 3), (0, \text{undefined}), (1, 15),$ and $(3, 3)$

44. $(-3, -17), (-1, -7), (0, -2), (1, 3),$ and $(3, 13)$ **45.** $(-3, 4), (-1, 6), (0, 7), (1, 8),$ and $(3, 10)$

46. $\left(-3, \dfrac{6}{13}\right), (-1, \text{undefined}), (0, 0), (1, 2),$ and $\left(3, \dfrac{3}{7}\right)$ **47.** $\left(-3, -\dfrac{1}{2}\right), \left(-1, -\dfrac{1}{2}\right), (0, 0), \left(1, \dfrac{1}{2}\right),$ and

$\left(3, \dfrac{1}{2}\right)$ **48.** $(-3, -7), (-1, -45), (0, \text{undefined}), (1, -27),$ and $(3, -1)$ **49.** $\left(-3, \dfrac{5}{9}\right), (-1, 35),$

$(0, \text{undefined}), (1, 65),$ and $\left(3, \dfrac{95}{9}\right)$ **50.** $\left(-3, -\dfrac{23}{8}\right), \left(-1, -\dfrac{7}{2}\right), (0, 5), \left(1, \dfrac{7}{4}\right),$ and $\left(3, \dfrac{23}{10}\right)$

51. $\left(-3, -\dfrac{5}{3}\right), \left(-1, -\dfrac{1}{2}\right), \left(0, -\dfrac{1}{3}\right), (1, -1),$ and $(3, \text{undefined})$

52. $(-3, -2), (-1, 4), (0, 7), (1, 10)$ and $(3, 16)$ **53.** $(-3, -3), (-1, 1), (0, 3), (1, 5),$ and $(3, 9)$

54. $\left(-3, \dfrac{5}{3}\right), (-1, 7), (0, \text{undefined}), (1, -1),$ and $(3, -1)$

55.

56.

57.

58.

59.

60.

61.

62.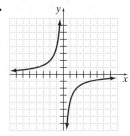

63. (a) $T(x) = \dfrac{26}{x} + \dfrac{110}{x + 20}$

(b)

(c) The total time is approximately 6.7 hours.

(d) The average speeds for running and bicycling are approximately 6.6 mph and 26.6 mph, respectively.

64. (a) $T(x) = \dfrac{1}{x - 2} + \dfrac{1}{x + 2}$

(b)

(c) It will take approximately 2.2 hours.

(d) He should swim at approximately 2.8 mph.

65.

66.

Experiencing Algebra the Calculator Way

1. $(4, 6.8571), (8, 1.7455)$, and $(10, 1.3187)$ **2.** $(-6, -3), (-1, 2), (0, 3), (2, 5), (3, \text{undefined}), (5, 8)$
3. $(-6, -5), (-1, -2.5), (0, -3), (2, -13), (3, \text{undefined}), (5, 17)$ **4.** $(-5, -20), (-2, -8), (0, \text{undefined})$,
$(1, 4), (3, 12), (6, 24)$ **5.** $(-5, -0.05), (-2, -0.125), (0, \text{undefined}), (1, 0.25), (3, 0.08333), (6, 0.04167)$
6. $(-2.5, 4.3333), (-1.3, 17.667), (0, -4), (1.8, -0.7857), (2.7, -0.3514), (5.9, 0.27536)$
7. $(-2.5, 4.3333), (-1.3, 17.667), (0, -4), (1.8, -0.7857), (2.7, -0.3514), (5.9, 0.27536)$

PROBLEM SET 12.2

Experiencing Algebra the Exercise Way

1. $\dfrac{2xz}{3y^3}$ **2.** $\dfrac{3y^3}{5x^2z^2}$ **3.** $-\dfrac{2a}{3c}$ **4.** $-\dfrac{11b^3c}{8a^2}$ **5.** $\dfrac{3(x - 3)}{2(3x - 1)}$ **6.** $\dfrac{2(x + 2)}{3(2x + 1)}$ **7.** -1 **8.** -1

9. $\dfrac{y(x + 2y)}{3 - 4x}$ **10.** $\dfrac{x(5 - 3x)}{y(2x + y)}$ **11.** $\dfrac{-2x + 3y - z}{x - 7y + z}$ **12.** $\dfrac{-x + 4y - 2z}{2x - y + z}$ **13.** $\dfrac{x - 2}{x - 4}$ **14.** $\dfrac{x - 3}{x - 7}$

15. $\dfrac{x - 3}{x + 7}$ **16.** $\dfrac{x + 8}{x - 5}$ **17.** $\dfrac{x + 2}{x - 4}$ **18.** $\dfrac{x + 5}{x - 9}$ **19.** $\dfrac{3x - 2}{2x - 3}$ **20.** $\dfrac{5x - 4}{4x - 5}$ **21.** $\dfrac{(x + 1)(2x + 1)}{2(x - 2)(3x + 1)}$

22. $\dfrac{2(x + 1)(2x - 1)}{3(x + 2)(3x - 1)}$ **23.** $\dfrac{2x - y}{3x + y}$ **24.** $\dfrac{5x - y}{4x + y}$ **25.** $-\dfrac{1}{x + 2}$ **26.** $-\dfrac{1}{x + 3}$ **27.** $\dfrac{2x + 3}{x^2 + 11}$

28. $\dfrac{3x + 4}{x^2 + 9}$ **29.** $\dfrac{28ac}{45b}$ **30.** $\dfrac{9a^2}{10b^2d^2}$ **31.** $-\dfrac{3x^2}{4}$ **32.** $-\dfrac{2y^2}{13x^2}$ **33.** $\dfrac{8.06x^3}{y^2}$ **34.** $\dfrac{21x^2y}{2z}$ **35.** $\dfrac{2a^2}{9b}$

36. $\dfrac{14a^3}{15b^2}$ **37.** $\dfrac{x^2(x+5)}{x+4}$ **38.** $\dfrac{x(x+15)}{x-11}$ **39.** $\dfrac{x-4}{x+4}$ **40.** $\dfrac{x+7}{x-7}$ **41.** $\dfrac{(x+7)(5x+2)}{x(2x+1)}$

42. $\dfrac{(3x+5)(x+4)}{x(2x+9)}$ **43.** $\dfrac{(x-3)(x-1)}{(x+1)(x+3)}$ **44.** $\dfrac{(x+5)(x+2)}{(x-2)(x-5)}$ **45.** $\dfrac{x(x-2y)}{(x+3y)(x-y)}$

46. $\dfrac{y(x+y)}{(x+2y)(x+5y)}$ **47.** $\dfrac{3a^2}{2}$ **48.** $\dfrac{7a}{8b}$ **49.** $-3xyz$ **50.** $-\dfrac{3}{x^2y^2z}$ **51.** $\dfrac{4c}{b}$ **52.** $3ab^2c^2$

53. $-\dfrac{7x}{yz^3}$ **54.** $-\dfrac{2x}{y^3z^2}$ **55.** $\dfrac{1}{5(3a-1)}$ **56.** $\dfrac{7}{6a+1}$ **57.** $(x-4)(5y+2)$ **58.** $(x-7)(4y-3)$

59. $\dfrac{(2x+1)(x-3)}{(x+2)(3x+1)}$ **60.** $\dfrac{(x-4)^2}{(x-1)(3x+2)}$ **61.** $\dfrac{1}{2x+1}$ **62.** $\dfrac{1}{3x-2}$ **63.** $\dfrac{3x+4}{2x+1}$

64. $\dfrac{5x-2}{2x-5}$ **65.** $\dfrac{x+7}{3x-5}$ **66.** $\dfrac{5(2x+1)}{7(4x+3)}$ **67.** $\dfrac{x(x-y)}{y(x+y)}$ **68.** $\dfrac{y(x+2y)}{x(x-2y)}$ **69.** $\dfrac{2(x+2y)}{x-4y}$

70. $\dfrac{4(x+7y)}{3(x-2y)}$ **71.** $\dfrac{170}{x}$ hours; $(x-10)\left(\dfrac{170}{x}\right)$ miles; The distance is 136 miles. **72.** $\dfrac{155}{x}$ hours;

$(x+8)\left(\dfrac{155}{x}\right)$ miles; The distance is $182\dfrac{5}{9}$ miles. **73.** The length is $(5x-1)$ inches.; height: 4 inches;

width: 14 inches; length: 19 inches **74.** The height is $(6x-5)$ inches.; The height is 4 inches.

75. (a) $C(x)=300+5x$; $R(x)=25x$ **(b)** $\dfrac{5x}{60+x}$ **(c)** The ratio is 2.

76. (a) $C(x)=175+25x$; $R(x)=75x$ **(b)** $\dfrac{7+x}{3x}$ **(c)** The ratio is $\dfrac{57}{150}$.

Experiencing Algebra the Calculator Way

1. $x=3$; $x+3$; yes **2.** $x=3$; $\dfrac{x^2+9}{x-3}$; no **3.** $x=0$; $4x$; yes **4.** $x=0$; $\dfrac{1}{4x}$; no **5.** $x=0$; $x-2$; yes

6. $x=0,\dfrac{5}{2}$; $\dfrac{2x-3}{2x-5}$; no **7.** $x=4$; -1; yes **8.** $x=-5,-1$; $\dfrac{x-4}{x+1}$; no **9.** $x=0$; $\dfrac{x^2-6x-16}{2}$; no

10. $x=4$; $2x+5$; yes

PROBLEM SET 12.3

Experiencing Algebra the Exercise Way

1. $\dfrac{13}{x}$ **2.** $\dfrac{12}{x}$ **3.** $-\dfrac{3}{x}$ **4.** $\dfrac{6}{x}$ **5.** $\dfrac{1}{y}$ **6.** $\dfrac{1}{a}$ **7.** $\dfrac{2x}{x+6}$ **8.** $\dfrac{3x}{x+12}$ **9.** $\dfrac{2}{b-5}$ **10.** $\dfrac{3}{z-7}$

11. 3 **12.** 4 **13.** 2 **14.** 3 **15.** $a+3$ **16.** $5+c$ **17.** $\dfrac{5}{x+3}$ **18.** $\dfrac{7}{x+1}$ **19.** $\dfrac{9x+7}{6x^2}$

20. $\dfrac{3(6x+1)}{10x^3}$ **21.** $\dfrac{7x-2}{2(x-6)}$ **22.** $\dfrac{5x-4}{2(x+9)}$ **23.** $\dfrac{2x+3}{2x-3}$ **24.** $\dfrac{2x-3}{5x+2}$ **25.** $\dfrac{3(11x+5)}{(3x-5)(3x+5)}$

26. $\dfrac{6(4x-1)}{(2x-3)(2x+3)}$ **27.** $\dfrac{2(4x-17)}{(x-5)^2}$ **28.** $\dfrac{5x-12}{(x-8)^2}$ **29.** $\dfrac{2(b^2+8b+32)}{b(b+8)}$ **30.** $\dfrac{5a^2-6a+9}{2a(a-3)}$

31. $\dfrac{x^2+3x+10}{4(x+3)(x-3)}$ **32.** $\dfrac{2x^2-2x-1}{3(x+2)(x-2)}$ **33.** $\dfrac{2(11x+2)}{(x+5)(x-3)(x+4)}$ **34.** $\dfrac{-x^2+6x-2}{(x+7)(x+1)(x-2)}$

35. $\dfrac{a^2+5ab-b^2}{a^2b^2}$ **36.** $\dfrac{p^2+q^2}{p^2q^2}$ **37.** $\dfrac{3x-4y}{x-2y}$ **38.** $\dfrac{x-3y}{5x-y}$ **39.** $\dfrac{11x-16y}{(x-3y)(x+3y)}$

40. $\dfrac{2(8x+11y)}{(2x-3y)(2x+3y)}$ **41.** $\dfrac{2(5x-9z)}{(x+3z)^2(x-3z)}$ **42.** $\dfrac{4(2x+y)}{(x+2y)^2(x-2y)}$ **43.** $-\dfrac{5}{d}$ **44.** $-\dfrac{8}{b}$

45. $\dfrac{1}{x}$ **46.** $-\dfrac{1}{y}$ **47.** $\dfrac{x}{x+9}$ **48.** $\dfrac{3(x-1)}{x+8}$ **49.** 2 **50.** 2 **51.** $\dfrac{-x+11}{x+11}$ **52.** $\dfrac{-2x+9}{x+13}$

53. $z - 4$ **54.** $c - 7$ **55.** $\dfrac{3}{c + 3}$ **56.** $\dfrac{5}{b + 2}$ **57.** $\dfrac{2(x + 2)}{2x + 3}$ **58.** $\dfrac{-2x + 3}{3x - 4}$ **59.** $\dfrac{4(2x + 1)}{x - 2}$

60. $\dfrac{3x + 1}{x - 7}$ **61.** $\dfrac{3}{x - 2}$ **62.** $\dfrac{5}{a - 6}$ **63.** $\dfrac{x}{x + 5}$ **64.** $\dfrac{8x + 17}{3(2x + 3)}$ **65.** $\dfrac{-4(x - 20)}{(2x - 5)(2x + 5)}$

66. $\dfrac{15x + 13}{(3x - 1)(3x + 1)}$ **67.** $\dfrac{-x(2x + 13)}{(x + 6)^2}$ **68.** $\dfrac{-x^2 + 11x - 25}{(x - 7)^2}$ **69.** $\dfrac{16(x - 4)}{x(8 - x)}$ **70.** $\dfrac{-20(x - 5)}{x(x - 10)}$

71. $\dfrac{x - 1}{3(x + 4)}$ **72.** $\dfrac{-2x + 27}{x(x + 3)(x - 3)}$ **73.** $\dfrac{15b + 34}{(b + 3)(b - 3)(2b + 5)}$ **74.** $\dfrac{19a - 31}{(a - 5)(a + 5)(2a + 1)}$

75. $\dfrac{14a - 15b - 15a^2b}{10a^2b^2}$ **76.** $\dfrac{15y - 4xy - 56x}{48x^2y^2}$ **77.** $\dfrac{3(p - q)}{p + 3q}$ **78.** $\dfrac{x + 3z}{x + 5z}$ **79.** $\dfrac{5x - 27y}{(x + 3y)^2(x - 3y)}$

80. $\dfrac{5(x - 11y)}{(x + 5y)^2(x - 5y)}$ **81.** $\dfrac{x - 4}{x - 5}$ **82.** $\dfrac{2z + 3}{z + 9}$ **83.** $\dfrac{2x + 1}{x + 10}$ **84.** $\dfrac{10x + 3}{3x + 1}$ **85.** $\dfrac{10x + 31}{2x + 7}$

86. $\dfrac{4}{x + 4}$ **87.** $\dfrac{x - 10}{x + 7}$ **88.** $\dfrac{-31x + 16}{9x - 2}$ **89.** $\dfrac{x^2 + 8x + 18}{x + 3}$ **90.** $\dfrac{x^2 + 4x + 5}{x + 1}$ **91.** $\dfrac{2x^2 - 7x - 7}{x - 4}$

92. $\dfrac{-10x(2x - 1)}{4x - 1}$ **93. (a)** The total width is $\dfrac{65}{L}$ feet. **(b)** The total width is $\dfrac{5(17L - 20)}{L(2L - 5)}$ feet.

94. (a) The difference is $\dfrac{8}{L}$ inches. **(b)** The difference is $\dfrac{4(4L - 15)}{L(2L + 5)}$ inches.

95. The perimeter is $\dfrac{96(2x - 1)}{(x - 1)(x + 1)}$ feet. **96.** The perimeter is $\dfrac{x^2 + 246x + 117}{2x(x + 3)}$ inches.

97. (a) The ratio is $\dfrac{11x}{20 + 5x}$. **(b)** The ratio is $\dfrac{2x}{40 + x}$. **(c)** $\dfrac{x(x + 400)}{5(4 + x)(40 + x)}$ **(d)** $\dfrac{125}{182}$

98. (a) The ratio is $\dfrac{x(25 - x)}{5(x + 2)}$. **(b)** The ratio is $\dfrac{20 - x}{4}$. **(c)** $\dfrac{(x + 20)(x - 10)}{20(x + 2)}$ **(d)** $\dfrac{10}{11}$

99. The sum is $\dfrac{s + 2}{s(s + 1)}$. **100.** The sum is $\dfrac{10(s + 3)}{s(s + 1)}$.

Experiencing Algebra the Calculator Way

1. $\dfrac{2x^2 - 3}{x(x - 1)}$ **2.** $\dfrac{4x - 3}{x(x - 1)}$ **3.** $\dfrac{x^2 + 5x + 2}{(x - 2)(x + 2)}$ **4.** $\dfrac{x^2 + 3x + 6}{(x + 2)(x - 2)}$ **5.** $\dfrac{2}{x - 2}$ **6.** 0

PROBLEM SET 12.4

Experiencing Algebra the Exercise Way

1. rational **2.** not rational **3.** rational **4.** not rational **5.** not rational **6.** rational
7. not rational **8.** not rational **9.** rational **10.** rational **11.** rational **12.** rational
13. not rational **14.** rational **15.** rational **16.** rational **17.** -7 and 7 **18.** -9 and 9
19. -2 and 3 **20.** 5 **21.** 6 **22.** 1 **23.** 3 **24.** 4 **25.** 6 **26.** 2 and 3 **27.** 2 **28.** -3
29. 6 **30.** 5 **31.** 10 **32.** -38 and 3 **33.** 3 **34.** -2 **35.** 4 **36.** -2 **37.** -2 and 3
38. 0 and 1 **39.** all integers not equal to -1 or 1 **40.** all integers not equal to -3 or 3 **41.** no solution

42. no solution **43.** 4 **44.** 7 **45.** $\dfrac{1}{2}$ and 10 **46.** -3 and $1\dfrac{1}{3}$ **47.** $\dfrac{1}{3}$ **48.** 2 **49.** 0.8 **50.** 0.5

51. 3.5 **52.** $1\dfrac{2}{3}$ **53.** approximately -2.8117 and 2.3117 **54.** approximately -6.6714 and 5.1714

55. 8 and 15 **56.** -4 and -1 **57.** approximately -2.5811 and 0.5811
58. approximately -1.5774 and -0.4226 **59.** approximately -1.8019, -0.4450, and 1.2470
60. approximately -0.8810 and 0.6810 **61.** approximately 0.1878 and 1.7752
62. approximately 0.3077 and 1.5 **63.** approximately -0.3024 and 1.2399
64. approximately -0.2758 and 3.4187 **65.** approximately -0.4066 and 0.6086

66. approximately -0.3548 and 0.7878 **67.** no solution **68.** no solution

69. all real numbers except $b = 2$ and $b = 1$ **70.** all real numbers except $x = -\dfrac{3}{2}$ and $x = 2$

71. $\dfrac{85.56}{x} = \dfrac{53.22}{x - 1200}$; His monthly salary is \$3174.77. **72.** $\dfrac{3000}{x} = \dfrac{4000}{x + 8000}$; Her current salary is \$24,000 and her new salary is \$32,000. **73.** $\dfrac{132}{x} = \dfrac{225}{x + 1.6}$; His first time is 2.3 hours and his second time is 3.9 hours.

74. $\dfrac{17}{x} = \dfrac{21}{x + 0.3}$; Her first time was 1.275 hours and her second time was 1.575 hours.

75. The interest on the first account is 6.5% and on the second account is 4.5.%. **76.** The first investment was for 2 years and the second for 3.5 years. **77.** The resistance of the second vessel is 26.2 dynes. **78.** The constant for the second spring is 2 pounds per square inch.

Experiencing Algebra the Calculator Way

Answers will vary.

PROBLEM SET 12.5

Experiencing Algebra the Exercise Way

1. $\dfrac{9}{11}$ **2.** $\dfrac{63}{8}$ **3.** -21 **4.** $\dfrac{30}{7}$ **5.** 8 **6.** -24 **7.** 18 **8.** 14 **9.** 12 **10.** 2 **11.** 22

12. 15 **13.** -7 **14.** $\dfrac{3}{2}$ **15.** 12 **16.** 5 **17.** 5 **18.** $\dfrac{19}{3}$ **19.** 9 **20.** -5 **21.** 7 **22.** 11

23. $\dfrac{3}{4}$ **24.** $\dfrac{4}{7}$ **25.** -6 **26.** -4 **27.** 1 **28.** -2 and 5 **29.** ± 4 **30.** ± 9 **31.** ± 7 **32.** ± 8

33. -2 and 5 **34.** -7 and 4 **35.** 4 **36.** $-\dfrac{1}{4}$ **37.** -3 **38.** 6 **39.** -6 and -2 **40.** -8 and -5

41. 4 and 8 **42.** 1 and 6 **43.** -4 and 9 **44.** -3 and 5 **45.** 7 **46.** 6 **47.** $\dfrac{1}{2}$ and 8 **48.** -5

49. $\dfrac{1}{12}$ **50.** 2 **51.** -15 **52.** $\dfrac{56}{11}$ **53.** $\pm \dfrac{1}{3}$ **54.** $\pm \dfrac{1}{4}$ **55.** -6 and 10 **56.** -7 and 2

57. no solution **58.** -13 **59.** 11 **60.** -8 **61.** 5 **62.** -7 and 6 **63.** -9 and 1 **64.** -9

65. -4 and 8 **66.** -3 and 5 **67.** all real numbers not equal to 1 **68.** no solution **69.** no solution

70. all real numbers not equal to 6 **71.** -2 **72.** no solution **73.** $-\dfrac{11}{2}$ and 6 **74.** -11 and 3

75. The resistance of the resistors is 10 ohms and 15 ohms, respectively.
76. The resistance of the resistors is 5 ohms and 20 ohms, respectively.
77. They should raise and spend \$27.27. **78.** He must raise another \$50.
79. The height should be increased by 6 feet. **80.** Jim should add 4.5 feet to the width.

Experiencing Algebra the Calculator Way

Answers will vary.

PROBLEM SET 12.6

Experiencing Algebra the Exercise Way

1. It will take them 1.75 hours working together. **2.** It will take them 18 minutes working together.
3. It takes Jacques 10 hours and Simone 5 hours. **4.** It will take Joe about 2.58 hours and Mary Lynne about 3.58 hours. **5.** It will take 3.6 hours working together. **6.** It will take 9.375 minutes working together.
7. It will take approximately 2.55 hours for both pipes together. **8.** It will take 3 hours to drain when both

are used. **9.** It takes Line A 8 hours and Line B 12 hours. **10.** It will take the first line about 8.3 hours and the second line about 9.8 hours. **11.** He can buy 28.35 shares for $1800. **12.** He recovered $972.04.

13. There must be an additional 15 points. **14.** An additional $\frac{1}{3}$ liter of pure vinegar should be added.

15. $\overline{XY}$ measures 4 inches; $\overline{PR}$ measures 18 inches **16.** $\overline{MN}$ measures 2 mm; $\overline{KL}$ measures 28 mm
17. $\overline{PQ}$ measures 10.075 cm; $\overline{YZ}$ measures 1.76 cm **18.** $\overline{JK}$ measures 16.56 yards; $\overline{MO}$ measures 18.3 yards
19. $\overline{QR}$ measures $4\frac{3}{8}$ feet; $\overline{XZ}$ measures $2\frac{1}{4}$ feet **20.** $\overline{JL}$ measures $29\frac{1}{4}$ feet; $\overline{NO}$ measures $9\frac{1}{4}$ feet
21. The estimated height is 48.125 feet. **22.** The flag pole is 15 feet high.

Experiencing Algebra the Calculator Way

1. $P(x) = 2x + 2\left(\dfrac{25}{x}\right)$; The dimensions are $\dfrac{5}{2}$ feet by 10 feet. **2.** It will take Becky 12 hours and Tom
6 hours. **3.** It will take an additional $9\frac{1}{3}$ hours. **4.** $f(x) = \dfrac{9 + 0.55x}{x}$; She should bake 45 dozen.

CHAPTER 12 REVIEW

Reflections

1–6. Answers will vary.

Exercises

1. rational expression **2.** non-rational expression **3.** rational expression **4.** rational expression

5. $0; x \neq 0$ **6.** -8 and $3; x \neq -8, x \neq 3$ **7.** no restricted values; all real numbers

8. $\pm\dfrac{3}{2}; x \neq -\dfrac{3}{2}, x \neq \dfrac{3}{2}$ **9.** $(-2, 30), (-1, 150), (0, \text{undefined}), (1, 210),$ and $(2, 60)$

10. $\left(-2, \dfrac{1}{4}\right), (-1, \text{undefined}),$ **11.** **12.**
$\left(0, -\dfrac{3}{2}\right), (1, -2),$ and
$(2, \text{undefined})$

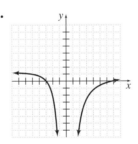

13. (a) $t(x) = \dfrac{125}{10 + x} + \dfrac{80}{x}$ **(c)** The trip took 5.8 hours. **14.** $-\dfrac{4x}{9y^2}$ **15.** $\dfrac{p - 3}{3p + 5}$ **16.** $-\dfrac{1}{2x}$

(b) **(d)** Gretchen's speed was 40 mph **17.** $\dfrac{2x - 5}{4x + 1}$ **18.** $\dfrac{b - 7}{b^2 + 2}$

and Bob's speed was 50 mph. **19.** $-\dfrac{3y}{14x^2}$ **20.** $\dfrac{a^2 + 6a + 5}{a - 4}$

21. $\dfrac{4}{(m + 5)(2m + 7)}$ **22.** -1

23. $-\dfrac{x}{6y^2}$ **24.** $-\dfrac{1}{15}$ **25.** $-\dfrac{6yz^2}{5x}$

26. $\dfrac{6a^3b^3}{c^3d^2}$ **27.** $\dfrac{(x + 3)(x + 1)^2}{5(x - 2)}$ **28.** $\dfrac{3x}{2z^4}$ **29.** $14ac^2$ **30.** $\dfrac{x + 2}{x^2 + 4}$ **31.** $(x + 1)(2x + 3)$

32. $\dfrac{(a+3)(a+4)}{(a+6)(a+2)}$　　**33.** 1　　**34.** His average speed is $\dfrac{220}{t}$ mph.; His new distance is $\dfrac{110(t+2)}{t}$ miles.

35. The height is $(x+3)$ inches.　　**36. (a)** $C(x)=500+40x$; $R(x)=80x$　　**(b)** The ratio is $\dfrac{25+2x}{4x}$.

37. $\dfrac{y(3+7y)}{5x}$　　**38.** $\dfrac{b(5b^2-2)}{7a}$　　**39.** 2　　**40.** $\dfrac{10x^2+10x+3}{(2x-3)(2x+3)}$　　**41.** $\dfrac{12y+7x}{15x^3y^2}$

42. $\dfrac{x(7x+4)}{(x-8)(x+4)}$　　**43.** $\dfrac{44}{(2x-1)(x+5)}$　　**44.** $\dfrac{3}{x-y}$　　**45.** $\dfrac{2(13x+4)}{5(3x-4)(3x+4)}$

46. $\dfrac{29x-3}{(2x+1)(x-3)(3x-2)}$　　**47.** $\dfrac{x+55}{2(x-9)(x+9)}$　　**48.** $\dfrac{10(2x-1)}{(2x-3)(x+2)(3x-2)}$

49. $\dfrac{5(x-9)}{(x+5)(x-5)}$　　**50.** $\dfrac{37x^2-32x-44}{6x(x+2)}$　　**51.** The perimeter is $\dfrac{5x^2-4x-5}{2x(x+1)}$ units.

52. The length is $\dfrac{4x+3}{x}$ units.　　**53.** not rational　　**54.** rational　　**55.** rational　　**56.** not rational

57. rational　　**58.** rational　　**59.** -8 and 4　　**60.** all integers equal to -3　　**61.** -4 and 4　　**62.** no solution
63. -8 and 8　　**64.** no solution　　**65.** -3 and 5　　**66.** all real numbers except 0　　**67.** -4 and 0.75

68. $\dfrac{70}{x}=\dfrac{91}{x+0.6}$; The times were 2 hours and 2.6 hours.　　**69.** The resistance of the two resistors are

44 ohms and 93 ohms.　　**70.** 7　　**71.** -3 and $\dfrac{1}{2}$　　**72.** 5　　**73.** ±10　　**74.** -5 and 6　　**75.** -4

76. $\pm\dfrac{1}{5}$　　**77.** -3 and 4　　**78.** no solution　　**79.** -3 and $\dfrac{9}{2}$　　**80.** no solution　　**81.** 5　　**82.** -4

83. all real numbers except -4　　**84.** $-\dfrac{3}{2}$ and 4　　**85.** The resistances of the two resistors are 20 ohms and

30 ohms.　　**86.** She should add another \$40.　　**87.** It will take them $\dfrac{24}{7}$ hours or approximately 3.4 hours.

88. It will take Viv 55.4 minutes and Lucy 65.4 minutes.　　**89.** It will take 6 minutes working together.

90. It will take the high speed line $5\dfrac{1}{4}$ hours and the other line $10\dfrac{1}{2}$ hours working alone.

91. He will earn \$61.67.　　**92.** Another 2 cups should be added.

93. (a) $\overline{GI}$ measures 12 in.; $\overline{KL}$ measures 14 in.　　**(b)** $\overline{HI}$ measures $7\dfrac{3}{4}$ feet; $\overline{JL}$ measures $9\dfrac{3}{4}$ feet

(c) $\overline{GH}$ measures 7.52 feet; $\overline{JL}$ measures 3.52 feet　　**94.** The bluff is 48 feet high.
95. The tree's shadow was 96 feet long.

CHAPTER 12 MIXED REVIEW

1. $(-2, 3.75)$, $(-1, 30)$, $(0, \text{undefined})$, $(1, 60)$, and $(2, 18.75)$

2. $\left(-2, -\dfrac{3}{2}\right)$, $(-1, \text{undefined})$, $\left(0, \dfrac{5}{4}\right)$, $\left(1, \dfrac{3}{5}\right)$, and $\left(2, \dfrac{7}{18}\right)$

3.

4.

5. -7 and 3　　**6.** no solution

7. all real numbers except -3

8. ±8　　**9.** all real numbers except 0

10. -1 and $\dfrac{4}{5}$　　**11.** -9 and 9　　**12.** no solution

13. -7 and 2

14. no restricted values; all real numbers

15. $\pm\dfrac{5}{3}; x \neq -\dfrac{5}{3}, x \neq \dfrac{5}{3}$ **16.** $0; x \neq 0$ **17.** -2 and $\dfrac{4}{3}; x \neq -2, x \neq \dfrac{4}{3}$ **18.** $\dfrac{3x+4}{2x+3}$ **19.** $\dfrac{k+5}{k^2+6}$

20. $-\dfrac{3x^3}{4y^4}$ **21.** $\dfrac{q-3}{2(q+2)}$ **22.** $\dfrac{-2x}{3(x+2)}$ **23.** $\dfrac{x-25}{(3x+2)(x-3)}$ **24.** $\dfrac{5}{a-b}$ **25.** $\dfrac{b(7+5b)}{3a}$

26. $\dfrac{p(3p-2)}{4m}$ **27.** $\dfrac{5+2y^2}{4x^2y^3}$ **28.** $\dfrac{x(5x+7)}{(x+3)(x-5)}$ **29.** $\dfrac{8x+5}{3(2x-5)(2x+5)}$

30. $\dfrac{31x+9}{(2x-1)(x+3)(3x+2)}$ **31.** 2 **32.** $\dfrac{2x-1}{5x+4}$ **33.** $\dfrac{x-30}{(x+6)(x-6)}$ **34.** $\dfrac{x^2-9x-6}{4x(x+1)}$

35. $\dfrac{x-27}{2(x+5)(x-5)}$ **36.** $\dfrac{7x-2}{(4x-5)(x-3)(5x-4)}$ **37.** $\dfrac{3(m+6)}{2m+5}$ **38.** -1 **39.** $-\dfrac{10b^2}{9a^3}$

40. $\dfrac{(2c+3)(c+7)}{c+3}$ **41.** $-\dfrac{a}{3b^2}$ **42.** $-\dfrac{1}{4}$ **43.** $-\dfrac{4g^4k}{3h^2}$ **44.** $\dfrac{6p^3q^7}{5m^3n^4}$ **45.** $\dfrac{75m^2p^3}{2}$ **46.** $\dfrac{2x-3}{4x^2+9}$

47. $\dfrac{(x+2)^2}{2}$ **48.** $\dfrac{5b^2}{3c^7}$ **49.** $\dfrac{(z-3)(z+8)}{(z-6)(z+4)}$ **50.** 1 **51.** $(x+5)(2x+1)$ **52.** 4 **53.** 4

54. -3 **55.** 6 **56.** approximately -0.51 and 4.71 **57.** -2 **58.** 0 **59.** $\dfrac{1}{3}$ and 8 **60.** 5

61. $-\dfrac{1}{7}$ and $\dfrac{1}{5}$ **62.** no solution **63.** $-\dfrac{7}{4}$ **64.** 15 **65.** -4 **66.** $\dfrac{7}{2}$ **67.** 5

68. approximately -4.01 and 6.51 **69.** all real numbers except 3 **70.** It will take them $\dfrac{70}{17}$ hours or

approximately 4.1 hours. **71.** Another $\dfrac{1}{7}$ pint of glue is needed. **72.** She would earn \$70.

73. His average rate of speed is $\dfrac{120}{t}$ mph.; The new distance is $\dfrac{80(t+1)}{t}$ miles. **74.** The tree is 24 feet high.

75. The height is $(2x+1)$ inches. **76.** It would take the first line 6 hours and the second line 7.5 hours

working alone. **77.** The perimeter is $\dfrac{(4x-3)(x-1)}{x(x-3)}$ units. **78.** She needs an additional \$20.

79. She drove 273 miles. **80.** Each resistor is approximately 45 ohms and 57 ohms.

CHAPTER 12 TEST

1. -3 and $0; x \neq -3, x \neq 0$ **3.**
2. -4 and $9; x \neq -4, x \neq 9$

4. $\dfrac{8}{3x-7}$ **5.** $\dfrac{2z(z-3)}{z^2+9}$ **6.** $\dfrac{7x-15}{x(x+4)(x-3)}$

7. $\dfrac{1}{2}$ **8.** $\dfrac{x^2+15x+5}{x(x+5)^2}$ **9.** $\dfrac{9(x-2y)}{2x(x+y)}$

10. **(a)** -1 and 5 **(b)** -1 and 5 **(c)** -1 and 5

11. $11 \pm 4\sqrt{7}$ **12.** no real number solutions

13. ± 15 **14.** -2 and $-\dfrac{1}{3}$ **15.** 3 **16.** 0

17. $-4, -1.34$, and 0.5 **18.** The height is $21\dfrac{2}{3}$ feet. **19.** Jill can rake the leaves in 4 hours.

20. Answers will vary.

Chapter 13

PROBLEM SET 13.1

Experiencing Algebra the Exercise Way

1. 9 **2.** 7 **3.** 1.2 **4.** 1.3 **5.** $\dfrac{2}{3}$ **6.** $\dfrac{5}{6}$ **7.** $\dfrac{-1}{3}$ **8.** $\dfrac{-2}{3}$ **9.** -5 **10.** -7

11. not a real number **12.** not a real number **13.** 6 **14.** 11 **15.** -6 **16.** -11 **17.** -6 **18.** -11
19. 10.488 **20.** 14.142 **21.** -10.488 **22.** -14.142 **23.** not a real number **24.** not a real number
25. 4.791 **26.** 5.848 **27.** -4.791 **28.** -5.848 **29.** 1.821 **30.** 1.710 **31.** 2.321 **32.** 2.921
33. $\sqrt{36} = 6$ **34.** $\sqrt{100} = 10$ **35.** $\sqrt[3]{216} = 6$ **36.** $\sqrt[3]{729} = 9$ **37.** $-\sqrt[4]{81} = -3$
38. $-\sqrt[4]{625} = -5$ **39.** $\sqrt[4]{-81}$, not a real number **40.** $\sqrt[4]{-625}$, not a real number **41.** $-\sqrt[3]{8} = -2$

42. $-\sqrt[3]{27} = -3$ **43.** $\sqrt[3]{-8} = -2$ **44.** $\sqrt[3]{-27} = -3$ **45.** $\dfrac{1}{\sqrt{36}} = \dfrac{1}{6}$ **46.** $\dfrac{1}{\sqrt{100}} = \dfrac{1}{10}$

47. $\dfrac{1}{\sqrt[3]{216}} = \dfrac{1}{6}$ **48.** $\dfrac{1}{\sqrt[3]{729}} = \dfrac{1}{9}$ **49.** $\dfrac{1}{\sqrt[4]{81}} = \dfrac{1}{3}$ **50.** $\dfrac{1}{\sqrt[4]{625}} = \dfrac{1}{5}$ **51.** $-\dfrac{1}{\sqrt[4]{81}} = -\dfrac{1}{3}$

52. $\dfrac{1}{\sqrt[4]{-625}}$, not a real number **53.** $\dfrac{1}{\sqrt[3]{8}} = \dfrac{1}{2}$ **54.** $\dfrac{1}{\sqrt[3]{27}} = \dfrac{1}{3}$ **55.** $\dfrac{1}{\sqrt[3]{-8}} = -\dfrac{1}{2}$ **56.** $\dfrac{1}{\sqrt[3]{-27}} = -\dfrac{1}{3}$
57. $\sqrt{522} \approx 22.847$ **58.** $\sqrt[3]{478} \approx 7.819$ **59.** $\sqrt[4]{522} \approx 4.780$ **60.** $\sqrt[5]{478} \approx 3.435$

61. $\dfrac{1}{\sqrt[3]{522}} \approx 0.124$ **62.** $\dfrac{1}{\sqrt{478}} \approx 0.046$ **63.** $\dfrac{1}{\sqrt[5]{522}} \approx 0.286$ **64.** $\dfrac{1}{\sqrt[4]{478}} \approx 0.214$ **65.** $(\sqrt[3]{27})^4 = 81$

66. $(\sqrt{25})^3 = 125$ **67.** $(\sqrt[3]{-27})^4 = 81$ **68.** $(\sqrt{-25})^3$, not a real number **69.** $\dfrac{1}{(\sqrt[3]{27})^4} = \dfrac{1}{81}$

70. $\dfrac{1}{(\sqrt{25})^3} = \dfrac{1}{125}$ **71.** $-\dfrac{1}{(\sqrt[3]{27})^4} = -\dfrac{1}{81}$ **72.** $-\dfrac{1}{(\sqrt{25})^3} = -\dfrac{1}{125}$ **73.** $(\sqrt{4})^5 = 32$

74. $(\sqrt{9})^3 = 27$ **75.** $(\sqrt[3]{8})^7 = 128$ **76.** $(\sqrt[3]{125})^5 = 3125$ **77.** $\dfrac{1}{(\sqrt{4})^7} = \dfrac{1}{128}$ **78.** $\dfrac{1}{(\sqrt{16})^5} = \dfrac{1}{1024}$

79. $-(\sqrt{16})^3 = -64$ **80.** $-(\sqrt{64})^3 = -512$ **81.** $(\sqrt{-9})^3$, not a real number

82. $(\sqrt{-4})^3$, not a real number **83.** $-\dfrac{1}{(\sqrt{81})^3} = -\dfrac{1}{729}$ **84.** $-\dfrac{1}{(\sqrt{36})^3} = -\dfrac{1}{216}$ **85.** $(\sqrt[4]{28})^5 \approx 64.409$

86. $(\sqrt[4]{36})^5 \approx 88.182$ **87.** $(\sqrt[3]{-21})^4 \approx 57.937$ **88.** $(\sqrt[3]{-15})^2 \approx 6.082$ **89.** $\dfrac{1}{(\sqrt[3]{5})^2} \approx 0.342$

90. $\dfrac{1}{(\sqrt[3]{7})^2} \approx 0.273$ **91.** $-\dfrac{1}{(\sqrt[3]{42})^2} \approx -0.083$ **92.** $-\dfrac{1}{(\sqrt[3]{36})^2} \approx -0.092$ **93.** $(\sqrt[8]{-88})^3$, not a real number
94. $(\sqrt[6]{-66})^5$, not a real number **95. (a)** The length of the side is 17 ft. **(b)** The length of the side is
9.5 inches. **(c)** The length of the side is approximately 10.724 mm **96. (a)** The length of the side is 23 yards.
(b) The length of the side is 10.5 cm. **(c)** The length of the side is approximately 6.708 feet.

97. (a) The length of the radius is 14 inches. **(b)** The length of the radius is $\dfrac{7}{\pi} \approx 3.949$ yards.

(c) The length of the radius is $\sqrt{\dfrac{108}{\pi}} \approx 5.863$ meters. **98. (a)** The length of the radius is 15 dm.

(b) The length of the radius is $\dfrac{19}{\sqrt{\pi}} \approx 10.720$ ft **(c)** The length of the radius is $\sqrt{\dfrac{200}{\pi}} \approx 7.979$ cm.

99. (a) The length of the side is 12 inches. **(b)** The length of the side is 4.93 meters.
100. (a) The length of the side is 21 cm. **(b)** The length of the side is 7.94 feet.
101. (a) The radius is 6 dm and the diameter is 12 dm.
    (b) The radius is approximately 3.908 yards and the diameter is approximately 7.816 yards.

102. (a) The radius is 9 inches and the diameter is 18 inches.
(b) The radius is approximately 6.204 meters and the diameter is approximately 12.407 meters.
103. The radius and diameter are approximately 36.126 ft and 72.252 ft, respectively.
104. The side is approximately 614 feet.

Experiencing Algebra the Calculator Way

6257; 7883; 9024; 9932; 10,699; 11,370; 11,969; 12,514; 13,015; 13,480; 13,915; 14,325

PROBLEM SET 13.2

Experiencing Algebra the Exercise Way

1. nonradical   **2.** radical   **3.** radical   **4.** radical   **5.** radical   **6.** radical   **7.** radical
8. nonradical   **9.** nonradical   **10.** nonradical   **11.** all real numbers less than 3; $[3, \infty)$
12. all real numbers less than 0; $[0, \infty)$ **13.** no restricted values; $(-\infty, \infty)$ **14.** all real numbers greater
than $\frac{5}{4}$; $\left(-\infty, \frac{5}{4}\right]$ **15.** no restricted values; $(-\infty, \infty)$ **16.** no restricted values; $(-\infty, \infty)$
17. all real numbers greater than $\frac{7}{2}$; $\left(-\infty, \frac{7}{2}\right]$ **18.** all real numbers less than $\frac{1}{3}$; $\left[\frac{1}{3}, \infty\right)$
19. all real numbers less than 0; $[0, \infty)$ **20.** no restricted values; $(-\infty, \infty)$ **21.** all real numbers less than
3; $[3, \infty)$ **22.** all real numbers less than $-\frac{5}{3}$; $\left[-\frac{5}{3}, \infty\right)$ **23.** no restricted values; $(-\infty, \infty)$
24. no restricted values; $(-\infty, \infty)$ **25.** all real numbers less than $-\frac{2}{3}$; $\left[-\frac{2}{3}, \infty\right)$ **26.** all real numbers less
than $\frac{5}{7}$; $\left[\frac{5}{7}, \infty\right)$ **27–40.** Answers will vary. Possible answers follow.   **27.** $(-3, 2), (2, 3), (9, 4),$ and $(10, 4.123)$
28. $(-5, 9), (0, 6), (1, 5.1962),$ and $(4, 0)$ **29.** $(-2, 2.224), (-1, 2.519), (0, 2.7589),$ and $(1, 2.9625)$
30. $(-1, 2), (0, -3), (3, -8),$ and $(8, -13)$ **31.** $(9, 1), (10, 7), (13, 13),$ and $(18, 19)$
32. $(-1, 2), (0, 3), (1, 4),$ and $(8, 5)$ **33.** $(-4, 7.4833), (-3, 6.6332), (-2, 5.6569),$ and $(0, 2.8284)$
34. $\left(-\frac{1}{2}, 0\right), (0, 1), (1, 1.7321),$ and $(4, 3)$ **35.** $\left(\frac{1}{2}, 2\right), (1, 3), (3, 4.2361),$ and $(5, 5)$ **36.** $(0, 9), (4, 1),$
$(9, -3),$ and $(16, -7)$ **37.** $(-3, 5), (-2, 0), (-1, 5),$ and $(6, 20)$ **38.** $.(-6, -8), (1, -2), (2, 0),$ and $(3, -2)$
39. $(1, 0), (2, -2), (5, -16),$ and $(10, -54)$ **40.** $(-1, 0), (0, 4), (3, 32),$ and $(8, 108)$

41.

42.

43.

44.

45.

46.

47.

48.

49.

50.

51.

52.

53.

54.

55.

56.

57.

58.

59. 3.1623, 4.4721, 5.4772, 6.3246, 7.0711, 7.746, 8.3666, 8.9443, 9.4868, and 10

60. 1.7841, 2.5231, 3.0902, 3.5682, 3.9894, 4.3702, 4.7203, 5.0463, 5.3524, and 5.6419

61.

There should be 16 rows in the table.

62.

The variability is about 43.

63.

The velocity should be about 55 mph.

64.

The velocity would be about 46 mph.

Experiencing Algebra the Calculator Way

Answers will vary.

PROBLEM SET 13.3

Experiencing Algebra the Exercise Way

1. $\dfrac{1}{3}$ **2.** $\dfrac{1}{3}$ **3.** 2 **4.** 2 **5.** 243 **6.** 512 **7.** 8 **8.** 8 **9.** 5 **10.** 4 **11.** 6 **12.** 5

13. $\dfrac{2}{3}$ **14.** $\dfrac{9}{25}$ **15.** $\dfrac{4}{3}$ **16.** $\dfrac{8}{27}$ **17.** $\dfrac{1}{8}$ **18.** $\dfrac{1}{16}$ **19.** $\dfrac{1}{x^{2/3}}$ **20.** $\dfrac{1}{x^{5/6}}$ **21.** $12y^{3/4}$ **22.** $2y^{4/7}$

23. $z^{17/12}$ **24.** $z^{13/8}$ **25.** $p^{1/6}$ **26.** $\dfrac{1}{x^{1/9}}$ **27.** $b^{2/3}$ **28.** $z^{3/8}$ **29.** $x^{3/2}y^{3/4}$ **30.** $p^{5/6}q^{5/2}$ **31.** $\dfrac{x^{5/3}}{y^{5/2}}$

32. $\dfrac{a^{7/3}}{b^{7/4}}$ **33.** $\dfrac{b^{1/3}}{a^{1/3}}$ **34.** $\dfrac{n^{3/4}}{m^{3/4}}$ **35.** $\dfrac{1}{c^{1/5}}$ **36.** $k^{2/7}$ **37.** $4a^{10/3}b^4$ **38.** $8c^{2/3}d^{3/2}$ **39.** $10a^{13/12}b^{4/5}$

40. $-6x^{4/5}y^{7/12}$ **41.** $\dfrac{m^{10/7}}{4}$ **42.** $64z^{7/3}$ **43.** $\dfrac{8a^{10/3}c^{13/6}}{9b^{13/4}}$ **44.** $\dfrac{z^3}{2y^{7/4}}$ **45.** $x^{11/12} - x^{21/20}$ **46.** $z^{11/12} - z$

47. $2x^{3/5} + 6x^{2/5}y^{2/5}$ **48.** $15a^{3/7} - 5a^{2/7}b^{4/7}$ **49.** $3a^{1/4}b^{1/3} - a^{3/4}b^{7/6}$ **50.** $x^{3/4}y^{9/8} - 4x^{1/4}y^{3/4}$
51. $x^{5/6} + x^{1/2}y^{1/3} - x^{1/3}y^{1/2} - y^{5/6}$ **52.** $c^{7/6} + c^{2/3}d^{1/2} - c^{1/2}d^{2/3} - d^{7/6}$ **53.** $x^{1/2} - y^{1/2}$ **54.** $p^{3/2} - q^{3/2}$
55. $x^{5/2} - x^2y^{1/2} + x^{1/2}y^2 - y^{5/2}$ **56.** $a^{5/3} - a^{2/3}b + ab^{2/3} - b^{5/3}$ **57.** $x^{2/3} - 4$ **58.** $16 - z^{1/2}$
59. $x^{1/2} + 4x^{1/4} + 4$ **60.** $x^{2/3} + 6x^{1/3} + 9$ **61.** $x^2 - 2xy^{1/2} - y$ **62.** $x - 2x^{1/2}y - y^2$
63. $a + 2a^{1/2}b^{1/2} + b$ **64.** $c - 2c^{1/2}d^{1/2} + d$ **65.** The side length should be doubled.
66. The side length should be tripled. **67.** The time is increased by about $0.1824d^{1/2}$ seconds.
68. The time is increased by about $0.2492d^{1/2}$ seconds.

Experiencing Algebra the Calculator Way

1. x^2 **2.** $\dfrac{1}{x^2}$ **3.** $x^{7/4}$ **4.** $\dfrac{1}{x^{3/2}}$ **5.** $x^{9/4} - x^{17/12}$ **6.** $x^{2/3} - 1$

PROBLEM SET 13.4

Experiencing Algebra the Exercise Way

1. $2\sqrt{7}$ **2.** $5\sqrt{3}$ **3.** $-7\sqrt[3]{2}$ **4.** $-4\sqrt[3]{3}$ **5.** $2\sqrt[4]{7}$ **6.** $7\sqrt[4]{3}$ **7.** $-5\sqrt[5]{2}$ **8.** $-3\sqrt[5]{8}$
9. $2x^2yz\sqrt{5y}$ **10.** $2xy^4z^4\sqrt{3xy}$ **11.** $2mn^3\sqrt[3]{9m^2}$ **12.** $3p^2q^2\sqrt[3]{4pq^2}$ **13.** $3xy\sqrt[4]{2y}$
14. $2ab^2\sqrt[4]{5a^2}$ **15.** $3ab^2\sqrt[5]{2ac^2}$ **16.** $3yz^3\sqrt[5]{3x^2y^3}$ **17.** $(x + 3)\sqrt{5}$ **18.** $(x + 1)\sqrt{3x}$
19. $7\sqrt{2xy}$ **20.** $6\sqrt{2xy}$ **21.** $14xy\sqrt{2x}$ **22.** $-6p^2q\sqrt{21p}$ **23.** $(x + y)\sqrt{21}$ **24.** $(p + 2q)\sqrt{3p}$
25. $(x + 2)\sqrt{x + 1}$ **26.** $(x - 7)\sqrt{x + 1}$ **27.** $(x - 1)\sqrt{(x + 2)(x + 4)}$
28. $(x + 4)\sqrt{(x + 2)(x - 4)}$ **29.** $-2xy\sqrt[3]{3x^2}$ **30.** $-5x^2y^2\sqrt[3]{2y^2}$ **31.** $-\dfrac{6}{7}$ **32.** $-\dfrac{5}{9}$ **33.** $\dfrac{11}{12}$
34. $\dfrac{13}{14}$ **35.** $-\dfrac{2\sqrt{6}}{9}$ **36.** $-\dfrac{3\sqrt{15}}{25}$ **37.** $\dfrac{\sqrt[3]{4}}{5}$ **38.** $\dfrac{\sqrt[3]{5}}{8}$ **39.** $-\dfrac{\sqrt[3]{45}}{5}$ **40.** $-\dfrac{\sqrt[3]{70}}{7}$ **41.** $\dfrac{\sqrt[5]{2}}{2}$
42. $\dfrac{\sqrt[5]{3}}{3}$ **43.** $\dfrac{2x}{3y}$ **44.** $\dfrac{5x}{7y}$ **45.** $\dfrac{\sqrt{3x}}{5y}$ **46.** $\dfrac{\sqrt{5p}}{7q}$ **47.** $\dfrac{2\sqrt{5xyz}}{5z}$ **48.** $\dfrac{6\sqrt{7abc}}{7c}$ **49.** $\dfrac{x\sqrt{3}}{3}$
50. $\dfrac{z^2\sqrt{5}}{5}$ **51.** $\dfrac{3x}{y^2}$ **52.** $\dfrac{-4x^2y}{z^3}$ **53.** $\dfrac{\sqrt[3]{15x}}{5x}$ **54.** $\dfrac{\sqrt[3]{42a}}{6a}$ **55.** $\dfrac{\sqrt[3]{75xy^2z^2}}{5yz}$ **56.** $\dfrac{\sqrt[3]{196ac^2}}{7c}$
57. $\dfrac{\sqrt{5x}}{x}$ **58.** $\dfrac{\sqrt{10y}}{y}$ **59.** $\dfrac{\sqrt{2y}}{2y}$ **60.** $\dfrac{\sqrt{3b}}{3b}$ **61.** $\dfrac{z\sqrt{2z}}{4}$ **62.** $\dfrac{p\sqrt{3p}}{9}$ **63.** $\dfrac{b\sqrt{ab}}{a}$ **64.** $\dfrac{\sqrt{cd}}{cd^2}$
65. $\dfrac{\sqrt{3x}}{6}$ **66.** $\dfrac{p\sqrt{2q}}{6q}$ **67.** $\dfrac{\sqrt[3]{3x}}{x}$ **68.** $\dfrac{\sqrt[3]{7a}}{a}$ **69.** $\dfrac{\sqrt[3]{2y^2}}{2y}$ **70.** $\dfrac{\sqrt[3]{2a^2}}{2a}$ **71.** $\dfrac{-2\sqrt[3]{9x^2z}}{3x}$

72. $\dfrac{-3\sqrt[3]{25b^2c}}{5b}$ **73.** The period is approximately 2.9 seconds.   **74.** The period is approximately 3.8 seconds.

75. It takes approximately 1.92 seconds.   **76.** It takes approximately 1.4 seconds.

77. The current 6 amperes.   **78.** The current is 9 amperes.   **79.** The current is approximately 6.52 amperes.

80. The current is approximately 7.66 amperes.

Experiencing Algebra the Calculator Way

1. $6x$ **2.** $18a^3\sqrt{2}$ **3.** $x + 5$ **4.** $(b + 3)\sqrt{b}$ **5.** $(x - 1)\sqrt{2}$ **6.** $\dfrac{2\sqrt{3x}}{3x}$

PROBLEM SET 13.5

Experiencing Algebra the Exercise Way

1. $\sqrt{7}$ **2.** $7\sqrt{6}$ **3.** $\dfrac{9}{10}\sqrt{10}$ **4.** $\dfrac{14}{13}\sqrt{13}$ **5.** $-2\sqrt[3]{3}$ **6.** $13\sqrt[3]{2}$ **7.** $23\sqrt{3}$ **8.** $12\sqrt{5}$

9. $14\sqrt{x}$ **10.** $-2\sqrt{bc}$ **11.** $11\sqrt{x}$ **12.** $20\sqrt{p}$ **13.** $-3x\sqrt{2x}$ **14.** $-y^2\sqrt{3y}$ **15.** $(3 + 4a)\sqrt{a}$

16. $(11b - 4)\sqrt{b}$ **17.** $14a\sqrt{b}$ **18.** $x\sqrt{y}$ **19.** $7\sqrt{pq} + 7\sqrt[3]{pq}$ **20.** $6\sqrt[3]{ab} - 8\sqrt{ab}$

21. $6xy\sqrt{xy}$ **22.** $-cd\sqrt{cd}$ **23.** $-xy\sqrt[3]{x^2yz}$ **24.** $7xy\sqrt[4]{xyz^2}$ **25.** $\sqrt{35} - 7$ **26.** $\sqrt{30} + 5$

27. $\sqrt{3x} - \sqrt{15}$ **28.** $2\sqrt{35} + 2\sqrt{5a}$ **29.** $6a - 15\sqrt{a}$ **30.** $24c + 32\sqrt{c}$ **31.** $8x - 12\sqrt[3]{x^2}$

32. $35\sqrt[3]{a^2} - 14a$ **33.** $6 + 2\sqrt{6} - 30\sqrt{2} - 20\sqrt{3}$ **34.** $3\sqrt{30} - 36\sqrt{2} + 2\sqrt{5} - 8\sqrt{3}$

35. $\sqrt{6} + \sqrt{3x} - \sqrt{2x} - x$ **36.** $\sqrt{10} + \sqrt{2z} - \sqrt{5z} - z$ **37.** 19   **38.** -1 **39.** $144 - p$

40. $169 - q$ **41.** $2x - 3y$ **42.** $6x - 3y$ **43.** $a + 8\sqrt{a} + 16$ **44.** $bc + 10\sqrt{bc} + 25$

45. $9b - 12\sqrt{b} + 4$ **46.** $81c - 54\sqrt{c} + 9$ **47.** $x - 2\sqrt{xy} + y$ **48.** $2x - 2\sqrt{6xy} + 3y$

49. $\sqrt{3x} - \sqrt{2}$ **50.** $\sqrt{2x} + \sqrt{6}$ **51.** $1 - \dfrac{12\sqrt{a}}{a}$ **52.** $\dfrac{9\sqrt{b}}{b} + 1$ **53.** $1 + \dfrac{\sqrt{xy}}{x} + \dfrac{\sqrt{xz}}{x}$

54. $\sqrt{a} - \dfrac{\sqrt{abc}}{b} + \sqrt{c}$ **55.** $6(\sqrt{6} - \sqrt{3})$ **56.** $3(\sqrt{10} - \sqrt{2})$ **57.** $5 + 2\sqrt{6}$ **58.** $5 - 2\sqrt{6}$

59. $\dfrac{3x\sqrt{x} + 6x}{x - 4}$ **60.** $\dfrac{12w + 4w\sqrt{w}}{9 - w}$ **61.** $\sqrt{3b} + 2$ **62.** $\sqrt{ab} - 1$ **63.** $\dfrac{x + 6\sqrt{x} + 9}{x - 9}$

64. $\dfrac{36 - 12\sqrt{p} + p}{36 - p}$ **65.** -1 **66.** -1 **67.** It will require $8\sqrt{10} \approx 25.3$ inches more of material.

68. It is $4\sqrt{6} \approx 9.8$ inches larger.   **69.** The difference is $4\sqrt[3]{14} \approx 9.6$ inches.

70. The difference is $20\sqrt[3]{2} \approx 25.2$ inches.

Experiencing Algebra the Calculator Way

Students should check the results by one of the methods presented.

1. $4\sqrt[3]{x} + 6\sqrt{x} + 7$ **2.** $\sqrt{x} - 2$ **3.** $6\sqrt[3]{2x^2} + 10\sqrt[3]{x}$ **4.** $8x + 5x\sqrt{2}$ **5.** $\sqrt{x} - 4$

6. $\dfrac{21\sqrt{x} + 147}{x - 49}$ **7.** $3x - 13\sqrt{x} - 41$

PROBLEM SET 13.6

Experiencing Algebra the Exercise Way

1. radical   **2.** nonradical   **3.** nonradical   **4.** nonradical   **5.** radical   **6.** nonradical   **7.** nonradical

8. radical   **9.** nonradical   **10.** radical   **11.** radical   **12.** radical   **13–18.** Students can set up a table to solve the radical equations numerically on a calculator.   **13.** 12   **14.** all real numbers greater than or equal to $-\dfrac{7}{2}$ **15.** all real numbers   **16.** 7   **17.** all real numbers less than or equal to $\dfrac{5}{2}$

18. all real numbers   **19.** 9   **20.** 16   **21.** 11   **22.** 9   **23.** 5   **24.** 4   **25.** 6   **26.** 4

27. $-1, 0,$ and 1 **28.** $-\dfrac{1}{2}, 0,$ and $\dfrac{1}{2}$ **29.** -2 and -1 **30.** $1, 2,$ and 3 **31.** $-\dfrac{1}{2}$ and 0 **32.** 4 and 5

33. no solution   **34.** no solution   **35.** all real numbers   **36.** all real numbers   **37.** all real numbers greater than or equal to 3 **38.** all real numbers greater than or equal to 0 **39.** 0 **40.** 4 **41.** 7 **42.** 2.57 **43.** -5 **44.** -1.375 **45.** -8 **46.** 1.24 **47.** 17.89 **48.** 11.35 **49.** -0.97 **50.** 0.46 **51.** 1.04 **52.** 2.43 **53.** no solution   **54.** no solution   **55.** all real numbers greater than or equal to $-\dfrac{2}{3}$ **56.** all real numbers less than or equal to $\dfrac{5}{2}$ **57.** The width is 4 inches and the length is 6 inches.   **58.** The width is 6 inches and the length is 9 inches.   **59.** The height is approximately 550 feet.   **60.** The height is approximately 1249.6 feet.

Experiencing Algebra the Calculator Way

1. 2 **2.** 1 **3.** -2 **4.** -3 **5.** 3.25 **6.** -3.606 and 3.606 **7.** 1.514 **8.** -3.275 and 4.275 **9.** 3.5 **10.** 9 **11.** -2.5 **12.** approximately -2.84 and 8 **13.** 20 **14.** 4 **15.** -3

PROBLEM SET 13.7

Experiencing Algebra the Exercise Way

1. 64 **2.** 49 **3.** 7.84 **4.** 38.44 **5.** no solution   **6.** no solution   **7.** 12 **8.** 28 **9.** $\dfrac{9}{2}$

10. $\dfrac{3}{2}$ **11.** $\dfrac{3}{2}$ **12.** 3 **13.** 4 **14.** 22 **15.** 10 **16.** $\dfrac{8}{3}$ **17.** 20 **18.** 12 **19.** 1 **20.** 6

21. 5 **22.** $\dfrac{9}{2}$ **23.** -1 **24.** -2 **25.** 5 **26.** 7 **27.** 4 **28.** -2.42 and 2.75

29. all real numbers less than or equal to 7 **30.** all real numbers less than or equal to $\dfrac{3}{2}$

31. approximately 3.83 **32.** -4.70 **33.** 8 **34.** 12 **35.** 36 **36.** 64 **37.** 16 **38.** 1

39. no solution   **40.** no solution   **41.** no solution   **42.** 6 **43.** -72 **44.** $-\dfrac{9}{2}$ **45.** 5000 **46.** 133

47. -16 **48.** -27 **49.** -8 **50.** 8 **51.** 256 **52.** 81 **53.** 13 **54.** -22 **55.** 21 **56.** 88 **57.** 124 **58.** 11 **59.** -8 and 1 **60.** -27 and 3 **61.** 9 **62.** 3 **63.** 10 **64.** 52 **65.** 3

66. 2 **67.** 0 **68.** 0 **69.** no solution   **70.** no solution   **71.** 2 **72.** $\dfrac{1}{2}$ **73.** 2 **74.** 1 **75.** ± 8

76. ± 125 **77.** -38 and 26 **78.** -72 and 56 **79.** 85 **80.** 25 **81.** $\pm\dfrac{1}{8}$ **82.** $\dfrac{1}{81}$ **83.** $\dfrac{406}{81}$

84. 155 **85.** $-\dfrac{122}{5}$ and $\dfrac{128}{5}$ **86.** $\dfrac{257}{6}$ **87.** no real-number solution   **88.** no real-number solution   **89.** 16 **90.** 243 **91.** 5 units   **92.** 8 units   **93.** 8 units   **94.** 7 units   **95.** $\sqrt{106}$ units   **96.** $\sqrt{185}$ units   **97.** -8 and 16 **98.** -10 and 5 **99.** -10 and 6 **100.** 4 and -2 **101.** no solution   **102.** no solution   **103.** The energy was approximately 2.875×10^{17} ft-lb.   **104.** The energy was 1.5625×10^{16} ft-lb.   **105.** The crushing load was 100 tons.   **106.** The crushing load was 324 tons.

Experiencing Algebra the Calculator Way

1. 40 **2.** 10 **3.** 20 **4.** -0.307 and 1.412 **5.** 2.462 **6.** -1.291 and 20.920

Reflections

1–7. Answers will vary.

Exercises

1. 15 **2.** 1.7 **3.** $\dfrac{7}{8}$ **4.** $-\dfrac{3}{5}$ **5.** -6 **6.** not a real number **7.** 12.247 **8.** -3.271 **9.** 2.627

10. $\sqrt[3]{-64} = -4$ **11.** $-\sqrt[4]{16} = -2$ **12.** $\sqrt[4]{-16}$, not a real number **13.** $-\dfrac{1}{\sqrt[3]{64}} = -\dfrac{1}{4}$

14. $-(\sqrt[3]{64})^4 = -256$ **15.** $(\sqrt{-64})^3$, not a real number **16.** $\dfrac{1}{(\sqrt[4]{16})^3} = \dfrac{1}{8}$

17. $\dfrac{1}{(\sqrt[4]{-16})^3}$, not a real number **18.** 11 inches **19.** $\dfrac{5}{6}$ yard **20.** The approximate radius is 2.5 cm and

the diameter is 5 cm. **21.** all real numbers less than $\dfrac{7}{2}$; $\left[\dfrac{7}{2}, \infty\right)$ **22.** no restricted values; $(-\infty, \infty)$

23. all real numbers less than $-\dfrac{9}{4}$; **24.**

$\left[-\dfrac{9}{4}, \infty\right)$

25.

26. The variability is 6.78. **27.**

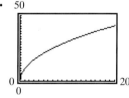

The approximate speed is 36.7 mph.

28. 2 **29.** 128

30. $(\sqrt[3]{9})^5 \approx 38.9$ **31.** $\dfrac{27}{8}$

32. $\dfrac{1}{27}$ **33.** 8 **34.** $\dfrac{1}{x^{1/6}}$

35. $y^{1/10}$ **36.** $z^{1/3}$ **37.** $\dfrac{b^{5/2}}{a^{5/4}}$

38. $16x^8y^{12}$ **39.** $6a^{13/12}b$ **40.** The new side should be $\sqrt{5}$ times larger than the old side. **41.** $30\sqrt{7}$

42. $-4\sqrt[3]{5}$ **43.** $3\sqrt[4]{2}$ **44.** $3x^2y^3z\sqrt{5y}$ **45.** $-4y^2\sqrt[3]{x^2y}$ **46.** $(2x - 3)\sqrt{3}$ **47.** $4x^2$

48. $-2ab^2\sqrt[3]{5a}$ **49.** $(x - 2y)\sqrt{3x}$ **50.** $\dfrac{5}{8}$ **51.** $\dfrac{\sqrt{13}}{17}$ **52.** $\dfrac{3\sqrt{21}}{49}$ **53.** $\dfrac{\sqrt[3]{30}}{5}$ **54.** $\dfrac{\sqrt{30}}{6}$

55. $\dfrac{5a}{8b^2}$ **56.** $\dfrac{4\sqrt{5m}}{5}$ **57.** $\dfrac{z\sqrt[3]{6xy^2}}{2xy}$ **58.** $\dfrac{a\sqrt{2b}}{6b}$ **59.** The period is approximately 1.9 seconds.

60. $7\sqrt{5}$ **61.** $11\sqrt{11}$ **62.** $\dfrac{16}{15}\sqrt{15}$ **63.** $7\sqrt[3]{2}$ **64.** $2\sqrt{x}$ **65.** $5ab\sqrt{ab}$ **66.** $7\sqrt{2} - 7$

67. $6\sqrt{2a} + 2a$ **68.** $3 - 2\sqrt{5}$ **69.** $5x - 7y$ **70.** $x + 16\sqrt{x} + 64$ **71.** $6x + 3\sqrt[3]{x^2}$

72. $\sqrt{3x} - \sqrt{6}$ **73.** $1 - \dfrac{5\sqrt{z}}{z}$ **74.** $24\sqrt{5} - 48$ **75.** $\dfrac{x + 4\sqrt{x} + 4}{x - 4}$ **76.** -1 **77.** $\sqrt{2x} + 3$

78. It will require $24\sqrt{5}$ inches more material. **79.** 7 **80.** no solution **81.** all real numbers greater

than or equal to -5 **82.** $\dfrac{7}{2}$ and 4 **83.** all real numbers greater than or equal to -1 **84.** no solution

85. -0.683 and 1.62 **86.** The width is 12 in. and the length is 18 in.   **87.** It fell from a height of 579.6 feet.

88. 12   **89.** 7   **90.** 11   **91.** 10   **92.** no solution   **93.** -32 **94.** 78   **95.** -39 and 25   **96.** $\dfrac{1}{4}$

97. $\pm 3\sqrt{3}$ **98.** 10 units   **99.** 9 units   **100.** 5 units   **101** 12 units   **102.** -6 and 2

103. The skid mark would be approximately 152.4 feet long.

CHAPTER 13 MIXED REVIEW

1. 14   **2.** 2.1   **3.** $-\dfrac{3}{4}$ **4.** 4   **5.** not a real number   **6.** -3.072 **7.** $\sqrt{121} = 11$ **8.** $\sqrt[3]{-125} = -5$

9. $-\sqrt[4]{81} = -3$ **10.** $\sqrt[4]{-81}$, not a real number   **11.** $(\sqrt[6]{729})^5 = 243$ **12.** $(\sqrt[6]{-729})^5$, not a real number

13. $\dfrac{1}{(\sqrt[3]{-8})^2} = \dfrac{1}{4}$ **14.** $\dfrac{1}{(\sqrt[4]{-81})^3}$, not a real number   **15.** 3   **16.** 2187   **17.** $(\sqrt[3]{6})^5 \approx 19.812$ **18.** 6

19. $\dfrac{64}{27}$ **20.** $\dfrac{1}{(\sqrt{6})^3} \approx 0.068$ **21.** $-\dfrac{6}{7}$ **22.** $\dfrac{\sqrt{15}}{12}$ **23.** $\dfrac{5}{13}$ **24.** $-\dfrac{4}{5}$ **25.** $5\sqrt{6}$ **26.** $-4\sqrt[3]{7}$

27. $2\sqrt[4]{3}$ **28.** $-3\sqrt[5]{2}$ **29.** $5\sqrt{21}$ **30.** $-\dfrac{4}{21}\sqrt{21}$ **31.** $12\sqrt{13}$ **32.** $11\sqrt{7}$ **33.** $3\sqrt{2} - 3$

34. $60 - 2\sqrt{3}$ **35.** 5   **36.** $34\sqrt[3]{3}$ **37.** $\dfrac{1}{x^{1/12}}$ **38.** $\dfrac{1}{z^{9/10}}$ **39.** $\dfrac{q^{5/2}}{p^{5/4}}$ **40.** $81x^{12}y^{16}$ **41.** $6x^3yz^2\sqrt{2y}$

42. $-4y^2\sqrt[3]{x^2y}$ **43.** $6xy\sqrt{2y}$ **44.** $-3a^2b^2\sqrt[3]{2b}$ **45.** $(2x + 7y)\sqrt{5}$ **46.** $\dfrac{6x}{7y^2}$ **47.** $\dfrac{5\sqrt{3z}}{3}$

48. $\dfrac{-3\sqrt[3]{a}}{b}$ **49.** $\dfrac{\sqrt{2b}}{2b}$ **50.** $\dfrac{\sqrt{xy}}{xy^2}$ **51.** $2\sqrt{x}$ **52.** $14cd\sqrt{cd}$ **53.** $a + 18\sqrt{a} + 81$

54. $3\sqrt{6a} + 6a$ **55.** $3x - 2y$ **56.** $6x + 10x\sqrt[3]{x}$ **57.** $\sqrt{3x} - \sqrt{7}$ **58.** $1 - \dfrac{9\sqrt{m}}{m}$

59. $6(\sqrt{7} - 2)$ **60.** $\dfrac{9 + 6\sqrt{x} + x}{9 - x}$ **61.** -1 **62.** $5 + \sqrt{7x}$

63. restricted values are all real numbers less than 0;

64. restricted values are all real numbers less than 0;

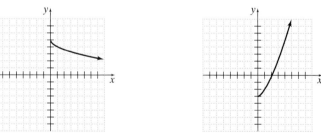

65. all real numbers greater than or equal to -4 **66.** 2 and 3
67. all real numbers greater than or equal to -3 **68.** 2.681
69. -0.429 and 1.061 **70.** 81
71. 45   **72.** 8   **73.** 7   **74.** 4
75. no solution   **76.** -72 **77.** 79
78. -248 and 238   **79.** $\dfrac{1}{9}$
80. $\pm 3\sqrt{3}$

81. The side is 23 inches.   **82.** The variability is approximately 7.937.   **83.** It fell from a height of 257.6 feet.
84. The period is approximately 2.08 seconds.   **85.** 10 units   **86.** 6 units   **87.** 5 units   **88.** $\sqrt{58}$ units
89. no solution   **90.** -1 and 5

CHAPTER 13 TEST

1. 14   **2.** 1.5   **3.** 2.141   **4.** not a real number   **5.** $-\dfrac{2}{5}$ **6.** 512   **7.** 9   **8.** 16   **9.** $\dfrac{9}{4}$

10. $\sqrt{x}$ **11.** $2x - 5y$ **12.** $3x^2y\sqrt{10y}$ **13.** $\dfrac{z\sqrt{6xz}}{2xy}$ **14.** $\dfrac{5\sqrt{y}}{7x}$ **15.** $7\sqrt{x}$ **16.** $10x + 15\sqrt[3]{x^2}$

17. $\dfrac{x + 3\sqrt{x} - 4}{x - 1}$ **18. (a)** -5 **(b)** -5 **(c)** -5 **19.** 36 **20.** 5

21. all real numbers greater than or equal to -5 **22.** 3

23. restricted values are all real numbers less than -7 **24.** 7 units   **25.** $\sqrt{58}$ units   **26.** It will require $20\sqrt{5}$ inches more border.

27. Answers will vary.

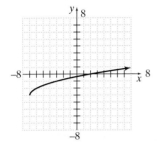

CUMULATIVE REVIEW CHAPTERS 1–13

1. $\dfrac{y^2}{x}$ **2.** $9xy^{3/2}$ **3.** $\dfrac{27t^3}{64s^6}$ **4.** $5x^3 + 6x^2y + 2xy^2$ **5.** $-2.8a^2 - 6.31ab + 4.4b^2$ **6.** $-13.6m^3n^3p$

7. $6a^2 + 10ab - 4b^2$ **8.** $4x^2 - 9$ **9.** $4x^2 + 12x + 9$ **10.** $-5xy^2$ **11.** $1 + \dfrac{2}{m} - \dfrac{4n}{m^2}$ **12.** $\dfrac{x - 1}{x - 3}$

13. $\dfrac{x^2 + x + 6}{(x + 2)(x - 2)}$ **14.** $-\dfrac{3x^2 + 22x + 42}{(x + 2)(x - 3)(x + 4)}$ **15.** $\dfrac{2a - 1}{2a + 5}$ **16.** $\dfrac{x + 5}{2xy(2x + 1)}$ **17.** $-3\sqrt{2y}$

18. $5a\sqrt[3]{a^2b^2}$ **19.** -2 **20.** $\dfrac{c}{a}\sqrt{3c}$ **21.** $\dfrac{x + 3\sqrt{x} + 2}{x - 1}$ **22.** $x^{7/6} - x^{5/4}$ **23.** $(4a + 5b)(4a - 5b)$

24. $(x - 4)(x + 2)$ **25.** $3(x - 5)(x + 2)$ **26.** -11

27.

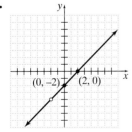

Domain: all real numbers
Range: all real numbers

28.

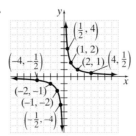

Domain: all real numbers
Range: all real numbers ≥ 2.

29.

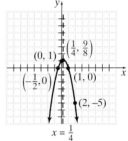

Domain: all real numbers
Range: all real numbers $\leq \dfrac{9}{8}$

30.

Domain: all real numbers $\neq -2$
Range: all real numbers $\neq -4$

31.

Domain: all real numbers $\neq 0$
Range: all real numbers $\neq 0$

32.

Domain: all real numbers ≥ 0
Range: all real numbers ≥ 0

33.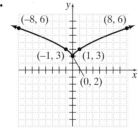

Domain: all real numbers
Range: all real numbers ≥ 2

34. 6   **35.** all real numbers   **36.** -5 and 3   **37.** $\dfrac{-3 \pm \sqrt{41}}{4}$

38. -5 **39.** $\pm 2\sqrt{7}$ **40.** $\dfrac{19}{2}$ **41.** $\left(-\dfrac{3}{2}, 6\right)$ **42.** $(5, 3)$

43. $y = -x - 2$ **44.** $y = \dfrac{3}{2}x + 4$ **45.** $y = x^2 + 3x - 4$

46. The rectangle is 12 feet by 16 feet.   **47.** The possible y-coordinates are 0 or 8.   **48.** Yes, they can finish raking the leaves.

49. The company must sell at least 1429 items in order to break-even.

50. The skydiver was free-falling for about 21.65 seconds.

Chapter 14

PROBLEM SET 14.1

Experiencing Algebra the Exercise Way

1. $10i$ **2.** $12i$ **3.** $\dfrac{4}{7}i$ **4.** $\dfrac{6}{11}i$ **5.** $4\sqrt{2}i$ **6.** $5\sqrt{3}i$ **7.** $10\sqrt{2}i$ **8.** $-21\sqrt{2}i$ **9.** $7i$

10. $14i$ **11.** $-5i$ **12.** $-i$ **13.** $60i$ **14.** $26i$ **15.** $13i$ **16.** $26i$ **17.** $\dfrac{4}{5}$ **18.** $\dfrac{4}{5}$ **19.** $-20i$

20. $-15i$ **21.** $\sqrt{2} + 2\sqrt{3}$ **22.** $\sqrt{15} - 2\sqrt{2}$ **23.** 2   **24.** 8   **25.** real number; real part is $\dfrac{5}{7}$; imaginary part is 0   **26.** pure imaginary number; real part is 0; imaginary part is $5\sqrt{3}$ **27.** pure imaginary number; real part is 0; imaginary part is 2   **28.** real number; real part is $2\sqrt{3} - \sqrt{5}$; imaginary part is 0

29. imaginary number; real part is $\sqrt{3}$; imaginary part is -5 **30.** real number; real part is $\dfrac{\sqrt{3}}{2}$; imaginary part is 0   **31.** real number; real part is -6; imaginary part is 0   **32.** imaginary number; real part is 7; imaginary part is $\sqrt{3}$ **33.** pure imaginary number; real part is 0; imaginary part is $2\sqrt{5}$ **34.** pure imaginary number; real part is 0; imaginary part is -14 **35.** real number; real part is $-4\sqrt{7} + \sqrt{11}$; imaginary part is 0
36. real number; real part is -17; imaginary part is 0   **37.** $-5 + 4i$ **38.** $-2 - 9i$ **39.** $3 - i$
40. $9 + 9i$ **41.** $-5 + 14i$ **42.** $-4 + 16i$ **43.** 1   **44.** $6i$ **45.** $1 + i$ **46.** $-2 + 2i$

47. $13 + 5i$ **48.** $18 - 7i$ **49.** $\dfrac{7}{2} + \dfrac{13}{3}i$ **50.** $\dfrac{1}{2} - i$ **51.** $1.62 + 11.38i$ **52.** $17.3 + 9.07i$
53. $7\sqrt{3} + \sqrt{2}i$ **54.** $-2\sqrt{5} - 7\sqrt{3}i$ **55.** $-28 - 63i$ **56.** $-35 - 55i$ **57.** $10 + 40i$ **58.** $84 - 21i$
59. $39 + 2i$ **60.** $69 - 6i$ **61.** 74   **62.** 130   **63.** 37   **64.** 29   **65.** $11.76 - 48.72i$

66. $-28.2 + 15.04i$ **67.** $4.76 - 17.35i$ **68.** $5.04 + 2.58i$ **69.** $\dfrac{43}{75} - \dfrac{1}{5}i$ **70.** $\dfrac{121}{180} - \dfrac{3}{20}i$

71. $-\sqrt{6} + 2i$ **72.** $-9\sqrt{5} - 9\sqrt{2}i$ **73.** 8   **74.** 31   **75.** $1 + 3i$ **76.** $2 + 6i$ **77.** $-\dfrac{19}{10} + \dfrac{17}{10}i$

78. $9 - i$ **79.** $-\dfrac{5}{2} - 3i$ **80.** $-\dfrac{3}{2} + 2i$ **81.** $-5 - 6i$ **82.** $1.5 - 2.1i$ **83.** $4 - 3.2i$
84. $2.5 + 3i$ **85.** $\sqrt{3} + \sqrt{7}i$ **86.** $-\sqrt{7} - \sqrt{5}i$ **87.** $\sqrt{3} + 2\sqrt{2}i$ **88.** $3\sqrt{5} - 2\sqrt{2}i$
89. The magnitude of the total voltage is approximately 37.336 volts.   **90.** The total voltage is $42 + 2i$ volts.
91. The magnitude of the current is 5 amperes.   **92.** The magnitude of the current is approximately 8.2 amperes.

Experiencing Algebra the Calculator Way

1. $\sqrt{-25}$ **2.** $\sqrt[3]{-27}$ **3.** $\sqrt[4]{-64}$ **4.** $\sqrt[5]{-32}$ **5.** $\sqrt[4]{-324}$ **6.** $\sqrt[4]{-40000}$ **7.** $1.5 - 3.5i$
8. $0.4 + 3.2i$ **9.** $-1.8i$ **10.** $6 + 8i$ **11.** $6 - 8i$ **12.** $2 - 5i$ **13.** 22   **14.** $-7i$ **15.** $\sqrt{3}i$

Experiencing Algebra the Exercise Way

1. $x = \pm 3i$ **2.** $x = \pm 5i$ **3.** $a = \pm\sqrt{7}i$ **4.** $b = \pm\sqrt{11}i$ **5.** $z = \pm 2i$ **6.** $m = \pm 4i$ **7.** $p = \pm 5i$
8. $q = \pm 4i$ **9.** $d = \pm\sqrt{3}i$ **10.** $c = \pm\sqrt{2}i$ **11.** $t = -1 \pm 3i$ **12.** $s = 3 \pm 6i$ **13.** $x = 5 \pm \sqrt{5}i$

14. $x = -3 \pm 2\sqrt{2}i$ **15.** $x = -\dfrac{5}{2} \pm i$ **16.** $y = \dfrac{1}{2} \pm \dfrac{5}{2}i$ **17.** $y = \pm 1.2i$ **18.** $z = \pm 2.4i$

19. $x = 1.2 \pm 0.6i$ **20.** $x = -2.7 \pm 1.1i$ **21.** $z = -2.5 \pm 2.3i$ **22.** $y = 1.4 \pm 1.6i$ **23.** $x = \pm\dfrac{3}{4}i$

24. $x = \pm\dfrac{5}{7}i$ **25.** $b = \dfrac{1}{2} \pm \dfrac{1}{2}i$ **26.** $c = -\dfrac{2}{3} \pm \dfrac{3}{4}i$ **27.** $x = -1 \pm \sqrt{3}i$ **28.** $x = 3 \pm \sqrt{5}i$

29. $b = 5 \pm \sqrt{2}i$ **30.** $x = -7 \pm \sqrt{2}i$ **31.** $y = -\dfrac{1}{2} \pm i$ **32.** $x = -\dfrac{4}{3} \pm \dfrac{1}{3}i$ **33.** $p = \dfrac{2}{3} \pm \dfrac{2}{3}i$

34. $z = \dfrac{1}{4} \pm \dfrac{\sqrt{6}}{4}i$ **35.** $x = 1.2 \pm \sqrt{2}i$ **36.** $m = -2.1 \pm \sqrt{3}i$ **37.** $y = \dfrac{1}{2} \pm \dfrac{3}{5}i$ **38.** $z = -0.6 \pm 0.3i$

39. $x = \dfrac{1}{3} \pm \dfrac{1}{2}i$ **40.** $x = -\dfrac{1}{4} \pm \dfrac{1}{3}i$ **41.** $z = -\dfrac{1}{6} \pm \dfrac{1}{6}i$ **42.** $x = -\dfrac{1}{6} \pm \dfrac{1}{4}i$ **43.** $x = 1 \pm 3i$

44. $a = -\dfrac{3}{2} \pm \dfrac{3\sqrt{15}}{2}i$ **45.** $y = -\dfrac{5}{2} \pm \dfrac{\sqrt{159}}{2}i$ **46.** $b = 1 \pm 2\sqrt{13}i$ **47.** $z = -\dfrac{7}{8} \pm \dfrac{3\sqrt{39}}{8}i$

48. $c = -\dfrac{3}{4} \pm \dfrac{3\sqrt{23}}{4}i$ **49.** $s = -1 \pm i$ **50.** $s = -\dfrac{3}{2} \pm \dfrac{\sqrt{7}}{2}i$ **51.** $r = 1.335 \pm \dfrac{\sqrt{3.8711}}{2}i$

52. $r = 1.335 \pm \dfrac{\sqrt{6.8711}}{2}i$

Experiencing Algebra the Calculator Way

1. $x = 5 \pm 3i$ **2.** $x = -7 \pm 4i$ **3.** $x = -\dfrac{5}{2} \pm \dfrac{1}{2}i$ **4.** $x = \dfrac{1}{4} \pm \dfrac{3}{4}i$

CHAPTER 14 REVIEW

Reflections

1–7. Answers will vary.

Exercises

1. $8i$ **2.** $\dfrac{5}{7}i$ **3.** $2.5i$ **4.** $5\sqrt{2}i$ **5.** $\dfrac{9\sqrt{2}}{2}i$ **6.** $-20\sqrt{2}i$ **7.** $12i$ **8.** $4i$ **9.** $66i$ **10.** $4i$

11. $\dfrac{13}{15}$ **12.** $-30i$ **13.** $-2\sqrt{3} + 5\sqrt{6}i$ **14.** $4\sqrt{2}$ **15.** 4 **16.** pure imaginary number; real part is 0;

imaginary part is $-\sqrt{3}$ **17.** real number; real part is $\dfrac{\sqrt{11}}{3}$; imaginary part is 0 **18.** imaginary number;

real part is $\sqrt{13}$; imaginary part is -2 **19.** real number; real part is $4\sqrt{2} + 1$; imaginary part is 0
20. imaginary number; real part is 3; imaginary part is -17 **21.** real number; real part is -43;
imaginary part is 0 **22.** $29 - 2i$ **23.** $-90 - 45i$ **24.** $11 - 4i$ **25.** $-26 - 7i$ **26.** 130
27. $4 - 12i$ **28.** $4 + 5i$ **29.** $3 + 2i$ **30.** $7 + 3i$ **31.** $1 - 3i$ **32.** $-1.22 - 1.21i$

33. $8\sqrt{7} + 6\sqrt{13}i$ **34.** $6 + 3\sqrt{2}i$ **35.** $\dfrac{8}{15} - \dfrac{7}{90}i$ **36.** $11.6 + 11.02i$ **37.** $\sqrt{2} + \sqrt{15}i$

38. $\sqrt{2} - 4\sqrt{3}i$ **39.** The magnitude of the total voltage is 59.0 volts. **40.** The magnitude of the
impedance is $5\sqrt{2}$ ohms. **41.** $x = \pm 10i$ **42.** $y = \pm\sqrt{15}i$ **43.** $z = \pm 3i$ **44.** $t = \pm 5i$

45. $a = \pm\sqrt{11}i$ **46.** $r = 5 \pm 6i$ **47.** $x = -2 \pm \sqrt{3}i$ **48.** $x = -\frac{1}{4} \pm \frac{3}{4}i$ **49.** $u = \pm 2.2i$

50. $v = 3.4 \pm 1.8i$ **51.** $c = \pm\frac{6}{11}i$ **52.** $m = -\frac{2}{5} \pm \frac{4}{5}i$ **53.** $x = 5 \pm 2i$ **54.** $y = -\frac{1}{2} \pm \frac{3}{2}i$

55. $z = -8 \pm \sqrt{47}$ **56.** $x = \frac{2}{3} \pm 2i$ **57.** $x = 1.2 \pm 1.1i$ **58.** $x - 0.5 \pm 1.1i$ **59.** $x = \frac{3}{4} \pm \frac{1}{4}i$

60. $x = \frac{3}{2} \pm \frac{1}{3}i$ **61.** $x = \frac{9}{2} \pm \frac{\sqrt{119}}{2}i$ **62.** $y = -\frac{1}{2} \pm \frac{\sqrt{383}}{2}i$ **63.** $b = -\frac{11}{4} \pm \frac{\sqrt{71}}{4}i$

64. $s = -4 \pm \sqrt{14}i$

CHAPTER 14 MIXED REVIEW

1. real number; real part is $-\frac{\sqrt{23}}{5}$; imaginary part is 0   **2.** imaginary number; real part is $\sqrt{29}$; imaginary part is 5   **3.** imaginary number; real part is 16; imaginary part is 22   **4.** real number; real part is $-3\sqrt{5} - 7$; imaginary part is 0   **5.** pure imaginary number; real part is 0; imaginary part is $\sqrt{31}$ **6.** real number; real part is $-\pi$; imaginary part is 0   **7.** $13i$ **8.** $\frac{8}{9}i$ **9.** $\frac{5\sqrt{6}}{6}i$ **10.** $40\sqrt{5}i$ **11.** $2.5i$ **12.** $-6\sqrt{3}i$

13. $30.85 - 4.23i$ **14.** $10i$ **15.** $4i$ **16.** $\frac{4}{3} - \frac{23}{18}i$ **17.** $-6 - 4.35i$ **18.** $59i$ **19.** $-24i$

20. $\sqrt{15} + 8\sqrt{2}$ **21.** 4   **22.** $14 - 2i$ **23.** $-72 + 54i$ **24.** 148   **25.** $-5 - 4i$ **26.** $-3 + 2i$

27. $-3 - 2i$ **28.** $7 + 6i$ **29.** $\frac{5}{3} - 6i$ **30.** $2\sqrt{5} + 5\sqrt{2}i$ **31.** $\sqrt{5} + 2\sqrt{3}i$ **32.** $\sqrt{2} + \sqrt{5}i$

33. $\frac{17}{29}$ **34.** $\frac{53}{10} \pm \frac{\sqrt{1049}}{10}$ **35.** $x = \pm 3.2i$ **36.** $m = -7 \pm 5i$ **37.** $y = 3 \pm \sqrt{6}i$

38. $x = 8 \pm \sqrt{3}i$ **39.** $y = -\frac{5}{3} \pm \frac{\sqrt{7}}{3}i$ **40.** $a = \pm 9i$ **41.** $b = \pm\sqrt{13}i$ **42.** $x = -1.5 \pm 0.7i$

43. $x = -\frac{5}{8} \pm \frac{\sqrt{3}}{8}i$ **44.** $y = \frac{3}{2} \pm \frac{\sqrt{281}}{2}$ **45.** $y = -\frac{3}{7} \pm \frac{5}{7}i$

46. The magnitude of the current is approximately 5.8 amperes.   **47.** $s = -\frac{13}{4} \pm \frac{\sqrt{71}}{4}i$

CHAPTER 14 TEST

1. $11i$ **2.** $16i$ **3.** $-28i$ **4.** $-\sqrt{14} - 4\sqrt{7}i$ **5.** $\frac{15}{17}$ **6.** 7   **7.** $-42 - 2i$ **8.** $3 + 7i$

9. $10.27 - 6.28i$ **10.** $-5\sqrt{3} + 3\sqrt{5}i$ **11.** $8 - 22i$ **12.** $\frac{4}{5} + \frac{1}{90}i$ **13.** $x = \pm 14i$

14. $t = -2 \pm \sqrt{15}i$ **15.** $d = \pm\frac{2}{7}i$ **16.** $z = \pm 1.2i$ **17.** $x = 3 \pm 2\sqrt{2}i$ **18.** $x = \frac{1}{3} \pm \frac{\sqrt{6}}{3}i$

19. $y = \frac{3}{8} \pm \frac{\sqrt{215}}{8}i$ **20.** The magnitude of the total voltage is approximately 97.4 volts.

21. Answers will vary.

Chapter 15

Experiencing Algebra the Exercise Way

1. $h^{-1} = \{(5, -3), (4, -2), (3, -1), (2, 0), (1, 1), (0, 2)\}$ **2.** $d^{-1} = \{(25, 5), (16, 4), (9, 3), (4, 2), (1, 1), (0, 0)\}$

3. $A^{-1} = \{(6, 3), (7, 2), (8, 1), (8, 0), (7, -1), (6, -2)\}$ **4.** $J^{-1} = \{(1, -4), (2, 3), (1, -2), (2, 1), (1, 0),$

$(2, -1)\}$ **5.** $M^{-1} = \left\{\left(1.3, \frac{1}{5}\right), \left(2.3, \frac{3}{5}\right), (3.3, 1), \left(4.3, \frac{7}{5}\right), \left(5.3, \frac{9}{5}\right), \left(6.3, \frac{11}{5}\right)\right\}$

6. $P^{-1} = \{(0.2, 14), (0.4, 24), (0.6, 34), (0.8, 44), (1.0, 54)\}$ **7.** $y = \frac{1}{2}x + 4$ **8.** $y = \frac{1}{3}x - 2$

9. $y = -\frac{1}{3}x + \frac{2}{3}$ **10.** $y = -\frac{1}{2}x + \frac{5}{2}$ **11.** $y = \frac{4}{3}x - 12$ **12.** $y = -\frac{3}{2}x + 2$ **13.** $y = 8x + 20$

14. $y = -2.5x + 4.5$ **15.** $y = \pm\sqrt{x + 2}$ **16.** $y = \sqrt[3]{x} - 1$ **17.** function **18.** not a function

19. not a function **20.** function **21.** yes **22.** no **23.** no **24.** yes **25.** yes **26.** yes

27. $g^{-1}(x) = \frac{1}{3}x + 2$ **28.** $f^{-1}(x) = -\frac{1}{4}x + \frac{1}{2}$ **29.** $y^{-1} = \frac{3}{2}x + 6$

30. $y^{-1} = -\frac{5}{2}x + 10$ **31.** $h^{-1}(x) = \pm\sqrt{x + 1}$ **32.** $r^{-1}(x) = \pm\sqrt{2 - x}$

33. $y^{-1} = \sqrt[3]{3x + 12}$ **34.** $y^{-1} = \sqrt[3]{4x - 8}$ **35.** $f(x) = 1500 + 0.02x$
$f^{-1}(x) = 50x - 75,000$
The inverse function represents the amount of Julia's transactions in terms of her monthly income.

36. $f(x) = 125 + 0.15x$
$f^{-1}(x) = 6\frac{2}{3}x - 833\frac{1}{3}$
The inverse function represents the amount of Harvey's sales in terms of his weekly income.

37. $f(x) = 55x$
$f^{-1}(x) = \frac{x}{55}$
The inverse function represents the time in terms of the distance traveled.

38. $f(x) = 30x$
$f^{-1}(x) = \frac{x}{30}$
The inverse function represents the number of hours in terms of the number of pairs in jeans.

39. $f(x) = 2000 + 10x$
$f^{-1}(x) = \frac{1}{10}x - 200$
The inverse function represents the number of months in terms of the total amount to repay.

40. $f(x) = 1500 + 6x$; $f^{-1}(x) = \dfrac{1}{6}x - 250$; The inverse function represents the number of months in terms of the amount earned.

Experiencing Algebra the Calculator Way

1. $y^{-1} = \pm\sqrt{\dfrac{x + 4}{0.3}}$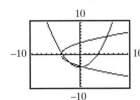

2. $f^{-1}(x) = \sqrt[3]{\dfrac{x - 2}{0.1}}$

3. $g^{-1}(x) = \left(\dfrac{x + 1.5}{5}\right)^2$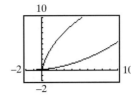

4. $y^{-1} = \dfrac{1}{x - 2}$

PROBLEM SET 15.2

Experiencing Algebra the Exercise Way

1. exponential **2.** not exponential **3.** exponential **4.** exponential **5.** not exponential
6. not exponential **7.** exponential **8.** exponential **9.** not exponential **10.** exponential

11. exponential **12.** exponential **13.** 4096 **14.** 65,536 **15.** $\dfrac{1}{256}$ **16.** $\dfrac{1}{16}$ **17.** 4 **18.** 8

19. ≈ 50.453 **20.** 1 **21.** ≈ 0.875 **22.** 0.512 **23.** ≈ 1.160 **24.** ≈ 0.689 **25.** ≈ 1.880 **26.** ≈ 0.369

27. $Y1 = 4^x$

28. $Y1 = 3^x$

29. $Y1 = 4^{-x}$

30. $Y1 = 3^{-2x}$

31. $Y1 = 4^{2x}$

32. $Y1 = 3^{2x-1}$

33. $Y1 = 4^{1/2x}$

34. $Y1 = 3^{x/4}$

35. $Y1 = 4^{x-1}$

36. $Y1 = 3^x + 1$

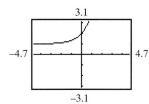

37. $Y1 = 4^x - 1$

38. $Y1 = 3^{x+1}$

39. $Y1 = e^{1/2x}$

40. $Y1 = e^{0.2x}$

41. $Y1 = \dfrac{1}{2}e^x$

42. $Y1 = 0.2e^x$

43. $Y1 = e^{-1/2x}$

44. $Y1 = e^{-0.2x}$

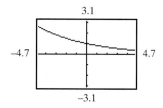

45. $Y1 = e^x + \dfrac{1}{2}$

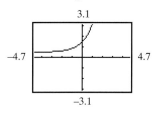

46. $Y1 = e^{0.2x} + 0.2$

47. $Y1 = \dfrac{1}{2}e^{1/2x}$

48. $Y1 = 0.2e^{0.2x}$

49. $A = 6000(1.055)^t$

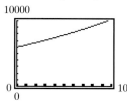

The investment was worth $8728.08.

50. $A = 3000(1.062)^t$

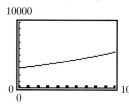

The investment was worth $3816.10.

51. $A = 8000e^{0.048t}$

20000

0
0   10

She will have earned $2169.99.

52. $A = 4500e^{0.075t}$

20000

0
0   20

The investment will be worth $9526.50.

53. $y = (281.49)1.047^x$

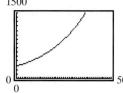

1500

0
0   50

The number of passenger miles will be 887.42 billion.

54. $y = (78.16)1.115^x$

2500

0   50
0

The expenditures are predicted to be $2047.53 billion.

Experiencing Algebra the Calculator Way

1. (a)

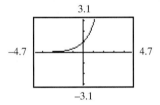

3.1

−4.7   4.7

−3.1

(b)

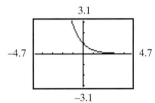

3.1

−4.7   4.7

−3.1

2. (a)

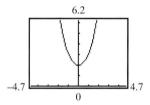

6.2

−4.7   4.7

0

(b)

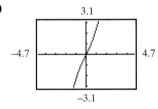

3.1

−4.7   4.7

−3.1

3. (a)

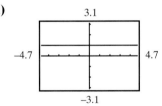

3.1

−4.7   4.7

−3.1

(b)

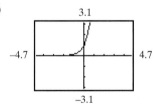

3.1

−4.7   4.7

−3.1

4. (a)

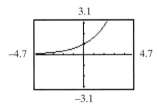

3.1

−4.7   4.7

−3.1

(b)

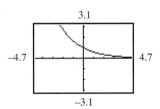

3.1

−4.7   4.7

−3.1

5. (a)

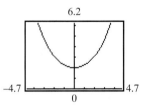

6.2

−4.7   4.7

0

(b)

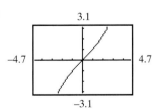

3.1

−4.7   4.7

−3.1

6. (a)

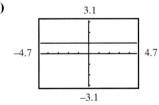

3.1

−4.7   4.7

−3.1

(b)

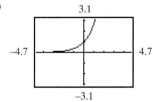

3.1

−4.7   4.7

−3.1

Experiencing Algebra the Exercise Way

1. $f^{-1}(x) = \log_{11}x$ **2.** $h^{-1}(x) = \log_{15}x$ **3.** $g^{-1}(x) = \log_6 x$ **4.** $p^{-1}(x) = \log_{29}x$ **5.** $H^{-1}(x) = \log_k x$
6. $J^{-1}(x) = \log_b x$ **7.** 6   **8.** 7   **9.** 5   **10.** 6   **11.** 4   **12.** 3   **13.** -3 **14.** -2 **15.** -1
16. -3 **17.** -4 **18.** -3 **19.** 1   **20.** 4   **21.** -4 **22.** -6 **23.** 3   **24.** 7   **25.** -5 **26.** -8
27. -5 **28.** -7 **29.** ≈ 1.176 **30.** ≈ 1.362 **31.** ≈ -1.079 **32.** ≈ -1.279 **33.** ≈ 0.130
34. ≈ 1.097 **35.** ≈ 2.639 **36.** ≈ 3.296 **37.** ≈ 1.047 **38.** ≈ 2.451 **39.** ≈ -1.609 **40.** ≈ -2.708
41. ≈ 1.792 **42.** ≈ 2.070 **43.** ≈ 3.322 **44.** ≈ 3.322 **45.** ≈ 0.657 **46.** ≈ 2.447 **47.** ≈ -0.252
48. ≈ -0.465 **49.** ≈ 1.302 **50.** ≈ 1.984 **51.** ≈ 1.616 **52.** ≈ 0.679 **53.** ≈ -1.209 **54.** ≈ -0.442

55. $Y1 = \dfrac{\log x}{\log 5}$ **56.** $Y1 = \dfrac{\log x}{\log 7}$ **57.** $Y1 = \log(x + 2)$

58. $Y1 = \log(x - 2)$ **59.** $Y1 = \ln(x + 2)$ **60.** $Y1 = \ln(x - 2)$

61. The hydrogen ion concentration is 0.0000006 moles per liter.   **62.** The hydrogen ion concentration is 0.001 moles per liter.   **63.** The pH is approximately 8.5.   **64.** The pH is approximately 6.4.
65. The larger earthquake's intensity was 63095.7 times as great as the smaller earthquake's intensity.
66. The larger earthquake's intensity was 39.8 times as great as the smaller earthquake's intensity.

Experiencing Algebra the Calculator Way

1.

2.

3.

4.

5.

6.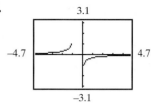

Answers will vary.

PROBLEM SET 15.4

Experiencing Algebra the Exercise Way

1. $\log 12 + \log a$ **2.** $\ln 25 + \ln c$ **3.** $3 \ln x$ **4.** $3 \log z$ **5.** $\log_5 x - 1$ **6.** $1 - \log_7 y$

7. $\log 2 + 2 \log x - \log y$ **8.** $2 \log x - \log 5 - 3 \log y$ **9.** $3 \log_3 x + 2 \log_3 y$ **10.** $2 \log_2 a + 4 \log_2 b$

11. $\dfrac{1}{3} \ln x + \dfrac{2}{3} \ln y$ **12.** $\dfrac{3}{4} \log x + \dfrac{1}{4} \log y$ **13.** $\dfrac{1}{2} \log 2 + \dfrac{1}{2} \log x - \dfrac{1}{3} \log y$

14. $\dfrac{1}{3} \ln 3 + \dfrac{2}{3} \ln x - \dfrac{1}{2} \ln 2 - \dfrac{1}{2} \ln y$ **15.** $1 + \log_3 a$ **16.** $1 + \log_5 z$ **17.** $\log_5 10 + \log_5 x + \log_5 y$

18. $\log_3 x + \log_3 y - \log_3 6$ **19.** $1 + 2 \log_a b$ **20.** $\log_6 3 + \log_6 a + 2 \log_6 b$ **21.** $\log x(x + 5)$

22. $\log (x^2 - 1)$ **23.** $\ln x^2 y^3$ **24.** $\ln \dfrac{b^3}{c^2}$ **25.** $\log_3 \dfrac{(x + 3)^2}{x - 1}$ **26.** $\log_5 (a - 5)^5 a^2$ **27.** $\ln \dfrac{\sqrt{x}}{\sqrt[5]{x + 1}}$

28. $\log \dfrac{\sqrt[4]{z}}{\sqrt[3]{z + 5}}$ **29.** $\log \dfrac{y}{z}$ **30.** $\log pq^2$ **31.** The power gain is approximately 11.249 decibels.

32. The power gain is approximately 11.761 decibels.   **33.** The depth is approximately 15.033 units.
34. The depth is approximately 17.918 units.   **35.** It will take approximately 22 years.   **36.** It will take

approximately 15.4 years.   **37.** It will take approximately 15.4 years.   **38.** It will take approximately $12\dfrac{1}{2}$ years.

Experiencing Algebra the Calculator Way

1.

2.

3.

4.

5. no   **6.** no
7. The logarithm of a sum is not equivalent to the sum of the logarithms.
8. The logarithm of a difference is not equivalent to the difference of the logarithms.

Experiencing Algebra the Exercise Way

1. logarithmic **2.** exponential **3.** neither **4.** logarithmic **5.** exponential **6.** neither **7.** neither
8. neither **9.** 2 **10.** 2 **11.** ≈ 0.693 **12.** ≈ 0.231 **13.** 0 **14.** ≈ -0.631 **15.** ≈ 0.405

16. ≈ -0.693 **17.** 1 **18.** $\dfrac{1}{2}$ **19.** 3 **20.** 4 **21.** $\dfrac{1}{2}$ and 3 **22.** 1 and 4 **23.** -2 and 5

24. -5 and $\dfrac{3}{2}$ **25.** no solution **26.** no solution **27.** all real numbers **28.** all real numbers **29.** 2

30. 11 **31.** $-\dfrac{1}{2}$ **32.** 5 **33.** -3 and $\dfrac{1}{2}$ **34.** -2 and $\dfrac{1}{3}$ **35.** ≈ 2.773 **36.** ≈ 0.602 **37.** ≈ 1.984

38. ≈ 1.228 **39.** 3125 **40.** 16 **41.** 1 **42.** 10 **43.** 1 **44.** ≈ 7.389 **45.** 9 **46.** 625

47. $\dfrac{1}{125}$ **48.** $\dfrac{1}{81}$ **49.** 7 **50.** 5 **51.** ≈ 1.649 **52.** ≈ 0.135 **53.** $\dfrac{1}{100}$ **54.** 100 **55.** 1

56. ≈ 2.718 **57.** 3 **58.** 5 **59.** 8 **60.** 11 **61.** all real numbers greater than 0

62. all real numbers greater than 0 **63.** no solution **64.** 0 **65.** 4 **66.** $\dfrac{3}{4}$ **67.** $\dfrac{2}{3}$ **68.** 2

69. 2 **70.** 7 **71.** $A(t) = 121.6e^{0.011t}$; The prediction is 178.7 million. **72.** $A(t) = 6.98e^{0.131t}$;
The prediction is 210.4 million households in the year 2010. **73.** It will double its value in the year 2012.
74. It will be 1.5 times its value in the year 2003. **75.** The decay factor is ≈ -0.154; It will take approximately
0.131 billion years. **76.** It will take approximately 0.684 billion years.

Experiencing Algebra the Calculator Way

Students should read graphing techniques.

Reflections

1–7. Answers will vary.

Exercises

1. $h^{-1} = \{(4.5, 2), (3.5, 4), (2.5, 6), (1.5, 8), (0.5, 10)\}$ **2.** $y^{-1} = \dfrac{1}{3}x + 3$ **3.** $y^{-1} = \pm\sqrt{x - 1}$

4. $y^{-1} = \sqrt[3]{x + 1}$ **5.** not a function **6.** function **7.** no **8.** yes **9.** no

10. $f^{-1}(x) = \dfrac{4}{3}x + 4$ **11.** $y^{-1} = \sqrt[3]{x - 8}$ **12.** $f(x) = 570 + 0.03x$;

$f^{-1}(x) = 33.\overline{3}x - 19{,}000$, which represents the value of all sales in terms of Motomo's weekly salary.

13. $f(x) = 15x$; $f^{-1}(x) = \dfrac{x}{15}$, which represents the number of hours in terms of the number of problems

solved. **14.** exponential **15.** not exponential **16.** 1.4641 **17.** ≈ 0.826 **18.** 1 **19.** 1.1 **20.** ≈ 1.059
21. ≈ 1.309

22.

23.

24.

25. $A = 1000(1.04)^t$

26. The expenditures are expected to be \$3528.6 billion. **27.** $h^{-1}(x) = \log_8 x$

28. $A^{-1}(x) = \dfrac{1}{k} \ln \dfrac{x}{A}$ **29.** 2 **30.** 4 **31.** -3 **32.** ≈ 0.176 **33.** 4

34. ≈ 2.303 **35.** -2 **36.** ≈ -0.222 **37.** ≈ 1.683

After 4 years the investment was worth \$1169.86.

38. $Y1 = \dfrac{\log x}{\log 3}$

39. $Y1 = \ln(x - 2)$

40. The pH is approximately 2.208.

41. The hydrogen ion concentration is 3.98×10^{-8} moles per liter.

42. $4 \log 2 + 4 \log x$

43. $1 + \log_7 x - \log_7 y$

44. $\ln 25 + 2 \ln x + 3 \ln y + \ln z$

45. $\dfrac{1}{3} \ln 2 + \dfrac{2}{3} \ln x + \dfrac{1}{3} \ln y - \dfrac{1}{2} \ln y - \dfrac{1}{2} \ln z$ **46.** $\log (x^2 - 9)$ **47.** $\ln \dfrac{x^5}{y^3}$ **48.** $\log \dfrac{\sqrt[3]{x}}{\sqrt{y}}$ **49.** $\log ad$

50. It will take approximately 18.3 years. **51.** exponential **52.** neither **53.** logarithmic **54.** neither

55. exponential **56.** neither **57.** 4 **58.** ≈ -0.322 **59.** 0 **60.** $\dfrac{3}{2}$ **61.** no solution

62. -3 and 1 **63.** all real numbers **64.** ≈ 0.262 **65.** 2.569×10^{41} **66.** 19,683 **67.** ≈ 2.718

68. 1 **69.** $\dfrac{1}{1000}$ **70.** $\dfrac{1}{4}$ **71.** ≈ 1.396 **72.** -5 and $\dfrac{3}{2}$ **73.** 5 **74.** no solution

75. all real numbers greater than 0 **76.** $A(t) = 697.5e^{0.077t}$; The estimated expenditures in the years 2000, 2005, and 2010 are \$1506.44 billion, \$2213.88 billion, and \$3253.55 billion, respectively.

77. The time since the skeleton's demise is 3351 years.

CHAPTER 15 MIXED REVIEW

1. -3 **2.** 3 **3.** -6 **4.** ≈ 0.708 **5.** -3 **6.** ≈ 4.605 **7.** 1 **8.** ≈ -0.560 **9.** ≈ 3.262

10. $\log 3 + 2 \log x + \log y$ **11.** $2 + \log_3 a - \log_3 b$ **12.** $\ln 100 + 3 \ln p + 2 \ln q + \ln r$

13. $\frac{1}{5}\log 6 + \frac{3}{5}\log x - \frac{1}{2}\log x - \frac{1}{2}\log y$ **14.** $\log(x-3)$ **15.** $\log\frac{c^2}{d^5}$ **16.** $\ln\frac{\sqrt{x}}{y^3}$ **17.** $\log 6y^2$

18. $y^{-1} = 5 - x$ **19.** $y^{-1} = \pm\sqrt{1-x}$ **20.** $y^{-1} = \sqrt[3]{4-x}$ **21.** $y^{-1} = -\frac{5}{4}x + \frac{5}{2}$

22. $m^{-1}(x) = \log_5 x$ **23.** $G^{-1}(x) = \log_b\left(\frac{x}{a}\right)$ **24.** ≈ 1.088 **25.** $\frac{13}{4}$ **26.** 2   **27.** $1\frac{2}{3}$

28. ≈ 1.296 **29.** ≈ 5.074

30.

31.

32.

33.

34.
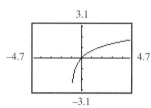

35. 6^{216} **36.** 27   **37.** 10   **38.** 1

39. $\frac{1}{20,000}$ **40.** 243   **41.** ≈ 3.162

42. -3 and $\frac{3}{2}$ **43.** -1

44. no solution

45. all real numbers greater than 0   **46.** 6   **47.** 0   **48.** ≈ 0.514 **49.** $-\frac{5}{3}$ **50.** no solution

51. -1 and 4   **52.** all real numbers   **53.** ≈ 0.530 **54.** $f(x) = 1200 + 0.025x$; $f^{-1}(x) = 40x - 48,000$; The inverse function represents her total sales in terms of her monthly income.

55. $f(x) = 95x$ **56.** $A = 8500(1.065)^t$ **57.** The model predicts that there will be

$f^{-1}(x) = \frac{x}{95}$;

The inverse function represents the number of hours in terms of the distance traveled.

The investment was worth $15,955.67.

36.755 thousand (or 36,755) cable systems in the year 2010.

58. The pH is approximately 3.796.

59. The hydrogen ion concentration is approximately 2.5×10^{-2} moles per liter.   **60.** It will take approximately 12.4 years.

61. $A(t) = 96.9e^{0.076t}$; The estimated revenues for 2000, 2005, and 2010 are (in billions) $443.0, $647.9, and $947.4, respectively.   **62.** It has been about 7573 years since the organism died.

CHAPTER 15 TEST

1. $f(x) = x^3$
$f^{-1}(x) = \sqrt[3]{x}$

2.

3.
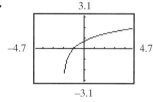

4. $F^{-1}(x) = \frac{1}{2}x + 4$ **5.** $\frac{1}{4}$ **6.** 1   **7.** 256   **8.** ≈ 1.516

9. ≈ 11.036 **10.** $\log 3 + 2 \log x + 3 \log y + \log z$

11. $2 + 2 \log_3 a - \log_3 b$ **12.** $\log x^2(x - 4)$ **13.** $\ln \dfrac{\sqrt{x}}{y^2}$

14. (a) 1   **(b)** 1   **(c)** 1   **15.** $\dfrac{5}{3}$ **16.** ≈ 4.771 **17.** all real numbers greater than 0   **18.** ≈ 0.732

19. (a) $f(x) = 400 + 0.03x$ **(b)** $f^{-1}(x) = 33.\overline{3}x - 13,333.\overline{3}$ **(c)** The inverse function represents the value of weekly sales in terms of his weekly income.   **20.** $f(x) = 2000(1.05)^x$; The investment was worth approximately \$5306.60.   **21.** It will take approximately 9.24 years.   **22.** Answers will vary.

CUMULATIVE REVIEW CHAPTERS 1–15

1. $\dfrac{y^2}{25}$ **2.** $\dfrac{4y^4}{x^6}$ **3.** $16x^2$ **4.** $-0.8a^2 - 5.2ab + 2.7b^2$ **5.** $-9x^2y^3z$ **6.** $9x^2 - 4y^2$ **7.** $4x^2 + 6x - 18$

8. $x^2 - 8x + 16$ **9.** $-5xy^3z$ **10.** $r + 2 - \dfrac{4s}{r}$ **11.** $\dfrac{x + 2}{x + 3}$ **12.** $\dfrac{x^2 + 2x + 5}{(x + 2)(x - 2)}$

13. $-\dfrac{(x + 2)(x + 1)}{(x + 4)(x - 2)}$ **14.** 1   **15.** $\dfrac{4(y - 5)}{xy^2(y - 3)}$ **16.** $6\sqrt{2x}$ **17.** $4ab\sqrt[3]{2b}$ **18.** -1 **19.** $\dfrac{2}{x}\sqrt{yz}$

20. $\dfrac{x + 7\sqrt{x} + 12}{x - 9}$ **21.** $x^{17/12} - x$ **22.** $(5m + 6n)(5m - 6n)$ **23.** $2(x - 4)(x + 2)$

24. does not factor

25.

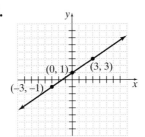

Domain: all real numbers
Range: all real numbers

26.

Domain: all real numbers

Range: all real numbers $\geq -\dfrac{9}{4}$

27.

Domain: all real numbers $\neq -2$
Range: all real numbers ≤ -9.66
or ≥ 1.66

28.

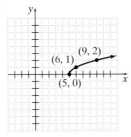

Domain: all real numbers ≥ 5
Range: all real numbers ≥ 0

29.

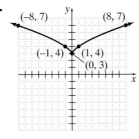

Domain: all real numbers
Range: all real numbers ≥ 3

30.

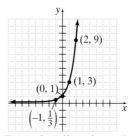

Domain: all real numbers
Range: all real numbers > 0

31.

Domain: all real numbers > 3
Range: all real numbers

32. -6 **33.** no solution

34. 6 and -4 **35.** $\dfrac{5}{2} \pm \dfrac{\sqrt{11}}{2}i$

36. $-\dfrac{5}{3}$ **37.** 8   **38.** 2

39. $\sqrt{5}$ **40.** $(9, \infty)$

41. $(-\infty, -1 - \sqrt{3}] \cup [-1 + \sqrt{3}, \infty)$ **42.** $(4, 4)$ **43.** $y = -\dfrac{3}{5}x + \dfrac{4}{5}$ **44.** $y = 4x + 9$

45. $y = \dfrac{3}{2}x^2 + \dfrac{9}{2}x - 6$ **46.** $f^{-1}(x) = \dfrac{3}{2}x - 9$

47. The company must sell 53 books in order to break-even.   **48.** The dimensions are 9 feet by 12 feet.
49. It will take the drains about 2.5 hours to drain the tank.
50. It will take about 24.4 years for the money to triple.

Answers to Check Up Exercises

Chapter 1

Section 1.1

1   **1.** $15, \dfrac{6}{3}$ (or 2), 1 billion   **2.** all of the numbers   **3.** $15, -3, 0, \dfrac{6}{3}$ (or 2), 1 billion, -180

4. $15, 0, \dfrac{6}{3}$ (or 2), 1 billion   **2**   **1.** $-12°C$ **2.** $36°C$ **3.** $-5\dfrac{1}{2}°C$ **4.** $18.75°C$

3   **1.**

   4   **1.** $>$ **2.** $<$ **3.** $=$ **4.** $>$ **5.** false   **6.** false

7. true   **8.** $15 > 5$ **9.** $-2 < 6$ **10.** $\dfrac{11}{4} = 2.75$

5   **1.** 15   **2.** 3.3   **3.** $\dfrac{2}{7}$ **4.** $\dfrac{5}{3}$ **5.** $|-126.9|$ **6.** MATH ▶ 1 (−) (3 + 3 ÷ 4)) ENTER ; 3.75

6   **1.** $-3\dfrac{1}{3}$ **2.** $\dfrac{1}{2}$ **3.** 15   **4.** -35 **5.** $-\dfrac{4}{7}$ **6.** 0   **7.** $-(11.9) = -11.9$ percent

Section 1.2

2   **1.**

   2.

3.

   4.

3   **1.** 34   **2.** -5.75 **3.** 4.5   **4.** -4 **5.** $\dfrac{1}{28}$ **6.** 43   **7.** $-\dfrac{29}{24}$

4 $455.76 + (-12.56) + (-35.78) + (-255.65) + (-267.87) = -116.10$; Bob must deposit $116.10 in order to not have his account overdrawn.

Section 1.3

2   **1.**

   2.

3.

   4.

3   **1.** -24 **2.** 34   **3.** -11.75 **4.** -4.5 **5.** $-\dfrac{41}{28}$ **6.** $\dfrac{4}{3}$ **7.** -1 **8.** -15.35 **9.** $\dfrac{5}{24}$

4   **1.** 7   **2.** $-\dfrac{3}{10}$ **3.** 22.2

5 $897.63 + 355 + 572 - 120 - 300 - 185.23 - 104.50 - 231.97 - (-231.97) - 10$; The current balance in Beverly's account is $1104.90.

Section 1.4

2   **1.** 16, 12, 8, 4, 0, −4, −8, −12   **2.** −16, −12, −8, −4, 0, 4, 8, 12   **3**   **1.** 72   **2.** 224   **3.** $\dfrac{1}{4}$

4. −0.144   **5.** $-\dfrac{1}{3}$ **6.** −96   **7.** −3   **8.** [(−)] [( ] [2] [+] [3] [÷] [7] [ )] [×] [( ] [3] [+] [5] [÷] [8] [ )] [MATH] [1] [ENTER]; $-\dfrac{493}{56}$

5   **1.** −48   **2.** 600   **3.** 0   **4.** $\dfrac{1}{11}$ **5.** $-\dfrac{64}{21}$ **6.** 0   **7.** 0   **8.** 0

6   **1.** ($215 per week) · (4 weeks) = $860; Sara's paycheck shows her gross earnings are $860.
2. Instant Game = 3 · $3 = $9; Big Jackpot = 2 · $4 = $8; Monster Millions = 2 · $5 = $10; Weekly total = $27; Yearly amount = $27 · 52 = $1404; She would have to win $1404 in order to break even.

Section 1.5

1   **1.** positive   **2.** negative   **3.** zero   **4.** undefined result   **5.** indeterminate result
3   **1.** (a) −2   (b) −2   (c) 3   (d) −3   **2.** (a) 0.6   (b) −0.6   (c) −0.6   (d) 0.6

3. (a) −4.1   (b) 36   (c) 0   **4.** (a) $\dfrac{8}{7}$ (b) $-\dfrac{9}{7}$ (c) $\dfrac{5}{9}$ (d) $-\dfrac{1}{5}$ **5.** (a) $\dfrac{3}{14}$ (b) $\dfrac{4}{9}$

(c) $-\dfrac{27}{16}$ (d) undefined   **6.** [(−)] [( ] [2] [+] [3] [÷] [7] [ )] [÷] [( ] [3] [+] [5] [÷] [8] [ )] [MATH] [1] [ENTER]; $-\dfrac{136}{203}$

4   **1.** 125   **2.** $-\dfrac{1}{15}$ **3.** −11.76   **5**   **1.** Total = 11 + (−4) + 8 + (−2) + 0 + 4 + 12 = 29;

average = 29 ÷ 7 ≈ 4.1°F; The average daily low temperature for the week was about 4.1°F.

2. Rate = 700 ÷ 4 = 175 mph; distance = 175 · $2\dfrac{1}{2}$ = 437.5 miles; At the same rate, you could send a message 437.5 miles.

Section 2.1

1   **1.** 3^7 **2.** $\left(\dfrac{2}{3}\right)^4$ **3.** $(1.3)(1.3) = 1.69$ **4.** $0 \cdot 0 \cdot 0 \cdot 0 \cdot 0 \cdot 0 = 0$

5. $\left(\dfrac{2}{5}\right)\left(\dfrac{2}{5}\right)\left(\dfrac{2}{5}\right)\left(\dfrac{2}{5}\right)\left(\dfrac{2}{5}\right) = \dfrac{32}{3125}$ **6.** (a) $(-6)(-6) = 36$ (b) $-6 \cdot 6 = -36$
7. (a) $(-6)(-6)(-6) = -216$ (b) $-6 \cdot 6 \cdot 6 = -216$

8. [( ] [(−)] [( ] [2] [+] [1] [÷] [3] [ )] [ )] [^] [4] [MATH] [1] [ENTER]; $\dfrac{2401}{81}$; 29.64   **2**   **1.** 7   **2.** −7   **3.** −7   **4.** 1

5. 1   **6.** −1   **3**   **1.** $\dfrac{1}{3^3} = \dfrac{1}{27}$ **2.** $-\dfrac{1}{3^3} = -\dfrac{1}{27}$ **3.** $-\dfrac{1}{(-3)^3} = \dfrac{1}{27}$ **4.** $\dfrac{1}{(0.5)^4} = 16$ or

$\left(\dfrac{1}{2}\right)^{-4} = 2^4 = 16$ **5.** $\left(\dfrac{4}{3}\right)^3 = \dfrac{64}{27}$ **6.** $\dfrac{1}{\left(-1\frac{3}{7}\right)^2} = \dfrac{49}{100}$ or $\left(-\dfrac{10}{7}\right)^{-2} = \left(\dfrac{7}{10}\right)^2 = \dfrac{49}{100}$

7. [( ] [(−)] [( ] [3] [+] [1] [÷] [3] [ )] [ )] [^] [(−)] [4] [MATH] [1] [ENTER]; 0.0081, calculator may not display fraction form; the fraction form may take more characters than the calculator screen will allow.   **4**   The volume of the box is 5832 cubic inches.

Section 2.2

1   **1.** 5×10^6 **2.** -1.589×10^7 **3.** 3.67×10^{-4} **4.** -5.037×10^{-7}
2   **1.** $6.5 \times 10^7 = 65{,}000{,}000$ **2.** $-8.33 \times 10^{13} = -83{,}300{,}000{,}000{,}000$ **3.** $9.3 \times 10^{-3} = 0.0093$
4. $-3.12 \times 10^{-4} = -0.000312$
3   **1.** 299,792,458; 300 million meters per second would be a useful approximation.
2. $(6.74 \times 10^4)(2) = 1.348 \times 10^5$. It would take about 134,800 calories to change 250 g of water at 100°C to steam at 100°C.

Section 2.3

1 **1.** 7   **2.** 0.9   **3.** $\dfrac{5}{6}$ **4.** -4 **5.** not a real number

6. $\boxed{\text{2nd}}\ \boxed{\sqrt{}}\ \boxed{1}\ \boxed{4}\ \boxed{4}\ \boxed{\div}\ \boxed{1}\ \boxed{6}\ \boxed{9}\ \boxed{)}\ \boxed{\text{MATH}}\ \boxed{1}\ \boxed{\text{ENTER}};\ \dfrac{12}{13}$ **7.** 4 and 5; 4.123105626   **8.** -3 and -4; -3.872983346

2 **1.** 4.642   **2.** 3   **3.** -4 **4.** not a real number   **5.** -3 **6.** $\dfrac{2}{5}$ **7.** 2.5

3 **1.**

4 The length of a side is $5\dfrac{3}{4}$ feet.

Section 2.4

2 **1.** $256^{1/4} = 4$ **2.** $243^{1/5} = 3$ **3.** $(-256)^{1/4} =$ not a real number   **4.** $(-243)^{1/5} = -3$

5. $25^{1/3} \approx 2.924$ **6.** $(-25)^{1/3} \approx -2.924$ **7.** $(2.8561)^{1/4} = 1.3$ **8.** $\left(\dfrac{16}{81}\right)^{1/4} = \dfrac{2}{3}$

9. $(1.95)^{1/4} \approx 1.182$ **10.** $\left(\dfrac{4}{9}\right)^{1/5} \approx 0.850$ **3** **1.** Each side of the tank measures 7 feet.

2. The diagonal walkway should be 14.72 feet long.

Section 2.5

1 **1.** b   **2.** f   **3.** d   **4.** c   **5.** e   **6.** a   **7.** Opposites: $-4, 17, -\dfrac{5}{7}, \dfrac{8}{9}$; Reciprocals: $\dfrac{1}{4}, -\dfrac{1}{17}$,

$\dfrac{7}{5}, -\dfrac{9}{8}$ **2** **1.** d   **2.** b   **3.** a   **4.** c   **5.** $-42 + (-11)$ **6.** $(5 + 9)4$ or $4(9 + 5)$ or $(9 + 5)4$

7. $-102 \cdot 125$ **8.** $[-4 + (-3)] + 11$ **9.** $[-5 \cdot (-3)] \cdot (-2)$ **3** **1.** $5 \cdot 3 + 5 \cdot 7$

2. $4(-7) + 18(-7)$ **3.** $17 \cdot 5 - 25 \cdot 5$ **4.** $\dfrac{-46}{2} + \dfrac{62}{2}$ **5.** $-5 - 9$ **6.** $5 - 9$ **7.** $5(12 + 17)$

8. $13(17 - 22)$ **9.** $-6(7 + 11)$ **10.** $-12(11 - 14)$ **4** **1.** 6   **2.** 31   **3.** 3   **4.** -97 **5.** 2
6. -17 **7.** -5 **8.** -65 **5** **1.** $[71 + (71 + 0.50) + 69.50 + (69.50 - 0.25) + 72] \div 5 = 70.65$;
The average closing price of the stock was \$70.65.   **2.** The distance from New York are:
Philadelphia $=$ 100 miles; Boston $=$ 206 miles; Baltimore $=$ 196 miles; Chicago $=$ 802 miles;
Cleveland $=$ 473 miles; Los Angeles $=$ 2786 miles.; The greatest distance between the cities is the distance between
Los Angeles and Philadelphia which is (at least) 2686 miles.

Section 3.1

1 **1.** Let $n =$ the number; $n + 13$ **2.** Let a and b be the numbers; $2(a + b)$ **3.** Let $n =$ the number;
$8n - 6$ **4.** Let $n =$ the number; $6 - 8n$ **5.** Let $b =$ the length of the base, $h =$ the height, $A =$ the area;
$A = bh$ **2** **1.** The product of a number and -27.   **2.** Twenty-five less than twice a number.
3. The perimeter of a triangle is equal to the sum of the lengths of its three sides.   **3** **1.** 52   **2. (a)** 16

(b) $\dfrac{4}{25}$ **3. (a)** 24   **(b)** -24 **(c)** 24   **(d)** 288   **(e)** -288 **4. (a)** -24 **(b)** 24   **(c)** -24

(d) 288   **(e)** -288 **5.** $\boxed{(-)}\ \boxed{1}\ \boxed{2}\ \boxed{\text{STO}\blacktriangleright}\ \boxed{\text{X,T,}\theta\text{,n}}\ \boxed{\text{ALPHA}}\ \boxed{:}\ \boxed{3}\ \boxed{\text{X,T,}\theta\text{,n}}\ \boxed{+}\ \boxed{1}\ \boxed{5}\ \boxed{\text{ENTER}};\ -21$

4 Let $b =$ the length of the base, $h =$ the height, and $A =$ the area of the triangle. Then $A = \dfrac{1}{2}bh$.

The area of the given triangle is 35 square inches.

Section 3.2

1 **1.** 3 terms; $4x^2, -3x, 7$ **2.** 4 terms; $5x^2, 3xy, -2y^2, 11$ **3.** 3 terms; $2(x - 4), -6x, 12$ **4.** $12, -17, 29$
5. $-2.3, 1.6, -4.1$ **6.** $5, -1$ **7.** none   **8.** $3(p + q)$ and $-5(p + q), 13$ and -6 **9.** none

2   **1.** $35x$ **2.** $12z$ **3.** $14a$ **4.** 0 **5.** $2x^3 + 2x^2 - 4x$ **6.** $6xy - 2yz$ **7.** $\dfrac{25}{12}x + \dfrac{13}{12}y$
3   **1.** $-2a + 5$ **2.** $5.9b - 6$ **3.** $6x + 6$ **4.** $4x^2 + 2x + 12$ **5.** $-3a - 5$ **6.** $0.4x + 11.2$
7. $3y + 14$ **8.** $-x + y - 6z + 16$ **4**   **1.** Let the sides measure x, y and z. Let $p =$ the perimeter.
Then $p = x + y + z$. The perimeter of the garden is 36 feet.   **2.** Let $e =$ the length of an edge of a cube.
Let $S =$ the surface area of the cube. Then $S = 6e^2$. The surface area of the box is 4374 square inches.

Section 3.3

1   **1.** $72ab$ **2.** $18x + 45$ **3.** $-6x^2 - 8xy$ **4.** $\dfrac{11a}{2}$ **5.** $\dfrac{x}{4}$ **6.** $2x + 3y - 8$ **2**   **1.** $50p + q$
2. $x - 13$ **3.** $-18a - 14b - 4c$ **4.** $-8y + 43$ **5.** $20p + 204$ **6.** $7x + 53$
3 $p = 2W + 2(W + 25)$; $p = 4W + 50$; The perimeter of the desktop is 170 inches.

Section 3.4

1   **1.** equation   **2.** expression   **3.** expression   **4.** equation   **5.** equation   **6.** expression
2   **1.** false   **2.** true   **3.** false   **4.** true   **5.** yes   **6.** no   **7.** no

3   **1.** $2\left(\dfrac{21}{3}\right) = 2 + 3\cdot 4$ **2.** Let $x =$ the number; $3(x + 4) = 4x$ **4**   Let $r =$ the length of the
radius of the circle, and $A =$ the area of the circle. Then $A = \pi r^2$.

Section 3.5

1   **1.** $A = 7$ square inches   **2.** $C \approx 15.08$ inches; $\boxed{\text{2nd}}\ \boxed{\pi}\ \boxed{\text{x}}\ \boxed{4}\ \boxed{.}\ \boxed{8}\ \boxed{\text{ENTER}}$ 15.07964474 inches
2   **1.** The volume of the cube is 50.653 cubic inches, and the surface area is 82.14 square inches.
2. The volume of the can is approximately 78.54 cubic inches and the surface area is approximately
102.10 square inches.   **3**   **1.** The third angle measures 55°.   **2.** The second angle measures 31°.
4   **1.** The hypotenuse is 17 cm.   **5**   **1.** The equatorial circumference of Mercury is approximately
15,331 km.   **2.** The packing crate requires 1376 square inches of plywood, not including scrap.

Section 3.6

1   **1.** The simple interest is $1700.   **2.** The compounded amount is $11,853.05 and the interest is $1853.05.
2   **1.** The temperature at the center of the Earth's core could be 3982°C.   **2.** The temperatures on the
moon range from 273°F to −274°F.   **3**   The distance traveled is 175 miles   **4**   The height of the
apple is 150 feet above the ground.   **5**   The period of the pendulum is approximately 2.832 seconds.
6   **1.** The length of time for one stride is approximately 1.9238 seconds. Steve's walking speed is
approximately 3.12 feet per second.   **2.** Simple interest totals $400; annually compounded interest totals
$398.05; monthly compounded interest totals $392.83. Pete should choose the third option.

Section 4.1

1   **1.**

F	C
86	30
77	25
68	20
59	15
50	10
41	5
32	0

2.

t	A
4	$5254.70
8	$5522.40
12	$5803.80
16	$6099.40
20	$6410.20

3.

b	a
−3	25
−2	19
−1	13
0	7
1	1
2	−5
3	−11

2   **1.** Temperature ordered pairs: (86, 30), (77, 25), (68, 20), (59, 15), (50, 10), (41, 5), (32, 0); Investment
ordered pairs: (4, 5254.70), (8, 5522.40), (12, 5803.80), (16, 6099.40), (20, 6410.20); Ordered pairs for (b, a):
(−3, 25), (−2, 19), (−1, 13), (0, 7), (1, 1), (2, −5), (3, −11)   **3**   **1.** domain is {5, 10, 15}; range is {15, 30, 45}
2. domain is {0, 1, 2, 3, ...} or the whole numbers; range is {4, 6, 8, 10, ...} or all even integers 4 or larger
3. domain is all real numbers; range is all real numbers   **4.** domain is all real numbers ≥ -4;
range is all real numbers ≥ 0 **5.** domain is all real numbers $\neq -1$; range is all real numbers $\neq 0$

6. domain is all positive real numbers; range is all positive real numbers

2.

n	r
2	672
3	803
4	934
5	1065

3. $(2, 672), (3, 803), (4, 934), (5, 1065)$

4   **1.** $r = 410 + 131n$

Section 4.2

1   **1.**

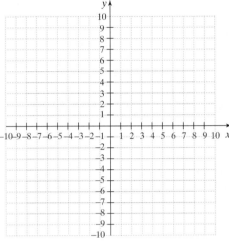

The graph corresponds to the setting of ZStandard.

ZOOM 6

2.

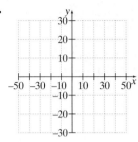

The graph corresponds to the setting of ZInteger.

ZOOM 6 ZOOM 8 ENTER

2   **1–2.**

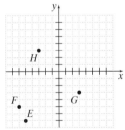

3. Answers may vary.
4. $A(-5, -2), B(5, 5), C(-1, 1), D(0, 4), E(4, -3), F(-3, 0)$
5. (a) II   **(b)** I   **(c)** IV   **(d)** III   **(e)** origin   **(f)** x-axis
(g) y-axis

6.

7.

8.

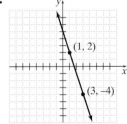

$(1, 2)$

$(3, -4)$

9.

3   **1.** domain is $\{-3\}$; range is all real numbers   **2.** domain is all real numbers ≥ -4; range is all real numbers   **3.** domain is all real numbers; range is all real numbers   **4.** domain is all real numbers ≤ 0; range is all real numbers ≥ 0 **4**   **1.** Domain is $\{1, 2, 3, 4, 5, 6, 7\}$ or day of the week; range is $\{60, 65, 68, 70, 64, 55, 50\}$ or the number of nondefective parts produced each day.

Section 4.3

1 **1.** yes **2.** yes **3.** no **4.** no **2** **1.** yes **2.** yes **3.** no **4.** yes **5.** yes
3 **1.** yes **2.** yes **3.** no **4.** no
5. | ZOOM | 6 | ZOOM | 4 | Y= | 2 | − | 3 | X,T,θ,n | x^2 | GRAPH |

6. | ZOOM | 6 | ZOOM | 4 | Y= | 3 | X,T,θ,n | − | 2 | GRAPH |

4 **1.** $f(4)$ is not a real number; $f(-4) = 9$ **2.** $h(1) = -3; h(0) = -8; h(-1) = -17$
3. $g(b) = 4b - 8; g(1) = -4; g(b + 1) = 4b - 4$ **5** **1.** $c(d) = 5 + 10d$ **2.** $c(4) = 45$

Section 4.4

1 **1.** x-intercept is $(5, 0)$; y-intercept is $(0, 3)$ **2.** x-intercepts are $(-2, 0), (-1, 0), (1, 0)$; y-intercept is $(0, -1)$ **3.** x-intercepts are $(2, 0)$ and $(-2, 0)$; y-intercept is $(0, -4)$ **4.** x-intercept is $(-0.5, 0)$ and the y-intercept is $(0, 1)$ **2** **1. (a)** $(-\infty, -2)$ **(b)** $(3, \infty)$ **(c)** $(-2, 3)$ **2. (a)** The relative maximum 2 occurs at $(-6, 2)$; the relative maximum of 4 occurs at $(-1, 4)$. **(b)** The relative minimum of -3 occurs at $(-4, -3)$; the relative minimum of -7 occurs at $(4, -7)$. **3. (a)** $(-\infty, -1)$ **(b)** $(-1, \infty)$ **(c)** relative maximum of 0 at $(-1, 0)$ **(d)** no relative minimum **4. (a)** $(1, \infty)$ **(b)** $(-\infty, 1)$ **(c)** no relative maximum **(d)** relative minimum of -1 at $(1, -1)$ **5. (a)** $(-1, 1.5)$ and $(3, \infty)$ **(b)** $(-\infty, -1)$ and $(1.5, 3)$ **(c)** relative maximum of 45.9375 at $(1.5, 45.9375)$ **(d)** relative minima of -40 at $(-1, -40)$ and 24 at $(3, 24)$ **3** **1.** $(1, 0)$ and $(4, 3)$ **2.** $(5, -5)$ **3.** $(-1, -3)$ and $(2.5, 2.25)$ **4** **1.** $c(x) = 55 - x$ **2.** $r(x) = (55 - x)x$ **3.** $(0, 27.5)$ **4.** $(27.5, \infty)$ **5.** $x = 27.5$

6. To maximize revenue sell 27 seats or 28 seats.
7. The maximum revenue for selling 27 or 28 seats will be \$756.

Section 5.1

1 **1.** linear **2.** nonlinear **3.** linear **4.** nonlinear **5.** nonlinear **2** **1.** -2
2. any real number **3.** 3 **4.** no solution **3** **1.** 1 **2.** any real number **3.** no solution
4. -3.5 **4** **1.** The cost of production will equal the revenue received when 10 baskets are produced and sold. **2.** Phillipe must score a 96 in order to achieve an average of 90.

Section 5.2

1 **1.** $455 = 455$ **2.** $a = 44.93$ **3.** $p - \dfrac{3}{4} = -\dfrac{1}{8}$ **2** **1.** 31 **2.** $\dfrac{6}{35}$ **3.** 15 **4.** 22

3 **1.** $24.8 + 23.4 = 48.2$ **2.** $x = -0.9$ **3.** $z = -\dfrac{5}{3}$ **4** **1.** 28 **2.** -1 **3.** -325 **4.** -33

5. $\dfrac{2}{15}$ **6.** 5 **5** **1.** There were 215 adult admissions. **2.** Ayse's balance was \$917.99 before writing

the check. **3.** Each side of Cheryl's garden will be 9.5 feet long. **4.** The height of the triangle is $5\dfrac{1}{2}$ feet.

Section 5.3

1 **1.** 3 **2.** $-\dfrac{13}{2}$ **3.** any real number **4.** no solution **5.** $-\dfrac{56}{15}$ **6.** -3 **7.** 13

2 **1.** The monthly payments will be \$75. **2.** The break even point is any real number since the cost will always equal the revenue. **3.** The mixture used 10 cc's of the 40% alcohol solution.

Section 5.4

1 **1.** $h = \dfrac{2A}{b}$ **2.** $a = 4A - b - c - d$ **3.** $x = \dfrac{5}{3}y + \dfrac{5}{6}$ **4.** $y = -2x + \dfrac{5}{2}$ **5.** $y = \dfrac{7}{3}x + 9$

2 **1.** $c = 0.12x + 49.95$ **2.** $x = \dfrac{25}{3}c - \dfrac{1665}{4}$ **3.** You can drive approximately 1250 miles if your vacation budget is \$200. **4.** For \$150 you can drive approximately 834 miles; for \$250 approximately 1667 miles; for \$500 approximately 3750 miles.

Section 5.5

1 **1.** The integers are 12, 14, and 16. **2.** The lengths Jim needs to cut are 3 inches, 4 inches, 5 inches, 6 inches and 7 inches. **2** **1.** The angles measure 40°, 80°, and 60°. **2.** The sand box will have two sides of 3.5 feet and a third side of 5 feet. **3** **1.** You will actually receive \$2752.29. The interest paid on the loan will be \$247.71. **2.** Zeke will borrow \$4000 at 7% and \$1000 at 8.5%.
4 The room charge before adding the surcharge is \$62.50.

Section 5.6

1 **1.** linear **2.** linear **3.** nonlinear **4.** linear **2** **1.** two solutions; $x = 10$ and $x = 8$
2. no solutions **3.** one solution; $x = 9$ **3** **1.** 1 and $-1.666\ldots$ **2.** 1 and -1 **3.** 5 and -7
4. no solutions **5.** $-1.666\ldots$ and 3 **4** **1.** 9 **2.** 1 and $-1.666\ldots$ **3.** 1 and -1 **4.** 5 and -7
5. no solutions **6.** $-1.666\ldots$ and 3 **5** $|72 - h| = 3$; $h = 69$ and $h = 75$; The smallest height for drivers will be 69 inches (or 5 feet 9 inches) and the largest height will be 75 inches (or 6 feet 3 inches).

Section 6.1

1 **1.** nonlinear **2.** linear; $2x - 5y = -7$; $a = 2, b = -5, c = -7$ **3.** linear; $x = -\dfrac{3}{8}$; $a = 1, b = 0$,
$c = -\dfrac{3}{8}$ **4.** linear; $8.2x - y = 3.6$; $a = 8.2, b = -1, c = 3.6$ **5.** nonlinear **6.** linear;
$\sqrt{3}x - \sqrt{2}y = 0$; $a = \sqrt{3}, b = -\sqrt{2}, c = 0$ **7.** nonlinear **2** **1.** no **2.** yes **3.** yes **4.** yes

3 **1.**

x	y
0	6
1	6
2	6

2.

x	y
0	-1
1	3
2	7

3.

x	$g(x)$
0	2
5	5
-5	-1

4.

x	y
2	-7
4	-10
6	-13

5.

6.

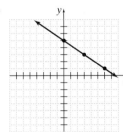

4 Answers may vary.
1. $(0, -2), (1, -3), (2, -4)$ for example
2. $(0, 4), (4, 1), (8, -2)$ for example

5   **1. (a)** $(1, 3), (3, 7), (5, 11)$

(b)

Charge (dollars) vs Weight (pounds)

(c) The cost for an 8 pounds package is $17.
(d) Answers may vary.
2. $(2, 120), (3, 180), (4, 240)$, for example; the first ordered pair indicates that after 2 hours, Tom is 120 miles from Cincinnati; the second ordered pair indicates that after 3 hours, Tom is 180 miles from Cincinnati; the third ordered pair indicates that after 4 hours, Tom is 240 miles from Cincinnati.

Section 6.2

1   **1.** The x-intercept is $(4, 0)$ and the y-intercept is $(0, -2)$.   **2.** The x-intercept is $(2, 0)$ and the y-intercept is $(0, 5)$.   **3.** The x-intercept is $(1, 0)$ and the y-intercept is $(0, 1)$.   **4.** The x-intercept is $(2.5, 0)$ and the y-intercept is $(0, 5)$.   **5.** The x-intercept is $(2, 0)$ and the y-intercept is $(0, 12)$.

6. The x-intercept is $\left(-\dfrac{11}{5}, 0\right)$ and the y-intercept is $(0, 11)$.   **7.** $y = 7x - 15$, the y-intercept is $(0, -15)$.

8. $y = -\dfrac{4}{3}x + 8$; the y-intercept is $(0, 8)$.   **2**   **1.** The x-intercept is $(16, 0)$.   **2.** The x-intercept and the y-intercept occur at the origin, $(0, 0)$.   **3.** The x-intercept and the y-intercept occur at the origin, $(0, 0)$.

4. The y-intercept is $(0, -1)$.   **5.** The y-intercept is $\left(0, \dfrac{3}{5}\right)$.   **6.** The x-intercept is $\left(\dfrac{3}{2}, 0\right)$.

3   **1.**

2.

4   The x-intercept is $(24, 0)$ and the y-intercept is $(0, 6)$. The x-intercept indicates that after 24 hours of use, the tank will be empty; the y-intercept indicates that at the start, the tank is full.;
; After 8 hours of use, there are 4 gallons of gas remaining in the tank.

Gallons of Butane Gas vs Hours of Use, point $(8, 4)$

Section 6.3

1   **1.** The slope is zero.   **2.** The slope is $\dfrac{2}{5}$.   **3.** The slope is $-\dfrac{7}{2}$.   **4.** The slope is undefined.

2   **1.** $m = \dfrac{3}{2}$ **2.** $m = 0$ **3.** $m =$ undefined   **4.** $m = -\dfrac{4}{3}$ **3**   **1.** $m = -\dfrac{7}{11}$ **2.** $m = -\dfrac{8}{3}$

3. $m = 0$ **4.** $m =$ undefined   **4**   **1.**   **2.**

3.   **4.**   **5.**

6.   **7.**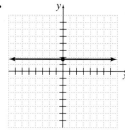

5   **1. (a)** $m = 4.55$ **(b)** Let $x =$ the number of years after 1970; $y = 4.55x + 169$

(c)   **(d)** For 1980, $x = 10$ and $y = 214.5$; this estimate is off by 10.5, which is a small error of less than 5%.   **(e)** In the year 2000, $x = 30$ and $y = 305.5$; if the trend continues, there will be about 306 corporate listings in the year 2000.

2. $m = 10$; her average rate of ascent is 10 feet per minute.

Section 6.4

1   **1.** coinciding   **2.** coinciding   **3.** not coinciding   **4.** not coinciding   **2**   **1.** parallel
2. not parallel   **3.** parallel   **4.** parallel   **3**   **1.** intersecting and perpendicular   **2.** neither intersecting nor perpendicular   **3.** intersecting   **4.** neither intersecting nor perpendicular   **4**   **1.** Let $x =$ the number of lawns for which Tim cares. $y = 8.50x + 6.50x + 85.$ **2.** $y = 20x$ **3.** Since the slopes are different, the lines intersect, and there is a break-even point.   **4.** If the revenue function is $y = 15x$, the slopes are the same, but the y-intercepts are different, and the lines are parallel. Tim will never break-even.
5. 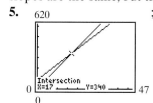 ; The break-even point is (17, 340) which means Tim will make a profit if he cares for more than 17 lawns.

Section 6.5

1   **1.** $y = -\dfrac{1}{4}x + 2$ **2.** $x = 2$ **3.** $y = -3$ **4.** $y = 5x - 4$ **5.** $y = 4x - 1$

6. $y = -\dfrac{2}{5}x + 3.2$ **2**   **1.** $y = 2x + 3$ **2.** $y = \dfrac{3}{4}x - \dfrac{9}{2}$ **3**   **1.** $y = \dfrac{2}{3}x + \dfrac{5}{3}$ **2.** $y = -4x - 1$

3. $y = \dfrac{3}{2}$ **4.** $x = -\dfrac{5}{2}$ **4**   **1.** $y = x - 1$ **2.** $y = -\dfrac{3}{2}x + \dfrac{13}{2}$ **3.** $y = -\dfrac{5}{2}x + \dfrac{3}{2}$

5   **1. (a)** $m = -0.625$ **(b)** $y = -0.625x + 90$ **(c)** $y(91) = 33.125$; The prediction was very close, off by less than 5%.

(d) $y(99) = 28.125$; The predicted rate of accidental deaths for 1999 is 28.1 deaths per 100,000 population.

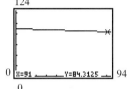

2. (a) $m = \dfrac{5}{9}$ **(b)** $C = \dfrac{5}{9}(F - 32)$

(c) $C(75) \approx 23.9$; The Celsius temperature corresponding to 75°F is approximately 23.9°C.

Section 7.1

1   **1.** The coordinate pair is a solution.   **2.** The coordinate pair is not a solution.   **3.** The coordinate pair is not a solution.   **4.** The coordinate pair is a solution.   **2**   **1.** $(1, 1)$ **2.** $(4, -5)$ **3.** $(-2, -3)$ **4.** no solution   **5.** infinitely many solutions; any coordinate pair satisfying $y = 2x + 3$ **6.** no solution   **3**   **1. (a)** $C(x) = 255 + 2.50x$; $R(x) = 20x$ **(b)** approximately $(14.6, 291.4)$ **(c)** The solution represents the break-even point where the cost of making the cakes equals the revenue received from selling the cakes. **(d)** 14 or less   **(e)** 15 or more   **2.** Let $x =$ the width of the current garden and $y =$ its length.; $2x + 2y = 64$; $4x + 2y + 30 = 118$; The solution is $(12, 20)$. The current garden measures 12 feet by 20 feet; the future garden will be 24 feet by 35 feet.

Section 7.2

1   **1.** $(1, -1)$ **2.** $\left(\dfrac{1}{4}, -\dfrac{9}{2}\right)$ **3.** $\left(\dfrac{2}{11}, -\dfrac{26}{11}\right)$ **4.** infinitely many solutions; any coordinate pair where $y = 5x - 3$ **5.** no solution   **2**   **1. (a)** Let $x =$ the length of a side of the garden, and $x + 2 =$ the length of a side of the walkway. Let $y =$ the perimeter of the walkway.; $4x = 46$; $y = 4(x + 2)$

(b) The solution of the system of equations is $\left(11\dfrac{1}{2}, 54\right)$. The dimensions of the garden are $11\dfrac{1}{2}$ feet on each side. The outside dimensions of the walkway are $13\dfrac{1}{2}$ feet on each side.   **(c)** The outside perimeter of the walkway is 54 feet.   **2.** Let $x =$ the measure of the first angle and $y =$ the measure of the second angle.; $x + y = 180$; $y = 2x + 15$; The solution of the system of equations is $(55, 125)$. The first angle measures 55° and the second angle measures 125°.

Section 7.3

1   **1.** $(6, 4)$ **2.** $(2, -6)$ **3.** $(1, -1)$ **4.** $\left(\dfrac{1}{4}, \dfrac{8}{5}\right)$ **5.** no solution   **6.** infinitely many solutions; any coordinate pair where $y = 5x + 12$ **2**   Let $x =$ the number of cans of cashews sold and $y =$ the number of cans of peanuts sold; $x + y = 262$; $6.50x + 4.00y = 1240.50$; The solution of the system of equations is $(77, 185)$. The Indian Maidens sold 77 cans of cashews and 185 cans of peanuts.

Section 7.4

1 **1.** Let x = Patty's time on the road and y = the distance she traveled when her dad caught up with her. Her dad's distance would also be y and his time on the road is 0.5 hours less than Patty's time.; $y = 55x$; $y = 65(x - 0.5)$; The solution is (3.25, 178.75). Patty's dad must travel for $3.25 - 0.5 = 2.75$ hours before catching up with Patty. They will have traveled 178.75 miles before he catches her. **2.** Let x = the speed of the canoe in still water, and y = the speed of the current.; $4(x - y) = 16$; $2(x + y) = 16$; The solution is (6, 2). The girls can paddle 6 miles per hour in still water, and the speed of the current is 2 miles per hour.

2 **1.** Let x = the number of pounds of coarse fescue in the mix, and y = the number of pounds of Kentucky blue grass in the mix.; $x + y = 100$; $0.75x + 1.25y = 1.00(100)$; The solution is (50, 50). The mix must contain 50 pounds of each type of grass seed. **2.** Let x = the number of dimes Rosita saved, and y = the number of quarters.; $x + y + 120 = 498$; $0.05(120) + 0.10x + 0.25y = 63.75$; The solution is (245,133). Rosita had saved 245 dimes and 133 quarters. **3.** Let x = the amount of 25% solution and y = the amount of 5% solution in the mix.; $x + y = 1$; $0.25x + 0.05y = 0.10(1)$; The solution is $\left(\dfrac{1}{4}, \dfrac{3}{4}\right)$. The mix should contain 0.25 liters of the 25% solution and 0.75 liters of the 75% solution.

Section 8.1

1 **1.** linear   **2.** linear   **3.** nonlinear   **4.** nonlinear   **5.** nonlinear

2 **1.** [number line from −4 to 4, open circle at −2, shaded right]   **2.** [number line from −4 to 4, closed dot at 3, shaded left]

3. [number line from −2 to 6, closed dot at 2, open circle at 5]   **3** **1.** $(-2, \infty)$ **2.** $(-\infty, 3]$ **3.** $[1, 5)$

4. [number line from −4 to 4, open circle at −3, shaded right] ; $(-3, \infty)$ **5.** $x \leq 0$; $(-\infty, 0]$

6. $-4 \leq x < 1$; [number line from −4 to 4, closed dot at −4, open circle at 1]

4   Let x = the number of CD's Joseph can order.; $6.99x + 5.99 \leq 50.00$

Section 8.2

1 **1.** $x > -1$ **2.** $z > -1$ **2** **1.** $x < -1$ **2.** [number line from −4 to 4, closed dot at −1, shaded left]   **3.** $(-\infty, 2)$

4. $(-\infty, 2.5)$ **5.** no solution   **6.** all real numbers   **7.** all real numbers   **3** **1.** $(2, \infty)$ **2.** $z \geq 3$

3. [number line from 0 to 8, open circle at 7.52]   **4.** no solution   **5.** $(-\infty, \infty)$

4   Let x = number of hours Maria can work; $1275 + 7.50x \leq 3000$; $x \leq 230$; Maria can work no more than 230 hours.

Section 8.3

1 **1.** linear; $7x - y < 10$; $a = 7, b = -1, c = 10$ **2.** linear; $x - 3y < 12$; $a = 1, b = -3, c = 12$
3. nonlinear   **4.** linear; $4x + y < 10$; $a = 4, b = 1, c = 10$ **5.** nonlinear   **6.** nonlinear
3 **1.**   **2.**   **3.**

4.

4 **1.**

2.

3.

4.

5 **1. (a)** Let x = the number of payments Lana makes and y = the number of payments her parents make.; $60x + 125y \leq 1500$

(b)

(c) Yes, see the graph.
(d) No, see the graph.

2. Let x = the number of word processing packages sold and y = the number of spread sheet packages sold. $225x + 75y \geq 3600$; 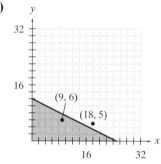 ; $(0, 60)$ indicates selling 60 spread sheet packages; $(20, 0)$ indicates selling 20 word processing packages; $(20, 20)$ indicates selling 20 of each package. (See figure.)

Section 8.4

1 **1.**

2.

3.

4.

5.

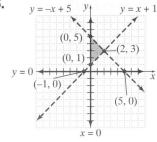

2

1. $Y1 = x - 3$
$Y2 = 2x + 1$

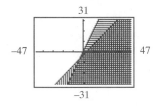

2. $Y1 = -3x + 4$
$Y2 = -x + 2$

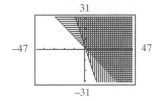

3. Note: Set window to first quadrant to achieve last two inequalities.

$Y1 = \dfrac{2}{3}x + 1$

$Y2 = -\dfrac{3}{4}x + 5$

3

1.

The solution set is all ordered pairs located below the line $y = \dfrac{1}{3}x + 2$ and above or on

2.

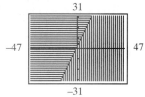

The solution set is the set of all coordinate pairs located on the line $y = 2x + 3$.

the line $y = \dfrac{1}{3}x - 3$.

3.

There are no ordered pairs that satisfy this system.

4.

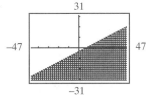

The solution set is the set of all coordinate pairs located

below the line $y = \dfrac{1}{2}x - 4$.

5.

The solution set is all points whose x-coordinate is greater than or equal to 1.

4 **1.** Let x = the number of rag dolls and y = the number of sculptured dolls produced; $1.5x + 4y \leq 30$; $1.5x + y \leq 24$;
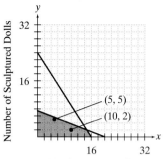
; Possible combinations: $(5, 5)$ indicates they produce 5 of each doll; $(10, 2)$ indicates they produce 10 rag dolls and 2 sculptured dolls; see points on figure.

2. Let x = the number of adult tickets sold and y = the number of child tickets sold; $x + y \leq 150$; $3x + 2y \geq 250$;
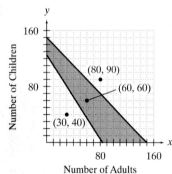
; Sales of 60 adult tickets and 60 child tickets will meet his criteria; sales of 80 adult and 90 child tickets will not meet his criteria; sales of 30 adult and 40 child tickets will not meet his criteria; see points on figure.

Section 9.1

1 **1.** polynomial   **2.** polynomial   **3.** not a polynomial   **4.** not a polynomial   **5.** polynomial
6. not a polynomial   **2** **1.** polynomial   **2.** binomial   **3.** trinomial   **4.** monomial
3 **1.** The degrees of the terms are 2, 4, and 3; the degree of the polynomial is 4.   **2.** The polynomial simplifies to $-2x^2 + 5x + 1$; the degrees of the terms are 2, 1, and 0; the degree of the polynomial is 2.
3. The degrees of the terms are 10 and 9; the degree of the polynomial is 10.
4

descending order	ascending order
1. $2x^3 - x^2 - 5x + 3$	$3 - 5x - x^2 + 2x^3$
2. $y + 12$	$12 + y$

5 **1. (a)** 172   **(b)** 11   **2. (a)** -214.08 **(b)** -355.76 or $-\dfrac{8894}{25}$

6 **1.** Let x = length of a side of the cabin, a = length of the lot, b = width of the lot, A = area not covered by the cabin.   **(a)** $A = ab - x^2$ **(b)** If $x = 35$, $a = 200$ and $b = 150$, then $A = 28{,}775$ square feet.
2. Let x = the number of tables made and sold, y = the number of birdhouses made and sold, R = the revenue for sales, and C = the cost of making the items.   **(a)** $R = 12x + 15y$
(b) $C = 47 + 4.25x + 5.85y$ **(c)** If $x = 22$, $y = 19$, $R = \$549$, $C = \$251.65$, and the net return is $\$297.35$.

Section 9.2

1 **1.**

x	y
-3	0
-2	4
-1	0
0	-6
1	-8
2	0

2. x; y; all real numbers   **2** **1.**

3 **1.** all real numbers   **2.** all real numbers less than or equal to 9   **3.** all real numbers
4. all real numbers greater than or equal to -12.69 (approximately)   **4** **1. (a)** 36   **(b)** 60   **(c)** 10
(d) 0   **(e)** 0   **(f)** 0   **(g)** 33.292

5 **1.**

# attending	Revenue
5	$650
10	$1100
15	$1350
20	$1400
25	$1250
30	$900
35	$350
40	−$400

2. The revenue will be at most $1406.   **3.** Answers will vary.

Section 9.3

1 **1.** quadratic   **2.** quadratic   **3.** nonquadratic   **4.** quadratic   **5.** nonquadratic   **6.** nonquadratic

2

	a	b	c	w/n	u/d	vertex	axis
1.	−3	0	2	narrow	down	$(0, 2)$	$x = 0$
2.	4	−8	5	narrow	up	$(1, 1)$	$x = 1$
3.	0.25	1	−2	wide	up	$(-2, -3)$	$x = -2$
4.	$\frac{2}{3}$	1	0	wide	up	$\left(-\frac{3}{4}, -\frac{3}{8}\right)$	$x = -\frac{3}{4}$

3 **1.**

2.

4 **1.**

The maximum height the balloon reaches is approximately 80 meters. By tracing on the graph, the balloon will return to the ground in approximately 5.5 seconds.

2.

The area will be maximized when the width is 100 feet. The maximum area will be 10,000 square feet.

Section 9.4

1   **1.** $y = -\frac{2}{3}x^2 - \frac{4}{3}x + 2$ **2.** $y = 0.75x^2 + 2.75x - 1$ **2**   **1.** $y = x^2 + x - 6$

2. $y = \frac{1}{2}x^2 + x - 2$ **3**   Let $t =$ the time in seconds after release and $s(t) =$ position of the case in feet

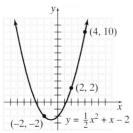

above the water. $s(t) = -16t^2 - 30t + 1500$; The case will reach the water in approximately 8.8 seconds.

Section 10.1

1   **1.** $3 \cdot 3 \cdot x \cdot x \cdot x$ **2.** $(-2x)(-2x)(-2x)$ **3.** $(a - b)(a - b)(a - b)(a - b)$ **4.** $q \cdot q \cdot q \cdot q$

5. $\frac{1}{x^4}$ **6.** y^2 **7.** $\frac{y^2}{x^4}$ **8.** $\frac{8a^4b^3}{25}$ **9.** $\frac{q^5}{p^5}$ **2**   **1.** a^9 **2.** $\frac{1}{z^3}$ **3.** $(x + y)^8$

3   **1.** a^4 **2.** b^9 **3.** $\frac{1}{c^5}$ **4.** $(x + 5)^2$ **4**   **1.** x^{12} **2.** $\frac{1}{y^{10}}$ **3.** z^{12} **5**   **1.** $64a^6$ **2.** $\frac{y^9}{x^9}$

3. $a^{18}b^{18}$ **4.** $\frac{-64x^3y^3}{z^3}$ **5.** $\frac{q^4}{16p^4}$ **6**   The volume of the original box is x^3. The volume of the new box

is $\frac{1}{8}x^3$. The volume of the new box is one-eighth as large as the volume of the original box. If the original box measures 1.5 meters on a side, its volume is 3.375 cubic meters and the volume of the new box is 0.421875 cubic meters.

Section 10.2

1   **1.** $8x^3 - 3x^2 - x + 9$ **2.** $7x^3 - x^2y - 7xy^2 + 5y^3$ **3.** $a^3 - 7a^2 + 15$

4. $4a^4 + 3a^3b - 9a^2b^2 + 5ab^3 + 2b^4$ **2**   **1.** $-25a^5c$ **2.** $-4m^5n + 20m^4n^2 - 4m^3n^3$ **3**   **1.** $\frac{3b^3c}{a^2}$

2. $\frac{3x^2y^8}{2}$ **3.** $\frac{1}{4a^2}$ **4.** $\frac{3x}{y} + \frac{3}{2} - \frac{9y}{4x} - \frac{y^2}{2x^2}$ **4**   **1.** Let $x =$ the number of box lunches made and sold

in a day.   **(a)** $C(x) = 15 + 1.25x$ **(b)** $R(x) = 4.50x$ **(c)** $P(x) = 3.25x - 15$ **(d)** $A(x) = 3.25 - \frac{15}{x}$

(e) Her average profit for each is $3.00.   **2.** Let x be the length of one side of the square floor, and $A(x)$ be the area of the office less the storage space. $A(x) = x^2 - 2x$. Let $C(x)$ be the cost of carpeting the floor. $C(x) = 21(x^2 - 2x)$.

x	$A(x)$	$C(x)$
6.0	24 ft^2	$504.00
6.5	29.25 ft^2	$614.25
7.0	35 ft^2	$735.00
7.5	41.25 ft^2	$866.25
8.0	48 ft^2	$1008.00

; Bridgett should build a 7 yard by 7 yard office, which will cost $735 to carpet.

Section 10.3

1   **1.** $7a^2 + 50a + 7$ **2.** $4y^2 - 1$ **3.** $x^2 - 10x + 25$ **2**   **1.** $3x^3 + 4x^2 - 12x - 16$
2. $x^3 + 3x^2y + 3xy^2 + y^3$ **3**   **1.** $9y^2 - 49$ **2.** $9y^2 - 42y + 49$ **3.** $9y^2 + 42y + 49$
4   **1.** Let $A(s)$ be the area of the new garden. $A(s) = 2s^2 + 11s + 12$. If the garden measured 5 feet on a side, the area of the new garden will be 117 square feet.   **2.** Let x be the height of the box, and $V(x)$ be the volume of each compartment.; $V(x) = 2x^3 + 18x^2 + 32.5x$; If the height of the box is 10 inches, the volume of each section is 4125 cubic inches, so the volume of the box is twice this, or 8250 cubic inches.
3. Let x be the width of the garden; $3x$ is the length of the garden; $x + 4$ is the width of the garden and walkway, and $3x + 4$ is the length of the garden and walkway. If $A(x)$ is the area of the walkway, $A(x) = (3x + 4)(x + 4) - 3x(x)$. Thus, $A(x) = 16x + 16$. If $N(x)$ is the number of bricks, $N(x) = A(x) \div 0.4$, and $N(x) = 40x + 40$.

Section 10.4

1   **1.** $6a^2bc$ **2.** $42x^3y^3z^2$ **3.** $11p$ **2**   **1.** $6a^2b^2(a - 2b + 4)$ **2.** $-4xy(2xy^2z + 6x^2y - 9z)$
3   **1.** $(2a + b)(7a + 4b)$ **2.** $(3x - 2)(4x^2 - 3)$ **4**   **1.** $(3x - 5)(2x + 3)$ **2.** $(y^2 + 1)(2y^2 - 5)$
3. $5a(3a - 4)(a + 7)$ **4.** $(x + y)(a + b)$ **5**   **1.** Let x = the amount Katie received the first month. Let $T(x)$ = the total amount of money Katie will receive. $T(x) = 6x + 180$ **2.** $T(x) = 6(x + 30)$; $(x + 30)$ is the average monthly amount Katie will receive, if she stops smoking for (6) months.
3. $T(50) = 480$; Katie will receive $480.   **4.** Katie's average monthly receipt is $80, and this does check with the interpretation from exercise 2.

Section 10.5

1   **1.** $(b - 7)(b - 5)$ **2.** $(c - 8)(c + 3)$ **3.** $6(d + 7)(d + 3)$ **4.** $(y^2 - 3)(y^2 + 1)$
2   **1.** $(2x + 1)(x - 5)$ **2.** Does not factor.   **3.** $5(2x + 3)(3x + 2)$ **4.** $(2x^2 - 5)(3x^2 - 4)$
3   Note: These exercises have the same answers as those in **2** directly above.   **4**   **1.** Since the polynomial factors as $(w + 13)(w + 5)$, the outside dimensions are $(w + 5)$ feet wide and $(w + 13)$ feet long. Comparing these dimensions with the inside width of w feet and length of $w + 9$ ft, the walk is 2.5 feet wide along the pool's length, and 2 feet wide along its width.   **2. (a)** The polynomial factors as $\frac{1}{2}(3x - 4)(x - 4)$. The sides of the reduced garden measure $(3x - 4)$ and $(x - 4)$ feet.
(b) Carri reduced each of the two sides of the garden by 4 feet.

Section 10.6

1   **1.** $(y - 2)(y + 2)$ **2.** $(5x - 4y)(5x + 4y)$ **3.** $2(z - 3)(z + 3)$ **4.** Does not factor.
5. $(c - 2)(c + 2)(c^2 + 4)$ **2**   **1.** $(z + 6)^2$ **2.** $(7a + 3b)^2$ **3.** $5(x - 6)^2$ **4.** Does not factor.
5. $(y - 2)^2(y + 2)^2$ **3**   **1.** $(a + 2)(a^2 - 2a + 4)$ **2.** $(a - 2)(a^2 + 2a + 4)$
3. $(2x + 3y)(4x^2 - 6xy + 9y^2)$ **4**   **1.** $5(2z - 5)(z + 6)$ **2.** $2a(3a + 1)(a + 4)$
3. Does not factor.   **4.** $6x(x - 5y)(2x - y)$ **5.** $-6(a - 2)(a + 2)$ **6.** $(3x - 2)^2(3x + 2)^2$
7. $(4 + h)(3 - 5h)$ or $-1(5h - 3)(h + 4)$ **5**   **1. (a)** Let P = the length of a side of the square patio; $A(p)$ = the area to be landscaped. $A(p) = 16^2 - p^2$.   **(b)** $A(p) = (16 - p)(16 + p)$. An equivalent rectangular area will be one that is 9 feet by 23 feet.   **(c)** The package covers an area of 48 square feet. The landscaped area will be 207 square feet. The package is not large enough.

2. The polynomial factors as $x(7 - 2x)(5 - 2x)$. Therefore, the height is x inches, the width is $5 - 2x$ inches, and the length is $7 - 2x$ inches. If the height is 1 inch, the width is 3 inches, and the length is 5 inches.

Section 11.1

1   **1.** A quadratic polynomial.   **2.** Not a polynomial.   **3.** Not a polynomial.   **4.** A cubic polynomial. **5.** A quadratic polynomial.   **6.** A cubic polynomial.   **2**   **1.** 2 and -3 **2.** $-2, -1$, and 2 **3.** Noninteger solutions between -1 and 0 and between 0 and 1.   **4.** Contradiction, no solution. **5.** Not a contradiction, no real number solution.   **6.** Solution set is all real numbers.   **3**   **1.** -7 and 3 **2.** $-2, -1$, and 1   **3.** -0.2 and 0.75   **4.** No solution, contradiction.   **5.** No real number solution, not a contradiction.   **6.** Solution set is all real numbers, identity.   **4**   **1.** The banana would hit the ground after approximately 8.8 seconds.   **2.** Let $x =$ the height and width of the crate. $x^2(x + 7) = 1300$. The crate measures approximately 9 inches by 9 inches by 16 inches.

Section 11.2

1   **1.** -7 and $\dfrac{3}{4}$ **2.** $0, 1$, and $\dfrac{5}{4}$ **2**   **1.** Contradiction, no solution.   **2.** -9 and 9

3. $-\dfrac{3}{4}$, double root.   **4.** $\dfrac{5}{4}$ and 3   **5.** -6 and 4   **6.** Does not factor, $x \approx -5.193$, $x \approx 0.193$

7. Identity, solution set is all real numbers.   **3**   **1. (a)** The dimensions of the tray are 1 inch by 5 inches by 7 inches.   **(b)** The dimensions of the posterboard are 7 inches by 9 inches.   **2.** The dimensions of the box are 2 inches by 2 inches by 4 inches.   **3.** The height of the sail is 12 feet and the hypotenuse is 15 feet. **4.** The nozzle diameter is 2 inches.

Section 11.3

1   **1.** $7\sqrt{2}$ **2.** 6   **3.** $10\sqrt{3}$ **2**   **1.** $\dfrac{\sqrt{7}}{8}$ **2.** $\dfrac{8\sqrt{7}}{7}$ **3.** $\dfrac{5\sqrt{2}}{3}$ **3**   **1.** ± 4

2. $\pm\dfrac{5}{3}$ **3.** No real number.   **4.** 0 and 8   **5.** $1 \pm \sqrt{3}$ or ≈ -0.732 and ≈ 2.732

6. $-1 \pm \sqrt{6}$ or ≈ 1.499 and ≈ 3.449 **4**   **1.** They would free fall about 24 seconds, ignoring wind resistance and maneuvering.   **2.** The vertical distance between the two hookups is 2.1 feet. **3.** Sales will reach 3500 million dollars in 7.3 years after 1991, which would be in 1999.

Section 11.4

1   **1.** 16   **2.** $\dfrac{49}{4}$ **3.** $\dfrac{4}{25}$ **2**   **1.** $-4 \pm 3\sqrt{2}$ or ≈ -8.243 and ≈ 0.243 **2.** $\dfrac{2 \pm \sqrt{29}}{5}$ or ≈ -0.677

and ≈ 1.477 **3.** No real number solution.   **4.** -3 and $\dfrac{3}{2}$ **5.** 8, a double root   **3**   **1.** Let $x =$ the

number of items purchased. $x(60 - 2x) = 200$.; $x = 15 \pm 5\sqrt{5}$ or $x \approx 3.81$ and $x \approx 26.18$. Since the minimum price is \$35, the number to be purchased must be 4, and the cost will be \$208.   **2.** $x = 15.6 \pm \sqrt{157.36}$ or $x \approx 3.06$ and $x \approx 28.14$. The price to the nearest dollar which meets the other conditions is \$3 per item.

Section 11.5

1   **1.** -2 and 1.5   **2.** $\approx \dfrac{-1 \pm \sqrt{29}}{2}$ or ≈ -3.193 and ≈ 2.193 **3.** $\dfrac{2}{3}$, a double root

4. No real number solutions.   **2**   **1.** Discriminant is 0.08; there are two irrational solutions. **2.** Discriminant is zero; there is one rational solution.   **3.** Discriminant is 400; there are two rational solutions. **4.** Discriminant is -25; there is no real number solution.   **3**   **1.** Tommy must realize an equivalent annual interest rate of 17.5%.   **2.** $x = 10$ and $x = 115$. The reasonable solution appears to be $x = 10$, which means the dealer would buy 35 items at a price of \$140 each.

Section 11.6

1 **1.** The height is approximately 5.0 feet and the base is approximately 15.0 feet. **2.** The forward distance of the pass is approximately 16 yards. **2** **1.** The congruent legs are $3\sqrt{2}$ or approximately 4.2 mm long. **2.** The catcher must throw the ball 127.3 ft. **3.** The horizontal distance of the ramp is $3\sqrt{3}$ feet (or approximately 5.2 feet), and the ramp's length is 6 feet. **3** **1.** $s = \sqrt{A}$ **2.** $a = \sqrt{c^2 - b^2}$

3. $r = \dfrac{-\pi h + \sqrt{\pi^2 h^2 + \pi A}}{\pi}$ or $r = -h + \sqrt{h^2 + \dfrac{A}{\pi}}$

Section 11.7

1 **1.** yes **2.** yes **3.** no **4.** no **2** **1.** All integers less than or equal to -3 or all integers greater than or equal to 4. **2.** The integers between -3 and 1 exclusive, that is $x = -2, -1$ and 0. **3.** All integers less than -2 or all integers greater than 1. **3** **1.** $x \le -3$ or $x \ge 4$ or $(-\infty, -3] \cup [4, \infty)$

2. $-3 < x < \dfrac{1}{2}$ **3.** $x < -2.562$ or $x > 1.562$ **4.** $x = 0$ **5.** $x \ne 2$ or $(-\infty, 2) \cup (2, \infty)$ **6.** $x = 2$

4 Same answers as **3** directly above. **5** **1.** Let $t =$ the time the baseball is no lower than the top of the tower. $0 \le t \le 3.125$; The baseball is no lower than the top of the tower for the first 3.125 seconds of its flight. **2.** If the revenue must be at least \$7500, the value of x is between 5 and 15 inclusive. Therefore, the number of computers ordered must be between 15 and 25 inclusive. **3.** The function will be greater than 30 when x is greater than 52.14 approximately. The population will first exceed 30 million people in the year 2003.

Section 12.1

1 **1.** A rational expression; an algebraic fraction. **2.** Not a rational expression. **3.** A rational expression; an algebraic fraction. **4.** A rational expression; not an algebraic fraction. **5.** A rational expression; an algebraic fraction. **6.** A rational expression; an algebraic fraction. **2** **1.** The restricted value is -4. The domain is all real numbers not equal to -4. **2.** The restricted values are -4 and 3. The domain is all real numbers except -4 and 3. **3.** There are no restricted values. The domain is all real numbers. **4.** The restricted value is 1.5. The domain is all real numbers except 1.5. **3** **1.** $-36, 36, 6.75$ **2.** $-1, 0, \dfrac{1}{3}$

4 **1.**

2.

3.

4.

5 **(a)** $T(x) = \dfrac{60}{x} + \dfrac{210}{2x - 10}$ **(b)**

(c)

The total time of the delivery trip is approximately 5.2 hours.

(d)

The average speed on the rural roads was 31 mph and on the interstate was 52 mph.

Section 12.2

1 **1.** $\dfrac{3y}{7x}$ **2.** $\dfrac{a-2}{3a+4}$ **3.** $\dfrac{x-2}{x-6}$ **4.** $-\dfrac{5+x}{x^2+7}$ **2** **1.** $\dfrac{2y^2}{5x^2}$ **2.** $\dfrac{(x-1)(x+4)}{x^2(x+1)}=\dfrac{x^2+3x-4}{x^3+x^2}$

3. $\dfrac{2}{(x-4)^2}=\dfrac{2}{x^2-8x+16}$ **3** **1.** $\dfrac{5x^2z}{4y}$ **2.** $\dfrac{3(x^2+1)}{2}=\dfrac{3x^2+3}{2}$ **3.** $\dfrac{x+4}{(x-2)(x+2)}=\dfrac{x+4}{x^2-4}$

4 **1.** Let $x=$ a student's age and $y=$ the resulting number.; $y=\dfrac{2x+6}{2}+7$ which simplifies to

$y=x+10$. When a student gives Glenda a number, she just subtracts 10 from it and obtains the student's age.

2. (a) Let $R(x)=$ Reza's average speed. $R(x)=\dfrac{150}{x}$. **(b)** New rate $=\dfrac{300}{x}$. New time $=x+1$.

New distance $=\dfrac{300(x+1)}{x}$.

Section 12.3

1 **1.** $\dfrac{5xy-7x}{3z}=\dfrac{x(5y-7)}{3z}$ **2.** 3 **3.** $\dfrac{1}{x+4}$ **4.** $\dfrac{x}{(x+6)(x-3)}$ **2** **1.** $60x^2y^3$

2. $(x+4)(x-5)$ **3.** $(5x-1)(5x+1)(3x-1)$ **4.** $x-5$ or $5-x$ **3** **1.** $\dfrac{-16x^2}{12x^2y^2}$

2. $\dfrac{2x(x+4)}{(x+5)(x+4)}=\dfrac{2x^2+8x}{x^2+9x+20}$ **3.** $\dfrac{(2x+1)(x+7)}{(x^2-16)(x+7)}=\dfrac{2x^2+15x+7}{x^3+7x^2-16x-112}$

4. $\dfrac{-7x}{-x(x-5)}=\dfrac{-7x}{5x-x^2}$ **4** **1.** $\dfrac{27x+5y}{6x^2y^2}$ **2.** $\dfrac{7x^2-31x}{x^2-11x+24}=\dfrac{x(7x-31)}{(x-3)(x-8)}$ **3.** $\dfrac{8}{x-4}$

4. $\dfrac{x^2+8x+21}{(x+3)(x+5)(x+7)}$ **5.** $\dfrac{x+3}{x-4}$ **5** **1.** $\dfrac{16x+4}{15x}$ **2.** $\dfrac{7x+5}{x}$ **3.** The second perimeter is

larger than the first by $\dfrac{89x+71}{15x}$.

Section 12.4

1 **1.** Not a rational equation. **2.** A rational equation. **3.** Not a rational equation.
4. A rational equation. **5.** A rational equation. **6.** A rational equation. **2** **1.** -6 and 6
2. -5 and 1 **3.** 3 **4.** A noninteger solution exists between -4 and -3. **5.** No solution.
6. All real numbers except -1. **3** **1.** -6 and 6 **2.** -5 and 1 **3.** 3 **4.** -3.5
5. No solution. **6.** All real numbers except -1. **4** **1.** Let $x=$ the interest rate for the 3 year period.
Then $\dfrac{225}{3x}+\dfrac{225}{2(x-0.005)}=4000$ and $x=0.05$. The interest rate for the 3 year investment was 5% and for

the two year investment was 4.5%. **2.** Let $x=$ the additional hours. Then $\dfrac{35}{1.5}=\dfrac{56}{1.5+x}$ and $x=0.9$. Joey

will need an extra 0.9 hours to complete the competition trail.

Section 12.5

1 **1.** 4 **2.** Contradiction, no solution. **3.** The solution is extraneous since it is the same as the
restricted value. **4.** Identity, solution is all real numbers except -1.
5. -5 (3 is an extraneous solution.) **2** **1.** Let $x=$ the first resistor's resistance. Then $\dfrac{1}{12}=\dfrac{1}{x}+\dfrac{1}{x+10}$.
$x=20$. The two resistances are 20 ohms and 30 ohms.

Section 12.6

1 **1.** Let $x=$ the time it will take to do the lawn together. Then $\dfrac{1}{2}+\dfrac{1}{1.6}=\dfrac{1}{x}$. $x=\dfrac{8}{9}$. It will take them $\dfrac{8}{9}$ of

an hour to do the lawn together. **2.** Let $x=$ the time to fill an empty tank. Then $\dfrac{1}{5}=\dfrac{1}{x}-\dfrac{1}{2}$. $x=\dfrac{10}{7}$. It will

take $1\frac{3}{7}$ hours to fill an empty tank if no water is pumped out. **2** **1.** Let $x =$ the amount earned for an 8 hour shift. Then $\frac{55.13}{4.5} = \frac{x}{8}$. $x = 98.01$. Jose will earn \$98.01 for an 8 hour shift. **2.** Let $x =$ the number of consecutive baskets she must make. Then $\frac{6 + x}{10 + x} = \frac{75}{100}$. $x = 6$. Michelle must make 6 consecutive baskets to average 75%. **3** **1.** Side AC measures 22.8 inches Side EF measures 6.1 inches.
2. The antenna is 10 feet tall.

Section 13.1

1 **1.** 3   **2.** -3 **3.** Not a real number.   **4.** -4 **5.** 4   **6.** 10.817   **2**   **1.** $\sqrt[4]{16} = 2$

2. $-\sqrt[4]{16} = -2$ **3.** $\sqrt[4]{-16}$, not a real number.   **4.** $\frac{1}{\sqrt[3]{125}} = \frac{1}{5}$ **5.** $-\frac{1}{\sqrt[3]{125}} = -\frac{1}{5}$ **6.** $\frac{1}{\sqrt[3]{-125}} = -\frac{1}{5}$

7. 4.729   **8.** 0.115   **3**   **1.** $(\sqrt{16})^3 = \sqrt{16^3} = 64$ **2.** $(\sqrt[3]{-125})^5 = \sqrt[3]{(-125)^5} = -3125$

3. $(\sqrt{15})^3 = \sqrt{15^3} \approx 58.095$ **4.** $-\frac{1}{(\sqrt[3]{125})^5} = -\frac{1}{\sqrt[3]{125^5}} = -\frac{1}{3125}$; Note: $-3.2E - 4$ on the calculator

4   **1.** Let $s =$ the length of one side. $s = \sqrt{A} = \sqrt{5,600,000} \approx 2366$; The length of one side is approximately

2366 feet or 0.45 miles.   **2.** $r = \sqrt{\dfrac{A}{\pi}} = \sqrt{\dfrac{19,360}{\pi}} \approx 78.5$; The radius of the dome is approximately 78.5 feet.

The diameter is approximately 157 feet.
3. The number of employees in the year 2000 is estimated to be 14,325.

Section 13.2

1   **1.** Radical   **2.** Nonradical   **3.** Radical   **4.** Nonradical   **5.** Radical   **6.** Radical
2   **1.** There are no restricted values. The domain is all real numbers. $(-\infty, \infty)$ **2.** The restricted values are all real numbers less than -2. The domain is all real numbers greater than or equal to -2, or $[-2, \infty)$.
3. The restricted values are all real numbers less than 3. The domain is all real numbers greater than or equal to 3, or $[3, \infty)$.   **4.** The restricted values are all real numbers less than 4. The domain is all real numbers greater than or equal to 4, or $[4, \infty)$.
3   **1.** $-3, -6.708, -9, -10.82$ **2.** Not a real number, $0, 0.66667, 1.8856, 5.333$
3. $1, 2.5304, 3$ **4.** $48, 3, 0, 48$
4   **1.**

2.

3.

4.

5   **1. (a)**

A	r
1	0.56
2	0.80
3	0.98
4	1.13
5	1.26
6	1.38
7	1.49
8	1.60
9	1.69
10	1.78

(b)

(c)

The radius is approximately 1.64 feet.

2.

The absolute luminosity values are 1, 128, 16,384, and 2,097,152. As the mass increases by a factor of four, the absolute brightness increases by a factor of 128, or $4^{3.5}$.

Section 13.3

1   **1.** 6   **2.** 2   **3.** 3   **4.** $\dfrac{729}{125}$ **2**   **1.** x^3 **2.** $x^{1/6}$ **3.** $z^{1/2}$ **4.** $\dfrac{q^{3/5}}{p^{3/5}}$ **5.** $2ab^{3/2}$ **6.** $8x^4$

7. $a^{3/4} - a^{7/6}$ **3**   **1. (a)** The radius increases by a factor of $\sqrt{2}$.   **(b)** The radius increases by a factor of $\sqrt{3}$.   **(c)** The ratio of the length of the larger radius to the smaller is 2.   **2. (a)** $V = (128.8h)^{0.5}$
(b) $V_2 - V_1 = (\sqrt{128.8} - \sqrt{64.4})h^{0.5} \approx 3.324\sqrt{h}$

Section 13.4

1   **1.** $8\sqrt{3}$ **2.** $-2\sqrt[3]{5}$ **3.** $3\sqrt[4]{2}$ **4.** $7x^2yz^4\sqrt{2yz}$ **5.** $30ab\sqrt{a}$ **6.** $(x+2)\sqrt{10}$

7. $72x^2y^4\sqrt[3]{2y^2}$ **2**   **1.** $\dfrac{\sqrt{13}}{4}$ **2.** $\dfrac{3\sqrt{15}}{10}$ **3.** $\dfrac{3\sqrt[3]{4}}{2}$ **4.** $\dfrac{5\sqrt{2xyz}}{2z}$ **5.** $\dfrac{3\sqrt{7ab}}{7}$ **6.** $\dfrac{\sqrt[3]{75xyz^2}}{5yz}$

7. $\dfrac{\sqrt{2y}}{2y}$ **8.** $\dfrac{b\sqrt{5a}}{15a}$ **9.** $\dfrac{\sqrt[3]{2c^2}}{2d}$ **3**   **1.** The period of the pendulum is 1.28 seconds.
2. The current passing through the circuit is 18.3 amps.

Section 13.5

1   **1.** $-\sqrt{ab} + 7\sqrt[4]{ab}$ **2.** $4p\sqrt{q}$ **3.** $(5m+2)\sqrt[3]{mn}$ **4.** $13\sqrt{3}$ **5.** $-xy\sqrt{xy}$ **6.** $\dfrac{2}{3}\sqrt{3}$

2   **1.** $35x + 28\sqrt[3]{x^2}$ **2.** $\sqrt{21} + \sqrt{3ab} - \sqrt{7ab} - ab$ **3.** 5   **4.** $121 - z$ **5.** $15 + 10\sqrt{2}$

6. $z - 10\sqrt{z} + 25$ **3**   **1.** $\sqrt{2x} + \sqrt{5}$ **2.** $\dfrac{\sqrt{65} - \sqrt{26}}{3}$ **3.** $2 + \sqrt{3}$ **4.** $\dfrac{8x - 17\sqrt{3x} + 6}{x - 12}$

4   **1.** Let s = the length of a side of the square floor, and A = the area of the square floor. $s = \sqrt{A}$. The perimeter of the floor is $p = 4s = 4\sqrt{A}$. The perimeter of Sandra's floor is $p_1 = 4\sqrt{350}$, and of Julie's floor is $p_2 = 4\sqrt{224}$. The difference is $d = p_1 - p_2 = 4\sqrt{350} - 4\sqrt{224} = 4\sqrt{14}$. This is approximately 15 feet.

Section 13.6

1   **1.** Nonradical   **2.** Radical   **3.** Radical   **2**   **1.** $-3, -1$, and 1   **2.** 25
3. There is a noninteger solution between 2 and 3.   **4.** There appears to be no solution.
5. All real numbers greater than or equal to zero.   **3**   **1.** $-3, -1$, and 1   **2.** 25   **3.** 2.5
4. no solution   **5.** all real numbers ≥ -0.5
4   The unknown sides are 6 feet and 12 feet long. The perimeter of the garden is 27 feet.

Section 13.7

1   **1.** $\dfrac{4}{5}$ **2.** 4. Note: $x = -3$ is an extraneous solution.   **3.** 5 and 4   **4.** 2

5. No solution. $z = -5$ is an extraneous solution.   **6.** 16   **7.** No solution. $x = \dfrac{21}{4}$ is an extraneous

solution.   **8.** Identity; the solution set is all real numbers in the domain of the functions; $[-3, \infty)$.

2   **1.** 2   **2.** 19   **3.** -9 and 3   **3**   **1.** 32   **2.** 4   **3.** $\dfrac{17}{16}$ **4.** There is no real number solution.

4   **1.** 9   **2.** 7   **3.** $\sqrt{34} \approx 5.831$ **4.** $y = -1, y = 11$

Section 14.1

1   **1.** $7i$ **2.** $\dfrac{2}{9}i$ **3.** $3\sqrt{3}i$ **4. (a)** -4 **(b)** $4i$; Answers may vary.   **2**   **1.** $10i$ **2.** $-5\sqrt{5}i$

3. $\dfrac{10}{11}$ **4.** $-30i$ **5.** $7\sqrt{3} - 4\sqrt{10}$ **3**   **1.** This is a real number; the real part is $\sqrt{3} - 2\sqrt{5}$ and the imaginary part is zero.   **2.** This is a pure imaginary number; the real part is zero and the imaginary part is 12. **3.** This is a real number; the real part is 1244 and the imaginary part is zero.   **4.** This is a real number; the real part is $\dfrac{\sqrt{7}}{8}$ and the imaginary part is zero.   **5.** This is an imaginary number; the real part is 9 and the imaginary part is $-\sqrt{6}$.   **6.** This is a pure imaginary number; the real part is zero and the imaginary part is $-2\sqrt{17}$.   **4**   **1.** $26 - 5i$ **2.** $6 + 3i$ **3.** $-8 + 20i$ **4.** $-3 + 12i$ **5.** $80 - 20i$ **6.** 58

7. $4 - 3i$ **8.** $-4 - \dfrac{7}{2}i$ **9.** $\dfrac{8 + i}{13}$ **5**   **1.** The magnitude of the total voltage across the circuit is approximately 26.1 volts.   **2.** The magnitude of the current across the circuit is approximately 2.485 amperes.

Section 14.2

1   **1.** $a = \pm 2\sqrt{2}i$ **2.** $x = \pm 2i$ **3.** $x = 4 \pm 3\sqrt{3}i$ **4.** $z = \dfrac{-1 \pm \sqrt{2}i}{3}$

2   **1.** $x = \dfrac{-3 \pm 3\sqrt{19}i}{10}$ **2.** $x = \dfrac{-10 \pm 2\sqrt{19}i}{2}$ **3** $s = \dfrac{-5 \pm \sqrt{23}i}{4}$

Section 15.1

1   **1.** $g^{-1} = \{(0.5, 1), (1, 2), (1.5, 3), (2, 4), (2.5, 5), (3, 6)\}$

2. $K^{-1} = \left\{ \left(3, \dfrac{1}{2}\right), \left(4, \dfrac{2}{3}\right), \left(5, \dfrac{3}{4}\right), \left(4, \dfrac{4}{5}\right), \left(3, \dfrac{5}{6}\right) \right\}$ **3.** $y = -\dfrac{1}{4}x + \dfrac{1}{4}$ **4.** $y = \pm\sqrt{\dfrac{1}{3}x - 2}$

2   **1.** The inverse is a function since this function is one-to-one.   **2.** The inverse is not a function since this function is not one-to-one.   **3.** The graph represents a one-to-one function.
4. The graph does not represent a one-to-one function since it fails the horizontal line test.
5. The graph does not represent a one-to-one function since it fails the vertical line test.

3   **1.**

4   **1.** $f^{-1}(x) = -\dfrac{1}{2}x + 3$ **2.** $g^{-1}(x) = \sqrt[3]{x}$

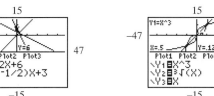

5   **(a)** $I(x) = 60x$ **(b)** $I^{-1}(x) = \dfrac{x}{60}$ **(c)** The inverse function represents the number of years over which Dimitri must invest \$1200 at 5% simple interest per year in order to earn x dollars in interest.

Section 15.2

1   **1.** not an exponential function   **2.** exponential function   **3.** not an exponential function

2   **1.** 64   **2.** $\dfrac{1}{64}$ or 0.015625   **3.** 8   **4.** approximately 11.036

3 1.

2.

4 1.

2.

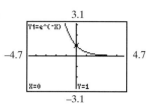

5 1. After 4 years, Cindy will have $6312.38.

2. After 4 years, Cindy would have had $6356.25.

3.

The expenditures for the year 2000 are estimated to be 862.5 billion dollars.

Section 15.3

1 1. $f^{-1}(x) = \log_3 x$ **2.** $h^{-1}(x) = \log_{13} x$ **2 1.** 4 **2.** −3 **3.** 3 **4.** −3 **5.** undefined
6. 4 **7.** −4 **8. (a)** 1.52832 **(b)** 1.52832

3 1.

x	$f(x)$
0.001	−6.288
0.01	−4.192
0.1	−2.096
0.5	−0.6309
1	0
2	0.6309
3	1
4	1.2619
5	1.465

2.

x	$f(x)$
0.001	−2.523
0.01	−1.523
0.1	−0.5229
0.5	0.1761
1	0.4771
2	0.7782
3	0.9542
4	1.0792
5	1.1761

3.

x	$f(x)$
0.001	−5.809
0.01	3.507
0.1	−1.204
0.5	0.4055
1	1.0986
2	1.7918
3	2.1972
4	2.4849
5	2.7081

4 1. The hydrogen in concentration of pure water is 10^{-7} moles per liter. **2.** The ratio of the intensity of the 1964 Alaskan earthquake to the intensity of the 1989 San Francisco earthquake is $\dfrac{10^{9.2}}{10^{7.1}}$ or approximately 126. The Alaskan quake was 126 times as great as the 1989 San Francisco quake. **3.** The ratio of the intensity of the downgrade earthquake to the original intensity is $\dfrac{10^{7.9}}{10^{8.3}}$ or approximately 0.40. The intensity is downgraded to 0.40 of its original intensity.

Section 15.4

1 **1.** $\log_5 11 + \log_5 x$ **2.** $\ln x - \ln y$ **3.** $\log\left(\dfrac{xy}{z}\right)$ **4.** $\ln(x^{-3}) = \ln\left(\dfrac{1}{x^3}\right)$ **5.** $1 + 2\log_5 x$

2 **1.** $\ln A = \ln \pi + 2\ln r$ **2.** $\log A = \log b + \log h - \log 2$ **3. (a)** $y = c\ln\left(\dfrac{I_0}{I}\right)$

(b) The depth is 9.3 units below the surface.

Section 15.5

1 **1.** neither **2.** logarithmic **3.** exponential **4.** neither **2** **1.** -2 **2.** any real
number greater than zero, the domain of the functions. **3.** 5 **4.** There does not appear to be a
solution. **5.** There appears to be a noninteger solution between one and two. **3** **1–4.** have the same
answers as those given in Section 15.5 **2** above. **5.** ≈ 1.582 **4** **1.** 4 **2.** $\ln 3$ or ≈ 1.099

3. $\ln 7 - \ln 2$ or ≈ 1.253 **4.** $\dfrac{3}{2}$ **5.** $\dfrac{100}{3}$

6. This is an identity. The solution set is all positive real numbers.
7. This is a contradiction. No solution exists. **5** **1.** Let $A(t)$ represent the total female population t years
after 1990. Then $A(t) = 127.798e^{0.009t}$. In the year 2020, $t = 30$, and the total female population of the U.S. is

predicted to be 167.411 million. **2.** The Gross National Product will triple in value in 31 years according to

this prediction. **3.** $A(t) = A_0 e^{-0.000428t}$. When $A(t) = 0.9A_0, t = \dfrac{\ln(0.9)}{-0.000428}$ or $t \approx 246$.; The radium-226 will

diminish to 90 percent of its original amount in 246 years. **4.** Let $T(t)$ represent the temperature of the

liquid after t minutes in the freezer. The solution is $t = \dfrac{\ln\left(\dfrac{1}{5}\right)}{-0.0277}$ or $t \approx 58.1$. The water will cool to 20°C after

58 minutes.

Index

Photo Credits

Chapter 1 CO Steven Frame/Stock Boston   **p. 15** Bob Jacobson/International Stock Photography, Inc.
p. 27 Randy Ury/The Stock Market   **p. 38** NASA Headquarters   **p. 39** James M. McCann/Photo
Researchers, Inc.   **p. 49** Richard Lord/The Image Works   **p. 51** Andy Lyons/Allsport Photography
(USA), Inc.   **p. 75** Paramount/Kobal Collection
Chapter 2 CO Bill Horsman/Stock Boston   **p. 78** Tom and Michele Grimm/International Stock
Photography Ltd.   **p. 88** Tom Pantages   **p. 91** Hirmer Fotoarchiv   **p. 98** Calvin Larsen/Photo
Researchers, Inc.   **p. 115** Udo Weitz/AP/Wide World Photos
Chapter 3 CO Israel Government Tourist Office   **p. 146** (c) Namikawa Foundation, Shimane.
p. 168 Paolo Koch/Photo Researchers, Inc.   **p. 210** David Taylor/Allsport Photography (USA), Inc.
Chapter 4 CO Lee Snider/The Image Works   **p. 234** Roy Morsch/The Stock Market
Chapter 5 CO Owen Franken/Stock Boston   **p. 314** John Elk III/Stock Boston   **p. 316** Susanne
Buckler/Gamma-Liaison, Inc.   **p. 341** Stacy Pick/Stock Boston   **p. 352** Kent Knudson/Stock Boston
p. 362 Donna Binder/Impact Visuals Photo & Graphics, Inc.   **p. 368** Chris Bensley/Stock Boston
p. 382 Boyd Norton/The Image Works   **p. 387** W. Cody/Westlight
Chapter 6 CO Matthew Stockman/Allsport Photography (USA), Inc.   **p. 412** Photri, Inc.   **p. 422** Ross
Kinnaird/Allsport Photography (USA), Inc.   **p. 428** Robert Aschenbrenner/Stock Boston
p. 448 Carolina Kroon/Impact Visuals Photo & Graphics, Inc.   **p. 480** Monique Salaber/NASA/The
Image Works
Chapter 7 CO Brian J. Gill/Impact Visuals Photo & Graphics, Inc.   **p. 518** Glenn Short/Gamma-Liaison, Inc.
p. 523 Australian Picture Library/Nick Rains/Westlight   **p. 553** Nathan Bilow/Allsport Photography
(USA), Inc.
Chapter 8 CO Matthew Borkoski/Stock Boston   **p. 559** Charles Thatcher/Tony Stone Images
p. 605 Elise Amendola/AP/Wide World Photos   **p. 621** C. Takagi/Impact Visuals Photo & Graphics, Inc.
Chapter 9 CO NASA/Johnson Space Center/The Image Works   **p. 661** Randy Faris/Westlight
p. 691 Chris Beeson/Allsport Photography (USA), Inc.   **p. 696** Richard Renaldi/Impact Visuals Photo &
Graphics, Inc.
Chapter 10 CO Esbin-Anderson/The Image Works   **p. 722** Paul Griffin/Stock Boston   **p. 725** Jeff
Vanuga/Westlight   **p. 746** Salaber/The Image Works   **p. 774** Hulton Getty Picture Collection/Tony
Stone Images
Chapter 11 CO John Coletti/Stock Boston   **p. 811** Robert Frerck/Odyssey/Chicago   **p. 811** Robert
Frerck/Odyssey Productions   **p. 834** Guy Sauvage/Agence Vandystadt/Allsport Photography (USA), Inc .
p. 835 Ron Sherman/Stock Boston   **p. 844** David Bartruff/FPG International   **p. 859** Bill
Horsman/Stock Boston
Chapter 12 CO Rhoda Sidney/Stock Boston   **p. 897** NASA/Science Photo Library/Photo Researchers, Inc.
p. 930 Brown Brothers   **p. 975** Sonia Boulton/Photo Researchers, Inc.
Chapter 13 CO Tom Hanson/AP/Wide World Photos   **p. 1002** Bill Gallery/Stock Boston
p. 1002 Eunice Harris/Photo Researchers, Inc.   **p. 1004** Lawrence Migdale/Photo Researchers, Inc.
p. 1004 Romer/Explorer/Photo Researchers, Inc.   **p. 1006** Robert Frerck/Odyssey/Chicago
p. 1006 Will and Deni McIntyre/Photo Researchers, Inc.   **p. 1008** Joe Sohm/Chromosohm/Stock Boston
p. 1023 NASA/AP/Wide World Photos   **p. 1031** AP/Wide World Photos   **p. 1032** Rick Stewart/Focus
West/Allsport Photography (USA), Inc.   **p. 1046** Ronald Sheridan/The Ancient Art & Architecture
Collection   **p. 1071** Francois Gohier/Photo Researchers, Inc.
Chapter 14 CO Joseph Schuyler/Stock Boston   **p. 1092** Adam Hart-Davis/Science Photo Library/Photo
Researchers, Inc.   **p. 1106** Michael W. Davidson/Photo Researchers, Inc.   **p. 1111** NIBSC/Science Photo
Library/Photo Researchers, Inc.   **p. 1114** Gregory Sams/Science Photo Library/Photo Researchers, Inc.
p. 1114 Gregory Sams/Science Photo Library/Photo Researchers, Inc.
Chapter 15 CO David Bartruff/Stock Boston   **p. 1119** Vincent Yu/AP/Wide World Photos
p. 1144 E. De Malglaive/Explorer/Photo Researchers, Inc.   **p. 1146** Tom Chargin/Impact Visuals Photo &
Graphics, Inc.   **p. 1156** Linc Cornell/Stock Boston   **p. 1158** Simon Fraser/Science Photo Library/Photo
Researchers, Inc.   **p. 1160** Courtesy of Sony Electronics Inc.   **p. 1178** Sinclair Stammers/Science
Photo Library

Slope of a Line (m)

$$m = \frac{y_2 - y_1}{x_2 - x_1}$$

(x_1, y_1) and (x_2, y_2) are coordinates of two points on a line

Linear Equation in Two Variables

Standard Form

$$ax + by = 0$$

a, b, and c are real numbers and a and b are not both equal to zero

Slope-Intercept Form

$$y = mx + b$$

m is the slope of its graphed line and b is the y-coordinate of the y-intercept of the graph

Point-Slope Form

$$y - y_1 = m(x - x_1)$$

m is the slope of the graphed line and (x_1, y_1) are coordinates of a point on the line

Standard Form for a Quadratic Function

$$f(x) = ax^2 + bx + c$$

a, b, and c are real numbers and $a \neq 0$

Calculator Windows

This text uses the following notation to identify the calculator window setting:

(x minimum value, x maximum value, x scale, y minimum value, y maximum value, y scale, x resolution)

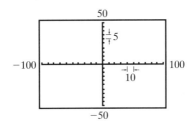

$(-100, 100, 10, -50, 50, 5, 1)$

A shorter version may not include the x scale, y scale, or x resolution:

(x minimum value, x maximum value, y minimum value, y maximum value)

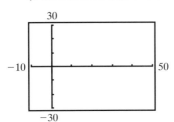

$(-10, 50, -30, 30)$

Sample Functions

Linear Function

$$f(x) = ax, a > 0$$

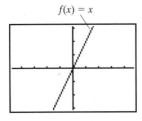

$(-47, 47, -31, 31)$

$$f(x) = ax, a < 0$$

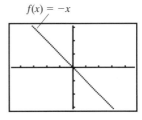

$(-47, 47, -31, 31)$